THE ROUGH GUIDE TO

South Africa
Lesotho & Swaziland

written and researched by

**Tony Pinchuck, Barbara McCrea, Donald Reid and
Ross Velton**

with additional contributions by

Hilary Heuler, Jeroen van Marle and Lone Mouritsen

**ROUGH
GUIDES**

roughguides.com

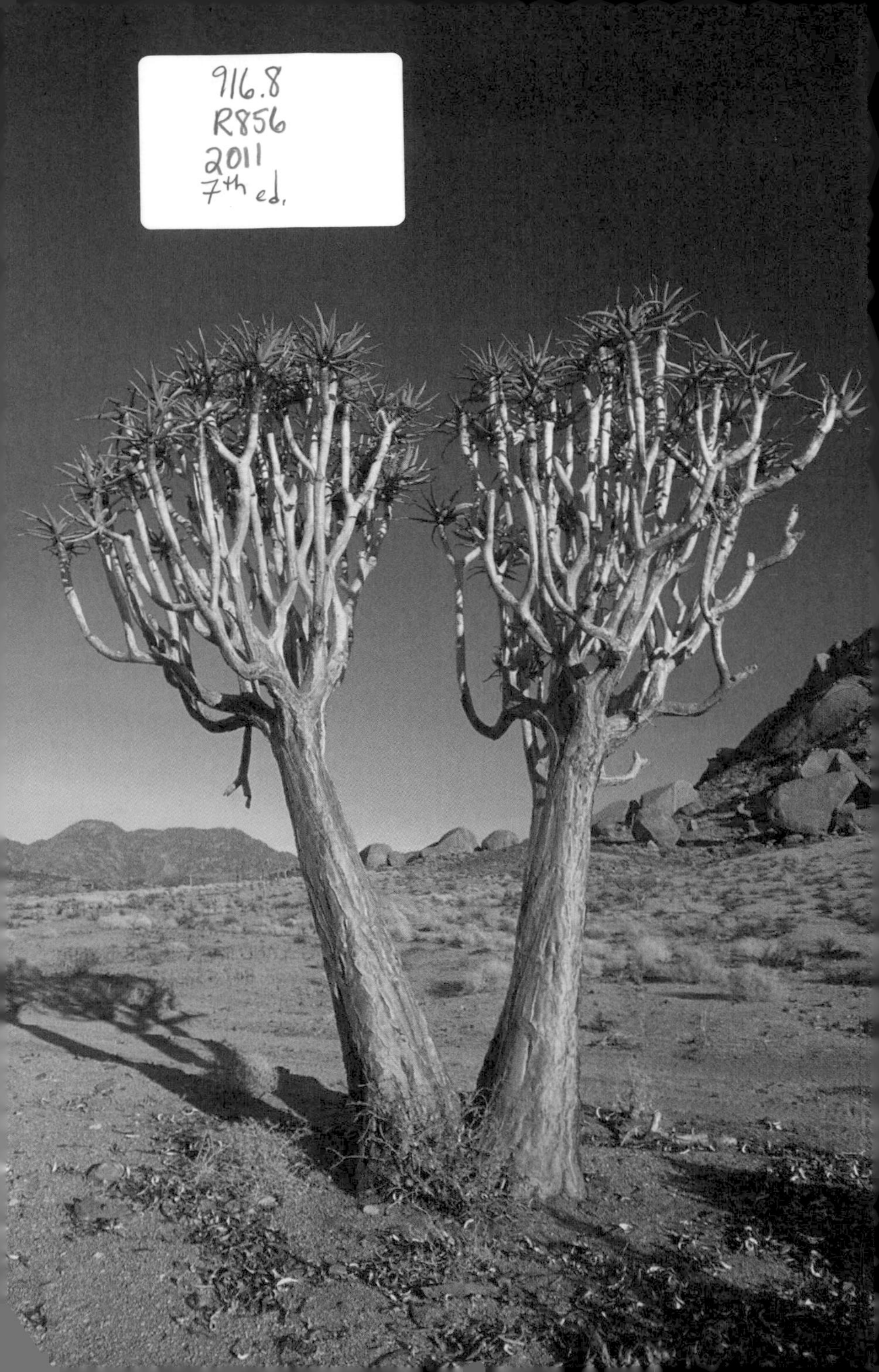

Contents

Introduction to
South Africa

South Africa is a large, diverse and incredibly beautiful country. The size of France and Spain combined, and roughly twice the size of Texas, it varies from the picturesque Garden Route towns of the Western Cape to the raw subtropical coast of northern KwaZulu-Natal, with the vast Karoo semi-desert across its heart and one of Africa's premier safari destinations, Kruger National Park, in the northeast. It's also one of the great cultural meeting points of the African continent, a fact obscured by decades of enforced racial segregation, but now manifest in the big cities.

Many visitors are pleasantly surprised by South Africa's excellent **infrastructure**, which draws favourable comparison with countries such as Australia or the United States. Good air links and bus networks, excellent roads and a growing number of first-class B&Bs and guesthouses make South Africa a perfect touring country. For those on a budget, mushrooming backpacker hostels and backpacker buses provide cost-efficient means of exploring.

Yet, despite all these facilities, South Africa is also something of an enigma; after nearly two decades of non-racial democracy, the **"rainbow nation"** is still struggling to find its identity. Apartheid may be dead, but its heritage still shapes South Africa in a very physical way. Nowhere is this more evident than in the layout of towns and cities; the African areas – generally poor – are usually tucked out of sight.

South Africa's **population** doesn't reduce simply to black and white. The majority are **Africans** (79.5 percent of the population); **whites** make up nine percent, followed by **coloureds** (just under nine percent) – the descendants of white settlers, slaves and Africans, who speak English and Afrikaans and comprise the majority in the Western Cape. The rest (2.5 percent), resident mainly in KwaZulu-Natal, are descendants of **Indians**, who came to South Africa at the beginning of the twentieth century as indentured labourers.

Even these statistics don't tell the whole story. A better indication of South Africa's diversity is the plethora of official languages, most of which represent a distinct culture with rural roots in different parts of the country. In each region you'll see distinct styles of architecture, craftwork and sometimes dress. Perhaps more exciting still are the cities, where the whole country comes together in an alchemical blend of rural and urban, traditional and thoroughly modern.

Crime isn't the indiscriminate phenomenon that press reports suggest, but it is an issue. Really, it's a question of perspective – taking care but not becoming paranoid. Statistically, the odds of becoming a victim are highest in downtown Johannesburg, where violent crime is a daily reality. Other cities present a reduced risk – similar to, say, some parts of the United States.

Where to go

While you could circuit South Africa in a matter of weeks, a more satisfying approach is to focus on one section of the country. Each of the nine provinces has compelling reasons to visit, although, depending on the time of year and your interests, you'd be wise to concentrate on either the **west** or the **east**.

The **west**, best visited in the warmer months (Nov–April), has the outstanding attraction of **Cape Town**, worth experiencing for its matchless setting beneath Table Mountain. Half a day's drive from here can take you to any other destination in the **Western Cape**, a province that owes its distinctive character to the longest-established colonial heritage in the country. You'll find gabled Cape Dutch architecture, historic towns and vineyard-covered mountains in the **Winelands**; forested coast along the **Garden Route**; and a dry interior punctuated by Afrikaner *dorps* (towns) in the **Little Karoo**.

FACT FILE

• South Africa has a **population** of 51 million and eleven official **languages**: Zulu, Xhosa, Afrikaans, Pedi, English, Ndebele, Sotho, Setswana, siSwati, Venda and Tsonga.

• The country is a **multiparty democracy**, the head of state being President Jacob Zuma. Parliament sits in Cape Town, the **legislative capital**, while Pretoria is the **executive capital**, from where the president and his cabinet run the country. Each of the nine provinces has its own government.

• The **highest point** in South Africa is Njesuthi, in the Drakensberg, at 3408m. The highest point in Lesotho and Southern Africa is also in the Drakensberg: Thabana Ntlenyana, at 3482m.

• South African President **Jacob Zuma**'s three-spouse household is modest compared to the fourteen-wife ménage of Swazi King Msawati; King Letsie of Lesotho has been married just once.

• **Nelson Mandela**'s wife, Graça Machel, who was previously married to the late president of Mozambique, Samora Machel, is the only woman to have been first lady of two different countries.

If the west sounds too pretty and you're after a more "African" experience, head for the **eastern** flank of the country, best visited in the cooler months (May–Oct). **Johannesburg** is likely to be your point of entry to this area: its frenetic street life, soaring office blocks and lively mix of people make it quite unlike anywhere else in the country. Half a day away by car lie **Limpopo** and **Mpumalanga** provinces, which share the mighty **Kruger National Park**. Of South Africa's roughly two dozen major parks, Kruger is unrivalled on the continent for its cross section of mammal species.

A visit to Kruger combines perfectly with KwaZulu-Natal to the south, and an excellent short cut between the two is through tiny, landlocked **Swaziland**, which has a unique Swazi culture and a number of well-managed game parks. **KwaZulu-Natal** itself offers superb game and birdlife; **Hluhluwe-Imfolozi Park** is the best place in the world to see endangered rhinos, and there are several other outstanding small game reserves nearby, such as Ithala, Mkhuze and Ndumo. For hiking and nature, the high point of the province – literally – is the soaring **Drakensberg**, half a day's drive from Durban. After Cape Town, **Durban** remains the only city in South Africa worth visiting in its own right: a busy cultural melting pot with a bustling Indian district and lively beachfront. The long stretch of **beaches** north and south of Durban is the most developed in the country, but north towards the Mozambique border lies South Africa's wildest stretch of coast.

Long sandy **beaches**, developed only in pockets, are characteristic of much of the 2798km of shoreline that curves from the cool Atlantic along the Northern Cape round to the subtropical Indian Ocean that foams onto KwaZulu-Natal's shores. Much of the **Eastern Cape** coast is hugely appealing: for strolling, sunbathing or simply taking in backdrops of mountains and hulking sand dunes. **Scuba diving**, especially in KwaZulu-Natal, opens up a world of coral reefs rich with colourful fish, and, south of the Western Cape winelands, along the **Whale Coast**, is one of South Africa's major wildlife attractions – some of the best shore-based **whale-watching** in the world.

FROM TOP WHITE RHINOS, EASTERN CAPE; BEACH VOLLEYBALL, CAMPS BAY, CAPE TOWN >

With time in hand, you might want to drive through the sparse but exhilarating **interior**, with its open horizons, switchback mountain passes, rocks, scrubby vegetation and isolated *dorps*. The **Northern Cape** and **North West Province** can reveal surprises, such as the Martian landscapes of the Richtersveld and the lion country of the remote but thrilling Kgalagadi Transfrontier Park.

From the staunchly Afrikaner heartland of **Free State**, you're well poised to visit the undeveloped kingdom of **Lesotho**, set in the mountains between Free State and KwaZulu-Natal. Lesotho has few vestiges of royalty left, but does offer plenty of spectacular highland scenery, best explored on a sturdy, sure-footed Basotho pony.

When to go

South Africa is predominantly sunny, but when it does get cold you feel it, since everything is geared to fine weather. **Midwinter** in the southern hemisphere (the reverse of the north) is in June and July, and **midsummer** is during December and January, when the country shuts down for its annual holiday.

South Africa has distinct climatic zones. In **Cape Town** and the **Garden Route** coastal belt, summers tend to be warm, mild and unpredictable; rain can fall at any time of the year and winter days can be cold and wet. Many Capetonians regard March to May as the perfect season, when the winds drop; it's beautifully mild and the tourists have gone. Subtropical **KwaZulu-Natal** has warm, sunny winters and tepid seas; in common with the **Lesotho** highlands, the province's Drakensberg range has misty days in summer and mountain snow in winter. **Johannesburg** and **Pretoria** lie on the highveld plateau and have a near-perfect climate; summer days are hot and frequently broken by dramatic thunder showers; winters are dry with chilly nights. East of Johannesburg, the **lowveld**, the low-lying wedge along the Mozambique border that includes the **Kruger National Park** and much of **Swaziland**, is subject to similar summer and winter rainfall patterns to the highveld, but experiences far greater extremes of temperature because of its considerably lower altitude.

HOUSE OF THE SPIRITS

For thousands of years, San Bushman shamans in South Africa decorated rock faces with powerful religious images. These finely realized paintings, found in mountainous areas across South Africa, include animals, people, and humans changing into animals. Archeologists now regard the images as metaphors for religious experiences, one of the most significant of which is the healing trance dance, still practised by the few surviving Bushman communities. Rockfaces can be seen as portals between the human and spiritual world: when we gaze at Bushman rock art, we are looking into the house of the spirits.

Author picks

Having returned to his home country after two decades, our author, Tony, is still constantly amazed by South Africa, where he's watched a whale breach over his morning coffee, trodden grapes with a high-court judge and run into a baboon during a morning jog. Chance encounters aside, here are some of the other things that make his home so special.

Oldest artistic tradition The haunting rock paintings of the Drakensberg hark back to a mythological time of shamans, animals and shape-shifters. **See p.406**

In the raw Taking an outdoor shower at one of the Kruger's private lodges is an unforgettable way to experience the African wild. **See p.562**

Soweto on spokes Bike tours of South Africa's largest township get you out of the bus and onto the street. **See p.480**

Walk with leviathans The five-day Whale Trail in De Hoop Nature Reserve is stunningly beautiful throughout the year – and sublime in season when there are whales around every corner. **See p.212**

Mother of all asteroids The Vredefort dome is part of the world's oldest, widest and deepest meteorite impact crater. **See p.454**

Glass menagerie The see-through bedroom walls at boutique-hotel-in-the-bush, *Kwandwe Ecca Lodge*, one of the lodges at Kwandwe Private Game Reserve, are all that separates you from the Big Five. **See p.327**

Wettest seafood The small deck at *Harbour House Restaurant* in Kalk Bay jetties out over the crashing surf, with the risk of a drenching at high tide. **See p.149**

Switched on switchbacks Few drives are more dramatic than taking the Swartberg Pass, which carves through mountains to reach the Karoo hamlet of Prince Albert. **See p.183**

Our author recommendations don't end here. We've flagged up our favourite places – a perfectly sited hotel, an atmospheric café, a special restaurant – throughout the guide, highlighted with the ★ symbol.

28

things not to miss

It's not possible to see everything that South Africa, Lesotho and Swaziland has to offer in one trip – and we don't suggest you try. What follows is a selective and subjective taste of the country's highlights, including outstanding national parks, spectacular wildlife, adventure sports and beautiful architecture. All entries have a page reference to take you straight into the guide, where you can find out more. Coloured numbers refer to chapters in the Guide section.

1

2 HLUHLUWE-IMFOLOZI PARK
Page 412
KwaZulu-Natal's finest game reserve offers an unsurpassed variety of wildlife-spotting activities, from night drives to self-guided walks and even donkey trails.

8

5 THE DRAKENSBERG
Page 398

Hike in the "dragon mountains", which harbour South Africa's highest peaks, plus waterfalls, rock art and awesome panoramas.

6 VERNACULAR ARCHITECTURE
Page 448

Beautifully decorative Basotho huts are characteristic of the eastern Free State's Maloti Route.

7 ADDO ELEPHANT NATIONAL PARK
Page 314

Encounter elephants and the rest of the Big Five at the end of the Garden Route.

8 TRADITIONAL ARTS AND CRAFTS
Page 583

Find traditional handicrafts in rural and urban areas alike, such as the Venda region of Limpopo.

9 WINE ROUTES
Page 168

The Cape's wine estates combine stunning scenery, Cape Dutch architecture and some fine vintages.

9

10 THE SANI PASS
Page 402

The most precipitous pass in Southern Africa, connecting Lesotho to KwaZulu-Natal.

11 GAME TRAILS
Page 557

Spot wildlife on a guided hike in Kruger National Park.

12 CAPE POINT
Page 127

The rocky promontory south of Cape Town is one of the most dramatic coastal locations on the continent.

13 STORMS RIVER MOUTH
Page 242

The Garden Route's most spectacular coastline, where you can cross Storms River Mouth by footbridge.

14 KGALAGADI TRANSFRONTIER PARK
Page 284

View cheetahs, meerkats and other desert dwellers amid the harsh beauty of the Kalahari.

15 WILD FLOWERS
Page 290

Following the winter rains, Namaqualand's normally bleak landscape explodes with colour.

16 THE BO-KAAP
Page 102

Cape Town's oldest residential area is filled with colourful Cape Dutch and Georgian architecture.

22

23

24

25

26

27

28

Itineraries

The following itineraries take you from South Africa's southwestern corner to its northeastern extent, covering the classic attractions – such as Cape Town and Kruger National Park – as well as far less-visited sights. Stitched together, the three itineraries could constitute a two-month grand tour, sweeping across the country's major themes, from safaris, beaches and epic landscapes to ethnic art and culture, colonial architecture and urban life.

WESTERN CAPE CIRCUIT

South Africa's oldest urban centres are in the Western Cape, a province that packs a huge variety. You could cover its highlights in three weeks, but four would be more comfortable.

❶ **Cape Town** Southern Africa's oldest, most beautiful and most unmissable city has it all: an extraordinary natural setting, beautiful historic architecture and a buzzing urban life. **See p.82**

❷ **Winelands** Limewashed Cape Dutch manors planted among vineyards beneath mauve mountains and the country's best restaurants and guesthouses in the country. **See p.168**

❸ **Whale Coast** Monumental dunes and wild surf are reason enough to visit De Hoop Nature Reserve, but it's also one of the world's top spots for land-based whale-watching. **See p.197**

❹ **Garden Route** South Africa's quintessential self-drive route follows the N2 through pretty coastal towns, such as Sedgefield and Knysna, as well as national parks proclaimed for their ancient forests and dramatic coastline. **See p.214**

❺ **Little Karoo** The R62, the mountainous inland counterpart to the Garden Route, cuts through the semi-arid Little Karoo's mountain passes, taking in sculptural rock formations, hot springs and some lovely historic villages. **See p.183**

❻ **Swartland** The closest place to Cape Town to see the veld glowing with wild flowers in spring is Darling. **See p.246**

❼ **Cederberg** San rock-art sites and grotesque gargoyle-like rock formations give the Western Cape's mountain wilderness its otherworldly atmosphere. **See p.255**

THE EAST

The eastern flank of the country most easily conforms to stereotypical Africa: game reserves, beaches and ethnic culture. You'll need three weeks for this tour.

❶ **Johannesburg** Africa's economic powerhouse buzzes with a thriving arts scene, well-established café culture and Soweto, the country's most populous township. **See p.460**

❷ **Kruger National Park** The size of a small country and brimming with wildlife, Kruger is up there with the continent's top game reserves. **See p.551**

❸ **Swaziland** One of the world's few remaining absolute monarchies retains its tribal traditions through a number of ceremonies. **See p.622**

❹ **iSimangaliso Wetland** UNESCO World Heritage Site that offers scuba diving in the subtropical waters of Sodwana Bay and where loggerhead and leatherback turtles come ashore to nest in summer. **See p.415**

❺ **KwaZulu-Natal game reserves** Hluhluwe-Imfolozi is the province's premier game reserve, roamed by big cats, rhinos and elephants; a number of minor reserves such as Ithala, Mkhuze and Phinda also have a lot to offer. **See p.410**

❻ Zulu heartland Geometrically patterned basketry and several festivals, including Shaka Day, keep alive the proud traditions of KwaZulu-Natal's dominant ethnic group. **See p.428**

❼ Ukhahlamba Drakensberg The dramatic landscapes make for breathtaking hikes and the chance to see the rock art of the San. **See p.398**

❽ Durban The subtropical vegetation, popular beachfront and cocktail of Zulu, Indian and English colonial cultures make Durban a compelling stay for a couple of days. **See p.365**

THE FRONTIER

Discover the dry interior of the Great Karoo and the contrastingly verdant Wild Coast. Allow three weeks to explore these historic stomping grounds of Dutch trekboers, English settlers and Xhosa herders.

❶ Port Elizabeth Four thousand English settlers made landfall here in 1820 and today their descendants' families are drawn to its safe sandy beaches. **See p.308**

❷ Big Game Country Addo, the only Big Five national park in the southern half of the country, is also close to Shamwari and Kwande, two of the top private game reserves. **See p.314**

❸ Graaff Reinet Totally surrounded by the mountainous Camdeboo National Park, whose highlight is the deep Valley of Desolation, this eighteenth-century Cape-Dutch Karoo outpost is perfect for exploring on foot. **See p.332**

❹ Cradock The atmospherically dusty frontier town sits on the west bank of the Great Fish River, the fractious nineteenth-century border between the English-governed Cape Colony and the traditional Xhosa chiefdoms. **See p.328**

❺ Grahamstown Edgy blend of cultured university town and rural backwater, the Settler City glories in extensive Georgian- and Victorian-colonial streetscapes. **See p.323**

❻ Hogsback Cultivated fantasies of Little England abound in this lush Afromontane highland resort elevated above baking valleys where herders graze their livestock. **See p.340**

❼ Madiba Country Boys still herd cattle, just as Nelson Mandela did, around Qunu, the village where he grew up; at nearby Mthatha, a museum tells the story of his life. **See p.355**

❽ Wild Coast Immerse yourself in Xhosa culture and life at Bulungula Lodge, in an unspoilt region of traditional villages, undulating hills, lush forests and hundreds of kilometres of undeveloped sandy beaches. **See p.344**

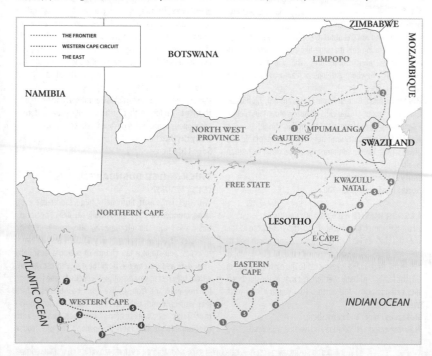

Wildlife

Apart from Kruger, Kgalagadi Transfrontier, Hluhluwe-Imfolozi, Addo Elephant, the Pilanesberg and a number of private parks, where you'll see the Big Five (lion, leopard, buffalo, elephant and rhino), over a hundred other reserves offer numerous smaller predators and dozens of herbivores, including endangered species, in invariably beautiful settings.

This field guide provides a quick reference to help you identify some of the **mammals** most likely to be encountered in South Africa. It includes species found throughout the country as well a number whose range is more restricted. The photos show easily identified markings and features. The notes give pointers about the kind of habitat in which you are likely to see each mammal; its daily rhythm; the kind of social groups it usually forms; and some of the reserves you're most likely to find it in.

PRIMATES

Southern Africa has the lowest diversity of primates on the continent, a mere five species excluding Homo sapiens. They include two varieties of bushbaby, two monkeys and one species of baboon – the largest and most formidable of the lot. Great apes such as gorillas and chimpanzees aren't found in the wild in Southern Africa.

CHACMA BABOON *PAPIO (URSINUS) CYNOCEPHALUS*
Apart from humans, baboons are the primates most widely found in South Africa. Males can be intimidating and are bold enough to raid vehicles or accommodation in search of food, undeterred by the presence of people. Troops are led by a dominant male and are governed by complex social relations in which gender, precedence, physical strength and family ties determine status. Every adult male enjoys dominance over every female. Grooming forms part of the social glue and you'll commonly see baboons lolling about while performing this massage-like activity. Baboons are highly opportunistic omnivores who will tuck into a scorpion or a newborn antelope as readily as raid a citrus farm for oranges.
Reserves Addo, Garden Route (Tsitsikamma), Hluhluwe-Imfolozi, Kruger, Marakele, Mkhuze, Mountain Zebra, Pilanesberg, Table Mountain (Cape of Good Hope).
Habitat Open country with trees and cliffs; adaptable, but always near water; sometimes venture close to human habitation.
Daily rhythm Diurnal.
Social life Troops of 15–100.

LESSER BUSHBABY *GALAGO MOHOLI*
Of the half-dozen or so bushbaby species endemic to Africa, only the thick-tailed bushbaby (below) and, about half its size, the lesser bushbaby are found south of the Limpopo. While the thick-tailed is restricted to the eastern fringes of SA, the lesser bushbaby overlaps its range in the northeast and extends across the north of the country into North West Province.
Reserves Kruger and Pilanesberg.
Habitat Woodland savanna and riverine woodland.

Daily rhythm Nocturnal.
Social life Small family groups.

SAMANGO (OR SYKES') MONKEY
CERCOPITHECUS MITIS
In striking contrast with the cheekier, upfront disposition of vervets, the rarer samango monkeys are shy and may only give themselves away through their loud explosive call or the breaking of branches as they go about their business. Samangos are larger than vervets and have long cheek hair. Like vervets, they're highly social and live in troops of females under the proprietorship of a dominant male, but unlike their relatives they are more inclined to fan out when looking for food.
Reserves Isimangaliso, Hluhluwe-Imfolozi and Ndumo.
Habitat Prefer higher reaches of gallery forest; occasionally venture into the open to forage.
Daily rhythm Diurnal.
Social life Troops.

THICK-TAILED BUSHBABY *OTOLEMUR CRASSICAUDATUS*
With their large, soft, fluffy pelts, huge, saucer-like eyes, large, rounded ears and superficially cat-like appearance, bushbabies are the ultimate in cute, cuddly-looking primates. If you're staying at any of the KwaZulu-Natal reserves, you stand a fair chance of seeing a bushbaby after dark as they emerge from the dense forest canopy, where they rest in small groups, for spells of lone foraging for tree gum and fruit. Unlike other bushbabies, which leap with ease and speed, the thick-tailed is a slow mover that hops or walks along branches, often with considerable stealth. Even if you don't see one, you're

bound to hear their piercing scream cut through the sounds of the night. Bushbabies habituate easily to humans and will sometimes come into lodge dining rooms, scavenging for titbits.

Reserves Hluhluwe-Imfolozi, Isimangaliso, Kruger.
Habitat Dry and riverine woodland; arboreal.
Daily rhythm Nocturnal.
Social life Small groups of a mating pair or one or two females with young; males territorial with ranges that overlap several female ranges.

VERVET MONKEY *CERCOPITHECUS AETHIOPS*

A widespread primate you may see outside reserves, living around nearby farms and even on suburban fringes, where opportunities for scavenging are promising. Vervets are principally vegetarians but are not averse to eating invertebrates, small lizards, nestlings and eggs, as well as biscuits and sweets. Vervet society is made up of family groups of females and young, defended by associate males, and is highly caste-ridden. A mother's rank determines that of her daughter from infancy, and lower-ranking adult females risk being castigated if they fail to show due respect to these "upper-crust" youngsters.

Reserves Eastern half of SA: virtually every game reserve in Northwest, Limpopo, Mpumalanga and KwaZulu-Natal, as well as along the coast from Mossel Bay to northern KwaZulu-Natal.
Habitat Will forage in grasslands, but rarely far from woodland; particularly along river courses; arboreal and terrestrial.
Daily rhythm Diurnal.
Social life Troops.

DOG-RELATIVES AND ALLIED SPECIES

AARDWOLF *PROTELES CRISTATUS*

The hyena-like aardwolf is far smaller than the spotted hyena and far lighter, as well as being less shaggy, with vertical dark stripes along its tawny body. It is further distinguished from other hyenas by its insectivorous diet and its particular preference for harvester termites, which it laps up en masse (up to 200,000 in one night) with its broad sticky tongue. Far more widely distributed in South Africa than hyenas, but shy and not often seen.

Reserves Addo, Bontebok, Isimangaliso, Kruger and Pilanesberg.
Habitat Most habitats, except dense forest.
Daily rhythm Nocturnal; sometimes active in the cooler hours just before dusk or after dawn.
Social life Solitary.

BAT-EARED FOX *OTOCYON MEGALOTIS*

The bat-eared fox can easily be distinguished from the jackals by its outsized ears, its shorter, pointier muzzle and its considerably smaller-size. The bat-eared fox's black Zorro mask helps distinguish it from the similar-sized Cape fox, *Vulpes chama*, which inhabitats an overlapping range. Like other dogs, the bat-eared fox is an omnivore, but it favours termites and larvae, which is where its large radar-like ears come in handy. With these it can triangulate the precise position of dung-beetle larvae up to 30cm underground and dig them out.

Reserves Addo, Bontebok, Karoo, Kgalagadi, Kruger, Mountain Zebra and Pilanesberg.
Habitat Open countryside; short-scrubland; lightly forested areas.
Daily rhythm Nocturnal and diurnal.
Social life Family groups of 2–6.

BLACK-BACKED JACKAL *CANIS MESOMELAS*

The member of the dog family you're most likely to see is the black-backed jackal, found especially in the country's reserves. It bears a strong resemblance to a small, skinny German Shepherd, but with a muzzle more like that of a fox, and is distinguished from the grey, side-striped jackal (see below) by the white-flecked black saddle on its back, to which it owes its name. Jackals are omnivorous scavenger-hunters, who get most of their food from catching small creatures such as insects, lizards, snakes or birds, but will also tackle baby antelope and larger birds, and they are cheeky enough to steal pieces of prey from under the noses of lions or hyenas at a kill.

Reserves Addo, Hluhluwe-Imfolozi, Karoo, Kgalagadi, Kruger, Mkhuze, Mountain Zebra, Pilanesberg.
Habitat Broad range, from moist mountain regions to desert; avoid dense woodland.
Daily rhythm Normally nocturnal, but diurnal in safety of game reserves.
Social life Mostly monogamous pairs, but also seen singly and in small family groups.

SIDE-STRIPED JACKAL *CANIS ADJUSTUS*

Like its black-backed relative, the side-striped jackal is omnivorous, with a diet that takes in carrion, small animals, reptiles, birds and insects, as well as wild fruit and berries. The fact that the black-backed jackal seeks a drier habitat, in contrast to the side-striped's preference for well-watered woodland, is an identification pointer.

Reserves Isimangaliso, Kruger.
Habitat Well-watered woodland.
Daily rhythm Mainly nocturnal.
Social life Solitary or pairs.

SPOTTED HYENA *CROCUTA CROCUTA*

The largest carnivores after lions are hyenas, and apart from the lion, the spotted hyena is the meat-eater you will most often see. Although considered a scavenger *par excellence*, the spotted hyena is a formidable hunter, most often found where antelope and zebra are present. Exceptionally efficient consumers, with immensely strong teeth and jaws, spotted hyenas eat virtually every part of their prey, including bones and hide and, where used to humans, often steal shoes, unwashed pans and refuse from tents. They are most active at night, when they issue their unnerving whooping cries. Clans of twenty or so are dominated by females, who are larger than the males and compete with each other for rank.

Reserves Addo, Hluhluwe-Imfolozi, Kruger and Kgalagadi.
Habitat Wide variety of habitat apart from dense forest.
Daily rhythm Generally nocturnal from dusk, but diurnal in many parks.
Social life Highly social, usually living in extended family groups.

WILD DOG *LYCAON PICTUS*

Once the widely distributed hunters of the African plains, wild dogs have been brought to the edge of extinction. The world's second most threatened dog relative, the South African population consists of just five hundred individuals, of which two hundred are in the Kruger National Park. For many years they were shot on sight, having gained an unjustified reputation as cruel and wanton killers of cattle and sheep. More recent scientific evidence reveals them to be economical and efficient hunters – and more successful at it than any other African species. Capable of sustaining high speeds (up to 50km/h) over long distances, wild dogs lunge at their prey en masse, tearing it to pieces – a gruesome finish, but no more grisly than the suffocating muzzle-bite of a lion. The entire pack of ten to fifteen animals participates in looking after the pups, bringing back food and regurgitating it for them.

Reserves Kruger (best place) as well as Hluhluwe-Imfolozi, Madikwe, Pilanesberg, Marakele, Tswalu and Mkhuze.
Habitat Open savanna in the vicinity of grazing herds.
Daily rhythm Diurnal.
Social life Nomadic packs.

CATS

Apart from lions, which notably live in social groups, cats are solitary carnivores. With the exception of the cheetah, which is anatomically distinct from the other cats, the remaining members of the family are so similar, says mammal ecologist Richard Estes, that big cats are just "jumbo versions" of the domestic cat, "distinguished mainly by a modification of the larynx that enables them to roar".

CARACAL *CARACAL CARACAL*

Although classified as a small cat, the caracal is a fairly substantial animal. An unmistakeable and awesome hunter, with great climbing agility, it's able to take prey, such as adult impala and sheep, which far exceed its own weight of 8–18kg kilos. More commonly it will feed on birds, which it pounces on, sometimes while still in flight, as well as smaller mammals, including dassies (see p.40).

Reserves Addo, Karoo, Kgalagadi, Kruger, Mountain Zebra (one of the best places), Table Mountain (Cape of Good Hope).
Habitat Open bush and plains; occasionally arboreal.
Daily rhythm Mainly nocturnal.
Social life Solitary.

CHEETAH *ACINONYX JUBATUS*

In the flesh the cheetah is so different from the leopard that it's hard to see how there could ever be any confusion. Cheetahs are the greyhounds of the big-cat world, with small heads, long legs and an exterior decor of fine spots. Unlike leopards, cheetahs never climb trees, being designed rather for activity on the open plains. Hunting is normally a solitary activity, down to keen eyesight and an incredible burst of speed that can take the animal up to 100km/h for a few seconds. Because they're lighter than lions and less powerful than leopards, cheetahs can't rely on strength to bring down their prey. Instead they resort to tripping or knocking the victim off balance by striking its hindquarters, and then pouncing.

Reserves Addo, Kruger, Kgalagadi, Hluhluwe-Imfolozi, and Mountain Zebra.
Habitat Savanna in the vicinity of plains game.
Daily rhythm Diurnal.
Social life Solitary or temporary nuclear family groups.

LEOPARD *PANTHERA PARDUS*

The lion may be king, but most successful and arguably most beautiful of the large cats is the leopard, which survives from the southern coastal strip of Africa all the way to China. Highly adaptable, they can subsist in extremes of aridity or cold, as well as in proximity to human habitation, where they happily prey on domestic animals – which accounts for their absence in the sheep-farming regions of central South Africa, due to extermination by farmers. Powerfully built, they can bring down prey twice their weight and drag an impala (see p.37) their own weight up a tree. The chase is not part of the leopard's tactical

repertoire; they hunt by stealth, getting to within 2m of their target before pouncing.

Reserves Kruger, Hluhluwe-Imfolozi, Kruger, Pilanesberg and Marakele; best places are the private reserves in Sabi Sands, abutting Kruger, which trade on their leopards being highly accustomed to humans; also present in rugged, mountainous southern W. Cape, but secretive and rarely seen.

Habitat Highly adaptable; frequently arboreal.

Daily rhythm Nocturnal; also cooler daylight hours.

Social life Solitary.

LION *PANTHERA LEO*

The most compelling and largest of the cats for most safari-goers are lions, the most massive predators in Africa. It's fortunate then that, despite having the most limited distribution of any cat in South Africa, lions are the ones you're most likely to see. Lazy, gregarious and sizeable, lions rarely attempt to hide, making them relatively easy to find, especially if someone else has already found them – a gathering of stationary vehicles frequently signals lions. Their fabled reputation as cold, efficient hunters is ill-founded, as lions are only successful around thirty percent of the time, and only if operating as a group. Males don't hunt at all if they can help it and will happily enjoy a free lunch courtesy of the females of the pride.

Reserves Healthy populations in Kruger and Kgalagadi; limited numbers in Addo, Hluhluwe-Imfolozi, Mapungubwe, Marakele and Pilanesberg.

Habitat Wherever there's water and shade except thick forest.

Daily rhythm Diurnal and nocturnal.

Social life Prides of three to forty, more usually around twelve.

SERVAL *FELIS SERVAL*

Long-legged and spotted, servals bear some resemblance to, but are far smaller than, cheetahs and are more rarely seen. Efficient hunters, servals use their large rounded ears to pinpoint prey (usually small rodents, birds or reptiles), which they pounce on with both front paws after performing impressive athletic leaps.

Reserves Hluhluwe-Imfolozi, Ithala, Kruger, Pilanesberg, Ukhahlamba Drakensberg.

Habitat Reed beds or tall grasslands near water.

Daily rhythm Normally nocturnal, but can be seen during daylight hours.

Social life Usually solitary.

SMALLER CARNIVORES

CIVET *CIVETTICTIS CIVETTA*

The civet (or African civet) is a stocky animal resembling a large, terrestrial genet. Civets were formerly kept in captivity for their musk (once an ingredient in perfume), which is secreted from glands near the tail. Civets aren't often seen, but they're predictable creatures, wending their way along the same path at the same time, night after night. Civets are omnivores that will scavenge for carrion and feed on small rodents, birds, reptiles and even fruit. Found in Northern SA, Mpumalanga and extreme north of KwaZulu-Natal.

Reserves Kruger and Pilanesberg.

Habitat Open, especially riverine, woodland.

Daily rhythm Nocturnal.

Social life Solitary.

HONEY BADGER *MELLIVORA CAPENSIS*

The unusual honey badger, related to the European badger, has a reputation for defending itself extremely fiercely. Primarily an omnivorous forager, it will tear open bees' nests (to which it is led by a small bird, the honey guide), its thick, loose hide rendering it impervious to stings.

Reserves Addo, Karoo, Kgalagadi, Kruger, Hluhluwe-Imfolozi and Pilanesberg.

Habitat Wide range except forest.

Daily rhythm Mainly nocturnal.

Social life Solitary, sometimes pairs.

SMALL-SPOTTED GENET *GENETTA GENETTA*

Small-spotted genets are reminiscent of slender elongated cats, and were once domesticated around the Mediterranean (but cats turned out to be better mouse hunters). In fact, they are viverrids, related to mongooses, and are frequently seen after dark around national-park lodges, where some live a semi-domesticated existence. They're difficult to distinguish from the less widely distributed, large-spotted genet, *Genetta tigrina*, which has bigger spots and a black (instead of white) tip to its tail.

Reserves Addo, Bontebok, Karoo, Kgalagadi, Kruger, Mountain Zebra, Pilanesberg, Table Mountain (Cape of Good Hope).

Habitat Wide range: light bush country, even arid areas; partly arboreal.

Daily rhythm Nocturnal. But becomes active at dusk.

Social life Solitary.

WATER MONGOOSE *ATILAX PALUDINOSUS*

Most species of mongoose, of which there are nearly a dozen in South Africa, are also tolerant of humans and, even when disturbed, can usually be observed for some time. If you keep your eyes peeled when driving on the open road, you'll often see mongooses darting across your path. Social arrangements differ from species to species, some being solitary while others live in packs. The water mongoose, one of the most widely distributed of the mongooses, resembles

an otter, but is a lot smaller and lighter. Foragers, they'll root for anything edible – mostly crabs and amphibians, but also invertebrates, eggs, lizards and small rodents. Water mongooses are found in a deep swathe across Southern Africa, sweeping down from Mpumalanga in the northeast to the Cape Peninsula in the southwest.
Reserves Bontebok, Hluhluwe-Imfolozi, Karoo, Kruger, Mkhuze, Table Mountain (Cape of Good Hope).
Habitat Well-watered areas, such as alongside streams, rivers and lakes.
Daily rhythm Mainly nocturnal, but also active at dusk and dawn.
Social life Solitary.

ANTELOPE

South Africa has roughly a third of all antelope species in Africa, and antelope are the most regularly seen family of animals in the country's game reserves. You'll even spot some on farmland along the extensive open stretches that separate interior towns. South African antelope are subdivided into a number of tribes, and like buffalo, giraffe and domestic cattle, they are ruminants – animals that have four stomachs and chew the cud.

BLACK WILDEBEEST *CONNOCHAETES GNOU*
Black wildebeest were brought to the edge of extinction in the nineteenth century and now number around three thousand in South Africa, though you will find them in one or two parks in the country. You can tell them apart from their blue relatives by their darker colour (brown rather than the black suggested by their name) and long white tail. Black wildebeest appear to be under threat again, this time not from hunting, but hybridization, since black and blue wildebeest can interbreed and produce fertile offspring. Conservationists fear that the rarer black species will be bred out of existence. The problem is taken so seriously by KwaZulu-Natal wildlife authorities that no park in the province is stocked with both species.
Reserves Karoo, Mountain Zebra and Ukhahlamba Drakensberg.
Habitat Low scrub and open grassland.
Daily rhythm Diurnal.
Social life Cows and offspring wander freely through bull territories; during rut bulls try to keep females within their territory.

BLUE DUIKER *PHILANTOMBA MONTICOLA*
The smallest South African antelope, the blue duiker, weighs in at around 4kg, has an arched back and stands 35cm at the shoulder (roughly the height of a domestic cat). Pairs stick together and remain vigilant as a defence against predators, which can include leopards, baboons and even large birds of prey. Duiker are found in the forested areas of coastal strip from George in the Western Cape to northern KwaZulu-Natal, but are extremely shy and so seldom seen.
Reserves Garden Route (Knysna), Isimangaliso and Ndumo.
Habitat Forests and dense bushland.
Daily rhythm Mainly diurnal.
Social life Monogamous couples.

BLUE WILDEBEEST *CONNOCHAETES TAURINUS*
All hartebeest are sociable but the exemplar of this is the blue wildebeest (sometimes known as the brindled gnu), which, in East Africa, gather in hundreds of thousands for their annual migration. You won't see these numbers in South Africa, but you'll see smaller herds. Blue wildebeest are often seen in association with zebra.
Reserves Hluhluwe-Imfolozi, Ithala, Kgalagadi, Kruger, KwaZulu-Natal, Mapungubwe and Mkhuze.
Habitat Grasslands.
Daily rhythm Diurnal, occasionally nocturnal.
Social life Intensely gregarious in a wide variety of associations from small groups to sizeable herds.

BONTEBOK *DAMALISCUS DORCAS DORCAS* P.213
Better-looking version of the tsessebe, from which it's distinguished by its chocolate-brown colouring and white facial and rump markings. Bontebok, which were historically limited to a small range in the southern Cape, teetered on the edge of extinction, but their survival is now secured on several reserves and farms. A subspecies, the blesbok, *Damaliscus dorcas phillipsi*, is found in the Free State and northern Eastern Cape.
Reserves Bontebok, De Hoop, Table Mountain (Cape of Good Hope), West Coast.
Habitat Coastal plain where Cape fynbos occurs.
Daily rhythm Diurnal.
Social life Rams hold territories; ewes and lamb herds numbering up to ten wander freely between territories.

BUSHBUCK *TRAGELAPHUS SCRIPTUS*
Despite a distinct family resemblance, you could never confuse a kudu with a bushbuck, which is considerably shorter and, in the males, has a single twist to its horns, in contrast to the kudu's two or three turns. They also differ in being the only solitary members of the tribe, one reason you're less likely to spot them. Often seen in thickets or heard crashing through them. Not to be confused with the larger nyala.

1 BUSHBUCK; 2 NYALA; 3 ELAND >

Reserves Addo, Garden Route (Wilderness and Knysna), Isimangaliso, Kruger, Mapungubwe, Pilanesberg; also most reserves (even minor ones) in KwaZulu-Natal.
Habitat Thick bush and woodland near water.
Daily rhythm Mainly nocturnal, but also active during the day when cool.
Social life Solitary, but casually sociable; sometimes graze in small groups.

COMMON (OR GREY) DUIKER *SYLVICAPRA GRIMMIA*

Of the duikers, the one you're most likely to see is the common duiker (sometimes called the grey duiker, reflecting its colouring), which occurs all over South Africa and is among the antelopes most tolerant of human habitation. When under threat it freezes in the undergrowth, but if chased will dart off in an erratic zigzagging run designed to throw pursuers off balance. The common duiker has a characteristic rounded back, is about 50cm high at the shoulder, and rams have short, straight horns.
Reserves Addo, Bontebok, Karoo, Kruger, Ithala, Hluhluwe-Imfolozi, Mountain Zebra, Mkhuze, Table Mountain (Cape of Good Hope) and Pilanesberg.
Habitat Adaptable; prefers scrub and bush.
Daily rhythm Nocturnal and diurnal.
Social life Mostly solitary, but sometimes in pairs.

ELAND *TAUROTRAGUS ORYX*

Eland, the largest living antelope, is built like an ox and moves with the slow deliberation of one, though it's also a superb jumper. Once widely distributed, herds now survive only in pockets of northeast SA and protected areas of the Drakensberg in KwaZulu-Natal; also small introduced populations in numerous other reserves.
Reserves Addo, Ithala, Karoo, Kgalagadi, Kruger, Marakele, Mountain Zebra, Pilanesberg and Table Mountain (Cape of Good Hope).
Habitat Highly adaptable; semi-desert to mountains, but prefers scrubby plains.
Daily rhythm Nocturnal and diurnal.
Social life Non-territorial herds of up to sixty.

GEMSBOK (OR ORYX) *ORYX GAZELLA* P.287

If you encounter a herd of these highly gregarious grazers, you should be left in no doubt as to what they are. Gemsbok are highly adapted for survival in the arid country they inhabit, able to go for long periods without water, relying instead on melons and vegetation for moisture. They tolerate temperatures above 40°C by raising their normal body temperature of 35°C above that of the surrounding air, losing heat by conduction and radiation; their brains are kept cool by a supply of blood from their noses.

Reserves Addo, Augrabies, Karoo, Kgalagadi, Mokala, Pilanesberg and Tankwa Karoo.
Habitat Open grasslands; waterless wastelands; tolerant of prolonged drought.
Daily rhythm Nocturnal and diurnal.
Social life Highly hierarchical mixed herds of up to fifteen, led by a dominant male.

IMPALA *AEPYCEROS MELAMPUS*

Larger and heavier than springbok, which they superficially resemble, impala are elegant and athletic. Prodigious jumpers, they have been recorded leaping distances of 11m and heights of 3m. Only the males carry the distinctive lyre-shaped pair of horns. They are so common in the reserves of the northeast and of KwaZulu-Natal that some jaded rangers look on them as the goats of the savanna – a perception that carries more than a germ of truth, as these flexible feeders are both browsers and grazers.
Reserves Hluhluwe-Imfolozi, Ithala, Kruger, Mapungubwe, Marakele, Mkhuze and Pilanesberg.
Habitat Open savanna, near light woodland cover.
Daily rhythm Diurnal.
Social life Large herds of females overlap with several male territories; during the rut (first five months of the year) dominant males will cut out harem herds of around twenty and expend considerable amounts of effort driving off the any potential rivals.

KLIPSPRINGER *OREOTRAGUS OREOTRAGUS*

Another dwarf antelope (about 60cm at the shoulder) you could well see is the stocky klipspringer, whose Afrikaans name (meaning "rock hopper") reflects its goat-like adaptation to living on *koppies* and cliffs – the only antelope to do so, making it unmistakable. It's also the only one to walk on the tips of its hooves. They occur sporadically throughout SA where there are rocky outcrops.
Reserves Addo, Augrabies, Garden Route (Tsitsikamma), Karoo, Kruger, Mapungubwe, Mkhuze, Mountain Zebra, Pilanesberg and Table Mountain (Cape of Good Hope).
Habitat Rocky terrain.
Daily rhythm Diurnal; most active in morning and late afternoon.
Social life Monogamous pairs or small family groups.

KUDU *TRAGELAPHUS STREPSICEROS* P.540

The magnificent kudu is more elegantly built than the eland, and males are adorned with sensational spiralled horns that can easily reach 1.5m in length. Known for their athleticism, kudu can vault over a 2m fence with no difficulty.
Reserves Northern Limpopo and North West provinces, and in Mpumalanga and northeastern KwaZulu-Natal;

Addo, Ithala, Hluhluwe-Imfolozi, Karoo, Kgalagadi, Kruger, Marakele, Mountain Zebra and Pilanesberg.

Habitat Semi-arid, hilly or undulating bush country; tolerant of drought.

Daily rhythm Diurnal when secure, otherwise nocturnal.

Social life Males usually solitary or in small transient groups; females in small groups with young.

NYALA *TRAGELAPHUS ANGASII*

Nyalas are midway in size between the kudu and bushbuck, with which they could be confused at first glance. Telling pointers are their size, the sharp vertical white stripes on the side of the nyala (up to fourteen on the male, eighteen on the female), orange legs, and, in the males, a short stiff mane from neck to shoulder. Females tend to group with their two last offspring and gather with other females in small herds, rarely exceeding ten. Males become more solitary the older they get.

Reserves Kruger and around three dozen reserves in KwaZulu-Natal, of which Mkhuze, Ndumo and Hluhluwe-Imfolozi have the largest populations.

Habitat Dense woodland near water.

Daily rhythm Mainly nocturnal with some diurnal activity.

Social life Non-territorial; basic unit is female and two offspring.

ROAN *HIPPOTRAGUS EQUINUS*

The roan looks very similar to but is larger than a sable (it's Africa's second-largest antelope), with less impressive horns and lighter colouring. You're more likely to see them in open savanna than sables.

Reserves Kruger NP.

Habitat Tall grassland near water.

Daily rhythm Nocturnal and diurnal; peak afternoon feeding.

Social life Small herds led by dominant bull; herds of immature males; sometimes pairs in season.

SABLE *HIPPOTRAGUS NIGER*

The magnificent sable has a sleek, black upper body set in sharp counterpoint to its white underparts and facial markings, as well as its massive backwardly curving horns, making it the thoroughbred of the ruminants, particularly when galloping majestically across the savanna.

Reserves Kruger and Marakele reserves.

Habitat Open woodland with medium to tall grass near water.

Daily rhythm Nocturnal and diurnal.

Social life Highly hierarchical female herds of up to three dozen; territorial bulls divide into sub-territories, through which cows roam.

SPRINGBOK *ANTIDORCAS MARSUPIALIS*

Springboks are South Africa's only gazelle. Their characteristic horns and dark horizontal patch on their sides, separating their reddish tawny upper body from their white underparts, are definitive identifiers. Springbok are recorded as having reached nearly 90km/h and are noted for "pronking", a movement in which they arch their backs and straighten their legs as they leap into the air. Indigenous to the (often arid) northern reaches of South Africa, where they once could be seen in their hundreds, they are now more widespread in reserves and on farms where they are raised for their venison and hides.

Reserves Addo, Augrabies, Chelmsford NR (biggest population in KZN), Golden Gate, Karoo, Kgalagadi, Mountain Zebra, Pilanesberg, Tankwa Karoo and West Coast.

Habitat Wide range of open country, from deserts to wetter savanna.

Daily rhythm Seasonally variable, but usually cooler times of day.

Social life Highly gregarious, sometimes in huge herds of hundreds or even thousands; various herding combinations of males, females and young.

TSESSEBE *DAMALISCUS LUNATUS*

Somewhat ungainly in appearance because, according to legend, it arrived late when the Creator was dishing out the goodies, the tsessebe turns out to be a thoroughbred when it comes to speed. One of the fastest antelope on the African plains, a fleeing tsessebe can reach 70km/h. Males often stand sentry on termite hills, marking territory against rivals (rather than defending it against predators). Tricky customers, tsessebe bulls will sometimes falsely give an alarm signal to deter females from wandering out of their territory.

Reserves restricted to northern extremities of SA; best place is Kruger NP; also present in Ithala, Marakele and Pilanesberg.

Habitat Savanna woodland.

Daily rhythm Diurnal.

Social life Females and young form permanent herds usually of about half a dozen, but up to thirty individuals with a territorial bull.

WATERBUCK *KOBUS ELLIPSIPRYMNUS*

Waterbuck are largest of the near-aquatic Kob tribe, which live close to water. They are sturdy animals – 1.3m at the shoulder, and a distinctive white horseshoe marking on their rump. Only the males have horns. Unable to reach or sustain significant speed, they rely on cover to evade predators. It is also claimed that the oily, musky secretion and powerful odour waterbuck emit from their hair is distasteful to predators and acts as a

deterrent. They are common and rather tame where they occur predominantly in KwaZulu-Natal, Limpopo and Mpumalanga.

Reserves Hluhluwe-Imfolozi, Isimangaliso, Ithala, Kruger, Mapungubwe, Marakele and Mkhuze.

Habitat Open woodland and savanna, near permanent water.

Daily rhythm Nocturnal and diurnal.

Social life Sociable animals, they usually gather in small herds of up to ten, and occasionally up to thirty.

OTHER HOOFED RUMINANTS

Alongside cattle, sheep, goats and antelope, buffalo and giraffe are also hoofed ruminants. Bacteria in their digestive systems process plant matter into carbohydrates, while the dead bacteria are absorbed as protein – a highly efficient arrangement that makes them economical consumers, far more so than non-ruminants such as elephants, which pass vast quantities of what they eat as unutilized fibre. Species that concentrate on grasses are grazers; those eating leaves are browsers.

BUFFALO *SYNCERUS CAFFER*

You won't have to be in the Kruger or most of the other reserves in South Africa for long to see buffalo, a common safari animal that, as one of the Big Five, appears on every hunter's shopping list. Don't let their resemblance to domestic cattle or water buffalo (to which they are not at all closely related) or apparent docility lull you into complacency; lone bulls, in particular, are noted and feared even by hardened hunters as dangerous and relentless killers.

Herds consist of clans and you'll be able to spot distinct units within the group: at rest, clan members often cuddle up close to each other. There are separate pecking orders among females and males, the latter being forced to leave the herd during adolescence (at about three years) or once they're over the hill, to form bachelor herds, which you can recognize by their small numbers. To distinguish males from females, look for their heavier horns bisected by a distinct boss, or furrow. Once found throughout South Africa, natural populations survive in the Eastern Cape, KwaZulu-Natal and Mpumalanga and have been widely reintroduced elsewhere.

Reserves Addo, Hluhluwe, Isimangaliso, Karoo, Kruger and Mountain Zebra.

Habitat Wide range of habitats, always near water.

Daily rhythm Nocturnal and diurnal, but inactive during heat of the day.

Social life Buffalo are non-territorial and gather in large herds of hundreds or even sometimes thousands. Herds under one or more dominant bulls consist of clans of a dozen or so related females under a leading cow.

GIRAFFE *GIRAFFA CAMELOPARDALIS*

Giraffe are among the easiest animals to spot because their long necks make them visible above the low scrub. The tallest mammals on earth, they spend their daylight hours browsing on the leaves of trees too high up for other species; combretum and acacias are favourites. Their highly flexible lips and prehensile tongues give them almost hand-like agility and enable them to select the most nutritious leaves while avoiding deadly-sharp acacia thorns. At night they lie down and spend the evening ruminating. If you encounter a bachelor herd, look out for young males testing their strength with neck wrestling. When the female comes into oestrus, which can happen at any time of year, the dominant male mates with her. She will give birth after a fourteen-month gestation. Over half of all young, however, fall prey to lions or hyenas in their early years.

Reserves Hluhluwe-Imfolozi, Ithala, Kgalagadi, Kruger, Mapungubwe, Mkhuze and Pilanesberg.

Habitat Wooded savanna and thorn country.

Daily rhythm Diurnal.

Social life Loose, non-territorial, leaderless herds.

NON-RUMINANTS

Non-ruminating mammals have more primitive digestive systems than animals that chew the cud. Although both have bacteria in their gut that convert vegetable matter into carbohydrates, the less efficient system of the non-ruminants means they have to consume more raw material and process it faster. The upside is they can handle food that's far more fibrous.

AFRICAN ELEPHANT *LOXODONTA AFRICANA*

Elephants were once found throughout South Africa. Now you'll only see them in a handful of reserves. When encountered in the flesh, elephants seem even bigger than you would imagine. You'll need little persuasion from those flapping warning ears to back off if you're too close, but they are at the same time amazingly graceful. In a matter of moments a large herd can merge into the trees and disappear, silent on their padded, carefully placed feet, their presence betrayed only by the noisy cracking of branches as they strip trees and uproot saplings. Elephants are the most engaging of animals to watch, perhaps because their

1 GIRAFFE; 2 BUFFALO >

interactions, behaviour patterns and personality have so many human parallels. Like people, they lead complex, interdependent social lives, growing from helpless infancy through self-conscious adolescence to adulthood. Babies are born with other cows in close attendance, after a 22-month gestation. Calves suckle for two to three years. Basic family units are composed of a group of related females, tightly protecting their young and led by a venerable matriarch. Bush mythology has it that elephants become embarrassed and ashamed after killing a human, covering the body with sticks and grass. They certainly pay much attention to the disposal of their own dead relatives, often dispersing the bones and spending time near the remains. Old animals die in their 70s or 80s, when their last set of teeth wears out and they can no longer feed.

Reserves Addo (the only population to survive naturally in the southern two-thirds of the country), Hluhluwe-Imfolozi, Ithala, Kruger, Mkhuze, Pilanesberg and Tembe.

Habitat Wide range of habitats, wherever there are trees or water.

Daily rhythm Nocturnal and diurnal; sleeps as little as four hours a day.

Social life Highly complex; cows and offspring in herds headed by matriarch; bulls solitary or in bachelor herds.

ROCK DASSIE (OR HYRAX) *PROCAVIA CAPENSIS*

Dassies look like they ought to be rodents but, amazingly, despite being fluffy and rabbit-sized, their closest relatives (admittedly from some way back) are elephants. Their name (pronounced like "dusty" without the "t") is the Afrikaans version of *dasje*, meaning "little badger", given to them by the first Dutch settlers.

Like reptiles, hyraxes have poor body control systems and rely on shelter against both the cold and hot sunlight. They wake up sluggish and seek out rocks to catch the early morning sun – this is one of the best times to look out for them. One adult stands sentry against predators and issues a low-pitched warning cry in response to a threat. Dassies are found throughout South Africa (except the Northern Cape, and KwaZulu-Natal coastal belt) and are frequently sighted.

Reserves Bontebok, Garden Route (Tsitsikamma), Karoo, Kruger, Mountain Zebra, Pilanesberg, Table Mountain (Cape of Good Hope), Ukhahlamba Drakensberg.

Habitat Rocky areas, from mountains to isolated outcrops and coastal cliffs.

Daily rhythm Diurnal.

Social life Colonies of a dominant male and eight or more related females and their offspring.

RHINOS

Hook-lipped" and "square-lipped" are technically more accurate terms for the two rhinos. "Black" and "white" are based on a linguistic misunderstanding – somewhere along the line, the German "weid", which refers to the square-lipped's wide mouth, was misheard as "white". The term has stuck, despite both rhinos being a greyish muddy colour.

The shape of their lips is highly significant as it indicates their respective diets and consequently their favoured habitat. Rhinos give birth to a single calf after a gestation period of fifteen to eighteen months, and the baby is not weaned until it is at least a year old, sometimes two. Their population grows slowly compared with most animals, another factor contributing to their predicament.

BLACK RHINO *DICEROS BICORNIS*

The cantankerous, far rarer and smaller black rhino has the narrow prehensile lips of a browser, suited to picking leaves off trees and bushes. A solitary animal, it relies on the camouflage of dense thickets, which is why you'll find them so much more difficult to see. South Africa's 1600 individuals make up about a third of Africa's remaining black rhinos.

Reserves Addo, Augrabies, Hluhluwe-Imfolozi, Isimangaliso, Ithala, Karoo, Kruger, Marakele, Mkhuze and Pilanesberg.

Habitat Thick bush.

Daily rhythm Active day and night, resting between periods of activity.

Social life Solitary.

HIPPOPOTAMUS *HIPPOPOTAMUS AMPHIBIUS*

Hippos are highly adaptable animals that once inhabited South African waterways from the Limpopo in the north to

the marshes of the Cape Peninsula in the south. Today they're far more restricted. You'll see them elsewhere, in places where they've been reintroduced. Hippos need fresh water deep enough to submerge themselves, with a surrounding of suitable grazing grass. By day, they need to spend most of their time in water to protect their thin, hairless skin. After dark, hippos leave the water to spend the whole night grazing, often walking up to 10km in one session. Their grunting and jostling in the water may give the impression of loveable buffoons, but throughout Africa they are feared, and rightly so, as they are reckoned to be responsible for more human deaths on the continent than any other animal. When disturbed, lone bulls and cows with calves can become extremely aggressive. Their fearsomely long incisors can slash through a canoe with ease; on land they can charge at speeds up to 30km/h, with a tight turning circle.

Reserves Addo, Kruger, Isimangaliso and Pilanesberg.

Habitat Slow-flowing rivers, dams and lakes.

Daily rhythm Principally nocturnal, leaving the water to graze at night.

Social life Bulls solitary; others live in family groups known as pods, headed by a matriarch.

WHITE RHINO *CERATOTHERIUM SIMUM*

Twice as heavy as its black counterpart, the white rhino is also aggressive. Diet and habitat account for the greater sociability of the white rhino, which relies on safety in numbers under the exposure of open grassland; while its wide, flatter mouth is well suited to chomping away at grasses like a lawnmower. By the end of the nineteenth century, the only place white rhinos survived was the Hluhluwe-Imfolozi reserve (where they still thrive), but they have since been introduced to a number of reserves.

Reserves Hluhluwe-Imfolozi, Ithala, Kruger, Mkhuze, Marakele, Ndumo, Pilanesberg and Tembe.

Habitat Savanna.

Daily rhythm Active day and night, resting between periods of activity.

Social life Mother/s and calves, or small same-sex herds of immature animals; old males solitary.

ZEBRAS

Zebras are closely related to horses and, together with them, donkeys and wild asses, form the equid family. Of the three species of zebra, two live in South Africa. Zebras congregate in family herds of a breeding stallion and two mares (or more) and their foals. Unattached males will often form bachelor herds. Among plains zebras, offspring leave the family group after between one and two years, while mountain zebras are far more tolerant in allowing adolescents to remain in the family.

BURCHELL'S ZEBRA *EQUUS QUAGGA*

A highly successful herbivore that can survive in a variety of grassland habitats, which accounts for its geographical range, the Burchell's or plains zebra has small ears and thick, black stripes, with lighter "shadows".

Reserves Addo, Hluhluwe-Imfolozi, Isimangaliso, Ithala, Kruger, Mapungubwe, Mkhuze, Pilanesberg.

Habitat Savanna, with or without trees.

Daily rhythm Active day and night, resting intermittently.

Social life Harems of several mares and foals, led by a dominant stallion, usually group together in large herds; harems highly stable and harem mares typically remain with the same male for life.

CAPE MOUNTAIN ZEBRA *EQUUS ZEBRA ZEBRA*

The Cape mountain zebra only narrowly escaped extinction, but now survives in healthy if limited numbers in a number of reserves in the southern half of SA, wherever there is suitably mountainous terrain. Characteristics that distinguish the two zebras are the dewlap on the mountain

RHINOS: LAST CHANCE TO SEE?

Two species of rhinoceros are found in Africa: the hook-lipped or black rhino and the much heavier square-lipped or white rhino. Both have come close to extinction in the African wild and have all but disappeared. Until recently, South Africa had bucked this continental trend, and, despite a recent spike in poaching in the country, South Africa, with over 19,000 white and roughly 1600 black rhinos (the biggest populations in Africa by far), is still the best place on the planet to see black and white rhinos in the wild.

Alarmingly, though, in 2008 there was a sharp increase in rhino poaching, when 83 animals were slain for their horns; in 2009 and 2010 the numbers rose to 122 and 333.

The main market for rhino horn is in Asia, where a single horn can fetch up to US$70,000 , as an ingredient in traditional medicine. So lucrative is the trade that sophisticated criminal syndicates have moved in, using helicopters and night-vision equipment to slaughter the mammals under cover of night.

The battle of the rhinos isn't entirely one-sided: 162 suspected poachers were arrested and five were killed in a shoot-out with game rangers in the Kruger National Park in 2010. But this may not be enough to save the animals, who are now being killed faster than they can reproduce.

Dr David Mabunda, CEO of South African National Parks, is committed to saving the animals: "We have worked hard as a country to bring this species back from the brink of extinction and we will continue to defend it even if we become the last man standing".

Some conservationists argue that more resources need to be thrown at the problem, while others argue for more innovative tactics, such as injecting poison into the horns, making them unusable, or even removing them altogether, as is being done in Zimbabwe.

zebra's lower neck, its absence of shadow stripes, its larger ears, and stripes that go all the way down to its hooves – the Burchell's stripes fade out as they progress down its legs.

Reserves Bontebok, Karoo, Mountain Zebra, Table Mountain (Cape of Good Hope) and Tankwa Karoo.

Habitat Mountainous areas and their immediate surrounds.

Daily rhythm Active by day.

Social life Harems of stallions with four or five mares and their foals.

OTHER MAMMALS

AARDVARK *ORYCTEROPUS AFER* P.440

One of Africa's – indeed the world's – strangest animals, a solitary mammal weighing up to 70kg. Its name, Afrikaans for "earth pig", is an apt description, as it holes up during the day in large burrows that are excavated with remarkable speed and energy. It emerges at night to visit termite mounds within a radius of up to 5km, digging for its main diet. It's most likely to be common in bush country that's well scattered with termite mounds. Found throughout South Africa, but rarely seen.

Reserves Addo, Hluhluwe-Imfolozi, Karoo, Kgalagadi, Kruger, Mapungubwe and Mountain Zebra.

Habitat Open or wooded termite country; softer soil preferred.

Daily rhythm Nocturnal.

Social life Solitary.

PANGOLIN *MANIS TEMMINCKII*

Equally unusual – scale-covered mammals, resembling armadillos and feeding on ants and termites. Under attack they roll themselves into a ball. Pangolins occur widely in South Africa, north of the Orange River.

Reserves Kgalagadi and Kruger.

Habitat Wide range apart from desert and forest.

Daily rhythm Nocturnal.

Social life Solitary.

PORCUPINE *HYSTRIX AFRICAEAUSTRALIS*

The most singular and largest (up to 90cm) of the African rodents is the porcupine, which is quite unmistakeable with its coat of many quills. Porcupines are widespread and present in most reserves but, because they're nocturnal, you may only see shed quills. Rarely seen, but common away from croplands, where it is hunted as a pest.

Reserves Virtually all.

Habitat Adaptable to a wide range of habitats.

Daily rhythm Nocturnal; sometimes active at dusk.

Social life Family groups.

SPRINGHARES *PEDETES CAPENSIS*

If you go on a night drive in the Kruger or one of several other reserves in the north of the country, you'd be most unlucky not to see the glinting eyes of spring hares which, despite their resemblance to rabbit-sized kangaroos, are in fact true rodents.

Reserves Kgalagadi, Kruger, Mountain Zebra and Pilanesberg.

Habitat Savanna; softer soil areas preferred.

Daily rhythm Nocturnal.

Social life Burrows, usually with a pair and their young; often linked into a network, almost like a colony.

WARTHOG *PHACOCHOERUS AETHIOPICUS*

If you're visiting the Kruger, Pilanesberg or the KwaZulu-Natal parks, families of warthogs will become a familiar sight, trotting across the savanna with their tails erect like communications antennae. Boars join family groups only to mate; they're distinguished from sows by their prominent face warts, which are thought to be defensive pads protecting their heads during often violent fights.

Reserves Addo, Hluhluwe-Imfolozi, Isimangaliso, Ithala, Mkhuze, Kruger, Pilanesberg.

Habitat Savanna.

Daily rhythm Diurnal.

Social life Family groups usually consist of a mother and her litter of two to four piglets, or occasionally two or three females and their young.

CAPE TOWN INTERNATIONAL JAZZ FESTIVAL

Basics

Getting there

As sub-Saharan Africa's economic and tourism hub, South Africa is well served with flights from London and the rest of Europe. The majority of these touch down at Johannesburg's OR Tambo International, but there are also frequent flights into Cape Town. From North America there are a relatively small number of nonstop flights into Johannesburg.

Airfares depend on the **season**, with the highest prices and greatest demand in June, July, August, December and the first week of January. You get the best prices during the low season in October and November and from the last three weeks of January until March.

Flights from the UK and Ireland

From London there are nonstop flights with British Airways (Wwww.ba.com), South African Airways (Wwww.flysaa.com) and Virgin Atlantic (Wwww.virgin-atlantic.com) to Johannesburg and Cape Town. Flying time from the UK is around eleven hours to Jo'burg, about an hour longer to Cape Town; nonstop fares from London start from £800 in high season and £500 in low season. You can save up to £200 by flying via mainland Europe or the Middle East, and changing plane at least once.

From the Republic of Ireland, a number of European carriers fly out of Dublin to South Africa via their hub airports.

Flights from the US and Canada

From the US there are three nonstop **flights** a week from New York (JFK) to Johannesburg operated by South African Airways (SAA) in partnership with United Airlines (Wunited.com). These take between fifteen and sixteen hours. Most other flights stop off in Europe, the Middle East or Asia and involve a change of plane. There are no direct flights **from** Canada; you'll have to change planes in the US, Europe or Asia on hauls that can last up to thirty hours.

On the direct flights from the US to Jo'burg, expect the high/low season fare to start from $2600/1700 for a round trip; you might save from $100 to as much as $700 if you fly **via Europe**. Fares from Vancouver to Jo'burg start at Can$2200.

Flights from Australia and New Zealand

There are nonstop flights **from Sydney** (which take 12hr) and **Perth** (just under 10hr) to Johannesburg, with onward connections to Cape Town. Flights **from New Zealand** tend to be via Sydney. South African Airways and Qantas (Wqantas.com) both fly nonstop to South Africa from Australia; several Asian, African and Middle Eastern airlines fly to South Africa via their hub cities, and tend to be less expensive, but their routings often entail long stopovers.

Direct flights from Sydney to Johannesburg start at Aus$2800 in high season and Aus$1800 in low; a flight to Europe with a stopover in South Africa, or even a round-the-world ticket, may represent better value than a straightforward return.

AGENTS AND OPERATORS

Abercrombie & Kent Australia ☎ 1300/851 800, Wwww.abercrombiekent.com.au; UK ☎ 0845/618 2202, Wwww.abercrombiekent.co.uk; US ☎ 1-800/554-7016, Wwww.abercrombiekent.com. Classy operator whose packages feature Cape Town, Johannesburg, Kruger and luxury rail travel.

Absolute Africa UK ☎ 020/8742 0226, W www.absoluteafrica.com. Adventure camping overland trips.

Acacia African Adventures UK ☎ 020/7706 4700, Wwww.acacia-africa.com. Camping-based trips along classic South African routes.

Adventure Center US ☎ 1-800/228 8747, Wwww.adventurecenter.com. Wide variety of affordable packages.

Adventures Abroad US ☎ 1-800/665-3998, Wwww.adventures-abroad.com. Small-group and activity tours, including family-friendly trips.

A BETTER KIND OF TRAVEL

At Rough Guides we are passionately committed to travel. We feel that travelling is the best way to understand the world we live in and the people we share it with – plus tourism has brought a great deal of benefit to developing economies around the world over the last few decades. But the growth in tourism has also damaged some places irreparably, and climate change is exacerbated by most forms of transport, especially flying. All Rough Guides' trips are carbon-offset, and every year we donate money to a variety of charities devoted to combating the effects of climate change.

Africa Travel Centre UK ☎ 0845/450 1520, ⓦ www
.africatravel.co.uk. Experienced Africa specialists, who are agents for
many South Africa-based overland operators.

Bales Worldwide UK ☎ 0845/057 1819, ⓦ www
.balesworldwide.com. High-quality escorted tours.

Classic Safari Company Australia ☎ 1300/130 218 or
☎ 02/9327 0666, ⓦ www.classicsafaricompany.com.au. Luxury
tailor-made safaris to southern Africa.

Cox & Kings UK ☎ 020/7873 5000, ⓦ www.coxandkings.co.uk;
US ☎ 1-800/999-1758. Packaged self-drive holidays in South Africa as
well as pick-and-mix tailor-made tours.

Dragoman UK ☎ 01728/861 133, ⓦ www.dragoman.co.uk.
Extended overland journeys in purpose-built vehicles, plus shorter
camping and hotel-based safaris.

Exodus UK ☎ 020/8675 5550, ⓦ www.exodus.co.uk. Small-group
adventure tour operator with plenty of South Africa offerings, including
activity packages.

Expert Africa UK ☎ 020/8232 9777, ⓦ www.expertafrica.com.
Small-group tours for independent travellers, as well as tailor-made trips.
Strong on Cape Town and the Western Cape.

Explore Worldwide UK ☎ 0845/013 1537, ⓦ www.explore.co
.uk. Good range of small-group tours, treks, expeditions and safaris.

GAP Adventures Canada ☎ 1-416/260 0999, ⓦ www
.gapadventures.com. Canadian agent for a multitude of adventure
companies.

Guerba Expeditions UK ☎ 020/3147 7777, ⓦ www.guerba.co
.uk. Trans-African overland travel, plus shorter packages exploring parts
of South Africa.

Joe Walsh Tours Ireland ☎ 01/241 0800, ⓦ www
.joewalshtours.ie. Budget airline fares as well as beach and safari
packages.

Journeys International US ☎ 1-800/255-8735, ⓦ www
.journeys-intl.com. Small-group trips with a range of safaris.

Journeys Worldwide Australia ☎ 07/3221 4788, ⓦ www
.journeysworldwide.com.au. Escorted tours.

Kumuka Expeditions Australia ☎ 1300/667 277, ⓦ www
.kumuka.com.au; UK ☎ 0800/092 9595, ⓦ www.kumuka.co.uk;
US ☎ 1-800/517-0867, ⓦ www.kumuka.com. Five-week journeys
from Nairobi to Cape Town and short tours around South Africa.

Kuoni Travel UK ☎ 01306/747 002, ⓦ www.kuoni.co.uk. Flexible
package holidays, including safaris, escorted tours and golfing packages.
Good deals for families.

North South Travel UK ☎ 01245/608 291, ⓦ www
.northsouthtravel.co.uk. Discounted airline fares worldwide. Profits are
used to support projects in the developing world, especially the
promotion of sustainable tourism.

Oasis Overland UK ☎ 01963/363 400, ⓦ www.oasisoverland
.co.uk. One of the smaller overland companies, often running budget
trips through Africa.

Okavango Tours and Safaris UK ☎ 020/8347 4030,
ⓦ www.okavango.com. Fully flexible and individual tours across
South Africa.

On the Go Tours UK ☎ 020/7371 1113, ⓦ www.onthegotours
.com. Group and tailor-made tours to Africa.

Rainbow Tours UK ☎ 020/7226 1004, ⓦ www.rainbowtours
.co.uk. Knowledgeable and sensitive South Africa specialists whose trips
emphasize eco-friendly and community-based tourism.

Safari Consultants UK ☎ 01787/888 590, ⓦ www
.safari-consultants.co.uk. Individually tailored and fairly upmarket
holidays across southern Africa, with particular expertise in activity-based
holidays, including walking safaris.

STA Travel Australia ☎ 134 782, New Zealand ☎ 0800/474 400,
South Africa ☎ 0861/781 781, UK ☎ 0871/2300 040, US
☎ 1-800/781-4040; ⓦ statravel.com. Worldwide specialists in
independent travel; also sell student IDs, travel insurance, car rental, rail
passes, and more. Good discounts for students and under-26s.

Trailfinders Australia ☎ 1300/780 212, Ireland ☎ 01/677 7888,
UK ☎ 0845/058 5858; ⓦ trailfinders.com. One of the best-informed
and most efficient agents for independent travellers.

Tribes UK ☎ 01728/685 971, ⓦ www.tribes.co.uk. Unusual and
off-the-beaten-track fair-trade safaris and cultural tours.

Twohigs Ireland ☎ 01/648 0800, ⓦ www.twohigs
.com. Long-haul specialist offering South Africa packages.

Travel CUTS Canada ☎ 1-866/246-9762, US ☎ 1-800/592-2887;
ⓦ travelcuts.com. Canadian youth and student travel firm.

USIT Ireland ☎ 01/602 1906, Northern Ireland ☎ 028/9032 7111;
ⓦ usit.ie. Ireland's main student and youth travel specialists.

Wilderness Travel US ☎ 1-800/368-2794, ⓦ www
.wildernesstravel.com. Hiking, cultural and wildlife adventures.

Wildlife Worldwide UK ☎ 0845/130 6982, ⓦ www
.wildlifeworld wide.com. Tailor-made trips for wildlife and wilderness
enthusiasts.

World Travel Centre Ireland ☎ 01/416 7007, ⓦ www
.worldtravel.ie. Competitive fares to South Africa.

Getting around

**Despite the large distances, travelling
around most of South Africa is fairly
straightforward, with a reasonably well-
organized network of public transport,
a good range of car rental companies,
the best road system in Africa, and the
continent's most comprehensive
network of internal flights. The only
weak point is public transport in urban
areas, which is almost universally poor
and often dangerous. Urban South
Africans who can afford to do so tend to
use private transport, and if you plan to
spend much time in any one town, this
is an option seriously worth considering. It's virtually impossible to get to
the national parks and places off the
beaten track by public transport; even if
you do manage, you're likely to need a
car once you're there.**

Buses

South Africa's three established intercity bus companies are **Greyhound** (☎083 915 9000, ⓦwww .greyhound.co.za), **Intercape** (☎086 128 7287, ⓦwww.intercape.co.za) and **Translux** (☎086 158 9282, ⓦwww.translux.co.za); between them, they reach most towns in the country. Travel on these buses is safe, good value and comfortable, and the vehicles are usually equipped with air conditioning and toilets. **Fares** vary according to distance covered and time of year, with peak fares corresponding approximately to school holidays; at other times you can expect about thirty percent off. As a rough indication, you can expect to pay the following fares from Cape Town: to Paarl, R185; Mossel Bay, R225; Port Elizabeth, R315; East London, R400; Mthatha, R470; Durban, R535; and Johannesburg R575.

Translux, Greyhound and Intercape also operate the no-frills **budget buslines** City to City, Cityliner and Budgetliner, whose schedules and prices are listed on their main websites.

Baz Bus (☎021 21 422 5202, ⓦwww.bazbus .com) operates an extremely useful hop-on/hop-off system aimed at backpackers and budget travellers,

with intercity buses stopping off at backpacker accommodation en route. Its services run up and down the coast in both directions between Cape Town and Port Elizabeth (1 daily), and between Port Elizabeth and Durban (5 weekly). Inland, it runs buses between Durban and Johannesburg (5 weekly). A number of independently run **shuttle services** connect with Baz services and go in the Western Cape to: Stellenbosch, Hermanus and

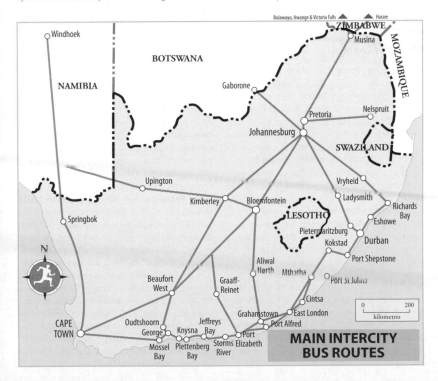

MAIN INTERCITY BUS ROUTES

DISTANCE CHART

Figures are given in kilometres

	Bloemfontein	Cape Town	Durban	East London	George	Graaff-Reinet	Johannesburg
Bloemfontein	–	998	628	546	764	422	396
Cape Town	998	–	1660	1042	436	672	1405
Durban	628	1660	–	667	1240	945	598
East London	546	1042	667	–	630	388	992
George	764	436	1240	630	–	342	1168
Graaff-Reinet	422	672	945	388	342	–	826
Johannesburg	396	1405	598	992	1168	826	–
Kimberley	175	960	842	722	734	501	467
Maseru	150	1187	476	516	837	503	415
Mbabane	614	1483	394	802	1189	922	310
Mthatha	527	1181	436	231	851	509	866
Nelspruit	754	1779	689	1214	1509	1167	358
Port Elizabeth	676	756	927	300	330	251	1062
Pretoria	454	1324	656	322	1226	895	58
Skukuza	880	1888	809	1334	1616	1274	478
Upington	576	821	1243	958	857	667	875

Oudtshoorn; in the Eastern Cape to: Hogsback, Coffee Bay, Mpande and Port St Johns; in KwaZulu-Natal to: additional points in Durban, Southern Drakensberg, Southbroom; and in Gauteng to Pretoria. In addition to the website, tickets can also be bought through hostels or the Baz offices at Cape Town and Durban's central tourist offices.

Minibus taxis

Minibus taxis provide transport to two-thirds of South Africans, travelling absolutely everywhere in the country, covering relatively short hops from town to town, commuter trips from township to town and back, and routes within larger towns and cities. However, the problems associated with them – unroadworthy vehicles, dangerous drivers and violent feuds between the different taxi associations competing for custom – mean that you should take local advice before using them. This is particularly true in cities, where minibus taxi ranks tend to be a magnet for petty criminals. The other problem with minibus taxis is that there is rarely much room to put **luggage**. However, despite the drawbacks, don't rule out using this form of transport altogether. In 2005 the government began a seven-year programme of replacing the country's creaking taxi fleet with new vehicles, which has at least improved the comfort and safety of many of the vehicles. Short of renting a car, minibus taxis will often be your only option for getting around in **remote areas**, where you're unlikely to encounter trouble. You should, however, be prepared for some long waits, due to their infrequency.

Fares are low and comparable to what you might pay on the inexpensive intercity buses. Try to have the exact change (on shorter journeys particularly), and pass your fare to the row of passengers in front of you; eventually all the fares end up with the conductor, who dishes out any change.

It's advisable to ask locals which taxi routes are safe to use.

Trains

Travelling by **train** is just about the slowest way of getting around South Africa: the journey from Johannesburg to Cape Town, for example, takes 29 hours – compared with 19 hours by bus. **Overnighting** on the train, though, is more comfortable than the bus and does at least save you the cost of accommodation en route. Families with children get their own private compartment on the train, and under-5s travel free.

The **Passenger Rail Agency of South Africa (Prasa)** runs most of the intercity rail services. Its standard service, Shosholoza Meyl (☎086 000 8888, ⓦshosholoza-meyl.co.za), offers Tourist Class travel in two- or four-person compartments equipped with washbasins. The seats are comfortable and convert into **bunks**; you can rent sheets and blankets for the night (R40 per person), which are brought around by a bedding attendant who'll make up your bed in the evening. It's best to buy your bedding voucher when you book your train ticket. Services run between Johannesburg and Cape Town, Port Elizabeth and Durban, as well as between Cape Town and Durban.

Kimberley	Maseru	Mbabane	Mthatha	Nelspruit	Port Elizabeth	Pretoria	Skukuza	Upington
175	150	614	527	754	676	454	880	576
960	1187	1483	1181	1779	756	1324	1888	821
842	476	394	436	689	927	656	809	1243
722	516	802	231	1214	300	322	1334	958
734	837	1189	851	1509	330	1226	1616	857
501	503	922	509	1167	251	895	1274	667
467	415	310	866	358	1062	58	478	875
–	326	684	779	832	763	525	952	401
326	–	326	402	620	660	473	707	734
684	489	–	626	96	1001	300	257	1008
779	402	626	–	983	490	903	1099	1178
832	620	96	983	–	1373	328	120	1144
763	660	1001	490	1373	–	1119	1459	902
525	473	300	903	328	1119	–	436	813
952	707	257	1099	120	1459	436	–	1252
401	734	1008	1178	1144	2902	813	1252	–

Prasa also runs the twice-weekly, upmarket air-conditioned **Premier Classe** (☎086 000 8888, ⓦwww.premierclasse.co.za) service between Johannesburg and Cape Town, and Johannesburg and Durban. The trains offer a choice of single, double, triple and four-person compartments, with gowns and toiletries provided, and four-course lunches and five-course dinners served in a luxury dining car – all included in the fare.

The fare from Johannesburg to Cape Town in Premier Classe is R2210 per person (roughly half that to Durban). Tourist Class fares range from roughly R300 per person from Johannesburg to Durban (the shortest route) and R740 from Cape Town to Durban (the longest route) but vary slightly depending on the time of year. Tickets must be booked in advance at train stations or online.

South Africa offers a handful of **luxury trains**, worth considering if you want to travel in plush surroundings and don't mind paying through the nose for the privilege. The celebrated **Blue Train** (ⓦwww.bluetrain.co.za) runs between Cape Town and Pretoria; fares start at R10,930 per person, sharing a double berth for the 29-hour journey. Passengers must be dressed in "smart casual" clothes during the day and appear in formal wear for the evening meal. Bookings can be made through the website, with Blue Train's central reservations in Pretoria (☎012 334 8459) or through the Cape Town reservations office (☎021 449 2672).

Another luxury rail option is offered by **Rovos Rail** (Cape Town ☎021 421 4020; Pretoria ☎012 315 8242; ⓦwww.rovos.co.za), which runs trips between Pretoria and Cape Town (from R12,000), Durban

(R12,000) and Victoria Falls in Zimbabwe (R13,750), at three levels of luxury, with prices to match.

A word of warning about **security** on trains: as thieves work the stations, especially around Gauteng, don't leave your valuables unattended in your compartment unless you have some way of locking it, and make sure you close the window if leaving the carriage for a while, even if it is locked.

Domestic flights

Flying between destinations in South Africa is an attractive option if time is short. It also compares favourably with the cost of covering long distances in a rental car, stopping over at places en route, and, with several competing **budget airlines**, you can sometimes pick up good deals.

By far the biggest airline offering domestic flights is **South African Airways** (SAA), with its two associates **SA Airlink** and **SA Express** (reservations for the three go through SAA). SAA's main direct competitor is British Airways Comair, but there are also the no-frills budget airlines: Kulula, 1Time, Velvet Sky and Mango, which have more limited networks than the big airlines, but generally offer better deals on the major routes.

On SAA and its associates, you can pick up a one-way tourist-class fare for under R1000 from Johannesburg to Cape Town or from Cape Town to Durban. On the Johannesburg to Cape Town route you'll generally pick up **fares** for around R700 on the budget airlines provided you book well ahead and sometimes for as little as half that when there are special offers.

SOUTH AFRICAN DOMESTIC AIRLINES

1Time ☎ 011 086 8000, Ⓦ www.1time.aero. Budget flights on a network that covers Johannesburg, Cape Town, Durban, East London, George and Port Elizabeth, and beyond South Africa's border to Livingstone, Maputo and Zanzibar.

British Airways Comair ☎ 086 043 5922, Ⓦ www.ba.com. Flights that cover Bloemfontein, Cape Town, Durban, East London, George, Hoedspruit, Johannesburg, Nelspruit (for Kruger National Park) and Port Elizabeth.

Kulula ☎ 086 158 5852, Ⓦ www.kulula.com. Budget flights that cover Cape Town, Durban, George, Johannesburg, Nelspruit (for Kruger National Park) and Port Elizabeth, as well as destinations in Mauritius, Mozambique, Namibia, Tanzania, Zambia and Zimbabwe.

Mango ☎ 086 116 2646, Ⓦ www.flymango.com. SAA's budget airline provides cheap flights from Johannesburg to Bloemfontein, Cape Town and Durban; and from Cape Town to Jo'burg, Durban and Bloemfontein.

South African Airways ☎ 086 135 9722, Ⓦ www.flysaa.com. Together with SA Airlink and SA Express, SAA serve the major hubs of Johannesburg, Cape Town and Durban. Other destinations served include Bloemfontein, East London, George, Hoedspruit, Kimberley, Margate, Mmabatho, Mthatha, Nelspruit (for Kruger National Park), Phalaborwa, Pietermaritzburg, Plettenberg Bay, Polokwane, Sun City, Ulundi and Upington.

Velvet Sky ☎ 031 582 8722, Ⓦ www.flyvelvetsky.co.za. At the time of its launch in 2011 services were limited to flights between Johannesburg and Durban or Cape Town.

Driving

Short of joining a tour, the only way to get to national parks and the more remote coastal areas is by **car**. Likewise, some of the most interesting places off the beaten track are only accessible in your own vehicle, as buses tend to ply just the major routes.

South Africa is ideal for driving, with a generally **well-maintained** network of highways and a high proportion of secondary and tertiary roads that are tarred and can be driven at speed. **Renting a vehicle** is not prohibitively expensive and, for a small group, it can work out to be a cheap option.

Filling stations are frequent on the major routes of the country, and usually open 24 hours. Off the beaten track, though, stations are less frequent, so fill up whenever you get the chance. Stations are rarely self-service; instead, poorly paid attendants fill up your car, check oil, water and tyre pressure if you ask them to, and often clean your windscreen even if you don't. A **tip** of R5 or so is always appreciated.

Parking is pretty straightforward, but due to the high levels of car break-ins, attendants, known as "car guards", are present virtually anywhere you'll find parking, for example at shopping malls. You're not obliged to give them anything, but a tip of R2–5 (depending on how long you've been parked) is generally appreciated.

Rules of the road and driving tips

Foreign driving licences are valid in South Africa for up to six months provided they are printed in English. If you don't have such a licence, you'll need to get an **International Driving Permit** (available from national motoring organizations) before arriving in South Africa. When driving, you are obliged by law to carry your driving **licence** and (unless you're a South African resident) your passport (or certified copies) at all times, although in reality, in the very rare event of your being stopped, the police will probably let you off with a warning if you're not carrying the required documents.

South Africans drive on the **left-hand side** of the road; speed limits range from 60km/h in built-up areas to 100km/h on rural roads and 120km/h on highways and major arteries. In addition to roundabouts, which follow the British rule of giving way to the right, there are four-way stops, where the rule is that the person who got there first leaves first. Note that traffic lights are called **robots** in South Africa.

The only real challenge you'll face on the roads is other drivers. South Africa has among the world's worst road **accident** statistics – the result of recklessness, drunken drivers (see p.74) and unroadworthy, overloaded vehicles. Keep your distance from cars in front, as domino-style pile-ups are common. Watch out also for overtaking traffic coming towards you: overtakers often assume that you will head for the **hard shoulder** to avoid an accident (it is legal to drive on the hard shoulder, but be careful as pedestrians frequently use it). If you do pull into the hard shoulder to let a car overtake, the other driver will probably thank you by flashing the hazard lights. If oncoming cars flash their headlights at you, it probably means that there is a speed trap up ahead.

Another potential **hazard** is animals on the road in rural areas; this can be especially dangerous at night, so drive slowly at that time. Also, the large distances between major towns mean that falling asleep at the wheel, especially when travelling through long stretches of flat landscape in the Karoo or the Free State, is a real danger. Plan your car journeys to include breaks and stopovers. Finally, in urban areas, there's a small risk of being car-jacked; see p.73 for safety hints.

South Africa's motoring organization, the **Automobile Association** (AA; ☎ 083 843 22, Ⓦ www.aa.co.za), provides useful information about road conditions as well as maps.

Car rental

Prebooking your **rental car** with a travel agent before flying out is the cheapest option, and will provide more favourable terms and conditions (such as unlimited mileage and lower insurance excesses). Don't rely on being able to just arrive at the airport and pick up a vehicle without reserving in advance as rental firms do run out of cars, especially during the week.

As a rough guideline, for a **one-week rental** you can expect to pay from R250 a day (with a R7000 insurance excess) including two hundred free kilometres a day. Most companies stipulate that drivers must be a minimum age of 23 and must have been driving for two years at least. Note that to collect your vehicle, you will need to produce a credit (not debit) card.

The advantage of renting through major companies is that you don't have to return the car to where you hired it, but can deposit it in some other major centre instead – though rental companies usually levy a charge for this. If you're planning to drive into **Lesotho** and **Swaziland**, check that the company allows it – some don't. **Insurance** often doesn't cover you if you drive on unsealed roads, so check for this too. Local firms are almost always cheaper than chains, but usually have restrictions on how far you can take the vehicle.

Camper vans and **4WD vehicles** equipped with rooftop tents can be a good idea for getting to remote places where accommodation is scarce. Expect to pay from R1000 a day for a vehicle that sleeps two. Some companies offer **standby rates** that knock fifteen to twenty percent off the price if you book at short notice (one week or less in advance). Vans come fully equipped with crockery, cutlery and linen and usually a toilet. The downside of camper vans and 4WDs is that they struggle up hills and guzzle a lot of fuel (15 litres per 100km in the smaller vans), which could partly offset any savings on accommodation.

RENTAL AGENCIES

Cheap Motorhome Rental ⓦ www.cheapmotorhomes.co.za. Booking agency that sources competitive motorhome rentals.

Drive Africa Cape Town ☎ 021 447 1144, ⓦ www.driveafrica .co.za. Competitive motor-home deals and cheap car rental. If you're planning to be on the road for three months or longer, consider their rental-purchase agreement, under which you buy a car and they guarantee to buy it back for an agreed price.

Kea Rentals ⓦ www.kea.co.za. Good-value motor-home rental.

Maui ⓦ www.maui.co.za. One of the biggest rental outlets for camper vans and 4WDs.

Tempest ☎ 086 003 1666, ⓦ www.tempestcarhire.co.za. Offers some very competitive rates.

Cycling

It's easy to see why **cycling** is popular in South Africa: you can get to stunning destinations on good roads unclogged by traffic, many towns have decent cycle shops for spares and equipment, and an increasing number of backpacker hostels rent out mountain bikes for reasonable rates, making it easy to do plenty of cycling without having to transport your bike into the country. You'll need to be fit though, as South Africa is a hilly place, and many roads have punishing gradients. The **weather** can make life difficult, too: if it isn't raining, there is a good chance of it being very hot, so carry plenty of liquids. Cycling on the main intercity roads is not recommended.

Hitching

Generally speaking, **hitching** in most areas of South Africa is not a good idea, particularly in large towns and cities. Even in rural areas it's **risky** and, while you might encounter wonderful hospitality and interesting companions, it's generally advisable not to hitch at all.

If you must hitchhike, avoid hitching alone and being dropped off in isolated areas between *dorps* (small towns). Ask drivers where they are going before you say where you want to go, and keep your **bags** with you: having them locked in the boot makes a hasty escape more difficult. Check the **notice boards** in backpacker lodges for people offering or looking to share lifts – that way, you can meet the driver in advance.

Accommodation

Relative to what's on offer in other developing countries, accommodation in South Africa may seem expensive, but standards are generally high and you get exceptional bang for your buck. Even the most modest backpacker lodge will provide a minimum of fresh sheets and clean rooms. Other than in the very cheapest rooms, a private bath or shower is almost always provided, and you'll often have the use of a garden or swimming pool. You're in luck if you're looking for something special as South Africa has some outstanding boutique hotels, luxury guesthouses, lodges and country retreats – invariably in beautiful

settings – at fairly reasonable prices by developed world standards. The country's national parks and reserves themselves feature a range of accommodation, from fairly basic restcamps to incredibly slick game lodges (see p.67).

The continuing growth of **backpacker accommodation** means you'll find a hostel in most areas, and many offer excellent facilities. For **camping** and **self-catering**, you'll be spoilt for choice.

Advance booking is vital if you're travelling in high season or if you plan to stay in a national park or in popular areas such as Cape Town or the Garden Route. South Africa's **peak season** is during the midsummer Christmas school holiday period, which coincides with many foreign tourists piling in to catch their winter tan. The Easter school holiday is a less intense period, when South African families migrate to the coast and inland resorts. At both Christmas and Easter, **prices** for budget and mid-priced accommodation (but not backpacker lodges or camping) can double, and most places get booked up months ahead (see p.77).

Hotels

Most of South Africa's **budget hotels** are throwbacks to the 1950s and 1960s. Most have degenerated into watering holes, earning most of their keep from the bar.

Mid-range hotels usually charge from R800 a room. Along the coastal holiday strips such as the Garden Route, southern KwaZulu-Natal and all the major seaside towns in between, these hotels are ubiquitous and frequently offer rooms on the **beachfront**. Many of the mid-priced hotels – especially those on main routes in the interior – are fully booked during the week by travelling salesmen, but over the weekend, when they're often empty, you can usually negotiate reasonable **discounts**.

A large number of mid-range and upmarket establishments belong to large hotel **chains**, of which Protea (ⓦwww.proteahotels.com) is the largest in the country. Other groups include Southern Sun (ⓦwww.southernsun.com), Holiday Inn (ⓦwww.ichotels.com) and Three Cities (ⓦwww.threecities.co.za), all of which offer reliable but sometimes soulless accommodation.

Country lodges and boutique hotels

If you're after somewhere special to stay and have a little money to burn you can get incredible value in South Africa at small, characterful establishments – something the country really excels at. You'll find hip **boutique hotels** in the cities and *dorps* and luxurious **country lodges** in exceptional natural surroundings: eco-lodges in the middle of forests, places perched on the edges of cliffs and magical hideaways in the middle of nowhere. For a really memorable stay expect to pay from R1500 a room, but more usually from R2000. At these places you can expect to be **pampered** and there will often be a spa on site. There are also numerous first-rate **safari camps** and **game lodges**, which fulfil all those Out-of-Africa fantasies (see p.67).

B&Bs and guesthouses

The most ubiquitous form of accommodation in South Africa is in **B&Bs** and **guesthouses**. The official difference between the two is that the owner lives on site at a B&B. The most basic B&Bs are just one or two rooms in a private home, with washing facilities shared with the owners. In reality, the distinction is a little hazy once you move up a notch to B&Bs and guesthouses that provide en-suite rooms (as is usually the case). **Rates** for en-suite rooms in both start at around R400, for which you can expect somewhere clean, comfortable and relaxed, but usually away from the beach or other action. Moving up a notch, you'll be paying from R600 for a room with a bit extra, and anything from R1000 upwards should offer the works: a great location, comfort and good service.

For decades the homes of black South Africans were deliberately kept hidden from tourist trails, a situation that has changed dramatically with the proliferation of **township tours**. Since the late 1990s, township dwellers have begun offering accommodation, opening up new possibilities for experiencing South Africa. **Township B&Bs** are still few in number, but we've tried to cover as many as possible in the Guide; expect to pay from R500 per room per night for this type of accommodation.

Along many roads in the countryside you will see signs for "**Bed en Ontbyt**" (Afrikaans for "bed and breakfast"), signalling **farmstay** accommodation. These offer rooms in the main homestead or in a cottage in its garden. Some offer hiking, horse-riding, and other **activities** and excursions – there are some real gems dotted about, which we've listed in this Guide. Tourist offices almost always have lists of farms in the area that rent out rooms or cottages.

ONLINE ACCOMMODATION RESOURCES

B&BS, GUESTHOUSES AND SELF-CATERING

ⓦ **www.budgetgetaways.co.za** The best resource for affordable (under R350/person) self-catering accommodation in the Western Cape.

ⓦ **www.greenwoodguides.com/south-africa** Although properties pay to be listed, this site's handpicked selection is interesting and quirky.

ⓦ **www.portfolioofplaces.co.za** The online presence of Portfolio Collection, in which properties pay through the nose to be listed, but also have to meet fairly rigorous standards.

ⓦ **www.safarinow.com** One of the oldest and best South African online booking sites covers all types of accommodation – not just safaris – with user reviews and rankings.

BACKPACKERS

ⓦ www.backpackingsouthafrica.co.za Internet presence of the South African Youth Travel Confederation, a non-profit organization that represents various players in the youth travel sector. Good accommodation links.

ⓦ **www.bazbus.co.za** Website of South Africa's biggest backpacker bus service also provides links to lodges with an online booking facility.

ⓦ **www.hihostels.com** Hostelling International acts as a booking agent for a large number of South Africa's backpacker lodges.

ⓦ **www.hostelbookers.com** International website with clear navigation and good coverage of South African hostels, including user reviews and ratings.

CAMPING AND CARAVAN PARKS

ⓦ **www.sa-venues.com** General accommodation website that has a good section on camping and caravan parks.

Caravan parks, resorts and camping

Caravanning was once the favourite way to have a cheap family holiday in South Africa, and this accounts for the very large number of caravan parks dotted across the length and breadth of the country. However, their popularity has declined and with it the standard of many of the country's municipal caravan parks and campsites. Today, **municipal campsites** are generally pretty scruffy, though you may find the odd pleasant one in rural areas, or near small *dorps*. Staying in a municipal campsite adjoining a city or large town is often more grief than it's worth; not only will facilities be run-down, but theft is a big risk. Municipal sites cost around R80 per tent.

All in all, you're best off heading for the privately owned **resorts**, where for roughly the same price you get greater comfort. Although private resorts sometimes give off a holiday-camp vibe, they usually provide good washing and cooking **facilities**, self-catering chalets, shops selling basic goods, braai stands and swimming pools.

Virtually all **national parks** – and many provincial reserves – have campsites, and in some of the really remote places, such as parts of KwaZulu-Natal, camping may be your only option. Use of a **campsite** will cost R150–250 per site depending on the popularity of the park and the facilities. At national parks you can expect well-maintained washing facilities and there are often communal kitchen areas or, at the very least, a braai stand and running water, as well as a decent communal shower, toilet and washing facilities (known locally as "ablutions").

Camping rough is not recommended anywhere in the country.

Backpacker lodges

The cheapest beds in South Africa are in **dormitories** at backpacker lodges (or hostels), which go for around R120 per person. These are generally well-run operations with clean linen and helpful staff. In the cities and tourist resorts you'll have a number of places to choose from and virtually any town of any significance has at least one.

Apart from dorm beds, most also have **private rooms** (R200–300) – sometimes even with private bathrooms – and an increasing number have **family rooms** that work out at around R125 per person. They usually have communal kitchens, an on-site restaurant, TV, internet access and often other facilities such as bike rental. When choosing a hostel, it's worth checking out the **ambience** as some are party joints, while others have a quieter atmosphere.

The lodges are invariably good meeting points, with a constant stream of travellers passing through, and useful **notice boards** filled with advertisements for hostels and backpacker facilities throughout the country. Many lodges operate reasonably priced **excursions** into the surrounding areas, and will pick you up from train stations or bus stops (especially Baz Bus stops) if you phone in advance.

Self-catering cottages and apartments

Away from the resorts and caravan parks, **self-catering accommodation** in cottages, apartments and small complexes provides the cheapest option apart from staying in a backpackers' lodge. One of the best things about self-catering is the wide **choice** of location: there are self-catering places on farms, near beaches, in forests and in wilderness areas, as well as in practically every town and city.

There's a wide range of this type of accommodation starting from under R500 a night. **Apartments** often sleep up to six, and because rates are mostly quoted for entire units, this can be very economical if you're travelling as a family or in a group. You can save a lot of money by cooking for yourself, and you'll get a sense of **freedom** and **privacy** which is missing from even the nicest guesthouse or B&B. Standards are high: cottages or apartments generally come fully equipped with crockery and cutlery, and even microwaves and TVs in the more modern places. Linen and towels are often provided; check before you book in.

Eating and drinking

South Africa doesn't really have a coherent indigenous cuisine, although attempts have been made to elevate Cape Cuisine to this status. The one element that seems to unite the country is a love of meat. It's also well worth paying attention to South Africa's vast array of seafood (see box, p.58), which includes a wide variety of fish, lobster (crayfish), oysters and mussels. Locally grown fruit and vegetables are generally of a high standard.

There is no great tradition of street food and people on the move tend to pick up a pie or chicken and chips from one of the fast-food chains. Drinking is dominated by South Africa's often superb wines and by a handful of unmemorable lagers. In the cities, and to a far lesser extent beyond them, there are numerous excellent restaurants where you can taste a spectrum of international styles.

Breakfast, lunch and dinner

South Africa's daily culinary timetable follows the British model. Most B&Bs, hotels and guesthouses serve a **breakfast** of eggs with bacon and usually some kind of sausage. Muesli, fruit, yoghurt, croissants and pastries are also becoming increasingly popular. **Lunch** is eaten around 1pm and **dinner** in the evening around 7pm or 8pm; the two can be pretty much interchangeable as far as the menu goes, usually along the lines of meat, chicken or fish and veg: in fact, any of the dishes mentioned below.

Styles of cooking

Traditional African food tends to focus around stiff grain **porridge** called *mielie pap* or *pap* (pronounced: "pup"), made of maize meal and accompanied by meat or vegetable-based sauces. Among white South Africans, Afrikaners have evolved a style of cooking known as **boerekos** (see opposite), which can be heavy-going if you're not used to it.

Some of the best-known South African **foods** are mentioned below, while there's a list of South African culinary terms, including other local foods, in the Language section (see p.683).

Braais

Braai (which rhymes with "dry") is an abbreviation of *braaivleis*, an Afrikaans word translated as "meat grill". More than simply the process of cooking over an outdoor fire, however, a braai is a cultural event arguably even more central to the South African identity than barbecues are to Australians. A braai is an intensely social event, usually among family and friends and accompanied by gallons of **beer**. It's also probably the only occasion when you'll catch an unreconstructed South African man cooking.

You can braai anything, but a traditional barbecue meal consists of huge slabs of **steak**, **lamb cutlets** and **boerewors** ("farmer's sausage"), a South African speciality. Potatoes, onions and butternut squash wrapped in aluminium foil and placed in the embers are the usual accompaniment.

Potjiekos and boerekos

A variant on the braai is **potjiekos** – pronounced "poy-key-kos" – (pot food), in which the food is cooked in a three-legged cast-iron cauldron (the

VEGETARIAN FOOD

While not quite a **vegetarian** paradise, South Africa is nevertheless vegetarian-savvy and you'll find at least one concession to meatless food on most menus. Even steakhouses will have something palatable on offer and generally offer good salad bars. If you're self-catering in the larger cities, delicious dips and breads can be found at delis and Woolworths and Pick 'n Pay supermarkets.

potjie), preferably outdoors over an open fire. In a similar vein, but cooked indoors, is **boerekos**, (literally "farmer's food"), a style of cooking enjoyed mainly by Afrikaners. Much of it is similar to English food, but taken to cholesterol-rich extremes, with even the vegetables prepared with butter and sugar. *Boerekos* comes into its own in its variety of over-the-top **desserts**, including *koeksisters* (plaited doughnuts saturated with syrup) and *melktert* ("milk tart"), a solid, rich custard in a flan case.

Cape Cuisine

Styles of cooking brought to South Africa by **Asian** and **Madagascan** slaves have evolved into **Cape Cuisine** (sometimes known as Cape Malay food). Characterized by mild, semi-sweet **curries** with strong Indonesian influences, Cape Cuisine is worth sampling, especially in Cape Town, where it developed and is associated with the Muslim community. Dishes include *bredie* (stew), of which *waterblommetjiebredie*, made using water hyacinths, is a speciality; *bobotie*, a spicy minced dish served under a savoury custard; and *sosaties*, a local version of kebab using minced meat. For **dessert**, dates stuffed with almonds make a light and delicious end to a meal, while *malva* pudding is a rich combination of milk, sugar, cream and apricot jam.

Although Cape Cuisine can be delicious, there isn't that much **variety** and few restaurants specialize in it. Despite this, most of the dishes considered as Cape Cuisine have actually crept into the South African diet, many becoming part of the Afrikaner culinary vocabulary.

Other ethnic and regional influences

Although South Africa doesn't really have distinct **regional** cuisines, you will find changes of emphasis and local specialities in different parts of the country. KwaZulu-Natal, for instance, particularly around Durban and Pietermaritzburg, is especially good for **Indian** food. The South African contribution to this great multifaceted tradition is the humble **bunny chow**, a cheap takeaway consisting of a hollowed-out half-loaf of white bread originally filled with curried beans, but nowadays with anything from curried chicken to sardines.

Portuguese food made early inroads into the country because of South Africa's proximity to Mozambique. The Portuguese influence is predominantly seen in the use of hot and spicy peri-peri seasoning, which goes extremely well with braais. The best-known example of this is delicious peri-peri chicken, which you will find all over the country.

Eating out

Restaurants in South Africa offer good value compared with Britain or North America. In every city you'll find places where you can eat a decent main course for under R100, while for R200 you can splurge on the best. All the cities and larger towns boast some restaurants with imaginative menus. **Franschhoek**, a small town in the Winelands (see p.170), has established itself as a culinary centre for the country, where you'll find a number of fine eating places in extremely close proximity to each other. As a rule, restaurants are **licensed**, but Muslim establishments serving Cape Cuisine don't allow alcohol at all.

An attractive phenomenon in the big cities, especially Cape Town, has been the rise of continental-style **cafés** – easy-going places where you can eat just as well as you would in a regular restaurant, but also drink **coffee** all night without feeling obliged to order food. Service tends to be slick and friendly, and a reasonable meal in one of these cafés is unlikely to set you back more than R75.

Don't confuse these with traditional South African cafés, found in even the tiniest country town. The equivalent of **corner stores** elsewhere, they commonly sell a few magazines, soft drinks, sweets, crisps and an odd collection of tins and dry goods, though no sit-down meals.

If popularity is the yardstick, then South Africa's real national cuisine is to be found in its **franchise restaurants**, which you'll find in every town of any size. The usual international names like **KFC** and **Wimpy** are omnipresent, as are South Africa's own home-grown offerings, such as the American-style steakhouse chain, **Spur**, and the much-exported **Nando's** chain, which grills excellent Portuguese-style chicken, served under a variety of spicy sauces.

Expect to pay around R40 for a burger and chips or chicken meal at any of these places, and twice that for a good-sized steak. Note that quite a few restaurants don't have well-defined hours of business, in which case we have stated in the Guide which meals they tend to open for. Phone numbers are given where **booking** a table might be a good idea.

Drinking

White South Africans do a lot of their drinking **at home**, so, for them, pubs and bars are not quite the centres of social activity they are in the US or the UK, though in the African townships **shebeens** (informal bars) do occupy this role. Having said that, in recent years South African drinking culture has seen a shift with a plethora of sports bars springing up, with huge screens that draw in crowds when there's a big match on, though at other times they are relaxed places for a drink. You'll also find drinking spots in city centres and suburbs that conform more to European-style café-bars than British pubs, and which serve booze, coffee and light meals. The closest thing to British-style pubs is the themed restaurant-bar franchises, such the *Keg* chain or *O'Hagans Irish Pub and Grill*.

Beer, wines and spirits can by law be sold from Monday to Saturday between 9am and 6pm at **bottle stores** (the equivalent of the British off-licence) and also at most supermarkets, although you'll still be able to drink at a restaurant or pub outside these hours.

There are no surprises when it comes to **soft drinks**, with all the usual names available. What does stand out is South African **fruit juice**, the range amounting to one of the most extensive selections of unsweetened juices in the world. One unusual drink you might well encounter in the country's tearooms is locally produced rooibos (or redbush) tea, made from the leaves of an indigenous plant (see box, p.258).

Beer

Although South Africa is a major wine-producing country, **beer** is indisputably the national drink. Beer is as much an emblem of South African manhood as the braai and it cuts across all racial and class divisions. South Africans tend to be fiercely loyal to their brand of beer, though they all taste pretty much the same, given that the vast majority of beer in the country is produced by the enormous **South African Breweries** monopoly. In fact, so big is SAB that in 2002 it bought Miller Brewing, the second-largest beer producer in the US, and formed SABMiller, one of the biggest brewers in the world. The advantage for South Africans was that a number of international labels became available to supplement the pretty undistinguished and indistinguishable local offerings dominated by Castle, Hansa and Carling Black Label lagers, which are likely to taste a bit thin and bland to a British palate, though they can be refreshing drunk ice-cold on a sweltering day. According to local beer aficionados, the SAB offerings are given a good run for their money by Windhoek Lager, produced by Namibian Breweries. Other widely available SAB offerings from their international subsidiaries are Peroni, Miller Genuine Draft, Grolsch and, the best of the lot, Pilsner Urquell.

GREEN AROUND THE GILLS: SUSTAINABLE SEAFOOD

Overfishing has brought global fish stocks to the brink – if it isn't controlled, stocks will collapse within a generation.

In South Africa, the Southern Africa Sustainable Seafood Initiative (SASSI) is a programme set up by the World Wildlife Fund South Africa to educate consumers about this issue and to encourage them to use seafood responsibly. SASSI places seafood on one of three lists:

- Red – endangered species which are illegal to sell or buy; avoid.
- Orange – species you can buy, but about which there are environmental concerns; think twice.
- Green – the list you are encouraged to choose from, because populations are healthiest and most sustainable.

HOW GREEN IS MY FISH?

Many restaurants, fishmongers and supermarkets in South Africa are aware of the issue and try as far as possible to sell only green-list fish, but as this is a relatively new initiative not all restaurant staff are aware of the issue. This isn't an obstacle, since you can use your mobile phone to find out which list a fish species is on, by texting its name to ☏079 499 8795 and waiting for an automatic text response; or visiting ⓦwwfsassi.mobi or ⓦwwfsassi.co.za.

There are one or two **microbreweries**, best known of which are Mitchell's in Knysna, which produces some distinctive ales, and Birkenhead in Stanford. Their beers can be found at some bottle stores and bars between Cape Town and Port Elizabeth.

Wine

South Africa is one of the world's top ten winemaking countries by volume. In 2010 it overtook France to become the UK's biggest wine supplier. Despite South Africa's having the longest-established New World winemaking tradition (going back over 350 years), this rapid rise is remarkable in having taken place within the past two post-apartheid decades. Before that, South Africa's isolation had led to a stagnant and inbred industry that produced heavy Bordeaux-style wines. After the arrival of democracy in 1994, winemakers began producing fresher, fruitier New World wines, but many quaffers still turned their wine-tasting noses up at them. It's over the last ten years that things have really started to rev up, and some South African winemakers are developing excellent wines that combine the best of the Old and New Worlds.

South Africa produces wines from a whole gamut of major cultivars. Of the **whites**, the top South African Sauvignon Blancs can stand up with the best the New World has to offer, and among the **reds** it's the blends that really shine. Also look out for red wine made from Pinotage grapes – a somewhat controversial curiosity unique to South Africa – which its detractors, perhaps unfairly, say should stay on the vine. **Port** is also made, and the best vintages come from the Little Karoo town of Calitzdorp along the R62 (see p.193). There are also a handful of excellent **sparkling wines**, including Champagne-style, fermented-in-the-bottle bubbly, known locally as **methode cap classique** (MCC).

Wine is available throughout the country, although prices rise as you move out of the Western Cape. **Prices** start at under R30 a bottle, and you can get something pretty decent for twice that – the vast bulk of wines cost less than R100 – but you can spend upwards of R250 for a truly great vintage. All this means that anyone with an adventurous streak can indulge in a bacchanalia of sampling without breaking the bank.

The best way to sample wines is by visiting **wineries**, some of which charge a small tasting fee to discourage freeloading. The oldest and most rewarding wine-producing regions are the **Constantia estates** in Cape Town (see p.110) and the region known as **the Winelands** around the towns of Stellenbosch (see p.168), Paarl (see p.174) and Franschhoek (see p.178), which all have well-established **wine routes**. Other wine-producing areas include **Robertson** (see p.185), the **Orange River** (see p.279) and **Walker Bay** (see p.206).

The media

South Africa lacks a strong tradition of national newspapers and instead has many regional publications of varying quality. Television delivers a mix of imported programmes and home-grown soaps heavily modelled on US fare, as well as the odd home-grown reality TV show and one or two watchable documentary slots. Radio is where South Africa is finding it easiest to meet the needs of a diverse and scattered audience, and deregulation of the airwaves has brought to life scores of small new stations.

Newspapers

Of the roughly twenty daily **newspapers**, most of which are published in English or Afrikaans, the only two that qualify as nationals are *Business Day* (🌐 www.businessday.co.za), which is a good source of serious national and international news, and *The New Age* (🌐 www.thenewage.co.za), which is aligned with the government.

Each of the larger cities has its own English-language **broadsheet**, most of them published by South Africa's largest newspaper publisher, **Independent News & Media**, a subsidiary of the Irish company that owns London's *Independent* newspaper and the *Irish Independent*. In Johannesburg, **The Star** (🌐 www.thestar.co.za), the group's South African flagship, has a roughly equal number of black and white readers and offers somewhat uninspired Jo'burg coverage, padded out with international bits and pieces piped in from Dublin and London. Cape Town's morning **Cape Times** (🌐 www.capetimes.co.za) and **Cape Argus** (🌐 www.capeargus.co.za), published in the afternoon, follow broadly the same tried (and tired) formula, as do the **Pretoria News** (🌐 www.pretorianews.co.za), the **Herald** (🌐 www.theherald.co.za) in Port Elizabeth and the **Daily News** (🌐 www.dailynews.co.za) in Durban.

The country's biggest-selling paper is the **Daily Sun**, a Jo'burg-based tabloid that taps into the concerns of township dwellers, with a giddy cocktail of gruesome crime stories, tales of witchcraft and the supernatural, and coverage of the everyday problems of ordinary people. Another Jo'burg tabloid is the **Sowetan** (W www.sowetan .co.za), which has been going since the 1980s, but is a far more serious publication than the *Sun*. In Cape Town, the studiedly sleazy **Voice** attempts to emulate the *Sun* in the coloured community, with a downbeat mixture of crime, the supernatural and sex advice.

Unquestionably the country's intellectual heavyweight, the **Mail & Guardian** (W www.mg.co.za), published every Friday, frequently delivers nonpartisan and fearless investigative journalism, but at times tends towards the turgid.

The Sunday Times (W www.sundaytimes.co.za), on the other hand, can attribute its sales – roughly half a million copies – to its well-calculated mix of investigative reporting, gossipy stories and rewrites of salacious scandal lifted from foreign tabloids, while the **Sunday Independent** (W www.sunday independent.co.za), from the *Independent* stable, projects a more thoughtful image but is a bit thin.

The easiest places to buy newspapers are corner stores and newsagents, especially the **CNA** chain. These outlets also sell **international publications** such as *Time*, *Newsweek*, *The Economist* and the weekly overseas editions of the British *Daily Mail*, the *Telegraph* and the *Express* – you'll also find copies of the daily and weekend international editions of the *Financial Times*.

Television

The **South Africa Broadcasting Corporation**'s three TV channels churn out a mixed bag of domestic dramas, sport, game shows, soaps and documentaries, filled out with lashings of familiar imports. SABC 1, 2 and 3 share the unenviable task of trying to deliver an integrated service, while having to split their time between the **eleven official languages**. English turns out to be most widely used, with SABC 3 (W www.sabc3.co.za) broadcasting almost exclusively in the language, with a high proportion of British and US comedies and dramas, while SABC 2 (W www.sabc2.co.za) and SABC 1 (W www.sabc1.co.za) spread themselves thinly across all the remaining ten languages with a fair amount of English creeping in too. SABC 1, with its high proportion of sports coverage, has the most viewers.

South Africa's first and only free-to-air independent **commercial channel** e.tv (W www .etv.co.za) won its franchise in 1998 on the promise of providing a showcase for local productions, a pledge it has signally failed to meet.

There is no **cable TV** in South Africa, but DSTV (W www.dstv.co.za) offers a satellite television subscription service with a selection of sports, movies, news and specialist channels, some of which are piped into hotels.

Radio

Given South Africa's low literacy rate and widespread poverty, it's no surprise that **radio** is its most popular medium. The SABC operates a national radio station for each of the eleven official language groups. The English-language service, SAfm (W www.safm.co.za), is increasingly degenerating into tedious wall-to-wall talk shows interspersed with news. The SABC also runs 5FM Stereo, a national pop station broadcasting Top 40 tracks, while its Radio Metro is targeted at black urban listeners.

To get a taste of what makes South Africans tick, tune into the privately owned **Gauteng talk station 702** (in Jo'burg 92.7 FM and in Pretoria 106 FM; W www.702.co.za) or its Cape Town sister station **CapeTalk** (567 AM; W www.capetalk.co.za), both of which are a lot livelier than the state stations and broadcast news, weather, traffic and sports reports. Apart from these, there are scores of regional, commercial and community stations, broadcasting a range of music and other material, which makes surfing the airwaves an enjoyable experience, wherever you are in the country.

Festivals

South Africa has no shortage of events – there are over eighty music festivals each year, nine of them over the Easter weekend alone. Apart from these there are umpteen minor events in countless small towns. Diverting as these may be, you aren't going to plan your trip around them, but there are a number of more significant events (listed below) that may be worth pencilling into your holiday diary. Although Johannesburg and Cape Town tend to dominate, the country's two biggest cultural events, the National Arts Festival and the Klein Karoo Nasionale Kunstefees, both take place in small Karoo towns (Grahamstown and Oudtshoorn respectively) that, once things get humming, swell to twice their normal size.

JANUARY

Cape Town Minstrel Carnival Cape Town South Africa's longest and most raucous annual party brings over ten thousand spectators to watch the parade through the city centre on January 2 for the Tweede Nuwe Jaar or "Second New Year" celebrations. Brightly decked-out minstrel troupes parade, and vie in singing and dancing contests. Tickets (R30–60) can be reserved through Computicket (Ⓦ computicket.com).

Maynardville Shakespeare Festival Cape Town Ⓦ maynardville.co.za. A usually imaginative production of one of the Bard's plays is staged each year in the beautiful setting of the Maynardville Open Air Theatre in Wynberg.

FEBRUARY

Cape Town Pride Pageant Ⓦ capetownpride.co.za. Series of gay-themed events over two weeks, taking in a bunch of parties and a street parade.

FNB Dance Umbrella Johannesburg Ⓦ at.artslink.co.za/~arts /umbrella. The country's leading contemporary dance festival showcases a diversity of local forms from mid-February to mid-March.

MARCH

Cape Argus Pick 'n Pay Cycle Tour Cape Town (see p..000). The largest, and arguably most spectacular, individually timed bike race in the world, much of it along the ocean's edge, draws many thousands of spectators.

Cape Town International Jazz Festival Cape Town Ⓦ www .capetownjazzfest.com. Initiated in 2000 as the Cape Town counterpart of the world-famous North Sea Jazz Festival, this event is held over the last weekend of the month and draws leading local and international performers.

APRIL

Out in Africa South African Gay & Lesbian Film Festival Cape Town and Johannesburg Ⓦoia.co.za. Purportedly the most popular movie festival in the country, screening gay- and lesbian-themed international and local productions over the first ten days of the month.

Klein Karoo Nasionale Kunstefees Oudtshoorn, Western Cape Ⓦ kknk.co.za. South Africa's largest Afrikaans arts and culture festival turns the otherwise dozy Karoo *dorp* of Oudtshoorn into one big jumping party with a significant English-language component.

Two Oceans Marathon Cape Town Ⓦ twooceansmarathon .org.za. Another of the Western Cape's big sporting events is this 56-kilometre ultra-marathon, which bills itself as "the world's most beautiful marathon", with huge crowds lining the route to cheer on participants.

Splashy Fen Music Festival Underberg, KwaZulu-Natal Ⓦ www.splashyfen.co.za. Held during the second half of the month, South Africa's oldest music festival draws thousands of punters to a beautiful farm in the Drakensberg foothills, with a spread of mainstream and alternative rock and pop and a kids' programme too.

Pink Loerie Mardi Gras Knysna, Western Cape Ⓦ www .pinkloeriemardigras.com. Five-day gay pride celebration of parties, contests, cabaret, drag shows and performance in South Africa's oyster capital.

MAY

Franschhoek Literary Festival Franschhoek, Western Cape Ⓦ flf.co.za. Three day celebration of books, writers and wine, featuring leading local and international writers, editors and cartoonists.

Good Food & Wine Show Cape Town Ⓦ gourmetsa.com. Celebrity chefs from around the world cooking live is just one of the compelling attractions that make this the foodie event of the year. There are also hands-on workshops, delicious nibbles and wine as well as kitchen implements and books for sale. The event is also held in Johannesburg (Sept) and Durban (July).

Comrades Marathon Durban/Pietermaritzburg, KwaZulu-Natal Ⓦ www.comrades.com. A national institution, held at the end of the month. The Comrades, run along the 80km between Durban and Pietermaritzburg, attracts around thirteen thousand runners, many of them international competitors, and is followed by a huge TV audience.

JUNE

National Arts Festival Grahamstown, Eastern Cape (see p.326). The largest arts festival in Africa, with its own fringe festival – ten days of jazz, classical music, dance, cabaret and theatre spanning every conceivable type of performance.

Encounters South African International Documentary Film Festival Johannesburg and Cape Town Ⓦ encounters.co.za. Fortnight-long showcase of documentary film-making from South Africa and the world.

UN Comedy Festival Johannesburg. Spin-off of the older Cape Town Comedy Festival (see p.62).

JULY

Knysna Oyster Festival Knysna, Western Cape Ⓦ oysterfestival .co.za. Ten days of carousing and oyster-eating along the Garden Route with lots of wine-tasting and other satellite events in between.

Good Food & Wine Show Durban Ⓦ gourmetsa.com. See May.

Durbs Comedy Festival Durban. Spin-off of the older Cape Town Comedy Festival (see p.62).

AUGUST

Oppikoppi Bushveld Festival Northam, North West Province Ⓦ oppikoppi.co.za. South Africa's scaled-down answer to Woodstock, Oppikoppi (Afrikaans for "on the hill") brings the bushveld hills alive with the sound of music, as some sixty local and foreign bands rock the bundu (equivalent of Aussie "outback") for four days and nights.

Joy of Jazz Johannesburg Ⓦ joyofjazz.co.za. Jo'burg's flagship jazz festival offers three days of varied music in the Newtown precinct.

SEPTEMBER

Arts Alive Johannesburg Ⓦ artsalive.co.za. Jo'burg's largest arts event features a month of dance, visual art, poetry and music at venues in Newtown, the cultural precinct in the inner city.

Hermanus Whale Festival Hermanus, Western Cape Ⓦ whalefestival.co.za. To coincide with the peak whale-watching season, the southern Cape town of Hermanus (see p.203) stages its annual festival over several days towards the end of the month with plays, a craft market, a children's festival and live music.

Out of the Box Festival Cape Town ⓦ unimasouthafrica.org. Extraordinary week-long event that brings together exciting puppetry from all over the subcontinent and beyond with family, adult and film programmes.

Cape Town Comedy Festival Cape Town ⓦ comedyfestival .co.za. .Africa's biggest comedy festival brings the world's hottest acts to the Mother City for a week.

Good Food & Wine Show Johannesburg ⓦ gourmetsa.com. See May.

NOVEMBER TO MARCH

Kirstenbosch Summer Sunset Concerts Cape Town ☎021 799 8783. Popular concerts held on the magnificent lawns of the botanical gardens at the foot of Table Mountain. Performances begin at 5.30pm and cover a range of genres. Come early to find a parking place, bring a picnic and some Cape bubbly, and kick back. Tickets available at the gate.

DECEMBER

Mother City Queer Projects Cape Town (see p.154). A hugely popular party attracting thousands of gay revellers. Outlandish get-ups, multiple dancefloors and a mood of sustained delirium make this event a real draw.

Carols by Candlelight at Kirstenbosch Cape Town ☎ 021 799 8783. The botanical gardens' annual carol-singing and Nativity tableaux – staged on the Thursday to the Sunday before Christmas – is a Cape Town institution, drawing crowds of families with their picnic baskets. Gates open at 7pm and the singing kicks off at 8pm.

Franschhoek Cap Classique and Champagne Festival Franschhoek ⓦ webtickets.co.za. Popular three-day bacchanalia of bubbly sampling – a vast selection of local and French sparkling wine is on hand – and gourmandizing in the Cape Winelands.

DECEMBER TO MARCH

Spier Summer Festival Spier Wine Estate, Stellenbosch, Western Cape ⓦ spier.co.za. Four months of major arts events, which are increasingly taking on an African flavour, featuring music, opera, dance, stand-up comedy and theatre.

Activities and outdoor pursuits

South Africa's diverse landscape of mountains, forests, rugged coast and sandy beaches, as well as kilometres of veld and game-trampled national parks, make the country supreme outdoor terrain. This fact hasn't been overlooked by South Africans themselves, who have been playing outdoors for decades. The result is a well-developed infrastructure for activities, an impressive national network of hiking trails and plenty of commercial operators selling adventure sports.

Hiking trails

South Africa has an incredibly comprehensive system of **footpaths** (inspired by the US Appalachian Hiking Trail). Wherever you are – even in the middle of Johannesburg – you won't be far from some sort of trail. The best ones are in wilderness areas, where you'll find **waymarked paths**, from half-hour strolls to major hiking expeditions of several days that take you right into the heart of some of the most beautiful parts of the country.

Overnight trails are normally well laid out, with painted route markers, and campsites or huts along the way. Numbers are limited on most, and many trails are so popular that you may need to book months (up to eleven months in some cases) in advance to use them (details are given in the Guide).

There are also **guided wilderness trails**, where you walk in game country accompanied by an armed guide. These walks should be regarded as a way to get a feel for the wild rather than actually see any wildlife, as you'll encounter far fewer animals on foot than from a vehicle. Specialist trails include mountain biking, canoeing and horseback trails. A handful of trails have also been set up specifically for people with disabilities, mostly for the visually impaired or people confined to wheelchairs.

Watersports

South Africa has some of the world's finest **surfing** breaks. The country's perfect wave at Jeffrey's Bay was immortalized on celluloid in the 1960s cult movie *Endless Summer*, but any surfer will tell you that there are equally good, if not better, breaks all the way along the coast from Namibia to Mozambique.

Surfers can be a cliquey bunch, but the South African community is reputedly among the friendliest in the world and, provided you pay your dues, you should find yourself easily accepted. Some of the world's top shapers work here, and you can pick up an excellent **board** at a fraction of the European or US price. **Boogie-boarding** and **body-surfing** make easy alternatives to the real thing, require less skill and dedication and are great fun. **Windsurfing** (or sailboarding) is another popular sport you'll find at many resorts, where you can rent gear.

On inland waterways, South African holidaymakers are keen **speedboaters**, an activity that goes hand in hand with **waterskiing**. **Kayaking** and **canoeing** are also very popular, and you can often

BEACH CONDITIONS

Don't expect balmy Mediterranean seas in South Africa: of its 2500km of coastline, only the stretch along the Indian Ocean seaboard of KwaZulu-Natal and the northern section of the Eastern Cape can be considered **tropical**, and along the entire coast an energetic surf pounds the shore. In Cape Town, sea bathing is only comfortable between November and March. Generally, the further east you go from here, the warmer the water becomes and the longer the **bathing season**. Sea temperatures that rarely drop below 18°C make the KwaZulu-Natal coast warm enough for a dip at any time of year.

A word of warning: dangerous **undertows** and **riptides** are present along the coast and you should try to bathe where lifeguards are present. Failing that (and guards aren't that common away from main resorts out of season), you should follow local advice, never swim alone, and always treat the ocean with respect.

rent craft at resorts or national parks that lie along rivers. For the more adventurous, there's **whitewater rafting**, with some decent trips along the Tugela River in KwaZulu-Natal and on the Orange River.

Diving and snorkelling

Scuba diving is popular, and South Africa is one of the cheapest places in the world to get an internationally recognized open water certificate. **Courses** start at around R3300 (including gear) and are available at all the coastal cities as well as a number of other resorts. The most rewarding diving is along the St Lucia Marine Reserve on the northern KwaZulu-Natal coast, which hosts 100,000 dives every year for its coral reefs and fluorescent fish.

You won't find corals and bright colours along the Cape coast, but the huge number of sunken vessels makes **wreck-diving** popular, and you can encounter the swaying rhythms of giant kelp forests. There are a couple of places along the southern Cape and Garden Route where you can go on **shark-cage dives** and come face to face with deadly great whites.

KwaZulu-Natal is also good for **snorkelling** and there are some underwater trails elsewhere in the country, most notable of which is in the Tsitsikamma National Park.

Other activities

Fishing is another well-developed South African activity and the coasts yield 250 species caught through rock, bay or surf angling. Inland you'll find plenty of rivers and dams stocked with freshwater fish, while trout fishing is extremely well established in Mpumalanga, the northern sections of the Eastern Cape and the KwaZulu-Natal Midlands.

There are ample opportunities for aerial activities.

In the Winelands you can go **ballooning**, while **paragliding** offers a thrilling way to see Cape Town, by diving off Lion's Head and riding the thermals. More down-to-earth options include **mountaineering** and **rock climbing**, both of which have a huge following in South Africa. In a similar vein is **kloofing** (or canyoning), in which participants trace the course of a deep ravine by climbing, scrambling, jumping, abseiling or using any other means.

If you can't choose between being airborne and being earthbound, you can always bounce between the two by **bungee jumping** off the Gouritz River Bridge near Mossel Bay – the world's highest commercial jump.

Horseriding is a sport you'll find at virtually every resort, whether inland or along the coast, for trips of two hours or two days. Take your own hat, as not everyone provides them. **Birdwatching** is another activity you can do almost anywhere, either casually on your own, or as part of a guided trip with one of the several experts operating in South Africa. Among the very best birdwatching spots are Mkhuze and Ndumo game reserves in KwaZulu-Natal.

Golf lovers will have a fabulous time in South Africa as courses are prolific and frequently in stunningly beautiful locations. Finally, if you decide to go **skiing** at one or two resorts in the Eastern and Western Cape, you'll be able to go home with a quirky experience of Africa.

Spectator sports

South Africa is a nation obsessed by sport, where heights of devotion are reached whenever local or international teams take to the field. Winning performances, controversial selections and scandals commonly dominate the front

as well as the back pages of newspapers, and it can be hard to escape the domination of sport across radio, television and advertising media. The major spectator sports are football, rugby and cricket, and big matches involving the international team or heavyweight local clubs are well worth seeing live.

Football

Football is the country's most popular game, with a primarily black and coloured following, and it is now starting to attract serious money.

The professional **season** runs from August to May, with teams competing in the **Premier Soccer League** (ⓦwww.thepsl.co.za) and a couple of knock-out cup competitions. Unlike rugby teams, football teams do not own their own grounds and are forced to rent them for specific fixtures. In Gauteng, the heartland of South African football, all the big clubs use the same **grounds**, which has prevented the development of the kind of terrace fan culture found elsewhere. Nonetheless, football **crowds** are generally witty and good-spirited. The very big games, normally involving Johannesburg's two big teams, **Kaizer Chiefs** and **Orlando Pirates**, do simmer with tension, though violence is rare. Although Chiefs and Pirates are both Sowetan clubs, they have a nationwide following, and their derbies are the highlight of the PSL's fixture list.

Games are played on weekday evenings (usually at 7.30pm or 8.30pm) and at 3pm on Saturdays. **Tickets** cost about R40 to watch top teams play. The **national squad**, nicknamed Bafana Bafana (literally "boys boys" but connoting "our lads"), qualified for the World Cup finals in both 1998 and 2002, but in 2006 the national team bit the dust when they were brought down by a decisive 3–0 defeat to Ghana in their second match.

Erratic performers, Bafana are imaginative and strong on spectacular athletic feats, but less impressive when it comes to teamwork and resilience. Even games the team should win have an element of **unpredictability** that makes for great spectator sport. Indeed, at the 2010 World Cup, Bafana delivered an entertaining draw against Mexico in the opening match, but against Uruguay suffered the worst defeat (3–0) for a host nation since 1970 (when Mexico lost to Italy). The hosts went on to put up a spirited performance against France, whom they beat 2–0, but it wasn't enough to prevent Bafana from being eliminated.

Rugby

Rugby is hugely popular with whites, though attempts to broaden the game's appeal, particularly to a black audience, have struggled. South Africa's victory against England at the 2007 World Cup final in Paris did for a brief spell bring the whole country together. The strength of emotion almost matched that shown in 1995 when South Africa hosted the event. Coming shortly after the advent of democracy, it attracted fanatical attention nationwide, particularly when the Boks triumphed and President **Nelson Mandela** donned a green Springbok jersey (long associated exclusively with whites) to present the cup to the winning side – as depicted in the 2009 Clint Eastwood movie Invictus, starring Matt Damon and Morgan Freeman.

Following that, the goodwill dissipated, to be replaced by an acrimonious struggle to transform the traditionally white sports (cricket and rugby) into something more representative of all race groups, particularly following the government's policy of enforcing **racial quotas** in national squads.

Despite these problems, the country's two World Cup victories in twelve years testify to the fact that South Africa is extraordinarily good at rugby, and you are likely to witness high-quality play when you watch either inter-regional or international games. The main domestic competition is the **Currie Cup**, with games played on weekends from March to October; admission to one of these matches costs from R55.

More recently this has been overshadowed by the **Super 14** competition, involving regional teams from **South Africa**, **New Zealand** and **Australia**. Matches are staged annually from late February to the end of May in all three countries, and in South Africa you'll catch a fair bit of action in the major centres of Johannesburg, Cape Town and Durban, though smaller places such as Port Elizabeth, East London and George sometimes get a look-in.

International fixtures involving the **Springboks** are dominated by visiting tours by northern-hemisphere teams and by the annual **Tri-Nations** competition, in which South Africa plays home and away fixtures against Australia and New Zealand. These are normally played from June to August, and you will need to get tickets well in advance to attend.

Cricket

Cricket was for some years seen as the most progressive of the former white sports, with development programmes generating support and discovering talent among black and coloured communities. The sport was rocked to its foundations in 2000, however, when it was revealed that the South African national captain, **Hansie Cronje**, had received money from betting syndicates hoping to influence the outcome of one-day matches. Cronje was banned for life, the credibility of the sport took a dive and the national team, the **Proteas** (formerly the Springboks), struggled for years to raise itself, successfully clawing its way back by 2009 to a respectable number two in international test-match rankings, a position it still held in 2011.

The **domestic season** of inter-regional games runs from October to April, and the main competitions are the four-day **Supersport Series**, the series of one-day, forty-overs matches, the MTN40, and the shorter twenty-overs **Standard Bank Pro20**. The contests see six regional squads slogging it out for national dominance. Games are played throughout the week, and admission is from R50. In the international standings, South Africa is one of the world's top teams, and you stand a good chance of being around for an international test or one day series if you're in the country between November and March. Expect to pay from R100 for an international, which are played in all the major cities.

Running and cycling

South Africa is very strong at long-distance **running**, a tradition that reached its apotheosis at the 1996 Atlanta Olympics when Josiah Thugwane won the marathon, becoming the first black South African ever to bag Olympic gold. The biggest single athletics event in South Africa, the **Comrades Marathon**, attracts nearly fifteen thousand participants, among them some of the world's leading international ultra-marathon runners. The ninety-kilometre course crosses the hilly country between Durban and Pietermaritzburg, with a drop of almost 800m between the town and the coast. Run annually towards the end of May, the race alternates direction each year and is notable for having been non-racial since 1975, although it wasn't until 1989 that a black South African, Samuel Tshabalala, won it. Since then, **black athletes** have dominated the front rankings. Almost as famous is the **Two Oceans ultra-marathon**, which attracts ten thousand competitors each April to test themselves on the 56-kilometre course that spectacularly circuits the Cape Peninsula.

Traversing a 109-kilometre route, the **Pick 'n Pay Cape Argus Cycle Tour** also includes the Cape Peninsula in its routing. The largest – and most spectacular – individually timed cycle race anywhere, it attracts 35,000 participants from around the world each year in March.

Horse racing

You'll find huge interest among rich and poor South Africans in **horse racing**, with totes and tracks in all the main cities. Its popularity is partly due to the fact that for decades this was the only form of public gambling that South Africa's Afrikaner Calvinist rulers allowed – on the pretext that it involved skill not chance. The highlight of the racing calendar is the **Durban July Handicap** held at Durban's Greyville racecourse. A flamboyant event, it attracts huge crowds, massive purses, socialites in outrageous headgear and vast amounts of media attention.

Parks, reserves and wilderness areas

No other African country has as rich a variety of parks, reserves and wilderness areas as South Africa. Literally hundreds of game reserves and state forests pepper the terrain, creating a bewildering but enticing breadth of choice. While there are dozens of unsung treasures among these, the big destinations amount to some two dozen parks geared towards protecting the country's wildlife and wilderness areas.

With a few exceptions, these fall under **Ezemvelo KZN Wildlife** (☎033 845 1000, ⓦ www.kznwildlife .com), which controls most of the public reserves in KwaZulu-Natal, and **South African National Parks** (☎012 428 9111, ⓦ www.sanparks.org), which covers the rest of the country. In addition to the state-run parks there are **private reserves**, frequently abutting onto them and sharing the same wildlife population.

Only some national parks are game reserves (see p.68). While most people come for South Africa's superb **wildlife**, don't let the **Big Five** (buffalo, elephant, leopard, lion and rhino) blinker you into missing out on the marvellous wilderness areas that take in dramatic landscapes and less publicized animal life. There are parks protecting marine and coastal areas, wetlands, endangered species, forests, deserts and mountains, usually with the added attraction of assorted animals, birds, insects, reptiles or marine mammals – South Africa is one of the top destinations in the world for land-based **whale watching**.

If you had to choose just one of the country's top three parks, **Kruger**, stretching up the east flank of Mpumalanga and Limpopo Province, would lead the pack for its sheer size (it's larger than Wales and roughly the size of Massachusetts), its range of animals, its varied lowveld habitats and unbeatable game-viewing opportunities. After Kruger, the **Tsitsikamma** in the Western Cape attracts large numbers of visitors for its ancient forests, cliff-faced oceans and the dramatic Storms River Mouth as well as its Otter Trail, South Africa's most popular hike. For epic mountain landscapes, nowhere in the country can touch the **Ukhahlamba Drakensberg Park**, which takes in a series of reserves on the KwaZulu-Natal border with Lesotho and offers gentle hikes along water-

courses as well as ambitious mountaineering for serious climbers.

The unchallenged status of Kruger as the place for packing in **elephants**, **lions** and casts of thousands of animals tends to put the KwaZulu-Natal parks in the shade, quite undeservedly. As well as offering the best places in the world for seeing **rhino**, these parks feel less developed than Kruger, and often provide superior accommodation at comparable prices. Both Kruger and KwaZulu-Natal parks offer guided wildlife trails and **night drives**, a popular way to catch sight of the elusive denizens that creep around after dark.

Also worth a mention is the **Addo Elephant National Park** in the Eastern Cape, which has become Big Five country and is being expanded – the only such major game reserve in the southern half of the country. Addo has a lot more in its favour as well: it has the most diverse **landscape** of any

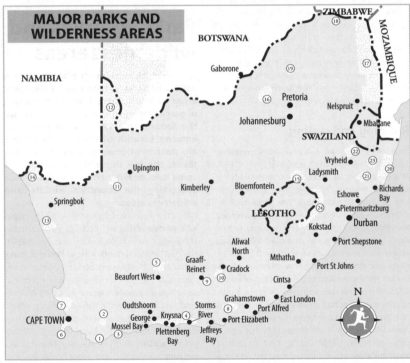

MAJOR PARKS AND WILDERNESS AREAS

Addo Elephant NP	8	Golden Gate Highlands NP	15	Marakele NP	19
Agulhas NP	1	Hluhluwe-Imfolozi GR	21	Mkhuze GR	23
Ai-Ais Richtersveld Transfrontier Park	14	iSimangaliso Wetland Park	20	Mountain Zebra NP	10
Augrabies Falls NP	11	Ithala GR	22	Namaqua NP	13
Bontebok NP	2	Karoo National Park	5	Pilanesberg NP	16
Camdeboo NP	9	Kgalagadi Transfrontier Park	12	Table Mountain NP	6
De Hoop Nature Reserve	3	Kruger NP	17	Ukhahlamba Drakensberg Park	24
Garden Route NP	4	Mapungubwe NP	18	West Coast NP	7

PARK FEES, RESERVATIONS AND ENQUIRIES

Fees given in our park accounts are generally conservation fees, payable daily. The most expensive places are Kruger National Park and Kgalagadi Transfrontier Park, for which foreign visitors pay a conservation fee of R180 per person, followed by Addo Elephant National Park where the fee is R140. The majority of the rest charge R100, but some of the smaller parks charge a lot less.

As a rule of thumb, foreign visitors aged 12 and under pay half the adult rate; South African residents pay a quarter of the foreign adult fee, while citizens of the Southern Africa Development Community, to which many countries in the region belong, pay half the foreign adult fee.

Accommodation at most of South Africa's major national parks can be booked in advance (to stay in high season, do so several months in advance) through South African National Parks, except at Pilanesberg (see p.520) and the KwaZulu-Natal reserves, for which you book through Ezemvelo KZN Wildlife. Note that if you try booking with South African National Parks over the phone you could well be in for a long wait; contacting them online is recommended (see p.65).

reserve in the country; it is a day's drive from Cape Town; and it is the only major game reserve in the country that is **malaria-free**.

Park accommodation

Accommodation at national parks includes **campsites** (expect to pay R150–200 per tent); **safari tents** at some of the Kruger and KwaZulu-Natal restcamps (clusters of accommodation, including chalets, safari tents and campsites, in game reserves, from R260 per tent); one-room **huts** with shared washing and cooking facilities (from R500); one-room en-suite **bungalows** with shared cooking facilities (from R700); and self-contained **cottages** with private bath or shower and cooking facilities (from R750). For groups of four there are self-contained family cottages with private bath and kitchen. In national parks accommodation (excluding campsites) you're supplied with bedding, towels, a fridge and basic cooking utensils. Some restcamps have a **shop** selling supplies for picnics or braais, as well as a **restaurant**.

The ultimate wildlife accommodation is in the **private game reserves**, most of which are around the Kruger National Park. Here you pay big bucks for accommodation, which is almost always luxurious, in large en-suite walk-in tents, or small thatched **rondavels**, or – in the larger and most expensive lodges – plush rooms with air conditioning. A couple of places have "bush-showers" (a hoisted bucket of hot water with a shower nozzle attached) behind reed screens but open to the sky – one of the great treats of the bush is taking a shower under the southern sky. Some chalets or tents have gaslights or lanterns in the absence of **electricity**. Food is usually good and plentiful, and vegetarians

can be catered for. Expect to pay upwards of R2000, rising to several times that amount at the most fashionable spots. It's worth remembering that, high as these **prices** are, all your meals and game drives are included, and as numbers are strictly limited, you get an exclusive experience of the bush in return.

Game viewing

Spotting game takes skill and **experience**. It's easier than you'd think to mistake a rhino for a large boulder, or to miss the king of the beasts in the tall grass – African game has, after all, evolved with **camouflage** in mind. Don't expect the volume of animals you get in wildlife documentaries: what you see is always a matter of **luck**, patience and skill. If you're new to the African bush and its wildlife, consider shelling out for at least two nights at one of the luxurious lodges on a private reserve (for example, those abutting Kruger); they're staffed by well-informed **rangers** who lead game-viewing outings in open-topped 4WDs.

The section on Kruger National Park (see p.551) gives more advice on how to go about spotting game and how to enjoy and understand what you do see – whether it's a brightly coloured lizard in a rest camp, head-butting giraffes at a waterhole or dust-kicking rhinos. Numerous **books** are available that can enhance your visit to a game reserve – especially if you plan a self-drive safari (see p.674).

Self-drive safaris

The least expensive way of experiencing a game park is by **renting a car** and driving around a national park, taking advantage of the self-catering and camping facilities. You'll have the thrill of spotting game yourself and at your own pace

MAJOR PARKS AND WILDLIFE AREAS

PARK	FOCUS	DESCRIPTION AND HIGHLIGHTS
1. Agulhas NP (see p.209)	Marine and coastal	Rugged southernmost tip of Africa with rich plant biodiversity and significant archeological sites
2. Bontebok NP (see p.201)	Endangered species	At the foot of rugged mountains, the park provides refuge to bontebok and Cape mountain zebra
3. De Hoop Nature Reserve (see p.212)	Marine and coastal, endangered species, and coastal vegetation	One of the world's top spots for *land*-based whale watching with epic coastline and *fynbos* grazed by rare mountain zebras
4. Garden Route National Park (see p.223)	Marine and coastal/ endangered species	Focused on three sections: Wetlands and coast around Wilderness; Knysna's forests and lagoon; and Tsitsikamma's cliffs, gorges and ancient forests
5. Karoo NP (see p.197)	Desert reserve	Arid mountainous landscape with fossils, herbivores and wild flowers in spring
6. Table Mountain NP (see p.127)	The natural areas of the peninsula	Extraordinarily rich and diverse flora and fauna that thrives in the wilderness that is Cape Town's back yard
7. West Coast NP (see p.249)	Marine and coastal	Wetland wilderness with birding and watersports
8. Addo Elephant NP (see p.314)	Game reserve	The only Big Five national park in the southern half of the country
9. Camdeboo NP (see p.334)	Desert reserve	Karoo semi-desert landscape in the foothills of the Sneeuberg range with 120m-high dolerite pillars plus 43 species of herbivore
10. Mountain Zebra NP (see p.331)	Endangered species	Dramatic hilly landscape in otherwise flat country with rare mountain zebras and other herbivores
11. Augrabies Falls NP (see p.288)	Desert reserve	Notable for the dramatic landmark from which the park takes its name, where the Orange River plummets down a deep ravine; also great for desert scenery, antelope and prolific birdlife

rather than relying on a ranger, and for people with **children** a self-drive safari is the principal way to see a game reserve, as most of the upmarket lodges don't admit under-12s. The one real disadvantage of self-driving is that you can end up jostling with other cars to get a view, especially when it comes to lion-watching. Also, you may not know what animal signs to look for, and unless you travel in a minibus or 4WD vehicle you're unlikely to be high enough off the ground to be able to see across the veld.

The KwaZulu-Natal game reserves – foremost among them Hluhluwe-Imfolozi, Mkhuze and Ithala – offer rewarding opportunities for **self-drive touring**. The same applies to the Pilanesberg Game Reserve in North West Province, while the remote Kgalagadi Transfrontier Park that stretches across the border into Botswana promises truly exciting wilderness driving. You might choose to cover a route that combines the substantial Kruger National Park with the more intimate reserves of KwaZulu-Natal province.

12. **Kgalagadi Transfrontier Park** (see p.284)	Desert/game reserve	Remote desert with rust-red dunes, desert lions, shy leopards and thousands of antelope
13. **Namaqua NP** (see p.293)	Marine and coastal	Mountainous and coastal region renowned for its estimated 3500 plant varieties, among them beautiful spring wildflowers
14. **Ai-Ais Richtersveld Transfrontier Park** (see p.300)	Mountain and desert	Craggy *kloofs*, high mountains and dramatic landscapes, sweeping inland from the Orange River, which sustain a remarkable range of reptiles, birds, mammals and plant life.
15. **Golden Gate Highlands NP** (see p.449)	Mountain enclave	Resort at the foot of rich sandstone formations in the heart of the Maluti Mountains
16. **Pilanesberg NP** (see p.520)	Game reserve	Mountain-encircled grassland trampled by the Big Five, accessible from Johannesburg
17. **Kruger NP** (see p.551)	Game reserve	The largest, best-stocked and most popular game reserve in the subcontinent
18. **Mapungubwe NP** (see p.583)	Archeology/game reserve	World Heritage Site listed for its significance as the location of a highly developed Iron Age culture. Also noted for its landscape and biodiversity, which supports a large variety of mammals
19. **Marakele NP** (see p.577)	Game reserve	Striking landscape of peaks, plateaus and cliffs, home to lions, elephants, rhinos and a variety of other mammals
20. **Isimangaliso** (see p.415)	Coastal wetland	Vast patchwork of wetlands, wilderness, coast and game reserves
21. **Hluhluwe-Imfolozi GR** (see p.412)	Game reserve	KwaZulu-Natal's hillier, smaller answer to Kruger is among the top African spots for rhinos
22. **Ithala GR** (see p.426)	Game reserve	Lesser-known small gem of a game reserve in mountainous country
23. **Mkhuze GR** (see p.419)	Game/bird reserve	Top birding venue and excellent for rhinos and other herbivores; walks in wild fig forest
24. **Ukhahlamba Drakensberg Park** (see p.398)	Mountain reserve	A series of parks covering the highest, most stirring and most dramatic peaks in South Africa

If you plan to self-drive, consider investing in good animal and bird **field guides**, and a decent pair of **binoculars** – one pair per person is recommended if you want to keep your relationships on a friendly footing. Finally, whether you're cooking or not, it's worth taking a flask for tea and a cool bag to keep water cold.

Escorted safaris

It's possible to book places on a **safari excursion** – such packages are often organized by backpackers'

lodges located near reserves, and occasionally by hotels and B&Bs. On the downside, these don't give you the experience of waking up in the wild, and entail spending considerably more time on the road than if you were based inside a reserve. But during South African school holidays, when Kruger, for example, is booked to capacity, you may have no other option.

Mostly, you get what you pay for as regards game-viewing packages. Be wary of any cheap deals on **"safari farms"** in the vicinity of Kruger.

These are generally fine if you want to see animals in what are essentially huge zoos and make an acceptable overnight stop en route to Kruger, but are no substitute for a real wilderness experience – sooner or later you hit fences and gates on your game drive. Some of the better places in this category are listed in the relevant chapters.

Safaris on private reserves

If you choose well, the ultimate South African game experience has to be in a **private reserve**. You can relax while your game-viewing activities are organized, and because you spend time in a small group you get a stronger sense of the wild than you ever could at one of the big Kruger restcamps. Best of all, you get the benefit of knowledgeable **rangers**, who can explain the terrain and small-scale wildlife as they drive you around looking for game.

Privately run safari lodges in concessions inside Kruger and some other national parks, such as Addo, operate along similar lines. The smaller private reserves accommodate between ten and sixteen guests; larger **camps** often cater to two or three times as many people, and resemble hotels in the bush. Many safari lodges have their own **water-holes**, overlooked by the bar, from which you can watch animals drinking. Nowhere are the private reserves more developed than along the west flank of the Kruger, where you'll find the top-dollar prestigious lodges as well as some places offering more bang for fewer bucks.

A typical day at a private camp or lodge starts at **dawn** for tea or coffee followed by guided **game viewing** on foot, or driving. After a mid-morning brunch/breakfast, there's the chance to spend time on a **viewing platform** or in a **hide**, quietly watching the passing scene. Late-afternoon game viewing is a repeat of early morning but culminates with **sundowners** as the light fades, and often turns into a **night drive** with spotlights out looking for nocturnal creatures.

Prices, which include accommodation, meals and all game activities, vary widely. The ultra-expensive camps offer more luxury and social cachet, but not necessarily better game viewing. You might find the cheaper camps in the same areas more to your taste, their plainer and wilder atmosphere more in keeping with the bush.

Health

You can put aside most of the health fears that may be justified in some parts of Africa; run-down hospitals and bizarre tropical diseases aren't typical of South Africa. All tourist areas boast generally high standards of hygiene and safe drinking water. The only hazard you're likely to encounter, and the one the majority of visitors are most blasé about, is the sun. In some parts of the country there is a risk of malaria, and you will need to take precautions.

Public hospitals in South Africa are fairly well equipped, but they are facing huge pressures under which their attempts to maintain standards are unfortunately buckling. Expect **long waits** and frequently indifferent treatment. **Private hospitals** or clinics, which are well up to British or North American standards, are usually a better option for travellers. You're likely to get more personal treatment and the **costs** are nowhere near as high as in the US – besides which, the expense shouldn't pose a problem if you're adequately insured (see p.76). Private hospitals are listed in the town and city listings throughout the Guide.

Dental care in South Africa is well up to British and North American standards, and is less expensive. You'll find dentists in all the cities and most smaller towns, listed after doctors at the beginning of each town in the telephone directory.

Inoculations

Although no specific **inoculations** are compulsory if you arrive from the West, it's wise to ensure that your **polio** and **tetanus** vaccinations are up to date. A **yellow fever** vaccination certificate is necessary if you've come from a country where the disease is endemic, such as Kenya, Tanzania or tropical South America.

In addition to these, the Hospital for Tropical Diseases in London recommends, depending on which parts of the country you're visiting, a course of shots against **typhoid** and an injection against **hepatitis A**, both of which can be caught from contaminated food or water. This is a worst-case scenario, and in any case, typhoid is eminently curable and few visitors to South Africa ever catch it.

Vaccination against **hepatitis B** is essential only for people involved in health work; the disease is spread by the transfer of blood products, usually dirty needles.

It's best to start organizing to have jabs **six weeks** before departure. If you're going to another African country first and need the yellow fever jab, note that a yellow fever certificate only becomes valid ten days after you've had the shot.

MEDICAL RESOURCES FOR TRAVELLERS

Canadian Society for International Health ☎ 613/241-5785, ⓦ csih.org. Extensive list of travel health centres.
CDC ☎ 1-800/232 4636, ⓦ cdc.gov/travel. Official US government travel health site.
Hospital for Tropical Diseases Travel Clinic ⓦ thehtd.org . UK.
International Society for Travel Medicine ☎ 1-404/373-8282, ⓦ istm.org. Has a full list of travel health clinics.
MASTA (Medical Advisory Service for Travellers Abroad) ⓦ masta.org. For information on the nearest clinic in the UK.
The Travel Doctor – TMVC ☎ 1300/658 844, ⓦ tmvc.com.au. Lists travel clinics in Australia and New Zealand.
Travel Doctor ☎ 0861/300 911, ⓦ www.traveldoctor.co.za. Lists travel clinics in South Africa.
Tropical Medical Bureau ⓦ tmb.ie. Ireland.

Stomach upsets

Stomach upsets from food are rare. Salad and ice – the danger items in many other developing countries – are both perfectly safe. As anywhere, though, don't keep food for too long, and be sure to wash fruit and vegetables as thoroughly as possible.

If you do get a stomach bug the best cure is lots of **water** and **rest**. Papayas – the flesh as well as the pips – are a good tonic to offset the diarrhoea. Otherwise, most chemists should have name-brand anti-diarrhoea remedies, such as Lomotil.

Avoid jumping for **antibiotics** at the first sign of illness. Instead keep them as a last resort – they don't work on viruses and annihilate your "gut flora" (most of which you want to keep), making you more susceptible next time round. Most tummy upsets will resolve themselves if you adopt a sensible **fat-free diet** for a couple of days, but if they do persist without improvement (or are accompanied by other unusual symptoms), then see a **doctor** as soon as possible.

The sun

The **sun** is likely to be the worst hazard you'll encounter in Southern Africa, particularly if you're fair-skinned.

Short-term effects of **overexposure** to the sun include burning, nausea and headaches. Make sure you wear adequate **sunscreen** and you don't stay too long in the sun – especially when you first arrive.

Take particular care with **children**, who should ideally be kept well covered at the seaside, prefer-ably with UV-protective sun suits. Don't be lulled into complacency on cloudy days, when UV levels can still be high.

Bilharzia

One ailment that you need to take seriously throughout sub-Saharan Africa is **bilharzia** (schisto-somiasis), carried in most freshwater lakes and rivers in South Africa except in the mountains. Bilharzia is spread by tiny, parasitic worm-like flukes which leave their water-snail hosts and burrow into human skin to multiply in the bloodstream; they then work their way to the walls of the intestine or bladder, where they begin to lay **eggs**.

The chances are you'll avoid bilharzia even if you swim in a suspect river, but it's best to avoid **swimming** in dams and rivers where possible. If you go **canoeing** or can't avoid the water, have a test for bilharzia when you return home.

Symptoms may be no more than a feeling of lassitude and ill health. Once the infection is estab-lished, abdominal pain and blood in the urine and stools are common. Fortunately, although no **vaccine** is available, bilharzia is easily and effectively treatable.

Malaria

Most of South Africa is free of **malaria**, a potentially lethal disease that is widespread in tropical and subtropical Africa, where it's a major killer. However, **protection** against malaria is essential if you're planning to travel to any of these areas: northern and northeastern Mpumalanga, notably the Kruger National Park; northern KwaZulu-Natal; the border regions of North West and Limpopo provinces. The highest **risk** is during the hot, rainy months from November to April. The risk is reduced during the cooler, dry months from May to October, when some people decide not to take prophylactic medication.

Malaria is caused by a parasite carried in the saliva of the female anopheles mosquito. It has a variable incubation period of a few days to several weeks, so you can become ill long after being bitten. The first symptoms of malaria can be mistaken for **flu**, starting off relatively mildly with a variable combination that includes fever, aching limbs and shivering, which come in waves, usually beginning in the early evening. Deterioration can be rapid as the parasites in the bloodstream prolif-erate. Malaria is not **infectious**, but can be fatal if not treated quickly: get medical help without delay if you go down with flu-like symptoms within a week of entering or three months of leaving a malarial area.

Doctors can advise on which kind of **anti-malarial tablets** to take. It's important to keep to the prescribed dose, which covers the period before and after your trip. Consult your **doctor** or **clinic** several weeks before you travel, as you should start taking medication a week or two before entering the affected region – depending on the particular drug you're using.

Whatever you decide to take, be aware that no antimalarial drug is totally effective – your only sure-fire protection is to **avoid getting bitten**. Malaria-carrying mosquitoes are active between **dusk** and **dawn**, so try to avoid being out at this time, or at least cover yourself well. Sleep under a **mosquito net** when possible, making sure to tuck it under the mattress, and burn **mosquito coils** (which you can buy everywhere) for a peaceful, if noxious, night. Electric mosquito-destroyers which you fit with a pad every night are less pungent than mosquito coils, though note that you may not have access to a power supply at some safari lodges, or if you're camping. Mosquito "buzzers" are useless. Whenever the mosquitoes are particularly bad – and that's not often – cover your exposed parts with **insect repellent**; those containing diethyltoluamide (DEET) work well. Other locally produced repellents such as Peaceful Sleep are widely available.

Bites and stings

Bites, **stings** and **rashes** in South Africa are comparatively rare. **Snakes** are present, but hardly ever seen as they move out of the way quickly. The sluggish puff and berg adders are the most dangerous, because they often lie on paths and don't move when humans approach. The best **advice** if you get bitten is to note what the snake looked like and get yourself to a clinic or hospital. Most bites are not fatal and the worst thing you can do is to panic: desperate measures with razor blades and tourniquets risk doing more harm than good.

Tick-bite fever is occasionally contracted from walking in the bush, particularly in long wet grass. The offending ticks can be minute and you may not spot them. **Symptoms** appear a week later – swollen glands and severe aching of the bones, backache and fever. The disease will run its course in three or four days. Ticks you may find on yourself are not dangerous, just repulsive at first. Make sure you pull out the head as well as the body (it's not painful). A good way of removing small ones is to

smear **Vaseline** or grease over them, making them release their hold.

Scorpion stings and **spider bites** are painful but almost never fatal, contrary to popular myth. Scorpions and spiders abound, but they're hardly ever seen unless you turn over logs and stones. If you're collecting wood for a campfire, knock or shake it before picking it up. Another simple **precaution** when camping is to shake out your shoes and clothes in the morning before you get dressed.

Rabies is present throughout Southern Africa, with **dogs** posing the greatest risk, although the disease can be carried by other domestic or wild animals. If you are bitten you should go immediately to a clinic or hospital. Rabies can be treated effectively with a course of **injections**.

Sexually transmitted diseases

HIV/AIDS and venereal diseases are widespread in Southern Africa among both men and women, and the danger of catching the virus through sexual contact is very real. Follow the usual precautions regarding **safer sex**. There's no special risk from medical treatment in the country, but if you're travelling overland and you want to play it safe, take your own needle and transfusion kit.

Tuberculosis

TB is a serious problem in South Africa, but most travellers are at low risk. At higher risk are healthcare workers, long-term travellers and anyone with an impaired immune system, such as people infected with HIV.

A **BCG vaccination** is recommended for children, most of whom should already have received one in infancy, but it's not routinely given to adults since it can mask latent symptoms should you later become infected. Adults should take medical advice on the question of **immunization** if they feel they may be at risk.

Crime and personal safety

Despite horror stories of sky-high crime rates, most people visit South Africa without incident; be careful, but don't be paranoid. This is not to underestimate the issue – crime is probably the most serious

problem facing the country. However, once you realize that crime is disproportionately concentrated in the poor African and coloured townships, the scale becomes less terrifying. Violent crime is a particular problem not just in the townships but also in Johannesburg, where the dangers are the worst in the country.

Protecting property and "security" are major national obsessions, and it's difficult to imagine what many South Africans would discuss at their dinner parties if the problem disappeared. A substantial percentage of middle-class homes subscribe to the services of armed private security firms. The other obvious manifestation of this obsession is the huge number of **alarms**, high walls and electronically controlled gates you'll find, not just in the suburbs, but even in less deprived areas of some townships. **Guns** are openly carried by police – and often citizens.

If you fall victim to a **mugging**, you should take very seriously the usual advice not to resist and do

SAFETY TIPS

IN GENERAL:

- try not to look like a tourist.
- dress down.
- don't carry a camera or video openly in cities.
- avoid wearing jewellery or expensive watches.
- leave your designer shades at home – they are sometimes pulled off people's faces.
- if you are accosted, remain calm and cooperative.

WHEN ON FOOT:

- grasp bags firmly under your arm.
- don't carry excessive sums of money on you.
- don't put your wallet in your back trouser pocket.
- always know where your valuables are.
- don't leave valuables exposed (on a seat or the ground) while having a meal or drink.
- develop an awareness of what people in the street around you are doing.
- don't let strangers get too close to you – especially people in groups.
- in big cities, travel around in pairs or groups.

ON THE ROAD:

- lock all your car doors, especially in cities.
- keep rear windows sufficiently rolled up to keep out opportunistic hands.
- never leave anything worth stealing in view when your car is unattended.

AT ATMS:

Cash machines are favourite hunting grounds for sophisticated con men who use cunning rather than force to steal money. Never underestimate their ability and don't get drawn into any interaction at an ATM, no matter how well-spoken, friendly or distressed the other person appears. If they claim to have a problem with the machine, tell them to contact the bank. Don't let people crowd you or see your personal identification number (PIN) when you withdraw money; if in doubt, go to another machine. Finally, if your card gets swallowed, report it without delay.

WHEN PAYING WITH A CARD:

- beware skimming (where the information stored in your card's magnetic strip is copied to create a clone).
- never let your plastic out of your sight.
- at a restaurant, ask for a portable card reader to be brought to your table.
- at the till, keep an eye on your card.

as you're told. The chances of this happening can be greatly minimized by using common sense and following a few simple rules (see box, p.73).

Drugs and drink-driving

Dagga (pronounced like "dugger" with the "gg" guttural, as in the Scottish pronunciation of "loch") is **cannabis** in dried leaf form, South Africa's most widely produced and widely used drug. Grown in hot regions like KwaZulu-Natal (the source of Durban Poison), Swaziland (Swazi Gold) and as a cash crop in parts of the former Transkei, it is fairly easily available and the quality is generally good – but this doesn't alter the fact that it is **illegal**. If you do decide to partake, you should take particular care when scoring, as visitors have run into trouble dealing with unfamiliar local conditions. Strangely, for a country that sometimes seems to be on one massive binge, South Africa has laws that prohibit **drinking** in public – not that anyone pays any attention to them. The drink-drive laws are routinely and brazenly flouted, making the country's **roads** the one real danger you should be concerned about. People routinely stock up their cars with booze for long journeys, and even at filling stations you'll find places selling liquor. Levels of alcohol consumption go some way to explaining why during the Christmas holidays over a thousand people die in an annual orgy of carnage on the roads.

Sexual harassment

South Africa's extremely high incidence of **rape** doesn't as a rule affect tourists. However, at heart the majority of the country's males, regardless of race, hold on to fairly **sexist attitudes**. Sometimes your eagerness to be friendly may be taken as a sexual overture – always be sensitive to potential crossed wires and unintended signals.

Women should avoid travelling on their own, nor should they hitchhike or walk alone in deserted areas. This applies equally to cities, the countryside or anywhere after dark. Minibus taxis should be ruled out as a means of transport after dark, especially if you're not exactly sure of local geography.

The police

Poorly paid, shot at (and frequently hit), underfunded, badly equipped, barely respected and demoralized, the police in South Africa keep a low profile. If you ever get stopped, at a **roadblock** for example (one of the likeliest encounters), always be

courteous. And if you're driving, note that under South African law you are required to carry your driver's **licence** at all times.

If you are **robbed**, you will need to report the incident to the police, who should give you a case reference for insurance purposes – though don't expect too much crime-cracking enthusiasm, or to get your property back.

Travel essentials

Climate

Although South Africa is predominantly a dry, sunny country, bear in mind that the chart opposite shows average maximums. **June and July** temperatures can drop below zero in some places; be prepared for average minimums of 4°C in Johannesburg, 7°C in Cape Town and 11°C in Durban.

Costs

The most expensive thing about visiting South Africa is getting there. Once you've arrived, you're likely to find it a relatively **inexpensive** destination. How cheap will depend partly on exchange rates at the time of your visit – in the decade after becoming fully convertible (after the advent of democracy in South Africa) the rand has seen some massive fluctuations against sterling, the dollar and the euro.

When it comes to daily budgets, your biggest expense is likely to be **accommodation**. If you're willing to stay in backpacker dorms and self-cater, you should be able to sleep and eat for under £22/$36/€25 per person a day. If you stay in B&Bs and guesthouses, eat out once a day, and have a snack or two, you should budget for at least double that. In luxury hotels expect to pay upwards of £150/$250/€175 a day, while luxury safari lodges in major game reserves will set you back from £200/$325/€230 a day to way beyond. **Extras** such as car rental, outdoor activities, horseriding and safaris will add to these figures substantially. While most museums and art galleries impose an **entry fee**, it's usually quite low: only the most sophisticated attractions charge more than £1/$1.50/€1.

Electricity

South Africa's electricity supply runs at 220/230V, 50Hz AC. **Sockets** take unique round-pinned plugs; see Ⓦ www.kropla.com for details. Most hotel rooms have sockets that will take 110V electric shavers, but for other appliances US visitors will need an **adaptor**.

Emergencies

Police and **fire** ☎1011, **ambulance** ☎10177. **Netcare 911** private hospital network ☎082 911.

Entry requirements

Nationals of the EU, the US, Canada, Australia and New Zealand don't require a **visa** to enter South Africa. As long as you carry a **passport** that is valid for at least six months and has at least two empty pages you will be granted a temporary visitor's permit, which allows you to stay in South Africa for up to 90 days. All visitors should have a valid return ticket; without one, you may be required to pay the authorities the equivalent of your fare home (the money will be refunded after you have left the country). Visitors may also need to prove that they have sufficient funds to cover their stay.

Applications for **visa extensions** must be made at one of the main offices of the Department of Home Affairs, where you will be quizzed about your inten-

tions and your funds. In Cape Town, go to 56 Barrack St (☎021 468 4500); in Johannesburg, the office is at the corner of Plein and Harrison streets (☎011 639 4000). The Department also has offices in a number of towns – check in the telephone directory or on its website (🅦www.dha.gov.za/Service%20Centers.html), and make sure that the office you're intending to visit is able to grant extensions.

SOUTH AFRICAN DIPLOMATIC MISSIONS ABROAD

Australia Corner of State Circle and Rhodes Place, Yarralumla, Canberra, ACT 2600 ☎02/6272 7300, 🅦wahc.org.au.
Canada 15 Sussex Drive, Ottawa, Ontario K1M 1M8 ☎613/744-0330, 🅦southafrica-canada.ca.
Ireland 2nd Floor, Alexandra House, Earlsfort Centre, Earlsfort Terrace, Dublin ☎01 661 5553.
New Zealand c/o the High Commission in Australia, see above.
UK Consular Section, 15 Whitehall, London SW1A 2DD ☎020/7925 8900, 🅦southafricahouseuk.com.
US 4301 Connecticut Ave, NW, Van Ness Building Suite 220 Washington, DC 20008 ☎202/232-4400, 🅦www.southafrica-newyork.net/homeaffairs/index.htm. Consulates: 333 E 38th St, 9th floor, New York, NY 10016 ☎212/213-4880; 6300 Wilshire Blvd, Suite 600, Los Angeles, CA 90048 ☎323/651-0902.

AVERAGE DAILY MAXIMUM TEMPERATURES

CAPE TOWN

	Jan	Feb	Mar	Apr	May	Jun	Jul	Aug	Sep	Oct	Nov	Dec
Max (°C)	27	27	26	23	20	19	17	18	19	22	24	26
Max (°F)	81	81	79	73	68	66	63	64	66	72	75	79

DURBAN

	Jan	Feb	Mar	Apr	May	Jun	Jul	Aug	Sep	Oct	Nov	Dec
Max (°C)	27	28	27	26	24	23	22	22	23	24	25	26
Max (°F)	81	82	81	79	75	73	72	72	73	75	77	79

JOHANNESBURG

	Jan	Feb	Mar	Apr	May	Jun	Jul	Aug	Sep	Oct	Nov	Dec
Max (°C)	26	26	24	22	19	16	16	20	23	25	25	26
Max (°F)	79	79	75	72	66	61	61	68	73	77	77	79

SKUKUZA (KRUGER NATIONAL PARK)

	Jan	Feb	Mar	Apr	May	Jun	Jul	Aug	Sep	Oct	Nov	Dec
Max (°C)	31	31	30	29	27	25	25	26	29	29	30	30
Max (°F)	88	88	86	84	81	77	77	79	84	84	86	86

MASERU (LESOTHO)

	Jan	Feb	Mar	Apr	May	Jun	Jul	Aug	Sep	Oct	Nov	Dec
Max (°C)	20	17	14	11	9	7	7	9	11	14	17	20
Max (°F)	68	63	57	52	48	45	45	48	52	57	63	68

Gay and lesbian travellers

South Africa has the world's first gay- and lesbian-friendly constitution, and Africa's most developed and diverse gay and lesbian scene. Not only is homosexuality **legal** for consenting adults of 18 or over, but the constitution outlaws any **discrimination** on the grounds of sexual orientation. This means that, for once, you have the law on your side. Outside the big cities, however, South Africa is a pretty **conservative** place, where open displays of public affection by gays and lesbians are unlikely to go down well; many whites will find it un-Christian, while blacks will think it un-African.

South African Tourism, on the other hand, is well aware of the potential of pink spending power and actively woos **gay travellers** – an effort that is evidently paying off, with Cape Town ranking among the world's top gay destinations. The city is South Africa's – and indeed, the African continent's – gay capital. Like many things in the city, Cape Town's gay scene (see p.154) is white dominated, though there are a few gay-friendly **clubs** starting to emerge in the surrounding townships. The gay scene is a lot more multiracial in Johannesburg, especially in the clubs. The Pretoria gay and lesbian scene has grown enormously over the past few years. There are also gay scenes in Port Elizabeth and Durban and you'll find a growing number of gay-run or gay-friendly establishments in small towns all over the country. There are **gay pride** festivals in Cape Town in February–March (ⓦcapetownpride.org) and in Jo'burg in September (ⓦjoburgpride.org), while the South African Gay and Lesbian Film Festival (ⓦoia .co.za) takes place in Cape Town and Johannesburg in October/November.

Insurance

It's wise to take out an **insurance** policy to cover against theft, loss and illness or injury prior to visiting South Africa. A typical travel insurance policy usually provides cover for the loss of baggage, tickets and – up to a certain limit – cash or cheques, as well as cancellation or curtailment of your journey. Most of them exclude so-called dangerous sports unless an extra **premium** is paid: in South Africa this can mean scuba diving, whitewater rafting, windsurfing, horseriding, bungee jumping and paragliding. In addition to these, it's well worth checking whether you are covered by your policy if you're hiking, kayaking, pony trekking or game viewing on safari, all activities people commonly take part in when visiting South Africa. Many policies can be chopped and changed to exclude **coverage** you don't need – for example, sickness and accident benefits can often be excluded or included at will. If you do take medical coverage, ascertain whether benefits will be paid as treatment proceeds or only after you return home, and if there is a 24-hour medical emergency number. When securing baggage cover, make sure that the per-article limit will cover your most valuable possession. If you need to make a **claim**, you should keep receipts for medicines and medical treatment, and in the event you have anything stolen, you must obtain an official statement from the **police**.

Internet

Finding somewhere to access the **internet** will seldom be a problem in South Africa: cybercafés are found even in relatively small towns, and most backpacker hostels and hotels have internet and email facilities. Expect to pay R25–40 an hour for online access. If you are carrying your own computer or palm-top device you'll also be able to take advantage of the **wireless hotspots** at a small (but growing) number of cafés and accommodation.

Mail

The deceptively familiar feel of South African **post offices** can lull you into expecting an efficient

British- or US-style service. In fact, post within the country is slow and unreliable, and money and valuables frequently disappear en route. Expect domestic **delivery times** from one city to another of about a week – longer if a rural town is involved at either end. International airmail deliveries are often quicker, especially if you're sending or receiving at Johannesburg or Cape Town – the cities with direct flights to London. A letter or package sent by surface mail can take up to six weeks to get from South Africa to London.

Most towns of any size have a post office, generally open Monday to Friday 8.30am to 4.30pm and Saturday 8am to 11.30am (closing earlier in some places). The ubiquitous private **PostNet** outlets (Ⓦwww.postnet.co.za) offer many of the same postal services as the post office and more, including courier services. Courier companies like **FedEx** (Ⓣ0800 033 339, Ⓦwww.fedex.com/za) and **DHL** (Ⓣ086 034 5000, Ⓦwww.dhl.co.za) are more expensive and available only in the larger towns, but they are far more reliable than the mail.

Stamps are available at post offices and also from newsagents, such as the CNA chain, as well as supermarkets. Postage is relatively inexpensive – it costs about R5 to send a postcard or small letter by airmail to anywhere in the world. You'll find **poste restante** facilities at the main post office in most larger centres, and in many backpackers' hostels.

Maps

Many **place names** in South Africa were changed after the 1994 elections – and changes are still being made – so if you buy a **map** before leaving home, make sure that it's up to date. Bartholomew produces an excellent map of South Africa, including Lesotho and Swaziland (1:2,000,000), as part of its World Travel Map series. The **Rough Guide Map**: South Africa, Lesotho & Swaziland covers the same turf with the advantage that it's rip-proof and waterproof. Also worth investing in are MapStudio's "Miniplan" maps of major cities such as Cape Town, Durban and Pretoria: these are a convenient size and have useful details, such as hotels, cinemas, post offices and hospitals. **MapStudio** also produces good regional maps, featuring scenic routes and street maps of major towns, and a fine Natal Drakensberg map which shows hiking trails, picnic spots, campsites and places of interest.

South Africa's motoring organization, the **Automobile Association** (AA; see p.52), sells a wide selection of good regional maps (free to members) that you can pick up from its offices.

For travel around the Western Cape (including the Cape Peninsula) and the Eastern Cape's Wild Coast, the most accurate, up-to-date and attractive touring and hiking maps – the best bar none – are those produced by local cartographers **Slingsby Maps** (Ⓦslingsbymaps.com), which you buy from bookshops.

Money

South Africa's currency is the **rand** (R), often called the "buck", divided into 100 **cents**. Notes come in R10, R20, R50, R100 and R200 denominations and there are coins of 5, 10, 20 and 50 cents, as well as R1, R2 and R5. At the time of writing, the **exchange rate** was hovering at around R11 to the pound sterling, R7 to the US dollar, R10 to the euro and R7 to the Australian dollar.

All but the tiniest settlement will have a **bank** where you can change money swiftly and easily. Banking hours are Monday to Friday 9am to 3.30pm, and Saturday 9am to 11am; the banks in smaller towns usually close for lunch. In major cities, some banks operate **bureaux de change** that stay open until 7pm. Outside banking hours, some hotels will change money, although this entails a fairly hefty **commission**. You can also change money at branches of American Express and Rennies Travel.

Cards and travellers' cheques

Credit and **debit cards** are the most convenient way to access your funds in South Africa. Most international cards can be used to withdraw money at **ATMs**. Plastic can come in very handy for hotel bookings and for paying for more mainstream and upmarket tourist facilities, and is essential for car rental. **Visa** and **Mastercard** are the cards most widely accepted in major cities.

Travellers' cheques make a useful backup as they can be replaced if lost or stolen. American Express, Visa and Thomas Cook are all widely recognized brands; both US dollar and sterling cheques are accepted in South Africa.

Travellers' cheques and plastic are useless if you're heading into remote areas, where you'll need to carry **cash**, preferably in a safe place, such as a leather pouch or waist-level money belt that you can keep under your clothes.

Opening hours and holidays

The **working day** starts and finishes early in South Africa: shops and businesses generally open on

weekdays at 8.30am or 9am and close at 4.30pm or 5pm. In small towns, many places close for an hour over **lunch**. Many shops and businesses close around noon on Saturdays, and most shops are closed on Sundays. However, in every neighbourhood, you'll find small shops and supermarkets where you can buy groceries and essentials after hours.

Some establishments have summer and winter opening times. In such situations, you can take **winter** to mean April to August or September, while **summer** constitutes the rest of the year.

School holidays in South Africa can disrupt your plans, especially if you want to camp, or stay in the national parks and the cheaper end of accommodation (self-catering, cheaper B&Bs, etc), all of which are likely to be booked solid during those periods. If you do travel to South Africa over the school holidays, book your accommodation well in advance, especially for the national parks.

The longest and busiest holiday period is **Christmas** (summer), which for schools stretches over most of December and January. Flights and train berths can be hard to get from December 16 to January 2, when many businesses and offices close for their annual break. You should book your **flights** – long-haul and domestic – as early as six months in advance for the Christmas period. The inland and coastal provinces stagger their school holidays, but as a general rule the remaining school holidays roughly cover the following periods: Easter, mid-March to mid-April; winter, mid-June to mid-July; and spring, late September to early October. Exact **dates** for each year are given on the government's information website: ⓦ www.info.gov.za/aboutsa/schoolcal.htm.

Phones

South Africa's **telephone** system, dominated by Telkom, generally works well. Public phone booths are found in every city and town, and are either coin- or card-operated. While international calls can be made from virtually any phone, it helps to have a **phone card**, as you'll be lucky to stay on the line for more than a minute or two for R20. Phone cards come in R20, R50, R100 and R200 denominations, available at Telkom offices, post offices and newsagents.

Mobile phones (referred to locally as cell phones or simply cells) are extremely widely used in South Africa, with more mobile than landline handsets in use. The competing networks – Vodacom, MTN, Cell C and VirginMobile – cover all the main areas and the national roads connecting them.

You can use a GSM/tri-band phone from outside the country in South Africa, but you will need to arrange a **roaming** agreement with your provider at home; be warned that this is likely to be expensive. A far cheaper alternative is to buy a **local SIM card** that replaces your home SIM card while you're in South Africa. (For this to work, you'll need to check that your phone hasn't been locked to your home network.) The local SIM card contains your South African phone number, and you pay for airtime. Very inexpensive starter packs (R100 or less) containing a SIM card and some airtime can be bought from the ubiquitous mobile phone shops and a number of other outlets, including supermarkets and the CNA chain of newsagents and supermarkets.

Another option is to **rent** just a South African SIM card or a phone and SIM card when you arrive. Cards start at R5 a day and phones at R7. Phone (and GPS) rental can also be arranged when you arrange car rental. Among the companies that offer this are Avis, Budget, Hertz and National (see p.53) as does the Baz backpacker bus (see p.49). There are rental outlets at the major airports: Johannesburg, Cape Town, Port Elizabeth, Durban and George.

PHONE RENTAL COMPANIES

Rent a Mobile ⓦ rentamobile.co.za. Rental operation of MTN.

SOUTH AFRICAN PUBLIC HOLIDAYS

Many shops and tourist-related businesses remain open over public holidays, although often with shorter opening hours. Christmas Day and Good Friday, when most of the country shuts down, are the only exceptions. The main holidays are:

New Year's Day (Jan 1)

Human Rights Day (March 21)

Good Friday, **Easter Monday** (variable)

Freedom Day (April 27)

Workers' Day (May 1)

Day of Goodwill (Dec 26)

Youth Day (June 16)

National Women's Day (Aug 9)

Heritage Day (Sept 24)

Day of Reconciliation (Dec 16)

Christmas Day (Dec 25)

Vodashop Renta Fone Ⓦ rentafone.net. Vodacom's phone rental wing.

CALLING HOME FROM SOUTH AFRICA

To dial out of South Africa, the international access code is Ⓣ 00. Remember to omit any initial zero in the number of the place you're phoning.

Australia international access code + 61
New Zealand international access code + 64
UK international access code + 44
US and Canada international access code + 1
Republic of Ireland international access code + 353

Taxes

Value-added tax (**VAT**) of fourteen percent is levied on most goods and services, though it's usually already included in any quoted price. Foreign visitors older than seven can claim back VAT on goods over R250. To do this, you must present an official tax receipt with your name on it for the goods, a non-South African passport and the purchased goods themselves, at the **airport** just before you fly out. You need to complete a VAT refund control sheet (VAT 255), which is obtainable at international airports. For further information contact the VAT Refund Administrator (Ⓣ 011 394 1117, Ⓦ www.taxrefunds.co.za).

Time

There is only one **time zone** throughout the region, two hours ahead of GMT year-round. If you're flying from anywhere in Europe, you shouldn't experience any jet lag.

Tipping

Ten to fifteen percent of the tab is the normal **tip** at restaurants and for taxis – but don't feel obliged to tip if service has been shoddy. Keep in mind that many of the people who'll be serving you rely on tips to supplement a meagre wage on which they support huge extended families. **Porters** at hotels normally get about R5 per bag. At South African garages and filling stations, someone will always be on hand to fill your vehicle and clean your windscreen, for which you should tip around R5. It is also usual at **hotels** to leave some money for the person who services your room. Many establishments, especially private game lodges, take (voluntary) communal tips when you check out – by far the fairest system, which ensures that all the low-profile staff behind the scenes get their share.

Tourist information

Given South Africa's booming tourism industry, it's not surprising that you'll have no difficulty finding **maps**, **books** and **brochures** before you leave. South African Tourism, the official organization promoting the country, is reasonably efficient: if there's an office near you, it's worth visiting for its free maps and **information** on hotels and organized tours. Alternatively, you can check out its **website** Ⓦ www.southafrica.net, which includes content specific to users in South Africa, the UK, the US, Canada, Germany and France.

In South Africa itself, nearly every town, even down to the sleepiest *dorp*, has some sort of **tourist office** – sometimes connected to the museum, municipal offices or library – where you can pick up local maps, lists of B&Bs and travel advice. In larger cities such as Cape Town and Durban, you'll find several branches offering everything from hotel bookings to organized safari trips. We've given precise opening hours of tourist offices in most cases; they generally adhere to a standard schedule of Monday to Friday 8.30am to 5pm, with many offices also open on Saturdays and Sundays. In smaller towns some close between 1pm and 2pm, while in the bigger centres some have extended hours.

In this fast-changing country the best way of finding out what's happening is often by word of mouth, and for this, backpacker **hostels** are invaluable. If you're seeing South Africa on a budget, the useful notice boards, constant traveller traffic and largely helpful and friendly staff in the hostels will greatly smooth your travels.

To find out what's on, check out the entertainment pages of the daily **newspapers** or better still buy the *Mail & Guardian*, which comes out every Friday and lists the coming week's offerings in a comprehensive pullout supplement.

TRAVEL ADVISORIES

Australian Department of Foreign Affairs Ⓦ dfat.gov.au.
British Foreign & Commonwealth Office Ⓦ fco.gov.uk.
Canadian Department of Foreign Affairs Ⓦ international .gc.ca.
Irish Department of Foreign Affairs Ⓦ foreignaffairs.gov.ie.
New Zealand Ministry of Foreign Affairs Ⓦ mfat.govt.nz.
US State Department Ⓦ state.gov.

Travellers with disabilities

Facilities for **disabled travellers** in South Africa are not as sophisticated as those found in the developed world, but they're sufficient to ensure

NAME CHANGING

After the birth of **democracy** in South Africa in 1994, the government began changing place names, particularly ones with apartheid associations – a process that still continues. Practically, this means you may still find inconsistencies between maps and reality, so it's worth using maps that are as up to date as you can find.

you have a satisfactory visit. By accident rather than design, you'll find pretty good **accessibility** to many buildings, as South Africans tend to build low (single-storey bungalows are the norm), with the result that you'll have to deal with fewer **stairs** than you may be accustomed to. As the car is king, you'll frequently find that you can drive to, and park right outside, your destination. There are organized **tours** and **holidays** specifically for people with disabilities, and activity-based packages for disabled travellers to South Africa are increasingly available. These packages offer the possibility for wheelchair-bound visitors to take part in safaris, sport and a vast range of adventure **activities**, including whitewater rafting, horseriding, parasailing and zip-lining. Tours can either be taken as self-drive trips or as packages for large groups. The contacts below will be able to put you in touch with South Africa travel specialists.

If you want to be more **independent** on your travels, it's important to know where you can expect help and where you must be self-reliant, especially regarding **transport** and **accommodation**. It's also vital to know your limitations, and to make sure others know them. If you do not use a wheelchair all the time but your walking capabilities are limited, remember that you are likely to need to cover greater distances while travelling (often over rougher terrain and in hotter temperatures) than you are used to. If you use a **wheelchair**, have it serviced before you go and take a repair kit with you.

USEFUL CONTACTS

Ⓦ **www.disabledtravel.co.za** Website of occupational therapist Karin Coetzee aimed at disabled travellers with listings of accommodation, restaurants and attractions personally evaluated for accessibility, as well as hugely useful links to everything from car rental and tours to orthopedic equipment.

Ⓦ **www.access-able.com** US-based website aimed at travellers with disabilities that includes some useful information about South Africa.

Travelling with children

Travelling with **children** is straightforward in South Africa, whether you want to explore a city, relax on the beach, or find peace in the mountains. You'll find local people friendly, attentive and accepting of babies and young children. The following is aimed mainly at families with under-5s.

Although children up to 24 months only pay ten percent of the adult **airfare**, the illusion that this is a bargain rapidly evaporates when you discover that they get no seat or baggage allowance. Given this, you'd be well advised to secure bulkhead seats and reserve a basinet or sky cot, which can be attached to the bulkhead. **Basinets** are usually allocated to babies under six months, though some airlines use weight (under 10kg) as the criterion. When you reconfirm your flights, check that your seat and basinet are still available. A child who has a **seat** will usually be charged fifty percent of the adult fare and is entitled to a full baggage allowance.

For getting to and from the aircraft, and for use during your stay, take a lightweight collapsible **buggy** – not counted as part of your luggage allowance. A child-carrier backpack is another useful accessory.

Given the size of the country, you're likely to be **driving** long distances. Aim to go slowly and plan a route that allows frequent stops – or perhaps take trains or flights between centres. The Garden Route, for example, is an ideal drive, with easy stops for picnics, particularly on the section between Mossel Bay and Storms River. The route between Johannesburg and Cape Town, conversely, is tedious.

Game viewing can be boring for young children, since it too involves a lot of driving – and disappointment, should the promised beasts fail to put in an appearance. Furthermore, of course, toddlers won't particularly enjoy watching animals from afar and through a window. If they are old enough to enjoy the experience, make sure they have their own **binoculars**. To get in closer, some animal parks, such as Tshukudu near Kruger, have semi-tame animals, while snake and reptile parks are an old South African favourite.

Family accommodation is plentiful, and hotels, guesthouses, B&Bs and a growing number of backpacker lodges have rooms with extra beds or interconnecting rooms. Kids usually stay for half-price. Self-catering options are worth considering, as most such establishments have a good deal of space to play in, and there'll often be a **pool**. A number of resorts are specifically aimed at families with older children, with suitable activities offered. The pick of the bunch is the **Forever** chain (Ⓦ www .foreversa.co.za), which has resorts in beautiful settings, including Keurboomstrand near Plettenberg Bay, and two close to the Blyde River Canyon in Mpumalanga. Another excellent option is full-board family hotels, of which there are a number along the Wild Coast (see p.344), where not only are there playgrounds and canoes for paddling about lagoons, but also often **nannies** to look after the kids during meals or for the whole day. Note that many **safari camps** don't allow children under 12, so you'll have to self-cater or camp at the national parks and those in KwaZulu-Natal.

Eating out with a baby or toddler is easy, particularly if you go to an outdoor venue where they can get on unhindered with their exploration of the world. Some restaurants have highchairs and offer small portions. If in doubt, there are always the ubiquitous family-oriented **chains** such as Spur, Nando's or Wimpy.

Breast-feeding is practised by the majority of African mothers wherever they are, though you won't see many white women doing it in public. Be discreet, especially in more conservative areas – which is most of the country outside middle-class Cape Town, Johannesburg or Durban. There are relatively few **baby rooms** in public places for changing or feeding, although the situation is improving all the time and you shouldn't have a problem at shopping malls in the cities. You can buy disposable **nappies** wherever you go (imported brands are best), as well as wipes, bottles, formula and dummies. High-street chemists and the Clicks chain are the best places to buy baby goods. If you run out of **clothes**, the Woolworths chain has good-quality stuff, while the ubiquitous Pep stores, which are present in even the smallest towns, are an excellent source of extremely cheap, functional clothes.

Malaria (see p.71) affects only a small part of the country, but think carefully about visiting such areas as the preventatives aren't recommended for under-2s. Avoid most of the major **game reserves**, particularly the Kruger National Park and those in KwaZulu-Natal, North West and Limpopo provinces, and opt instead for malaria-free reserves – Addo Elephant National Park in the Eastern Cape is an excellent choice. Malarial zones carry a considerably reduced risk in winter, so if you are set on going, this is the best time. **Tuberculosis** (TB) is widespread in South Africa, mostly (but by no means exclusively) affecting the poor, so make sure your child has had a **BCG jab**. Sun protection is another important consideration (see p./1).

USEFUL CONTACTS

Ⓦ **www.familytravelsa.co.za** Information on child-friendly accommodation and activities throughout South Africa.

Ⓦ **www.capetownkids.co.za** Resources for parents and children in Cape Town.

Ⓦ **www.jozikids.co.za** Resources for parents and children in Johannesburg.

Cape Town and the Cape Peninsula

VIEW OF LION'S HEAD AND THE TWELVE APOSTLES

1

Cape Town and the Cape Peninsula

Cape Town is Southern Africa's most beautiful, most romantic and most visited city. Its physical setting is extraordinary, something its pre-colonial Khoikhoi inhabitants acknowledged when they referred to Table Mountain, the city's most famous landmark, as Hoerikwaggo – the mountains in the sea. Even more extraordinary is that so close to the national park that extends over much of the peninsula, there's a pumping metropolis with a nightlife that matches the city's wildlife. You can hang out with baboons and zebras at Cape Point in the morning, dine at an Atlantic seaboard bistro for lunch, tipple at a Constantia wine estate in the afternoon and party the night away in a Long Street club. All in a Cape Town day.

More than a scenic backdrop, **Table Mountain** is the solid core of Cape Town, dividing the city into distinct zones with public gardens, wilderness, forests, hiking routes, vineyards and desirable residential areas trailing down its lower slopes. Standing on the tabletop, you can look north for a giddy view of the **city centre**, its docks lined with matchbox ships. To the west, beyond the mountainous Twelve Apostles, the drop is sheer and your eye sweeps across Africa's priciest real estate, clinging to the slopes along the chilly but spectacularly beautiful **Atlantic seaboard**. To the south, the mountainsides are forested and several historic vineyards and the marvellous Botanical Gardens creep up the lower slopes. Beyond the oak-lined suburbs of Newlands and Constantia lies the warmer **False Bay seaboard**, which curves around towards **Cape Point**. Finally, relegated to the grim industrial east, are the coloured **townships** and black **ghettos**, spluttering in winter under the smoky pall of coal fires – your stark introduction to Cape Town when driving in from the airport on the eastern outskirts of the city.

PENGUINS AT BOULDERS BEACH

Highlights

❶ The Bo-Kaap One of Cape Town's oldest residential areas, its streets characterized by colourful nineteenth-century Cape Dutch and Georgian terraces. **See p.102**

❷ Gold of Africa Museum A major collection of exquisite historic African works of art, wrought from the glittering precious metal. **See p.103**

❸ Robben Island The infamous island prison that was Nelson Mandela's home for nearly two decades. **See p.106**

❹ Kirstenbosch Gardens Picnic or amble in one of the world's loveliest gardens with its matchless rear wall – Table Mountain. **See p.110**

❺ Rotate up Table Mountain The revolving cable car is the city's best route to breathtaking views, without getting short of breath. **See p.112**

❻ Swim with penguins Boulders Beach offers wonderful bathing and is home to a colony of African penguins. **See p.126**

❼ Cape Point The dramatically rocky southernmost section of the Cape Peninsula offers spectacular views and walks. **See p.127**

❽ Township tour See where most Capetonians live on a gospel tour jazz safari. **See p.132**

❾ Long Street nightlife Party till the early hours along the city centre's café, pub and nightclub strip. **See p.150**

HIGHLIGHTS ARE MARKED ON THE MAP ON P.86

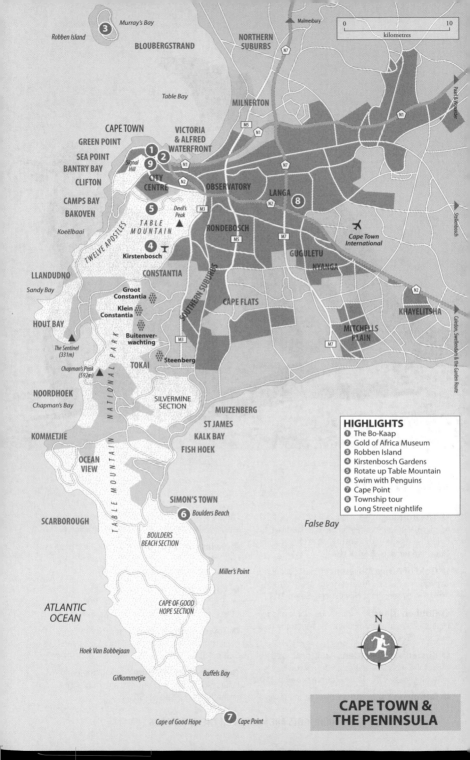

Robben Island Murray's Bay

BLOUBERGSTRAND

NORTHERN SUBURBS

Malmesbury

Table Bay

MILNERTON

CAPE TOWN

GREEN POINT

VICTORIA & ALFRED WATERFRONT

SEA POINT

BANTRY BAY

Signal Hill

CLIFTON

CITY CENTRE

OBSERVATORY

LANGA

CAMPS BAY

BAKOVEN

Devil's Peak

TABLE MOUNTAIN

Koeëlbaai

TWELVE APOSTLES

Kirstenbosch

RONDEBOSCH

GUGULETU

NYANGA

Cape Town International

LLANDUDNO

CONSTANTIA

Sandy Bay

SOUTHERN SUBURBS

CAPE FLATS

KHAYELITSHA

Groot Constantia

HOUT BAY

Klein Constantia

Buitenverwachting

MITCHELLS PLAIN

The Sentinel (331m)

Chapman's Peak (592m)

Steenberg

NATIONAL PARK

TOKAI

NOORDHOEK

Chapman's Bay

SILVERMINE SECTION

MUIZENBERG

ST JAMES

KOMMETJIE

KALK BAY

FISH HOEK

OCEAN VIEW

TABLE MOUNTAIN NATIONAL PARK

SIMON'S TOWN

Boulders Beach

SCARBOROUGH

BOULDERS BEACH SECTION

False Bay

Miller's Point

ATLANTIC OCEAN

CAPE OF GOOD HOPE SECTION

Hoek Van Bobbejaan

Gifkommetjie

Buffels Bay

Cape of Good Hope

Cape Point

N

HIGHLIGHTS

❶ The Bo-Kaap
❷ Gold of Africa Museum
❸ Robben Island
❹ Kirstenbosch Gardens
❺ Rotate up Table Mountain
❻ Swim with Penguins
❼ Cape Point
❽ Township tour
❾ Long Street nightlife

CAPE TOWN & THE PENINSULA

kilometres

Paarl & Worcester

Stellenbosch

Caledon, Swellendam & the Garden Route

WINDY CITY

Weather is an abiding obsession of Capetonians, particularly the **southeaster**, the cool summer wind that blows in across False Bay. It can singlehandedly determine the kind of day you're going to have, and when it gusts at over 60km/h you won't want to be outdoors, let alone on the beach. Conversely, its gentler incarnation as the so-called **Cape Doctor** brings welcome relief on humid summer days, and lays the famous cloudy tablecloth on top of Table Mountain.

To appreciate Cape Town you need to spend time **outdoors**, as Capetonians do: they hike, picnic or sunbathe, often choose mountain bikes in preference to cars, and turn **adventure activities** into an obsession. Sailboarders from around the world head for Table Bay for some of the world's best windsurfing, and the brave (or unhinged) jump off Lion's Head and paraglide down close to the Clifton beachfront. But the city offers sedate pleasures as well, along its hundreds of paths and 150km of beaches.

Cape Town's rich urban texture is immediately apparent in its diverse **architecture** (see p.108): an indigenous Cape Dutch style, rooted in northern Europe, seen at its most diverse in the Constantia wine estates, which were influenced by French refugees in the seventeenth century; Muslim dissidents and slaves, freed in the nineteenth century, added their minarets to the skyline; and the English, who invaded and freed these slaves, introduced Georgian and Victorian buildings. In the tightly packed terraces of the present-day Bo-Kaap and the tenements of District Six, coloured descendants of slaves evolved a unique, evocatively Capetonian brand of jazz, which is well worth catching live if you can.

Brief history

San hunter-gatherers, South Africa's first human inhabitants, moved freely through the Cape Peninsula for tens of millennia before being edged into the interior some two thousand years ago by the arrival of sheep-herding **Khoikhoi** migrants from the north. Over the following 1600 years, the Khoikhoi held sway over the Cape pastures. **Portuguese** mariners, in search of a stopoff point en route to East Africa and the East Indies, first rounded the Cape in the 1480s, and named it Cabo de Boa Esperanza (Cape of Good Hope), but their attempts at trading with the Khoikhoi were short-lived.

The Cape goes Dutch

Europeans did not seriously attempt to create a permanent stopping-off point at the Cape until the **Dutch East India Company** (VOC) cruised into Table Bay in 1652 and set up shop.

The VOC, the world's largest corporation at the time, planned little more than a halfway house, to provide fresh produce to their ships trading between Europe and the East. Their small landing party, led by **Jan van Riebeeck**, built a mud fort where the Grand Parade now stands and established **vegetable gardens**, which they hoped to work with indigenous labour.

The Khoikhoi were understandably none too keen to swap their freedom for a nine-to-five job, so Van Riebeeck began to import **slaves** in 1658, first from West Africa and later the East Indies. The growth of the Dutch settlement alarmed the Khoikhoi, who in 1659 tried to drive the Europeans out; however, they were defeated and had to cede the peninsula to the colonists. By 1700, the settlement had grown into an urban centre, referred to as "Kaapstad" (Cape Town).

During the early eighteenth century, Western Cape Khoikhoi society disintegrated, **German** and **French** religious refugees swelled the European population, and slavery became the economic backbone of the colony, now a minor colonial village of canals and low, whitewashed, flat-roofed houses. By 1750, Cape Town was a town of over a thousand buildings, with 2500 inhabitants.

1

Goodbye slavery, hello segregation

In 1795, **Britain**, deeply concerned by Napoleonic expansionism, grabbed Cape Town to secure the strategic sea route to the East. This displeased the settlement's Calvinist Dutch burghers, but was better news for the substantially Muslim slave population, as Britain ordered the **abolition of slavery** in 1834. The British also allowed **freedom of religion**, and South Africa's first mosque was soon built by freed slaves, in Dorp Street in the Bo-Kaap.

By the turn of the nineteenth century, Cape Town had become one of the most cosmopolitan places in the world and a seaport of major significance, growing under the influence of the British Empire. The Commercial Exchange was completed in 1819, followed by department stores, banks and insurance company buildings. In the 1860s the docks were begun, Victoria Road from the city to Sea Point was built, and the suburban railway line to Wynberg, one of the southern suburbs, was laid. Since slavery had been abolished, Victorian Cape Town had to be built by **convicts** and prisoners of war transported from the colonial frontier in the Eastern Cape (see p.308). Racial segregation wasn't far behind, and an outbreak of bubonic plague in 1901 gave the town council a pretext to establish **N'dabeni**, Cape Town's first black location, near Maitland.

In 1910, Cape Town was drawn into the political centre of the newly federated South Africa when it became the **legislative capital** of the Union (see p.654). Africans and coloureds, excluded from the cosy deal between Boers and the British, had to find expression in the workplace. In 1919, they flexed their collective muscle on the docks, forming the mighty **Industrial and Commercial Workers Union**, which boasted two hundred thousand members in its heyday.

Competing nationalisms

Increasing industrialization brought an influx of black workers to the city, who were housed in the locations of **Guguletu** and **Nyanga**, built in 1945. Three years later, the whites-only National Party came to power, promising a fearful white electorate that it would reverse the flow of Africans to the cities. In Cape Town it introduced a policy favouring coloureds for employment, rather than Africans, and among Africans, only men who had jobs were admitted to Cape Town (the women were excluded altogether), and the construction of family accommodation for Africans was forbidden.

Langa township, a few kilometres east of the city's southern suburbs, became a stronghold of the exclusively black **Pan Africanist Congress** (PAC), which organized a peaceful anti-pass demonstration in Cape Town on April 8, 1960. During the demonstration, police fired on the crowd, killing three people and wounding many more. As a result, the government declared a state of emergency and banned anti-apartheid opposition groups, including the PAC and ANC.

In 1966, the notorious **Group Areas Act** was used to uproot whole coloured communities from District Six and move them to the desolate **Cape Flats**. Here, rampant gangsterism took root and remains one of Cape Town's most pressing problems today. To compound the issue, the National Party stripped away coloured representation on the town council in 1972.

Resistance resumes

Eleven years later, at a huge meeting on the Cape Flats, the extra-parliamentary opposition defied government repression and re-formed as the **United Democratic Front**, heralding a period of intensified opposition to apartheid. In 1986, one of the major pillars crumbled when the government was forced to scrap influx control; blacks began pouring into Cape Town seeking work and erecting shantytowns, making Cape Town one of the fastest-growing cities in the world. On February 11, 1990, the city's history took a neat twist when, just hours after being released from prison, **Nelson Mandela** made his first public speech from the balcony of City Hall to a jubilant crowd

1

spilling across the Grand Parade, the very site of the first Dutch fort. Four years later, he entered the formerly whites-only Parliament, 500m away, as South Africa's first democratically elected president.

Transformation

One of the anomalies of the 1994 election was that while most of South Africa delivered an **ANC landslide**, the Western Cape returned the **National Party**, the party that invented apartheid, as its provincial government. Politics in South Africa were not, it turned out, divided along a faultline that separated whites from the rest of the population as many had assumed; the majority of coloureds had voted for the party that had once stripped them of the vote, regarding it with less suspicion than the ANC. Apart from the period between 2002 and 2006, when Capetonians elected an ANC administration, the Western Cape and its capital have consistently bucked South Africa's national trend of overwhelming ANC dominance. Since 2006 both have been governed by the liberal Democratic Alliance (DA), which increased its proportion of the vote in the 2011 local elections.

During the ANC's first term in national government under Mandela (1994–99), affirmative action policies and a racial shift in the economy led to the rise of a **black middle class**, but even so this represented a tiny fraction of the African and coloured population, and many people felt that transformation hadn't gone far enough. Indeed after nearly two decades of non-racial democracy, Cape Town is still a very divided city and one that is becoming increasingly so.

A tale of two cities

On the one hand, the Mother City has been titivating itself for tourists and investors, with the post-apartheid period bringing a wave of economic confidence expressed by investors in a number of monumental developments, among them the megalomaniacal **Century City** (1997) in the northern suburbs, a retail, residential, office-complex, theme-park, wannabe-city-in-itself, with Tuscan architecture and Venice-inspired canals. More tasteful was the expansion of the V&A Waterfront to include the hugely symbolic **Nelson Mandela Gateway** (2001) occupying a prime site and the nearby **Cape Town International Convention Centre** (2003), which finally gave the Mother City the world class conference facility it so badly needed. As part of South Africa's successful hosting of the 2010 FIFA World Cup, the iconic **Cape Town Stadium** (2009) went up on Green Point Common and Cape Town International Airport got a brand-new **Central Terminal Building** (2009), at last providing a facility that can cope with the city's expanding air traffic. To cap it all, the state-of-the-art **Cape Town Film Studio** (2010) was already attracting major projects by 2011, kicking off with the production of 3D extravaganza *Judge Dredd*.

On the other hand, as the biggest city within over a thousand kilometres, Cape Town continued (and continues) to attract a steady **influx** of people seeking a better life, mostly from the rural Eastern Cape, but also from all over Africa, with shacks proliferating wherever there are available open spaces in the townships. The city estimates that nearly a quarter of its households live in so-called "**informal dwellings**" or shacks. In 2005, the ANC national housing minister launched the **N2 Gateway Project**, to substitute brick buildings for some of the shacks that lined the N1 from the airport to the city. Whether it was a serious attempt to alleviate the housing shortage or just grandstanding for the electorate and eye candy for tourists arriving by air in the Mother City is a moot point. Either way, housing is still one of the biggest problems facing the metropolis (and the whole of South Africa), and a growing one: between 1998 and 2008 Cape Town's housing **backlog** grew from 150,000 to 300,000.

The housing shortage means that hundreds of thousands of Capetonians have limited **access to services**, such as running water, waterborne-sewerage and electricity. It's also symptomatic of the city's slew of other problems: poverty, unemployment, rampant

1

CITY CENTRE & SUBURBS

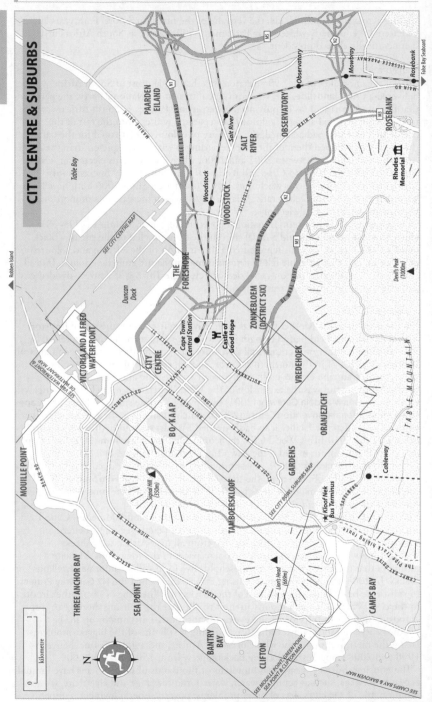

THE LANGUAGE OF COLOUR

It's striking just how un-African Cape Town looks and sounds. Halfway between East and West, Cape Town drew its population from Africa, Asia and Europe, and traces of all three continents are found in the genes, language, culture, religion and cuisine of South Africa's coloured population. Afrikaans (a close relative of Dutch) is the mother tongue of over half the city's population. Having said that, a very substantial number of Capetonians are born English-speakers and English punches well above its weight as the local lingua franca, which, in this multilingual society, virtually everyone can speak and understand.

Afrikaans is the mother tongue of a large proportion of the city's **coloured** residents, as well as many whites. The term "coloured" is contentious, but in South Africa it doesn't have the same tainted connotations as in Britain and the US; it refers to South Africans of mixed race. Most brown-skinned people in Cape Town (over fifty percent of Capetonians) are coloureds, with Asian, African and Khoikhoi ancestry.

crime, and high infection rates for HIV and TB. Planners project that within the next twenty years the city's **population** will grow from its present 3.5 million to anywhere between five and seven million inhabitants.

Industry has long been the route for urbanizing societies to rapidly create **employment**. But industrialization comes at an environmental cost and Cape Town's environment is one of its greatest assets: a tangible source of income and employment through tourism. But on its own, tourism is not enough. The city's planners and politicians face some tough choices.

The City Centre

Strand Street marks the edge of Cape Town's original beachfront (though you'd never guess it today), and all urban development to its north stands on reclaimed land. To its south is the **Upper City Centre**, containing the remains of the city's 350-year-old historic core, which has survived the ravages of modernization and apartheid-inspired urban clearance, and emerged with enough charm to make it South Africa's most pleasing city centre. The entire area from Strand Street to the southern foot of the mountain is a collage of Georgian, Cape Dutch, Victorian and twentieth-century architecture (see p.108), as well as being the place where Europe, Asia and Africa meet in markets, alleyways and mosques. Among the drawcards here are **Parliament**, the **Company's Gardens** and many of Cape Town's major **museums**. North of Strand Street to the shore, the **Lower City Centre** takes in the still-functional **Duncan Dock**.

The Upper City Centre

Adderley Street, running from the train station in the north to the Gardens in the south, is the obvious orientation axis here. To its east, and close to each other just off Strand Street, are the **Castle of Good Hope**, the site of **District Six**, the **Grand Parade** and the **City Hall**. The district to the west of Adderley Street is the closest South Africa gets to a European quarter – a tight network of streets with cafés, buskers, bookshops, street stalls and antique shops congregating around the pedestrianized **St George's Mall** and **Greenmarket Square**. The **Bo-Kaap**, or Muslim district, three blocks further west across Buitengragt (which means the Outer Canal, but is actually a street), exudes a piquant contrast to this, with its minarets, spice shops and cafés selling curried snacks.

Southwest of Adderley Street, where it takes a sharp right into Wale Street, is the symbolic heart of Cape Town, with **Parliament**, museums, archives and De Tuynhuys – the Western Cape office of the President – arranged around the **Company's Gardens**.

1

CITY CENTRE

● SHOPS	
Book Lounge	2
Neighbourgoods Market	1

■ ACCOMMODATION	
iKhaya Lodge	2
Rouge on Rose	1

■ BARS & CLUBS	
The Assembly	2
Evol	5
Perserverance Tavern	4
Thirtyone	3
Vaudeville	1

● RESTAURANTS & CAFÉS	
Biesmiellah	4
Bizerca Bistro	1
Charly's Bakery	5
Col'Cacchio	2
Sinn's	6
Vaudeville	3

Duncan Dock

THE FORESHORE

DUNCAN ROAD

Cape Town International Conference Centre

COEN STEYTLER AVE

HERTZOG BOULEVARD
HERTZOG BOULEVARD

WHARF STREET

THIBAULT SQUARE

HANS STRIJDOM AVE

PRESTWICH

HOSPITAL
PRESTWICH
SOMERSET ROAD

WATERKANT

Gold of Africa Museum

Cape Quarter

Evangelical Lutheran Church

STRAND

SEE AROUND LONG ST & THE COMPANY GARDENS MAP

Cape Town Tourism Visitors' Centre

Train Station

STRAND STR. EXTN.

Castle of Good Hope

GRAND PARADE

HOUT

BO-KAAP

Bo-Kaap Museum

DARLING

City Hall

LONGMARKET

Fugard Theatre

CALEDON

District Six Museum

ZONNEBLOEM (DISTRICT 6)

Cape Technikon

WALE

DORP

LEEUWEN

UPPER

PEPPER

BLOEM

BUITEN

COMMERCIAL

ROELAND

VREDEHOEK

The Company Gardens

ORPHAN

BUITENSINGEL

Bertram House

ORANGE

ORANJEZICHT

GARDENS

0   500
metres

Cable Station, Camps Bay & Atlantic Seaboard

Adderley Street

Once the place to shop in Cape Town, **Adderley Street**, lined with handsome buildings from several centuries, is still worth a stroll today. Its attractive streetscape has been blemished somewhat by a series of large 1960s and 1970s shopping centres but, just minutes from crowded malls, among the streets and alleys around Greenmarket Square, you can still find some human scale and historic texture.

1

THE NAMING OF ADDERLEY STREET

Although the Dutch used Robben Island as a political prison (see p.106), the South African mainland only narrowly escaped becoming a second Australia, a **penal colony** where British felons and enemies of the state could be dumped. By the 1840s, "respectable Australians" were lobbying for a ban on the transportation of criminals to the Antipodes, and the British authorities responded by trying to divert convicts to the Cape.

In 1848, the British ship *Neptune* set sail from Bermuda for Cape Town with a cargo of 282 prisoners. When news of its departure reached Cape Town there was outrage; five thousand citizens gathered on the Grand Parade the following year to hear prominent liberals denounce the British government. When the ship docked in September 1849, governor Sir Harry Smith forbade any criminal from landing while, back in London, politician **Charles Adderley** successfully addressed the House of Commons in support of the Cape colonists. In February 1850, the *Neptune* set off for Tasmania with its full complement of convicts, and grateful Capetonians renamed the city's main thoroughfare **Adderley Street**.

One of the ugliest buildings erected in the 1970s is the **Golden Acre** shopping complex, dominating the north (harbour) end of Adderley Street, which is a hub for much of Cape Town's public transport. Although the mall itself and its environs are anything but picturesque, here you do get an authentic taste of ordinary Capetonians doing their shopping – something you won't find at the sanitized V&A Waterfront (see p.104). Among the pavements and pedestrianized sections outside, which run down to the station, there's a closely packed **flea market** offering curios, crafts and electronic goods (but watch your wallet).

A little further south lies the **Adderley Street Flower Market** at Trafalgar Place, in Adderley Street between Strand and Darling streets, run by members of the Bo-Kaap Muslim community, who are known for their sharp wit. Continuing south, two grandiose bank buildings stand on opposite sides of Adderley Street; the fussier of the two, the erstwhile **Standard Bank**, fronted by Corinthian columns and covered with a tall dome – a temple to the partnership of empire and finance – is now an upmarket **restaurant** and coffee shop. The **First National Bank**, completed in 1913, was the last South African building designed by Sir Herbert Baker (see box, p.473).

The Slave Lodge

Mon–Sat 10am–5pm • R20 • audio headset R20 • ☎ 021 467 7229, ⊚ iziko.org.za/slavelodge

At the top corner of Adderley Street, just as it veers sharply northwest into Wale Street, **The Slave Lodge** was built in 1679 to house the human chattels of the Dutch East India Company (VOC) – the largest single slaveholder at the Cape.

For nearly two centuries – more than half the city's existence as an urban settlement – Cape Town's economic and social structures rested on slavery (see box, p.94). By the 1770s, almost a thousand slaves were held at the lodge. Under VOC administration (see p.87), the lodge also became the Cape Colony's main brothel, its doors thrown open to all comers for an hour each night. In 1810 the British administration decided to use the lodge as the Supreme Court, a function it retained for over a century. To clear out the government-owned slaves, it auctioned most off to private individuals, while the remaining two hundred were moved to smaller accommodation in the Company's Gardens, where they remained until they were freed in 1827, nearly ten years earlier than the rest of the slaves at the Cape. From 1914, the building was used as government offices, and now houses an exhibition, still evolving, about slavery. Taking an audio headset allows you to follow the footsteps of German salt trader Otto Mentzl as he is taken on a tour of the lodge in the 1700s, which gives you a good idea of the miserable conditions at the time.

SLAVERY AT THE CAPE

Slavery was officially **abolished** at the Cape in 1838, but its legacy lives on in South Africa. The country's coloured inhabitants, who make up fifty percent of Cape Town's population, are largely descendants of slaves and indigenous Khoisan people, and some historians argue that apartheid was a natural successor to slavery.

By the end of the eighteenth century, the almost 26,000-strong slave population of the Cape exceeded that of the free burghers (citizens, mostly of European extraction). Despite the profound impact this had on the development of social relations in South Africa, it remained one of the most neglected topics of the country's history, until the publication in the 1980s of a number of studies on slavery. There's still a reluctance on the part of most coloureds to acknowledge their slave origins.

Few, if any, slaves were captured at the Cape for export, making the colony unique in the African trade. Paradoxically, while people were being captured elsewhere on the continent for export to the Americas, the Cape administration, forbidden by the VOC from enslaving the local indigenous population, had to look further afield. Of the 63,000 slaves imported to the Cape before 1808, most came from East Africa, Madagascar, India and Indonesia, representing one of the broadest cultural mixes of any slave society. This diversity initially worked against the establishment of a unified group identity, but eventually a **Creolized culture** emerged which, among other things, played a major role in the development of the Afrikaans language.

Long Street

Parallel to Adderley Street, buzzing one-way **Long Street** is one of Cape Town's most diverse thoroughfares, best known as the city's **main nightlife strip**. When it was first settled by Muslims some three hundred years ago, Long Street marked Cape Town's boundary; by the 1960s, it had become a sleazy thoroughfare of drinking holes and whorehouses. Miraculously, it's all still here, but with a whiff of gentrification and a rather boring section of discount furniture shops and fast-food joints; it deserves exploration from the Wale Street intersection onwards.

Mosques still coexist with bars, *dagga* (weed) is readily available, and antique dealers, craft shops, bookshops and cafés do a good trade. The street is packed with backpacker hostels and a couple of upmarket hotels, though it can be very noisy into the early hours from the nightclubs. At night it's safe enough to pub or club crawl, and you'll always be able to find taxis. Street vendors sell boerewors rolls and from 8pm till the early hours music blares from Mohammed's street *schwarma* stand.

Long Street Baths

Long and Orange sts • Daily 7am–7pm • Turkish baths men: Tues 1–7pm, Wed & Fri 8am–7pm, Sun 8am–noon • Women: Mon, Thurs & Sat 9am–6pm • R40/hour • Pool R12 • ☎ 021 400 3302

The **Long Street Baths** is an unpretentious and relaxing historic Cape Town institution, established in 1908 in an Edwardian building that occupies the top of the road, where it hits Buitensingel. For a quiet swim and steam, avoid lunchtime, when local office workers pile in for a quick dip. The Turkish baths are open separately to men and women. If you're after a luxury spa hangout, however, you'd be better off heading for the *Mount Nelson Hotel*, up the road in Orange Street (see p.147).

Palm Tree Mosque

185 Long St • Not open to the public

An unmistakable landmark on Long Street, just south of where it crosses Leeuwen Street, the **Palm Tree Mosque** is fronted by a lone palm tree, its fronds caressing the upper storey. Significant as the only surviving eighteenth-century house in the street, it was bought in 1807 by members of the local Muslim community, who turned the upper floor into a mosque and the lower into living quarters.

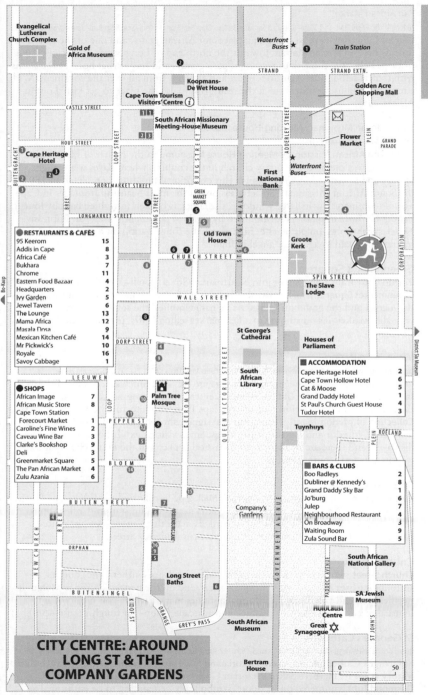

1

Evangelical Lutheran Church Complex

Gold of Africa Museum

Waterfront Buses ★ ❶

Train Station

STRAND

STRAND EXTN.

Koopmans-De Wet House

Golden Acre Shopping Mall

Cape Town Tourism Visitors' Centre ℹ️

CASTLE STREET

South African Missionary Meeting-House Museum

Flower Market

GRAND PARADE

HOUT STREET

LOOP STREET

BURG STREET

ADDERLEY STREET

PLEIN STREET

BUITENGRACHT

Cape Heritage Hotel

First National Bank

Waterfront Buses ★

BREE

SHORTMARKET STREET

LONGMARKET STREET

GREEN MARKET SQUARE

LONG STREET

Old Town House

LONGMARKET STREET

Groote Kerk

ST GEORGE'S MALL

PARLIAMENT STREET

CORPORATION

CHURCH STREET

WALE STREET

SPIN STREET

The Slave Lodge

● RESTAURANTS & CAFÉS

95 Keerom	15
Addis in Cape	8
Africa Café	3
Bukhara	7
Chrome	11
Eastern Food Bazaar	4
Headquarters	2
Ivy Garden	5
Jewel Tavern	6
The Lounge	13
Mama Africa	12
Masala Dosa	9
Mexican Kitchen Café	14
Mr Pickwick's	10
Royale	16
Savoy Cabbage	1

DORP STREET

St George's Cathedral

Houses of Parliament

South African Library

LEEUWEN

Palm Tree Mosque

QUEEN VICTORIA STREET

● SHOPS

African Image	7
African Music Store	8
Cape Town Station Forecourt Market	1
Caroline's Fine Wines	2
Caveau Wine Bar	3
Clarke's Bookshop	9
Deli	3
Greenmarket Square	5
The Pan African Market	4
Zulu Azania	6

LOOP

PEPPER ST

BLOEM

LEEUWEN STREET

■ ACCOMMODATION

Cape Heritage Hotel	2
Cape Town Hollow Hotel	6
Cat & Moose	5
Grand Daddy Hotel	1
St Paul's Church Guest House	4
Tudor Hotel	3

Tuynhuys

PLEIN

ROELAND

BUITEN STREET

Company's Gardens

GOVERNMENT AVENUE

■ BARS & CLUBS

Boo Radleys	2
Dubliner @ Kennedy's	8
Grand Daddy Sky Bar	1
Jo'burg	6
Julep	7
Neighbourhood Restaurant	4
On Broadway	3
Waiting Room	9
Zula Sound Bar	5

ORPHAN

NEW CHURCH

BREE

South African National Gallery

PADDOCK AVENUE

SA Jewish Museum

Long Street Baths

BUITENSINGEL

Holocaust Centre

Great Synagogue ✡

ST JOHN'S

KLOOF ST

ORANGE

GREY'S PASS

South African Museum

Bertram House

0 ___ 50

metres

Bo-Kaap

District Six Museum

CITY CENTRE: AROUND LONG ST & THE COMPANY GARDENS

1

Pan African Market

76 Long St • Oct–April Mon–Fri 8.30am–5.30pm & Sat 9am–3.30pm, May–Sept Mon–Fri 9am–5pm & Sat 9am–3pm • ⓦ panafrican.co.za

One of Cape Town's most intriguing places for African crafts, and one of the easiest to miss, is the **Pan African Market**, towards the north end of Long Street. Its inconspicuous frontage belies the three-floor warren of passageways and rooms that burst at the seams with traders selling vast quantities of art and artefacts from all over the continent. With a team of in-house seamstresses at the ready, this is also the place to get kitted out in African garb.

South African Missionary Meeting-House Museum

40 Long St • Mon–Fri 9am–4pm • Free

The **South African Missionary Meeting-House Museum**, on the corner of Hout Street and Long, was the first missionary church in the country, where slaves were taught literacy and instructed in Christianity. This exceptional building, completed in 1804 by the South African Missionary Society, has one of the most beautiful frontages in Cape Town. Dominated by its large windows, the facade is broken into three bays by four slender Corinthian pilasters surmounted by a gabled pediment. Inside, an impressive Neoclassical timber **pulpit** perches high above the congregation on a pair of columns, framing an inlaid image of an angel in flight.

Greenmarket Square

Turning east from Long Street into Shortmarket Street, you'll skim the edge of **Greenmarket Square**, which is worth a little exploration to take in the cobbled streets, the market and the grand buildings. As its name implies, the square started as a vegetable market; it's now home to a flea market selling crafts, jewellery and hippie clobber.

Michaelis Collection

Old Town House, Greenmarket Square • Mon–Fri 10am–5pm, Sat 10am–4pm • Free • ☎ 021 481 3933, ⓦ iziko.org.za/michaelis

On the western side of Greenmarket Square are the solid limewashed walls and small shuttered windows of the **Old Town House**, entered from Longmarket Street. Built in the mid-1700s, this beautiful example of Cape Dutch architecture houses the **Michaelis Collection** of predominantly minor but still significant Dutch and Flemish portrait, townscape, interior and landscape paintings. Small visiting exhibitions are also displayed, and there are regular evening classical concerts in the Frans Hals room; the website lists forthcoming events.

St George's Mall

East of Greenmarket Square is **St George's Mall**, a pedestrianized road that runs northeast from Wale Street to Thibault Square, near the train station. Coffee shops, snack bars and lots of street traders and buskers make this a more pleasant route between the station and Company's Gardens than Adderley Street.

Church Street

Church Street (which crosses St George's Mall towards its southern end) and its surrounding area abound with antique dealers, and on the pedestrianized section at its northeastern end you'll find an informal antiques market where you may pick up unusual pieces of jewellery, bric-a-brac and Africana (Mon–Sat roughly 9am–4pm).

St George's Cathedral

Queen Victoria and Wale sts • Mon–Fri 8.30am–5pm, Sat 8am–12.30pm, Sun open only for church services: 7am, 8am, 10am & 7pm

St George's Cathedral, at Queen Victoria and Wale streets, is interesting as much for its history as for its Herbert Baker Victorian Gothic design; on September 7, 1986, **Desmond Tutu** hammered on its doors, symbolically demanding to be enthroned as

South Africa's first black archbishop. Three years later, he heralded the last days of apartheid by leading thirty thousand people from the cathedral to the City Hall, where he coined his now famous slogan for the new order: "We are the rainbow people!" he told the crowd, "We are the new people of South Africa!"

Government Avenue and around

A stroll down pedestrianized **Government Avenue**, the southwest extension of Adderley Street, makes for one of the most serene walks in central Cape Town. This oak-lined boulevard runs past the rear of Parliament through the gardens, and its benches are frequently occupied by snoring tramps.

South African Library

5 Queen Victoria St • Mon, Tues, Thurs & Fri 9am–6pm, Wed 10am–5pm • Free

At the northern end of Government Avenue, the **South African Library** houses one of the country's best collections of antiquarian historical and natural history books, covering Southern Africa. Built with the revenue from a tax on wine, it opened in 1822 as one of the first free libraries in the world.

Company's Gardens

Queen Victoria St

Stretching from the South African Library to the South African Museum, the **Company's Gardens** were the initial *raison d'être* for the Dutch settlement at the Cape. Established in 1652 to supply fresh greens to Dutch East India Company ships travelling between the Netherlands and the East, the gardens were initially worked by imported slave labour. At the end of the seventeenth century, the gardens were turned over to botanical horticulture for Cape Town's growing colonial elite. Ponds, lawns, landscaping and a crisscross web of oak-shaded walkways were introduced. Today the gardens are full of local plants, the result of long-standing European interest in Cape botany, and are a pleasant place to meander, featuring a pleasantly shady outdoor café.

Tuynhuys

Government Avenue

You can see the grand buildings and tended flowerbeds of **Tuynhuys**, about fifty metres south of the South African Library along Government Avenue. Now the Cape Town office (but not residence) of the president, it started off as a Dutch building, but was remodelled under the instructions of **Lord Charles Somerset** during his governorship (1814–26). The energy Somerset put into implementing an official policy of Anglicization at the Cape was matched only by this private obsession with architecture. This saw the demolition of the two Dutch wings of the residence to bring it into line with contemporary English taste and the reinvention of the entire garden frontage with a Colonial Regency facade. Among the features he introduced was the veranda sheltering under an elegantly curving canopy, supported on slender iron columns.

South African National Gallery

Government Avenue, Company's Gardens • Daily 10am–5pm • R20 • ⓦ iziko.org.za/sang

The **South African National Gallery** is an essential port of call for anyone interested in the local art scene, and includes a small but excellent permanent collection of contemporary South African art. Be sure to take in Jane Alexander's *Butcher Boys* sculpture, which figuratively portrays South Africa's inherent menace and violence.

You'll also find a fine display of traditional works from the southeast of the continent, based around a small collection donated by the German government. The exhibits, which include beadwork, carvings and craft objects, were chosen for their aesthetic qualities and rarity, and represent the gallery's policy of focusing on neglected parts of South Africa's heritage. In addition, another room contains minor works by British

1

artists including George Romney, Thomas Gainsborough and Joshua Reynolds, as well as some Pre-Raphaelite paintings. The gallery has a **café** serving light lunches and snacks, as well as an **excellent craft shop** selling embroidered textiles, basketry, wire products and fine beadwork from South Africa.

South African Jewish Museum

88 Hatfield St • Sun–Thurs 10am–5pm, Fri 10am–2pm • R50 • ⓦ sajewishmuseum.co.za

The **South African Jewish Museum** is partially housed in South Africa's first synagogue, built in 1863. One of Cape Town's most ambitious and successful permanent exhibitions, it tells the story of South African Jewry from its beginnings over 150 years ago to the present – a narrative that starts in the Old Synagogue, from which visitors cross, via a gangplank, to the upper level of a new two-storey building, symbolically re-enacting the arrival by boat of the first Jewish immigrants at Table Bay in the 1840s. Multimedia interactive displays, models and Judaica artefacts follow three threads: "**Memories**", looking at the roots and experiences of the immigrants; "**Reality**", covering their integration into South Africa; and "**Dreams**", examining a diversity of views about the role of Jews in South Africa, their relationship to Israel and their position in the world.

The **basement level** houses a wonderfully executed walk-through reconstruction of a Lithuanian village (most South African Jews have their nineteenth-century roots in Lithuania). A good restaurant, shop and auditorium are also housed in the museum complex.

Cape Town Holocaust Centre

88 Hatfield St • Mon–Thurs & Sun 10am–5pm, Fri 10am–1pm • Free • ⓦ ctholocaust.co.za

Opened in 1999, the **Holocaust Exhibition** is one of the most moving and brilliantly executed museums in Cape Town. Housed upstairs in the Holocaust Centre (in the same complex as the Jewish Museum), it resonates sharply in a country that only recently emerged from an era of racial oppression – a connection that the exhibition makes explicitly. Exhibits trace the history of anti-Semitism in Europe, culminating with the Nazis' Final Solution; they also look at South Africa's Greyshirts, who were motivated by Nazi propaganda during the 1930s and were later absorbed into the National Party. The story is told through text, photographs, artefacts (such as a concentration camp uniform), film clips, soundtracks, multimedia and interactive video.

The Great Synagogue

88 Hatfield St (entrance through same gate as Jewish Museum) • Mon 10am–1pm, Tues–Thurs & Sun 10am–4pm

The **Great Synagogue** is one of Cape Town's outstanding religious buildings. Designed by the Scottish architects Parker & Forsyth and completed in 1905, its facade features two soaring towers after the style of central European Baroque churches. The interior is dominated by an impressive copper-clad dome that arches over an alcove containing religious objects and beautifully decorated with golden mosaics.

The South African Museum

25 Queen Victoria St • Daily 10am–5pm • R15 • ⓦ iziko.org.za/sam

The nation's premier museum of natural history and human sciences, the **South African Museum**, west of Government Avenue, is notable for its **ethnographic galleries** which contain some very good displays on the traditional arts and crafts of several African groups and some exceptional examples of rock art. Upstairs, the **natural history galleries** display mounted mammals, dioramas of prehistoric Karoo reptiles, and Table Mountain flora and fauna. A highlight is the four-storey "whale well", in which a collection of beautiful whale skeletons hang like massive mobiles, accompanied by the eerie strains of their song.

1

The Planetarium

25 Queen Victoria St • Shows daily 11am–3pm & also Tues 8pm, closed first Mon of month outside school holidays • R20 • Ⓦ iziko.org.za /planetarium

The **Planetarium**, attached to the South African Museum, is recommended if you want to see the constellations of the southern hemisphere, accompanied by informed commentary. There's also a changing programme of shows covering topics such as San sky myths. Leaflets at the museum provide a list of forthcoming attractions (or check the website), and you can buy a monthly chart of the current night sky.

Bertram House

Hiddingh Campus, Orange St • Mon & Fri 10am–5pm • R10 • Ⓦ iziko.org.za/bertram

At the southernmost end of Government Avenue, you'll come upon **Bertram House**, whose beautiful two-storey brick facade looks out across a fragrant herb garden. Built in the 1840s, the museum is significant as the only surviving brick Georgian-style house in Cape Town, and displays typical furniture and objects of a well-to-do colonial British family in the first half of the nineteenth century.

Bertram House was extensively restored to its current state in the 1980s (and again in 2010): imported face brick and Welsh slate were used to re-create the original facade, while the interior walls were redecorated in their earlier dark green and ochre, based on the evidence of paint scrapings. The reception rooms are decorated in the Regency style, while the porcelain is predominantly nineteenth-century English.

Houses of Parliament

120 Plein St • National Assembly tours Mon–Fri on the hour 9am–noon • Free • Book one week in advance & bring passport or ID • ☎ 021 403 2266, ✉ tours@parliament.gov.za • Ⓦ parliament.gov.za

South Africa's **Houses of Parliament**, on Parliament Street, are a complex of interlinking buildings, with labyrinthine corridors connecting hundreds of offices, debating chambers and miscellaneous other rooms. Many of these are relics of the 1980s reformist phase of apartheid when, in the interests of racial segregation, there were three distinct legislative complexes sited here to cater to different "races".

The original wing, completed in 1885, is an imposing Victorian Neoclassical building that first served as the legislative assembly of the Cape Colony. After the Boer republics and British colonies amalgamated in 1910, it became the parliament of the Union of South Africa. This is the old parliament, where over seven decades of repressive legislation, including apartheid laws, were passed.

The new chamber was built in 1983 as part of the **tricameral parliament**, P.W. Botha's attempt to avert majority rule by trying to co-opt Indians and coloureds – but in their own separate debating chambers. The "tricameral" chamber, where the three non-African "races" on occasions met together, is now the **National Assembly**, where you can watch sessions of parliament. One-hour **tours** leave from the Plein Street entrance to Parliament; this is also where you buy day tickets to the debating sessions, the most interesting of which is question time (Wed from 3pm) when ministers are quizzed by MPs.

Castle of Good Hope

Buitenkant & Darling sts, opposite the Grand Parade • **Castle** Daily 9am–4pm • R28 • **Guided tours** Mon–Sat 11am, noon & 2pm • Free • Ⓦ castleofgoodhope.co.za

From the outside, South Africa's oldest official building looks somewhat miserable, and its position on Darling Street, behind the train station and city-bus terminal, does nothing to dispel this. Nevertheless, the **Castle of Good Hope** is well worth the entrance fee; inside, a meticulous ten-year restoration has returned the decor to the British Regency style introduced in 1798. But the Castle has also shaken off a dour historical image, and has some **fine contemporary exhibitions** – check the website for current details.

Completed in 1679, the castle replaced Van Riebeeck's earlier mud and timber fort, which stood on the site of the Grand Parade. It was built in accordance with seventeenth-century European principles of fortification, comprising strong bastions from which the outside walls could be protected by crossfire.

The entrance is a fine example of seventeenth-century Dutch classicism and, in the tower above, the bell cast in Amsterdam in 1697 still hangs from its original wooden beams. For 150 years, the castle remained the symbolic heart of the Cape administration, and the centre of social and economic life.

Inside the castle are three interesting collections. The **Military Museum** has displays on the conflicts that dogged the early settlement; the **Secunde's House** has furnishings, paintings and *objets d'art* that filled the living space of the deputy governor; and the **William Fehr Collection**, one of the country's most important exhibits of decorative arts, includes paintings of the settlement, eighteenth- and nineteenth-century Dutch and Indonesian furniture, and seventeenth- and eighteenth-century Chinese and Japanese porcelain. Guided tours are useful for orientation and cover the main features of the castle. In the elegant courtyard there is a very pleasant teashop, with Table Mountain looming over the west wall.

The Grand Parade and the City Hall

The **Grand Parade** is a large open area, to the west of the Castle of Good Hope, which has been used for markets, parking and political rallies – and, of course, originally for military parades.

The Grand Parade appeared on TV screens throughout the world on February 11, 1990, when one hundred thousand people gathered to hear **Nelson Mandela** make his first speech after being released from prison, from the balcony of the adjoining **City Hall**. A slightly fussy Edwardian building dressed in Bath stone, City Hall manages, despite its drab surroundings, to look impressive against Table Mountain.

District Six

South of the castle, in the shadow of Devil's Peak, is a vacant lot shown on maps as the suburb of **Zonnebloem**. Before being demolished by the apartheid authorities, it was an inner-city slum known as **District Six**, an impoverished but lively community of 55,000 predominantly coloured people. Later mythologized as the erstwhile soul of Cape Town, the district harboured a rich cultural life in its narrow alleys and crowded tenements.

In 1966, apartheid ideologues declared District Six a **White Group Area** and the bulldozers moved in, taking fifteen years to drive its presence from the skyline, leaving only the mosques and churches. But, in the wake of the demolition, international and domestic outcry was so great that the area was never developed apart from a few luxury town houses on its fringes and the hefty Cape Technikon, a college that now occupies nearly a quarter of the former suburb. After years of negotiation, a few of the original residents have moved back under a scheme to develop low-cost housing in the district, but much of the area remains empty land as conflicting parties vie for a piece of the pie.

District Six Museum

25a Buitenkant St • Mon 9am–2pm, Tues–Sat 9am–4pm • R20 • Ⓦ districtsix.co.za

Few places in Cape Town speak more eloquently of the effect of apartheid on the day-to-day lives of ordinary people than the **District Six Museum**. Situated on the northern boundary of District Six, on the corner of Buitenkant and Albertus streets, the museum occupies the former **Central Methodist Mission Church**, which offered solidarity and ministry to the victims of forced removals right up to the 1980s, and became a venue for anti-apartheid gatherings. Today, it houses a series of fascinating displays that include everyday household items and tools of trades, such as hairdressing implements, as well as documentary photographs, which evoke the lives of the

1

individuals who once lived here. Occupying most of the floor is a huge map of District Six as it was, annotated by former residents, who describe their memories, reflections and incidents associated with places and buildings that no longer exist. There's also an almost complete collection of original street signs, secretly retrieved at the time of demolition by the man entrusted with dumping them into Table Bay. Their **coffee shop** sells snacks, including traditional, syrupy *koeksisters*.

The Bo-Kaap

On the slopes of Signal Hill, the **Bo-Kaap** is one of Cape Town's oldest and most fascinating residential areas. Its streets are characterized by brightly coloured nineteenth-century Dutch and Georgian terraces, which conceal a network of alleyways that are the arteries of its **Muslim community**. The Bo-Kaap harbours its own strong identity, made all the more unique by the destruction of District Six, with which it had much in common. A particular dialect of Afrikaans is spoken here, although it is steadily being eroded by English. Long-time residents have sold off family properties, and, with the closing of a landmark halal butchery, the area is set for substantial change. A number of trendy outsiders have moved in, and some guesthouses have started up, capitalizing on the outstanding central city position, poised between Long Street distractions and the buzzing Waterkant district.

Bo-Kaap residents are descended from dissidents and slaves imported by the Dutch in the sixteenth and seventeenth centuries. They became known collectively as "**Cape Malay**", although most originated from Africa, India, Madagascar and Sri Lanka, with fewer than one percent actually from Malaysia.

The easiest way to get to the Bo-Kaap is by foot along Wale Street, which trails up from the south end of Adderley Street and across Buitengragt, to become the main drag of the Bo-Kaap.

Bo-Kaap Museum
71 Wale St • Mon–Sat 10am–5pm • R15 • ⓦ iziko.org.za/bokaap

One of the best introductions to Bo-Kaap history and traditions is the **Bo-Kaap Museum**, near the Buitengragt end of Wale Street. It consists mainly of the family house and possessions of Abu Bakr Effendi, a nineteenth-century religious leader brought out from Turkey by the British in 1862 as a mediator between feuding Muslim factions. He became an important member of the community, founded an Arabic school and wrote a book in the local vernacular – now regarded as possibly the first book to be published in what can be recognized as Afrikaans. The museum also has exhibits exploring the local brand of Islam, which has its own unique traditions and nearly two dozen *kramats* (shrines) dotted about the peninsula.

Auwal Mosque
43 Dorp St

One block south of the museum is the **Auwal**, South Africa's first official mosque, founded in 1795 by Tuan Guru, a Muslim activist. Ten more mosques, whose minarets

---

BO-KAAP TOURS

The Bo-Kaap is best explored on a **tour** that walks you around the district and takes in the museum (see above). The most reliable (and cheapest, at R150 including the museum entrance fee) is run by **Bo-Kaap Guided Tours** (☎021 422 1554 or ☎082 423 6932, ✉shireen .narkedien@gmail.com). It lasts two hours and is operated by residents of the area, whose knowledge goes beyond the standard tour-guide script. The same outfit also offers a similar tour for R300 that culminates at the house of a Bo-Kaap resident for lunch, and where you get to watch the Cape Muslim meal being prepared and cooked. For this, you need to book at least two days in advance.

give spice to the quarter's skyline, now serve the district's ten thousand residents. Very little of the mosque's original structure remains and it blends in with the single-storey Georgian terraced houses it abuts, distinguished only by its large minaret.

De Waterkant

South of the V&A Waterfront and rubbing up against the west side of the city centre and Bo-Kaap is **De Waterkant**, with attractive Georgian terraced streets, some great restaurants and coffee spots and, notably, the "pink square" – the city's self-proclaimed gay quarter with clubs, pubs and saunas. With its elevated setting, cobbled streets, attractive terraces and harbour views, De Waterkant is supremely suited for just wandering around.

Strand Street

A major artery from the N2 freeway to the central business district, **Strand Street** neatly separates the upper from the lower city centre. Between the mid-eighteenth and mid-nineteenth centuries, Strand Street was one of the most fashionable streets in Cape Town because of its proximity to the shore. Its former cachet is now only discernible from the handful of quietly elegant national monuments left standing amid the roar of traffic: **Martin Melck House** (accommodating the **Gold of Africa Museum**), the **Evangelical Lutheran Church** and **Koopmans-De Wet House**.

Evangelical Lutheran Church

Corner of Buitengragt and Strand St • Mon, Wed & Fri 9am–noon • Free

Converted in 1785 from a barn, the **Evangelical Lutheran Church**'s facade includes Classical details such as a broken pediment perforated by the clock tower, as well as Gothic features like arched windows. Inside, the magnificent **pulpit**, supported by two life-size Herculean figures, is one of Cape Dutch architect Anton Anreith's masterpieces.

The establishment of a Lutheran church in Cape Town in the late eighteenth century struck a significant blow against the extreme **religious intolerance** when Protestantism was the only form of worship allowed and the Dutch Reformed Church held an absolute monopoly over saving people's souls.

Gold of Africa Museum

96 Strand St, just off Buitengragt • Mon–Sat 9.30am–5pm • R35 • ⓦ goldofafrica.com

Since the discovery of gold near Johannesburg in the late nineteenth century, South Africa has been closely associated in the Western mind with the precious metal and the riches it represents. However, the outstanding **Gold of Africa Museum** focuses on a completely different side to gold – the exquisite **artworks** crafted by nineteenth- and twentieth-century **African goldsmiths** from Mali, Senegal, Ghana and the Cote d'Ivoire. Arguably the most important such collection in the world, it traces Africa's ancient gold routes, and includes several hundred beautiful items including precious masks, crocodiles, birds, a gold crown and human figures; the highlight is the sculpted **Golden Lion** from Ghana, which is the symbol of the museum.

There's also a small auditorium with a continuous **film show** about the history of gold, a restaurant that serves pan-African cuisine with Malian puppets performing between courses, a **studio** where goldsmiths practise their art and where you can learn smithing, and a **shop** selling postcards, gold leaf and beautiful little souvenirs.

Koopmans-De Wet House

35 Strand St • Mon–Fri 10am–5pm • R10 • ⓦ iziko.org.za/koopmans

Sandwiched between two office blocks, **Koopmans-De Wet House** is an outstanding eighteenth-century pedimented Neoclassical town house and museum, accommodating a very fine collection of antique furniture and rare porcelain.

1

The earliest sections of the house were built in 1701 by **Reyner Smedinga**, a well-to-do goldsmith who imported the building materials from Holland. The house changed hands more than a dozen times over the following two centuries, with minor additions made in the 1760s and a second storey added between 1774 and 1790. In 1806, it came into the hands of the De Wet family, eventually becoming the home of **Marie Koopmans-De Wet** (1834–1906), a prominent figure on the Cape social and political circuit.

The building's **facade** has been attributed to Louis Thibault and Anton Anreith, but there's no proof of this. Whoever was responsible, the house represents a fine synthesis of Dutch elements (sash windows and large entrance doors) with the demands of local conditions; the huge rooms, lofty ceilings and shuttered windows reflect the high summer temperatures, while the front *stoep* has plastered masonry seats at each end. The **lantern** in the fanlight of the entrance to the house was a feature of all Cape Town houses in the eighteenth and early nineteenth centuries, its purpose to shine light onto the street and thus hinder slaves from gathering at night to plot.

The inexpensive **guide** booklets at the entrance give a good introduction to the background to the house and its history.

The V&A Waterfront

The **Victoria and Alfred Waterfront**, known simply as the Waterfront, is Cape Town's original Victorian harbour. After two decades of stagnation, it was redeveloped in the 1990s and incorporates the city's most popular central shopping area, an always busy complex of shops, restaurants, cinemas, waterside walkways and a functioning harbour, with magnificent Table Mountain rising beyond. The Waterfront is where you set sail for Robben Island (see p.106), embarking at the very same spot as many of South Africa's anti-apartheid activists on their way to incarceration and hard labour.

The Marina and the Victoria and Alfred basins

Victoria Basin, the smaller **Alfred Basin** to its west, and the **Marina** beyond, create the northwestern half of the Waterfront's geography of piers and quays. The shopping focus of the Waterfront is **Victoria Wharf**, an enormous flashy mall on two levels, extending along Quays Five and Six. It's here that most visitors to the Waterfront arrive. With outdoor seating, the restaurants and cafés on the mall's east side have fabulous views across the busy harbour to Table Mountain.

Alfred Mall Shopping Centre and the Old Port Captain's Office

Along the Alfred Basin's North Quay, **Alfred Mall Shopping Centre** is a complex of touristy curio shops, boutiques and restaurants. East of the Alfred Shopping Mall, the Pierhead is dominated by the **Old Port Captain's Office**, a gabled Arts and Crafts building erected in 1904, with an imposing presence that reflects its status as the nerve centre of the harbour in the early twentieth century.

THE BREAKWATER

Throughout the first half of the nineteenth century, arguments raged in Cape Town over the need for a proper dock. The Cape was often known as the **Cape of Storms** because of its tempestuous weather, which left Table Bay littered with wrecks. Clamour for a harbour grew in the 1850s with the increase in sea traffic arriving at the Cape, reaching its peak in 1860, when the Lloyd's insurance company refused the risk of covering ships dropping anchor in Table Bay. The British colonial government dragged its heels due to the costs involved, but eventually conceded and, on a suitably stormy September day in 1860, at a huge ceremony, the teenage Prince Alfred tipped the first batch of stones into Table Bay to begin the **Breakwater**, the westernmost arm of the harbour. In 1869, the dock – consisting of two main basins – was completed.

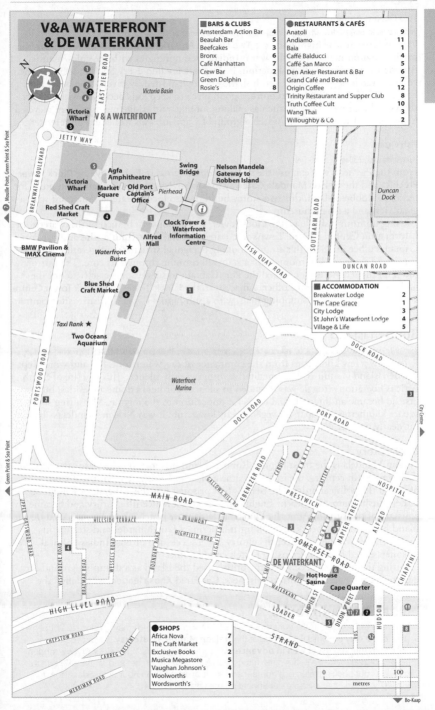

V&A WATERFRONT & DE WATERKANT

BARS & CLUBS

Amsterdam Action Bar	4
Beaulah Bar	5
Beefcakes	3
Bronx	6
Café Manhattan	7
Crew Bar	2
Green Dolphin	1
Rosie's	8

RESTAURANTS & CAFÉS

Anatoli	9
Andiamo	11
Baia	1
Caffé Balducci	4
Caffé San Marco	5
Den Anker Restaurant & Bar	6
Grand Café and Beach	7
Origin Coffee	12
Trinity Restaurant and Supper Club	8
Truth Coffee Cult	10
Wang Thai	3
Willoughby & Co	2

ACCOMMODATION

Breakwater Lodge	2
The Cape Grace	1
City Lodge	3
St John's Waterfront Lodge	4
Village & Life	5

SHOPS

Africa Nova	7
The Craft Market	6
Exclusive Books	2
Musica Megastore	5
Vaughan Johnson's	4
Woolworths	1
Wordsworth's	3

1

Two Oceans Aquarium

Dock Rd at the Marina's North Wharf • Daily 9.30am–6pm • R96 • ⓦ aquarium.co.za

One of Cape Town's highlights, the **Two Oceans Aquarium** showcases the Cape's unique marine environment, where the warm Indian Ocean mingles with the cold Atlantic. Among the highlights of the aquarium is the **shark feeding** every Sunday at 3pm, when you can watch *raggies* (ragged-tooth sharks) being hand-fed by divers. The **basement** houses the **AfriSam Children's Centre**, a good place to keep kids occupied with puppet shows and creative activities, such as making mobiles and fridge magnets from recycled materials, and where you can watch a group of Cape fur seals frolicking underwater.

Fish Quay

Swing bridge daily 7.30am–5.30pm • Free

From the Pierhead you can use the **swing bridge** to cross to **Fish Quay**, the **Clock Tower Precinct** and the **Nelson Mandela Gateway to Robben Island**. The embarkation point for ferries to Robben Island, this two-storey building also incorporates a restaurant with a great view and a small museum.

Rising up from Fish Quay, the **Clock Tower**, which houses a branch of the Waterfront Information Centre, is Cape Town's finest architectural folly. Built as the original Port Captain's office in 1882, this strange-looking octagonal structure with Gothic windows consists of three stacked rooms with a stairwell running through its core. The mirror room on the second floor enabled the Port Captain to survey all the activities of the harbour without leaving his office. Adjacent to the Clock Tower, the **Clock Tower Centre** is a compact two-storey shopping mall, with a substantial Cape Tourism visitor centre.

Robben Island

Boats daily 9am, 11am, 1pm & 3pm • R200, including boat trip, island entry and 3hr 30min tour • ☎ 021 413 4233, ⓦ robben-island.org.za

Lying only a few kilometres from the commerce of the Waterfront, flat and windswept **Robben Island** is suffused by a meditative, otherworldly silence. This key site of South Africa's liberation struggle was intended to silence apartheid's domestic critics, but instead became an international focus for opposition to the regime. Measuring six square kilometres and sparsely vegetated by low scrub, it was Nelson Mandela's "home" for nearly two decades.

Brief history

Nelson Mandela is the most famous Robben Island prisoner, but he wasn't the first. In the seventeenth century, the island became a place of banishment for those who offended the political order. The island's first prisoner was the indigenous Khoikhoi leader **Autshumato**, who learnt English in the early seventeenth century and became an emissary of the British. After the Dutch settlement was established, he was jailed on the island by Jan van Riebeeck in 1658 for murdering a Dutch herder and stealing his cattle. The rest of the seventeenth century saw a succession of East Indies political prisoners exiled here for opposing Dutch colonial rule.

During the nineteenth century, the **British** used the island as a dumping ground for deserters, criminals and political prisoners. Captured **Xhosa leaders** who defied the

---

ROBBEN ISLAND TOURS

A number of vendors at the Waterfront sell tickets for cruises, which may go close to Robben Island, but only the official ones sold at the **Nelson Mandela Gateway** will get you onto it. Bookings must be made **well in advance** with a credit card (☎ 021 413 4233, ⓦ www.robben -island.org.za) as the boats are often full, especially around December and January. Be sure to present your booking reference number and arrive at least half an hour before departure to collect your ticket. All trips are dependent on the weather.

empire during the Frontier Wars of the early to mid-nineteenth century were transported by sea from the Eastern Cape to be imprisoned here. In 1846, the island's brief was extended to include a whole range of the **socially marginalized**; criminals and political detainees were joined by vagrants, prostitutes, lunatics and the chronically ill. In the 1890s, a leper colony existed alongside the social outcasts. Lunatics were removed in 1921 and the lepers in 1930.

Robben Island's greatest era of notoriety began in 1961, when it was taken over by the **Prisons Department**. When Nelson Mandela arrived, it had become a maximum security prison, and prisoners were only allowed to send and receive one letter every six months. Harsh conditions, including routine beatings and forced hard labour, were exacerbated by geographical location: icy winds routinely blow in from the South Pole, and inmates wore only shorts and flimsy jerseys. Like every other prisoner, Mandela slept on a thin mat on the floor and was kept in solitary confinement in a cell measuring two metres square for sixteen hours a day.

Amazingly, the prisoners found ways of **protesting**, through hunger strikes, publicizing conditions when possible (by visits from the International Committee of the Red Cross, for example) and, remarkably, by taking legal action against the prison authority to stop arbitrary punishments. They won improved conditions over the years, and the island also became a university behind bars, where people of different political views and generations met; it was not unknown for prisoners to give academic help to their warders. The last political prisoners were released from Robben Island in 1991 and the remaining common-law prisoners were transferred to the mainland in 1996. On January 1, 1997, control of Robben Island was transferred from the Department of Correctional Services to the Department of the Arts, Culture, Science and Technology, which has now established it as a museum. In December 1999, the entire island was declared a **UNESCO World Heritage Site**.

The island

The ferry trip from the Waterfront takes about half an hour to reach the island. After arrival you are taken on a **bus tour** around the island and a **tour of the prison**. The bus tour stops off at several historical landmarks, the first of which is a beautiful shrine built in memory of Tuan Guru, a Muslim cleric from present-day Indonesia who was imprisoned here by the Dutch in the eighteenth century. On his release, he helped to establish Islam among slaves in Cape Town. The tour also passes a **leper graveyard** and **church** designed by Sir Herbert Baker.

Robert Sobukwe's house is perhaps the most affecting relic of incarceration on the island. It was here that Sobukwe (see p.332), leader of the Pan Africanist Congress (a radical offshoot of the ANC), was held in solitary confinement for nine years. No other political prisoners were allowed to speak to him, but he would sometimes gesture his solidarity with them by letting sand trickle through his fingers as they walked past. After his release in 1969, Sobukwe was restricted to Kimberley under house arrest, until his death from cancer in 1978.

Another stopoff is the **lime quarry** where Nelson Mandela and his fellow inmates spent countless hours of hard labour.

The Maximum Security Prison

The Maximum Security Prison, a forbidding complex of unadorned H blocks on the edge of the island, is introduced with a tour through the famous **B-Section**; you'll be guided by a former inmate, after which you're free to wander. **Mandela's cell** has been left exactly as it was, without embellishments or display, but the rest have been left locked and empty.

In the nearby **A-Section**, the "Cell Stories" exhibition skilfully suggests the sparseness of prison life; the tiny isolation cells contain personal artefacts loaned by former prisoners, plus quotations, recordings and photographs.

1

Towards the end of the 1980s, cameras were sneaked onto the island, and inmates took snapshots of each other, which have been enlarged to almost life size and mounted as the **Smuggled Camera Exhibition** in the D-Section communal cells. The **Living Legacy** tour in F-Section involves ex-political prisoner guides describing their lives here and answering your questions.

The southern suburbs

Away from Table Mountain and the city centre, the bulk of Cape Town's residential sprawl extends east into South Africa's interior. It's here that the **southern suburbs**, the formerly whites-only residential areas, stretch out down the east side of Table Mountain, ending at Muizenberg on the False Bay coast, with Claremont and Newlands acting as the central pivotal point.

From anywhere in the southern suburbs you can see Table Mountain. The area offers some quick escapes from the city into forests, gardens and vineyards, all hugging the eastern slopes of the mountain and its extension, the Constantiaberg. The quickest way of reaching the southern suburbs from the city centre, Waterfront or City Bowl suburbs is the **M3 highway**. Alternatively, you can travel **by train** to Woodstock, Salt River, Observatory, Mowbray, Rosebank and Rondebosch, and all the stations southwards to Fish Hoek and Simon's Town.

Woodstock

First and oldest of the suburbs as you take an easterly exit from town is **Woodstock**, unleafy and windblown, but redeemed by some nice Victorian buildings, originally occupied by working-class coloureds, and now gentrifying and home to arty folk. The focus of the revival is the **Old Biscuit Mill** in Albert Road (see p.160) with its terrific Saturday-morning market where you can eat your fill, wander about craft shops and visit art galleries.

Salt River and Observatory

To the east of Woodstock, **Salt River** is a harsh, industrial, mainly coloured area, built initially for workers and artisans, while **Observatory**, abutting its southern end, is generally regarded as Cape Town's bohemian hub, a reputation fuelled by its proximity to the University of Cape Town, Groote Schuur Hospital Medical School and a number of NGOs. The refreshingly unrestored peeling arcades on Observatory's Lower Main Road, and the streets off it, have some nice places to chill, including a great organic food shop and café (see p.153), and lively bars. The huge Groote Schuur Hospital, which overlooks the freeway that sweeps through Observatory, was the site of the world's first heart transplant in 1967.

CAPE DUTCH ARCHITECTURE

Cape Dutch style, which developed in the Western Cape countryside from the seventeenth to the early nineteenth century, is so rooted in the Winelands that it has become an integral element of the landscape. Limewashed walls glisten in glowing green vineyards, while thatched roofs and curvilinear gables mirror the undulations of the surrounding mountains. The signature element of Cape Dutch manors is their central gables set into the long side of the roof. Gables became more and more elaborate and became an expression of wealth and status.

In central Cape Town, the gable only survived until the 1830s, to be replaced by buildings with flush facades and flat roofs – a response to a series of great fires in Cape Town and Stellenbosch. With pitched roofs gone, the urban gable withered away, surviving symbolically in some instances as minimal roof decoration; an example of this is the wavy parapet on the **Bo-Kaap Museum** (1763–68) in Wale Street.

IRMA STERN

Born in a backwater town in South Africa in 1894 to German Jewish parents, Irma Stern studied at Germany's Weimar Academy. In reaction to the academy's conservatism, she adopted **expressionist distortion** in her paintings, some of which were included in the Neue Sezession Exhibition in Berlin in 1918. Stern went on several expeditions into Zanzibar and the Congo in the 1940s and 1950s, where she found the source for her intensely sensuous paintings, which shocked South Africa at the time.

Although Stern's work was appreciated in Europe, when she returned to South Africa after World War II critics claimed that her style was simply a cover for technical incompetence. South African art historians now regard her as the towering figure of her generation. One of her most famous works is the much reproduced *The Eternal Child* (1916), a simple but vibrant portrait of a young girl, while *The Wood Carriers* (1951) uses raw ochres, browns and oranges to create an exoticized portrayal of a pair of African women.

The Irma Stern Museum
Cecil Rd, Rosebank • Tues–Sat 10am–5pm • R10 • ⓦ irmastern.co.za

Irma Stern is acknowledged as one of South Africa's pioneering artists of the twentieth century, more for the fact that she brought modern European ideas to the colonies than for any huge contribution she made to the art world. The **UCT Irma Stern Museum** was the artist's home for 38 years until her death in 1966 and is worth visiting if only to see Stern's collection of Iberian, African, Oriental and ancient artefacts. The whole house, in fact, reflects the artist's fascination with exoticism, starting with her own Gauguinesque paintings of "native types", the fantastic carved doors she brought back from Zanzibar, and the very untypical garden that brings a touch of the tropics to Cape Town with its exuberant bamboo thickets and palm trees.

Rondebosch and the Rhodes Memorial
Tea Garden daily 9am–5pm

South of Rosebank, neighbouring **Rondebosch** is home to the **University of Cape Town** (UCT), whose nineteenth-century buildings are handsomely festooned with creepers and sit grandly on the mountainside, overlooking Main Road and the M3 highway. Next to the campus, north towards the city, is the conspicuous **Rhodes Memorial**, built to resemble a Greek temple. The monument celebrates Cecil Rhodes with a sculpture of a wildly rearing horse, and the empire-builder's bust is planted at the top of a towering set of stairs. Herds of wildebeest and zebra nonchalantly graze on the slopes around the Memorial as cars fly past on the M3, and the **Tea Garden** offers terrific views of Cape Town. Rhodes' large estate, **Groote Schuur**, bordering on Main Road, became the official prime-ministerial residence of the Cape, then of South Africa, and when the country switched to a presidential system it became the home of the president. Below the Memorial, alongside the M3, is the incongruous **Mostert's Mill**, a windmill built two centuries ago when there were wheat fields here.

Newlands and Claremont

Continuing south from Rondebosch along the Van der Stel Freeway (the M3) or along the more congested Main Road, you pass some of Cape Town's most established, genteel suburbs. **Newlands**, almost merging with Rondebosch, is home to the city's famous rugby and cricket stadiums.

The well-heeled suburb of **Claremont**, south of Newlands, is an alternative focus to the city centre for shopping and entertainment, with two cinema complexes and plenty of shops at **Cavendish Square Mall**.

1

Bishopscourt and Wynberg

A little further south, beyond the signpost to Kirstenbosch Gardens, is **Bishopscourt**. As its name suggests, it's home to the Anglican bishop of Cape Town, and is full of luxurious mansions with enormous grounds.

Further down the line, **Wynberg** is known for its Maynardville Shakespearean open-air theatre (see p.156) and its quaint row of shops and restaurants in Wolfe Street, known as **Little Chelsea**.

By contrast, Wynberg's Main Road offers a distinctly less genteel shopping experience, an interesting stroll past street vendors and fabric shops, as well as food outlets catering to the large number of workers travelling between Wynberg and Khayelitsha.

Kirstenbosch National Botanical Gardens

Rhodes Drive • Daily: April–Aug 8am–6pm; Sept–March 8am–7pm • R37 • ☎ 021 799 8783, ⓦ sanbi.org

Five kilometres south of Rondebosch, the **Kirstenbosch National Botanical Gardens** are one of the planet's great natural treasure houses, a status acknowledged in 2004 when they became part of South Africa's sixth UNESCO World Heritage Site – the first botanical garden in the world to achieve this. The listing recognizes the international significance of the *fynbos* plant kingdom (see opposite) that predominates here.

Kirstenbosch is the oldest and largest botanical garden in South Africa, created in 1895 by Cecil Rhodes, whose camphor and fig trees are still here. Today, over 22,000 indigenous plants – and a research unit and library – attract researchers and botanists from all over the world. There's a nursery selling local plants, while characteristic Cape plants, found nowhere else in the world, are cultivated on the slopes. The gardens are magnificent, glorying in lush shrubs and exuberant blooms.

The gardens trail off from the lower gardens, which are formally organized, into wild vegetation, covering a huge expanse of the rugged eastern slopes and wooded ravines of Table Mountain. The setting is quite breathtaking – this is a great place to have tea and stroll around gazing up at the mountain, or to wander along the paths, which meander steeply to the top with no fences cutting off the way. Two popular paths, starting from the Contour Path above Kirstenbosch, are **Nursery Ravine** and **Skeleton Gorge** (see p.115); note that there have been muggings in the isolated reaches of Kirstenbosch and on Table Mountain, and women and hikers are advised to walk in groups and avoid carrying valuables.

Constantia and its winelands

South of Kirstenbosch lie the elegant suburbs of **Constantia** and the Cape's oldest **winelands**. Luxuriating on the lower slopes of Table Mountain and the Constantiaberg, with tantalizing views of False Bay, the winelands are an easy drive from town, not more than ten minutes off the Van der Stel Freeway (the M3), which runs between the centre and Muizenberg.

UP THE GARDEN PATH

In Kirstenbosch, there is a free **walking tour** Mon–Sat at 10am, and **shuttle-car tours** (R45) every hour on the hour, both departing from the Information Desk at the Visitors' Centre (Gate 1). If you're visiting the gardens in summer, one of the undoubted delights is to bring a picnic for a Sunday-evening **open-air concert** (late Nov–March 5.30pm), where you can lie back on the lawn, sip Cape wine and savour the mountain air and sunsets. There's an outdoor coffee shop open daily for breakfast, lunch and tea, plus a restaurant with a fire going for winter days. Eating out here is more about the fabulous location than the food or service.

If you don't have a car and don't want to take an **organized tour**, the best way to get to Kirstenbosch is by rikki or one of the local taxi services, a couple of which usually rank outside the garden. If you're **driving**, take the M3 and leave it at the signposted Rhodes Drive turn-off (M63), close to Newlands.

FYNBOS

Early Dutch settlers were alarmed by the lack of good timber on the Cape Peninsula's hillsides, which were covered by nondescript, scrubby bush they described as *fijn bosch* (literally "fine bush") and which is now known by its Afrikaans name **fynbos** (pronounced "fayn-bos"). The settlers planted exotics, like the oaks that now shade central Cape Town, and over the ensuing centuries their descendants established pine forests on the sides of Table Mountain in an effort to create a landscape that fulfilled their European idea of the picturesque. It's only relatively recently that Capetonians have come to claim *fynbos* proudly as part of the peninsula's heritage. Amazingly, many bright blooms in Britain and the US, including varieties of geraniums, freesias, gladioli, daisies, lilies and irises, are hybrids grown from indigenous Cape plants.

Fynbos is remarkable for its astonishing variety of plants, its 8500 species making it one of the world's biodiversity hot spots. The Cape Peninsula alone, measuring less than 500 square kilometres, has 2256 plant species (nearly twice as many as Britain, which is five thousand times bigger). The four basic types of *fynbos* plants are **proteas** (South Africa's national flower); **ericas**, amounting to six hundred species of heather; **restios** (reeds); and **geophytes**, including ground orchids and the startling flaming red disas, which can be seen in flower on Table Mountain in late summer.

The winelands started cultivated life in 1685 as the farm of **Simon van der Stel**, the governor charged with opening up the fledgling Dutch colony to the interior. Thrusting himself wholeheartedly into the task, he selected for his own use an enormous tract of the choicest land set against the Constantiaberg, the section of the peninsula just south of Table Mountain. He named the estate after his daughter Constancia, and this is now (with a minor change of spelling) the name of Cape Town's oldest and most prestigious residential area, shaded by oak forests and punctuated with stables, the Cape Dutch-style Constantia Mall and, of course, the vineyards.

Constantia grapes have been making wine since Van der Stel's first output in 1705. After his death in 1712, the estate was divided up and sold off as the modern **Groot Constantia**, **Klein Constantia** and **Buitenverwachting**. All three estates are open to the public and offer tastings; they're definitely worth visiting if you aren't heading to the Winelands proper.

There is no public **transport** to Constantia, but Groot Constantia features on most organized tours of Cape Town or the peninsula.

Groot Constantia

Groot Constantia Rd • Daily: May–Sept 10am–4.30pm; Oct–April 9am–5.30pm • Cellar tours daily on the hour: 10am–4pm • Wine tasting R35 including five wines and a souvenir glass • ☏ 021 794 5128, ⊚ grootconstantia.co.za

Groot Constantia is the largest wine estate in Constantia and the one most geared to tourists. Its big pull is that it retains the rump of Van der Stel's original estate, as well as the original buildings, though its portrayal of life in a seventeenth-century colonial chateau makes scant reference to the slave labour that underpinned its operations. The **manor house**, a quintessential Cape Dutch building, was Van der Stel's original home, modified at the end of the eighteenth century by the French architect Thibault. Walking straight through it, down the ceremonial axis, you'll come to the cellar, fronted with a carved pediment, depicting a riotous bacchanalia, which represents fertility. The substantial grounds of Groot Constantia also make for good walks.

Klein Constantia

Klein Constantia Rd • Mon–Fri 9am–5pm, Sat 9am–3pm • Free • ⊚ www.kleinconstantia.com

Smaller in scale than Groot Constantia, **Klein Constantia** offers free wine tasting in less regimented conditions than at the bigger estate and, although the buildings are far humbler, the setting is equally beautiful. Klein Constantia has a friendly atmosphere and produces some fine wines. Something of a curiosity is its **Vin de Constance**, the re-creation of an eighteenth-century Constantia wine that was a favourite of Napoleon,

1

Frederick the Great and Bismarck. It's a delicious dessert wine, packaged in a replica of the original bottle, and makes a unique souvenir.

Buitenverwachting

Klein Constantia Rd · **Buildings** Mon–Fri 9am–5pm, Sat 9am–1pm · Free · **Picnic lunches** Nov–April Mon–Sat noon–4pm · R110 · Booking essential – contact Adrienne ☎ 021 794 1012 or ☎ 083 257 6083 · ⊕ www.buitenverwachting.co.za

Buitenverwachting (roughly pronounced "bay-tin-fur-vuch-ting" with the "ch" as in the Scottish rendition of loch) is a bucolic place in the middle of the suburbs, with sheep and cattle grazing in the fields as you approach the main buildings, making it an inviting spot for a picnic lunch or an amble. The architecture and setting at the foot of the Constantiaberg are as good reasons to come here as the estate's impressive list of top-ranking wines, among them the classy Christine, an outstanding Bordeaux blend that has retained its edge for yonks. Overlooking the vineyards and backing onto the garden, the homestead was built in 1794 and features an unusual gabled pediment broken by an urn motif.

Table Mountain

Table Mountain, a 1087-metre flat-topped massif with dramatic cliffs and eroded gorges, dominates the northern end of the Cape Peninsula. Its north face overlooks the city centre with the distinct formations of **Lion's Head** and **Signal Hill** to the west and **Devil's Peak** to the east. The west face is made up of a series of gable-like formations known as the **Twelve Apostles**; the southwest face towers over Hout Bay and the east face over the southern suburbs. The mountain is a compelling feature in the middle of the city, a wilderness where you'll find wildlife and 1400 species of flora. Indigenous mammals include baboons, dassies (see box, p.115) and porcupines.

Reckoned to be the most-climbed massif in the world, Table Mountain has suffered under the constant pounding of **hikers** – although the damage isn't always obvious. Every year the mountain strikes back, taking its toll of lives. One of the commonest causes of difficulties is people losing the track (often due to sudden mist falling) and becoming trapped. If you plan to tackle one of the hundreds of its walks or climbs, go properly prepared. There are also **full-day guided hikes** tailored to your level of fitness (see p.158). You may choose to come back the easy way by cable car, or partially abseil.

The cable car

Daily every 10–15min: Jan & Dec 8am–9pm; Feb & March 8.30am–7.30pm; April 8.30am–5.30pm; May–Oct 8am–6pm; Nov 8am–7pm · R180 · Operations can be disrupted by bad weather or maintenance work · For information on current schedules call ☎ 021 424 8181, or check ⊕ www.tablemountain.net

The least challenging, but certainly not least interesting, way up and down the mountain is via the highly popular **cable car** at the western table, which offers dizzying views across Table Bay and the Atlantic. The state-of-the-art Swiss system is designed to complete a 360-degree rotation on the way, giving passengers a full panorama. Cars leave from the **lower cableway station** on Tafelberg Road. You can make a real outing of it by going up for breakfast or a sunset drink and meal at the vamped-up eco-restaurant; the upper station is an incomparable spot to watch the sun go down.

ARRIVAL AND DEPARTURE

By public transport You can get to the lower cableway station by rikki, metered taxi, or in one of the minibus taxis that ply the route here from Adderley St. The open-top Cape Town Explorer bus also serves the cableway (p.134).

By car If you're driving, you'll find parking along Tafelberg Rd, but you may be in for a bit of a walk in peak season – the stretch of parked cars can extend several hundred metres.

FROM TOP STREET PERFORMERS AT THE WATERFRONT; ST JAMES BEACH HUTS >

1

Walks and viewpoints

Climbing the mountain will give you a greater sense of achievement than being ferried up by the cable car, but proceed with extreme caution: it may look sunny and clear when you leave, but conditions at the top could be very different. There are fabulous hikes up and along Table Mountain (see p.158), but they are best done guided, both for mountain safety and because there have been some random muggings of tourists.

Signal Hill and Lion's Head

From the roundabout at the top of Kloofnek, a road leads all the way along **Signal Hill** to a car park and lookout, with good views over Table Bay, the docks and the city. A cannon was formerly used for sending signals to ships at anchor in the bay, and the Noon Gun, still fired from its slopes daily, sends a thunderous rumble through the Bo-Kaap and city centre below. Halfway along the road is a sacred Islamic *kramat* (see box below), one of several dotted around the peninsula that "protect" the city. You can also walk up **Lion's Head**, a non-strenuous hike that seems to bring out half the population of Cape Town every full moon, but it should always be done in a group, as it is potentially unsafe to walk alone. Google "Lion's Head full moon" and you'll find a group to walk with.

Platteklip Gorge

The first recorded ascent to the summit of Table Mountain was by the Portuguese captain Antonio de Saldanha, in 1503. He wisely chose **Platteklip Gorge**, the gap visible from the front table (the north side), which, as it turned out, is the most accessible way up. A short and easy extension will get you to Maclear's Beacon which, at 1086m, is the highest point on the mountain. The Platteklip route starts out at the lower cableway station and has the added advantage of ending at the upper station, so you can descend in a car.

From the lower station, walk east along Tafelberg Road until you see a high embankment built from stone and maintained with wire netting. Just beyond and to the left of a small dam is a sign pointing to Platteklip Gorge. A steep fifteen-minute climb brings you onto the **Upper Contour Path**. About 25m east along this, take the path indicated by a sign reading "Contour Path/Platteklip Gorge". The path zigzags from here onwards and is very clear. The gorge is the biggest cleavage on the whole mountain, leading directly and safely to the top, but it's a very steep slog that will take two to three hours in total if you're reasonably fit. Once on top, turn right and ascend the last short section onto the **front table** for a breathtaking view of the city. A sign points the way to the upper cableway station – a fifteen-minute walk along a concrete path thronging with visitors.

Maclear's Beacon

Maclear's Beacon is about 35 minutes from the top of the Platteklip Gorge on a path leading eastward, with white squares on little yellow footsteps guiding you all the way.

SACRED CIRCLE

A number of **Muslim holy men and princes** were exiled from the East Indies by the Dutch during the late seventeenth and early eighteenth centuries and brought to the Cape, where some became revered as **auliyah** or Muslim saints. The **kramats**, of which there are nearly two dozen in the province, are their burial sites, shrines and places of pilgrimage. The Signal Hill *kramat* is a shrine to **Mohamed Gasan Galbie Shah**, a follower of Sheik Yusuf, a Sufi scholar, who was deported to the Cape in 1694 with a 49-strong retinue. According to tradition, he conducted Muslim prayer meetings in private homes and slave quarters, becoming the founder of Islam in South Africa. **Sheik Yusuf**'s *kramat* on the Cape Flats is said to be one of a sacred circle of six *kramats*, including one on Robben Island, that protect Cape Town from natural disasters.

DASSIES

The outsized fluffy guinea pigs you'll encounter at the top of Table Mountain are **dassies** or hyraxes (*Procavia capensis*), which, despite their appearance, aren't rodents at all, but the closest living relatives of elephants. Their name (pronounced like "dusty" without the "t") is the Afrikaans version of *dasje*, meaning "little badger", a name given to them by the first Dutch settlers. Dassies are very widely distributed, having thrived in South Africa with the elimination of predators, and can be found in suitably rocky habitats all over the country. They live in colonies consisting of a dominant male and eight or more related females and their offspring.

Dassies have poor body temperature control and, like reptiles, rely on shelter against both hot sunlight and the cold. They wake up sluggish and seek out rocks where they can catch the early morning sun – this is one of the best times to look out for them. One adult stands sentry against predators and issues a low-pitched warning cry in response to a threat.

The path crosses the front table with Maclear's Beacon visible at all times. From the top you'll get views of False Bay and the Hottentots Holland Mountains to the east.

Skeleton Gorge and Nursery Ravine

You can combine a visit to the gardens at Kirstenbosch (see p.110) with an ascent up Table Mountain via one route and a descent down another, ending at the Kirstenbosch National Botanical Gardens' **restaurant** for tea. Starting at the restaurant, follow the **Skeleton Gorge** signs, which lead you onto the **Contour Path**. At the Contour Path, a plaque indicates that this is **Smuts' Track**, the route favoured by Jan Smuts, the Boer leader and South African prime minister. The plaque marks the start of a broad-stepped climb up Skeleton Gorge, involving wooden steps, stone steps, wooden ladders and loose boulders. Be prepared for steep ravines and difficult rock climbs – and under no circumstances stray off the path. This route requires reasonable fitness, and takes about two hours.

Skeleton Gorge is not recommended for the descent, as it can be very slippery; rather use **Nursery Ravine**. At the top of Skeleton Gorge, walk a few metres to your right to a sign indicating **Kasteelspoort**. It's just 35 minutes from the top of Skeleton Gorge along the Kasteelspoort path to the head of Nursery Ravine. The descent returns you to the 310-metre Contour Path, which leads back to Kirstenbosch. This entire walk lasts about five hours.

The Atlantic seaboard

Table Mountain's steep drop into the ocean along much of the western peninsula forces the suburbs along the **Atlantic seaboard** into a ribbon of developments clinging dramatically to the slopes. The sea washing the west side of the peninsula can be very chilly, far colder than on the False Bay seaboard. Although not ideal for bathing, the Atlantic seaboard offers mind-blowing views from some of the most incredible coastal roads in the world, particularly beyond **Sea Point**, and there are opportunities for whale-spotting (see p.124). The coast itself consists of a series of bays and white-sanded beaches edged with smoothly sculpted bleached rocks; inland, the Twelve Apostles, a series of rocky buttresses, gaze down onto the surf. The beaches are ideal for sunbathing, or sunset picnics – it's from this side of the peninsula that you can watch the sun sink into the ocean, creating fiery reflections on the sea and mountains behind as it slips away. Making the most of the views, and beautiful people-watching, are some of the city's trendiest outdoor cafés and bars.

Mouille Point and Green Point

Just to the west of the V&A Waterfront, Mouille Point and its close neighbour, Green Point, are among the suburbs closest to the city centre. **Mouille** ("moo-lee") **Point** is

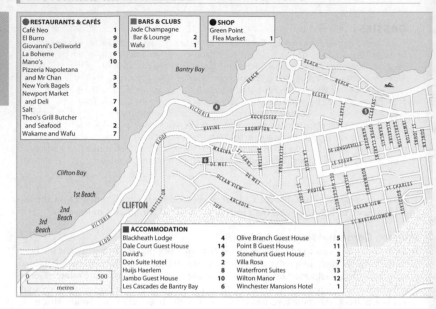

● RESTAURANTS & CAFÉS	
Café Neo	1
El Burro	9
Giovanni's Deliworld	8
La Boheme	6
Mano's	10
Pizzeria Napoletana and Mr Chan	3
New York Bagels	5
Newport Market and Deli	7
Salt	4
Theo's Grill Butcher and Seafood	2
Wakame and Wafu	7

■ BARS & CLUBS	
Jade Champagne Bar & Lounge	2
Wafu	1

● SHOP	
Green Point Flea Market	1

■ ACCOMMODATION			
Blackheath Lodge	4	Olive Branch Guest House	5
Dale Court Guest House	14	Point B Guest House	11
David's	9	Stonehurst Guest House	3
Don Suite Hotel	2	Villa Rosa	7
Huijs Haerlem	8	Waterfront Suites	13
Jambo Guest House	10	Wilton Manor	12
Les Cascades de Bantry Bay	6	Winchester Mansions Hotel	1

known principally for its squat rectangular Victorian lighthouse, commissioned in the 1820s, and painted like a children's picture-book lighthouse, with diagonal red and white stripes.

Mouille Point merges with the larger suburb of **Green Point**, which continues both inland from it and west along the ragged Atlantic shore. Green Point's proximity to the Waterfront – an easy ten-or-so minutes' walk away – and its position along the coast has turned it into a humming area of good accommodation and cafés.

Cape Town Stadium

Fritz Zonneneberg Rd

Described by British architecture critic Jonathan Glancey as "a stunning white apparition … in a sublime setting", **Cape Town Stadium** is arguably the jewel in South Africa's 2010 FIFA World Cup crown. The 68,000-seat stadium is fifteen floors high, with parking for twelve thousand cars in the basement. It relies on natural light, and at night the open-meshed roof can glow to resemble an ethereal UFO landed in Green Park.

In 2011, once the final World Cup whistle had been blown, the **Ajax Cape Town** football team used it as their home ground and, in the same year, it was packed to the rafters when Irish rockers U2 came to town. In a less sublime outing for Neil Diamond, they actually removed some of the seats.

But it isn't all rock and roll: with the FIFA World Cup party over, Capetonians woke up to a nasty hangover in November 2010 when it was revealed that it will cost nearly R50 million a year to run the stadium, and that **taxpayers** will most likely be footing the bill. On top of that, in February 2011 it was revealed that there had been **corruption** in the tender process for the project, which was initially quoted at R2.9 billion (US$400 million) but had ballooned to R4.4 billion (US$600 million) by completion. It's alleged that the six major construction companies involved in building the World Cup stadiums and infrastructure around the country had colluded in **bid rigging** to share out bloated contracts among themselves.

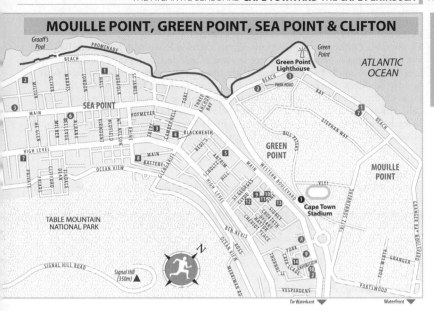

Sea Point

West along Main Road, Green Point merges with **Sea Point**, a cosmopolitan area crammed with apartment blocks, the odd Victorian house, tourist accommodation and restaurants. The Sea Point promenade is the best way to appreciate the rocky coastline and salty air, along with pram-pushing mothers, grannies, power walkers and joggers. People picnic or play ball games on the grassy parkland beside the walkway. The restaurants and shops are along Main Road, a busy thoroughfare, one block nearer Lion's Head than the Promenade.

Sea Point Pavilion Swimming Pool

Lower Beach Rd • Daily: May–Nov 9am–5pm; Dec–April 7am–7pm • R15

At the westernmost end of Sea Point Promenade is a set of four unheated saltwater/chlorine **pools**, which its fans breathlessly claim is the most beautifully located pool in the world, set as it is alongside the crashing surf. The largest of the four is Olympic-sized, making it a popular training tank for many of Cape Town's long-distance swimmers. There are also two kids' splash pools and a fully equipped diving pool for the brave. Gloriously unmodernized since it was built in the 1960s – a large part of its attraction – the complex was slated by its owners, the city council, for demolition with permission for an upmarket hotel to go up on the prime site. Happily, after a three-year battle that culminated in the Supreme Court of Appeal in 2011, lobby group Seafront for All stayed the developer's hand and saved the much-adored institution for the community.

Bantry Bay

At the westernmost edge of Sea Point lies **Bantry Bay**, combining the density of Sea Point with the wealth of the Atlantic suburbs; mansions rake back from the Atlantic shore on steep slopes, guarded by the granite boulders of Lion's Head. The upmarket resort hotels and self-catering apartment blocks are just far enough for comfort from the hubbub of Sea Point, but close enough should you want to walk to a restaurant.

Clifton

Hout Bay buses go to Clifton from the city centre several times a day • 30min

Fashionable **Clifton**, on the next cove along Victoria Road (the M6) from Bantry Bay, sits on the most expensive real estate in Africa, studded with fancy seaside apartments and with four sandy **beaches**, reached via steep stairways separated by clusters of granite boulders. The sea here is good for surfing and safe for swimming, but bone-chillingly cold. Bring your own refreshments as there's only one overpriced café, although adjacent Camps Bay (see below) is packed with them. The beaches here are sheltered from the wind and popular with muscular ball-players and families alike, and are especially recommended on summer evenings to enjoy the sunset and cool of the day.

Camps Bay

The suburb of **Camps Bay** climbs the slopes of Table Mountain and is scooped into a small amphitheatre, bounded by the Lion's Head and the Twelve Apostles sections of the Table Mountain range. This, and the airborne views across the Atlantic, makes Camps Bay one of the most desirable places to live in Cape Town. The main drag, Victoria Road, skirts the coast and is packed with trendy restaurants, a couple of nightspots and some upmarket accommodation, while the wide sandy beach is accessible by bus and is consequently enjoyed by families of all shapes and colours. However, the beach is exposed to the southeaster, and there's the usual Atlantic chill and an occasional dangerous backwash.

Llandudno

There's little development between Camps Bay and the exclusive cove of **Llandudno**, 20km from Cape Town along Victoria Road (not served by public transport). Here a steep and narrow road winds down past smart homes to the shore, where the sandy beach is punctuated at either end by magnificent granite boulders and rock formations. This is a good sunbathing spot and a choice one for bring-your-own sundowners. The small car park frequently spills over into the suburban streets at peak periods.

Sandy Bay

Isolated **Sandy Bay**, Cape Town's main nudist beach, can only be reached via a twenty-minute walk from Llandudno; a signposted path leads from the south end of the Llandudno car park.

In the apartheid days, the South African police went to ingenious lengths to trap nudists, but nowadays the beach is relaxed, so feel free to come as undressed as feels comfortable. It's a prime gay cruising spot too.

Hout Bay

Although no longer the quaint fishing village it once was, **Hout Bay** still has a functioning fishing harbour and is the centre of the local crayfish industry. Some 20km

TOURS OF IMIZAMO YETHU

Although it is unsafe to wander into ImiZamo Yethu by yourself (see p.120), you can take a fun, two-hour **walking tour** (daily at 10.30am, 1pm & 4pm; R75; ❶ 083 719 4870, ⓦ suedafrika.net/imizamoyethu) with enthusiastic and accomplished guide Afrika Moni, who knows the place and its history inside out. He walks you through his home township, stopping to chat to proprietors of informal "spaza" shops, sipping traditional beer at a *shebeen*, as well as popping into shacks and brick houses. Tours start from the police station at the entrance to the township, where there are reserved parking places for visitors; the City Sightseeing bus comes out here too, as will the MyCiTi bus from mid-2012.

1

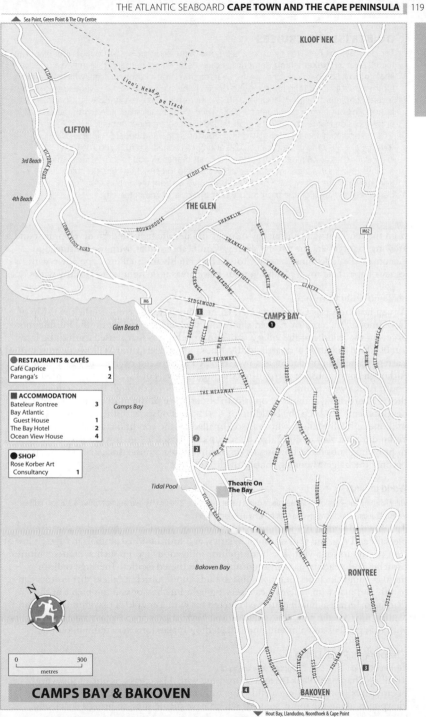

Sea Point, Green Point & The City Centre

KLOOF NEK

Lion's Head Pipe Track

CLIFTON

3rd Beach

4th Beach

KLOOF NEK

THE GLEN

ROUNDHOUSE

SHANKLIN

SHANKLIN

M62

LOWER KLOOF ROAD

THE CHEVIOTS

THE GRANGE

THE MEADOWS

CRANBERRY

SHANKLIN

BLAIR

ATHOL

COMRIE

GENEVA

M6

SEDGEMOOR

1

CAMPS BAY
1

ATHOL

Glen Beach

BERKLEY

LINCOLN

PARK

THE FAIRWAY

CENTRAL

CLIFFORD

GENEVA

CRAMOND

MEDBURN

PRIME

RHINECLIFFE

1

THE MEADWAY

FILLANS

WOODFORD

Camps Bay

RESTAURANTS & CAFÉS
Café Caprice   **1**
Paranga's   **2**

ACCOMMODATION
Bateleur Rontree   **3**
Bay Atlantic
  Guest House   **1**
The Bay Hotel   **2**
Ocean View House   **4**

SHOP
Rose Korber Art
  Consultancy   **1**

THE DRIVE

2
2

RONALD

STRATHEARN

UPPER TREE

DONKIN

Tidal Pool

Theatre On
The Bay

VICTORIA ROAD

FIRST

FIRST BAY

WILLIAMSON

FINCHLEY

Bakoven Bay

RONTREE

HOUGHTON

IKON

CHAS BOOTH

SUSAN

ROTTINGDEAN

PILLOCHRY

ROTTINGDEAN

ICHNUS

TUSSEN

FULHAM

RONTREE

3

N

0   300
metres

4

BAKOVEN

CAMPS BAY & BAKOVEN

Hout Bay, Llandudno, Noordhoek & Cape Point

1

DUIKER ISLAND CRUISES

The best way to take in the landscape is on one of the short cruises just out of Hout Bay, from the harbour to **Duiker Island**, sometimes called "seal island" because it's home to a massive **seal colony**. South African, or Cape, fur seals are the largest of the fur seals, which accounts for their popularity among hunters, who began harvesting them in the seventeenth century, severely depleting the population by 1893 when restrictions were introduced. Controlled hunting in South Africa continued till 1990 when it was finally suspended, with the exception of two culls on Malgas island in 1999 and 2000 to protect gannet populations.

Of the operators that run tours (10 daily departures all year round; 45 min; R65) Nauticat (☎021 790 7278, ⓦnauticatcharters.co.za) and Circe Launches (☎021 790 1040, ⓦcircelaunches.co.za) have glass-bottomed boats that allow you to see the seals and other marine denizens in action under water, as well as kelp forests when conditions are clear. Apart from the seals, the outings also provide fabulous views from the water of the Sentinel, the distinctive formation on the promontory that guards one side of the bay.

from the centre, it's a favourite day outing, and despite ugly modern development and a growing shantytown, the natural setting is quite spectacular, with the Sentinel and Chapman's Peak defining the entry to the bay. Highly unusual for Cape Town with its legacy of apartheid town planning, poor black areas nose right up to wealthy white ones.

ImiZamo Yethu township

As you head towards Constantia Nek from Hout Bay, you come to the township of ImiZamo Yethu, a tightly packed shackland settlement crawling up the hillside more or less in the middle of the village. ImiZamo Yethu was first settled during the late 1980s, the dying days of apartheid, by Xhosa job seekers from Willowvale in the rural Eastern Cape. Its population is now estimated at between twelve and thirty thousand. Although conditions are pretty dire (the highest levels of E. Coli ever recorded in South Africa were found in the Disa River which flows through the settlement), there's a surprising amount of optimism about. One of the most positive recent developments has been the building of 450 brick houses with the help of Irish millionaire Niall Mellon, who was so appalled by the conditions he saw in ImiZamo Yethu during a visit in 2002 that he set up the Niall Mellon Township Trust dedicated to providing subsidized housing in townships across South Africa and which has now become the biggest housing charity in the country.

World of Birds

Valley Rd • Daily 9am–5pm • R70 • Monkey jungle daily 11.30am–1pm & 2–3.30pm • Penguin feeding 11.30am & 3.30pm • Pelican feeding 12.30pm • Birds of prey feeding 4.30pm • ⓦworldofbirds.org.za

The **World of Birds** is home to more than three thousand birds, housed in surprisingly pleasant and peaceful walk-through aviaries, and four hundred animals in cages; allow at least two hours for a visit. The birds include indigenous species such as cranes, vultures, ostriches and pelicans, as well as a number of feathered exotics. The large walk-in monkey jungle includes among its inhabitants cute squirrel monkeys that visitors can handle and play with. There's a café serving light lunches, or you can picnic at the Flamingo Terrace. Children are well catered for with a couple of playground areas, and feeding time for the penguins, pelicans and birds of prey are a likely winner. The setting with lush gardens and a mountainous backdrop makes for a very tranquil outing.

Chapman's Peak Drive

Toll charge R30 • ☎ 021 791 8222, ⓦchapmanspeakdrive.co.za

Thrilling **Chapman's Peak Drive**, a 9km route with 114 curves, is one of the world's best ocean drives, winding along a cliff-edge to Noordhoek. There are a number of safe viewpoints along the route, some of which have picnic sites, so bring a snack and refreshments and stop to enjoy the spectacular view. The road is occasionally closed due to rockfall, so it's advisable to phone or visit their website in advance to check out the current situation.

Noordhoek and Noordhoek Farm Village

Noordhoek, a fast-developing settlement at the southern end of the descent from Chapman's Peak Drive, consists of smallholdings and riding stables in a gentle valley planted with oaks. The **Noordhoek Farm Village**, close to the signposted Chapman's Peak exit or entry point, is a centre of sorts, with some great places to eat, some decent craft shops and a children's play area. From here, a long white, wide, untamed beach stretches 6km across Chapman's Bay to Kommetjie. The sands are fantastic for walking and **horseriding**, but can resemble a sandblaster when the southeaster blows. Swimming is cold, though surfers relish the rough waters around the rocks to the north. Signposted on the left if you're heading south is the *Red Herring* restaurant and pub (see p.153), which has views of the beach; it's set back from the sea, about ten minutes' walk from the car park. Also signposted in the vicinity is *Monkey Valley Resort* (see p.143), which welcomes non-guests for reasonably priced meals with great views.

Kommetjie

Although only a few kilometres south of Noordhoek along the beach, getting to the tiny settlement of **Kommetjie** by road involves a fifteen-kilometre detour inland. Facilities are limited and one of the main reasons to come here is for the superb walks, either around the rocky shore near Slangkop lighthouse, or across the extensive sands of Long Beach towards Noordhoek. The beach walk takes you past the well-preserved wreck of the *Kakapo*, which ran aground in 1900 and whose boiler, rudders and ribs are still visible above the sands. The *Kakakapo* had a bit-part in the David Lean film *Ryan's Daughter*, where Long Beach stood in for the windswept Irish coast in some scenes. Another major draw of Kommetjie is its powerful surf, though riding the waves in these parts is only for the very experienced. If you want to learn to surf, Muizenberg is the place (p.123).

Scarborough

The developing and idyllic village of **Scarborough** is the most far-flung settlement along the peninsula, with turquoise, cold water and white sands. The drive here from Simon's Town is an easy and lovely one, winding over the spine of the peninsula, and onto Cape Point.

The False Bay seaboard

In summer the waters of **False Bay** are several degrees warmer than those on the Atlantic seaboard, which is why Cape Town's oldest and most popular seaside development is along this flank of the peninsula. A series of village-like suburbs, backing onto the mountains, each served by a Metrorail station, is dotted all the way south from **Muizenberg**, through **St James**, **Kalk Bay**, **Fish Hoek** and down to **Simon's Town**. Each has its own character with restaurants, shops and places to stay while

---

ON THE BEACH

Don't take valuables, including car keys, onto Muizenberg beach (see p.122). Instead, leave them with one of the beachfront establishments such as *Knead* coffee shop, which will happily look after them.

1

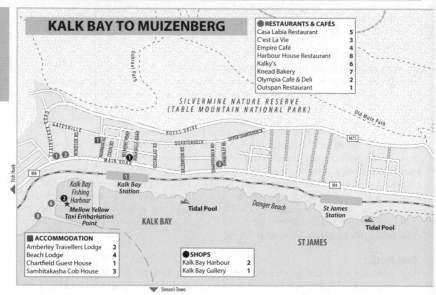

KALK BAY TO MUIZENBERG

● **RESTAURANTS & CAFÉS**
Casa Labia Restaurant	5
C'est La Vie	3
Empire Café	4
Harbour House Restaurant	8
Kalky's	6
Knead Bakery	7
Olympia Café & Deli	2
Outspan Restaurant	1

■ **ACCOMMODATION**
Amberley Travellers Lodge	2
Beach Lodge	4
Chartfield Guest House	1
Samhitakasha Cob House	3

● **SHOPS**
Kalk Bay Harbour	2
Kalk Bay Gallery	1

Simon's Town, one of South Africa's oldest settlements, is worth taking in as a day-trip and makes a useful base for visiting the Cape of Good Hope section of the **Table Mountain National Park** and **Cape Point** (see p.127).

GETTING TO FALSE BAY

By train From Muizenberg, Main Rd and the railway line spectacularly hug the shore all the way to Simon's Town; indeed, the train ride to Simon's Town, taking an hour from Cape Town, is reason enough to visit, and most stations from Muizenberg are situated close to the surf. If you're travelling by train to Simon's Town (see p.125) you can arrange to be collected by Rikki's (☎072 387 4366); they charge R10/km for up to four people: a one-way trip to Boulders will set you back R40; an excursion to Cape Point, returning you to the station, costs R500.

By car Driving here from Cape Town, it is best to take the M3 south.

By water taxi Mellow Yellow Water Taxi runs an hourly service (☎073 473 7684, ⊛ watertaxi.co.za; 9am–4pm; R100 one way, R150 return per person; around 20min) between *Kalky's Fish and Chips*, Kalk Bay Harbour (leaving on the half-hour) and Simon's Town public jetty at the marina (leaving on the hour). Although tickets can be bought on the boat, it's best to book ahead as the vessel takes a maximum of ten passengers and services are subject to the weather and whales crossing.

Muizenberg

Once South Africa's most fashionable beachfront, **Muizenberg** is now a bit run-down, though nothing detracts from the fact that it has a long, safe and fabulous beach that shelves gently, making it the most popular spot along the peninsula for swimming. It also has some terrific beachfront coffee shops that draw the crowds, especially over weekends.

The brightly coloured bathing boxes along the beach are reminders of a more elegant heyday, when the resort was visited by the likes of Agatha Christie, who enjoyed riding its waves while holidaying here in the 1920s: "Whenever we could steal time off," she wrote, "we got out our surf boards and went surfing."

The Historical Mile

A short stretch of the shore, starting at Muizenberg station, is known as the **Historical Mile**, dotted with a run of notable buildings. **Muizenberg Station**, an Edwardian-style edifice completed in 1913, with its lovely ornate clock tower, is now a National

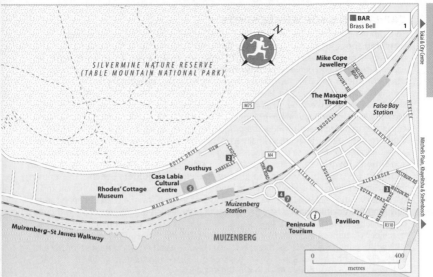

Monument, while the **Posthuys** is a rugged whitewashed and thatched building dating from 1673 and a fine example of the Cape vernacular style – and purportedly the oldest European building in South Africa. **Rhodes' Cottage Museum**, 246 Main Road (Tues–Sun 10am–1pm & 2–5pm; free), was bought in 1899 by the millionaire empire builder who died here in 1902. It is interesting for some personal memorabilia and period furniture.

Casa Labia Cultural Centre

192 Main Rd · Tues–Sun 10am–4pm · Free · ☎ 021 788 6068, ⓦ casalabia.co.za.

The most idiosyncratic of the buildings along the Historical Mile, and closest to St James, **Casa Labia** was completed in 1930 as the residence of the Italian consul, Count Natale Labia. Built in the eighteenth-century Venetian style, it's a glorious piece of architectural bling on Main Road and worth popping into just for the *palazzo*'s film-set **interiors**. It also houses a **cultural centre** that puts on concerts and talks, a **gallery** that features contemporary South African art, and a rather opulent café.

St James

St James is more upmarket than neighbouring Muizenberg, its mountainside homes accessed mostly up long stairways between Main Road and Boyes Drive. The best reason to hop off the train here is for the **sheltered tidal pool** and the twenty-minute walk along the **paved coastal path** that runs along the rocky shore to Muizenberg – one of the peninsula's easiest and most rewarding walks, with panoramas of the full sweep of False Bay. Look out for seals and, in season, whales.

ALL ABOARD

Bathing aside, there's also good **surfing** in Muizenberg's breakers, with the opportunity for adults and children to take surfing lessons from several beachfront surf schools.

Gary's Surf School 34 Balmoral Building, Beach Rd ☎ 021 788 9839, ⓦ www.garysurf.com. R380 for a two-hour lesson including gear rental.

Surf Shack Muizenberg Corner, Beach Rd ☎ 021 788 9286, ⓦ www.urfshack.co.za. R340 for a two-hour lesson or four lessons for R800.

1

CAPE TOWN'S TOP WHALE SPOTS

The commonest whales around Cape Town are southern rights, and the best **whale-watching spots** are on the warmer **False Bay** side of the peninsula, from August to November. You could also try your luck on the **Atlantic seaboard** at **Chapman's Peak** towards Hout Bay, and between **Llandudno** and **Sea Point**, where the road curves along the ocean. Whichever seaboard you're visiting, remember to have **binoculars** handy.

Along the False Bay seaboard, look out for whale signboards, indicating good places for sightings. **Boyes Drive**, running along the mountainside behind Muizenberg and Kalk Bay, provides an outstanding vantage point. To get there by car, head out on the M3 from the city centre to Muizenberg, taking a sharp right into Boyes Drive at Lakeside, from where the road begins to climb, descending finally to join Main Road between Kalk Bay and Fish Hoek.

Alternatively, sticking close to the shore along Main Road, the stretch between **Fish Hoek** and **Simon's Town** is recommended, with a particularly nice spot above the rocks at the south end of Fish Hoek Beach, as you walk south towards Glencairn. **Boulders Beach** at the southern end of Simon's Town has a whale signboard and smooth rocky outcrops on which to sit and gaze out over the sea. Even better vantage points are further down the coast between Simon's Town and **Smitswinkelbaai**, where the road goes higher along the mountainside. Without a car, you can get the train to Fish Hoek or Simon's Town and whale-spot from the Jager's Walk beach path that runs along the coast from Fish Hoek to Sunny Cove, just below the railway line.

It's worth noting that there are more spectacular whale-spotting opportunities further east, especially around Hermanus and Walker Bay (see p.205). For information on the latest whale sightings in False Bay, contact Alan on ☎072 930 4798.

The compact St James beach draws considerable character from its much-photographed Victorian-style bathing boxes, whose bright, primary colours catch your eye as you pass by road or rail. The beach tends to be overcrowded at weekends and during school holidays; occasionally, African Christian groups carry out jubilant baptizing ceremonies here, wading fully dressed into its waters.

Kalk Bay

One of the most southerly of Cape Town's suburbs, **Kalk Bay** centres around a lively working harbour with wooden fishing vessels, mountain views, and a strip of shops packed with collectibles, antique shops, trendy coffee shops and restaurants. Kalk Bay somehow managed to slip through the net of the Group Areas Act, making it one of the few places on the peninsula with an intact coloured community, and Kalk Bay and the larger Hout Bay are the only harbour settlements still worked by coloured fishermen. It is well known for its artistic and alternative community too, living up cobbled streets, and there is a fair bit of visitor accommodation available.

The village is arranged around the small docks, where you can watch the boats come in; you can also buy fresh fish, which are flung onto the quayside, sold in spirited auctions, gutted for a small fee and the innards then thrown to waiting seals. Kalk Bay is busiest on Saturdays and Sundays when Capetonians descend to breakfast or lunch at one of the excellent cafés, wander the shops and harbour, or have a drink right on the water's edge.

Silvermine Nature Reserve

Dawn–dusk • R20 • The picnic sites and dam are reached via the Ou Kaapseweg (the M64) to Noordhoek, signposted at the southern end of the M3 • Access from Boyes Drive Free

Rising up behind Kalk Bay village, **Silvermine Nature Reserve** runs across the peninsula's spine. Part of the Table Mountain chain, it offers walks with fabulous views of both sides of the peninsula and the opportunity for picnics by its lake, and is highly recommended if you're travelling with children (see p.128). At the payment point, you'll be given a sketchy map of the reserve with walks shown. From Kalk Bay, several trails, which lead off Boyes Drive, strike out along beautiful routes into the mountains behind the village (there are no gates on the Boyes Drive side). All the walks are accurately detailed on the

Slingsby Silvermine & Hout Bay Map (ⓦwww.slingsbymaps.com), the best map of the reserve by a mile, which is available at outdoor and book shops.

Fish Hoek

Fish Hoek, south of Kalk Bay, boasts one of the peninsula's finest family **beaches** along the False Bay coast. The best and safest swimming is at its southern end, where the surf is moderately warm, tame and much enjoyed by boogie boarders. Thanks to the beach, there's a fair amount of accommodation (see p.143), but this is otherwise one of the dreariest suburbs along the False Bay coast. An obscure bylaw banning the sale of alcohol in supermarkets or bottle stores boosts the town's image as the Mother Grundy capital of the peninsula.

From the west side of the beach, **Jager's Walk** skirts the rocky shoreline above the sea for 1km to Sunny Cove; from there, it continues for 6km as an unpaved track to Simon's Town. The walkway provides a good vantage point for seeing whales.

Simon's Town

The country's third-oldest European settlement, and also South Africa's principal naval base, **Simon's Town** isn't the hard-drinking, raucous place you might expect. It's exceptionally pretty, with a near perfectly preserved historic streetscape, slightly marred on the ocean side by the domineering **naval dockyard**. On the other hand, glimpses of naval squaddies square-bashing behind the high walls or strolling to the station in their crisp white uniforms, are part of the place's distinct character. Just 40km from Cape Town, roughly halfway down the coast to Cape Point, Simon's Town is a favourite stop-off point on peninsula tours, but it's also a good option for a holiday base, with sweeping vistas of False Bay and the Hottentots Holland Mountains. A few kilometres to the south is **Boulders Beach**, with its colony of cute **African penguins** – reason enough alone for a Simon's Town visit.

Brief history

Founded in 1687 as the winter anchorage of the Dutch East India Company, Simon's Town was one of several places in and around Cape Town modestly named by **Governor Simon van der Stel** after himself. Its most celebrated visitor was Lord Nelson, who convalesced here as a midshipman while returning home from the East in 1776. Nineteen years later, the British sailed into Simon's Town and occupied it as a bridgehead for their first invasion and occupation of the Cape. They left after just seven years, only to return in 1806. Simon's Town remained a British base until 1957, when it was handed over to South Africa.

There are fleeting hints, such as the occasional mosque, that the town's predominantly white appearance isn't the whole story. In fact, the first **Muslims** arrived

---

SHARK COUNTRY

False Bay is one of the best places in the country to see **Great White Sharks**. For one thing, the False Bay sharks are on average about a third bigger than their Gansbaai (see p.208) counterparts.

One of the best ways to see these giants is with **Apex Shark Expeditions** (ⓣ021 786 5717, ⓦapexpredators.com; Feb–March R1350, April–May R1700, June–Aug R2400), operated by naturalists Chris and Monique Fallows, who have worked with National Geographic and the BBC. They operate a range of marine trips in False Bay, among them shark-cage diving. Their emphasis is on observing shark behaviour – and that of other marine creatures that you'll encounter on the trip out to Seal Island – rather than the adrenaline rush. Numbers of passengers are strictly limited to twelve, which means you have a pretty personalized experience and get twenty to thirty minutes in the cage. Trips leave from the Simon's Town pier and prices vary according to season and likelihood of encountering a shark.

1

from the East Indies in the early eighteenth century, imported as slaves to build the Dutch naval base. After the British banning of the slave trade in 1807, ships were compelled to disgorge their human cargo at Simon's Town, where one district became known as Black Town. In 1967, when Simon's Town was declared a White Group Area, there were 1200 well-established coloured families living here, who were descended from these slaves. By the early 1970s, the majority had been forcibly removed under the Group Areas Act to the township of Ocean View, whose inspiring name belies its desolation.

Simon's Town Museum

Court Rd • Mon–Fri 10am–4pm, Sat 10am–1pm • R10

The building now housing the **Simon's Town Museum** was once the Old Residency, built in 1772 for the Governor of the Dutch East India Company, and has also served as the slave quarters (the dungeons are in the basement) and town brothel. The museum's motley collection includes maritime material and an inordinate amount of information and exhibits on Able Seaman Just Nuisance, a much-celebrated seafaring Great Dane. He enjoyed drinking beer with the sailors he accompanied into Cape Town, and was adopted as a mascot by the Royal Navy during World War II.

Jubilee Square and St George's Street

In the centre of Simon's Town, a little over 1km south of the station, lies **Jubilee Square**, a palm-shaded car park just off St George's Street. Flanked by some cafés and shops, the street has on its harbour-facing side a broad walkway with a statue of the ubiquitous Able Seaman Just Nuisance and a few curio sellers. A couple of sets of stairs lead down to the **Marina**, a modest development of shops and restaurants set right on the waterfront.

Boulders Beach

2km from Simon's Town Station • Daily: Feb–March 8am–6.30pm; April–Sept 8am–5pm; Oct–Nov 8am–6.30pm; Dec–Jan 7am–7.30pm • R40

Boulders Beach takes its name from its huge granite rocks, which create a cluster of little coves with sandy beaches and clear sea pools, which are gorgeous for swimming. However, the main reason people come to Boulders' fenced seafront reserve is for the **African penguins** (formerly known as jackass penguins). African penguins usually live on islands off the west side of the South African coast, and the Boulders birds form one of only two mainland colonies in the world. This is also the only place where the endangered species are actually increasing in numbers, and provides a rare opportunity to get a close look at them.

Access to the Boulders reserve is through two gates, one at the Boulders Beach, (eastern) end, off Bellevue Road and the other at the **Seaforth Beach** (western) side, off Seaforth Road. Both entrances are signposted along Main Road between Simon's Town and Cape Point. At Seaforth, there's a small visitors' centre and deck, from which two boardwalks lead to either end of Foxy Beach where you'll see hundreds of penguins. Most people walk from Seaforth to Boulders, looking at all the penguins in the bushes along the paths, where there are masses of burrows for nesting. At Seaforth itself, there is safe swimming on the beach, which is bounded on one side by the looming grey mass of the naval base. While there are no facilities of any kind on Boulders Beach,

---

WHALE-WATCHING IN FALSE BAY

Simon's Town Boat Company (☎083 257 7760, ⊛www.boatcompany.co.za) is the only outfit licensed to do False Bay boat-based **whale-watching trips** (R750); they also do cruises around Cape Point (R350), to Seal Island (R250), and guided history tours that include a visit to the Naval Dockyard and a **tour of a submarine** (R80).

1

there is a restaurant with outdoor seating and fresh fish on the menu at both of the entrances to Boulders.

Table Mountain National Park – Cape of Good Hope

Daily: April–Sept 7am–5pm; Oct–March 6am–6pm • R80 • ☎ 021 780 9526, ⓦ tmnp.co.za, ⓦ capepoint.co.za

Most people come to the **Cape of Good Hope section** of the Table Mountain National Park to see the southernmost tip of Africa at **Cape Point**. In fact, the continent's real tip is at Cape Agulhas, some 300km southeast of here (see p.209), but Cape Point is a lot easier to get to and a hugely dramatic spot. The reserve sits atop massive sea cliffs with huge views, strong seas and, when it's blowing southeast, gales that whip off caps and sunglasses as visitors gaze southwards from the old lighthouse buttress.

From the car park, the famous viewpoint is a short, steep walk up a series of stairs to the original lighthouse. A **funicular** (R45 return) runs the less energetic to the top, where there's a curio shop.

ARRIVAL

There's no public transport to the reserve, but numerous **tours** take it in as part of a package of peninsula highlights; Day Trippers (☎ 021 511 4766, ⓦ daytrippers.co.za) runs fun tours for R545 (including a picnic lunch), some of which give you the option of cycling part of the way. For general tours that take in the reserve, see p.135. However you get there, go as early as you can in the day, unless you enjoy crowds; and the chance of the wind gusting up increases as the day progresses.

INFORMATION

Tourist information Buffelsfontein Visitors' Centre, 8km from the entrance gate, has attractive displays about the local fauna and flora as well as video screenings on the ecology of the area (daily 7.30am–5pm).

Cape Point and around

Cape Point is the treacherous promontory of rocks, winds and swells braved by navigators since the Portuguese first "rounded the Cape" in the fifteenth century. Plenty of wrecks lie submerged off its coast, and at **Olifantsbos** on the west side you can walk to a US ship sunk in 1942, and a South African coaster that ran aground in 1965. The **Old Lighthouse**, built in 1860, was too often dangerously shrouded in cloud, and failed to keep ships off the rocks, so another was built lower down in 1914. It's not always successful in averting disasters, but is still the most powerful light beaming onto the sea from South Africa.

Walking

Most visitors make a beeline for Cape Point, seeing the rest of the reserve through a vehicle window, but walking is the best way to appreciate the dramatic landscape and **flora**.

FURRY FELONS

Baboons may look amusing, but be warned: they can be a menace. Keep your car windows closed, as it's not uncommon for them to invade vehicles, and they're adept at swiping picnics. You should lock your car doors even if you only plan to get out for a few minutes to admire the view as there are growing reports of baboons opening unlocked car doors while the vehicle owner's back is turned. Avoid unwrapping food or eating or drinking anything if baboons are in the vicinity. Feeding them is illegal and provocative and can incur a fine. Authorized baboon-chasers are in evidence in several places, warding them off.

1

CAPE TOWN FOR KIDS

Cape Town is an excellent place to travel with children, with plenty of outdoorsy activities. Car rental companies will give you child seats, but only if you organize this in advance. A good **website** for finding out what's on is Cape Town Kids (ⓦ www.capetownkids.co.za). For **babysitters**, or even nannies, to accompany you on trips, try Sitters4U (☎ 083 691 2009, ⓦ www.sitters4u.co.za) or Super Sitters (☎ 021 552 1220, ⓦ www.supersitters.net).

BEACHES AND SWIMMING POOLS

Cape Town's **beaches** are a classic summer weekend family outing. Most beaches are pretty undeveloped, so it's best to take what you need in the way of food and drinks with you. Get to the beach as early as possible to leave by 11am when the sun gets too strong, and to avoid the wind which often gusts up in the late morning. Beach, in Cape Town, is not synonymous with warm water.

On the False Bay seaboard, **Boulders Beach** (see p.126) is one of the few beaches to visit when the southeaster is blowing, and gorgeous at any time. It has safe, flat water, making it ideal for kids – and its resident penguin-breeding colony is an added attraction. **Fish Hoek** (see p.125) is one of the best peninsula beaches, with a long stretch of sand and a playground. The paved Jager's Walk which runs along the rocky coast here is suitable for pushchairs. **St James** (see p.123) boasts a safe tidal pool with a small sandy beach and photogenic bathing boxes, though it is seriously overcrowded on summer weekends. From here you can walk to Muizenberg along a pushchair-friendly coastal pathway.

The **Atlantic seaboard** is too cold for swimming, but does have some lovely stretches of sand, boulders and rock pools – and astonishing scenery. The beaches here are excellent for picnics, and on calm summer evenings idyllic at sunset. The closest stretch of coast to the centre ideal for prams – and rollerblading – is the paved **Sea Point promenade**, stretching 3km from the lighthouse in Mouille Point to Sea Point Pavilion, with the draw of playgrounds en route. The tidal pool and small rock pools of **Camps Bay** (see p.118) make this popular beach very child-friendly, and it's easily reached from the centre by car or bus. Finally, the six-kilometre stretch of white sand from **Noordhoek** to **Kommetjie** (see p.121) provides fine walking, kite-flying and horseriding opportunities, with stupendous views of Chapman's Peak. It has a sheltered area among the rocks on the Noordhoek side. If you're heading for Kommetjie you can go camel-riding at Imhoff Farm Village (see opposite).

As regards child-friendly swimming pools, **Newlands Pool** (see p.158) has a toddlers' pool and a little playground in large grounds, while the marvellous **Sea Point Pool** at Sea Point Pavilion (see p.117) has two paddling pools for children, and lawns to laze on.

INDOORS AND ENTERTAINMENT

Planet Kids 3 Wherry Rd, Muizenberg, behind False Bay Station; daily 10am–6pm; R30/hr; ☎ 021 788 3070, ⓦ planetkids.co.za. A great indoor play centre for kids up to 12, designed by an occupational therapist, which is loads of fun, as well as offering healthy snacks and a calmer environment than the usual plastic, sugar-crazed scene. With good assistants on hand, you can drop off your child, or wait with a cup of tea and a home-bake. Kids of all abilities welcome.

SA Museum and Planetarium See p.100. A great choice for rainy days, especially for 5- to 12-year-olds, who'll enjoy the four-storey whale well and

---

There are several waymarked **walks** in the Cape of Good Hope Nature Reserve. If you're planning a big hike it's best to set out early, and take plenty of water, as shade is rare and the wind can be foul. One of the most straightforward **hiking routes** is the signposted forty-minute trek from the car park at Cape Point to the more westerly **Cape of Good Hope**. For exploring the shoreline, a clear path runs down the Atlantic side, which you can join at **Gifkommetjie**, signposted off Cape Point Road. From the car park, several sandy tracks drop quite steeply down the slope across rocks, and through bushes and milkwood trees to the shore, along which you can walk in either direction. The **Hoerikwaggo Table Mountain Trail** is a popular four-day, five-night hike from Table Mountain to Cape Point along the Peninsula spine. There are overnight huts along the way and you can do just one or more of

African animal dioramas, as well as the dinosaur displays. Its Discovery Room (Mon–Fri 10am–3pm, Sat & Sun 11am–4.30pm) features live ants, massive spiders and a crocodile display. The Planetarium has special children's shows over weekends and in school holidays; for schedule see ⓦiziko.org.za /planetarium.

Scratch Patch Dido Valley, Simon's Town ⓣ021 786 2020; Dock Rd, Waterfront ⓣ021 419 9429; daily 9am–5pm; ⓦwww.scratchpatch.co.za. Mounds of shiny semi-precious stones to pick through and fill whichever sized container you decide on. R15 for the smallest and R90 for a great big bag of "jewels".

Ratanga Junction Century City, Sable St exit, off N1; daily 10am–5pm; ⓣ086 120 0300, ⓦratanga. co.za. Popular theme park with a variety of thrilling rides which provides a very good day out, though it only operates during Cape school holidays and at weekends during the summer; best to check their dates and times when you're in town.

Two Oceans Aquarium See p.106. Not only one of Cape Town's most rewarding museums, the aquarium also features loads of interest to children. Kids can actually handle a few species in the touch pool – sometimes this includes a small shark or sea urchins – while the Alpha Activity Centre usually has puppet shows or face painting as well as computer terminals where older kids can learn about marine ecology.

OUTDOOR AND PICNIC SPOTS

The Barnyard Farmstall Steenberg Rd (M42), next to Steenberg Estate, between Tokai Rd and the Ou Kaapseweg. An excellent place, if you're en route to the Southern Peninsula or Cape Point, for an outdoor snack or cup of coffee at a small farmyard, with ducks and chickens wandering around, and an unusually good kids' playground.

Imhoff Farm Kommetjie Rd, South Peninsula, opposite the Ocean View turn-off ⓣ021 783 4545, ⓦwww.imhofffarm.co.za. A conglomeration of activities including camel rides, pony rides, horseriding on the beach, paintball, a farmyard petting zoo and reptile park. There's also a good café and farmers' shop. Daily 10am–5pm.

Kirstenbosch National Botanical Gardens See p.110. Top of the list for an outdoor family outing, with extensive lawns for running about, trees and rocks to climb and streams to paddle in. There's no litter, no dogs, it's extremely safe and you can push a pram all over the walkways; it's also great for picnics or to have tea outdoors at the café. For older kids there are short waymarked walks.

Newlands Forest 9km south of the centre, off the M3 to Muizenberg. Gentle walks in and around pine forests and streams on the wooded southern slopes of Table Mountain, with a flattish pathway suitable for pushchairs. Safest at weekends and in the afternoons when the joggers and dog walkers are out. Use the access point off the M3 signposted "Forestry Office", where there's ample parking. Dawn–dusk; free.

Silvermine Nature Reserve See p.124. A good place to stroll around the lake, paddle and picnic with small children; however, it is exposed, and not recommended in heavy winds or mist. For older children there are some mountain-top walks with relatively gentle gradients, which give spectacular views over both sides of the peninsula. Bring your own drinking water and food. Elephant's Eye Cave walk is recommended, signposted from the car park.

Tokai Forest Arboretum Take the M3 Southbound Tokai exit, then turn right and continue a couple of kilometres towards the mountain, until the tarred road ends, then turn left. A peaceful outdoor, country place with a thatched teashop and a great place for young children to explore, with logs to jump off, a gentle walk to a stream and, best of all, it's sheltered when it's blowing everywhere else.

the 17–18km sections (from R42/person a night; ⓣ021 683 7826, ⓦwww .hoerikwaggotrail.org).

The beaches

A single main road runs from the Cape Point entrance to the car park, restaurant and funicular. A number of roads branch off this, each leading to one of the series of beaches on either side of the peninsula. The sea is too dangerous for swimming, but there are safe tidal pools at the **Buffels Bay** and **Bordjiesrif beaches**, which are adjacent to each other, midway along the east shore. Both have braai stands, but more southerly Buffels Bay is the nicer, with big lawned areas and some sheltered spots to have a picnic.

1

CAPE FAUNA

Along with indigenous plants and flowers, you may well spot some of the animals living in the *fynbos* habitat on Cape Point. **Ostriches** stride through the low *fynbos*, and occasionally **African penguins** come ashore. A distinctive bird on the rocky shores is the **black oystercatcher** with its bright red beak, jabbing limpets off the rocks. You'll also see **Cape cormorants** in large flocks on the beach or rocks, often drying their outstretched wings. Running up and down the water's edge (where, as on any other beach walk in the Cape, you'll see piles of shiny brown *Ecklonia* kelp) are **white-fronted plovers** and **sanderlings**, probing for food left by the receding waves.

As for mammals, **baboons** lope along the rocky shoreline, and grazing on the heathery slopes are **bontebok**, **eland** and **red hartebeest**, as well as **Cape rhebok** and **grysbok**. If you're very lucky, you may even see some of the extremely rare **Cape mountain zebras**.

What you will undoubtedly see are rock agama lizards, black zonure lizards and rock rabbits (*dassies*).

The Cape Flats and the townships

East of the northern and southern suburbs, among the industrial smokestacks and the windswept **Cape Flats**, reaching well beyond the airport, is Cape Town's largest residential quarter, taking in the **coloured districts**, **African townships** and shantytown **squatter camps**. The Cape Flats are exactly that: flat, barren and populous, exclusively inhabited by Africans and coloureds in separate areas, with the M5 acting as a dividing line between it and the southern suburbs.

Brief history

The African townships were historically set up as dormitories to provide labour for white Cape Town, not as places to build a life, which is why they had no facilities and no real hub. The **men-only hostels**, another apartheid relic, are at the root of many of the area's social problems. During the 1950s, the government set out a blueprint to turn the tide of Africans flooding into Cape Town. No African was permitted to settle permanently in the Cape west of a line near the Fish River, the old frontier over 1000km from Cape Town; women were entirely banned from seeking work in Cape Town and men prohibited from bringing their wives to join them. By 1970 there were ten men for every woman in Langa.

In the end, apartheid failed to prevent the influx of work-seekers desperate to come to Cape Town. Where people couldn't find legal accommodation they set up **squatter camps** of makeshift iron, cardboard and plastic sheeting. During the 1970s and 1980s, the government attempted to demolish these and destroy anything left inside – but no sooner had the police left than the camps reappeared, and they are now a permanent feature of the Cape Flats. One of the best known of all South Africa's squatter camps is **Crossroads**, whose inhabitants suffered campaigns of harassment that included killings by apartheid collaborators and police, and continuous attempts to bulldoze it out of existence. Through sheer determination and desperation its residents hung on, eventually winning the right to stay. Today, the government is making attempts to improve conditions in the shantytowns by introducing electricity, running water and sanitation, as well as building tiny brick houses to replace the shacks.

Langa

Langa is the oldest and most central township, lying just east of the white suburb of Pinelands and north of the N2. In this relentlessly grey place, without the tiniest patch of green relief, you'll find women selling sheep and goats' heads, alongside

1

TOWNSHIP TOURS AND HOMESTAYS

Several projects are under way to encourage tourists into the townships but, as a high proportion of Cape Town's nearly two thousand annual murders take place here, the recommended way to visit is on one of the **tours** listed in the box on p.135. All of these tours are operated by residents of the Cape Flats, or in cooperation with local communities, and emphasize face-to-face encounters with ordinary people. They include visits to *shebeens*, nightclubs and a township restaurant, chats with residents of squatter camps and the Langa hostels, and meetings with traditional healers and music makers, township artists and craftworkers. Some tours also take in "sites of political struggle", where significant events in the fight against apartheid occurred. If you want to really get under the skin of the townships, there's no better way than staying in one of the **township B&Bs** which offer pleasant, friendly and safe accommodation; for more information, see box, p.143.

state-of-the-art public phone bureaus run by enterprising township businessmen from inside recycled cargo containers. Families live in fairly smart suburban houses while, not far away, there are former men-only hostels where as many as three families share one room.

Mitchell's Plain

South of the African ghettos is **Mitchell's Plain**, a coloured area stretching down to the False Bay coast (you'll skirt Mitchell's Plain if you take the M5 to Muizenberg). More salubrious than any of the African townships, Mitchell's Plain reflects how, under apartheid, lighter skins meant better conditions, even if you weren't quite white. But for coloureds the forced removals were no less tragic, many being summarily forced to vacate family homes because their suburb had been declared a White Group Area. Many families were relocated here when District Six was razed (see p.101), and their communities never fully recovered – one of the symptoms of dislocation and poverty is the violent gangs that have become an everyday part of Mitchell's Plain youth culture.

ARRIVAL AND DEPARTURE

BY PLANE

Cape Town International Airport, the city's international and domestic airport (CPT; ⓦwww.acsa .co.za), lies 22km east of the city centre. All domestic airlines fly to and from Cape Town including 1Time, British Airways, Kulula, Mango, South African Airways, SA Airlink and Velvet Sky. Metered 24-hour **taxis** operated by *Touch Down Taxis* (☎021 919 4659), an association of independent cab companies officially authorized by the airport, rank in reasonable numbers outside both terminals and charge around R250 for the trip into the city. The cheapest transport from the airport is the **MyCiTi bus** (every 20min; 4.20am–9pm; R50; ☎0800 65 64 63, ⓦwww.capetown.gov.za/myciti), operated by the city, which goes to the Civic Centre on Hertzog Boulevard, opposite the central train and bus station. More expensive but considerably more convenient are the **door-to-door shuttle services** which offer transport around Cape Town, including airport transfers. Rikkis (☎086 174 5547, ⓦrikkis.co.za; see p.135) offer airport shuttles (R200 to/ from the city centre for the first passenger with discounts after that), and the Backpacker Bus (pre-booking

CAPE TOWN AND THE CAPE PENINSULA

recommended: ☎021 439 7600 or ☎082 809 9185, ⓦbackpackerbus.co.za; see p.135) also offers a well-priced airport shuttle service with two buses plying the route to and from Cape Town International (8am–5pm; R160 for the first person with discounts after that). All the major **car rental** chains have branches at the airport, though for the best deals book in advance.

Destinations: Bloemfontein (4 daily; 1hr 35min); Durban (23 daily; 2hr); East London (6 daily; 1hr 30min); George (2 daily; 1hr); Hoedspruit (2 weekly; 3hr); Johannesburg (55 daily; 2hr); Kimberley (1 daily; 2hr); Port Elizabeth (11 daily; 1hr 30min); Upington (1 daily; 1hr 50min). There are also direct flights to Cape Town from a significant number international cities (see p.147).

BY TRAIN

Cape Town's mainline station is in the centre of town on the corner of Strand and Adderley sts. All mainline trains arrive and depart here including services between Cape Town and Johannesburg (26–27hr) on state-run **Shosholoza Meyl** Tourist Class (daily) and Premier Classe (twice weekly) trains. The Tourist Class service stops at Matjiesfontein

(5hr), Kimberley (16hr 30min) and Bloemfontein (23hr). The **luxury** Blue Train (3–5/month) and Rovos Rail (4–6/month) ply the Cape Town–Pretoria route (27hr).

BY BUS

Intercity buses operated by Greyhound, Intercape and Translux terminate at the train station (see p.132).

Destinations: Bloemfontein (3 daily; 13hr); Cradock (daily; 10hr); Durban (3 daily; 20hr); East London (daily; 15hr 40min); George (5 daily; 6hr); Graaff-Reinet (daily; 9hr); Grahamstown (daily; 12hr 25min); Johannesburg (6 daily; 17hr); Kimberley (2–3 daily; 11hr 45min); Knysna (5 daily; 6hr 50min); Montagu (daily; 4hr); Mossel Bay (5 daily; 5hr 15min); Oudtshoorn (change at Mossel Bay; daily; 6hr 15min); Plettenberg Bay (5 daily; 7hr 30min); Port Elizabeth (5 daily; 10hr); Pretoria (6 daily; 18hr); Sedgefield (5 daily; 6hr 45min); Springbok (daily; 6hr 30min);

Stellenbosch (3 daily; 1hr); Storms River (5 daily; 10hr 10min); Umtata (3 daily; 18hr); Upington (daily; 10hr 30min); Wilderness (5 daily; 6hr 30min); Windhoek (Namibia; 1–2 daily; 16hr 30min).

BY BAZ BUS

The backpacker Baz Bus has daily services along the Garden Route to Port Elizabeth (about 14hr) making stops at all the major tourist destinations along the N2 including: Bot River (1hr 30min); George (7hr; change here for shuttle bus to Oudtshoorn); Jeffrey's Bay (12hr 15min); Knysna (8hr 30min); Mossel Bay (6hr); Plettenberg Bay (9hr 30min); Storms River (10hr 30min); Swellendam (3hr); Wilderness (7hr 30min). From Port Elizabeth there are onward connections to the Wild Coast, Durban and Johannesburg.

GETTING AROUND

Although Cape Town's city centre is compact enough to get around on foot, many of the major attractions are spread along the considerable length of the peninsula and require transport to get there. Viable public transport is limited, but should improve with the phasing in of the **MyCiTi rapid bus service** from 2011 and its further expansion in mid-2012. Apart from that, the only recommended system is **Metrorail**, a single train line down the peninsula. It's easy and well used during the day, but should be avoided after dark. With the exception of a couple of specific routes, forget about **Golden Arrow buses**, whose services are limited, slow and irregular. Most visitors consequently rent a car or rely on shuttle buses, tours and taxis. The **Golden Acre** shopping complex, at the junction of Strand and Adderley sts in the heart of Cape Town, can be a confusing muddle, but this is where all rail and most bus transport (both intercity and from elsewhere in the city) and most minibus taxis converge. Everything you need for your next move is within two or three blocks of here, including tourist information (see p.136).

MYCITI CENTRAL ROUTES

INNER CITY INTERIM CIRCULAR ROUTE

This is a temporary service that will run until the launch of the new network in mid-2012 (see p.134). Buses operate every twenty minutes Mon–Fri 6am–8pm, Sat 7am–8pm & Sun 8am–8pm. Services are every ten minutes on Mon–Fri 6.30–9am & 3.30–6pm.

Loop 1: Civic Centre–Cape Town International Convention Centre–Cape Town Stadium–Watefront–Civic Centre.
Loop 2: Civic Centre–train station–Strand St–Long St–Orange St–Gardens Centre– Loop St–Adderley St–Civic Centre.

ROUTES TO BE LAUNCHED AROUND MID-2012

A new network for the city centre, City Bowl, Sea Point, Waterfront and the Atlantic Seaboard to Hout Bay is planned for mid-2012. Buses are expected to be pretty frequent with at least one every twenty minutes during the day:

F01 Hout Bay to Cape Town via Camps Bay and Sea Point taking in Clifton and Camps Bay as well as a number of stops within Hout Bay including ImiZamo Yethu township
F02 Waterfront to Camps Bay via the city centre and Kloof Nek
F03 Sea Point to Gardens via the city centre and Vredehoek
F04 Sea Point to Fresnaye and Cape Town
F05 Bo Kaap to Salt River via city centre and Zonnebloem
F06 Civic Centre to City Bowl via Long St, Kloof St, Gardens and Oranjezicht
F07 Civic Centre to Gardens Centre via Zonnebloem and Vredehoek
F08 Highlands Estate to city centre via Vredehoek and Gardens
F65 Tamboerskloof to city centre via Gardens

1

GO TOPLESS

The open-top, hop-on, hop-off red **Cape Town Sightseeing Bus** (☎ 021 511 6000, ⓦ citysightseeing.co.za; 1 day ticket R120) is an extremely useful way of getting to the major sights. Buses leave from the Two Oceans Aquarium at the Waterfront (see p.106), but you can hop on or off at any point. The City Centre Tour (daily every 15min: mid-March to mid-Oct 9.10am–4.30pm; mid-Oct to mid-March 9.10am–5.15pm) includes stops at Cape Town Tourism in Burg St, St George's Cathedral, SA Museum, *Mount Nelson Hotel*, Jewish Museum, District Six Museum, Castle of Good Hope, Gold Museum, Cableway, Camps Bay and Sea Point. The Mini Peninsula Tour (daily every 35 min; 9am–3.25pm) stops at Cape Town Tourism in Burg St, *Mount Nelson Hotel*, Kirstenbosch, World of Birds, Mariner's Wharf in Hout Bay, Camps Bay and Sea Point. For full itineraries see the website.

BUSES

Cape Town has two public bus services: the well-established and slow Golden Arrow service, and the MyCiTi rapid bus system launched in 2011 that should dramatically improve public transport around the centre and its immediate suburbs, and which will be expanded in 2012 to cover the Atlantic seaboard down to Hout Bay.

MYCITI BUSES

MyCiTi buses are part of a government initiative to improve public transport in South Africa's major centres. In Cape Town, the bus rapid transport network emulates a rail system, with stations along dedicated trunk roads served by express buses. The initial phase was launched in 2011, at the time of this edition's research period, with three main routes running from the **Civic Centre bus station** on the Foreshore. These go to **Table View** (northern suburbs), the **airport** and around the **city centre**. This Inner City Interim Service is the most useful for visitors as it serves major places of interest in the city centre and the Waterfront. The city authorities have said that this service will be incorporated into a comprehensive network of nine routes in mid-2012, expanding over the city centre, the Waterfront, the City Bowl suburbs and the Atlantic seaboard as far as Hout Bay (see box, p.133). **Tickets** are sold at bus stops or on buses. Fares hadn't been finalised at the time of writing, but are expected to be competitive with minibus taxis. For further details and up-to-date information contact the Cape Town Transport information line ☎ 0800 65 64 63 or visit the MyCiTi website ⓦ capetown.gov.za/en/myciti.

GOLDEN ARROW BUSES

Golden Arrow buses ply Cape Town's main roads and tend to be slow, often getting snarled up in congested traffic. The only frequent and reliable Golden Arrow services are those from the centre to the Waterfront, Sea Point and down the Atlantic seaboard to Hout Bay. The **Waterfront bus** (Mon–Fri every 10min, Sat & Sun every 15min) leaves from Adderley St outside the train station with stops en route in Riebeeck and Buitengragt sts; and the one to **Sea Point** (Mon–Sat 20 daily) leaves from the Golden Acre terminal and runs along Main Rd through **Mouille Point** and **Green Point**. The bus service down the Atlantic seaboard goes about twice an hour during the day via Camps Bay as far as Hout Bay. Buses to the southern suburbs are best avoided: the train is much quicker and more efficient. **Tickets** are sold by the driver: state your destination to them, and pay when you get on. **Fares** are cheap: a ticket for the station to the Waterfront is R6. For timetables, enquire at the Golden Arrow information booth (toll-free ☎ 0800 65 64 63, ⓦ gabs.co.za) at the Golden Acre bus terminal.

TAXIS, MINIBUS TAXIS, SHUTTLE BUSES AND CYCLECABS

The term **"taxi"** refers, somewhat confusingly, to conventional metered cars, jam-packed minibuses and rikkis. Regulated **metered taxis** don't cruise up and down looking for fares; you'll need to go to the taxi ranks around town, which include the Waterfront, the train station and Greenmarket Square, or phone to be picked up (see below). Taxis must have the driver's name and identification clearly on display and the meter clearly visible. Fares work out at around R10–12 per kilometre.

TAXI

Excite Taxis ☎ 021 448 4444, ⓦ excitetaxis.co.za. Reliable, reputable and prompt service from a company that runs a fleet of fifty metered taxis and has a 24-hour call centre. Fares are R9 a kilometre within their normal operating area (city centre to southern suburbs), but there may be an additional charge if your pick-up or drop-off point is further flung than this.

Marine Taxis ☎ 021 434 0434, ⓦ marinetaxis.co.za. The largest and one of the oldest taxi outfits in the Mother City operates 24 hours a day, seven days a week and can accommodate up to seven passengers. Fares are R11 a kilometre, charged from your pickup point, and they have the facility in the cab to take card payments.

MINIBUS TAXIS

Minibus taxis are cheap, frequent and bomb up and down the main routes at tearaway speeds. They can be hailed from the street – you'll recognize them from the hooting, booming music and touting – or boarded at the central taxi rank, adjacent to the train station. Once you've boarded, pay the assistant, who sits near the driver, and tell him when you want to get off. Fares for most trips should be under R10. As well as risky driving, be prepared for pickpockets working the taxi ranks.

RIKKIS AND SHUTTLES

Rikkis are ex-London taxi cabs, operating all hours and aimed principally at tourists; you need to book them by telephone (☎086 174 5547, ⓦrikkis.co.za). They operate within three distinct areas: central (City Bowl and the Atlantic seaboard as far as Hout Bay; private R35–50, shared R25–35); southern suburbs (Claremont and Constantia; R65–75); plus in and around Hout Bay (R60). In the same vein but a little cheaper, the **Backpacker Bus** (pre-booking recommended: ☎021 439 7600 or ☎082 809 9185, ⓦbackpackerbus.co.za) offers transport from backpacker lodges to Kirstenbosch and Stellenbosch.

CYCLECABS

Cyclecabs – two-passenger vehicles drawn by pedal power – are a great, relaxed way of getting around the city centre when the weather is fine. The distinctive tricycles operate in the vicinity of the Company's Gardens, the

---

TOURS

One of the best Cape Town orientations at the start of a visit is to take a two-and-a-half- to three-hour **walking tour** through central Cape Town. The two companies listed below depart mid-morning daily, except Sundays, from the Visitor Information Centre in Burg Street, but need to be booked.

A number of smaller companies offer **niche cultural tours**; the most popular of these are townships tours, the safest way to see the African and coloured areas that were created under apartheid. Almost all companies will pick you up from your accommodation and drop you off again at the end of the day, and tours generally start from R600, less for classic township tours.

WALKING TOURS

Cape Town on Foot ☎021 462 4252, ⓦwanderlust.co.za. Run by an ex-teacher and writer, takes in the city centre as well as the Bo-Kaap, and can be taken in English or German (R150).

Footsteps to Freedom ☎083 452 1112, ⓦfootstepstofreedom.co.za. Runs a tour that takes in historical sights and buildings with a conscious politico/socio slant (R150).

CULTURAL TOURS

Andulela Tours ☎021 790 2592, ⓦandulela.com. Fabulous selection of under the skin tours that could get you drumming, bead-making or cooking in the African townships, doing a soccer tour, or learning more about baboons with a conservationist at Cape Point. They can also take you further afield to the Cederberg to look at rock art.

Bonani Our Pride ☎021 531 4291 or ☎082 446 7974, ⓦbonanitours.co.za. Tours that get you onto the streets to meet local people and visit sites of political significance in the townships. They offer township evening tours, gospel tours where you visit Xhosa churches on a Sunday morning and Xhosa folklore tours.

Coffee Beans Routes ☎021 424 3572, ⓦcoffeebeansroutes.com. Music and cultural specialists who are the people to go with for a Cape Town Jazz Safari, soccer route tour, or to find out what's happening in the poetry/performance scene in the townships.

Off Beat Tours ☎021 788 6613, ⓔsimric1@gmail.com. Simric Yarrow, a teacher and professional storyteller and musician, takes an ecological slant on his entertaining tours of Cape Town.

GENERAL TOURS

Day Trippers ☎021 511 4766, ⓦdaytrippers.co.za. An excellent company if you want an active Peninsula and Cape Point day tour that will include cycling and hiking. They also go further afield to hike and cycle in the Cederberg, Little Karoo and Winelands.

Cape Convoy ☎021 531 1928, ⓦcapeconvoy.com. Tours in a canopied Land-Rover with a passionate and fun Brit, Rob Salmon, who offers a reduced rate (R1000) if you book the two most popular tours: the full-day Cape Point and the Table Mountain and Robben Island tour. Trips can also be arranged to the Winelands and to the nearest safari park to see some wildlife, a couple of hours out of Cape Town.

1

Castle, the Foreshore and the V&A Waterfront. Cyclecabs cruise around and also rank outside the Slave Lodge in Adderley St as well as the South African Museum. You can call one on ☎ 0861 967 537 or ☎ 072 907 7333 or hail one in the street. Fares are negotiated with the cabbie, but expect to pay from R5 for a short hop from the station to the Company's Gardens.

TRAINS

Cape Town's suburban train service is run by **Metrorail** (☎ 080 065 64 63). The only route likely to be useful to tourists is the relatively reliable if slightly run-down line going through the southern suburbs and all the way down to False Bay seaboard from Cape Town station. Three other lines run east from Cape Town to Strand (through Bellville), to the Cape Flats, and to the outlying towns of Stellenbosch and Paarl; however, the journeys aren't recommended, as they run through some less safe areas of the Flats. Even on a Simon's Town train, avoid boarding an empty carriage.

The service to the **False Bay seaboard** is one of the great urban train journeys of the world. It reaches the coast at Muizenberg and continues south to Simon's Town, sometimes so spectacularly close to the ocean that you can feel the spray and peer into rock pools. The stretch of the line to Fish Hoek is well served, with several trains an hour (Mon–Fri 5am–8pm roughly every 15min, Sat 6.20am–6.45pm every 20min, Sun 5.50am–6.30pm roughly hourly, though more frequently during the summer). Services to Simon's Town go every forty to sixty minutes.

Trains run overground, and there are no signposts to the stations on the streets. If you're staying in the southern suburbs, ask for directions at your accommodation. **Tickets** must be bought at the station before boarding. You're best off in the **first-class** carriages, which are reasonably priced (for example, Cape Town–Muizenberg is about R12 one-way); curiously, there's no second class. Third class tends to be more crowded, and in the mornings frequently ring out with the harmonies of domestic workers singing on their way to work.

DRIVING

Given Cape Town's scant public transport, renting a vehicle is the only convenient way of exploring the Cape Peninsula, and needn't break the bank. Cape Town has good roads and several fast freeways that, outside peak hours (7–8.30am

& 4–6pm), can whisk you across town in next to no time. The obvious landmarks of Table Mountain and the two seaboards make orientation straightforward, particularly south of the centre.

The usual precautions for defensive and alert driving in South Africa are in order (see p.73). An unwritten rule of the road is that minibus taxis have the right of way – and will change lanes or push in front of you without warning. There's often little notice of branches off to the suburbs, with only the final destination of the freeway being signed. Your best bet is to plan your journey, and make sure you know exactly where you're going.

Car parks are dotted all over the place in this car-friendly city. To park on the street you'll frequently need to pay a parking attendant (with a luminous yellow bib), from whom you purchase parking time. Elsewhere, apart from parking garages, you'll almost invariably be expected to tip the car guards who are supposed to look after parked vehicles and, annoying as they may be, are dependent on this for their livelihood.

CAR AND MOTORBIKE RENTAL

There are dozens of competing **car rental companies** to choose from. To get the best deal, either pick up one of the brochures at the Cape Town Tourism office or book beforehand (often cheaper) with an international company. Many backpacker hostels also have cheap deals with agencies. Aroundaboutcars (☎ 021 422 4022, ⓦ aroundaboutcars.com) is an independent national rental company based in Cape Town offering good package deals and flexible pricing. Another inexpensive option is Vineyard Car Hire (☎ 021 761 0671, ⓦ vineyardcarhire.co.za). Allen's Car Hire (☎ 021 701 8844, ⓦ allenscarhire.co.za) is reasonable, reliable and of a similar price. Staff can deliver a car to you, or meet you at the airport when you land. For details of the larger, national agencies, see Basics, p.53. For **bike rental**, Downhill Adventures (☎ 021 422 0388, ⓦ downhilladventures.co.za) has rentals from R160 for 24hr. For **motorbike rental**, Le Cap Motorcycle Hire, B9 Edgemead Business Park, on the corner of Link Way & Southdale Rd, Edgemead (☎ 072 259 0009, ⓦ lecap .co.za), provides all the necessary gear and rents out serious bikes (from R470 daily, plus R1/km; weekly rental available). They also offer motorbiking tours with pre-arranged accommodation.

INFORMATION

Tourist Information Cape Town Tourism (ⓦ www .tourismcapetown.com) has two excellent information bureaus: the city-centre visitor centre (April–Sept Mon–Fri 8.30am–5pm, Sat & Sun 8.30am–1pm; Oct–March Mon–Fri 8am–6pm, Sat 8am–2pm & Sun 8.30am–1pm; ☎ 021 426 4260), at the corner of Burg and Castle sts, a

five-minute walk two blocks west of the station; and Cape Town Routes Unlimited – Gateway Visitor Centre and the Clocktower Precinct visitor centre (daily 9am–9pm; ☎ 021 405 4500) at the V&A Waterfront, next to the Nelson Mandela Gateway to Robben Island. Both centres operate comprehensive accommodation and activity booking services, have a coffee shop, bookshop and cybercafé, and dish out lots of brochures and cheap city maps. Bookings for national parks can also be made.

Events listings The best events listings is in the *Mail & Guardian's* Friday supplement, which injects some attitude into its reviews and listings, but *The Next 48 Hours* (ⓦwww.48hours.co.za), a free supplement you'll find distributed on Thursdays at a variety of city-centre coffee shops, tourist offices and branches of *Exclusive Books* (found in most malls), is best for clubs and theatre.

Maps and books If you're planning to explore beyond the city centre, it's advisable to get one of the detailed street atlases, found at most bookshops. MapStudio's *A to Z Streetmap* is the cheapest; it's adequate for the centre and most of the suburbs, but doesn't cover Simon's Town. The best detailed maps to the peninsula and large parts of the Western Cape and beyond are Slingsby Maps (see p.125).

ACCOMMODATION

Cape Town has plenty of accommodation to suit all budgets, though booking ahead is recommended to guarantee the kind of place you want, especially over the Christmas holidays (mid-Dec to mid-Jan). Cape Town is a long peninsula and there are many different locations which all have their hotly debated advantages and varying physical beauties. You'll need to choose whether you want to be central, with nightlife on your doorstep, or would prefer a quieter setting closer to the ocean, in which case you'll travel further to get into the city. The greatest concentration of accommodation is in the City Centre, City Bowl and the Atlantic seaside strip as far as Camps Bay. If you find everything booked up, Cape Town Tourism (see opposite) has an efficient **accommodation booking** desk, and can be contacted before you arrive.

CITY CENTRE

Cape Town's liveliest street for clubs and restaurants is **Long Street**. There are a number of **backpacker lodges** and a couple of hotels on Long St itself, and several places east of Long St around the museum complex and the Company's Gardens. From here you can walk to all the museums, trawl Cape Town's best nightlife spots, and find transport easily out of the centre or to the Waterfront. Expect rooms fronting Long St to be noisy.

★ **Cape Heritage Hotel** 90 Bree St ☎021 424 4646, ⓦcapeheritage.co.za; map p.95. An exceptionally stylish, elegant and tastefully restored boutique hotel, dating back to 1771, located in Cape Heritage Square, just below the Bo-Kaap. The rooms have an enchantingly beautiful mix of antique Cape furniture, with the finest contemporary hand-crafted objects and furnishings. The rooftop jacuzzi is another draw. R1800

Cape Town Hollow Boutiique Hotel 88 Queen Victoria St ☎021 423 1260, ⓦcapetownhollow.co.za; map p.95. A multistorey hotel with the usual facilities, and in a great central location, close to the South African Museum and National Gallery. Rooms are done out in creams and beiges with white linen; it's worth paying more for a mountain-facing room. R2370

Cat & Moose 305 Long St ☎021 423 7638, ⓦcatandmoose.co.za; map p.95. The most stylish of the Long St lodges, housed in an eighteenth-century building a couple of doors from Long St baths at the south end of the city centre. Timber floors, rugs, earthy reds and ochres, as well as some African masks, imbue it with a warm ethnic feel. The dorms, triples and double rooms are arranged around a small leafy courtyard, with a plunge pool. Dorm R110, double R360

The Grand Daddy Hotel 38 Long St ☎021 424 7247, ⓦdaddylonglegs.co.za; map p.95. A feature of the *Grand Daddy* is the seven retro-cool American Airstream trailers, decorated by local artists, that sit on the roof, linked by wooden walkways. Besides staying in a snug trailer on the rooftop, the hotel has double rooms, also imaginatively decorated, colourful and funky, with queen-sized beds. R1500

iKhaya Lodge Wandel St, Dunkley Square ☎021 461 8880, ⓦikhayalodge.co.za; map p.92. A guesthouse three short blocks away from the museums and close to trendy restaurants. There are en-suite rooms as well as some luxury lofts, all with ethnically inspired decor. You can choose between mountain or (cheaper) city views. There's 24hr reception, satellite TV and wi-fi throughout. R1205

Rouge on Rose 25 Rose St/corner Hout St ☎021 426 0298, ⓦrougeonrose.co.za; map p.92. Nine suites in a modern Bo-Kaap guesthouse – one of the very few places to stay in this much photographed area, where you will hear the calls to mosque from your room, each with self-catering facilities for nights in. Great views across to Signal Hill, and a short walk to the action in Long St or De Waterkant. Free internet access. R1200

St Paul's Guest House 182 Bree St ☎021 423 4420, ⓦstpaulschurch.co.za; map p.95. A charming,

---

TOP 5 B&BS

Blackheath Lodge Sea Point, p.141
Chartfield Guesthouse Kalk Bay, p.143
Cob House Muizenberg, p.143
Stonehurst Guesthouse Sea Point, p.142
Welgelegen Boutique Guesthouse
    City Bowl Suburbs, p.140

1

well-managed and inexpensive guesthouse in a Georgian building (formerly a maternity hospital) on a calm street on the city-centre fringes, within easy striking distance of the sights. The rooms are large, comfortable and light with huge windows, and shared bathrooms. R650

Tudor Hotel 153 Longmarket St ☎021 424 1335, ⊚tudorhotel.co.za; map p.95. The most centrally located hotel you could find, and prices are reasonable to boot. En-suite B&B rooms, with contemporary finishes and refurbished bathrooms, overlook cobbled Greenmarket Square. R1090

V&A WATERFRONT AND DE WATERKANT

Accommodation here tends to be upmarket; there are, however, a couple of reasonably priced places to stay. Staying at the **Waterfront** is a good idea if you like shopping in a self-contained safe area, and you want to walk to restaurants and cafés, with transport readily available. On a hillside, less than 1km from the Waterfront, adjacent to the Bo-Kaap and a short hop to Green Point or the city centre, **De Waterkant** is a most desirable place to stay, full of restored Victorian terraces on narrow, well-kept cobbled streets. Though known as Cape Town's pink quarter, it is by no means exclusively so. Many of the historical cottages are for rent, and include family or group accommodation.

Breakwater Lodge Portswood Rd, Waterfront ☎021 406 1911 (ask for Lodge Reservations), ⊚breakwaterlodge.co.za; map p.105. Once a nineteenth-century prison, this lodge provides the most affordable, if characterless, place to stay in the Waterfront, favoured by conference groups. Wireless hotspots throughout and ample parking. R1215

The Cape Grace West Quay, Waterfront ☎021 410 7100, ⊚capegrace.com; map p.105. One of South Africa's most expensive and exclusive hotels, in a perfect location on the Waterfront, and deserving of every accolade. Each room has harbour or Table Mountain views, there's a large heated pool for laps, a spa and a perfectly-positioned-for-the-view jacuzzi on the top floor. Non-guests can also use its fabulous quayside bar for lunch or cocktails. R6000

City Lodge On the corner of Alfred and Dock rds, Waterfront ☎021 419 9450, ⊚citylodge.co.za; map p.105. A perfectly adequate if rather austere hotel, part of a national chain, and less than 1km from both the Waterfront and the city centre. The rooms have TV and there's a small swimming pool. Rates are cheaper Fri–Sun, and you can also pick up discounts using the hotel's room auction site ⊚www.bid2stay.co.za. R1500

St John's Waterfront Lodge 6 Braemar Rd ☎021 439 1404, ⊚stjohns.co.za; map p.105. The closest hostel to the Waterfront (a 10min walk away), well run by helpful

staff. Accommodation is in four dorms sleeping eight to nine people, as well as thirteen doubles, three of which are en suite. There are two swimming pools, a great garden and a bar. There's also free internet access, a coin-operated washing machine and a travel centre. Dorm R120, double R400

★ **Village and Life** 1 Loader St, De Waterkant ☎021 409 2500, ⊚villageandlife.com; map p.105. Self-catering accommodation in upmarket restored, historical cottages in Waterkant, Loader, Dixon and Napier sts of varying sizes, from one to three bedrooms; some have garages, swimming pools and roof gardens with harbour or mountain views. *Village and Life's* extensive portfolio of properties also includes two smart bed and breakfast guesthouses, and self-catering apartments for rent in the Waterfront itself. R1000

CITY BOWL SUBURBS

The City Bowl suburbs are a popular choice for accommodation as they are quieter and leafier than the city centre, especially the further up the mountainside you go, with gardens, good views and swimming pools at the more comfortable guesthouses. The most northerly sections are just ten minutes' walk from the Company's Gardens and the museums. A few backpacker lodges can be found along **Kloof St**, the continuation of Long St and home to some great cafés and restaurants. There's no public transport out to the City Bowl suburbs, but most of the places listed below are under 3km from Cape Town centre and it's easy enough to find taxis or use Rikki's.

African Sun 3 Florida Rd, Vredehoek ☎021 461 1601, ✉afpress@iafrica.com; map p.139. A small self-catering apartment, attached to a family house a little over 1km from the city centre. Furnished with simple ethnic decor, it's run by friendly, well-informed owners, both well-known writers who also offer literary evenings and tours as an extra. Good value. R590

Ashanti Lodge and Guest House 11 Hof St, Gardens ☎021 423 8721, ⊚ashanti.co.za; map p.139. This massive, two-storey Victorian mansion has marbling and ethnic decor, soaring ceilings, a nicely kept front garden, and a swimming pool with sun terrace. The private rooms (with twin or double beds) and dorms (sleeping 6–8) are furnished with custom-made wrought-iron bunks and beds. The bar is very lively, so if you are not a party animal, head for their guesthouses in nearby Union St (R600). Dorm R140, double R420

The Backpack 74 New Church St, Tamboerskloof ☎021 423 4530, ⊚backpackers.co.za; map p.139. An excellent lodge in four interconnected houses, on the cusp of the City Bowl suburbs and the city centre, and easily walkable to both. It's furnished with bold colours and ethnic fabrics, with plenty of outdoor space, including a pool terrace in

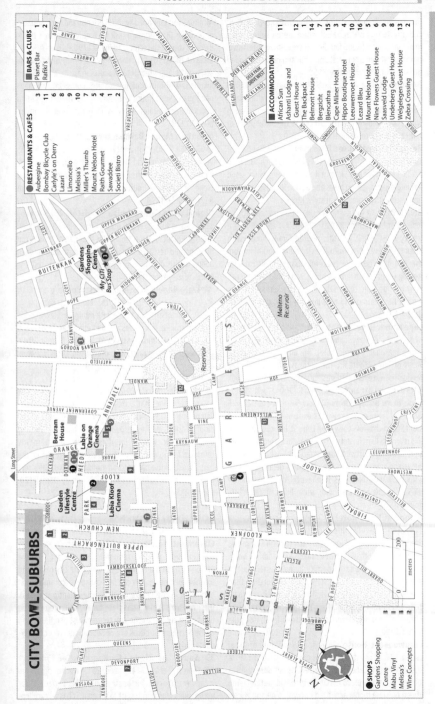

CITY BOWL SUBURBS

■ **BARS & CLUBS**
Planet Bar	1
Rafiki's	2

● **RESTAURANTS & CAFÉS**
Aubergine	3
Bombay Bicycle Club	11
Carlyle's on Derry	6
Lazari	8
Limoncello	9
Melissa's	10
Miller's Thumb	7
Mount Nelson Hotel	5
Raith Gourmet	4
Sawaddee	1
Societi Bistro	2

■ **ACCOMMODATION**
African Sun	11
Ashanti Lodge and Guest House	12
The Backpack	1
Belmont House	14
Bergzicht	7
Blencathra	15
Cape Milner Hotel	3
Hippo Boutique Hotel	4
Leeuwenvoet House	10
Lezard Bleu	16
Mount Nelson Hotel	5
Nine Flowers Guest House	6
Saasveld Lodge	9
Underberg Guest House	8
Welgelegen Guest House	13
Zebra Crossing	2

● **SHOPS**
Gardens Shopping Centre	3
Mabu Vinyl	1
Melissa's	4
Wine Concepts	2

1

the garden. Accommodation is in dorms (sleeping 4–8) and private rooms (several of which are en suite); some rooms are suitable for families. There's an on-site travel centre, a 24hr internet café, and a bar and restaurant open till late. Dorm R145, double R550

Belmont House 10 Belmont Ave, Oranjezicht ☎021 461 5417, ⓦcapeguest.com; map p.139. A tastefully restored 1920s house with seven good-sized rooms, each with its own shower or bath. Either take the B&B option, or self-cater in the communal kitchen. R700

Bergzicht Guesthouse 5 Devonport Rd, Tamboerskloof ☎021 423 8513, ⓦbergzichtguesthouse.co.za; map p.139. Friendly and informal guesthouse with good mountain views, caring hosts and a pool. Rooms are simply furnished with no pretence at style. R995

Blencathra On the corner of De Hoop and Cambridge aves, Tamboerskloof ☎021 424 9571, ⓦblencathra .co.za; map p.139. A large, relaxed family house with mountain views, 2km from the city centre and 4km from the Atlantic. There are peaceful, spacious self-catering rooms, six of which are en suite, attracting a youngish crowd who want to avoid the backpacker scene. The garden has seating and a swimming pool. Dorm R130, double R800

Cape Milner Hotel 2a Milner Rd, Tamboerskloof ☎021 426 1101, ⓦwww.capemilner.com; map p.139. A smart, reasonably priced hotel. The airy rooms all boast views of Table Mountain, the decor is minimal, and the service is excellent. There's also a swimming pool, restaurant and bar on the premises. R1300

Cape Town Backpackers 81 New Church St ☎021 426 0200, ⓦcapetownbackpackers.com; map p.139. Just off Kloof St, which is less noisy than Long St, but close enough, this is an excellent hostel with a variety of accommodation, a breakfasting courtyard, roof terrace with Table Mountain views and tours on offer. There are also deluxe en suites with their own balconies in the next-door guesthouse (R650). Rooms are clean with white linen. Dorm R130, double R575

Hippo Boutique Hotel 5–9 Park Rd, Gardens ☎021 423 2500, ⓦwww.hippotique.co.za; map p.139. A trendy hotel in a good location. Each spacious room has its own kitchenette and coffee maker, a PC and free wi-fi. With convenience and modernity being at the heart of the style here, you don't have to walk further than downstairs for a Mexican or Thai meal, which can also be delivered to your room, or if you're wanting cocktails and a steak, *Greens Restaurant*, also at street level, does the trick. R1290

Leeuwenvoet House 8 Kloofnek Rd, Tamboerskloof ☎021 424 1133, ⓦleeuwenvoet.co.za; map p.139. A lovely, tranquil Cape Dutch gabled guesthouse with a fantastic view of Table Mountain from its wide veranda. The fifteen en-suite rooms are kitted out with pine and wicker

furniture and equipped with TV, phones and fans. Situated on a major thoroughfare (ask for a quieter room if traffic disturbs you) with secure parking. R1290

Lezard Bleu 30 Upper Orange St, Oranjezicht ☎021 461 4601, ⓦlezardbleu.co.za; map p.139. Seven luxurious and immaculate en-suite rooms, in a spacious open-plan 1960s house with Afro-chic styling. The sliding doors from each room open onto a garden and swimming pool. R1220

Mountain Manor Backpackers 17 Breda St, Gardens ☎021 461 7200, ⓦmountainmanor.co.za; map p.139. Very central dorms and two doubles in a Victorian house, with a communal kitchen and the usual young backpacker scene, including a rooftop deck for chilling out. Dorm R120, double R790

Nine Flowers Guest House 133 Hatfield St, Gardens ☎021 462 1430, ⓦwww.nineflowers.com; map p.139. In a convenient location, on a quiet street, this German-run nine-roomed restored Victorian guesthouse has wooden floors, white linen, contemporary furnishings and is immaculately kept. R1050

★ **Welgelegen Boutique Guest House** 6 Stephen St, Gardens ☎021 426 2373, ⓦwelgelegen.co.za; map p.139. A Victorian guesthouse with mountain views, styled with a luxurious mix of classical and ethnic, and with a spa treatment room and massages for guests. There is also a DVD library. The owners are green and socially aware, unusual in the tourist industry. R1850

Zebra Crossing 82 New Church St ☎021 422 1265, ⓦzebra-crossing.co.za; map p.139. Cape Town's only backpacker lodge that actually boasts about being quiet. Comprising two Victorian houses, it's an easy walk to the Kloof St cafés, and has its own café-bar and two pleasant terraces under vines. The doubles are basic, mostly courtyard facing and not en suite, but they are cheap; the best has access to a balcony and mountain views. Off-street parking, communal kitchen and child-friendly. Dorm R120, double R350

SOUTHERN SUBURBS

Cape Town's gracious southern suburbs – **Rosebank**, **Claremont**, **Newlands** and **Rondebosch** – are on the forested side of the mountain, convenient for the university and on a train line between the city centre and southern peninsula. You can find cheaper accommodation here than in the centre or along the Atlantic seaboard. **Observatory** is the only place for nightlife here, and is the closest suburb to the city centre. Most people staying in the Southern Suburbs are on work-, sports- or family-related trips.

33 South Boutique Backpackers 48 Trill Rd, Observatory ☎021 447 2423, ⓦ33southbackpackers .com. A spacious Victorian house that's perfect for backpackers who don't want to rough it. It has an excellent location in a quiet street, a couple of minutes from the train station and vibrant Lower Main Rd with its nightlife and cafés. They offer rooms in other parts of Cape Town of a similar standard – for example in Kalk Bay, Bo-Kaap and Khayelitsha – so that you can explore different aspects of the city. R120

Carmichael House 11 Wolmunster Rd, Rosebank ☎021 689 8350, ⓦcarmichaelhouse.co.za. A two-storey guesthouse in a building dating from the turn of the last century, with six spacious rooms. There's a peaceful garden, swimming pool and secure parking, plus internet facilities. The Rondebosch shops are 1km away. R820

Gloucester House Bed & Breakfast 54 Weltevreden Ave, Rondebosch ☎021 689 3894. A private house with two double bedrooms and a spacious kitchen/diner for self-catering. Guests may also use the large garden, swimming pool and barbecue area, and you can get breakfast if you don't feel like self-catering. R500

Ivydene Off Glebe Rd, Rondebosch ☎021 685 1747, ⓔivydene@mweb.co.za. Five self-catering flats in a delightful old house near the university, with a garden, swimming pool and friendly atmosphere. There are discounts for stays of a week or more. R450

★ **The Vineyard** On the corner of Colinton and Protea rds, Newlands ☎021 657 4500, ⓦvineyard .co.za. One of the city's top hotels, situated in a restored country villa. The public spaces are decorated in elegant Cape Dutch style, with contemporary artworks, and you can soak up the outstanding panorama of Table Mountain from the extensive and gorgeous grounds. There's a spa, heated pool and gym at one end of the garden. R1900

ATLANTIC SEABOARD

Down the Atlantic seaboard lie the seaside suburbs of Mouille Point, Green Point, Three Anchor Bay and Sea Point. Historically Cape Town's hotel and high-rise land, this is packed with a range of accommodation, making it a good alternative to the City Bowl if you want to be close to the city centre.

South from Sea Point along Victoria Drive, the well-heeled mountainside suburb of **Camps Bay** has soaring views over the Atlantic, with the advantage of being close to the city centre, and with its own restaurants and shops. Though nearby **Llandudno** lacks shops or restaurants, it can boast similar vistas and a supremely beautiful beach with clusters of granite boulders at either end. **Hout Bay** is the main urban concentration along the lower half of the peninsula, with a harbour, pleasant waterfront development and the only public transport beyond Camps Bay. South of Hout Bay is the semi-rural settlement of **Noordhoek**, close to Table Mountain National Park, with good horseriding, beach walks and surfing.

GREEN POINT

Dale Court Guest House 1 Exhibition Terrace Rd ☎021 439 8774, ⓦdalecourt.co.za; map pp.116–117. A conveniently located, very reasonably priced B&B for this area, directly opposite the V&A Waterfront, with simple and clean rooms which don't get prizes for imaginative decor. The guesthouse owners also manage the eight-storey block opposite, which comprises functional self-catering apartments for families. R950

David's 12 Croxteth Rd ☎021 439 4649, ⓦdavids .co.za; map pp.116–117. An elegant, affordable and airy gay-run B&B in a quiet residential street in trendy Green Point, just off the main road. It also has some self-catering apartments. R900

Jambo Guest House 1 Grove Rd ☎021 439 4219, ⓦjambo.co.za; map. Small, atmospheric establishment with four luxury en-suite rooms and one garden suite, in a quiet cul-de-sac off Main Rd. The lush, leafy exterior and enclosed garden with pond are delightfully relaxing and the service is excellent. A lavish buffet breakfast is included. R1300

Point B Guest House 14 Pine Rd ☎021 434 0902 or ☎083 627 5583, ⓦpointb.co.za; map pp.116–117. Four rooms inside, and another in the garden of a 1900s house, all brightly decorated, with wicker furniture. Great personal service, and there's lovely poolside seating on a bricked terrace. R1000

Wilton Manor 15 Croxteth Rd ☎021 434 2572, ⓦwiltonmanor.co.za; map pp.116–117. A quiet and friendly guesthouse with a homely atmosphere in a Victorian house close to the city centre. Of the seventeen B&B rooms, five are en suite; the cheaper rooms share a bathroom, though each room has its own hand basin. The service is good, and there's also a small garden. R1200

SEA POINT AND BANTRY BAY

★ **Blackheath Lodge** 6 Blackheath Rd ☎021 439 2541, ⓦblackheathlodge.co.za; map pp.116–117. Superb owner-run guesthouse, in a grand Victorian home, that gets everything right. The ten rooms are large and airy (some with views of Lion's Head) and the king-sized beds are the most comfortable you'll find in Cape Town. Breakfast is served on a courtyard-garden deck overlooking the pool. Situated down a quiet backstreet, it's close to the Sea Point action. R1550

Don Suite Hotel 249 Beach Rd, Sea Point ☎021 434 1083, ⓦdon.co.za; map pp.116–117. A five-storey block of 27 self-catering apartments across the road from the beachfront promenade and 300m from the lively Main Rd restaurant strip. All the flats are modern and well equipped; rates vary depending on whether or not you get a view. R1500

Huijs Haerlem 25 Main Drive ☎021 434 6434, ⓦwww.huijshaerlem.co.za; map pp.116–117. Elegant

1

and friendly guesthouse in two adjacent houses furnished with Dutch antiques. Each of its eight rooms has a sea view, a vista of Signal Hill or overlooks the lovely garden. R1450

Les Cascades de Bantry Bay 48 De Wet Rd, Bantry Bay ☎ 021 434 5209, ⓦ lescascades.co.za; map pp.116–117. One of the city's most beautiful guesthouses, perched above the Atlantic. Every room has a full sea view and deck or balcony and features Balinese-influenced decor in warm earthy tones. Unusually for such an upmarket, honeymoon destination, they do take children and there's also a sister establishment down the road. R2150

★ **Stonehurst Guest House** 3 Frere Rd, Sea Point ☎ 021 434 9670, ⓦ stonehurst.co.za; map pp.116–117. An airy tin-roofed Victorian residence with original fittings and furnished with an attractive melange of antiques and collectibles by friendly antique-dealer owner, Jan. There's a kitchen for self-catering and a guest lounge. Most rooms are en suite, and some have balconies. Great value and location, a couple of roads back from busy Main Rd. R650

Villa Rosa 277 High Level Rd, Sea Point ☎ 021 434 2768, ⓦ villa-rosa.com; map pp.116–117. A friendly eight-room guesthouse in a brick-red two-storey Victorian house on the lower slopes of Signal Hill, two blocks from the beachfront promenade. Decorated with simplicity and style, all rooms have TVs, phones and safes, but only some, on the upper floor, have sea views. R975

Winchester Mansions Hotel 221 Beach Rd, Sea Point ☎ 021 434 2351, ⓦ www.winchester.co.za; map pp.116–117. A self-consciously colonial-style 1920s hotel, in a prime spot across the road from the seashore, with an atmosphere straight from the pages of Agatha Christie – though the rooms themselves are fresh and contemporary in furnishing. Palm trees at the front of the three-storey Cape Dutch Revival building hint at the interior: rooms have ceiling fans, and the cool Italianate courtyard restaurant is overlooked by balconies draped in luxuriant creepers. R2400

CAMPS BAY AND BAKOVEN

Bateleur Rontree 12 Rontree St, Camps Bay ☎ 021 438 4783, ⓦ bateleurshouse.co.za; map p.119. Straightforward guesthouse notable for its friendly service and spectacular sea views from the pool deck and some rooms. The simply furnished en-suite rooms with tiled floors flow out onto a wooden deck to make the most of outdoor living. R990

Bay Atlantic Guest House 3 Berkley Rd ☎ 021 438 4341, ⓦ thebayatlantic.com; map p.119. Supremely laid-back double-storey family home-turned-guesthouse offering personal service from the friendly, informal owners. Rooms range from a small, but comfortable, box room with no view (probably the cheapest guesthouse room in Camps Bay; R700) to more luxurious ones with decks and superb views of the Atlantic. R1500

Bay Hotel Victoria Rd, Camps Bay ☎ 021 438 4444, ⓦ thebay.co.za; map p.119. Glitzy five-star hotel on the fashionable beachfront strip. Its late 1980s construction blends neo-Cape Dutch with Mediterranean styles and its crisp, stylishly simple decor, to conjure up a laidback beachside fantasy. Rooms vary from small but well-appointed Traveller's Rooms to a luxury penthouse suite, and everything in between. R2800

Leeukop 25 Sedgemoor Rd, Camps Bay ☎ 021 438 1361, ⓦ leeukop.co.za; map p.119. Near the beach and cafés, offering one stylishly arty and comfortable apartment adjoining the cheerful proprietor's home, with mountain views and a small patio garden. The flat is fully equipped, and you can either self-cater or stay on a B&B basis. R1000

Ocean View House 33 Victoria Rd, Bakoven ☎ 021 438 1982, ⓦ oceanview-house.com; map p.119. A river runs through the grounds of this family-run, eccentrically blue and yellow boutique hotel, set in 3000 square metres of gorgeous garden that borders a *fynbos* reserve. The fourteen spacious rooms are comfortably furnished in a contemporary style and have either sea or mountain views. R1950

HOUT BAY AND LLANDUDNO

★ **Hout Bay Hideaway** 37 Skaife St, Hout Bay ☎ 021 790 8040, ⓦ houtbay-hideaway.com. An outstanding guesthouse that has a genuine verve – Persian rugs, stunning Art Deco armchairs and huge beds. Each of the four rooms has views of the mountains or sea and outdoor decks on which your private breakfast is served. At the back there's a saltwater pool in a lovely *fynbos* garden with the mountain rising up behind. R1500

Houtkapperspoort 1 Hout Bay Main Rd, 7km from Hout Bay ☎ 021 794 5216, ⓦ houtkapperspoort.co.za. The 26 charming one- to four-bedroom stone-and-timber self-catering cottages here are set against the mountain in a rural setting, close to Constantia Nek. You can hike, play tennis or take a dip in the solar-heated pool. Highly recommended. R1300

Sunbird Mountain Retreat & Lodge Boskykloof Rd, Hout Bay ☎ 021 790 7758, ⓦ sunbirdlodge.co.za. Four pleasant, spacious self-catering apartments (R600) and a guesthouse that includes a family unit, all nestling in a forest high up on the mountainside. All of the rooms have great views and there's a secluded swimming pool. R90

★ **Sunset on the Rocks** 11 Sunset Ave, Llandudno ☎ 021 790 2103, ⓦ sunsetontherocks.co.za. A magical hideaway clinging to the hillside of one of the loveliest coves on the peninsula. Set among a *fynbos* garden, the three compact self-contained flats, one of which incorporates a massive granite boulder in the wall, all have superb sea views and are attached to the house of Brian and Helen Alcock. Despite the sense of remoteness, neighbouring Hout Bay is less than 10min away by car. **R600**

NOORDHOEK

★**Ekogaia Farm Cottages** 2 Nthombeni Way, Noordhoek ☎021 789 1751 or ☎083 403 2623, ⓦwww.ekogaia.co.za. Two thatched self-catering cottages on an attractive organic smallholding, each built with a low ecological footprint design, with outdoor patios, mountain and sea views, plenty of privacy and picnic and play areas for children. **R650**

Monkey Valley Beach Nature Resort Mountain Rd, Noordhoek ☎021 789 8000, ⓦmonkeyvalleyresort .com. An attractive group of mainly wooden and thatched two-storey chalets spread over several acres on Chapman's Peak, 40km south of the city centre. Overlooking Noordhoek Beach, the site is surrounded by indigenous vegetation, though there are no monkeys. The cottages sleep six to eight people, and work out reasonably for a group. You can either eat in the restaurant, self-cater or stay on a B&B basis. **1500**

FALSE BAY SEABOARD

This is the area to look in if you want to swim every day, surf and walk on the beach, as well as enjoy excellent eateries – though the city centre is some 20km away by car, or connected by train during the day. **Muizenberg**, the oldest of Cape Town's seaside suburbs, was once hugely popular, though is now a bit run-down. To its south is salubrious **St James**, while the jewel in the crown is **Kalk Bay** with its working harbour, quirky shops and arty cafés. **Fish Hoek**, further south, is recommended for its beach, while **Simon's Town**, 45 minutes' drive from the city, is regarded by many as a separate village, which it originally was, although it's definitely part of the metropolis now. There are far fewer guesthouses than on the Atlantic side, and a worthwhile option, especially for popular Kalk Bay, is to take a self-catering apartment, the best source being ⓦsafarinow .com or Peninsula Tourism, Beach Rd Pavilion, Muizenberg (Mon–Fri 8am–5pm, Sat 9am–1pm; ☎021 787 9140, ⓦcapetown.travel).

MUIZENBERG TO FISH HOEK

Amberley Travellers Lodge 15 Amberley Rd, Muizenberg ☎021 788 7032; map p.122–123. A restored two-storey house, off Main Rd, with gleaming wooden floors, a self-catering kitchen, and the cheapest double rooms you'll find this close to the ocean. **R280**

Beach Lodge Surfers Corner, Muizenberg ☎021 788 1771, ⓦthebeachlodge.co.za; map pp.122–123. Right on the beachfront, above a surfing shop, with clean, bright budget rooms, some big enough for families, the best of which have balconies fronting the promenade. You'll hear the surf pounding, wherever you are. **R360**

Chartfield Guest House 30 Gatesville Rd, Kalk Bay ☎021 788 3793, ⓦchartfield.co.za; map pp.122–123. Comfortable accommodation, 100m from Kalk Bay station, in a well-kept rambling house halfway up the hill overlooking the harbour, with terrific sea views. The best rooms are the one in the loft with its own balcony, and the two semicircular corner ones with 180-degree views. **R900**

★**Cob House** 13 Watson Rd, Muizenberg ☎021 788 6613, ⓦcobhouse.co.za; map pp.122–123. The greenest B&B in Cape Town, run by an exceptionally friendly family, and just 200m from the beach. Teacher/storyteller/ musician Simric Yarrow also runs excellent tours around the city. The comfy en-suite guest room (just one) can sleep up to four, and the reasonable rate includes an organic breakfast served in your room. **R700**

The Mountain House 7 Mountain Rd, Clovelly ☎083 455 5664, ⓦthemountainhouse.co.za. Beautiful

---

AFRICAN TOWNSHIP HOMESTAYS

One of the best ways of getting a taste of the African townships is by spending a night there, something you can do for the price of a regular township tour (see p.132). The number of township residents offering **B&B accommodation** in their homes is still small, but growing. You'll have a chance to experience the warmth of *ubuntu* – traditional African hospitality – by staying with a family with whom you'll generally eat breakfast and dinner; they can also usually take you around their area to *shebeens*, music venues, churches or just to meet the neighbours.

A number of the township B&Bs will send someone to meet you at the airport, while many people are dropped off at their accommodation by tour operators. If you're driving, your accommodation will give you detailed directions or arrange to meet you at a convenient landmark, such as a garage or police station. Township homestays are considerably cheaper than staying in central Cape Town, with prices around R500–600 per room.

To book a township B&B, contact **Cape Town Tourism Centre**, corner NY1 & NY4, Gugiletu (Mon–Fri 9am–5.30pm, Sat 9am–2pm; ☎021 637 8449, ⓦcapetown.travel). The Tourism Centre also serves as a stop-off point for tourists, with a historical photographic exhibition and an arts and crafts shop.

1

accommodation equidistant from Fish Hoek and Kalk Bay with distant views of False Bay and the Atlantic seaboards. Built in the garden of local architect Carin Hartford, this two-bedroom, self-catering cottage has windows everywhere to capitalize on the mountain setting, and the living space flows out to a timber deck. R900

Tranquility Guest House 25 Peak Rd, Fish Hoek ☎ 021 782 2060, ⓦ tranquil.co.za. Warm and welcoming guesthouse on Fish Hoek mountainside, with ocean views (the beach is within walking distance). There are four cosy B&B en-suite rooms, plus a self-catering apartment with its own entrance (R900), and you can soak up the views from the outdoor jacuzzi. R1200

SIMON'S TOWN AND AROUND

Blue Bay 48 Palace Hill Rd ☎ 021 786 1700, ⓦ bbay .co.za. A luxurious self-catering home with stupendous ocean views and a tranquil ambience, 1km from the centre of Simon's Town. You can take the whole place as a couple,

or install your family since it sleeps up to six. Discounts are available for longer stays. R1000

Simon's Town Backpackers 66 St George's St ☎ 021 786 1964, ⓦ capepax.co.za. Conveniently located in the heart of Simon's Town, within walking distance of the station. The renovated 1802 building with wooden floors, and clean spacious rooms, offers dorms and doubles (some en suite), the best of which have French doors leading onto a balcony and harbour view. You can rent bicycles for a ride to Cape Point or paddle in a kayak past the penguin colony. Dorm R140, double R380

Topsail House 176 St George's St ☎ 021 786 5537, ⓦ topsailhouse.co.za. A converted old convent school with more space than the average backpacker lodge, though a tad staid. There are various accommodation options, including an extraordinary bedroom in a chapel, which is self-catering, though the en-suite doubles, with balconies, upstairs in the main building are the nicest rooms. Five minutes' walk to the centre of town, with secure parking. R420

EATING

Eating out is one of the highlights of visiting Cape Town, and the city is home to a large number of relaxed and convivial restaurants, which generally serve imaginative food of a high standard. Prices are inexpensive compared with much of the developed world, and you can eat innovative food by outstanding chefs in upmarket restaurants for the kind of money you'd spend on a pizza back home. This is the place to splash out on whatever takes your fancy, and you'll find the quality of meat and fish very high, with many vegetarian options available as well. There are a couple of restaurants dedicated to **Cape** or **African Cuisine** (see opposite), though it's not the thing to concentrate on when you're choosing something to eat since other genres are done a lot better. You can expect fresh **Cape fish** at every good restaurant as well as seafood from warmer waters. Fish stocks are declining worldwide, however, and to be ecologically responsible, go for a delicious Cape fish like Yellow Tail which is not endangered (see box on p.58 for more details).

CITY CENTRE
AROUND LONG STREET

95 Keerom 95 Keerom St ☎ 021 422 0765; map p.95. Flash, fabulous and expensive, with fresh and light Italian nouvelle cuisine, such as grilled beef, butternut ravioli or seared tuna (R150), though the decor is a little stark. Mon–Sat 7–9.30pm, Thurs & Fri noon–2.30pm.

Addis in Cape 41 Church St ☎ 021 424 5722; map p.95. Delicious traditional Ethiopian dishes and yummy *injera* (flat bread) to soak up the flavours and eat with your fingers, served in a friendly and casual atmosphere (mains around R100). Mon–Sat noon–3pm & 6–10.30pm.

Africa Café 108 Shortmarket St, Cape Heritage Square ☎ 021 422 0221. ⓦ africacafe.co.za; map p.95. Probably the best tourist restaurant in Cape Town for African cuisine, with a fantastic selection of dishes from across the continent. Given that you're served a communal feast of sixteen dishes, and that you can have as many extra helpings as you like, the R250-per-head price tag is pretty reasonable. It is also open for breakfast and African tapas lunches. Booking essential. Mon–Sat 8am– 2pm & 6.30–10pm.

★ **Bird's Café** 127 Bree St ☎ 021 426 2534; map p.95. A great daytime spot to sit with a good coffee at trestle

tables on upturned crates. Their conical chicken pies are recommended, as well as the lemonade and fresh bakes, and they use organic produce where possible (mains around R60). Portions can be big enough for two, but service can be sluggish. Mon–Fri 7am–5pm, Sat 8am–2pm.

Bukhara 33 Church St ☎ 021 424 0000; map p.95. A popular upmarket North Indian restaurant, with green marble floors and a show kitchen where you can watch the chefs at work. The food is superb, though expensive (R110), but portions are large and there is creative use of local meat cooked with traditional Indian spices such as ostrich tikka. Booking essential. Daily noon–3pm & 6–11pm.

★ **Eastern Food Bazaar** Wellington Fruit Growers Building, 96 Longmarket ☎ 021 461 2458; map p.95. Good cheap canteen-style place serving Indian and Cape Malay food, including freshly made faloodas and lassis (R35). You queue up to order – expect long waits at lunchtime. No alcohol or smoking permitted. Daily 11am–10pm.

Headquarters Heritage Square, 100 Shortmarket St ☎ 021 424 6373; map p.95. This trendy, yuppy place is a bit of a destination restaurant, with one thing on the menu

– prime free-range Namibian sirloin steak and butter sauce, with perfect matchstick chips and salad (R165). On Friday nights they have a DJ with relaxing beats, hotting up around 10pm when the tables are pushed back for dancing. Monday nights you get two meals for the price of one. Booking always essential. Mon–Sat 11.30am–10.30pm.

Jewel Tavern 101 St George's Mall ☎021 422 4041; map p.95. Once an unpretentious Taiwanese sailors' eating house, *Jewel Tavern* still serves superb food, though it has lost its charming harbour atmosphere in a central, though far more convenient, venue. Try the great hot and sour soup and spring rolls, sometimes made while you watch (R95). Daily 11am–3pm & 5–10pm.

Mama Africa 178 Long St ☎021 424 8634; map p.95. Food from around the continent, including a mixed grill of springbok, impala, kudu, ostrich and crocodile (mains around R90). You can also sit at the 12m bar – in the form of a green mamba – and listen to live African music in the evening. Mon & Sat 6.30–11pm, Tues–Fri 11am–4pm & 6.30–11pm.

Masala Dosa 167 Long St ☎021 424 6772; map p.95. Inexpensive and fast South Indian cuisine with a touch of Bollywood decor. Worth visiting just for the qinger and apple lassi and yummy dosas (R70). Daily noon–10pm.

Mexican Kitchen Café 13 Bloem St ☎021 423 1541; map p.95. A casual restaurant serving good-value burritos, enchiladas, nachos and calamari fajitas, with some fine vegetarian options and deli-style takeaways (R70), and the best frozen margaritas in town. Fun atmosphere, with sombreros to wear and pictures of Frida Kahlo outside. Sun–Thurs 11am–11pm, Fri & Sat 11am–midnight.

Mr Pickwick's 158 Long St; map p.95. The place to go for midnight munchies. Hearty and cheap "tin-plate" meals (R50), including a challenging range of hot and cold foot-long sandwiches. Mon–Sun 8am–2am.

Royale 273 Long St ☎021 422 4536; map p.95. A hip hangout serving gourmet burgers that pack a surprise with unusual combinations, such as served with brie or roasted vegetables. Choose from lamb, beef, chicken and seven vegetarian patties including tofu (around R75). Packed, so book ahead if you want a balcony seat looking out onto Long St. Mon–Sat noon–10.30pm.

Savoy Cabbage 101 Hout St ☎021 424 2626; map p.95. Sophisticated and innovative European-style peasant food, madly expensive (mains around R140) but worthwhile for one of the best gourmet meals in town. The seasonally influenced menu changes all the time, but their tomato tart with goat's milk cheese and caramelised onion is a hit and you will find it difficult to choose between all the delectable meat offerings. Mon–Fri noon–2pm & 7–10pm, Sat 7–10pm.

ELSEWHERE IN THE CENTRE

Biesmiellah In the Bo-Kaap, on the corner of Upper Wales and Pentz sts ☎021 423 0850; map p.92. One of the oldest restaurants in the city for traditional Cape Muslim cuisine; rather than a sit-down meal, join local residents in the queue for their takeaway samosas and delicious savoury, meat-filled wraps called *salomes* (R35). No alcohol. Mon–Sat 7am–10pm.

★ **Bizerca Bistro** 15 Jetty St, Foreshore ☎021 418 0001; map p.92. You are unlikely to eat better in Cape Town than at this inner-city gourmet bistro with a modern, funky feel. The food, from French chef Laurent Deslandes, is light, elegant and creative, using local ingredients and arrayed on the blackboard, with meat and fish choices and incredible desserts. Not cheap (mains R110), but you never feel ripped off and service is excellent. Booking essential. Mon–Fri noon–2.30pm & 6–10pm, Sat 6–10pm.

Charly's Bakery 38 Canterbury St; map p.92. The most spectacular cakes and cupcakes in Cape Town, but don't

---

AFRICAN FOOD

Around the centre of Cape Town you will find a couple of restaurants offering African food, but these are geared towards tourists – you would never find a full-blooded Xhosa worker eating in Long Street. The best way to experience the African food in the **townships** is by staying in one of the B&Bs (see box, p.143), or by taking a tour that incorporates an organized township meal or a drink in a *shebeen* (see p.132).

You are not going to find authentic places to eat and drink if you just drive about in the townships, which would be unwise and unsafe in any event, but there is one notable exception: *Mzoli's*, in the closest township to the centre and within easy driving distance, has even caught the attention of Jamie Oliver, who adored the **barbecued meat**.

Mzoli's NY 115, Gugulethu, N2 Modderdam Rd offramp, close to the airport ☎021 638 1355. Best at lunchtime (you need to book a table and phone for directions), when you can join a local crowd and devour tasty meat barbecued (*tshisanyama* – "chi-san-knee-yama") for you out the back (R100). Serves meat and more meat, ranging from chops, boerewors sausage, cuts of beef and lamb served with dumplings, *pap* (thick maize porridge), meat sauce and *chakalaka*, a tomato salad. Not suitable for vegetarians or those with small appetites.

1

expect anything from the decor. Try the Death by Chocolate – a very rich, moist cake – or the double chocolate cheesecake (R50). Also does breakfasts and light lunches. Mon–Fri 8am–5pm, Sat 8.30am–3pm.

Col'Cacchio Seeff House, 42 Hans Strijdom Ave; map p.92. An offbeat pizza restaurant, part of a chain, which also serves pasta and salads and has a range of low-fat and heart-friendly pizzas, perfect if you're feeling guilty. There are over forty different designer pizza toppings, such as smoked salmon, sour cream and rocket (R95). Mon–Fri 9am–10.30pm, Sat & Sun 6–10.30pm.

Sinn's Wembley Square, McKenzie Rd ☎ 021 465 0967; map p.92. A busy, all-day spot, in a trendy complex, with a decidedly Continental air and good food (mains R90), from rye sandwiches and salad to bouillabaisse, served promptly to a hip, young crowd. It is family friendly too, with a menu for under-12s, and it's also known for excellent cocktails and snacks. Daily 9am–11pm.

Truth Coffee Cult Prestwich Memorial, Somerset Rd ☎ 021 419 2945; map p.92. Coffee as good as it gets in a tranquil café with white umbrellas and a shady tree outside. A great breakfast or lunch spot for some calm, and good, reasonably priced sandwiches and coffee (R60). Mon–Fri 7am–5pm, Sat 7am–3pm, Sun 9am–2pm.

V&A WATERFRONT AND DE WATERKANT

THE WATERFRONT

Baia Upper Level, Quay 6 ☎ 021 421 0935; map p.105. Sit on the terraced balcony and take in the views of Table Mountain while dining on masterfully cooked fresh fish and seafood. The spicy seafood bouillabaisse is worth a try (R140). Daily noon–11pm.

Caffe Balducci Quay 6 ☎ 021 421 6002; map p.105. An upmarket café-restaurant with a fresh feel, lovely harbour views and interesting Californian/Italian food with South African overtones. Try the biltong salad with blue cheese and caramelised nuts (R110). Expensive but worth it, with a popular sushi bar just outside the front door. Daily 9am–midnight.

Caffé San Marco Piazza level, Victoria Wharf ☎ 021 418 5434; map p.105. A coffee shop-bar on the piazza, offering an all-day breakfast menu, good sandwiches on Italian breads and fresh salads. The grilled calamari with garlic and chilli is delicious (R90). They also serve eighteen flavours of ice cream and sorbet. Daily 8.30am–11.30pm.

Grand Café and Beach Haul Rd, off Beach Rd, Granger Bay ☎ 021 425 0551; map p.105. There's a French Riviera atmosphere to this waterside venue where a beach has been artificially created. Not as kitsch as it sounds, it is a jolly place, largely for a beautiful people crowd. The food is good (mains around R150), though service is sketchy. The fusion menu has Asian and Portuguese influence, and

includes a huge pizza to feed a group of six. Wed–Sat noon–midnight, Sun noon–11pm.

Wang Thai Shop 2, 61 Victoria Wharf ☎ 021 421 8702; map p.105. Possibly Cape Town's best Thai restaurant, serving such delights as hot and spicy prawn soup, steamed fish with lemon juice and chilli, and its special – thinly sliced, seared sirloin (R85). Daily 11am–10.30pm.

Willoughby & Co Shop 6182, Lower Level, Victoria Wharf ☎ 021 418 6115; map p.105. The best fish restaurant at the waterfront, serving fantastic sushi and seafood (mains around R100), with a lively atmosphere that makes up for the lack of views. Daily noon–11pm.

DE WATERKANT

★ **Anatoli** 24 Napier St ☎ 021 419 2501; map p.105. A Turkish restaurant in an early twentieth-century warehouse that buzzes with atmosphere. The excellent *meze* includes exceptionally delicious *dolmades*, and there are superb desserts such as pressed dates topped with cream (mains around R90). Great for vegetarians. Mon–Sat 7–10.30pm.

Andiamo Cape Quarter piazza, Dixon St ☎ 021 421 3688; map p.105. Busy Italian deli with a courtyard restaurant serving salads, pastas and sandwiches. The deli itself does a great selection of meats, cheeses, salads, dips and fresh breads – phone ahead and they'll put a picnic or platter together for you. Daily 9am–11pm.

Origin Coffee 28 Hudson St ☎ 021 421 1000; map p.105. Home-roasted coffees from across Africa, as well as Asia and Latin America. Their range of teas is equally appealing and your drink can be accompanied with a sandwich or pastry (R70), but the food is secondary to the quality of the beans. Mon–Fri 7am–5pm, Sat 9am–2pm.

CITY BOWL SUBURBS

Aubergine 39 Barnet St ☎ 021 465 4909; map p.139. Unbeatable choice, country wide, for a five-star dinner, with a garden to sit in to enjoy the top-quality Afro-Asian cooking of chef Harald Bresselschmidt. Expensive, but memorable (mains around R160). The menu changes all the time, but you may get to eat wild boar leg with creamy Kalahari truffle sauce. If you aren't up for a full-on dinner, they also do fabulous tapas and sundowners. Mon–Sat 7–10pm. Wed–Fri noon–2pm. Tapas Mon–Sat 5–7pm.

Bombay Bicycle Club 158 Kloof St ☎ 423 6805; map p.139. Don't expect Indian cuisine, but a totally fun place for a great evening out, with things to play with in every area, whether it's sitting at a table with swings, or wearing silly hats. Food includes grills, soups, pastas and carpaccio (mains around R100). Booking essential. Mon–Sat 6–11pm, though the bar is open from 4pm.

Carlyle's on Derry 17 Derry St, Gardens ☎ 021 461 8787; map p.139. A friendly place where you can munch

1

on gourmet thin-base pizzas, such as fig and blue cheese, Thai chicken and coriander or lemon-infused ham and rocket (R70). Book ahead. The bar is open from 4.30pm. Daily 6–10.30pm.

Daily Deli 110 Kloof St, Gardens; map p.139. Pavement café in a row of attractive Victorian houses, with mountain views and popular with the local creative set. Great for coffee and cake, croissants, sandwiches and breakfast which can even be served at supper time (R60). Always chock-a-block. Daily 10am–10pm.

Lazari Corner of Upper Maynard St and Vredehoek Ave ☎021 461 9865; map p.139. A meeting place for City Bowl residents, serving fresh, interesting breakfasts all day (R70), as well as lunches, including bangers and mash, salads, pasta and falafels, plus home-made cakes and biscuits. There's a sister branch in De Waterkant, on the corner of Jarvis and Napier sts. Mon–Fri 7.30am–4pm, Sat 8am–3pm, Sun 8.30am–2.30pm.

Limoncello 8 Breda St, Gardens ☎021 461 5100; map p.139. Small Italian trattoria serving unfailingly excellent pastas and pizzas, with an emphasis on fresh foods. Serves possibly the best calamari in Cape Town and a great risotto of the day (R90). Mon–Fri noon–3.30pm & 6.30–11pm, Sat & Sun 6.30–11pm.

Melissa's 94 Kloof St, Gardens; map p.139. Interesting breakfasts, light meals (around R60) and fine desserts in the small café, attached to the food emporium, which sells freshly made Mediterranean food. Mon–Fri 7.30am–9pm, Sat & Sun 8am–9pm.

Miller's Thumb 10b Kloof Nek Rd ☎021 424 3838; map p.139. Consistently good seafood dishes, in a friendly place, with a selection of line-fish served in a variety of ways (R120). A great choice if it's fish you're after, though they also do steaks. Mon & Sat 6.30–10.30pm, Tues–Fri 12.30–2pm & 6.30–10.30pm.

Mount Nelson Hotel 76 Orange St, Gardens; map p.139. The colonial-style afternoon tea (R170) in Cape Town's oldest and most gracious hotel is definitely one of the city's culinary highlights, with the large tea table piled high with hot and cold pastries, classic savouries like smoked salmon sandwiches, and cakes. Daily 2.30–5.30pm.

Raith Gourmet Gardens Shopping Centre, Mill St, Gardens; map p.139. Meat-focused deli and café with an exceptional selection of foods and some marvellous sandwiches; German specialities include sauerkraut fried with strips of bacon (R60). Mon–Fri 8.30am–6pm, Sat 8.30am–1pm.

Societi Bistro 50 Orange St ☎021 424 2100; map p.139. Friendly bistro with a great atmosphere and good Italian-style food, in a lovely restored building and garden virtually opposite the *Mount Nelson* hotel. Sometimes they do special deals if you are going to the nearby Labia cinema, and there is a fireplace for winter evenings. Their

risotto is always a hit (R110), and starters include ox tongue, roasted bone marrow and lamb liver. Mon–Sat noon–11pm.

SOUTHERN SUBURBS

Buitenverwachting Klein Constantia Rd, Constantia ☎021 794 3522. Expensive restaurant on a beautiful wine estate that's ideal for an elegant, special (though not stiflingly formal) occasion with beautifully plated food. Seafood and venison feature regularly, or you can opt for a variety of titillating flavours from their four- or seven-course degustation menu (R250 and R365, respectively). Tues–Sat noon–3pm & 7–9.30pm.

Chandani 85 Roodebloem Rd, Woodstock ☎021 447 7887. Great North Indian food (mains R80). Aside from the more expensive and centrally located *Bukhara*, you are unlikely to do better in Cape Town for Indian dining. Vegetarians can breathe a sigh of relief at the array of dishes on offer. Set in a tastefully restored Victorian house, in a gritty neighbourhood. Mon–Sat noon–3pm, 6–10.30pm.

★ **The Kitchen** 111 Sir Lowry Rd, Woodstock ☎021 462 2201. Run by one of the stallholders at the Neighbourhood Goods Market (see p.160), using fresh ingredients to create fabulous, creative sandwiches on artisanal bread, with salads made up of lentils, chickpeas and couscous (R45). This is one of the best places in town, especially if you are vegetarian, for a casual, cheap lunch. Mon–Fri 8am–4pm.

Gardener's Cottage 31 Newlands Ave, Montebello Estate, Newlands. Browse outstanding arts and crafts and enjoy croissant and egg breakfasts, baked potatoes, line fish or pasta (R70), within a complex of old farm buildings under shady pines and oaks. It is recommended for tea and cake, and while the food is fine, it's a place to choose for the craft shopping, shady trees and mountain outlook. Tues–Fri 8am–4.30pm, Sat & Sun 8.30am–4.30pm.

★ **Kirstenbosch Tea Room** Rhodes Drive, Newlands ☎021 797 4883. The gorgeous park setting as well as pleasing, fresh and creative Cape country food (R80) – particularly the pickled fish or home-made burgers – is the draw here. Though the large self-service place by the main entrance is ideal for kids to roam around as you drink tea by the river, avoid it if you want a meal and head instead for the tearoom by the upper entrance to the Gardens. They have some good options for vegetarians and you can order a gourmet picnic. Daily 8.30am–5pm.

Olive Station Levantine Restaurant & Deli Rondebosch Village Shopping Centre, Main Rd, Rondebosch ☎021 686 8224. Fabulous Middle-Eastern breakfasts, wood-fired pitta pockets, breads, pastries and *meze* (R60), as well as a nice range of olives, Cape olive oils

1

and deli products to purchase. Mon–Fri 8am–6pm, Sat 8am–2pm.

River Café Constantia Uitsig Wine Estate, Spaanschemat River Rd ☎021 794 3010. An outstanding lunch – or breakfast stop (their eggs Benedict has a reputation up and down the peninsula) – at the Uitsig Wine Estate. The ambience among the vineyards is tranquil and, in keeping with the rural setting, the food is fresh and imaginative country bistro style (mains around R110). Sit indoors or eat alfresco with views of the mountains. Daily 8.30–11am, 12.30–3pm & 6.30–9pm.

ATLANTIC SEABOARD

GREEN POINT

El Burro 81 Main Rd, Green Point ☎021 433 2364; map pp.116–117. Decent Mexican food, which isn't too cheesy or oily, with a good view from the balcony of Green Point Stadium (mains around R80). Casual and fun. Mon–Sat noon–11.30pm.

★ **Giovanni's Deliworld** 103 Main Rd; map pp.116–117. With indoor and pavement seating, this friendly, buzzing Italian deli/coffee shop is a handy stop for coffee, excellent made-to-order sandwiches (R60), salads and dips, as well as good pre-packaged meals. Daily 8am–9pm.

Mano's 39 Main Rd ☎021 434 1090; map pp.116–117. Popular with model-types and generally beautiful people, this place serves Italian staples (R90), exciting salads and one of the best *crème brûlées* in town. After dinner, the party continues in champagne bar *Jade*, upstairs (see p.153). Mon–Sat noon–10.30pm.

Theo's Grill Butcher and Seafood 163 Beach Rd ☎021 439 3494; map pp.116–117. Right on the beachfront, with pub-style outdoor seating, *Theo's* offers superb Greek-style meat and seafood dishes (R95). A good choice for families. Daily 11.30am–10pm.

MOUILLE POINT

Café Neo 129 Beach Rd; map pp.116–117. Deli-style food with a Greek influence (R60), which can be enjoyed with views of Green Point stadium and lighthouse. There's outdoor seating with umbrellas for shade, unless the wind is up. Daily 7am–7pm.

Newport Market and Deli 47 Beach Rd; map pp.116–117. A light, airy deli with views onto Table Bay, and serving coffee, excellent gourmet sandwiches, salads and some hot dishes such as Thai green curry on noodles, or burgers. Their smoothies and power pack blends make a welcome change from breakfast fry-ups and toasted sandwiches – just right if you are walking or jogging along the Sea Point promenade. Daily 7am–10pm.

Wakame and Wafu 47 Beach Rd ☎021 433 2377; map pp.116–117. Contemporary Asian fusion food with killer desserts – try the chocolate and banana spring rolls. Every table has a view of the ocean and upstairs is *Wafu*, a popular contender for the drinking spot with the best sea views in Cape Town. *Wafu* offers a tapas and dim sum menu (R90), while *Wakame* serves more formal meals (R110). Each place has its own sushi bar too. Booking essential. Daily noon–3pm & 6–10pm.

SEA POINT

La Boheme Wine Bar & Bistro 341 Main Rd ☎021 434 6539; map pp.116–117. Interesting, well-presented French country-style food and lovely wines by the glass, with at least sixty to choose from. Dishes include ostrich meatballs with tagliatelle, potato gnocchi and roasted pork belly (mains around R80). There's pavement seating for people- watching. An enjoyable and inexpensive night out. Next door is their sister espresso and tapas bar, if you want just a sandwich with brilliant coffee. Mon–Sat noon–2.30pm & 7.30–10.15pm.

Chan 178a Main Rd ☎021 439 2239; map pp.116–117. Decent Chinese restaurant, serving happy customers for the last twenty years with excellent Hong Kong-style beef, prawns, roast duck, and for vegetarians braised bean curd and mixed vegetable (mains around R80). Daily noon–2.30pm & 6–10.30pm.

New York Bagels 51 Regent Rd; map pp.116–117. Deli with a mix of Eastern European and Mediterranean Jewish food. Choose from an array of bagels and home-made fillings, from chopped liver to herring, and salads to take away (R30). Outstanding choice for filling a sunset picnic basket, or to munch on at the Sea Point Pool lawns, a block away. Daily 7am–8pm.

Pizzeria Napoletana 178 Main Rd ☎021 434 5386; map pp.116–117. Family-styled, real Italian restaurant with hearty, good-value cooking and a slightly old-age home feel, but the food is delicious and reasonable (mains R70). Mon–Sat 6.30–10pm.

CAMPS BAY AND SOUTHWARDS

Café Caprice 37 Victoria Rd, Camps Bay ☎021 438 8315; map p.119. Directly opposite Camps Bay beach, this lively, albeit pretentious, Mediterranean-style restaurant is a great place to soak up street life and sunshine (mains around R90). Daily 9am–midnight.

Café Roux Noordhoek Farm Village ☎021 789 2538. Wholesome and healthy food with a contemporary feel, offering breakfasts, gourmet sandwiches, fish and chips and other simple fare (mains around R60), with a menu (and garden) that caters to children. Sit under umbrellas, gaze at the mountains and have tea after doing Chapman's Peak. Tues–Sun 8.30am–5pm.

★ **Food Barn** Noordhoek Farm Village ☎021 789 1390. Gourmet French food from an acclaimed chef, Franck Dangereux, served at reasonable prices compared to the other top restaurants in the city centre (mains around R120). The food is great, and worth suffering the slow service. Kids are welcome and you can sit on a sunny veranda in beautiful rural Noordhoek surrounds. Booking essential. Tues noon–2.30pm, Wed–Sat noon–2.30pm & 7–9.30pm.

La Cuccina Food Store Victoria Mall, Victoria Rd, Hout Bay. High-quality, delicious deli and café food in pleasant surrounds, though without sea views. At lunchtime they have a buffet of quiches, salads and lasagne (R70). Daily 8am–7pm.

Mariners Wharf Bistro The Harbour, Hout Bay. A relaxed, well-run place with terrace seating overlooking the harbour. The views outshine the seafood, which you can eat in or take away (R80). Daily 10am–9pm.

Paranga's Shop 1, The Promenade, Victoria Rd, Camps Bay ⓣ 021 438 0404 pp.116–117. Right on the beach, this is a place to see and be seen while you munch on salads, seafood, pasta or sushi (mains R155). There's a variety of champagne on offer while you watch the sun sinking into the ocean. Daily 9.30am–10.30pm.

Salt Ambassador Hotel, 34 Victoria Rd, Bantry Bay ⓣ 021 439 7258. The top chef here creates food with a French influence; their braised lamb in a herb crust is recommended, or try the orange-glazed line fish (R160). The views couldn't be better, with the plush hotel built on a rocky cliffside, fronting the Atlantic ocean. Expensive, but if you don't want to eat you can always just sink a beer and watch the sunset, or alternatively eat at their street-level deli across the road, which lacks the position but is far cheaper and less pretentious. Daily 12.30–2.30pm & 6.30–10pm.

FALSE BAY SEABOARD

MUIZENBERG

Casa Labia 192 Main Rd Muizenberg ⓣ 021 788 6068; map pp.122–123. Contemporary Italian food and English-style teas in *palazzo* surroundings (R60), with oil paintings, antiques and beautiful table linen. Courtyard dining comes with mountain views. Tues–Sun 10am–4pm.

Empire Café 11 York Rd ⓣ 021 788 1250; map pp.122–123. Coffee, including organic, and pastries while you sit upstairs and gaze at passing trains and the blue ocean beyond, or work at your computer, use free wi-fi and wait for the surf to come up. Their tasty pastas make a wholesome lunch (R50), and your waiter may slide down the banisters to despatch your order. Daily 8am–4pm.

Knead Muizenberg Beachfront ⓣ 021 788 2909; map pp.122–123. People come here in droves to sample the first-rate breads, crusty sandwich platters (R60) and cakes at this vibrant venue right at Surfer's Corner. Gusty outdoor seating as well as an indoor counter from which you can still admire the ocean, but service is consistently chaotic and slow. Daily 7.30am–5pm.

KALK BAY

★ **C'est La Vie** Rosmead Ave, Kalk Bay ⓣ 083 676 7430; map pp.122–123. Unassuming, charming French-style bakery up a cobbled street serving breakfast on the pavement, real baguettes, croissants and excellent coffee. Wed–Sun 7am–3pm.

Harbour House Restaurant At the harbour ⓣ 021 788 4133; map pp.122–123. Seafood and Mediterranean dishes (R130), served in a spectacular position on the breakwater of Kalk Bay harbour; book a table with bay views or enjoy sundowners on the deck. There's a fireplace and comfortable sofas for winter. Daily noon–10pm for drinks, food noon–4pm & 6–10pm.

Kalky's At the harbour; map pp.122–123. For years, this totally unpretentious eating place has been serving the best traditional fish and chips (R40) on the peninsula, and great-value seafood platters; fish is hauled off the boats and straight into the frying pan. You sit at benches to eat, though takeaway is available. Daily 10am–8pm.

★ **The Olympia Café & Deli** Main Rd; map pp.122–123. One of the few places that draws parochial uptown Capetonians down to the False Bay seaboard, serving great coffee accompanied by lovely freshly baked goods. Gourmet lunch menus, often featuring local fish, are chalked up (R80). Always buzzing, if a tad scruffy, and has good views of the harbour. Arrive early for dinner. Daily 7am–9pm.

Outspan Restaurant Main Rd/Corner of Boyes Drive; map pp.122–123. In an unpretentious setting with a few umbrellas and outdoor seating, close to the harbour and railway line, this is an excellent spot to eat barbecued fish (R70), with the appetizing smell of fish cooking on open fires wafting about the tables. Daily noon–9pm.

FISH HOEK

Fish Hoek Galley Fish Hoek Beach ⓣ 021 782 3354, ⓦ fishhoekgalley.com. Friendly family restaurant right on the beach that makes a good lunch stop, with outdoor seating and a large interior that lives up to its name by packing in the seating. Although they do meat and poultry, seafood's what you eat here (and the menu is extensive): line fish starts at R80, or if you don't have a conscience about depleting fish stocks you can go the whole hog and gorge on their Royal Flush Seafood Extravaganza that includes prawns, lobster, mussels, oysters, fish and calamari for R400. Daily 11am–10pm.

SIMON'S TOWN

Black Marlin Main Rd, south of Simon's Town ⓣ 021 786 1621, ⓦ blackmarlin.co.za. Every kind of sea denizen, apart from its namesake, is on the menu at this hugely popular restaurant on the road to Cape Point. (Tour buses pull in here for lunch, but their passengers are corralled off into a separate section.) The clifftop views from the outdoor tables make up for any lack of culinary fireworks – especially

1

when there are whale sightings. Main courses R150–250. Mon–Fri noon–10pm, Sat & Sun 8am–10pm.

The Meeting Place 98 St George's St ☎021 786 5678. At street level, sofas and newspapers are perfect props for a lazy deli–style breakfast or toasted sarnies lunch. Upstairs, with a harbour view balcony, is a more upmarket restaurant and bar, serving more expensive fare, such as fresh line fish and steaks (mains around R50 downstairs, R90 upstairs). Tues & Sun 9am–4pm, Wed–Sat 9am–9pm.

Salty Sea Dog Waterfront ☎021 7861918. This is a contender for the freshest fish and chips in town (R55), with adventurous delicacies for the jaded palate, such as crunchy deep-fried squid heads. Mon–Sat 10am–8pm, Sun 10am–4.30pm.

Tibetan Teahouse 2 Harrington Rd, Seaforth Beach ☎021 786 1544. Traditional Tibetan recipes, with a yak-free lentil stew (R55), as the menu's completely vegetarian. You'll find the venue signalled by its prayer flags. Tues–Sun 10am–5pm.

CAPE POINT

Two Oceans Cape Point ☎021 702 0703, ⊛two-oceans.co.za. The real star of the show at this primarily seafood-focused restaurant is the totally sublime views from its alfresco deck that jetties out seemingly to float above the ocean, taking in the whole of False Bay and its mountains (it's a great place to see whales in season). As well as fish and chips, calamari, lobster and seafood platters, they also have tapas and kids' menus, and serve bacon-and-egg breakfasts till 11am. Main course R80–250. Daily 9am–5pm.

BARS AND CLUBS

Being a hedonistic city – especially in the summer – Cape Town has plenty of great places to drink and party, especially along **Long Street** where it's safe and busy, and there are taxis to get you home. In the summer, the Atlantic Seaboard, notably **Camps Bay**, is a great option, especially for sundowners. When the dust has settled after Saturday's hedonism, Sunday nights are notably quiet, though there are a couple of welcoming options. Most liquor **licences** stipulate that the last round is served at 2am, but this is far from strictly followed; bars often stay open until the last customer leaves. You'll find that many drinking places are also **restaurants**, and may be better known as the latter; in a city where wine is produced, food and wine definitely go together. Drink **prices** obviously depend on the venue – a local beer in a sports bar might set you back R15, with international brews costing upwards of R20. A smart bar will charge up to R40 for a cocktail, while glasses of delicious Cape wine begin at R25. **Clubs** get going after 10pm and are pretty international in flavour, with **DJs** mixing house hits you're bound to recognize. Some may have a **cover charge**, but this is usually only when they have live music on and it's never more than R100. It's really not a good idea to walk around late at night, so take a **taxi number** out with you (see p.134). Many bars and clubs offer food as well, for those hungry moments before or after dancing. When it comes to **live music**, the best-known South African musicians are sadly better appreciated, and better remunerated, abroad than in their own country. Live music generally happens at a few restaurant/bars, where you may expect a small cover charge if live music is featured. If anyone good is in town, you will pick that up on posters or in a listings magazine. Cape Town is known for its brand of Cape Jazz, but there is nowhere regular to pick that up, though the best jazz event of the year happens in late March at the annual **Cape Town International Jazz Festival**. When you are in town, check out what is on at the Baxter and Artscape (see p.155), which are likely venues for any good musical offerings.

CITY CENTRE
AROUND LONG STREET

Boo Radleys 62 Hout St ☎021 424 3040, ⊛booradleys.co.za; map p.95. Classic cocktails are the signature of this slick and sociable, bustling New York-style bistro with a long, polished bar counter, and black and white chequerboard floor. Great for lunch too or an after-show meal, with salads, creative sandwiches

---

NEW YEAR, NEW YEAR – SO GOOD THEY DO IT TWICE

A long-standing tradition in Cape Town is **Tweede Nuwe Jaar** (second New Year) on January 2 – until recently an official public holiday. Historically, this was the only day of the year slaves were allowed off, and the day has persisted as a holiday of epic proportions. If you're in Cape Town over this period, Tweede Nuwe Jaar sees Cape Minstrels from the coloured community dancing through the streets of the city centre performing a traditional form of singing and riotous banjo playing. Expect each troupe to be dressed up in matching outfits, often featuring outrageous colour combinations. Some roads in the centre are blocked off during the day for the festivities, which process through the city and end up at Green Point Stadium.

V&A WATERFRONT >

1

and heavier meals on offer at reasonable prices (R100). Mon–Sat 10am till late.

Caveau Wine Bar and Deli Heritage Square, 92 Bree St ☎021 422 1367; map p.95. An appealing and tranquil courtyard setting in a listed building, off a busy road. The wide variety of Cape wines sold by the glass, in addition to the sushi on offer, is a good enough reason to stop off for lunch or dinner, though it's a popular breakfast spot too. Mon–Sat 7am–10pm.

Dubliner@Kennedy's 251 Long St ☎021 424 1212 ⓦthedubliner.co.za; map p.95. Crammed, wildly popular traditional Irish pub with Guinness and pilsner on tap. Upstairs you can relax with a pint, pub meal and sing-a-long with a honky-tonk piano player. Flat screens for sporting events and a pool table. Noon–midnight daily.

Grand Daddy Sky Bar Grand Daddy Hotel, 38 Long St ⓦgranddaddy.co.za; map p.95. Roof-top Bedouin tent style bar with sofas and deckchairs amid seven trailer home hotel rooms. Recommended for the views and the amazing cocktails, which include fresh juices and herbal infusions, and crafted beers. Daily noon–8.30pm.

Jo'burg 218 Long St ☎021 422 0142; map p.95. A good, if crowded, place to hang out, grooving to funky soundtracks or playing pool in the company of a young, hip and racially mixed crowd. Most people end up here, at some part of a night out on Long St, and it's one of the few places open on Sunday nights. Cool off on the open-air patio out back. Mon–Sat noon–4am, Sun 6pm–4am.

★ **Julep** 2 Vredenburg Lane, off Long St ☎021 423 4276; map p.95. The best cocktails and snacks in town in a small, but lively two-room bar, discreetly tucked away down an alley. Gives you the feeling of being in a friend's living room, with comfy couches and intimate table lamps. Tues–Sat 5.30pm–2am.

Neighbourhood 163 Long St ☎021 424 7260; map p.95. Lively sports bar, perfect for guzzling beers and watching sports on the giant screen in the lounge. The balcony is great from sundowner time onwards, and the bar serves a good selection of local and imported beers, as well as reasonably-priced bar food. Daily noon–2am.

Planet Bar Mount Nelson Hotel, 76 Orange St; map p.95. A smart sundowner bar, popular with well-heeled Capetonians, particularly on Friday nights after work. Emerge through an old-fashioned lobby into a modern

salon with couches in elegant surroundings, with gardens and views of Table Mountain. No shorts allowed. Daily noon–11pm.

Rafiki's 13b Kloof Nek ☎021 426 4731; map p.95. A laidback bar with a wrap-around veranda where you can hang out all day slowly getting sozzled, cheering on sports teams on the big screen or making use of the wi-fi. There are roaring fires during the winter months, and it's always popular with backpackers and locals alike. Try their chilli-poppers and everything-on-it pizzas. Daily noon–2am.

Waiting Room 273 Long St ☎021 422 4536 ⓦroyaleeatery.co.za; map p.95. Upstairs from the *Royale Eatery* is this busy, funky, retro-cool bar and dance floor with a roof deck to cool down on. While music is mostly courtesy of DJs, there is usually a live band once a week. Mon–Sat 6pm–2am.

Zula Sound Bar 194 Long St ⓦzulabar.co.za; map p.95. Live, local talent of variable quality, showcased every night (music, comedy, odd poetry reading), and a well-priced restaurant with nachos, salads, chicken wings and burgers. Also a balcony to relax on, with Cape wines, as well as a games room. One of the top Long St spots. Mon–Thurs, Sat & Sun 4pm–4am, Fri noon–4am.

ELSEWHERE IN THE CENTRE

The Assembly 61 Harrington St, Zonnebloem ☎021 465 7286 ⓦtheassembly.co.za; map p.92. One of the most popular places in town to party away the night, this spacious ex-factory has plenty of tequila and DJs who rock the crowd with indie, rock, pop and electronica, as well as live bands. Sat 9pm–4am.

Evol 69 Hope St ☎083 562 2583; map p.92. The only place in town for DJ'd alternative, electro, punk and particularly indie music, with a committed crowd. The place is named after a Sonic Youth album. Good dancing though it's a bit of a grungy venue. Fri 10pm till late.

Perserverance Tavern 83 Buitenkant St, Gardens ☎021 461 2440; map p.92. The oldest pub in Cape Town, dating back to 1836 when sailors and soldiers frequented it, is now worth a visit if for no other reason than to look at the restoration work, wooden floors and original fittings, then to sink some cheap beers and fries, before moving on to *The Assembly* or the like. Mon–Sat noon till late.

Thirtyone 31st Floor, Absa Centre, 2 Riebeeck St ☎021 421 0581 ⓦthirtyone.co.za; map p.92. One of the most stylish clubs, set at the top of one of the city's tallest buildings, providing views of the city below. It's smart and rather exclusive, providing a blend of funky house from the decks, and occasionally closes to the public to host a celebrity party. Fri & Sat 10pm–4am.

THE WATERFRONT

Alba Cocktail Lounge Pierhead, above the Hilderbrand Restaurant ☎021 425 3385; map p.105.

TOP 5 DRINKS WITH A VIEW

Alba Cocktail Lounge V&A Waterfront, see opposite

Brass Bell Kalk Bay, see opposite

Grand Daddy Sky Bar City Centre, see above

La Med Clifton, see opposite

Thirtyone City Centre, see above

Cocktails and snacks in the stunning setting of a lounge-bar, equipped with sofas and a fireplace for winter, looking out over the Waterfront. In summer, enjoy an Albatizer (jellytots & gin) on the outdoor deck. Daily 11am–midnight. Sometimes closed when hired for private events.

Den Anker Pierhead; map p.105. A quayside pub and Continental-style bistro, patronised by tourists and well-heeled locals, *Den Anker* specializes in imported Belgian beers, both on tap and bottled, and Cape wines by the glass. Not cheap, but good quality. Daily 11am–midnight.

GREEN POINT

Jade Champagne Bar and Lounge 39 Main Rd, above Manos Restaurant, Green Point ☎ 021 439 4108; map pp.116–117. Plush sofas, chandeliers, two bars and a semi-enclosed balcony to relax on, patronized by a laidback crowd. Pasta dishes are on offer. DJs play on Wednesdays. Wed–Sat 8pm–2am.

Trinity Restaurant and Super Club 15 Bennett St, Green Point ☎ 021 421 1367, ⓦ trinitycapetown .co.za; pp.116–117. Sophisticated and contemporary brick warehouse with several levels of places to eat, drink, watch sport or dance. It is a major jazz venue in Cape Town, with big bands on Monday evenings. Mon–Sat noon–4am.

Vaudeville 11 Mechau St (off Lower Bree) ☎ 021 419 7000, ⓦ vaudeville.co.za; map p.92. Offering a full evening out, from 6pm pre-dinner cocktails in the *Fez Bar*, followed by á la carte dinner in the chic 1920s interior of the *Brasserie Restaurant*, where you may be entertained as you dine by anything from flyline artist and acrobats to dancers and musicians. From 10.30pm the *Fez Club* opens for late-night dancing to the tunes of at least six DJs. R75 entertainment surcharge. Brasserie hours 7–10pm, *Fez Club* Fri & Sat 10.30 till late.

SOUTHERN SUBURBS

Brass Bell Kalk Bay station, Main Rd ☎ 021 788 5455, ⓦ brassbell.co.za. One of the city's best-loved spots, *Brass Bell* has arguably the best location on the peninsula, with False Bay's waves breaking against the wall of its outdoor terrace, though the bland seafood meals can't match the magnificent setting. Stick to simple fish and chips. Children are welcome at the restaurant, and prices are reasonable. Daily 11am–2am.

Caveau at the Mill 13 Boundary Rd, off Main Rd, Newlands ☎ 021 685 5140. A great place if you want to try quality Cape wines by the glass – there are over seventy to choose from, from budget to expensive – and match them with some good cheese, meat or a more substantial meal. It's open for breakfast too; sit at tables under trees by the river at the historical Josephine Mill. Tues–Sat 7am–10pm, Sun 10am–3pm.

Foresters' Arms 52 Newlands Av, Newlands ☎ 021 689 5949. Preppie students and professionals gather to quaff draught beer at the very popular and busy *Forries* in the heart of leafy Newlands. A big wood-panelled pub, it boasts a beautiful hedged-in courtyard where you can grab a bench for a lazy afternoon pint. It's a good place for match-cheering or post-match wind-downs. Mon–Sat 10am–11pm, Sun 10am–6pm.

Obz Café Lower Main Rd, Observatory. A great place to start an exploration of the different spots along Lower Main Rd, this has been a meeting point forever in Obs, with a good bar, big windows for people-watching and acceptable food. Daily 7am–1am.

Tiger Tiger Stadium 103 Main Rd, Claremont ⓦ tigertiger.co.za. Reliable for parties, Saturday nights are especially good, with six luxurious bars and a spacious dance floor with commercial music pumped out of a state-of-the-art sound system. Tues & Thurs–Sat 8pm–4am.

ATLANTIC SEABOARD

Café Caprice 37 Victoria Rd, Camps Bay ☎ 021 438 8315; map p.119. A beach-facing, beautiful people's hangout, just right for cocktails, celebs and wannabes. Families are welcome during the day for breakfast and lunch, but the pace increases at sunset and pavement tables are like gold dust. They show major sporting events on big screens and DJs feature nightly during the summer, winding down to weekend nights only during the rest of the year. Tues–Sun 8am till late, Mon closed.

Dizzy Jazz Café 41 Camps Bay Drive, Camps Bay ☎ 021 438 2686. A crowded and lively pub, ideal for beer drinkers with its selection of draughts, and for getting a last one in when everywhere else is closed. It has a big veranda, pub meals, a tiny dance floor and features a variety of live music nightly, with a R30 cover charge. Daily noon–4am (music from 9.30pm).

Dunes 1 Beach Rd, Hout Bay ☎ 021 790 1876. Right on Hout Bay beach, this is a popular drinking spot, especially on sunny weekend afternoons when kids roar about. You can eat in the bar upstairs, or downstairs in the no-smoking restaurant. Daily 9am–10pm for dining, winter from 10am.

La Med Bar and Restaurant Glen Country Club, Victoria Rd, Clifton ☎ 021 438 5600. A great sundowner venue overlooking the rocks at Clifton Beach, drawing a sporty, mainstream crowd. This is a favourite spot for hang-gliders from Lion's Head, after they've landed in the adjacent field. Big screens are great for matches and there are fireplaces for winter, plus they have live music at the weekend. Mon–Fri noon till late, Sat & Sun 9.30am till late.

Red Herring On the corner of Pine and Beach rds, Noordhoek ☎ 021 789 1783. An informal, friendly pub and restaurant, with an outdoor deck overlooking the panoramic Noordhoek Valley, popular with families, surfers, beachgoers and their dogs. Particularly busy on warm weekend afternoons, and live music gets going on Sunday evenings. Daily 11am–11pm.

1

GAY AND LESBIAN CAPE TOWN

Cape Town is South Africa's – and indeed, the African continent's – gay capital. The city has always had a vibrant gay culture, and is on its way to becoming an African Sydney, attracting gay travellers from across the country and the globe. Cape Town's **gay village**, with B&Bs, guesthouses, pubs, clubs, cruise bars and steam baths, is concentrated along the entertainment strips of Somerset Road and in the interconnected inner-city suburbs of Green Point, Sea Point and, particularly, the chic De Waterkant, adjacent to the centre. The **Pink Map**, (ⓦpinksa.co.za), published by A&C Maps, lists gay-friendly and gay-owned places in Cape Town and is distributed at the visitor centres, and viewable online.

Cape Town hosts a hugely popular annual **gay costume party**, organized by Mother City Queer Projects (ⓦwww.mcqp.co.za), a ten-day festival held each December the week before Christmas. People dress as outrageously as possible according to the official yearly theme (past ones have included Kitchen Kitsch, The Twinkly Sea Project and Lights, Camera, Action) and the event seeks to rival Sydney's Mardi Gras. There's also an annual **gay pride festival** in February (ⓦcapetownpride.org).

RESOURCES

Besides the South African gay **websites** and resources listed on p.76, it's worth having a look at ⓦwww.gaynetcapetown.co.za, aimed specifically at gay and lesbian travellers to Cape Town, with restaurants and gay accommodation listings, as well as information about HIV/AIDS. In the De Waterkant, **Health4Men** at 24 Napier St (ⓦhealth4men.co.za) provides free sexual health services to men, including access to free ARV treatment for men living with HIV.

The best listings magazine is *Out Africa Magazine*, available from the bars and restaurants in De Waterkant, and from GAP Leisure (ⓦgapleisure.com), on the corner of Napier and Waterkant streets, an agency that specializes in finding gay accommodation in the De Waterkant and countrywide.

Though there are many lesbians living in Cape Town, there are no dedicated lesbian bars or clubs, but the lesbian publication *L Magazine* (ⓦlmag.co.za) is a good way to discover anything up-and-coming. Regular parties for women are arranged monthly at different venues; for more information, look at ⓦlushcapetown.co.za.

BARS

Amsterdam Action Bar 12 Cobern St, off Somerset Rd, De Waterkant. Old school gay bar with a more mature crowd, some Leather Men and Bears, no disco and a pool table. Women are not welcome. Daily 4pm till late.

Bar Code 18 Cobern St, De Waterkant ☎021 421 5305 ⓦwww.leatherbar.co.za. A men-only leather, uniform and jeans bar with darkrooms and an outdoor deck. It's worth finding out what the evening's dress code is beforehand, in case they're having a themed night. Opening hours and days vary, but usually from 10pm until late. R50.

Beefcakes 40 Somerset Rd, Green Point ☎021 425 9019 ⓦwww.beefcakes.co.za. A seriously camp burger bar, with pink flamingo wallpaper and

CAPE FLATS

West End and Club Galaxy College Rd, Rylands ☎021 637 9132, ⓦsuperclubs.co.za. Definitely the most happening places on the Flats – your ears will never be the same again. These two long-established nightclubs, with four dance floors in one building, featuring pumping mainstream house at *Galaxy* and contemporary-fusion at *West End*, draw a smart young crowd. *Galaxy* Thurs–Sat 9pm–4am, *West End* Fri & Sat 5pm–4am.

ENTERTAINMENT

There is a satisfying range of dramatic and musical performances on offer in Cape Town that are easily accessed as theatres are scarcely full, and easily affordable compared to the prices you'd pay in London or New York. Despite the virtual lack of arts funding by the government, there is a creative and lively arts scene. The best strategy in finding out what's on in Cape Town is to check out the offerings at the two major arts venues, the **Baxter** and **Artscape**, where you are likely to find something appealing, whether a play, a classical concert, opera, contemporary dance or comedy. The daily *Cape Times* and *Argus* carry listings and reviews, and the *021* listings magazine (ⓦwww.021cape.com), on sale at *Vida e Caffe* stores and local bookshops, has a comprehensive selection of cultural listings, as well as wine festivals, sporting events, art exhibitions and lectures.

feathers, where you can create your own delicious burger if you like, and wear a sequined cowboy hat. There is a range of live entertainment from Drag Divas to "Bitchy Bingo", on varying nights. Great for cocktails. Mon–Sat 11am till late, Sun 6pm–late.

Bubbles Bar 125a De Waterkant St, opposite Manhattan. Small, relaxed venue with a cheap tequila special during the week that ensures loyalty. Besides tequila, it's known as the Drag Show mecca, with shows run by Drag Queen Lola Lou from France, now married to a South African. Shows Wed–Sun. Daily 5pm–2am.

Bronx Action Bar 22 Somerset Rd, corner of Napier St, Green Point ⓦwww.bronx.co.za. Cape Town's most popular gay bar and longest-standing dancing venue, the *Bronx Bar* is a wildly busy, nightly meat market with pumping pop music and bare-chested barmen. Straight and gay women also use this club. Small cover charge. Daily 8pm till late.

Cafe Manhattan 74 Waterkant St, De Waterkant, and 247 Main Rd, Sea Point ⓦwww.manhattan.co.za. A buzzing bar-restaurant chain with an affordable and largely meat-orientated menu. The De Waterkant branch has an attractive terrace under oak trees, while the Sea Point branch is ideal for people-watching on a busy street. Always bustling and lively, especially when the weather is good. Patrons of all genders and orientation can feel comfortable too, though it is primarily a gay venue. Daily 10am–2am.

Crew Bar 30 Napier St, Green Point ⓦwww.bronx.co.za. Stylish bar with topless barmen and sexy go-go dancers. The verandas are packed in the summer, and it's a good choice for a party. Small cover charge. Daily 7pm till late.

★ **Lazari Food Gallery** Corner of Jarvis & Napier St, Green Point ☎021 419 9555. A popular spot, great for coffee and cocktails – the best in the village–and good for business or quiet meetings. The balcony is especially nice for people-watching. Breakfast is served until 3pm and you can get ciabatta, meze and Mediterranean fare. Mon & Tues 8am–4pm, Wed–Sun 8am–10pm.

Navigaytion 22 Somerset Rd, corner of Napier St, Green Point ⓦwww.bronx.co.za. Above *Bronx Action Bar*, and styling itself as slightly more exclusive, this popular club prefers less commercial dance music and is avowedly a place where gay men and boys, as well as adventurous straight men and women, can lose all their inhibitions on the dance floor. Tues–Sun 5pm–2am.

Rosie's Corner of De Waterkant St and Chiappini, De Waterkant. An intimate bar attracting black and coloured guys – one of the few places in the village known for this, and women are also welcome. Drinks are quite a bit cheaper here than at the other bars. Its drag shows on Sunday nights are extremely popular. Daily 4pm till late.

SAUNA

The Hothouse 18 Jarvis St, Green Point ⓦwww.hothouse.co.za. A luxurious, men-only pleasure and total relaxation complex, and the only one of its kind in Cape Town, with all manor of jacuzzis and steam rooms, as well as a sundeck boasting superb views. There's also a bar (complete with fireplace). Entrance R90–110 depending on days and times. Mon–Wed noon–2am, Thurs noon–4am, Fri–Sun noon–6am.

CLASSICAL MUSIC AND AFRICAN OPERA

Classical music has a relatively small but faithful following, with symphony concerts at the City Hall and Baxter Theatre. There are free lunchtime concerts, often showcasing the work of students from Cape Town University's **South African College of Music**, on Thursdays at 1pm; these take place at the **Baxter Theatre** (ⓦbaxter.co.za) or at the college itself (☎021 650 2640, ⓦweb.uct.ac.za/depts/sacm). Many recitals by visiting soloists and chamber ensembles are put on by an organization called **Cape Town Concert Series** (ⓦctconcerts.co.za), and there are regular and excellent performances in different churches by Cape Town's only Baroque ensemble, **Camerata Tinta Barocca** (ⓦctbmusic.co.za). It's a treat to catch one of the performances by **Cape Town Opera** (ⓦcapetownopera.co.za) to hear black South Africans, who dominate opera in Cape Town (and South Africa), injecting some powerful new voices and energy into a programme that still predominantly features European works.

THEATRES

Tickets for all of the venues and performances listed are available from Computicket (☎083 915 8000, ⓦcomputicket.com). You'll find that most ticket prices are very reasonable at R90–150.

Artscape Adderley St, Foreshore ☎021 410 9838, ⓦartscape.co.za. Cape Town's most central and largest arts venue, where major productions are staged. Catch some contemporary dance, ballet or opera here, with some

1

adventurous new dramas appearing periodically. Don't be intimidated by the monumental 1970s apartheid architecture.

Baxter Theatre Centre Main Rd, Rondebosch ☎ 021 685 7880, ⓦ baxter.co.za. This mammoth brick theatre complex – its design inspired by Soviet Moscow's central train station – is the cultural heart of Cape Town, mounting an eclectic programme of innovative plays, comedy festivals, jazz and classical concerts and kids' theatre. It's the first place to check out what's on when you hit town.

Maynardville Open Air Theatre On the corner of Church and Wolfe sts, Wynberg ⓦ maynardville.co.za. Under the summer stars in Maynardville Park, every year in January and February, an imaginative production of a Shakespeare play is staged by the cream of Cape Town's young actors and designers.

On Broadway 44 Long St, city centre ☎ 021 424 1194, ⓦ onbroadway.co.za. One of the few venues committed to the city's small cabaret scene is this fun bar-restaurant with live performances, comedy and music every night of the week. Ticket prices are appealingly lower than mainstream venues. Daily 6.30pm–late.

Jou Ma Se Comedy Club River Club, Liesbeek Parkway, Observatory ⓦ joumasecomedy.com. The only dedicated comedy venue in Cape Town, run by comedian Kurt Skoonraad, who has a regular Thursday-evening gig. Their website also carries info about any other comedy events and clubs in Cape Town, in a relatively new scene.

Fugard Theatre Corner of Caledon and Harrington sts ☎ 021 461 4554, ⓦ thefugard.com. Great new initiative on the east side of town in the old District Six, with a cross-section of interesting productions that are well worth checking out. The venue, a stylishly renovated church, has a very nice ambience for a pre- or post-show drink.

CINEMAS

Labia 69 Orange St & Lifestyles on Kloof Centre, Kloof St ☎ 021 424 5927, ⓦ labia.co.za. Despite the porno-sounding name, the retro Labia (Lah-bia) shows an intelligent mix of art films, cult classics and new releases. The cinema in Orange St is the original Labia, with its sister cinema round the corner in Kloof; ticket prices are appealingly cheap, and half that of mainstream cinemas.

Ster-Kinekor Cinema Nouveau Waterfront ☎ 082 16789, & Cavendish Square Mall ☎ 021 657 5600, ⓦ www.sterkinekor.com. If you want to catch a movie, simply pitch up at the Waterfront or Cavendish Square. Each of these Malls has two cinemas, one for mainstream popular releases, and a Cinema Nouveau, with an art-house selection, each showing films three times a day. Tickets are under R100, with cheap nights on Tuesdays.

SOUTH AFRICAN THEATRE AND COMEDY

Athol Fugard is the best known of South African playwrights internationally. Some of his finest plays include *Boesman and Lena* and *Master Harold and the Boys*, and there is now a theatre in Cape Town named after him. Most controversial of contemporary playwrights is the brilliant **Brett Bailey**, a white man more "township" than many blacks, who creates electrifying, chaotic visual and physical theatre, often using untrained actors and dancers in his **Third World Bunfight** company (ⓦ thirdworldbunfight.co.za). The company puts on theatre productions, installations, house music shows and opera, mostly concerned with the post-colonial landscape of Africa. You are as likely to catch his work in Europe as you ever are in Cape Town – the schedules appear on his website – but try to go to anything at all which may be on while you're in the city.

Cape Town's premier physical theatre company, **Magnet** (ⓦ magnettheatre.co.za), produces consistently excellent, politically conscious, non-didactic physical theatre. Magnet sometimes collaborates with **Jazzart** contemporary dance/theatre company (ⓦ jazzart.co.za) where you'll see the finest black dancers in town, who have forged a fusion of Western and African dance in their work. Cape Town-born RSC actor **Sir Anthony Sher** is the city's most famous son, appearing occasionally in the mother city in some fabulous productions, including an Africanized *Tempest* in 2009 and Arthur Miller's *Broken Glass* in 2011.

South Africa's best-known stage satirist is **Pieter Dirk Uys**, whose character Evita Bezuidenhout, South Africa's answer to Dame Edna Everidge, has relentlessly roasted South African society since apartheid days. He often performs in Cape Town, though the best place to catch him is on a dedicated day out, over the weekend, in Darling, an hour out of Cape Town (see p.247). New generation home-grown comedians to look out for include **Marc Lottering**, a coloured Capetonian who derives his material from his own community; **Nik Rabinowitz**, an irreverent middle-class Jewish boy who uses his fluency in Xhosa to poke fun at cultural stereotypes; and **Riyaad Moosa**, a Muslim doctor turned comedian. If he is visiting from Gauteng, catch **Trevor Noah**, one of the most talented young South African stand-ups.

1

CAPE TOWN MUSIC

One of Cape Town's musical treasures is **Cape jazz**, a local derivative of the jazz genre with distinctive African flavours. Its greatest exponent is the internationally acclaimed **Abdullah Ibrahim**. Born and raised in District Six, Ibrahim is a supremely gifted pianist and composer, who has for decades produced an hypnotic fusion of African, American and Cape idioms. Some of his renowned recordings include *Mannenberg* and *African Marketplace*, combining the fluttering rhythms of *ghoema* – traditional Cape carnival music – with the call-and-answer structure of African gospel. Other Cape Jazz legends include a triumvirate of distinctive saxophonists: the late Basil Coetzee, a phenomenal tenor saxophonist; Robbie Jansen, alto player with a raunchy and original style; and Winston Mankunku, schooled on Coltrane and Wayne Shorter, and his unique brand of African inflections. One reliable spot to hear Cape jazz is the Waterfront's *Green Dolphin*. The Monday-night jam session at *Swingers* in Lansdowne (1 Wetton Rd ❶ 021 762 2443) is an institution in Cape Town and you can see some of the best local talent on show here. Go under your own steam or as part of a Jazz Tour (❻ www.coffeebeans.co.za).

The annual **Cape Town International Jazz Festival** (April) features some of the world's most renowned musicians. **Ghoema** is the rhythm played on a *ghoema* drum, a sound that, for many generations, has been the basis for the popular *moppies* (comic songs) and *ghoemaliedjies* (picnic songs). The term *ghoema* comes from the barrel-shaped drum made out of a tin can without a bottom. Cape Town's colourful minstrel troops occupy the streets of the city over New Year, when the hugely popular Rio-style *nagtroepe* (literally night-time marchers) and armies of lookers-on fill the city's streets from January 1 onwards and *ghoema* troupes compete for honours in festival gatherings. Catch the Christmas Bands and Malay Choirs in this same season for **marching music** in the Mother City.

At other times of year, personalized township or jazz tours will take you to musicians' homes (see p.135).

OUTDOOR ACTIVITIES AND SPORT

One of Cape Town's most remarkable features is the fact that it melds with the Table Mountain National Park, a patchwork of mountains, forests and coastline – all on the city's doorstep. There are few, if any, other cities in the world where outdoor pursuits are so easily available and affordable. You can try activities such as sea kayaking, abseiling, rock climbing and scuba diving for little more than the price of a night out back home. Alternatively, just let everyone else get on with it while you sink a few beers and watch the cricket, rugby or football.

SPECTATOR SPORTS

The best place to find out what major fixtures are on, and to book for them, is ❻ computicket.com. Expect to pay R25–75 for local rugby, football or cricket, and upwards of R500 for international games.

Cricket Keenly followed by a wide range of Capetonians. The city's cricketing heart is at Newlands Cricket Ground (also known after its sponsors as Sahara Park), 61 Campground Rd, Newlands (❶ 021 657 2003). One of the most beautiful grounds in the world, Newlands nestles beneath venerable oaks and the elegant profile of Devil's Peak, and plays host to provincial, test and one-day international matches.

Football Though football matches aren't as well attended as cricket or rugby fixtures, Cape Town football is burgeoning with talent and more prominent since the 2010 World Cup. The dusty streets of the Cape Flats have produced superb young footballers such as Benni McCarthy (Porto, Ajax Amsterdam, Celta Vigo) and Quinton Fortune (Atletico Madrid, Manchester United). The most ambitious and professional club in the city is Ajax (pronounced "I-axe") Cape Town (❻ www.ajaxct.org), jointly owned by its Amsterdam

namesake. The most exciting games to attend are those between a local outfit and one of the Soweto glamour teams, Orlando Pirates and Kaizer Chiefs. Matches take place at the Green Point Stadium; Athlone Stadium, off Klipfontein Rd, Athlone; and Newlands Rugby Stadium (see below).

Rugby The Western Cape is one of the world's rugby heartlands, and the game is followed religiously here. Provincial, international and Super 12 contests are fought on the hallowed turf of Newlands Rugby Stadium, Boundary Rd, Newlands (❶ 021 659 4600).

PARTICIPATION SPORTS AND OUTDOOR ACTIVITIES

Abseiling You can abseil off Table Mountain with Abseil Africa (❶ 021 424 4760, ❻ www.abseilafrica.co.za) for around R695. A guided summit walk up Platteklip Gorge costs R250.

Birdwatching The peninsula's varied habitats and pelagic populations, including the highly endangered (from fishing trawlers) albatross, boost numbers up to four hundred different species of birds. Pelagic trips virtually guarantee sightings of four species of albatross. Good

1

places for birdwatching include Lion's Head, Kirstenbosch Gardens and the Cape of Good Hope Nature Reserve, as well as at Kommetjie and Hout Bay; you can find out about birding trips in Cape Town from Birding Africa (☎ 021 531 9148, ⊛ www.birdingafrica.com), and pelagic tours by boat from Anne Grey (☎ 083 311 1140).

Cycling Cycling (for rental outlets see p.136) is popular all over the peninsula, and is a great way to take in the scenery. For information about the annual, spectacular Argus Cycle Tour, in March, right around the peninsula, contact Pedal Power Associates (☎ 021 689 8420, ⊛ www.cycletour .co.za), which also organizes fun rides from Sept—May.

Golf The Milnerton golf course, Bridge Rd, Milnerton (☎ 021 552 1047), is tucked in between a lagoon and Table Bay, and boasts classic views of Table Mountain. Other popular local courses are Rondebosch Golf Club, Klipfontein Rd, Rondebosch (☎ 021 689 4176), and Westlake Golf Club, Westlake Ave, Lakeside (☎ 021 788 2020).

Gyms Virgin Active clubs run upmarket, well-appointed gyms dotted around the peninsula, all with large swimming pools and spotless changing rooms. Contact their call centre (☎ 086 020 0911, ⊛ virginactive.co.za) to find out about visitor rates.

Horseriding Horse Trail Safaris, Indicator Lodge, Skaapskraal Rd, Ottery (east of Wynberg across the M5; ☎ 021 703 4396, ⊛ horsetrailsafaris.co.za), offers riding through the dunes to the coast (R350), though you are only on the actual beach for ten minutes. Sleepy Hollow Horse Riding, Sleepy Hollow Lane, Noordhoek (☎ 021 789 2341 or ☎ 083 261 0104), covers the spectacular Noordhoek Beach, as does Imhoff Farm (☎ 082 774 1191). Both charge around R350 for two hours. If you are an intermediate/advanced rider, do find out if there are rides which are for advanced riders only, otherwise you may be stuck walking.

Kayaking Real Cape Adventures (☎ 021 790 5611 or ☎ 082 556 2520, ⊛ seakayak.co.za) offers a range of half- or full-day sea-kayaking packages that include trips around Cape Point, to the penguin colony at Boulders Beach and around Hout Bay. Downhill Adventures, on the corner of Kloof and Orange sts in the city centre (☎ 021 422 0388, ⊛ www.downhilladventures.co.za), offers trips from Mouille Point or Simon's Town from R500 per half-day.

Mountain biking Day Trippers (☎ 021 511 4766, ⊛ daytrippers.co.za) offers expert mountain-bike tours, including one from Scarborough to Cape Point. Downhill Adventures (see above) offers similar tours, including Tokai Forest.

Paragliding Cape Town has great air thermals for paragliding: the usual spot is from Lion's Head, drifting down to Camps Bay. Para-Taxi (☎ 082 966 2047, ⊛ para-taxi.com) does tandem jumps from R695. Wallend-Air School (☎ 021 762 2441, ⊛ wallendair.com), run by Peter Wallend (one of SA's paragliding champs), offers courses to get your paragliding licence.

Rock climbing High Adventure (☎ 021 689 1234 or ☎ 082 437 5145, ⊛ www.highadventure.co.za) will take you to unusual and unique locations depending on your ability. Packages are tailor-made, with a minimum of two people. For an indoor wall, try City Rock Indoor Climbing Centre, 21 Anson Rd, Observatory (☎ 021 447 1326, ⊛ cityrock.co.za).

Sandboarding Downhill Adventures (see "Mountain biking", above) is the pioneer of this ski-related adventure sport. Boards, boots and bindings are provided, as well as expert instruction for beginners. Sunscene Outdoor Adventures (☎ 021 783 0203, ⊛ sunscene.co.za) offers sandboarding as well as surfing, and is good at teaching kids. Expect to pay from R500 for a day out.

Scuba diving While the Cape waters are cold, they're also good for seeing wrecks, reefs and magnificent kelp forests. The Scuba Shack, 289 Long St (☎ 021 424 9368, ⊛ scubashack.co.za), arranges land and boat dives, from R520 for the dive and equipment, as well as dives in the fish tank at the Aquarium (see p.106), or in the Kelp Forest, which teems with non-biting fish. If you don't want to dive, you can snorkel with Cape fur seals off the coast. You can also take an internationally recognized PADI open-water diving qualification through them.

Skydiving The ultimate way to see Table Mountain and Robben Island is from a tandem jump 3000m up; contact Skydive Cape Town, situated 20min from Cape Town along the R27 West Coast Rd (☎ 082 800 6290, ⊛ skydivecapetown.za.net; R1550).

Surfing Top surfing spots include Big Bay at Bloubergstrand (competitions are held here every summer), Llandudno, Muizenberg and Long Beach near Kommetjie and Noordhoek. For information on competitions check out ⊛ wavescape.co.za, the best place on the web for everything you want to know about surfing in SA, including what the waves are up to. Muizenberg is the best place to learn to surf; try Gary's or Surf Shack (see p.123).

Swimming In the summer there are surf lifesaver patrols on duty at Milnerton, Camps Bay, Llandudno, Muizenberg and Fish Hoek beaches. For pools, try Long St Baths, Long St (☎ 021 400 3302; daily 7am—7pm), Cape Town's only public heated indoor pool; or Newlands Swimming Pool, corner of Main and San Souci roads, Newlands (☎ 021 674 4197; Oct—Easter 9.30am—5pm; R15), an Olympic-sized chlorinated pool. The ocean-side Sea Point Swimming Pool on Beach Rd (☎ 021 434 3341; summer 7am—7pm, winter (unheated) 8.30am—5pm; R15) is an Olympic-sized chlorinated seawater pool.

Walking The best places for gentle strolls are in Kirstenbosch Gardens, Newlands Forest and the beaches. There are limitless opportunities for hiking. Head for anywhere on Table Mountain, Tokai Forest, Silvermine Nature Reserve or Cape Point Nature Reserve – these are best done as guided half-day or day trips with Margie (☎ 021 715 6136, ⊛ tablemountainwalks.co.za), a registered Table Mountain Guide who offers the classic Table Mountain ascents, as well as other gorgeous routes on the peninsula. She will pick you up for free from your accommodation, and provide refreshments and lunch. High Adventure (see "Rock climbing", opposite) also runs similar guided hikes up Table Mountain, geared to your level of fitness and with experienced guides. Both charge from R450 for a shorter hike, up to R900 for a full-day Table-top ascent.

Windsurfing and kitesurfing While most Capetonians moan about the howling southeaster in summer, it's heaven if you're into windsurfing; Langebaan, a 75min drive north of town, is one of the best spots, as the enormous lagoon offers better conditions than the ocean around Cape Town, which has a bigger swell and is choppier. Cape Sport Centre, Langebaan (☎ 022 772 1114, ⓦ capesport.co.za), offers a variety of watersports and has accommodation along the same street. Prices for windsurfing start at R500 for a lesson and two hours on the water; a two-day kitesurfing package costs from R2400, including gear and instruction.

SHOPPING

The **V&A Waterfront** is the city's most popular shopping mall, with good reason: it has a vast range of shops, the setting on the harbour is lovely and there's a huge choice of places to eat and drink when you want to rest your feet. The city centre also offers variety and, for some people's taste, a grittier and more interesting venue for browsing, especially if you're looking for collectibles, antiques and secondhand books. For crafts and gifts, wander about Kalk Bay's Main Rd or Long Street, while the most sophisticated central shopping area – small, modern and full of desirable goods with great cafés, is the Cape Quarter in the Waterkant. Don't expect much to be open on Sunday afternoons, except at the Waterfront.

MALLS AND SHOPPING CENTRES

Cavendish Square Claremont station, Vineyard Rd, Claremont. An upmarket multistorey complex, this is the major shopping focus for the southern suburbs. Mon–Sat 9am–7pm, book and music shops open till 9pm, Sun 10am–5pm.

Gardens Shopping Centre Mill St, Gardens. A small shopping mall in the City Bowl, very close to the city centre, with a large supermarket, excellent deli and most of the shops you'll need. Mon–Fri 9am–7pm, Sat 9am–5pm, Sun 10am–2pm.

V&A Waterfront A vast range of upmarket shops packed into the Victoria Wharf Shopping Centre, including outlets of all the major South African chains, selling books, clothes, food and crafts. Mon–Sat 9am–9pm, Sun 10am–9pm.

CRAFT SHOPS

Africa Nova Cape Quarter, Waterkant St, De Waterkant ⓦ africanova.co.za. A better-than-average selection of ethnic crafts and curios as well as contemporary African textiles and artwork, with an emphasis on the individual and handmade. Mon–Sat 10am–5pm, Sun (summer only) 10am–2pm.

African Image Corner Church/Burg St, City Centre. One of the best places for authentic traditional and contemporary African arts and crafts, from fabrics and antique sculpture to pieces using recycled materials and South African beadwork. Mon–Fri 9am–5pm, Sat 9am–1pm.

Ethno Bongo Main Rd, Hout Bay ⓦ dolceandbanana .com. A charming shop selling wonderful and well-priced crafts, jewellery and accessories. They use natural materials, gemstones, shells and reclaimed wood, and also sell ethnic clothing – highly recommended for unique gifts and souvenirs. Mon–Fri 9.30am–5.30pm, Sat 9.30am–4pm, Sun 10am–2pm.

Monkeybiz 43 Rose St, Bo-Kaap ⓦ monkeybiz .co.za. Colourful animals and beaded figures made at a non-profit income-generating project. Good place to buy quality craft work which is uniquely South African and helps a good cause. Mon–Fri 9am–5pm, Sat 9am–1pm.

Rose Korber Art Consultancy 48 Sedgemoor Rd, Camps Bay ☎ 021 438 9152, ⓦ rosekorberart.com. This should be the first stop for the serious collector, with an exceptional selection of contemporary arts and crafts, including ceramics and beadwork from around the continent. Mon–Fri 9am–5pm. Weekends by appointment.

Street Wires 77 Upper Shortmarket St, Bo-Kaap ⓦ www .streetwires.co.za. Large range of wire and beadwork, made in the studio of their orange-coloured premises, where you can buy small beaded animals or beautiful tableware and lamps. Mon–Fri 9am–5pm, Sat 9am–1pm.

MARKETS

Green Point Flea Market Outside Green Point Stadium. A massive open-air market displaying everything from African arts and crafts to plants, car parts, and anything home-made. Sun 9am–4pm.

The Craft Market Next to the Aquarium, V&A Waterfront. Handmade products and African crafts, ranging from kitsch ostrich eggs to clothing and accessories. Daily 9am–6pm.

Greenmarket Square Burg St. Open-air market in a beautiful cobbled square where you can pick up knick-knacks, souvenir crafts from all over Africa and CDs. This is also the best place in town for *kikois* from Tanzania (beach clothes). Most of the traders are West African or Zimbabwean. Mon–Fri 9am–4pm, Sat 9am–2pm.

1

★ **Neighbourgoods Market** 373–375 Albert Rd, Old Biscuit Mill, Woodstock, ⓦ www.theoldbiscuitmill .co.za. The city's best weekly food experience – sample artisanal cheeses and wood-fired breads, coffee, luxury beers, fresh flowers, fruit and veg in a sky-lit Victorian warehouse. Not cheap, but the finest natural/organic/fresh food on offer in Cape Town. Sat 9am–2pm.

The Pan African Market 76 Long St. A multicultural hothouse of township and contemporary art, artefacts, curios and crafts in the heart of the city centre's antiques and art precinct. There's also music, a café specializing in African cuisine, a bookshop, a Cameroonian hairbraider and West African tailors for your custom-made garments. Mon–Fri 9am–5pm, Sat 9am–3pm.

Sivuyile Craft Centre On the corner of NY1 and NY4, Guguletu, Cape Flats ☎ 021 637 8449. Township market attached to the Guguletu Information Centre close to the N2 freeway, where bead-workers, wire-workers and other artists make traditional and modern crafts. Telephone for directions. Mon–Fri 9am–5pm, Sat 9am–1pm.

BOOKS

★ **Book Lounge** 71 Roeland St ⓦ booklounge.co.za. The most congenial central bookshop with comfy sofas and a downstairs café with an excellent selection of local books and an imaginative selection of imported titles. The literary heart of Cape Town, there are poetry readings, discussions and launches of new South African books, often on Thursdays at 5.30pm. Mon–Fri 8.30am–7.30pm, Sat 9.30am–6pm, Sun 10am–4pm.

Clarke's Bookshop 211 Long St ⓦ clarkesbooks.co.za. The best place in Cape Town for South African books, with a huge selection of local titles covering literature, history, politics, natural history and the arts. They also deal in collectors' editions of South African books. Very well-informed staff. Mon–Fri 9am–5pm, Sat 9am–1pm.

Kirstenbosch Shop Kirstenbosch National Botanical Gardens (see p.110). A good selection of natural history books, field guides and travel guides covering Southern Africa, as well as a range of titles for kids. You won't need a gardens ticket to browse. Daily 9am–6pm.

MUSIC

African Music Store 134 Long St. A small, centrally located shop specializing in African music from around the continent. Mon–Fri 9am–5pm, Sat 9am–2pm.

Look & Listen Cavendish Square, Claremont. Cape Town's largest music store, stocking local jazz and a respectable selection from all over the African continent. Daily 9am–7pm.

Mabu Vinyl 2 Rheede St, Gardens. The aficionado's choice for a great selection of secondhand CDs and records, covering many genres. Mon–Thurs 9am–8pm, Fri 9am–7pm, Sat 9am–6pm, Sun 11am–3pm.

Musica Megastore V&A Waterfront. One of the best ranges of African music in the city, as well as classical music, and the usual pop/rock/jazz offerings, not to mention DVDs. Daily 9am–9pm.

FOOD AND PROVISIONS

The most convenient **supermarkets** in central Cape Town are the Pick 'n Pay (daily 8am–10pm) and Woolworths (daily 9am–9pm) in the V&A Waterfront, both of which have far longer trading hours than anywhere else in the city.

Andiamo Cape Quarter, Dixon St, De Waterkant ☎ 021 421 3688. Italian Deli with an excellent selection of meats, cheeses, salads, dips, *meze* and fresh breads. Phone ahead and they'll put a picnic together for you. Daily 9am–10pm.

Fish Market Mariner's Wharf, Hout Bay Harbour. Fresh seafood from South Africa's original waterfront emporium, but slicker and less atmospheric than Kalk Bay Harbour. Mon–Fri 9am–5.30pm, Sat & Sun 9am–6pm.

Giovanni's 103 Main Rd, Green Point. Excellent breads and delicious Italian foods to take away. Daily 8.30am–9pm.

Kalk Bay Harbour Harbourside, Kalk Bay. Buy fresh fish directly from the fishermen and have it gutted and scaled on the spot. Your best bet is lunchtime, especially at weekends.

Melissa's Fine Food Deli 94 Kloof St, Gardens and Lower Level, Waterfront. Highly delectable imported and local specialities. Gardens Mon–Fri 7.30am–8pm, Sat & Sun 8am–9pm; Waterfront 9am–10pm.

Organic Zone Lakeside Shopping Centre, Main Rd, Lakeside. Always fresh and well-stocked organic veggies and fruit, plus grains, honey, bread, and dairy products. Mon–Fri 9am–6pm, Sat 9am–2pm.

Quensch Organic Deli 42 Lower Main Rd, Observatory. Organic restaurant and shop, with a recycling service and veggie box delivery schemes. Mon–Fri 7.30am–5pm, Sat 7.30am–4pm.

WINE

Caroline's Fine Wines 62 Strand St; and King's Warehouse, V&A Waterfront. Caroline Rillema has been in the wine business since 1979 and carries the Cape's finest and most exclusive wines. Mon–Fri 9am–5.30pm; Waterfront also Sat 9am–1pm.

Vaughan Johnson's Dock Rd, V&A Waterfront. One of Cape Town's best-known wine shops, stocking a huge range of labels from all over the country, though it can be a bit pricey. Mon–Fri 9am–6pm, Sat 9am–5pm, Sun 10am–5pm.

Wine Concepts 50 Kloof St; and Castle Building, on the corner of Kildare Rd and Main Rd, Newlands. An excellent selection of South African and foreign wines from a knowledgeable and helpful outfit. Mon–Thurs 9am–7pm, Fri 9am–8pm, Sat 9am–5pm.

DIRECTORY

Banks and exchange Main bank branches with ATMs are easy to find in the shopping areas of the city centre, the middle-class suburbs and at the Waterfront. For foreign exchange transactions outside normal banking hours, try one of the following: American Express, Shop 11a, Alfred Mall, Waterfront (Mon–Fri 9am–7pm, Sat 9am–5pm, Sun 9am–5pm); Rennies Foreign Exchange, Victoria Wharf, V&A Waterfront (Mon–Sat 9am–9pm, Sun 10am–9pm); or Master Currencies, Cape Town International Airport (Mon–Sun 6.30am–10pm).

Consulates Canada, 60 St George's Mall ☎ 021 423 5240; UK, Southern Life Centre, 8 Riebeeck St ☎ 021 405 2400; USA, 2 Reddam Ave, Westlake ☎ 021 702 7300.

Dental care Dentists, listed in the *Yellow Pages* telephone directory, are well up to international standards, and generally less expensive.

Hospitals and doctors The two largest hospital groups are the Netcare (emergency response ☎ 082 911) and Medi-Clinic chains, with hospitals all over the Cape Peninsula. Most central of Netcare's hospitals is the Christian Barnard Hospital, 181 Longmarket St (☎ 021 480 6111) – you'll get to see a doctor quickly and costs are not excessive for simple procedures. Avoid the state system at all times if you possibly can – waits can be excessive, and they are overcrowded and understaffed. The largest state hospital is Groote Schuur, Hospital Drive, Observatory (☎ 021 404 9111), just off the M3.

Laundry Most backpacker hostels have coin-operated washing machines, while guesthouses, hotels and B&Bs will usually offer a laundry service for a charge.

Mobile phone rental Available from Cellucity, Shop 6193, V&A Waterfront (☎ 021 418 1306). Rentals can also be done at the airport when you arrive, from Vodashop Rentafone (ⓦ rentafone.net) or Cellucity (ⓦ cellucity.co.za).

Pharmacies Chemists with extended opening hours include: Hypermed Pharmacy, corner York and Main rds, Green Point (☎ 021 434 1414; Mon–Fri 8.30am–7pm, Sat & Sun 9am–7pm); Sunset Pharmacy, Sea Point Medical Centre, Kloof Rd, Sea Point (☎ 021 434 3333; daily 8.30am–9pm); and Tamboerskloof Pharmacy, 16 Kloof Nek Rd, Tamboerskloof (☎ 021 424 4450; daily 9am–8.30pm). Homeopathic remedies are available from **White's Chemist** (☎ 021 465 3332; Mon–Fri 7.30am–5pm, Sat 8am–12.30pm).

Police Emergencies ☎ 10 111. The central station is on Caledon Square, Buitenkant St ☎ 021 467 8079.

Post office The main branch is on Parliament St (Mon, Tues, Thurs & Fri 8am–4.30pm, Wed 8.30am–4.30pm, Sat 8am–noon).

Travel agents The largest travel franchise in the country is Sure Travel, which has about two dozen offices across Cape Town (call ☎ 0800 221 656 for the nearest), try also One World Travel Centre, 309 Long St (☎ 021 423 0777). There are several agencies up and down Long St and some hostels have dedicated travel desks.

The Western Cape

OSTRICH FARM, OUDTSHOORN (P.190)

The Western Cape

The most mountainous and arguably the most beautiful of South Africa's provinces, the Western Cape is also the most popular area of the country for foreign tourists. Curiously, it's also the least African province. Visitors spend weeks here without exhausting its attractions, but frequently leave slightly disappointed, never having quite experienced an African beat. Of South Africa's nine provinces, only the Western Cape and the Northern Cape don't have an African majority; one person in five here is African, and the largest community, making up 55 percent of the population, are coloureds – people of mixed race descended from white settlers, indigenous Khoisan people and slaves from the East.

Although the Western Cape appears to conform more closely to the developed world than any other part of the country, the impression is strictly superficial. Beneath the prosperous feel of the Winelands and the Garden Route lies a reality of poverty in **squatter camps** on the outskirts of well-to-do towns, and on some farms where nineteenth-century labour practices prevail, despite the end of apartheid. Nevertheless, you can't fail to be moved by the sensuous beauty of the province's mountains, valleys and beaches. **The Winelands**, less than an hour from Cape Town, are all about eating, drinking and visual feasting on gabled homesteads among vineyards backed by slatey crags.

The best-known feature of the Western Cape is the **Garden Route**, a drive along the N2 that extends between Cape Town and Port Elizabeth (see p.308). **Public transport**

CAPE DUTCH ARCHITECTURE STELLENBOSCH

Highlights

❶ **The Winelands** Quaff fine vintages on beautiful wine estates. **See p.168**

❷ **Route 62** This mountainous inland route takes you through dozy villages, across spectacular passes and through semi-desert. **See p.183**

❸ **De Hoop Nature Reserve** Massive dunes and edge-to-edge whales make this arguably the most exciting provincial nature reserve in the country. **See p.212**

❹ **Ocean safaris** Learn about whales and dolphins on an excursion around Plettenberg Bay. **See p.238**

❺ **Storms River Mouth** A dramatic section of coast, where hillside forests drop away to rocky coastline and the Storms River surges out of a gorge into the thundering ocean. **See p.242**

❻ **Canopy Tour** Swing from tree to tree among the highest boughs of the Tsitsikamma Forest's arboreal giants. **See p.245**

❼ **Seafood** Feast on endless courses of fish and lobster at one of the casual beachside eating places along the West Coast. **See p.246**

❽ **Oudrif** An exceptional and remote retreat lodge on the edge of a gorge in the dry and dramatic redstone back country of the Cederberg. **See p.260**

HIGHLIGHTS ARE MARKED ON THE MAP ON PP.166–167

along the Garden Route is better than anywhere in the country, partly because the route is a single stretch of freeway, and tour operators along the way have turned it into the country's most concentrated strip for packaged **adventure sports** and **outdoor activities**.

To the east of the Winelands, the **Breede River Valley** is a region usually bypassed along the N1 en route to Johannesburg, but featuring among its functional fruit-farming towns are some hideaways favoured by Capetonians as weekend retreats.

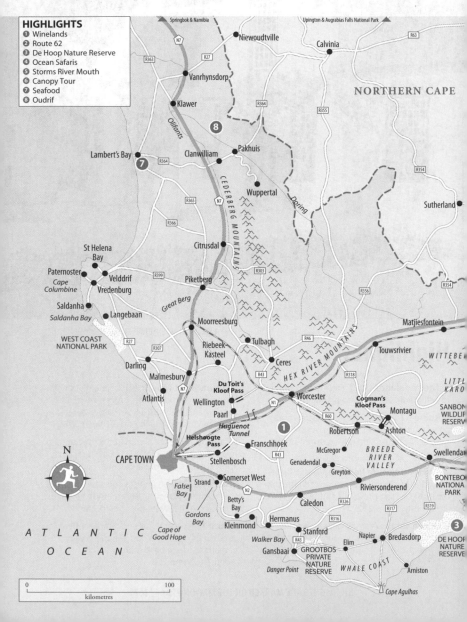

HIGHLIGHTS
1 Winelands
2 Route 62
3 De Hoop Nature Reserve
4 Ocean Safaris
5 Storms River Mouth
6 Canopy Tour
7 Seafood
8 Oudrif

Though the region was neglected by visitors in the past, some creative marketing has now literally put it on the map as **Route 62**, most of which consists of the intriguing eponymous back road tracing its way through the interior, linking **Little Karoo** towns between Cape Town and Port Elizabeth.

The **Overberg** – roughly the area between Arniston and Mossel Bay along the coast, and inland to Swellendam – is another region that remains hidden behind the mountains. West of here, the **Whale Coast** is the best area in the country for

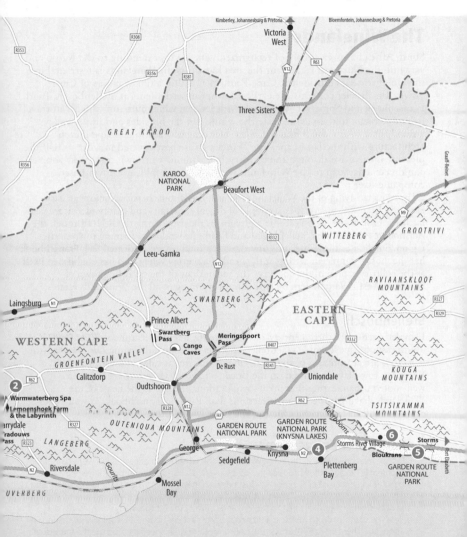

WESTERN CAPE

shore-based whale-watching, and a couple of pleasant coastal towns lie off the main routes. North of Cape Town, the less popular, remote and windswept **West Coast** is usually explored during the wild-flower months of August and September, when visitors converge on its centrepiece, the West Coast National Park. Its other major draw, 200km north of Cape Town on the N7, is the Cederberg, a rocky wilderness with hikes and hidden rock-art sites – the work of indigenous **San people**, who were virtually extinguished in the nineteenth century.

The Winelands

South Africa has over a score of recognized wine routes extending to the Karoo and way into the Northern Cape, but the area known as the **Winelands** is restricted to the oldest wineries outside the Cape Peninsula, within a 60km radius of Cape Town. The district contains the earliest European settlements at Stellenbosch, Paarl, Franschhoek and Somerset West, each with its own **wine route**, on which you travel from one estate to the next to taste the wines. On the hillsides and in the valleys around these towns you'll find a flawless blending of traditional Cape Dutch **architecture** with the landscape. The Winelands are best covered in a car, as half the pleasure is the drive through the countryside; without your own transport, you could take a day-trip to the Winelands with one of several Cape Town-based companies (see p.135).

The most satisfying of the Winelands towns is **Stellenbosch**, which enjoys an easy elegance, beautiful streetscapes, a couple of decent museums and plenty of visitor facilities. One of the region's scenic highlights is the drive along the R310 through the **Helshoogte Pass** between Stellenbosch and **Paarl**, the workaday farming town of the region. Smallest of the Winelands towns, with a rural yet sophisticated feel, **Franschhoek** has the most magnificent setting at the head of a narrow valley, and has established itself as the culinary capital of the country. The major draw of the sprawling town of **Somerset West** is **Vergelegen**, by far the most stunning of all the Winelands estates.

Stellenbosch

Dappled avenues of three-century-old oaks are the defining feature of **STELLENBOSCH**, 46km east of Cape Town – a fact reflected in its Afrikaans nickname *Die Eikestad* (the oak city). Street frontages of the same vintage, pavement cafés, water furrows and a European town layout centred on the Braak, a large village green, add up to a well-rooted urban texture that invites exploration. The city is the heart of the Winelands, having more urban attractions than Paarl or Franschhoek, as well as being at the hub of the largest and oldest of the Cape **wine routes**.

TACKLING THE WINELANDS

Of the several hundred estates in the Winelands, the **wineries** in our selection were chosen not primarily because they produce the best wine (although some do), but for general interest – beautiful architecture or scenery – or just because they are fun. When planning, bear in mind that although all the wineries offer **tastings**, many offer a lot more, such as restaurants, picnics and horseriding. Choose an area to explore and don't try to visit too many wineries in a day unless you want to return home in a dizzy haze. Most estates charge a fee for a wine-tasting session (anywhere up to R40) and some only have tastings at specific times; see the individual accounts for more details.

The definitive and widely available John Platter's **South African Wine Guide** (also available as an iPhone app) is a useful companion, which provides ratings of the produce of pretty well every winery in the country.

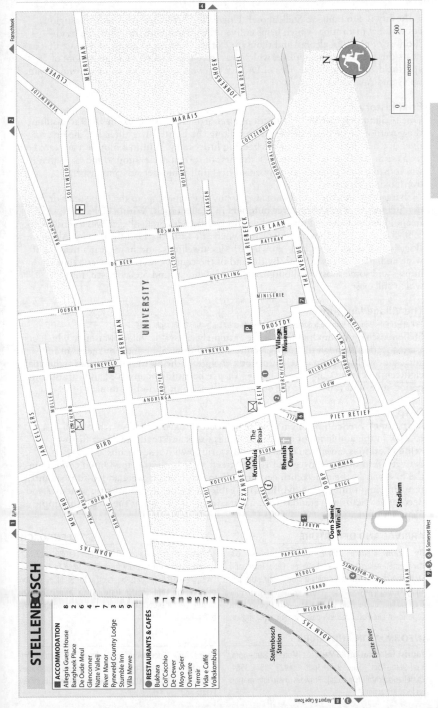

STELLENBOSCH

■ ACCOMMODATION

Allegria Guest House	8
Banghoek Place	2
De Oude Meul	6
Glenconner	4
Natte Vallеij	1
River Manor	7
Ryneveld Country Lodge	3
Stumble Inn	5
Villa Merwe	9

● RESTAURANTS & CAFÉS

Bukhara	4
Col'Cacchio	2
De Oewer	3
Moyo Spier	8
Overture	7
Terroir	6
Vida e Caffè	5
Volkskombuis	1

The city is also home to Stellenbosch University, Afrikanerdom's most prestigious educational institution, which helps enliven the atmosphere. But even the heady promise of plentiful alcohol and thousands of students hasn't changed the fact that at heart this is a conservative place, which was once the intellectual engine room of apartheid, and fostered the likes of Dr H.F. Verwoerd, the prime minister who dreamed up Grand Apartheid.

Brief history

One of **Simon van der Stel**'s first actions after arriving at the Cape in 1679 to assume the governorship was to explore the area along the Eerste River (literally "the first river"), where he came upon an enchanting little valley. Within a month it appeared on maps as Stellenbosch ("Stel's bush"), the first of several places around the Cape that he was to name after himself or members of his family; another was Simonsberg overlooking the town.

Charged by the Dutch East India Company with opening up the Cape interior, Van der Stel soon settled the first **free burghers** in Stellenbosch. Within eight years, sixty freehold grants had been made and within two decades Stellenbosch was a prosperous, semi-feudal society dominated by landowners. In 1702 the Danish traveller, Abraham Bogaert, admired how it had "grown with fine dwellings, and how great a treasure of wine and grain is grown here". By the end of the century there were over a thousand houses and some substantial burgher estates in and around Stellenbosch, many of which still exist.

The Village Museum

18 Ryneveld St • Mon–Sat 9am–5pm, Sun Sept–Feb 10am–4pm & March–Aug 10am–1pm • R25

Stellenbosch's museum highlight is the extremely enjoyable **Village Museum**, which cuts a cross section through the town's architectural and social heritage by means of four adjacent dwellings from different periods, including the **Blettermanhuis**, an archetypal eighteenth-century Cape Dutch house. They're beautifully conserved and furnished in period style, and you'll meet the odd worker dressed in period costume.

Dorp Street

Dorp Street, Stellenbosch's best-preserved historic axis, is well worth a stroll just to soak in the ambience of buildings, gables, oaks and roadside water furrows. **Krige's Cottages**, an unusual terrace of historic town houses at nos. 37–51, between Aan-de-Wagenweg and Krige Street, were built as Cape Dutch cottages in the first half of the nineteenth century; Victorian features were added subsequently, resulting in an interesting hybrid, with gables housing Victorian attic windows and decorative Victorian verandas with filigree ironwork fronting the elegantly simple Cape Dutch facades.

ARRIVAL AND DEPARTURE   STELLENBOSCH

By train Metrorail trains (☎0800 65 64 63, ⓦ capemetrorail.co.za) travel between Cape Town and Stellenbosch roughly every ninety minutes during the day, and take about an hour.

By bus Infrequent (and expensive) intercity buses from Cape Town and Port Elizabeth pass through Stellenbosch,

calling at the train station. The Baz Bus (☎0861 229 287, ⓦ bazbus.co.za) runs daily from Cape Town to Somerset West, where it drops passengers off at the BP filling station next to the Lord Charles Hotel. Some hostels operate shuttle services from there, but you must arrange this beforehand.

INFORMATION AND TOURS

Tourist information 36 Market St (Mon–Fri 8am–6pm, Sat 9am–4pm, Sun 9am–3pm; ☎021 883 3584, ⓦ stellenboschtourism.co.za). Provides basic information on local attractions.

Tours Easy Rider Wine Tours, based at *Stumble Inn* backpacker lodge (see opposite), offers daytime packages to four wineries (R400), with cheese tasting at Fairview Estate and lunch thrown in.

ACCOMMODATION

Allegria Guest House Cairngorm Rd, Stellenbosch ☎ 021 881 3389, ⓦ allegria.co.za; map p.169. Small, well-run establishment on a country estate 8km west of Stellenbosch between two wine farms. Under the warm proprietorship of hospitable Dutch couple Jan and Annemarie, the guesthouse offers six rooms with three levels of luxury, a swimming pool and great views. R1100

Banghoek Place 193 Banghoek Rd ☎ 021 887 0048, ⓦ banghoek.co.za; map p.169. Slightly more upmarket sister hostel to *Stumble Inn* (see below), with mostly en-suite double, twin and triple rooms that offer terrific value, and also three small dorms. Discount packages available that include two nights' accommodation plus a wine tour. Dorm R120, double R400

De Oude Meul 10a Mill St (off Dorp St) ☎ 021 887 7085, ⓦ deoudemeul.com; map p.169. Located in the middle of town on a fairly busy street, above an antique shop, these pleasing rooms are good value. Ask for accommodation at the back to ensure a quiet night's sleep. R850

Glenconner Jonkershoek Rd, 4km from centre ☎ 021 886 5120, ⓔ glenconner@icon.co.za; map p.169. Pretty, tranquil cottages on a farm in a spectacular valley, and close to the walks in the Jonkershoek Nature Reserve. Breakfast can be taken under an old oak tree. R750

Natte Valleij On the R44, 12km north of town ☎ 021 875 5171, ⓦ nattevalleij.co.za; map p.169. Guests have a choice of a large cottage sleeping six, a smaller one-bedroom unit attached to an old wine cellar, or an en-suite room with its own entrance. There's a swimming pool, and breakfast is served on the veranda. R500

River Manor 6–8 The Ave ☎ 021 887 9944, ⓦ rivermanor.co.za; map p.169. Enjoy a totally romantic, if formal, stay in two historic houses with rose-petal-strewn beds, oil lamps, plush dressing gowns and wicker chairs to laze on in the sun around the pool, and with spa facilities on site for extra pampering. R1900

Ryneveld Country Lodge 67 Ryneveld St ☎ 021 887 4469, ⓦ ryneveldlodge.co.za; map p.169. Gracious late nineteenth-century building, now a National Monument and furnished with Victorian antiques. The rooms are spotless, with the two best rooms upstairs leading onto a wooden deck. There are also three family cottages that sleep up to four (R650 per person), and a pool. R900

Stumble Inn 12 Market St ☎ 021 887 4049, ⓦ stumbleinnstellenbosch.hostel.com; map p.169. The town's best and oldest established hostel in two houses from the turn of the last century, with friendly, switched-on staff and a relaxed atmosphere. Just down the road from the tourist office, the hostel offers doubles and dorms, and is also noted for its good-value tours (see opposite). Dorm R100, double R280

Villa Merwe 6 Cynaroides Rd, Paradyskloof ☎ 021 880 1185, ⓦ villamerwe.co.za; map p.169. Three immaculate and comfortable rooms in the owner's modern house, each with its own entrance and bathroom, with a lounge, pool and garden. It's a 5min drive from the centre. R800

EATING

You'll be spoilt for choices of good places to eat in and around Stellenbosch – some of the town's establishments (including *Terroir*, *Overture* and the restaurant at Jordan Vineyards) made the Eat Out (South African foodie Oscars) Top 10 restaurants in 2010. Many of the wine estates also have good restaurants, some of which are covered under Stellenbosch Wine Estates (see p.172).

Bukhara Corner of Dorp and Bird sts ☎ 021 882 9133, ⓦ bukhara.com; map p.169. Succulent North Indian dishes prepared in a kitchen behind a glass wall, in full view of diners. Prices are moderate or even steep, though portions are large (mains R110–175). Favourites include butter chicken and tandoori lamb chops. Service is excellent and the ambience relaxed. Daily noon–3pm & Sat 6–10.30pm.

Col'Cacchio Shop 8, Simonsplein Centre, Plein St ⓦ colcacchio.co.za; map p.169. Better than average pizzeria, popular with students. Try the Morituri, topped with bacon, chicken, feta, red pepper and avocado. Mains R45–90. Daily noon–11pm.

Moyo Spier Lynedoch Rd (R310) ☎ 021 809 1133, ⓦ moyo.com; map p.169. An extravaganza of an eating place (one of four restaurants at Spier) in the gardens of one of the Western Cape's largest and most tourist-friendly wine estates. It's made to feel like a cross between an African village and a bedouin encampment, with seating for 1200 in gazebos, tents and tree houses, and the vast all-you-can-eat buffet for R200 brings together a dazzling array of flavours and dishes from across Africa. With live performance and optional face painting thrown in, you can't help but enjoy yourself. Daily noon till late.

★ **Overture** Hidden Valley Wine Estate, Annandale Rd, Stellenbosch ☎ 021 880 2646, ⓦ dineatoverture .co.za; map p.169. Top of the town in more ways than one, *Overture* looks down magnificently from the hills into the Annandale Valley, but it also bagged gold for South Africa's Best Chef, Best Restaurant and Best Service in the Eat Out 2010 Awards. Based on classical French cuisine, the dishes offer interesting contemporary twists. Select four-or-so courses (R350), or sample the works with the eight-course tasting menu (R600). Tues–Sun noon–5pm, Thurs & Fri 6.30pm–midnight.

Terroir Kleine Zalze Wine Estate, Strand Rd (R44) ☎ 021 880 8167, ⓦ kleinezalze.com; map p.169. Some

2

WINERIES AROUND STELLENBOSCH

Stellenbosch was the first locality in the country to wake up to the marketing potential of a **wine route**. It launched its wine route in 1971 to huge success; today tens of thousands of visitors are drawn here annually, making this the most toured area in the Winelands. Although the region accounts for only a fraction of South Africa's land under vine, its wine route is the most extensive in the country, approaching three hundred establishments; apart from the tiny selection below (all of which produce creditable wines and are along a series of roads that radiate out from Stellenbosch), there are scores of other excellent places, which taken together would occupy months of exploration. All the wineries are clearly signposted off the main arteries; see map p.173.

Delaire Graff Estate On the Helshoogte Pass, 6km east of Stellenbosch along the R310 to Franschhoek ☎ 021 885 8160, ⓦ delairewinery.co.za; map p.173. The highly regarded Delaire Graff restaurant has possibly the best views in the Winelands, looking through pin oaks across the Groot Drakenstein and Simonsig mountains and down into the valley. Tasting Mon–Sat 10am–5pm & Sun 10am–4pm; summer sundowners with musical accompaniment Fri & Sat 5–9pm; three wines R30, five wines R50, six wines R60.

Jordan Vineyards 11.5km west of Stellenbosch off the R310 ☎ 021 881 3441, ⓦ jordanwines.com; map p.173. A pioneer among the new-wave Cape wineries, Jordan's hi-tech cellar and modern tasting room are complemented by its friendly service. The drive there is half the fun, taking you into a *kloof* bounded by vineyards that get a whiff of the sea from both False Bay and Table Bay, which has clearly done something for its output – it has a list of outstanding wines as long as your arm and an award-winning restaurant. Tasting daily 9.30am–4.30pm; R25 for six wines, refundable with purchases.

Morgenhof 4km north of Stellenbosch on the R44 ☎ 021 889 5510, ⓦ morgenhof.com; map p.173. French-owned chateau-style complex on the slopes of the vine-covered Simonsberg, owned by Anne Cointreau-Huchon (granddaughter of the founder of Remy Martin cognac). Morgenhof has a light and airy tasting room with a bar. Delicious light lunches are served outside, topped off with ice cream on the lawns. Tasting May–Oct Mon–Fri 9am–4.30pm, Sat & Sun 10am–3pm; Nov–April Mon–Fri 9am–5pm, Sat & Sun 10am–5pm; R20 for five wines.

Neethlingshof 6.5km west of Stellenbosch on Polkadraai Rd (the R306) ☎ 021 883 8988, ⓦ neethlingshof.co.za; map p.173. Centred around a beautifully restored Cape Dutch manor dating back to 1814, reached down a kilometre-long avenue of stone pines, Neethlingshof's first vines were planted in 1692. There's a restaurant and for R95 you can try their "flash food" light lunch – pairings of six wines with six bite-sized takeaways (booking essential). The estate has two labels: Premium and Short Story reserve range, which consists of a Pinotage, a red blend and a flagship Noble

Late Harvest white. Tasting Mon–Fri 9am–5pm, Sat & Sun 10am–4pm; R30 for six wines.

Overgaauw 6.5km west of Stellenbosch, off the M12 ☎ 021 881 3815, ⓦ overgaauw.co.za; map p.173. Notable for its elegant Victorian tasting room, this pioneering estate was the first winery in the country to produce Merlots, and it's still the only one to make Sylvaner, a well-priced, easy-drinking dry white. Tasting Mon–Fri 9am–5pm, Sat 10am–3.30pm; free.

Rustenberg Wines Rustenberg Rd, 5km north of Stellenbosch ☎ 021 809 120, ⓦ rustenberg.co.za; map p.173. One of the closest estates to Stellenbosch, Rustenberg is also one of the most alluring, reached after a drive through orchards, sheep pastures and tree-lined avenues. An unassuming working farm, it has a romantic pastoral atmosphere, in contrast to its architecturally stunning, hi-tech tasting room in the former stables. Tasting Mon–Fri 9am–4.30pm, Sat 10am–1.30pm; free.

Simonsig Estate 9.5km north of Stellenbosch, off Kromme Rhee Rd, which runs between the R44 and the R304 ☎ 021 888 4900, ⓦ www.simonsig.co.za; map p.173. The winery has a relaxed outdoor tasting area under vine-covered pergolas, offering majestic views back to Stellenbosch of hazy stone-blue mountains and vineyards. The first estate in the country to produce a bottle-fermented bubbly some three decades back, it also produces a vast range of first-class still wines. Tasting Mon–Fri 8.30am–5pm, Sat 8.30am–4pm, Sun 11am–3pm; R25 for five wines and a bubbly.

★ **Uva Mira** About 8km south of Stellenbosch, off Annandale Rd, which spurs off the R44 ☎ 021 880 1683, ⓦ uvamira.co.za; map p.173. Enchanting boutique winery that punches well above its weight, and worth visiting just for the winding drive halfway up the Helderberg. The highly original tasting room, despite being fairly recently built, gives the appearance of a gently decaying historic structure, and there are unsurpassed views from the deck across mountainside vineyards to False Bay some 50km away – on a clear day you can even see Robben Island. Tasting Mon–Fri 8am–5pm, Sat & Sun 10am–4pm; R20 for Cellar selection (four wines), R30 for Vineyard selection (two premier wines), R40 for all six wines.

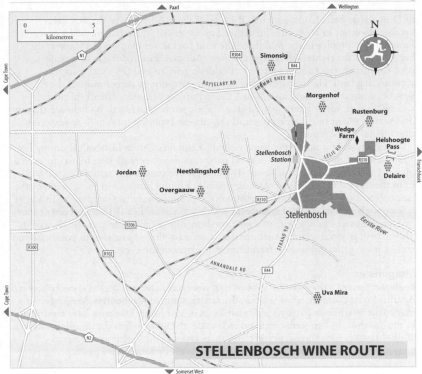

STELLENBOSCH WINE ROUTE

12.5km from Stellenbosch on a wine and golf estate, *Terroir* has a surprisingly relaxed dining room (for a nationally fêted restaurant) and tables outside under shady oaks. The expensive French-inspired menu (mains R160–200) is based as far as possible on local seasonal produce, with signature dishes that include pork trotters and oxtail. Mon–Sat 12.30–2.30pm & 7–9.30pm, Sun 12.30–2.30pm.

Vida e Caffé Corner of Bird and Kerk sts; map p.169. Vibey Portuguese-style coffee shop in the middle of town. Part of a national chain, it boasts excellent service and

coffee and is also a good bet for quick, inexpensive Portuguese-style sandwiches and rolls (R25–40). Mon–Sat 8am–5pm & Sun 9am–4pm.

Volkskombuis Aan-de-Wagenweg, off Dorp St ☎021 887 2121, ⓦ volkskombuis.co.za; map p.169. Popular spot on the banks of the Eerste River in a beautiful Cape Dutch house. If you want to sample traditional Cape cuisine, then this is the place to head, with starters that include *snoek* samosas, and main courses such as Boland *bobotie* and braised oxtail (R65–130). Daily noon–2.30pm & 6.30–10pm; winter Sun noon–2.30pm only

Somerset West and around

The only compelling reasons to trawl out to the unpromising town of **SOMERSET WEST**, 50km east of Cape Town along the N2, are for **Vergelegen** on Lourensford Road, and its immediate neighbour **Morgenster**, which are officially part of the Helderberg wine route, but can easily be included as an extension to a visit to Stellenbosch, 14km to the north.

Vergelegen

Buildings Daily 9.30am–4pm • R10 • **Wine tasting** Nov–April daily 10.30am, 11.30am & 3pm; May–Oct daily 11.30am & 3pm • R30 for six wines • ☎ 021 847 1337, ⓦ vergelegen.co.za

An absolute architectural treasure as well as producing a stunning range of wines, **Vergelegen** represents a notorious episode of corruption at the Cape in the early years of Dutch East India Company rule. Built by Willem Adriaan van der Stel, who became governor in 1699 after his father Simon retired, the estate formed a grand Renaissance complex in the middle of the wild backwater that was the Cape at the beginning of the eighteenth century. Willem Adriaan acquired the land illegally and used Company slaves and resources to build Vergelegen and farm vast tracts of surrounding land. He also abused his power as governor to corner most of the significant markets at the Cape. When the Company became aware of this, they sacked Willem Adriaan and ordered that Vergelegen be destroyed. It's believed that the destruction wasn't fully carried out and the current building is thought to stand on the original foundations.

Vergelegen was the only wine estate visited by Britain's Queen Elizabeth II during her 1995 state visit to South Africa – a good choice, as there's enough here to occupy even a monarch for an easy couple of hours. The **interpretive centre**, just across the courtyard from the shop at the building entrance, provides a useful history and background to the estate. Next door, the **wine-tasting centre** offers professionally run sampling with a brief talk through each label. The **homestead**, which was restored in 1917 to its current state by Lady Florence Phillips, wife of a Johannesburg mining magnate, can also be visited. The massive grounds, planted with chestnuts and camphor trees and with ponds around every corner, make this one of the most serene places in the Cape.

Morgenster

Mon–Fri 10am–5pm, Sat & Sun 10am–4pm • R20 for wine tasting, R20 for olive product tasting • ☎ 021 852 1738, ⓦ www.morgenster.co.za

Apart from its exquisite rustic setting, the tasting room at **Morgenster**, Vergelegen's immediate neighbour, has a veranda that looks onto a lovely lake with hazy mountains in the distance. Its two stellar blended reds aside, the estate offers the unusual addition of olive tasting, with three types of olive, three types of oil (including an award-winning cold-pressed extra virgin olive oil) and some delicious olive paste.

Paarl

Although **PAARL** is attractively ensconced in a fertile valley brimming with historic buildings, at heart it's a parochial *dorp*, lacking the sophistication of Stellenbosch or the striking setting of Franschhoek. It can claim some virtue, however, from being a prosperous farming centre that earns its keep from the agricultural industries – grain silos, canneries and flour mills – on the north side of town, and the cornucopia of grapes, guavas, olives, oranges and maize grown on the surrounding farms.

Brief history

In 1657, five years after the establishment of the Cape settlement, a party under **Abraham Gabbema** arrived in the Berg River Valley to look for trading opportunities with the Khoikhoi, and search for the legendary gold of Monomotapa. With treasure on the brain, they awoke after a rainy night to see the silvery dome of granite dominating the valley, which they dubbed Peerlbergh (pearl mountain), which in its modified form, **Paarl**, became the name of the town.

Thirty years later, the commander of the Cape, Simon van der Stel, granted strips of the Khoikhoi lands on the slopes of Paarl Mountain to French Huguenot and Dutch settlers. By the time Paarl was granted town status in 1840, it was still an outpost at the edge of the Drakenstein Mountains, a flourishing wagon-making and last-stop provisioning centre. The town holds deep historical significance for the two competing political forces that forged modern South Africa. **Afrikanerdom** regards Paarl as the hallowed ground on which their language movement was born in 1875 (see box, p.176), while the **ANC** and everyone else remember it as the place from which Nelson Mandela made the final steps of his long walk to freedom, when he walked out of **Groot Drakenstein Prison** (then called Victor Verster) in 1990.

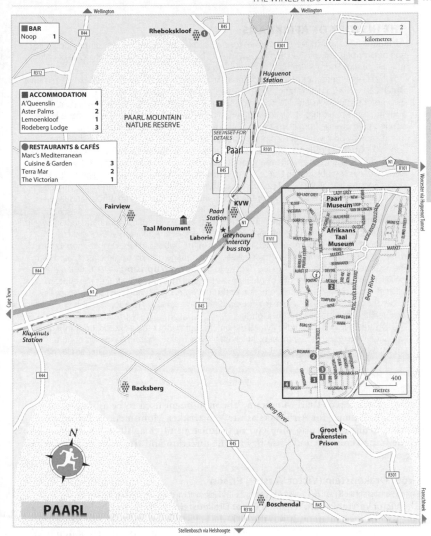

Paarl Museum

303 Main St • Mon–Fri 9am–5pm, Sat 9am–1pm • R5

Housed in a handsome, thatched Cape Dutch building with one of the earliest surviving gables (1787) in the "new style", characterized by triangular caps, the contents of the **Paarl Museum** don't quite match up to its exterior. It does include some reasonably enlightening panels on the architecture of the town, and several eccentric glass display cases of Victorian bric-a-brac. There's also some coverage of the indigenous Khoisan populations of the area and the changes that came with European colonization, including slavery.

Taal Monument

Daily 9am–5pm • Free • To get here, drive south along Main St and follow the signs to your right up the slope of the mountain

The only other sight of any interest in Paarl itself is the grandiose **Taal Monument**, the apartheid-era memorial to the Afrikaans language, standing just outside the

2

THE HISTORY OF AFRIKAANS

Afrikaans is South Africa's third mother tongue, spoken by fifteen percent of the population and outstripped only by Zulu and Xhosa. English, by contrast, is the mother tongue of only nine percent of South Africans.

Signs of the emergence of a new Southern African dialect appeared as early as 1685, when a Dutch East India Company official from the Netherlands complained about a "distorted and incomprehensible" version of Dutch being spoken around modern-day Paarl. By absorbing English, French, German, Malay and indigenous words and expressions, the language continued to diverge from mainstream Dutch, and by the nineteenth century was widely used in the Cape by both white and coloured speakers, but was looked down on by the elite.

In 1905, **Gustav Preller**, a young journalist from a working-class Boer background, set about reinventing Afrikaans as a "white man's language". He aimed to eradicate the stigma of its "coloured" ties by substituting Dutch words for those with non-European origins. Preller began publishing the first of a series of populist magazines written in Afrikaans and glorifying Boer history and culture. Pressure grew for the recognition of Afrikaans as an official language, which came in 1925.

When the **National Party** took power in 1948, its apartheid policy went hand in hand with promoting the interests of its Afrikaans-speaking supporters. Afrikaners were installed throughout the civil service and filled most posts in the public utilities. Despite there being more coloured than white Afrikaans speakers, the language quickly became associated with the apartheid establishment. This led directly to the **Soweto uprising** of 1976, when the government attempted to enforce Afrikaans as the sole medium of instruction in African schools. At the same time, the repression of the 1970s and 1980s and the forced removals under the Group Areas Act led many coloured Afrikaans speakers to adopt English in preference to their tainted mother tongue.

There are few signs that Afrikaans will die out, though. Under the new constitution, existing language rights can't be diminished, which effectively means that Afrikaans will continue to be almost as widely used as before. But it is now as much with coloured as white people that the future of the **taal** (language) rests.

---

centre on the top of Paarl Mountain. The monument used to be as important a place of pilgrimage for Afrikaners as the Voortrekker Monument in Pretoria. From the coffee and curio shop you can admire a truly magnificent panorama across to the Cape Peninsula and False Bay in one direction and the Winelands ranges in the other.

Groot Drakenstein (Victor Verster) Prison

Roughly 9km south of the N1 as it cuts through Paarl, along the R301 (the southern extension of Jan van Riebeeck St)

The **Victor Verster Prison**, renamed **Groot Drakenstein** in 2000, was Nelson Mandela's last place of incarceration. It was through the gates at Victor Verster that he walked to his freedom on February 11, 1990, and it was here that the first images of him in 27 years were broadcast (under the Prisons Act, not even old pictures of him could be published during his incarceration). The working jail looks rather like a boys' school fronted by rugby fields beneath hazy mountains.

ARRIVAL AND DEPARTURE   PAARL

By train Metrorail and Spoornet services from Cape Town (18 daily; 1hr 15min) pull in at Huguenot Station in Lady Grey St at the north end of town, near to the central shops.

By bus Daily Greyhound intercity buses from Cape Town (1hr) and Johannesburg (17hr) stop at the Monument Shell Garage, on the corner of Main Rd and South St.

INFORMATION

Tourist information 216 Main St, on the corner with Plantasie St (Mon–Fri 8am–5pm, Sat 9am–2pm & Sun 10am–2pm; ☎ 021 872 0860, ⓦ paarlonline.com). Offering a selection of good maps and can help with finding accommodation.

ACCOMMODATION

A'Queenslin 2 Queen St ☏ 021 863 1160, ✉ aqueenslin@
telkomsa.net; map p.175. Two en-suite rooms with their
own entrances and garden spaces, and three double rooms
that share a bathroom, in a split-level family home set in a
quiet part of town, bounded on one side by vineyards and
towered over by Paarl Rock. Limited self-catering is possible
– there's a fridge and microwave. **R450**

Aster Palms 3 Patriot St ☏ 021 872 0895,
ⓦ asterpalms.co.za; map p.175. Hospitable B&B in a
1920s house a couple of blocks from the tourist office, with
four airy double rooms and a lovely back garden with a
solar-heated swimming pool. **R550**

Lemoenkloof 396a Main St ☏ 021 872 3782,
ⓦ www.lemoenkloof.co.za; map p.175. A comfortable
and tranquil owner-run guesthouse in a National
Monument, with 1820s Cape Dutch and Victorian
features, a TV and fridge in each room, and a secluded
swimming pool. **R920**

Rodeberg Lodge 74 Main St ☏ 021 863 3202,
ⓦ rodeberglodge.co.za; map p.175. Plain period
furnishing gives the six en-suite rooms (three doubles and
three family rooms) in this huge, centrally located Victorian
town house a cool, spacious atmosphere. Ask for a room at
the back if traffic noise bothers you. **R540**

EATING AND DRINKING

Marc's Mediterranean Cuisine & Garden 129 Main
St ☏ 021 863 3980; map p.178. One of Paarl's most
popular casual restaurants, *Marc's* dishes up a moderately
priced, simple but tasty menu that includes paella,
Lebanese meze, couscous, seafood and lamb (mains R70–
120), served in a converted historic house with a large

outdoor area dotted with sun umbrellas and lemon trees.
Daily noon–2.30pm, Mon–Sat 6.30–9.30pm.

Noop 127 Main St, ⓦ noop.co.za; map p.175. A super-
cool wine bar with pavement seating with a dauntingly
long menu and equally long list of wines by the glass and
some great takes on simple favourites such as burgers,

WINERIES AROUND PAARL

There are a couple of notable wineries in Paarl itself, but most are on farms in the surrounding
countryside. Boschendal, one of the most popular of these, is officially on the Franschhoek
wine route (see p.172), but is within easy striking distance of Paarl.

Backsberg Estate 22km south of Paarl on
Simondium Rd (WR1) ☏ 021 875 5141, ⓦ backsberg
.co.za. Notable as the first carbon-neutral wine estate
in South Africa, Backsberg produces some top-ranking
red blends, and a delicious Chardonnay, in its Babylons
Ioren and Black Label ranges. Outdoor seating, with
views of the rose garden and vineyard on the slopes of
the Simonsberg, makes this busy estate a nice place to
while away some time. There's also a restaurant and a
maze to get lost in. Tasting Mon–Fri 8am–5pm, Sat &
Sun 9.30am–4.30pm; R15 for five wines.

Fairview Suid Agter Paarl Rd, on the southern
fringes of town ☏ 021 863 2450, ⓦ fairview.co.za.
One of the most fun of all the Paarl estates (especially
for families), with a resident population of goats who
clamber up the spiral tower at the entrance, featured
in the estate's emblem. A deli sells sausages and cold
meats for picnics on the lawn, and you can also
sample and buy the goat's, sheep's and cow's cheeses
made on the estate. As far as wine tasting goes,
Fairview is an innovative, family-run place, but it can
get a bit hectic when the tour buses roll in. Tasting
Mon–Fri 8am–5pm, Sat 9am–4pm, Sun 10am–4pm;
cheese selection R15, six wines and cheese selection
R25, eight wines plus cheese and olive oil selection
R60.

Laborie Taillefert St ☏ 021 807 3390,
ⓦ laboriewines.co.za. One of the most impressive Paarl
wineries, all the more remarkable for being right in
town. The beautiful manor is fronted by a rose garden,
acres of close-cropped lawns, historic buildings and oak
trees all towered over by the Taal Monument. There's a
truly wonderful tasting room with a balcony that jetties
out over the vineyards trailing up Paarl Mountain, as well
as a great restaurant with terrace seating under oaks
with gobsmackingly good views of the town vineyards
and mountains. Tasting Mon–Sat 9am–5pm, Sat
10am–5pm, Nov–April Sun 11am–3pm; R25.

Rhebokskloof Signposted off the R45, 11.5km
northwest of Paarl ☏ 021 869 8386, ⓦ rhebokskloof
.co.za. A highly photogenic wine estate, a popular
wedding venue, and a great place to bring kids,
Rhebokskloof sits at the foot of sculptural granite
koppies overlooking a shallow *kloof* that borders on the
mountain nature reserve. The estate's renowned
restaurant (see p.178) overlooks an artificial lake with
swans. For those too young to legally imbibe, there's a
kids' playground, pony rides and remote-controlled
boats on the lake, among the extensive offerings. Horse
and quad-bike trails for adults are also operated from
Rhebokskloof (see box, p.178). Tasting daily 9am–5pm;
R50 for five wines.

biryanis and pies, inspired, says the owner, by the old French stock pot (mains R90–185). Mon–Fri 11am–11pm, Sat 10am–3pm.

Terra Mare 90a Main St ☎ 021 863 4805; map p.175. Italian and Mediterranean influenced dishes, such as Karoo lamb chops with spring rolls or pasta and pesto (R80–140), using local ingredients and infused with considerable flair, served in a glass-and-steel restaurant with great sweeping views of the Paarl Valley. Tues–Sat 10am–2pm & 6–10pm, Sun 10am–2pm.

The Victorian Rhebokskloof winery, Rhebokskloof Minor Rd ☎ 021 869 8386, ⓦ rhebokskloof.co.za; map p.175. An intimate outdoor establishment, recommended for the outstanding setting as well as the food. Overlooking a lake, it has a shaded terrace for summer lunches, offering expensive gourmet meals. Meat is the house speciality, done with thrilling combinations of flavours, both Cape and international (R90–110). It's also a good place for morning or afternoon teas. Tues–Sat 9.30am–9pm, Sun–Mon 9.30am–5pm.

Franschhoek

If eating, drinking and sleeping is what the Winelands is really about, then **FRANSCHHOEK**, 33km from Stellenbosch and 29km from Paarl, is the place that does it best. Despite being a fairly small *dorp*, it has managed to establish itself as the culinary capital of the Western Cape, if not the whole country. Its late Victorian and more recent Frenchified rustic architecture, the terrific setting (hemmed in on three sides by mountains), the vineyards down every other backstreet, and some vigorous myth-making have created a place you can really lose yourself in, a set piece that unashamedly draws its inspiration from Provence.

Between 1688 and 1700, about two hundred **French Huguenots**, desperate to escape religious persecution in France, accepted a Dutch East India Company offer of passage to the Cape and the grant of lands. They made contact with the area's earliest settlers, groups of **Khoi herders**, whom the white settlers gradually dispossessed. By 1713 white hegemony was established and the area was known as *de france hoek*. Though French-speaking died out within a generation, many of the estates are still known by their original French names. Franschhoek itself occupies parts of the original farms of La Cotte and Cabrière and is relatively young, having been established around a church built in 1833.

The Huguenot Museum and the monument

Lambrechts Rd • Mon–Sat 9am–5pm & Sun 2–5pm • R10

If you drive through Franschhoek, you can't really miss the **Huguenot Memorial Museum** because it's adjacent to the town's most obvious landmark, the **Huguenot Monument**, set in a prime position at the head of Huguenot Road, the main road through town. The monument consists of three skinny, interlocking arches symbolizing the Holy Trinity, while the museum gives comprehensive coverage of Huguenot history, culture and of their contribution to modern South Africa.

EQUESTRIAN TOURS IN THE WINELANDS

A great way to take in the beauty of the winelands (and some wine) is in the saddle – a few operators offer guided **equestrian tours**. Prices of wine-tasting tours include the wine.

Delta Crest Stables Based at Solms Delta Wine Estate (see p.182; contact Rayanne ☎ 083 300 4368). Three-hour wine-tasting rides (R350) that take in Solms Delta and Allée Bleue wineries; scenic outrides are R170 an hour.

Paradise Stables Roberstvlei Rd, Franschhoek (☎ 021 876 2160, ⓦ paradisestables.co.za). Visits the same wineries as Delta Crest Stables, but does so over four hours (2hr 30 min in the saddle; R550) and uses thoroughbred Arabians; their outrides cost R200 an hour.

Wine Valley Horse Trails Based at Rhebokskloof wine estate (see p.177; ☎ 021 869 8687 or ☎ 083 226 8735, ⓦ horsetrails-sa.co.za). Offers one- to four-hour equestrian trails for novices and experts through the surrounding countryside – a choice spot for some riding. Prices start from R300 for a one-hour trail. Longer trails are restricted to experienced riders, but a half-day package (R650) of a ride plus a conducted wine tasting at the estate is available to novices.

■ ACCOMMODATION			Le Quartier Français	4	● RESTAURANTS & CAFÉS			The Tasting Room	5
Akademie Guest			The Map Room	7	Bread & Wine	6		The Restaurant at	
Houses	1		Plumwood Inn	8	Cabriére at Haute	2		Grande Provence	7
Bird Cottage &			Residence Klein		La Fromagerie at				
Frog Lodge	6		Oliphants Hoek	2	La Grange	8			
Cook's Cottage	3		Rusthof Country		La Petite Ferme	1			
La Bourgogne			House	5	Le Bon Vivant	3			
Riverside Cottages	9		Sep se Plek	10	Reuben's	4			

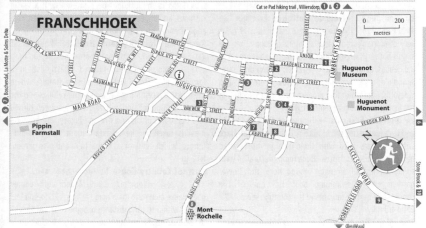

Museum van de Caab

Solms Delta Wine Estate, 12km north of Franschhoek along the R45 • Sun–Thurs 9am–5pm, Fri & Sat 9–6pm • Free • ⊕ solms-delta.co.za

The highly recommended **Museum van de Caab** gives a condensed and riveting slice through South African vernacular history as it happened on the farm and its surrounds. Housed alongside the atmospherically understated tasting room in the original 1740s gabled Cape Dutch cellar, the display begins with Stone Age artefacts found on the site and goes on to trace the arrival of the aboriginal Khoisan people, their colonization by Europeans, the introduction of slavery and how this eventually evolved into the apartheid system and its eventual demise.

INFORMATION
FRANSCHHOEK

Tourist information 70 Huguenot Rd (May–Aug Mon–Fri 9am–5pm, Sat & Sun 9am–4pm; Sept–April Mon–Fri 9am–6pm, Sat & Sun 9am–5pm; ☎ 021 876 3603, ⊕ franschhoek.org.za). Can provide activities in the area and some excellent maps of the village and its winelands.

ACCOMMODATION

On the whole, guesthouse accommodation here is on the pricey side, but the rooms are of high quality and frequently in unparalleled settings; budget accommodation is hard to find, but there are a couple of reasonably priced self-catering cottages (listed here).

★ **Akademie Street Boutique Hotel and Guest House** 5 Akademie St ☎ 021 876 3027, ⊕ aka.co.za; map above. Luxury guesthouse offering total privacy in each of its tastefully decorated and spacious suites in five Cape Dutch-style buildings set in beautiful gardens. Facilities include free wi-fi access, DVDs and CDs to use in your room, a fridge stocked with free drinks and a long saltwater swimming pool. Gourmet breakfasts with regional specialities are served at the poolside by the charming hosts who'll happily recommend a restaurant for dinner and book a table for you. R2600

Bird Cottage and Frog Lodge Verdun Rd, 4.5km from town ☎ 021 876 2136, ✉ cindy@kingsley.co.za; map above. Two very artistically furnished cottages surrounded by beautiful indigenous gardens, close to the mountains, in the midst of farmland. About as remote as you'll find this close to Franschhoek as well as being thoroughly laidback and exceptional value. R460

2

Cook's Cottage Corner of De La Rey and Van Wyk sts ☎021 876 4229, Ⓦexplorersclub.co.za; map p.179. A spacious, beautifully decorated double-storey Victorian house in the centre of town with two bedrooms and a huge open-plan kitchen, dining room and lounge with a fireplace. Sleeps up to four people. R1600

La Bourgogne Riverside Cottages Excelsior Rd ☎021 876 3245, Ⓦlabourgogne.co.za; map p.179. Six very comfortable converted labourers' cottages that are simply but very tastefully furnished. The cottages are set in indigenous gardens along a river on a working farm surrounded by plum and olive groves. There are also vineyards, from which they produce three wines, including the highly rated Progeny semillon. R800

Le Quartier Français 16 Huguenot Rd ☎021 876 2151, Ⓦlequartier.co.za; map p.179. A magical place with six suites (two with their own private walled garden and pool) and fifteen huge rooms decorated with sunny fabrics, all arranged around herb and flower gardens and a swimming pool. Has one of the consistently best restaurants in the country (see p.182). Child-friendly. R3700

The Map Room Cabrière St ☎021 876 4229, Ⓦexplorersclub.co.za; map p.179. Imaginatively decorated double-storey self-catering cottage in the centre of the village. Two raised ground-floor bedrooms, one of them enormous, sleep up to four people, with the living space upstairs. Six folding glass doors open onto a terrace with vineyard and mountain views. R1700

Plumwood Inn 11 Cabrière St ☎021 876 3883, Ⓦplumwoodinn.com; map p.179. An unfailingly excellent boutique guesthouse that makes a break from Franschhoek's Francophilia with its ethnic African-inspired decor. Detail is everything – from the custom-made cotton tablecloths to the luxurious beds covered with a sea of cushions, and impeccable service from Dutch owners Roel and Lucienne Rutten. R1150

Residence Klein Oliphants Hoek 14 Akademie St ☎021 876 2566, Ⓦkleinoliphantshoek.co.za; map p.179. Atmospheric eight-roomed guesthouse in a former double-storey Victorian mission station, where the massive reception room has soaring ceilings and the classrooms and missionary's quarters have been turned into bedrooms of varying size and luxury. The morning meal is taken in the breakfast room and adjoining terrace, which overlooks a formal herb and rose garden. R1240

Rusthof Country House 12 Huguenot St ☎021 876 3762, Ⓦrusthof.com; map p.179. Modern eight-roomed guesthouse along the main drag (although it doesn't feel like it), within spitting distance of some of Franschhoek's top restaurants. Rooms open onto a rose garden. Service is superb. R1700

Sep se Plek Excelsior Rd ☎083 459 9534 Ⓔladboer @mweb.co.za; map p.179. Possibly the only bargain you'll find in Franschhoek, in the form of three fully equipped, two-bedroom cottages on the edge of a small tranquil tree-lined lake on a working fruit farm. R400

EATING AND DRINKING

Eating and drinking is what Franschhoek is all about, so plan on sampling at least one or two of its excellent restaurants, some of which rate among the Cape's best. Franschhoek's cuisine tends to be French-inspired, but includes salmon trout as a local speciality. Restaurants in town are concentrated along Huguenot Rd, but there are a number of excellent alternatives in the more rustic environment of the surrounding wine estates.

Bread & Wine Moreson Farm, Happy Valley Rd, La Motte ☎021 876 3692, Ⓦmoreson.co.za; map p.179. Signposted off the R45, this genial and child-friendly venue is surrounded by lemon orchards and vineyards. It specializes in charcuterie accompanied by breads and the estate's own wines. Main courses range from R95 to R160. Daily noon–3pm.

La Fromagerie at La Grange 13 Daniel Hugo St ☎021 876 2155, Ⓦlagrange.co.za; map p.179. Sample platters of South African cheeses accompanied by local wines in the gardens here, overlooking vineyards, or sit down for tea or lunches that include savoury tarts, terrines and soufflés. On summer weekends this family-friendly spot becomes a buzzing jazz venue. Daily noon–4pm.

La Petite Ferme Franschhoek Pass Rd ☎021 876 3016, Ⓦlapetiteferme.co.za; map p.179. Gorgeous views across a vineyard-covered valley and an equally outstanding lunch menu unfailingly pull in accolades and diners – both locals and visitors – in their numbers. Local heritage is there, but always with a twist, in dishes such as kudu fillet medallions with courgette-wrapped cous cous roulade (mains R95–150). Influences include tastes from Asia, the Mediterranean and North Africa. Meals are served with wines made in the restaurant's cellar. Daily noon–4pm.

Le Bon Vivant 22 Dirkie Uys St ☎021 876 2717, Ⓦlebonvivant.co.za; map p.179. Well-priced and consistently excellent establishment serving two- to five-course nouvelle cuisine set meals as well as an à la carte menu with a splash of Dutch influence. The menu includes goat cheese and beetroot dumplings, seared tuna served with mango salad, and beef fillet with truffle dumplings (mains R90–160). Daily except Wed noon–3pm & 6.30pm till late.

VINEYARDS OF THE WINELANDS >

2

WINERIES AROUND FRANSCHHOEK

Franschhoek's **wineries** are small enough and sufficiently close together to make it a breeze to visit two or three in a morning. Heading north through town from the Huguenot Monument, you'll find most of the wineries signposted off Huguenot Road and its extension, Main Road; the rest are off Excelsior Road and the Franschhoek Pass Road.

Boschendal Pniel Rd, just after the junction of the R45 and R310 to Stellenbosch ☎021 870 4272, ⓦ boschendalwines.com. One of the world's longest-established New World wine estates, Boschendal draws busloads of tourists – 200,000 visitors a year – with its impressive Cape Dutch buildings, tree-lined avenues, restaurants and cafés, and of course its wines. Tasting takes place at the Cellar Door Tasting Centre, where you can sit indoors or sip under shady trees. Informal tasting daily 8.30am–4.30pm, R20 for five wines; conducted tasting daily Oct–March 8.30am–6pm & April–Sept 8.30am–4.30pm; R30.

Cabriére at Haute Cabriére About 2km from town along the Franschhoek Pass Rd ☎021 876 8500, ⓦ cabriere.co.za. Atmospheric winery notable for its Pinot Noirs and colourful wine-maker Achim von Arnim, whose presence guarantees an eventful visit; try to catch him or, more commonly now, his son Takuan, when they demonstrate *sabrage* – slicing off the upper neck of a bubbly bottle with a French cavalry sabre. Tasting Mon–Fri 9am–4.30pm, Sat 10am–4pm, Sun 11am–4pm; R10 per wine or R30 for five.

GlenWood Robertsvlei Rd, signposted off the R45 ☎021 876 2044, ⓦ www.glenwoodvineyards.co.za. Small winery in a beautiful setting that produces outstanding wines year after year. Although only ten-or-so minutes' drive from the village throng, it feels surprisingly remote; vineyard and cellar tours are frequently conducted by the owner. Tasting Mon–Fri

11am–4pm plus Sept–April Sat & Sun 11am–3pm; tasting R30 (three whites and three reds).

Mont Rochelle Dassenberg Rd ☎021 876 2770, ⓦ www.montrochelle.co.za. Set against the Klein Dassenberg, Mont Rochelle has one of the most stunning settings in Franschhoek and an unusual cellar in a converted nineteenth-century fruit-packing shed, edged by eaves decorated with fretwork, stained-glass windows and chandeliers. Tasting daily 10am–6pm; R25.

★ **Solms Delta** 13km north of Franschhoek along the R45 ☎021 874 3937, ⓦ solms-delta.co.za. The pleasingly bucolic Solms Delta produces unusual and consistently outstanding wines which, on a summer's day, you can taste under ancient oaks at the edge of the vineyards. You can also order a picnic basket to enjoy on the banks of the stream that traces the estate's boundary. There's a fine museum here, too (see p.179). Half the profits from the wines produced go into a trust that benefits residents of the farm and the Franschhoek Valley. Tasting Sun–Thurs 9am–5pm, Fri & Sat 9am–6pm; R10 (refunded if you buy wine).

Stony Brook Vineyards About 4km from Franschhoek, off Excelsior Rd ☎021 876 2182, ⓦ stonybrook.co.za. A family-run boutique winery, with just 140,000 square metres under vine, that produces first-rate wines, including its acclaimed flagship Ghost Gum Cabernet Sauvignon, which takes its name from a magnificent old tree outside the house. Tastings are convivial affairs conducted by the owners. Mon–Fri 10am–3pm & Sat 10am–1pm; R20.

The Restaurant at Grande Provence Grande Provence Estate, Main Rd ☎021 876 8600, ⓦ www.grandeprovence.co.za; map p.179. A great lunchtime venue on an historic estate, with tables under shady oaks and seriously stylish country cuisine with an edge – which bagged it an *Eat Out* magazine Top 10 award for 2010. Indoors, you sit on leather-backed chairs and the ambience is elegant, but relaxed. Three courses R295, four courses R380, 5 courses R450. Daily noon–2.30pm & 7–9.30pm.

Reuben's 19 Huguenot Rd ☎021 876 3772, ⓦ reubens.co.za; map p.179. Minimalist chic decor and a relaxed ambience set the tone at one of Franschhoek's top restaurants (one of only two in town nominated for *Eat Out's* Top 10), with an inspired, eclectic menu that varies from day to day. Venison features big among the main

courses (R95–170) and there's always poultry, lamb, pork, seafood and a vegetarian option, all spiced up with a touch of Indian, Japanese and other Asian accents. Daily noon–3pm & 7–9pm.

★ **The Tasting Room** Le Quartier Français, 16 Huguenot Rd ☎021 876 2151, ⓦ lequartier.co.za; map p.179. The place that made Franschhoek synonymous with food yonks ago, and has never put a foot wrong since, is irrepressibly one of South Africa's very best restaurants (rated among *Eat Out's* Top 10 in South Africa and one of San Pellegrino's World's 50 Best in 2010), offering excellent formal evening meals and relaxed lunches with a contemporary, global flavour. Main courses range between R90 and R170 and there are always vegetarian options and delicious desserts. Daily 7–10pm.

Route 62 and the Little Karoo

One of the most rewarding journeys in the Western Cape is an inland counterpart to the Garden Route (see p.214) – the **mountain route** from Cape Town to Port Elizabeth, largely along the R62, and thus often referred to as **Route 62**. Nowhere near as well known as the coastal journey, this trip takes you through some of the most dramatic mountain passes in the country and crosses a frontier of *dorps* and drylands. This "back garden" of the Little Karoo is in many respects more rewarding than the actual Garden Route, being far less developed, with spectacular landscapes, quieter roads and some great small towns to visit.

The most likeable of these towns are the historic spa town of Montagu, rural and arty Barrydale, and the port capital Calitzdorp. Oudtshoorn and the Cango Caves mark the convergence of the mountain and coastal roads; over the most dramatic of all passes in the Cape – the unpaved **Swartberg Pass**, 27km of spectacular switchbacks and zigzags through the Swartberg Mountains – is **Prince Albert**, a Karoo village whose spare beauty and remarkable light make it popular with artists.

From Prince Albert, the hinterland of the **Great Karoo** opens up, the semi-desert that covers one-third of South Africa's surface. The fruit farms of the **Little Karoo** spread out into treeless plains, vegetated with low, wiry scrub, and dotted with flat-topped hills. The best of the Karoo can be found in the **Karoo National Park**, while, in **Sutherland**, the clear, clean air provides some of the best stargazing opportunities in the world.

Worcester

The best part of the journey from Cape Town to **WORCESTER**, 110km east, is taking the **Huguenot Toll Tunnel** on the N1, burrowing through high mountains that give onto a magnificent valley. Worcester, a relatively large town for this part of the world, is an agricultural centre with a number of factories and smelly chicken farms. It's at the centre of a wine-making region, consisting mostly of cooperatives producing bulk plonk that makes up about a fifth of national output.

Karoo Botanic Gardens

As you enter Worcester on the N1 • Daily 7am–7pm • R16 • Restaurant Mon & Sun 9am–5pm, Tues–Sat 9am–8pm • ☎ 023 347 0785

The **Karoo Botanic Gardens**, sister reserve to Kirstenbosch in Cape Town (see p.110), is

---

PASSES AND POORTS OF THE LITTLE KAROO

The Little Karoo is hemmed in by a gauntlet of rugged mountains and steep-sided valleys (or *poorts*) that for centuries made this area virtually impassable for wheeled transport. In the nineteenth century, the British began to tackle the problem and dozens of passes were built through the Cape's mountains, 34 of which were engineered by the brilliant road-builder Andrew Geddes Bain and his son Thomas. In fact, whatever the Little Karoo lacks in museums and art galleries is amply compensated for by the towering drama of these Victorian masterpieces. We've listed a selection of some of the best of the passes below.

Cogman's Kloof Pass Between Ashton and Montagu. A five-kilometre route that's at its most dramatic as it cuts through a rock face into the Montagu Valley (see box, p.188).

Gamkaskloof Pass Also called Die Hel (The Hell; see box, p.195), reached from the summit of the Swartberg Pass. Arguably the most awesome of all the passes leading into a dramatic and lonely valley, all on gravel.

Meiringspoort A tarred road through a gorge in the Swartberg, which can be taken to reach Prince Albert, which keeps crossing a light-brown river, while huge slabs of folded and zigzagging rock rise up on either side.

Prince Alfred's Pass On the R339, between the N2, just east of Knysna, and Avontuur on the R62. A dramatic dirt road twisting through mountains, past a few isolated apple farms.

Swartberg Pass Between Oudtshoorn and Prince Albert. Over-the-Swartberg counterpart of Meiringspoort, with 1:7 gradients on narrow untarred roads, characterized by precipitous hairpins.

known for its show of indigenous spring flowers and succulents, and is a worthwhile place to stop, have a walk to admire the mountain backdrop, and recharge at the pleasant *Kokerboom* restaurant.

Worcester Museum

Just outside the centre of town at Kleinplasie – to get here, head east along High St and turn right onto the road to Robertson • Mon–Sat 8am–4.30pm, Sun 10am–3pm • R15

The absorbing **Worcester Museum** depicts life on the Karoo frontier between 1690 and 1900, and is made up of about two dozen reconstructed buildings, with staff in old-style workshops engaged in crafts and home industries. Keep a lookout in particular for the corbelled shepherd's hut, which represents a vernacular style unique to the Karoo, using domed stone roofs rather than beam and lintel construction – a response to the dearth of timber in the treeless expanse.

Tulbagh

You could easily drive into town, down Van der Stel Street and out the other end, and assume from this unexceptional main street that **TULBAGH** was just another humdrum *dorp*. But one block west, on **Church Street**, is the most perfectly restored eighteenth- and nineteenth-century streetscape. Only a fraction of what you see here is original (the town was flattened in 1969 by an earthquake), yet this is no Disneyland; the restoration of the buildings used salvaged materials from the ruins, following photographic and hand-drawn records. The best way to enjoy Tulbagh is to stroll up Church Street and take in the houses, gardens and gables, which are an essential element of Cape Dutch architecture. At least six different styles can be distinguished just along this short road. At no. 23, **Paddagang** (frog passage) was originally a *taphuis* (wine house); today it's a restaurant with a wine house attached (see opposite), recommended for its wonderful labels, all featuring comical frogs, rather than for the liquor itself.

ARRIVAL AND INFORMATION   TULBAGH

By car Situated 120km from Cape Town, Tulbagh is easily visited as a day-trip. If you've time, you might consider approaching via the beautiful Bain's Kloof Pass, on the R303 from Paarl, though the most direct way is on the N1 to Paarl, and then the R44.

Tourist information 4 Church St (Mon–Fri 9am–5pm, Sat & Sun 10am–3pm; ☎ 023 230 1348, ⓦ tulbaghtourism .co.za).

ACCOMMODATION

Acre Laan Farm Cottages 5km south of town, 1km off the Wolseley Rd ☎ 023 230 2991, ✉ fanie@cfconstruksie .co.za. Two self-catering cottages on a working farm, with brass beds and fireplaces, sleeping four. R500
Wild Olive Farm 6km south of town, heading towards Wolseley; a signposted turn-off leads you 2km down a

bumpy track ☎ 023 230 1160, ⓦ wildolivefarm.com. Olive-oil producing farm with accommodation in six fully equipped, self-catering cottages with fireplaces and braai stands. You can swim in a mountain-stream dam on the property. R500

TULBAGH WINERIES

Several new **wine farms** have become established around Tulbagh, making wine tasting and buying a notable activity. The Tulbagh wine route (ⓦ tulbaghwineroute.com) has some reputable cellars, among them **Twee Jonge Gezellen** (Mon–Fri 9am–4pm, Sat 10am–2pm; free), with lovely bubbly, and the very contemporary **Saronsberg** (Mon–Fri 8.30am–5pm, Sat 10am–2pm; free). The tourist office provides an excellent map of the wine farms with opening times. In and around town, you can buy local wines at the **Paddagang Wine House** and the **Manley Wine Lodge** cellar, or at **Things I Love** in Van der Stel Street, which carries a full selection of local wines (☎ 023 230 1742, ⓦ thingsilove.co.za).

EATING AND DRINKING

Paddagang Restaurant and Wine House 23 Church St ☎ 023 230 0242. Established in 1821 as one of the first taverns in the Cape, *Paddagang* serves acceptable regional cooking with stews, bakes and local fish (around R90), including *waterblommetjiebredie smoorsnoek* and *bobotie*, and locally produced wines. The situation is better than the food; you can sit outside under vines in the garden. Mon & Wed–Sat 8.30am–9pm, Tues & Sun 8.30am–9pm.

Readers 12 Church St ☎ 023 230 0087. A small eating place in an eighteenth-century cottage with a veranda once used by the church's sick comforter or "reader". The lunch and dinner menu consists of Cape country cuisine with unusual blends – so you'll find lamb cooked with citrus and served with roasted garlic, and gazpacho with avocado sorbet. Wed–Mon noon–9.30pm.

Robertson

ROBERTSON, approached either from the N1 or N2 from Cape Town, is the largest town in the attractive stretch of the Breede River Valley, known locally as the Robertson Valley. The acidity level of the soil is ideal for growing grapes – indeed, the Robertson Valley is responsible for some ten percent of South Africa's vineyards – but irrigation is necessary as the climate is hot and dry. The best wines here tend to be Chenin Blancs and Colombards, and some good Muscadels are conjured up too.

The only conceivable reason for visiting this fruit-picking town is to taste and buy wine, which tends to be cheaper than around the winelands closer to Cape Town, and very good.

ARRIVAL AND INFORMATION   ROBERTSON

By car Robertson, best approached via the N1, is 160km from Cape Town, with no public transport.

Tourist information Voortrekker St (Mon–Fri 8am–5pm, Sat 9am–2pm, Sun 10am–2pm; ☎ 023 626 4437, ⓦ robertsontourism.co.za).

WINERIES IN AND AROUND ROBERTSON

The Robertson Valley's **wine route** extends to McGregor in the south and to Bonnievale in the east; we've picked out the best of its nearly three dozen wineries. If you don't have time to meander, you can purchase wine from **La Verne Wine Boutique** (Mon–Thurs 9am–5.30pm, Fri 9am–6pm, Sat 9am–5pm, ⓦ lavernewines.co.za), situated in a converted railway cottage, next to the Robertson Art Gallery as you enter town from the west on the R60, which represents most of the local wine cellars. You can taste wine here, as well as buy by the case or just the odd bottle. La Verne also has a map of the wine areas to make your ramblings easier.

Bon Courage Roughly 10km southeast of Robertson along the R317 ⓦ boncourage.co.za. Producer of some great sweet whites, especially Muscadel, with a tasting room in a beautiful old homestead along the Breede River. Its *Café Maude* serves breakfast and light lunches. Mon–Fri 8am–5pm, Sat 9am–3pm; free.

De Wetshof About 12km southeast of town along the R317 ⓦ dewetshof.com. Top-notch estate with photogenic mountain and vineyard views, producing several excellent whites, including its flagship Bateleur Chardonnay. Mon–Fri 8.30am–4.30pm, Sat 9.30am–12.30pm; free.

Graham Beck About 7km west of Robertson along the R60 ⓦ grahambeckwines.co.za. A modern, high-flying estate making an international splash, with orders from British supermarket giants for its vast range of reds and whites, many of them in the top rank. The

tasting room is daringly modern. Mon–Fri 9am–5pm, Sat 10am–3pm; free.

Robertson Winery In town, just off the R60 ⓦ robertsonwinery.co.za. Producer of some good-value and highly drinkable Chardonnays and Colombards, sold cheaper here than in the shops. Mon–Fri 8am–5pm, Sat & Sun 9am–3pm; free.

Springfield A few kilometres southeast of Robertson on the R317 ⓦ springfieldestate.com. Stellar estate that produces a range of really outstanding reds and whites, a number of which are among South Africa's frontrunners. Mon–Fri 8am–5pm, Sat 9am–4pm; free.

Van Loveren 15km northwest of Bonnievale along the R317 ⓦ www.vanloveren.co.za. Wine tasting in a lovely garden at a winery known for its hugely quaffable wines, including River Red, South Africa's classic plonk that offers consistently good value. Mon–Fri 8.30am–5pm, Sat 9.30am–1pm; free.

2

ACCOMMODATION

Robertson Backpackers 4 Dordrecht Ave ☏ 023 626 1280, ⓦ robertsonbackpackers.co.za. Situated in a spacious Victorian house, this is one of the best backpackers in the Western Cape, with its own reasonably priced wine tour, a fireplace for chilly winter nights and a nice garden. They also do a good river-rafting day out. Camping R60, dorm R100, double R280

McGregor

McGregor is an attractive place, with thatched, whitewashed cottages glaring in the summer daylight amid the low, rusty steel-wool scrub, vines and olive trees, and a quiet, relaxed atmosphere that has attracted a small population of spiritual seekers and artists. It makes a great weekend break from Cape Town, with a couple of decent restaurants, plenty of well-priced accommodation, and a beautiful retreat centre with reasonably priced massage. Spending a day wine tasting around McGregor and Robertson is another drawcard, as long as it's not a Sunday when almost everything is closed.

McGregor gained modest prosperity in the nineteenth century by becoming a centre of the whipstock industry, supplying wagoners and transport riders with long bamboo sticks for goading oxen. There aren't too many ox-drawn wagons today, and tourism, though developing, is still quite limited. A great draw is to walk the **Boesmanskloof Traverse** (see box, p.199), which starts 14km from McGregor and crosses to Greyton on the other side of the mountain. From McGregor you can walk a section of trail, hiking to the main waterfall and back to the trailhead, which is a three- to four-hour round hike of exceeding beauty through the river gorge (*kloof* in Afrikaans).

ARRIVAL AND INFORMATION   MCGREGOR

By car McGregor is fifteen minutes to the south of Robertson, at the end of a minor road signposted off the R60, and 180km from Cape Town. Don't be tempted by an approach from the south which may look like a tempting back route – you would need a 4WD for this.

Tourist information Voortrekker St (Mon–Fri 9am–1pm & 2–4.30pm, Sat & Sun 9am–2pm; ☏ 023 625 1954,

ⓦ www.tourismmcgregor.co.za). Issues permits for walking the whole Boesmanskloof Traverse or simply for the waterfall section (R30). Staff will also direct you to artists' studios in town, and where you can get a massage or take a yoga class.

ACCOMMODATION

All the central accommodation is in Voortrekker St or clearly indicated off it along the town's gravel roads. The switched-on tourist office (see above) offers a free booking service and has a list of accommodation on its website.

The Barn Grewe St; book through the tourist office. A beautifully restored barn sleeping five in three rooms, with a Victorian bath, antique Cape furniture, fireplace and wood-burning stove. The barn is taken as a whole, which is a bit pricey if there are only two of you. R1000

Langewater Farm 2km outside town towards Boesmanskloof; book through the tourist office. Three no-frills, very reasonably priced self-catering cottages on a working farm. Ideal for families, with plenty of animals and space to run about. R400

McGregor Country Cottages Voortrekker St ☏ 023 625 1816, ⓦ www.mcgregor.co.za/countrycottages. Tranquil self-catering in a complex of cottages with traditional reed ceilings and fireplaces, surrounded by gardens, orchards and vegetable patches. There's also a pool. A separate honeymoon house is available and worth the price (R600). Wheelchair- and child-friendly. R550

McGregor Country House Voortrekker St ☏ 023 625 1656. B&B in a Victorian cottage on the main road with a pretty garden, three en-suite rooms, swimming pool and cosy Irish-style pub. Delicious Continental breakfasts are served by the friendly hostess Carol Smith. R600

Onverwacht At the trailhead of the Boesmanskloof Traverse ☏ 023 625 1667. Basic semi-equipped huts with spectacular views, no electricity and river pools for swimming – bring your own sleeping bag, towels and supplies. R100

Rhebokskraal Farm Cottages 2km south of town ☎ 023 625 1787, ✉ info@rhebokskraalolives.co.za. Secluded cottages, each on a different part of this beautiful fruit, olive and grape farm, which is within easy reach of the restaurants in town. **R440**

Temenos Country Retreat On the corner of Bree and Voortrekker sts ☎ 023 625 1871, ⓦ temenos.org.za. A holistic retreat centre with cottages dotted about beautiful gardens and walkways, a lap-length swimming pool, a library and meditation spaces. Safe and peaceful, it's also ideal for solo women. **R700**

EATING AND DRINKING

★ **Tebaldi's** *Temenos Country Retreat*, corner of Bree and Voortrekker sts. Delicious tapas, cheeses, Italian fare and local wines served in a tranquil garden setting or at street-side tables. Stylish and friendly. Tues–Sun 9.30am–4.30pm, Wed–Sat 7–10pm.

Forty One Voortrekker St ☎ 072 423 8378. A good spot for daytime snacks and teas (R80), with a veranda from which to watch the passing scene, and home-made olives, preserves and organic fruit nectars for sale. Tues–Sat 10am–9pm.

DeliGirls Voortrekker St. Great for picnic supplies with home-made bread, smoked fish, cheese, chocolate and other tempting goodies; it also serves coffee and light lunches too, if you are not stocking up. Daily 9am–4.30pm.

2

Montagu

As you approach **Montagu**, soaring mountains rise up in vast arches of twisted strata that display reds and ochres; in spring, the town, known for its fruit growing, is full of peach and apricot blossoms. Montagu is certainly very pleasing, with sufficient Victorian architecture to create an historic character, and worth a night at least.

The town was named in 1851 after **John Montagu**, the visionary British Secretary of the Cape, who realized that the colony would never develop without decent communications and was responsible for commissioning the first mountain passes connecting remote areas to Cape Town. The grateful farmers of Agter Cogman's Kloof (literally: "behind Cogman's Kloof") leapt at the chance of a snappier moniker for their village and named it after him.

Montagu is best known for its **hot springs**, but serious **rock climbers** come for its cliff faces, which are regarded as among the country's most challenging. One of South Africa's top climbers runs *De Bos Guest Farm* (see p.188), which you could use as a base for climbing. You can also explore the mountains on a couple of trails or, easiest of all, on a tractor ride onto one of the peaks. Montagu is also conveniently positioned for excursions along both the Robertson and Little Karoo **wine routes** (see p.185). On Saturday mornings, don't miss the local **farmers' market** at the church, where you can get local olives and olive oil, bread, cheese, almonds and dried fruit from the surrounding farms – all exceptionally well priced.

Montagu Springs Resort

About 3km northwest of town on the R318 (or reached on foot by following the Keisie River, which flows along the north edge of town) • Daily 8am–11pm • R60 • ☎ 023 614 1050, ⓦ www.montagusprings.co.za

Montagu's main draw is the **Montagu Springs Resort**; several chlorinated open-air pools of different temperatures and a couple of jacuzzis are spectacularly situated at the foot of cliffs – an effect spoilt by the neon lights of a hotel complex and fast-food restaurant. It's a fabulous place to take kids, but the weekends become a mass of splashing bodies. If you want a quiet time, go first thing in the morning or last thing at night. The temperatures in winter are not hot enough to be entirely comfortable, when you're better off heading to the springs at Caledon (p.198) or Warmwaterberg (p.190), which are much hotter and quieter.

ARRIVAL AND INFORMATION   MONTAGU

By car Montagu is 190km from Cape Town, via the N1. The approach from the south through Cogman's Kloof Gorge numbers among the most dramatic arrivals in the country: a five-kilometre winding road cuts through a rock face into

2

MONTAGU ACTIVITIES

Three **hikes** begin from the Old Mill at the north end of Tanner Street; maps for the hikes are available from Montagu's tourist office (see below). Shortest is the **Lover's Walk**, a stroll of just over 2km through Bath Kloof (or Badkloof; daily 7am–6pm) that follows the Keisie River to the hot springs, while the other two are day-long hikes.

If you don't feel like walking up the **Langeberg Mountains**, you can still get to the top on a recommended three-hour **tractor ride** (Wed & Sat 10am & 2pm; book at the Montagu tourist office) from Protea Farm, which is 29km along the Koo/Touws River road (R318). Remember to take warm clothes.

a narrow valley dramatically opening out onto the town. **Tourist information** 24 Bath St (Mon–Fri 8am–6pm, Sat 9am–5pm, Sun 9.30am–5pm; ☎023 614 2471).

ACCOMMODATION

⭐ **Aasvoelkrans** 1 Van Riebeeck St ☎023 614 1228, ⓦaasvoelkrans.co.za. Four exceptionally imaginative garden rooms at a comfortable guesthouse, situated on an Arabian stud farm – where you can see, but not ride, horses – in a pretty part of town. R950

Cynthia's 3 Krom St ☎023 614 2760, ⓦwww.cynthias-cottages.co.za. Seven self-catering cottages dotted around the west side of town, all in old houses, with gardens and braai areas, and near the starting point for hiking trails. R320

De Bos Guest Farm 8 Brown St ☎023 614 2532, ⓦwww.debos.co.za. Camping, dorms and basic doubles on a farm at the western edge of town, run by rock climbers, where you can be taken on guided climbs. While they do have some equipment to hire, it's best if you have your own, and book in advance. There are also hikes on the doorstep. Camping R40, dorm R80, double R360

Montagu Rose Guest House 19 Kohler St ☎023 614 2681, ⓦmontagurose.co.za. In a modern home, with friendly and helpful hosts. All rooms have baths and mountain views. Well run and good value. R700

Montagu Springs Signposted off the R62, west of town ☎023 614 1050, ⓦwww.montagusprings.co.za. Large resort with fully equipped, very decent self-catering chalets, some more luxurious than others, sleeping four. It is worth staying here if your focus is going to the hot springs and relaxing. R680

⭐ **Squirrel's Corner** On the corner of Bloem and Jouberts sts ☎023 614 1081, ⓦsquirrelscorner.co.za. B&B with four comfortable, spotless en-suite rooms in a friendly family house, as well as a garden suite that is two blocks from the main road. R550

EATING AND DRINKING

Die Stal 8km out of town on the R318 ☎082 324 4318. A thoroughly pleasant venue on a farm serving breakfast, lunches and teas, en route to the obligatory tractor ride. A good destination venue if you want to see something of the surrounding orchards and farmlands. Try their peppermint crisp tart (R60). Tues–Sun 9am–5pm.

Jessica's 28 Bath St ☎023 614 1805. Small and friendly, named after the proprietors' boxer dog and decorated with period dog prints. Here you'll get fairly pricey, refined, cosmopolitan bistro-style dishes and a top selection of Robertson wines; the cajun-roasted baby chicken on wild rice with *peri-peri* cream is recommended, as is the vegetable curry (R110). Daily 6.30–9.30pm; closed Tues in winter.

Preston's Restaurant & Thomas Bain Pub Bath St ☎023 614 3013. Small, intimate local pub that remains open till late and is recommended for its pub rather than its food. It is primarily the local pub. Daily 11am–2.30pm & 5.30pm till late.

Templetons@Four Oaks 46 Long St ☎023 614 2778. Pub and restaurant with meat and fish dishes, and a nice shady courtyard in a beautiful thatched house. Vegetarians can get a good spinach and goat's cheese ravioli, and meat-eaters can try marinated lamb rump in a port sauce (R110). Summer daily 12.30–2.30pm & 6–9pm, winter Mon–Sat 6–9pm.

Barrydale and around

BARRYDALE, 240km from Cape Town, is perfect for a couple of days of doing very little other than experiencing small-town life in the Little Karoo. There's a distinct rural feel about the town: vineyards line the main road, farm animals are kept on large plots of land behind dry-stone walling, and you'll find fig, peach and quince trees thriving in the dryness; unsurprisingly, its beauty and tranquillity have made it an artists' haven. West of town you'll find big game – and correspondingly high rates – at the magnificent **Sanbona Wildlife Reserve**, though day visitors are not accepted. To the east, you can totally relax at the Warmwaterberg hot springs.

ARRIVAL AND INFORMATION BARRYDALE

By car Allow two to three hours for the journey from Cape Town, either taking the N1 and R62, or the N2, and cutting inland on the R324 just east of Swellendam for the lovely drive through Suurbraak and the Tradouw Pass. Both routes are equally recommended for the scenery and ease of travel.

Tourist information On the R62 (Mon–Fri 8.30am–1.15pm & 2–5pm; ☎ 028 572 1572).

ACCOMMODATION

Goose and Gum Villiers St, phone for directions ☎ 028 572 1419, ✉ nigel@tugshill.co.za. Two tasteful, compact, self-catering cottages in a garden setting, at the home of Nigel and Linda, two Barrydale artists. One cottage has an outdoor shower and the garden leads to a dam with lots of birdlife. **R250**
★ **Tradouw Guest House** 46 van Riebeeck St ☎ 028 572 1434, ⊛ home.intekom.com/tradouwguesthouse.

One of the best accommodation places along the R62 is the friendly *Tradouw Guest House*, with four simple, homely rooms opening onto a courtyard shaded by vines where you can breakfast, and two onto the appealing large garden. Rates are extremely reasonable, and during the day you can eat at their on-site café or get a picnic. **R550**

EATING AND DRINKING

Blue Cow Signposted off the eastern side of the R62. The setting, overlooking fields and a dam, is restful and they serve delicious cakes and light meals (R50), with freshly picked peaches in summer. This is the best place if you are travelling with children and they need to run around. Mon–Sat 8am–5pm.
★ **Garden Café at the Tradouw Guest House** 46 van Riebeeck St. For real coffee, fresh salads, quiche and toasted bacon and egg sarnies (R60), served on the veranda with the friendliest hosts in town, the perfect place for watching the world go by. Daily 8am–8pm.
Jam Tarts On the R62. Of the several places strung along the R62, which are good options if you are driving through,

the best place for coffee and light meals is *Jam Tarts*, where you can also pick up local olives and delicious jams. Dishes include delicious soups, pizzas and other light meals (R80). Daily 8am–5pm, Mon also 6–9pm.
★ **Mez** On the corner of Van Riebeeck and Laing sts ☎ 028 572 1259. Excellent, eclectic Mediterranean food – try their light tapas meals or their lamb speciality (R80). Their bright-pink rose-water ice cream, served with pistachios and fresh mint, is always delightful. Sit outside on the wooden benches for some street surveying, or inside where it's decorated with Persian rugs and batiks. Tues–Sat 6–10pm.

Sanbona Wildlife Reserve

R4800 • ☎ 028 572 1365, ⊛ sanbona.com

Twenty kilometres west of Barrydale, Sanbona Wildlife Reserve is the amalgamation of 21 farms that together create a massive wilderness area. The landscape is gorgeous – rocky outcrops, mountains and semi-desert vegetation with luxurious all-inclusive lodges, *Dwyka Tented Lodge* and *Gondwana Family Lodge*. *Dwyka* is closer to where most of the game is to be found and has the more spectacular setting, while *Gondwana* is great if you are travelling with kids. The price includes two game drives a day, but, owing to the vegetation, the game is far sparser here than in the major game-viewing areas such as the Kruger National Park. Having said that, it is the only place in the Western Cape with free-roaming lions and cheetahs and there's a herd of elephants. Sanbona is worth considering only if you are set on seeing some big game and don't have time for Kruger. A two-night stay is recommended and day visitors are not allowed – check for specials and cheaper winter rates.

WARMWATERBERG SPA

Thirty kilometres east of Barrydale is **Warmwaterberg Spa** (☎028 572 1609, ⊛ warmwaterbergspa.co.za), a Karoo farm blessed with natural hot water siphoned into two unchlorinated hot pools and surrounded by lush green lawns and lofty palms. Primarily aimed at South Africans, it gets rather crowded and noisy during school holidays and over weekends. Indeed, the best time of day to enjoy the baths is after dark, when the steam rises into the cold, starry Karoo sky.

Accommodation is basic, reasonably priced and all self-catering – in wooden cabins or rooms in the main farmhouse, each of which has an indoor spa bath (R535). There are also some campsites (R255), a bar, and a restaurant serving dinners and breakfasts.

Oudtshoorn

OUDTSHOORN, 420km from Cape Town and an arid, mountainous 180km from Barrydale, styles itself as the ostrich capital of the world; the town's surrounds are indeed crammed with ostrich farms, several of which you can visit, and the local souvenir shops keep busy dreaming up 1001 tacky ways to recycle ostrich parts as comestibles and souvenirs. The town's main interest visually lies in its Victorian and Edwardian sandstone buildings, some of which are unusually grand and elegant for a Karoo dorp; Oudtshoorn's primary draw is as the base for visiting the nearby **Cango Caves** (see p.192).

Brief history

Oudtshoorn started out as a small village named in honour of Geesje Ernestina Johanna van Oudtshoorn, wife of the first civil commissioner for George. By the 1860s **ostriches**, which live in the wild in Africa, were being raised under the ideal conditions of the Oudtshoorn Valley. The quirky Victorian fashion for large feathers had turned the ostriches into a source of serious wealth, and by the 1880s hundreds of thousands of kilograms of feathers were being exported. On the back of this boom, the labourers drew the shortest straw of all – mostly coloured descendants of the Outeniqua and Attaqua Khoikhoi and trekboers, who received derisory wages supplemented by rations of food, wine, spirits and tobacco. In the early twentieth century, the most successful farmers and traders built themselves feather palaces, ostentatious sandstone Edwardian buildings that have become the defining feature of Oudtshoorn.

C.P. Nel Museum

Corner of Baron van Reede St and Voortrekker Rd • Mon–Fri 8am–5pm, Sat 9am–1pm • R15

The C.P. Nel Museum is a good place to start your explorations. A handsome sandstone building, it was built in 1906 as a boys' school, but now houses an eccentric collection of items relating to ostriches.

Le Roux Town House

Corner of Loop and High sts • Mon–Fri 9am–5pm • R15

A perfectly preserved family town house, and the only way to get a glimpse inside one of the much-vaunted feather palaces. The beautifully preserved furnishings were all imported from Europe between 1900 and 1920, and there is plenty to stroll around and admire.

Buffelsdrift Game Lodge

7km out of town on the Cango Caves Rd • R180 • ☎044 272 0106

Though not hugely traditional for Oudtshoorn, **Buffelsdrift Game Lodge** offers the opportunity to feed and touch elephants. Book ahead for a really worthwhile experience where you get to stroke elephants under the guidance of their handlers, and watch them at training and play. From the lodge's restaurant on the large dam (see p.192), you are likely to see hippos, and may be lucky to see other animals coming to drink. It's also possible to stay here (see below).

ARRIVAL AND DEPARTURE OUDTSHOORN

By bus Intercity buses pull in at Queens Mall, off Voortrekker St, where you'll also find the Pick 'n Pay supermarket, internet café and chemist. It's a six-hour drive from Cape Town, one- and- a- half hours from George, and fourteen hours from Gauteng, routes traversed by national coach companies. A daily shuttle from George collects guests for *Backpacker's Paradise*.

INFORMATION AND TOURS

Tourist information Next to the *Queens Hotel*, Baron van Reede St (Mon–Fri 8am–6pm, Sat 9.30am–1pm; ☎ 044 279 2532, ⓦ oudtshoorn.com). Good for information about the caves, ostrich farms and local accommodation.

Tours *Backpacker's Paradise* (see below) rents out bikes and also arranges spectacular adventurous cycling trips down the Swartberg Pass, chaperoned with motor vehicle backup.

ACCOMMODATION

Oudtshoorn has a number of large hotels catering mainly to tour buses, plus plenty of good-quality B&Bs and guesthouses, a centrally located campsite with chalets, and one of the country's best-run backpacker lodges. Some of the nicest places to stay are in the attractive countryside en route to Cango Caves. The tourist office offers a free accommodation booking service.

Backpacker's Paradise 148 Baron van Reede St ☎ 044 272 3436, ⓦ backpackersparadise.net. A well-run two-storey hostel along the main drag, which makes an effort to go the extra few centimetres with three-quarter beds, en-suite doubles and family rooms as well as three small dorms. There are nightly ostrich or veg-friendly braais, too, and a daily shuttle from the Baz Bus drop-off in George to the hostel. The on-site adventure centre organizes cycle trips in the Swartberg Pass and there's a daily shuttle to the caves, ostrich farm and wildlife ranch. Dorm **R110**, double **R350**

Berluda On the R328, 15km from Oudtshoorn, en route to Cango Caves ☎ 044 272 8518, ⓦ berluda.co.za. An avenue of trees leads up to a fairly modern-looking farmhouse with five bedrooms and two self-catering cottages in a lovingly tended garden. The friendly owners can organize ostrich farm tours on their property 8km away, and there is a pool to cool off in. **R650**

Buffelsdrift Game Lodge 7km from town on the road to the caves ☎ 044 272 0106, ⓦ buffelsdrift.com. The town's top stay, in luxurious en-suite safari tents overlooking a large dam with hippo in it, and a grand thatched dining area. Game drives or horseback rides to

view rhino, buffalo, elephant, giraffe and various antelope are included in the price. No kids under 12 can be accommodated, though families can visit during the day for a meal or game activity (see opposite). **R2110**

De Oue Werf Signposted off the R328 to Cango Caves, 12km north of Oudtshoorn ☎ 044 272 8712, ⓦ www .ouewerf.co.za. Luxurious and well-priced garden rooms on a working farm, run by the very welcoming sixth generation of the family. Green lawns run down to a dam which has a swinging slide and raft to play on, and lots of birdlife. There's also a coffee shop and deli. A great option if you're visiting the caves and want to stay in the country. **R900**

Gum Tree Lodge 139 Church St ☎ 044 279 2528, ⓦ www.gumtreelodge.co.za. Six rooms in a peaceful B&B, conveniently a few minutes' walk from the centre, fronting onto a river with good birdlife. **R630**

Kleinplaas Holiday Resort 171 Baron van Reede St ☎ 044 272 5811, ⓦ www.kleinplaas.co.za. Well-run, spick-and-span shady camping and fully equipped self-catering brick chalets, conveniently close to town, with a swimming pool and launderette. B&B is available. Camping **R185**, chalet **R380**

OSTRICH TOURS

Many people come to Oudtshoorn to see, or even ride, **ostriches**. You don't actually have to visit one of the ostrich farms to view Africa's biggest bird, as you're bound to see flocks of them as you drive past farms in the vicinity or past truckloads of them on their way to the slaughterhouse (feathers being no longer fashionable, these days ostriches are raised for their low-cholesterol flesh). A number of show farms offer **tours** (45–90min) costing around R60 per adult, which include the chance to sit on an ostrich and the spectacle of jockeys racing the birds. Best of the bunch is **Cango Ostrich and Butterfly Farm** (☎ 044 272 4623; tours every 30min; R70), on the main road between Oudtshoorn and the Cango Caves, which takes only one group of visitors (or individuals) at a time.

2

EATING AND DRINKING

Oudtshoorn has a choice of several places to eat, mostly strung out along Baron van Reede St and catering to the tourist trade, with the obligatory ostrich on the menu.

Bello Cibo 146 Baron van Reede St. Relaxed and reasonably priced Italian place with indoor and outdoor seating, making it a good choice for children. Besides pizza and pasta, there are some creative ostrich offerings (R80). Mon–Sat 12.30–3.30pm & 6–10pm. R80

Buffelsdrift Game Lodge 7km out of town towards Cango Caves ☎044 272 0106. Have a great breakfast or lunch (R80) on a wooden deck overlooking the waterhole, and do a spot of game-viewing at the same time. The lodge is open to non-guests for meals, and you could combine it with an elephant encounter or other game activity (see p.190). Daily 7am–3pm.

Jemima's 94 Baron van Reede St ☎044 272 0808. An imaginative and good-value menu including boerewors-stuffed ravioli, butternut cheesecake, game dishes and other tasty, light food (mains around R120). Mon–Fri 11am–3pm, daily 6pm till late.

★ **Kalinka's** 93 Baron van Reede St ☎044 279 2596. A sandstone house with a fountain outside, specializing in game dishes, with Russian black bread at every meal, and imported vodka. Service is good and food well presented, fresh and delicious (mains around R120). The baked cardamom and date brandy pudding is great, and there are some creative choices for vegetarians. Book an outside table in the rose garden on summer evenings. Daily 6–10pm.

Paljas 109 Baron van Reede St ☎044 272 0982. With a heavy emphasis on meat and a pan-African menu, this is a good choice for ostrich steaks (R80). Daily 6–10pm.

Cango Caves

29km from Oudtshoorn on the R328 • Tours daily 9am–4pm • Standard tour on the hour • R65 • Adventure tour on the half-hour • R80 • ☎044 272 7410, ⓦ www.cangocaves.co.za

The **Cango Caves** number among South Africa's most popular attractions, drawing a quarter of a million visitors each year to gasp at their fantastic cavernous spaces, dripping rocks and rising columns of calcite. In the two centuries since they became known to the public, the caves have been seriously battered by human intervention, but they still represent a stunning landscape growing inside the Swartberg foothills. Don't go expecting a serene and contemplative experience, though: the only way of getting inside the caves is on a guided tour accompanied by a commentary.

Cango is a Khoi word meaning a wet place – accurate enough, given that the caves' awesome formations are the work of water constantly percolating through rock and dissolving limestone on the way. The solution drips from the roof of the cave and down the walls, depositing calcium carbonate that gradually builds up. Although the caves are many millions of years old, the calcite formations that you see today are geological youngsters, dating back a mere 100,000 years.

The caves must be visited on a **tour**. The one-hour Standard Tour takes you through the first six chambers, but if you're an adrenaline junkie the ninety-minute Adventure Tour is a must; this takes you into the deepest sections open to the public, where the openings become smaller and smaller. Squeezing through the tight openings, with names like Lumbago Walk, Devil's Chimney and The Letterbox, is not recommended for the overweight, faint-hearted or claustrophobic, and you should wear clothes you don't mind getting dirty and shoes with a grip to negotiate the slippery floors. The **visitors' complex** includes an interpretive centre with quite interesting displays about geology, people and wildlife connected with the caves, and a decent restaurant. Below the complex you'll find shady **picnic sites** at the edge of a river that cuts its way into the mountains and along which there are hiking trails.

Brief history

San hunter-gatherers sheltered in the entrance caves for millennia before white settlers arrived, but it's unlikely that they ever made it to the lightless underground chambers. **Jacobus van Zyl**, a Karoo farmer, was probably the first person to penetrate beneath the surface, when he slid down on a rope into the darkness in July 1780, armed with a lamp. Over the next couple of centuries the caves were visited and pillaged by growing numbers of callers, some of whom were photographed cheerfully carting off wagonloads of limestone columns.

In the 1960s and 1970s, the caves were made accessible to mass consumption when a **tourist complex** was built, the rock-strewn floor was evened out with concrete, ladders and walkways were installed and the caverns were turned into a kitsch extravaganza with coloured lights, piped music and an indecipherable commentary that drew hundreds of thousands of visitors each year. Even apartheid put its hefty boot in: under the premiership of Dr Hendrik Verwoerd, the arch-ideologue of racial segregation, a separate non-whites entrance was hacked through one wall, resulting in a disastrous through-draught that began dehydrating the caves. Fortunately, the worst excesses have now ended; concerts are no longer allowed inside the chambers, and the coloured lights have gone.

Calitzdorp

The tiny Karoo village of **CALITZDORP** hangs in a torpor of midday stillness, with attractive, unpretentious Victorian streets and a handful of wineries which produce the best port and fortified wines in the land.

INFORMATION
CALITZDORP

Tourist information At the Shell Garage in Voortrekker St (Mon–Fri 9am–5pm, Sat & Sun 10am–5pm; ☎ 044 213 3775, ⓦ www.calitzdorp.co.za).

ACCOMMODATION

Die Dorpshuis Opposite the church ☎ 044 213 3453, ⓦ www.diedorpshuis.co.za. Airy, no-frills rooms in a nineteenth-century house that offer exceptional value. Conveniently there is a restaurant on-site, serving reasonably priced sandwiches, teas, light meals and heavier traditional Karoo food, such as stews and lamb. R370
Port-Wine Guest House On the corner of Queen and Station sts ☎ 044 213 3131, ⓦ www.portwine.net. The smartest and most comfortable guesthouse in town, in a renovated early nineteenth-century homestead overlooking the Boplaas Estate, with a nice veranda. R840
Welgevonden Guest House St Helena Rd ☎ 044 213 3642, ⓦ www.welgevondenguesthouse.co.za. A comfortable and country-style guesthouse, on a small Chardonnay farm 300m from the main road. The four en-suite bedrooms in an 1880 outbuilding are furnished with brass or wooden bedsteads, patchwork quilts and wooden family heirloom furniture. R500

The Groenfontein Valley

A circuitous minor route diverts off the R62, just east of Calitzdorp, and drops into the highly scenic **Groenfontein Valley**. The narrow dirt road twists through the Swartberg foothills, past whitewashed Karoo cottages and farms and across brooks, eventually joining the R328 to Oudtshoorn. Winding through these back roads is also an option to reach Cango Caves (see opposite) and Prince Albert (see p.194), one of the best drives you'll ever do in South Africa. Many of the roads are unsealed but are perfectly navigable in an ordinary car if taken slowly.

> ### SOUTH AFRICAN PORT
> Some of South Africa's best **ports** are produced at the three modest wineries in Calitzdorp. The most highly recommended is **Die Krans Estate** (☎ 044 213 3314, ⓦ dekrans.co.za; Mon–Fri 8am–5pm, Sat 9am–3pm; free), where you can sample its wines and ports (its vintage reserve port is reckoned to be among the country's top three), and stretch your legs on a thirty-minute vineyard walk in lovely countryside. **Boplaas Estate** (Mon–Fri 8am–5pm, Sat 9am–3pm; free tasting; ☎ 044 213 3326, ⓦ www.boplaas.co.za) also produces some fine ports and is worth a quick look to see its massive reed-ceiling tasting room, which looks like a cantina that fell off the set of a spaghetti western.

2

Kruis Rivier Guest Farm 17km off the R62 (signposted turn-off 14km east of Calitzdorp) on a good, wide gravel road ☎044 213 3788, ⓦkruisrivier.co.za. Homely cottages right underneath the mountains, with lovely streams and waterfalls, which make an excellent base for hiking, with a policy of keeping prices absolutely affordable. The owners will also do breakfast on request, and provide braai packs, home-made bread, and wood. R400

Red Stone Hills 6km off the R62 (signposted turn-off 14km east of Calitzdorp) ☎044 213 3783, ⓦredstone .co.za. This place has four lovely period-furnished Victorian cottages on a working farm in an open landscape full of red rock formations. The owners can provide dinners on request, as well as breakfast. Besides walking and cycling trails, there is birdwatching and four horses on the farm that can be ridden. R680

★ **Retreat at Groenfontein** 20km from Calitzdorp ☎044 213 3880, ⓦgroenfontein.com. This isolated Victorian colonial farmstead borders the 2300-square-kilometre Swartberg Nature Reserve, an outstandingly beautiful area of gorges, rivers and dirt tracks. Accommodation is in comfortable en-suite rooms, each with its own fireplace, and rates include a very good dinner, with vegetarians well catered for, and extremely hospitable and helpful owners who turn every evening into a dinner party. R1420

Prince Albert and around

Isolation has left intact the traditional rural architecture of **PRINCE ALBERT**, an attractive little town 70km north of Oudtshoorn, across the loops and razorbacks of the Swartberg Pass – one of the most dramatic drives and entries to a town imaginable. Although firmly in the thirstlands of the South African interior, on the cusp between the Little and Great Karoo, Prince Albert is all the more striking for its perennial spring, whose water trickles down furrows along its streets – a gift that propagates fruit trees and gardens.

The town's essence is in the fleeting impressions that give the flavour of a Karoo *dorp* like nowhere else: the silver steeple of the Dutch Reformed church puncturing a deep-blue sky, and residents sauntering along or progressing slowly down the main street on squeaky bikes. Prince Albert is known for its **mohair products**: rugs, socks, scarves and other garments; check out Karoo Looms at 55 Church Street, which has some funky, bright designs, or, further down Church Street, the more traditional Wolskuur Spinnerst.

Prince Albert Gallery

57 Church St • Mon–Fri 10am–4pm, Sat & Sun 10am–1pm • Free • ⓦ www.princealbertgallery.co.za

The town's beauty has attracted a number of artists to live here; at the excellent **Prince Albert Gallery**, housed in an airy Victorian building, you can browse and purchase paintings, sculpture, beadwork, jewellery, ceramics and etchings by local artists.

Gay's Guernsey Dairy

Upper Church St, southern end of town • Daily 7am–9am & 4–6pm • Free • ☎ 023 541 1274, ⓦ www.princealbert.org.za/dairy

Gay's Guernsey Dairy sells fantastic, award-winning home-made cheeses, which you can taste before buying, as well as yoghurts and cream. If you're travelling with children,

---

ACTIVITIES IN PRINCE ALBERT

One of the most exciting things you can do in Prince Albert, if not in South Africa, is to watch the **night skies** with resident astronomer Hans Daehne (weekends & school holidays only, at new moon; R250; ☎072 732 2950; ⓦastrotours.co.za). The Karoo sky is heaven for astronomers, with no pollution and few lights, and you get some of the southern hemisphere's sharpest views of the firmament from here. He also runs guided trips to Sutherland (see p.196).

You can also visit **rock-art sites** with one of the country's top paleontologists and archeologists, the now retired Dr Judy Maguire (☎023 541 1713, ✉questar@icon.co.za), on her farm at the start of the Swartberg Pass. It's a highly recommended way to spend an afternoon, but you'll need to book beforehand to arrange it.

Mountain biking and **hiking** trips are offered by *Dennehof Guest House* (see opposite) – you're driven up the Swartberg, and descend the terrifying 18km on your own two wheels.

GO TO HELL

Prince Albert is one of the best places to begin a trip into **Die Hel** (also known as Hell, The Hell or Gamkaskloof), a valley that's part of the **Swartberg Nature Reserve**. Die Hel is not on the way to anywhere and, although it doesn't look very far on the map, you'll need to allow two- and- a- half hours in either direction to make the spectacular but tortuous drive into it along a rough dirt road. Call **CapeNature** (☎023 541 1736, ⒲capenature.co.za) in the valley for up-to-date road conditions.

The attraction of the place is the silence, isolation and birdlife. If you don't want to go it alone, Lisa from *Onse Rus B&B* (see below) organizes full-day tours, for a minimum of two people, and you can get picked up if you want to hike a section of the road (4–12km), instead of driving it.

There's accommodation in the centre of the valley in the form of spick, nicely restored Cape Nature cottages (☎021 483 0190; R550). The valley has no electricity supply, and no shops or any other facilities, though you can order picnic baskets and cooked breakfasts and dinners from Annetje Joubert, a third-generation Kloof dweller who will deliver (☎023 541 1107).

2

you can take them to watch the milking at sunrise, and walk around the farm looking at other farm animals.

ARRIVAL AND DEPARTURE
PRINCE ALBERT

By car The most direct route is via the N1 which avoids the mountain passes, but by far the most scenic is via Calitzdorp or Oudtshoorn across the Swartberg Pass.

By train The Cape Town–Johannesburg train stops at Prince Albert Rd Station, 45km from the hamlet, where you could arrange to be collected by your guesthouse, if they are willing. The trains are often late, and Prince Albert Rd Station has absolutely no facilities.

INFORMATION

Tourist information Church St (Mon–Fri 9am–5pm, Sat 9am–1pm; ☎023 541 1366, ⒲patourism.co.za). Supplies maps with accommodation, restaurants and craft shops, and can point you to other activities in the area.

ACCOMMODATION

★ **Cactus Blue Cottages** Church St, behind the National Centre, opposite the Swartberg Hotel ☎076 339 0888, ⒲cactusbluecottages.co.za. Two modern, funky cottages full of space, light and pleasing colours, overlooking a small vineyard. There is a stripy day bed to loll on, a collection of DVDs to watch, and a double mattress on an outside deck if you fancy a night under the stars. R700

Dennehof Guest House Off Christina de Wit St, on the outskirts of town ☎023 541 1227, ⒲dennehof.co.za. Five B&B rooms in a homestead that is a National Monument, full of farm furniture and collectibles. R800

Karoo Lodge 66 Church St ☎023 541 1467 or ☎082 692 7736, ⒲karoolodge.com. Reasonably priced, spacious accommodation in a B&B run by keen hosts who'll show you the ropes. They also have a good restaurant on site serving a variety of traditional Afrikaans/Cape Malay dishes. R800

Karoo Views Margrieta Prinsloo Rd ☎023 541 1929, ⒲www.karooview.co.za. Upmarket, comfortable self-catering in two modern Karoo-style cottages on the edge of town, with views of the Swartberg and surrounding countryside, but close enough to walk into town. R700

Mai's Guest House 81 Church St ☎023 541 1188, ⒲maisbandb.co.za. A comfortable stay in a restored nineteenth-century house with great linen, a/c and a pool, plus fab breakfasts under the vines, dished up by a full- of- beans Irish owner. R800

★ **Onse Rus** 47 Church St ☎023 541 1380, ⒲onserus .co.za. Cool, thatched B&B rooms attached to a restored Cape Dutch house, with welcoming and informed owners who serve you tea and chocolate cake on arrival, and do delicious home-made muesli and local yoghurt breakfasts, as well as the usual eggs. They also run tours to Gamkaskloof and into the Swartberg range. R840

EATING

Cafe Albert 44 Church St ☎023 541 1175. Quiche, salad, scones, muffins and a variety of coffees on the *stoep*. Interesting dishes include tortillas filled with kudu steak and home-made chicken pies (R50). Tues–Sun 8am–4pm.

2

★**Gallery Cafe** Church St ☎082 749 2128. Imaginative dishes by passionate chef Brent, who creates a relaxed ambience above the gallery, with balcony seating – first choice for an evening in Prince Albert, and best booked beforehand. Vegetarians and vegans are catered for, there are delightful starters, meat dishes such as kudu, springbok and chicken and home-made ice creams (mains around R90). Daily 10am–10pm.

Karoo Kombuis 18 Deurdrift St ☎023 541 1110.

Traditional fare from this part of the country, with a home-cooked feel and meat galore (mains R70). It has a nice atmosphere and is a little cheaper than the *Gallery*. Mon–Sat 6–10pm.

Ladida Farmstall At the south end of the main road. Snacks, excellent dried fruit and rusks, as well as local olives that are among the best in South Africa. In late summer you can buy boxes of freshly picked figs. Daily 8am–5pm.

Matjiesfontein

One of the quirkier manifestations of Victorian colonialism lies 250km northeast of Cape Town at the historic village of **MATJIESFONTEIN** (pronounced "Mikey's-fontayn"). Little more than two dusty streets beside a train track, the village resembles a film set rather than a Karoo *dorp*: every building, including the grand train station, is a classic period piece, with tin roofs, pastel walls, well-tended gardens and Victorian frills. At the eastern end of the main street is the centrepiece, the *Lord Milner*, a hotel decked out with turrets and balconies and fountains by the entrance. If you're passing by, make sure you stop at least for a look around.

The origins of this curious place lie in the tale of a young Scottish entrepreneur, **Jimmy Logan**, who came to Cape Town to work on the railways. He built Matjiesfontein as a health resort – making much play on the clean Karoo air – and it became a gathering point for the wealthy and influential around the turn of the last century.

Today the village is doing brisk trade as a treasured relic. You can still come here in the classical manner on the train from Cape Town to Jo'burg/Pretoria (see p.50).

ACCOMMODATION MATJIESFONTEIN

Lord Milner ☎023 561 3011, ⓦmatjiesfontein.com. Inside the *Lord Milner*, there are huge portraits on the wall, grand staircases, polished brass fittings and, perhaps taking the theme a touch too far, rather surly service from waitresses dressed in black and white, with doilies on their heads. For eating and drinking, the hotel has a dimly lit dining room and an aged and creaking bar. **R700**

Sutherland

Remote **SUTHERLAND**, fearfully known to South Africans as the coldest spot in the country and featured on every weather report, is actually most notable for its clear, unpolluted skies, and it's one of the handful of places in the world where scientists can study Deep Space. You can do a tour (see below) to see the Observatory – actually a hilltop covered with huge silver domes, housing massive telescopes where experts from all over the world spend freezing nights, extending human knowledge. The largest of all is **SALT** (the **South African Large Telescope**), the second-largest telescope in the southern hemisphere.

Observatory

18km east of Sutherland • Tours Mon–Fri & Sun 10.30am & 2.30pm, Sat 11.30am & 2.30pm (R30) • Mon, Wed, Fri & Sat 7pm (R50) • ☎023 571 2436

Day-time tours of the Observatory start from the informative visitors' centre and take you to see **SALT** – an extremely valuable and massive machine behind protective glass, which is powerful enough, with its 91 hexagonal mirrors, to be able to see just one candle were it placed on the moon, though only scientists at the Observatory actually get to look through it. The night tours, though, do provide telescopes for visitors and give you a talk on the stars.

INFORMATION AND ACCOMMODATION   SUTHERLAND

INFORMATION

Tourist information Main Rd (Mon–Fri 8am–5pm, Sat

9am–noon; ☎ 023 571 1265, ⓦ karoohoogland.co.za).

ACCOMMODATION

★ **Kambrokind B&B** 19 Piet Retief St ☎ 023 571 1405, ⓦ sutherlandinfo.co.za. Comfortable and warm rooms in a house where the big attraction is that the owner amateur astronomer Jurg Wagener sets up telescopes in

the garden for guests and gives a nightly stargazing talk. There is also an agreeable café on site, the Halley se Kom Eet (Halley's come eat). **R670**

Karoo National Park

Entrance gate is 2km south of Beaufort West • R100 • Gate daily 5am–10pm • Reception daily 7am–7pm • ☎ 023 415 2828, ⓦ sanparks .org/parks/karoo

With an unusually mountainous setting for the generally flattish and parched Karoo, the **Karoo National Park**'s attraction is in the landscape and the serene atmosphere – and it scores highly as a place to break the long drive between Johannesburg and Cape Town.

Near the main restcamp there is an environmental **education centre**, along with three **trails**: an 11km day-walk; a short but informative tree trail; and a very imaginative fossil trail (designed to accommodate wheelchairs and incorporating Braille boards), which tells the fascinating 250-million-year geological history of the area and shows fossils of the unusual animals that lived here in the times when the Karoo was a vast inland sea. While there are some **black rhino**, big game is limited, although there are some impressive raptors, including the **black eagle**.

Park reception 10km into the park. There's a shop selling basic foodstuffs and a restaurant (breakfast and dinner daily), with a pool nearby.

ACCOMMODATION   KAROO NATIONAL PARK

★ **Main Rest Camp** Entrance 2km south of Beaufort West ☎ 023 415 2828, ⓦ sanparks.org/parks/karoo. Thirty fully equipped chalets and cottages strung out on either side of the main complex, all positioned with lovely outlooks onto the Karoo landscape ; the rate is for a minimum of two people and includes breakfast in the restaurant, which is open to day as well as overnight visitors. The campsite is hidden away over a rise. Camping **R215**, double **R810**

★ **Matoppo Inn** On the corner of Bird and Meintjies sts, Beaufort West ☎ 023 415 1055, ⓦ www .matoppoinn.co.za. Elegant rooms with brass beds and antique furniture, as well as standard rooms with more modern furnishing, in the town's old *drostdy*, or magistrate's house. The gardens are beautiful – it's a green oasis in the deserty Karoo – and there's a pool, good food all day, and a tranquil atmosphere. **R640**

The Overberg interior and the Whale Coast

East of the Winelands lies a vaguely defined region known as the **Overberg** (Afrikaans for "over the mountain"). In the seventeenth century, when Stellenbosch, Franschhoek and Paarl were remote outposts, everywhere beyond them was, to the Dutch settlers, a fuzzy hinterland drifting off into the arid sands of the Karoo.

Of the two main routes through the Overberg, the **N2** strikes out across the interior, a four- to five hour stretch of sheep, wheat and mountains. North of the N2 is **Greyton**, a charming, oak-lined village used by Capetonians as a relaxing weekend retreat, and the starting point of the **Boesmanskloof Traverse** – a terrific two-day trail across the mountains into the Karoo. The historic Moravian mission station of **Genadendal**, ten minutes down the road from Greyton, has a strange Afro-Germanic ambience that offers a couple of hours' pleasant strolling. **Swellendam**, with its well-preserved streetscape with serene Cape Dutch buildings and superb country museum, is favoured for the first night's stop on a Garden Route tour.

2

The real draw of the area is the **Whale Coast**, close enough for an easy outing from Cape Town, yet surprisingly undeveloped. The exception is popular **Hermanus**, which owes its fame to its status as the whale-watching capital of South Africa. The whole of this southern Cape coast is, in fact, prime territory for land-based whale-watching. Also along this section of coast is **Cape Agulhas**, the southernmost point on the continent, where rocks peter into the ocean. Nearby, and more exclusive, is **Arniston**, one of the best-preserved fishing villages in the country, and a little to its east the **De Hoop Nature Reserve**, an exciting wilderness of bleached dunes, craggy coast and more whales.

Greyton

GREYTON, a small, peaceful village 145km from Cape Town, is a favourite weekend destination for Capetonians, based around a core of Georgian and Victorian buildings, shaded by grand old oaks, and tucked away at the edge of the Riviersonderend (meaning "river with no end") Mountains. It offers good guesthouses, cafés, restaurants and places to walk, most notably the **Boesmanskloof Traverse** hike, which crosses the mountains to a point 14km from McGregor.

ARRIVAL AND INFORMATION   GREYTON

By car The best route to drive here is the sealed R406 from just west of Caledon; don't attempt the untarred route from Riviersonderend, which will hammer your suspension.

Tourist information 29 Main St (Mon–Fri 9am–5pm, Sat 9am–3pm, Sun 9am–1pm; ☎ 028 254 9414, ⓦ www .greyton.net).

ACCOMMODATION

It's worth staying somewhere with a fireplace if you're here in winter, as it can be cold in this mountainous terrain, and conversely look for a pool in summer.

Auberge Greyton Corner of Oak St and Main Rd ☎ 028 254 9192. Simple, uncluttered farm-style rooms – if you're planning on hiking and just need a bed for the night or two, this is the place to stay. **R350**

Barnards Boutique Hotel 16 Main Rd ☎ 028 254 9394, ⓦ barnardshotel.co.za. Modern and comfortable rooms in a fashionable establishment with a lovely pool and a great bar. The cheaper doubles are more functional, above the bar, while the duplexes at the back (R950) are quieter and have some self-catering facilities. **R600**

★ **Blue Hippo Tipi Village** 4km outside Greyton on the road to Riviersonderend ☎ 028 254 9595, ⓦ www .bluehippo.co.za. Fruit orchards surround a shady,

spacious campsite next to a river. You can pitch your own tent, or even better, sleep in a large, stand-up tepee that sleeps five on futons. There is a fully kitted-out communal kitchen, ropes and swings in the trees and several fireplaces. You can walk to a dam for swimming and picnics, and they have a herd of horses for fabulous riding. Camping **R100**, tepee **R300**

High Hopes 89 Main Rd ☎ 028 254 9898, ⓦ www .highhopes.co.za. One of the best B&Bs in town, in a beautiful country-style home set in large gardens with a swimming pool. Besides four rooms, there's a self-contained unit with a kitchen, which can be taken on a B&B or self-catering basis. A variety of therapies, including massage, is on offer too. **R800**

EATING

The town has a short Saturday market at the corner of Main Rd and Cross Market St (10am–noon), to which locals bring their produce: organic vegetables, fabulous and well-priced cheeses, decadent cakes, breads, biscuits and preserves.

CALEDON SPA

The thermal springs at **Caledon Spa and Casino** (Tues–Sun 8am–7pm; R150; ☎ 028 214 5100), signposted off the N2, make a fun day-trip out of Cape Town, or a restorative stop off the N2. The Victorians built a pool filled with steamy, naturally brown water where the Khoi people had once had wallowing holes, and now there is a series of pools of varying temperatures to luxuriate in. There's also a steam room and sauna, but bring your own towel and robe.

THE BOESMANSKLOOF TRAVERSE

The 14km **Boesmanskloof Traverse** takes you from the gentle, oak-lined streets of Greyton across the Riviersonderend mountain range to the glaring Karoo scrubland around the town of McGregor (see p.186). No direct roads connect the two towns; to drive from one to the other involves a circuitous two-hour journey.

The classic way to cover the Traverse is to walk from Greyton to **Die Galg** (14km from McGregor), where people commonly spend the night, returning the same way to Greyton the following day. The Traverse rises and falls a fair bit, so you'll have to contend with a lot of strenuous uphill walking. If you're based in Greyton and don't want to do the whole thing, walk to **Oak Falls**, 9km from Greyton, and back. Composed of a series of cascades, it's the highlight of the route, its most impressive feature being a large pool where you can rest and swim in cola-coloured water.

TRAIL PRACTICALITIES

You're free to walk the first 5km of the trail and back, but to walk to Oak Falls or Die Galg, or to complete the whole route from Greyton to Die Galg, you will need a permit (R35 per person per day), booked in advance from the Greyton tourist information office (see opposite).

Barnard's Boutique Hotel 16 Main Rd ☎028 254 9394. Nice setting for a sundowner, or champagne, on the veranda or by the fireplace inside. The food is contemporary country, such as caramelized onion with gnocchi (R100), and the big screen at the pub draws sports fans. There are pavement braziers in the evening, livening up the street. Daily 8am–10pm.

Oak and Vigne Café Ds Botha St ☎028 254 9037. An extremely popular restaurant situated in an old cottage with an oak-shaded terrace where you can savour Mediterranean-influenced country breakfasts, teas and gourmet lunches – including home-made ice cream with locally made chocolate for pudding (R60). Mon, Wed & Sun 8am–5pm, Thurs–Sat 8am–10.30pm.

Peccadillo's 23 Main Rd ☎028 254 9066. You're unlikely to eat better than at this bistro, with its seasonal blackboard specials. The food has a strong Mediterranean influence; try the local trout dishes, or fish pie with capers (R85). This is also a good place to try boutique wines, which the owner collects from winelands excursions. Children can be accommodated. Daily noon–2pm, Thurs–Mon 7.30–10pm.

Via's Deli 31 Main Rd ☎028 254 9190. Vegetarian buffet lunches sold by weight and a reliable outlet for deli food and organic vegetables. Great salads, soups and stews. Tues–Sun 9am–4pm.

Genadendal

GENADENDAL, whose name means "valley of grace", was founded in 1737 by Moravians, and some of the ochre and earthy-pink architecture hints at Central European influences. Just 6km from Greyton, it's definitely worth roaming around. The village's focus is around **Church Square**, dominated by a very Germanic church building dating back to 1891. The old bell outside dates back to the eighteenth century, when it became the centre of a flaming row between the local farmers and the mission station. The scrap broke out when missionary Georg Schmidt annoyed the local white farmers by forming a small Christian congregation with impoverished Khoi – who were on the threshold of extinction – and giving refuge to maltreated labourers from local farms. What really got the farmers' goat was the fact that while they, white Christians, were illiterate, Schmidt was teaching native people, whom they considered uncivilized, to read and write. The Dutch Reformed Church, under the control of the Dutch East India Company, waded in when Schmidt began baptizing converts, and prohibited the mission from ringing the bell which called the faithful to prayer.

In 1838 it established the first teacher training college in the country, which the government closed in 1926, on the grounds that coloured people didn't need tertiary education and should be employed as workers on local farms – a policy that effectively ground the community into poverty. In 1995, in recognition of the mission's role, Nelson Mandela renamed his official residence in Cape Town "Genadendal".

Swellendam

SWELLENDAM is an attractive historic town at the foot of the Langeberg, 220km from Cape Town. With one of the best country museums in South Africa, it's a congenial stop along the N2 between Cape Town and the Garden Route. And because of its ample supply of good accommodation and its position – poised between the coastal De Hoop Nature Reserve and the Langeberg – it's a suitable base for spending a day or two exploring this part of the Overberg, with the Bontebok National Park, stomping ground of an attractive type of antelope, close at hand to the south. The town is built along a very long main road with no traffic lights; it's most attractive at either end, with a mundane shopping area in the middle. The eastern end is dominated by the museum complex which serves as a tourist centre of sorts.

Brief history

South Africa's third-oldest white settlement, Swellendam was established in 1745 by Baron Gustav van Imhoff, a visiting Dutch East India Company bigwig. He was deeply concerned about the "moral degeneration" of burghers who were trekking further and further from Cape Town and out of Company control. Of no less concern to the Baron was the loss of revenue from these "vagabonds" who were neglecting to pay the Company for the right to hold land and were fiddling their annual tax returns. The town grew into a prosperous rural centre known for its wagon-making, and for being the last "civilized" port of call for trekboers heading out into the interior. The income generated from this helped build Swellendam's gracious homes, many of which went up in smoke in the fire of 1865, which razed much of the town centre.

Oefeningshuis

36 Voortrek St

The only building in the centre to survive the town's 1865 fire was the Cape Dutch-style **Oefeningshuis**. Built in 1838, it was first used as a place for religious activity, then as a school for freed slaves, and has surreal-looking clocks with frozen hands carved into either gable end, below which there's a real clock.

Dutch Reformed church

Voortrek St

The imposing **Dutch Reformed church**, dating from 1910, incorporates Gothic windows, a Baroque spire, and Cape Dutch gables into a wedding cake of a building that agreeably holds its own, against the odds, and certainly still draws a good crowd on Sundays.

Drostdy Museum

18 Swellegrebel St • Mon–Fri 9am–4.45pm, Sat & Sun 10am–3.45pm • R15

On the east side of town, a short way from the centre, is the excellent **Drostdy Museum**, a collection of historic buildings arranged around large grounds, with a lovely nineteenth-century Cape garden. The centrepiece is the *drostdy* itself, built in 1747 as the seat of the *landdrost*, a magistrate-cum-commissioner sent out by the Dutch East India Company to control the outer reaches of its territory. The building conforms to the beautiful limewashed, thatched and shuttered Cape Dutch style of the eighteenth century, but the furnishings are of nineteenth-century vintage.

HORSERIDING IN SWELLENDAM

One of the best things to do in Swellendam is to go **horseriding** in the forests and mountains at the eastern edge of town, securely seated in a Western-style saddle. **Two Feathers Horse Trails** (☎ 082 494 8279, ⓦ www.twofeathers.co.za) offers riding by the hour for R200.

ARRIVAL AND INFORMATION
SWELLENDAM

By bus Buses between Cape Town and Port Elizabeth, including the Baz Bus, pull in diagonally opposite the *Swellengrebel Hotel*, 91 Voortrek St, in the centre of town. Tickets for buses can be purchased from Oasis Supermarket, close to the hotel.

By car Swellendam is an easy 220km drive along the N2 from Cape Town.

Tourist information 36 Voortrek St (Mon–Fri 9am–5pm, Sat & Sun 9am–1pm; ☎028 514 2770, ⓦwww.swellendamtourism.co.za).

ACCOMMODATION

★ **Augusta de Mist** 3 Human St ☎028 514 2425, ⓦwww.augustademist.co.za. A 200-year-old homestead with three beautifully renovated cottages, two garden suites and a family unit, mostly with fireplaces. A rambling terraced garden and a pool complete the picture. There is a good restaurant on site for dinner, but you need to book in advance. R1000

★ **Cypress Cottage** 3 Voortrek St ⓦwww .cypresscottage.info. Seven charming rooms, decorated with antiques, in the back garden of a grand house, one of the oldest in town, as well as two rooms inside the main house. The friendly owner is an excellent gardener. Great value. R700

Eenuurkop Huisie 8km from town on the Ashton Rd ☎028 514 1447. Two self-catering cottages, one with three bedrooms, the other with one, in a stunning setting with great views and access to mountain walks. R650

Hermitage Huisies 3km from town on the R60 to Ashton ☎028 514 2308/082 380 2080, ⓦwww .wildebraam.co.za. Two restored labourers' self-catering cottages, sleeping four or five people, plus a flatlet for two, on a smallholding with a duck pond and grazing sheep and horses, ideal for families. On the next-door farm, *Wildebraam* (same contact details) has a couple more cottages, which are a little more upmarket. If you

want to ride, you can arrange in advance to be taken up the mountain, plus there is berry picking in Nov & Dec and a liquor-tasting cellar at *Wildebraam*. R470

Klippe Rivier Homestead Signposted off the western end of town ☎028 514 3341, ⓦwww.klipperivier.com. Swellendam's most formal and luxurious accommodation, in a beautiful 1825 Cape Dutch homestead with six utterly comfortable country-style bedrooms, each with a patio or veranda. There's also a secluded cottage and saltwater swimming pool, gorgeous gardens and fabulous breakfasts. No under-8s. R1990

Lulu's B&B 10 Voortrek St ☎028 514 2202 or ☎082 343 4648. A well-run B&B, centrally located, with two en-suite rooms and a self-catering loft apartment (sleeping up to eight) above. It's a good choice on a tight budget. R400

Swellendam Backpackers 5 Lichtenstein St ☎028 514 2648, ⓦwww.swellendambackpackers.co.za. Swellendam's only hostel is a friendly place, well situated near the Marloth Nature Reserve and museum, with a large campsite, dorms and decent doubles; staff can also arrange activities including horseriding and hiking permits for Marloth. Children are welcome, as there's lots of space, and while this isn't a big party place, there is a bar on the premises. Dorm R90, doubles R410

EATING

De Kolonie 26 Swellengrebel St ☎083 286 6303. Set in a historic thatched building at the Museum complex, this is a good place to rest your legs and have a salad, sandwich or a traditional Afrikaans-styled dish (R80). Mon–Sat 9am–5pm, Thurs & Fri till 10pm.

The Old Gaol Coffee Shop Church Square, 8a Voortrek St ☎028 514 3847. A great place with indoor and outdoor seating where you can get milk tart in a copper pan (R40) and *roosterkoek*, traditional bread made on an open fire, with nice fillings. Daily 8.30am–5pm.

Pennantwing Café and Gift Shop 5 Swellengrebel, near the bridge, east end ☎028 514 3957. This café has the best coffee in town, with great scones and cakes, combined with the opportunity to browse around unusual, locally-made crafts and art pieces. Mon–Sat 8.30am–4.30pm.

Woodpecker Deli Voortrek St, west end ☎028 514 2924. Pizzas, pasta, soups, sandwiches and light meals are on the menu here, plus great burgers (R70). This is a good choice if you are in town for one night and don't want a formal or expensive meal. Mon–Sat 9.30am–9pm, Sun 9.30am–3pm.

Bontebok National Park

Just 6km south of Swellendam along the Breede River • Daily: May–Sept 7am–6pm; Oct–April 7am–7pm • R50, overnight visitors free • ☎028 514 2735, ⓦsanparks.org/parks/bontebok

Bontebok National Park is a compact 28-square-kilometre reserve at the foot of the Langeberg range that makes a relaxing overnight stop between Cape Town and the Garden Route. The park was established in 1931 to save the Cape's dwindling population of bontebok, an attractive antelope with distinctive cappuccino, chocolate-brown and white markings on its forehead and hindquarters. By 1930, hunting in the area had reduced the number of animals to a mere thirty. Their survival has happily been secured and there are now three hundred of them in the park, as well as populations in other game and nature reserves in the province. There are no big cats in the park, but **mammals** you might encounter include rare Cape mountain zebra, red hartebeest and grey rhebok, and there are more than 120 **bird species**. It's also a rich environment for **fynbos**, with nearly five hundred species here, including erica, gladioli and proteas. Apart from game viewing, there are opportunities to swim in the Breede River, hike a couple of short nature trails and fish.

ACCOMMODATION   BONTEBOK NATIONAL PARK

★ **Park accommodation** Self-catering accommodation is available in ten fully equipped chalets, or you can camp. A shop at the park entrance sells drinks and sweets, but you'll need to bring your own food with you as there is no restaurant. Swimming in the river, close to the chalets, is delightful. Camping R180, chalet R775

Pringle Bay and Betty's Bay

Stony Point Penguin Colony along the R44 • Daily sunrise–sunset • R10

The coastal drive along the R44 from Cape Town to Hermanus via Pringle and Betty's Bay is spectacular – one of the most beautiful drives in the country – though this stretch is home to a series of rather unattractive, ever developing settlements, including **Pringle Bay** and **Betty's Bay**. The only reason to stop in the latter is for its colony of African (jackass) penguins, at **Stony Point Penguin Colony**, which can be seen from the well-signposted wooden boardwalk.

Harold Porter National Botanical Garden

In the mountains just above Betty's Bay • Mon–Fri 8am–4pm, Sat & Sun 8am–5pm • R15 • ☎ 028 272 9311

Harold Porter National Botanical Garden is a wild sanctuary of coastal and montane *fynbos* that makes a good stop along the R44, if only to picnic or have tea at its outdoor café. The relatively compact botanical garden extends over two square kilometres from the mountains, through marshland down to coastal dunes. Once here, you'll probably get lured at least some of the way up the *kloof* that runs through the reserve; as you get higher up, you're treated to sea views in one direction and rugged mountains in the other.

Although wildlife in the form of small **antelope**, **baboons** and **leopards** is present, they are rarely sighted and it's more worthwhile to look out instead for the birds and blooms. Four **trails** of between one and three hours meander through the gardens, but you can just as easily take yourself off on an impromptu stroll, up and across the red-stained waters (the colour stems from phenols and tannins leaching from the *fynbos*) running through Disa Kloof.

ACCOMMODATION   PRINGLE BAY AND BETTY'S BAY

★ **Moonstruck on Pringle Bay** 264 Hangklip Rd, Pringle Bay ☎ 028 273 8162, ⓦ moonstruck.co.za. This romantic and palatial modern guesthouse offers four huge rooms with sea-facing balconies. It's a short walk from the guesthouse to a bay with good swimming. R1600

EATING

★ **Hook, Line and Sinker** Off Pass Rd, Pringle Bay ☎ 028 273 8688. The best place to eat in the area, and an event in itself, run by a husband-and-wife team in their own home. There is only seasonal fish and steak on the menu, cooked on an open fire by larger-than-life Stephan, who has spent years deep-sea diving along the West Coast. Prices are moderate, and you won't eat better fish in the country; you can also buy the catch of the day to take home. Reservations essential, and directions are given to reach the restaurant when you book. Lunch Tues–Sun from noon, dinner daily from 7pm.

Hermanus

On the edge of rocky cliffs and backed by mountains, **HERMANUS**, 112km east of Cape Town, sits at the northernmost end of Walker Bay, an inlet whose protective curve attracts calving whales as it slides south to the promontory of Danger Point. From about July, southern right whales (see box, p.205) start appearing in the warmer sheltered bays of the Western Cape, and the town trumpets itself as the **whale capital** of South Africa. To prove it, an official whale crier (purportedly the world's only one) struts around armed with a mobile phone and a dried kelp horn through which he yells the latest sightings.

There is still the barest trace of a once-quiet cliff-edge fishing village around the historic harbour and in some understated seaside cottages, but for the most part the town has gorged itself on its whale-generated income. An almost continuous five-kilometre cliff path through coastal *fynbos* hugs the rocky coastline from the old harbour to Grotto Beach in the eastern suburbs, and it's from this path that you will spot whales.

Main Road, the continuation of the R43, meanders through Hermanus, briefly becoming Seventh Street. Market Square, just above the old harbour and to the south of Main Street, is the closest thing to a centre, and it's here you'll find the heaviest concentration of restaurants, craft shops and flea markets – the principal forms of entertainment in town when the whales are taking time out.

Old Harbour Museum

At the Old Harbour • Mon–Sat 9am–4.30pm, Sun noon–4pm • R20

The **Old Harbour Museum**, just below Market Square, is home to some rather uncompelling displays, among which you'll find lots of fishing tackle and some

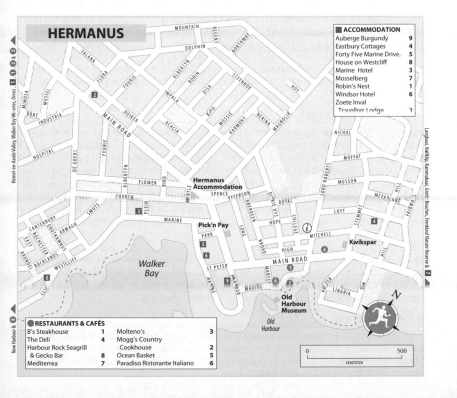

■ ACCOMMODATION	
Auberge Burgundy	9
Eastbury Cottages	4
Forty Five Marine Drive	5
House on Westcliff	8
Marine Hotel	3
Mosselberg	7
Robin's Nest	1
Windsor Hotel	6
Zoete Inval	
Travellers Lodge	2

● RESTAURANTS & CAFÉS			
B's Steakhouse	1	Molteno's	3
The Deli	4	Mogg's Country	
Harbour Rock Seagrill		Cookhouse	2
& Gecko Bar	8	Ocean Basket	5
Mediterrea	7	Paradiso Ristorante Italiano	6

sharks' jaws. Outside, a few colourful boats, used by local fishermen from the mid-eighteenth to mid-nineteenth centuries, create a photogenic vignette in the tiny harbour.

New Harbour
A couple of kilometres west of town along Westcliff

The **New Harbour** is a working fishing harbour, dramatically surrounded by steep cliffs, projecting a gutsy counterpoint to the more manicured central area. The whales sometimes enter the harbour – and there's nowhere better to watch them than from the *Harbour Rock* (see p.206).

Beaches and swimming

Just below the *Marine Hotel* on Marine Drive, a beautiful tidal pool offers the only sea swimming around the town centre's craggy coast. For sandy beaches, you have to head out east to the suburbs, where you'll find a decent choice, starting with secluded Langbaai, closest to town, a cove beneath cliffs at the bottom of Sixth Avenue that has a narrow strip of beach and is excellent for swimming. Voelklip, at the bottom of Eighth Avenue, has grassed terraces, toilets, a nearby café for tea and is great for picnics if you prefer your sandwiches unseasoned with sand. Adjacent is Kammabaai, with the best surfing break around Hermanus, and 1km further east, Grotto Beach, which marks the start of a 12km curve of dazzlingly white sand that stretches all the way to De Kelders.

Fernkloof Nature Reserve
On the east side of town, off Main Rd on Theron St • Daily dawn–dusk • Free

The **Fernkloof Nature Reserve** encompasses fifteen square kilometres of mountainous terrain and offers sweeping views of Walker Bay. It has some 40km of **waymarked footpaths**, including a 4.5-kilometre circular nature trail. Visiting is an excellent way to get close to the astonishing variety of delicate *fynbos* (over a thousand species have been identified in the reserve), much of it flowering species that attract scores of birds, including the brightly coloured sunbirds and sugarbirds endemic to the area.

ARRIVAL AND DEPARTURE | HERMANUS

By car The N2 from Cape Town, cutting south onto the R43 at Bot River, is more direct (1hr 30min) than the winding road that hugs the coast from Strand, leaving the N2 just before Sir Lowrie's Pass, which is a lot more scenic (2hr). Hermanus is 140km from Cape Town.

By shuttle There is no public transport, but a couple of shuttles run between Hermanus and Cape Town International airport or Cape Town central (both

R350–R700/person depending on number of people): Splash Bus (☎028 316 4004, ✉splash@hermanus.co.za) and Bernardus Shuttle Service (☎028 316 1093 or ☎083 658 7848). There is no timetable; you book the transport to suit your needs, or fit in with the schedule of other passengers, for a cheaper price.

By Baz Bus The Baz Bus stops off at Bot River and your hostel can arrange for a pick-up from there.

INFORMATION

Tourist information At the old station building in Mitchell St (Mon–Sat 9am–5pm; ☎028 312 2629). Stocks maps, useful brochures about the area and has an internet café, and they also operate a free accommodation-finding

service and can take bookings for boat-based and aerial whale-watching, as well as shark-cage diving trips. In September, check out the popular whale festival; ⓦwhalefestival.co.za.

ACCOMMODATION

The most popular coastal destination outside Cape Town, Hermanus is awash with accommodation. If you want something a little more countrified, head off to Stanford, twenty minutes' drive away around the curve of the bay, though there are no beaches. Alternatively, head further along the coast to Gansbaai (see p.208), an ugly place, but one with great whale-viewing in season from the windows of any sea-facing room.

SOUTHERN CAPE WHALE-WATCHING

The Southern Cape, including Cape Town, provides some of the easiest and best places in the world for **whale-watching**. You don't need to take a pricey boat tour to get out to sea; if you come at the right time of year, whales are easily visible from the shore, although a good pair of binoculars will come in useful.

All nine of the great whale species of the southern hemisphere pass by South Africa's shores, but the most commonly seen are **southern right whales** (their name derives from being the "right" one to kill because of their high oil and bone yields and the fact that, conveniently, they float when dead). Southern right whales are black and easily recognized from their pale, brownish callosities. These unappealing patches of raised, roughened skin on their snouts and heads have a distinct pattern on each animal, which helps scientists keep track of them.

Female whales come inshore to calve in sheltered bays, and stay to nurse their young for up to three months. **July to October** is the best time to see them, although they start appearing in June and some stay around until December. When the calves are big enough, the whales head off south again, to colder, stormy waters, where they feed on enormous quantities of plankton, making up for the nursing months when the females don't eat at all. Though you're most likely to see females and young, you may see males early in the season boisterously flopping about the females, though they neither help rear the calves nor form lasting bonds with females.

What gives away the presence of a whale is the **blow or spout**, a tall smoky plume which disperses after a few seconds and is actually the whale breathing out before it surfaces. If luck is on your side, you may see whales **breaching** – the movement when they thrust high out of the water and fall back with a great splash.

THE WHALE COAST'S HOTTEST WHALE SPOTS

In **Hermanus**, the best vantage points are the concrete cliff paths which ring the rocky shore from New Harbour to Grotto Beach. There are interpretation boards at three of the popular vantage points (Gearing's Point, Die Gang and Bientang's Cave). At their worst, the paths can be lined two or three deep with people.

Aficionados claim that **De Kelders** (see p.208), some 39km east of Hermanus, is even better, while **De Hoop Nature Reserve** (see p.212), east of Arniston, is reckoned by some to be the ultimate place along the entire Southern African coast.

WHALE-WATCHING BY BOAT

Several operators offer **boat trips** from Hermanus; they're all essentially the same, so your choice of whom to go with will depend more on the time and day than the reliability of the operator. For starters, try **Hermanus Whale Cruises** (☎028 313 2722, ⓦhermanus-whale-cruises.co.za; R550), a coloured fishing village community project. Boats go out five times daily from the New Harbour from June 1 to Dec 31.

Marine Dynamics (☎028 384 0406, ⓦwhalewatchsa.com) is another reputable operator; whale-watching trips of two-and-a-half hours go out daily from Kleinbaai at Gansbaai at 9.15am, 11.45am and 2.15pm (R900).

Auberge Burgundy 16 Harbour Rd ☎028 313 1201, ⓦauberge.co.za; map p.203. A Provençal-style country house in the town centre, with a stylish Mediterranean feel. The rooms are light and airy with imported French fabrics, and there's a lavender garden. **R1300**

Eastbury Cottages 36 Luyt St ☎028 312 1258, ⓦeastburycottage.co.za; map p.203. Three very reasonably priced, fully equipped self-catering cottages close to the *Marine Hotel*. Prices vary depending on group size, and you can add breakfast for R60. **R450**

Forty Five Marine Drive 45 Marine Drive ☎028 312 3610, ⓦhermanusesplanade.com; map p.203. Cliffside self-catering apartments of varying sizes and prices, with terrific views across the bay. At their sister establishment, the *Esplanade*, on Marine Drive, there are cheaper self-catering units as well as some backpacker rooms. Backpacker room **R190**, apartment **R3F0**

House on Westcliff 96 Westcliff Rd ☎028 313 2388, ⓦwestcliffhouse.co.za; map p.203. This B&B is situated just out of the centre near the new harbour and boasts six bedrooms in a classic Cape-style house with a protected, tranquil garden and a solar-heated pool and jacuzzi. All rooms are en suite and have their own entrance off the garden. **R800**

2

Marine Hotel Marine Drive ☎028 313 1000, Ⓦwww.marine-hermanus.co.za; map p.203. Treat yourself to pure luxury at this five-star Relais & Chateaux Hotel. The tastefully decorated seafront rooms are set in verdant gardens, and there's also an expensive spa on site. R4200

Mosselberg Tenth Ave, Voelklip ☎086 111 9000, Ⓦmosselberg.co.za; map p.203. Five-star, five-roomed guesthouse right at the beach with a mellow atmosphere and superbly designed spaces. It's particularly worth checking out during low season, when rooms are far cheaper. R2800

Robin's Nest 10 Meadow Ave ☎028 316 1597; map p.203. Three fully equipped, self-catering studio flats above a garage in a garden, 4km west of the centre. Reached through the Hemel-en-Aarde shopping village,

these purpose-built, two-storey flats sleep two and have good mountain views. R450

Windsor Hotel 49 Marine Drive ☎028 312 3727, Ⓦwindsorhotel.co.za; map p.203. This seafront hotel offers a full range of accommodation right on the cliff edge. It's ideally situated in the centre of Hermanus and guests can whale-watch from the dining room, lounges and almost half of the bedrooms. R1360

Zoete Inval Travellers Lodge 23 Main Rd ☎028 312 1242, Ⓦzoeteinval.co.za; map p.203. A quiet and relaxing hostel, with a distinct lack of party vibe, comprising dorms, doubles and family suites and extras such as good coffee, a jacuzzi and a fireplace. They'll organize all tours and outings, and arrange transport to and from the Baz Bus drop-off in Bot River. Dorm R120, double R400

EATING AND DRINKING

Seafood is the obvious thing to eat in Hermanus – and you'll find plenty of restaurants serving it – though the views are generally better than the food. Book well ahead at weekends; without a booking, you can always get fish and chips at the harbour.

B's Steakhouse Hemel-en-Aarde Village ☎028 316 3625; map p.203. A friendly and buzzing independent steakhouse serving brilliantly prepared and reasonably priced slabs of beef (R90). Its formidable wine list and child-friendliness makes it an obvious choice for families. Tues–Sun noon–10pm.

The Deli Main Rd ☎028 313 2137; map p.203. This friendly café is a good spot for coffee, breakfasts and light meals (R50). Their cheese soufflé is particularly recommended. Mon–Fri 8am–5pm, Sat & Sun 8am–2pm.

Harbour Rock Seagrill & Gecko Bar New Harbour ☎028 312 2920; map p.203. This very busy, trendy

restaurant serves up fish and chips and other seafood dishes (R130); the stunning views from the cliffs make it an excellent place for sundowners and sushi. It's always packed and has occasional live music, which makes Friday nights, in particular, quite raucous. Summer daily 9am–10pm; winter Mon–Fri noon, Sat & Sun 9am–10pm.

Mediterrea 83 Marine Drive ☎028 313 1685; map p.203. A great gourmet restaurant with good views of Walker Bay. The Mediterranean-style food is expensive (mains R130), but you pay for the location right on the seafront and its reputation – booking is essential in season. Daily 7–10pm, Sun also 12.30–2.30pm.

WALKER BAY WINERIES

Some of South Africa's top wines come from the **Hemel-en-Aarde Valley**, about fifteen minutes' drive west of Hermanus. Even if you have no time for tasting, Hermanus has possibly the best wine shop in South Africa, the **Wine Village** (Hemel-en-Aarde Village, corner R43 and R320; ☎028 316 3988, Ⓦwww.wine-village.co.za; Mon–Sat 9am–6pm & Sun 10am–3pm), home to a staggering selection of labels from all the country's various wine-producing districts, covering a vast price range. You can drive through the valley, stopping off at the different wineries.

Hamilton Russell ☎028 312 3595, Ⓦwww.hamiltonrussellvineyards.com. The longest established of the Walker Bay wineries, which produces some of South Africa's priciest wines. Mon–Fri 9am–5pm, Sat 9am–1pm.

Bouchard Finlayson ☎028 312 3515, Ⓦwww.bouchardfinlayson.co.za. Adjacent to Hamilton Russell, this is another establishment with a formidable reputation, and a wider range of wines

than its neighbour. Mon–Fri 9am–5pm, Sat 10.30am–12.30pm.

Newton Johnson 8km from the Hemel-en-Aarde turn-off ☎028 312 3864, Ⓦwww.newtonjohnson.com. Furthest from Hermanus is this family-run winery. It's worth the visit for their estate restaurant, Heaven (Tues–Sun noon–3pm), which is rated for a good blackboard-menu lunch and superb views of the valley and vineyards. Mon–Fri 9am–4pm, Sat 9am–noon.

Molteno's Viljoen St, On Rus ☎028 316 2658; map p.203. Friendly staff, reasonable prices, generous portions and consistently reliable Italian-style food (mains R100) make this a good bet, though it is out of town and without a sea view. Open Mon & Wed–Sat 6–10pm, Sun noon–2.30pm.

★ **Mogg's Country Cookhouse** Hemel-en-Aarde Valley, 12km from Hermanus along the R320 to Caledon ☎028 312 4321; map p.203. A most unlikely location for one of Hermanus's most successful restaurants – a farm cottage – with superb views across the valley. *Mogg's* is an intimate place that's always full and unfailingly excellent, serving whatever country-cooking surprises take the fancy of chefs Jenny Mogg and her daughter Julia

(mains around R90). Booking essential. Wed–Sun noon–2.30pm, Fri & Sat also 7–9.30pm.

Ocean Basket Fashion Square, 137 Main Rd ☎028 312 1313; map p.203. Moderately priced and consistently reliable seafood chain restaurant in a fabulous setting, often with queues outside. Mains around R65. Daily 11.30am–2.30pm & 6–9pm.

Paradiso Ristorante Italiano 83 Marine Drive ☎028 313 1153; map p.203. Situated behind the village square, near the water in a zone of tourist restaurants, this Italian place offers a number of veal, chicken and prawn dishes (R75), in addition to delicious pizza and pasta. Mon–Fri noon–5pm & 5.30–10pm, Sat & Sun 11.30am–10pm.

Stanford

East of Hermanus, the R43 takes a detour inland around the attractive Klein River Lagoon, past the pretty riverside hamlet of **STANFORD**. Despite its proximity to hyped-up Hermanus, this historic village, established in 1857, has become something of a refuge for arty types seeking a tranquil escape from the urban rat race. Stanford's principal attraction is its streetscape of simple **Victorian architecture** that includes limewashed houses and sandstone cottages – as well as an Anglican church – with thatched roofs that glow under the late afternoon sun.

The town's northern boundary is the attractive Klein River, and there are a couple of great places to stay out of town along the river. There's rich birdlife in and among the rustling reed beds lining the river banks, where you stand a chance of spotting the flashy malachite kingfisher; a great boat trip for birdwatching is run by Platanna River Cruises (☎084 583 5389; R100). For canoe or kayak hire, try Ernie (☎083 310 0952).

Birkenhead Brewery

Across the R43 from Stanford, along the R326 • Tasting tours Wed–Fri 11am or 3pm • Free • Beer tasting and sales Wed–Sun 11am–5pm • Pub Mon–Sun 10am–4pm • ☎028 341 0183, ✆www.birkenhead.co.za

Although the **Birkenhead Brewery** bills itself as a craft brewery, the gleaming stainless-steel pipes and equipment inside soon dispel any images of bloodshot hillbillies knocking up a bit of moonshine on the quiet. This is a slick operation and a great place to go for a pub lunch or to buy beers that put those of SAB, South Africa's big brewing near-monopoly, in their place.

ARRIVAL AND INFORMATION   STANFORD

By car Stanford is 173km from Cape Town, and 33km east of Hermanus. There is no public transport to Stanford.
Tourist information Next to the library and opposite the

Spar mini-supermarket in the middle of the village (Mon–Fri 8am–4pm & Sat 9am–5pm, Sun 9am–1pm; ☎028 341 0340, ✆www.stanfordinfo.co.za).

STANFORD CHEESE AND WINE

Two kilometres beyond Birkenhead brewery, and 7km from Stanford, is the **Klein River Cheese Farm** (Mon–Fri 9am–5pm, Sat 9am–1pm), which offers tastings of its famous Gruyère, Leiden, Colby and Dando, or you can buy one of its picnic baskets to have under the trees next to the river (Sept 15 to May 15 daily 11am–3pm).

As everywhere else in the Cape, more and more vineyards are opening; Stanford's best wine is sold by **Raka Winery** (Mon–Fri 9am–4.30pm, Sat 10am–2.30pm), 17km from town along the R326. To visit other wineries, ask at the tourist office (see above) for a map of wine routes.

2

ACCOMMODATION

B's Cottage 17 Morton St ☎ 028 341 0430, ⓦ stanford-accommodation.co.za. A small, open-plan, self-catering thatched house, sleeping two, in an English-style country garden. It's popular and central, so book well ahead. **R450**

Klein River Cheese Farm Cottage On the R326, 7km from Stanford ☎ 028 341 0693. This is a charming three-bedroomed/two-bathroomed Victorian cottage on the river, complete with a fireplace for the winter. There's a minimum stay of two nights. **R410**

Mosaic Farm 10km from the centre, exit from Queen Victoria St ☎ 028 313 2814, ⓦ mosaicfarm.net. You'll find stone, canvas and thatch self-catering chalets on the

river here, with 4km of lagoon frontage and canoeing and walks on the farm. They also run the half-board *Lagoon Lodge* on the same site, which has a luxury safari-lodge feel (R2800). They can make you picnic-basket lunches and dinners for a bit extra. **R800**

★ **Stanford River Lodge** 4km from the centre, exit from Queen Victoria St ☎ 028 341 0444 or ☎ 082 378 1935, ⓦ stanfordriverlodge.co.za. Sunny, spacious and modern self-catering cottages with river and mountain views. It's a lovely, upmarket spot with river swimming and canoeing in summer. Owners John and Valda Finch will provide breakfast for a bit extra. **R700**

EATING

Madres Kitchen Robert Stanford Estate, 1km outside Stanford ☎ 028 341 0647. Farm-style eating with a menu that changes daily. Home-made bread, pies, pâtés and cheeses (R70), plus some South African signature dishes and wines from their own estate (which they also sell in their on-site shop). It is great for children, with lawns, a jungle gym and dam. Daily except Wed 8am–4pm.

★ **Mariana's Bistro and Home Deli** Du Toit St ☎ 028 341 0272. The innovative and reasonably priced country food served at this Victorian cottage is good enough to draw Cape Town gourmands out for the day.

Food and wines are local (mains around R75), and many of the vegetables are picked from owners Mariana and Peter's garden. It is so popular that you'll need to book a couple of months beforehand, though cancellations are always a possibility. No children under 10. Thurs–Sun noon–4pm.

Stanford Gallery Art Café Queen Victoria St. You can enjoy espressos and cake, and the best pizza in Stanford, surrounded by artworks by local artists at this pleasant café. There are daily specials too, including fish from Gansbaai. Tues–Sun 8am–9pm.

Gansbaai and De Kelders

GANSBAAI, 39km from Hermanus, is a workaday place, economically dependent on its fishing industry and the seafood canning factory at the harbour, which gives the place a gutsier feel than the surrounding holidaylands, but there's little reason to spend time here unless you want to engage in **great white shark safaris** (see box opposite), Gansbaai's other major industry. It is an appropriately competitive and cut-throat business, with operators engaged in a blind feeding frenzy to attract punters.

DE KELDERS, a couple of kilometres further east, is a suburb of Gansbaai. The De Kelders holiday homes and mansions are for the most part bland and ostentatious, but its rocky coast provides outstanding whale-watching and there is access to a beautiful, long sandy beach at the Walker Bay Nature Reserve, known by everyone as "Die Plat", where you can clamber over rocky sections and walk for many kilometres. Swimming is rather dangerous though, so best not to venture in more than knee-high.

ARRIVAL AND INFORMATION

GRANSBAAI AND DE KELDERS

By tour Many people come for the day to shark-cage dive on organized trips from Cape Town's backpacker hostels.

By car Take the Hermanus off-ramp from the N2 (about 90km from Cape Town), and follow the R43 for another 85km through Hermanus and Stanford.

Tourist information In the Gateway Centre on Kapokblom St, Gansbaai (Mon–Fri 9am–1pm & 2–5pm, Sat 10am–2pm; ☎ 028 384 1439, ⓦ gansbaaiinfo.com).

ACCOMMODATION

Ama-Krokka 28 Vyfer St, De Kelders ☎ 028 384 2776, ⓦ ama-krokka.co.za. This homely B&B has two suites, each with its own patio, situated nice and close to the beach. Each room has a microwave and the owners

will let you make a braai. There is also a swimming pool. **R900**

Cliff Lodge 6 Cliff St, De Kelders ☎ 028 384 0983, ⓦ clifflodge.co.za. A stylish seafront guesthouse, perched

DYER ISLAND, SHARK ALLEY AND DIVING FOR DENIZENS

How a black American came to be living on an island off South Africa in the early nineteenth century is something of a mystery. But, according to records, Samson Dyer arrived here in 1806 and made a living collecting guano on the island that subsequently took his name.

Now, **Dyer Island** is home to substantial African penguin and seal breeding colonies, both of which are prized morsels among great white sharks. So shark-infested is the channel between the island and the mainland at some times of year that it is known as Shark Alley, and these waters are used extensively by shark-cage diving operators.

WHALE-WATCHING AND SHARK-CAGE DIVING OPERATORS

African Wings ☎028 312 2701, ⬡africanwings .co.za. This operator, based in Hermanus, sells popular whale-watching plane flights over the bay. A two-hour flight for two to six people costs from R3700.

Marine Dynamics and Dyer Island Cruises Geelbek St, Kleinbaai, between De Kelders and Gansbaai ☎028 384 0406, ⬡whalewatchsa.com. Whale sightings by boat and shark-cage diving, around Dyer Island. Boat trips are 2hr 30min long, and preceded by an introductory talk (R950), and you may see southern right whales, Cape fur seals, sharks, humpback whales and African penguins. If you want to see Great Whites close up and underwater, trips cost from R1400 per person, and you stand the best chance of seeing them in the winter.

on the cliffs of De Kelders, with breathtaking views from all four luxurious bedrooms and a spacious penthouse suite, plus a deck for whale-watching and a pool for your own splashing. R1500

★ **Crayfish Lodge** Killarney St, De Kelders ☎028 384 1898, ⬡www.crayfishlodge.net. This is the top stay in town; a palatial guesthouse with sea views and an individual patio or courtyard for all five rooms. If you're treating yourself, book the upstairs suites with jacuzzis. A path leads down to a rocky beach with a channel for bathing and there's a heated swimming pool. R1920

Grootbos Private Nature Reserve On the hills 6km before reaching De Kelders ☎028 384 8000, ⬡www .grootbos.co.za. A tasteful, luxurious eco-lodge, providing whale-watching safaris and guidance into Cape flora and fauna. This is undoubtedly the top stay along the Whale Coast, but day visitors are also allowed. Two-night minimum stay. R6000

EATING AND DRINKING

Benguela Corner of Church & Harbour St, Gansbaai ☎028 384 2120. An upmarket restaurant offering a range of specialities, from seafood and meat to vegetarian options, where every plate is picture perfect. The desserts are recommended, prices reasonable (mains R110) and the host, Jonathan, is very welcoming and friendly. Mon & Wed–Fri 6–10pm, Sat & Sun 11am–2.30pm & 6–10pm.

Coffee on the Rocks Cliff St, De Kelders ☎028 384 2017. A very popular small bistro that does great coffee, cakes and light meals (R65), with a deck in an unsurpassed position for whale-watching, and a great spot for leisurely Sunday roasts. Booking is absolutely essential. Wed–Sun 10am–5pm.

★ **Grootbos Nature Reserve** On the hills 6km before reaching De Kelders ☎028 384 8000. This is the culinary highlight of the area – fine-dining traditional cuisine with a modern twist. Set menu only: 3-course lunch R155, 6-course dinner R320. Daily 1–3pm & 6.30–9pm.

Cape Agulhas

Along the east flank of the Danger Point promontory, the rocky and shallow coastline with heavy swells and strong currents makes this one of South Africa's most treacherous stretches of coast – one that has claimed over 250 wrecks and around 2500 lives. Its rocky terrain also accounts for the lack of a coastal road from Gansbaai to **Cape Agulhas**, the southernmost tip of Africa.

The actual tip of the continent is marked by a rock and plaque about 1km from the landmark of Agulhas lighthouse, towards Suiderstrand. Following the dirt road to **Suiderstrand** itself takes you to some beautiful, undeveloped beaches with rock pools to explore, and is definitely the best part of Agulhas.

L'AGULHAS, the rather windblown settlement associated with the southern tip, consists of a small collection of holiday houses and a few shops. It's a much quieter coastal destination

2

ELIM MISSION STATION

A good reason to venture along the network of dirt roads that crisscrosses the Whale Coast interior is to visit **Elim**, a Moravian mission station 40km northwest of Agulhas, founded in 1824. The whole village is a National Monument of streets lined with thatched, whitewashed houses and fig trees. Tours, arranged by the tourist office in Church Street (Mon–Sat 9am–12.30pm & 1.30–5pm; ☏ 028 482 1806), take in the oldest house in the settlement, the church, the restored water mill where wheat is still ground, and the pottery studio. There's also a memorial commemorating the emancipation of slaves in 1834, the only such monument in South Africa; its presence reflects the fact that numerous freed slaves found refuge in mission stations like Elim. The only accommodation is the community-run Elim Guesthouse (☏ 028 482 1715; R400; dinner available on request), a renovated 1901 thatched home.

than anywhere along the Garden Route, though. The centre of Agulhas, if you can call it a centre, is along Main Road, where you'll find a couple of restaurants, a small supermarket and a craft shop. **Struisbaai**, about 6km east of Agulhas, off the R319, with an attractive harbour and long sandy beaches, is little more than a small collection of holiday homes.

Agulhas Lighthouse

Daily 9am–5pm • R20 • Restaurant Mon–Sat 9am–10pm, Sun 9am–5pm • ☏ 028 435 7580

The red and white **Agulhas Lighthouse**, commissioned in 1849, offers vertiginous views from its top, reached by a series of steep ladders. The appeal of lonely lighthouses on rocky edges beaming out signals to ships at night is explored in interesting exhibits about lighthouses around South Africa. It's worth absorbing the lighthouse atmosphere at the restaurant, but stick to tea and *koeksisters* – the food is no draw.

ARRIVAL AND DEPARTURE
CAPE AGULHAS

By car Agulhas is 230km from Cape Town. Take the N2 to Caledon (115km), then the R316 to Bredasdorp, where the road splits; the more westerly branch (the R319) continuing 43km on to Agulhas.

INFORMATION AND TOURS

Tourist information At the Agulhas Lighthouse (Mon–Sun 9am–5pm, ☏ 028 435 7185, ⊚ www.discover capeagulhas.co.za). It produces an excellent guide book *Discover Cape Agulhas* (free), which is useful if you want a map to explore several new vineyards and wineries that have opened up in the area. The Wine Boutique (☏ 082 567 7858) in the Main Rd next to Angelo's Trattoria stocks wines of the region.

Tours For tours of the region, to Arniston or Agulhas and other scenic areas, you can take a full-day tour with Coastal Tours from Agulhas (⊚ www.coastaltours.co.za; R480) or with Pieter in Swellendam from Fynbus Tours (☏ 028 514 3303/083 621 8503, ⊚ www.fynbus.co.za). They will drive you to the major sites, and organize the day depending on the interests of the group involved.

ACCOMMODATION

Agulhas Country Lodge Main Rd, L'Agulhas ☏ 028 435 7650, ⊚ agulhascountrylodge.com. Housed in a rather grand stone building perched halfway up a hillside, all rooms have sea views from private balconies, and some from the beds themselves. The excellent, if pricey, seafood dinners provide another inducement to stay. **R1400**
Cape Agulhas Backpackers Corner of Duiker & Main Rd, L'Agulhas ☏ 082 372 3354, ⊚ capeagulhas backpackers. com. The only budget place around Agulhas has camping, dorms, doubles and self-catering cottages with a pool, garden and good bedding throughout. It's run by a couple who are big on helping you enjoy the outdoors and will organize boating, surfing lessons, kiteboarding, horseriding and other activities

around Struisbaai, and also arrange pick-ups from Botrivier or Swellendam for those without their own transport. Camping **R50**, dorm **R100**, double **R320**
★ **Pebble Beach** Follow signs to the Southern Tip of Africa and then 4km beyond ☏ 028 435 7270 or ☏ 082 774 5008, ⊚ pebble-beach.co.za. Uniquely positioned on the edge of the Agulhas National Park, with kilometres of undeveloped beach to explore to the west, this sea-facing guesthouse run by Chris and Peta has two en-suite rooms in a modern thatched house, featuring white beds and wooden floors, with the scent of *fynbos* wafting in from the dunes. Guests also have the choice of a special upstairs bedroom with bath and large balcony overlooking the sea (R1120). **R790**

Southermost B&B On the corner of Van Breda and Lighthouse sts, L'Agulhas ☏028 435 6565, ⓦsouthermost.co.za. A well-loved and rather dilapidated historic beach cottage, run by the welcoming Meg, opposite the tidal pool with an indigenous garden sloping down to the water's edge. It is an easy walk from here to the centre to get an evening meal. Closed in winter. R700

EATING

Agulhas Seafoods Main Rd. The best fish and chips (R55) in the region. Mon–Sat 11.30am–7pm, Sun 11.30am–3pm.

Pelican's Hawe Rd, Struisbaai ☏072 742 5824. Struisbaai's best seafood grill restaurant (mains around R85), in a good position at the harbour. It's a lovely spot to watch the sun go down with a chilled glass of wine, although it can get uncomfortably busy in peak season. Daily 9am–10pm.

Pot Pouri Main Rd. Outdoor seating under umbrellas and a well-stocked curio & craft shop are a good enough reason to stop here for a light lunch of sandwiches and salad (R45). Mon–Sat 9am–5pm.

Zuidste Kaap 99 Main Rd ☏028 435 7838. Straightforward cooking with no fancy presentation in an elegant thatched restaurant with an open feel, but no sea views. Recommended dishes include stuffed chicken breasts and line fish (R80). Daily 10am–10pm.

Arniston

After the cool deep blues of the Atlantic to the west, the azure of the Indian Ocean at **ARNISTON** is startling, made all the more dazzling by the white dunes interspersed with rocky ledges. This is one of the best places to stay in the Overberg – if you want nothing more than beach life. The colours may be tropical, but the wind can howl unpredictably here, as anywhere else along the Cape coast, and when it does, there's nothing much to do. The village is known to locals by its Afrikaans name, Waenhuiskrans ("wagon-house cliff"), after a cliff containing a huge cave 1500m south of town, which trekboers reckoned was spacious enough for a wagon and span of oxen (the largest thing they could think of). The English name derives from a British ship, the *Arniston*, which hit the rocks here in 1815.

The shallow seas, so treacherous for vessels, provide Arniston with the safest swimming waters along the Whale Coast. You can swim next to the slipway or at **Roman Beach**, the main swimming beach, just along the coast as you head south from the harbour. Apart from sea bathing, the principal attraction is **Kassiesbaai**, a district of starkly beautiful limewashed cottages, now declared a National Monument and home to coloured fishing families that have for generations made their living here. But Kassiesbaai sits a little uneasily as a living community, as it's also a bit of a theme park for visitors stalking the streets with their cameras.

Heading north through Kassiesbaai at low tide, you can walk 5km along an unspoilt beach unmarred by buildings until you reach an unassuming fence – resist the temptation to climb over this, as it marks the boundary of the local testing range for military material and missiles. Heading south of the harbour for 1500m along spectacular cliffs, you'll reach the vast **cave** after which the town is named. The walk is worth doing simply for the *fynbos*-covered dunes you'll cross on the way. From the car park right by the cave, it's a short signposted walk down to the dunes and the cave, which can only be reached at low tide. The rocks can be slippery and have sharp sections, so be sure to wear shoes with tough soles and a good grip.

ARRIVAL AND DEPARTURE
ARNISTON

By car The town is reached on the R316, 24km southeast of Bredasdorp, and 220km from Cape Town. There's no public transport to Arniston.

ACCOMMODATION

The holiday accommodation is in the modern section of town, adjacent to the traditional fishing village quarter of Kassiesbaai, where you'll find a number of exclusive holiday homes all built in a whitewashed, thatched-roof cottage style.

2

Arniston Lodge 23 Main Rd ☎028 445 9175, ⓦarnistonlodge.co.za. In the residential area, this B&B offers four rooms in a double-storeyed thatched home with a pool. The downstairs rooms have no views, while the upstairs ones have sea views as well as better bathrooms. R620

Arniston Seaside Cottages Huxham St, signposted as you arrive from Bredasdorp ☎028 445 9772, ⓦarniston-online.co.za. This reliable place is one of the nicest of the self-catering options in Arniston, offering a clutch of limewashed cottages, fully equipped, clean and serviced. R560

★ **Arniston Spa Hotel** Beach Rd ☎028 445 9000, ⓦarnistonhotel.com. Dominating the seafront, this luxurious spa hotel boasts every comfort, including a spa with massage and beauty treatments. The best rooms have a fireplace, or a balcony with sea views. It is one of the best-set beach hotels in the country, and the only one in town. R1185

EATING

Arniston Hotel Beach Rd ☎028 445 9000. Outdoor seating to take in the sea views, and serves blow-out breakfasts, and pleasing fresh fish dinners (from R90). It is also home to the town's only bar, which serves burgers and the like and has sport on TV. Daily 8–10am & 7–10pm.

★ **Willeen's Meals Arts and Crafts House** C26, Kassiesbaai ☎028 445 9995. This is an authentic fisherman's cottage where you'll be served traditional Cape Malay meals by family members. You can try *bobotie*, a seafood platter (R100) or fried fish. They have a BYO booze policy, though soft drinks are available. You can also just have tea and scones in the garden that boasts sea views. Daily 8am–10pm.

De Hoop Nature Reserve

Daily 7am–6pm • R30

De Hoop is the **wilderness highlight** of the Western Cape and one of the best places in the world for land-based whale-watching from July to October, with the greatest numbers of whales to be seen in August and September. There's no need to take a boat or use binoculars; in season you'll see whales blowing or breaching – leaping clear of the water – or perhaps slapping a giant tail. Although the reserve could technically be done as a day-trip from Agulhas, Arniston or Swellendam, you'll find it far more rewarding to come here for a night or more. The **Whale Trail** hike is one of South Africa's best walks and among the finest wildlife experiences in the world (6 days; 54km).

The breathtaking coastline is edged by bleached sand dunes standing 90m high in places, and rocky formations that at one point open to the sea in a massive craggy arch. The flora and fauna are impressive, too, encompassing 86 species of mammal, 260 different birds and 1500 varieties of plants. Inland, rare **Cape mountain zebra**, **bontebok** and other **antelope** congregate on a plain near the reserve accommodation.

ARRIVAL AND DEPARTURE   DE HOOP NATURE RESERVE

By car De Hoop is signposted off the N2, the Spitskop Rd, 13km west of Swellendam; this is the quickest route from Cape Town. Alternatively, if you are in the Overberg, take the signposted dirt road that spurs off the R319 as it heads out of Bredasdorp, 50km to its west.

By tour Without your own car, you can take a full-day tour with Coastal Tours from Agulhas (ⓦwww.coastaltours .co.za; R480) or with Pieter from Fynbus Tours in Swellendam (☎028 514 3303/ 083 621 8503, ⓦwww .fynbus.co.za).

ACCOMMODATION

De Hoop Cottages Accommodation ☎0861 334 667 or ☎021 422 4522, ⓦdehoopcollection.co.za. The De Hoop Collection offers an array of options in the reserve, none of them cheap, apart from camping and some small rondavels. The most convenient is at *De Opstel*, situated by the information office and restaurant, and a twenty-minute drive from the coast.

Best of all, if you're in a group of six, is the splendidly isolated beach house at *Koppie Allene* (R4800), on the beach itself. The site couldn't be more thrilling, overlooking a bay full of whales and huge rock pools. Camping R295, cottage R600

Verfheuwel Farm Off the road signposted Whale Trail and Potberg, outside the reserve. ☎028 542 1038 or

☎082 767 0148, ✉verfheuwel@whalemail.co.za. Cottage attached to the main farmhouse here, run by hospitable Afrikaner farming folk who can bring dinner to your cottage if you ask in advance. The country-style cottage sleeps a couple, with beds in the living area for children. The garden is beautiful and has a swimming pool. **R500**

EATING

Fig Tree Restaurant Close to reception ☎028 542 1254. There are no food supplies at De Hoop, bar a small shop selling basics, so be sure to stock up with everything before you come. If you don't want to self-cater, the *Fig Tree Restaurant* is your only option (mains around R185). Daily noon–3pm & 7–8.30pm.

The Garden Route

The **Garden Route**, a slender stretch of coastal plain between Mossel Bay and Storms River Mouth, has a legendary status as South Africa's paradise – reflected in local names such as **Garden of Eden** and **Wilderness**. This soft, green, forested swath of nearly 200km is cut by rivers from the mountains to the north, tumbling down to its southern rocky shores and sandy beaches.

The Garden Route coast is dominated by three inlets, of which the closest to Cape Town is **Mossel Bay**, an industrial centre of some charm, marking the official start of the Garden Route. **Knysna**, though younger, exudes a well-rooted urban character but has a major drawback – unlike **Plettenberg Bay**, its eastern neighbour, it has no beach of its own. A major draw, though, is the **Knysna forest** covering some of the hilly country around Knysna, the awe-inspiring remnants of once vast ancient woodlands.

Between the coastal towns are some ugly modern holiday developments, but also some wonderful empty beaches and tiny coves, such as **Victoria Bay** and **Nature's Valley**. Best of all is the **Tsitsikamma** section of the Garden Route National Park, which has it all – indigenous forest, dramatic coastline, the pumping **Storms River Mouth** and South Africa's most popular hike, the **Otter trail**.

Brief history

Khoi herders who lived off the Garden Route's natural bounty considered the area a paradise, calling it *Outeniqua* ("the man laden with honey"). Their Eden was quickly

GETTING AROUND THE GARDEN

The Garden Route is probably the best-served stretch of South Africa for **transport**.

BAZ BUS

Most user-friendly among the public transport options is the daily Baz Bus service between Cape Town and Port Elizabeth (☎021 439 2323, ⊕bazbus.co.za), which picks up passengers daily in Cape Town (7.15–8.30am) and Port Elizabeth (6.45–7.30am). It provides a door-to-door service within the central districts of all the towns along the way, and has the advantage over the large intercity lines that it will happily carry outdoor gear, such as surfboards or mountain bikes. Although the buses take standby passengers if there's space available, you should book ahead to secure a seat.

INTERCITY BUSES

Intercape, Greyhound and Translux intercity buses (see p.49) from Cape Town and Port Elizabeth are cheaper than the Baz Bus for direct journeys, stopping only at Mossel Bay, George, Wilderness, Sedgefield, Knysna and Storms River (the village, but not the Mouth, which is some distance away). These buses often don't go into town, letting passengers off at filling stations on the highway instead.

FLIGHTS

If time is tight, you may want to fly to George at the western end of the Garden Route, served by scheduled flights from Cape Town, Johannesburg, Durban and Port Elizabeth.

GARDEN ROUTE ADVENTURE ACTIVITIES: THE HIGHLIGHTS

The Garden Route is no longer just a place for sun-soaking or communing with nature. Now adrenaline-junkies go expressly to throw themselves off bridges, to gape into the jaws of great white sharks and to freewheel down scary mountain passes. The choice is broad – and widely spread across the entire length of the Garden Route. To help you plan, here are some highlights.

Abseiling Drop down a cliff face at the private Featherbed Nature Reserve (see box, p.227), the entrance to the Knysna lagoon, or along the Kaaimans River gorge in Wilderness (p.222).

Blackwater Tubing Get wet and wild riding the rapids of the Storms River gorge (see p.245).

Bungee jumping The world's highest commercial jump is at Bloukrans Bridge (see p.240).

Canopy tours and ziplining Swing from tree to tree in an indigenous forest, 30m above the forest floor, or zing over waterfalls and across a river gorge (see box, p.245).

Hiking There's a terrific circular one-day hike along the edge of the Robberg Peninsula (p.239), with a chance of seeing whales, dolphins and seals. Otherwise, there are quite a few longer and more challenging trails to attempt.

Horseriding Sit cowboy-style in a deep saddle at *Southern Comfort Western Horse Ranch*, between Knysna and Plettenberg Bay (see p.229). Or head out with an English saddle through African countryside near Plettenberg Bay, for *fynbos* and forest trails.

Mountain biking Tear down the hair-raising Swartberg Pass, starting out from Knysna or Oudtshoorn (p.191), or pedal your way in a slightly calmer fashion round the Homtini Cycle Route in the Knysna forest (p.231).

River boat Go for a leisurely ferry ride down the spectacular Keurbooms River estuary where birdlife is in abundance (p.240).

Sandboarding Pit yourself against the "Dragon Dune", the longest runnable stretch of sand in South Africa, just outside Mossel Bay (see p.218).

Scenic excursions The Outeniqua Power Van, a diesel-powered, single cab train, climbs into the Outeniqua Mountains along the train tracks east of George (see p.220). With your own transport, try taking the old road just east of The Crags, winding your way down the fantastically scenic route to Nature's Valley (see p.241).

Whale, dolphin and shark encounters Take to the water on a well-informed eco-tour that could encounter a variety of whales and dolphins at Plettenberg Bay (p.238), or enter a shark cage for a first-hand encounter with Jaws at Mossel Bay (see p.218).

Wildlife spotting There's family fun in the forest, looking for apes from around the world at Monkeyland (p.239) or avifauna at the adjacent Birds of Eden; or coming face to face with the world's largest land mammal at the Elephant Sanctuary (see p.239) and the Knysna Elephant Park (see p.233).

Ziplining See canopy tours (above).

destroyed in the eighteenth century with the arrival of Dutch **woodcutters**, who had exhausted the forests around Cape Town and set about doing the same in Outeniqua, killing or dispersing the Khoi and San in the process. Birds and animals suffered too from the encroachment of Europeans. In the 1850s, the Swedish naturalist Johan Victorin shot and feasted on the species he had come to study, some of which, including the endangered narina trogon, he noted were both "beautiful and good to eat".

Despite the dense appearance of the area, what you see today are only the remnants of one of Africa's great **forests**; much of the indigenous hardwoods have been replaced by exotic pine plantations, and the only milk and honey you'll find now is in the many shops servicing the Garden Route coastal resorts.

Mossel Bay

MOSSEL BAY, a midsized town 397km east of Cape Town, gets a bad press, mainly because of the huge industrial facade it presents to the N2. Don't panic – the historic centre is a thoroughly pleasant contrast, set on a hill overlooking the small working harbour and bay, with one of the best swimming beaches along the southern Cape coast and an interesting museum. While Mossel Bay's modest attractions are unlikely to hold you for more than a night, it has some decent accommodation.

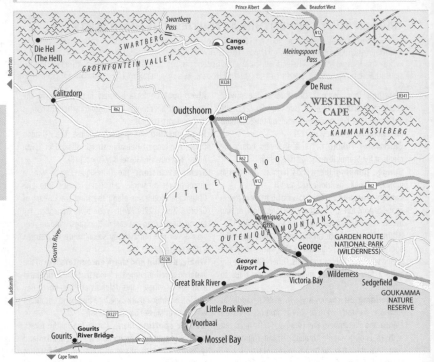

Brief history

Mossel Bay bears poignant historical significance as the place where indigenous Khoi cattle herders first encountered Europeans in a bloody spat. A group of Portuguese mariners under captain **Bartholomeu Dias** set sail from Portugal in August 1487 in search of a sea route to India, and months later rounded the Cape of Good Hope. In February 1488, they became the first Europeans to make landfall along the South African coast, when they pulled in for water at an inlet they called Aguado de Saõ Bras ("watering place of St Blaize"), now Mossel Bay. The Khoikhoi were organized into distinct groups, each under its own chief and each with territorial rights over pastures and water sources. The Portuguese, who were flouting local customs, saw it as "bad manners" when the Khoikhoi tried to drive them off the spring. The Portuguese retaliated with crossbow fire that left one of the herders dead.

Bartholomeu Dias Museum Complex

1 Market St • Maritime Museum Mon–Fri 9am–4.45pm, Sat & Sun 9am–3.45pm • R10 • Dias caravel R15

Mossel Bay's main urban attraction is the **Bartholomeu Dias Museum Complex**, housed in a collection of historic buildings well integrated into the small town centre, all near the tourist office and within a couple of minutes' walk of each other. The highlight is the **Maritime Museum**, a spiral gallery with displays on the history of European, principally Portuguese, seafaring, arranged around a full-size replica of Dias' original caravel. The ship was built in Portugal and sailed from Lisbon to Mossel Bay in 1987 to celebrate the five-hundredth anniversary of Dias' historic journey.

The **Post Office Tree**, just outside the Maritime Museum, purportedly may be the very milkwood under which sixteenth-century mariners left messages for passing ships in an

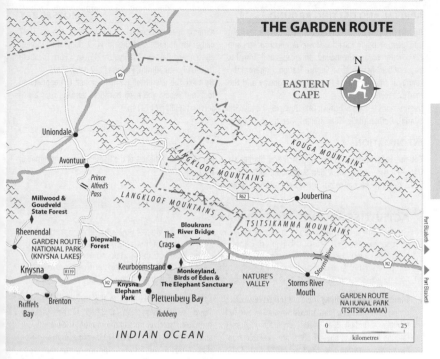

THE GARDEN ROUTE

2

old boot. You can post mail here in a large, boot-shaped letterbox and have it stamped with a special postmark. Of the remaining exhibitions, the Shell Museum and Aquarium next to the Post Office Tree is the only one worth taking time to visit. This is your chance to see some of the beautiful shells found off the South African coast, as well as specimens from around the world.

Santos Beach

North side of town, a short walk north down the hill from the Maritime Museum

Santos Beach, the main town strand, is north-facing – extremely unusual for South Africa – which gives it exceptionally long sunny afternoons. Adjacent to the small town harbour, the beach provides some of the finest swimming along the Garden Route, with uncharacteristically gentle surf, small waves and a depth perfect for practising your crawl.

The Point and St Blaize Lighthouse

East of the harbour, the coast bulges south towards the **Point**, which has several restaurants and a popular bar/restaurant (see p.219) with a deck at the ocean's edge, from which you may see dolphins cruising past.

A couple of hundred metres to the south at the top of some cliffs, the **St Blaize Lighthouse**, built in 1864, is still in use as a beacon to ships. Below it, the **Cape St Blaize Cave** is both a marvellous lookout point and a significant archeological site. A boardwalk leads through the cave past three information panels describing the history of the interpretation of the cave, where in 1888 excavations uncovered stone tools and showed that people had been using the cave for something close on 100,000 years. The path leading up to the cave continues onto the Cape St Blaize trail (see p.218).

2

ARRIVAL AND GETTING AROUND

MOSSEL BAY

By bus Of all the buses, only the daily Baz Bus comes right into town, dropping you off at *Mossel Bay Backpackers* and *Park House Lodge*. Greyhound, Intercape and Translux buses stop at Shell Voorbaai Service Station, 7km from the centre, at the junction of the national highway and the road into town.

Destinations (intercity buses): Cape Town (6–7 daily; 5hr 30min); Durban (daily; 18hr 30min); George (6–7 daily;

45min); Johannesburg (1–2 daily; 14hr); Knysna (6–7 daily; 1hr 15min); Oudtshoorn (1–2 daily; 1hr 15min); Plettenberg Bay (6–7 daily; 2hr 15min); Port Elizabeth (6–7 daily; 4hr 30min); Pretoria (1–2 daily; 15hr).

By taxi The town itself is small enough to negotiate on foot, but should you need transport, Jordaan runs a taxi service (☎ 082 673 7314).

INFORMATION

Tourist information Corner of Church and Market sts (Mon–Fri 8am–6pm, Sat & Sun 9am–4pm; ☎ 044 691 2202, ⓦ visitmosselbay.co.za). Shelves of brochures about

Mossel Bay and the rest of the Garden Route, and a map of the town.

ACTIVITIES AROUND MOSSEL BAY

Great White Sharks are a major reason many visitors come to Mossel Bay, which has one of the southern coast's more reputable shark-cage diving operations. The town is also a springboard for other popular activities, including skydiving, surfing instruction, sandboarding and deep-sea fishing, all of which can be booked through the Garden Route Adventure Centre at *Mossel Bay Backpackers* (☎ 044 691 3182, ⓦ gardenrouteadventures.com).

Diving and snorkelling There are several rewarding diving and snorkelling spots around Mossel Bay, and full facilities, including Open Water certification courses (around R2400) and one-off dives, are available from Electro Dive (☎ 044 690 3402 or ☎ 082 561 1259, ⓦ electrodive.co.za). If you haven't the time or inclination to go the whole hog, you can take a scuba crash course (R500) that allows you to go out on a dive with an instructor. Electro Dive rents out gear and provides shore-based and boat-based dives (R300/340 including kit); it also does parasailing and jet-skiing. These aren't tropical seas, so don't expect clear warm waters, but with visibility usually between 4m and 10m you stand a good chance of seeing octopus, squid, sea stars, soft corals, pyjama sharks and butterfly fish.

Hiking On the mainland you can check out the coast on the St Blaize hiking trail, an easy 15km walk (roughly 4hr each way; a map is available from the tourist office) along the southern shore of Mossel Bay. The route starts from the Cape St Blaize Cave, just below the lighthouse at the Point, and heads west as far as Dana Bay, taking in magnificent coastal views of cliffs, rocks, bays and coves.

Sandboarding and surfing Mossel Bay is one of the best places in the country for sandboarding: the dunes are big, the sand is moist and fine, and you pay roughly half what you would in Cape Town. Billeon Surf and Sandboarding, at the Surf Factory in Fields St (☎ 044 691 3811 or ☎ 082 97 11 405,

ⓦ billeon.com), take trips to the so-called "Dragon Dune", which they claim, at 320m, is the longest runnable stretch of sand in the country. The activity is suitable for all levels, from beginner to extreme – the dune tends to run faster during the winter months. They also offer surfing instruction, and Mossel Bay has a good beach break suitable for novices. All gear is included in the price for both activities (R350; group discounts available).

Shark encounters One of the better shark-cage operations in the country is White Shark Africa, located on the corner of Church and Market sts (☎ 044 691 3796, ⓦ whitesharkafrica.co.za), who let you watch from a boat or go underwater in a cage for R1300. The best months for sightings are March to November, but at no time are encounters guaranteed.

Whale watching and Seal Island cruises Cruises around Seal Island, about 10km northwest of Santos Beach, to see the African penguin and seal colonies can be taken on the *Romonza* (hourly 10am–3pm, peak season 10am–4pm; R120; ☎ 044 690 3101), a medium-sized yacht that launches from the yacht marina in the harbour. The Romonza is also the only registered vessel allowed to run boat-based whale-watching cruises (R600; 2–3hrs) in Mossel Bay. As elsewhere along this coast, the whale season is variable, with southern rights appearing from June till late October. If you're extremely lucky, you may also see a humpback whale.

ACCOMMODATION

Mossel Bay has a range of accommodation, including a number of reasonable B&Bs that can be booked through the tourist office should our recommendations be full.

Edward Charles 1 Sixth Ave ☎044 691 2152, ⓦedwardcharles.co.za. An upmarket two-storey guesthouse in a central location overlooking Santos Beach with a swimming pool. There are fifteen en-suite rooms all with satellite television and phones, and there's a courtesy shuttle to take you to the town restaurants if you don't have your own car. **R850**

Huijs Te Marquette 1 Marsh St ☎044 691 3182, ⓦmarquette.co.za. Twelve guest rooms in a very well-run establishment near the Point. The decor is simple and fairly impersonal, and half the suites have doors opening out onto a patio garden and swimming pool. **R760**

Mossel Bay Backpackers 1 Marsh St ☎044 691 3182, ⓦmosselbayhostel.co.za. Well-run lodge with squeaky-clean rooms, only 300m from the sea and attached to *Huijs Te Marquette* (see above). They also do adventure activity

bookings and there's a swimming pool in the garden. Dorm **R120**, double **R320**

Park House Lodge 121 High St ☎044 691 1937, ⓦparkhouse.co.za. Top-notch budget accommodation in twenty rooms distributed across three buildings, one of which is a beautiful nineteenth-century sandstone manor house. Some rooms have private entrances leading onto the lush garden. Dorm **R160**, double **R440**

Protea Hotel Mossel Bay Bartholomeu Dias Museum Complex, Market St ☎044 691 3738, ⓦproteahotels .com/mosselbay. Opposite the tourist office, in an old Cape Dutch manor house, this quaint place has breakfast served at *Café Gannet*, Mossel Bay's nicest restaurant. Rooms are smart and fairly formally furnished with exposed rafters that give an airy atmosphere. Most have sea or harbour views. **R1100**

EATING AND DRINKING

You don't come to Mossel Bay for the food, but there are a number of reasonable places to eat, some of them with superb sea views. The small Point Village shopping development at the north end has a couple of inexpensive to mid-priced family restaurants, opening daily from the morning until 11pm-ish.

Café Gannet Market St ☎044 691 1885, ⓦoldposttree .co.za. Close to the Bartholomew Dias Museum Complex, Mossel Bay's smartest restaurant offers straightforward seafood dishes that will set you back R60–160 for a main course. Meals are served in a stylish garden with glimpses across the harbour, and this is a good spot for sundowners. Daily 7am–11pm.

Delfino's Espresso Bar and Pizzeria Point Village ☎044 690 5247. Pasta, pizza (R30–60) and steak (R85) as well as decent coffee, with great views of the sea. Try their scrambled egg and bacon pizza for a breakfast that will set you up for the day. Daily 7am–11pm.

Jazzbury's 11 Marsh St ☎044 691 1923. Traditional South African main courses for around R165, such as *bobotie*, Karoo lamb and mixed ostrich grill served with maize meal and sweet potato, at a relaxed venue that's popular with locals. There's seating inside the atmospheric stone building as well as alfresco. Daily 6–11pm.

King Fisher Point Village ☎044 690 6390, ⓦthekingfisher.co.za. A relaxed joint that, as its name suggests, specializes in seafood from humble fish and chips (R60) to lobster thermidor (R280) and everything in between. There's also a kids' menu. Its position above *Delfino's* means it has excellent sea views. Daily 10.30am–5pm & 6–11.30pm.

Robinson Pass to Oudtshoorn

Heading inland towards Oudtshoorn from Mossel Bay on the R328 takes you over the forested coastal mountains on the **Robinson Pass** into the desiccated Little Karoo. Close to the top, and a compelling stop for a meal or drink, is the *Eight Bells Mountain Inn* (see p.220). Out of school holidays, it remains a restful stop-off with lovely gardens and extensive grounds.

Botlierskop Private Game Reserve

About 7km north of Little Brak River • ☎044 696 6055, ⓦbotlierskop.co.za

There are no serious Big Five game reserves in the Western Cape and certainly none that can offer anything like you'll get on a safari in the Kruger or a stay in one of the reserves near Port Elizabeth at the eastern end of the Garden Route. Having said that, Botlierskop is probably the best safari you're going to find this close to Cape Town. There's nothing wild about it, but the tented accommodation does work hard at providing the atmosphere and you will mostly (although not always) see lions in their huge enclosure. In addition, there's a good chance of spotting rhinos, elephants, giraffes and antelope. The whole package is professionally put together and includes a number of activities for both day and overnight visitors.

<table>
<tr><td>**ACCOMMODATION**</td><td>**BOTLIERSKOP PRIVATE GAME RESERVE**</td></tr>
</table>

Botlierskop Private Game Reserve ☎ 044 696 6055, ⓦ botlierskop.co.za. A range of tented suites – luxury, deluxe, executive and family – with prices to match the number of bells and whistles laid on. All are decorated in a colonial style and have decks and fabulous views. Full-board rates include high tea with the elephants and two game drives. **R2331**

Eight Bells Mountain Inn 35km from Mossel Bay ☎ 044 631 0000, ⓦ eightbells.co.za. A firm favourite with well-heeled families wanting a fully catered hotel-style holiday with all sorts of activities laid on for children, and rest time for adults. The atmosphere is friendly and it's superbly run with special meals and meal times for younger children, plus horseriding, swimming, tennis and walking. **R1100**

George

There's little reason to visit **GEORGE**, 66km northeast of Mossel Bay, unless you need what a big centre offers – airport, hospital and shops – and it does lie conveniently halfway between Cape Town and Port Elizabeth. If you're pushed for time, flying here drops you at the western end of the Garden Route.

A large inland town, surrounded by mountains, George is a 5km detour northwest off the N2, and 9km from the nearest stretch of ocean at Victoria Bay. Sadly, all that's left of the forests and quaint character that moved Anthony Trollope, during a visit in 1877, to describe it as the "prettiest village on the face of the earth" are some historic buildings, of which the beautiful Dutch Reformed Church in Davidson Street is the most notable. Other than that, George's claim to recent fame (or notoriety) is that it was the parliamentary seat of former State President **P.W. Botha** (see box opposite), the last of South Africa's apartheid hardliners.

<table>
<tr><td>**ARRIVAL AND DEPARTURE**</td><td>**GEORGE**</td></tr>
</table>

By plane Kulula, 1Time and SAA fly between Johannesburg and the small George airport, 10km west of town on the N2, at least once daily (1hr 50min). SAA also flies here at least once a day from Cape Town (50min) and Durban (90min). Most tourists flying in rent a car from one of the rental companies here and set off down the Garden Route.
By bus Intercape, Translux and Greyhound intercity buses pull in at George station, adjacent to the railway museum.

Destinations: Cape Town (6–7 daily; 6hr); Durban (1 daily; 18hr); Johannesburg (1–2 daily; 15hr); Knysna (6–7 daily; 1hr); Mossel Bay (6–7 daily; 45min); Oudtshoorn (3–4 daily; 1hr 30min); Plettenberg Bay (6–7 daily; 1hr 30min); Port Elizabeth (6–7 daily; 4hr 30min); Pretoria (1–2 daily; 16hr). The **Baz Bus** drops off at *Outeniqua Backpackers* on Merriman St on its daily run between Cape Town and Port Elizabeth.

ACCOMMODATION

10 Caledon Street 10 Caledon St ☎ 044 873 4983, ⓦ 10caledon.co.za. The pick of the mid-priced B&Bs, in a spotless guesthouse in a quiet street around the corner from the museum, featuring balconies with mountain views and a garden. The owners are superb hosts and provide an excellent breakfast. The B&B is an easy walk to the city centre. **R800**
Die Waenhuis 11 Caledon St ☎ 044 874 0034, ⓦ www .diewaenhuis.co.za. Mid-nineteenth-century home that has retained its period character with eleven spacious en-suite rooms, a beautiful garden and gracious hosts. English breakfasts, included in the price, are served in a sunlit dining room. **R700**
Fairview Historic Homestead 36 Stander St ☎ 082 226 9466, ⓦ fairviewhomestead.com. Stately Cape

Georgian homestead with five B&B rooms filled with lovely Victoriana and set in extensive, beautiful formal gardens. Despite the obvious attention to detail, there's nothing precious about this welcoming, child-friendly establishment. **R650**
Mount View Resort & Lifestyle Village York St ☎ 044 874 5205, ⓦ mountviewsa.co.za. Modern complex that lacks much character, but offers great value in its one-, two- and three-bedroom en-suite chalets and rondavels. The gardens are well kept and pleasant and the complex also houses a wellness and beauty salon, a ten-pin bowling alley and a pool hall. **R390**
Outeniqua Backpackers 115 Merriman St ☎ 082 316 7720, ⓦ outeniqua-backpackers.com. Friendly hostel in

PRESIDENT BOTHA AND APARTHEID'S LAST STAND

Pieter Willem Botha was the last and most rabid of South Africa's apartheid enforcers. A National Party hack from the age of 20, Botha worked his way up through the ranks, becoming an MP in 1948 and subsequently **Minister of Defence**, a position he used in 1978 to unseat Prime Minister John Vorster. Botha set about streamlining apartheid, modifying his own role from that of a British-style prime minister, answerable to parliament, to one of an executive president taking vital decisions in the secrecy of a President's Council heavily weighted with army top brass.

Informed by the generals that apartheid couldn't be preserved purely through force, Botha embarked on his **Total Strategy**, reforming peripheral aspects of apartheid while fostering a black middle class as a buffer against the ANC. He also pumped vast sums into building an enormous military machine that crossed South Africa's borders to bully or crush neighbouring countries harbouring anti-apartheid activists. At home, security forces were free to murder, maim and torture **opponents of apartheid**.

Botha's iron fist proved his undoing when, in 1985, he responded to international calls for change by hinting that he would announce significant political reforms at his party congress. In the event, out of fear of a white backlash, or just bloody-minded intransigence, he shrank away from meaningful concessions. The result was an immediate and devastating flight of capital from the country, a withdrawal of credit by Chase Manhattan Bank and intensified sanctions.

Botha blustered on through the late 1980s, while his bloated military sucked the state coffers dry. Even National Party stalwarts realized that his policies were leading to ruin, and in 1989, when he suffered a stroke, the party was quick to replace him with **F.W. de Klerk**, who swiftly announced reforms.

Botha lived out his unrepentant retirement near George, declining ever to apologize for the political crimes committed by his administration. Curiously, when he died in 2006, he was given an uncritical, high-profile state funeral, broadcast on national television and attended by members of the government, including then-president, Thabo Mbeki.

a bright and airy suburban house with comfortable dorms and doubles, some with mountain views. There's a swimming pool, and they rent out bikes and provide free airport pickups. The Baz Bus pulls in here. Dorm R120, double R400

EATING AND DRINKING

Het Vijfde Seizoen 3 Maitland St ☎044 870 7320. Cosy restaurant that serves Belgian-influenced international-fusion cuisine with some traditional South African touches. Main courses, which range from R70 to R100, include Flemish-style mussel pot, Moroccan lamb shanks on a bed of couscous and Cape Malay lamb pot. Mon 8–10am, Tues–Sat 8–10am, noon–3pm & 6.30pm till late, Sun (booking essential) noon–3pm.

Kafe Serefe 60 Courtenay St ☎044 884 1012. Hugely popular venue that serves South African cuisine that, like the Wednesday- and Friday- night belly dancing, comes with a Turkish twist. Meat main courses (R65–100) are the speciality; try the oven-roasted lamb in a red wine sauce or pork with goat's cheese and a brandy fig sauce. There's also a good choice of meze. Mon 10am–4.30pm, Tues–Fri 10am–4.30pm & 7pm–late, Sat 10.30am–2.30pm.

La Capannina 122 York St ☎044 874 5313. Italian restaurant that, in addition to excellent pizzas and pasta (around R65), has other tricks up its sleeve such as beef fillet on a bed of polenta for R90 and distinctly un-Italian fare such as ostrich jambalaya with a hint of curry. Mon–Fri noon–2pm & 6–10pm, Sun 6–10pm.

The Old Town House Corner of York and Market sts ☎044 874 3663. Home style cooking with a contemporary edge in a cosy historic town house, which specializes in venison and beef (R60–120). Despite the place's carnivorous inclination, vegetarians are catered for. Mon–Fri 12.30–3pm & Mon–Sat 6–10pm.

Zanzibar Sports Café Next to the museum, in two old railway carriages. Zanzibar's big screen, Sunday deck parties, Monday metal nights, and, of course, amber nectar, make it a popular spot for a lively night out. Mon–Sat 11am till late.

Victoria Bay

Some 9km south of George and 3km off the N2 lies the minuscule hamlet of **VICTORIA BAY**, on the edge of a small sandy beach wedged into a cove between cliffs, with a grassy sunbathing area, safe swimming and a tidal pool. During the December holidays

2

and over weekends, the place packs out with day-trippers, and rates as one of the top **surfing** spots in South Africa. Because of the cliffs, there's only a single row of buildings along the beachfront, home to some of the most dreamily positioned guesthouses along the coast (and, therefore, some of the priciest).

ARRIVAL AND DEPARTURE   VICTORIA BAY

By car Arriving by car, you'll encounter a metal barrier as you drop down the hill to the bay, and you'll have to try and park in the car park, which is frequently full (especially in summer). If you're staying at one of the B&Bs, leave your car at the barrier and collect the key from your lodgings to gain access to the private beach road.

By bus The daily Baz Bus, which provides the only public transport to Victoria Bay, drops passengers at the *Victoria Bay Surf Lodge*.

ACCOMMODATION

Land's End Guest House The Point, Beach Rd ☎ 044 889 0123, ⓦ www.vicbay.com. En-suite rooms in what claims to be "the closest B&B to the sea in Africa", as well as self-catering accommodation a few doors away at Bay House, which sleeps four, and Sea Cottage, which sleeps five. R1035

Sea Breeze Holiday Resort Along the main road into the settlement ☎ 044 889 0098, ⓦ seabreezecabanas .co.za. A variety of budget self-catering units, including modern two-storey holiday huts and wooden chalets, sleeping two, four or eight people. The huts have no sea views, but it's an easy stroll to the beach. R750

Victoria Bay Surf Lodge Behind *Spencer's Sandwich Café* at the entrance to Vic Bay ☎ 072 593 1741, ⓦ vicbaysurflodge.com. Former municipal workers' accommodation transformed into a squeaky-clean backpacker lodge that sleeps up to 26 in dorms or private rooms (only available off-peak). They also run the adjacent Lank Small Surf Shop, which rents out all the gear you might need to make the most of the water: surfboards, body boards, wetsuits, snorkelling kit and fishing equipment. Dorm R120, double R30

The Waves 6 Beach Rd ☎ 044 889 0166, ⓦ www .thewavesvictoriabay.co.za. Three comfortable and pleasantly furnished B&B suites, all with sea views and opening onto a patio, in a high-ceilinged Victorian house, as well as three self-catering units, which come with stoves, microwaves and fridges. R1500

EATING

Spencer's Sandwich Café Just after the boom at the entrance to Victoria Bay ☎ 044 889 0212. Unpretentious restaurant that delivers to a tee what a casual beach café ought to: a relaxed atmosphere that feels right in flip-flops and shorts, and a straightforward menu covering standards such as toasted sandwiches (R30), fish and chips (R40–70) and burgers (R40–70). April–Aug Mon–Thurs 9am–7pm & Fri–Sun 9am–9pm; Sept–March daily 7.30am–9pm.

Wilderness

East of Victoria Bay, across the Kaaimans River, the beach at **WILDERNESS** is so close to the N2 that you can pull over for a quick dip and barely interrupt your journey, though you'll struggle to find African wilderness among the sprawl of retirement homes, holiday houses and thousands of beds for rent in the vicinity. The beach, renowned for its long stretch of sand, is backed by tall dunes, blighted by holiday houses. Once in the water, stay close to the shoreline: the coast here is notorious for its unpredictable currents.

The main attraction, though, is the Wilderness section of the Garden Route National Park (see opposite), whose river is lovely to paddle along, with good bird-spotting.

ARRIVAL AND DEPARTURE   WILDERNESS

By bus Greyhound, Intercape and Translux buses stop at the Caltex Garage, on the corner of South St and the N2. The daily Baz Bus stops at Fairy Knowe Backpackers.
Destinations: Cape Town (6–7 daily; 7hr 40min); Knysna (6–7 daily; 40min); Mossel Bay (6–7 daily; 1hr); Plettenberg Bay (6–7 daily; 1hr 10min); Port Elizabeth (6–7 daily; 4hr 30min); Sedgefield (6–7 daily; 20min); Storms River Bridge (6–7 daily; 2hr).

INFORMATION

Tourist information Milkwood Village Mall, Beacon Rd, off the N2 opposite the Caltex Garage (Mon–Fri 7.45am–4.30pm, Sat 9am–1pm; ☎ 044 877 0045, ⓦ visitgeorge.co.za).

2

ACTIVITIES IN AND AROUND WILDERNESS

Abseiling, canoeing, cycling and kloofing Eden Adventures (☎044 877 0179 or ☎083 628 8547, ⓦeden.co.za) offers daily kloofing adventures (8am–1pm, R475) and abseiling (1.30–4.30pm, R365); a full day taking in both activities costs R750. Explore the river yourself by renting a two-seater canoe from them (R70/hr).

Horse Trails Black Horse Trails (contact Lindsay ☎082 494 5642, ⓦblackhorsetrails.co.za) runs mountain and forest horseriding tours (R250 for 90min or R390 for 3hr).

Paragliding To see it all from the air, sign up with the recommended Cloudbase Paragliding Adventures (☎044 877 1414, ⓦcloudbase-paragliding.co.za) for a tandem paragliding jump that starts from R450 for a minimum of fifteen minutes. You'll only be taken up when the weather offers absolutely safe conditions. They also offer a one-day introductory course for R950.

ACCOMMODATION

The Albatross Sixth Ave, take South St exit off the N2 ☎044 877 1716. A B&B in an elevated position that provides great views and makes for perfect dolphin-watching from its balconies. Of the three colour-coordinated rooms (pink, blue and ocean), only one has sea views. It's an easy walk to the beach down a boardwalk. R600

Fairy Knowe Backpackers 6km from the village, follow signs from the N2 east of Wilderness ☎044 877 1285, ⓦwildernessbackpackers.com. The oldest home (built 1897) in the area, with a wraparound balcony and set in the quiet woodlands near the Touws River, though nowhere near the sea. The Baz Bus drops off here. Dorm R100, double R300

Island Lake Holiday Resort Lakes Rd, 2km from the Hoekwil/Island Lake turn-off on the N2 ☎044 877 1194, ⓦislandlake.co.za. Camping and self-catering bungalows that sleep four, in one of the quietest and prettiest spots on the lakes. Camping R185, bungalow R370

Mes-Amis Homestead Buxton Close, signposted off the N2 on the coastal side of the road, directly opposite the national park turn-off ☎044 877 1928, ⓦmesamis.co.za. Nine terrifically positioned double rooms, each of which has its own terrace, offering some of the best views in Wilderness. R1300

The Tops Hunts Lane, on a hill about 500m from the tourist office ☎044 877 0187 or ☎083 631 2339, ⓦthetops.co.za. Four airy en-suite bedrooms, three of which have sea views and French doors opening onto a deck, as well as four self-catering studio flats (R900). R650

Wilderness Bush Camp Heights Rd (follow Waterside Rd west for 1600m up the hill) ☎044 877 1168, ⓦboskamp.co.za. Six self-catering timber units with loft bedrooms, thatched roofs and ocean views. The camp is part of a conservation estate that you're free to roam around. R300

EATING

Pomodoro Corner of George and Layla rds ☎044 877 1403. Good pastas and pizzas are among the Italian standards at this trattoria that's a popular family venue with a pleasant ambience. For something more substantial, try the lamb shanks, which are slow roasted in the pizza oven. Main courses range between R60 and R120. Daily 7.30am–10.30pm.

The Girls George Rd ☎044 877 1648, ⓦthegirlsrestaurant.co.za. Deservedly one of the most popular restaurants in the village, fusing classic French fare, such as steak tartare, with North African flavours and Middle Eastern dishes. The prawns (spiced up with cajun, lemongrass, Moroccan or sesame seasoning, among others) are fantastic, they do a mean steak and even vegetarians get a decent look-in (mains R80–180). Tues–Sun 6pm till late.

Wilderness Grill George Rd. A casual venue offering a range of dishes that might include smoked salmon omelette, pizza or steak (mains around R70). Seating outside under parasols or, in winter, indoors by the fire. Daily 8am–11pm.

Garden Route National Park: Wilderness Section

Reception open 24hr • R80 • ☎044 877 0046

Stretching east from Wilderness village is the **Wilderness National Park**, the least aptly named national park in South Africa, as it never feels very far from the rumbling N2.

Although the park takes in beach frontage, it's the **forests** you should come for, as well as the 16km of inland waterways; the variety of habitats here includes coastal and montane *fynbos* and wetlands, attracting 250 species of **birds** – as well as many holidaymakers.

There are five waymarked **trails** in the Wilderness Section of between two and five kilometres. A map of the trails, which also shows the location of three bird hides, is available at reception or you can download it from the SANParks website (⬢ sanparks.org).

ACCOMMODATION	GARDEN ROUTE NATIONAL PARK: WILDERNESS SECTION

The park has two restcamps, *Ebb & Flow North* and *Ebb & Flow South*, both on the west side of the park and clearly signposted off the N2.

Ebb and Flow North Right on the river, the north camp is cheap, old-fashioned and away from the hustle. It offers camping, fully equipped two-person bungalows with their own showers, and ones with communal washing and toilet facilities. Camping R210, bungalow R280

Ebb and Flow South The south camp is the smarter and more modern of the park's accommodation, offering spacious log cottages on stilts and brick bungalows for up to four people. There are also en-suite forest huts with communal kitchens for two people, and camp sites. Camping R210, cabin R540, cottage R1015

Sedgefield

The drive between Wilderness and Sedgefield gives glimpses on your left of dark-coloured lakes that eventually surge out to sea, 21km later, through a wide lagoon at **SEDGEFIELD**. A pleasantly old-fashioned holiday village – one of the last of its kind along the Garden Route – Sedgefield is a few kilometres off the road, with long stretches of beautiful beaches. In fact, so proud is the village of its lack of pizzazz that it has had itself registered as a "slow town", affiliated to the Cittaslow towns of Italy with its emblem of a tortoise.

ARRIVAL AND DEPARTURE	SEDGEFIELD

By bus Greyhound, Intercape and Translux buses stop in the middle of the village at the Sedgefield Garage, Main Rd, a service road running parallel to the N2, which passes through the town's shopping area.

Destinations: Cape Town (6–7 daily; 8hr); Knysna (6–7 daily; 20 min); Mossel Bay (6–7 daily; 40min); Plettenberg Bay (6–7 daily; 50min); Port Elizabeth (6–7 daily; 4hr); Storms River Bridge (6–7 daily; 2hr).

ACCOMMODATION

Coral Reef Guesthouse 28 Coral Reef Crescent, Cola Beach, Sedgefield ☎ 044 343 3133, ⬢ coralreef.co.za. Two double rooms, a triple and a family unit, all brightly decorated, and just two minutes' walk from the beach. There's a saltwater pool and a comfortable relaxing area. R700

Ganzvlei Cottage 12km east of Sedgefield along the N2 ☎ 083 373 3880, ✉ cmeterlerkamp@ganzvlei.co.za. An exceptional rustic retreat in a hundred-year-old cottage on Ganzvlei dairy farm. The cottage is effectively on an island, cut off from the rest of the property by the oxbowing Goukamma River, and massive dunes that abut the Goukamma Nature Reserve (see below). There's no electricity – lighting is by paraffin lamps and generator, and cooking is on a wood stove – and transport to the cottage is via a pont across the water. The cottage has three bedrooms, sleeps six and must be taken for a minimum of three nights. R500

★ **Teniqua Treetops** 23km northeast of Sedgefield ☎ 044 356 2868, ⬢ teniquatreetops.co.za. Genuinely unique and romantic retreat in the boughs of a beautiful piece of virgin forest well off the beaten track, between Sedgefield and Knysna, with four kilometres of woodland walks and a river and pools you can swim in. Accommodation is in luxury tents mounted on raised timber decks, where, if you feel so inclined, you can leave the flaps open and wake up to dappled light filtering through the leaves. There are four honeymoon suites and a pair each of one- and two-bedroom units, one of which is wheelchair accessible. Apart from being a chilled hideout, this is a fascinating example of sustainable living in practice – not a single tree was felled to build Teniqua – with recycled materials used where possible. Water is gravity fed, showers are solar heated and toilets use a dry composting system that preserves water. R1045

Goukamma Nature Reserve

Daily 8am–6pm • R30 • Overnight visitors free • ☎ 044 383 0042

An unassuming sanctuary of around 220 square kilometres, Goukamma starts near Sedgefield and stretches east to **Buffalo Bay** (also known as Buffels Bay) to take in

Groenvlei Lake and approximately 18km of beach frontage, some of the highest vegetated dunes in the country, and walking country covered with coastal *fynbos* and dense thickets of milkwood, yellowwood and candlewood trees.

Away from the water, you stand a small chance of spotting one of the area's mammals, including bushbuck, grysbok, mongoose, vervet monkeys, caracals and otters. Because of the diversity of coastal and wetland habitats, over 220 different kinds of birds have been recorded here, while offshore, southern right whales often make an appearance during their August to December breeding season, and dolphins show up at any time of year.

2

ARRIVAL AND DEPARTURE

GOUKAMMA NATURE RESERVE

By car Two roads off the N2 provide access to the reserve. The entrance and office are on the Buffalo Bay side accessed via the Buffalo Bay Rd, halfway along which is the reserve office. There are no public roads within the reserve. At the westernmost side, a dirt road that runs down to Platbank Beach takes you past the tiny settlement of Lake Pleasant on the south bank of Groenvlei, which consists of little more than a hotel and holiday resort.

ACCOMMODATION

CapeNature (☎0861 227 362 8873, ⓦcapenature.co.za) run two fully equipped bush camps, Groenvlei and Mvubu, on the Groenvlei side of the reserve, and three thatched rondavels on the east. Over weekends, expect to pay roughly 25 percent more than prices quoted.

Groenvlei A timber bush camp, set in a milkwood forest with two double-storey sleeping units, each with two bedrooms, one with a double and the other two single beds. A walkway leads to a jetty where two double canoes are moored for guests' use. **R580**

Mvubu Thatched timber and reed bush camp on stilts at the edge of Groenvlei in a stand of milkwood trees, with just two en-suite bedrooms, both of which have doors opening onto a deck that overlooks the lake. **R670**

Rondavels Three basic double units at the Buffalo Bay side of the reserve that sleep four to five people. Each has a double bed and single or bunk beds, and the rondavels overlook the river and estuary. **R280**

Knysna

KNYSNA (pronounced "nize-na"), 102km east of Mossel Bay, stands at the hub of the Garden Route, its lack of ocean beaches compensated for by its hilly setting around the Knysna lagoon, its ancient forests, good opportunities for adventure sports and a pleasant **waterfront** development. Knysna wraps around the lagoon, which opens out to the sea at a narrow mouth guarded by a pair of steep rocky promontories named The Heads, the western side being a private nature reserve and the eastern one an exclusive residential area along dramatic cliffs above the ocean.

On the north side of the lagoon, a small historic core of Georgian and Victorian buildings gives the town a distinctive character absent from most Garden Route holiday towns. Coffee shops, craft galleries, street traders and a modest nightlife add to the attractions, and you may find yourself tempted to stay longer than just one night.

ACTIVITIES IN THE GOUKAMMA

Apart from angling and birdwatching, the Goukamma offers a number of other self-guided activities, including safe swimming in Groenvlei. There are several day-long **hiking trails** that enable you to explore different habitats. A beach walk, which takes around four hours one-way, traverses the 14km of crumbling cliffs and sands between the Platbank car park on the western side of the reserve and the Rowwehoek one on the eastern side. Alternatively, you can go from one end of the reserve to the other via a slightly longer inland trek across the dunes. There's also a shorter circular walk from the reserve office through a milkwood forest.

You can also **canoe** on the Goukamma River on the eastern side of the reserve; a limited number of canoes can be hired from the reserve office during the week or at the gate over the weekend. Single/double canoes cost R60/100 a day.

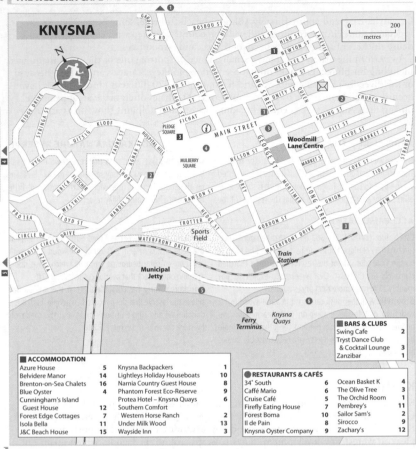

KNYSNA

SEE MAP ABOVE FOR DETAIL

BARS & CLUBS

Swing Cafe	2
Tryst Dance Club & Cocktail Lounge	3
Zanzibar	1

ACCOMMODATION

Azure House	5
Belvidere Manor	14
Brenton-on-Sea Chalets	16
Blue Oyster	4
Cunningham's Island Guest House	12
Forest Edge Cottages	7
Isola Bella	11
J&C Beach House	15
Knysna Backpackers	1
Lightleys Holiday Houseboats	10
Narnia Country Guest House	8
Phantom Forest Eco-Reserve	9
Protea Hotel – Knysna Quays	6
Southern Comfort Western Horse Ranch	2
Under Milk Wood	13
Wayside Inn	3

RESTAURANTS & CAFÉS

34° South	6
Caffé Mario	6
Cruise Café	5
Firefly Eating House	7
Forest Boma	10
Il de Pain	8
Knysna Oyster Company	9
Ocean Basket K	4
The Olive Tree	3
The Orchid Room	1
Pembrey's	11
Sailor Sam's	2
Sirocco	9
Zachary's	12

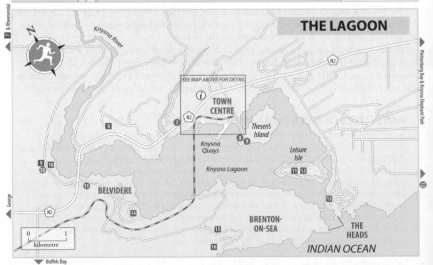

THE LAGOON

Brief history

At the beginning of the nineteenth century, the only white settlements outside Cape Town were a handful of towns that would have considered themselves lucky to have even one horse. Knysna, an undeveloped backwater hidden in the forest, was no exception. The name comes from a Khoi word meaning "hard to reach", and this remained its defining character well into the twentieth century. One important figure was not deterred by the distance – **George Rex**, a colonial administrator who placed himself beyond the pale of decent colonial society by taking a coloured mistress. Shunned by his peers in Britain, he headed for Knysna in the early 1800s in the hope of making a killing exporting hardwood from the lagoon.

When Rex died in 1839, Knysna had become a major **timber centre**, attracting white labourers who felled trees with primitive tools for miserly payments, and looked set eventually to destroy the forest. The forest narrowly escaped devastation by far-sighted and effective conservation policies introduced in the 1880s.

By the turn of the twentieth century, Knysna was still remote, and its forests were inhabited by isolated and inbred communities made up of the impoverished descendants of the woodcutters. As late as 1914, if you travelled from Knysna to George you would have to open and close 58 gates along the 75-kilometre track. Fifteen years on, the passes in the region proved too much for **George Bernard Shaw**, who did some impromptu off-road driving and crashed into a bush, forcing Mrs Shaw to spend a couple of weeks in bed at Knysna's *Royal Hotel* with a broken leg.

Knysna Quays

At the end of Grey Street

Knysna Quays, the town's waterfront complex and yacht basin, was built at the end of the 1990s; the elegant two-storey steel structure with timber boardwalks resembles a tiny version of Cape Town's V&A Waterfront. Here you'll find the luxury *Protea Hotel* (see p.228), some clothes and knick-knack shops, and a couple of good places to eat.

Thesen's Island

Reached by a causeway at the south end of Long St

Thesen's Island is home to a number of stylish shops and restaurants, among them the *Knysna Oyster Company* (see p.230), one of the best spots in town for feasting on shellfish, set on the edge of the lapping lagoon.

Mitchell's Brewery

Arend Rd, off George Rex Drive via Vigilance and Sandpiper rds • Tasting Mon–Fri 10am–4pm • R30 • Tours Mon–Fri 10.30am & 3pm • R50, including tasting of four beers • Ⓦ mitchellsbrewery.com

A twenty-minute walk from the centre, in the town's industrial area, Mitchell's Brewery offers tours on which you get to sample its excellent beers – Forester's Lager, Bosun's

---

KNYSNA CRUISES

One of the obligatory excursions around Knysna is a **cruise** across the lagoon to The Heads. Knysna Featherbed Company (Ⓣ 044 382 1693, Ⓦ knysnafeatherbed.com) runs a number of trips a day from Knysna Quays to The Heads, the shortest of which takes 75 minutes (R85). For travel beyond The Heads, you can take a sailing trip (1hr 30min; R250) and a sunset cruise (2hr 30min; R490) with delicious food and wine. The only way to reach the private **Featherbed Nature Reserve** on the western side of the lagoon is on a four-hour Featherbed Nature Tour (R420), which includes the boat there, a 4WD shuttle to the top of the Western Head and a buffet meal. There's a slightly shorter version (3hr 30min) which excludes the meal. **Bookings** are essential, and can be made at the kiosk on the north side of Knysna Quays; **departures** are from the Waterfront Jetty and municipal jetty on Remembrance Avenue, 400m west of the quays and station.

Bitter, Ninety Shilling Ale and Raven Stout – which have miles more character than the generally insipid offerings of South Africa's mega-brewery (see p.58).

Leisure Isle and Eastern Head

The main reasons to head for **Leisure Isle**, off the eastern suburbs, are the excellent swimming in the lagoon and the views out to sea through the gap between The Heads. The best bathing spots are along the southern shore of the island, particularly the western section along Bayswater Drive, but the swimming is only good around high tide in summer.

Continuing south along George Rex Drive brings you to the web of roads winding through the small suburban areas of The Heads and Coney Glen to the top of the **Eastern Head**. Around *Paquitas* restaurant there are fantastic views out to sea; for an even better viewpoint head along the short walkway starting outside the restaurant, taking you along the cliff edge.

The beaches

Don't come to Knysna for a beach holiday: the closest beach is 20km from town at **Brenton-on-Sea**. A tiny settlement on the shores of Buffels Bay, it does admittedly have a quite exceptional beach. In the opposite direction from Knysna, the closest patch of sand is at **Noetzie**, a town known more for its eccentric holiday homes built to look like castles than for its seaside.

ARRIVAL AND DEPARTURE

KNYSNA

By bus Greyhound, Intercape and Translux buses connect Knysna with Cape Town (6–7 daily; 7hr); Durban (daily; 17hr); George (6–7 daily; 1hr); Johannesburg (1–2 daily; 16hr); Mossel Bay (6–7 daily; 1hr 15min); Oudtshoorn (1–2 daily; 2hr); Plettenberg Bay (6–7 daily; 1hr 30min); Port Elizabeth (6–7 daily; 4hr 30min); Pretoria (1–2 daily; 17hr); and all Garden Route towns along the N2. The bus terminus is at the train station (trains no longer run from here) in Remembrance Avenue opposite Knysna waterfront. The Baz Bus travels daily in each direction between Cape Town and Port Elizabeth along the N2. It drops passengers off at *Knysna Backpackers*.

INFORMATION

Tourist information Knysna Tourism, 40 Main St (Mon–Fri 8am–5pm, Sat 8.30am–1pm; ☎044 382 5510, ⓦ visitknysna.co.za), provides maps and runs a desk for booking activities around Knysna – including cruises to and abseiling down The Heads, and bungee jumping from the Bloukrans River Bridge. They can also help with booking accommodation.

ACCOMMODATION

The best places to stay in Knysna are away from the main road, with views of the lagoon and The Heads. Out of town there are some excellent establishments as well as reasonably priced self-catering cottages right in the forest. For somewhere quieter on the lagoon, make for the western edge at Brenton-on-Sea.

TOWN CENTRE AND KNYSNA QUAYS

Knysna Backpackers 42 Queen St ☎044 382 2554, ⓦ knysnabackpackers.co.za; map p.226. Spotless, well-organized hostel in a large, rambling and centrally located Victorian house that has been declared a National Monument. This tranquil establishment has five rooms rented as doubles (but able to sleep up to four people) and a dorm that sleeps eight. Dorm R90, double R280

Protea Hotel – Knysna Quays Waterfront Drive ☎044 382 5005, ⓦ proteahotels.com; map p.226. A 122-room, nautically themed luxury hotel in a fabulous spot on the waterfront, within walking distance of the centre. Rooms either have views of the lagoon and the yacht basin or of the train station. R1630

Wayside Inn Pledge Square, 48 Main Rd ☎044 382 6011, ⓦ www.waysideinn.co.za; map p.226. A smart overnight right in the centre, done out in sisal matting, wicker furniture and white linen on black wrought-iron bedsteads. A continental breakfast is served in your room or on the deck outside. R780

EASTERN SUBURBS, LEISURE ISLE AND THE HEADS

Cunningham's Island Guest House 3 Kingsway, Leisure Isle ☎044 384 1319, ⓦ islandhouse.co.za;

map p.226. Purpose-built two-storey, timber-and-glass guesthouse with eight suites, decked out in dazzling white, relieved by a touch of blue and some ethnic colour (stripy cushions and African baskets). Each room has its own entrance leading to the garden, which has a swimming pool shaded by giant strelitzias. Stylish and comfortable, its only drawback is the lack of views. R760

Isola Bella 21 Hart Lane, Leisure Isle ✆ 044 384 0049, ⊛ isolabella.co.za; map p.226. You can't help but gasp at The Heads views through the huge windows of this imposing guesthouse at the lagoon's edge. You'll either love or loathe the mildly operatic decor – repro furniture, lots of oil paintings and some floral fabrics. Either way, the rooms are undeniably luxurious. Breakfast is served on the spectacularly positioned balcony overlooking the water. R3320

Under Milk Wood George Rex Drive, The Heads ✆ 044 384 0745, ⊛ milkwood.co.za; map p.226. Luxury self-catering accommodation on the lagoon at the foot of The Heads with its own private beach – safe for swimming – and terrific views of the mountains and water. The two-bedroom self-catering units, with their own sun decks, are surrounded by milkwood trees; rates vary depending on whether the unit is on the lagoon, the hillside or between. There are also two B&B rooms. R1185

WEST OF TOWN

Azure House 65 Circular Drive, ✆ 044 382 1221, ⊛ azurehouse.com; map p.226. Lime-washed whites, blues and pale yellows are the signature colours in these upmarket self-catering rooms, each en suite, with a small lounge. Breakfast (optional) is served on a wicker tray on your private balcony overlooking the lagoon. R850

Blue Oyster Corner of Rio and Stent sts ✆ 044 382 2265, ⊛ blueoyster.co.za; map p.226. Hospitable three-storey, vaguely Greek-themed B&B set high on one of the hills that rise up behind Knysna, offering fabulous panoramas across the lagoon to The Heads. The four comfortable double rooms, of which the ones on the top floor have the best views, are done out in white and blue. R940

Lightleys Holiday Houseboats Moored at the Belvidere turn-off from the N2 ✆ 044 386 0007, ⊛ houseboats.co.za/knysna; map p.226. For something different, you can rent a fully equipped houseboat with interiors resembling those of caravans and which lets you explore the lagoon's 20km of navigable water. R1450

★ Narnia Country Guest House Signed off Welbedacht Lane, 3km west of Knysna ✆ 044 382 1334, ⊛ www.narnia.co.za; map p.226. On a hillside with views of the lagoon, this is an immensely fun stone and rough-hewn timber farmhouse in a glorious garden. Two en-suite B&B rooms upstairs have their own balconies and swinging chairs and are decorated in a rustic-chic style, as is a comfortable semi-detached two-bedroom cottage downstairs which has a lounge, fireplace and kitchenette. The *Pool House* (so called either because it opens onto a swimming pool or because its spacious lounge has its own pool table) is a one-bedroom cottage not far from the house. Walks on the property include one down to a small lake. R1050

Phantom Forest Eco-Reserve Phantom Pass Rd, west of town off the N2 ✆ 044 386 0046, ⊛ phantomforest.com; map p.226. Breathtaking, tranquil forest lodge making extensive use of timber and glass, set on a hill in indigenous forest, with fabulous lagoon views. African fabrics and pure cotton linen reinforce the sense of unbridled luxury. Timber boardwalks wind through the forest to connect the suites to the main buildings, which feature a safari-style dining room, an open-air hot tub, a massage suite and a jacuzzi. The swimming pool teeters on the edge of the hill, cocooned by vegetation, with vervet monkeys frolicking in the forest canopy. R3400

THE FOREST

Forest Edge Cottages Rheenendal turn-off, 16km west of Knysna on the N2 ✆ 082 456 1338, ⊛ forestedge.co.z; map p.226. Ideal if you want to be close to the forest itself, these traditional tin-roofed, two-bedroomed cottages have verandas built in the vernacular tin-roofed style. Self-contained, fully equipped and serviced, the cottages sleep four. Forest walks and cycling trails start from the cottages, and you can also rent mountain bikes. R650

Southern Comfort Western Horse Ranch 3km along the Fisanthoek Rd, 17km east of Knysna en route to Plettenberg Bay ✆ 044 532 7885, ⊛ schranch.co.za; map p.226. Very basic double rooms, dorms and a tree house, on a farm adjacent to the eastern section of the Knysna forest; staff can pick you up from the N2. Horseriding (one-hour R200, two-hour R300) and massages for the saddle-weary are on offer. You can self cater or take the meals provided. Dorm R100, double R260

BELVIDERE AND BRENTON-ON-SEA

Belvidere Manor Duthie Drive, Belvidere Estate ✆ 044 387 1055, ⊛ belvidere.co.za; map p.226. A collection of tin-roofed repro Victorian cottages, nicely positioned on the water's edge. The only accommodation in this exclusive leafy area, with its lush gardens and replica Norman Church, built in the 1850s. R2340

Brenton-on-Sea Chalets C.R. Swart Drive, Brenton beachfront ✆ 044 381 0081, ⊛ abalonelodges.co.za; map p.226. A 15min drive from Knysna and overlooking the long curve of Brenton beach, which swings round to Buffels Bay. The three-bedroom, self-catering chalets sleep

2

six people, and are well equipped and comfortably furnished. R780
J&C Beach House 116 Watsonia Ave, Brenton ☎044 381 0107, ⍟jcbeachhouse.co.za; map p.226. Simple

and elegant rooms, each with views of the ocean from the balcony. You can sun yourself at the pool or on nearby Brenton beach. R900

EATING

Oysters are an obvious choice in Knysna, with the Knysna Oyster Company here being one of the world's largest oyster farms, but you'll also find a lot of good restaurants catering to other palates and one or two excellent coffee shops.

★ **34° South** Knysna Quays, ⍟34-south.com; map p.226. An outstanding deli, café, restaurant, bar, and sushi joint with imported groceries, home-made food and an extensive menu that includes seafood in all its guises, whether peri-peri calamari heads, red Thai curry mussel pot or game fish salad (mains from R70); from here you can watch the drawbridge open to let yachts sail through. Daily 8.30am–10pm.
Caffé Mario Knysna Quays ☎044 382 7250; map p.226. An intimate Italian waterside restaurant with outdoor seating, and *paninoteca* and *tramezzini* on its snack menu as well as great pizza and pasta (around R70). Consistently great food and excellent value. Daily 7.30am–10pm.
Cruise Café Featherbed Ferry Terminal, off Waterfront Drive; map p.226. A relaxed joint that fuses African and Asian flavours to create starters such as *bobotie* spring rolls. Main courses (R80–175) include Karoo lamb with mint and cranberry reduction and great seafood offerings. The waterside deck here is one of the best places in town to sink a drink while watching the setting sun. Daily 11am–3pm & Mon–Sat 5–11pm.
Firefly Eating House 152a Old Cape Rd ☎044 382 1490, ⍟fireflyeatinghouse.com; map p.226. Relaxed little bistro whose fiery red decor and sparkling fairy lights match the spicy menu (mains around R70). Dishes draw their inspiration from Malaysia, Thailand and East and South Africa. Tues–Sun 6.30–10pm.
Forest Boma *Phantom Forest Eco-Reserve*, Phantom Pass Rd ☎044 386 0046; map p.226. Eating is secondary to being in one of the most beautiful places in South Africa, in a forest with views of the whole estuary. The six-course Pan-African set menu (R290) ranges from kudu and prune *sosatie* (skewered pieces of meat) with herb polenta to pan-fried ostrich in black cherry sauce with Knysna cheese,

and tempting desserts such as brandy snap baskets. Daily 6.30–8.30pm.
Il de Pain Thesen Island ⍟iledepain.co.za; map p.226. Trendy restaurant in a bakery, with an inexpensive menu of salads, baguettes, oysters and pastas (R45–90), written up on a blackboard. Try the thick crusty bread baked in a woodfired oven with butter and preserve for breakfast, or settle for one of the delicious pastries with coffee. Tues–Sat 8am–3pm & Sun 9am–1.30pm.
Knysna Oyster Company Thesen Island; map p.226. Run by the firm of the same name, this well-established restaurant serves oysters harvested by the parent company from beds in the Knysna River Estuary. Don't worry if you're not an oyster eater – they also serve medium-priced steaks, chicken and freshly caught fish (mains around R90). Daily 9am–5pm (closes 9pm in high season).
The Olive Tree 12 Wood Mill Lane, Main Rd; map p.226. This local favourite offers a great buffet lunch, where the choice depends on the whim of the chef and the availability of ingredients, but could consist of spicy chickpeas, chicken wings and a range of fresh salads. À la carte dinners are strongly Mediterranean-influenced (mains around R50). Excellent offerings for vegetarians. Mon & Tues 8am–4pm, Wed–Fri 8am–4pm & 6.30pm till late, Sat 9am–1pm.
Pembrey's Brenton Rd, Belvidere ☎044 386 0005; map p.226. Small, unpretentious and highly rated restaurant that fuses country cooking with haute cuisine. You'll find venison, duck confit and prawns on the changing menu that's written up daily on a blackboard (mains R90–140). Booking essential. Wed–Sun 6.30pm till late.
★ **Sailor Sam's** Main Rd, opposite the post office; map p.226. A warm-hearted, old-fashioned chippy that offers incredible value, brilliant fish and chips (R30) and the cheapest oysters (R9) in town (but don't tell a soul: the

---

TOWNSHIP TOURS AND HOMESTAYS

Get a taste of Knysna's African and coloured **townships** by joining one of the warts-and-all tours operated by Eco Afrika (daily 9.30am & 2pm; R350; booking essential ☎082 558 9104). Tours go to five areas, where you'll be given some historical background and get a chance to walk around and chat to people. You can also include lunch with a township family as part of the package (an additional R50 paid directly to your hosts).

Eco Afrika also arrange **homestays** in one of the townships, where you stay with a family in a corrugated iron shack (R150 paid to your hosts). Eco Afrika will drop you off and pick you up the next morning.

delicious shellfish aren't local, they're shipped in from the West Coast). Mon–Sat 11am–8.30pm & Sun 11am–3pm. **Zachary's** *Pezula Resort Hotel and Spa*, Lagoonview Drive, Eastern Head ☎ 044 302 3300, ⊛ zacharys.co.za; map p.226. Fine dining at the only place in Knysna to be

nominated in 2010 for an *Eat Out* Top 10 Award. Though the service and ambience are formal, the pitch-perfect food – South African with a global twist – is worth traipsing out for if the prices don't put you off (mains R130–210). Daily 7–10.30am & 6.30–10pm.

DRINKING AND NIGHTLIFE

Swing Cafe 3 Sun Centre, Templeman Square, ⊛ theswingcafe.co.za; map p.226. One of the Garden Route's more serious live music venues aims at a mature audience and features local performers three nights a week (and every night during the December holidays). It also has an all-day snack menu and decent bar food and drinks. Mon–Sat 9am till late.

Zanzibar Corner of St George's and Main rds ☎ 044 382 0386; map p.226. Knysna's longest-established nightclub occupies the premises of the Old Barnyard Theatre and, in addition to a range of sounds from commercial to house, it continues with the Barnyard's tradition of occasional live acts that include bands, cabaret and comedy. Wed, Fri & Sat 9pm–2am.

DIRECTORY

Emergencies General emergency number from landline ☎ 107, from mobile phone ☎ 112; Police ☎ 044 302 6600; National Sea Rescue ☎ 082 990 5956.

Hospital Life Knysna Private Hospital, Hunters Drive (☎ 044 384 1083), is well run and has a casualty department open to visitors.

The Knysna forests

The best reason to come to Knysna is for the **forests** just north of town. Shreds of a once magnificent **woodland** that was home to **Khoi** clans and harboured a thrilling variety of wildlife, including significant **elephant** and **buffalo** herds, the forests attracted European explorers and naturalists. In their wake came woodcutters and gold-diggers, all bent on making their fortunes. The last buffalo was shot in 1883 and the elephants were reduced to their present handful (see box p.234), but the forests were saved from destruction when their exploitation was stopped in 1939 and controlled harvesting introduced in 1965. The remaining 568-square-kilometre patchwork is still impressive – and dense enough to lose yourself in. It represents Africa's southernmost (and South Africa's tallest) **Afromontane forest**, relics of ancient tropical forest that thrived thousands of years ago when the subcontinent was warmer and moister.

The Knysna forests owe their continued existence to the area's mild coastal temperatures and year-round rainfall. Among the arboreal giants, you'll come across South Africa's national tree, the beautiful real yellowwood (*Podocarpus latifolius*) with its tall straight trunk, long thin strips of peeling bark and spreading canopy. The tallest yellowwood in the vicinity is the 40m (about as high as a fifteen-storey building) Big Tree in the Diepwalle Forest (see p.233). The height and density of trees in some parts of the forests create a subdued, dappled light that lends itself to fantasies about fairies and water sprites, but in reality you stand a good chance of seeing vervet monkeys, small antelope and a substantial range of forest birds.

Goudveld State Forest

Just over 30km northwest of Knysna • Daily sunrise–sunset • R8 if attendant is present, otherwise by self-issued free permit

The beautiful **Goudveld State Forest** is a mixture of plantation and indigenous woodland.

EXPLORING THE FORESTS

Knysna Forest Tours and Mountain Biking Africa (Tony Cook ☎ 082 783 8392, ⊛ mountainbikingafrica.co.za, ⊛ knysnaforesttours.co.za) is an adventure company offering guided forest and coastal **hikes**, **trail-running**, **mountain biking** and **canoe trips** in the area, as well as birdwatching and fly fishing. You can also combine two activities into a full-day trip. Half-day hikes start at R400 per person and biking trips at R530 including refreshments.

It takes its name from the gold boom (*goudveld* is Afrikaans for goldfields) that brought hundreds of prospectors to the mining town of **Millwood** in the 1880s. The boom was short-lived, and bust followed in 1890 after most of the mining companies went to the wall. Today, the old town is completely overgrown, apart from signs indicating where the old streets stood. The forest itself is still lovely, featuring tall, indigenous trees, a delightful valley with a stream, and plenty of swimming holes and picnic sites.

Hiking in the Goudveld

A number of clearly **waymarked hikes** traverse the Goudveld. The most rewarding (and easy going) is along **Jubilee Creek**, which traces the progress of a burbling brook for 3.5km through giant woodland to a gorgeous, deep rock pool – ideal for cooling off after your effort. Along the way you'll see miners' excavations scraped or blasted out of the hillside. Some of the old mine works have been restored, as have the original **reduction works** around the cocopan track, used to carry the ore from the mine to the

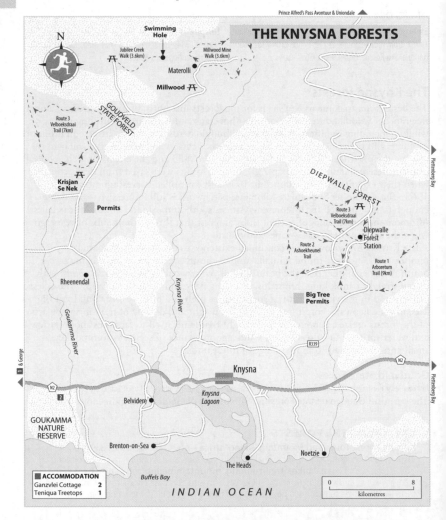

works, which is still there after a century. Jubilee Creek is also an excellent place to encounter **Knysna louries**; keep an eye focused on the branches above for the crimson flash of their flight feathers as they forage for berries. You can pick up a **map** directing you to the creek from the entrance gate to the reserve; note that the waymarked trail is linear, so you return via the same route. There's a pleasant **picnic site** along the banks of the stream at the start of the walk.

A more strenuous option is the circular **Woodcutter Walk**, though you can choose either the 3km or the 9km version. Starting at **Krisjan se Nek**, another picnic site not far past the Goudveld entrance gate, it meanders downhill through dense forest, passing through stands of tree ferns, and returns uphill to the starting point. The tourist office has maps of the area.

2

ARRIVAL AND DEPARTURE   GOUDVELD

By car To get to the Goudveld from Knysna, follow the N2 west toward George, turning right onto the Rheenendal Rd just after the Knysna River, and continue for about 25km, following the Bibby's Koep signposts until the Goudveld sign.

Diepwalle Forest
Just over 20km northeast of Knysna • daily 6am–6pm • R15

The **Diepwalle Forest** is the last haunt of Knysna's almost extinct elephant population. The only elephants you're guaranteed seeing are on the painted markers indicating the three main hikes through these woodlands. However, if you're quiet and alert, you do stand a chance of seeing vervet monkeys, bushbuck and blue duiker. Diepwalle ("deep walls") is one of the highlights of the Knysna area and is renowned for its impressive density of huge trees, especially **yellowwoods**.

Hiking in Diepwalle
Diepwalle's **Elephant Walk** consists of three looped hiking routes covering 7km, 8km and 9km of terrain respectively. They pass through flat to gently undulating country covered by indigenous forest and montane *fynbos*. If you're moderately fit, the hikes should each take three to three-and-a-half hours. All three loops start and end at the **Diepwalle Forest Station** (see below).

The 9km **Route 1**, marked by black elephants, descends through an **arboretum** to a stream edged with tree ferns. Across the stream you'll come to the much-photographed **Big Tree**, a 600-year-old Goliath yellowwood. The easy 8km **Route 2**, marked by white elephants, crosses the Gouna River, where there's a large pool allegedly used by real pachyderms. Most difficult of the three hikes is the rewarding 7km **Route 3**, marked by red elephants, which passes along the foothills of the Outeniquas. Take care here to stick to the elephant markers, as they overlap with a series of painted footprints marking the Outeniqua Trail, for which you need to have arranged a permit to use. Just before the Veldboeksdraai picnic site stands another mighty yellowwood regarded by some as the most beautiful in the forest.

ARRIVAL AND DEPARTURE   DIEPWALLE FOREST

By car To get to Diepwalle Forest from Knysna, follow the N2 east towards Plettenberg Bay, turning left onto the R339 after 7km. Heading in the direction of Avontuur and Uniondale, continue for 17km, after which you'll reach the clearly signposted turn-off on your right to the Diepwalle Forest Station, where there's designated parking.

Knysna Elephant Park
N2, 9km west of Plettenberg Bay • Daily 8.30am–5pm • Tours daily 8.30am–4.30pm • R190 • Elephant ride R815 • Booking essential • ☎ 044 532 7732, ⓦ knysnaelephantpark.co.za

Heading east from Knysna along the N2, you come to the **Knysna Elephant Park**. The park was established in 1994 to provide a home for abandoned, orphaned and abused young elephants, and opened to the public in 2003. The youngest of its charges are

2

THE KNYSNA ELEPHANTS

Traffic signs warning motorists about elephants along the N2 between Knysna and Plettenberg Bay are rather optimistic: there are few indigenous **pachyderms** left and, with such a large forest, sightings are rare. But such is the mystique attached to the Knysna elephants that locals tend to be a little cagey about just how few they number. By 1860, the thousands that had formerly wandered the once vast forests were down to five hundred, and by 1920 (twelve years after they were protected by law), there were only twenty animals left; the current estimate is three. Loss of habitat and consequent malnutrition, rather than full-scale hunting, seems to have been the principal cause of their decline.

The only elephants you're guaranteed to see near Knysna are at the **Knysna Elephant Park** (see p.233) or the **Elephant Sanctuary** (see p.239), both near Plettenberg Bay.

---

reared by park staff, who hand-feed them forty litres of baby formula a day, and sleep next to them at night. Of the activities on offer, the most popular are the roughly hour-long tours, which leave every half hour, where you'll get the chance to touch and feed one of the pachyderms. You can also take a two-hour ride on an elephant or a guided nature walk of the same duration alongside one.

ACCOMMODATION   **KNYSNA ELEPHANT PARK**

Self-catering units The park offers accommodation in upmarket self-catering units, set on an upper storey, above the elephant boma, which means you'll hear the pachyderms and the sounds of their stalls being cleaned in the morning. R1260

Plettenberg Bay

Over the Christmas holidays, tens of thousands of residents from Johannesburg's wealthy northern suburbs decamp to **PLETTENBERG BAY** (usually called Plett), 33km east of Knysna, the flashiest of the Garden Route's seaside towns. Plett's town centre, at the top of the hill, consists of a conglomeration of supermarkets, swimwear shops, estate agents and restaurants aimed largely at the holiday trade. It's wise to give it a miss during peak season, when available accommodation is scarce and prices correspondingly double.

Yet, during low season, the banal suburban development on the surrounding hills somehow doesn't seem so bad because the bay views really are stupendous. Further afield, the deep-blue **Tsitsikamma Mountains** drop sharply to the inlet and its large estuary, providing a constant vista to the town and its suburbs. The bay curves over several kilometres of white sands separated from the mountains by forest, which makes this a green and temperate location with rainfall throughout the year.

Southern right whales appear every winter, and are a seriously underrated attraction, while **dolphins** can be seen throughout the year, hunting or riding the surf, often in substantial numbers. **Swimming** is safe, and though the waters are never tropically warm they reach a comfortable temperature between November and April. On the east of the bay lies the seaside resort of **Keurboomstrand** and beyond that **The Crags** (both of them more or less suburbs of Plett) with its trio of wildlife parks: Monkeyland, Birds of Eden and the Elephant Sanctuary, all worth a visit, especially if you're travelling with kids.

ARRIVAL AND DEPARTURE   **PLETTENBERG BAY**

By bus Intercape, Greyhound and Translux intercity buses stop at the Shell Ultra City filling station, just off the N2 in Marine Way, 2km from the town centre. Between them they service the route along the N2 between Plettenberg Bay and Cape Town (6–7 daily; 7hr 30min); Durban (daily; 16hr); George (6–7 daily; 1hr 30min); Knysna (6–7 daily; 1hr 30min); Mossel Bay (6–7 daily; 2hr 15min); Port Elizabeth (6–7 daily; 2hr 30min). As there's no transport around town, if you don't have your own car, you'll need to arrange for your guesthouse to collect you from the petrol station. The Baz Bus drops passengers off at accommodation in town.

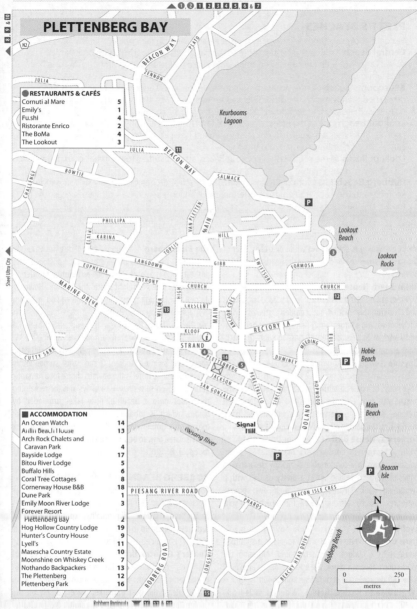

PLETTENBERG BAY

● RESTAURANTS & CAFÉS

Cornuti al Mare	5
Emily's	1
Fu.shi	4
Ristorante Enrico	2
The BoMa	4
The Lookout	3

■ ACCOMMODATION

An Ocean Watch	14
Anlin Beach House	13
Arch Rock Chalets and	
Caravan Park	4
Bayside Lodge	17
Bitou River Lodge	5
Buffalo Hills	6
Coral Tree Cottages	8
Cornerway House B&B	18
Dune Park	1
Emily Moon River Lodge	3
Forever Resort	
Plettenberg Bay	2
Hog Hollow Country Lodge	19
Hunter's Country House	9
Lyell's	11
Masescha Country Estate	10
Moonshine on Whiskey Creek	7
Nothando Backpackers	13
The Plettenberg	12
Plettenberg Park	16

INFORMATION

Tourist information Shop 35, Mellville Corner, Main St (Mon–Fri 8.30am–5pm, Sat 9am–1pm; ☎ 044 533 4065, ⓦ plettenbergbay.co.za). Stocks maps of the town and may be able to help with finding accommodation.

ACCOMMODATION

THE TOWN

An Ocean Watch 21 Plettenberg St ☎ 044 533 1700, ⓦ anoceanwatchguesthouse.co.za; map above. A beautifully decorated beach-style home in which just

2

PLETT'S BEACHES

Visitors principally come to Plett for its beaches – and there's a fair choice.

Central Beach Right at the central shore of the bay, this is where the fishing boats and seacats anchor a little out to sea. The small waves here make for calm swimming, making it an ideal family spot.

Keurbooms Beach On the northern side of the Keurbooms Lagoon, the beach feels less developed than those on the other side and stretches for over 10km along a section of coastline where you can see groups of dolphins playing in big breakers.

Lookout Beach One of the nicest stretches of sand for bathers, body-surfers or sun lizards, Lookout Beach has a marvellously located restaurant (see p.238), from which you can often catch sight of dolphins cruising into the bay.

Lookout Rocks To the southeast of Lookout Beach, attracts surfers to the break off a needle of rocks known as the Point.

Robberg Beach Just south of Beacon Island, the beach stretches for roughly six soft, sandy kilometres to the Robberg Peninsula, offering excellent long beach walks. It's also accessible by road at several points along the way.

about everything is shimmering white or cream. Four of the six rooms have sea views, as does the heated swimming pool. **R990**

Anlin Beach House 33 Roche Bonne Ave ☎ 044 533 3694, ⓦ anlinbeachhouse.co.za; map p.235. Two stylish and comfortably kitted-out garden studios with kitchenettes, and a larger family unit with three bedrooms and a kitchen, in a garden setting close to Robberg Beach. Units are serviced daily. **R1110**

Bayside Lodge 5 Sanganer Ave ☎ 044 533 0601, ⓦ baysidelodge.co.za; map p.235. Modern two-storey brick house in a quiet suburban area about 500m from the beach with four en-suite rooms and a self-contained cottage. Breakfast is served inside or on the patio overlooking the garden and saltwater pool. **R900**

Cornerway House B&B 61 Longships Drive ☎ 044 533 3190, ⓦ cornerwayhouse.co.za; map p.235. Seven en-suite rooms in a comfortable bungalow decorated in English cottage style and set in a pretty garden with a swimming pool. All rooms have their own private entrances. There's also a lovely three-bedroom self-catering cottage. **R990**

Lyell's 59 Beacon Way ☎ 044 533 5692; map p.235. Three sparkling white en-suite B&B rooms in a suburban house, plus a budget self-catering unit. Although the rooms don't have sea views, the upstairs lounge area does have 180-degree vistas of the ocean and lagoon. **R600**

★ **Nothando Backpackers** 5 Wilder St ☎ 044 533 0220, ⓦ nothando.com; map p.235. Top-notch child-friendly hostel run by a former schoolteacher. A five-minute walk from Plett's main drag, the single-storey suburban house has seven luxury double rooms (five of which are en suite) as well as three dorms (two with four beds, the other with eight). Breakfast (of cereal, cheese, bread, muffins and yoghurt, as well as bacon and eggs) is available for R35. Dorm **R130**, double **R400**

The Plettenberg 40 Church St, Lookout Rocks ☎ 044 533 2030, ⓦ plettenberg.com; map p.235. Plett's poshest hotel is a large, luxurious establishment offering unbeatable views straight onto the ocean. However, despite the sky-high rates, you could still end up in a room overlooking the car park. **R4000**

★ **Plettenberg Park** Near the end of Robberg Rd ☎ 044 533 9067, ⓦ plettenbergpark.co.za; map p.235. Set in a private nature reserve and perched on a cliff edge above the swirling Indian Ocean, this stupendously located boutique hotel is the obvious choice for a romantic getaway. Seven suites have sea views and the remaining three look onto a beautiful little lake surrounded by *fynbos*, which is inhabited by small game. A set of meandering timber steps leads down from the pool deck to an isolated private beach far below with a lovely natural rock pool. **R5120**

ROBBERG BEACH AND WEST OF PLETT

Coral Tree Cottages Off the N2, 11km west of Plettenberg Bay ☎ 044 532 7822, ⓦ coraltreecottages .co.za; map p.235. High-quality, spacious thatched cottages sleeping up to four, though unfortunately the roar of the N2 is never absent. **R600**

Hunter's Country House Off the N2, 10km west of Plett on the way to Knysna ☎ 044 532 7818, ⓦ hunterhotels.com; map p.235. Set in a woodland area, this is one of the best upmarket places to stay on the Garden Route, with an emphasis on country comfort rather than seaside glitz. Garden suite accommodation is in thatched cottages set in well-established gardens, each with an open fireplace, private patio, underfloor heating and a/c, while the forest suites are larger and more sumptuous, each with its own private pool. **R2890**

Masescha Country Estate 1km north off the N2, signposted 12km west from Plettenberg Bay

☎ 044 532 7647, **ⓦ** masescha.co.za; map p.235. Six units, from a small self-catering chalet to a five-bedroom house, on an aquaponic farm, with outdoor sitting areas surrounded by pleasant gardens and a forest. Good for both families and couples, it also has a swimming pool. R400

KEURBOOMSTRAND AND EAST OF PLETT
Arch Rock Chalets and Caravan Park Arch Rock **☎** 044 535 9409, **ⓦ** archrock.co.za; map p.235. Seventeen fully-equipped chalets with either one or two bedrooms. Apart from the forest chalets and log cabins, which are set back among trees, the rest are close to the beach and have sea views. R610

Bitou River Lodge Bitou Valley Rd (the R340), about 4km from the N2 **☎** 044 535 9577, **ⓦ** bitou.co.za; map p.235. A great-value place, in a lovely spot on the banks of the Bitou River. The five bedrooms at this intimate lodge are comfortable but unfussy and overlook a pretty garden with a lily pond. Rate includes use of canoes on the river. R1150

Buffalo Hills Rietvlei Rd, Wittedrif Village **☎** 044 535 9739, **ⓦ** buffalohills.co.za; map p.235. Farm turned game lodge on the banks of the Bitou River, a 15min drive from Plett. No substitute for seeing the Big Five at one of the major game reserves, it nonetheless provides a thoroughly entertaining experience. The package includes a game drive and guided walk on which you stand a chance of seeing rhino, buffalo, giraffe, zebra, bontebok and a number of other antelope.

Accommodation is an old-style African farmhouse with four double rooms, a stone cottage that sleeps four, and nine huge, luxury walk-in tents, pitched on their own decks, with spa baths. R1800

Dune Park Keurboomstrand Rd, leading off the N2 and running along the shore to Keurbooms **☎** 044 535 9606, **ⓦ** www.dunepark.co.za; map p.235. Luxury hotel with airy bedrooms that are simple and stylishly furnished with crisp white linen, as well as two-bedroom self-catering cottages built on top of high dunes to provide great views (R750), within spitting distance of the sea. R695

Emily Moon River Lodge Rietvlei Rd, off the N2 (turn off at Penny Pinchers) **☎** 044 533 2982, **ⓦ** emilymoon.co.za; map p.235. That the owner of this highly imaginative and luxurious lodge, perched on a ridge looking across the Bitou Wetlands, is a dealer in ethnic art is plain to see. The place is not only littered with Batonga sculptures and Swazi crafts, it has in places been constructed out of artworks, such as the intricate Rajasthani arched screen that is the entrance to the magnificently sited restaurant. Each of its chalets jetties out of the hillside to offer views from a private deck (and bathroom) of the oxbowing Bitou, along which small game can occasionally be seen. All chalets have fireplaces and TVs. There is a family suite that sleeps four in which kids are accommodated at a very discounted rate. R2540

Forever Resort Plettenberg Bay 6km east of Plett and signposted off the N2 near Keurboomstrand

WHALING AND GNASHING OF TEETH
For conservationists, the monumental 1970s eyesore of the *Beacon Island Hotel*, on a promontory on the southern side of the Piesang River mouth, may not be such a bad thing, since previously the island was the site of a whale-processing factory established in 1806 – one of some half-dozen such plants erected along the Western Cape coast that year. Whaling continued at Plettenberg Bay until 1916. Southern right whales were the favoured species, yielding more oil and **whalebone** – an essential component of Victorian corsets – than any other. In the nineteenth century, a southern right would net around three times as much as a humpback caught along the Western Cape coast, leading to a rapid decline in the southern right population by the middle of the nineteenth century.

The years between the establishment and the closing of the Plettenberg Bay factory saw worldwide whaling transformed by the inventions of the Industrial Revolution. In 1852, the explosive harpoon was introduced, followed by the use of steam-powered ships five years later, and the **cannon-mounted harpoon** in 1868. In 1913, Plettenberg Bay was the site of one of seventeen shore-based and about a dozen floating factories between West Africa and Mozambique, which that year between them took about ten thousand whales.

Inevitably, a rapid decline in humpback populations began; by 1918, all but four of the shore-based factories had closed due to lack of prey. The remaining whalers now turned their attention to fin and blue whales. When the South African fin whale population became depleted by the mid-1960s to twenty percent of its former size, they turned to sei and sperm whales. When these populations declined, the frustrated whalers started hunting minke whales, which at 9m in length are too small to be a viable catch. In 1979 the South African government banned all activity surrounding whaling.

2

WHALE- AND DOLPHIN-WATCHING IN PLETTENBERG BAY

Elevated ocean panoramas give Plettenberg Bay outstanding vantages for watching **southern right whales** during their breeding season between June and October. An especially good vantage point is the area between the wreck of the *Athene* at the southern end of Lookout Beach and the Keurbooms River. The Robberg Peninsula is also excellent, looming protectively over this whale nursery and giving a grandstand view of the bay. Other good town viewpoints are from Beachy Head Road at Robberg Beach; Signal Hill in San Gonzales Street past the post office and police station; the *Beacon Island Hotel* on Beacon Island; and the deck of *The Lookout* restaurant on Lookout Beach.

Outside Plett, the Kranshoek viewpoint and hiking trail offers wonderful whale-watching points along the route. To get there, head for Knysna, taking the Harkerville turn-off, and continue for 7km. It's also possible to view the occasional pair (mother and calf) at Nature's Valley, 29km east of Plett on the R102, and from Storms River Mouth. For more information about whales, see the box on p.240.

☎044 535 9309, ⍟foreverplettenberg.co.za; map p.235. A sizeable family resort, with camping (up to four people R550) on the shady banks of the Keurbooms River, away from the sea, and a range of self-catering log cabins, some with river views. Canoes and motorboats are available to rent, and there's a swimming pool. R675

Hog Hollow Country Lodge Askop Rd, 18km east of Plettenberg Bay (turn south off the N2 at the signpost) ☎044 534 8879, ⍟hog-hollow.com; map p.235. A touch of luxury on a private reserve where each of the chalets, done out in earthy colours and spiced up with African artefacts, has a bath or shower and its own

wooden deck with vistas across the forest and Tsitsikamma Mountains; superb food is served as well. R3040

Moonshine on Whiskey Creek 14km east of Plettenberg Bay along the N2, signposted north of the N2 ☎044 534 8515 or ☎072 200 6656, ⍟whiskeycreek .co.za; map p.235. Fully equipped bungalows, three wooden cabins and one creatively renovated labourers' cottage, nestled in indigenous forest, with a children's play area. One of the best reasons to come here is the access to a secluded natural mountain pool and waterfall at the bottom of the nearby gorge. R590

EATING AND DRINKING

Restaurants come and go in Plett at a similar lick to the tides, but one or two long-standing establishments have managed to remain afloat. Locally caught fresh fish is the thing to look out for. And because the town is built on hills, you should generally expect terrific views.

Cornuti al Mare Seaview Properties, 1 Perestrella St ☎044 533 1277; map p.235. Terrific pizzas (R60–120) – the best along the Garden Route – and also great pasta dishes that won't break the bank, plus endless views of sea and sky. Daily noon–10pm.

Emily's *Emily Moon River Lodge,* Rietvlei Rd, off the N2 (turn off at Penny Pinchers) ☎044 533 2982; map p.235. Enchanting restaurant attached to *Emily Moon River Lodge* that many regard as the best in the area, offering stunning views of the Bitou Wetland and classical French cuisine with an edge. The menu changes daily as everything is based on what seasonal ingredients are available locally on the day, but there's always a choice of five or six starters and mains with a small range of desserts. Booking is essential. Mains R80–120. Tues– Sun noon–3pm & daily 6.30–10pm.

Fu.shi The Upper Deck, 3 Strand St ☎044 533 6489; map p.235. Asian-fusion restaurant bang in the centre of town, surrounded by picture windows to make the

most of the elevated views. Sushi is on the menu, as are various coquettishly named dishes, such as Nuggets of Pleasure (wasabi prawns with cashew salad) and Concubine's Whisper (chilli chocolate fondant with pistachio brittle). Mains R85–110. Daily noon–5pm & 6–9.30pm.

The Lookout Lookout Beach; map p.235. Marvellous bay views – if you're lucky, you'll see whales and dolphins rollicking in the surf – at this casual bar-restaurant focusing on seafood, including crayfish. They also do meat, poultry, pasta, salads and English breakfasts. Mains R70– 130. Daily 9am–11pm.

Ristorante Enrico Main Beach, Keurboomstrand ☎044 535 9818; map p.235. Great, mid-priced Italian standards – thin-based pizzas (from R55), pasta and veal – to enjoy alfresco on the beach or in the stylish indoor restaurant. Try the delicious line fish baked with garlic for a substantial main course (R130), or kudu with avocado for an unusual starter. Daily 11.30am–10.30pm.

Robberg Marine and Nature Reserve

8km southeast of Plett's town centre • Daily: Feb–Nov 7am–5pm; Dec & Jan 7am–8pm • R25 • There's no public transport to the reserve; to drive there, take Strand St towards Beacon Isle, turn right into Piesangs Valley Rd, and 200m further on turn left into Robberg Rd; follow the airport signs, continuing for 3.5km – look out for the Robberg turn-off to your left.

One of the Garden Route's nicest walks is the four-hour, 9km circular route around the spectacular rocky peninsula of **Robberg**. Here you can completely escape Plett's development and experience the coast at its wildest, with its enormous horizons and lovely vegetation. Much of the walk takes you along high cliffs, from where you can often look down on seals surfacing near the rocks, dolphins arching through the water and, in winter, whales further out in the bay.

If you don't have time for the full circular walk, there is a shorter two-hour hike and a thirty-minute ramble. A **map** indicating these is available at the reserve gate when you pay to enter. You'll need sturdy walking shoes, as the terrain is rocky and steep in parts, and the walk involves some serious rock-hopping on the west side. Bring a hat and a bottle of water, as there's no drinking water for much of the way.

Keurboomstrand

Some 14km east of Plettenberg Bay by road, across the Keurbooms River, is the uncluttered resort of **KEURBOOMSTRAND** (Keurbooms for short), little more than a suburb of Plett, sharing the same bay and with equally wonderful beaches, but less safe for swimming. The safest place to take the waves is at **Arch Rock**, in front of the caravan park, though **Picnic Rock Beach** is also pretty good. A calm and attractive place, Keurbooms has few facilities, and if you're intending to stay here (see p.237) you should stock up in Plettenberg Bay beforehand. One of Keurbooms' highlights is **canoeing** or, if you feel less energetic, taking a ferry ride or motorboat up the Keurbooms River (see box, p.240).

The Crags

The Crags, 2km east of Keurbooms, is a collection of smallholdings along the N2, a bottle store and a few other shops on the forest edge, but the reason most visitors pull in here is for the Elephant Sanctuary, Monkeyland and Birds of Eden. To reach them, look out for the BP filling station, then take the Monkeyland/Kurland turn-off and follow the Elephant Sanctuary/Monkeyland signs for 2km.

Elephant Sanctuary

Daily 8am–5pm; Trunk-in-Hand daily on the hour 8am–noon & 1.30–3.30pm • R29 • Elephant rides R670 • ☎ 044 534 8145, ⓦ elephantsanctuary.co.za

The **Elephant Sanctuary** offers a chance of close encounters with its half dozen pachyderms, all of which were saved from culling in Botswana and the Kruger National Park. On the popular one-hour Trunk-in-Hand programme you get to walk with an elephant, holding the tip of its trunk in your hand, and also to stroke, feed and interact with it. The programme includes an informative talk about elephant behaviour. Fifteen-minute elephant-back rides are among the other packages on offer.

Monkeyland

Daily 8am–5pm • Viewing deck free • Safaris into the forest R125 • Combined ticket with Birds of Eden R200 • ☎ 044 534 8906, ⓦ monkeyland.co.za

Monkeyland is 400m beyond the Elephant Sanctuary and brings together primates from several continents, all of them orphaned or saved from a dismal life as pets. The place is a sanctuary, so none of the animals has been taken from the wild – and most wouldn't have the skills to survive there. Life is made as comfortable as possible for them and they are free to move around the reserve, looking for food and interacting

WHALE-WATCHING AND OTHER ACTIVITIES

A number of outfits run trips to see whales from the water, offering the chance of close encounters with a variety of whales and several dolphin species. Only **permitted whale-watchers** are allowed to go within 50m of a whale; everyone must maintain a distance of 300m. In Plett, only Ocean Safaris and Ocean Blue (listed below) hold permits. Air-based trips have the additional attraction of spectacular aerial views of bays and river inlets.

Dolphin Adventures Central Beach ☎083 590 3405, ⓦ dolphinadventures.co.za. Sea kayaking is one of the best ways to watch whales, and this outfit offers unforgettable trips with experienced and knowledgeable guides in two-person kayaks (2hr–2hr 30min; R250, including all equipment). Out of whale season it's still worth going out to see dolphins and seals.

Ocean Blue Central Beach ☎044 533 4897 or ☎083 701 3583, ⓦ oceanadventures.co.za. Sea-kayaking (R300) and boat-based whale-watching (R650) are among the offerings of this licensed outfit, which also runs township tours (see below).

Ocean Safaris Shop 3, Hopwood St ☎044 533 4963, ⓦ oceansafaris.co.za. Tailor-made cruises from a licensed whale-watching company. Apart from southern rights, the trips run into common, bottlenose and humpback dolphins, as well as Bryde's and humpback whales – and the occasional minke and killer whale. The Close Encounter with Whales outing costs R650 per person and virtually guarantees sightings between July and November; the Discovery Cruise, which costs R400, is principally a dolphin-viewing excursion.

OTHER ACTIVITIES

Bungee jumping If you fancy swinging through the air, then pull in at Tsitsikamma Forest Village, 20km east of The Crags and Monkeyland turn-off along the N2, where you'll find the registration office for the world's highest commercial bungee jump. The jump takes place off the 216m Bloukrans River Bridge, 2km beyond the village down a signposted road that also brings you to a viewpoint. There's no need to book ahead for the jump, which costs R690 (including video) for the seven-second descent. For the not so brave there's a mesh catwalk over the jump site (R100). For further information, contact Bloukrans Bungy (aka Face Adrenalin) at the bridge (☎042 281 1458, ⓦ faceadrenalin.com).

Canoeing If you can tear yourself away from the beach, canoeing up the Keurbooms River gives an alternative perspective on the area. CapeNature on the east side of the Keurbooms River Bridge along the N2 (☎044 533 2125) rents out fairly basic craft (R130 per day for a two-person canoe).

Elephant encounters The Knysna Elephant Park (see p.233) and Elephant Sanctuary (see p.239) offer the opportunity of close encounters with the large mammals.

Ferry trips and motorboating Keurbooms River Ferries (ⓦ ferry.co.za), signposted on the east side of the Keurbooms River Bridge, runs guided upriver boat trips (☎044 532 7876; R120) with knowledgeable guides skilled at spotting rare birds, and also rents out motorboats (☎082 487 3355; R350 per half-day, R500 per full day). Be sure to bring a picnic for any of the boat trips; the river is dotted with little beaches that are a good place to stop for a swim and walk. The indigenous forest comes right down to the river edge, and the journey gets better the higher up you go, the gorge narrowing and the pleasure boats and waterskiers now left behind.

Skydiving If you fancy a bit of an adrenaline rush, you can go tandem skydiving (no experience required) with Skydive Plettenberg Bay (☎082 905 7440, ⓦ skydiveplett.com; R1600).

Township tours Ocean Blue, Central Beach (☎044 533 5083 or ☎083 701 3583, ⓦ oceanadventures .co.za), arranges relaxed tours into Plett's township with a guide who is a member of the community. Outings cost R150 per person and all the takings go into a development trust, which, among other things, pays teachers' salaries and funds a crèche.

with each other and their environment in as natural a way as possible. For your own safety and that of the monkeys, you are not allowed to wander around alone. Guides take visitors on walking "**safaris**", during which you come across water holes, experience a living indigenous forest and have chance encounters with creatures such as ringtail lemurs from Madagascar and squirrel monkeys from South America. One of the sanctuary's highlights is crossing the Indiana Jones-esque rope bridge spanning a canyon to pass through the upper reaches of the forest canopy. For refreshments or meals, there's a restaurant with a forest deck at the day lodge.

Birds of Eden
Daily 8am–5pm • R125 • Combined ticket with Monkeyland R200 • ☎ 044 534 8906, ⓦ birdsofeden.co.za

Under the same management as Monkeyland and right next door, **Birds of Eden** is a huge bird sanctuary. Great effort has been taken to place netting over a substantial tract of virgin forest with as little impact as possible. The result is claimed to be the largest free-flight aviary in the world. As with Monkeyland, most of Birds of Eden's charges were already living in cages and are now free to move and fly around within the confines of the large enclosure (so large in fact that you can easily spend an hour slowly meandering along its winding, wheelchair-friendly, wooden walkway). Most of the birds are exotics, some impossibly brightly coloured, but you'll also see a number of locals, such as the Knysna lourie and South Africa's national bird, the blue crane. A restaurant by one of the lakes sells light meals and refreshments.

Tsitsikamma

The **Tsitsikamma section** of the Garden Route National Park, roughly midway between Plettenberg Bay and Port Elizabeth, is the highlight of any Garden Route trip. Starting from just beyond Keurboomstrand in the west, the section extends for 68km into the Eastern Cape along a narrow belt of coast, with dramatic foamy surges of rocky coast, deep river gorges and ancient hardwood forests clinging to the edge of tangled, green cliffs. Don't pass up its main attraction, **Storms River Mouth**, the most dramatic estuary on this exhilarating piece of coast. Established in 1964, Tsitsikamma is also South Africa's oldest marine reserve, stretching 5.5km out to sea, with an **underwater trail** open to snorkellers and licensed scuba divers.

Tsitsikamma itself has two sections: **Nature's Valley** in the west and **Storms River Mouth** in the east. Each section can only be reached down a winding tarred road from the N2 (apart from hiking, there's no way of getting from one to the other through the park itself). Nature's Valley incorporates the most low-key settlement on the Garden Route, with a fabulous sandy beach stretching for 3km. South Africa's ultimate hike, the five day **Otter Trail** (see p.244), connects the two sections of the park.

The nearest settlement to Storms River Mouth, some 14km to its north at the top of a steep winding road, is the confusingly named **Storms River Village**, which is outside the national park and some distance from any part of the river, but makes a convenient base for adventure activities in the vicinity and day-trips down to Storms River Mouth.

Nature's Valley
Nature's Valley, at the western end of the Tsitsikamma section of the Garden Route National Park, extends inland into a rugged and hilly interior incised with narrow valleys and traversed by a series of footpaths. It also incorporates a pleasingly old-fashioned settlement on the stunningly beautiful Groot River Lagoon with 20km of beach. Bypassed by the N2, and by intercity buses and tour parties, Nature's Valley is the supreme destination if you're after a relaxed retreat along the Garden Route.

Walks
There are plenty of good **walks** at Nature's Valley, many starting from the national park campsite, 1km north of the village, where you can pick up maps and information about birds and trees. One of the loveliest places to head for is **Salt River Mouth**, 3km west of Nature's Valley, where you can swim and picnic – though you'll need to ford the river at low tide. This walk starts and ends at the café at Nature's Valley. Also recommended is the circular 6km **Kalanderkloof trail**, which starts at the national park campsite, ascends to a lookout point, and descends via a narrow river gorge graced with a profusion of huge Outeniqua yellowwood trees and Cape wild bananas.

2

ARRIVAL AND DEPARTURE

NATURE'S VALLEY

Nature's Vally is 29km east of Plettenberg Bay, down the lovely winding Groot River pass (along which you'll often encounter baboon troops). If you're self-catering, stock up on supplies before you get to Nature's Valley, since their supplies are basic.

INFORMATION

Tourist information Nature's Valley Trading Store, corner of Forest and St Michael sts (☎044 531 6835, ⓦwww .cyberperk.co.za/naturesvalley) is effectively the village centre and acts an informal but excellent information bureau.

ACCOMMODATION

Accommodation in Nature's Valley itself is pretty limited, which contributes to its low-key charm, but you'll find some choice options on the road leading off the N2 into the village, just before the switchbacks begin. Apart from the places listed below, self-catering accommodation can be rented through Meyer van Rooyen (☎082 772 2972), who handles a number of houses (R550–900 per house) in and around Nature's Valley – most of which sleep between six and eight people.

Four Fields Farm Nature's Valley Rd; 3km from the N2 along the R102 and 6km from Nature's Valley ☎044 534 8708, ⓦfourfields.iowners.net. A welcoming, charmingly unpretentious former dairy farm, less than 10mins' drive from the sea. Five en-suite bedrooms, simply furnished with beautiful old pieces, have French doors leading to their own private decks, which in turn open onto a lovely garden surrounded by fields. There's also a self-catering unit sleeping four (R720). R910

Froggy Pond Second house on the right as you enter Nature's Valley ☎044 531 6835, ⓦwww .cyberperk.co.za/naturesvalley/froggypond.htm. Self-catering accommodation in a two-storey timber and brick cottage. Downstairs is a self-contained flatlet with a double bedroom and living area that can sleep two adults and two children (R450; discounts for stays of 4 days or longer); upstairs are two basic double rooms with en-suite showers. R350

Lily Pond Lodge 102 Nature's Valley Rd; 3km from the N2 along the R102 and 6km from Nature's Valley ☎044 534 8767, ⓦlilypond.co.za. Probably the most memorable accommodation in the vicinity of Nature's Valley, which distinguishes itself through its sharp sense of style and its commitment to luxury. The four en-suite rooms have sound systems, TV, wi-fi access ands French doors opening onto private terraces, while the two spacious luxury suites also have their own lounge, underfloor

heating and king-sized beds. There are a further three even more luxurious garden suites and a honeymoon suite that has its own private garden. R1380

Nature's Valley Guest House 411 St Patrick's Ave ☎044 531 6805, ⓦnaturesvalleyguesthouse.co.za. A well-located and well-priced B&B with six doubles, three of them en suite. A snooker table, TV lounge, canoe, surfboard and windsurfer are available for guests, and you can set out from the guesthouse on two- to six-hour hikes along the beaches or through the forest. R580

Nature's Valley Restcamp 1km to the north of the village; book through South African National Parks (☎012 428 9111, ⓦsanparks.org), or if you're already in Nature's Valley area, the camp supervisor (☎044 531 6700). Camp sites tucked into indigenous forest, and basic two-person forest huts with communal ablution facilities. Camping R170, hut R390

Tranquility Lodge 130 Saint Michael's St (next to the shop) ☎044 531 6663, ⓦtranquilitylodge.co.za. If Nature's Valley has a centre then this comfortable lodge, next to the village's only shop, is bang in the middle of it. A two-storey brick and timber building set in a garden that feels as if it's part of the encroaching forest, it is just 50m from the beach. Breakfast is served on an upstairs deck among the treetops. All rooms are en suite, and there's a larger honeymoon suite with a spa bath, double shower, fireplace and private deck. R1180

EATING AND DRINKING

Nature's Valley Trading Store Forest and St Michael sts ☎044 531 6835, ⓦwww.cyberperk.co.za/ naturesvalley. The only place in the village that does food and booze is a pretty informal and convivial spot for

seafood, steaks, burgers and toasted sandwiches, and provides the only nightlife – a large-screen TV – apart from gazing at the stars. Daily 9.30am–8.45pm.

Storms River Mouth

55km east of Plettenberg Bay • Daily 6am–7.30pm • R108 • ☎042 281 1607

In contrast to the languid lagoon and long soft sands of Nature's Valley, **Storms River**

KNYSNA LAGOON (P.225) >

2

Mouth presents the elemental face of the Garden Route, with the dark Storms River surging through a gorge to do battle with the surf. **Storms River Mouth Restcamp**, sited on tended lawns, is poised between a craggy shoreline of black rocks pounded by foamy white surf and steeply raking forested cliffs, and is without a doubt the ultimate destination along the southern Cape coast. Don't confuse this with **Storms River Village** just off the N2, which is nowhere near the sea. Even if your time is limited and you can't spend the night at Storms River Mouth, it's still worth nipping down for a meal, a walk or a swim in the summer.

Walks

Walking is the main activity at the Mouth, and at the visitors' office at the restcamp you can get maps of short, waymarked coastal trails that leave from here. These include steep walks up the forested cliffs, where you can see 800-year-old yellowwood trees with views onto a wide stretch of ocean. Most rewarding is the **three-kilometre hike** west from the restcamp along the start of the Otter Trail to a fantastic **waterfall** pool at the base of 50m-high falls where you can swim right on the edge of the shore. Less demanding is the kilometre-long **boardwalk stroll** from the restaurant to the suspension bridge to see the river mouth. On your way to the bridge, don't miss the dank **strandloper** (beachcomber) **cave**. Hunter-gatherers frequented this area between 5000 and 2000 years ago, living off seafood in wave-cut caves near the river mouth. A modest display shows an excavated midden, with clear layers of little bones and shells.

If you're desperate to walk the **Otter Trail** (5 days; 42km; book through SAN Parks), which begins at Storms River, and have been told that it is full, don't despair. A single person or a couple do stand a chance of getting in on the back of a last-minute cancellation, so it may be worth hanging out at the Mouth for a night or two.

Swimming

Swimming at the Mouth is restricted to a safe and pristine little sandy bay below the restaurant, though conditions can be icy in summer if there are easterly winds and cold upwellings of deep water from the continental shelf.

ARRIVAL AND DEPARTURE   STORMS RIVER MOUTH

By car Storms River Mouth is 18km south of Storms River Bridge, on the N2. Most people stop at the bridge to gaze into the deep river gorge and fill up at the most beautifully located filling and service station in the country.

By shuttle *Tsitsikamma Backpackers* can arrange a shuttle service for their guests from Storms River Village to the Mouth (R100 per person; minimum three passengers).

INFORMATION

Tourist information The visitor's office at the park reception is open daily 7.30am–6pm, and a shop (daily 6am–6pm) here sells souvenirs and basic commodities, such as tinned foods, wine and beer. There's also a self-service launderette.

ACCOMMODATION

Storms River Mouth Restcamp Book through South African National Parks ☎012 428 9111, ⓦsanparks.org. A variety of accommodation, all with sea views, is available at the restcamp; all are heavily subscribed in season, so book in advance. The camping area is superbly located, just metres from where the surf breaks on the rocks. The two-person forest huts are definitely a notch up and offer great value, although they are quite small and basic. Bedding and towels are provided, but you share washing and cooking facilities with other guests. There are also comfortable one-bedroom, fully-equipped self-catering cabins mostly with two single beds, although some have doubles, and oceanettes right on the ocean's edge, plus two-bedroom family cottages sleeping four; all have their own kitchens and bathrooms. Camping R235, forest huts R340, chalets R690, family cottage R1215

EATING

Tsitsikamma Restaurant The only place to eat at Storms River Mouth has such startling views that it can be forgiven its workaday fare of traditional English breakfasts, toasted sandwiches, burgers, pastas and steak. They also do a reasonable range of seafood dishes. Daily 8.30am–10pm.

Storms River Village

About a kilometre south of the national road, STORMS RIVER VILLAGE is a tranquil place crisscrossed by a handful of dirt roads and with about forty houses, enjoying mountain vistas. The main attraction of the village is as a centre for adventure activities, of which the Canopy Tour is the really substantial drawcard.

2

ACCOMMODATION   STORMS RIVER VILLAGE

The Armagh Fynbos Ave ☎ 042 281 1512, ⓦ thearmagh.com. A hospitable guesthouse in a beautiful garden that drifts off into the *fynbos*. The rooms include two budget rooms, three standard ones, two garden cottages (R1450) and a honeymoon room, all of which open onto the garden. There's also a decent restaurant. R750

At the Woods Guest House 49 Formosa St, along the main drag into town ☎ 042 281 1446, ⓦ atthewoods .co.za A friendly, modern guesthouse that's the nicest place in town, with traditional reed ceilings and large, comfortable rooms with king-sized beds and French doors that open onto garden verandas or, upstairs, onto private decks with mountain views. Three-course home-cooked dinners can be arranged. R990

Tsitsikamma Backpackers 54 Formosa St ☎ 042 281 1868, ⓦ tsitsikammabackpackers.co.za. Well-run hostel set in a beautiful garden that claims environmentally friendly and fair-trade credentials. You can self-cater or order a reasonably priced breakfast or dinner, and there's a bar. They offer a shuttle service to local attractions and pick up guests for free from the Storms River Bridge. Dorm R120, double R300

Tsitsikamma Lodge A couple of kilometres east of town along the N2, 8km east of the Storms River Bridge ☎ 042 280 3802, ⓦ www.riverhotels.co.za /tsitsikamma. Thirty cosy A-frame cabins with their own decks and connected by boardwalks that traverse beautifully kept gardens. Most cabins have their own jacuzzi, and there are a number of forest walks. There's also a restaurant serving South African cuisine. R1380

Tsitsikamma Village Inn Darnell St, along the road into the village and left at the T-junction ☎ 042 281

STORMS RIVER ACTIVITIES

Storms River Village makes a good base for numerous local adventure activities as well as those further afield.

Blackwater Tubing *Tube 'n Axe Backpackers* (see p.246) operate trips down the Storms River gorge, where during the high-water season (generally winter) you ride the river and its rapids buoyed up by a small inflatable.

Boat trips SANParks (☎ 042 281 1607) runs trips (every 45min; 9.30am–2.45pm; R66) about 1km up Storms River leaving from near the dive shop, just beneath the Storms River Mouth restcamp restaurant.

Mountain biking A 22km mountain trail winds through the forest on the edge of the village and offers terrific views of the river gorge and coastline. *Blackwater Daakpackers* rent out mountain bikes for the day (R100).

Quad biking Bikes can be rented for R350 an hour from Tsitsikamma Falls Adventures (☎ 042 5280 3770, ⓦ tsitsikammaadventure.co.za), 8km east of the Storms River Bridge on the N2.

Woodcutters' Journey A relaxed jaunt organized by Storms River Adventures (☎ 042 281 1836, ⓦ stormsriver.com; teatime trip R140, lunch trip R200), which has its headquarters next to the Storms River Village post office. The trip takes you down through the forest to the river along the old Storms River Pass in a specially designed trailer, drawn by a tractor.

Zipline Run by Storms River Adventures (see Woodcutters' Journey, above), the Canopy Tour (R450) through the treetops gives a bird's-eye view of the forest as you travel 30m above ground along a series of interconnected cables attached to the tallest trees. The system has been constructed in such a way that not a single nail has been hammered into any tree. A faster, higher alternative, geared more to adrenaline junkies, ir the zipline tour across the Kruis River at Tsitsikamma Falls Adventures (☎ 072 030 4367, ⓦ tsitsikamma adventure.co.za; R350), which at times is 50m above the ground and crisscrosses an awesome ravine, zipping over three waterfalls, with the longest slide measuring 211m.

1711, ⓦ village-inn.co.za. A charmingly old-fashioned hotel – part of the huge *Protea* chain – in the village with 49 rooms in eleven cottages, each differently themed and surrounding a manicured garden. **R850**
Tube 'n Axe On the corner of Darnell and Saffron sts ⓣ 042 281 1757, ⓦ tubenaxe.co.za. A lively place that works hard to compete with the bright lights of Knysna and Plett by offering backpackers drumming nights, a pool table and loads of laughs. Accommodation, besides the usual dorms and doubles, includes two-person elevated tents (R150). Dorm **R125**, double **R300**

EATING

De Oude Martha *Tsitsikamma Village Inn*, Darnell St. Adequate, if unexceptional, hotel restaurant that serves up unpretentious breakfasts, lunches and dinners, and still dines out on the fact that the *New York Times* rated it the "best restaurant in the Tsitsikamma" in 1991. Daily 7am–10pm.

Rafters The Armagh, Fynbos Avenue. The dinner menu has an emphasis on the local: South African cuisine using organic vegetables grown in the village, fish from Plettenberg Bay and meat sourced nearby. Cape Muslim sweet and mild curries feature big on the menu. They also do a set or à la carte breakfast and lunch. Daily 8am–2.30pm & 6–8.30pm.

The West Coast

The **West Coast** of South Africa – remote, windswept and bordered by the cold Atlantic, demands a special appreciation. For many years the black sheep of Western Cape tourism, it has been set upon by developers who seem all too ready to spoil the bleached, salty emptiness that many people have just begun to value. The sandy soil and dunes harbour a distinctive coastal *fynbos* vegetation, while the coastline is almost devoid of natural inlets or safe harbours, with fierce southeasterly summer winds and dank winter fogs, though in spring **wild flowers** ever-miraculously appear in the veld. The southern 200km of the region, by far the most densely populated part of the coast, has many links to Namaqualand to the north (see p.290) – not least the flowers.

Outside the flower months of August and September, this part of the West Coast has a wide range of attractions, particularly during summer when the lure of the sea and the cooler coast is strong. The area is well known for a wide range of activities, most popularly various types of watersports, hiking and some excellent **birdwatching** (see box opposite).

A highlight of a number of West Coast towns is the casual but sumptuous **seafood** feast served in **open-air restaurants**, with little more than a canvas shelter held up with driftwood and lengths of fishing twine or a simple wind-cheating brush fence as props. The idea is to serve up endless courses of West Coast delicacies right by the ocean, in the style of a beach braai.

Swartland

The N7 highway north from Cape Town leads quickly into the pleasing and fertile **Swartland** landscape. Swartland means "black country", but while the rolling countryside takes on some attractive hues at different times of year, it's never really black. The accepted theory is that before the area was cultivated, the predominant vegetation was a grey-coloured bush called **renosterbos** (rhinoceros bush) which, seen from the surrounding ranges of hills, gave the area a complexion sufficiently dark to justify the name.

Bordered to the west by the less fertile coastal strandveld and to the east by the tall mountain range running from Wellington to the Cederberg, Swartland is known best as a wheat-growing area, although it also supports dairy farms, horse studs, tobacco crops and vineyards famous for earthy red wines. The N7 skirts a series of towns on its way north, including the largest in the region, **Malmesbury**. If you're travelling south towards Cape Town, look out for some unusual views of Table Mountain, and also for tortoises, which you should take care to avoid as they cross the road.

2

BIRDWATCHING ON THE WEST COAST

The **West Coast** is a twitchers' dream, where you can tick off numerous wetland species. The most rewarding viewing time is just after **flower season** in early summer, which heralds the arrival of around 750,000 migrants on their annual pilgrimage from the northern hemisphere, many from as far off as the Arctic Circle. They spend about eight months fattening up on delicacies from the tidal mudflats before their arduous journey back to their breeding grounds. **Langebaan** in the West Coast National Park is the best place in the country for such sightings and is considered the fifth most important wetland in the world, hosting over 250 bird species, more than a quarter of South Africa's total. The Berg River estuary and saltworks at **Velddrif** are another vital feeding ground for waders.

The coastal lake of **Verlorenvlei**, meaning "the lost marsh", is one of the most important wetlands in South Africa; it stretches 13.5km from its mouth at Eland's Bay (25km south of Lambert's Bay) to its headwaters near Redelinghuys. Look out here for the purple gallinule, a colourful, shy wader, and the African marsh harrier, a raptor that may be declining in numbers. Here species more fond of arid conditions merge with the waders, and there have been some rare sightings including a black egret and a palm-nut vulture. At **Bird Island**, Lambert's Bay, a sunken hide makes it convenient to view the garrulous behaviour of the breeding colony of Cape gannets.

Darling and around

The small country town of **DARLING** is famous for its rolling countryside, vineyards and dairy products, and also for its displays of wild flowers in spring, but far more so as the home to one of South Africa's best-loved comedians, Pieter Dirk-Uys, who regularly performs on weekends.

Easily reached from Cape Town via the coastal R27 route on a day-trip, Darling boasts some handsome old buildings and is known as an **artists' colony**.

Evita se Perron

At the old train station in the centre of town • ☎ 022 492 3930, ⓦ www.evita.co.za

Pieter Dirk-Uys, South Africa's most famous comedian, has established his best-known and loved character, **Evita Bezuidenhout** (South Africa's answer to Dame Edna Everidge), as the hostess of a weekend cabaret show here. Taking in lunch and a show here is one of the best days out from Cape Town you can have. Book in advance.

!Khwa Ttu San Culture and Education Centre

Some 20km west of Darling, along the R27, 70km from Cape Town • Mon–Sun 9am–5pm • Free • Tours 10am & 2pm, daily; R240 • ☎ 022 492 2998, ⓦ www.khwattu.org

If you'd like some knowledge and contact with "bushmen" or San, !**Khwa Ttu San Culture and Education Centre** is the place to go. The centre is run by descendants of Northern Cape San people in partnership with a Swiss NGO, with profits returned to San communities. There is an excellent exhibition of photographs, authentic crafts for sale and a restaurant, all appealingly situated on a hilltop. With a couple of hours in hand, you can take one of their tours to a replica San village and see tracking and hunting techniques. It's possible to stay overnight here (see below).

INFORMATION	DARLING AND AROUND

Tourist information Located inside the museum (Mon–Fri 9am–1pm & 2–4pm, Sat & Sun 10am–3pm; ☎ 022 492 3361, ⓦ www.darlingtourism.co.za).

ACCOMMODATION

Darling Lodge 22 Pastorie St ☎ 022 492 3062, ⓦ www.darlinglodge.co.za. A restored Victorian house, with six en-suite rooms. There's a pool and three rooms around it, and a garden big enough to relax and lose yourself in. **R880**

!Khwa Ttu San Culture and Education Centre Some 20km west of Darling, along the R27 ☎ 022 492 2998, ⓦ www.khwattu.org. Accommodation comprises a tented camp, with communal facilities, and a

---

WEST COAST FLOWERS

During August and September you'll find displays of **wild flowers** across the West Coast region, with significant displays starting as far south as **Darling**. Excellent displays are also found in the **West Coast National Park** and the hazy coastal landscapes around **Cape Columbine** and **Lambert's Bay**, while inland, **Clanwilliam** is the centre of some good routes. An incredible four thousand flower species are found in the region, most of them members of the daisy and mesembryanthemum groups. For up-to-date advice and guidance, contact the helpful tourist offices in Darling, Saldanha and Clanwilliam; for further tips on flower-viewing, see p.291.

---

two-bedroomed self-catering house with a fireplace inside. The centre, on a lovely farm, makes a good base for an exploration of Darling and the West Coast National Park. Tented camp R200, house R770

★ **Trinity Guest Lodge** 19 Long St ☎ 022 492 3430, ☺ www.trinitylodge.co.za. A charming Victorian guest-house set in gracious large grounds, with wooden shutters and a verandah. They also offer a two-night package (R1500 pp) that includes a ticket to a Pieter Dirk-Uys show at Eva se Perron (see p.247), and a wine-tasting and lunch at the historic Groote Post Wine Estate just out of town. R800

EATING

Bistro Seven Restaurant and Coffee Bar 7 Main Rd ☎ 022 492 3626. Bakery and coffee shop that serves cakes, tarts, pasties and sandwiches. Evening meals (R70) include steaks, line fish, salads and tomato *bredie* (stew), and there's a bar open from 5pm. Mon & Wed–Sun 9am–3.30pm & 6–9pm.

Hilda's Kitchen Groote Post Wine Estate, Darling Hills Rd ☎ 022 492 2825. Modern country cooking including hearty soups, fish cakes with Asian flavours, and rich lamb pie (R90), in a beautiful eighteenth-century house, complemented by wines from the estate; booking essential. Children are welcome to roam in the extensive grounds. Wed–Sun noon–2.30pm.

Cloof Winery Twenty minutes' drive towards Malmesbury from Darling ☎ 022 492 2839. Reasonably priced light lunches including Caesar salad, chicken wrap and butternut ravioli (R70), plus a menu for children. Tues–Sat 11am–3pm.

Langebaan

Once the home to the largest whaling station in the southern hemisphere, and for a while Cape Town's long-haul passenger flight terminus (when seaplanes from Europe touched down on the lagoon during World War II), **LANGEBAAN** now sells itself as the gateway to the **West Coast National Park**, though it has become depressingly overdeveloped. If you're after a small-town West Coast experience, avoid it in favour of Paternoster (see p.251). The only reason to stay here is if you want to spend time in small but precious West Coast National Park itself, where there is almost zero accommodation. On the other hand, if you're into windsurfing, kitesurfing or sailing and have been wondering how to harness the big southeasterly summer winds, the excellent conditions here mean Langebaan could be just your thing. Right off the beach the water is flat, the sailing winds – as the ragged flags above the centre testify – anywhere from fresh to fearsome and, unless you catch a fast-running tide out towards the Atlantic, it's all reasonably safe.

ARRIVAL AND INFORMATION   LANGEBAAN

By bus A daily bus, run by Elwierda (☎ 086 100 1094), leaves Cape Town Station at 4.45pm. Book in advance.

Tourist information In the municipal building on Bree St (Mon–Fri 8.30am–4.30pm, Sat 9am–2pm; ☎ 022 772 1515, ☺ www.langebaaninfo.com).

ACCOMMODATION

Friday Island Next to Cape Sport, on the beach ☎ 022 772 2506, ☺ www.fridayisland.co.za. Perfect for the watersports enthusiast wanting a more upmarket place to stay, offering fresh and light units with small kitchenettes, wooden decks and outdoor courtyards opening from the bathroom to hang up wet gear. Sea-facing rooms are more expensive (R800). There's also an in-house restaurant and pub. R600

HITTING THE WATER IN LANGEBAAN

If you want to try your hand at any of the **watersports** on offer in Langebaan, the friendly Cape Sport Centre (daily 9am–5pm; ☎022 772 1114, ⓦwww.capesport.co.za), on the beach on the northern edge of town, is the place to head to for **windsurfing**, **hobiecat sailing** and **kitesurfing** tuition. **Sailing courses** are offered by Ocean Sailing Academy (☎021 425 7837, ⓦwww.oceansailingacademy.co.za).

Olifantskop Opposite the Club Mykonos turn-off on the coast road, halfway between Langebaan and Saldanha ☎022 772 2326, ⓦwww.oliphantskop .co.za. An out-of-town option offering both en-suite rooms and self-contained cottages, plus a restaurant and bar if you don't want to cook. There's also a swimming pool

and an equestrian centre where you can do beach or hill outrides. R380

Puza Moya On the corner of North and Suffern sts ☎022 772 1114. Cheerful en-suite rooms with a shared kitchen and courtyard for braais. A good option if you like to socialize in a relaxed environment after an active day. R500

EATING

★ **Die Strandloper Restaurant and Beach Bar** On the beach just beyond the Cape Sport Centre on the road to Saldanha ☎022 772 2490 or ☎083 227 7195. A good example of the West Coast's lively open-air seafood restaurants, with sand on your feet and fishing nets above. Committed to sustainable seafood, this is a good place to try West Coast fish delicacies like *bokkoms*, *harders* and dried *snoek*. R215 for ten-course set menu; booking essential. Mid-Jan to mid-Nov Sat & Sun 12.30–3.30pm;

mid-Nov to mid-Jan daily 12.30–3.30pm, 6.30–9.30pm.

Froggy's 29 Main Rd ☎022 772 1869. Delicious curries, including Thai green fish curry, as well as meat stews and their signature mussels in Pernod (R110). Booking essential. Tues–Sat 6.30–10.30pm.

Pearly's On the main beach. Crowded eating, drinking and ogling spot with outside tables, in a great location for watching the sunset, and enjoying pizza, pasta, seafood or their speciality of grilled steak (R90). Daily 9.30am–midnight.

West Coast National Park

Daily: April–Aug 7am–6pm; Sept–March 7am–7pm • R72 • ☎022 772 2144

The **West Coast National Park** is one of the best places to savour the charm of the West Coast, which elsewhere is being devoured by housing developments. The park protects over forty percent of South Africa's remaining pristine strandveld and 35 percent of the country's salt marshes, and incorporates both the majority of Langebaan Lagoon and a Y-shaped area of land immediately around and below it.

Much of the park's appeal lies in uplifting views over the still lagoon to an olive-coloured, rocky hillside, the sharp, saline air, and the calling gulls and Atlantic mists vanishing in the harsh sunlight. This isn't a game park – a few larger antelope are located in the Postberg section of the park, an area open only during the spring flower season – but there are huge numbers of **birds**, including some seventy thousand migrating waders, ostriches, and tortoises galore. A number of well organized interpretive walking trails lead through the dunes to the long, smooth, wave-beaten Atlantic coastline, offering plenty of opportunity to learn about the hardy *fynbos* vegetation that so defines the look and feel of the West Coast region. The best time to visit the park is in **spring**, when the sun is shining and the flowers are out, although this is, inevitably, also the busiest period. Like much of the West Coast, the national park is chilly and wet in winter, and hot and wind-blasted in summer.

On the southern tip of the lagoon is the effective centre – a large old farmhouse called **Geelbek**. If you continue from Geelbek up the peninsula on the western side of the lagoon you'll come to **Churchhaven**, a tiny village still without electricity, closed to day visitors, and two signposted beaches with picnic areas, Priekstool and Kraalbaai.

A little further on is the demarcated **Postberg area**, open only during flower season (see box opposite), but worth visiting at that time to see **zebra**, **gemsbok** and **wildebeest** wandering through fields of wild flowers.

2

ARRIVAL AND DEPARTURE

WEST COAST NATIONAL PARK

By car There are two entrance gates to the park: one on the R27, roughly 10km north of the turning to Yzerfontein, and the other south of Langebaan. The park isn't huge – if you're driving you'll cover the extent of the roads in a couple of hours.

INFORMATION

Tourist information The Geelbek Information Centre in the Geelbek Cape Dutch House (Mon–Fri 8.30am–4pm, Sat & Sun 9am–1pm) can direct you to the bird hides nearby, or give you information about walks in the area.

ACCOMMODATION

Duinepos 1km from Geelbek (signposted) ☎ 022 707 9900, ✆ www.duinepos.co.za. Eleven self-catering chalets, close to the lagoon, but with no access to the water because of bird breeding. There's a swimming pool on site, or lagoon swimming possibilities at Priekstool or Kraalbaai, some 12 to 15km away. **R650**

EATING

★ **Geelbek Restaurant** Geelbek ☎ 022 772 2134. Magnificent setting in a graceful Cape Dutch building on the lagoon, where you can sit outside and see flamingos if you are lucky. South African dishes (R90), such as *bobotie*, ostrich burgers, *snoek* salad and Cape Malay curries, are their speciality. Booking essential during flower season. Daily 9am–5pm.

Vredenburg

North of Saldanha lies a sizeable inland farming centre, **VREDENBURG**, an unremarkable town in a featureless setting. Vredenburg has well-stocked supermarkets and is a good place to buy fuel – many of the smaller towns nearby don't have filling stations.

West Coast Fossil Park

About 10km southeast of Vredenburg, on the R45 • Mon–Fri 8am–5pm, Sat 10am–2pm • R35 • Guided tours daily 11.30am

Founded in 1998 on the site of a decommissioned phosphate mine, and still being developed, the West Coast Fossil Park is a relatively low-key affair, but interesting and highly recommended nevertheless. Displays include thousands of fossils and modern animal bones, and also information panels about the extinct species dating back about five million years ago that were found on site. Finds include fossils from sabre-toothed cats, two species of extinct elephant, and sivatheres – long-horned, short-necked, giraffe-like browsers. Perhaps strangest of all are the extinct giant bears, *Agriotherium africanum*, which weighed in at 750kg (compared to 150kg for a large lion), making them the heftiest predators – and the only known bears – to have roamed sub-Saharan Africa in the past 65 million years. It's best to take a tour, though you can wander around by yourself.

ARRIVAL AND DEPARTURE

VREDENBURG

By bus A daily bus, operated by Elwierda (☎ 086 100 1094), leaves Cape Town Station at 4.45pm, and departs at 5.45am from Vredenberg for Cape Town.

INFORMATION

Tourist information The West Coast Peninsula Tourism Bureau is in the Atrium Building on Main Rd (Mon–Fri 9am–5pm; ☎ 022 715 1142, ✆ www .capewestcoastpeninsula.co.za).

ACCOMMODATION

Windstone Backpackers Just past the main crossroads of the R45 from Vredenburg and the R27 from Cape Town ☎ 022 766 1645 or ☎ 083 477 1756, ✆ www .windstone.co.za. With four- and six-bed dorms and one room suitable for families, plus some doubles, *Windstone* makes a friendly base for exploring the region. The owners also run a horseriding centre, with outrides in the adjoining fossil park and nature reserve (R200). The lodge is on the route of the daily Elwierda bus (☎ 021 418 4673), between Cape Town and Saldanha. Dorm **R100**, double **R280**

Paternoster

The best of the West Coast is to be found at the village of **PATERNOSTER**, a favourite seaside weekend away from Cape Town. Small-scale angling and crayfish netting is the principal economic activity of the village, and most of the fishermen live in the whitewashed cottages of the coloured district to the west of the hotel. When they're not out at sea, their small, brightly painted boats lie beached at the water's edge.

Unfortunately, Paternoster has become a bit of a building site of late, with lots of people building houses in this idyllic spot. Nevertheless, the coast itself is beautiful, saved from development by the Columbine Nature Reserve, 3km to the west (see below), where huge waves smash against large granite rocks as smooth as whales' backs.

2

Columbine Nature Reserve

3km to the west of Paternoster, along an unpaved road • Nature reserve daily sunrise to sunset • R20 • Columbine lighthouse tours on request • R15 • ☎ 022 752 2705

A small area set aside to conserve the sandveld-*fynbos* heathland indigenous to the region, the **Columbine Nature Reserve** makes a stunning change from the salty flats that typify the West Coast. Large vegetated dunes sweep down to a shoreline of massive pink granite boulders and little coves, with beaches that are blue-tinged, a result of mussel shells being washed up and finely crushed into the sands. It's best to park at **Tieties Bay** (camping is allowed here, right by the ocean), from where you can simply follow the marked path over the rocks and along the dunes to explore the area.

Besides rambling, there are some excellent coastal **hiking trails** through the reserve, including two long day-trails (details from Vredenburg tourist office, see opposite). Along the road from Paternoster to the reserve you'll pass the **Cape Columbine lighthouse**, built in 1936 on Castle Rock. Usually the first lighthouse to be sighted by ships from Europe rounding Africa, it emits a single white flash every fifteen seconds.

ARRIVAL AND INFORMATION

PATERNOSTER

By car There is no public transport to Paternoster. The town is 15km northwest of Vredenburg and 160km from Cape Town, on the R27.

Tourist information Next to the fish market at the beach, signposted from the main road as you enter town (Fri & Sat 10am–5pm; ☎ 022 752 2323).

ACCOMMODATION

Baywatch Villa 8 Ambyl Rd ☎ 022 752 2039, ⓦ www.baywatchvilla.co.za. Five luxurious self-catering thatched fisherman's-style cottages, just two minutes' walk from Long Beach, in the quiet part of town to the north. **R775**

Beach Camp Signposted from Paternoster in Cape Columbine Reserve ☎ 082 926 2267, ⓦ www.ratrace .co.za. Right on the beach, in its own bay, *Beach Camp* has walk-in tents and small A-frames, some of which can sleep children. This is where you launch for sea-kayaking, when the swell is not too strong. They offer pick-ups from the Elwierda Bus from Vredenburg (☎ 021 418 4673), which

departs Cape Town daily at 5pm, and there's a bar where you can breakfast on the terrace, and fish braais are available if requested in advance. Otherwise, bring your own supplies to self-cater. **R560**

Blue Dolphin 12 Warrelklip St, right on the beach ☎ 022 752 2001, ⓦ www.bluedolphin.co.za. Four comfortable en-suite rooms in a modern building. The owner, George, is very informative and prepares excellent and beautifully presented breakfasts. **R900**

Die Opstal Sonkwasweg ☎ 083 988 4645, ⓦ www .paternoster-villas.co.za. Three self-catering flats and a studio, all with separate entrances. The building is one row

---

SEA KAYAKING IN PATERNOSTER

An adventure highlight of Paternoster is **sea kayaking**. When the swell is not too big, you launch from Beach Camp at Columbine Nature Reserve, or from the Main Beach, with **Kayak Paternoster** (☎ 082 824 8917, ⓦ www.ratrace.co.za; no under 16s; closed in winter). The one-hour trips cost R150 and are as much about observing and learning about birds, whales, dolphins and seals as about paddling.

2

behind the beachside properties, and it is cheaper than other options as it lacks beachfront views. R550

Light House Keeper Cottages Cape Columbine Reserve ☎ 021 449 2400. Self-catering is offered in three former lighthouse keepers' cottages around the lighthouse itself, on a prominent headland in the Cape Columbine reserve. The cottages are kitted out with all mod cons, and have two or three bedrooms. R700

Mosselbank On the corner of Trappiesklip and Mosselbank sts ☎ 022 752 2027, ⊛ www.weskus.com. An hospitable B&B in a suburban development, with sea views from five en-suite rooms in the northern part of town, close to Long Beach. R730

Oystercatchers' Haven 48 Sonkwasweg ☎ 022 752 2193, ⊛ www.oystercatchershaven.com. A beautiful guesthouse with three romantic rooms, situated on the beach, on the edge of Columbine Reserve. The views are wonderful, with a swimming pool and loungers close to the beach. R1600

★ **The Paternoster Dunes** 18 Sonkwas St ☎ 083 560 5600, ⊛ www.paternosterdunes.co.za. A gorgeous guesthouse with contemporary beachhouse-style rooms leading onto the sand, and everything designed to inspire and delight the senses. The pool, in the central courtyard, is protected from the wind. Make sure you have a seaview room, rather than a courtyard-facing one. R1800

EATING AND DRINKING

Gaaitjie Off Sampson Rd ☎ 022 752 2242. The top-notch chef here produces creative seafood-based dishes (R120) in a great beachside location. Book in advance for a sea-facing table. The chef can produce something delicious on request for vegetarians. Thurs–Mon lunch and dinner. Closed in winter.

Noisy Oyster St Augustine Rd ☎ 022 752 2196. You'll find creamy oysters and crayfish (R100), as well as meat dishes and options for vegetarians, at this informal restaurant just off the main drag. What it lacks in setting, it makes up for in ambience and good food. Wed–Sat lunch

and dinner, Sun lunch only. Closed June & July.

Oep Ve Koep St Augustine Rd ☎ 022 752 2105. A good choice for imaginative lunches (R75) in a wind-sheltered garden, made by a chef who is inspired by local fare. Daily breakfast and lunch.

Paternoster Hotel St Augustine Rd ☎ 022 752 2703. Known for their West Coast seafood platters (R460 for two), and if you book in advance they can organize a seafood braai. Also in the hotel is the *Panties Bar*; the roof is festooned with assorted knickers and the odd trophy bra. Daily 8am–9.30pm.

Velddrif

At the northern end of the R27 from Cape Town is **VELDDRIF**, a fishing town situated at the point where the Great Berg River meets the sea. Each year the Berg River **canoe marathon** (which starts near Ceres, 49km north of Worcester) ends here at a marina development called Port Owen. During the last few years, the town has outgrown its fishing industry origins and is now dominated by a modern suburbia of brick bungalows. The town's setting on the meandering Berg and the surrounding wetlands – as well as the vision of some locals, who have managed to stay the eager hand of the demolition crews – has resulted in Velddrif retaining a little of its historic character.

In the quieter backwaters near the Velddrif bridge, you can still see individual fishermen in small boats landing catches of mullet or horse mackerel. The fish are then dried and salted to make *bokkoms*, called by some a delicacy, but essentially a source of cheap protein for fishermen and farm workers on the West Coast. To see the rickety wooden jetties where the boats tie up, and the frames and sheds by the shore where *bokkoms* are strung up to dry, turn right at the roundabout just over the bridge coming into town on the R27, and after 1km or so take the first right-hand turn down to the riverside. Turning left over the same bridge takes you to Pelican Harbour, where a number of coffee and craft shops are housed in a renovated fishing factory.

There is a wealth of **birdlife**, including pelicans and flamingos, along both banks of the river (see box, p.247). You can take a pleasant **boat trip** into the wetlands with well-informed birder Dan Ahlers (☎ 082 951 0447; 30min trip R40), who takes excursions up the Berg River. He also leads bay cruises on which you stand a chance of seeing marine mammals.

INFORMATION

Tourist information Voortrekker Rd (Mon–Fri 8.30am–1pm, 2–5pm, Sat 9am–1pm; ☎ 022 783 1821).

ACCOMMODATION

★ **Kersefontein Guest Farm** 25km south of Velddrif on the Berg River ☎ 022 783 0850, ⓦ kersefontein .co.za. A definite highlight of the West Coast region, this is a working farm grazed by wild horses that dates back to the eighteenth century, and boasts several handsome Cape Dutch listed buildings, complete with antiques, some of which have been converted into stylish accommodation. Julian Melck, the eighth-generation owner, treats guests to lively tales of adventures on a South African farm. **R960**

Kuifkopvisvanger 5km from town on the other side of the river ☎ 022 783 0818, ⓦ kuifkop.co.za. There

are just seven charming, rustic fishermen's cottages here, with views of the river and marshlands. In addition, camping is available, and in the summer you can use the canoes to explore or swim in the river. Camping **R120**, cottage **R480**

Riviera 136 Voortrekker Rd ☎ 022 783 1137, ⓦ eigevis .com. The *Riviera* has well-equipped self-catering chalets, sleeping six, each with a patio and set on the water's edge; there's also a restaurant and bar. Flamingos and many other water birds can be seen from the restaurant/bar balcony, and the food is good. **R800**

EATING AND DRINKING

Eigevis Fish Shop Jameson St, close to the *Laaiplek Hotel*. If you're self-catering, this is the place to stock up on frozen seafood, including lobster, or to come for fresh fish and chips. Mon–Sat 9am–5pm.

The Laaiplek Hotel Jameson St ☎ 022 783 1116. A long-established old-fashioned harbour hotel, great for a drink with views of large boats, fish factories and cranes, as well as birds. They offer seafood and steaks and huge Sunday lunches (mains from R90). Mon–Sat 7.30am–9.30pm, Sun 7.30am–2.30pm.

Vishuis About 3km west of Velddrif along the atmospheric riverside dirt road from the Velddrif bridge ☎ 022 783 1183. Housed in a restored traditional fish-drying factory, with outdoor seating offering views across the wetlands, *Vishuis* serves well-priced English breakfasts and excellent fish-and-chips lunches (R90). Book ahead for dinner. Tues–Sat 11am–3pm & 6–9pm, Sun 9am–3pm.

Elands Bay

Elands Bay (more commonly known as Elands) is a popular weekend destination, with a couple of guesthouses and restaurants, some fine bushman rock paintings on the south-side cliffs, and exceptional birdwatching. It's probably a place to catch before it's developed, though, like most of the West Coast, the water is freezing, and the coastline spare, windswept and harsh – the tide spewing mounds of kelp, shells and dried-out seal bones onto the deserted beaches.

Elands is divided into north and south sides by the **Verlorenvlei** ("lost wetland"), which supports over two hundred bird species. The nicer side is the south, where the surfers hang out. Above here, the Bobbejaanberg ridge runs into the sea. Where the road ends under the cliffs lies the harbour, and the path up to a large cave with rock art, including some big eland and hundreds of handprints, which are thought to be connected to rites of passage – when adolescents imprinted their hands as they walked through the site. Spring flowers in this vicinity are also phenomenal.

ARRIVAL AND DEPARTURE

By car A lonely 70km drive joins Velddrif with Elands, but it's tarred all the way. It's a two-and-a-half-hour drive from

Cape Town, approximately 200km

ACCOMMODATION

Elands Bay Guest House 184 Kreef Rd, South Side ☎ 022 972 1755, ⓦ elandsbayguesthouse.co.za. No frills self-catering accommodation principally geared to groups of surfers, sleeping up to four people, with

a communal kitchen and lots of wetsuits drying in the sun. **R750**

Elands Bay Hotel North Side Beachfront ☎ 022 972 1640, ⓦ elandsbayhotel.co.za. Reasonably priced

2

accommodation right at the beach, with double rooms – go for sea-facing with splendid views – as well as backpackers' rooms and camp sites. Camping R150, backpacker room R200, double R420
Vensterklip 5km from Elands Bay ☎022 972 1340,

⑩vensterklip.co.za. Self-catering in restored, historic cottages, as well as camping, including tents for hire, and a good restaurant on-site, on this farm on the *vlei*. Day visitors can hire kayaks to nose around the *vlei*, or for free if you are a guest. Camping R100, cottage R700

EATING

Elands Bay Hotel North Side Beachfront. The only central option for reasonably priced seafood meals, grills and steak (R75), or pop in for a drink with brilliant views. Breakfasts are popular after a long surfing bout. Daily 8am–10pm.
Tin Kitchen Country Restaurant 5km from Elands Bay

☎022 972 1340. The best bet for food, though only at weekends, serving meals using organic ingredients wherever possible, both farm meat and seasonal vegetables (R80). Friday nights are their popular and lively pizza nights (not served on other nights). Fri & Sat 8am–10pm, Sun 9am–3pm.

Lambert's Bay

LAMBERT'S BAY is the only settlement of any note between Velddrif and Port Nolloth, the latter almost at the Namibian border. This is an important fishing port, although by the sights and sounds of the harbour you soon become aware that even the fishermen have to stand aside for the impressive colony of **gannets** on **Bird Island**, in the centre of the bay.

Bird Island

Daily dawn–dusk • R30

It's possible to walk out to the island on the causeway for a closer look at the tightly packed, ear-piercing mass of petulant gannets from the bird hide, along with a few disapproving-looking penguins and cormorants, though viewing is not always guaranteed outside of breeding season. The bay plays host to a resident pod of around seven **humpback whales** during their breeding season from July to November. This is also the southernmost area ranged by **Heaviside's dolphins** – small, friendly mammals with wedge-shaped beaks (rather than the longer ones more commonly associated with dolphins), with a white, striped patterning reminiscent of killer whales. You may be lucky and view the cavorting mammals on trips from the fishing port.

ARRIVAL AND INFORMATION   LAMBERT'S BAY

By car Lambert's Bay is some 27km north of Elands Bay, and 70km due west of Clanwilliam by tarred road.

Tourist information Main Rd (Mon–Fri 9am–5pm, Sat 9am–12.30pm; ☎027 432 1000, ⑩www.lambertsbay .co.za).

ACCOMMODATION

Donkieskraal Guest Lodge and Private Game Reserve Between Lambert's Bay and Clanwilliam ☎083 235 4717, ⑩www.donkieskraal.co.za. A potato and game farm with chalets built right into the rocks to give a furnished cave experience, plus four safari tents nestling into the rocky hillside, and a campsite. While it's self-catering, the owner can offer meals on request. Camping R90, safari tent R450, chalet R800

Lamberts Bay Hotel Voortrekker St ☎027 432 1126, ⑩www.lambertsbayhotel.co.za. Smack in the centre of town, this conventional and rather old-fashioned hotel offers neat and reasonably priced rooms, a swimming pool at the back, and help with organizing boat trips, or activities such as birding, beach riding or spring flower trips. R650

EATING

Isabella's Restaurant and Coffee Shop Harbour ☎027 432 1177. A favourite choice, largely for its location right at the waterfront with plastic tables and chairs outdoors to take in the harbour atmosphere and views. It offers the whole gamut, from coffee and cake to fish and chips, prawns or a pot of mussels, but is renowned for its

blowout cooked English or West Coast breakfast (R80). Daily 8am–10pm.
★ **Muisboskerm** Elands Bay Rd, 5km from Lamberts Bay ☎027 432 1017. The original West Coast open-air seafood restaurant scores on location – right on the edge of the ocean, on a deserted beach, and rated by many as one

of the top ten things to do on a visit to South Africa. A massive buffet (R185) is on offer, with fish baked, smoked or grilled, potato bread baked in a clay oven and traditional *waterblommetjie* stew, complete with Afrikaans *boeremusiek* in the background. It is not open every day (phone to enquire), and you will need to book in advance. Lunch from 12.30pm, dinner from 6.30pm.

The Cederberg

A bold and jagged outcrop of the Western Cape fold escarpment, the **Cederberg range** is one of the most magical wilderness areas in the Western Cape. Rising with a striking presence on the eastern side of the Olifants River Valley, around 200km north of Cape Town, these high sandstone mountains and long, dry valleys manage to combine accessibility with remote harshness, offering something for hikers, campers, naturalists and rock climbers.

The **Cederberg Wilderness Area**, flanking the N7 between Citrusdal and Clanwilliam, was created to protect the silt-free waters of the Cederberg catchment area, but it also provides a recreational sanctuary with over 250km of hiking trails. In a number of places, the red-hued sandstone has been weathered into grotesque, gargoyle-like shapes and a number of memorable natural features. Throughout the area there are also numerous **San rock-art** sites, an active array of Cape mountain fauna, from baboon and small antelope to leopard, caracal and aardwolf, and some notable montane *fynbos* flora, including the gnarled and tenacious Clanwilliam cedar and the rare snow protea.

The Cederberg is easily reached from Cape Town on the N7: the two main, though very small, towns of **Citrusdal** and **Clanwilliam** lie just off the highway near, respectively, the southern and northern tips of the mountain range, but are not in the mountains themselves, and are not the places to base yourself if you want to hike.

Citrusdal

North of Piketberg on the N7, a long, flat plain reaches out to the line of Olifantsrivierberg Mountains, which the highway crosses by way of the impressive Piekenierskloof Pass, forged in 1857 by the indomitable road engineer Thomas Bain. CITRUSDAL appears in the rolling countryside of the Olifants River Valley, with the dramatic mountainscape of the Cederberg behind, though it is bypassed by the N7. Strange as it may seem now, early Dutch explorers saw huge herds of elephants here as they travelled north towards Namaqualand, hence the river's name.

One of the principal attractions of this area is the natural hot springs 16km from Citrusdal that you can visit as a day visitor or stay overnight (see p.256).

ARRIVAL AND INFORMATION CITRUSDAL

By car Citrusdal is a couple of kilometres off the N7, 170km from Cape Town.

Tourist information 39 Voortrekker St (Mon–Fri 8.30am–5pm, Sat 9am–noon; ☎022 921 3210, ⓦwww .citrusdal.info).

INTO THE MOUNTAINS

You have to **hike** to actually get into the Cederberg mountains themselves; short walks are possible from a few properties, but if you want to do any serious walking you should be properly equipped and experienced as this is rough country, and weather conditions can be harsh throughout the year.

One of the best ways to get into the mountains is with **professional mountaineer**, Mike Wakeford, who offers tailor-made multi-day trekking trips that depart from Cape Town (☎083 402 0288, ⊖guidedbymike@gmail.com). Prices depend on the number of people and days.

2

ACCOMMODATION

★ **Petersfield Mountain Cottages** 4km from Citrusdal ☎ 022 921 3316, ⊛ www.petersfieldfarm .co.za. On a working rooibos and citrus farm, with some of the best self-catering cottages you'll find anywhere; each secluded cottage has its own private pool and you can hike and swim. For weekends, though, you'll have to book a year in advance. R850

The Baths South off the road leading into Citrusdal from the N7, then 16km down a good tarred road ☎ 022 921 8026, ⊛ www.thebaths.co.za. A pleasantly old-fashioned, if rather rule-bound, mineral spa resort with one large hot pool (43°C), a cold pool and several large indoor spa baths. Day visitors pay R70 to use the amenities, which are included in the accommodation price for guests. The place is set in a beautiful wooded glen with camp sites, chalets, and self-catering rooms in some large old stone buildings. There's also restaurant with passable food, though most people self-cater. Camping R95, double R570

The Cederberg Wilderness Area

The main route into the Cederberg, and Algeria, the forest station that serves as a focal point for the area, heads east off the N7, 28km north of Citrusdal, and connects all the way towards Ceres in the east. The 710-square-kilometre **Cederberg Wilderness Area** features many designated trails, including the two main peaks, **Sneeuberg** (2027m) and **Tafelberg** (1969m), and the awesome rock formations of the huge **Wolfberg Arch** in the southeast of the reserve, and a 30m-high freestanding pillar shaped like (and known as) the **Maltese Cross**, to its south.

ARRIVAL AND INFORMATION   THE CEDERBERG WILDERNESS AREA

By car The main route into the Cederberg, clearly signposted to Algeria, is a rough dirt road, normally known as the Algeria Rd, but fine in an ordinary car if you take it fairly slowly.

Information You'll need permits to hike, which are easy and cheap to get from the CapeNature Office in Algeria (see below).

ACCOMMODATION

Algeria Campsite 18km east on Algeria Rd, signposted off the N7 ☎ 0861 227 362 8873, ⊛ capenature.org.za. A pretty riverside site, with a gorgeous river pool and hikes leaving from the campsite itself into the surrounding mountains. It can be quite crowded and nosiy during school hols but kids will have a ball. There are also, a couple of self-catering chalets here, and isolated cottages a few kilometres away, which have paraffin lamps rather than electricity. Camping R100, chalet R550

Cederberg Oasis 62km east of Algeria, but approach via N1 Worcester and Ceres, rather than Algeria ☎ 027 482 2819, ⊛ cederbergoasis.co.za. Accommodation geared to backpackers is in basic rooms, doubles and dorms, plus there's camping on the lawn. It has a licensed restaurant, serving meals of gigantic proportions. This area is great for the sandstone formations and rock art at Tanjieskraal and Stadsaal Caves, and owner Gerrit will hand-draw you a map when you plan your day's outing, and sell you permits. R125 per person

---

CEDERBERG ROCK ART

The Cederberg has around 2500 known **rock-art sites**, estimated to be between one and eight thousand years old. They are the work of the first South Africans, hunter gatherers known as San or **Bushmen**, the direct descendants of some of the earliest Homo sapiens who lived in the Western Cape 150,000 years ago.

One of the best ways to see rock art is on a self-guided 4km walk from *Traveller's Rest Farm* (see p.260) along the Sevilla Trail, which takes in ten sites.

Another way to see paintings is on a half-day tour to Warmhoek site near Clanwilliam, run by the excellent Living Landscape Project, 18 Park St in Clanwilliam (☎ 027 482 1911, ⊛ www.cllp .uct.ac.za), and led by competent local guides. The project is the brainchild of archeologist John Parkington, from the University of Cape Town, whose books on rock art in the Cederberg (*The Mantis and the Moon* and *Cederberg Rock Paintings*) offer the best interpretation of the puzzling and beautiful images you'll see delicately painted on rocks and overhangs.

2

Jamaka Organic Farm Cottages and Campsite Signposted and accessed just before Algeria, on the Algeria Rd ☎ 027 482 2801, ⓦ jamaka.co.za. The campsite on this organic citrus and mango farm has a lovely setting, and, in contrast to *Algeria*, strict rules about partying, though for good hikes you will need to drive over to *Algeria*. If you want a roof over your head, the best of their reasonably priced cottages is the stone one next to the river. Camping R100, cottage R360

Kromrivier 50km south of Algeria ☎ 027 482 2807, ⓦ cederbergtourist.co.za. Fourteen fully equipped chalets, some with their own baths and cheaper ones without, sleeping four, with bedding available for a small charge. They also have a café on site if you don't feel like cooking, and camp sites near river pools for swimming. Camping R120, chalet R500

Mount Ceder Via Ceres and Worcester on the N1 ☎ 023 317 0113, ⓦ mountceder.co.za. A luxurious mountain retreat with self-catering cottages, some of which have jacuzzis. It's set along a perennial river, in a gorgeous area, and there are some good horseriding trails for beginners as well as experienced riders (R250). R680

★ **Sanddrif** About 26km south of Algeria, along the same dirt road ☎ 027 482 2825, ⓦ cederbergwine .com. Fully equipped chalets with one to three rooms (bring your own bedding), on a farm where there are natural river pools and good walks, as well as camping. *Sanddrif* also sells permits for the classic walks on its property – the Maltese Cross and Wolfberg Arch and Cracks. Camping R120, chalet R650

Clanwilliam

At the northern end of the Cederberg, **CLANWILLIAM** is an attractive and assured small town. It carries off with some aplomb its various roles as a base for the majestic Cederberg Wilderness Area, a centre for spring flowers, a service centre for surrounding farms, and the place to head for if you want to see good **rock art** within easy striking distance of Cape Town.

Established in the last years of the eighteenth century, Clanwilliam is one of the older settlements north of Cape Town and features a number of historic buildings around town.

ARRIVAL AND DEPARTURE   CLANWILLIAM

By bus The daily Intercape bus from Cape Town to Windhoek stops 7km away at a garage on the N7, though there are no means of getting to the town itself.

INFORMATION

Tourist information On Main Rd (mid-Aug to mid-Sept daily 8am–5pm; mid-Sept to mid-Aug Mon–Fri 8.30am–5pm, Sat 8.30am–12.30pm; ☎ 027 482 2024, ⓦ www.clanwilliam.info).

ROOIBOS TEA

Few things in South Africa create such devotion or aversion as **rooibos** (literally, "red bush") **tea**. Still sown and harvested by hand on many farms, rooibos is a type of *fynbos* plant grown only in the mountainous regions around Clanwilliam and Nieuwoudtville. The caffeine-free, health tea brewed from its leaves has been a South African drink ever since it was developed by Asian slaves two centuries ago. In homes and cafés throughout South Africa, rooibos is now firmly entrenched alongside regular tea and coffee, and now even comes as an espresso, known as Red Espresso, which you can buy in powdered form from supermarkets or order as a brew at an increasing number of cafés.

Should you want to see how the tea is grown and processed on a farm, take one of the **tours** offered by Elandsberg Eco Tours (☎ 027 482 2022, ⓦ www. elandsberg.co.za; R75), which start from their premises 20km west of Clanwilliam, on the Lambert's Bay road. Otherwise, it is easy enough to visit the country's main rooibos **tea-processing factory** in Clanwilliam itself, in Ou Kaapse Weg, which shows videos of the manufacturing process (Mon–Fri 10am, 11.30am, 2pm & 3.30pm), as well as rooibos tea and rooibos-inspired cosmetics for sale; while you can peek into the factory, there are no tours as such.

ACCOMMODATION

Blommenberg Guest House 1 Graafwater Rd ☎027 482 1851, ⓦwww.blommenberg.co.za. An easy-to-find guesthouse, opposite the garage as you come into Clanwilliam, with good-value rooms of a consistent standard. R750

Living Landscape 18 Park St ☎027 482 1911. Acceptable place to stay, and the only backpacker accommodation in the centre of Clanwilliam, with dorms in the suburban house next door to the community project. It is mostly geared towards school and university groups on rock-art projects. R100

Ndedema Lodge At the end of Park St ☎027 482 1314, ⓦwww.ndedemalodge.co.za. A romantic Victorian B&B with an upmarket feel, four antique-filled rooms and a charming garden with pool. R900

EATING

The Palms Restaurant Clanwilliam Lodge, Graafwater Ave ☎027 482 1009. A good choice for a refuelling stop – kick back by the fire in winter, or outside by the pool in summer. Their food is predominantly meat-based, with some salads on the menu (R90). Daily 8.30am–10pm.

Nancy's Tea Room 33 Main Rd ☎027 482 2661. The outdoor garden here is a peaceful place for breakfast or lunch; they serve creative toasted sandwiches and good coffee, as well as heavier lunch dishes such as *bobotie* (R65). Daily 8am–4.30pm.

Olifants Huis 1 Main Rd ☎027 482 2301. The best choice for an evening meal, in a cosy manor house, with a wood-fired pizza oven and a good reputation for steaks (R80). The chef uses local, seasonal ingredients and one dish uses rooibos tea-leaves to smoke ostrich fillets. Mon–Sat 6.30–9.30pm.

Yellow Aloes 1 Park Rd ☎027 482 2018. Primarily open for tea and light lunches, or you can enjoy a romantic dinner under the trees with a view of the mountain (three courses R120), but only if you book it in advance. Daily 8am–5pm.

The Boskloof

About 1km east of Clanwilliam along the Pakhuis Pass road, a good dirt road heads south and drops into the **Boskloof**, through which the Jan Dissels River traces its course. Although less than 10km from the town, and 290km from Cape Town, the valley feels a very long way from anywhere and is a relaxed spot where you can spend time lolling about along the riverbank, swimming in its natural pools or just walking along the dirt road that twists through the mountains. From the valley you can hike up into the Cederberg Mountains on the **Krakadouw hiking trail**, which starts at **Krakadouw Cottages** in the valley, where you can buy permits. Hikes can last up to a week, though you can also do shorter day or half-day hikes along a section of the trail.

ACCOMMODATION   THE BOSKLOOF

Boskloof Swemgat Boskloof Rd, 13km from Clanwilliam ☎027 482 2522, ⓦboskloofswemgat .co.za. Accommodation is in eight simple, self-catering cottages without a great deal of privacy, in an open, grassy area, right on the river. The draw of this place is the excellent river swimming and reasonable prices. R550

★ **Karukareb** Boskloof Rd, 15km from Clanwilliam ☎027 482 1675, ⓦkarukareb.co.za. This luxury bushcamp and guest lodge is situated along the river, in one of the loveliest and wildest valleys in the Western Cape. The best way to appreciate the wilderness is in one of five luxury safari tents along the river, rather than at the lodge itself. Each tent has its own section of river to swim in and wooden decks to relax on. Best of all are the baths positioned by windows, where you can relax, glass in hand, and watch the sunset reddening the mountains. Rates include board and activities. R2300

Klein Boschkloof Chalets Boskloof Rd, 9km from Clanwilliam ☎027 402 2441, ⓦkleinboschkloof.co.za. A reasonably priced collection of 250-year-old Cape Dutch farm buildings converted into guest cottages. The thatched chalets stand in the middle of fragrant citrus groves, and are finished to a high standard, with cooking gear, bed linen and towels. Breakfast and dinner can be provided by prior arrangement. R650

Northern Cederberg and the Pakhuis Pass

The **R364** northeast from Clanwilliam winds over the **Pakhuis Pass**, a drive worth taking for its lonely roadside scenery and inspiring views. This area is said to be one of the two best places in the world for **bouldering**, so expect to see plenty of lithe climbers going to and from the graded routes, particularly in the milder winter months.

Although you are below the Cederberg massifs, the rocks, rivers, valleys and sense of space make this area very appealing, with the added attraction of access to the finest rock art in the Western Cape (see below).

ACCOMMODATION   NORTHERN CEDERBERG AND THE PAKHUIS PASS

All the accommodation in this area is along the Pakhuis Pass Rd. The road is now tarred, though it peters out beyond Bushman's Kloof into a network of dirt roads leading to farms.

Alpha Excelsior Guest Farm and Winery ☎ 027 482 2700, ⓦ alphaexcelsior.co.za. Three cottages, the nicest of which, Weaver, is nearest to the river and sleeps two; the others sleep more, and there's an attic room in one house for dorm beds, often taken up by rock climbers. The farm, run by friendly folk, has its own small winery too, with bottles for sale. Dorm R90, cottage R350

Bushman's Kloof ☎ 027 482 2627, bookings ☎ 021 685 2598, ⓦ bushmanskloof.co.za. A luxury lodge, which has won international hotel accolades, set in a wilderness area with game drives and rock art, with over 125 recorded sites on the property. The rangers are trained in both wildlife guiding and rock-art interpretation. The rate includes all meals, game drives and guided rock-art trails. R8000

De Pakhuys ☎ 027 482 1468, ⓦ www.depakhuys .co.za. Three large garden cottages of varying sizes on a rooibos farm with marked hiking trails, starting near the secluded campsite, plus a farm dam for swimming. The Krugers are exceptionally obliging and you also have the use of their swimming pool and braai facilities. Camping R40, cottage R700

Traveller's Rest Farm 36km northeast of Clanwilliam on the R364 ☎ 027 482 1824, ⓦ travellersrest.co.za. Twelve self-catering cottages at different locations on a passion fruit, rooibos and sheep farm, where there are plenty of walks. Meals for groups can be pre-arranged and there is a well-stocked farm stall which also serves daytime meals. The main attraction is the 4km Sevilla bushman painting trail, starting right beside the farm. The trail takes in nine separate rock-art sites, and provides an easy and varied introduction to rock art; if you're pushed for time, you can restrict yourself to the first six, which are the best. Horse trails may be arranged, and there are river pools for summer swimming. R380

Wuppertal and the Biedouw Valley

One of the best drives you can do in the Western Cape is along the mountainous R364 dirt road, pretty awful and steep in parts, which winds through remote valleys to reach historic **WUPPERTAL**. Set deep in the tunefully named Tra-tra Valley, the Moravian mission station is one of the oldest in the Western Cape and, with a tiny collection of thatched cottages in the small centre and along the river, it remains one of the most untouched settlements in South Africa. Run by the church elders and with an entirely coloured population, the mission is famous for making **velskoene** (literally "hide shoes"), the suede footwear commonly known as *vellies* and part of Afrikaner national dress. You can see the shoes being made and, of course, buy them at the little shop at De Werf – the centre that clusters around the church.

OUDRIF

An exceptional retreat lodge in the Cederberg back country, ★ **Oudrif** (booking essential; ☎ 027 482 2397, ⓦ www.oudrif.co.za; R1500) occupies inspiring countryside in the transitional zone between the foothills of the mountains and the dry Karoo, with redstone gorges and a wide valley incised by the Doring River. Although there are wonderful **guided walks** through *fynbos* to San rock-art sites and paddling opportunities on the river, this is as much a place to chill out – the only rule enforced by the co-owner and manager Bill Mitchell, and his wife Janine, is that there are no rules. The multi-talented Mitchell is also a qualified chef and does all the cooking at this full-board establishment.

    Accommodation is in five straw-bale houses. The cream-coloured chalets have an uneven hewn quality that befits their isolation on the edge of the gorge that falls away to the Doring River. Each is stylishly equipped with retro furniture and has a double and a three-quarter bed; the power for lighting is provided by solar panels, and showers are heated. *Oudrif* is 48km from Clanwilliam, some of it along rough dirt roads.

On the way to Wuppertal you can turn into the **Biedouw Valley**, which only sees traffic during the spring, when the valley floor is carpeted with flowers.

| INFORMATION | WUPPERTAL |

Tourist information Housed in one of the oldest buildings in Wuppertal (☎027 492 3410, ⓦtourismwupperthal.co.za).

ACCOMMODATION

Enjolife Biedouw Valley Rd ☎027 482 2869, ⓦsoulcountry.info. The best reason to visit the Biedouw Valley is to stay at this isolated 200-year-old farmhouse, run by a young German couple who offer lovely self-catering chalets at backpacker prices, as well as camping. The emphasis here is on enjoying nature, and in the hot summer you can swim at the farm dam. Due to its isolation, it's a place to spend a few days, rather than simply overnight. Access is only on dirt roads. Dinners can be booked on request and flights arranged by the former Lufthansa pilot owner. Camping R50, chalet R350

Wuppertal Cottages ☎027 492 3410. Modest self-catering cottages in the village, run by the tourist office. Meals can be ordered from the *Lekkerbekkie Tea Room*, as there is nowhere for dinner or breakfast. R260

2

The Northern Cape

QUIVER TREES IN RICHTERSVELD TRANSFRONTIER PARK

The Northern Cape

The vast Northern Cape, the largest and most dispersed of South Africa's provinces, is not an easy region to tackle as a visitor. From the lonely Atlantic coast to Kimberley, the provincial capital on its eastern border with the Free State, it covers over one-third of the nation's landmass, an area dominated by heat, aridity, empty spaces and huge travelling distances. The miracles of the desert are the main attraction – improbable swaths of flowers, diamonds dug from the dirt and wild animals roaming the dunes.

3

The most significant of these surprises is the **Orange** (or Oranje) **River**, flowing from the Lesotho Highlands to the Atlantic where it marks South Africa's border with Namibia. The river separates the **Kalahari** and the **Great Karoo** – the two sparsely populated semi-desert ecosystems that fill the interior of the Northern Cape. On its banks, the isolated northern centre of **Upington** is the main town in the Kalahari region, the gateway to the magnificent **Kgalagadi Transfrontier Park** and the smaller **Augrabies Falls National Park**.

In **Namaqualand**, on the western side of the province, the brief winter rains produce one of nature's truly glorious transformations when in August and September the land is carpeted by a magnificent display of wild flowers. A similar display of blossoming succulents can be seen at the little-visited **Richtersveld Transfrontier Park**, a mountain desert tucked around a loop in the Orange River either side of the Namibian border.

Despite these impressive natural attractions, most of the traffic to the Northern Cape is in its southeastern corner, through which the two main roads between Johannesburg and Cape Town, the **N1** and the **N12**, pass. However, given the uninspiring nature of this area, it isn't covered in this book. A less obvious way to get from Johannesburg to Cape Town involves taking the **N14** through Upington, passing the atmospheric old mission station at **Kuruman**, then driving on to **Springbok** and following the scenic **N7** down the coast. This route is around 400km longer than the N1 or N12 but, while the N14 has more than its fair share of long, empty landscapes, the sights along the way are more interesting.

Getting around by **public transport** can be a pain. While the main towns of Kimberley, Springbok and Upington lie on Intercape's bus routes (with connections to Windhoek in Namibia), many services arrive and depart at night and thus miss the scenery. Minibus taxis cover most destinations several times a day during the week, but are much reduced or nonexistent at weekends. Taxis don't serve the national parks (take an organized tour instead). Details of the most useful routes are given in the text.

Highlights

❶ **The Big Hole** The vast hand-dug crater that dominates Kimberley is an awesome testament to South Africa's pioneer diamond hunters. **See p.270**

❷ **Kgalagadi Transfrontier Park** Discover lion, gemsbok and suricate among the parched red sand dunes of the Kalahari. **See p.284**

❸ **Augrabies Falls** Marvel at Africa's second-biggest waterfall, where the Orange River thunders into an echoing gorge carved out of the desert. **See p.288**

❹ **Namaqualand flowers** In August and September the veld bursts into colour with a superb natural floral display, and boasts a fascinating variety of unusual succulents year-round. **See p.291**

❺ **Driving down the N7** The province's most scenic drive stretches south from Springbok through rocky mountains and peaceful *dorps*. **See p.293**

❻ **Richtersveld Transfrontier Park** South Africa's only mountain desert, a hot, dry and forbidding place that can only be explored by 4WD or by drifting down the Orange River in an inflatable canoe. **See p.300**

HIGHLIGHTS ARE MARKED ON THE MAP ON PP.266–267

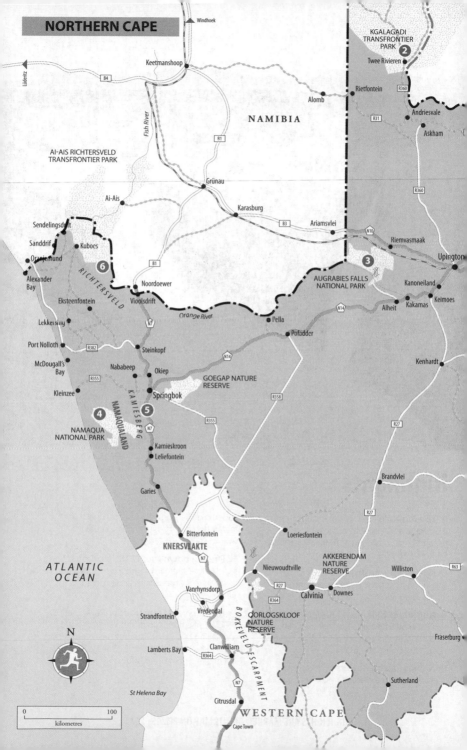

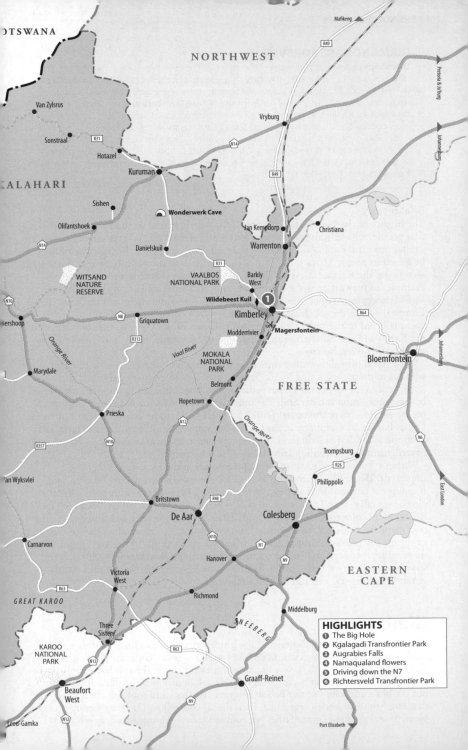

HIGHLIGHTS
1. The Big Hole
2. Kgalagadi Transfrontier Park
3. Augrabies Falls
4. Namaqualand flowers
5. Driving down the N7
6. Richtersveld Transfrontier Park

DIAMONDS ARE FOREVER

Diamonds originate as carbon particles in the Earth's mantle, which are subjected to such high pressure and temperature that they crystallize to form diamonds. Millions of years ago the molten rock, or magma, in the mantle burst through weak points in the Earth's crust as volcanoes, and it is in the pipe of cooled magma – called **kimberlite**, after Kimberley – that diamonds are found. Finding kimberlite, however, isn't necessarily a licence to print money – in every one hundred tonnes there will be about twenty carats (4g) of diamonds.

The word "carat" derives from the carob bean – dried beans were used as a measure of weight. (Carat has a different meaning in the context of gold, where it is a measure of purity.) De Beers estimates that fifty million pieces of diamond jewellery are bought each year – which represents a lot of marriage proposals.

Brief history

The history of the Northern Cape area is intimately linked to the **San**, South Africa's first people, whose hunter-gatherer lifestyle and remarkable adaptations to desert life exert a powerful fascination. Although no genuine vestiges of the San way of life can be found in South Africa (only tiny pockets remain in the Namibian and Botswanan sections of the Kalahari desert), their heritage is most visible in the countless examples of **rock art** across the province, and, to a lesser extent, in their ancient legends and place names. The movement of Africans from the north and east, and Europeans from the southwest, drove the San from their hunting grounds and eventually led to their extinction; yet for both sets of newcomers, the semi-desert of the Karoo and the Kalahari at first appeared to offer little more than hopelessness and heartbreaking horizons.

What it did provide – wealth under the dusty ground – the Europeans pursued without restraint, beginning in 1685, soon after the Dutch first established their settlement in the Cape, with an expedition into Namaqualand to mine for copper led by **Governor Simon van der Stel**. The other Europeans who made an early impression on the province were **trekboers**, Dutch burghers freed from the employment of the Dutch East India Company in the Cape who wanted to find new lands to farm away from the authoritarian company rule, and **missionaries**, who established a framework of settlement and communication used by all who came after.

Within a few years of the discovery of **diamonds** in the area, a settlement of unprecedented size had grown up around Kimberley. The town soon boasted more trappings of civilization than most of the southern hemisphere, with public libraries, electric streetlights and tramways, as well as South Africa's first urban "location" for Africans and coloureds. The British authorities in the Cape were quick to annexe the new diamond fields – a move which didn't endear them to either the Orange Free State or the mainly coloured **Griqua** people, who both claimed this ill-defined region. It was no surprise, therefore, that at the outbreak of the **Anglo-Boer War** in 1899, rich and strategic Kimberley was one of the first towns besieged by the Boer armies. Many reminders of the war can still be seen in the area.

Kimberley

Although it's a provincial capital and the historic centre of production of one of the world's most valuable materials, **KIMBERLEY** itself is neither large nor glamorous. During the diamond rush, it was the fastest-growing city in the southern hemisphere and Cecil Rhodes held in his grip not only the fabulously wealthy diamond industry, but the heart and mind of the British Empire; yet status and sophistication have been draining from Kimberley ever since. Even the all-controlling De Beers Group (sometimes called the "grandfather" of Kimberley for the number of people it has

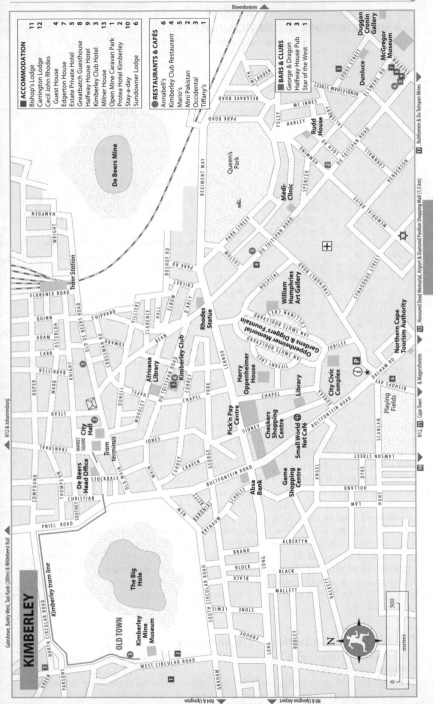

A SHORT HISTORY OF THE DIAMOND FIELDS

The area now known as the **Diamond Fields** was once unpromising farmland, marked by occasional *koppies* inhabited by pioneer farmers and the Griquas, an independent people of mixed race. In 1866 this changed forever, when a 15-year-old boy noticed a shiny white pebble on the banks of the Orange River near Hopetown, about 120km southwest of Kimberley. Just as word of that discovery was spreading, another Hopetown resident, Schalk van Niekerk, acquired from a Griqua shepherd a massive 83.5-carat diamond. These two stones became known, respectively, as "**Eureka**" and "**The Star of South Africa**"; the latter was described at the time – with some justification – by the British Colonial Secretary as the "rock on which the future success of South Africa will be built". Certainly in the short term, the discoveries provoked wild optimism: thousands of prospectors made the gruelling trek across the Karoo to sift through the alluvial deposits along the banks of the Orange and Vaal rivers, and by 1873 there were an estimated fifty thousand people living in the area.

Although plenty of diamonds were found in the rivers, **prospectors** also began scratching around in the dry land between them, encouraged by tales of diamonds found in farmhouse bricks made from local earth. Two of the most promising "dry diggings" were on a farm owned by two brothers, Johannes Nicolas and Diederick Arnoldus de Beer. In 1871 the brothers sold the farm, which they had bought a few years previously for £50, to prospectors for the sum of £6300. The two sites subsequently became the **Kimberley Mine**, or Big Hole, and the **De Beers Mine**, situated on either side of the centre of Kimberley. The Big Hole was the focus of the most frenetic mining activity of the early years, and the shantytown that grew up around it, **New Rush**, was the origin of the present city.

Kimberley in those days was a heady, rugged place to live, with little authority or structure, but with prizes rich enough to attract bold men with big ideas. Of these, two very different, if equally ambitious, men rose to prominence in the new settlement. **Barney Barnato**, a flamboyant Cockney, established his power base at the Kimberley Mine, while **Cecil Rhodes** (see box opposite), a parson's son who had come out to join his brother in South Africa to improve his health, gradually took control of the De Beers Mine. The power struggle between the two men was intense, culminating in the formation in 1888 of the **De Beers Consolidated Mines Limited**, an agreement involving the transfer from Rhodes to Barnato of over £5 million, an astronomical sum in those days. This consolidation laid the foundation for De Beers' monopoly of the diamond industry in South Africa.

directly and indirectly employed) closed its Kimberley mines in 2005 as part of a process to streamline the company, and the city lives in the chilly shadow of the day when the diamonds dry up altogether.

However, Kimberley's legacy gives it an historic flavour few other cities in South Africa can match. It's worth spending a few hours seeking out some of the many old buildings, not forgetting to peer into the depths of the Big Hole just west of the centre, the remarkable, hand-dug chasm that takes up almost as much land area as the city's central business district (CBD).

The fact that the Big Hole is underground doesn't make orientation immediately easy; a useful landmark is the stern-looking skyscraper, **Harry Oppenheimer House** (often referred to as HOH), near the tourist office. Many of Kimberley's other main sights lie on or near **Du Toitspan Road**, which slices diagonally across the city centre and becomes one of the main arteries out of town to the southeast. The central business district (CBD) sits at Du Toitspan Road's northern end, to the south of Lennox Road.

The Big Hole: Kimberley Mine Museum

On the western side of the hole along West Circular Rd • **Museum** Daily 8am–5pm • R75 • **Tram** Hourly 9.15am–4.15pm • R10 • ⓦ thebighole.co.za

Although the 500-metre-wide **Big Hole**, just west of the city centre, is neither the only nor even the biggest hole in Kimberley, it remains the city's principal attraction. In

1871, with diamonds known to be in the area (see box opposite), a group of workers known as the Red Cap Party were scratching around at the base of **Colesberg koppie**, a small hill on the De Beers brothers' farm. The story goes that they sent one of their cooks to the top of the hill as a punishment for being drunk, telling him not to return until he'd found a diamond. The unnamed servant duly came back with a peace offering, and within two years there were over fifty thousand people in the area frantically turning Colesberg *koppie* inside out. In its heyday, tens of thousands of miners swarmed over the mine to work their ten-square-metre claim, and a network of ropes and pipes crisscrossed the surface; each day saw lives lost and fortunes either discovered or squandered. Once the mining could go no further from the surface, a shaft was dug to allow further excavations beneath it to a depth of over 800m. Incredibly, the hole was dug to a depth of 240m entirely by pick and shovel, and remains one of the largest manmade excavations in the world. By 1914, when De Beers closed the mine, some 22.6 million tonnes of earth had been removed, yielding over 13.6 million carats (2722kg) of diamonds.

The only official way to see the Big Hole is from inside the **Kimberley Mine Museum**, which you can reach either on foot or via a delightfully rickety, open-sided tram that runs from the City Hall. The museum gives a comprehensive insight into Kimberley's main claim to fame. The Big Hole itself is viewed from a suspended platform, from which you can peer down into nothingness. An informative film puts it all into context, as do other displays, from a re-creation of a nineteenth-century mineshaft to a vault full of real diamonds.

The Old Town

West Circular Rd • Daily 8am–5pm • free

This impressive collection of **historic buildings**, many originating from the days of Rhodes and Barnato, is scattered around the entrance to the Mine Museum and can be wandered through without paying the museum entry fee. The old shops, churches, pub, banks and sundry other period institutions were moved here from the city centre when development and demolition threatened; now there's enough here to create a fairly complete settlement, and most of the fixtures, fittings and artefacts are genuine.

CECIL JOHN RHODES

When **Cecil Rhodes** first arrived in the Kimberley Diamond Fields he was a sickly 18-year-old, sent out to join his brother for the sake of his health. Soon making money buying up claims, he returned to Britain to attend Oxford University, where his illnesses returned and he was given six months to live. He came back out to South Africa, where he was able to improve both his health and his business standing, allowing him to return to Oxford and graduate in 1881. By that point he had already founded the **De Beers Mining Company** and been elected an MP in the **Cape Parliament**.

Within a decade, Rhodes controlled ninety percent of the world's diamond production and was champing at the bit to expand his mining interests north into Africa, with the British Empire in tow. With much cajoling, bullying, brinkmanship and obfuscation in his dealings with imperial governments and African chiefs alike, Rhodes brought the regions north of the Limpopo under the control of his **British South African Company** (BSAC). This territory – now Zimbabwe and Zambia – became known as **Rhodesia** in 1895, the same year as a Rhodes-backed invasion of the Transvaal Republic, the **Jameson Raid**, failed humiliatingly. Rhodes was forced to resign as prime minister of the Cape Colony, a post he had assumed in 1890 at the age of 37, while the Boers and the British slid towards war. He spent the first part of the war in besieged Kimberley, trying to organize the defences and bickering publicly with the British commander. A year after the end of the war, Rhodes died at Muizenberg near Cape Town, aged only 49 and unmarried; he was buried in the Matopos Hills near Bulawayo in Zimbabwe.

River digging

Daily 8am–5pm • R30

One of the more engaging features in the Old Town is an area where you can buy a bucket of **alluvial river diggings** and sift through it on old sorting tables, in the hope of finding one of the mock diamonds planted among the gravel. The rocks can be exchanged for various prizes, and the price of the bucket includes a shot at some old-fashioned ten-pin bowling as well.

Market Square and around

At the heart of the city centre is **Market Square**, dominated by the white, Corinthian-style City Hall. During the early diamond days, the square was the hub of buying and selling. Around the square, the sense of movement and commerce is perpetuated by a large taxi rank and an assortment of scruffy but colourful stalls and traders. One block west of Market Square along the tramline, at **36 Stockdale St**, lies the head office of De Beers, a dignified but unremarkable old building (not open to the public) rather swallowed up by the city around it.

The Kimberley Club

70–72 Du Toitspan Rd • ☎ 053 832 4224, ⓦ kimberleyclub.co.za

Not far southwest of Market Square is the two-storey **Kimberley Club**, founded in 1881 by the new settlement's movers and shakers. The club was modelled on London's gentlemen's clubs, but its colourful, enterprising members made the place dynamic rather than stuffy. As well as leather armchairs in the smoking lounge and marble in the hallway, there are plenty of fine antiques and a few quirky pieces. It's possible to look around or go for a meal at the restaurant (see p.276), though you'll get a much less chilly welcome if you introduce yourself at the reception and respect the club's dress code, which includes no T-shirts or shorts in the dining room and bar.

The Africana Library

Du Toitspan Rd • Mon–Fri 8am–12.45pm & 1.30–4.30pm • ☎ 053 830 6247

The small but engrossing **Africana Library**, across the road from the Kimberley Club, specializes in historical material relevant to Kimberley and the Northern Cape. Opened in 1887, it retains many original features, and one of the librarians will show you around if you ask nicely. There are also historical books and copies of weathered, evocative old photos for sale; all proceeds go towards supporting the library's conservation work.

The CBD

At the junction of Du Toitspan and Lennox roads stands a statue of **Cecil Rhodes** astride a horse. The **CBD** area begins across Lennox Street, where the **Oppenheimer Memorial Gardens** contain a bust of mining magnate Sir Ernest Oppenheimer and the Diggers' Fountain; the latter depicts five miners holding aloft a massive sieve, and looks particularly impressive when floodlit after dusk. The tall building overlooking the gardens is **Harry Oppenheimer House** (HOH), the offices of De Beers' DTC (Diamond Trading Company; not open to the public), on the upper floors of which all of the company's South African-mined diamonds are assessed for caratage, colour, clarity and shape. To allow this to take place in the best natural light, the building faces south, with special windows to eliminate glare; there are no windows on the other faces other than small ones along the stairwell.

KIMBERLEY TOURS

While the cessation of operations at the De Beers mines has brought to an end the fascinating underground tours of a working diamond mine, Kimberley still offers a series of informative and entertaining local tours. The **Diamantveld Visitor Centre** (see p.275) maintains a list of accredited guides; alternatively, contact the recommended **Diamond Tours Unlimited** (☎053 832 9756 or ☎084 645 7754, ⓦdiamondtours.co.za).

GHOST TOURS

If you're brave enough to hear the stories of restless spirits, or simply like the idea of poking around some of Kimberley's most interesting buildings after hours, join a **Ghost Tour** (R80) of the city. You'll be shown scenes of strange encounters at places such as the Africana Library, the Regimental headquarters and spooky Rudd House in Belgravia. Tours begin just before sunset at the Honoured Dead Memorial, and last three to four hours; book through Diamond Tours Unlimited (see above).

TOWNSHIP TOURS

Kimberley was the first settlement in South Africa to establish "locations" on its fringes to house the African and coloured labourers working in the mines. A tour of **Galeshewe**, named after a rebellious nineteenth-century chief, offers an insight into a typical modern South African township with its mix of shacks, simple government houses and the more ostentatious homes of locals-made-good. The tour takes in some alternative historic sights, including the grave of **Sol Plaatje** (see box, p.527) and the house where **Robert Sobukwe** (see box, p.332), founder of the Pan-African Congress, lived under house arrest after his release from Robben Island in 1969. Most tours finish with the post-apartheid **Northern Cape Provincial Legislature complex** – an extraordinary construction combining elements of traditional African design with silver polygonal slabs.

3

William Humphreys Art Gallery

On the opposite side of the gardens to HOH, in the Civic Centre • Mon–Fri 8am–4.45pm, Sat 10am–4.45pm, Sun & holidays 2–4.45pm • R5 • ☎053 831 1724, ⓦwhag.co.za

The **William Humphreys Art Gallery**, one of South Africa's few top-notch art galleries, is an unexpected gem. Although dominated by European Old Masters when it opened in 1952, the collection has always moved with the times and now houses an impressively well-balanced representation of South African art, including both traditional and contemporary work and some excellent modern sculpture. The gallery was one of the first places in the world to display **San rock paintings** as works of art rather than anthropological museum pieces. At the back of the gallery is a very pleasant **tea room**, which serves breakfasts and light lunches on a terrace beside a small garden (see p.276).

Belgravia

Du Toitspan Rd

Belgravia, the residential suburb where most of Kimberley's wealthy families lived during the boom years, lies about 1km southeast of the CBD. The focus of the area is at the junction of Du Toitspan and Egerton roads, where you'll find the historic **Halfway House Pub**. The pub takes its name from its location halfway between the De Beers and Bultfontein mines, and gained fame as a drive-in (or, in those days, ride-in) pub, a custom started by Cecil Rhodes who liked to tipple while in the saddle. Nowadays you can still drive up and blow your horn to attract the bartender.

McGregor Museum

Atlas Rd • Mon–Sat 9am–5pm, Sun 2–5pm • R12 • ☎053 839 2700, ⓦmuseumsnc.co.za

The fabulous **McGregor Museum**, named after an early mayor of Kimberley, is housed in a magnificent Victorian mansion. The highlight here is the extensive and imaginative Ancestors Display, which draws on archeological evidence to piece together an

absorbing and – unusual still in South Africa – well-balanced exhibition on the various ancestral roots of today's inhabitants of the Northern Cape, going right back to evidence of the earliest hominids millions of years ago. There's also an evocative section on the siege of Kimberley.

Duggan-Cronin Gallery

Egerton Rd • Mon–Fri 9am–5pm • Donation • ☎ 053 839 2700

The **Duggan-Cronin Gallery**, adjacent to the McGregor Museum, includes over eight thousand endearingly unsophisticated photographs portraying the lifestyles of the indigenous people of South Africa between the two world wars. They were taken by Alfred Duggan-Cronin, a night watchman for De Beers.

Lodge Road houses

Lodge Rd • Arrange a guide from the McGregor Museum to visit Rudd House and Dunluce • R20 for each house

A trio of elegantly restored Belgravia houses, all on Lodge Road, are redolent of the atmosphere of old Kimberley and give a sense of the kind of wealth the city once attracted: **Rudd House** at no. 5 was the mansion of mining magnate and partner of Rhodes, Charles Dunnell Rudd; at no. 7 the Edwardian estate birthplace of Harry Oppenheimer, now the *Estate Private Hotel* (see opposite), was the family's last Kimberley home before they moved to Johannesburg in 1915; and **Dunluce** at no. 10 is an elegant late Victorian home, the former residence of one of the mayors of Kimberley.

ARRIVAL AND DEPARTURE   KIMBERLEY

By plane Kimberley's airport (☎ 053 838 3337) lies 7km to the west of the city, along the N8 to Upington. South African Express (☎ 053 838 3337) and South African Airlink (☎ 053 838 3339), both based at the airport, operate flights to Johannesburg and Cape Town respectively. There's no regular transport into town, so phone for a taxi (see opposite). All of the major car rental agencies are based at the airport, including Avis (☎ 053 851 1082), Budget (☎ 053 851 1183), Hertz (☎ 053 830 2200), Imperial/Europcar (☎ 053 851 1131) and National (☎ 053 851 1131).

Destinations: Cape Town (1–2 daily; 1hr 35min); Johannesburg (5–6 daily; 1hr 25min).

By bus Intercity buses stop outside the tourist office, which is handy when arriving on overnight Greyhound and Translux services from Cape Town, but to be avoided on daytime departures from Cape Town or Jo'burg, which arrive at night when the place is deserted. You can either arrange for a hotel to pick you up, ask to be dropped off at one of the hotels along the N12 (Bishops Avenue) just south of the centre, or alight at the Ultra City service station 6km north of town, which is a much safer place to call a taxi. Information and tickets for the four main intercity bus companies (Intercape, Greyhound, SA Roadlink and Translux) are available at the Tickets for Africa bureau inside the Diamantveld Visitor Centre (see opposite; Mon–Fri 8am–7.30pm, Sat 8am–12.30pm; ☎ 053 832 6040); most buses depart from just outside. Intercape services go to Upington and Bloemfontein, while Greyhound, Translux and SA Roadlink (☎ 083 918 3999)

all have services to Jo'burg. Greyhound also operates a daily service to Cape Town.

Destinations: Bloemfontein (2 weekly; 2hr 30min); Bloemhof (4 daily; 2hr); Cape Town (daily; 11hr 30min); Christiana (4 daily; 1hr 30min); Johannesburg (4 daily; 6hr 30min–7hr 40min); Klerksdorp (4 daily; 3hr 45min); Potchefstroom (4 daily; 4hr 30min); Upington (2 weekly; 5hr).

By train The train station (☎ 053 838 2709) is just off Quinn St on the northeastern edge of town.

Destinations: Beaufort West (1–2 daily; 9hr); Bloemfontein (Mon; 3hr); Cape Town (1–2 daily; 18hr 30min); Christiana (daily; 2hr); De Aar (1–2 daily; 4hr); Durban (Mon; 19hr 15min); Johannesburg (daily; 9hr); Klerksdorp (daily; 4hr 30min); Krugersdorp (daily; 8hr); Ladysmith (Mon; 13hr 20min); Laingsburg (1–2 daily; 12hr); Pietermaritzburg (Mon; 17hr); Potchefstroom (daily; 5hr 30min); Worcester (1–2 daily; 15hr 15min).

By minibus taxi Minibus taxis operate from Pniel Rd (the northern extension of Bultfontein Rd), 1.5km from the tourist office. To be sure of a ride in daylight, arrive at 6.30am (7am winter); most destinations also have early afternoon departures, but on these you risk being dropped off at night. Services on all routes are reduced on Saturday, and often nonexistent on Sunday. Frequencies given below refer to weekdays. Except to Barkly West (for which you pay on board), fares are paid at an office on Pniel Road beside the long-distance rank.

Destinations: Barkly West (hourly; 30min); Kuruman (1–2 daily; 2hr 30min); Upington (3–4 daily; 5hr).

GETTING AROUND

Central Kimberley is fairly walkable, but take **taxis** at night; reliable outfits include Alpha Taxis (☎073 925 8695) and Rikkis (☎053 842 1764). Note that around town, many street names are written on the curbside rather than on signs.

INFORMATION

Tourist office The Diamantveld Visitor Centre is at 121 Bultfontein Rd (Mon–Fri 8am–5pm, Sat 8am–noon; ☎053 832 7298, ⓦsolplaatje.org.za). The staff can provide city plans, lists of places to stay, detailed driving itineraries in the province, information on local tours (see box, p.273) and self-guided walking tours of Kimberley.

Northern Cape Tourism Authority On Dalham Rd, a few hundred metres southeast of the tourist office (Mon–Fri 7.30am–4pm; ☎053 833 1434, ⓦnorthern cape.org. za) can provide more information about the province, particularly wildlife parks and reserves.

ACCOMMODATION

The bulk of the town's hotels, guesthouses and B&Bs lie in the southern suburbs, most within a kilometre or two of the centre. The most atmospheric places – occupying historic buildings – are clustered in and around the upmarket Belgravia suburb.

HOTELS AND GUESTHOUSES

Bishop's Lodge 9 Bishops Ave ☎053 831 7876, ⓦbishopslodge.co.za; map p.269. Close to the tourist office, this quiet, modern affair offers spotless twin rooms and keenly priced self-catering apartments (R750), plus a suite with wheelchair access. There's a swimming pool, but no meals except breakfast. R600

Carrington Lodge 60 Carrington Rd, at the corner with Oliver Rd ☎053 831 6448, ⓦcarringtonlodge .co.za; map p.269. Friendly guesthouse on the edge of Belgravia, with two pools and a pleasant garden with a braai area. The stylish rooms have a/c, while ramps provide good wheelchair access. Book ahead weekdays. R615

Cecil John Rhodes Guest House 138 Du Toitspan Rd ☎053 830 2500, ⓦceciljohnrhodes.co.za; map p.269. The most central of the historic guesthouses, built in 1895, with seven airy and elegantly furnished rooms with all mod cons, plus a shady tea garden facing the road. Dinner on request. R740

Edgerton House 5 Egerton Rd ☎053 831 1150, ⓦedgertonhouse.co.za; map p.269. An ornate Belgravia option in an attractive Edwardian house kitted out with crystal chandeliers and gold-plated bathroom fittings. There are thirteen elegant rooms, plus a pool and tea garden. R750

★ Estate Private Hotel 7 Lodge Rd ☎053 832 2668, ⓦtheestate.co.za; map p.269. Six attractive wheelchair-friendly rooms with all mod cons in the Oppenheimers' lavish former Belgravia home, open to visitors by day (see p.272). There's also a pool, a shady tea garden and restaurant, and cooking courses are available at the chefs' school on site. Excellent value. R550

Halfway House Hotel Du Toitspan Rd, at the corner with Egerton Rd ☎053 831 6324, ⓦwww .halfwayhousehotel.co.za; map p.269. Large and airy en-suite rooms around a paved beer garden behind the historic boozer. A handy place to crash after sampling the pub's nocturnal delights, but be prepared for noisy evenings. R550

Kimberley Club Boutique Hotel 70–72 Du Toitspan Rd ☎053 832 4224, ⓦkimberleyclub.co.za; map p.269. This local landmark was recently refurbished to include 21 spacious rooms, some with balconies. Best of all, staying in one gives you temporary club membership, with access to the members' bar and other facilities. Book ahead for weekdays. R1600

Milner House 31 Milner St ☎053 831 6405, ⓦmilner house.co.za; map p.269. Another Belgravia guesthouse, this one more modest and down-to-earth than the others, with six comfortable rooms decorated in refreshing whites, and a swimming pool set in a shady garden. R660

Protea Hotel Kimberley West Circular Rd ☎053 802 8200, ⓦproteahotels.com; map p.269. Perched on the edge of the Big Hole, Kimberley's newest luxury hotel is furnished with all the mod cons. Still, some effort has been made to make the place look suitably antique, with brick walls and a pool shaped like a cattle trough. R950

Sundowner Lodge 1 Bishops Ave ☎053 831 1145, ⓔsundowner@telkomsa.net; map p.269. Within shouting distance of the tourist office, this friendly family-run place has a vaguely colonial feel (perhaps it's the boggle-eyed wildlife trophies adorning the walls), and offers fourteen huge rooms in rows of chalets. R620

CAMPSITES AND BUDGET LODGING

Open Mine Caravan Park West Circular Rd ☎053 830 6322; map p.269. The only central campsite, located among the old mine heaps, over the road from the Big Hole. Lush and neat, although the shade from the trees isn't generous. Office open daily 6am–4pm. R85

Greatbatch Guesthouse 3 Egerton Rd ☎053 832 1113, ⓦgreatbatchguesthouse.co.za; map p.269. Elegant guesthouse and backpackers (the only one within

3

walking distance of the centre) occupying the former home of the architect who created Dunluce (see p.274) and other notable Kimberley buildings. There are attractive, antique-filled rooms in the main house; the dorm is a little cramped, but quirky old miners' bunks make up for the lack of space. Dorm **R150**, double **R500**

Stay-a-day 72 Lawson St ☎053 832 7239, ✉stayaday@lantic.net; map p.269. Ongoing renovations should spruce up the currently rather stark rooms – which are en suite and wheelchair accessible – at this friendly place. A revenue earner for an orphanage, it's 1km south of the tourist office in a residential district. **R300**

EATING, DRINKING AND NIGHTLIFE

Apart from a handful of historic pubs (use a taxi at night), there's little in the way of nightlife in Kimberley. For live **music**, ask at the tourist office about *Destiny*, a township nightclub that hosts old-time jazz bands.

RESTAURANTS AND CAFÉS

Annabell's Du Toitspan Rd, next to Halfway House Pub ☎053 831 6324; map p.269. Offers a similar range of pub food as the *Halfway House* next door, but served in a more elegant atmosphere, with a few pizzas and pasta dishes thrown in (around R55). The pleasant roof terrace is a great place for sundowners. Mon–Sat 6–10pm.

Kimberley Club Restaurant 70–72 Du Toitspan Rd ☎053 832 4224; map p.269. One of the town's most sophisticated restaurants, serving a mix of local and international dishes – everything from Cape salmon and springbok steak to Thai curry – for unexpectedly reasonable prices (R65–90), along with a hefty wine list. Daily 7–10am, noon–2.30pm & 6–9.30pm.

★ **Mario's** 159 Du Toitspan Rd ☎053 831 1738; map p.269. Bright, cheery and easy-going Italian place that's justifiably one of the most popular restaurants in town, with friendly staff and an extensive menu ranging from light lunches and pizzas to more elaborate meals (mains R60–95). There's also a good – if expensive – wine list. Mon–Fri noon–3pm & 6pm–late; Sat 6pm–late.

Mini Pakistan Market Square, facing the post office ☎053 832 3628; map p.269. A bustling little halal canteen dishing out inexpensive curries (around R22), *bunnies*, rotis and *pap* to diners preoccupied with the cricket on TV. Open 7am–8pm (till 3pm on Sun).

Occidental At the Big Hole ☎053 830 4418; map p.269. Unlike the other museum buildings in the Old Town, this is a fully functioning bar and restaurant with a good though small menu – try the excellent Karoo lamb chops (mains around R60). Mon–Fri 9am–7pm, Sat 9am–6pm, Sun 9am–5pm.

Palette Tearoom In the William Humphreys Art Gallery, Civic Centre; map p.269. Modest little tearoom serving healthy food like fruit shakes, teas and fresh salads – a nice change from the meaty fare you find elsewhere. Daily 10am–4pm.

Tiffany's The Savoy hotel, 15 De Beers Rd ☎053 832 6211; map p.269. Formerly Kimberley's foremost dining experience, this formal place lacks windows and is ageing fast, though the food – mostly steaks and game – is still good, albeit a little pricey (mains R60–110). Daily 6.30am–10pm.

BARS

George & Dragon Du Toitspan Rd ☎053 833 2075; map p.269. Popular English theme pub and sports bar. The food – from steaks to bobotie – tends to be rather hit or miss, but the portions are large and prices reasonable (mains around R50). Also features the town's best selection of draught beers. Daily 11am–late.

★ **Halfway House Pub** Corner of Du Toitspan and Egerton rds ☎053 831 6324; map p.269. Cecil Rhodes' old refreshment stop, known as "the Half" and still a favourite for its unpretentious atmosphere. There are more tables in a paved courtyard out the back, and two pool tables. Also serves good, cheap British pub food (mains from R48). Mon–Sat 8.30am–late.

Star of the West West Circular Rd, at the corner of North Circular Rd ☎053 832 6463; map p.269. Kimberley's oldest pub remains a defiantly local dive, complete with eccentric locals propping up the bar. It also receives its fair share of tourists, who enjoy drinking a beer or eating a decent, cheap pub meal in the beer garden. Tends to host live bands on Fri or Sat nights. Daily 10am–late.

DIRECTORY

Banks Quickest for changing money is the foreign exchange counter at Absa, corner of Bultfontein Rd and Long St. Standard has branches opposite Absa on Bultfontein Rd and on Old Main Rd.

Emergencies Call ☎053 831 1954 for an ambulance.

Hospitals and doctors Best-equipped is the 24hr Medi-Clinic, 177 Du Toitspan Rd (☎053 838 1111; emergencies ☎0800 053 053). There are good doctors at Medicross (☎053 833 4200), corner of Long and Stone sts.

Internet access Small World Net Café, 42 Sidney St, near

the tourist office, opposite the library (Mon–Fri 8am–6pm, Sat 9am–2pm).

Pharmacies Piet Muller Pharmacy, 52 Market Square (☎053 831 1787; Mon–Fri 8am–8.30pm, Sat 8am–1pm & 5.30–8.30pm, Sun 10am–12.30pm & 5.30–8.30pm); Medpark, 142 Du Toitspan Rd (☎053 831 1737; Mon–Fri 8am–6pm, Sat 8am–1pm).

Post The post office is on the eastern side of Market Square (Mon–Fri 8.30am–4.30pm, Sat 9am–noon).

Around Kimberley

A couple of interesting places lie on or near the R31, which runs northwest out of Kimberley in the direction of Kuruman: there is some fascinating San rock art at **Wildebeest Kuil**, while the area around Barkly West was where some of the first **diamond camps** sprang up in the 1860s. South of Kimberley along the N12, the mostly unremarkable landscape around Magersfontein was the setting for one of the most dramatic campaigns of the **Anglo-Boer War**.

Wildebeest Kuil

Around 15km from Kimberley along the road to Barkly West • Tues–Fri 8.30am–5.30pm, Sat & Sun 11am–4pm • R20 • ☎ 053 833 7069, ⓦ wildebeestkuil.itgo.com • Coming from Kimberley, you can catch one of the frequent minibus taxis to Barkly West and ask to be dropped at the signposted turning – the site is close by.

Wildebeest Kuil is a small *koppie* of ancient andesite rock. This is an important rock-art site, unusual in that the images are engraved (rather than painted) and are found on loosely scattered rocks and small boulders, rather than cave walls or overhangs. A number of boardwalks have been built to allow access without disturbing the engravings, and trained guides from the local community are on hand to show you around. The visitor centre at the base of the *koppie* provides an introductory display and shows a video.

Under South Africa's programme of land restitution, ownership of the site has been given to the local !Xun and Khwe San communities. Originally from Angola and Namibia, they were recruited as trackers by the South African Defence Force during the war fought in those countries in the 1970s and 1980s. When Namibia became independent in 1990, 370 of these soldiers and their families chose to relocate to South Africa. Largely ignored and forgotten thereafter, and subsisting on meagre military pensions, they established various projects to generate income.

THE KIMBERLEY CAMPAIGN

At the outbreak of the **Anglo-Boer War**, the Boer forces identified diamond-rich Kimberley as an important strategic base and quickly besieged the city, trapping its residents, including Cecil Rhodes, inside. In response, the British deployed an army under **Lord Methuen** to relieve the city. The size of the army and lack of knowledge of the terrain compelled them to advance from the coast along the line of the railway so that a supply of troops, water, food and equipment could be ensured.

Methuen first encountered Boer forces at Belmont; this was followed by further battles at Graspan and the Modder River, from which the Boers made a tactical withdrawal to Magersfontein, a range of hills 30km south of Kimberley. Here the Boer generals, under the leadership of General Cronjé and the tactical direction of **Koos de la Rey**, decided to dig a line of trenches along the bottom of the *koppie* rather than defend the top of the ridge of hills, as was their usual tactic.

In the early hours of December 11, 1899, the British advanced on Magersfontein, fully expecting the enemy to be lined along the ridge. The British were led by the **Highland Regiment**, fresh from campaigns in North Africa and India, and considered the elite of the British army. Just before dawn, as they fanned out into attack formation, four thousand Boers in the trenches just a few hundred metres away opened fire. The use of trenches was, at that point, a rare tactic in modern warfare, and the element of surprise caused devastation in the ranks. Those not killed or wounded in the first volleys were pinned down by snipers for the rest of the day, unable to move in the coverless veld and suffering appallingly under the hot sun. The next day the British withdrew to the Modder River, and the relief of Kimberley was delayed for two months. The defeat was one in a series of three the British suffered within what became known as "Black Week", news of which sent shock waves through the British public who had been expecting their forces to overrun the "crude farmers" before Christmas.

Magersfontein

32km south of Kimberley along the N12 • Daily 8.30am–5pm • R10 • Visitor's Centre ☎ 053 833 7115

The Anglo-Boer War battlefield at **Magersfontein** provides a poignant reminder of the area's blood-spattered past. This is where Boer forces put trench warfare into effect against British troops, with devastating results (see box, p.277). Signs at the battlefield point the way to the **visitor's centre** and its small **museum**, which has some vivid exhibits, including an audiovisual re-creation of the battle. You can also hike up to various monuments situated on the western end of the line of hills. Out on the battlefield itself – now open veld with springbok grazing and the occasional car throwing up a plume of dust along the dirt road – the lines of **trenches** and other memorials can still be seen, including a pair of granite crosses marking the graves of Scandinavian soldiers who fought on the Boer side.

One of the most enjoyable ways of finding out more about the history of the area is to book a one-day battlefield tour with Steve Lunderstedt (☎083 732 3189) or Frank Higgo (☎082 591 5327), both enthusiastic and entertaining military historians. Their tours provide a vivid picture of the campaign, with trips to battlefields, fortifications and gun positions, and walks to get a sense of the terrain and look for old shells and other evidence of the fighting. Alternatively, pick up a "Diamond Fields Battlefields Route" brochure from the tourist office in Kimberley (see p.275) for detailed self-drive directions.

The Kalahari

While the Northern Cape has no shortage of dry, endless expanses, the most emotive by far is the **Kalahari**. The very name holds a resonance of sun-bleached, faraway spaces and the unknown vastness of the African interior, both harsh and magical. The name derives from the word *kgalagadi* (saltpans, or thirsty land), and describes the semi-desert stretching north from the Orange River to the Okavango delta in northern Botswana, west into Namibia and east until the bushveld begins to dominate in the catchment areas of the Vaal and Limpopo rivers.

The Kalahari in the Northern Cape is characterized by surprisingly high, thinly vegetated red or orange sand dunes, scored with dry river beds and large, shimmering saltpans. Although this is, strictly speaking, semi-desert, daytime temperatures are searingly hot in summer and nights are numbingly cold in winter. North of the Orange, South Africa's largest river, the land is populated by tough, hard-working farmers and communities largely descended from the indigenous San hunter-gatherers

---

KALAHARI TOURS

To save yourself driving the vast distances of the Kalahari region – and to take advantage of specialized knowledge of the area's distinctive flora, fauna, landscapes and climate – it's worth considering joining a **guided tour**. Most of the tours incorporate a visit to **Augrabies Falls** and the **Kgalagadi Transfrontier Park**, although customized itineraries are also available. Prices start at R1000 per person per day for a party of two; costs can be kept to a minimum by asking to join a pre-booked safari. For a bird's-eye view of the Kalahari, it's possible to go **paragliding** at Kuruman (see p.281).

The following is a list of reliable, knowledgeable and well-organized tour operators offering a range of Kalahari-based tours:

Diamond Tours Unlimited 71 Jacobson Ave, Kimberley ☎ 053 832 9756, ⓦ diamondtours.co.za.

Kalahari Outventures based near *Augrabies Falls Backpackers*, Augrabies Village (see p.289) ☎ 082 476 8213, ⓦ kalahari.co.za.

Kalahari Safaris 3 Orange St, Upington ☎ 054 332 5653 or ☎ 082 435 0007, ⓦ www.kalaharisafaris.co.za.

Kalahari Tours and Travel 12 Mazurka Curve, Upington ☎ 082 493 5041, ⓦ kalahari-tours.co.za.

and nomadic Khoi herders. For many land-users, there is an increasing realization that **eco-tourism** may be the only viable option on huge areas where stock farming and hunting provide at best a marginal living.

Upington, the main town in the area, stands on the northern bank of the Orange at the heart of an irrigated corridor of intensive wheat, cotton and, most prominently, grape farms. At the far end of the farming belt, about an hour's drive west, the Orange picks up speed, frothing and tumbling into a huge granite gorge at **Augrabies Falls**, the focus of one of the area's two national parks. The other is the undoubted highlight of this area, the **Kgalagadi Transfrontier Park**. A vast desert sanctuary rich in game and boasting a magnificent landscape of red dunes and hardy vegetation, it's well worth the long trek to get there.

Upington

As an inevitable focus of trips to Kgalagadi and Augrabies, as well as those to and from Namaqualand and Namibia, **UPINGTON**, just over 400km west of Kimberley, is a good place to stop for supplies, organize a park tour or onward accommodation, or simply draw breath. Situated on the banks of the Orange River, central Upington is compact and easy to get around, with most of the activity on the three main streets running parallel to the riverbank. It can be a mellow spot, with plenty of greenery softening the arid landscape that surrounds it – a result of the irrigation that allows Upington to be surrounded by vineyards. However, the savage summer temperatures mean you probably won't want to linger.

The Orange River

Sakkie se Arkie cruise Sept–April daily, by prior arrangement in winter if the river is sufficiently high • R60 • ☎ 082 564 5447 or ☎ 082 575 7285, Ⓦ arkie.co.za

Upington's obvious highlight is the **Orange River**, but unless you're staying at one of the riverside guesthouses (see p.281), it tends to be hidden from view. The terrace behind the *Irish Pub* (see p.281) is a good place to admire the river and its swans. Better still, take a cruise with Sakkie se Arkie on its strange two-tier barge; it's based on the riverbank at the east end of Park Street.

The vineyards

Upington's **vineyards** produce ten percent of the country's grapes – mostly table grapes and raisins, though wine is also made. Wine tasting is offered by Orange River Wine Cellars (Mon–Fri 8am–5pm, Sat 9am–noon; free; ☎054 337 8800, Ⓦowk.co.za) in the industrial estate 3km west of the town centre off Industria Street. Alternatively, you can sample or buy its output at *Le Must Restaurant* (see p.281), or at the Kalahari Dried Fruit & Coffee Shop (Mon–Fri 8am–5pm, Sat 8am–1pm), which also sells other local produce, including raisins (a major export crop), conserves and pickles.

ARRIVAL AND DEPARTURE
UPINGTON

By plane The airport, to which there is no public transport, lies 7km north of town along Diedericks Rd (☎054 337 7900). South African Airlink (☎054 332 2161), based at the airport, flies from here to Cape Town (daily except Sat; 1hr 50min) and Johannesburg (1–2 daily; 1hr 35min). To get to town from here, call Shawn Scott (☎076 045 4719) or Tata Ma Tata tours (☎054 339 1112), both of whom run a transfer service.

By bus The only major bus company operating from Upington is Intercape, based at Lutz St (Mon–Fri 6am–7pm, Sat 6am–1pm & 5–6pm, Sun 6–8am &

4–7pm; ☎086 128 7287). There's a daily 8am service to Johannesburg (10hr 50min) and Pretoria (11hr 50min) via Kuruman, Vryburg and Klerksdorp; daily 7pm buses to Cape Town (11hr 45min) via Springbok; daily 7.30am buses to Kimberley (5hr) and Bloemfontein (7hr) on Thurs & Sat; and a 6.30am bus to Windhoek in Namibia (12hr) on Tues, Thurs, Fri & Sun. Big Sky also serves Kimberley and Bloemfontein, leaving on Sunday at 1pm (book on ☎053 832 2006). All buses, including Big Sky, arrive and depart from the Intercape office in the town centre. If you're likely to arrive at night, it's best to

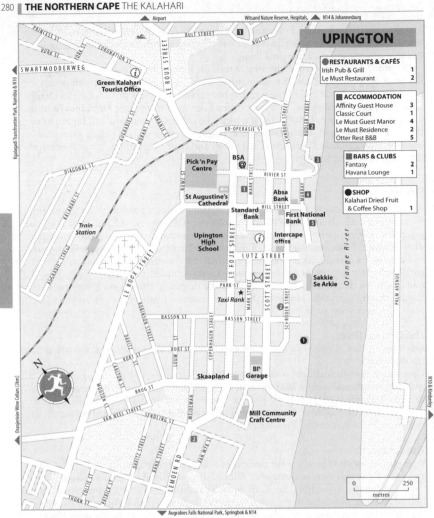

UPINGTON

Airport ▲
Witsand Nature Reserve, Hospitals, ▲ N14 & Johannesburg

RESTAURANTS & CAFÉS
Irish Pub & Grill 1
Le Must Restaurant 2

ACCOMMODATION
Affinity Guest House 3
Classic Court 1
Le Must Guest Manor 4
Le Must Residence 2
Otter Rest B&B 5

BARS & CLUBS
Fantasy 2
Havana Lounge 1

SHOP
Kalahari Dried Fruit
& Coffee Shop 1

Augrabies Falls National Park, Springbok & N14 ▼

0 — 250 metres

reserve a room and get your accommodation to pick you up when you arrive (usually R20). That said, some enterprising drivers are usually on hand to meet tourists arriving by bus, or you could try ringing one of the two transfer services (see p.279).

By minibus taxi Minibus taxis use the rank on Park St, between Le Roux and Mark sts. There are regular daily minibus services (fewer on Sun) to Kimberley, but only one daily to Springbok, one to two daily to Johannesburg and Kuruman, and four a week to Cape Town (via Calvinia). There are also two to three a day to Windhoek in Namibia. Bays are marked for local destinations; for long-distance runs, ask at the booking office, where you must also buy tickets.

INFORMATION

Tourist information Upington has two tourist offices. The one on Mark St (Mon–Fri 7.30am–5pm, Sat 9am–noon; ☎054 338 7151, ⓦkharahais.gov.za), behind the municipality building, deals only with the town and its immediate surroundings, and provides brochures, an accommodation list and details of local tours. For regional information, including details of Augrabies and Kgalagadi, head to the Green Kalahari Tourist Office at the start of Swartmodder Rd (Mon–Fri 7.30am–4.30pm; ☎054 337 2952, ⓦupington.com), which has even more brochures, including detailed driving itineraries.

Internet BSA, Rivier St (Mon–Fri 8am–5pm, Sat 8am–noon).

KALAHARI KUIERFEES

In late September, Die Eiland resort, across the river from Upington, plays host to the **Kalahari Kuierfees** (last Thursday to Saturday; ⓦ kalahari-kuierfees.co.za). A chance for the local Afrikaner community to come together to celebrate their culture, language and food, the event combines flea markets and craft stalls with a triathlon, arts, live Afrikaner music and dance.

ACCOMMODATION

Accommodation in Upington tends to be concentrated along the river, where you'll find no shortage of guesthouses to chose from – the ones on Budler St and Murray Avenue are particularly recommended, so long as guard dogs and a sometimes starchy neo-colonial tenor don't faze you. Book ahead during August and September, though reservations are advisable at all times of year to ensure that someone's there when you arrive.

Affinity Guest House 4 Budler St ☎ 054 331 2101, ⓦ affinityguesthouse.co.za; map p.280. The largest of the riverfront choices, offering reasonable en-suite rooms in a functional pink two-storey building, all with TV, a/c and fridge. Many of the rooms have access to a common balcony overlooking the river, and there's a small swimming pool and braai area. Staff can arrange tours and safaris. **R580**

Classic Court 26 Josling St ☎ 054 332 6142, ⓦ www .classiccourt.co.za; map p.280. Reliable guesthouse with nicely decorated, good-value en-suite rooms with wooden floors and microwaves. No river views, but there is a tiny pool. **R400**

Le Must Guest Manor and Residence 12 Murray Ave & 14 Budler St ☎ 054 332 3971, ⓦ lemustupington.com; map p.280. Two Cape Dutch houses on the riverbank with elegant, comfortable rooms and large gardens (the lavishly -decorated Residence is more upscale), offering luxury and sophistication rarely encountered in the Northern Cape. **R730**

Otters Rest B&B 4 Murray Ave ☎ 054 332 6327 or ☎ 082 399 2705, ⓔ riverlodge@upington.net; map p.280. One of the most attractive places along the river, in an old Cape Dutch house guarded by noisy dogs. There is just a single self-catering apartment, with three beds in two bright rooms, plus a swimming pool, canoes and fishing equipment. **R360**

EATING, DRINKING AND NIGHTLIFE

As the only large town for hundreds of kilometres, Upington seems like culinary heaven compared to the *dorps* you pass through to get here. Aside from the franchised steakhouses lined up in the town centre, you'll also find a couple of more interesting local options.

Fantasy Less than 1km southwest of the centre in the Lemoen Drie area, just off Lemoen Rd; map p.280. The town's main night club – good for contemporary music, though it's best to go with a local. Cover charge R30. Fri & Sat 7pm till late.

Havana Lounge 35 Mark St ☎ 082 773 5188; map p.280. Slick restaurant and bar with a Latin-flavoured tapas menu, including pork belly and stuffed jalapeno peppers (R35), as well as a leathery cigar lounge and decent cocktails. Daily 7am–11pm.

Irish Pub & Grill 20 Schröder St ☎ 054 331 2005; map p.280. The best place in town to down a beer, with real

Guinness and a lovely terrace at the back overlooking the river. There's also a meat-heavy menu of food, on which you'll find things like ostrich schnitzel and springbok carpaccio (R80–120). Mon–Sat 8am–midnight, Sun 9am–11pm.

★ **Le Must Restaurant** 11a Schröder St ☎ 054 332 6700; map p.280. One of the most outstanding restaurants in the region, offering the likes of Kalahari lamb cutlets and rump steak with feta alongside Afrikaner delicacies such as baked sheep's head and biltong soup (R95–110). Paired with a superb list of local wines and great service, it makes for an unexpectedly sophisticated dining experience. Mon–Fri noon–10pm; Sat & Sun 6–10pm.

Kuruman

The Eye daily 7am–7pm • R10

Around 265km east of Upington, lying near the border between the Northern Cape and North West Province, the historic settlement of **KURUMAN** is an important landmark along the main N14 route to and from Gauteng. The settlement grew up around **The Eye** ("Die Oog" in Afrikaans), a natural spring which, since time immemorial and through drought and flood, has consistently delivered twenty million litres a day of crystal-clear water. The Eye was the focal point for a rather

unsettled Tswana clan called the **Batlhaping**, whose chief, Mothibi, first invited missionaries to live among his people in the early nineteenth century. It was a decision that led to the building of the famous **Mission Station** by Robert Moffat, and the establishment of Kuruman as the "Gateway to the Interior" of darkest Africa.

These days Kuruman's centre is pretty scruffy, dominated by cut-price chain stores, faceless supermarkets and litter-strewn minibus-taxi ranks. You can visit **The Eye**, next to the tourist office, though there isn't much to look at: a moss-covered slab of rock dribbling water and a lily-covered pond surrounded by a high green fence. More interesting is the Moffat Mission Station some 4km north of town (see below).

Moffat Mission Station

About 5km north of town, on Moffat Lane • daily 8am–5pm • R10 • ☎ 053 712 2645

Kuruman's main attraction is **Moffat Mission Station**, where a large, often gruff, energetic Scot, Robert Moffat, and his demure but equally determined wife, Mary, established a mission (see box below) where they lived for fifty years. During this time they produced and printed the first Tswana Bible, and saw their eldest daughter, also called Mary, married to the missionary/explorer David Livingstone. Charmingly overgrown and shaded by tall acacia and camelthorn trees, the atmospheric old village looks much as it did in the nineteenth century. It includes the Moffat homestead, with the original printing press on display, along with a collection of furniture, portraits and a wagon used by the missionaries. In front of the homestead is the furrow that Robert dug to bring water from The Eye.

Witsand Nature Reserve

Halfway between Kuruman and Upington, reached by heading south off the N14 from Olifantshoek • Daily 8am–6pm • R40 • ☎ 053 313 1061–2, ⓦ witsandkalahari.co.za • For organized trips, contact Kalahari Safaris in Upington (see box, p.278)

The **Witsand Nature Reserve** is famous for its pristine white "roaring" dunes: in summer a curious rumbling sound occurs when the dunes, 9km in extent, are disturbed, possibly by ground water. While the reserve isn't exactly teeming with wildlife, it does have an abundance of desert bird species, and with patience you may also be rewarded by springbok, duikers and ground squirrels. It's also possible to stay here (see opposite).

ARRIVAL AND DEPARTURE   **KURUMAN**

By bus Getting to Kuruman is easiest from Upington or North West Province, with daily Intercape buses running to and from Jo'burg (7hr 20min) and Pretoria (8hr 20min) via Vryburg, Klerksdorp and Potchefstroom. The buses stop at Leach Toyota on Main St, 1.5km west of the tourist office (☎ 053 712 1031), and tickets can be bought next door at DJ's Beads. Moving on, the Intercape bus to Upington passes through Kuruman at 3pm and to Jo'burg at 11.25am.

THE MOFFATS AND THEIR MISSION

Robert and Mary Moffat, newly married envoys of the London Missionary Society, arrived in the Kuruman area in 1820, initially at a place rather charmingly mistranslated by early explorers as Lattakoo about 14km from Kuruman. As a former market gardener, however, Moffat soon saw the advantages of irrigating the flow of The Eye of Kuruman, and began to build his mission on the closest land wide and flat enough to plough.

Moffat didn't clock up too many converts – by the time he had built his eight-hundred-seater "Cathedral of the Kalahari", in 1838, he had just nine – but the challenge of preaching and establishing a school inspired him not only to learn the local language, which he did by living for a period in a remote Tswana village, but also to attempt the daunting task of **translating the Bible** into Tswana, which he then published on an imported iron printing press. The mission at Kuruman, meanwhile, carried on until the passing of the Group Areas Act of 1950, which brought about the end of the school and the church as a functioning place of (multiracial) worship.

By minibus taxi To Kimberley (2–3 daily; 2hr), minibus taxis are the only option; in Kuruman they stop at the rank on Voortrekker St, just south of Main St. Minibus taxis for Upington (1–2 daily; 2hr 45min) leave from the sprawling taxi rank on Tsening Rd north of Main St – note, however, that services on all routes are reduced on Saturday and often nonexistent on Sunday.

INFORMATION

Tourist information In the old *drostdy* (magistrate's house) on Main St just west of The Eye (Mon–Fri 7.30am–1pm & 2–4.30pm; ☎078 296 3046, ⓦkurumankalahari.co.za).

ACCOMMODATION

Die Mynhuis 10 Botha St ☎053 712 2546 or ☎082 412 0045, ⓦdiemynhuis.co.za. Six rooms surrounding a garden, each with its own entrance and decor vaguely reminiscent of the mine after which it was named. There are also two larger family suites and a braai area, with meals available on request. **R580**

Moffat Mission Moffat Lane, 5km north of town ☎053 712 2645. The cheapest beds in town are in these dorms in the conference centre, just behind the old homestead. There are no self-catering facilities, although meals can be arranged in advance. **R100**

Red Sands Country Lodge In the Kuruman Hills 15km along the N14 towards Upington ☎053 712 0033 or ☎082 801 4414, ⓦredsands.co.za. A pleasant option outside weekends and school holidays (when it gets very busy). Besides camping facilities, they have characterful thatched stone rondavels and comfy self-catering chalets sleeping up to four. There's also a good German/South African restaurant, though it's only open for dinner. Camping **R70**, rondavels & chalets **R700**

Riverfield Guest House 12 Seodin Rd ☎053 712 0003, ⓦriverfield.co.za. Situated 2km northeast of the centre: from the tourist office, walk east along Main St, then left up Livingstone St. A tranquil retreat on the riverbank, with a gorgeous swimming pool, shady gardens and restaurant. **R660**

Witsand Nature Reserve Off the N14, between Kuruman and Upington ☎053 313 1061–2, Wwitsandkalahari.co.za. There are some superb self-catering air-conditioned chalets to stay in at the nature reserve, each sleeping up to six, and rustically done up with thatched roofs and outdoor fireplaces. A campsite is also available. Camping **R80**, chalet **R960**

EATING

Aside from the usual line-up of fast-food chains and steak joints, Kuruman hasn't got much to offer in terms of restaurants.

Palermo Main St, across from the Spar supermarket. Worth a visit to sample their wide range of breakfasts or to grab a refreshing smoothie. They also offer grilled meats and the like, as well as some Afrikaner dishes like stewed oxtail (mains around R60). Mon–Sat 7am–10pm.

DIRECTORY

Banks To change money, try Absa bank at the corner of Main and Livingstone sts; other banks also have central branches.

Hospital On Main St, 1km east of the tourist office (☎053 712 0044).

Post office On Church St, two blocks north and one block west of the tourist office.

Tswalu Kalahari Reserve

On the R31, 100km northwest of Kuruman • ☎053 781 9311, reservations ☎011 274 2299, ⓦtswalu.com

The upmarket Tswalu Kalahari Reserve centres on an impeccably stylish game lodge not far from the tiny settlement of Sonstraal, on the R31 100km northwest of Kuruman. Tucked under the 1500-metre Korannaberg Mountains, this is the largest privately owned game reserve in South Africa. Some R50 million was spent bringing over nine thousand head of game to this desert setting, including some highly endangered desert black rhino, sable, roan antelope and cheetah. The price for accommodation (R14,000) includes game drives, horseriding and full board.

Wonderwerk (Miracle) Cave

Along the R31, 43km south of Kuruman • Mon–Sat 8.30am–1pm & 2–5pm, Sun 8.30am–1pm & 2–4pm • R7 • ☎ 082 832 7226

This intriguing limestone **cave**, burrowing 139m into the hillside, is thought to be one of the longest-inhabited caves on Earth. A major archeological site, it has yielded important evidence of human occupation in various eras dating back over 800,000 years, including fossils, animal teeth, San rock paintings and engraved stones. There is a small visitor's centre on the site and some basic accommodation (R375). Sometimes there are archeologists working in the cave, but if there's no one around, you'll have to ask at the farm for the gate to be unlocked.

Kgalagadi Transfrontier Park

Opening hours vary from month to month, roughly following first and last light• R180 • ☎ 054 561 2000, Ⓦ sanparks.org/parks/kgalagadi

Africa's first official transfrontier park, named **KGALAGADI TRANSFRONTIER PARK** after the ancient San name for the Kalahari (it's pronounced "kha-la-khadi", the kh as in the Scottish "loch"), is the result of the formalization of a long-standing joint management arrangement between South Africa's Kalahari-Gemsbok National Park and Botswana's neighbouring Gemsbok National Park. The local **Mier** and **San** communities have agreed that their land be jointly managed by themselves and South African National Parks, so that the land remains part of the wildlife sanctuary. In keeping with the agreement, tourism opportunities for the local community are being explored, including training people as trackers and rangers. The park is run as a single ecological unit and gate receipts are shared, although the tourist facilities in South Africa and Botswana are still run autonomously. Almost all visitors to the park will, however, encounter only the South African section, where all the established tourist facilities are found.

Kgalagadi covers an area of over 37,000 square kilometres – nearly twice the size of Kruger National Park – and although the South African side is by far the smaller section, it still encompasses a vast 9500 square kilometres. Be prepared to clock up some serious mileage here; the shortest circular game drive is over 100km long, not far short of the distance to **Mata-Mata restcamp** on the western edge of the reserve. The park is bounded on its western side by the Namibian border, and to the south by

---

KGALAGADI WILDLIFE

The **game-viewing highlights** in Kgalagadi Transfrontier Park are, inevitably, the predators, headed by the **Kalahari lion** and, enjoying rare status alongside the Big Five, **gemsbok**, the large, lolloping antelope with classically straight, V-shaped horns. You won't find buffalo, elephant or rhino, but the other animals more than compensate. Of the remaining Big Five, **leopards**, as elsewhere, are not uncommon, but remain elusive. Kalahari lions commonly have much darker manes than those found in the bushveld, and studies have shown their behavioural and eating patterns to be distinctively well adapted to the semi-desert conditions here.

Beyond the Big Five, there are various species of **antelope, hyena, jackal, bat-eared fox, cheetah** and some extravagant **birdlife**, including vultures, eagles, the dramatic bateleur (which takes its name from the French word for an acrobatic tumbler), bustards and ostrich. There's also a good chance you'll see family groups of **suricate**, a relative of the mongoose and squirrel, striking their characteristic pose of standing tall on their hind legs, looking round nervously for signs of danger.

The best time to take your game drives is as early as possible in the **morning**, when you're more likely to see animals out in the open. Drives normally take at least four to five hours, so an early start means you can avoid the desert sun at its zenith. The last couple of hours of light in the afternoon are also a good time for game (and for taking photographs), but it's a lot more relaxing to go out for a little foray from your base than to be en route to a new camp, destined to arrive just as it's getting dark. The middle of the day, especially during summer, is a necessarily inactive time for both animals and humans, so don't plan too full a programme.

the dry Auob River and a strip of land running parallel to this. The national boundary with **Botswana** follows the dry Nossob river bed, as does one of the few roads in the park. No fences exist along this line, allowing game undisturbed access to the ancient migration routes so necessary for survival in the desert. The main roads follow the river beds, and this is where the game – and their predators – are most likely to be. Water flows very rarely in the two rivers, but frequent boreholes have been drilled to provide water for the game. Larger trees such as camelthorn and witgat (shepherd's tree) offer a degree of shade and nutrition, and desert-adapted plants, including types of melon and cucumber, are a source of moisture for the animals.

Much of the park is dominated by **red sand dunes**, which, when seen from the air, lie strung out in long, wave-like bands. From a car, the perspective is different, as you are in the valley of the river bed, but this doesn't prevent the path from offering one of the finest **game-viewing** experiences in South Africa – not only for the animals, but for the setting, with its broad landscapes, the crisp light of morning and the huge open skies. The clear viewing and wonderful light are ideal for **photography**, as shown by the exhibition at the visitor centre at *Twee Rivieren Camp*.

When to visit

In a place where ground temperatures in the **summer** can reach a scorching 70ºC, timing your visit is everything. The best period to be in the park is **between March and May**, when there is still some greenery left from the summer rain and the sun is not so

intense. **Winter** can be very cold at night, while **spring**, though dry, is a pleasant time before the searing heat of summer.

ARRIVAL AND DEPARTURE — KGALAGADI TRANSFRONTIER PARK

By car Coming from Gauteng, the longer approach to the park is via the R31, which is surfaced only between Kuruman and Hotazel – the remainder is a long, bleak dirt road which should only be tackled in a sturdy vehicle.

Alternatively, you can drive further along the N14 to Upington and turn onto the R360, which is surfaced all the way to Andriesvale (about 200km) before becoming a sand road for the 45km to the park entrance at *Twee Rivieren*.

Whichever way you travel, the journey is a hot and weary one. You'll see plenty of the classic red dunes of the Kalahari, and every so often a huge, crazily paved grey saltpan, but the vegetation has been largely denuded, and the landscape is filled with desolate images, such as broken windmills and rusting frames of motor cars drowning in the desert sand.

By plane and tour The two alternatives to making the long drive to Kgalagadi are to go on a package tour (see box, p.278) or to fly to *Twee Rivieren* by private charter plane (arrange this through Walker Flying Service in Upington; ☎ 054 332 3685, ✉ newtonw@intekom.co.za), from where you can pick up a car by prior arrangement with Avis.

GETTING AROUND

The **park roads** are also sand. While you can travel in a normal car, bear in mind that the higher the clearance the better – a car packed with four adults might struggle. It's also a good idea to reduce the pressure in your tyres by about half a bar before setting off and to play the steering to maintain traction. You might find it's often easier to drive either side of the "road" along tracks left by other drivers. If you're in a rental car, check the small print as it may exclude cover for damaged wheels, undercarriage and paintwork. In the event of a breakdown you just have to sit it out until someone else passes; a park vehicle patrols most roads each day. Fuel is available at the restcamps at Twee Rivieren, Mata-Mata and Nossob. Entry to the Botswana side of Kgalagadi is only allowed by 4WD, and you must exit through the same gate you entered if you don't want to show your passport and complete immigration formalities. The Botswana section has 974km of dirt roads comprising two access routes, two self-guided 4WD trails and a game-viewing trail.

INFORMATION AND ACTIVITIES

Tourist information The visitor's centre at *Twee Rivieren* (☎ 054 561 2000) has exhibitions and slide shows worth checking out.

Permits For safety reasons you'll be given a permit on arrival, and you have to sign in and out whenever you are leaving or arriving at a restcamp. If you stay longer than anticipated (unlikely, as accommodation is often fully booked), pay for the additional time when you leave.

Activities The focus in Kgalagadi Transfrontier Park is on self-guided game drives. Activities inside the park are limited to the exacting three-day Nossob 4WD trail over the duneveld (book this in advance at the *Twee Rivieren camp*), night and day game drives and day walks, which can be booked on arrival at the *Nossob, Twee Rivieren* or *Mata-Mata* camps. Look out for details posted at the restcamp offices about what's happening on any given day. There are no guides for hire other than for these activities.

ACCOMMODATION

INSIDE THE PARK

It's vital to **book** park accommodation, even for campsites, as early as you can through South African National Parks (see p.65). The park has a choice of cottages and camping in two broad types of site: fenced restcamps at *Twee Rivieren, Mata-Mata* and *Nossob*, which have electricity (even in the campsites) and creature comforts such as kitchens, fans or air conditioning, braai areas and shops; and six far more basic and remote unfenced wilderness camps, for which you need to be completely self-sufficient. It's worth staying at least a night at a park restcamp away from *Twee Rivieren* to taste the raw flavour of the desert. If time is limited an excursion to *Mata-Mata* makes sense, but *Nossob, although further off,* is better for atmosphere and game viewing: as well as hearing the lions roaring at night, you'll probably have your best chance of seeing them in this area. The roads to *Nossob* and *Mata-Mata* follow river beds, and so are good for spotting game. On the Botswana side, facilities are limited to campsites at *Mabuasehube, Two Rivers, Rooiputs* and *Polentswa;* visitors here need to be completely self-sufficient. For reservations, contact the Botswana Parks and Reserves Reservation Office in Gaborone (☎ 09 267 318 0774, ✉ dwnp@gov.bw).

Bitterpan Wilderness Camp A peaceful spot near the centre of the park on a 4WD trail between *Nossob* and *Mata-Mata* (access by 4WD only), with four unfenced reed cabins perched on the edge of a saltpan. R945

Gharagab Wilderness Camp Four log cabins in an unfenced area in the remote far north, a four-hour drive from *Nossob* (access by 4WD), with elevated views onto a landscape of dunes and thornveld savannah. R965

Grootkolk Wilderness Camp This unfenced desert camp near Union's End at the very northern tip of the South African section is in prime predator country; its four chalets come fully equipped with cooking supplies, linen and fans, and they're usually booked solid months in advance. R1050

★ **Kalahari Tent Camp** Guarded by an armed guide, this unfenced site has comfortable, fully equipped, self-catering tents built of sandbags and canvas (including one luxurious "honeymoon tent"), all decorated in desert tones with views over the Auob River. There's also a swimming pool. R1070

Kieliekrankie Wilderness Camp This is the closest wilderness camp to *Twee Rivieren* (41km), and is accessible to ordinary vehicles; it offers four unfenced cabins sunk into

a red sand dune, providing lovely panoramic views of the desert. R1050

Mata-Mata Camp A fenced restcamp 120km northwest of *Twee Rivieren* on the (closed) Namibian border, at the end of the road that follows the course of the Auob River. Accommodation is in fully equipped family cottages (sleeping six), comfortable two-person bungalows and a campsite. Other amenities include a water hole lit up at night, a shop and fuel. Camping R180, bungalow R615

Nossob Camp On the Botswana border, 160km north of *Twee Rivieren* along the Nossob River Rd, this is the most remote of the three fenced restcamps. It has fifteen simple chalets, better family-size guesthouses (sleeping four), a cottage and a campsite. There's also a supply shop, fuel, plus a predator information centre (the place is famed for nocturnal visits by lions). Camping R180, chalet R630

Twee Rivieren Camp The first, and most developed, of the three fenced restcamps, right by the entrance, offering over thirty pleasant self-catering chalets with thatched roofs and nice patio areas, a sizeable campsite (with or without electricity), a mediocre restaurant, a pool, fuel, and a shop selling souvenirs and simple foodstuffs. Camping R145, chalet R715

Urikaruus Wilderness Camp Roughly halfway between *Twee Rivieren* and *Mata-Mata*, with an attractive setting among camelthorn trees overlooking the Auob River; the four two-person cabins, all equipped with solar power and kitchen supplies, are built on stilts and connected by a plank walkway. R1050

OUTSIDE THE PARK

On the approach road to Kgalagadi there are a number of places to stay. However, with morning being the best time for game viewing, staying en route to the park isn't really an option if you're on a tight schedule.

Rooiduin Guest Farm 30km south of Twee Rivieren ☏082 589 6659. The closest accommodation to the entrance is at this community-run campsite, which has become famous for sand-surfing (a bit like snow-sledging, sitting on a strip of plastic) down the face of one of the large nearby red sand dunes. Camping R50

Molopo Kalahari Lodge 55km from Twee Rivieren, in Andriesvale ☏054 511 0008, ⌨molopolodge .co.za. A smart, well-run place with over thirty comfortable en-suite chalets around a pool, as well as luxury bush tents, campsites, a bar and a decent restaurant. Andriesvale has a filling station and a small shop. Camping R75, chalet R58

Askham Post Office Guesthouse In the nearby settlement of Askham ☏054 511 0040, ⌨post officeguesthouse.com. This B&B offers three spacious and clean en-suite rooms on the site of the old post office. Book well in advance. R400

Augrabies Falls National Park

Daily 7am–7pm · R100 · ☏054 452 9200, ⌨sanparks.org/parks/augrabies

One of the undoubted highlights of any trip to the Northern Cape is **AUGRABIES FALLS NATIONAL PARK**, 120km west of Upington. Roaring out of the barren semi-desert, sending great plumes of spray up above the brown horizon, the falls – still known by their Khoikhoi name, *Aukoerabis*, "the place of great noise" – are the most spectacular moment in the two-thousand-kilometre progress of the Orange River. At peak flow, the huge volume of water plunging through the narrow channel actually compares with the more docile periods at Victoria Falls and Niagara, although Augrabies lacks both the height and the soul-wrenching grandeur of its larger rivals. But in its eerie desert setting under an azure evening sky, the falls provide a moving and absorbing experience. The sides of the canyon are shaped like a smooth parabola, and there are many tales of curious visitors venturing too far to peer at the falls and sliding helplessly into the seething maelstrom below. Despite the odd miraculous survival, several dozen people have died here since the national park was created in 1966.

Visiting the park

The **falls** are viewed from behind a large fence, while a boardwalk allows wheelchair access to the viewpoint. To see more of the **gorge**, walk the short distance to **Arrow Point** or drive on the link roads round to Ararat or Echo Corner. The atmosphere is at its best near **sunset**, when the sun shines straight into the west-facing part of the gorge.

The fairly inhospitable **northern section** of the park covers 184 square kilometres on both sides of the river. The land is dry and harsh, with sparse plants typical of arid areas, such as kokerboom (quiver tree), camelthorn and Namaqua fig. The landscape is

ACTIVITIES AT AUGRABIES FALLS

Various **adventure activities** are promoted within the park, though none really matches the adrenaline surge of the falls themselves. The half-day 3-in-1 **Gariep trail** (closed for maintenance at the time of writing) combines a short canoeing trip in the gorge with a walk and an eleven-kilometre mountain-bike ride back to the restcamp. The **Dassie nature trail** is a half-day hike out from the main restcamp, while the popular three-day **Klipspringer trail** (April–Sept only; R175) involves two overnight stops at simple huts; advance booking is essential. **Night game drives** are also on offer (R130), and there's a 56-kilometre **self-drive tourism route** (4WD only) in the park's northwestern section for viewing plains game.

Perhaps more instantly gratifying is the "**Augrabies Rush**", a half-day trip on small rafts down 8km of increasingly swift river immediately above the falls, run by Kalahari Outventures (see p.278; R315 per person with a minimum of four). The same company also runs four-day rafting trails taking you deep into the empty country downriver of the falls (R2950), while another three-day trip surges down the exciting rapids of the Oneepkans Gorge near Pella (R2850).

3

punctuated by various striking rock formations, notably **Moon Rock**, a huge dome of smooth, flaking granite rising out of the flat plains. If you drive on the (unsurfaced) roads in the park you'll probably spot some of the resident fauna – including eland, klipspringer and springbok – while you're likely to see dassie, mongoose and lizards around the falls and the camp.

The **best time to visit** Augrabies is from March to May, when the temperatures are slightly cooler and the river is at its maximum flow after summer rainfall up in the Lesotho catchment areas. With your own transport, the falls are easily visited as a day-trip from Upington, although there's plenty of reasonable accommodation both in the park itself and nearby.

Kakamas

The route to Augrabies from Upington is west along the N14, following the Orange River and its rich fringe of vineyards, orchards and alfalfa fields. Eighty kilometres southwest of Upington, **KAKAMAS** is the last town before the park and a handy base if you're driving. The settlement was founded in 1897 by the Dutch Reformed Church as a colony for livestock farmers rendered destitute by a prolonged drought; each farmer contributed manpower for a system of irrigation canals and tunnels, and was rewarded with a plot of irrigated land. Considered primitive by the experts of the day, their handiwork still funnels water to the land today. The inhabitants' ingenuity also saw expression in South Africa's first hydroelectric power station, modelled on an Egyptian temple and completed in 1914, which now houses a small museum. It's at the top of Voortrekker Street as you come in along the N14.

ARRIVAL AND DEPARTURE   AUGRABIES FALLS NATIONAL PARK

By bus and tour The closest you can get to the park on public transport is Alheit, on the N14 at the start of the turning to the park, 28km short of the entrance; however, most of the Kalahari tours out of Upington and elsewhere in the Northern Cape (see box, p.278) incorporate a visit to the falls.

INFORMATION AND EATING

The **park's reception**, just up the road from the entrance gate (daily 7am–7pm), has a shop, a self-service snack bar and a restaurant with views towards the gorge.

ACCOMMODATION

Augrabies Falls Backpackers In Augrabies village, 11km before the park gate ☎072 515 6079, ✉ augrabiesfallsbackpackers@gmail.com. Rustic, laid-back country house 2km down a dirt road (follow the signs from the main road to the falls). The rooms are simple, but the owner is full of tips on local activities and runs balloon trips from March to December. Dorm R125, double R250

Augrabies Falls Lodge 3km before the gate ☎054 451 7203, ⓦaugfallslodge.co.za. Pared-down backpacker accommodation and double rooms in a hotel that looks and feels a bit industrial, but is conveniently close to the falls. Meals available at the restaurant. Dorm R95, double R530

Falls Guesthouse On the R359, 2km before the park's main gate ☎082 928 7938, ⓦthefallsaugrabies .com. One of the more upmarket options in the area, this renovated farmhouse has big, cool rooms, nice furnishings and a generous veranda overlooking rows of vines. R680

Kalahari Gateway Hotel 19 Voortrekker St, Kakamas ☎054 431 0838, ⓦkalaharigateway.co.za. Large and a

bit tired looking, with the stuffy atmosphere of a conference venue. The rooms are adequate, though, and there's a swimming pool, two bars and a restaurant as well as a few self-catering apartments. R760

National Park Chalets At the park reception ☎054 452 9200, reserve through the National Park Service ☎012 428 9111. Comfortable brick chalets and family cottages (two of which are wheelchair accessible), within walking distance of the falls and with access to a pool. There is also a campground. Camping R165, chalet R655

Vergelegen Guesthouse & Restaurant About 3km east of Kakamas ☎054 431 0976, ⓦaugrabiesfalls .co.za. Sixteen neat and attractive rooms (two self-catering) on a farm by the main road, complete with a swimming pool; there's also a pleasant restaurant and information centre on site, which can arrange tours. R690

Namaqualand

NAMAQUALAND is another Northern Cape region whose name conjures up images of both desolation and magic. According to an oft-quoted saying about the area, in Namaqualand you weep twice: once when you first arrive and once when you have to leave. This is the land of Khoikhoi herders called the **Nama**: the Little Nama, who lived south of the Orange River, and the Great Nama, who lived north of the river in what is now Namibia. Sparsely populated, the region stretches south from the Orange to the empty **Knersvlakte** plains around Vanrhynsdorp, and from the **Atlantic coast** to the edge of the **Great Karoo**. Above all, Namaqualand is synonymous with the incredible annual display of brightly coloured **wild flowers** that carpet the landscape in August and September, one of South Africa's most compelling spectacles. Even outside flower season, swathes of orange, purple and white daisies emerge, and there is a tenacious beauty about this dry, empty landscape of mountain deserts, mineral-bearing granite hills and drought-defiant succulents.

The **N7** highway between Namibia and Cape Town cuts across Namaqualand, offering one of the most scenic drives in the country. At its northern end, at the junction with the dusty **N14** from Upington and the Kalahari, lies the region's capital, **Springbok**. This is the best base for flowers – the nearby **Namaqua National Park** provides reliable displays even in years of low rainfall, when displays elsewhere may be muted – and for visiting the Province's remote northwestern corner: the **Diamond Coast**, stretching from Port Nolloth to the Namibian border. The harsh but spectacular **Richtersveld Transfrontier Park** stretches inland, bisected by the Orange River – rafting on which ranks high among the region's attractions.

Springbok

The semi-arid expanse of northern Namaqualand is where the Karoo merges into the Kalahari, and both meet the ocean. If it weren't for the discovery of copper in the 1600s, and more recently of alluvial and offshore diamonds washed down from the Kimberley area by the Orange River, the region might well not have acquired any towns at all. Fresh water is scarce, and its presence here ensured the survival of SPRINGBOK, the region's capital, after its copper mines were exhausted.

Attractively hemmed in by hills, Springbok is the main commercial and administrative centre of Namaqualand, and an important staging post at the junction of the N7 and N14 highways. Lying 400km southwest of Upington, and just over 100km south of the

VIEWING THE FLOWERS OF NAMAQUALAND

The seeds of the spectacular **flowers of Namaqualand** – daisies, aloes, gladioli and lilies – lie dormant under the soil through the droughts of summer, waiting for the rain that sometimes takes years to materialize. About four thousand floral species are found in the area, a quarter of which are found nowhere else on Earth. Although it's difficult to predict where the best displays will occur, for more or less guaranteed flowers you can head for the Skilpad section of **Namaqua National Park** (see p.293) or to the **Richtersveld Transfrontier Park** (see p.300), with its ocean-mist-fed succulents.

One indication of where the displays will occur is **winter rainfall**; flowers follow the rain, so early in the season they will be out near the coast, moving steadily inland. **Temperature** is also a factor, meaning that on cool or cloudy days displays are muted.

PRACTICALITIES

Flower-viewing in Namaqualand means a lot of driving, simply because the distances are so great. **Cycling** is an option, although it can be frustrating if the best displays turn out to be 20km away from where you're based. Book **accommodation** well in advance, either on a farm (ideal if you don't have your own transport, as you can walk around the farm's own flower fields) or in a town like Springbok. Note that accommodation rates can increase substantially during flower season. The following tactics are worth keeping in mind:

• Plan your route before heading out – your hosts may have inside information about the best spots on a particular day.
• The flowers only open up around 10am, so you have time for a good breakfast. Because flowers turn to face the sun, it's best to drive westwards in the morning and eastwards in the afternoon.
• Take lots of pictures, but don't pick the flowers.

FLOWER TOUR OPERATORS

Diamond Tours Unlimited 71 Jacobson Ave, Kimberley ☎ 053 832 9756, ⍟ diamondtours.co.za.

Kalahari Tours and Travel 12 Mazurka Curve, Upington ☎ 054 338 0375, ⍟ kalahari-tours.co.za.

---

border with Namibia, it makes a pleasant base for visiting northern Namaqualand's flower fields in August and September (see above) or a springboard for visiting the coast, and it's a good place to arrange trips to the Richtersveld Transfrontier Park (see p.300).

Springbok's main action is centred on the mound of granite boulders next to the taxi rank in the town centre. Called **Klipkoppie** ("rocky hill"), this was the site of a British fort blown up by General Jan Smuts' commando during the Anglo-Boer War. A few hundred metres up from Klipkoppie, at the back of town, a gash in the hillside marks the **Blue Mine**, the first commercial copper mine in South Africa, sunk in 1852. Recent activity here has been in search of gemstones – previously ignored in the frantic hunt for copper ore – and zinc. A short trail wends up to a good **viewpoint** over town. You'll find a good selection of gemstones for sale at *Springbok Lodge*, together with an excellent display of mineralogical specimens from all over the globe.

ARRIVAL AND DEPARTURE   SPRINGBOK

By car Coming from Upington, the N14 eventually becomes Voortrekker St, the town's main drag, and veers south at the taxi rank to rejoin the N7 for Cape Town.

By bus Intercape buses pick up and drop off next to the Engen garage on Voortrekker St, 700m east of the taxi rank (buy tickets at Shoprite, 200m back towards town). There are daily services to Cape Town (11.25pm; 6hr 30min) and Upington (2.50am; 5hr), and buses to Windhoek run Tues, Thurs, Fri and Sun (6.25pm; 11hr 50min).

By minibus taxi Most minibuses leave from the taxi rank at Klipkoppie, but will pick you up at your hotel if you ring ahead (it's recommended in any case). Well-established minibus taxi companies running to Cape Town (6hr) include Titus (☎ 027 712 1381), Van Wyk's (☎ 027 713 8559) and Bezuidenhout (☎ 027 712 1271) – all leave at around 11am every day except Saturdays. There is also a 2pm taxi service to Port Nolloth and Alexander Bay (Mon–Sat; ☎ 082 972 9964). For Windhoek in Namibia, Namibian company Econolux (☎ 0264 61 258 961) runs Fridays and Sundays, leaving Springbok at 6.30pm (11hr 45min).

INFORMATION

Tourist information The helpful tourist office, doubling as the headquarters of the Namaqua Region Tourism Board (flower season Mon–Fri 7.30am–6pm, Sat & Sun 9am–noon; rest of year Mon–Fri 7.30am–4.15pm; ☎027 712 8035 or 8036, ⊚namaqualand.com), is on Voortrekker St 700m south of the taxi rank. Another source of local wisdom (and dour wit) is the *Springbok Lodge* on the corner or Voortrekker and Kerk sts. A hub for travellers and locals, it also sells an excellent selection of books, including plenty of titles on Namaqualand and its flowers, the history of copper mining and the Nama, the Richtersveld and rock art.

ACCOMMODATION

There's no shortage of rooms in Springbok, but you're still advised to book ahead in flower season. The notice board outside the tourist office has details and prices for most properties in and around town, and a map.

IN TOWN

★ **Annie's Cottage** 4 King St, signposted from Klipkoppie ☎027 712 1451, ⊚springbokinfo.com. Extremely stylish, comfortable and colourful rooms in a restored colonial house decorated with local artwork, with a swimming pool under jacaranda trees. There are hiking and biking trails in the vicinity, and the gregarious owner is a good source of information about where to see the best flowers. **R900**

Cat Nap Voortrekker St, opposite the tourist office ☎027 718 1905, ☎richtersveld.challen@kingsley .co.za. Attractive African-themed rooms, two with bathrooms, and twelve rudimentary pull-down bunks in the garage, with a kitchenette – there's even room for you to park your vehicle beside your bed. Dorm **R120**, double **R420**

Elkoweru Guest House 1 Bree St ☎027 718 1202, ⊚elkoweru.co.za. A modern two-storey guesthouse in vaguely Mediterranean style. The self-catering rooms are a bit small and ordinary, but the singles are particularly good value (R280), and there are also larger flats available. **R440**

Mountain View Guest House 2 Overberg Ave (turn-off is 100m south of tourist office, from where it's another 1km along Overberg Ave) ☎027 712 1438, ⊚mountview.co.za. Thirteen tasteful, colourfully African-themed rooms (one self-catering) in this stylish guesthouse, pleasantly situated on the fringe of the town, right by a short trail offering views over Springbok. **R650**

Springbok Lodge 37 Voortrekker St, entrance on Kerk St ☎027 712 1321, ⊚springboklodge.com. 32 guest cottages, all in distinctive white and yellow livery, and within walking distance of one another. The self-catering rooms are plain but reasonable, and there are also some larger apartments (R600). **R375**

OUTSIDE TOWN

Mùrewag Guest Farm 12km northwest of town, take the Kleinzee Rd and turn right after 8km towards Nababeep ☎084 408 0135. A pleasant working farm with plentiful flowers and succulents in season, some small game, three fully furnished guest rooms and a comfortable, old-fashioned cottage. The owners are happy to pick up guests from Springbok. **R300**

Naries Namaqua Retreat 27km west of town along the Kleinzee Rd ☎027 712 2462, ⊚naries.co.za. A homely, comfortable place to stay, with stylish rooms in an atmospheric Cape Dutch farmhouse, a self-catering cottage and three luxurious dome-shaped suites nestled among the boulders nearby. No under-12s allowed in the main farmhouse or the suites. The candlelight dinners are a big draw, and hiking and horseriding can be arranged. Rates include half board. **R600**

CAMPING

Springbok Caravan Park 2km southeast of town along the R355 ☎027 718 1584, ⊚spring bokcaravanpark.co.za. The closest campsite to town, *Springbok Caravan Park* is plain and shadeless; along with tent sites, it offers four-bed chalets, double rooms and a swimming pool. Camping **R60**, double **R165**, chalet **R550**

EATING AND DRINKING

El Dago Voortrekker St just south of the taxi rank ☎027 718 1475. Good for seafood and pizzas (R60), with a sunny street-facing balcony. Daily 6–11pm.

Springbok Lodge Restaurant ☎027 712 1321. Vaguely reminiscent of an American diner from the 1950s, serving an impressive selection of burgers and local wines (mains R50–80). Mon–Sat 7am–10pm, Sun 8am–10pm.

Tauren Steakranch Hospital St just north of the taxi rank ☎027 712 2717. Attractive African-style decor, and steaks dished up in a number of adventurous ways – topped with snails, for instance, or flambéed in brandy. Mains around R80. Mon–Sat 6–11pm.

Titbits Voortrekker St just south of the taxi rank ☎027 718 1455. The best place for a drink, notable for its impressive cocktail selection that includes chocolate Martinis and a house special involving ice cream. They also serve food, mainly pasta and lots of meat (mains R50–80). Mon–Sat 8am–10pm.

DIRECTORY

Bank You can change money at the Absa bank, on Namakwa St facing the taxi rank.

Camping and 4WD hire Fully equipped 4WDs and camping gear can be rented from Richtersveld Challenge, facing the tourist office (☎ 027 718 1905, ✉ richtersveld

.challenge@kingsley.co.za); you can also rent 4WD from Europcar (☎ 072 171 3081).

Internet access WS Computers on Lodge St just east of the taxi rank (Mon–Fri 8am–4pm).

Goegap Nature Reserve

Entrance on the R355, 15km east of Springbok • Daily 8am–6pm during flower season, otherwise 8am–4pm • R15

This **reserve** proclaims itself to be "Namaqualand in miniature". With close to six hundred indigenous flower species, it is a popular destination during flower season, and a garden showcasing some of the unusual, alien-like succulents endemic to the area makes it a good place to visit year-round. The reserve is also home to a number of animal species, including the Namaqualand sandgrouse, the bat-eared fox and the aardwolf.

Kamieskroon

About 70km south of Springbok, the village of **KAMIESKROON** is set among the Kamiesberg Mountains, beneath the rocky peak – or kroon – from which it takes its name. There isn't much to the village other than a pretty setting, the crisp air of the mountains and, in flower season, a sense of being at the heart of the garden of the gods.

Deeper into the mountains, at places east of Kamieskroon such as **Nourivier** and the old Moravian mission station of **Leliefontein**, the land is owned and farmed as a community project by the local Nama people. In places you'll see families living in traditional **matjieshuise** (reed huts); these settlements, many of which are still based around a mission, are connected by dirt roads, and so make good flower-viewing routes.

Namaqua National Park

17km northwest of Kamieskroon along a signposted gravel road • Daily 8am–6pm • R30 • ☎ 027 672 1948

A place worth going to in flower season, even if you're just passing through on the highway, is the Skilpad section of Namaqua National Park. The displays here, featuring great swathes of orange colour, tend to be more reliable than elsewhere, even in years with low rainfall. Butterfly fanatics and twitchers should be in for a treat, too. There's a circular five-kilometre drive around the reserve, two short walking trails and a scenic picnic site.

ACCOMMODATION   NAMAQUA NATIONAL PARK

KAMIESKROON

Kamieskroon Hotel To the right as you come off the N7 at Kamieskroon ☎ 027 672 1614, ⓦ kamieskroonhotel .com. A vibrant and creative place that runs photographic workshops during flower season, and has become the centre for a number of activities in the surrounding Kamiesberg. Rooms are simply decorated but comfortable, and there's also a caravan park and a restaurant (book meals in advance). R440

Randspaar Guest House 25 Church St, ☎ 027 672 1604 or ☎ 027 672 1729, ✉ alexroux.za@gmail.com. Comfortable guesthouse with a communal lounge and kitchen area, where you can stay on either a B&B or self-catering basis. The owners are informative about the region; they also run the supermarket across the road, where you'll go to pick up your key. R370

Gousblom B&B 95 De Waal St ☎ 027 672 1004 or ☎ 082 962 3213, ✉ eb@isat.co.za. A cosy little place offering bright, cheerful antique-filled rooms, along with a kitchen for self-caterers and a pleasant plant-filled patio area. R250

Kamieskroon B&B Charlotte St ☎ 027 672 1652 or ☎ 082 898 2759 ✉ jdmjvanwyk@gmail.com. There are five homey en-suite rooms at this family-style guesthouse, where the friendly hostess knows the area inside-out and serves up a good breakfast. R460

GARIES

If everywhere is booked up in Kamieskroon for flower season, consider staying at Garies, 45km further south along the N7; Sophie's Guesthouse is well worth the detour.

Garies Guesthouse Main St, across from Garies Hotel ☎ 027 652 1799 or ☎ 082 950 3050, ✉ selfcater@

telcomsa.net. Popular with groups of holidaying South Africans, this self-catering guesthouse supplies plenty of braai facilities and kitchenettes, as well as a couple of apartments for families and groups. R500

★ **Sophie's Guesthouse** 33 Main St ☎027 652 1069, ⌨sophiaguesthouse.co.za. A whimsically renovated old hotel from the 1930s, this is one of the best places to stay in the area. The cosy double rooms, kitchen and salon have all been lovingly decorated in colourful florals, and there's a charming self-catering cottage out back. The friendly owners are knowledgeable about the area and can help arrange onward travel. R260

NAMAQUA NATIONAL PARK

Skilpad Rest Camp In the Skilpad section of the park ☎012 428 9111, ⌨sanparks.org/parks/namaqua. Four 3-bed chalets in the rocky hills, all comfortably equipped with fireplaces, cooking supplies and enclosed verandas. R605

Vanrhynsdorp

Travelling south from Kamieskroon, the mountains gradually give way to the bleaker landscape of the pebble-strewn **Knersvlakte** – the "plains of the gnashing teeth", referring to the sound made by wagon wheels toiling across the harsh terrain. Around 190km from Kamieskroon lies the small agricultural town of **VANRHYNSDORP**, the most southerly of the Namaqualand towns. Although it's officially in the Western Cape, this is the gateway to the region if you're coming from Cape Town. It marks the crossroads between the N7 Cape Town–Namibia highway and the R27, which connects via the glorious **Bokkeveld Escarpment** with Calvinia and ultimately Upington, on the northern fringe of the Great Karoo. Set in the lee of the spectacular flat-topped Maskam Mountain, Vanrhynsdorp is pretty much deserted out of flower season.

Museums and historical sites

Vanrhynsdorp, dominated by the tall spire of its church, offers a surprising number of **local museums and historical sites** for a town of its size. The **Van Rhijn Museum** on Van Riebeeck Street (Mon–Fri 9am–6pm, Sat & Sun 9am–1pm; free) is diverting enough, featuring a collection of old military pieces and domestic paraphernalia from early Boer homesteaders. On the same side of Van Riebeeck Street is the **former prison** (daily 9am–5pm during flower season, open sporadically during the rest of the year; free), an attractive, low yellow building built in 1895; it now contains a small coffee shop and, making use of the old cells, various small crafts stalls displaying the woodwork and needlework of older members of the local Afrikaner population. Also in town is the quirky **Latsky Radio Museum**, behind the church, on the corner of Kerk and Olive streets (daily 9am–noon & 2–5pm during flower season, on request the rest of the year; free; ☎027 219 1032), nurturing a collection of some two hundred valve radios dating back to the 1920s. Venture about 500m out of town along Troe Troe Street and you'll find the town's dusty little **cemetery**, which contains the touchingly derelict graves of a number of casualties of the Anglo-Boer war – some marked by nothing more than piles of stones.

Kokerboom Kwekery

Voortrekker St, five blocks east of the church • Mon–Fri 8am–1pm & 2–5pm • R10 during flower season, free the rest of the year • ☎027 219 1119

This unusual **nursery** specializes in succulents, with a fascinating display of dozens of the more unusual varieties. Around a third of the world's succulent species grow in this area, many of them endemic. There's also a small café and shop, where you can obtain a permit for the **three-kilometre succulent hiking trail**, situated 25km north of town off the N7 – a worthwhile diversion if you're travelling that way.

ARRIVAL AND DEPARTURE   **VANRHYNSDORP**

Most **buses** and **taxis** running to and from Cape Town, Springbok or Upington stop at either the Shell or Caltex garages at the start of Van Riebeeck St after turning off the highway.

By minibus taxi Onward travel to Cape Town is easiest by minibus taxi, best at 2pm when the ones from Springbok pass through; ring ahead to be sure of a seat (see p.291). If you're going to Springbok, catch the vehicles returning from Cape Town in the afternoons. Note that there are no taxis in either direction on Saturdays.

By bus Intercape buses run daily to Cape Town (2.25am; 5hr) and Upington (11.45pm; 7hr) via Springbok, but the only way to buy tickets is either through the Intercape website or at Shoprite in the nearby town of Vredendal. Maasdorp Van Wyk minibus taxis (☏ 021 987 3191) cover the same routes, as well as running a daily service to Nieuwoudtville – phone ahead to reserve a place.

INFORMATION

Tourist information In the museum (Mon–Fri 9am–6pm, Sat & Sun 9am–1pm; ☏ 027 219 2935, ⓦ tourismvanrhynsdorp.co.za).

ACCOMMODATION

If you're planning on staying more than one night, you're probably best off looking for farm-based accommodation in the nearby mountains, for which you'll need a vehicle.

Gifberg Holiday Farm 29km north of Vanrhynsdorp ☏ 027 219 1555, ⓦ gifberg.co.za. A rural retreat with self-catering chalets that sleep 1–13 people, plus a swimming pool and an on-site coffee shop. But the real draw is the hiking in the area, which includes everything from beginners' trails to a 21km trek to San rock art sites. R280

Namaqualand Country Lodge 22 Voortrekker St, next to the church ☏ 027 219 1633 or ☏ 082 896 6444, ⓦ namaqualodge.co.za. A family-run lodge that has been in operation for over a century, with quirky, old-fashioned charm (think: taxidermied wildlife and the country's largest collection of neckties). There's a swimming pool, and a restaurant, *Mikie's*, next door. R400

Van Rhyn Guest House Van Riebeeck St ☏ 027 219 1429, ⓦ vanrhyngh.co.za. Calm, welcoming and artsy, with ten rooms, some in converted outhouses, which have

high ceilings and remain cool even during the summer heat; excellent meals can also be provided by prior arrangement. R600

Vanrhynsdorp Self-Catering Resort End of Lazarus St ☏ 027 219 1810 or ☏ 072 453 6766, ⊜ selfcater@telcomsa.net. These comfortable, self-catering chalets are somewhat impersonal, but they are good value and some have multiple bedrooms for families or groups. R350

CAMPSITES

Vanrhynsdorp Caravan Park 800m along Troe Troe St (which becomes Gifberg Rd) ☏ 027 219 1287 or ☏ 076 293 2578, ⓦ vanrhynsdorpcaravanpark.co.za. Reasonably quiet out of season, with a cheap campsite, basic en-suite chalets (four of them with kitchenettes) and a handful of simple double and single rooms. Camping R140, double R300, chalets R400

EATING

Aside from the options below, there are reasonable restaurants at both the Shell and Caltex garages catering mainly to passing motorists.

Mikie's Attached to Namaqualand Country Lodge. An unexciting place that is, nonetheless, one of the only proper restaurants in the town centre; offers a fairly standard menu of steaks, burgers and other meat-based offerings for around R70. Mon–Sat 8am–3pm.

ZAR In the Vanrhynsdorp Caravan Park. The best restaurant in town (mains R60–90), where well-prepared steaks are served up with snails, mussels and other interesting combinations, all in surprisingly refined surroundings. Mon–Sat 7–10am & 6–11pm.

Nieuwoudtville

Heading east from Vanrhynsdorp on the R27 you have a very clear impression of the sudden elevation of the land from the plains up to the **Bokkeveld Escarpment**, which the road tackles by way of Van Rhyn's Pass, complete with a couple of neck-achingly tight hairpins near the top. There's an excellent viewpoint overlooking the plains, signposted soon after you reach the plateau.

Eight kilometres on from the top of Van Rhyn's Pass, just over 50km from Vanrhynsdorp, the R27 passes just to the north of the picturesque *dorp* of **NIEUWOUDTVILLE** ("Knee-voet-vil"), with an attractive collection of tin-roofed, honey-coloured sandstone buildings and the sombre ruins of early settler homesteads on the outskirts. Founded just over a century ago, it's by far the most atmospheric place to stay in the region, full of character and history. The soil here has the highest concentration of bulb species on Earth, and there are several appealing nature reserves in the vicinity. Although most of the flowering species appear in August and September, a time of spectacularly colourful display, you're likely to find something in flower here any time between March and October.

Hantam National Botanic Garden

Oorlogskloof Rd • During flowering season, usually Aug–Oct: daily 8am–5pm • R12 • Rest of year: Mon–Fri 7.30am–4.30pm • Free • ☎ 027 218 1200

One of the best places in the country for seeing wild flowers is the **Hantam National Botanic Garden**. Formerly the farm Glenlyon, it has been described by botanist and former director of Kew Gardens Sir Ghillean Prance as "a botanical treasure of international importance". The BBC Natural History Unit and Sir David Attenborough visited twice in the 1990s to film footage of the garden's extraordinary flora for the documentary series *The Private Life of Plants*. While spring is obviously the best time to visit, you'll also find a number of early-blooming flowers in winter, and autumn features brilliant displays of pink candelabra lilies and yellow crossyne.

ARRIVAL AND DEPARTURE	NIEUWOUDTVILLE

By bus Public transport to Nieuwoudtville is limited to Maasdorp Van Wyk minibus taxis (see p.295), which run daily to and from Vanrhynsdorp.

INFORMATION

Information centre Operates out of the house in the attractively unkempt grounds of the church on Voortrekker Rd – the town's only sealed road (flower season Mon–Sat 9am–5.30pm, Sun 9am–2pm; other times Mon, Wed & Fri

---

NATURE RESERVES AROUND NIEUWOUDTVILLE

The area around Nieuwoudtville receives unusually high rainfall thanks to its location at the edge of the escarpment, and consequently boasts over three hundred different floral species; flowering starts after the first rains in April or May, and peaks in August and September. But even if you're here out of flower season, you'll still be privy to some fantastic scenery and a wealth of rare flora and fauna. The following reserves give a taste of what the area has to offer:

Nieuwoudtville Wildflower Reserve 3km east of Nieuwoudtville on the R27. This is the best place to see flowers, exhibiting an unparalleled variety of bulbs, notably the orange-flowered bulbinellas.

The Bokkeveld Nature Reserve 7km north of Nieuwoudtville. The main attraction of this reserve is the 30-metre waterfall which, when the Doring River is flowing between April and October, tumbles down into an impressive gorge where large raptors can sometimes be seen soaring around the tall cliffs.

Quiver Tree Forest 25km north of Nieuwoudtville, on the R357 towards Loeriesfontein. A dirt road leading towards Gannabos will take you to one of the area's botanical oddities, an extensive quiver tree forest, containing some of the tallest specimens of *Aloe dichotoma* (the kokerboom) found in South Africa. They flower in June and July.

Oorlogskloof Nature Reserve 16km west of the town; Department of Nature Conservation: Goedehoop St in Nieuwoudtville Mon–Fri 8am–4pm; permit R15 per day; ☎ 027 218 1159. Worthwhile for those who have a bit of time in the area, especially out of flower season, the reserve encompasses a series of deep ravines and natural swimming pools carved out by the Oorlogskloof River. Perched on the edge of the escarpment, it gives breathtaking views over the Knersvlakte plain to the northwest, the surrounding mountain ranges and the river. The reserve is known for rare breeding colonies of black-booted eagles, and is paradise for hikers and mountain bikers. Access is via a 10-kilometre gravel road that starts at the R27 near the top of Van Rhyn's Pass, 6km west of town. Before going, notify the Department of Nature Conservation (see above), which will issue you with a permit and give you the keys to the gate.

9am–2pm; ☎027 218 1336, ⓦnieuwoudtville.com).
Smidswinkel Restaurant & Information Centre In a large sandstone building on Neethling St (☎027 218

1535). Another good choice for reliable advice; staff can point you to the various hiking trails in the region, and to rock-art sites.

ACCOMMODATION

Olive Campsite Just over 1km out of town along Kerk St; book through the municipality office ☎027 218 8700. A large, pleasant campsite about 1km west of the town centre, with a big braai area, electricity and hot-water showers. R150
Papkuilsfontein Farm 23km south of town off the dirt road to Clanwilliam ☎027 218 1246. Particularly recommended as bases for visiting Oorlogskloof Nature Reserve (see opposite) are the three spotless, self-catering cottages run by the Van Wyk family, all within two hours' walk of the canyon. Tasty home-cooked meals are

available, and activities include hikes, birding and trips to the reserve. R660
Van Zijl guesthouses 1 Neethling St ☎027 218 1535, ⓦnieuwoudtville.co.za. A collection of attractive guesthouses located within walking distance of the Smidswinkel Restaurant. Most of the self-catering rooms are in restored traditional sandstone buildings, complete with fireplaces and cosy old furniture. There's also a double room tucked into a snug loft above the restaurant, and another in a restored wagon shed. R590

EATING

Smidswinkel Restaurant 1 Neethling St ☎027 218 1535. For somewhere to eat, you can't do better than this excellent restaurant, whose leg of lamb is famously good,

especially when washed down with the local wine. For less common Afrikaner specialities like baked sheep's heads and stuffed heart, give them a day's notice.

Calvinia

Despite its stern name, bestowed by an early dominee, **CALVINIA**, 70km east of Nieuwoudtville, has quite an appealing setting beneath the impressive Hantam Mountains. The town acts as a service centre for the western part of the **Great Karoo**, but it isn't a place you'll want to spend a lot of time in, unless you're here for the flowers in the surrounding area (*hantam* is Khoi for "where the red bulbs grow").

INFORMATION | CALVINIA

Tourist information Church St (Mon–Fri 7.30am–1pm & 1.45–4.30pm; ☎027 341 8100); can provide details of flower routes, various 4WD trails in

Hantam district, and two hiking trails in the magnificent Akkerendam Nature Reserve, just north of town in the lee of the mountains.

ACCOMMODATION

Hantam Huis 42–44 Hope St ☎027 341 1606, ⓦcalvinia.co.za. An atmospheric collection of restored old homes, turned into guesthouses and filled with beautiful

antique furniture. Self-catering is available, but there is also a restaurant serving traditional Afrikaner food, fresh bread, cakes and coffee. R520

The west coast and the Richtersveld

North from St Helena Bay, the hook of land 100km north of Cape Town, the long, lonely **west coast** of South Africa has two simple components: the cold, grey Atlantic Ocean, and the dominant sandveld vegetation, hardy but infertile. There isn't much more to the region: between the mouth of the Olifants River near Vanrhynsdorp, and the Orange River over 400km to the north, there is just one sealed road connecting the N7 highway to the coast. It leads to the only settlement of significance, **Port Nolloth**.

Namaqualand's first **diamonds** were discovered in 1925, confirming that diamonds could be carried the length of the Orange, washed out into the ocean and then dispersed by currents and the processes of longshore drift. Although initial prospecting was carried out along the course of the Orange and in the coastal dunes, the diamonds lying offshore on the sea bed are now more eagerly chased, mostly by boats operating with huge underwater "vacuum cleaners" and divers working in often dangerous conditions. Whereas much of Namaqualand's coast remains off-limits thanks to the presence of diamonds, the "**Diamond Coast**" from Port Nolloth to Alexander Bay, the mouth of the Orange River, is visitable. Springbok serves as a good access point.

During **flower season**, the rains fall first on the coastal areas, and you can often see displays beginning about 20km inland, making the few roads down to the coast from the N7 worthwhile detours. The dirt R355 road through the **Spektakel Pass** between Springbok and Kleinzee is one of the most spectacular drives in Namaqualand, and the **Anenous Pass** on the tarred R382 between Steinkopf and Port Nolloth is also impressive. Along this road you'll also see wandering herds of goats belonging to the pastoral **Nama** people living in the area, as well as the peaks and valleys of the **Richtersveld Transfrontier Park**, the mountain desert occupying the area immediately south of the Orange River. The area surrounding the park is home to several developing community tourism initiatives, providing an excellent introduction to the life of the Nama.

Port Nolloth

PORT NOLLOTH, 156km northwest of Springbok, is an odd but delightful place. In the hazy sunshine the horizons are never quite in focus, while the heavy morning mists shroud the town in a quiet eeriness. Populated by an eclectic mix of races and professions, including fishermen, diamond-boat owners, fortune-seeking commercial divers, diver-seeking girls and a significant Portuguese and Nigerian community, Port Nolloth is a place with a whiff of mystery and excitement, and tales are thick about "IDB" (illegal diamond buying). You should take care when broaching the subject – paranoia and illegal firearms make for a volatile combination. Attractions are limited and the Atlantic too cold for swimming, but a stroll to the **harbour** is always interesting. There are no tours on the diamond boats, but the guesthouses at McDougall's Bay, around 5km to the south, provide canoes and small boats for their guests.

ARRIVAL AND DEPARTURE   PORT NOLLOTH

Note that the border crossing to Oranjemund on the Namibian coast is closed; the only open border post is at Vioosldrift.

By minibus taxi The only public transport for Port Nolloth and Alexander Bay is the minibus taxi that runs Mon–Sat (☎ 082 972 9964) between Sanddrif on the Namibian border and Springbok. This passes through Alexander Bay at 7.45am, then Port Nolloth at 9am en route to Springbok, where it turns around at 2pm.

INFORMATION

Tourist information In the museum (Mon–Fri 8am–1pm & 1.45–4.30pm; ☎ 027 851 1111).

ACCOMMODATION

Bedrock Lodge 2 Beach Rd ☎ 027 851 8865, ⍟ bedrocklodge.co.za. A stylish, laid-back old beach house with period furniture that's a great place to stay, and a good source of local information. There is also a collection of self-catering cottages of various sizes, all with sea views. **R350**

McDougall's Bay Beach House Accommodation Haarder St, McDougall's Bay ☎ 027 851 8856, ⊜ beach accom@telkomsa.net. One of several beachfront houses at McDougall's Bay (be careful about walking there with luggage, as there have been muggings in the past). The simple rooms come with sea views; some are self-catering. **R550**

Port Indigo On Kamp St, McDougall's Bay ☎ 027 851 8012, ⍟ portindigo.co.za. One en-suite double in a B&B, plus a scattering of self-catering beachfront houses, of varying quality, with one to four bedrooms each. Can help to arrange local tours. **R550**

EATING

Anita's Tavern Opposite the Scotia Inn Hotel, Coastal Rd. This cosy pub is the best place in town to eat, serving good fish, meat and pasta dishes in a rustic beachside fisherman's hut decorated with nautical bric-a-brac. Mon–Sat noon–11pm.

Alexander Bay

The westernmost point of South Africa is **ALEXANDER BAY**, 85km north of Port Nolloth at the mouth of the Orange River, within a stone's throw of Namibia. Alluvial **diamonds** are the town's *raison d'être*, and their discovery in 1927 led to the site's appropriation by the state, which still runs the place. The largest stone ever found here, in 1944, was the Merensky Diamond, weighing in at a cool 211.5 carats; more recently, a 111-carat stone was found by divers contracted by the state **Alexkor** mining company, which controls most commercial activity in and around town.

The Richtersveld

Daily 8am–4pm • R120 • ☎ 027 831 1506

The **AI-AIS RICHTERSVELD TRANSFRONTIER PARK** in northwestern Namaqualand – commonly known as the Richtersveld – covers an area roughly bounded by the Orange River to the north, the N7 to the east, the R382 to Port Nolloth to the south and the Atlantic Ocean on its western side. Here, the starkly beautiful park was formed in 2003 by the merger of South Africa's Richtersveld National Park (by which name the new park is still known in South Africa) and Namibia's Ai-Ais Hot Springs Game Park. Tucked along either side of a loop in the Orange, the landscape is fierce and rugged; names such as Hellskloof, Skeleton Gorge, Devil's Tooth and Gorgon's Head indicate the austerity of the inhospitable brown mountainscape, tempered only by a broad range of hardy succulents, mighty rock formations, the magnificence of the light cast at dawn and dusk, and the glittering canopy of stars at night. Annual rainfall in parts of the park is under 50mm, making this the only true desert – and mountain desert at that – in South Africa. In summer the daytime heat can be unbearable – temperatures over 50°C have been recorded – while on winter nights temperatures drop below freezing.

The **best time to visit** is August and September, when the area's succulents – representing almost one-third of South Africa's species – burst into flower. There's little fauna in the park other than lizards and klipspringers, although leopards are present, if characteristically shy.

COMMUNITY TOURISM IN THE RICHTERSVELD

The Richtersveld area has several **community-based tourism initiatives**, combining basic accommodation (all around R150 per person, not including meals) – sometimes in the traditional *matjies* huts of the Nama – with opportunities to get to know the locals, eat traditional food and hike around the hills. **Access** – or lack thereof – is the main problem, as for most places you need your own wheels, and you'd do well to arrange things a week or so in advance by phone to be sure that places are open and food and water are available. For more information and updates, contact the tourist office in Springbok (see p.292).

Eksteenfontein (Xhobes) ☎ 027 851 7108. The oldest and most wide-ranging of the projects, this was started by local women whose husbands were away working in mines. It features the comfortable Eksteenfontein Guesthouse, with kitchen and shower, *matjies* huts to stay in, a coffee bar, a 4WD trail, meals, and plenty of excitable kids.

Lekkersing ☎ 027 851 8580. Over the hills west of Eksteenfontein, this offers the modern, self-catering Lekkersing Guesthouse, hiking, horseriding, donkey cart rides and even caving. The project also maintains a campsite at Koerdap.

Rooiberg ☎ 027 851 7108. Around 15km from Eksteenfontein at the base of a mountain, perfect for that middle-of-nowhere wilderness experience (bring water from Eksteenfontein). There's a guesthouse, campsite and hiking trails, for which you'll need a guide.

Sanddrift ☎ 027 831 1457. On the Orange River off the road from Alexander Bay to Sendelingsdrift, this is the departure point for the weekday minibus taxi to Springbok (see p.290), and is thus easily accessible. Accommodation is in Nama reed huts, and there are often performances of traditional music and dancing.

ACTIVITIES IN THE RICHTERSVELD

Between April and September it's possible to take **guided hikes** along designated trails and into the park with the help of the community tourism project at Kuboes (☎027 831 2013), although note that these trails are liable to closure if there are not enough qualified guides. Along the Orange River you'll find surprisingly rich **birdlife**, which is best enjoyed by taking a **canoeing trip** down the river – a gentle and relaxing jaunt rather than high-energy white-water rafting (by the time it reaches northern Namaqualand, the river is broad and the few rapids innocuous). Trips range from half-day tasters to full on six-day expeditions, with camps set up by the riverbank en route; costs start at around R400 for a full day, or R800 overnight. A recommended rafting company is **Bushwhacked Outdoor Adventure** (☎027 761 8953, ⓦbushwhacked.co.za), based at the riverside Fiddler's Creek campsite (R75) on the Namibian border, 10km along the south bank of the river from Vioolsdrif.

ARRIVAL AND DEPARTURE   THE RICHTERSVELD

Facilities are extremely limited – this is not the place for a casual visit, and there's **no public transport** either.

By tour Unless you're a skilled driver, probably the best way of seeing Richtersveld is as part of a tour. The most experienced operation is Richtersveld Challenge (see p.293), offering expeditions of varying lengths into the park as well as to Kgalagadi and Namibia. They can also incorporate hiking, abseiling or rafting along the Orange into their tours.

By car Ordinary cars are not allowed inside the park; the only way to explore is in a 4WD or a pick-up with a high enough clearance to handle the sandy river beds and rough mountain passes between the designated campsites. Pay

particular attention along the track linking the Richtersberg and De Hoop campsites, which is covered with thick sand and treacherously jagged rocks. If you are driving, it's recommended that you travel in a group of two vehicles, but note that no driving is allowed at night; fuel and limited supplies are available at the park headquarters at Sendelingsdrift (daily 8am–4pm), 94km from Alexander Bay. The Namibian section of the park can be reached via the Sendelingsdrift pontoon (daily 8am–4.15pm) across the Orange River, which marks the boundary between South Africa and its neighbour.

INFORMATION

Maps and guidebooks are sold at the park headquarters at Sendelingsdrift, and at *Springbok Lodge* (see p.292) in Springbok.

ACCOMMODATION

Campsites Inside the park at Kokerboomkloof, Potjiespram, Richtersberg and De Hoop ☎027 831 1506; ⓦsanparks.org. Four campsites spread throughout the park; they are very basic, though all but Kokerboomkloof come with cold showers. **R165**

Sendelingsdrift Rest Camp By the gate at Sendelingsdrift ☎027 831 1506; ⓦsanparks.org. Ten decent chalets sleeping between two and four people, each equipped with a/c, fridges and stoves. There are views

over the Orange River from the front porches, and a swimming pool on-site. **R575**

Tatasberg Wilderness Camp Inside the park at Tatasberg, on the Namibian border ☎027 831 1506; ⓦsanparks.org. Picturesque, two-person reed cabins that come with cooking facilities, set among dramatic boulders and enjoying lovely views of the surrounding mountains. Showers are provided, but bring your own drinking water. **R610**

The Eastern Cape

VIEW ACROSS THE KAROO (P.328)

The Eastern Cape

Sandwiched between the Western Cape and KwaZulu-Natal, South Africa's two most popular coastal provinces, the EASTERN CAPE tends to be bypassed by visitors – and for all the wrong reasons. The relative neglect it has suffered as a tourist destination and at the hands of the government is precisely where its charm lies. You can still find traditional African villages here, and the region's 1000km of undeveloped COASTLINE alone justifies a visit, sweeping back inland in immense undulations of vegetated dunefields. For anyone wanting to get off the beaten track, the province is, in fact, one of the most rewarding regions in South Africa.

Port Elizabeth is the province's commercial centre, principally used to start or end a trip along the Garden Route, though it's a useful springboard for launching out into the rest of South Africa – the city is the transport hub of the Eastern Cape. **Jeffrey's Bay**, 75km to the west, has a fabled reputation among surfers for its perfect waves. Around an hour's drive inland are some of the province's most significant game reserves, among them **Addo Elephant National Park**, a Big Five reserve where sightings of elephants are virtually guaranteed. Addo and the private reserves nearby are among the few game reserves in South Africa that are malaria-free throughout the year. The hinterland to the north takes in areas appropriated by English immigrants shipped out in the 1820s as ballast for a new British colony. Here, **Grahamstown** glories in its twin roles as the spiritual home of English-speaking South Africa and host to Africa's biggest arts festival.

The northwest is dominated by the sparse beauty of the **Karoo**, the thorny semi-desert stretching across much of central South Africa. The rugged **Mountain Zebra National Park**, 200km north of Port Elizabeth, is a stirring landscape of flat-topped mountains and arid plains stretching for hundreds of kilometres. A short step to the west, **Graaff-Reinet** is the quintessential eighteenth-century Cape Dutch Karoo town.

The eastern part of the province, largely the former Transkei, is by far the least developed, with rural Xhosa villages predominating. **East London**, the province's only other centre of any size, serves well as a springboard for heading into the Transkei, where the principal interest derives from political and cultural connections. **Steve Biko** was born here, and you can visit his grave in **King William's Town** to the west. Further west is **Fort Hare University**, which educated many contemporary African leaders. The only established resorts in this section are in the **Amatola Mountains**, notably Hogsback, where indigenous forests and mossy coolness provide relief from the dry scrublands below.

DANCERS AT THE GRAHAMSTOWN FESTIVAL

Highlights

❶ Port Elizabeth township tour Several guides run very accessible tours into the African areas of the province's largest city. **See p.312**

❷ Addo Elephant National Park See pachyderms and the rest of the Big Five in the best public game reserve in the malaria-free southern half of the country. **See p.314**

❸ Grahamstown Festival Africa's largest arts festival wakes up this pretty colonial university town. **See p.326**

❹ Nelson Mandela's birthplace, Qunu Follow the footsteps of South Africa's greatest hero to the village where he was born, attended school and learned from his elders, just outside Mthatha. **See p.355**

❺ The Tuishuise The historic frontier town of Cradock offers accommodation in a street of beautifully restored and furnished Victorian houses. **See p.328**

❻ Karoo farmstays Experience the sharp light and panoramic landscape of the Karoo semi-desert that sweeps across South Africa's interior. **See p.334**

❼ Bulungula Backpacker Lodge In a remote Wild Coast village, this brilliant base offers a vivid experience of Xhosa life and culture. **See p.353**

HIGHLIGHTS ARE MARKED ON THE MAP ON P.306–307

Tucked into the northeastern corner of the province, the **Drakensberg range**, more commonly associated with KwaZulu-Natal, makes a steep ascent out of the Karoo and offers trout-fishing and ancient San rock art. The focus of the area is the remote, lovely village of **Rhodes**. Further east, the **Wild Coast region** remains one of the least developed and most exciting regions in the country. The poorest part of the poorest province, the region is blessed with fabulously beautiful subtropical coast. From here, all the way to the KwaZulu-Natal border, dirt roads trundle down to the coast from

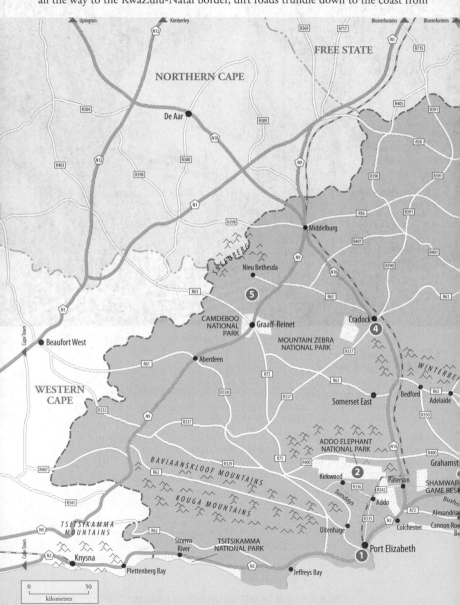

the N2 to dozens of remote and indolent hillside resorts, of which **Port St Johns** is the biggest and best known. In the rugged, goat-chewed landscape inland, Xhosa-speakers live in mud-and-tin homesteads, scraping a living herding stock and growing crops. Most visitors pass as quickly as possible through **Mthatha** (formerly Umtata), the ugly former capital of the Transkei – but if you're following in the footsteps of Nelson Mandela, the **Nelson Mandela Museum** in the centre of Mthatha, and **Qunu**, his birthplace southwest of the town, are obvious ports of call.

HIGHLIGHTS
❶ Port Elizabeth township tour
❷ Addo Elephant National Park
❸ Grahamstown Festival
❹ Tuishuise
❺ Karoo Farmstays
❻ Bulungula Backpacker Lodge

EASTERN CAPE

Brief history

The Eastern Cape was carved up into black and white territories under apartheid in a more consolidated way than anywhere else in the country. The stark contrasts between wealth and poverty were forged in the nineteenth century when the British drew the Cape colonial frontier along the **Great Fish River**, a thousand kilometres east of Cape Town, and fought over half a dozen campaigns (known as the **Frontier Wars**) to keep the **Xhosa** at bay on its east bank. In the 1820s, the British shipped in thousands of settlers to bolster white numbers and reinforce the line.

Even for a country where everything is suffused with politics, the Eastern Cape's identity is excessively **political**. South Africa's black trade unions have deep roots in its soil, which also produced many anti-apartheid African leaders, including former president **Nelson Mandela**, his successor **Thabo Mbeki**, and Black Consciousness leader **Steve Biko**, who died in 1977 at the hands of Port Elizabeth security police. The Transkei or Wild Coast region, wedged between the Kei and KwaZulu-Natal, was the testing ground for grand apartheid when it became the prototype in 1963 for the Bantustan system of racial segregation. In 1976 the South African government gave it notional "independence", in the hope that several million Xhosa-speaking South Africans, surplus to industry's needs, could be dumped in the territory and thereby become foreigners in "white South Africa". When the Transkei was reincorporated into South Africa in 1994 it became part of the new Eastern Cape, a province struggling for economic survival under the weight of its apartheid-era legacy and the added burden of widespread corruption.

4

Port Elizabeth and the western region

Port Elizabeth is the industrial centre of the Eastern Cape. In 1820 it was the arrival point for four thousand British settlers, who doubled the English-speaking population of South Africa and have left their trace on the architecture in the town centre. The port's industrial feel is mitigated by some outstanding city beaches and, should you end up killing time here, you'll find diversion in beautiful **coastal walks** a few kilometres from town and in the small **historical centre**.

However, the main reason most people wash up here is to start or finish a tour of the **Garden Route** – or head further up the highway to **Addo Elephant National Park** (see p.308), the most significant game reserve in the southern half of the country. Also within easy striking distance are several other smaller, and utterly luxurious, **private game reserves**.

East of Port Elizabeth, a handful of **resorts** punctuate the **R72 East London coast road**, where the roaring surf meets enormously wide sandy beaches, backed by mountainous dunes. The inland route to East London deviates away from the coast to pass through **Grahamstown**, a handsome university town, worth at least a night, and several during the National Arts Festival every July.

A couple of hundred kilometres north from Port Elizabeth, an area of flat-topped hills and treeless plains opens out to the **Karoo**, the semi-desert that extends across a third of South Africa. The oldest and best known of the settlements here is the picture-postcard town of **Graaff-Reinet**, a solid fixture on bus tours. Just a few kilometres away is the awesome **Valley of Desolation**, and the village of **Nieu Bethesda**, best known for its eccentric Owl House museum. Nearly as pretty as Graaff-Reinet, though not as architecturally rich, the town of **Cradock**, to its east, has the added attraction of the rugged **Mountain Zebra National Park**.

Port Elizabeth

At the western end of Algoa (aka Nelson Mandela) Bay, **PORT ELIZABETH**, commonly known as **PE**, is normally visited for Addo Park, and not for its own beauty. The

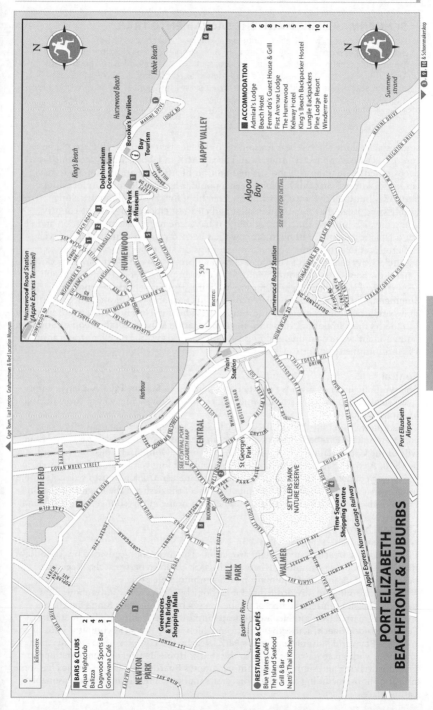

PORT ELIZABETH BEACHFRONT & SUBURBS

Cape Town, East London, Grahamstown & Red Location Museum

Humewood Road Station (Apple Express Terminal)

ACCOMMODATION	
Admiral's Lodge	9
Beach Hotel	6
Ferran'do's Guest House & Grill	8
First Avenue Lodge	7
The Humewood	3
Kelway Hotel	5
King's Beach Backpacker Hostel	1
Lungile Backpackers	4
Pine Lodge Resort	10
Windermere	2

BARS & CLUBS	
Aqua Nightclub	2
Balizza	4
Dagwood Sports Bar	3
Gondwana Café	1

RESTAURANTS & CAFES	
Blue Waters Café	1
The Island Seafood Grill & Bar	3
Natti's Thai Kitchen	2

HAPPY VALLEY

Brooke's Pavilion

Bay Tourism

Dolphinarium Oceanarium

Snake Park & Museum

HUMEWOOD

Humewood Beach

Hobie Beach

King's Beach

Algoa Bay

Summerstrand

CENTRAL

Train Station

St George's Park

Harbour

NORTH END

NEWTON PARK

MILL PARK

WALMER

SETTLERS PARK NATURE RESERVE

Time Square Shopping Centre

Greenacres & The Bridge Shopping Malls

Apple Express Narrow Gauge Railway

Port Elizabeth Airport

Baakens River

SEE CENTRAL PORT ELIZABETH MAP

SEE INSET FOR DETAIL

4

SCHOENMAKERSKOP AND THE SACRAMENTO TRAIL

From Summerstrand, Marine Drive continues 15km down the coast as far as the village of **Schoenmakerskop** (Schoenies to the locals), along impressive coastline that alternates between rocky shores and sandy beaches. From here you can walk the 8km **Sacramento Trail**, a shoreline path that leads to the huge-duned **Sardinia Bay**, the wildest and most dramatic stretch of coast in the area. To get there by road, turn right at the Schoenmakerskop intersection and follow the road until Sardinia Bay is signed, on the left. Always walk with others for safety.

---

smokestacks along the N2 bear testimony to the fact that the Eastern Cape's largest centre has thrived on heavy industry and cheap African labour, which accounts for its deep-rooted trade unionism and strong tradition of African nationalism. So it may come as a surprise that this has long been a popular holiday destination for white families – but then the town beachfront, stretching for several kilometres along Humewood Road, has some of the safest and cleanest **city beaches** in the country.

As a city, PE is pretty functional, though it has some terrific accommodation and reasonable restaurants. Although the town has been ravaged by industrialization and thoughtless modernization, one or two buildings do stand out in an otherwise featureless **city centre**, and a couple of classically pretty rows of Victorian terraces still remain in the suburb of **Central**, sliding into a revamped street of trendy cafés and restaurants. Holidaymakers head for the beachfront suburbs of **Humewood** and **Summerstrand** where there are places to stay plus bars and restaurants. There is little to draw you away from the beachfront, but further afield in **New Brighton**, you'll find Port Elizabeth's most important museum, the **Red Location Museum of the People's Struggle**, housed in an award-winning building, and there are also some excellent **tours** around PE and into the townships.

Central

The symbolic heart of town is the **City Hall**, standing in **Market Square**, a large, empty space surrounded by some striking mid-Victorian buildings, adjacent to the train and bus stations.

Heading west up hilly **Donkin Street**, you'll come upon a stone pyramid commemorating **Elizabeth Donkin**, after whom PE was named. Elizabeth was the young wife of the Cape's acting governor in 1820, Sir Rufane Donkin; she died of fever in India in 1818. As you stroll up Donkin Street, you could be forgiven for thinking you were in the wrong country, on the wrong continent: the nineteen **Donkin Houses** – double-storey terraces that are now National Monuments – reflect the desire of the English settlers in the mid-nineteenth century to create a home from home in this strange, desiccated land.

The beachfront

Baywold Museum and Snake Park daily 9am–4.30pm • R45

PE's wonderful **beaches** are its main attraction. The protection provided by Algoa Bay makes them safe for swimming (that said, it's best to do so between the lifeguard beacons), and clean enough to make **beachcombing** a pleasure.

The beachfront strip, divided from the harbour by a large wall, starts about 2km south of the city centre. The first of the beaches is beautiful, wide **King's Beach**, somewhat marred by a jumble of coal heaps and oil tanks behind it. To the southeast lies **Humewood Beach**, across the road from which is the Baywold complex, housing the missable **Bayworld Museum** and **Snake Park**. Nearby is a complex of restaurants, pubs and clubs with great views. Beyond, to the south, **Hobie Beach** and **Summerstrand** are great for walking and sunbathing. Summerstrand's **Boardwalk Casino Complex** has some pleasing shops, including an indigenous crafts market, cinemas and some reasonable eating places.

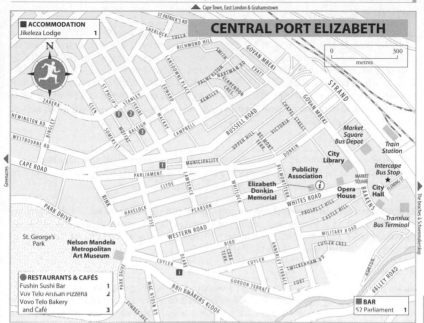

Red Location Museum of the People's Struggle

At the corner of Olof Palme and Singaphi sts, New Brighton, 7km north of central PE • Tues–Sat 9am–4pm • R12

The **Red Location Museum of the People's Struggle** is dedicated to recalling the experiences of the residents of Red Location, Port Elizabeth's oldest African township, established in 1902. The settlement took its name from the rusted corrugated-iron barracks, around which New Brighton developed, that had housed troops until the end of the Anglo-Boer War. A significant site of anti-apartheid resistance, New Brighton was the stomping ground of a number of significant South Africans, including Govan Mbeki (ANC stalwart and father of South Africa's ex-president), artist George Pemba, and internationally feted actor John Kani. Red Location was the first place in South Africa to stage a passive resistance campaign against the pass laws (see p.655) and was the birthplace of the first cell of MK (the ANC's armed wing).

This worthwhile museum is housed in a striking building awarded the 2006 Royal Institute of British Architects' **Lubetkin Prize** for the most outstanding work of architecture outside the European Union. Described by the judges as a *tour de force*, the building wears an industrial-style saw-toothed roof that evokes the area's strong association with trade unionism. Inside, four **permanent exhibitions** trace a century of Red Location's history from 1900.

ARRIVAL AND DEPARTURE   PORT ELIZABETH

By plane Port Elizabeth's airport (☎041 581 2984) is on the edge of Walmer suburb, 4km south of the CBD, with connections to the rest of the country, and with all the major car rental companies in attendance. It is approximately an hour's flight to Cape Town, Johannesburg and Durban. Taxis rank outside the airport and the fare to the city centre is around R70. Avis (☎041 501 7200), Budget (☎041 581 4242) and Hertz (☎041 508 6600) are based at the airport.

By train The train station (☎041 507 2662) is centrally located with a daily train to Johannesburg.

By bus The Baz Bus drops off anywhere in the centre, while Translux, Greyhound and Intercape intercity buses terminate at Greenacres shopping mall in Newton Park suburb, 3km from the centre, where you can find taxis to your final destination. The Minilux bus (☎043 741 3107) runs between East London and PE four days a week.

INFORMATION AND TOURS

Tourist information The Nelson Mandela Bay Tourism head office (Mon–Fri 8am–4.30pm; ☎041 582 2575, ⓦ nmbt.co.za) is on the corner of Mitchell St and Walmer Boulevard, South End. There are also offices at the airport (daily 7am–7pm; ☎041 581 0456); Shop 48 at the Boardwalk (daily 8am–7pm; ☎041 583 2030), Marine Drive, Summerstrand; and Donkin Reserve Lighthouse Building, Belmont Terrace, Central (Mon–Fri 8am–4.30pm,

Sat & Sun 9.30am–3.30pm; ☎041 585 8884).

Tours The best way to see Port Elizabeth is on one of the excellent bus tours, which shed light on a city shaped by layers of political history. Calabash Tours (☎041 585 6162 or ☎084 552 4414, ⓦ calabashtours.co.za) operates "Real City Tours" by day and *shebeen* tours by night, as well as day-trips to Addo, and the backpacker hostels run their own tours too, notably *Jikeleza*.

GETTING AROUND

If you're staying in Central, exploring the city on foot is a realistic possibility – try the self-guided **Heritage Walk** (shown on a map available at the tourist office). However, for any serious exploration of PE, or for getting to and from the beachfront, **renting a car** is your best option (see p.311).

By minibus taxi and taxi PE's minibus taxis run from town to the beachfront on a regular basis, but are the least recommended way to travel. Metered taxis don't have ranks so you'll need to phone to find a taxi; if you're

going to the airport or the bus or train stations, it's advisable to book ahead. Recommended companies include Hurters (☎041 585 5500) and Sisa (☎076 426 0145).

ACCOMMODATION

The obvious place to stay is the beachfront, with a wide choice of hotels, self-catering suites and B&Bs. During the December and January peak holiday period the beachfront becomes the focus for most of the city's action, while February, March and April are much quieter yet offer perfect beach weather. Note that PE can be subject to excoriatingly strong winds in the summer, which makes going to the beach unpleasant.

Admiral's Lodge 47 Admiralty Way, Summerstrand ☎041 583 1894 or ☎083 455 2072, ⓦ admiralslodge .co.za; map p.309. Spacious and stylish rooms at a good B&B, at the far end of Summerstrand about 7km from the centre. Airport transfers are available. R800

Beach Marine Drive, Humewood ☎041 583 2161, ⓦ beachhotel.co.za; map p.309. Across the road from popular Hobie Beach, and sited at the centre of the beachside action, with its own patio bar overlooking the ocean. It's worth paying more for a sea-facing room. R1400

Fernando's Guest House & Grill 102 Cape Rd, Mill Park ☎041 373 2823; map p.309. Purportedly South Africa's oldest guesthouse, in three separate Victorian houses decked out with period furniture and offering good value and a warm atmosphere. The busy Cape Rd does quieten down in the evening. R650

The Humewood 33 Beach Rd, Humewood ☎041 585 8961, ⓦ humewoodhotel.co.za; map p.309. A large, old-fashioned hotel with hints of 1950s family seaside holidays. The rooms are large and feature wicker furniture and summery floral prints. Service is excellent and includes laundry facilities and babysitting. Airport transfers available. R950

Jikeleza Lodge 44 Cuyler St, Central ☎041 586 3721, ⓦ highwinds.co.za; map p.309. A friendly backpacker place with dorms, doubles and a family room. Its adventure centre can help you sort out tour and travel bookings. Dorm

R120, double R310

Kelway Brookes Hill Drive, Humewood ☎041 584 0638, ⓦ thekelway.co.za; map p.309. Stylish hotel kitted out with timber panelling, seagrass chairs and handcrafted wooden tables. A variety of rooms is available at different prices, including family suites; opt for a sea view. R1300

King's Beach Backpacker Hostel 41 Windermere Rd, Humewood ☎041 585 8113, ⓔ kingsb@agnet.co.za; map p.309. Spotless, well-established hostel, a block away from the beach, with camping facilities, dorms and double rooms, plus an outside bar and braai area. The travel desk can book township, game park and other tours. Camping R60, dorm R100, double R300

Lungile Backpackers 12 La Roche Drive, Summerstrand ☎041 582 2042, ⓦ lungilebackpackers.co.za; map p.309. Large and popular hostel close to the beach, where you can party indoors or step out into the heart of PE's beachfront nightlife strip. Perched on a hill, it has facilities for camping, a large lawn to relax on, sea views, a pool table, bar and swimming pool. Camping R50, dorm R120, double R310

Pine Lodge Resort Off Marine Drive, Humewood ☎041 583 4004, ⓦ pinelodge.co.za; map p.309. Right on the beach, near the wonderful historic lighthouse and next to the Cape Recife Nature Reserve, where owls, mongooses and antelope make appearances. Offers various log cabin units, some with full kitchens, sleeping from four to eight people. R950

Windermere 35 Humewood Rd, Humewood ☏041 582 2245, ⊛thewindermere.co.za. A stylish hotel with just eight suites, given an almost Zen-like feel through the subtle use of off-white to oaty colours contrasted with dark hues. R1500

EATING, DRINKING AND NIGHTLIFE

A great area to focus on for trendy cafés and restaurants, open during the day as well as in the evening, is the newly developed Richmond Hill precinct, while having a meal or drink along the **beachfront** is another obvious choice – wander about and see what takes your fancy. For details of occasional concerts at the PE Opera House, next to the Donkin Memorial, check out the *Daily Herald*.

RESTAURANTS

Blue Waters Café Hobie Beach ☏041 583 4110; map p.309. This pleasant restaurant has great sea views, and serves good pasta (R90) and light snacks. Sipping an early evening cocktail on the terrace is recommended. Daily 8am–9pm.

Fushin Sushi Bar Stanley on Bain, Richmond Hill ☏082 865 2707; map p.311. Sit at the long counter for the most delicious sushi in town (R75), as well as salads and eastern-influenced tapas-style small dishes. Daily noon–10pm.

The Island Seafood Grill & Bar Pine Lodge Resort, Marine Drive ☏041 583 3789; map p.309. This place enjoys an appealing setting in coastal dunes with wooden walkways and decking, and boasts a patio bar, ideal for enjoying a cocktail, and an indoor restaurant serving a decent range of snacks and full meals. Every dish is named after an island, and, though the food is nicely presented, the range spans a fairly predictable selection of pastas, burgers and so on (mains around R80). Mon–Sat 11am–9pm, Sun 11am–8pm.

Natti's Thai Kitchen 5 Park Lane, Central ☏041 373 2763; map p.309. Unfailingly excellent restaurant, which has been going for years, serving reasonably priced authentic Thai cuisine in a relaxed atmosphere, with a BYO alcohol policy. Mon–Sat 6.30pm till late.

Vov Telo Artisan Pizzeria 24 Bain St, Richmond Hill ☏041 585 8225; map p.311. This industrial-chic restaurant with a pleasant outdoor patio serves up thin-based, wood-fired pizzas with interesting toppings (R60), though the menu stretches to antipastos, salads, coffee and dessert. It's a fun and laidback place, and the eco-conscious owners are quick to tell you that the wood burned is from infestations of wattle and other Australian trees, which leach the soil. Mon–Sat noon–10pm, Sun noon–9pm.

Vovo Telo Bakery and Café 16 Raleigh St, Richmond Hill ☏041 585 5606; map p.311. This is a great place for breakfast and lunch, with Italian and French breads and pastries, real coffee and balcony seating. It's just round the corner from its sister pizzeria. Mon–Sat 7.30am–3pm.

BARS AND CLUBS

52 Parliament 52 Parliament St, Central; map p.311. Late-night bar in a Victorian building decked out with interesting metal sculptures. DJs play house and other sounds, with occasional live music, though it does have a reputation for being rough. Wed, Fri & Sat.

Aqua Nightclub Corner of York St & Prince Alfred Rd, North End ☏072 057 7705, ⊛clubaqua.co.za; map p.309. Relaxed, racially mixed eatery by day that doubles up as a gay club by night; this is the only reliable gay spot in town if you are looking for a good night out. Tues–Sun 9am till late.

Balizza Times Square Shopping Centre, Walmer; map p.309. With two bars, three lounges and two dance floors, you are likely to have a fun night out here, with the DJs playing a mix of recent house and oldies. Daily 11am–2am.

Dagwood Sports Bar 76 Cape Rd, Newton Park ☏041 373 0936; map p.309. A fun bar-diner that has something on almost every night of the week, from one-man bands to karaoke on Saturday nights. Sunday nights are when it's really pumping, with house parties and drinking competitions until the early hours. Daily 11am till late.

Gondwana Café 2 Dolphin's Leap, Main Rd, Humewood; map p.309. This fun place is a casual, racially mixed restaurant that becomes a club in the evening. There's live jazz on Sunday afternoons. Tues–Sun 9am till late.

DIRECTORY

Cinemas You can catch the latest releases at Nu Metro, Walmer Park Shopping Centre, Walmer; or Cinema Starz at the Boardwalk Casino Complex at the beachfront.

Hospitals St George's (private), 40 Park Drive, Central (☏041 392 6111); Provincial (state), Buckingham Rd, Mount Croix (☏041 392 3911).

Pharmacy Mount Rd Pharmacy, 559 Govan Mbeki Ave, is open daily until 11pm (☏041 484 3838).

Post office Brookes Pavilion, Humewood (Mon–Fri 9am–3.30pm & Sat 8.30–11am).

Addo Elephant National Park

73km north of Port Elizabeth • Daily 7am–7pm • R140 • ☏042 2338600, ⊛addoelephantpark.com

A Big Five reserve, **Addo Elephant National Park** is just 73km north of Port Elizabeth,

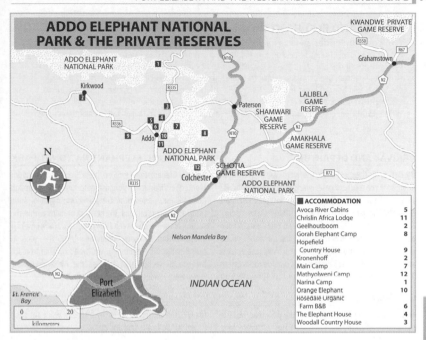

ADDO ELEPHANT NATIONAL PARK & THE PRIVATE RESERVES

KWANDWE PRIVATE GAME RESERVE

ADDO ELEPHANT NATIONAL PARK

Kirkwood

Grahamstown

LALIBELA GAME RESERVE

Paterson

SHAMWARI GAME RESERVE

AMAKHALA GAME RESERVE

Addo

ADDO ELEPHANT NATIONAL PARK

SCHOTIA GAME RESERVE

Colchester

ADDO ELEPHANT NATIONAL PARK

Nelson Mandela Bay

Port Elizabeth

INDIAN OCEAN

St. Francis Bay

■ ACCOMMODATION	
Avoca River Cabins	5
Chrislin Africa Lodge	11
Geelhoutboom	2
Gorah Elephant Camp	8
Hopefield	
Country House	9
Kronenhoff	2
Main Camp	7
Mathyolweni Camp	12
Narina Camp	1
Orange Elephant	10
Rosedale Organic	
Farm B&B	6
The Elephant House	4
Woodall Country House	3

and should be your first choice for an excursion – for just one day or for several. You can also stay at one of the nearby **private reserves** – especially if you just want to be pampered. On the N2 highway between PE and Grahamstown alone, there are three: **Shamwari**, **Amakhala** and **Lalibela**, while **Schotia**, 1km off the N10/N2 interchange, has exciting night drives and is the least upmarket. One big attraction of Addo and these private reserves is that, unlike the country's other major game parks, they benefit from the fact that the Eastern Cape is **malaria-free**.

Addo is currently undergoing an expansion programme that will see it become one of South Africa's three largest game reserves, and the only one including coastline. **Elephants** remain the park's most obvious drawcard, but with the reintroduction in 2003 of a small number of **lions**, in two prides (big cats last roamed here over a century ago), as well as the presence of the rest of the Big Five – **buffalo**, **hippos** and **leopards** – it has become a game reserve to be reckoned with. Spotted **hyenas** were also introduced in 2003 as part of a programme to re-establish predators in the local ecosystem. Other species to look out for include cheetah, black rhino, eland, kudu, warthog, ostrich and red hartebeest.

Wildlife watching

Daytime game drive R220; sunset game drive R330; night game drive R250 • Hop-on guide R150

The Addo bush is thick, dry and prickly, making it difficult sometimes to spot any of the 450 or so elephants and other game; when you do, though, it's often thrillingly close up. The best strategy is to ask where the pachyderms and the other four of the Big Five have last been seen (enquire with staff at the park reception), and also to head for the **water hole** in front of the restaurant to scan the bush for large grey backs quietly moving about. It also makes sense to go on a **guided game drive** in an open vehicle with a knowledgeable national parks driver. Two-hour outings leave throughout the day; book at **Main Camp**. The vehicles used are higher off the ground than a normal sedan to improve viewing opportunities. Alternatively, you can hire the exclusive services of a hop-on guide who joins you in your own car for two hours and will direct you to find game.

HORSE- AND ELEPHANT RIDES

Two-hour **horserides**, suitable for the not-so-experienced (8am; R220), and three-hour rides for experienced equestrians (2pm; R310) leave from just outside the main gate and run along the exterior of the park fence. All-day rides in the beautiful Zuurberg section, where there is not much game, but ample scenery to make up for it, is available for experienced riders, though you'll need a head for heights (R300). All horserides can be booked at *Main Camp*.

   Elephant-back safaris are operated from a farm abutting the northern boundary of Addo (R875; ☏042 235 1400, ⊛addoelephantbacksafaris.co.za), 90km from Port Elizabeth, off the R335.

ARRIVAL AND DEPARTURE   ADDO ELEPHANT NATIONAL PARK

By car By far the most straightforward way of getting to Addo is via the southern gate, which is accessed off the N2 at the village of Colchester, 43km northeast of Port Elizabeth. The gate is about 5km from *Matyholweni Camp*. To get to *Main Camp*, Addo's older and more established base, which is north of *Matyholweni*, you can either take a slow, scenic drive through the park, which will take at least an hour, or use the R335 Rd that runs outside the western flank of the park – take the N2 from Port Elizabeth east towards Grahamstown for 5km, branching off at the Addo/Motherwell/Markman signpost onto the R335 through Addo village. *Narina Bush Camp* is 22km north of *Main Camp* along a gravel road. The network of roads within the section of the park between *Main Camp* and *Mathyolweni* is untarred, but in good condition. Until the park is consolidated (not imminent), you won't be able to reach the coastal section that includes the Alexandria State Forest from inside the national park.

INFORMATION

Main camp reception has maps of the park that indicate the location of picnic and braai sites. The restaurant here (daily 6am–8pm) offers three meals a day, while the shop is well stocked with food and drink.

ACCOMMODATION

INSIDE THE PARK

Reservations for all accommodation in the park, except *Gorah*, can be made through SANParks (⊛addoelephant .com) or, less than 72 hours in advance, directly with Addo (☏042 233 8600). Reservations are essential in high season.
Gorah Elephant Camp 9km west along the Addo Heights Rd leading from the N10 to Addo village ☏044 501 1111, ⊛hunterhotels.com/gorahelephantcamp; map p.315. An ultra-luxurious outfit based around a Victorian homestead, decked out with the appropriate paraphernalia (mounted antelope skulls above the fireplace, evocative African landscapes, and polished tabletops you can see your reflection in). The suites are plush, there are opportunities to dine under the stars and there's a beautifully landscaped swimming pool. Rates include all meals and game drives. **R12700**
Main Camp Map p.315 The oldest and largest of the National Parks camps. Besides camping facilities, there are forest cabins that sleep two people and share cooking facilities in communal kitchens; and more luxurious two-person chalets (R900) with their own kitchenettes. Some of these units sleep up to four people (but the minimum charge is for two occupants). Also available are well-designed, spacious safari tents, perfect for summer, with decks right next to the perimeter fence. Camping **R165**, cabin **R420**
Matyoholweni Camp Map p.315 National Parks accommodation in a dozen fully equipped self-catering chalets with showers, each sleeping two. Set in a secluded valley surrounded by thicket that supports a wealth of birdlife, the chalets have decks from which you will be able to view game once a planned water hole is completed. There is no restaurant, but Colchester, a 15min drive away, has shops and basic places to eat. **R825**
Narina Camp Map p.315 Small National Parks bush camp in the mountainous Zuurberg section of Addo with four safari tents that sleep four people and share ablution and cooking facilities; bring your own provisions. Horseriding is available. **R855**

OUTSIDE THE PARK

Private B&Bs and guesthouses are in abundance around Addo, especially among the citrus groves of the Sundays River Valley. Many offer day and night drives in the game reserve.
Avoca River Cabins 13km northwest of Addo village on the R336 ☏042 234 0421, ⊛gardenroute.co.za/addo /avoca. Map p.315 Reasonably priced B&B and self-catering accommodation on a farm in the Sundays River Valley, ranging from budget cabins to more comfortable thatched huts (some on the banks of the river). Canoes are available to rent and there are walks on the farm. **R300**
Chrislin Africa Lodge 12km south of Addo main gate, off the R336 ☏042 233 0022, ⊛chrislin.co.za; map p.315. A quirky B&B with thatched huts built using traditional Xhosa construction techniques, with a lovely

4

lapa (courtyard) and pool, and hearty country breakfasts, as well as dinners on request. R800

★ **The Elephant House** 5km north of Addo village on the R335 ☎042 233 2462 or ☎083 799 5671, ⊛elephanthouse.co.za; map p.315. Just minutes from Addo is one of the Eastern Cape's top places to stay, a stunning thatch-roofed lodge filled with Persian rugs and antique furniture that perfectly balances luxury with a supremely relaxed atmosphere. The eight bedrooms and six garden cottages open onto a lawned courtyard. Candle-lit dinners are available, as well as game drives (R650 per person) into Addo and the surrounding reserves. R1200

Geelhoutboom 26 Market St, Kirkwood ☎042 230 1191, ⊛geelhoutboom.co.za; map p.315. A homely B&B with six a/c rooms, a twenty-minute drive from Addo main gate and shaded by a large yellowwood tree. Rooms all have fridges and simple self-catering facilities. R550

Hopefield Country House 20km southwest of Addo main gate ☎042 234 0333, ⊛hopefield.co.za; map p.315. An atmospheric 1930s farmhouse set in beautiful English-style gardens on a citrus farm. The five bedrooms are imaginatively furnished with period pieces in a style the owners (a pair of classical musicians who occasionally give impromptu concerts for guests) describe as "farmhouse eclectic". R1200

Kronenhoff On the R336 as you enter Kirkwood ☎042 230 1448, ⊛kronenhoff.co.za; map p.315. Situated in a small farming town, this is a hospitable, high-ceilinged Cape Dutch-style home, with spacious suites, polished wooden floors, large leather sofas and a sociable pub. In summer the sweet scent of orange blossom carries from the surrounding citrus groves. R1050.

Orange Elephant On the R335, 8km from the National Park gate ☎042 233 0023, ⊛addobackpackers.com; map p.315. Budget accommodation at a comfortable hostel, whose management will help you organize outings into the surrounding game reserves. In addition to dorms, they also offer two-bedroom cottages and en-suite rooms. Dorm R120, double R350

Rosedale Organic Farm B&B On the R335, 1km north of Addo village ☎042 233 0404 or ☎083 329 8775, ⊛rosedalebnb.co.za; map p.315. Very reasonably priced accommodation in six cottages on a certified organic farm that exports citrus to the EU. Hosts Keith and Nondumiso Finnemore are seriously committed to sustainable farming and tourism – water for the cottages is solar heated, the boilers for the outdoor showers are fired by uprooted exotic trees, and as far as possible breakfasts consist of organic produce. Keith offers a free one-hour walking tour of the farm to guests, on which you can get all those nagging questions about the state of the world's food industry answered. R650

Woodall Country House About 1km west of Addo main gate ☎042 233 0128, ⊛woodall-addo.co.za; map p.315. An excellent luxury guesthouse on a working citrus farm with eleven self-contained suites and rooms. There's a swimming pool, gymnasium, spa and sauna (massages are available, and there's a resident beautician), and the lovely sundowner deck overlooks a small lake full of swans and other waterfowl. Renowned for its outstanding country cuisine, its restaurant offers three- to six-course dinners. R2400

The private game reserves

Although driving through Addo can be extremely rewarding, nothing beats getting into the wild in an open vehicle with a trained guide – something the **private reserves** excel at. If you're strapped for cash or pushed for time, a good option is one of the day or half-day safaris that start at R600 per person offered by **Schotia** and **Amakhala**. If you want the works – game drives, outstanding food, uncompromising luxury and excellent accommodation, you'll find it at top-ranking **Shamwari**, with prices rising over R5000 per person a day. If you're in this league, it's also worth considering Kwandwe Game Reserve, another outstanding safari destination in the Eastern Cape, near Grahamstown.

ACCOMMODATION   PRIVATE GAME RESERVES

Amakhala Game Reserve Just 2km further along the N2 from the turn-off to Shamwari (see p.317) ☎042 235 1608, ⊛amakhala.co.za; map p.315. The far more affordable alternative to neighbouring *Shamwari*, and is family-friendly, too. Some lodges offer children's programmes, and the area is stocked with the Big Five as well as cheetah, giraffe, zebra, wildebeest and many antelopes. The Bushman's River meanders through the reserve, allowing for canoe safaris, accompanied by a ranger, and riverboat sundowner cruises. Day-visitor safaris must be booked in advance and include two game drives, a river cruise and lunch (R980). Accommodation comprises six independently owned lodges that make use of the existing farmhouses on the reserve, as well as a camp where there are beds inside restored ox wagons with private bathrooms – all with wonderful views. R4160

Lalibela Game Reserve 90km northeast of Port Elizabeth on the N2 to Grahamstown ☎041 581 8170, ⊛lalibela.co.za; map p.315. An excellent mid-range choice, *Lalibela Game Reserve* is home to the Big Five and a diversity of flora and fauna. Morning and evening safaris are included in the accommodation rate, along with all meals and drinks – you can dine on terrific Eastern Cape food and contemporary cuisine. There are three fabulous lodges with private viewing decks, swimming pools and *bomas* to choose from, and they also offer an African drumming and dancing session. **R6400**

Schotia Game Reserve On the eastern flank of Addo ☎ 042 235 1436, ⊛ schotia.com; map p.315. *Schotia* is the smallest and the busiest of the private reserves, on account of the excellent value it offers. While *Schotia* is not (quite) a Big Five reserve, it is still home to thirteen lions as well as giraffe, rhino, hippo and zebra, and is able to offer a Big Five experience with packages that include excursions to Addo Elephant National Park. **Day visitors** can arrange to be collected from Port Elizabeth or anywhere in the Addo vicinity; if you're driving, you're collected from a secure car park 2km up the N10 from the N2/N10 intersection. Full-day safaris (R1200 per person) involve a game drive through Addo followed by lunch and an evening game drive and dinner at *Schotia*, after which guests are returned to their accommodation. If you're pushed for time or money you can opt for the afternoon game drive (R660 per person). An overnight stay here is the cheapest among the private reserves, comprising a room in one of three bush lodges or eight double rooms, plus game drives into Addo. You pay even less if you don't go into Addo (R1400), but it's really not worth it without the elephants. **R4000**

Shamwari Game Reserve 65km north of Port Elizabeth on the N2 ☎ 042 203 1111, ⊛ shamwari.com; map p.315. The largest and best known of the Eastern Cape's private Big Five reserves, *Shamwari Game Reserve* has cultivated an image as a jetsetter destination, hosting such celebrities as Tiger Woods and John Travolta. It has an unbeatable reputation and in 2010 won the World's Leading Safari and Game Reserve Award at the World Travel Awards (tourism's Oscars) for the thirteenth year running. The accolades are justified in the reserve's diverse landscapes, good numbers of the requisite animals and high standards of game-viewing. Accommodation is in the colonial-style, family-friendly *Long Lee Manor* and five other attractive lodges and tented camps dotted around the reserve and furnished with every conceivable comfort; none is child-friendly. **R8470**

4 Jeffrey's Bay

Some 75km west of Port Elizabeth, off the N2, **JEFFREY'S BAY** (known locally as J Bay) is jammed during the holiday seasons, when thousands of visitors throng the beaches, surfing shops and fast-food outlets, giving the place a really tacky seaside resort feel.

For **surfing aficionados**, however, this is a trifling detail; J Bay is said by some to be one of the world's top three surfing spots. If you've come to surf, head for the break at **Super Tubes**, east of the main bathing beach, which produces an impressive and consistent swirling tube of whitewater, attracting surfers from all over the world throughout the year. Riding inside the vortex of a wave is considered the ultimate experience by surf buffs, but should only be attempted if you're an expert. Other key spots are at Kitchen Windows, Magna Tubes, the Point and Albatross. Surfing gear, including wet suits, can be rented from the multitude of surfing shops along Da Gama Road.

Dolphins regularly surf the waves here, and **whales** can sometimes be seen between June and October. The main **bathing areas** are Main Beach (in town) and Kabeljous-on-Sea (a few kilometres north), with some wonderful seashells to be found between Main and Surfer's Point.

ARRIVAL AND DEPARTURE   JEFFREY'S BAY

By Baz Bus The Baz Bus stops at J Bay on its daily trek in either direction between Cape Town and Port Elizabeth.

INFORMATION

Tourist information In the Shell Museum Complex on the corner of Da Gama and Dromedaris rds (Mon–Fri 8.30am–5pm, Sat 9am–noon; ☎ 042 293 2923, ⊛ www.jeffreysbaytourism.org).

ACCOMMODATION

With lots of hostels to choose from, J Bay is definitely backpacker territory – but there are also numerous good and inexpensive B&Bs and some self-catering places in town. To stay in December, in January or at Easter it's essential to book accommodation in advance. The off-season is very quiet except during the Billabong world-championship surfing competition, usually staged in July, when booking again becomes crucial.

A1 Kynaston 23 & 27 Chestnut Ave ☏ 042 296 1845, ⓦ www.a1kynaston.co.za. A friendly establishment offering rooms in two houses and a self-contained flat, 500m from the beach in a tranquil area, with outstanding views and mega-breakfasts. R570

Island Vibe 10 Dageraad St ☏ 042 293 1625, ⓦ islandvibe.co.za. Backpacker lodge built on a dune, with a wooden walkway onto the beach. Offers camping, dorms and doubles, with spectacular views. There's a lounge, bar, pool table and self-catering facilities. Breakfasts are available. Camping R80, dorm R120, double R420

Jeffrey's Bay Backpackers 12 Jeffrey St ☏ 042 293 1379, ⓦ jeffreysbaybackpackers.co.za. Two blocks away from the beach, this functional establishment has dorms and doubles. Guests can chill out in the bar, lounge and swimming pool. Board rental is available. Dorm R120, double R270

Lazee Bay 25 Mimosa St ☏ 082 657 2780, ⓦ lazeebay .co.za. A light and airy B&B offering good value with panoramic views. An informal place, it has a spacious communal lounge, a kitchen, plus a pool, sun deck and airy African-inspired decor. R400

Super Tubes Guest House 12 Pepper St ☏ 042 293 2957, ⓦ supertubesguesthouse.co.za. A beach house with modest en-suite rooms with old wooden bedsteads, all of which open onto a patio or garden. The Super Tubes beach is practically on the doorstep. R780

EATING

Walskipper Marina Martinique Seafront, Claptons Beach ☏ 042 292 0005. The town's top restaurant is incongruously housed in a weather-beaten wooden shack on the beach in Marina Martinique Harbour. Here you can tuck into lovely home-made bread, pâtés and jams while the main courses – including seafood (R105) – are cooked on an outside fire. Tues–Sun noon–9.30pm.

Alexandria State Forest

Alexandria Hiking Trail reservation • R140 • ☏ 041 468 0916, ✉ anya.vanvuuren@sanparks.org

A 50km tract of Eastern Cape beachfront, and the most deserted section of the coast, is protected by the **Alexandria State Forest**. Part of the **Woody Cape** section of the Addo Elephant National Park, it can be walked on the circular two-day **Alexandria Hiking Trail**, one of South Africa's finest coastal hikes, which winds through indigenous forest and crosses a landscape of great hulking sand dunes to the ocean.

The 35km trail starts at the Woody Cape office, 8km from the R72 (and not served by public transport), where you collect permits. If you're heading east, the signposted turn-off is on the right, just before you reach Alexandria, 86km from Port Elizabeth.

If you are picnicking rather than hiking, you can visit the forest and walk the 7km Tree Dassie Trail from the Woody Cape offices.

Kenton-on-Sea

Some 115km from Port Elizabeth and 56km from Grahamstown, the resort of **KENTON-ON-SEA** lies along two river valleys, perfect for a short beach holiday. A conglomeration of holiday houses served by a few shops and places to eat, Kenton is a good choice if you want to be somewhere undemanding and very beautiful – there's little to do except enjoy the sandy beaches, rocky coves and dunes. While you can swim in the rivers, avoid getting close to the entrance to the sea, as strong **riptides** occur and drowning is a real risk.

> ### PADDLING ABOUT
>
> If you want to spend time on Bushman's River, you can rent **canoes** from Kenton Marina (daily 8am–4pm; ☏ 046 648 1223; R150), well signposted off the R72, 300m up the R343 to Grahamstown. You can paddle 15km upriver on the two- to five-hour **Bushman's River Trail**, on which you pass through countryside lined with cycads and euphorbias, and filled with chattering birdlife.

Tourist information Signposted on the main road (Mon–Fri 9.30am–5pm, Sat 9.30am–1pm; ☏ 046 648 2411, ⓦ kentontourism.co.za). Erica McNulty, who ably runs the tourist office, is the coordinator of various interesting sustainable community projects run by Xhosa women.

ACCOMMODATION

Burke's Nest 38 Van der Stel Rd ☏ 046 648 1894 or ☏ 082 577 2142. A garden cottage and flatlet connected to a family home away from the beach, a short amble from the Kariega River, available with B&B or self-catering. R500

Dunwerkin 5 Park Rd ☏ 046 648 1173, ⓔ dunwerkin @imaginet.co.za. In a fine location, just two minutes' walk from the beach, this is the most upmarket of Kenton's self-catering options and can accommodate either one or two families in a spanking-new four-bedroomed house. R500

★ **Oribi Haven** Kasouga Farm, 9km from Kenton, on a gravel road off the R72 (turn right at the first cattle grid) ☏ 046 648 2043 or ☏ 084 477 1166, ⓦ oribihaven .co.za. Kasouga Farm sits on a hillside overlooking one of the best and least-known beaches in the country. The farm, which has been declared a Natural Heritage Site for its large population of Oribi antelope, has two well-equipped and spacious two-bedroom cottages, which can be taken on a B&B or self-catering basis. Farm game drives can be arranged, as can sundowners on the beach, and there is the use of sandboards for the dunes, or a canoe for the river. R480

Sebumo Tude On an inland farm between Kenton and Port Alfred, off the R72 and 15km from the coast ☏ 072 141 2375, ⓦ sebumotude.co.za. The African dream of a German couple who relish the isolation and beauty of the Eastern Cape bush. The secluded thatched chalets, each with its own deck overlooking treetops, are simply decorated yet luxurious, with magnificent bathrooms and showers outside for some romance under the stars. There's a bush restaurant serving good meals. R1980

Woodlands Country House and Tea Garden 2km from the centre along the R343 to Grahamstown ☏ 046 648 2867, ⓔ woodlands@accommodation-kenton .co.za. Acres of garden and bush leading down to the Bushman's River, with little cottages dotted along pathways cut through the vegetation. R450

EATING AND DRINKING

The Garden Main Rd ☏ 046 648 2239. During the day, you can get cooked breakfasts, teas and light lunches of toasted sandwiches and salads here (R40), though you are in town, and not at the beach. Mon–Fri 7.30am–4pm, Sat 8am–1pm.

Homewoods 1 Eastbourne Rd ☏ 046 648 2700. The best-located eating and drinking place in Kenton is *Homewoods*, a restaurant and pub at the mouth of the Kariega River. It has grand views, but the food is run-of-the-mill burgers, fish and chips, sandwiches and steaks (R70). Tues–Fri 11am–3pm & 6–9pm, Sat 10am–4pm & 6pm till late, Sun 9am–4pm.

Port Alfred

Of all the settlements between Port Elizabeth and East London – a largely undeveloped stretch of coast with huge dunes and exhilarating surf – only **PORT ALFRED**, midway between the two, can make any claims to a town life outside the holiday season, when for a few weeks the small centre is transformed into a hectic bustle. Like many other places along the coast, it is developing apace, with housing developments sprouting along its once lonely beaches. Besides beach walking and swimming, it's an excellent place to do some **canoeing**, **diving**, waterskiing, abseiling, deep-sea fishing and horseriding.

Nicknamed "Kowie" by locals, after the river, Port Alfred was named in honour of the second son of Queen Victoria, although he never actually made it here, since he chose to do an elephant hunt instead. Port Alfred's attractions are firmly rooted in its beaches and the Kowie River; the town itself has little else to offer. The rather expensive but obvious landmark *Halyards Hotel* and *Spur* restaurant constitute the town's ersatz caged-in waterfront; far more authentic, the river frontage on Wharf Street, next to the old bridge, has been revamped and the row of Victorian buildings spruced up, with the **Harbour Master and Brewery** offering its own home brew.

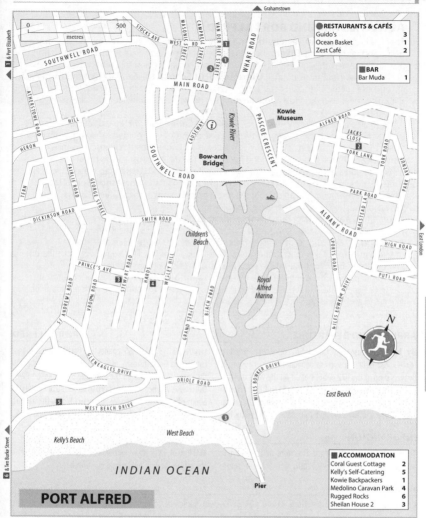

RESTAURANTS & CAFÉS
Guido's	3
Ocean Basket	1
Zest Café	2

BAR
Bar Muda	1

ACCOMMODATION
Coral Guest Cottage	2
Kelly's Self-Catering	5
Kowie Backpackers	1
Medolino Caravan Park	4
Rugged Rocks	6
Sheilan House 2	3

PORT ALFRED

The beaches

West Beach, where the river is sucked out to sea and the breakers pound in, makes a good start to exploring Port Alfred. From the café and stone pier you can watch the surfers and see fishing boats make dramatic entries into the river from the open ocean. Fifteen minutes' walk west along the beach lies **Kelly's Beach**, by far the most popular stretch, where you can swim safely in a gentle bay. **East Beach**, reached from the signposted road next to *Halyards Hotel*, is the nicest beach for walking, with a backdrop of hilly dunes popular for sandboarding, stretching to the horizon. For toddlers, the safest and most popular spot is **Children's Beach**, a stretch of sand close to the town centre along a shallow section of river, reached from Beach Road, a few hundred metres from the arched bridge.

ACTIVITIES AROUND PORT ALFRED

There's a host of **adventure activities** in Port Alfred, the best being canoeing, horseriding, diving and sandboarding. **Divers** shouldn't expect to see crystal waters and fluorescent fish around Port Alfred, though the slightly murky water contains colourful underwater denizens. The town is home to the reputable **Outdoor Focus School** (☏ 046 624 4432, ⓦ outdoorfocus .co.za), based at the Outdoor Focus Centre, next to the Kiddy's Beach, Beach Road, on the West Bank. They offer courses in just about anything to do with the sea, including scuba diving and skippering.

Outdoor Focus also takes bookings for the **Kowie Canoe Trail**, a 21km paddle up the Kowie River, a much-sought-after overnight trip and one of the few self-guided canoeing and hiking trails in South Africa. Much of its charm is the colourful birdlife, and the landscape – hills of dense, dry bush that slope down to the river. While the trip is almost always full at weekends, it's easy to find a place on weekdays out of school holidays, and is extremely reasonable at R150 per person. On the trip, you **stay overnight** in a hut in the **Horseshoe Bend Nature Reserve**, from where you can explore the forest on foot, and climb the steep escarpment to get an impressive view over the horseshoe.

Port Alfred is also great for beach **horseriding**. Book through Outdoor Focus, or sign up for the Three Sisters horse trail (signposted 14km east of Port Alfred off the R72 towards East London; ☏ 082 645 6345, ⓦ threesistershorsetrails.co.za; R300), which has access to one of the loveliest stretches of the coast in the region, and is recommended for beginners and children. There's also an overnight trail where you sleep in a treehouse (from R800).

Port Alfred's big sand dunes lend themselves to **sandboarding** – you can rent boards at Outdoor Focus, who also run some other activities especially **for children**, such as Kids' Scuba, kite flying and canoeing.

4

ARRIVAL AND DEPARTURE   PORT ALFRED

By bus The reasonably priced SA Connection minibus (☏ 043 722 0284, ⓦ www.saconnection.co.za) calls in at Beavers shop at the R72 petrol station on the west bank of town, on its way between Port Elizabeth and East London (Tues, Fri & Sun), and between Cape Town and East London (Tues & Fri). On Tuesdays and Thursdays, the Minilux bus

service (☏ 043 741 3107), connecting Port Elizabeth to East London via Grahamstown, pulls into the *Halyards Hotel*, off the main coastal road on the east side of the Kowie River. Otherwise, Wayne's Transport (☏ 046 624 2358 or ☏ 084 644 6060) offers a shuttle service from Port Elizabeth's airport, with times and drop-offs to suit passengers when you book.

INFORMATION

Tourist information On the riverfront at the Main St bridge (Mon–Fri 8.30am–4.30pm, Sat 8.30am–noon;

☏ 046 624 1235, ⓦ www.portalfred.co.za). Also home to the offices for Avis and Budget car rental.

ACCOMMODATION

Coral Guest Cottage Jack's Close ☏ 046 624 2849, ⓦ coralcottages.co.za; map p.321. A reasonably priced B&B on one of the East Bank hills, a 20min walk from East Beach. Comfortable rooms with bath in a restored corrugated-iron settler cottage, though the walls are not at all soundproof. Expect to be pampered by the ebullient owner. R600

Kelly's West Beach Drive, opposite Kelly's Beach ☏ 082 657 0345, ⓦ kellys.co.za; map p.321. As close to the main swimming beach as you could possibly be, these neat and clean self-catering apartments in a large face-brick house are good value. R480

Kowie Backpackers 13 Van Riebeeck St, off the R72, close to Beavers bus stop ☏ 046 624 3583/071 266 8899; map p.321. Comfortable, clean, affordable and friendly accommodation in a modern suburban house, with

a garden for camping. Convenient if you are travelling through, but a 20min walk from the beach. Camping R60, dorm R100, double R250

Medolino Caravan Park Prince's Ave, Kowie West ☏ 046 624 1651, ⓦ medolino.caravanparks.com; map p.321. A very efficiently run place in shady grounds behind the dunes, a 10min walk from Kelly's Beach. Good camping facilities, excellent wooden self-catering chalets and a swimming pool. Camping R100, chalet R550

Rugged Rocks Salt Vlei, 4km from the town centre ☏ 046 624 3112 or ☏ 082 781 4682, ⓦ rugged rocksbeachcottages.co.za; map p.321. A beachside property in sizeable grounds, offering fully equipped self-catering cottages, the older ones cheaper and tucked away in the coastal bush, the pricier, newer ones atop dunes with glorious views. R475

Sheilan House 27 Prince's Ave ☎046 624 4076 or ☎082 894 1851, ⓦsheilanhouse.co.za; map p.321. A well-run and friendly guesthouse, with four en-suite

bedrooms. Evening meals available on request, and the owners are happy to organize a multitude of activities. **R920**

EATING AND DRINKING

Bar Muda 25 Van der Riet St ☎046 624 8659. Over two hundred cocktails at a lovely riverside setting, where you can sit indoors or out, and eat seafood, steaks or schnitzels (R90). Daily 10am–9pm.

Guido's On the beach ☎046 624 5264. The only place right on the beach, though the pizzas and pasta dishes (R80) play second fiddle to the sundowners served on the deck. Daily 11am–9pm.

Ocean Basket In Port Frances House on Van der Riet St

☎046 624 1727. For fish and chips (R60), as well as sushi and a river view, head for *Ocean Basket* where the service is prompt and the food spot-on. Daily 11.30am–8.30pm.

★ **Zest Café** 48 Van der Riet St, The Courtyard ☎046 624 5783. Delicious, modern and imaginative lunches (R45) and coffee outdoors, from a kitchen in a wooden canteen that once stood at Grahamstown's railway station. Mon–Fri 8am–5pm, Sat 8am–3pm.

Grahamstown

Just over 50km inland from Port Alfred, **GRAHAMSTOWN** projects an image of a cultured, historic town, quintessentially English, Protestant and refined, with reminders of its colonial past in evidence in the well-preserved architecture.

Dominated by its cathedral, university and public schools, this is a thoroughly pleasant place to wander through, with well-maintained colonial **Georgian** and **Victorian buildings** lining the streets, and pretty suburban gardens. Every July, the town hosts an **arts festival**, the largest of its kind in Africa, and purportedly the second largest in the world (after Edinburgh; see box, p.326).

As elsewhere in South Africa, there are reminders of conquest and dispossession. Climb up Gunfire Hill, where the fortress-like 1820 **Settlers Monument** celebrates the achievement of South Africa's English-speaking immigrants, and you'll be able to see Makanaskop, the hill from which the **Xhosa** made their last stand against the British invaders. Their descendants live in desperately poor ghettos here, in a town almost devoid of industry.

Despite all this, and the constant reminders of poverty, Grahamstown makes a good stopover, and is the perfect base for excursions: a number of **historic villages** are within easy reach, some **game parks** are convenient for a day or weekend visit and, best of all, kilometres of **coast** are just 45 minutes' drive away.

Brief history

Grahamstown's sedate prettiness belies its beginnings as a **military outpost** in 1811. **Colonel Graham** made his – and the town's – name here, driving the Xhosa out of the Zuurveld, an area between the Bushman's and Fish rivers. The Fish River, 60km east of Grahamstown, marked the eastern boundary of the frontier, with Grahamstown as the capital. The ruthless expulsion of the Xhosa sparked off a series of nineteenth-century **Frontier Wars**.

The British decided to reinforce the frontier with a human barrier. With the promise of free land, they lured the dispossessed from a depressed Britain to occupy the lands west of the Fish River. In the migration mythology of English-speaking whites, these much-celebrated **1820 Settlers** came to take on a larger-than-life status as ancestors to whom many trace back their origins. However, far from discovering the hoped-for paradise, the

---

AFRICAN INSTRUMENTS

Reasonably priced *kalimbas*, handmade using high-quality timber, and many other instruments can be bought from African Musical Instruments on the corner of Cloncourt and Jarvis streets (☎046 622 6252 or ☎083 404 4567, ⓦwww.kalimba.co.za), *the* place in South Africa to buy an authentic instrument.

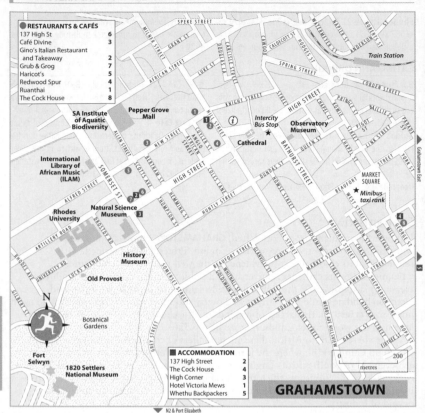

ill-equipped settlers found themselves in a nightmare. The plots given to them were subject to drought, flood and disease, and the threat of Xhosa attack was never far away.

Not surprisingly, many settlers abandoned their lands and headed to Grahamstown in the early 1820s. This brought prosperity and growth to the town, which enjoyed a boom in the 1840s, when it developed into the emporium of the frontier.

High Street and Rhodes University

High Street is Grahamstown's major shopping axis, with terraces of nineteenth-century buildings lending it a graceful air. Running from the station at its seedier east end, High Street continues past the cathedral at the junction of Hill Street, terminating at the 150-year-old Drostdy Arch, the whitewashed entrance gate to prestigious Rhodes University, named after Cecil John Rhodes (see box, p.271). Hawkers on the pavements sell small bags of fruit and vegetables. At the centre of the street is the **Cathedral of St Michael and St George**, opened in 1830. While High Street has most of the shops you'd need, many businesses have relocated, or opened up in the **Pepper Grove Mall**, five minutes' walk north of High Street, with entrances in African and Allen streets.

Natural Science Museum

Somerset St • Tues–Fri 9.30am–1pm & 2–5pm, Sat 9.30am–1pm • R10

If you've time for only one of the museums, head for the **Natural Science Museum**, just south of the university entrance. The display of Eastern Cape fauna and flora from 250 million years ago is excellent, with intriguing plant fossils and the bones of dinosaurs that once roamed these parts. The **History Museum** next door houses a dusty collection of 1820 settler memorabilia, nineteenth-century paintings and antique firearms, as well as Xhosa beadwork and traditional dress.

ILAM

Corner of Somerset and Prince Alfred sts • Mon–Fri 8.30am–12.45pm & 2.15–4.45pm • Free • ☎ 046 603 8557, ⓦ www.ilam.ru.ac.za

Beyond the Drostdy Arch, tucked behind some buildings, is **ILAM**, the International Library of African Music. The library is an absolute treasure trove of recordings of **traditional African music** from Southern Africa, as well as Zaire, Rwanda, Uganda and Tanzania.

SA Institute of Aquatic Biodiversity

Somerset St • Mon–Fri 8.30am–1pm & 2–5pm • Free • ⓦ www.saiab.ru.ac.za

The **SA Institute of Aquatic Biodiversity** was originally named after J.L.B. Smith, the Rhodes University scientist who shot to fame in 1939 after identifying the coelacanth, a "missing link" fish, caught off the East London coast and thought to have become extinct fifty million years ago. In the foyer are two huge stuffed specimens, with fins that look like budding arms and legs. The museum is worthwhile just to see the coelacanths.

Observatory Museum

Bathurst St • Mon–Fri 9am–1pm & 2–5pm; Sat 9.30am–1pm • Donation

The Observatory Museum is set in a restored building that was once the home and shop of a notable watchmaker and jeweller during the mid-1850s. The thing to see is the rooftop Victorian **camera obscura**, which projects magnified images of the streets below onto a wall. It's best seen on a clear day, when the reflections are crisp and clear.

ARRIVAL AND DEPARTURE   GRAHAMSTOWN

By bus Grahamstown is on the N2, 127km inland from Port Elizabeth, and is roughly twelve hours by bus from Cape Town, Johannesburg and Durban. Translux, Intercape and Greyhound buses stop outside the *Frontier Country Hotel* on the corner of Bathurst and High sts. East London and Port Elizabeth are connected to Grahamstown by the Minilux minibus, which also connects with the airport at Port Elizabeth; on Monday and Thursday, the minibus continues to Port Alfred, and to East London on Monday, Tuesday, Thursday and Friday. It stops at Settler City Motors in Beaufort St. Book through Go Travel in Peppergrove Mall, African St (☎ 046 622 2235). Intercity coaches can be booked through the tourist office (see below).

GETTING AROUND

Grahamstown is easily covered on foot, but if you want a **taxi**, use the reliable Roadtrip Shuttles (☎ 082 925 5971).

INFORMATION

Tourist information High St, next to City Hall (Mon–Fri 8.30am–5pm, Sat 9am–1pm; ☎ 046 622 3241, ⓦ www .grahamstown.co.za).

TOWNSHIP TOURS AND HOMESTAYS

Township tours are recommended with guide Mbuleli Mpokela (☎ 082 979 5906) who will take you in your own car around the township. Tours usually take three hours and include a Xhosa lunch at the Umthathi self-help project, which teaches people skills such as vegetable growing. You can also be taken to an arts and crafts project Egazini Outreach Project (ⓦ www .grahamstown.co.za/egazini.htm) in Joza township.

The town also provides the ideal opportunity for a **township homestay** without having to traipse far – the townships are less than ten minutes' drive from the centre. The tourism office has a list of fifteen houses (B&B R600) and can place you with a hospitable Xhosa family in Grahamstown East. Thabisa Xonxa (☎ 083 245 0496) offers a similar service (B&B R360). The rooms are mostly en suite, in brick houses with secure off-street parking.

4

THE GRAHAMSTOWN FESTIVAL

For ten days every July, Grahamstown bursts to overflowing as the town's population doubles, with visitors descending for the annual National Arts Festival – usually called the **Grahamstown Festival**. At this time, seemingly every home is transformed into a B&B and the streets are alive with colourful food stalls. Church halls, parks and sports fields become flea markets and several hundred shows are staged, spanning every conceivable type of performance.

This is the largest arts festival in Africa, and even has its own fringe festival. The hub of the event is the 1820 Settlers Monument, which hosts not only big drama, dance and operatic productions in its theatres, but also art exhibitions and free early-evening concerts. While work by African performers and artists is well represented, and is perhaps the more interesting aspect of the festival for tourists, the festival-goers and performers are still predominantly white.

The published **programme** – spanning jazz, classical music, drama, dance, cabaret, opera, visual arts, crafts, films and a book fair – is bulky, but absolutely essential; it's worth planning your time carefully to avoid walking the potentially cold July streets without seeing much of the festival proper. If you don't feel like taking in a show, the free art exhibitions at the museums, Monument and other smaller venues are always worth a look. For more **information and bookings**, contact the Grahamstown Foundation (☎ 046 622 3082, ⓦ www.nafest.co.za).

ACCOMMODATION

The most notable and choicest places to stay in Grahamstown are in historic houses, and there's a good selection of hotels. The only time you may have difficulty finding accommodation is during the festival in July, for when you'd be well advised to book as early as March. Several agencies specialize in finding accommodation during this period but the tourism office should be your first port of call.

137 High Street 137 High St ☎ 046 622 3242, ⓦ 137highstreet.co.za; map p.324. Reasonably priced rooms in a fabulously central location, above and behind a restaurant, in a house dating back to 1820. R750

The Cock House 10 Market St ☎ 046 636 1295, ⓦ cockhouse.co.za; map p.324. Plush rooms in a beautiful Victorian house with a top reputation for fine food, though not in the best location, being well away from the university and centre. R940

High Corner 122 High St ☎ 046 622 8284, ⓦ highcorner.co.za; map p.324. A beautiful historical home in a great location across the road from the university,

with six rooms furnished with Cape antiques and original art. R770

Whethu Backpackers 6 George St, on R67 to Port Alfred ☎ 046 636 1001, ⓦ whethu.com; map p.324. A spacious house with a garden and great views over the valley, and a 20min walk to the centre or university. Free internet, bicycles for hire, and evening meals available, often featuring local venison. Dorms sleep six or eight, and there are doubles and a family room. You can book trips there through Smileyface Tours (☎ 083 982 5966) to Addo Elephant National Park and the Fish River, or *shebeen* crawls and township tours. Camping R65, dorm R120, double R380

EATING

137 High St 137 High St ☎ 046 622 3242; map p.324. A favourite meeting place for students and academics for good coffee, sandwiches and great cheesecake (R70). Mon–Fri 7.30am–9.30pm, Sat 8am–2pm & 5–9.30pm, Sun 8am–2pm.

The Cock House Corner of Market and George sts ☎ 046 636 1295/87; map p.324. Grahamstown's best restaurant, serving country cuisine; its speciality is braised and marinated local lamb shank (R100). Daily 7–9pm, Tues–Sat also 7.30–9.30am & 12.30–2.30pm.

★ **Haricot's** 32 New St ☎ 046 622 2150; map p.324. French, European and Mediterranean food in a tranquil, secluded spot, which has contemporary decor and a central location. Great muesli and croissant breakfasts (R75). Mon–Sat 9am–9.30pm.

★ **Ruanthai** 7 New St ☎ 046 622 6788 or ☎ 072 701 6937; map p.324. A tiny restaurant with authentic family recipes, serving Thai and Asian food (R60) – a total novelty in the Eastern Cape. Wed and Fri are buffet evenings. Bring your own wine. Tues–Sat noon–2.30pm & 5–10pm.

ENTERTAINMENT

Despite being the home of the country's premier arts festival (see box above), and dominated by Rhodes University, Grahamstown's nightlife and entertainment scene is far less exciting than you might expect. Outside the hectic festival fortnight in July, the town relies on the **cinema** at the Pepper Grove Mall to deliver its only regular evening entertainment.

The two main venues for **live performances** are the Monument Theatre and the Rhodes University Theatre, where the Drama Department puts on productions from time to time. Look out for anything staged by Ubom First Physical Theatre Company, founded by Gary Gordon and Andrew Buckland, a local actor with an international reputation in physical theatre. To find out what's on, check the flyposters down High Street and also look in *Grocott's Mail*, the local rag, which comes out on Tuesday and Friday afternoons.

Bathurst

A significant centre in the nineteenth century, **BATHURST**, 45km south of Grahamstown, is today little more than a picturesque straggle of smallholdings, gardens and craft shops, anchored firmly around the Victorian landmark of the Pig and Whistle pub, an essential port of call.

ARRIVAL AND INFORMATION   BATHURST

By bus The twice-weekly Minilux bus between Grahamstown and Port Alfred stops at the *Pig and Whistle* (see p.328).

INFORMATION

Tourist information The *Pig and Whistle* (see p.328) provides maps and directions to historical sites.

EASTERN CAPE GAME RESERVES

The Eastern Cape is fast developing as a region for game viewing. Besides Addo Elephant National Park (p.314) and the private game reserves around Port Elizabeth, new game farms are opening all the time, many of them close to Grahamstown, or between Grahamstown and the coast. Several offer day-trips as well as overnight excursions. What follows is a selective list.

Great Fish River Reserve Complex On the R67, 34km north of Grahamstown; office daily 8am–4.30pm; day visitors R20 ☎ 043 701 9600, ⓦ ecparksboard.co.za. This is an amalgamation of three separate reserves covering 430 square kilometres situated along the banks of the Fish and Kat rivers. The catch is that although there is plenty of game, it is difficult to see, so if you want to tick off the Big Five, this reserve is not for you. In the southwestern section, closest to Grahamstown, there's accommodation in chalets for up to four people at *Mvubu*. R730

★ **Kwandwe Private Game Reserve** On the R67, 34km north of Grahamstown and 160km from Port Elizabeth ☎ 011 809 4300, ⓦ kwandwereserve .com; map p.315. This is the Eastern Cape's top wildlife destination, with 30km of Fish River frontage and the Big Five in attendance. Apart from twice-a-day game drives, *Kwandwe*'s safari activities include guided river walks, canoeing on the Great Fish, and rhino tracking, in which you follow one of the large mammals on foot. It also runs cultural tours with a resident historian who looks at the fascinating social and archeological past of the area. Some special activities are laid on for children, including family game drives, short bush walks and frog safaris. There are four lodges, ranging from a quintessential luxury lodge with nine suites and

thatched roofs, wooden walkways and French windows that afford panoramic views, to a funky boutique-hotel-in-the-bush ingeniously designed with glass walls that allow you to lie on your bed and feel you're totally alone in the middle of the wilderness. Others are for the exclusive use of single parties. R7800

Pumba Private Game Reserve 22km west of Grahamstown off the N2 ☎ 046 603 2000, ⓦ pumbagamereserve.co.za. A good bet if you want to see lions. The 7am game drive includes breakfast at the camp, while the 4pm game drive includes dinner, both at R960 per person. Drives are on a ten-seater Land-Rover, with no children under 8 permitted. The full safari experience includes luxury accommodation, meals, drives and drinks. R10, 680

Sibuya Game Reserve Access only by boat ☎ 046 648 1040, ⓦ sibuya.co.za. At the cheaper end of the spectrum, as it doesn't have lions, though you can still see zebra, giraffe, buffalo and rhinos on its recommended day tours which collect guests by boat from Kenton-on-Sea for a meander up the Kariega River, with a game excursion and picnic or braai (R795, or R445 without game excursion). If you stay overnight – and the rooms are comfortable–the rate includes all meals and game activities, as well as canoeing and walking. R4990

4

ACCOMMODATION

Palamino Cottage 387 Prince Phillip Rd ☎072 297 3060, ⓦpalamino.co.za. Nice and private, *Palamino Cottage* is a prettily furnished cottage on a rural smallholding, sleeping three, with a rooftop deck, braai facilities, horses to pat and the village common to walk around. **R580**

Pig and Whistle On the R67 as you drive into town ☎046 625 0673, ⓦpigandwhistle.co.za. A colonial Victorian village inn; the old rooms upstairs, furnished with period pieces, are best, and you can sit on the veranda with a beer, watching the world go by. It's a good place to meet locals. **R350**

EATING AND DRINKING

Pickwick's Pizza Corner of York & Trappes sts ☎046 625 0350. A cosy café-restaurant offering pasta, salads and pizza cooked in a wood oven (R50), and coffee and cake. There's a garden for summer meals and a fireplace for winter. Tues–Sun 9am–9pm.

Pig and Whistle On the R67 ☎046 625 0673 The *Pig and Whistle* pub is the place to down beers, while the restaurant offers traditional pub food, including breakfast, and Sunday roasts (R80). Daily 8am–9pm.

The Eastern Cape Karoo

Travelling between Grahamstown and the towns of Cradock and Graaff-Reinet (the Eastern Cape's two most-visited Karoo towns), you'll be heading into **sheep-farming country**, with the occasional *dorp* rising against the horizon, offering the experience of an archetypal Eastern Cape one-horse outpost. The roads through this vast emptiness are quiet, and lined with rhythmically spaced telephone poles. Dun-coloured sheep, angora goats and the occasional springbok graze on brown stubble, and you'll often see groups of charcoal-and-grey ostriches in the veld. Staying on a farm in this region is a highlight (see p.324).

Cradock, 240km north of Port Elizabeth, lies in the **Karoo** proper, and makes a great stopover on the Port Elizabeth to Johannesburg run, because of its excellent accommodation and its proximity to the beautiful **Mountain Zebra National Park**. Some 100km due west of Cradock, **Graaff-Reinet** is one of the oldest towns in South Africa, and much of its historical centre is intact. Surrounding the town is the **Camdeboo National Park**. For more of a sense of the Karoo's dry timelessness, head to **Nieu Bethesda**, 50km to the north of town.

ACCOMMODATION   THE EASTERN CAPE KAROO

★ **Cavers Country Guest House** Just outside of Bedford, an hour north of Grahamstown ☎046 685 0619, ⓦwww.cavers.co.za. One of the best farms to stay on in the region, this is a grand 1850 refurbished two-storey stone manor house with beautiful gardens on a working farm with a mountainous backdrop. The friendly owners cook delicious dinners. **R500**

Cradock

The silvery windmills on the surrounding sheep farms of **CRADOCK** have become an unofficial symbol of the town; as you enter town, Xhosa hawkers sell intricately crafted wire model windmills. The town itself has some handsome colonial architecture, with the main street dominated by the 1868 **Dutch Reformed Church**, based on London's St Martin-in-the-Fields.

But poverty has overshadowed Cradock since the Frontier Wars of the nineteenth century and the subjugation of the Xhosa people. Against this history of conquest the town has provided fertile grounds for **resistance**: ANC members in the vicinity almost single-handedly kept the organization alive during the 1930s. In 1985, Cradock hit the headlines when anti-apartheid activist **Matthew Goniwe** (his widow is the current mayor of Cradock) and three colleagues were murdered. It was only in 1997, during the **Truth and Reconciliation Commission** hearings, that five Port Elizabeth security policemen were named as the perpetrators.

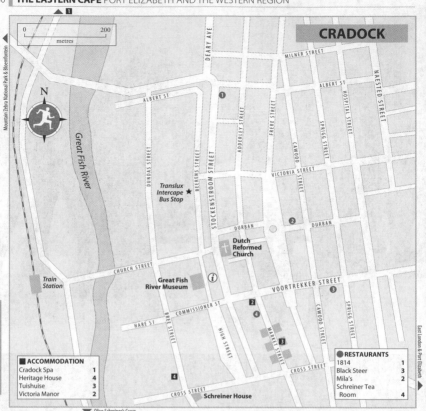

Schreiner House & Nursery

9 Cross St • Mon–Fri 8am–1pm & 2–4.30pm, weekends by appointment • Donation • ☎ 078 538 0555

Political controversy is the theme at Cradock's biggest attraction, **Schreiner House**. The house is dedicated to the life of the writer Olive Schreiner, best known for her ground-breaking novel *The Story of an African Farm* (1883), made into a film in 2004. It was remarkable enough for a woman from the conservative backwoods of nineteenth-century Eastern Cape to write a novel, but even more amazing that she espoused ideas considered dangerously radical even a century later, including universal franchise for men and women irrespective of race. Schreiner died in 1921 and is buried near Cradock on the Buffelskop Peak, with her one-day-old daughter and favourite dog. Her **burial site** has become something of a place of pilgrimage, and details of how to get there are available from Schreiner House. At the house there is also an interesting exhibition on Cradock's famous literary son, Guy Butler.

ARRIVAL AND DEPARTURE   CRADOCK

By bus Translux and Intercape buses from Port Elixabeth and Johannesburg pull in daily at Shoprite Checkers on Voortrekker St, where you can buy tickets and get information for onward travel.

By train Cradock is a daily stop on the Port Elizabeth–Johannesburg rail line; the station is on the west bank of the Great Fish River.

INFORMATION

Tourist information Stockenstroom St (Mon–Fri 8.30am–12.30pm & 2–4.30pm; ☎048 881 2383, Ⓦcradocktourism.co.za).

ACCOMMODATION

For a small town, Cradock offers some delightful accommodation; if you want to taste some Karoo country style, the *Tuishuise* is especially recommended.

Cradock Spa 4.5km north of town on the road to the signposted Mountain Zebra National Park ☎048 881 2709; map p.330. The best bet for budget accommodation, with self-catering, fully equipped chalets sleeping two to four, and a naturally warm, indoor swimming pool (though it's not quite warm enough in winter). R470

Heritage House 45 Bree St ☎048 881 5251 or 3210; map p.330. Set in a large tranquil garden, this Karoo-style Victorian homestead offers the weary traveller a welcome respite in peaceful surroundings. Each of the seven double en-suite bedrooms has a private entrance from the garden. R790

Tuishuise Market St ☎048 881 1322, Ⓦtuishuise .co.za; map p.330. Staying in this street of comfortable and very stylish one- to four-bedroomed Victorian houses gives an authentic sense of colonial domestic life over a century ago. Prices are very reasonable, given that you get what amounts to a mini-museum to yourself, each house kitted out with antique furniture and crockery. R880

Victoria Manor 36 Market St ☎048 881 1650, Ⓦtuishuise.co.za; map p.330. Effortlessly gracious, old-fashioned hotel with excellent service, bags of character and period fittings. The rooms are en suite, dining is off silverware and the breakfasts are among the best in the country. R650

EATING

Mila's 27 Durban St ☎048 881 0036; map p.330. A cosy, homely open-kitchen restaurant serving pizza, pasta, steaks and grills (R60). Local meat is always the thing to go for – Karoo lamb is free range and organic here. Bring your own wine. Mon–Sat 4–9pm.

Schreiner Tea Room Market St ☎072 381 3422; map p.330. The nicest place for tea, sandwiches and hot lunches of traditional *roostekoek* (bread grilled on an open fire) with various fillings, plus soups, pies and salads (R45). Mon–Sat 9.30am–5pm.

Mountain Zebra National Park

26km west of Cradock • Daily: May–Sept 7am–6pm; Oct–April 7am–7pm • R25 • ☎048 881 2427, Ⓦsanparks.org/parks/mountain_zebra

When the **Mountain Zebra National Park** was created in 1937, there were only five Cape **mountain zebras** left on its 65 square kilometres – and four were male. Miraculously, conservationists managed to cobble together a breeding herd from the few survivors on surrounding farms, and the park now supports several hundred.

For **game viewing**, the park has a couple of good part-tar, part-gravel loop roads forming a rough figure of eight. As well as zebra, keep an eye out for **springbok**, **blesbok** and **black wildebeest**. The introduction of **buffalo** in 1998 and plans to bring in cheetahs and rhinos add to the wildlife interest, but mean that hiking across the park isn't possible, since buffalo have a reputation for extreme aggression. There are, however, two **waymarked walks** near the camp.

ARRIVAL AND DEPARTURE   MOUNTAIN ZEBRA NATIONAL PARK

By car To reach the park, head north out of Cradock on the N10, turning west after about 6km onto the Graaff-Reinet Rd. After a further 5km, you turn left at the National Park

sign onto a good gravel road, which reaches the park gate after a further 16km.

INFORMATION

Services A small shop at reception sells basics, souvenirs, alcohol and soft drinks, but if you're staying for a few days you should stock up in Cradock. There's a reasonable

licensed à la carte restaurant (daily 7.30am–9pm), a post office, a filling station and a lovely swimming pool.

4

ACCOMMODATION

Park accommodation ☎ 048 881 2427, ⊕ sanparks .org/parks/mountain_zebra. There are three accommodation options in the park, either in two-bedroom cottages, all of which have outstanding mountain views and their own kitchens and bathrooms (R680), lovely camp sites (R155), and, ideal if there's a group of you, *Doornhoek,* a beautifully restored Victorian homestead for self-catering, set in splendid isolation, with great Karoo views across a small lake to the surrounding chain of scrubby hills. Extremely comfortable, it has three en-suite double rooms furnished with antiques, and is the unrivalled highlight of the park's lodgings. Camping R155, cottage R680, *Doornhoek* R1800

Graaff-Reinet

It's little wonder that tour buses pull in to **GRAAFF-REINET** in their numbers; this is a beautiful town and one of the few places in the Eastern Cape where you'd want to wander freely day and night, taking in historical buildings and the occasional little museum, and having a meal or a drink before strolling back to your accommodation.

Graaff-Reinet has a large population of Afrikaans-speaking coloured people, mostly living on the south side of town, some of slave origin, others the descendants of indigenous Khoi and San who were forced to work on frontier farms. The dry mountains surrounding the town are part of the **Camdeboo National Park** whose main attraction is the **Valley of Desolation**, a B-movie name for an impressive site. The rocky canyon, echoing bird calls and expansive skies of the valley shouldn't be missed.

Brief history

By the late eighteenth century, Dutch burghers had extended the Cape frontier northwards into the Sneeuwberg Mountains, traditionally the stomping ground of Khoi pastoralists and San hunter-gatherers. Little more than brigands, the settlers raided Khoi cattle and attacked groups of San, killing the men and abducting women and children to use as farm and domestic labourers. Friction escalated when the Khoi and San retaliated and, in 1786, the Cape authorities sent out a *landdrost* (magistrate) to **establish Graaff-Reinet**, administer the surrounding area and pacify the frontier.

Colonial control over the district was slowly consolidated, with vast tracts turned over to grazing sheep. The **wool boom** of the 1850s brought prosperity to the town and established a pattern of farming and land ownership which continues to this day.

The Dutch Reformed Church

Church St

Graaff-Reinet centres around the imposing 1886 **Dutch Reformed Church**, with its pointy steeple and cake-icing decoration. On either side of **Church Street**, the main

---

ROBERT SOBUKWE AND THE AFRICANISTS

One of Graaff-Reinet's most brilliant but often-forgotten sons is **Robert Managaliso Sobukwe**, founder of the Pan Africanist Congress (PAC). Born in 1923, Sobukwe went to Healdtown, a boarding school, then Fort Hare University (see p.341), where he joined the African National Congress Youth League. After graduating in 1947, he became a schoolteacher and then a lecturer at the University of the Witwatersrand. A charismatic member of the Africanist wing of the ANC – even the ultra-apartheid prime minister B.J. Vorster acknowledged him as "a man of magnetic personality" – Sobukwe questioned the organization's strategy of cooperating with whites, and formed the breakaway PAC in 1959. The following year he launched the nationwide **anti-pass protests**, which ended in the Sharpeville massacre and his imprisonment on Robben Island for nine years. In 1969, Sobukwe was released under a banning order to Kimberley, where he died in 1978. Five thousand people attended his funeral in Graaff-Reinet.

You can visit the Sobukwe home and grave on a **township tour** with Xolile Speelman (☎ 082 844 2897), who also accompanies people to traditional events, with music and the chance to meet members of Graaff-Reinet's African community.

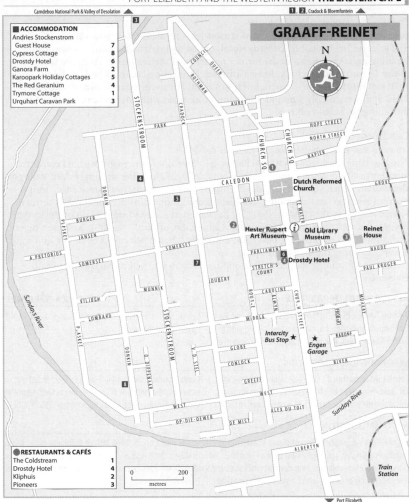

GRAAFF-REINET

ACCOMMODATION

Andries Stockenstrom Guest House	7
Cypress Cottage	8
Drostdy Hotel	6
Ganora Farm	2
Karoopark Holiday Cottages	5
The Red Geranium	4
Trymore Cottage	1
Urquhart Caravan Park	3

RESTAURANTS & CAFÉS

The Coldstream	1
Drostdy Hotel	4
Kliphuis	2
Pioneers	3

thoroughfare, little roads fan out, lined with whitewashed Cape Dutch, Georgian and Victorian buildings.

Old Library Museum

Church St • Mon–Fri 8am–12.30pm & 2–5pm, Sat 9am–3pm, Sun 9am–noon & 2–4pm • R10

The only, but spectacular, attraction at the **Old Library Museum**, one block south of the church, is the compelling collection of **fossil skulls** and skeletons of reptiles that populated the prehistoric Karoo, some 230 million years ago.

Hester Rupert Art Museum

Church St • Mon–Fri 9am–12.30pm & 2–5pm, Sat 9am–3pm, Sun 9am–noon • R10

The **Hester Rupert Art Museum**, in a restored 1821 mission church, features a representative selection of work by South African artists (primarily white) active in the mid-1960s. Much of it is dreary and derivative of European art, but a few pieces stand out.

The Drostdy Hotel and Reinet House

Drostdy Hotel, 30 Church St • Reinet House Mon–Fri 8am–12.30pm & 2–5pm, Sat 9am–3pm, Sun 9am–4pm • R10

The graceful, whitewashed **Drostdy Hotel**, opposite the Art Museum, is a historical building in its own right, as the former residence of the *landdrost*. From the front steps of the *Drostdy*, you can look down Parsonage Street, lined with Cape Dutch buildings, to **Reinet House**, Graaff-Reinet's finest museum. Formerly a parsonage, it was built in 1812 and is essentially a period house museum, filled with covetable furniture and intriguing household objects.

Camdeboo National Park

5km north of Graaff-Reinet, off the Marraysburg Rd • Daily dawn–dusk • R60

The low-lying **Camdeboo National Park** totally surrounds the town, with its entrance 5km north of the town centre. Its indisputable highlight is the strikingly deep **Valley of Desolation**, which you can gaze down into by driving the narrow tarred road from the reserve's entrance and ascending the bush-flecked mountainside; you'll pass a series of viewpoints up to the cliffs overlooking the valley. The views from the lip of the canyon, beyond the rocks and into the plains of Camdeboo, are truly thrilling, and even better if you tune into the echoing bird calls, especially when black eagles circle the dolomite towers, scanning the crevices for prey.

There's a 45-minute looped **walk** along the canyon lip, well marked with a lizard emblem.

ARRIVAL AND DEPARTURE
GRAAFF-REINET

By bus Translux buses between Johannesburg and Port Elizabeth, and Intercape buses connecting Jo'burg with the Garden Route towns, pull in daily at the Engen garage on Church St. For bus tickets and timetables, head to the tourist office (see below).

INFORMATION AND TOURS

Tourist information 13 Church St (Mon–Fri 8am–5pm, Sat 9am–noon; ☎049 892 4248, ⓦ graaffreinet.co.za). This is also the place for **maps** and accommodation lists.

Tours Ngomso township tours are a recommended way to experience the other side of Graaff-Reinet as well as some of its recent history; contact Isaac Ngomso (☎083 559 1207).

ACCOMMODATION

Graaff-Reinet has plenty of decent places to stay in the centre; the nicest are in listed historic buildings. If the Karoo landscape grabs you, you might want to head for one of the farmstays around here and Nieu Bethesda (see opposite), to witness some of the country's most dazzling night skies and spacious landscapes. December is the busiest month, and you should definitely book well ahead if you want to stay then.

Andries Stockenstrom Guest House 100 Cradock St ☎049 892 4575 or ☎083 5999 302, ⓦ www.asghouse .co.za; map p.333. This handsome listed house is one of the best upmarket stays in town, with seven very comfortable rooms, done out with white percale linen on kingsize beds, with leather and wood furnishings. There is a restaurant on the premises offering four-course slow food, primarily for overnight visitors. R1190

Cypress Cottage 80 Donkin St ☎049 892 3965 or ☎083 456 1795, ⓦ cypresscottage.co.za; map p.333. A restored Karoo house with six double en-suite rooms and a communal lounge and dining room. Families are welcome and the garden with swimming pool, trampoline and dolls' house is popular with kids. R900

Drostdy Hotel 30 Church St ☎049 892 2161, ⓦ drostdy .co.za; map p.333. An elegant Cape Dutch landmark in a

prime location, with a dining room lit by grand chandeliers, shady gardens and fountains. The rooms, in terraced artisan cottages behind the hotel, are comfortable but small; larger rooms are pricier (R1670). R975

Karoopark Holiday Cottages 81 Caledon St ☎049 892 2557, ⓦ wkaroopark.co.za; map p.333. A complex of self-catering cottages, set in a garden with a pool, plus dinky B&B units that are adequate for an overnight stay. R410

The Red Geranium 52 Stockenstrom St ☎049 892 2332; map p.333. Three decent historical cottages run by a friendly owner, at a reasonable price. They're equipped for self-catering, though light breakfast can be provided. R300

Trymore Cottage Wellwood Farm, 31km north of town, on the road to Nieu Bethesda ☎049 840 0302, ⓦ wellwood.co.za; map p.333. Self-catering, comfortable, four-bedroom house on a long-established, beautiful farm. Braai packs are available, as are evening dinners, with Karoo lamb or venison on the menu. The well-known private collection of Karoo reptile fossils here is absolutely stunning and is open to guests. R540

Urquhart Caravan Park On the outskirts of town, at the extension of Stockenstroom St, next to the Karoo

Nature Reserve ☏ 049 892 2136; map p.333. A large and well-maintained caravan park, with campsites and good-value rondavels, chalets and bungalows (R160). Linen is provided but you must bring your own towels. Camping R80, rondavel R120, chalet R400

EATING AND DRINKING

You'll find a couple of centrally located restaurants and tea shops catering for Graaff-Reinet's many visitors, though the town is pretty dead on Sundays.

The Coldstream 3 Church Square ☏ 049 891 1181; map p.333. Karoo lamb, as well as a considerable variety of local meats and venison. They are known for their generous snack platters, and there is some concession made for vegetarians. The venue is outstanding, in a handsome listed building, the old colonial Graaff-Reinet Club, with a big tree in the garden and veranda seating. (R100). Mon–Sat 9am till late.

Drostdy Hotel 30 Church St ☏ 049 892 2161; map p.333. The hotel has an unrivalled garden for drinks or tea, and a grand dining room for rather formal à la carte dinners; better value are the buffet breakfasts (R65–95).

There's also an atmospheric pub here, and the hotel should on no account be missed for a visit. Daily 9am–5pm & 6.30–10pm.

Kliphuis 46 Bourke St ☏ 049 892 2345; map p.333. Come here for full breakfast (R60), a light lunch at pavement tables, or in the evening for a three-course dinner (R160). There's a full liquor licence and a wine boutique. Tues–Sat 8am till late, Sun 6pm till late.

Pioneers 3 Parsonage St ☏ 049 892 6059; map p.333. A local pub with good venison pie, Karoo lamb and chops, chicken, hake and a platter for vegetarians (R120). Mon 5–10pm, Tues–Sun 10.30am–10pm.

Nieu Bethesda

In the mountains north of Graaff-Reinet, **NIEU BETHESDA** is drier and dustier than you might wish, especially in midsummer when it boils with harsh, bright light. There are no streetlamps, and on winter nights temperatures plummet to zero, the sky filled with icy stars. The Owl House aside (see below), the whitewashed **village** has plenty of charm. Once an archetypal conservative Karoo *dorp*, it has reinvented itself as a tiny artists' colony, attracting a growing number of visitors. Nearby, a few hundred coloured residents somehow manage to eke out a living in this harsh environment, though the non-profit organization Bethesda Arts Centre has provided some opportunities for craft workers and artists to get trained and to sell their work.

Owl House

River St • Daily April–Sept 9am–5pm; Oct–March 8am–6pm • R26

Most people who come to Nieu Bethesda do so in order to marvel – or shudder – at the **Owl House**, once the home of Helen Martins, a reclusive artist who expressed her disturbing and fascinating inner world through her work. Every corner of the house and garden has been transformed to meet her vision. The interior walls glitter with crushed glass, owls with large eyes gaze from the tin-roofed veranda, while at the back of the house, trapped by a stone wall and high chicken wire, are hundreds of glass and cement sculptures: camels, lambs, sphinxes and human figures.

ARRIVAL AND DEPARTURE   NIEU BETHESDA

By car Nieu Bethesda is 23km off the N9 between Graaff-Reinet and Middelburg, on a dirt road. No petrol is available

in Nieu Bethesda, so fill up in Graaff-Reinet; neither is there an ATM.

ACCOMMODATION

If you're self-catering, you should stock up elsewhere, though there is a village shop and butcher on the main road.

Huis Nommer Een Murray St, book through Suzette Pienaar on ☏ 049 841 1700. *Huis Nommer Een* has three

spacious rooms furnished in South African country style, a farm-style kitchen, and a handsome veranda. R460

4

Owl House Backpackers Lodge Martin St ☎049 841 1642, ⊛owlhouse.info. The only backpacker lodge, *Owl House* is friendly, laidback and well organized, with dorm beds, en-suite rooms (B&B or self-catering), two self-contained cottages (R490) and a restaurant, *The Karoo Lamb*, and pub, *The Ramstal*. They will collect you if you arrive in Graaff-Reinet without your own car. Dorm R110, double R370

Doornberg Farm 9km north of Nieu Bethesda ☎049 841 1401, ⊛nieubethesda.co.za. If you want to stay on a farm, try the friendly *Doornberg Farm*, which has a pub and serves evening meals, or you can self-cater; there's also a trampoline, pool, riding and hiking. The nicest place to stay on the farm is in *Die Vleihuisie*, a little cottage 4km away from the farmstead. R400

★ **Ganora Farm** Off the N9, 7km east of Nieu Bethesda ☎049 841 1302 or ☎082 698 0029, ⊛ganora .co.za. A working sheep farm whose owners arrange trips to climb Compassberg and to see Bushman rock shelters. There's also a small fossil collection. Accommodation is either B&B or in self-catering cottages (R780). Dinner can be ordered (R140 for a three-course meal). R680

EATING

Bethesda Arts Centre Muller St (opposite the police station), ⊛bethesdafoundation.org. In a building notable for its unusual tower (where you can also stay), the centre's restaurant is a good place for teas and coffee with hearty Karoo food such as venison stew and lamb chops, with the plus of looking at local crafts. Daily 8am–8pm.

The Brewery Across the dry Gats River, off New St ☎049 841 1602. A first-class choice for an unhurried lunch, serving its own cold beer accompanied by home-made cheese, bread, olives and salami (R55). Daily 10am–4pm.

East London and the central region

Between Port Alfred and East London lies some of the Eastern Cape's least-developed **coastline**, although it has now fallen into the hands of developers as more and more people discover the beauty of the region. **East London**, wedged uncomfortably between two ex-Bantustans, is the largest city in the central region of the province, with excellent beaches for surfing and swimming and good transport links to Johannesburg and along the coast. Inland, **Fort Hare University** near Alice has educated political leaders across the subcontinent, including Nelson Mandela, and has the country's finest collection of contemporary black South African art.

Sweeping up from Fort Hare's valley, the gentle, wooded **Amatola Mountains** yield to the dramatic landscapes of the **Eastern Cape Drakensberg**, which offer hiking, horseriding and even skiing opportunities. Before white settlers (or even the Xhosa) arrived, these towering formations were dominated by **San hunter-gatherers**, who decorated the rock faces with thousands of ritual **paintings**, many of which remain surprisingly vivid.

East London

EAST LONDON, the second-largest city in the Eastern Cape, is the obvious jumping-off point for exploring the Transkei. But without fine, warm weather, the city is dreary. What does happen takes place along the beachfront, where there's a plethora of places to stay, eat and drink. **Nahoon Beach** is a great **surfing spot**, and the town has a dedicated and lively surfing scene. It's also gradually becoming a place for black holidaymakers – a post-apartheid phenomenon. The beaches to the east of town are very beautiful, with long stretches of sand, high dunes, estuaries and luxuriant vegetation, and good swimming.

East London's drab city centre is dominated by **Oxford Street**, parallel to Station Street and the train station. Although a major traffic thoroughfare, it is largely deserted at night, when you shouldn't wander around alone. The newly upgraded **Vincent Park Centre** on Devereux Avenue is a popular shopping centre with cinemas and restaurants. It is 5km north of the city centre (leave the centre on Oxford St, and turn right into Devereux just beyond the museum), in the midst of the salubrious suburbs of Vincent and Stirling. This is the best place for **shopping**, or to find anything practical such as

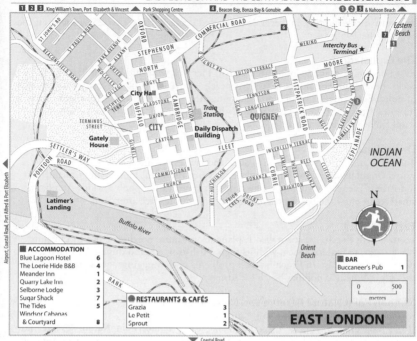

EAST LONDON

ACCOMMODATION

Blue Lagoon Hotel	6
The Loerie Hide B&B	4
Meander Inn	1
Quarry Lake Inn	2
Selborne Lodge	3
Sugar Shack	7
The Tides	5
Windsor Cabanas & Courtyard	8

RESTAURANTS & CAFÉS

Grazia	3
Le Petit	1
Sprout	2

BAR

Buccaneer's Pub	1

banks and the post office. Apart from a couple of handsome buildings, East London's Victorian heart has progressively been demolished, though the city centre's principal landmark, the splendid terracotta and lace-white **City Hall**, opened in 1899, remains. Over the road is a rather lifeless statue of martyred Black Consciousness leader **Steve Biko** (see box 340).

Away from the holiday strip, East London is dominated by an industrial centre served by **Mdantsane**, a huge African township 20km from the city towards King William's Town.

Brief history

Before the British, and even the Xhosa, the area was home to the **Khoikhoi** people, who called it Place of the Buffaloes. The Buffalo River once teemed with game, but the animals were gradually killed off with the arrival of British hunters. East London began life as a permanent British settlement during the nineteenth-century **Frontier Wars**, when it was used as a beachhead to land military supplies needed to push back the Xhosa. Taken by its strategic possibilities as a port, the British governor Sir Harry Smith optimistically called it **London** in 1848. Later it was changed to East London, because the port was on the east side of the Buffalo River.

Quigney and around

East of the city's train station is **Quigney**, best reached from Currie Street, an area of small colonial-style Victorian houses, now very run-down. Here you'll find the city's best curio outlet, Umzi Wethu Curio Shop, stocking handmade **African crafts**; it's at 110 Moore St, up the hill from the *Holiday Inn*.

East London Museum

Upper Oxford St • Mon–Thurs 9.30am–4.30pm, Fri 9am–4pm • R8

A few kilometres north of the city centre, the **East London Museum** has a stunning collection of South Nguni beadwork and contemporary wire sculpture. The museum's pride and joy, however, is its stuffed coelacanth (see p.325), caught off the coast in the 1950s.

The Esplanade

East London's **Esplanade** loops from Orient Pier in a wide and beautiful sweep of rocks, beach and sand dunes to Eastern Beach, marred only by the motley assortment of holiday apartments, hotels and restaurants lining the beachfront. It's about thirty minutes' walk from the city centre; buses here are sporadic, but it's easy enough to stroll from one end to the other.

Orient Beach

Tucked in next to Orient Pier, with dockland cranes poking their necks above the water, **Orient Beach** is a wonderful place to swim, though it looks a bit grim and industrial. There are changing rooms, and a couple of little pools for kids. You pay a small fee to enter the beach area during the day, but it's free after 5pm.

Eastern Beach

From Orient Beach, the sea-walled Esplanade continues northeast, along sand and black rocks, to **Eastern Beach**, with its high, bush-capped sand dunes. Although far more attractive, Eastern Beach has had problems with muggings, even during the day, though it remains a popular beach for surfers.

Nahoon Point Nature Reserve and Nahoon Beach

Visitor's Centre signposted off Epson Rd, Nahoon • Daily 8.30am–4pm • ☎ 083 232 5055 • Free

If you have time to visit one attraction, make it the **Nahoon Point Nature Reserve**, 5km from the centre of East London, where you can see the coastline from a good vantage point, visit the museum and have a coffee. In a building shaped like a footprint (commemorating the discovery of a young child's fossilized footprint 120,000 years old, in a nearby dune), the new Coastal Education and Visitors' Centre has a very worthwhile museum with displays on the town's surfing history, as well as an excellent section on the archeological finds of the area, including the famous footprint. There's also a café, serving a full range of light meals (daily 8am–5pm). From the Museum car park, there are nicely constructed wooden walkways along the coast where you can stroll or do longer hikes, to take in the best of the city's coastline.

Nahoon Beach, to the east of Nahoon Point, is a long stretch of sand, backed by dunes. This wonderful natural setting is superb for swimming and surfing, with some of the best waves in the country, and the nicest area to stay if you're looking for accommodation.

Bonza Bay and Gonubie Beach

East of the Nahoon River, 10km from the centre, the coast curves into **Bonza Bay**, with kilometres of beach walks and a lazy lagoon at the mouth of the Quinera River. Further on, **Gonubie Beach**, 18km northeast of the centre, at the Gonubie River Mouth, is still close enough to be considered part of East London, with some good accommodation, a beautiful beach and walks.

ARRIVAL AND DEPARTURE
EAST LONDON

By plane East London's small airport (☎ 043 706 0306), a few kilometres west of the centre on the R72, connects the city to all major centres. The airport shuttle, the Little Red Bus (☎ 082 569 3599), meets all flights and drops off at the Holiday Inn near the beachfront (R90). Imonti Tours (☎ 043 741 3884 or ☎ 083 487 8975) also do transfers from the airport to the city centre (R90).

By bus All three of the intercity buses – Translux (☎ 086 158 9282), Intercape (☎ 086 128 7287) and Greyhound (☎ 083 915 9000) – offer a frequent, comprehensive and inexpensive service connecting East London to major cities. The buses drop off at the coach terminal at Windmill Park on Moore St. The Minilux minibus, which connects Grahamstown with the airport at Port Elizabeth daily, goes on to Port Alfred on

Mondays and Thursdays, and East London on Mon/Tue/Thurs & Fri, and can be booked through Go Travel (☎ 046 622 2235).
By train The train station (☎ 086 000 8888) is on the eastern edge of East London's small business and shopping district. Metered taxis outside the station will get you to your accommodation, as there is no central accommodation.

GETTING AROUND

By car Like most South African cities, central East London is gridded; with uncongested roads and easy parking, it's far more geared to driving than walking.

By taxi For a taxi, call Deans Taxi Service (☎ 073 194 6367 or ☎ 079 293 5132).

INFORMATION AND TOURS

Tourist information 91 Western Ave in Vincent, opposite Impala Butchery (Mon–Fri 8am–4.30pm; ☎ 043 721 1346, ⓦ tourismbuffalocity.co.za). The Eastern Cape Tourism Board office (☎ 043 701 9600 ⓦ ectourism.co.za), where you can pick up information on the rest of the province, has unfortunately moved out to an inconvenient spot in Beacon Bay, quite a distance from town, at Ironwood House, Palm Square Business Park, Bonza Bay Rd.
Tours Township tours are best done via Imonti (☎ 043 741 3884 or ☎ 083 487 8975), who can also take you to a very good cultural village 30km out of town.

ACCOMMODATION

East London's beachfront sports graceless blocks of holiday apartments and functional hotels, redeemed only by their fabulous views of the Indian Ocean. The really cheap hotels are mostly filled with long-term residents, and are often rough drinking hangouts – best avoided. If the urban nature of the main beachfront doesn't appeal, your best bet is to head for the suburbs of Nahoon Mouth at the end of Beach Rd, Beacon Bay, Bonza Bay or Gonubie, close to the river and sea and reached via the N2 east of the city; without your own transport, you'll need to take a taxi or arrange to be picked up.

BEACHFRONT AND NORTHERN SUBURBS

Blue Lagoon Blue Bend Place, Beacon Bay ☎ 043 748 4821, ⓦ www.bluelagoonhotel.co.za; map p.337. Very pleasant accommodation surrounded by palm trees and close to the beach. Rooms are quiet and spacious, with balconies looking onto the river. R1005

The Loerie Hide B&B 2B Sheerness Rd, off Beach Rd, Nahoon ☎ 043 735 3206, ⓦ loeriehide.co.za; map p.337. Five reasonably priced en-suite rooms in the vicinity of Nahoon Beach at the bottom of a garden that gives way to indigenous bushland. R700

Meander Inn 8 Claredon Rd, Selborne ☎ 043 726 2310, ⓦ wildcoastholidays.co.za; map p.337. Five spacious, tastefully furnished rooms with white linen and ceiling fans, in a luxurious yet relaxed two-storey building. There's a swimming pool, patio and bar, and they offer airport transfer. R820

Quarry Lake Inn Quartzite Drive, off Pearce St, The Quarry ☎ 043 707 5400, ⓦ www.quarrylakeinn.co.za; map p.337. Spacious, well-appointed rooms in a lovely setting on the edge of a flooded disused quarry that has become home to abundant vegetation and birdlife. R1295

Selborne Lodge 18 Dawson Rd ☎ 043 743 2530, ⓦ selbornelodge.co.za; map p.337. A B&B with home comforts, dinner served on request, and four double en-suite rooms with private entrances and secure parking. There's also a swimming pool and tranquil garden. R400

Sugar Shack Eastern Beach ☎ 043 722 8240, ⓦ sugarshack.co.za; map p.337. A brilliantly located hostel, right on the beach, with terrific views. There's transport from the hostel to the mountain resort of Hogsback (see p.340). Dorm R110, double R270

Windsor Cabanas & Courtyard George Walker Parade ☎ 043 743 2225, ⓦ katleisure.co.za; map p.337. A Spanish-style block near Orient Beach, offering great views. The *Cabanas* has comfortable one-, two- and three-bedroom self-catering apartments, while the adjacent *Courtyard* offers basic accommodation with standard decor. Courtyard R350, Cabanas R870

★ **The Tides** 49 Harewood Drive, Nahoon ☎ 043 735 4454 or ☎ 073 198 9356; map p.337. Just above Nahoon Beach for early morning or evening walks, this comfortable B&B, with smart bathrooms and television, is run by the friendly Judy and Dave Fish who are well informed about the area and onward travel to the Wild Coast. R600

EATING AND DRINKING

East London has some good restaurants, a couple of them serving fresh fish in an outdoor setting. **Drinking** spots abound, from beachfront sleaze at lowlife hotels to lively surfers' hangouts and swanky places overlooking the ocean. Some of the pubs double up as **live music** venues, as well as offering a bite to eat.

Buccaneer's Pub Eastern Beach, next to Sugar Shack ☎ 043 743 5171; map p.337. A lively bar that buzzes till the early hours, with occasional live music. During the day there are fantastic views of the rodeo riders of the surf. Good pub fare includes fish and chips and, best of all, chicken schnitzel (R68). Daily 10am–10pm.

Grazia Upper Esplanade ☎ 043 722 2009; map p.337. A light and airy restaurant with stunning views of the sea, serving Italian-style food (mains R120). Their linguini alla marinara and layered vegetable gnocchi are recommended. Daily noon–10.30pm.

Le Petit 54 Beach Rd Shopping Centre, Nahoon ☎ 043 735 3685; map p.337. A highly regarded eating place serving rich Mediterranean/French-inspired food, with an emphasis on game, seafood and veal (mains around R115). Mon–Fri noon–2pm & 6–10pm, Sat 6–10pm.

★ **Sprout** 11 Beach Rd, Nahoon ☎ 043 735 3841; map p.337. Organic African and Portuguese food cooked with love. Their tapas are recommended, and lunch dishes include Portuguese sardines with olive oil and salad, Brazilian-styled pork with black beans (R95) and, best of all, some very healthy salads which can be eaten on a nice terrace. Mon 7.30am–5pm, Tues–Sat 7.30am–6pm.

The Amatola Mountains

Most visitors drive quickly through the scrubby, dry, impoverished area between East London and the **Amatola Mountains** proper, to reach the cool forests and holiday lands at **Hogsback**. However, it's worth deviating en route, to see the fine collection of African art at **Fort Hare University**, close to the little town of Alice, and to take in some peeling, but intact, colonial streetscapes in **King William's Town**.

Hogsback

Made sweeter by the contrast with the hot valleys below, the village of **HOGSBACK** in the Amatola Mountains, 32km north of Alice and 145km from East London, offers cool relief after hauling through prickly, overgrazed country. The name "Hogsback" applies to the area as much as to the village, and comes from the high rocky ridge (actually three peaks) resembling a bushpig's spine, which runs above the settlement.

Hogsback represents a corner of England, a fantasy fed by mists, pine plantations and exotic trees such as oak, walnut and azaleas, and snowfalls each winter. It's a great place to spend a relaxing couple of days, with plenty of walks and good air among the flowers, grasslands and forests, and there are many places to stay. The real attraction is

---

STEVE BIKO AND BLACK CONSCIOUSNESS

Steve Biko's brutal interrogation and death while in police custody triggered international outrage and turned opinion further against the apartheid regime.

Steven Bantu Biko was born in 1946 in King William's Town. His political ascent was swift, due to his eloquence, charisma and focused vision. While still a medical student at Natal University during the late 1960s, he was elected president of the exclusively black **South African Students' Organization** (SASO) and started publishing articles in their journal, fiercely attacking white liberalism, which they saw as patronizing and counter-revolutionary. In an atmosphere of repression, Biko's brand of **Black Consciousness** immediately caught on. He called for blacks to take destiny into their own hands, to unify and rid themselves of the "shackles that bind them to perpetual servitude". From 1973 onwards, Biko suffered banning, detention and other harassment at the hands of the state. In 1974, he defended himself in court, presenting his case so brilliantly that his international profile soared.

Barred from leaving King William's Town, Biko continued working and writing, frequently escaping his confinement. In August 1977 he was detained and taken to Port Elizabeth where he was interrogated and tortured. A month later he died from a brain haemorrhage, after a beating by security police. No one was held accountable. He is buried in King William's Town. The polished, charcoal-coloured tombstone sits midway through the graveyard, among the large patch of paupers' graves. To get there, take Cathcart Street south out of town (towards Grahamstown), turning left onto a road signposted to the cemetery, after the bridge (just before the Alice turn-off to the right).

FORT HARE UNIVERSITY

Despite decades of deliberate neglect, and its relegation after 1959 to a "tribal" university under apartheid, **Fort Hare**, 2km east of Alice on the R63, is assured a place in South African history. Established in 1916 as a multiracial college by missionaries, it became the first institution in South Africa to deliver tertiary education to blacks, and was attended by many prominent African leaders, including Zimbabwe's president Robert Mugabe and Tanzania's former president, Julius Nyerere. The most famous former student is Nelson Mandela (see box, p.355), making this an essential port of call if you're following his footsteps. **Free tours** of the university, its art gallery and the ANC archives are run during the week (Mon–Thurs 8am–4.30pm, Fri 8am–3.30pm; ☏040 602 2050 or 2239, ⓦufh.ac.za); book beforehand through the curator.

DE BEERS ART GALLERY

If you have even the slightest interest in African art, Fort Hare's **De Beers Art Gallery** (Mon–Fri 8am–4.30pm; free) is well worth a visit. A treasury of contemporary black Southern African art, it's one of the most significant and least publicized collections anywhere. The gallery also houses Fort Hare's **ethnographic collection** – a major museum of traditional crafts and artefacts, with many rare and valuable pieces.

---

the **Afro-montane cloud forest**, dense with yellowwood, stinkwood and Cape chestnut, singing with bird calls and gauzy waterfalls, and populated by the odd troop of **samango monkeys**, which survive on the steep slopes above the pine plantations. Note that Hogsback can be wet and cold, even in summer, so bring a warm pullover, sturdy shoes and rain gear.

The hamlet itself is strung out along 3km of tarred road, with gravel and fairly rough lanes branching out on either side to hotels and cottages. The closest thing to a **centre** is the small conglomeration of a general store, post office and filling station. Hogsback has its own **indigenous craft** found nowhere else in the country: prepare to be pestered by hawkers selling the characteristic unfired clay horses and hogs with white markings.

The trails

Amatola Trail R150 per day per section, complete trail R750 · Book through the Department of Forestry ☏ 043 642 2571, ⓦ amatola.co.za

Hogsback is prime **rambling** country, with short, relatively easy trails indicated by hogs painted onto trees. For a rewarding taste of indigenous forest, the Contour Path above the campsite makes an easy, one-hour walk. From this path, a route goes steeply up **Tor Doone**, which overlooks the settlement, and is the easiest summit to climb. One of the most rewarding waterfall trails is the one-hour steep downhill walk to the lovely **Madonna and Child Waterfall**. Walks are detailed in inexpensive **guidebooks** available at the information centre.

A much tougher hike, ranked among South Africa's best forested mountain walks, the **Amatola Trail** takes in numerous waterfalls, rivers and bathing pools en route. Starting at Maiden Dam in the Pirie Forest, some 21km north of King William's Town, the trail stretches 105km to end at Hogsback. There are huts with mattresses and braai facilities, some also with showers, at each designated night stop along the way, and you can do a day or two as well, by arrangement.

ARRIVAL AND DEPARTURE   HOGSBACK

By shuttle A cheap shuttle, on demand (☏043 722 8240), connects *Sugar Shack* in East London (see p.339) with Hogsback; *Away With The Fairies* and *Terra-Khaya* in Hogsback can make arrangements.

INFORMATION

Tourist information Main Rd (Mon–Sat 10am–4pm, Sun & Public Holidays 9am–3pm; ☏045 962 1245, ⓦ www.hogsback.com).

ON HORSEBACK AROUND HOGSBACK

Lowestoffe (❶045 843 1716) offers **horseriding** trails (R250) for beginners and experienced riders alike on a farm 25km outside Hogsback, where they breed appaloosas. The riding is on the large farm, through a wide valley and up mountain slopes. If you want **forested rides** at Hogsback itself, head for *Terra-Khaya Backpackers* (see below) where Shane, a superb horseman who rides bareback and barefooted, will take you on one of the best rides you can do anywhere, on well-schooled horses, for an hour or two (R250); overnight trails are available on request.

ACCOMMODATION

Places to stay are plentiful and of a high quality – everything trades on its lush, quiet garden setting, but the village tends to fill up during holidays and weekends, when you'll need to book ahead; and certainly stay for two nights at the very minimum.

Arminel Signposted along the main road ❶045 962 1005, ⓦkatleisure.co.za. The best of the hotels, with thatched buildings and large spaces. All the rooms lead directly onto the well-kept hotel gardens, and some have their own wooden decks. Rates include half board. R1000

Away With The Fairies Hydrangea Lane; down the first turning on your right and signposted as you drive into Hogsback ❶045 962 1031, ⓦawaywiththefairies .co.za. Unequivocally geared to the partying backpacker scene, this large converted house on a sizeable property has fabulous views of the Tyumi Valley. The small dorms sleep five to eight guests, and there are a number of twin and double rooms, some en suite and one with its own fireplace. One of the nicest features of the hostel is a platform in a tree for drinks and hanging out. Camping R60, dorm R110, double R320

Back O' The Moon Holiday Cottage Trewennan Lane ❶045 962 1017, ⓦbackofthemoon.hogsback.co.za. The ideal cottage for a group, with three comfortable bedrooms, a lounge with fireplace, large garden, veranda and fully equipped kitchen for self-catering, plus superbly obliging owners. R650

★ **The Edge** Signposted off Main Rd ❶045 962 1159, ⓦtheedge-hogsback.co.za. The best of the self-catering accommodation, with twenty cottages in separate locations a couple of kilometres off the main

road, plus ten B&B rooms. There are superb valley and forest views, and a restaurant on site. Booking is essential for the cottages. R500

Granny Mouse Country House Nutwood Drive ❶045 962 1259, ⓦgrannymousehouse.co.za. B&B and self-catering accommodation with country-style furnishings in an old home with a beautiful garden, with an owner who is organised and on-the-ball. R550

Lowestoffe Country Lodge Off Cathcart Rd ❶045 843 1716 or ❶083 654 5935, ⓦlowestoffecountrylodge .co.za. Three fairly modern cottages on a farm where you can horseride or fish for trout. The farm is 24km out on the unpaved road to Cathcart, so its draw is the dramatic and lonely mountain scenery. There are dams and mountain pools for swimming. R500

★ **Terra-Khaya** Off Plaatjieskraal Rd ❶082 897 7503, ⓦterrakhaya.co.za. Tucked into the backwoods is a wonderful and well-run backpackers, operating on traditional and alternative ecological techniques. While it is sociable and there is a lovely communal lounge and kitchen area where you can get meals or self-cater, this is not a party place, being more geared to outdoor and farm life. Free accommodation for your talents/labour is a possibility, as are free meals for cutting down water-guzzling alien trees. Phone to get directions. Camping R60, dorm R110, double R265

EATING AND DRINKING

All of the hotels do meals daily, and have pubs open with welcoming fireplaces. The oldest, and most atmospheric of the pubs, in the English tradition, is at *Hogsback Inn*.

Arminel Main Rd ❶045 962 1005. The hotel with the prettiest garden setting, great for a terrace lunch of sandwiches, steaks or burgers (R45), or tea or drinks, and with a roaring fireplace and screen for watching sport. Daily 11am–4pm.

Butterfly Bistro Main Rd, next to the tourist office ❶045 962 1326. Well regarded for its wood-fired pizza, pastas and salads (R65), with some deli items for sale if you

are picnicking. Thurs–Mon 9am–8pm, Tues & Wed 9am–6pm.

King's Lodge Hotel Main Rd ❶045 962 1024. Well-priced pub lunches, especially their three-course Sunday lunch buffet (R100), three-course set dinner (R120) and Tuesday-night buffet dinner special, which is so popular it needs booking in advance (R55). Daily 8am–8pm.

Tea Thyme at The Edge Signposted off Main Rd. The

best place in town for afternoon tea or lunch, though it's off the main road and so best combined with a walk along the edge of the escarpment or around the very beautifully set labyrinth. Their hot chocolate and carrot cake is legendary, and they serve three-course dinners for R160. Daily 8am–8pm.

The Eastern Cape Drakensberg

The **Eastern Cape Drakensberg** is the most southerly section of Southern Africa's highest and most extensive mountain chain, stretching east across Lesotho and up the west flank of KwaZulu-Natal into Mpumalanga. The obvious goal of this world of **San rock paintings**, sandstone **caves** and craggy sheep farms is **Rhodes**, one of the country's best-preserved and prettiest Victorian villages. Since there is no national park in the Eastern Cape Drakensberg, activities are all arranged through private farms. Very remote, Rhodes is reached from Barkly East, which itself is 130km from Aliwal North on the N6. The 60km dirt road to Rhodes from Barkly East is tortuous and rough, taking a good ninety minutes, with sheer, unfenced drops.

Rhodes and around

RHODES is almost too good to be true – a remote and beautiful village girdled by the Eastern Cape Drakensberg. Few people actually live here: like other villages in this region, Rhodes was progressively deserted as residents gravitated to the cities to make a living, leaving its Victorian tin-roofed architecture stuck in a very pleasing time warp. Today, its *raison d'être* is as a low-key holiday place for people who appreciate its isolation, wood stoves and restored cottages. Although electricity reached the village a few years ago, very few establishments have it, and paraffin lamps and candles are the norm. Given that Rhodes is not on the way to anywhere (on some maps it doesn't even appear), it is a place to dwell for a few days, rather than for an overnight stop. While nights are cool even in summer, in winter they are freezing, and there's no central heating, so pack warm clothes.

The village itself is not much more than a few crisscrossing gravel roads lined with pine trees. At the heart of the village is the *Rhodes Hotel*, a general shop and a garage; there's also a post office and payphone, but no banking facilities and no public transport in or out of the village.

Rhodes used to be busy in the winter, when **skiers** used it as a base for the artificial snowed Tiffendell slopes, but this activity has ceased due to mysterious legalities. The village is an hour's 4WD drive into the highest peaks of the Eastern Cape Drakensberg. December to May are the best months for swimming and hiking.

Rock-art sites

Martin's Dell ☎ 045 974 9201

Rhodes is a good base for exploring millennia-old **San rock paintings**, the majority of which are on surrounding private farms which can be visited with the farmers' permission (some farms also take guests). Rhodes locals can point you to nearby farms which have their own paintings.

Close to Rhodes, **Martin's Dell** farm, 16km from the village, is worth a visit, not just for the well-preserved, photogenic paintings, but for the lovely, lonely valley you have to drive through to get there. Make an appointment with Russie or Lookie Schmidt to see them. The signposted turn-off to Martin's Dell is 8km from Rhodes on the road to Barkly East. From the turn-off it's another 8km to the site, with parking and a couple of picnic tables.

Rock art had an essentially religious purpose, usually recording experiences of trance states (see p.10 for more); shamans' visions often included powerful animals like the eland, which you can see depicted at Martin's Dell.

INFORMATION

RHODES

Tourist information Dave Walker of *Walkerbouts* (see p.344) runs Highlands Information, 1 Vorster St (☎045 974 9290, ☻highlandsinfo.co.za), a service that can be used to book any sort of activities and accommodation in the area.

ACCOMMODATION

Gateshead Lodges ☎045 974 9303. A range of excellent cottages and a sandstone farmhouse on huge properties in marvellously remote and rugged territory, all within a large radius of Rhodes. R320

Rhodes Hotel Main Rd ☎045 974 9305. The only hotel in town, and a classic country village place, complete with an historical and restored pub, Victorian exterior, red tin roofs, an attractive wooden balustraded veranda and charming furnishings. R500

Rubicon Flats Old School House, signposted off Main Rd ☎045 974 9268, ☻rubiconflats.co.za. The

best-value, and the warmest, place in town, this handsome old schoolhouse has been converted into self-catering rooms, each with an anthracite burner, and there are also simple dorms. Good Afrikaans farm-style meals can be provided if you are staying here (R70). Dorm R100, double R460

Walkerbouts Inn Signposted off the main road ☎045 974 9290, ☻walkerbouts.co.za. A relaxed house with six en-suite guest rooms, on room-only or Dinner/B&B rates. The friendly owner, Dave Walker, knows a good deal about the area and can organize almost any activity (see above). R950

EATING AND DRINKING

Rhodes Hotel Main Rd ☎045 974 9305. A good place to pop into for a meal – the local trout is recommended (R80) – or tea. Don't miss a drink in the atmospheric, finely restored *Wydeman* pub. Daily 8am–10pm.

Walkerbouts Walkerbouts Inn, signposted off the main road. The best choice in town for food, offering home-cooked meals such as roast lamb, homemade pies, and rump steak (R70).

Naude's Nek

The most exhilarating drive out of Rhodes is on the R396 along **Naude's Nek,** the highest mountain-pass road in South Africa, connecting Rhodes with **Maclear** to the south, in a series of snaking hairpin bends and huge views. If you're chiefly looking for scenery, it's not essential to do the whole route to Maclear. Many people go from Rhodes to the top of the pass and back as a half-day trip, during which you can make a call from the highest phone (with a crank handle) in the country, in a corrugated-iron booth in the middle of a sheep pen at the top of the pass. Be sure to park your car facing into the wind, to ensure your car doors don't fly off, as the wind gets strong up here.

While it's only 30km from Rhodes, the journey can take a couple of hours to the Nek because so many changing vistas en route demand stops. You don't need a 4WD, but if you feel precious about your car don't attempt this route, as the road is harsh – and is definitely impassable after snow.

ACCOMMODATION

NAUDE'S NEK

Woodcliff 16km before Maclear ☎045 932 1550. *Woodcliff* offers self-catering accommodation, perfect if you're after a really remote mountain experience. Rooms in the farmhouse are available, or there's a three-bed cottage (R520). Meals are available on request, and they also offer

guided rock art and orchid trails, and hiking and fishing. To get here, turn right at the big sign that says Woodcliff, winding up into Joel's Hoek Valley for 7km until the road splits into three – take the middle road up to the farmhouse. R220

The Wild Coast region

The **Wild Coast region** is aptly named: this is one of South Africa's most unspoilt areas, a vast stretch of undulating hills, lush forest and spectacular beaches skirting a section of the Indian Ocean. Its undeveloped sandy beaches stretch for hundreds of kilometres, punctuated by rivers and several wonderful, reasonably priced hotels geared to family seaside holidays. The wildness goes beyond the landscape, for this is the former **Transkei** homeland, a desperately poor region that was disenfranchised during

THE WILD COAST

apartheid and turned into a dumping ground for Africans too old or too young for South African industry to make use of.

The Wild Coast region's inhabitants are predominantly Xhosa, and those in rural areas live mostly in traditional rondavels dotting the landscape for as far as the eye can see. The **N2** highway runs through the middle of the region, passing through the old Transkei capital of **Mthatha** and a host of scruffy, busy little towns along the way. To the south of the highway, the **coastal region** stretches from just north of East London to the mouth of the **Mtamvuna River**. With its succession of great beaches, hidden reefs, patches of subtropical forest, rural Xhosa settlements and the attractive little towns of **Coffee Bay** and **Port St Johns** (both popular with backpackers), this region offers the most deserted and undeveloped beaches in the country.

The Wild Coast, unlike the Western Cape Garden Route, is not a stretch that you can easily tour by car. There's no coastal road, and no direct route between one seaside resort and the next. Yet in this **remoteness** lies the region's charm. Resorts are isolated down long, winding gravel roads off the N2, which sticks to the high inland plateau. Choose one or two places to stay, and stay put for a relaxing few days. Most places along this stretch of coast are known simply by the name of the hotel that nominates the settlement, though you will also see the Xhosa name of the river mouth, on which each hotel is situated, on many maps.

Cintsa

Of the smattering of resorts between East London and the Kei River, one of the best is at **CINTSA**, where endless sandy beaches back up into forested dunes, sliced through by lagoons and rivers. Cintsa is actually two places, Cintsa East and Cintsa West, divided by a river; the whole place is gorgeous. **CINTSA EAST**, 45km from East

A WALK ON THE WILD COAST

Since there's no coastal road, the only way to explore stretches of the Wild Coast is **on foot**. Booking a package is a sensible option, not least because in most cases the tour operator takes care of transfers at the start and end of the package.

WILD COAST HIKING TRAILS

Walking **packages** include transfers between East London and the Wild Coast, accommodation, all meals, picnic lunches, and the services of guides. Expect to pay around R600 per person per night for a group of four. Hotels dotted along the coast where you might stay include the *Kob Inn*, *Mazeppa Bay*, *Wavecrest*, *Trennery's*, *Seagulls* and *Morgan Bay Hotel*. All you have to carry is your day pack, as porters and transport are available to take your luggage to the overnight stops. Book through Wild Coast Holiday Reservations (T 043 743 6181, W wildcoastholidays.co.za).

Wild Coast Hotel Meander A Green Flag 55km trail along pristine, wild coast from the *Kob Inn* at Qora Mouth to Morgan Bay, covered at an easy pace over six days (five nights). Optional side-trips include a canoe trip, and Trevor's Trail into the forests and gorges.

Wild Coast Amble Starting north of Kei River and heading south, this ends in Cintsa, covering terrain of moderate difficulty in 56km over five days (four nights).

Wild Coast Pondo Walk Five nights based at the *Mboyti River Lodge*, near Lusikisiki. Transfers aren't included, though you will be given maps and information to help you drive there and back. The hike entails two coastal walks and two inland trails. You might have to cover anything from 13km to 26km a day.

Hole in the Wall Walk Four nights and three days, from Presleys Bay, just north of Coffee Bay, to Hole in the Wall, with spectacular coastal scenery.

Strandloper Coastal Hiking Trail (T 043 841 1046, W strandlopertrails.org.za). Four-day, three-night, 58-km hiking trail between Kei Mouth and Gonubie (R400 per person). Varied terrain, well-planned stages, small coastal villages and friendly pubs en route make this a popular hike, suited to family groups. Overnight accommodation is provided in comfortable twelve-bunk self-catering cabins.

London, is an upmarket holiday village of some two hundred houses, while **CINTSA WEST** is famous for its beautiful tidal pool.

Haga-Haga

Just northeast of Cintsa, **HAGA-HAGA** is dominated by the box-like but perfectly positioned *Haga-Haga Resort* (see p.352). To reach a sandy beach from the hotel, take the 2km path to Pullens Bay, which is ideal for swimming among the breakers. A 4km walk takes you to Bead Beach, where vendors sell beads made from carnelian, and bits of pottery.

Morgan Bay

MORGAN BAY, 90km from East London, lies magnificently in an estuary at the confluence of two rivers carving their passage through forested dunes. A hike from the *Morgan Bay Hotel*, one of the best resorts along the Wild Coast (see p.352), leads over some grassy knolls to the 50m Morbay Cliffs, an excellent vantage point for spotting dolphins and, in season, whales. The bay is pounded by massive breakers, but the estuary provides a safe and tranquil place for toddlers to paddle.

Kei Mouth and Trennery's (Qholorha Mouth)

Pontoon daily: summer 6am–6pm; winter 7am–5.30pm

From Morgan Bay, it's a short, rough drive to the village of **KEI MOUTH** (it's not signposted, so get directions from *Morgan Bay Hotel*), though there's little point dallying. To get to beautiful **TRENNERY'S**, only 6km along the beach as the crow flies,

THE GREAT CATTLE KILLING

The 1850s were a low point for the **Xhosa** nation: most of their land had been seized by the British, drought had withered their crops, and cattle-sickness had decimated their precious herds. In 1856, a young woman called **Nongqawuse**, whose uncle Mhlakaza was a prophet, claimed to have seen and heard ancestral spirits in a pool on the Gxara River. The spirits told her the Xhosa must kill all their remaining cattle and destroy their remaining crops; if they did this, new cattle and crops would arise, along with new people who would drive the whites into the sea.

As news of her **prophecy** spread, opinion was sharply divided among the Xhosa – those whose herds had been badly affected by cattle-sickness were most inclined to believe her. A turning point came when the Gcaleka paramount chief Sarili became convinced she was telling the truth and ordered his subjects to start the cull. Thousands of cattle were killed, but when the "new people" failed to materialize, the unbelievers who had not killed their herds were blamed. By February 1857, the next date for the appearance of the new people, over 200,000 cattle had been slaughtered. When the new people failed once more to materialize, it was too late for many Xhosa. By July there was **widespread starvation**; 30,000 of an estimated population of 90,000 died of hunger.

The British administration saw the famine as a perfect way to force the destitute Xhosa into working on white settlers' farms. To speed up the process, the Cape governor Sir George Grey closed down the feeding stations established by missionaries and laid the blame for the disaster on the Xhosa chiefs, imprisoning many of them on Robben Island.

but considerably longer by road, cross the Kei River on a small pontoon (which you can take your car on); after disembarking, continue driving for another 17km to *Trennery's Hotel* (signposted; see p.352). From the hotel, it's a steep walk through luxuriant vegetation to the spectacular beach, where canoes and rowing boats are available.

Trevor's Trail

Daily 9am • ☎ 047 498 0006, or book through your hotel • R60

A recommended excursion from Trennery's is **Trevor's Trail**, a three-hour bush walk and boating trip to "The Gates" – the short corridor of rock face towering above the Qholorha River; it's run by local resident Trevor Wigley, who also runs a number of other trails that include a visit to a local **traditional healer**.

Wavecrest (Nxaxo Mouth)

Wavecrest, just north of Trennery's (though not drivable from there), is a tranquil location with mangrove swamps teeming with wildlife. It's an ideal place for hiking, shoreline fishing and general relaxation, as well as the more strenuous **activities** – canoeing, waterskiing and deep-sea fishing. All of this can be arranged through the resort's only **accommodation**, the *Wavecrest* (see p.352).

Mazeppa Bay

One of two good fishing and general chill-out spots on the Wild Coast (the other being by *Kob Inn*; see below), **MAZEPPA BAY** lies northeast of *Wavecrest* – a lovely spot surrounded by dunes and coastal forest. Swimming in the bay is safe, and the surfing is good.

Kob Inn (Qora Mouth)

Just northeast of Mazeppa, **KOB INN** is situated right on the sea front at the **Qora River Mouth**. Apart from the hotel (see p.352), there is nothing else at the settlement. A small ferry traverses the river mouth and takes you to some good hiking trails along the coast, through grassland and into nearby forest patches.

Bulungula (Nquileni)

Idyllically located at the mouth of the Bulungula River, the spread-out village of **NQILENI**, focused around *Bulungula Lodge* (see p.353), gives you the opportunity to experience rural Transkei life. The river winds its way to the sea through rolling green hills dotted with rondavels, maize fields and livestock, ending at a tranquil river mouth. Here, the coastline is carpeted in dense forest stretching into kilometres of soft, white beach.

Coffee Bay and around

The densely populated, gentle hills of **COFFEE BAY**, known to the Xhosa as Tshontini after a dense wood that grows there, mark the traditional boundary between the Bomvana and Pondo clans of the Xhosa nation. Coffee Bay, with its laidback, relaxed atmosphere, draws a growing number of visitors – yet retains its feeling of idyllic obscurity.

The **landscape** at Coffee Bay, dramatic high cliffs dropping to sandy beaches speckled with black pebbles, contrasts with the grasslands, forested sand dunes and lagoons further south. The main attraction here is the **coastal hikes**; the walk to Hole in the Wall is particularly outstanding. The **huts** here are also very distinctive: many are

---

SOME XHOSA TRADITIONS

The Wild Coast region is largely populated by **rural Xhosa**, who still practise traditions and customs that have faded in more urban areas. Many people, for example, still believe that the sea is inhabited by strange people who do not always welcome visitors, which explains the relative scarcity of the activities you would normally find thriving among seashore-dwelling people, such as fishing and diving.

Initiation for teenage boys and young men is still common. Young men usually leave their homes to stay in "circumcision lodges", dress in distinctive white paint and costumes and learn the customs of their clan. At the circumcision ceremony the young men are expected to make no sound while their foreskin is cut off (with no anaesthetic). After the ceremony, they wash off the paint and wrap themselves in new blankets, and all their possessions are thrown into a hut and set alight – they must turn away from this and not look back. There follows a feast to celebrate the beginning of manhood and the start of a year-long intermediary period during which they wear ochre-coloured clay on their faces. After this, they are counted as men.

Like other African peoples, although they believe in one God, **uThixo**, or uNhkulukhulu (the great one), many Xhosa also believe that their **ancestors** play an active role in their lives. However, the ancestors' messages are often too obscure to be understood without the aid of specialists, or *amaqgira*.

The Xhosa are patriarchal by tradition, with women's subordinate status symbolized by *lobola*, the **dowry** payment in cattle and cash that a prospective husband must make to her parents before he can marry her. If the woman is not a virgin, the man pays less. Married Xhosa women have the same right as men to smoke tobacco in **pipes**, and can often be seen doing so, the pipes' long stems designed to prevent ash falling on babies suckling at their breasts. Pipes are shared, but each person must have their own stem, not just for matters of hygiene but also to prevent witchcraft: bits of the body make the most effective poisonous medicines against people, and that includes hair, skin and spittle.

The Xhosa did not wear **cloth** until it was introduced by Europeans, when it was quickly adopted. Today, what is now seen as traditional Xhosa cloth is almost always worn by women, mostly in the form of long skirts, beautifully embroidered with horizontal black stripes placed at varying intervals. The breasts of unmarried women were traditionally uncovered, while those of married women were usually covered with beads or matching cloth. These days, most women wear T-shirts, though almost all still cover their heads with scarves intricately tied to form two peaks above the forehead.

4

THE EASTERN CAPE'S COASTAL NATURE RESERVES

The Eastern Cape has some undeveloped and beautiful **coastal reserves** that are reached on difficult dirt roads and suitable for a stay of a few days, rather than for the day. All accommodation is self-catering, and there are no shops or facilities in the reserve, so you need to be fully self-sufficient and stock up before you leave the N2.

All of the following reserves are **open daily** from 6am to 6pm, and charge R20 for entry. For **bookings** and further information, contact the Eastern Cape Parks Board (☎043 701 9600, ⓦ www.ecparks.co.za).

DWESA RESERVE

Situated between *Kob Inn* and Coffee Bay, **Dwesa Nature Reserve** has well-sited wooden chalets (R200), equipped with gas fridges and stoves, and is one of the best places to stay on the coast, boasting rare animals such as **tree dassies** and **samango monkeys**, as well as red hartebeest, blesbok, blue wildebeest and buffalo.

To get to the reserve, turn east off the N2 at Idutywa towards the coast and continue for 73km or so; the road forks right to *Kob Inn* and left to Dwesa.

HLULEKA NATURE RESERVE

One of the loveliest of the Wild Coast reserves, **Hluleka Nature Reserve** consists of coastal forest whose coral trees flower scarlet in July and August, a strip of grassland and outstanding **sandy beaches** interspersed with rocky outcrops tattooed with extraordinary wind-shaped rock formations. In the grassland strip, you're likely to see **wildebeest**, **zebra** and **blesbok**. Accommodation is in seven spacious self-catering chalets, on stilts overlooking the sea, sleeping up to four people (R600).

You can reach Hluleka along the difficult coastal road from Coffee Bay. Heading towards the N2 from Coffee Bay for a short distance, take the Mdumbi turn on the right, and continue for some 30km, when signs to Hluleka appear. Alternatively – and more easily – take the Hluleka turning 30km along the R61 from Mthatha to Port St Johns, and continue for another 57km to the coast.

MKHAMBATHI NATURE RESERVE

Largest of the Eastern Cape reserves, **Mkhambathi** consists almost entirely of grassland, flanked by the forested ravines of two rivers, and a ravishing **coastline** of rocky promontories and deserted beaches. There's plenty of **game**: you're likely to see eland, hartebeest, wildebeest and blesbok, as well as Cape vultures. The highlight, though, is the Mkhambathi River itself, which cuts through the middle of the reserve down a series of striking waterfalls, of which the **Horseshoe Falls** near the sea are the most spectacular.

Accommodation is at *Gwe Gwe River Lodge*, which is ideal for groups (R2060 for the whole place), with a further six more rondavels nearby sleeping two (R340).

To get to Mkhambathi, turn towards the coast at the Mkhambathi signpost at Flagstaff on the tarred R61. From Flagstaff, the reserve is 70km away on a dirt road, which is very variable in quality. Although the road to the reserve restcamp is fine, driving anywhere in the park except to the beach requires a high-clearance vehicle.

---

thatched with a topknot made from a tyre, coloured glass or even an aloe plant – said to discourage owls, harbingers of ill-omen, from roosting on roofs.

Village visits

An excellent community-run **village tour** can be organized through the impressive ANC Women's League veteran, Betty Madlalisa (R60, plus R100 per group to enter the kraal; ☎083 339 0454). Apart from visiting homesteads, the outing takes in the Masizame Women's Project (daily 8am–5pm), housed in a colourful building opposite the Bayview Store, 5km out of Coffee Bay on the Mthatha Road. The project is one of the very few outlets in South Africa where you can buy traditional Xhosa craftwork, including beaded bags and belts, traditional clothing, baskets, mats and blankets. With advance notice, they also offer Xhosa meals (R60) washed down with traditional beer.

Hole In The Wall

The settlement of **HOLE IN THE WALL**, 9km north west of Coffee Bay, has grown up on the shoreline near the large cliff that juts out of the sea, from which it gets its name. The cliff has a tunnel at its base through which huge waves pound during heavy seas, making a great crashing sound. As well as good fishing, safe swimming and snorkelling, there are several spectacular hikes, including a coastal walk northeast to Coffee Bay.

Mthatha River Mouth

The **Mthatha River** disgorges 6km north of Coffee Bay into another soothing lagoon. This is the site of the *Anchorage Hotel* (see p.353), one of the few places along the Wild Coast for self-catering and camping. An excellent way to see the surrounding area's gentle hills, coastal forest and shoreline is on **horseback**, which the hotel can arrange.

ARRIVAL AND DEPARTURE   THE WILD COAST

By car It's recommended to telephone your resort for up-to-the-minute directions, as roads, and road conditions, change. Be self-reliant and fill up before you leave the N2. Although some of the Wild Coast roads are being surfaced as part of an upgrading programme, most in the region remain untarred and, while generally passable in an ordinary car, it's best to carry a tool kit, a spare tyre and take the roads slowly. Watch out for livestock on all Wild Coast roads, including the N2, and avoid driving in rainy weather and at night. Do not park overnight anywhere that does not have security.

By bus The Baz Bus stops in Cintsa West and Mthatha; you can arrange to be met by hostels in Port St Johns and Coffee Bay, or in Butterworth for Mazeppa. Greyhound and other services ply the N2 between Durban and East London, stopping at Mthatha. Minibus taxis ply all routes, and you should be able to get from Mthatha quite easily to Coffee Bay or Port St Johns, both of which are along tarred and well-populated roads.

By plane If you are flying into East London and making for a specific resort, there is a useful shuttle service from East London run by Ken Black (☎ 043 740 3060) who will quote a price when you book, depending on how many people are travelling.

CINTSA

Cintsa East can be reached on a tarred road: turn off the N2 at the East Coast Resorts Rd (30km out of East London) then, after 8km, turn left at the sign to Cefane Mouth and *Michaela's Restaurant*, from where the village is 7km away. **Cintsa West** is on the Baz Bus Route, which drops off at *Buccaneers* (see p.352).

HAGA-HAGA

Haga Haga is 72km from East London, 27km of which is along a dirt road, signposted off the N2.

WAVECREST (NXAXO MOUTH)

To get to *Wavecrest*, follow the 34km of tarred road to Centani from the N2 at Butterworth. At Centani, take the

signposted road (to the left) to Nxaxo for 8km, then the dirt road for 24km to *Wavecrest* (on the right).

MAZEPPA BAY

To reach Mazeppa Bay, follow the 34km of tarred road to Centani from the N2 at Butterworth. At Centani, take the signposted road another 45km to Mazeppa.

KOB INN (QORA MOUTH)

To get to *Kob Inn* from the N2, take the signposted dirt road heading east for 34km from Idutywa, passing through grassy rolling hills and Xhosa villages.

BULUNGULA (NQULENI)

Bulungula Lodge runs a shuttle service (R70) from the Shell Ultra City in Mthatha (arrange this when booking). To drive to the lodge, make for Elliotdale (turn off the N2 at Jojweni, then about 500m beyond the edge of town), turn left onto a dirt road signposted for *Bulungula Lodge* and Madwaleni Hospital. Continue for another 30km until you reach the hospital, where you leave your car (secure parking R20/day). Lodge staff will collect you from there.

COFFEE BAY

Coffee Bay is easily reached on a tarred road that leaves the N2 14km south of Mthatha's Shell Ultra City.

HOLE IN THE WALL

A 9km gravel road – a scenic drive through traditional villages and along cliffs with sea views – links Coffee Bay with Hole In The Wall.

MTHATHA RIVER MOUTH

The best route to the *Anchorage* is the tarred Coffee Bay road: around 6km before you reach Coffee Bay, there's an *Anchorage* sign where you turn left and continue 14km on a periodically graded rough dirt road.

4

INFORMATION

Services Apart from Port St Johns, none of the places on the coast has a bank or ATM, so be sure to organize money in East London or Mthatha. Petrol is available in Coffee Bay and Port St Johns.

ACCOMMODATION

The **hotels** on the Wild Coast are typically run along old-fashioned, colonial lines, with set meals – old-fangled British fare features prominently – and tea at specific times. Most of the hotels offer full board – aside from Cintsa, and those at Port St Johns and Mthatha, there are no restaurants besides those provided by the accommodation establishments. If you're travelling with children, many hotels offer the services of experienced Xhosa nannies who can be employed for the whole day or for short stretches while you take a break to go to the beach or have a meal. There are a number of good backpacker lodges along the coast, and plenty of campsites, but **camping** in rural areas is not advisable, even if a beach looks idyllically deserted. It's wise to **book accommodation** in advance: the superbly well-informed Wild Coast Holiday Reservations (☎ 043 743 6181, ⓦ wildcoastholidays.co.za) is based in East London, and, apart from being able to arrange places to stay, is unsurpassed when it comes to organizing **activities** in the region.

CINTSA

Crawford's Lodge & Cabins Cintsa East ☎ 043 738 5000, ⓦ crawfordsbeachlodge.com; map p.346. Just a few minutes' walk from the beach, *Crawford's* offers guesthouse B&B accommodation; for a room with a spectacular view, expect to pay R1100. **R800**

Buccaneer's Backpackers Cintsa West ☎ 043 734 3012, ⓦ cintsa.com; map p.346. One of South Africa's most popular hostels, *Buccaneer's* has built its reputation on the excellence of its ten cottages of varying sizes, with fantastic sea and lagoon views, unspoilt beaches, and the plethora of activities they lay on. You can self-cater, or eat inexpensive breakfasts and dinners in the café and pub. It also lays on trips to a local African school and township. Dorm **R260**, double **R295**

HAGA-HAGA

Haga-Haga ☎ 043 841 1670 or ☎ 082 659 8881, ⓦ hagahagahotel.co.za; map p.346. This pleasant, rather old-fashioned hotel offers full board in hotel rooms, and self-catering in fourteen flatlets sleeping two or four. The en-suite rooms have balconies. A tidal swimming pool is sculpted into the rocky shoreline in front of the hotel. One of its advantages is being only 70km from East London with a mere 13km of dirt road. Flatlet **R650**, double **R1100**

MORGAN BAY

★ **Morgan Bay Hotel** ☎ 043 841 1062, ⓦ morganbayhotel.co.za; map p.346. This friendly, well-run place overlooks a gorgeous beach and is one of the best hotels along the Wild Coast, particularly for family holidays. It offers good food and fresh, airy rooms furnished with limewashed furniture; camping is also available. Rates include breakfast and dinner. It is close and accessible to East London with 70km on tar, and 6km on dirt roads. Camping **R180**, double **R1350**

TRENNERY'S (QHOLORHA MOUTH)

★ **Trennery's** ☎ 047 498 0095 or ☎ 082 908 3134, ⓦ www.trennerys.co.za; map p.346. This marvellous family hotel, founded in 1928, still has its heart somewhere in the 1950s or 1960s. Uniformed nannies accompany children around the playground and in the separate children's dining room. The en-suite chalets are slightly worn, while the English-style food is wholesome and well cooked. Rates include full board. **R1590**

WAVECREST (NXAXO MOUTH)

Wavecrest ☎ 047 498 0022, ⓦ wavecrest.co.za; map p.346. A cluster of pleasant bungalows and family rooms at arguably the most beautifully positioned of all the Wild Coast hotels. The charming thatched huts, with comfortable beds and linen, are right on the edge of a mangrove-lined estuary, where you can step out onto the gorgeous beach and sand dunes. Rates include full board. **R1200**

MAZEPPA BAY

Mazeppa Bay ☎ 047 498 0033, ⓦ mazeppabay.co.za; map p.346. This charming hotel offers full board in comfortable cabanas or family rooms, 39 steps up from the beach. Units are thatched and in a setting of palms and tropical plants. It has the added attraction of its own island (reached along a bridge), excellent game fishing and surfing. **R1180**

KOB INN (QORA MOUTH)

Kob Inn ☎ 047 499 0011/16, ⓦ kobinn.co.za; map p.346. Set away from the beach on a rocky shore close to the wide Mbashe River, with spacious and comfortable en-suite thatched bungalows, a good bar with views of the sea, a restaurant renowned for its seafood banquets, and a swimming pool built into the tidal rocks. Staff can arrange a boat and fishing tackle, or equip you for canoeing, waterskiing and boardsailing. There is also a tennis court and trampoline and satellite TV. Rates include full board. R1190

BULUNGULA (NQUILENI)

⭐ **Bulungula Backpackers Lodge** ☎ 047 577 8900, ⓦ bulungula.com; map p.346. Situated on the estuary of river and sea, *Bulungula* offers ten brightly painted rondavels (sleeping two or four) and camping with shared ablutions. It's a joint venture between the community and seasoned traveller Dave Martin, who spent many of his student years involved in community development projects. If you're looking for relaxation and an authentic cultural experience, you'll be hard pressed to find a better place to stay. Booking essential. Camping R140, rondavel R300

COFFEE BAY

Bomvu Paradise ☎ 047 575 2073 or ☎ 082 467 4494, ⓦ bomvubackpackers.com; map p.346. Popular and situated on the river, here you can attend yoga classes, make your own drum and participate in drumming sessions around an evening fire. There are also tours to the nearby village. Accommodation is in dorms and doubles, or you can camp, and there is tasty food available from the *Ubuntu Kitchen*. Camping R120, dorm R200, double R240

Coffee Bay Hotel 11 Main St ☎ 047 575 2051, ⓦ coffeebayhotel.co.za; map p.346. Just a 3min walk from the beach, with a pool and activities on offer. The rooms are simple yet comfortable with colourful decor. R720

Coffee Shack ☎ 047 575 2048, ⓦ coffeeshack.co.za; map p.346. Of the backpacker lodges in Coffee Bay, *Coffee Shack* is the liveliest, with dorm, double rooms and camping, and is well located on the Bomvu River. It has a restaurant, where a two-course dinner costs just R45. Its shuttle bus plies the route between Mthatha and Coffee Bay, meeting the Baz Bus on request. Camping R140, dorm R240, double R300

Ocean View ☎ 047 575 2005 or 2006, ⓦ oceanview .co.za; map p.346. The smartest accommodation in Coffee Bay, right on the sandy bay. It's a friendly place, with bright

rooms, terraced gardens, a pool area, and a trampoline and playground right next to the beach. The restaurant and bar serves English-styled food. Rates include full board. R1150

White Clay ☎ 047 575 0008; map p.346. One bay west of Coffee Bay, and set on a cliff high above the water, *White Clay* has en-suite double rooms and camping facilities. No one else lives on this bay, so you have it all to yourself, and the location couldn't be better, with gorgeous views. Whales can sometimes be seen between August and November, and dolphins all year round. They also have a fully licensed restaurant serving seafood specialities. Camping R150, double R435

HOLE IN THE WALL

Hole In The Wall ☎ 047 575 0009, ⓦ holeinthewall .co.za; map p.346. A conglomeration of white thatched rondavels on a small sandy bay and surrounded by lawns, with a pool, bar and playground. The hotel doesn't have a great reputation for food, accommodation or organization, but it is the only choice if you want to explore the area. There are well-equipped self-catering units sleeping two to eight people. R490

Hole In The Wall Backpackers ☎ 083 317 8786; map p.346. Owned by and run on the same site as the hotel, allowing guests to make use of hotel facilities. There isn't the same social scene here as at the Coffee Bay hostels, but the coastline is beautiful. Dorm R200, double R250

MTHATHA RIVER MOUTH

The Anchorage 70km from the N2 ☎ 047 575 9884, ⓦ anchoragehotel.co.za; map p.346. Though no great shakes as a resort, *The Anchorage* is worth considering for its setting between two rivers. It offers self-catering chalet accommodation, en-suite rooms in the hotel and camping, and a 3km walk along the beach from the Mthatha River Mouth, and also 3km from the Mdumbi River Mouth, with good fishing at both. There is a general store where you can buy bread, milk, eggs and braai packs. Camping R200, double R300

EATING

All of the resorts have their own restaurants; meals are often included in their rates. If you're self-catering, it's best to pick up supplies in Mthatha before heading to your accommodation. Otherwise, absolute basics can be purchased at trading stores you may find along the main roads, but don't rely on this.

CINTSA

Michaela's Steenbras Drive, Cintsa East ☎ 043 738 5139. Tapas and fresh seasonal seafood and game (mains around R130), with an incredible setting perched high on the dunes; the outside terrace offers almost 360° views of unspoilt coastline. Wed–Sun noon–10pm.

Mthatha and around

Straddling the Mthatha River and the N2 highway 235km from East London, the fractious, shambolic town of **MTHATHA** (formerly Umtata) is the erstwhile capital of the Transkei and the Wild Coast region's largest town. Unfortunately, it's a pretty ugly place, its crowded and litter-strewn streets lined with nondescript 1970s office buildings, with the odd older architectural gem, albeit dilapidated. However, the town is useful for stocking up and drawing money, all of which can be done at the Spar Centre or Shell Ultra City on the edge of town. The only reason to venture into the town centre is to visit the **Nelson Mandela Museum**.

Nelson Mandela Museum

Corner of Owen St and Nelson Mandela Drive • 9am–4pm • Free • ☎ 047 532 5110, ⓦ mandelamuseum.org.za

The **Nelson Mandela Museum** is housed in the old **parliament**, or *bungha*, built in 1927; however, it's closed for refurbishment until 2013. The most interesting display in the museum traces the great man's life with photos and other visual material. The museum co-ordinates guided **trips** to **Qunu** and **Mveso** (see opposite), Mandela's birthplace, from its sister museum, the Youth and Heritage Centre in Qunu (see below).

Qunu and the Nelson Mandela Youth and Heritage Centre.

500m from N2, 30km west of Mthatha • 9am–4pm • Free • Tours by arrangement • ☎ 047 538 0217, ⓦ mandelamuseum.org.za

Some 30km from Mthatha, on the East London side, are the scattered dwellings of **Qunu**, where Mandela grew up. The N2 thunders through it, but his large and rather plain mansion, which you may photograph but not enter, is clearly visible on the roadside. Signs from the N2 direct you to the **Nelson Mandela Youth and Heritage Visitors' Centre**, where you can pick up a tour by arrangement, and look around the craft centre. You can visit the remains of Mandela's primary school, the rock he used to slide down with friends, and the graveyard where his parents, son and daughter are buried. Qunu is a village where the women still wear traditional clothing and young boys herd the family cows, and you'll get some sense of the background and roots of the great man.

ARRIVAL AND DEPARTURE

MTHATHA AND AROUND

By plane The small Mthatha airport (❶ 047 536 0121) lies 10km west of town on the Queenstown Rd with daily flights to Jo'burg and East London. There is no public transport from the airport, but you can rent a car here from Avis or Budget.

By bus Greyhound and Translux buses pull in at Shell Ultra

City, 6km from the centre, on the N2, which is also served by the Baz Bus, and is the connecting point for backpackers to take organized shuttles to Port St Johns. There's an ATM here, and in the car park a little Eastern Cape Tourism Board caravan provides maps and basic information. Minibuses can take you into town.

INFORMATION

Tourist information 64 Owen St in the town centre (Mon–Fri 8am–4.30pm; ❶ 047 531 5290).

Self-catering supplies You can pick up groceries at the Spar Centre (daily 7am–9pm), 2.5km from town on the N2

(next to the *Wimpy* restaurant), or Pick 'n Pay (Mon–Fri 8.30am–7pm, Sat & Sun 9am–4pm) at the Southernwood Shopping Centre on Errol Spring Avenue.

ACCOMMODATION

MTHATHA

Mthatha is not somewhere you'd willingly choose to spend a night, but there's some decent accommodation catering mostly to people on business, predominantly on the quieter fringes of the city.

Ebony Lodge 22 Park Rd ❶ 047 531 3933 or ❶ 083 457 7507; map opposite. Close to the town centre, *Ebony* has 38 luxury en-suite rooms surrounded by lush gardens, a few swimming pools, and an à la carte restaurant open

daily for dinner (6.30–10pm). R750

Palm Lodge 19 Blakeway Rd ❶ 072 707 9847, ⓦ palmlodgemthatha.co.za; map opposite. Near the golf course, ten en-suite rooms with their own entrance, plus a swimming pool, garden and braai area. Dinner available on request. R740

The White House 5 Mhlobo St, South Ridge Park ❶ 047 537 0580 or ❶ 083 458 9810, ⓔ whitehouse @intekom.co.za; map opposite. Twenty five rooms,

4

NELSON MANDELA AND THE QUNU CONNECTION

Nelson Rolihlahla Mandela was born in the village of **Mveso**, close to Qunu (see opposite), on July 18, 1918. His father was a member of the Xhosa royal house – he was also chief of Mveso, until he crossed swords with the local white magistrate over a minor dispute. After his sacking, the family moved to a small kraal in Qunu, which Mandela remembers as consisting of several hundred poor households.

Mandela is often called **Madiba** – the name of his family's subclan of the Thembu clan. The name Nelson was given to him by a schoolteacher, and Rolihlahla means colloquially, "troublemaker". Mandela has said that at home he was never allowed to ask any questions, but was expected to learn by observation. Later in life, he was shocked to visit the homes of whites and hear children firing questions at their parents and expecting replies.

Shortly after his father died, Mandela was summoned from Qunu to the royal palace at Mqhakeweni, where he sat in on disputes in court and learned more about Xhosa culture. At 16 he was initiated into manhood before enrolling in Clarkebury, a college for the Thembu elite, then Healdtown at Fort Beaufort, and finally the celebrated **Fort Hare** in Alice (see p.341), which has educated generations of African leaders. Mandela was expelled from Fort Hare after clashing with the authorities, and returned to Mqhakeweni. In 1941, faced with the prospect of an arranged marriage, he ran away to Johannesburg and there immersed himself in politics.

It was only upon his release from prison in 1990 (at the age of 72) that Mandela was able to return to Qunu, visiting first the grave of his mother, who had died in his absence. He noted that the place seemed poorer than he remembered it, and that the children were now singing songs about AK47s and the armed struggle. However, he was relieved to find that none of the old spirit and warmth had left the community, and he arranged for a palace to be built there. This has become the venue for Mandela's holidays and family reunions and has a floor plan identical to that of the house in Victor Verster prison where Mandela spent the last few years of his captivity. In his autobiography he writes:

The Victor Verster house was the first spacious and comfortable home I ever stayed in, and I liked it very much. I was familiar with its dimensions, so at Qunu I would not have to wander at night looking for the kitchen.

eight en suite, in two adjoining suburban houses in a quiet area just off the N2, opposite the Shell Ultra City. An evening meal can be provided if booked beforehand. **R635**

QUNU
Nelson Mandela Youth and Heritage Centre Qunu (see p.354). Conference facilities that are also suitable for overnight stays are available at the Centre, comprising six simple doubles or family rooms with showers and a/c, and twelve dorms sleeping four in two double bunks. It's all self-catering and there are no restaurants in the area, though you could ask for dinner to be provided if you book in advance. Dorm **R140**, double **R300**

Jonopo Cultural Village 7km north of Mandela's house ☎ 083 503 3896. Basic B&B accommodation in rondavels with a washbasin in each room and shared outside toilet; a Xhosa dinner can be cooked if ordered in advance. The centre is open daily (8am–5pm; R10) and there are also good crafts for sale and some exhibitions of rural life. **R300**

EATING AND DRINKING

MTHATHA
Most guesthouses have their own restaurants, so you're unlikely to need to head out for food. The town has a thriving nightlife, with bars and *shebeens*, but exploring it without a local escort isn't recommended.

La Piazza Restaurant Country Club, Delville Rd ☎ 047 531 0795; map p.354. The à la carte *La Piazza Restaurant* in the Country Club is open to the public and has a thatch-covered deck overlooking the golf course (mains R100). Their steaks are recommended. Mon–Sat 11am–late.

Port St Johns

The 90km drive on the R61 to **PORT ST JOHNS** from Mthatha is one of the best journeys on the Wild Coast. After passing tiny **Libode**, with its small hotel and restaurant, you start the dramatic descent to the coast, past craggy ravines and epic vistas of forest and rondavel-spotted grassland. The road runs alongside the Mzimvubu River for the last few kilometres, giving you a perfect view of the Gates of St John, before reaching the town square and taxi rank. The big surprise, coming from the sparse hillsides around Mthatha, is how dramatic, hilly, lush and steamy it all is.

Initially the town is quite confusing – it meanders into three distinct localities, some kilometres apart. **First Beach**, where the river meets the sea, is along the main road from the post office and offers good fishing, but is unsafe for swimming. Close to First Beach is the rather run-down town centre, where you'll find shops and minibus taxis. **Second Beach**, 5km west along a tarred road off a right turn past the post office, is a fabulous swimming beach with a lagoon; it has a couple of nice places to stay close by. The area along the river around the **Pondoland Bridge** has some accommodation popular with anglers.

Port St Johns is a favoured destination for backpackers, drawn by its stunning location at the mouth of the Mzimvubu River, dominated by Mount Thesiger on the west bank and Mount Sullivan on the east. A further attraction for some visitors is the strong cannabis grown in the area, and the town's famously laidback atmosphere may tempt you to stay for longer than you intended. Port St Johns also has good fishing and swimming beaches, a wider choice of accommodation than anywhere else on the Wild Coast, and a good tarred road all the way into town. If you are looking for a stop-off along the Wild Coast, Port St Johns is the place to choose, rather than Mthatha.

For **crafts**, check out Pondo People on the east side of the Mzimvubu River across the Pondoland Bridge, easily the best craft shop on the Wild Coast.

The Gates of St John

Both the mountains of the **Gates of St John** merit a stiff climb to the top, from where you get a superb view of the lush surrounding landscape. To get here by car, drive up to the aircraft landing strip at the top of Mount Thesiger. Look out for the birds of prey, making use of the updraughts.

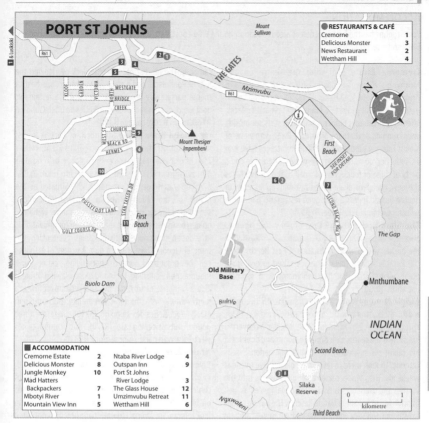

PORT ST JOHNS

Mount Sullivan

THE GATES

Mzimvubu

Mount Thesiger Impembeni

First Beach

SEE INSET FOR DETAILS

The Gap

● **RESTAURANTS & CAFÉ**

Cremorne	1
Delicious Monster	3
News Restaurant	2
Wettham Hill	4

Old Military Base

Buolo Dam

Bulule

Mnthumbane

INDIAN OCEAN

Second Beach

Silaka Reserve

Ngxwaleni

Third Beach

■ **ACCOMMODATION**

Cremorne Estate	2	Ntaba River Lodge	4
Delicious Monster	8	Outspan Inn	9
Jungle Monkey	10	Port St Johns	
Mad Hatters		River Lodge	3
Backpackers	7	The Glass House	12
Mbotyi River	1	Umzimvubu Retreat	11
Mountain View Inn	5	Wettham Hill	6

0 — kilometre — 1

Silaka Nature Reserve

Daily 6am–6pm • R20

Just south of town, the **Silaka Nature Reserve** is a small reserve with a dramatic coastline, and comprises the idyllic **Third Beach**, dense and beautiful tropical-forest areas with huge trees (through which there are good **trails**) and a handful of animals, including zebra and wildebeest. To get to the reserve, head down the Second Beach road from Port St Johns and then up the treacherously steep dirt road to the reserve's office. Some of the backpacker lodges can drop you in the reserve, and you can walk back along the coast. Accommodation is available on the reserve (see p.358).

ARRIVAL AND DEPARTURE | PORT ST JOHNS

By bus and minibus taxi The Baz Bus drops off at Shell Garage, from where you can catch a shuttle bus (pre-book through *Jungle Monkey* ☎ 047 564 1517), which drops off at their hostel; they will phone your accommodation to pick you up from there. If you're travelling from KwaZulu-Natal to Port St Johns by public transport, an alternative route is by minibus taxi via Port Edward, Bizana and Lusikisiki on the R61. This is also the route you should take if you're driving from Durban.

INFORMATION AND TOURS

Tourist information In an obvious building at the roundabout as you enter town (daily 8am–4.30pm; ☎ 047 564 1187). As well as maps, they provide information about local Xhosa homestays.

Tours Jimmy Gila and his brother (☎ 082 507 2256, ⊛ wildcoasthikes.com) run tours in the area.

ACCOMMODATION

Port St Johns has the best selection of accommodation on the Wild Coast, with a healthy number of backpacker lodges, B&Bs and resort complexes.

Cremorne Estate 5km from the centre on the Mzimvubu River, signposted from the Pondoland Bridge ☎047 564 1110 or 1113, ⓦcremorne.co.za; map p.357. One of Port St Johns' few upmarket places, offering self-catering timber cottages on stilts set on tidy lawns running down to the Mzimvubu River, with views of Mount Thesiger's red-slabbed cliffs. The cottages have two en-suite bedrooms, making them very affordable for a party of three or four. A row of small B&B doubles shares the view; cheaper still are some tiny cabins equipped with double bunks. There's a very good restaurant, bar, and a relaxing swimming pool area. R799

The Glass House Marine Drive; follow the signs to Second Beach ☎047 564 1242; map p.357. Nestled in the bushes within walking distance of First Beach, these comfortable wooden bungalows are raised to give good ocean views. Each unit has two rooms with separate entrances. R800

Jungle Monkey Berea Rd, second right off the main road after the post office ☎047 564 1517, ⓦjunglemonkey.co.za; map p.357. Hostel in a converted house near the centre, with camping, dorms and doubles in log cabins surrounded by forest. Accommodation is self-catering, though there's a restaurant, bar and live music at weekends. The owners can arrange guided trips into the villages and overnight visits to a traditional healer, as well as drive you to the Silaka Nature Reserve. The Baz Bus stops in Mthatha and they will pick you up from there. Camping R60, dorm R110, double R280

The Kraal Mpande ☎082 871 4964, ⓦthekraalbackpackers.co.za. One traditional dorm hut, a family hut (R400), and a double hut plus camping, on community land well off the beaten track. Efficiently run and wonderfully set right on the beach, it has no electricity, with biogas flushing toilets, hot-water showers and washing facilities in clay-brick thatched huts. You can opt to be self-catering (basic supplies are available for purchase) or order meals, often featuring crayfish, oysters and mussels, or visit the local traditional food restaurant. Activities include beach hikes, snorkelling, surfing and dolphin-watching (also whale-watching in season). A hostel bus connects with the Baz Bus at Shell Ultra City in Mthatha (book in advance by phone); driving, turn off at Tombo Stores, 70km from Mthatha on the Port St Johns Rd, and travel another 30min to the little village of Mpande. Camping R150, dorm 300, double R600

Mad Hatters Backpackers 2nd Beach Rd ☎047 564 8354, ⓦmadhattersbackpackers.com; map p.357. Funky backpackers providing en-suite cottages, dorms and camping. The hip bar has a serene deck overlooking the hills of Pondoland, and a stage for live music, and hosts a theme party every two weeks. There's also a restaurant, pool room, garden and loads of activities on offer. Camping R160, dorm R200, cottage R300

★ **Mbotyi River Lodge** Just north of Port St Johns; signposted off the R61, just before Lusikisiki; follow 7km of cement road to the end, and then turn right at Mbotyi sign and follow the dust road for 19km ☎082 674 1064, ⓦmbotyi.co.za; map p.357. Situated at the mouth of the Mbotyi River in complete wilderness, surrounded by green rolling hills, estuarine wetlands, golden beaches, forests and sheer cliffs. Accommodation is in wooden bungalows with balconies overlooking the tranquil lagoon. There is also a pub. A variety of activities can be organized, such as horseriding, canoe trips, mountain bikes, fishing, trails and game viewing. There is also a campsite nearby, run by Mbotyi Campsite Trust, a joint venture with the local community. Book through Mbotyi Lodge. Besides camping (R230), there are three pondo huts sleeping six (R770). The campsite has electricity, water and 24-hr security. R1310

Ntaba River Lodge On the banks of the Mzimvubu River ☎047 564 1707 or ☎032 941 5320, ⓦintabariverlodge.co.za; map p.357. A collection of chalets, with a restaurant and a huge variety of activities on offer. The friendly service is impeccable and you can look forward to *idombolo* (home-made bread). Signposted on the R61 from Mthatha, just before you reach Port St Johns. Rates include dinner and breakfast. R1180

Outspan Inn In the centre, past the town hall on the road to First Beach ☎047 564 1057, ⓦoutspaninn .co.za; map p.357. Two-storey ochre B&B with en-suite rooms set in an appealing large garden. Some rooms have unusually high beds that give a view of nearby First Beach. The pub and restaurant is open daily and there's a swimming pool. R700

Port St Johns River Lodge Mthatha Tar Rd ☎047 564 1459, ⓦportstjohnsriverlodge.co.za; map p.357. Wooden self-catering cottages on the riverside (R750) or B&B en-suite rooms in the lodge. There's also a swimming pool, ladies' bar and à la carte restaurant. R400

Silaka Nature Reserve Book through Eastern Cape Parks Board ☎043 701 9600, ⓦecparks.co.za. Accommodation in the reserve is in spacious, fully serviced self-catering thatched family bungalows surrounded by grassland, with fully fitted kitchens, sleeping four. R450

Umngazi River Bungalows Umngazi river mouth, west of Port St Johns ☎047 564 1115, ⓦumngazi .co.za. Unsurpassed as a Wild Coast holiday resort, *Umngazi* delivers probably the best beachside family holiday in the country. It's frequently fully booked, especially during school holidays, so reserve as far in advance as possible. It's signposted off the R61, about 10km before you reach Port St Johns from Mthatha; from the sign, continue another 11km along a potholed road. Alternatively, guests can arrange a private plane into Port St Johns and get picked up. Rates include full board. R1770

Umzimvubu Retreat Follow the road to First Beach; the entrance is clearly marked after the tar road ends ☎ 047 564 1741, ⊛ geocities.com/umzimvuburetreat; map p.357. Homely guesthouse set in a vast natural garden with scenic views. All rooms are en suite, and there is a R300 key deposit if you stay in a self-catering cottage. Book in advance for dinner at the restaurant (R80). R660

Wettham Hill 2 Mountain Drive, signposted from the tourist office ☎ 082 453 3944, ⊛ wetthamhill.co.za; map p.357. Port St Johns' nicest mid-range guesthouse with panoramic views of the town and a small restaurant open to the public (daily 7am–9pm). The rooms are comfortable and pleasantly furnished with white linen and curtains and the odd Art Deco piece. R475

EATING AND DRINKING

If you're self-catering, you can buy tempting local fruits by the roadside, and sometimes fresh fish is available too. In the centre, Boxer Supermarket has most foodstuffs you'll need, while Green Foods is the place for vegetables.

Cremorne Mzimvubu River; follow the signs from the Pondoland Bridge ☎ 047 564 1110 or ☎ 047 564 1113; map p.357. Port St Johns' poshest eating place, serving very good fish, steaks (R65) and puddings, in addition to having a pizza oven and pub. Daily 7–9.30am, noon–2.30pm & 6 8.30pm.

Delicious Monster Near Second Beach ☎ 083 997 9856; map p.357. A couple of tables in the owner's garden, where you can get breakfast, lunch and dinner made with seafood and fresh herbs from the garden, and home-baked goodies for tea (R60). Daily 9am–3pm & 6–9pm.

News Restaurant On the road to First Beach, next to Outspan Inn ☎ 073 359 4281; map p.357. A pub and seafood restaurant, with pub meals and fresh fish, also offering tea and cake and *koeksisters* (mains R75). Tues–Sun 9am–10pm.

Wettham Hill 2 Mountain Drive ☎ 082 453 3944; map p.357. A smart restaurant by Port St Johns standards, with fantastic views from its wraparound balcony. The menu changes every day, with offerings such as balsamic chicken and Mediterranean roast vegetables (R80). Daily 7am–9pm.

4

KwaZulu-Natal

SHAKALAND (P.434)

5

KwaZulu-Natal

KwaZulu-Natal, South Africa's most African province, has everything the continent is known for – beaches, wildlife, mountains and accessible ethnic culture. South Africans are well acquainted with KwaZulu-Natal's attractions; it's the leading province for domestic tourism, although foreign visitors haven't quite cottoned on to the incredible amount packed into this compact and beautiful region. The city of Durban is the industrial hub of the province and the country's principal harbour. British in origin, it has a heady mixture of cultural flavours deriving from its Zulu, Indian and white communities. You'll find palm trees fanning Victorian buildings, African squatters living precariously under truncated flyovers, high-rise offices towering over temples and curry houses, overdeveloped beachfronts, and everywhere an irrepressible fecundity.

To the north and south of Durban lie Africa's most developed beaches, known as the **North and South coasts**: stretching along the shore from the Eastern Cape border in the south to the Tugela River in the north, this 250km ribbon of holiday homes is South Africa's busiest and least enticing coastal strip. However, north of the Tugela River you'll find some of the most pristine shores in the country. Here, along the **Elephant Coast**, a patchwork of wetlands, freshwater lakes, wilderness and Zulu villages meets the sea at a virtually seamless stretch of sand that begins at the St Lucia Estuary and slips across the Mozambique border at Kosi Bay. Apart from southern **Lake St Lucia**, which is fairly developed in a low-key fashion, the Elephant Coast is one of the most isolated regions in the country, rewarding visitors with South Africa's best snorkelling and scuba diving along the coral reefs off **Sodwana Bay**.

KwaZulu-Natal's marine life is matched on land by its **game reserves**, some of which are beaten only by the Kruger National Park, and easily surpass the latter as the best place in the continent to see both black and white rhinos. Concentrated in the north, the reserves tend to be compact and feature some of the most stylish game-lodge accommodation in the country. Most famous and largest of the reserves is the **Hluhluwe-Imfolozi Park**, trampled by a respectable cross section of wildlife that includes all of the Big Five.

Since the nineteenth century, when missionaries were homing in on the region, the **Zulus** have captured the popular imagination of the West and remain one of the province's major draws for tourists. You'll find constant reminders of the old Zulu

HAWKSBILL TURTLE, SODWANA BAY (P.421)

Highlights

❶ Indian curries The tangy food of KwaZulu-Natal's second-largest ethnic group can be experienced in the heart of Durban. **See p.382**

❷ Ukhahlamba Drakensberg Towering peaks and ancient San (Bushman) rock paintings in one of KwaZulu-Natal's two World Heritage Sites. **See p.398**

❸ Sodwana Bay Swim with ragged-tooth sharks, sea turtles and bright tropical fish at South Africa's premier diving and snorkelling destination. **See p.421**

❹ iSimangaliso Wetland Park Declared a World Heritage Site in 1999, this reserve is home

to five ecosystems, full of marine life and wildlife. **See p.415**

❺ Hluhluwe-Imfolozi Park KwaZulu-Natal's most outstanding game park, and one of the best places in the world to see both black and white rhinos. **See p.412**

❻ Eshowe's authentic Zulu culture Be a guest at a traditional Zulu wedding or coming-of-age ceremony, or inspect Zulu baskets at the Vukani Zulu Cultural Museum. **See p.431**

❼ Battlefield tours Experience the drama of the Anglo-Zulu wars with world-renowned storytellers and guides. **See p.435**

HIGHLIGHTS ARE MARKED ON THE MAP ON P.362

5

kingdom and its founder Shaka, including an excellent reconstruction of the beehive-hutted capital at **Ondini** and the more touristy **Shakaland** near **Eshowe**. The interior north of the Tugela River was the heartland of the Zulu kingdom and witnessed gruesome battles between Boers and Zulus, British and Zulus, and finally Boers and British. Today, the area can be explored through **Battlefield tours**, a memorable way of taking in some of South Africa's most turbulent history.

From the Midlands, South Africa's highest peaks sweep west into the soaring **Ukhahlamba Drakensberg** range, protected by a chain of KZN Wildlife reserves. The area's restcamps are ideal bases for walking in the mountains or heading out for ambitious hikes; with relatively little effort, you can experience crystal rivers

HIGHLIGHTS

❶ Indian curries
❷ Ukhahlamba Drakensberg
❸ Sodwana Bay
❹ iSimangaliso Wetland Park
❺ Hluhluwe-Imfolozi Park
❻ Eshowe's authentic Zulu Culture
❼ Battlefield tours

KWAZULU-NATAL

> **5**
>
> ### KZN WILDLIFE
>
> Most of the public game parks and wilderness areas described in this chapter fall under the auspices of **Ezemvelo KwaZulu-Natal Wildlife**, also known as Ezemvelo KZN Wildlife or KZN Wildlife (PO Box 13053, Cascades 3202; ☎ 033 845 1000, ⓦ www.kznwildlife.com).
>
> **Accommodation** in these areas is best booked in advance through them; if you want to do so in person, one convenient location is their Durban office at Tourist Junction (☎ 031 274 1150; see p.380).

tumbling into marbled rock pools, awe-inspiring peaks and rock faces enriched by ancient San paintings.

KwaZulu-Natal experiences considerable variations in **climate**, from the occasional heavy winter snowstorms of the Ukhahlamba Drakensberg to the mellow, sunny days and pleasant sea temperatures a couple of hundred kilometres away along the **subtropical coastline**, which offers a temperate climate year-round. This makes the region a popular winter getaway, but in midsummer the low-lying areas, including Durban, the coastal belt and the game reserves, can be uncomfortably humid.

Brief history

Despite their defeats in battles with the Boers and the British during the nineteenth century, the Zulus have remained an active force in South African politics and are particularly strong in KwaZulu-Natal. The **Inkatha Freedom Party** (IFP), formed in 1975 by former ANC Youth League member **Mangosuthu Buthelezi** and currently the country's fourth-largest political party, has long been associated with Zulu nationalism and draws most of its support from Zulu-speaking people. The IFP and ANC were originally allies in the fight against apartheid, but the IFP's ardent nationalism soon proved to be a major hassle for the ANC, who responded with attacks on opposing IFP members. A bitter and violent conflict between the two parties ensued during the 1980s and 1990s, which, according to some, claimed around twenty thousand lives. Although the fighting is now restricted to isolated – and increasingly rare – incidents, the political rivalry continues. It is the ANC, however, which has gained the upper hand in KwaZulu-Natal and is currently in control of the provincial legislature. The South African president, **Jacob Zuma**, a Zulu from KwaZulu-Natal, has played an important role in trying to end the violence between the ANC and IFP. He often makes speeches in Zulu, and has retained strong support among his people despite his controversial political career.

Durban

Until the 1970s, **DURBAN** – South Africa's third-largest city and the continent's largest port – was white South Africa's quintessential seaside playground, thanks to its tropical colours and itinerant population of surfers, hedonists and holidaying Jo'burg families. Then, in the 1980s, the collapse of apartheid saw a growing stream of Africans flood in from rural KwaZulu-Natal, and shantytowns and cardboard hovels revealed the reality of one of the most unmistakably **African conurbations** in the country. The city's second-largest group is its **Indian population**, whose mosques, bazaars and temples are juxtaposed with the Victorian buildings of the colonial centre.

Although the **beachfront** pulls thousands of Jo'burgers down to "Durbs" every year, the city's main interest lies in its gritty urbanity, a seemingly endless struggle to reconcile competing cultures. However, most people come to Durban because it provides a logical springboard for visiting the region. The city is well connected to the

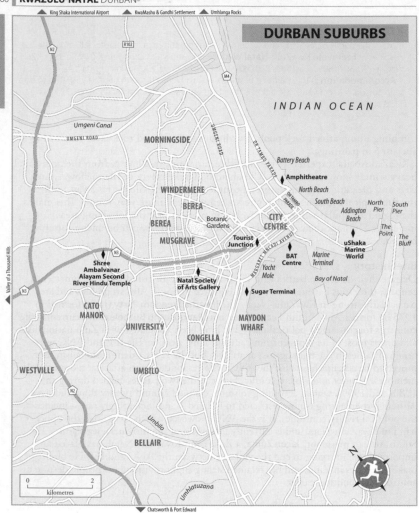

rest of South Africa, and with the opening of the King Shaka International Airport, the city is starting to attract international flights as well.

There's enough here to keep you busy for a few days. The pulsing warren of bazaars, alleyways and mosques that makes up the Indian area around Dr Yusuf Dadoo Street is ripe for exploration, and there are some excellent restaurants and nightlife around Durban's photogenic **harbour** area. Swanky **northern suburbs** such as the **Berea**, a desirable residential district perched on a cooler ridge, are replete with luxuriant gardens and packed with fashionable cafés, restaurants and bars.

Durban's **city centre** grew around the arrival point of the first white settlers, and the remains of the historical heart are concentrated around **Francis Farewell Square**. Durban's expansive **beachfront** on the eastern edge of the centre has one of the city's busiest concentrations of restaurants, a surfeit of tacky family entertainment, and a reputation for crime (which admittedly is improving).

Much further afield lie dormitory towns for blacks who commute to work, including the apartheid **ghettos** of KwaMashu and Inanda to the northwest. **Cato Manor**, the closest township to the city, provides an easily accessible vignette of South Africa's growing urban contradictions.

Brief history
Less than two hundred years ago Durban was known to Europeans as **Port Natal**, a lagoon thick with mangroves, eyed by white adventurers who saw business opportunities in its ivory and hides. In 1824, a British party led by **Francis Farewell** persuaded the Zulu king, **Shaka**, to give them some land. Not long after, the British went on to rename the settlement **Durban** after Sir Benjamin D'Urban, governor of the Cape Colony, whose support, they believed, might not go amiss later.

Britain's tenuous toehold looked threatened in 1839, when **Boers** trundled over the Ukhahlamba Drakensberg in their ox wagons and declared their Republic of Natalia nearby. Then, the following year, a large force of now-hostile Zulus razed the settlement, forcing the British residents to take refuge at sea in the brig *Comet*. Capitalizing on the British absence, a group of Boers annexed Durban, later laying siege to a British detachment. This provided the cue for a much-celebrated piece of Victorian melodrama when teenager **Dick King** heroically rode the 1000km from Durban to Grahamstown in ten days to alert the garrison there, which promptly dispatched a rescue detachment to relieve Durban.

Industrialization and apartheid
While Cape Town was becoming a cosmopolitan centre by the 1840s, Durban's population of barely one thousand lived a basic existence in a near wilderness roamed by lions, leopards and hyenas. Things changed after Britain formally annexed the **Colony of Natal** in 1843; within ten years, a large-scale immigration of settlers from the mother country had begun. The second half of the nineteenth century was marked by the city's considerable industrial development and major influxes of other groups. Indentured **Indian labourers** arrived to work in the KwaZulu-Natal cane fields, planting the seeds for South Africa's lucrative **sugar industry** and the city's now substantial Indian community; and **Zulus** headed south after their conquest by the British, in 1879, to enter Durban's expanding economy. In 1895, the completion of the railway connecting Johannesburg and Durban accelerated the process of migrant labour. This link to South Africa's industrial heartland, and the opening of Durban's harbour mouth to large ships in 1904, ensured the city's eventual pre-eminence as South Africa's principal harbour. In 1922, in the face of growing Indian and African populations, Durban's strongly English city council introduced **legislation** controlling the sale of land in the city to non-whites, predating Afrikaner-led apartheid by 26 years.

With the strict enforcement of **apartheid** in the 1950s, Durban saw a decade of ANC-led **protests**. And when it was banned in 1960, subsequently forming its armed wing, the ANC made plans for a nationwide **bombing campaign** that was initiated with an explosion in Durban on December 15, 1961. Durban scored another first in 1973 when workers in the city precipitated a wildcat strike, despite a total ban on black industrial action. This heralded the rebirth of South Africa's **trade unions** and reawakened anti-apartheid activity, sparking the final phase of the country's road to democracy.

The centre
Standing at the heart of colonial Durban, **Francis Farewell Square** is hemmed in by the centre's two main thoroughfares, Dr Pixley Kaseme (formerly West) Street and Anton Lembede (formerly Smith) Street. The square is a sultry palm-fringed garden overlooked by some fine old buildings, the focal point being the **Cenotaph**, a

5

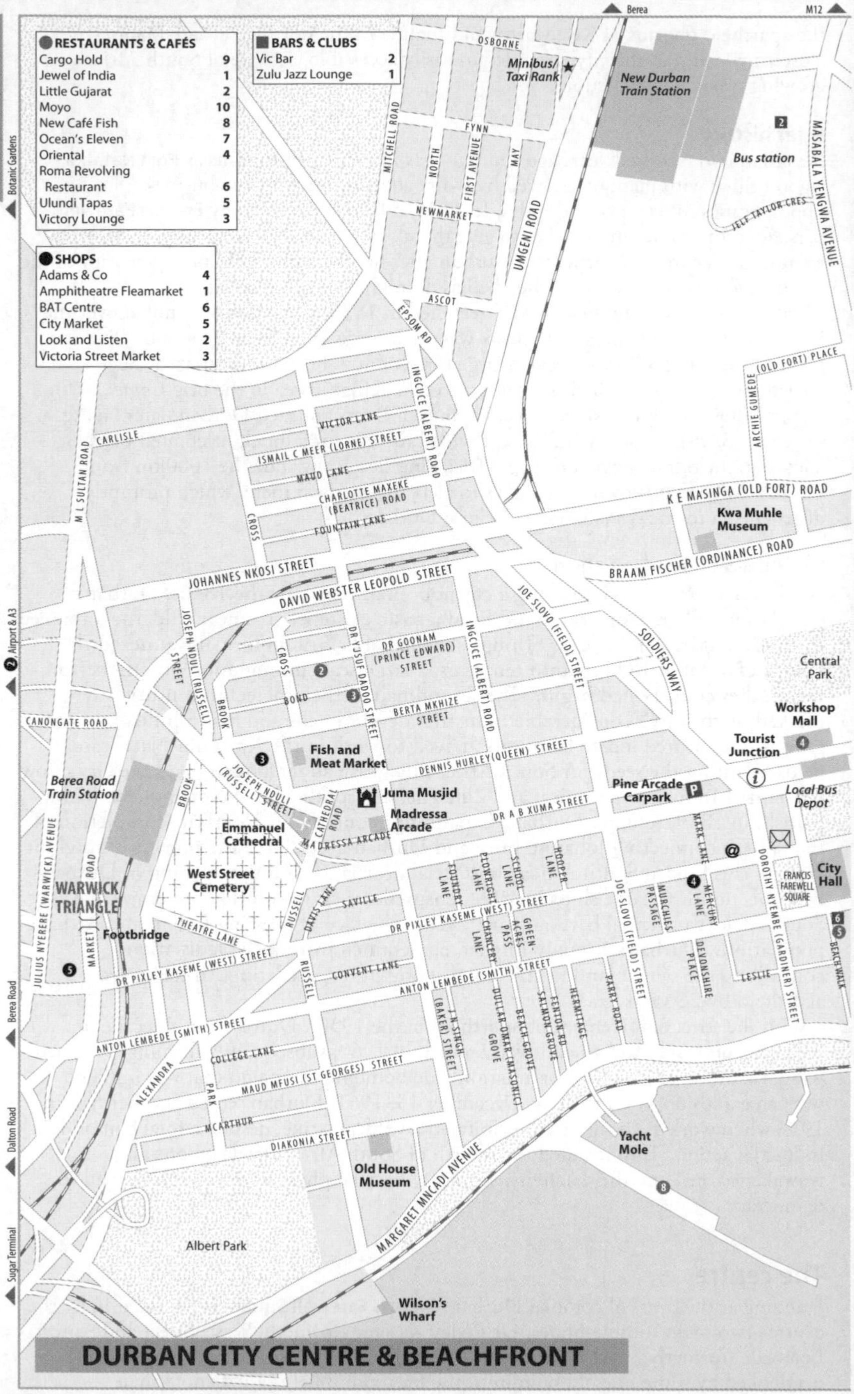

RESTAURANTS & CAFÉS
Cargo Hold 9
Jewel of India 1
Little Gujarat 2
Moyo 10
New Café Fish 8
Ocean's Eleven 7
Oriental 4
Roma Revolving Restaurant 6
Ulundi Tapas 5
Victory Lounge 3
SHOPS
Adams & Co 4
Amphitheatre Fleamarket 1
BAT Centre 6
City Market 5
Look and Listen 2
Victoria Street Market 3
BARS & CLUBS
Vic Bar 2
Zulu Jazz Lounge 1
Berea
M12
Botanic Gardens
Airport & A3
Berea Road
Dalton Road
Sugar Terminal
OSBORNE
Minibus/ Taxi Rank
New Durban Train Station
Bus station
MASABALA YENGWA AVENUE
JELF TAYLOR CRES
MITCHELL ROAD
FYNN
NORTH
FIRST AVENUE
MAY
NEWMARKET
UMGENI ROAD
ASCOT
EPSOM RD
INGCUCE (ALBERT) ROAD
(OLD FORT) PLACE
ARCHIE GUMEDE
VICTOR LANE
CARLISLE
ISMAIL C MEER (LORNE) STREET
MAUD LANE
CHARLOTTE MAXEKE (BEATRICE) ROAD
FOUNTAIN LANE
M L SULTAN ROAD
CROSS
K E MASINGA (OLD FORT) ROAD
Kwa Muhle Museum
BRAAM FISCHER (ORDINANCE) ROAD
JOHANNES NKOSI STREET
DAVID WEBSTER LEOPOLD STREET
JOE SLOVO (FIELD) STREET
SOLDIERS WAY
JOSEPH NDULI (RUSSELL) STREET
DR GOONAM (PRINCE EDWARD) STREET
DR YUSUF DADOO STREET
Central Park
BOND
BERTA MKHIZE STREET
Workshop Mall
BROOK
CANONGATE ROAD
Tourist Junction
Fish and Meat Market
DENNIS HURLEY(QUEEN) STREET
Berea Road Train Station
JOSEPH NDULI (RUSSELL) STREET
CATHEDRAL ROAD
Juma Musjid
Pine Arcade Carpark
Local Bus Depot
Emmanuel Cathedral
Madressa Arcade
MADRESSA ARCADE
DR A B XUMA STREET
MARK LANE
JULIUS NYERERE (WARWICK) AVENUE
WARWICK TRIANGLE
West Street Cemetery
FOUNDRY LANE
ELOWRIGHT LANE
SCHOOL LANE
HOOPER LANE
DOROTHY NYEMBE (GARDINER) STREET
City Hall
FRANCIS FAREWELL SQUARE
MURCHIES PASSAGE
MERCURY LANE
SAVILLE
DAVIS LANE
RUSSELL
DR PIXLEY KASEME (WEST) STREET
CHANCERY LANE
ACRES PASS
GREEN-
BEACH WALK
Footbridge
MARKET
THEATRE LANE
DEVONSHIRE PLACE
DR PIXLEY KASEME (WEST) STREET
CONVENT LANE
LESLIE
ANTON LEMBEDE (SMITH) STREET
PARRY ROAD
HERMITAGE
FENTON RD
SALMON GROVE
BEACH GROVE
DULLAR OMAR (MASONIC) GROVE
J N SINGH (BAKER) STREET
ANTON LEMBEDE (SMITH) STREET
ALEXANDRA
COLLEGE LANE
PARK
MAUD MFUSI (ST GEORGES) STREET
MCARTHUR
DIAKONIA STREET
Yacht Mole
Old House Museum
MARGARET MNCADI AVENUE
Albert Park
Wilson's Wharf
DURBAN CITY CENTRE & BEACHFRONT

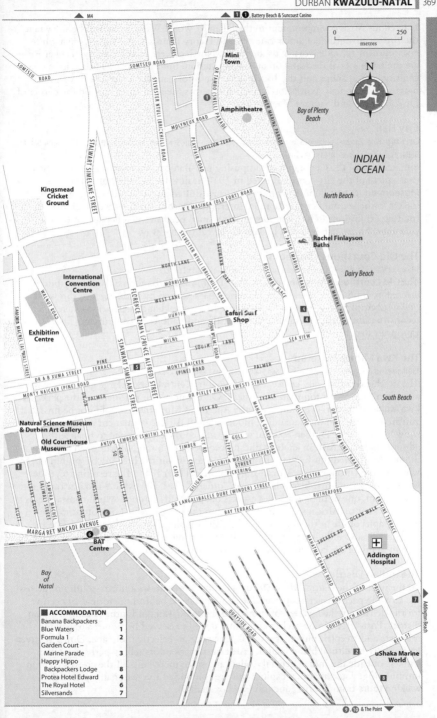

Mini Town

Amphitheatre

Bay of Plenty Beach

INDIAN OCEAN

North Beach

Rachel Finlayson Baths

Dairy Beach

South Beach

Kingsmead Cricket Ground

International Convention Centre

Exhibition Centre

Safari Surf Shop

Natural Science Museum & Durban Art Gallery

Old Courthouse Museum

BAT Centre

Bay of Natal

Addington Hospital

Addington Beach

uShaka Marine World

ACCOMMODATION

Banana Backpackers	5
Blue Waters	1
Formula 1	2
Garden Court – Marine Parade	3
Happy Hippo Backpackers Lodge	8
Protea Hotel Edward	4
The Royal Hotel	6
Silversands	7

❾, ❿ & The Point ▼

Streets labelled on map:

SOL HARRIS CRES
SOMTSEU ROAD
SOMTSEU ROAD
DR TAMBO (SNELL) PARADE
SYLVESTER NTULI (BRICKHILL) ROAD
MOLYNEUX ROAD
PAVILION TERR.
PLAYFAIR ROAD
STALWART SIMELANE STREET
LOWER MARINE PARADE
K E MASINGA (OLD FORT) ROAD
GRESHAM PLACE
SYLVESTER NTULI (BRICKHILL) ROAD
BAUMAN ROAD
BOSCOMBE PLACE
DR TAMBO MARINE PARADE
LOWER MARINE PARADE
NORTH LANE
MORRISON
WEST LANE
FLORENCE NZAMA (PRINCE ALFRED) STREET
HUNTER
EAST LANE
JOHN MILNE ROAD
MILNE
SOUTH LANE
SEA VIEW
PINE TERRACE
MONTY NAICKER (PINE) ROAD
PALMER
WALNUT ROAD
SAMORA MACHEL (ALIWAL) STREET
DR A B XUMA STREET
MONTY NAICKER (PINE) ROAD
UNION
PALMER
DR PIXLEY KASEME (WEST) STREET
TYZACK
MAHARMA GHANDI ROAD
GILLESPIE
DR TAMBO MARINE PARADE
PECK RD
ANTON LEMBEDE (SMITH) STREET
SOL
CATO
TIMBER
SCY RD
GULL
MAZEPPA
MASOBIYA MDLULI (FISHER) STREET
PICKERING
ROCHESTER
RUTHERFORD
MILLS LANE
JONSSON LANE
MONA ROAD
SAMORA MACHEL (ALIWAL) STREET
ACUTT
ALBANY GROVE
STALWART SIMELANE STREET
CREEK
GILLIGAN
DR LANGALIBALELE DUBE (WINDER) STREET
BAY TERRACE
OCEAN WALK
MARGARET MNCADI AVENUE
SHEARER RD
MASONIC RD
MAHARMA GHANDI ROAD
ERSKINE TERRACE
QUAYSIDE ROAD
HOSPITAL ROAD
PRINCE
SOUTH BEACH AVENUE
BELL ST

5

marvellous Art Deco monument to the fallen of World War I. It marks the site where the British adventurers Francis Farewell and Henry Fynn set up Durban's first white encampment to trade ivory with the Zulus. North of here at 160 Monty Naicker Rd are the remnants of the **Natal Great Railway Station**, built in 1894 and recycled a century later as shops and the Tourist Junction information centre. The city centre's main shopping mall, Workshop Mall, is just across the road from here on the corner of Dr A B Xuma and Samora Machel streets.

City Hall

City Hall Dr Pixley Kaseme St • Natural Science Museum Mon–Sat 8.30am–4pm, Sun 11am–4pm • Free • ☎ 031 311 1111 • **Durban Art Gallery** same hours • Free • ☎ 031 311 2264

Situated east of the Cenotaph, the imposing neo-Baroque **City Hall** is the monumental centrepiece of the city centre. Erected in 1910, it now houses the **Natural Science Museum** on its first floor, containing the usual stuffed animals and worth only a brief look. On the second floor is the more interesting **Durban Art Gallery**, which has rotating exhibitions in its main rooms and a small permanent collection of African paintings, prints, carvings and baskets in the central hallway.

The Old Courthouse Museum

99 Samora Machel St • Mon–Sat 8.30am–4pm, Sun 11am–4pm • Free • ☎ 031 311 2226

The **Old Courthouse Museum**, east of City Hall, was Durban's first two-storey building, erected in 1866 in the Natal Veranda style, characterized by wide eaves to throw off heavy subtropical downpours. Housed here in a somewhat austere atmosphere is a reconstruction of Henry Francis Fynn's wattle-and-daub cottage, Durban's first European structure.

The Kwa Muhle Museum

130 Braam Fischer Rd • Mon–Sat 8.30am–4pm, Sun 11am–4pm • Free • ☎ 031 311 2237

The north side of the city centre is dominated by **Central Park**, a large green space with a lovely mosaic water fountain as its focus. On the northern perimeter of the park, the **Kwa Muhle Museum** – also known as the Apartheid Museum – should not be missed if you are interested in understanding modern South Africa. Permanent exhibitions include one on the Durban System, which enabled the city council to finance the administration of African affairs without ever spending a rand of white ratepayers' money. It achieved this by granting itself a monopoly on the brewing of sorghum beer, which it sold through vast, African-only municipal beer halls. The resulting revenue was used to ensure that blacks lived in an "orderly" way. The exhibit also illustrates the Pass System, one of the most hated aspects of apartheid, through which constant tabs could be kept on Africans and their influx into the urban areas. Look out, too, for photographs of life in the single-sex, artificially tribalized worker hostels, which deliberately sowed divisions among blacks by creating separations, and so played its part in many of the current social problems in South Africa.

The Indian District

To the west of the centre, where **Dr Yusuf Dadoo Street** draws a north–south line across the city, the pace accelerates perceptibly, and you leave behind the formal city centre for the densely packed warren of shops and living quarters of Durban's central **Indian district**. Post-1910 Union-style architecture is well preserved here and, along with minarets and steeples, punctuates the skyline with an eclectic roofscape. Down at street level, the rich cultural blend includes African street vendors selling herbs, fruit and trinkets outside the Indian general dealers and spice merchants. If the crowds feel too intimidating, you can always explore this area on one of the reasonably priced daily **walking tours** from Tourist Junction (see box, p.380).

5

Juma Musjid and the Madressa Arcade
On the corner of Dr Yusuf Dadoo and Dennis Hurley sts

The gilt-domed minarets of **Juma Musjid** were completed in 1927. It's the largest mosque in the southern hemisphere and a focal point for the area, although Durban's Indian population is predominantly Hindu. You're welcome to enter the mosque, but make sure you leave your shoes at the door. The colonnaded verandas give way to the alley of the bazaar-like **Madressa Arcade** next door, heaving with Indian traders peddling kerosene lamps, tailor-made outfits and beads. The arcade emerges with a start into Cathedral Street, dominated by the **Emmanuel Cathedral**, built in 1902 in Gothic Revival style.

Victoria Street Market
North across Dennis Hurley St

The bright-pink **Victoria Street Market** (see p.385) is popular with tourists in search of a trinket or two, while the hectic fish and meat market opposite can provide drama, particularly on Sunday mornings when the stallholders compete to sell their stocks before the afternoon close-down.

Joseph Nduli Street and the West Street Cemetery

To the west of the Victoria Street Market, African hawkers gather on **Joseph Nduli Street** (formerly Russel St), where they do a brisk trade in *umuthi* (traditional herbal medicines). West of Joseph Nduli Street and jammed between the railway tracks to the west and the N3 into town on its northern side, **West Street Cemetery** is zoned according to religion, with many of the city's colonial big names buried here, such as Durban's first mayor, George Cato, and the Victorian documentary painter, Thomas Baines. In the Muslim section some tombstones are inscribed "*hagee*" or "*hafez*", the former indicating someone who has been to Mecca and the latter an individual who managed to memorize the entire Koran.

Warwick Triangle

In an Africanized *Bladerunner* setting west of Dr Yusuf Dadoo Street, concrete freeways run over chaotic roadways and minibus taxi ranks; here you'll find Durban's real urban heart of hawkers, shacks and *shebeens*. You'll need to be bold to explore the **Warwick Triangle**, which lies between King Dinizulu Road, Brook Street and Cannongate Road – walk with confidence, wear nothing easily snatched, and you should be fine.

The gateway to the triangle is across Brook Street – known until 1988 as Slaughterhouse Road because butchers slaughtered livestock here – through the hectic Berea station concourse full of pumping music and hawkers, and across the Market Road footbridge, where you'll come to the main **city market** (see p.385), which lies between Julius Nyerere Avenue and Market Road.

The harbour area

Margaret Mncadi Avenue (formerly Victoria Embankment), or the Esplanade, runs the length of Durban's harbour, the lifeblood of the city's economic power. Durban is one of the only cities in the world with a busy port a mere block from the city centre, but the harbour area is edged by a narrow strip of park that is too seedy to make for a very pleasant stroll. However, there are some good restaurants to be found in the area and a lively cultural scene at the BAT Centre at the eastern end, all of which are good spots from which to watch the sun glinting off the sparkling water and take in the mix of yachts and cargo ships chugging past.

The Sugar Terminal
51 Maydon Wharf Rd • Tours Mon–Fri 8.30am, 10am, 11.30am & 2pm • R15 • Make bookings at the SA Sugar Association Tour Centre • ☏ 031 365 8100

5

At the western edge of the harbour, where Margaret Mncadi Avenue joins Maydon Wharf Road, is a photogenic complex of functional industrial architecture, most notable of which are the three dramatic sugar silos at the **Sugar Terminal**. The terminal, whose design has been patented and used internationally, has become something of a tourist attraction; a tour gives you one hour of sugary history and access to half a million tonnes of sugar.

Old House Museum

31 Diakonia St • Mon–Fri 8.30am–4pm • Free • ☎ 031 311 2261

Margaret Mncadi Avenue and the streets around it were the prime residential areas during the city's early development in the nineteenth century, and working your way back east from Maydon Wharf Road there's a reminder of the city's colonial heritage at the **Old House Museum**, one block north of Margaret Mncadi Avenue. Once the home of Sir John Robinson, who became Natal's first prime minister in 1893, the two rooms of this renovated settler house are crammed full of period furniture and numerous ticking clocks.

Yacht Mole and the BAT

On the waterfront you'll find the **Yacht Mole**, a slender breakwater jutting into the bay and home to the Point and Royal Natal Yacht clubs. This is also the access point for the **BAT (Bartle Arts Trust) Centre**, an industrial-chic arts development and community venue boasting a concert hall, practical visual art workshops, classes and exhibition galleries (see p.383). The *Ocean's Eleven* restaurant upstairs (see p.382) provides a magnificent lookout for watching the passing harbour scene.

Ocean Terminal Building

Quayside Rd

The **Ocean Terminal Building**, which harks back to the romantic days of sea travel, is one of Durban's architectural masterpieces. Although you can't enter the building, the view from outside it at night, looking back onto the city, is spectacular. To get here, head east on Margaret Mncadi Avenue towards the Stalwart Simelane Street intersection, enter the Harbour at Port Entrance no. 3 and follow the signs.

The beachfront

Durban's **beachfront**, a high-energy holiday strip just east of the centre, is South Africa's most developed seaside; however, it's of limited appeal unless you enjoy unabashed kitsch and garish amusement parks. This 6km stretch from the Umgeni River in the north to the Point in the south was traditionally called the **Golden Mile**, but the prevalence of crime along the beachfront has earned it the moniker of Mugger's Mile. However, in the build-up to the 2010 football World Cup, concerted efforts were made to clean up the beachfront: the police presence has been increased significantly and CCTV cameras have been installed. These measures have improved security, although you should still exercise caution and use common sense during the day – for example, never leave valuables unattended on the beach – and avoid the beachfront altogether at night.

uShaka Marine World

Daily 9am–5pm • R99 to visit either Sea World or Wet 'n Wild, or R130 for both • ☎ 031 328 8000, ⓦ www.ushakamarineworld.co.za • uShaka Village Walk & uShaka Beach daily 9am–late

The big draw of Addington Beach – and the only really worthwhile attraction along the beachfront – is **uShaka Marine World**. This impressive water adventure wonderland is a tropical African theme park, complete with palm trees, fake rock formations and thatched *bomas*. The most appealing section is **uShaka Sea World**, designed in and around a superb mock-up of a wrecked 1920s cargo ship. The main entrance leads you down to the darkened hull with its broken wood, battered engine room, ropes and sloping floors. The walls of the hull serve as windows into the "ocean" (actually a series of large tanks), where turtles, stingrays, octopus, sharks and a host of other marine life can be seen. The complex also includes a dolphin stadium and a seal pool, where daily shows (three a day) feature these creatures, as well as **uShaka Wet 'n Wild**, a series of pools and water slides, including The Drop Zone, the highest water slide in Africa. The **uShaka Village Walk** development is home to plenty of restaurants, making it a great (and safe) night-time venue.

South Beach
Just north of uShaka Marine World lies **South Beach**, arguably South Africa's busiest beach, which heralds the start of the beachfront tourist tack. Further along OR Tambo Parade, you'll find paddling pools, stepping stones, an aerial cableway and amusement rides.

Dairy Beach and the Rachel Finlayson Baths
OR Tambo Parade • Rachel Finlayson Baths daily 6am–5pm • R7
Dairy Beach, the next along from South Beach, is so-called because of the milking factory that once stood here. It's now regarded as one of the country's best surfing beaches, and it's home to the saltwater **Rachel Finlayson Baths**, a good spot for sheltered swimming and sunbathing.

North Beach and the Bay of Plenty
Both **North Beach** and the adjacent **Bay of Plenty**, adjoining Dairy Beach, host an international professional surfing contest held every July (see p.384). Between OR Tambo Parade and the pedestrian walkway at the Bay of Plenty is the attractively landscaped **Amphitheatre**, the venue for Sunday flea markets (see p.385).

Mini Town
141 OR Tambo Parade • Daily: Feb–June, Aug, Oct & Nov 9.30am–4.30pm; Dec, Jan, July & Sept 9.30am–5pm • R15
Near the corner of OR Tambo Parade and KE Masinga Road, just north of North Beach, **Mini Town** is a scale replica of Durban's landmarks and great fun for kids; walkways lead you past hotels, beaches and the airport, giving you a bird's-eye view of the city.

Battery Beach and the Suncoast Casino
A kilometre north of the centre along Marine Parade, past **Battery Beach** (a good place for swimming), is the massive **Suncoast Casino**, a mock Art Deco entertainment complex with restaurants, gambling tables, eight cinemas and a pristine private beach.

The Berea
High on a north–south ridge overlooking the city centre, the **Berea** is Durban's oldest and most desirable residential district, where mansions and apartment blocks enjoy airy views of the harbour and the sea. Its palmy avenues provide an alternative to the torrid city centre and beachfront for accommodation, eating and entertainment. The term Berea actually has two meanings locally; the suburban area immediately north and west of the city centre is called the Berea, though within this is a suburb known as the Berea, as well as suburbs such as Morningside and Musgrave.

KwaZulu-Natal Society of Arts Gallery
166 Bulwer Rd • Tues–Fri 9am–5pm, Sat 9am–4pm, Sun 10am–3pm • Free • ☎ 031 277 1705, ⓦ nsagallery.co.za
South of the N3, which passes through the Berea to the city, and east of Peter Mokaba Road, in Bulwer Road, the **KwaZulu-Natal Society of Arts Gallery**, or NSA, adjacent to

5

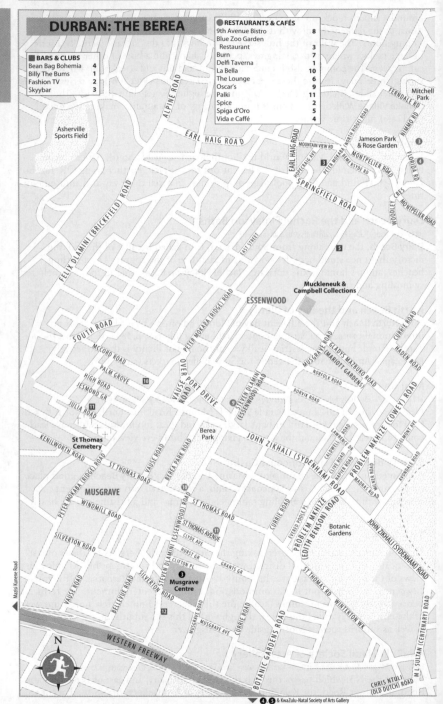

DURBAN: THE BEREA

BARS & CLUBS
Bean Bag Bohemia	4
Billy The Bums	1
Fashion TV	2
Skyybar	3

RESTAURANTS & CAFÉS
9th Avenue Bistro	8
Blue Zoo Garden Restaurant	3
Burn	7
Delfi Taverna	1
La Bella	10
The Lounge	6
Oscar's	9
Palki	11
Spice	2
Spiga d'Oro	5
Vida e Caffé	4

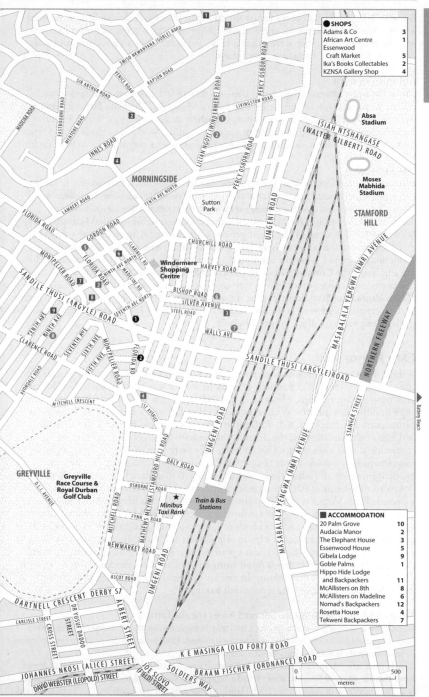

5

Bulwer Park, provides a breezy venue for taking in thrice-weekly exhibitions by local artists. Designed for the local climate, the 1990s building is a mass of interlinked spaces divided by a timber screen that forms a veranda. There's a good arts and crafts shop (see p.385) and a relaxing coffee shop.

Botanic Gardens

John Zikhali Rd, enter on St Thomas Rd • Daily 7.30am–5.15pm • Free • ☏ 031 309 1170, ⓦ www.durbanbotanicgardens.org.za

A little way northwest of the centre and east of Musgrave, Durban's **Botanic Gardens** were established in 1849. They're famous for their cycad collection, which includes *Encephalartos woodii*, one of the rarest specimens in the world. The gardens also boast cool paths, excellent picnic spots, a lovely tea house and a magnificent array of orchids.

Muckleneuk

Muckleneuk 220 Gladys Mazibuco Rd, corner of Steven Dlamini Rd • Campbell Collections Mon, Tues & Fri 9am–3pm, Sat 9am–noon • Tours by appointment R20 • ☏ 031 260 1720, ⓦ campbell.ukzn.ac.za • **Killie Campbell Africana Library and Museum** Mon–Fri 8.30am–4.30pm, Sat 9am–noon • Free • **Mashu Museum of Ethnology** Mon–Fri 8.30am–4.30pm, Sat 9am–noon • Free

The Cape Dutch-revival former homestead of sugar baron Sir Marshal Campbell, **Muckleneuk** houses one of the finest private collections of Africana in the country, including material relating to KwaZulu-Natal's ethnic heritage. The **Campbell Collections** comprise artworks and excellent examples of Cape Dutch furniture, while the adjacent **Killie Campbell Africana Library and Museum** is well known for its comprehensive collection of books, manuscripts and photographs. Also here is the **Mashu Museum of Ethnology**, consisting of a superb collection of Zulu crafts, including tools, weapons, beadwork and pottery. The entire complex is surrounded by a beautiful garden designed by Killie Campbell herself.

Cato Manor

A short drive west of the city centre takes you through **Cato Manor**, offering a graphic cross section of Durban's twentieth-century history, where you can see a juxtaposition of African squatter camps, Hindu temples and vegetation mingling in the heart of the city's middle-class suburbs. A large area in a valley below the Berea, Cato Manor was named after Durban's first mayor, **George Cato**, who arrived here in 1839. During the first half of the last century, the district was home to much of Durban's Indian community, who built temples on its hills. They were later joined by Africans, who were forced into crowded slums because of the shortage of housing. In 1949, an incident in which an Indian trader assaulted a Zulu man flared up into Durban's worst **riot**, with thousands of Africans attacking Indian stores and houses, leaving 142 dead.

Because Cato Manor was right in the middle of white suburbs, the apartheid government began enforcing the Group Areas Act here in the 1960s, moving Africans north to KwaMashu and Indians south to Chatsworth, leaving a derelict wasteland guarded only by the handful of Hindu temples left standing. The vacuum was filled again in the late 1980s, when Africans pouring into Durban built the closely packed tin shacks that line **Vusi Mzimela Road** (formerly Bellair Rd), winding its way through Cato Manor's valley. A drive along the road is undeniably interesting, though not altogether safe – carjackers are a potential hazard.

Shree Ambalvanar Alayam Second River Hindu Temple

890 Bellair Rd • Can be visited safely on a tour (see box, p.380) • Leave the city centre on the M13, take the Felix Dlamini Rd (formerly Brickfield Rd) exit and then turn left into the M10, which becomes Vusi Mzimela Rd; the temple is on the right if you're coming from town, just before Solomon Mahlangu Drive (formerly the Edwin Swales freeway)

While on Cato Manor's **Vusi Mzimela Road**, it's well worth stopping to visit the **Shree Ambalvanar Alayam Second River Hindu Temple**, a National Monument. The building is a 1947 reconstruction of the first Hindu temple in Africa, built in 1875 on the banks of the Umbilo River and subsequently destroyed by floods. The beautifully carved entrance doors are originals salvaged from the flood, while the facade is adorned with a pantheon of wonderfully garish Hindu deities. Around Easter every year the temple hosts a **firewalking festival** in which unshod devotees walk across red-hot coals, emerging unscathed. Visitors are welcome to join the thousands of worshippers who come to honour the goddess Draudpadi.

Umgeni River Bird Park

490 Riverside Rd, Durban North • Daily 9am–4.30pm • R30 • Bird shows daily 11am & 2pm • ☎ 031 579 4600 • Ⓦ umgeniriverbirdpark.co.za

The **Umgeni River Bird Park** is a tranquil place that's worth a visit for its fantastic free-flight bird shows. The park is home to a vast collection of indigenous and exotic birds, including flamingos, finches, magpies and macaws.

KwaMashu, Shembe and Inanda

Even though they're not hard to reach with your own wheels, some quintessential Durban experiences rarely make it into the pages of tourist brochures. Driving north of the city along the R102 (which becomes the M25), you can visit the place where Gandhi dreamed up passive resistance, and witness the epic religious ceremonies of the Zulu-Christian Shembe sect. A word of **warning**: driving through some of the areas covered here carries a certain risk, and you're advised to go with someone familiar with the road and local customs or on an organized tour (see box, p.380).

Aeroplane House

Head out of town towards the North Coast on the R102 and take the Inanda Phoenix exit along the M25; as you leave the R102 you'll see the suburb of Duff's Rd on the left – Aeroplane House is on the hillside

On the way out of Durban, you'll notice the bizarre sights of Dookie Ramdaari's **Aeroplane House** and his son's **Ship House** a few metres away. An affluent Indian bus builder with a taste for the unconventional, Ramdaari was a voracious traveller, a passion reflected in his first home built in the form of a ship, sailing east out of Duff's Road Indian township. Poised for take-off, the Aeroplane House – his current abode – has wings, an undercarriage, a television room with row seats in the tail and a superb lounge in the cockpit.

KwaMashu

Driving north along the M25 towards Inanda you'll pass the African township of **KwaMashu** on the left, established in the late 1950s to house residents of Cato Manor who had been forcibly resettled. It displays all the unimaginative planning typical of such low-cost housing schemes. The area is a sea of hills, vegetation and colour, which makes it tempting to romanticize the locality's poverty.

The Gandhi Settlement

Mon–Fri 8am–4.30pm, Sat 2am–2pm • Donation

A well-signposted turn off the M25 takes you to the **Gandhi Settlement**. On the eastern edge of the vast Inanda squatter camp, it's the site of a self-help scheme established by Mohandas Gandhi soon after his arrival in Durban in 1903. It was from here that Gandhi began to forge his philosophy of passive resistance; in a sad irony, violence brought it to ruin in 1985 when squatters from the adjacent camp looted and razed the settlement. With the help of the Indian Government, the settlement was rebuilt in time for its centenary celebration. A bronze bust of Gandhi now stands near the entrance to his house, **Sarvodaya** ("a place for the upliftment for all"), which is now a **museum** focusing on his time in South Africa and on Indian resistance to segregation.

5

Shembe

At **Ekuphakameni** ("the elated place"), west of the Gandhi Settlement along the M25, two "stars" laid in stone in the hilly landscape mark the spots where meteorites from the 1906 appearance of Halley's Comet struck the Earth. From here, you can continue to the Inanda police station at the top of the hill, then turn left to descend into the valley and cross the Umhlanga River bridge. At the next intersection, take the dirt road to the left, past the sports field, and turn left again to view the **Shembe settlement** at **Ebuhleni**. The settlement was established by the Holy Church of Nazareth as a refuge for Africans dispossessed as a result of the Land Act of 1913. According to the founding history of the Church, its prophet Isaya Shembe was "called" in 1910 to the summit of a mountain outside Durban, where he vowed before God to bring the Gospel to the Zulus. The Church's membership of tens of thousands was drawn initially from rural people whose lives had been devastated by colonization and who were eager to embrace Christianity, but were unwilling to give up traditional customs. The resulting religion was a rich synthesis that rejected drinking, smoking and cults, while encouraging a work ethic centred around crafts.

Every July devotees of the Holy Church of Nazareth gather in Ebuhleni for a month of worship. On these occasions, the men and women live on different sides of the village, and the unmarried maidens live in a separate enclosure. At the entrance gates to the settlement, rows of tables display what appear to be religious knick-knacks for sale to tourists – holographic images of Isaya Shembe and key rings with religious icons embedded in perspex – but which are actually religious artefacts revered by the converted of Shembe.

Leaving Ebuhleni, ignore the dirt road turn-off and head straight on to reach the Inanda Dam. The deep gorge to your left is the **Inanda Falls**, where the Shembe have baptismal ceremonies, which visitors are welcome to attend.

ARRIVAL AND DEPARTURE — DURBAN

BY PLANE

King Shaka International Airport Durban's international airport (☎032 436 6585) is located 35km north of the city in the village of La Mercy. A shuttle service to the city centre runs every 30min (daily 5am–10pm; ☎031 465 1660; R70) and will drop you at your accommodation. A metered taxi to the city should cost no more than R450. Several car-rental companies are based here (see opposite). Windermere Car Hire (see opposite) will collect you from the airport free of charge during office hours (Mon–Fri 8am–5pm, Sat 8am–noon) if you're renting one of their cars. There's an Absa Bank in the arrivals terminal (daily 7am–8pm) and a 24-hour ATM next to it. The following airlines are based at the airport: 1time ☎032 436 0260; British Airways ☎031 450 7000; Kulula ☎086 158 5852; Mango ☎086 116 2646; SA Airlink ☎011 451 7300; South African Airways ☎086 160 6606.

Destinations: Bloemfontein (2 daily; 1hr 5min); Cape Town (22 daily; 2hr 15min); East London (4 daily; 1hr 15min); George (1 daily; 1hr 50min); Johannesburg (around 50 daily; 1hr 10min); Nelspruit (2 daily; 1hr 20min); Port Elizabeth (8 daily; 1hr 20min).

BY TRAIN

New Durban Station The Trans-Natal service from Johannesburg and the Trans-Oranje service from Cape Town via Free State arrive at the grim main train station off Masabalala Yengwa Avenue, just north of the main commercial centre. The best option from here is to take one of the metered taxis that rank in front of the bus station that occupies the ground level of the station complex; a ride to the beachfront or Florida Rd costs R50.

Destinations: Cape Town (weekly; 38hr); Bloemfontein (weekly; 15hr 30min); Johannesburg (daily except Tues; 12hr 30min); Pietermaritzburg (daily except Tues; 2hr 10min).

BY BUS

Intercity buses Intercape (☎086 128 7287), Greyhound (☎031 334 9702), Translux (☎031 361 7670) and other intercity buses arrive at and depart from the Bus Station attached to the New Durban station complex. TCO also runs a thrice-weekly bus service to Maputo from here (Wed, Fri & Sun; ☎031 304 0997). The Margate Mini Coach (☎039 312 1406) from the South Coast pulls in here, and also outside domestic departures at King Shaka International Airport. The Umhlanga Explorer minibus shuttle from Umhlanga Rocks (☎031 561 2860) drops off at a number of points in Durban, including the airport and opposite Tourist Junction (see p.380) in the city centre.

Destinations: Ballito (daily; 45min); Bloemfontein (2 daily; 7hr); Cape Town (6 daily; 22hr); KwaDukuza (daily; 1hr); East London (2 daily; 9hr); Grahamstown (3 daily;

DURBAN'S NEW STREET NAMES

Many of Durban's main thoroughfares have been renamed to better reflect the cultural balance in the new South Africa. Well-known Durban streets, such as Point Road and West Street, now bear the names of famous and not-so-famous people who have contributed in one way or another to the democratization of South African society. However, this has been a controversial process. Some Durbanites question the merits of naming streets after foreigners such as Che Guevara and Samora Machel, and the changes have been challenged in court. Despite this, most of the proposed changes have been made and are reflected on new street signs around the city. On the maps for this edition, we have given the new name followed by the old name in brackets. Note, however, that people still commonly use the old names. You can pick up a list of the affected streets, along with their new names, at Tourist Junction (see p.380).

12hr); Harrismith (3 daily; 4hr 30min); Jeffrey's Bay (daily; 15hr 45min); Johannesburg (13 daily; 10hr); Knysna (3 daily; 17hr 30min); Ladysmith (2 daily; 3hr 30min); Maputo (3 weekly; 8hr 30min); Melmoth (daily; 4hr); Pietermaritzburg (14 daily; 2hr 15min); Plettenberg Bay (3 daily; 15hr 30min); Port Elizabeth (4 daily; 13hr 30min); Port Shepstone (3 daily; 1hr 30min); Pretoria (7 daily; 11hr 30min); Richards Bay (daily; 2hr 30min); Sedgefield (3 daily; 18hr); Umhlanga Rocks (daily; 20min); Umtata (2 daily; 6hr); Vryheid (daily; 6hr).

Baz Bus (☎ 086 122 9287, ⊕ www.bazbus.com) stops at most of the Durban backpacker hostels. For more about Baz Bus routes, see p.49.

Destinations: Amphitheatre (3 weekly; 5hr); Ballito (3 weekly; 45min); Bushlands (3 weekly; 6hr); Cintsa (5 weekly; 10hr); Coffee Bay (5 weekly; 7hr); East London (5 weekly; 11hr); Eshowe (3 weekly; 2hr); Johannesburg (3 weekly; 10hr); Kokstad (5 weekly; 4hr); Mthatha (5 weekly; 7hr); Mtubatuba (3 weekly; 6hr); Pietermaritzburg (3 weekly; 2hr); Port Alfred (5 weekly; 11hr); Port Elizabeth (5 weekly; 15hr); Port Shepstone (5 weekly; 3hr); Pretoria (3 weekly; 11hr); St Lucia (3 weekly; 6hr); Umkomaas (5 weekly; 1hr 30min); Umtentweni (5 weekly; 3hr); Umzumbe (5 weekly; 2hr).

GETTING AROUND

The easiest way to explore Durban is by car. **Cycling** is safe along the beachfront, but hazardous on any major road and not really recommended.

BY CAR

The city's freeways are well signposted and, with careful map-reading and advance planning, getting around is straightforward. There are several car rental companies in Durban, including Avis (☎ 031 310 9700), Budget (☎ 031 304 9023), Europcar/Imperial (☎ 031 337 3731), Hertz (☎ 031 335 2570), Tempest (☎ 031 368 5231) and Windermere (81 Windermere Rd; ☎ 031 312 0339); all except Windermere are based at the airport. The most convenient and central car parks are those at Pine Arcade, at the west end of Monty Naicker Rd, and in the Workshop Mall.

BY BUS

Durban's most useful urban transport is the cheap and regular bus system operated by Mynah, which covers the central districts, including the city centre, the beachfront, the Berea and Florida Rd. If you want to get to the more far-flung suburbs, the Aqualine buses are quite functional, although slightly the worse for wear. For information about times and routes for all of these companies, call ☎ 086 100 0834, or go to the bus depot on Monty Naicker Rd, which is adjacent to the Workshop Mall and is the starting point for most local bus services (you can also pick up bus schedules from the Tourist Junction). Fares in the centre range from R2.40 to R3.80 at peak time, with buses to the more distant suburbs more expensive. Useful routes include Mynah's Musgrave/Mitchell Park Circle buses, which either go along Florida Rd (on the Mitchell Park Circle bus) or Musgrave Rd (on the Musgrave Rd bus); and Aqualine's route #86/87, which goes to the KwaZulu-Natal Society of Arts Gallery, via Bulwer Rd. For travel within the city centre, the Durban People Mover (☎ 031 309 5942) operates modern buses along three routes linking the beachfront (from the Suncoast Casino to uShaka Marine World) with the centre as far east as Victoria St Market.

BY MINIBUS

Minibuses cover the entire city, and run with greater frequency than the buses. You can catch a minibus in the city centre going to Florida Rd from Field St, between Anton Lembele and Dr Pixley Kaseme sts.

BY TAXI

Reputable taxi companies in central Durban include Taxis Eagle (☎ 031 337 8333), Mozzies (☎ 086 066 9943) and Zippy (☎ 031 202 7067).

5

DURBAN TOURS AND HARBOUR RIDES

One of the safest and easiest ways to get under the skin of ethnic Durban is to take a **guided tour**. Standard three-hour tours cost around R250 per person and R400 for a full day; we've listed a few operators below. A good way to explore Durban's Indian areas is by joining the daily Walkabout Tour organized by the tourist office (book at Tourist Junction; R150, minimum of two people). You can also take a **harbour ride** with Isle of Capri Cruises, at Wilson's Wharf (daily on the hour 10am–4pm; R50; ☎ 031 305 3099).

Ethnic Tours ☎ 031 466 6549, ⓦ www.ethnic-tours .co.za. Half- and full-day city tours including a visit to a Hindu temple, as well as tours through Inanda following in Gandhi's footsteps.

Street Scene Tours ☎ 083 320 2675, ⓦ www .streetscenetours.co.za. One-day and overnight township and Durban tours with an emphasis on the "local" experience, which can include anything from

playing football with township kids to trawling through hip vintage clothing stores or trying your hand at brewing your own beer.

Tekweni Eco Tours ☎ 082 303 9112, ⓦ www .tekweniecotours.co.za. Durban city tours and visits to Zulu villages in the Valley of a Thousand Hills, for a Zulu meal and beer, traditional dancing and an encounter with a traditional healer.

INFORMATION

Tourist information The obvious first port of call for information is the central Tourist Junction at Old Station Building, 160 Pine St (Mon–Fri 8am–5pm, Sat 9am–2pm, Sun 9am–1pm; ☎ 031 304 4934, ⓦ durbanexperience .co.za), which houses Durban Africa (the city's tourist bureau) and Tourism KwaZulu-Natal (the province's excellent tourist bureau, ⓦ www.kzn.org.za). Also here are

KZN Wildlife and South African National Parks booking offices. There is another well-equipped tourist office at uShaka Marine World on the beachfront (daily 9am–9pm; ☎ 031 337 8099), and an excellent tourist information desk in the arrivals terminal at King Shaka international airport (Mon–Sat 8am–9pm, Sun 9am–9pm; ☎ 031 451 6758).

ACCOMMODATION

Durban's high-rise **accommodation** is concentrated along the beachfront and in the city centre, both convenient locations but less salubrious at night – taking taxis to your doorstep is recommended after dark. An alternative is the Berea residential area west and north of the centre, which boasts the best backpacker hostels in town, as well as guesthouses and B&Bs housed in beautifully renovated old homes. Durban has a selection of **township homestays** where you can experience the warmth of urban Zulu hospitality. Durban Africa at Tourist Junction (see above) can arrange your accommodation as well as transport into the townships.

CITY CENTRE

Banana Backpackers 61 Monty Naicker Rd, 1st floor, Ambassador House ☎ 031 368 4062, ⓦ bananaback packers.co.za; map pp.369–370. Simple dorms and doubles in an old Durban building that has seen better days, but there is a congenial courtyard with a plastic pool and it's very close to the beach, Tourist Junction and the Pine St bus terminal. Dorm R110, double R300

Formula 1 Directly opposite the bus station, near the corner of Masabalala Yengwa Ave and Jeff Taylor Crescent ☎ 031 301 1551, ⓦ hotelformula1.co.za; map pp.369–370. No-frills chain hotel that's tremendously convenient if you arrive late at night by train or bus. Rooms sleep up to three people. R409

The Royal Hotel 267 Anton Lembede St ☎ 031 333 6000, ⓦ theroyal.co.za; map pp.369–370. Once Durban's finest hotel, but now feels a little old-fangled. Smack in the centre of town and used mainly by business visitors, it's worth considering if you can afford five-star

splendour and fancy the liveried service. Discounts are often available. R1200

BEACHFRONT

Blue Waters 175 OR Tambo Parade ☎ 031 327 7000, ⓦ www.bluewatershotel.co.za; map pp.369–370. A delightful 1950s Durban landmark opposite Battery Beach, with great views onto the oceanfront. R920

Garden Court – Marine Parade 167 OR Tambo Parade ☎ 031 337 2231, ⓦ southernsun.com; map pp.369–370. All the rooms face the sea (those on the top floors are best), and the view from the thirtieth-floor swimming pool is fabulous. A cool through-breeze offers respite against the summer heat, and a back entrance across from Victoria Park provides handy access to the city centre. R600

Happy Hippo Backpackers Lodge 222 Mahatma Gandhi Rd ☎ 031 368 7181, ⓦ happy-hippo.co.za; map pp.369–370. Extremely spacious hostel a stone's throw from uShaka Marine World and the beach. The rooftop bar makes it popular with a younger crowd in the mood for a party. Dorm R120, room R310

Protea Hotel Edward OR Tambo Parade, at Seaview Rd ⓣ 031 337 3681, ⓦ proteahotels.com; map pp.369–370. Crystal chandeliers, a colonial-style ambience, sea-view balconies and a ladies' bar leading onto a cool veranda make this Art Deco mansion the *grande dame* of the beachfront. R1440

Silversands 16 Erskine Terrace, near the Addington Hospital ⓣ 031 332 1140, ⓦ goodersonvacations.com; map pp.369–370. These clean, comfortable and spacious self-catering apartments sleeping four to eight people are among the best value on the beach. Safe parking costs R60 per day. R800

THE BEREA

20 Palm Grove 367 Peter Mokaba Rd ⓣ 031 240 9140, ⓦ 20palmgrove.co.za; map pp.374–375. Well-equipped and comfortable self-catering units and B&B rooms, most with separate entrances, set in attractive gardens with two pools. It's close to public transport. R650

Audacia Manor 11 Sir Arthur Rd ⓣ 031 303 9520, ⓦ africanpridehotels.com; map pp.374–375. Luxurious guesthouse in a restored colonial mansion. The restaurant and bar on the veranda boast gorgeous sea views, and some of the rooms feature outdoor jacuzzi baths and showers. R1945

★ **The Elephant House** 745 Peter Mokaba Rd ⓣ 031 208 9580 or ⓣ 082 4522 574, ⓔ elephanthouse@mweb.co.za; map pp.374–375. If you like to feel as though you're staying in someone's home, this is one of the best B&Bs in South Africa. The home in question is the oldest in Durban, built in 1847 as a hunting lodge and oozing with character. The extremely kind and generous hosts love showing travellers around. Highly recommended and excellent value for money. R700

Essenwood House 630 Steven Dlamini Rd ⓣ 031 207 4547, ⓦ essenwoodhouse.co.za; map pp.374–375. This grand house with a sumptuous garden has seven large, comfortable rooms (the upstairs ones have sea views), an attractive pool and a good-natured, if somewhat eccentric, host. R895

Gibela Lodge 119 Ninth Ave, Morningside ⓣ 031 303 6291, ⓦ gibelabackpackers.co.za; map pp.374–375. Quiet hostel with a restful atmosphere, tastefully decorated rooms and single-sex dorms. The owner has a tremendous knowledge of Durban and the rest of the province. There's a strict no-smoking policy and no check-in after 9pm. Rates include a good breakfast. Dorm R180, double R480

Goble Palms 120 Smiso Nkwanyana Rd ⓣ 031 312 2598, ⓦ goblepalms.co.za; map pp.374–375. This house, built in 1900, features a sunny patio with sea views, a pool and an intimate on-site English-style pub, as well as pretty, restful rooms. R910

★ **Hippo Hide Lodge and Backpackers** 2 Jesmond Rd ⓣ 031 207 4366, ⓦ hippohide.co.za; map pp.374–375. A stunning, imaginative and cosy hostel in a beautiful tropical garden with a rock pool. It's clean and quiet, with a guesthouse feel, and conveniently located on the bus route to the centre (10min). One of the doubles is en suite, and there are also log cabins. Dorm R110, double R300

McAllisters on 8th 11 Eighth Ave ⓣ 031 303 4991, ⓦ 8thave.co.za; map pp.374–375. Stylish rooms built around a courtyard pool, all decked out in white linen, with flat-screen TVs, DVD players and microwaves. The sister guesthouse *McAllisters on Madeline* (92 Madeline Rd, same phone) offers accommodation of a similar standard and price. R850

Nomad's Backpackers 70 Steven Dlamini Rd ⓣ 031 202 9709 or ⓣ 082 920 5882, ⓦ nomadsbp.com; map pp.374–375. A short walk from the Musgrave Centre, this chilled-out hostel is good for nonsensical conversations at the bar or around the pool. The dorms are tidy and nicely decorated, though some of the bunks are triples. Meals available. Dorm R130, double R320

★ **Rosetta House** 126 Rosetta Rd ⓣ 031 303 6180, ⓦ rosettahouse.co.za; map pp.374–375. The fact that there are just four rooms, all warmly decorated, lends an intimate feel to this cosy guesthouse. There's a lush and tranquil garden in and the hosts maintain a high standard of service, serving one of the best breakfasts in town. R990

Tekweni Backpackers 169 Ninth Ave ⓣ 031 303 1433, ⓦ tekwenibackpackers.co.za; map pp.374–375. This large hostel near Florida Rd is spread over three houses and features plenty of communal areas, a pool and bar. Braais and other social gatherings cater to a young, energetic clientele. Monthly accommodation is also available. Dorm R125, double R400

EATING

Eating out is a favourite pastime in Durban, and although all types of cooking are found here, **Indian food** is what the city excels at – hardly surprising for a place with one of the largest Indian populations outside Asia. The Indian takeaways of the city centre are good places to try *bunny chow* – Durban's big contribution to the national fast-food scene – and the not-dissimilar *rotis* (Indian bread) stuffed with curries. **Shisanyama** outlets at the African markets and around the taxi ranks offer hunks of meat cooked over an open fire. For a more refined dining experience, the Berea has the city's best and most diverse range of restaurants; closing time for most is at around 10.30pm.

BEACHFRONT

Cargo Hold uShaka Marine World ⓣ 031 328 8065; map pp.369–370. A rather staid international menu – half of which consists of fish dishes (R85–120)

5

EATING INDIAN IN DURBAN

Inexpensive Indian **takeaways** – all open very early and usually shut by 5pm – abound in the city centre. *Little Gujarat*, 107 Dr Goonam St, and *Victory Lounge* on the corner of Dr Yusuf Dadoo and Bertha Mkhize streets are noted for their vegetarian food and traditional sweetmeats respectively. Otherwise, the *Oriental* takeaway at the Workshop Mall does a hotchpotch of fare – delicious Indian-style *shawarmas, bunny chows* and curries. If you're hankering for something much slicker in the heart of town, head to *Ulundi Tapas* at *The Royal Hotel* (see p.380), where you'll be served light *thali* curry dishes (R22–35 each; order a minimum of three) for lunch and dinner in a stylish and contemporary black-and-white dining room.

– although eating in front of the shark tank is a thrill. Daily noon–3pm & 6–10pm.

Jewel of India Southern Sun Elangeni, 63 OR Tambo Parade ☎031 362 1300; map pp.369–370. Two styles of food are served in this plush restaurant with Eastern decor: North Indian, including plenty of vegetarian options, and Chinese food with an Indian twist (ie spicier). Most curries cost R75–95. Daily noon–3pm & 6–10.30pm.

★ **Moyo** uShaka Marine World ☎031 332 0606; map pp.369–370. A large, breezy dining room overlooking the sea where you can order a great range of African specialities, from Moroccan *tajines* and Senegalese chicken *yassa* to crocodile kebabs and venison *potjie* (most mains R80–140). Light meals and drinks are available at the end of the pier opposite the restaurant; a good idea at sunset. Mon–Fri 11am–11pm, Sat & Sun 8am–11pm.

THE HARBOUR AREA

★ **New Café Fish** Yacht Mole, Margaret Mncadi Ave ☎031 305 5062; map pp.369–370. A beautiful restaurant looking out onto the harbour (the best views are from the bar upstairs), which specializes in great seafood (most mains R70–100). Daily noon–3pm & 6–10pm.

Ocean's Eleven BAT Arts Centre, Margaret Mncadi Ave ☎083 656 0974; map pp.369–370. This lively venue dishes up African fusion food like curcubita (butternut squash stuffed with vegetables), and ox tripe with steamed Zulu bread, all in the R30–50 range. Occasional live music and a great terrace overlooking the harbour add to the appeal. A good place to meet the locals. Tues–Sun noon–11pm.

Roma Revolving Restaurant John Ross House, Margaret Mncadi Ave ☎031 337 6707; map pp.369–370. No visitor to Durban should miss the view from the *Roma* as it revolves above the city. The international menu includes tasty mussel starters and mediocre Italian specialities, like gnocchi and veal dishes, plus an excellent dessert trolley. You pay for the view as much as for the food; count on around R90–110. Mon–Sat noon–2.30pm & 6–10.30pm.

THE BEREA

9th Avenue Bistro Shop 2, Avonmore Centre, Ninth Ave Morningside ☎031 312 9134; map pp.374–375.

One of the most highly regarded restaurants in Durban, serving refined French dishes – for example, duck confit in a cinnamon-orange demi glaze – from R100. Mon & Sat 6–10pm, Tues–Fri noon–2.30pm & 6–10pm.

Bean Bag Bohemia 18 Lilian Ngoyi Rd, Morningside ☎031 309 6019; map pp.374–375. A trendy, gay-friendly bar/bistro in a two-storey house, selling pizza, pasta and some adventurous tapas (R45–70) with plenty of art on the walls. The food is okay, but it's the bar (and people-watching) that's the main appeal. Daily 9am–late.

★ **Blue Zoo Garden Restaurant** 6 Nimmo Rd, Morningside ☎031 303 2265; pp.374–375. The varied and unusual menu features delicious Moroccan chicken, lamb shank in a port wine sauce, steaks, fish, and salads with mango-chilli dressing (mains R60–90). Beautifully located in Mitchell Park and great for kids. Daily 8am–5pm, also Tues–Sat 6–10.30pm.

★ **Delfi Taverna** 386 Lilian Ngoyi Rd, Morningside ☎031 312 7032; map pp.374–375. This cosy restaurant boasts excellent, authentic Greek dishes such as *kleffiko* (lamb shank) and *moussaka* (mains R40–60), and has a wonderfully congenial atmosphere created by friendly staff and plenty of regular customers – always a good sign. Wed–Mon 11am–3pm & 5pm–late.

La Bella Corner of Steven Dlamini and St Thomas rds ☎031 201 9176; map pp.374–375. Housed in a former power station, with outdoor seating that's good for a coffee or a stone oven-cooked pizza (R35–60), with imaginative toppings such as roast lamb. There's also live music on Friday evenings. Daily noon–3pm & 6–10pm.

Oscar's 339 Steven Dlamini Rd ☎031 208 5848; map pp.374–375. Casual café-cum-CD shop that's popular with the locals for its simple, delicious food, including sandwiches, burgers and great breakfasts (mains R55–80). There's also home-made bread to be had, a real treat in South Africa. Mon–Thurs & Sun 7.30am–9pm, Fri & Sat 7.30am–10pm.

Palki 225 Musgrave Rd, Musgrave ☎031 201 0019; map pp.374–375. The South African representative of a chain of restaurants based in the East, this has mouthwatering, authentic dishes (R50–65) mainly from South India – including *pooris* and *dosas* – created by chefs shipped in from other branches. Vegetarians are well catered for. Daily 11am–3pm & 6–11pm.

★ **Spice** 362 Lilian Ngoyi Rd, Morningside ☎031 303 6375; map pp.374–375. One of the city's finest restaurants, with excellent food that combines spicy curries (more aromatic than blisteringly hot) and inventive dishes such as roast duck with Amarula; mains start around R100. Tues–Sat noon–3pm & 6pm–late, Sun noon–3pm.

★ **Spiga d'Oro** 200 Florida Rd, Morningside ☎031 303 9511; map pp.374–375. Justifiably popular Italian restaurant serving several types of pasta dishes and pizza (R35–60), with outside tables on Florida Rd giving the place a European feel. The friendly and efficient service adds to the appeal. Tues–Sat 7am–late, Sun & Mon 7am–noon.

Vida e Caffé 446 Innes Rd, Morningside ☎031 312 4606; map pp.374–375. Small café with contemporary decor and a pleasant position in front of Mitchell Park. The coffee menu sticks to the basics, the better to focus on people-watching. Daily 7am–9pm.

DRINKING, NIGHTLIFE AND ENTERTAINMENT

Durban has a healthy nightlife scene, with a decent number of bars, clubs and music venues. For entertainment and nightlife listings, the *Mercury* is the better of Durban's two English-language dailies. Durban Africa also publishes a monthly events brochure, available from tourist offices.

BARS AND CLUBS

Billy The Bum's 504 Lilian Ngoyi Rd, Morningside ☎031 303 1988; map pp.374–375. Acrobatic barmen juggle bottles while mixing imaginative cocktails at this popular singles' watering hole. Food (burgers and the like for R50–70) is also available. Mon–Sat noon till late.

Skyybar 25 Silver Ave, Morningside ☎031 313 7424; map pp.374–375. This flashy club has a fabulous outdoor deck with views of the city, an emphasis on house music and a largely middle-class black clientele. Entrance R50. Fri & Sat 8pm–4am.

Fashion TV 153 Florida Rd ☎31 303 7631; map pp.374–375. Billing itself as a watering hole for Durban's beautiful people, this bar and nightclub can be entertaining in all its over-the-top sparkles and glitz. It hosts occasional live bands and fashion shows, and attracts top local DJs to the dancefloor upstairs. R50 cover Fri & Sat. Wed & Thurs 4–10pm, Fri & Sat 11am–10pm.

Vic Bar 241 Mahatma Gandhi Rd, the Point ☎031 337 4645; map pp.369–370. A down-to-earth neighbourhood bar, good for boozing and watching sport on TV. *Catembe* (cola and wine) is a house speciality, as is the excellent prawn curry (R60–90). Mon–Sat 10am–midnight.

LIVE MUSIC

You'll find plenty of live indie music on offer in Durban, much of it derivative of European or North American trends. More interesting, but less accessible, are some of the Zulu forms such as *iscathamiya* and *maskanda*. On the jazz scene, the city's most indigenous offering is a spicy combination of American mixed with township jazz and Zulu forms. As for classical music, the best place to hear concerts by the **KwaZulu-Natal Philharmonic** (☎031 369 9438, ⊛www.kznpo.co.za) is at a sundowner concert held in the Botanic Gardens. Check their website for the programme.

The BAT Centre Next to the harbour at 42 Maritime Place ☎031 332 0451, ⊛batcentre.co.za. This artsy cultural centre is your best bet for live concerts. The Centre's *Ocean's Eleven* restaurant also has jazz sundowners on Fridays and Sundays.

Burn 2nd Floor, Fidelity House, 16 Walls Ave, Morningside ☎082 876 8521. A good place to tap into Durban's indie music scene, where an alternative crowd of goths, punks and rockers gathers on Wednesday, Friday and Saturday nights.

Moyo uShaka Marine World ☎031 332 0606. Live jazz on Friday and Saturday evenings at this excellent restaurant (see opposite).

The Rainbow 23 Stanfield Lane in Pinetown, northwest of Durban ☎031 702 9161. A long-established restaurant offering monthly Sunday-lunchtime performances ranging from Afro-fusion to jazz, and more regular weekday sessions by up-and-coming bands.

Zulu Jazz Lounge 231 Anton Lembede St in the city centre ☎031 304 2373; map pp.369–370. Usually hosts evening jazz performances Thursdays to Saturdays.

THEATRE AND CINEMA

The best and most convenient cinemas are the multiscreen complexes at the Musgrave Centre, the Workshop Mall in

GAY DURBAN

Durban's **gay scene** is fairly well developed, although nothing like what you'll find in Cape Town. Among the smattering of gay or gay-friendly nightspots, the ★ **Bean Bag Bohemia** bar-restaurant (see pp.374–375) and The Lounge, 226 Mathews Meyiwa Rd, Morningside (☎031 303 9022), are two popular meeting places.

5

the city centre and the Suncoast Casino on the beachfront. The only place to see art-house movies is at Gateway Mall (see p.391), 15km north of town.

Playhouse Drama Theatre 231 Anton Lembede St ☎031 369 9555, ⍵playhousecompany.com. A mock-Tudor building that tends to host middle-of-the-road productions, but also sees performances by the resident progressive Playhouse Dance Company.

Elizabeth Sneddon Theatre University of KwaZulu-Natal, Mazisi Kunene Rd ☎031 260 2296. A modern venue for university and visiting productions.

OUTDOOR ACTIVITIES AND SPECTATOR SPORTS

Birdwatching, a major activity in the green fringes of the city, is being aided by the Durban Metropolitan Open Space System (DMOSS), a project linking all the city parks via narrow green corridors. Promising spots include the Manor Gardens area; the Botanic Gardens; the Berea; Burman Bush, to the north of the city; Pigeon Valley, below the University of KwaZulu-Natal; the Umgeni River Mouth; Virginia Bush, on the road to Umhlanga Rocks; and the Hawaan Forest in Umhlanga, where the spotted thrush and green coucal have been seen.

Golf is a popular and rewarding activity in Durban. Enclosed within the tracks of the Greyville Race Course (see below), the Royal Durban Golf Club (☎031 309 1373; R300 for eighteen holes) is notable for its unusual setting, while the Durban Country Club on Isiah Ntshangase Rd (☎031 313 1777; R400 for eighteen holes) is considered by many to be the finest course in South Africa.

Scuba diving is an obvious and pleasurable activity in KwaZulu-Natal's subtropical waters, but is somewhat limited immediately around Durban. The best diving sites are Vetches Pier at the southern tip of the beachfront, and Blood Reef at the tip of the Bluff (opposite the Point). Scuba-diving courses can be arranged through Underwater World, 251 Mahatma Gandhi Rd (☎031 332 5820, ⍵www.underwaterworld.co.za); a full six-day internationally recognized NAUI or PADI course costs R2500, including use of the main gear you'll need.

Kitesurfing has started to gain a following in Durban and you can take lessons (R800 for a half-day intro course) with an outfit called Kitesports (☎082 572 4163, ⍵www.kitesports.co.za) on the calm waters of La Mercy Lagoon.

Surfing Given Durban's seafront location, watersports are extremely popular, none more so than surfing. Night surfing competitions draw enormous crowds, as does the annual Mr Price Pro (formerly the Gunston 500), which, after the Rip Curl Pro at Bells Beach, Australia, is the world's longest-running professional surfing competition and is held in Durban every July. The favourite spot for surfers is North Beach, while a good place to pick up gear is the Safari Surf Shop, 43 Sylvester Ntuli Rd (☎031 337 2176), where Spider Murphy, South Africa's top board-shaper, will custom-build a world-class board for much less than a comparable order would cost in Europe or North America. Ocean Ventures at uShaka Marine World (☎031 332 9949, ⍵www.oceanventures.co.za), offers surfing lessons with experienced instructors (R200/hr, plus R100 for board rental).

Swimming Durban's largest pool is the heated King's Park Olympic Swimming Pool on Masabalala Yengwa Ave, between Sandile Thusi and Battery Beach rds in Stamford Hill (☎031 312 0404). The seawater Rachel Finlayson Baths on OR Tambo Parade are handy if you're staying near the beachfront. Entry to both is R4.40.

Cricket The Kingsmead Cricket Ground in the centre (☎031 335 4200) is the principal venue for local and international cricket matches and is home to the provincial cricket team.

Horse-racing The horse-racing season runs from May to August and centres around the Greyville Race Course, Avondale Rd, Greyville (☎031 314 1500). The annual Vodacom Durban July (⍵www.durbanjuly.info), which, as the name suggests, takes place during July, is South Africa's premier horse-racing event, drawing bets from across the length and breadth of the country.

Rugby You'll have plenty of opportunity to watch rugby in season at Absa Stadium, Isiah Ntshangase Rd, Stamford Hill (☎031 308 8400), home to the local Sharks. The spectacular new Moses Mabhida Stadium (see below; ☎031 582 8242) is just next door.

EXTREME SPORTS

Durban's newest architectural landmark, the **Moses Mabhida Stadium**, may have been designed with the 2010 football World Cup in mind, but city authorities seem determined to keep it from gathering dust. These days there are a number of activities on offer at the stadium, including mounting the striking 106m central arch by **cable car** for a 360-degree view of the city (daily 9am–6pm; R50), or strapping on safety equipment and scaling the arch on foot (Sat & Sun 10am, 1pm & 4pm; R80). Adrenaline junkies can also try the **Big Rush Big Swing**, which sends you plunging off one side of the stadium to swoop across in a 220m arc (daily 9am–5pm; R595; ⍵bigrush.co.za). For more information check ⍵mosesmabhidastadium.co.za.

ZULU CRAFTS AND CURIOS

Durban's huge range of galleries, craft shops and markets makes it one of the best places in the country to pick up **Zulu crafts**. Traditional works include functional items such as woven beer strainers and grass brooms, and basketry that can be extremely beautiful. Other traditional items are beadwork, pottery and Zulu regalia, of which *assegais* (spears), shields, leather kilts and drums are a few examples.

The availability of cheap plastic crockery and enamelware has significantly eroded the production of traditional ceramics and woven containers for domestic use. Even so, the effects of urbanization have led to the use of new materials, or new ways of using old materials. Nowadays you'll find beautifully decorated black-and-white sandals made from recycled rubber tyres, wildly colourful baskets woven from telephone wire, and *sjamboks* (whips) decorated with bright insulation tape. On the more frivolous side, industrial materials have been married with rural life or rural materials with industrial life. Attractive tin boxes made from flattened oil cans, chickens constructed from sheet plastic, and aircraft and little 4WD vehicles carved from wood are just some of the results.

SHOPPING

As one of South Africa's major cities, Durban is a good place to pick up general supplies and local books and records. But it's for **crafts and curios** that it scores particularly highly, with a dazzling range of handmade Zulu goods (see box above). The best places to browse for crafts are in the downtown markets, the weekend flea markets and the specialist shops around the city. Durban is littered with shopping malls of varying sizes, the two largest being the central Workshop Mall (see p.370) and the more upmarket Musgrave Centre in Musgrave

BOOKS

Adams & Co Shop 223 Musgrave Centre, Musgrave; map pp.374–375. Durban's oldest bookshop has an excellent selection of books on the history of Durban and KwaZulu-Natal. There's another branch in the city centre at 341 Dr Pixley Kaseme St. Mon–Thurs & Sat 8am–5pm, Fri 8am–6pm, Sun 10am–4pm.

★ **Ike's Books & Collectables** 48a Florida Rd, Morningside; map pp.374–375. A fascinating secondhand bookshop with an interesting range of items covering KwaZulu-Natal's history. Speciality areas include Africana and the Anglo-Boer War, travel and exploration, and South African politics. Mon–Fri 10am–5pm, Sat 9am–2pm.

MUSIC

Look and Listen Lower Level, Pavilion Shopping Centre, Westville; map pp.369–370. Well-stocked music shop offering a comprehensive range of indigenous music from the whole continent, including local favourites such as Ladysmith Black Mambazo and Hugh Masekela. Mon–Thurs 9am–7pm, Fri 9am–8pm, Sat 9.30am–6pm, Sun 9am–5pm.

CRAFTS AND CURIOS

African Art Centre 94 Florida Rd, Morningside Ⓦ www.afriart.org.za; map pp.374–375. A gallery and shop where many rural artists sell their work, well worth visiting for its traditional and modern Zulu and Xhosa beadwork, beaded dolls, wire sculptures, woodcuts and

tapestries. Mon–Fri 8.30am–5pm, Sat 9am–3pm.

BAT Centre Off Margaret Mncadi Ave, city centre; map pp.369–375. A grouping of several shops selling Zulu and other African crafts, with clothing and jewellery well represented. Mon–Fri 10am–5pm, Sat 9am–2pm.

KZNSA Gallery Shop KZNSA Gallery, Bulwer Rd, Berea; pp.374–375. This menagerie of contemporary hand-crafted goods includes a wonderful selection of functional art, including pewter cutlery, etchings and paintings. Tues–Fri 9am–5pm, Sat 9am–4pm, Sun 9am–3pm.

MARKETS

Amphitheatre Fleamarket OR Tambo Parade, beachfront; map pp.369–370. Crafts and beadwork sold both by local traders and by merchants from as far afield as Zimbabwe, Malawi and Kenya. Sun 8am–5pm.

City Market Between Julius Nyerere Ave and Market Rd, Warwick Triangle; map pp.369–370. Stock up with the cheapest fruit and veg in town, from aubergines and jackfruit to betel nut for red-stained lips and a two-minute rush.

Essenwood Craft Market Berea Park, Steven Dlamini Rd, Musgrave; map pp.374–375. Upmarket stalls in a beautiful park setting. Sat 9am–2pm.

Victoria Street Market Corner of Dennis Hurley and Joseph Nduli sts, city centre; map pp.374–375. Traders here sell all manner of stuff, from curios and jewellery to spices with labels like "mother-in-law exterminator". Touristy, but fun nonetheless.

5

DIRECTORY

Consulates Canada, 225 Musgrave Rd, Berea (☎ 0031 202 3432); Lesotho, West Guard House, corner of Dr Pixley Kaseme and Dorothy Nyembe sts, city centre (☎ 031 307 2323); UK, 86 Armstrong Ave, St Lucia Ridge (☎ 031 572 7259); US, Old Mutual Centre, 31st floor, 303 Dr Pixley Kaseme St, city centre (☎ 031 305 7600).

Currency exchange The First National Bank bureau de change, 306 Dr Pixley Kaseme St, city centre, will cash Visa travellers' cheques without commission (Mon–Fri 9am–3.30pm, Sat 8.30am–12.30pm). American Express, 151 Musgrave Rd, Musgrave (Mon–Fri 8.30am–4.30pm, Sat 8.30am–noon; ☎ 031 202 8733), replaces lost cheques and changes money.

Emergencies AA ☎ 083 84322.

Hospitals and medical centres The main state hospital is the Addington, Erskine Terrace, South Beach (☎ 031 327 2000), which offers a 24hr emergency ward. A better alternative is Entabeni Private Hospital, 148 Mazisi Kunene Rd, Berea (☎ 031 204 1300), which has a casualty unit and can also treat minor conditions, but where you'll have to pay a deposit on admission and settle up before leaving town. Travel Doctor, 45 Braam Fischer Rd, International Convention Centre, city centre (☎ 031 360 1122, ⊚ www .traveldoctor.co.za), is a clinic offering travel information and advice, as well as advise on malaria and the necessary jabs for venturing into African countries to the north.

Internet access Da-House, 320 Dr Pixley Kaseme Rd; iNet Café at 13 Gladys Mazibuko Rd, Berea.

Pharmacies Sparkport, corner of Anton Lembede and Dr Yusuf Dadoo sts (Mon–Sat 7.30am–8.30pm, Sun 9am–8pm; ☎ 031 304 9767).

Post The main post office, on the corner of Dorothy Nyembe and Dr Pixley Kaseme sts, has a poste restante and enquiry desk (Mon–Fri 8am–5pm, Sat 8am–1pm).

The South Coast

The **South Coast**, the 160km seaboard stretching from Durban to Port Edward on the Eastern Cape border, is a ribbon of seaside suburbs linked for most of its length by the **N2** and **R102** roads, running side by side. In the winter months it's much warmer and sunnier along this stretch than on any of the beaches between here and Cape Town. Away from the sea, the land is very hilly and green, dotted with sugar-cane fields, banana plantations and palm and pecan nut trees. Note that many beaches shelve steeply into the powerful surf, so only swim where it's indicated as safe.

   Margate, 133km from Durban, is the transport and holiday hub of the area, with plenty of resorts lying to the east and west of it. The highlight of the South Coast, however, lies just inland, where **Oribi Gorge Nature Reserve** has lovely forest hikes, breathtaking views and good-value accommodation.

ARRIVAL AND DEPARTURE   THE SOUTH COAST

By Car Driving from Durban, head for the N2, which runs south from the city as far as Port Shepstone before heading inland to Kokstad. From Port Shepstone to Southbroom, the South Coast Toll Rd is even faster and less congested.

By bus Margate Mini Coach (Gird Mowat Building, Marine Drive, Margate ☎ 039 312 1406), has two to three daily bus services departing from the Durban bus station (Greyhound terminal) and calling at King Shaka International Airport (domestic arrivals), Amanzimtoti (prebooked only), Scottburgh (prebooked only), Hibberdene, Port Shepstone (Shell Garage), Margate (Maroela Flats on Marine Parade), Sam Lameer (prebooked only) and Wild Coast Sun Casino (prebooked only). The Baz Bus between Durban and Port Elizabeth calls at Umkomaas, Umzumbe, Umtentweni and Port Shepstone five days a week.

Aliwal Shoal

The resorts that line the first 50km of coastline south of Durban – places such as **Amanzimtoti**, 27km down – feel more like beachside suburbs than towns in their own right. For diving enthusiasts, however, the faded town of **UMKOMAAS**, 20km further down the coast from Amanzimtoti, is the perfect point to set out for **Aliwal Shoal**, a scattered reef quite close to the shore and one of Southern Africa's top **dive sites**. Rewards for experienced divers include sightings of ragged-tooth and tiger sharks, and the chance to go wreck-diving to three stunning sites. The ideal time to dive is between June and October, when visibility is at its best.

RAGGED-TOOTH SHARK, SODWANA BAY (P.421) >

5

THE SARDINE RUN

Around June or July, the South Coast is witness to the extraordinary annual migration of millions of **sardines** moving northwards along the coast in massive shoals. They leave their feeding ground off the Southern Cape coast and move up the coast towards Mozambique, followed by about 23,000 dolphins, 100,000 Cape gannets and thousands of sharks and game fish, attracting fishermen from all over the province to join in the jamboree. The shoals appear as dark patches of turbulence in the water, and when they are cornered and driven ashore by game fish, hundreds of people rush into the water either to scoop them out with their hands or to net them. For updates on shoal co-ordinates and other information of use for sardine-spotting, call the Sardine Hotline on ☎083 913 9495 or visit ⓦshark.co.za.

ACTIVITIES   ALIWAL SHOAL

Various dive centres organize trips to Aliwal Shoal (expect to pay around R270, plus R220 for equipment rental), as well as PADI-certified four-day Open Water diving courses (around R3000, includes equipment); try Meridian Dive Centre (☎082 894 1625, ⓦscubadivesouthafrica.co.za) or Amatikulu Tours (☎039 973 2534, ⓦamatikulu.com).

ACCOMMODATION

Agulhas House 30 Barrow St, Umkomaas ☎039 973 1640, ⓦwww.agulhashouse.com. Centrally located B&B in a renovated doctor's clinic, whose simple en-suite rooms, with fridges and private entrances, are set around an attractive pool. R820

Oribi Gorge Nature Reserve

Daily 6.30am–7.30pm • R10 • ☎039 679 1644

A highly scenic area traversed by the fast-flowing Umzimkulu and Umzimkulwana rivers, with cliffs rising from vast chasms and forest, the **Oribi Gorge Nature Reserve**, 21km from Port Shepstone, signposted off the N2, is the South Coast's most compelling attraction. There are numerous idyllic picnic spots on the riverbanks (though avoid swimming here, as bilharzia parasites are present in the water) and waymarked **hikes** ranging from thirty-minute to day-long excursions, leading to dizzying lookout points or through the forest. A fine one-hour **walk** starts from the Umzimkulu car park, crosses the river and heads immediately up some steps into the forest. You'll only see the river when it opens out quite dramatically to reveal **Samango Falls** and a perfect little rock-bounded sandy beach.

Wildlife in the reserve includes bushbuck, common reedbuck and blue and grey duiker, but not oribi, which have left for the succulent shoots of the surrounding sugar-cane plantations. More difficult to see are the shy samango monkeys hiding in the high canopy of the forest, and leopards.

INFORMATION AND ACTIVITIES   ORIBI GORGE NATURE RESERVE

Tourist information KNZ Wildlife has an office at the main gate (daily 8am–12.30pm & 2–4.30pm; ☎039 679 1644).
Activities There are a few adventure activities on offer in the reserve, all run by Wild 5 (☎039 687 0253, ⓦoribigorge .co.za), who operate from the *Oribi Gorge Hotel* (see below).

There's an abseil (R300) with a tough half-hour walk out of the gorge afterwards; a gorge swing that requires you to leap off the top of the Lehrs Falls (R380); a gorge slide (R220), erected 160m above the gorge floor; plus rafting trips down the Umzimkulu River (R495).

ACCOMMODATION

KZN Wildlife huts ☎039 679 1644; book through KNZ Wildlife ☎033 845 1000, ⓦkznwildlife.com. The nicest accommodation is in the KZN Wildlife huts at the restcamp at the head of the Umzimkulwana Gorge, peering into the chasm of Oribi Gorge itself. There's a swimming pool here, and all crockery, cutlery and bedding is provided. R320

Oribi Gorge Hotel Some 16km from the restcamp, off the Oribi Flats Rd ☎039 687 0253, ⓦoribigorge .co.za. This colonial-style hotel has spectacular views, including of the famous overhanging rock, and offers spacious rooms, meals to suit most budgets and a pleasant outdoor tea area. R1140

The Hibiscus Coast

The 44km of coast from Port Shepstone to Port Edward has been dubbed the **Hibiscus Coast** because of its luscious, bright gardens, luxury suburbs, beachside developments and attractive caravan parks. It's also known as the **Golf Coast**: there are nine top courses on this short stretch of coastline, and many people come specifically for its golfing opportunities. Although the whole area, centred on Margate, is built up, the Hibiscus Coast gets nicer the further south you go.

Margate and Ramsgate

Some 14km south of Port Shepstone, the brash holiday town of **MARGATE**, with its high-rise apartments, fast-food outlets and ice-cream parlours, offers little in the way of undiscovered coves or hidden beaches, although it (and nearby Ramsgate) does have a reasonable choice of places to stay for all budgets (see below). Margate is also the liveliest town on the South Coast, with the best nightlife. Adjoining Margate to the south, **RAMSGATE** is quieter and slightly more refined – as evidenced by the Gaze Gallery (daily 9am–5pm; free; ☎039 314 4011), attached to the *Waffle House* restaurant (see p.390), just across the lagoon coming from Margate, which displays some reputable work by local artists.

Southbroom and Port Edward

Some 7km beyond Margate, **SOUTHBROOM** is known disparagingly as "Houghton-by-Sea" after one of Johannesburg's wealthiest suburbs, which allegedly relocates here en masse in December. The town is predominantly a sumptuous development of large holiday houses set in expansive gardens and centred on the pretty **Southbroom Golf Course** (R270 for eighteen holes; ☎039 316 6051). Huge dunes covered by lush vegetation sweep down to the sea, and there are good long walks along the shore. The best place for swimming is **Marina Beach**, 3km south of Southbroom Beach.

Heading on for another 10km or so brings you to **PORT EDWARD**, which marks the border with the Eastern Cape. The town has some nice sandy beaches, but its main interest lies in its proximity to the Umtamvuna Nature Reserve (see opposite).

ARRIVAL AND DEPARTURE | THE HIBISCUS COAST

By bus and minibus taxi The Margate Mini Coach runs between Durban and Margate two to three times a day (1hr 30min; see p.378), and minibus taxis connect Margate to Port Shepstone, Ramsgate, Southbroom and Port Edward. The only public transport heading west from Port Edward is the minibus taxis that form a lively rank on the R61 just outside town, collecting passengers for the Eastern Cape.

INFORMATION

Tourist information On the beachfront at Margate (Mon–Fri 8am–5pm, Sat 8am–1pm, Sun 9am–1pm; ☎039 312 2322, ⬩hibiscuscoast.kzn.org.za). Can provide details of accommodation and general information for the whole South Coast area.

ACCOMMODATION

Beachcomber Bay 75 Marine Drive, Ramsgate ☎039 317 4473, ⬩beachcomberbay.co.za. With splendid views of the seafront and private access to the beach, this comfortable, easy-going guesthouse has six rooms, a jacuzzi and sauna and is very close to Margate's restaurants and bars. R660

★ **BillsBest** Corner of Marine Dr and Penshurst Rd, Ramsgate ☎039 314 4837, ⬩billsbest.co.za. This recommended outfit offers a range of well-maintained and regularly serviced cabanas and self-catering units sleeping two to six people, all close to the beach and with good security. There's also B&B accommodation and the attractive *Rock Inn Lodge*, which is rented to large groups (up to 26) and idyllically located in a forest 300m from Ramsgate beach. R320

Ku-boboyi River Lodge Old Main Rd, Leisure Bay, Port Edward ☎072 222 7760, ⬩kuboboyi.co.za. An attractive backpacker hostel on a hilltop with sweeping views of the ocean, a relaxing atmosphere and a pool. Meals are also available. Dorm R110, double R400

Southbroom Traveller's Lodge 11 Cliff Rd, Southbroom ☎039 316 8448, ⬩southbroomtravellerslodge.co.za.

Budget accommodation in a quiet neighbourhood with a pool, a bright lounge area and free use of golf clubs. Rates include breakfast. R320

The Spot Backpackers 23 Ambleside Rd, Umtentweni, 4km north of Port Shepstone ☎039 695 1318, ⓦspotbackpackers.com. This collection of basic but comfortable dorms and cottages is right on the beach, which makes it a magnet for surfers. It's also on the Baz Bus route. Dorm R115, double R260

★ **Sunbirds** 643 Outlook Rd, Southbroom ☎039 316 8202, ⓦsunbirds.co.za. A classy, upmarket B&B offering immaculate rooms with modern decor, flat-screen TVs, DVD players and even iPod docking stations. The attentive hosts provide an imaginative, cooked-to-order breakfast and there's a lovely saltwater pool. R1150

EATING AND DRINKING

Flavours The Bistro Village, 1303 Marine Drive, Ramsgate ☎039 310 4437. One of the area's best restaurants, serving good prawns, paella and Moroccan lamb (most mains R90–115). Tues–Sat noon–2pm & 6–9pm, Sun noon–2pm.

★ **Pistols Saloon** Old Main Rd, Ramsgate ☎031 361 8463. A lively, slightly surreal cowboy-themed bar on the southern edge of Ramsgate, where the resident donkey is paraded in front of drinkers and there's live music (mostly from the 60s, 70s and 80s) on Friday nights. Daily 6pm–midnight.

Riptide Overlooking Southbroom Beach, Southbroom ☎039 316 6151. Perched on the edge of a cliff overlooking

water, this place serves reasonable seafood dishes (R50–75) and good fish and chips, but you really come here for the views. Wed–Sun 11am–9pm.

Trattoria La Terrazza Outlook Rd, Southbroom ☎087 805 9400. Solid Italian food (mains around R75–90) served in a lovely setting next to a lagoon where, at around sunset, thousands of swallows come home to roost. Tues–Sat 6.30–10pm, also Fri–Sun 12.30–2.30pm.

Waffle House Marine Drive, Ramsgate ☎039 314 9424. The best waffles in the province (R25–55), with elaborate toppings such as lemon meringue, ratatouille, and chicken and mushroom. There's also a nice wooden deck overlooking a lagoon. Daily 9am–5pm.

Umtamvuna Nature Reserve

About 8km north of Port Edward, signposted off the R61 to Izingolweni · Daily 7am–5pm · R15 · ☎039 311 2383

You'll find some of the best nature walks in the whole of KwaZulu-Natal at the **Umtamvuna Nature Reserve**. Extending 19km upstream along the tropical Umtamvuna River and the forested cliffs rising above it, the reserve is well known for its spring flowers, as well as the sunbirds and sugar birds that feed on the nectar. It's home to three hundred species of birds, including a famous colony of rare **Cape vultures**, though to see where they nest you'll have to be prepared for a whole day's walk. Waymarked paths are dotted throughout the reserve.

ACCOMMODATION   UMTAMVUNA NATURE RESERVE

Umtamvuna River Lodge Holiday Rd, inside the reserve ☎039 311 3583, ⓦboardalign.co.za. Eight rooms in tranquil, lushly forested surroundings on the banks of the river. Wakeboarding is also available, and there's a restaurant on-site. R700

Vuna Valley Ventures 9/10 Michelle Rd, 50m from the entrance to the reserve ☎039 311 3602, ⓦvunavalleyventures.co.za. This family-friendly budget guesthouse is handily located for forays into the reserve, with attractive rooms that can sleep between two and five people. R300

The North Coast

KwaZulu-Natal's **North Coast**, the 80km stretch along the coast north of Durban from Umhlanga Rocks to the mouth of the Tugela River, is also known as the **Dolphin Coast**. The combination of a narrow continental shelf and warm, shallow waters creates ideal conditions for attracting bottlenose dolphins, which come here to feed all year round. Though the chances of sighting a cetacean are fairly high, you'd be unwise to base a visit solely around this possibility.

Less tacky and developed than the South Coast, the North Coast attracts an upmarket breed of holidaymaker, especially to the main resort of **Umhlanga Rocks**, which is within easy striking distance of Durban. While the Dolphin Coast is still pretty much dominated by whites, the inland towns of **Tongaat** and **KwaDukuza**, linked by the old **R102** road, have substantial Zulu and Indian populations, with Indian temples at Tongaat and the Shaka memorial at KwaDukuza. Also on the R102 is the grave of one of the ANC's best-loved leaders, Albert Luthuli, at **Groutville**.

Umhlanga Rocks

With a permanent population of around 100,000, **UMHLANGA ROCKS** is 20km from the centre of Durban and merges with the suburb of Durban North. A swish resort, the town makes a good day out from the city, with a pleasant, sandy beach dominated by a red-and-white lighthouse. The town's shopping area along Chartwell Drive has a collection of smart, well-stocked malls, while a couple of kilometres up the hill on Umhlanga Ridge, the monster **Gateway Theatre of Shopping** has around four hundred shops, eighteen cinemas, a wave pool and an indoor climbing rock. To get there from Durban, follow the N2 and take the Umhlanga/Mount Edgecombe exit, then follow the signs.

KwaZulu-Natal Sharks Board

1a Herrwood Drive, signposted off the N2 · **Shark dissection** Tues, Wed & Thurs 9am & 2pm, Sun 2pm · R35 · ☎ 031 566 0400, ⓦ www .shark.co.za · **Boat trips** daily 6.30am · R250 · ☎ 082 403 9206 · Without your own transport, the best way to get to the Sharks Board is by minibus taxi or shuttle (see below)

A couple of kilometres north of Umhlanga's centre, the **KwaZulu-Natal Sharks Board** shows a multiscreen audiovisual about sharks and conducts a dissection of a recently caught shark, which disabuses any notions of these creatures as the hooligans of the oceans. It also plugs the board's work in maintaining the province's **shark nets**; although these nets protect swimmers all along the coast, they are controversial, as not just sharks but also endangered turtles and dolphins die in them, thus affecting the balance of the inshore ecosystem. The Sharks Board is investigating an electronic shark barrier that might improve the situation, while still ensuring safe swimming.

A trip on a Sharks Board boat allows you to look out for dolphins and whales. The trips depart from Wilson's Wharf in Durban; note that the weekday trips include an inspection of the shark nets.

ARRIVAL AND DEPARTURE   UMHLANGA ROCKS

By shuttle and minibus taxi The Umhlanga Explorer Shuttle Service (☎ 031 561 1846) runs trips on request to the Musgrave Centre in Berea and to Durban city centre, departing from near the tourist office (see p.380). Otherwise, minibus taxis make the trip to Gateway Mall from the taxi rank on Johannes Nkosi St.

INFORMATION

Tourist information 1A Chartwell Drive (Mon–Fri 8.30am–5pm, Sat 9am–1pm; ☎ 031 561 4257, ⓦ umhlangatourism.co.za).

ACCOMMODATION

Anchor's Rest 14 Stanley Grace Crescent ☎ 031 561 7380, ⓦ anchorsrest.co.za. Centrally located and elegant Mediterranean-style guesthouse with spacious and well-decorated self-catering suites, as well as an expansive veranda overlooking the pool. **R850**

Beverly Hills Hotel Lighthouse Rd ☎ 031 561 2211, ⓦ southernsun.com. The most upmarket place to stay in Umhlanga, occupying a prime location by the beach. All rooms have sea views, as does the restaurant – a good spot for a sundowner. **R3800**

Honeypot 11 Hilken Drive ☎ 031 561 3795, ⓦ honeypotguesthouse.co.za. An attractive B&B in a residential area, decorated in rustic style with limewashed furniture and African fabric. The rooms all look out onto a small pool. **R750**

★ **Jessica's B&B** 35 Portland Drive ☎ 031 561 3369, ⓦ jessicaskzn.co.za. Three comfortable self-contained cottages set in a rambling garden, ideal for families, plus a few double rooms in the main house. Good value, and the friendly owners will make you feel right at home. **R500**

5

EATING

Ile Maurice 9 McCausland Crescent ☎ 031 561 7609. A gastronomic Franco-Mauritian restaurant run by one of Durban's renowned chefs, where rabbit cooked in red wine meets octopus curry (mains R120–150). Tues–Sun noon–3pm & 6.30–10.15pm.

Olive & Oil 19 Chartwell Centre, on the 1st floor of the building next to the tourist office ☎ 031 561 2618. Particularly good for fish and seafood, though they also serve the usual Italian standbys; mains in the R70–95 range. Daily noon–3pm & 6–10pm.

★ **Razzmatazz** Cabana Beach Lifestyle Resort, 10 Lagoon Drive ☎ 031 561 5847. Enjoy ostrich fillet or tamarind fish curry from the great outdoor deck with ocean views. The three-course set menu is excellent value at R115. Daily 12.30–3.30pm & 6.30–10pm.

Tongaat

TONGAAT lies a few kilometres inland of Umhlanga Rocks across the N2 highway, a barrier between the coastal resorts and the workings of KwaZulu-Natal's sugar industry. The town, fronted by neglected imitation Cape Dutch cottages, has long associations with South Africa's Indian community and boasts a handful of temples. The most distinguished of these, a National Monument, is the small, whitewashed **Shri Jugganath Puri Temple**, built at the turn of the last century by the Sanskrit scholar Pandit Shrikishan Maharaj and dedicated to Vishnu. To get to the temple from the R102, turn west into Ganie Street, then left into Plane Street and left again into Catherine Street; the temple is at the junction of Catherine and Plane.

Ballito

There's nothing very African about **BALLITO**, a Mediterranean-style resort a further 10km up the coast from Tongaat, with a splurge of time-shares, high-rise holiday apartments and shopping malls by the sea. But it's a pleasant enough place nevertheless, with a beach offering safe swimming and full-time lifeguards.

ARRIVAL AND DEPARTURE BALLITO

By bus and minibus taxi One of the Greyhound bus routes between Durban and Johannesburg passes through Ballito (daily; 45min to Durban, 11hr 45min to Johannesburg). Otherwise, a number of minibus taxis trundle up the coast from Durban.

ACCOMMODATION

Dolphin Holiday Resort Five minutes' walk from the beach on the corner of Compensation Beach Rd and Hillary Drive ☎ 032 946 2187, ⓦ dolphinholidayresort .co.za. A good budget option, consisting of a well-shaded campsite and a collection of self-catering cottages. Camping R190, cottage R440

Zimbali Lodge 1km south of Ballito ☎ 032 538 5000, ⓦ fairmont.com/zimbalilodge. This is the swishest place to stay, with accommodation in luxury suites set in lush subtropical coastal forest in the heart of a network of wetlands. Even if you aren't staying, consider stopping here for a meal or a sundowner in the bar, raised on stilts overlooking the golf course, which rewards you with soaring views across the Indian Ocean. R1500

KwaDukuza

Head inland from Ballito and follow the R102 north for around 30km • KwaDukuza Interpretative Centre Mon–Fri 8am–4pm • Free • ☎ 032 552 7210

KWADUKUZA (still widely known by its pre-1994 election name, **Stanger**) has a special place in the cosmology of Zulu nationalists. This was the site of King Shaka's last kraal (the round formation of huts where the king lived), and it was the place where he was treacherously stabbed to death in 1828 by his half-brother Dingane, who succeeded him. The warrior-king is said to have been buried upright in a grain pit, and is commemorated by a small park and memorial on King Shaka Street, right in the centre of town. Near the memorial is a rock with a groove worn into it – supposedly where

Shaka sharpened his spears. At the rear of the park, the **KwaDukuza Interpretative Centre** has a small display on Shaka and a very good fifteen-minute audiovisual display. The park is also the venue of the **King Shaka Day** celebrations (see box, p.431), held every year on September 24 – which is also the Heritage Day public holiday.

Groutville

8km southwest of KwaDukuza on the R102, just across a rusty bridge over the Mvoti River

Tiny **GROUTVILLE** is remarkable mainly for the grave of **Albert Luthuli**, one of South Africa's greatest political leaders. A teacher and chief of the Zulus in Groutville, Luthuli became President General of the ANC in 1952. Advocating a non-violent struggle against apartheid, Luthuli was awarded the Nobel Peace Prize in 1960, which at home earned him a succession of banning orders restricting him to the KwaDukuza area. He died under mysterious circumstances in 1967 in KwaDukuza, apparently knocked down by a train. He is buried next to a whitewashed, nineteenth-century corrugated-iron mission church. Luthuli's life is recounted in the moving autobiography, *Let My People Go*.

ACCOMMODATION	KWADUKUZA AND GROUTVILLE

The best place to stay close to KwaDukuza and Groutville is Blythdale, the closest stretch of sand to KwaDukuza, where a ban on high-rise construction has preserved the deserted appearance of its endless beach.

Mini Villas 52 Umvoti Drive ☎ 032 551 1277, ⓦ minivillas.co.za. Simply decorated but well-equipped self-catering villas sleeping four to six people, some giving out onto a garden, with a nearby path leading down to the beach. **R460**

Palm Dune Beach Lodge 9 Umvoti Drive ☎ 032 552 1588, ⓦ palmdune.co.za. An upmarket resort where you can opt for a classy one-, two-, or three-bedroom chalet and partake of a wide range of activities, from jetskiing to beach volleyball. **R1410**

Harold Johnson Nature Reserve

Signposted 24km north of KwaDukuza off the N2 – take the Zinkwazi turn-off and turn left at Darnall • Daily 6am–6pm • R10 • Camping R150 • ☎ 032 486 1574

Abutting the Tugela River is KZN Wildlife's **Harold Johnson Nature Reserve**. With its well-preserved coastal bush, steep cliffs and gullies, this is a fine place to come for a day's visit or to camp overnight – there are no shops or facilities, so be sure to stock up before arrival. The reserve has several hiking **trails** that take you past various historical sites, most of them connected to the Anglo-Zulu War of 1879. These include the **Ultimatum Tree**: the wild fig tree where the British issued their ultimatum to King Cetshwayo in 1878, part of which required the Zulus to demobilize their standing army.

Valley of a Thousand Hills

The evocatively named **Valley of a Thousand Hills** (ⓦ 1000hills.kzn.org.za) makes for a picturesque drive along the edge of densely folded hills where Zulu people still live in traditional homesteads, and which visitors rarely venture into. However, the area is only worth a special trip if you're not exploring the KwaZulu-Natal interior, where scenes like this occur in abundance. While the valley, 45km from Durban, is best suited to touring in your own car (take the N3 from Durban, following the Pinetown signs), there are **daily tours** from Durban offered by Tekweni Eco Tours (see box, p.380) that take in the highlights. The trip to the valley and back can be done in half a day, but there are sufficient attractions laid on along the route to extend it to a full day's outing.

5

Vintage train trip

Last Sunday of the month • Two trips, at 8.30am and 12.30pm, from the Kloof Station, Stockers Arms, Old Main Rd • R150 • ☎ 082 353 6003, Ⓦ umgenisteamrailway.co.za

If you're in Durban on the last Sunday of the month, consider taking a **vintage train trip** with Umgeni Steam Railways, which boasts one of the largest collections of historic locomotives and coaches in the southern hemisphere. From Kloof, the trains chug for forty-five minutes along the edge of the Valley of a Thousand Hills, terminating at Inchanga Station and its crafts market.

Phezulu Safari Park

Old Main Rd • Daily 8.30am–4.30pm • R100 • Zulu dancing daily 10am, 11.30am, 2pm & 3.30pm • ☎ 031 777 1000, Ⓦ phezulusafaripark. co.za

Just south of the valley is **Phezulu Safari Park**, which brings you close to deadly serpents – tucked away in cramped little glass boxes – plus crocodiles and other penned animals. There's also a reconstruction of a pre-colonial Zulu village, where you can watch tourist-geared – but nonetheless spirited – displays of **Zulu dancing** set against the dramatic horizon of the valley.

Pietermaritzburg

Although **PIETERMARITZBURG** (often called Maritzburg), the provincial capital of KwaZulu-Natal, sells itself as the best-preserved Victorian city in South Africa, with strong British connections, little of its colonial heritage remains. It's actually a very South African city, with Zulus forming the largest community, followed by Indians, with those of British extraction a minority – albeit a high-profile one. This multiculturalism, together with a substantial student population, adds up to a fairly lively city that's also relatively safe and small enough to explore on foot, with most places of interest within easy walking distance of the centre's heart. Only 80km inland from Durban along the fast N3 freeway, Pietermaritzburg is an easy day's outing from the coastal city; it can be combined with visits to the Valley of a Thousand Hills (see p.393) along the Old Main Road (R103), or used as an overnight stop en route to the Ukhahlamba Drakensberg (see p.398) or the Battlefields in the vicinity of Ladysmith (see p.438).

Brief history

Pietermaritzburg's Afrikaner origins are reflected in its name; after slaughtering three thousand Zulus at the Battle of Blood River, the Voortrekkers established the fledgling Republic of Natalia in 1839, naming their capital in honour of the Boer leaders **Piet Retief** and **Gerrit Maritz**. The republic's independence was short-lived – Britain annexed it only four years later, and by the closing decade of the nineteenth century Maritzburg was the most important centre in the colony of Natal, with a population of nearly 10,000 (more than Durban at that time). Indians arrived at the turn of the last century, mostly as indentured labourers, but also as traders. Among their number was a young, little-known lawyer called Mohandas Gandhi, who went on to change the history of India. He later traced the embryo of his devastatingly successful tactic of passive resistance to an incident in 1893, when as a non-white he was thrown out of a first-class train compartment at Pietermaritzburg station.

Tatham Art Gallery

Corner of Chief Albert Luthuli and Langalibalele sts • Tues–Sun 10am–5pm • Free • ☎ 033 392 2801, Ⓦ tatham.org.za

Across from the imposing **City Hall**, a late Victorian red-brick building with an impressive 15m clock tower, you'll find the **Tatham Art Gallery**, another fine brick

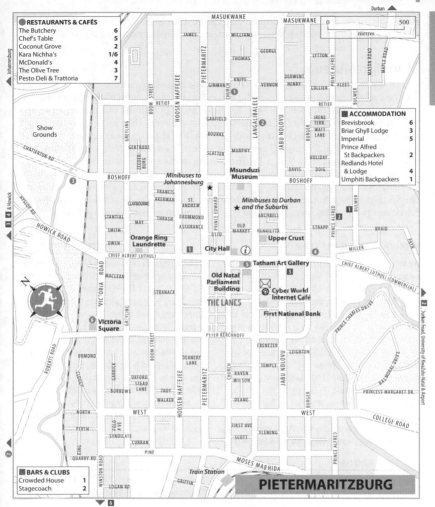

Durban ▲

5

● RESTAURANTS & CAFÉS
The Butchery	6
Chef's Table	5
Coconut Grove	2
Kara Nichha's	1/6
McDonald's	4
The Olive Tree	3
Pesto Deli & Trattoria	7

Johannesburg

Show
Grounds

MASUKWANE

MASUKWANE

0   500
metres

Minibuses to
Johannesburg

Msunduzi
Museum

Minibuses to Durban
★ and the Suburbs

■ ACCOMMODATION
Brevisbrook	6
Briar Ghyll Lodge	3
Imperial	5
Prince Alfred	
St Backpackers	2
Redlands Hotel	
& Lodge	4
Umphiti Backpackers	1

3 4 & Howick

HOWICK ROAD

Orange Ring
Laundrette

City Hall (i)

Upper Crust

Tatham Art Gallery

Old Natal
Parliament
Building

THE LANES

Cyber World
Internet Café

First National Bank

Victoria
Square

PETER KERCHHOFF

Train Station

PIETERMARITZBURG

■ BARS & CLUBS
Crowded House	1
Stagecoach	2

edifice, which was previously the Supreme Court of the Colony of Natal. This is the highlight of the city's attractions, housing one of the country's best collections of art. Pieces by black South Africans such as Zwelethu Mthethwa and Sam Nhlengethwa are exhibited alongside those by Marc Chagall, Georges Braque and Henri Matisse. A good way to enjoy the art is by attending the free **classical music concerts** that often take place at the gallery on Wednesday afternoons.

Old Natal Parliament Building, First National Bank and the Lanes

South of the Tatham on Langalibalele Street stands a series of attractive period buildings, including the typically imperial **Old Natal Parliament Building** and the **First National Bank**, which dates from 1903 and had its facade chosen from an Edwardian catalogue and shipped out from the mother country. Across from the First National Bank building is the mostly pedestrianized warren of alleyways known as **the Lanes**, which was the financial hub of Natal from 1888 to 1931 and housed four separate

5

stock exchanges. This area is enjoyable to explore during the day, but it's a notorious stamping ground for pickpockets, so stay alert and don't come here after dark.

Msunduzi Museum

Boshoff St • Mon–Fri 9am–4pm, Sat 9am–1pm • R8 • ☎ 033 394 6834, ⓦ voortrekkermuseum.co.za

The best of the town's museums is the **Msunduzi Museum**, which centres on the original Church of the Vow, built in 1838 by Boers in honour of their victory over the Zulus three years earlier at the Battle of Blood River. The church was their part of a bargain allegedly struck with God (see p.438). The museum connects with the Voortrekker roots of Pietermaritzburg and is worth a fleeting visit to gain some insight into life on a trek. The most interesting items are the home-made children's toys and beautifully embroidered *kappies* (hats) which the women used to shield themselves from the sun. Across the lovely courtyard garden is a reconstruction of the 1846 thatched house of **Andries Pretorius**, leader of the Voortrekkers at Blood River and the driving force behind the establishment of the Boer Republic of Natalia.

ARRIVAL AND DEPARTURE   PIETERMARITZBURG

By bus All intercity buses pull in at the *McDonald's* on the corner of Burger and Chief Albert Luthuli sts. Intercape (☎086 128 7287) and SA Roadlink (☎033 345 6890) have their own offices in the *McDonald's* parking lot, while Greyhound tickets can be bought at African Link Travel on Burger St (☎033 345 3175) and Translux tickets at the train station (see below; ☎033 345 0165).
Destinations: Bloemfontein (daily; 9hr 30min); Cape Town (daily; 21hr 45min); Durban (16 daily; 1hr 20min); Johannesburg (19 daily; 7hr); Ladysmith (daily; 2hr 15min); Pretoria (12 daily; 7hr 30min).

By Baz Bus The Baz Bus drops off at *Prince Alfred St Backpackers* in town.
Destinations: Amphitheatre (3 weekly; 3hr); Durban (3 weekly; 2hr); Johannesburg (3 weekly; 8hr); Pretoria (3 weekly; 9hr).

By plane Flights to Johannesburg (2–4 daily; 1hr 30min), used mainly by business travellers, depart from the city's Oribi Airport (☎033 386 9577), about 6km south of the centre. The only means of getting to and from the airport and the town centre is by taxi.

By train The train station (☎033 897 2201) lies at the unsavoury southwest end of Langalibalele St, one of the main city thoroughfares, from where it's advisable to arrange beforehand to be collected, particularly at night. Trains leave for Durban at 4.58am (Mon–Sat; 2hr 20min) and for Johannesburg at 9.36pm (Mon–Fri & Sun; 10hr).

By minibus taxi Minibuses to Durban and Johannesburg leave from ranks near the Msunduzi Museum in the centre.

GETTING AROUND

Taxi Metered taxis should be booked in advance, and in this compact city are unlikely to break the bank. One of the biggest firms is Yellow Cabs (☎033 397 1910); alternatively, try Ronnie's Taxis (☎033 387 4046).

ALAN PATON

Writer, teacher and politician **Alan Paton** was born in Pietermaritzburg in 1903. His visionary first novel, *Cry, the Beloved Country*, focused international attention on the plight of black South Africans and sold millions of copies worldwide. The book was published in 1948 – the same year the National Party assumed power and began to establish apartheid – and Paton subsequently entered politics to become a founder-member of the non-racial and fiercely anti-apartheid Liberal Party. He was president of the party from 1960 until 1968, when it was forced to disband by repressive legislation forbidding multiracial political organizations.

Paton died in Durban in 1988, having published a number of works, including two biographies and his own autobiography. The following year, the Alan Paton Centre was established at the University of KwaZulu-Natal's archives building on Milner Rd, Scottsville (visits by appointment; ☎033 260 5926). The Centre includes a re-creation of Paton's study, as well as personal memorabilia and documents.

INFORMATION

Tourist information Publicity House, on the corner of Langalibalele and Chief Albert Luthuli sts (Mon–Fri 8am–5pm, Sat 8am–1pm; ☎033 345 1348, ⓦwww .pmbtourism.co.za). Stocks an excellent selection of books, and also has information on the Ukhahlamba Drakensberg and other nearby attractions.

ACCOMMODATION

Brevisbrook 28 Waverleydale Rd, Boughton, 5km from centre ☎033 344 1402, ⓦbrevisbrook.co.za; map p.395. All rooms in this intimate little B&B have private entrances and bathtubs, and there's a wonderful woodsy braii area and a swimming pool. A self-catering option is available. R600

Briar Ghyll Lodge George MacFarlane Lane, off Howick Rd, Town Hill, 5km from centre ☎033 342 2664, ⓦbglodge.co.za; map p.395. A magnificent Victorian homestead on rolling lawns, with a tennis court and swimming pool. Choose between spacious suites in the main homestead or two self-contained cottages, with three-course dinners available on request. R790

Imperial 224 Jabu Ndlovu St, city centre ☎033 342 6551, ⓦproteahotels.com/imperial; map p.395. All the mod cons you'd expect, set in a lovely nineteenth-century building with a certain historical flair; Prince Louis Napoleon stayed here in 1879 before being killed in the Zulu Wars, and some of the decor is reminiscent of that era. It often books up, so reserve in advance. R1136

★ **Prince Alfred St Backpackers** 312 Prince Alfred St, city centre ☎033 345 7045, ⓦchauncey.co.za; map p.395. A notch above your average backpacker hostel; there are no dorms, just five attractive rooms (some en suite) which cost the same per person (R150) whether you're travelling alone or with someone. Calm, clean and highly recommended. Good breakfasts and dinners are available on request. R300

Redlands Hotel & Lodge 1 George MacFarlane Lane, Wembley, 3km from centre ☎033 394 3333, ⓦredlandshotel.co.za; map p.395. This upmarket boutique hotel has luxury finishes, a swimming pool and a tennis court. Besides rooms, they offer self-catering one- and two-bed apartments. R1080

Umphiti Backpackers 317 Bulwer St, city centre ☎033 394 3490, ⓦwww.umphiti.co.za; map p.395. A friendly, laidback hostel with a knowledgeable owner who can advise on things to do around town. Like *Prince Alfred St Backpackers*, single rooms are the same price per person as doubles (R140), making them good value for solo travellers. Dorm R120, double R280

EATING, DRINKING AND NIGHTLIFE

Pietermaritzburg has a fairly good choice of **restaurants**, as well as a handful of decent **pubs** and **nightclubs**. Around Boshoff St, at the heart of the city's Indian quarter, you'll find a concentration of shops selling cheap spicy snacks like *rotis* and *bunny chows*.

RESTAURANTS AND CAFÉS

The Butchery 101 Roberts Rd, Wembley ☎033 342 5239; map p.395. A good place not just for steaks, ribs and chicken (most mains R60–100), but also for salads and vegetarian dishes, and the Sunday lunch buffet is excellent value at R80. Daily noon–late.

Chef's Table Tatham Art Gallery, Chief Albert Luthuli St ☎033 342 8327; map p.395. A colourful little coffee shop that's the best place in town for light lunches, with sandwiches and curries for around R20–50. Tues–Sat 10am–4pm.

Coconut Grove 426 Langalibalele St ☎033 394 3337; map p.395. Popular with Indian families, serving cheap curries (under R40) and an extensive range of burgers, along with more substantial fare like seafood and roasts. Mon–Sat noon–3pm & 6–10.30pm.

★ **Kara Nichha's** 470 Church St ☎033 345 0228; map p.395. An excellent, very cheap vegetarian Indian takeaway (curries for R5), particularly good for filled *rotis* and Indian sweets. There's another branch at 151 Victoria Rd. Mon–Fri 8am–5.15pm, till 3pm Sat.

The Olive Tree McDonald's Garden Centre, Chatterton Rd ☎033 394 7033; map p.395. Occupying a tranquil, shaded spot overlooking the river, this pleasant café serves good breakfasts, imaginative salads and healthy lunches (R45–60). Daily 8am–4pm.

Pesto Deli & Trattoria 101 Roberts Rd, Wembley ☎033 342 2778; map p.395. A decent Italian restaurant offering the usual classics along with some more unusual dishes, such as roast lamb pizza. Mains R60–90. Daily noon–11pm.

BARS AND CLUBS

Crowded House Chief Albert Luthuli St ☎033 345 5977; map p.395. Centrally located nightclub that has been a firm favourite for years, attracting a mainly black crowd of university students and young professionals. Tues, Thurs & Sat; R40.

Stagecoach 44 Durban Rd, Scottsville ☎033 394 7727; map p.395. Close to the university, this lively student hangout hosts live bands every Monday and Wednesday, as well as serving tasty, good-value pub food. Daily 11am–11.30pm.

DIRECTORY

Emergencies AA ☎ 083 84322.

Hospital Pietermaritzburg Medi-Clinic, 90 Payn St (☎ 033 845 3911).

Internet access Cyber World Internet Café, Victoria Inn Arcade, Langalibalele St (daily 6.30am–8pm).

Pharmacy Medpharm, Victoria Mall, 157 Victoria Rd (Mon–Fri 8am–9pm, Sat 8am–8pm, Sun 8am–3pm; ☎ 033 342 3390).

The Midlands

For most travellers, the verdant farmland that makes up the **Midlands** is picture-postcard terrain, to be whizzed through on the two-hour journey from Durban or Pietermaritzburg to the Ukhahlamba Drakensberg. There's little reason to dally here, unless you fancy taking in the region's quaint, English-style country inns, tea shops and craft shops, several of which are on the so-called **Midlands Meander**, a route that weaves its way around the N3 on back roads between Pietermaritzburg and the **Mooi River** 60km to the northwest.

As you head north out of Pietermaritzburg on the N3 through the Midlands, you're roughly tracing the last journey of **Nelson Mandela** as a free man before his arrest in 1962. On the run from the police, Mandela had been continuing his political activities, often travelling in disguise – a practice that earned him the nickname of the "Black Pimpernel". **Howick**, 18km northwest of Pietermaritzburg, is recorded as the place where his historic detention began; the actual spot is on the R103, 2km north of a side road heading to the Tweedie junction. On this occasion, he was masquerading as the chauffeur of a white friend, when their car was stopped on the old Howick road, apparently because of a tip-off. A memorial unveiled by Mandela himself in 1996 marks the unassuming spot, amid farmland between a railway line and the road.

INFORMATION   **THE MIDLANDS**

A free **map** outlining the attractions on the Midlands Meander is available from most tourist offices in the vicinity.

ACCOMMODATION

For lists of self-catering accommodation in the area, contact KZN Wildlife or the Midlands Meander Association (☎ 033 330 8195, ⓦ midlandsmeander.co.za), which can make bookings on your behalf.

Granny Mouse Country House Old Main Rd, Balgowan, 28km northwest of Howick on the R103 ☎ 033 234 4071, ⓦ grannymouse.co.za. Stylishly renovated and offering rooms in thatched cottages decorated with rich-textured fabrics. There's a health spa, restaurant and loads of small lounges with large comfortable chairs to relax in. **R1640**

Loxley House South off the Lonteni/Sani Pass Rd in the hamlet of Nottingham Rd, 30km northwest of Howick on the R103 ☎ 033 266 6362, ⓦ loxleyhouse .com. Comfortable rooms in a small B&B with its own restaurant; electric blankets on request for chilly winter nights. **R1100**

Rawdon's Old Main Rd, Nottingham Rd ☎ 033 266 6044, ⓦ www.rawdons.co.za. Set in a gracious country estate looking onto its own trout lake, with welcoming log fires for cool misty days and airy verandas for hot summers. It also has an atmospheric pub with its own brewery on site. **R980**

The Ukhahlamba Drakensberg

Hugging the border with Lesotho, South Africa's premier mountain wilderness is mostly a vast national park officially known as the **Ukhahlamba Drakensberg Park**. The tallest range in Southern Africa, the "Dragon Mountains" (or, in Zulu, the "barrier of spears") reach their highest peaks along the border with Lesotho. The range is actually an escarpment separating a high interior plateau from the coastal lowlands of KwaZulu-Natal. Although this is a continuation of the same escarpment that divides the Mpumalanga highveld from the game-rich lowveld of the Kruger National Park

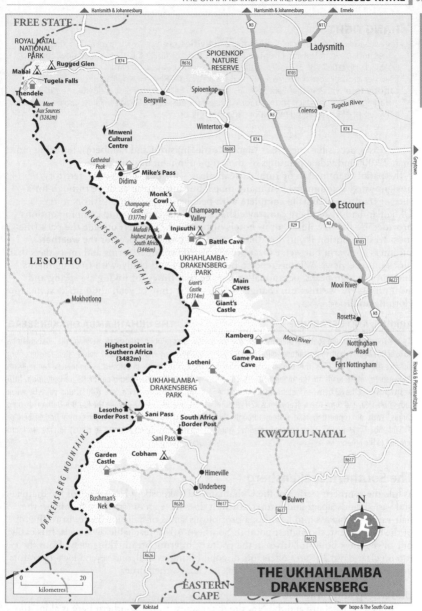

THE UKHAHLAMBA DRAKENSBERG

and continues into the northern section of the Eastern Cape, when people talk of the Berg, they invariably mean the range in KwaZulu-Natal.

For elating scenery – massive spires, rock buttresses, wide grasslands, glorious waterfalls, rivers, pools and fern-carpeted forests – the Ukhahlamba Drakensberg is unrivalled. Wild and unpopulated, it's a paradise for **hiking**. One of the richest **San rock-art** repositories in the world, the Ukhahlamba Drakensberg is also a World Heritage Site, with more than six hundred recorded sites hidden all over the mountains

5

HANG TIGHT

The Midlands offers a couple of **adventure activities**, both of which involve dangling from cables and ropes. In Howick, Over The Top Adventures organizes a 107m **abseil** down the Howick Falls (☎082 736 3651, ⓦoverthetop.co.za; R300 per person with a minimum charge of R900 per group). North of Howick, at the Karkloof Nature Reserve, you can undertake a **canopy tour** with Karkloof Canopy Tours (☎033 330 3415, ⓦkarkloofcanopytour.co.za; R450 including lunch), on which you're strapped into a harness and glide along steel cables between platforms erected high above the forest floor.

(three easily accessible ones are at **Giant's Castle**, **Injisuthi** and **Kamberg**), featuring more than 22,000 individual paintings by the original inhabitants of the area.

The park is hemmed in by rural African areas – former "homeland" territory, unsignposted and unnamed on many maps, but interesting to drive through for a slice of traditional **Zulu life** complete with beehive-shaped huts. Visitors to the Ukhahlamba Drakensberg can **stay** either in the self-catering and camping options provided by KZN Wildlife, or in hotels or backpacker hostels outside the park (the most feasible option if you don't have your own transport). As for the **weather**, summers are warm but wet; expect both dramatic thunderstorms and misty days that block out the views. Winters tend to be dry, sunny and chilly, with freezing nights and, on the high peaks, occasional snow. The best times for hiking are spring and autumn. As the weather can change rapidly at any time of year, always take sufficient clothing and food.

ARRIVAL AND DEPARTURE   THE UKHAHLAMBA DRAKENSBERG

By car You can reach the Southern Drakensberg using the R626 or R612/R617, both routes putting you within striking distance of Sani Pass. For the Central and Northern Drakensberg, most roads to the mountains branch off westwards from the N3 between Pietermaritzburg and the Ladysmith area, and come to a halt at various KZN Wildlife camps. With no connecting road system through the Ukhahlamba Drakensberg, it's not possible to drive from one end to the other.

By bus Public transport serving the Ukhahlamba Drakensberg is limited. Many hotels offer transfers from the bus terminals in Estcourt, a commercial centre 88km north of Pietermaritzburg on the N3, or Ladysmith. NUD Express shuttle service (see p.403) runs daily between Durban and Sani Pass, while the Baz Bus Durban–Jo'burg service goes via Winterton for the Central Drakensberg or *Amphitheatre Backpackers* (see p.409) for the Northern Drakensberg.

The Southern Drakensberg

While the southern section of the Ukhahlamba Drakensberg lacks some of the drama and varied landscape found further north, it does have an outstanding highlight: the hair-raising **Sani Pass** into Lesotho, a precipitous series of hairpins that twist to the top of the escarpment, the highest point in Southern Africa reachable on wheels. It is easily one of the most beautiful drives in the country, offering breathtaking views from the top on clear days. The area offers lots of good hiking as well, and several local operators organize pony trekking in the mountains just across the border.

Underberg and Himeville

From Pietermaritzburg and the N3, the main access to the Southern Berg is along the R617 (take the Bulwer/Underberg exit west off the N3). **UNDERBERG**, 150km west of Pietermaritzburg on the R617, is the main gateway to the Southern Drakensberg, with a good supermarket for stocking up on supplies. **HIMEVILLE**, 4km north from here, is the last village you'll find before heading up Sani Pass, and can make for a good place to stay en route.

5

Sani Pass

SANI PASS is the only place in the KwaZulu-Natal Ukhahlamba Drakensberg range where you can actually drive up the mountains using the only road from KwaZulu-Natal into Lesotho, connecting to the tiny highland outpost of **Mokhotlong**. It's the pass itself, zigzagging into the clouds, that draws increasing numbers into the High Berg.

Lotheni and Kamberg

Well off the beaten track, along dirt roads and seldom explored by foreign visitors, the two **KZN Wildlife camps** at Lotheni and Kamberg are worth venturing into for their isolated wilderness, good trout fishing and some exquisite San rock paintings.

In a valley in the foothills of the Berg and accessible by car either via Nottingham Road to the northeast or from Himeville to the southeast, **LOTHENI** is tranquil and beautiful, with waterfalls, grasslands and the lure of fishing in the Lotheni River, which flows through the reserve and is stocked with brown trout.

Apart from the superb fishing, the best reason to visit **KAMBERG**, 42km west of **Rosetta**, is for the rock art. At **Game Pass Cave** (one of the three caves in the Ukhahlamba Drakensberg open to the public, also known as Shelter Cave), images of stylized figures in trance states and large, polychrome eland dance across the wall. There are other less distinct paintings near the waterfall that you can visit at will. **Walks** from Kamberg are undemanding and very scenic, and include a 4km trail with handrails for wheelchair-users and the visually impaired.

HIKING AND OTHER ACTIVITIES

Whether you choose to take your time on easy walks or embark on a challenging three- or four-day trip into the mountains, **hiking** in the Ukhahlamba Drakensberg remains one of South Africa's top wilderness experiences. The marvel of setting out on foot in these mountains is that you're unlikely to encounter vehicles, settlements, or even other people, and the scenery is sublime.

The Ukhahlamba Drakensberg is divided into the High Berg and Little Berg, according to altitude. In the **High Berg**, you're in the land of spires and great rock buttresses, where the only places to sleep are in caves or, in some areas, huts. You'll need to be totally self-sufficient and obey wilderness rules, taking a trowel and toilet paper with you and not fouling natural water with anything – which means carrying water away from the streams to wash in. Both mountaineers' huts and caves must be booked with the KZN Wildlife office you start out from, and you'll also need to write down your route details in the mountain register. Slogging up the passes to the top of the mountains requires a high degree of fitness, some hiking experience and a companion or guide who knows the terrain.

The **Little Berg**, with its gentler summits, rivers, rock paintings, valleys and forests, is equally remote and beautiful. It's also easier (and safer) to explore if you're of average fitness. If you don't want to carry a backpack and sleep in caves or huts, it's feasible to base yourself at one of the KZN Wildlife camps and set out on day hikes, of which there are endless choices. It's also possible to do a two-day walk from one of the camps, spending one night in a cave. Two excellent bases for walking are **Injisuthi** in the Giant's Castle Game Reserve (see p.405), or **Thendele** in the Royal KwaZulu-Natal National Park (see p.408). If you want the luxury of spending the nights in a hotel, base yourself in the **Cathedral Peak** area at the *Cathedral Peak Hotel* (see p.408). With extensive grasslands, the Southern Berg is the terrain of the highly recommended **Giant's Cup Hiking Trail**, an exhilarating introduction to the mountains (see box, opposite).

KZN Wildlife offices sell books on Ukhahlamba Drakensberg walks, as well as trail maps they produce themselves (1:50,000). If you don't feel confident tackling the terrain, or are alone, you could contact Stef Steyn (☎033 330 4293, ⓦwww.kzntours.co.za), who specializes in **guided hikes** across the Ukhahlamba Drakensberg as well as scenic tours all over the province.

As for other activities, **angling** at Cobham Garden Castle or Giant's Castle costs R50 per day by permit only from KZN Wildlife, with a bag limit of ten trout per day. At Lotheni and Kamberg the permit costs R50–90, with a bag limit of two to ten trout, depending on where you fish. You'll need to bring all your own gear.

GIANT'S CUP HIKING TRAIL

The 60km, five-day **Giant's Cup Hiking Trail** (R75 per person per night, includes entrance fee to the reserve), part of which traverses a depression that explains the trail's name, is the only laid-out trail in the Ukhahlamba Drakensberg. It starts at the Sani Pass road, then leads through the foothills of the Southern Drakensberg and winds past eroded sandstone formations, overhangs with San paintings, grassy plains and beautiful valleys with river pools to swim in. No single day's hike is longer than 14km and, although there are some steep sections, this is not a difficult trail – you need to be fit to enjoy it, but not an athlete.

The **mountain huts** at the five overnight stops have running water, toilets, tables and benches, and bunks with mattresses. It's essential to bring a camping stove, food and a sleeping bag. The trail can be shortened by missing the first day and starting out at Pholela Hut, an old farmhouse where you spend the night, then terminating one day earlier at Swiman Hut close to the KZN Wildlife office at Garden Castle. You can also lengthen the trail by spending an extra night at Bushmen's Nek Hut, in an area with numerous caves and rock-art sites.

The trail is restricted to thirty people per day and tends to get booked out during holiday periods; **bookings** should be made through KZN Wildlife (**w** kznwildlife.com), where you can also get a map and a trail booklet.

ARRIVAL AND DEPARTURE   THE SOUTHERN DRAKENSBERG

SANI PASS

By bus For all its isolation, Sani Pass is fairly straightforward to get to. NUD Express (**☎** 033 701 2750, **w** underbergexpress .nudhosting.com) operates a shuttle service between Durban airport, Durban centre, Pietermaritzburg, Howick, Bulwer, Himeville and Sani Pass (dropping off at *Sani Lodge* – see

p.404). The fare from Durban's King Shaka airport to Sani Pass is R320 and the journey takes around three and a half hours.

By car If you intend to drive up to Sani Pass, it's preferable to use a 4WD vehicle, and you'll need your passport. The South African and Lesotho border posts are both open daily from 6am to 6pm.

INFORMATION AND TOURS

UNDERBERG

Tourist information In the centre of town, Southern Berg Escape (Mon–Fri 8am–4pm, Sat–Sun 9am–1pm; **☎** 033 701 1471, **w** www.drakensberg.org) is the best place to get information about the region.

SANI PASS

Tours Thaba Tours in Underberg (**☎** 033 701 2888, **w** thabatours.co.za) runs a daily jaunt into Lesotho, taking you by 4WD to the highest point on the Sani–Mokhotlong Rd to visit shepherds and learn about their lifestyle; it also organizes horseriding trails and walking trips to see rock art.

LOTHENI AND KAMBERG

Access and supplies Both Lotheni (**☎** 033 702 0540; R25) and Kamberg (**☎** 033 267 7251; R30) are open daily

April–Sept 6am–6pm, and Oct–March 5am–7pm. In Lotheni, there's a trading store about 10km before you reach the restcamp. At Kamberg, however, the nearest major supplies are at Rosetta, so it's best to bring all your own food and drink, though there's a very basic store just before you reach the reserve.

Tours and rock art In Kamberg, note that the paintings at Game Pass Cave can only be visited with a guide; arrange this beforehand, or join one of the guided tours departing daily from the restcamp at 9am (R50). The walk there and back takes around three hours, following a contoured path through the grasslands. There's also a rock-art centre at the Kamberg restcamp that's worth a visit.

ACCOMMODATION

HIMEVILLE

Himeville Arms Arbuckle St **☎** 033 702 1305, **w** himevillehotel.co.za. A decent country inn that makes a good stopover before the final haul to the mountains. It organizes 4WD trips, horseriding, fishing and golf, and also has dorm accommodation (R175) for backpackers. Dorm R175, double R880

Yellowwood Cottage 8 Mackenzie St **☎** 033 702 1065. One of the nicest B&Bs, set in a spectacular garden with

wonderful Berg views, with three en-suite rooms and a fully equipped kitchenette. R460

SANI PASS

Most accommodation is at the foot of the mountains, just before the pass hairpins its way up to the top.

Mkomazana Mountain Cottages 25km northwest of Underberg along the Sani Pass Rd **☎** 033 702 0340, **e** mkomazana@gmail.com. Self-catering in five cottages

5

sleeping two to six people. The lodge, on the site of an old trading post, is near the start of Giant's Cup Hiking Trail. Less ambitious walks into the mountains begin right on the property, which has its own river and waterfall, and a private dam with trout. R600

★ **Sani Lodge** 19km northwest of Underberg along the Sani Pass Rd ☎ 033 702 0330, ⓦ sanilodge.co.za. There are dorms, doubles and self-catering cottages at this popular backpacker hostel, some in picturesque thatched rondavels. The view from the veranda is stunning, and delicious home-made goodies are available at the café next door. It's a good base for walking to waterfalls and rock paintings – packed lunches can be supplied – and there are also tours up Sani Pass, guided hikes and 4WD excursions on offer. Dorm R100, double R300

Sani Pass Hotel 1km beyond Sani Lodge ☎ 033 702 1320, ⓦ sanipasshotel.co.za. A comfortable hotel offering full board in both rondavels and standard hotel rooms. There are also plenty of extras, including horseriding and free golf at the hotel's nine-hole course. R1680

Sani Top Chalet At the top of Sani Pass, just inside Lesotho ☎ 033 702 1069, ⓦ sanitopchalet.co.za. The only place to stay at Sani Top in Lesotho (see p.613) is the deservedly popular *Sani Top Chalet*, which makes much of its claim to be the highest pub in Africa, at 2874m above sea level. The cliff-edge setting is superb, with awesome views into KwaZulu-Natal, and there's also hearty food on offer, while in the evenings you can sit on the balcony and watch the sun set over the mountaintops. The rooms themselves are simple and sometimes chilly, though nicely furnished. The rondavels are very attractive with open fireplaces, and there's also camping available. Camping M80, dorm M175, double (half board) M1200

LOTHENI AND KAMBERG

Both restcamps can be booked through KZN Wildlife (☎ 033 845 1000, ⓦ kznwildlife.com).

Lotheni In a remote area of the park north of Sani Pass. A small campsite and fourteen comfortable self-catering chalets with two to six beds, as well as bathrooms and well-equipped kitchens. The pick of the bunch is *Simes Cottage* (R1800), a stone farmhouse with a majestic outlook, its own trout lake and grounds traversed by bushbuck and eland. The cottage sleeps ten, and there's a minimum charge for six people. You'll need to bring all your own supplies. Camping R140, chalet R425

Kamberg In the foothills of the Drakensberg, between Lotheni and Giant's Castle. The restcamp here consists of chalets and a rustic cottage; there's a communal kitchen but no campsite. There's trout fishing to be had nearby, as well as a number of scenic walks in the area. R350

The Central Drakensberg

The **Central Drakensberg** incorporates four distinct areas, all clearly signposted from the N3. **Giant's Castle**, the site of a beautiful game reserve, is where you'll find the popular lammergeier bird hide and access to important San rock paintings. More San art is at **Injisuthi** to the north, principally a hiking destination and the place to head for if you're after complete wilderness. Far more accessible and tourist-trammelled is **Champagne Valley**, which offers a healthy number of hotels with ample sporting facilities, while to the north, and out on a limb, the hotel at **Cathedral Peak** is the best place to base yourself for some serious walking.

Giant's Castle Game Reserve

Daily: April–Sept 6am–6pm; Oct–March 5am–7pm • R30 • ☎ 036 353 3718

Giant's Castle Game Reserve was created to protect the dwindling numbers of **eland**, which occurred in great numbers in the Ukhahlamba Drakensberg before the arrival of colonialists. Antelope of the montane zone are also found here – oribi, grey rhebok, mountain reedbuck and bushbuck – as well as four dozen other mammal species and around 160 bird species. The reserve is bordered to the west by three of the four highest peaks in South Africa: Mafadi (the highest at 3410m), Popple Peak (3325m) and the bulky ramparts of Giant's Castle itself (3314m). This is not a traditional game park – there are no roads inside the reserve apart from access routes, which terminate at the two main KZN Wildlife accommodation areas, **Giant's Castle** and **Injisuthi**; the only way to see the wildlife here is by hiking through the terrain.

The lammergeier hide

May–Sept • R645 for up to three people • Book as much as a year in advance through KZN Wildlife • ☎ 033 845 1000, ⓦ kznwildlife.com

One of the big attractions at the Giant's Head peak is the thrilling **lammergeier hide**

EN ROUTE TO THE BERG

The tiny hamlet of **Winterton**, some 90km north of Pietermaritzburg along the R74 as it deviates west off the N3, offers some pleasant **places to stay** if you're looking for a stopover on the way to the Central Drakensberg. One is *Lilac Lodge* at 8 Springfield Rd – the main drag as you drive into the town – (☎036 488 1025; R560), with accommodation in small cottages and its own coffee and arts and crafts shop. Another appealing choice is *Rolling M Ranch* (☎036 488 1751, ☻rollingmranch.co.za; R500), a working farm outside town on the banks of the Tugela River – to get there, head 2km north from Winterton on the R600, then turn right at the signposted Skietdrift road, the camp is around 15km down this route and has self-catering cabins and cottages as well as a bush camp. Since the farm is on the Battlefields route, there are trails from here to Spioenkop and Buller's Cross monuments.

If you fancy **whitewater rafting**, this is a good place to do it. The Tugela River east of the Drakensberg can be accessed from Winterton on trips run by Four Rivers Rafting and Adventures (☎036 468 1693, ☻www.fourriversadventures.co.za); its inflatable-raft forays into the river gorge last from one to five days and cost R460–4000.

where you may see the rare lammergeier, a giant, black and golden bird with massive wings and a diamond-shaped tail. A scavenger, the lammergeier is an evolutionary link between eagles and vultures and was thought extinct in Southern Africa until only a couple of decades ago. The bird is found only in mountainous areas such as the Himalayan foothills, and in South Africa only in the Ukhahlamba Drakensberg and Maloti mountains. In the locality you may also spot Cape vulture, black eagle, jackal buzzard and lanner falcon, attracted by the carcasses of animals put out by rangers during the winter.

Main Caves

Gates are opened daily on the hour from 9am–3pm • Self-guided tours with some interpretative materials are available on site

Giant's Castle has one of the three major **rock-art sites** open to the public in the Ukhahlamba Drakensberg, with more than five hundred paintings at **Main Caves**, about a half-hour's easy walk up the Bushman's River Valley.

Injisuthi

April–Sept 6am–6pm, Oct–March 5am–7pm • R20 • Guided visits to the San paintings (R235 for up to three people; 5hr) set out most days at 8.30am; book a day in advance through KZN Wildlife (see p.365) • ☎036 431 9000 • To get to the camp, take the indicated turning off the R615, which takes you along 30km of dirt road

In the northern section of the Giant's Castle Game Reserve, some 50km from both Winterton and Estcourt, **INJISUTHI** is a hiker's dream. You can walk straight out into the mountains, swim in the rivers or take in rock art. One of the best day walks, albeit a tough one, is up Van Heyningen's Pass to the viewpoint – the friendly staff at the main camp can direct you. There are ten different day hikes at Injisuthi, lasting from one to ten hours.

If you have even a passing interest in rock art, don't miss the paintings at **Battle Cave**, so-named because of a series of paintings that apparently depict an armed conflict between two groups of Bushmen. San art authority David Lewis-Williams has argued that these paintings are unlikely to depict a conflict over territory because there is no evidence that such conflicts took place in a society that was very loosely organized and un-territorial. Instead, he claims, the paintings are about the San spiritual experience and shamanic trance, the battles taking place in the spiritual realm where marauding evil shamans shoot arrows of "sickness", while good shamans attempt to fight them off. There are more than 750 beautifully painted people and animals in this extensive cave, though many are faded. The paintings are fenced off, and can be visited only on a guided walk in the company of a KZN Wildlife guide.

5

THE SAN AND THEIR ROCK PAINTINGS

Southern Africa's earliest inhabitants and the most direct descendants of the late Stone Age, the **San**, or Bushmen, lived in the caves and shelters of the Ukhahlamba Drakensberg for thousands of years before the arrival of the Nguni people and later the white farmers. There is still some disagreement over what to call these early hunter-gatherers. Many liberal writers use the word "Bushmen" in a strictly non-pejorative sense – though the word was originally deeply insulting. Several historians and anthropologists have plumped for "San", but as the term refers to a language group and not a culture, this isn't strictly accurate either. Since there is no agreed term, you'll find both words used in this book.

The San hunted and gathered on the subcontinent for a considerable period – paintings in Namibia date back 25,000 years. In the last two thousand years, the southward migration of Bantu-speaking farmers forced change on the San, but there is evidence that the two groups were able to live side by side. However, serious tensions arose when the white settlers began to annex lands for hunting and farming. As the San started to take cattle from farmers, whites came to regard these people as vermin; they felt free to hunt the San in genocidal campaigns in the Cape, and later in other areas, including the Ukhahlamba Drakensberg, until they were wiped off the South African map.

San artists were also **shamans**, and their paintings of hunting, dancing and animals mostly depict their religious beliefs rather than realistic narratives of everyday life in the Ukhahlamba Drakensberg. It's difficult to **date** the paintings with accuracy, but the oldest are likely to be at least 800 years old (although Bushmen lived in the area for thousands of years before that) and the most recent are believed to have been painted after the arrival of the whites towards the end of the nineteenth century. However, it's easy and rewarding to pick out some of the most significant elements in San paintings. The **medicine** or **trance dance** – journeying into the spiritual world in order to harness healing power – was the Bushmen's most important religious ritual and is depicted in much of their art. Look out for the postures the shamans adopted during the dance, including arms outstretched behind them, bending forward, kneeling, or pointing fingers. Dots along the spine often relate to the sensation of energy boiling upwards, while lines on faces or coming out of the nose usually depict nosebleeds – a common side effect of the trance state. Other feelings experienced in trance, such as that of elongation, attenuation or the sensation of flight, are expressed by feathers or streamers. The depictions of horses, cattle and white settlers, particularly in the Southern Berg, mark the end of the traditional way of life for the Ukhahlamba Drakensberg Bushmen, and it is possible that the settlers were painted by shamans as a supernatural technique to try to ward off their all-too-real bullets.

To enter the spirit world, shamans often tapped into the spiritual power of certain animals. You'll see the spiral-horned **eland** depicted in every cave – not because these antelope were prolific in the Berg, but because they were considered to have more power than any other animal. Sometimes the elands are painted in layers to increase their spiritual potency. In the caves open to the public, you can see depictions of human-like figures in the process of transforming into their power animal. Besides antelope, other animals associated with trance are honeybees, felines, snakes and sometimes elephants and rhinos.

Paintings weather and fade, and many have been vandalized. Well-meaning people dabbing water on them to make them clearer, or touching them, has also caused them to disappear – so never be tempted. One of the best and most up-to-date introductions to rock art is the slim **booklet** by David Lewis-Williams, *Rock Paintings of the Natal Drakensberg*, available from most decent bookshops in the area.

Champagne Castle

Champagne Castle, the second-highest peak in South Africa, provides the most popular view in the Ukhahlamba Drakensberg, with scores of resorts in the valley cashing in on the soaring backdrop. The name, so the story goes, derives from an incident in 1861, when a Major Grantham made the first recorded ascent of the peak accompanied by his batman, who inadvertently dropped the bottle of bubbly and christened the mountainside.

Champagne Valley
Monk's Cowl daily 6am–6pm • R35 • Overnight hiking R45 • ☎ 036 468 1103

Champagne Valley is an easy 32km from Winterton, and has shops, restaurants and facilities absent in other parts of the Ukhahlamba Drakensberg, all indicated along the route. This over-civilized but extremely pretty area, which lies outside the KZN Wildlife reserve, is best avoided if you want to **hike** from your doorstep – you'll have to drive west along the R600 through the valley to Monk's Cowl, from where plenty of hikes set off into the mountains.

Ardmore Ceramic Art Studio
20km from Winterton off the R600, signposted between the Nest Hotel and the Drakensberg Sun • Daily 8am–4.30pm • ☎ 033 234 4869, ⓦ www.ardmoreceramics.co.za

The Ardmore Ceramic Art Studio is one of the area's highlights, started in the 1980s by fine-arts graduate **Fée Halsted-Berning** with trainee **Bonnie Ntshalintshali**, a young Zulu girl suffering from polio. By 1990 they had collected a clutch of awards for their distinctive ceramic works, and the studio now has around forty people creating beautiful sculpture and crockery with wildly colourful and often impossibly irrational motifs, which have included rhinos dressed as preachers administering the sacrament to a congregation of wild animals. Bonnie died of AIDS in 1999, as have at least eight other artists at the studio, but the distinctive style she pioneered has been continued here and the works are well worth seeing and buying. There's also a less pricey local **curio shop** on the premises, selling works by other local artists.

Cathedral Peak
North of Monk's Cowl and the Champagne Valley resorts are the Mlambonja River Valley and **Cathedral Peak**, a freestanding pinnacle sticking out of the 5km-long basalt Cathedral Ridge. The peak looks nothing like a cathedral (its Zulu name, *Mponjwane*, means "the horn on a heifer's head").

Hiking trails
A number of **hiking trails** start right from the *Cathedral Peak Hotel* (see p.408), which can provide maps and books. One of the most popular day walks is to the beautiful **Rainbow Gorge**, an 11km round trip (4–5hr) following the Ndumeni River, with pools, rapids and falls to detain you. The hike can be wet, so wear proper walking boots. The hotel also operates nine-hour guided trips up to Cathedral Peak, which include plenty of time at the top to revel in the views. It's a very steep climb, and the final section beyond Orange Peel Gap should only be tackled by experienced climbers – you'll probably be quite satisfied to stop at this point.

Mike's Pass
Permit R30/person, R60/vehicle

The 24hr guardhouse at the park entrance is the place to buy a permit to drive up **Mike's Pass**, a 10km twisting forestry road that takes you to a car park from where, on a clear day, you'll get outstanding views of the entire region. There's a scale model on top to help identify the peaks. An ordinary car will make the journey when the weather is dry and the road is hard, but you'll need a 4WD when it's wet.

| **INFORMATION** | **THE CENTRAL DRAKENSBERG** |

Giant's Castle The reserve's only filling station is at the main entrance to Giant's Castle; you'll find the park's reception office and a shop 7km further on (Mon–Sat 8am–6pm, Sun 8am–4pm; ☎ 036 353 3718). The Cathedral Peak reception office is 1.5km from the park entrance (daily 7am–7pm; ☎ 036 488 8000).

5

ACCOMMODATION

GIANT'S CASTLE

Giant's Castle Camp Book through KZN Wildlife ☎ 033 845 1000, ⓦ kznwildlife.com. Comfortable self-contained two-, four- and six-bed chalets, some with wonderful picture windows looking out to the peaks, and cosy fireplaces. For food, there's the pleasant *Izimbali* buffet-style restaurant. You can buy frozen meat for braais and some tinned food at the curio shop in the reception area, though it's preferable to stock up before getting here. There are fabulous hiking trails from the camp, and Bannerman's Hut (R45), while basic, is one of the Berg's best-located hiking huts. **R630**

White Mountain Lodge Along the road to Giant's Castle hutted camp, 34km on a tarred road from Estcourt and 32km from the reserve ☎ 036 353 3437, ⓦ whitemountain.co.za. If the KZN Wildlife accommodation is full, this is the one hotel that gives access to the reserve. They offer full board as well as self-catering cottages, and it's located in the foothills and close to Zulu villages and farmlands, so while the area is pretty, it's neither grand nor remote. **R200**

INJISUTHI

Injisuthi Camp Book through KZN Wildlife ☎ 033 845 1000, ⓦ kznwildlife.com. Accommodation here includes comfortable self-catering chalets and safari tents , as well as campsites. However, most people come here with the express purpose of taking to the hills and camping in one of the designated caves, which have absolutely no facilities and must be booked at reception. **R290**

CHAMPAGNE VALLEY

Ardmore Guest Farm Signposted off the R600, midway between Winterton and Monk's Cowl ☎ 036 468 1314, ⓦ ardmore.co.za. A thoroughly hospitable farmstay with accommodation in en-suite rondavels or cottages, all with their own fireplaces. Guests eat together

from marvellous hand-crafted crockery made on the farm. Staff can arrange horse trails into Spioenkop Game Reserve through the Battlefields. Rates include full board. **R790**

Champagne Castle Along the R600 ☎ 036 468 1063, ⓦ champagnecastle.co.za. This old-fashioned hotel, the closest accommodation to the hiking trails beginning at Monk's Cowl, has comfortable en-suite rooms and self-catering chalets sleeping six set in lovely gardens with a swimming pool. Rates include full board. **R1460**

Graceland Cottage Signposted off the R600 ☎ 036 468 1011, ⓦ gracelandsa.com. A four-bedroom self-catering cottage with TV and fireplace as well as a smaller, two-bedroom cottage, the *Homestead*, perched right on the edge of a mountain with spectacular views. **R850**

Inkosana Lodge and Trekking Along the R600, midway between Winterton and Monk's Cowl ☎ 036 468 1202, ⓦ inkosana.co.za. Backpacker accommodation in unpretentious, ethnic-style rooms, with beautiful indigenous gardens and a retreat-centre feel. Breakfasts and dinners are also available. Dorm **R150**, double **R250**

CATHEDRAL PEAK

★ **Cathedral Peak Hotel** 44km from either Winterton or Bergville ☎ 036 488 1888, ⓦ www.cathedralpeak.co.za. The only hotel in the Cathedral Peak area and the closest in the Ukhahlamba Drakensberg to the mountains, and within the KZN Wildlife protected area, this is an excellent place to stay. The views are perfect and the rooms in thatched two-storey wings are comfortably furnished with pine and country-style floral fabrics. Rates include full board. **R2100**

Didima At the top of Mike's Pass; book through KZN Wildlife ☎ 033 845 1000, ⓦ kznwildlife.com. Self-catering chalets with satellite TV and fireplaces, as well as campsites. You'll also find the Didima San Art Centre (R55), which has displays on San rock art and shows a short film. Camping **R160**, chalets **R750**

The Northern Drakensberg

The dramatically beautiful **Northern Drakensberg** consists mainly of the **Royal Natal National Park** with a few resorts scattered around the fringes. The Tugela River and its bouldered gorge offer some of the most awe-inspiring scenery in the area, its most striking geographical feature being the **Amphitheatre**, the crescent-shaped 5km rock wall over which the Tugela plunges. With a complete cross section of accommodation, the Northern Berg is a very desirable area to visit. The best place to get a real feeling of these pristine mountains and valleys is at **Thendele**, the main KZN Wildlife camp, with chalets but oddly enough no camping.

Royal Natal National Park

Daily 6am–10pm · R30 · ☎ 036 438 6310

The **Royal Natal National Park**, 46km west of Bergville, is famed for its views of the Amphitheatre, which probably appears on more posters and postcards and in more books than any other single feature of the Ukhahlamba Drakensberg. Almost everyone does the **Tugela Gorge walk**, a fabulous six-hour round trip from Thendele, which gives close-up views of the **Amphitheatre** and the **Tugela Falls** plummeting over the 947m rock wall.

Established in 1916, the park only earned its royal sobriquet in 1947 when the Windsors paid a visit. The park is at the northern end of the Ukhahlamba Drakensberg, tucked in between Lesotho to the west and Free State province to the north. The three defining peaks are the Sentinel (3165m), the Eastern Buttress (3048m) and the Mont Aux Sources (3282m), which is also where five rivers rise – hence its name, given by French missionaries in 1878.

ARRIVAL AND DEPARTURE   THE NORTHERN DRAKENSBERG

Several of the resorts offer transfers from Bergville or the N3 if you book ahead and notify them, but they tend to be expensive.

By car Routes to the park are surfaced all the way. Coming from the south along the N3, take the Winterton/Berg resorts turn-off and follow the clear signposts through Bergville to the park entrance, some 46km away.

INFORMATION

Tourist information Contact the Drakensberg Tourism Association (daily 8am–5pm; ☎ 036 448 1557, ✉ info@drakensberg.org.za, ⊚ www.drakensberg.org.za) for information about the area and help booking accommodation, either by phone or email (they don't operate an actual tourism information office).
Supplies For supplies head to Bergville, the last place to stock up before heading into the park.

ACCOMMODATION

INSIDE THE PARK

KZN Wildlife offers some very reasonable campsites within the park, as well as some exceptional chalets. While you can book the KZN Wildlife chalets through their usual reservation system (see box, p.365), use of campsites here is best arranged by calling the sites concerned.
Mahai Campsite Along the river adjacent to the national park ☎ 036 438 6303. With facilities that cater for up to four hundred campers, *Mahai* attracts hordes of South Africans over school holidays and weekends. From here you can strike straight into the mountains for some of the best walks in the Berg. R160
Rugged Glen Campsite Signposted 4km from Mahai ☎ 036 438 6303. A smaller and quieter campsite than *Mahai*, though often only open during school holidays. The views and walks here aren't as good, though conveniently the *Orion Mont-Aux-Sources Hotel* is an easy walk away – handy if you want a substantial meal. R160
★ **Thendele Hutted Camp** At the end of the road into the Royal Natal National Park ☎ 036 438 6411. Right in the mountains, this is one of the most sought-after places to stay in South Africa, with splendid views of the Amphitheatre and excellent walks right from your front door. Accommodation is in comfortable two- and four-bed en-suite chalets, the cheapest of which have hotplates, fridges, kettles, toasters and eating utensils. If you opt for the more luxurious cottages or lodge, chefs are on hand to cook, though you need to bring the ingredients. There's a good curio and supply shop. R655

OUTSIDE THE PARK

Amphitheatre Backpackers On the R74, 21km west of Bergville ☎ 036 438 6675, ⊚ amphibackpackers .co.za. On the Baz Bus route, this place is convenient for those without their own transport who want to explore the Northern Drakensberg. Accommodation is in en-suite dorms, with a good range of private rooms also on offer. There's a bar and restaurant, and organized hiking trips and other activities such as horseriding and mountain biking are available. Dorm R125, double R280
The Cavern Off the R74, about 20km from the Royal Natal National Park ☎ 036 438 6270, ⊚ cavern.co.za. The most tucked-away of the hotels, the *Cavern* is family-run and has an old-fashioned feel, with adequate rooms. It's very much a South African weekend getaway with a swimming pool, horseriding and Saturday-night dances. Rates include full board. R1580
Hlalanathi Berg Resort About 10km from the Royal Natal National Park ☎ 036 438 6308, ⊚ hlalanathi .co.za. This family resort offers camping and self-catering thatched chalets, which sleep two to six people. There's also a swimming pool and trampolines, as well as a sit-down and takeaway restaurant serving cheap burgers, sandwiches and more substantial meals. R550
Mnweni Cultural Centre In the Mnweni Valley 30km west of Bergville along the Woodstock Dam/Rookdale rds ☎ 086 528 5841, ⊚ mnweni.org. Owed by the AmaNgwane and AmaZzizi communities, accommodation in this breathtaking valley is in simple four-bed thatched rondavels with shared ablutions and kitchen facilities.

5

Aside from hiking in the mountains (R35 per night), there are craft stalls, horseriding and some San rock paintings. **R120** per person

Orion Mont-Aux-Sources Hotel About 4km from the Royal Natal National Park ☎036 438 8000, ⓦ oriongroup.co.za. A smart but impersonal hotel with views of the Amphitheatre, as well as sports facilities that include tennis courts and horesriding. **R1600**

The Elephant Coast and Zululand game reserves

In startling contrast to the intensively developed 250km ribbon of coastline which runs north and south of Durban, the seaboard to the north of the Dolphin Coast drifts off into some of the wildest and most breathtaking sea frontage in South Africa – an area known as the **Elephant Coast**.

If you've travelled along the Garden Route and wondered where stereotypical Africa was, the answer is right here, in the northern reaches of the Elephant Coast – traditionally known as **Maputaland** – with its tight patchwork of wilderness and **ancestral African lands**. In this area hemmed in by Swaziland and Mozambique, **traditional life** continues: for example, there is one *nyanga* (traditional healer) for every 550 people, compared with one Western-style doctor to 18,000 people. Access can be difficult; St Lucia, Sodwana Bay and Kwa-Ngwanase are both reachable via tarred roads from the N2, but you'll still need a 4WD vehicle to visit any of the other idyllic spots along the Elephant Coast's 200km of virtually uninterrupted beachfront.

Further south, less than three hours' drive north on the N2 from Durban, is the big game country of **Hluhluwe-Imfolozi**, which rivals even the Kruger National Park for beautiful wilderness. Drive the same distance, but turn right instead of left at the Mtubatuba junction, and you'll hit the southernmost extent of South Africa's most satisfyingly "tropical" coast. It's protected all the way up to Mozambique by the country's third-largest protected area, the **iSimangaliso Wetland Park** (which includes Lake St Lucia, Cape Vidal, Charter's Creek, False Bay Park, Mkhuze Game Reserve, Sodwana Bay, Lake Sibaya and Kosi Bay). This 2750-square-kilometre patchwork encompasses wetland reserve, marine sanctuaries, a UNESCO World Heritage Site and some outstanding scuba diving and fishing opportunities around **Sodwana Bay**. The coast gets remoter and more exhilarating the further north you head, with one of South Africa's best upmarket beachside stays near Mozambique at **Kosi Bay**. Note that the northern KwaZulu-Natal coastal region is **malarial**.

Mtubatuba and Hluhluwe Village

Travelling north on the N2 from Durban and the main town in these parts, **Richards Bay**, a large industrial port 185km from Durban that's completely at odds with the remote and pristine coast to the north, you'll pass a few predominantly African villages that make adequate bases for exploring the Hluhluwe-Imfolozi Park.

Mtubatuba

Around 50km north of Richards Bay, **MTUBATUBA** (often shortened to Mtuba) is situated where the R618 intersects the N2, just twenty minutes from both the southern section of the Hluhluwe-Imfolozi Park and St Lucia. The town features lots of herbalists, traditional healers and a Zulu market, and is also a thriving centre

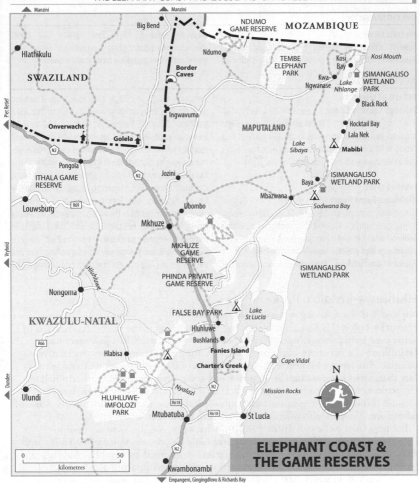

**ELEPHANT COAST &
THE GAME RESERVES**

for the local sugar-cane industry – both large commercial farms and small-scale African growers.

Hluhluwe

Just off the N2, about 20km north of Mtubatuba, is the straggling village of **HLUHLUWE** (pronounced "shla-shloo-wee"), which is handy for accessing the northern section of the Hluhluwe-Imfolozi Park, although it's the least attractive of the villages en route to the park. Five minutes' drive from Hluhluwe, *Ilala Weavers and The Fig Tree Restaurant* is a hub of community projects selling well-priced traditional **crafts** in a cheerful atmosphere, with a **restaurant** serving decent breakfasts, lunches and dinners, and cold beers.

ARRIVAL AND DEPARTURE	MTUBATUBA AND HLUHLUWE VILLAGE

By bus Greyhound buses from Durban (daily; 2hr 30min), Johannesburg (daily; 9hr 30min) and Pretoria (daily; 10hr) stop in Richard's Bay, from where you can catch regular minibuses on to Hluhluwe and Mtubatuba.

By plane There is an airport at Richard's Bay, from which six flights a day leave for Johannesburg (1hr 30min).

5

INFORMATION

HLUHLUWE
Tourist office The friendly Elephant Coast Tourism Association office is based at the Engen filling station on Main St (Mon–Fri 8am–2pm; ☎035 562 0966, ⓦelephantcoast.kzn.org.za), providing details of numerous lodges and game farms in the vicinity.

ACCOMMODATION

MTUBATUBA
Wendy's Country Lodge 3 Riverview Drive ☎035 550 0407 or ☎083 628 1601, ⓦwendybnb.co.za. Eight luxurious rooms in a house set in tropical gardens in a suburb of Mtubatuba, plus a cottage that sleeps five. There's also a swimming pool and a restaurant on site. R790

HLUHLUWE
Hluhluwe Guest House In the residential area behind the Engen garage ☎035 562 0838, ⓔhluguest@iafrica.com. Comfy, en-suite B&B accommodation with a pool and small bar, and meals on request. The guesthouse can arrange trips into Hluhluwe-Imfolozi Park. R830

Isinkwe Backpackers Bushcamp 20km south of Hluhluwe ☎035 562 2258, ⓦisinkwe.co.za. A well-run rustic hostel offering camping, wooden cabins for four and a traditional Zulu-style beehive hut dorm, as well as more comfortable doubles in the lodge. It serves reasonably priced meals (or you can self-cater), and arranges tours to Hluhluwe-Imfolozi Park and St Lucia. Dorm R155, double R420

Zulu Homestay ☎035 562 1329 or ☎082 953 5601, ⓦmbonise.com. This homestay, organized by Mbonise Cultural Concepts and Safaris, is the most interesting accommodation option in the area. Staying with the Mdaka family, you'll also be taken to visit the Nompondo Community adjacent to Hluhluwe-Imfolozi Park. The price includes meals, and you can pay extra for walking tours and the services of a Zulu guide or to witness Zulu dancing. R580

Hluhluwe-Imfolozi Park

Daily: March–Oct 6am–6pm; Nov–Feb 5am–7pm • R110 • ☎035 562 0848

Hluhluwe-Imfolozi is KwaZulu-Natal's most outstanding game reserve, considered by some even better than Kruger. While it certainly can't match Kruger's sheer scale (Hluhluwe is a twentieth of the size) or its teeming game populations, its relatively compact 960 square kilometres have a wilder feel. This has something to do with the fact that, apart from **Hilltop**, an elegant hotel-style restcamp in the northern half of the park, none of the other restcamps is fenced off, and wild animals are free to wander through. The vegetation, with subtropical forest in places, adds to the sense of adventure. The park also offers the best **trails** in the country.

The park used to be two distinct entities – hence its tongue-twisting double-barrelled name (pronounced something like "shla-shloo-wee-oom-fa-low-zee") – and the two sections retain their separate characters, reinforced by a public road slicing between them. The southern **Imfolozi section** takes its name from a corruption of *mfulawozi*, a Zulu word that refers to the fibrous bushes that grow along its rivers. The topography here is characterized by wide, deep valleys incised by the Black and White Imfolozi rivers, with altitudes varying between 60 and 650 metres. Luxuriant riverine vegetation gives way in drier areas to a variety of woodland, savannah, thickets and grassy plains. The notable feature of the northern **Hluhluwe section** is the river of the same name, a slender, slithering waterway, punctuated by elongated pools. The Hluhluwe rises in the mountains north of the park and passes along sandbanks, rock beds and steep cliffs in the game reserve before seeping away into Lake St Lucia to the east. The higher ground is covered by veld and dense thicket, while the well-watered ridges support the softer cover of ferns, lichens, mosses and orchids.

Brief history

Despite Hluhluwe-Imfolozi being the oldest proclaimed national park in Africa (it was created in 1895), its future as a game refuge has hung by a thread on several occasions in the last two hundred years. In the nineteenth century, Imfolozi was the private hunting preserve of the **Zulu** king, Shaka. During Shaka's reign between 1818 and 1828 the area saw the most sustained campaign of hunting in Zulu history, but this was nothing compared to the destruction caused by white farmers between 1929 and

1950, when a crusade of game **extermination** was launched to wipe out **nagama** disease, resulting in the slaughter of 100,000 head of game from sixteen species, with rhinos alone spared.

It was only in 1952, when the park was handed over to the newly formed organization now known as **KZN Wildlife**, that the slow process of resuscitating the threadbare game reserve began. The sense of pristine wilderness you now get at Hluhluwe-Imfolozi is the result of careful management, crowned by the brilliant success of re-establishing its white rhino population from twenty animals at the start of the twentieth century to 2500 today. The removal in 1994 of the **white rhino** from the World Conservation Union's endangered list was thanks mostly to conservationists in the Hluhluwe-Imfolozi Park, which has become the world's breeding bank for these animals.

ARRIVAL AND INFORMATION
HLUHLUWE-IMFOLOZI PARK

Day-trips and tours There is no public transport to Hluhluwe-Imfolozi. Without your own car, you can choose from any of the day-trips offered by accommodation within an hour's drive of the park, or from the tours operated by the Durban firms listed in the box on p.380.

By car Access to the park is via three gates. Just north of Mtubatuba, the R618 to Hlabisa and Nongoma reaches Nyalazi Gate after 21km, providing access to the southern section of the park. Further north, on the N3, an unclassified but signposted and tarred road near the turning for Hluhluwe takes you via Memorial Gate into the northernmost section of the park. A third gate, Cengeni, is accessible along a 30km tarred road from Ulundi to the west.

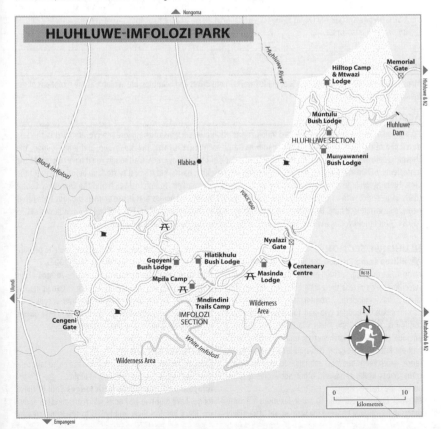

HLUHLUWE-IMFOLOZI PARK

5

GAME VIEWING AND ACTIVITIES IN HLUHLUWE-IMFOLOZI

Despite its compact size, Hluhluwe-Imfolozi is home to 84 mammal species and close to 350 varieties of birds. The Big Five are all here, and it's no exaggeration to say that this is the best place in the world to see **rhinos**, both black and white. Extinct in Imfolozi until 1958, **lions** have been reintroduced, and today they number around seventy, although they're not easy to see and their future hangs in the balance. Other **predators** present are cheetah, spotted hyena and wild dog. **Herbivores** include blue wildebeest, buffalo, giraffe, hippo, impala, kudu, nyala and zebra. When it comes to **birds**, there are over a dozen species of **eagle**, as well as other **raptors** including hawks, goshawks and honey buzzards. Other larger birds include ground hornbills, vultures, owls and herons. **Reptile** species number in the sixties, including crocodiles and several types of venomous snake, none of which you're likely to see. Along the Hluhluwe River, keep an eye open for the harmless monitor lizards.

Where Hluhluwe-Imfolozi really scores over the Kruger is in the variety of activities on offer. Apart from **self-driving** around the park, there are also **self-guided walks** near several of the restcamps, **guided trails** in the company of an armed field ranger, guided **night drives** and a **boat trip** on the Hluhluwe Dam. South Africa's first **wilderness trail** started in Imfolozi, and the reserve has remained the best place in South Africa for these (all are available from mid-March to mid-Dec). The three-night **Base Camp trail** (R3952 per person) involves day walks in the Wilderness Area, with nights spent at the Mndindini Trails camp not far from *Mpila*; the three-night **Primitive trail** (R2220 per person) departs from *Mpila* and requires you to carry your own gear and sleep under the stars, wherever the ranger chooses; and the **Short Wilderness trail** (R2180 per person) starts from *Mpila* at 1.30pm on Friday and ends on Sunday, also at *Mpila*. On all of these trails, which must be booked through the KZN Wildlife, you'll be accompanied by an armed ranger; and all gear – including linen and food – is included in the price.

INFORMATION

Maps and information, including details of guided walks, night drives and boat trips, are available at the receptions of the *Hilltop* and *Mpila* camps.

ACCOMMODATION

Accommodation is available in both the Imfolozi and Hluhluwe sections of the game reserve; Imfolozi is the less developed of the two. Hluhluwe's *Hilltop* camp has a pleasant **restaurant**, the *Mpunyane*, and a bar lounge, the *Usavolo*. Some of the lodges include the services of a cook to prepare your meals, although you'll have to provide the ingredients. *Hilltop* and *Mpila* camps also have small stores selling basics, but it's best to stock up before you enter the park. Hluhluwe village and Mtubatuba have well-stocked supermarkets. In Imfolozi you'll find the Centenary Centre (daily 8am–4pm), with a small takeaway restaurant, a craft centre, and *bomas* that house animals brought from other parks to be introduced here. **Bookings** are made through KZN Wildlife as usual (☎ 035 562 0848 for Hluhluwe, ☎ 035 550 8477 for Imfolozi, ☏ www.kznwildlife.com), though camping should be arranged locally.

HLUHLUWE SECTION

★ **Hilltop Camp** Probably the best publicly run safari camp in South Africa, set high on the edge of a slope with sweeping views across the park's hills and valleys. The camp has modern, comfortable and varied accommodation: budget two-bed rondavels that share communal ablutions and kitchen facilities; self-catering en-suite chalets with kitchenettes; and en-suite chalets without kitchens. The camp is surrounded by an electric fence, which keeps out most animals. You may, however, come across nyala, zebra and other herbivores grazing around the chalets. R480

Mtwazi Lodge Near Hilltop. Four luxurious en-suite rooms in the original home of the warden, set attractively in a secluded private garden. A chef is available to prepare meals. Minimum charge for five people. R4200

Muntulu and Munyawaneni bush lodges Four bedrooms with private verandas at each of two upmarket bush lodges overlooking the Hluhluwe River. A cook is on hand to cater and a field ranger is available to take guests on walks. Minimum charge for six people. R4200

IMFOLOZI SECTION

There are no fences around the Imfolozi camps, so take care when walking around, particularly at night.

Gqoyeni and Hlatikhulu bush lodges Both of these lodges have four two-bed units which are elevated above the Black Imfolozi River and linked to the living area by wooden walkways. Their field ranger can conduct walks in the area, and they have a chef to cook meals. Minimum charge for six people. Gqoyeni R5250, Hlatikhulu R4200 **Masinda Lodge** Near Nyalazi Gate, this renovated upmarket lodge has three en-suite bedrooms decorated with Zulu art, plus the services of a cook. Minimum charge for four people. R3000

Mpila Camp This camp in the centre of Imfolozi has excellent views of the surrounding wilderness from twelve one-roomed huts with two beds each, en-suite bathrooms and kitchenettes; two self-contained three-bedroom cottages for seven people (minimum charge for four people); and six self-catering chalets that accommodate five people (minimum charge for three people). There's also a safari camp with thirteen tents with two beds, and two with four. R750

Lake St Lucia

The most striking feature of the **iSimangaliso Wetland Park** is the 360-square-kilometre **Lake St Lucia**, South Africa's largest inland body of water, formed 25,000 years ago when the oceans receded. The lake is flanked by mountainous **dunes** covered by forest and grassland, whose peaks soar to an astonishing 200m above the beach to form a slender rampart against the Indian Ocean. Aside from the lake and dune ecosystems, the reserve protects a **marine zone** of warm tropical seas, coral reefs and endless sandy beaches; the **papyrus and reed wetland** of the Mkhuze swamps, on the north of the lake; and, on the western shore, dry **savannah** and **thornveld**. Any one of these would justify conservation, but their confluence around the lake makes this a world-class wilderness. The real prize of the area is **Cape Vidal** inside the wetland park, though the limited accommodation there may necessitate your making a day-trip from St Lucia town.

St Lucia

Once a rough and out-of-the-way anglers' hangout, **ST LUCIA**, which lies at the mouth of the **St Lucia Estuary** in the extreme south of the park, is in the process of reinventing itself as a well-organized eco-destination. The town's best feature is the **estuary**, the mouth of which was named Santa Lucia by Portuguese explorers when they reached it in 1576. During the second half of the eighteenth century, landlocked Boers made attempts to claim the mouth as a port, but were pipped at the post by the British, who sent HMS *Goshawk* in 1884 to annex the whole area, which then developed as a fishing resort. The estuary is hidden behind the buildings along the main drag, and it's easy to miss if you drive quickly through.

Situated at the end of the R618, 32km east of Mtubatuba, the town of St Lucia can become pretty hectic in midsummer when **angling** fanatics descend for the school holidays. There's not much to do in St Lucia itself, but it does provide an excellent base for a number of activities (see box, p.417), as well as having a good choice of accommodation. Facilities in St Lucia include filling stations, a supermarket, self-service laundries, banks and ATMs.

St Lucia Crocodile Centre

Beside the park gate about 2km north of town on the road to Cape Vidal • Daily 8am–4.30pm • R30 • Crocodile feeding Sat 2pm & Sun 11am • ☎ 035 590 1386

This isn't another of the exploitative wildlife freak-shows common throughout South Africa, but a serious educative spin-off of KZN Wildlife's crocodile conservation campaign. Up until the end of the 1960s, "flat dogs" or "travelling handbags" were regarded as pests, and this led to a hunting free-for-all that saw them facing extinction in the area. Just in time, it was realized that crocs have an important role in the ecological cycle, and KZN Wildlife began a successful **breeding programme**, returning the crocs to the wild to bolster their numbers. The Crocodile Centre aims to rehabilitate the reputation of these maligned creatures, with informative displays and an astonishing cross section of species lounging around enclosed pools (only the Nile crocodile occurs in the wild in South Africa).

5

ARRIVAL AND DEPARTURE
ST LUCIA

By taxi The taxi rank for Mtubatuba is situated at the Dolphin Centre on the corner of McKenzie St and the R618 as you enter the village.

INFORMATION

Tourist information The most helpful place is Advantage Tours at the Dolphin Centre on the corner of McKenzie St and the R618 as you enter the village (Mon–Fri 7.15am–4pm, Sat 7.15am–2pm, Sun 7.15am–1pm; ☎ 035 590 1259 or ☎ 035 590 1180). The local village of Khula, 7km west of St Lucia on the Mtuba Rd, has an excellent tourist office specializing in responsible eco-tourism on the Elephant Coast.

KZN Wildlife Has an office at the south end of Pelican Rd (daily 8am–12.30pm & 2–4pm; ☎ 035 590 1343), which is two blocks east of and parallel to McKenzie St.

ACCOMMODATION

Bib's International Backpackers 310 McKenzie St ☎ 035 590 1056, ⓦ bibs.co.za. This busy hostel offers camping, dorms, doubles and self-catering en-suite rooms, plus facilities such as laundry, pool tables and an internet café. A range of excursions is also available, including boat trips, cultural visits and overnight trails and drives. Camping R65 dorm R100, double R220

Elephant Lake Hotel 3 Mullet St ☎ 035 590 1001, ⓦ elephantlake.co.za. St Lucia's only hotel, complete with a pool and a fantastic deck for evening drinks and views of the estuary. Rates include breakfast. R1480

iGwalagwala Guest House 91 Pelican St ☎ 035 590 1069, ⓦ igwala.co.za. The spacious en-suite rooms here are elegantly decorated, and the leafy grounds are in a quiet part of town. Some rooms give directly onto the large garden and swimming pool. R640

Jo-a-Lize 116 McKenzie St ☎ 035 590 1224, ⓦ joalize .com. One of the cheaper places in town, offering a variety of accommodation ranging from self-contained, self-catering flats to en-suite B&B units set around a pool. Rates include breakfast. R530

Seasands Lodge 135 Hornbill St ☎ 035 590 1082, ⓦ seasands.co.za. Comfortable suites with patios and balconies overlooking lush gardens. Each suite is pleasantly decorated and comes with a fully equipped kitchen, and there's also a restaurant. R960

★ **St Lucia Wetlands B&B** 20 Kingfisher St ☎ 035 590 1098, ⓦ stluciawetlands.com. Six large, en-suite rooms fitted out with elegant wooden furnishings, and there's a pool and a classy bar for guests. Exceptional service and the friendly atmosphere created by congenial hosts makes this one of the best places to stay in St Lucia. A car-washing service is also available. R900

Sunset Lodge 154 McKenzie St ☎ 035 590 1197, ⓦ sunsetstlucia.co.za. Attractive self-catering log cabins sleeping two, four or five, with balconies and views of the estuary. Hippos occasionally feed on the grasslands in front of the wooden pool deck. Good value, and great for families. R550

CAMPSITE

Sugarloaf Campsite On Ski-Boat Club Rd, south of town; book through KZN Wildlife ☎ 033 845 1000, ⓦ kznwildlife.com. A sizeable campsite on the best site in St Lucia, right on the banks of the estuary, with plenty of fishing and birdwatching opportunities nearby. R170

EATING AND DRINKING

Ocean Basket Georgiou Centre ☎ 035 590 1241. Big seafood platters and grilled fish served up in the pan (R60–90) are the specialities of this casual, family-friendly restaurant. There's also a pleasant balcony. Daily 11am–9.30pm.

Braza Georgiou Centre ☎ 035 590 1242. Portuguese specialities like *espetada* (beef skewers with peppers) and chourico (pork sausage), plus plenty of grilled meat, including a "Portuguese steak" topped with a fried egg (mains R65–90). Daily 11.30am–10pm.

Fisherman's 61 McKenzie St ☎ 035 590 1257. A good place for fresh seafood is this friendly local hangout covered with fishing memorabilia. It serves good seafood baskets (R70–90), and at night it turns into a popular bar. Daily 8am till late.

Für Elize Near the boat jetty ☎ 035 590 2166. An agreeable outdoor setting and an appetizing menu (most mains R75–100), although many of the dishes are often not available and the food can be disappointing. Mon–Fri 11am–3pm & 6–9pm, Sat & Sun 10am–9pm.

Oasis McKenzie St next to Für Elize and Bib's ☎ 035 590 2166. A sports bar and nightclub that stays open late most nights, though it gets especially busy when there's a game on. Daily 6pm–late.

St Lucia Ski-Boat Club The end of Ski-Boat Club Rd ☎ 035 590 1376. This pub and grill has a nice patio with pleasant views of the estuary, making it a great place for sundowners. The food, mostly pizzas and burgers, is decent (R40–75). Daily noon–8.30pm.

ACTIVITIES AROUND ST LUCIA

Small as it is, St Lucia is the biggest settlement around the iSimangaliso Wetland Park, and the best place to organize activities. There are several excellent **hikes** in the park near St Lucia, but at the time of writing they were all closed due to a lack of adequately trained guides. For an update on this situation, contact the iSimangaliso Wetland Park Authority (☎035 590 1633). If you're using St Lucia as a base from which to visit the Hluhluwe-Imfolozi Park, informative half- and full-day game drives (R750–950) are conducted by St Lucia-based Maputaland Tours (☎035 590 1041 or ☎082 940 7380, ☜maputaland.com), which also organizes other tours in and around St Lucia.

BIKING

Birders on Bikes is the best-value cycling package in town, and one of the most interesting tours available. A two- to three-hour gentle cycle leads you through the southern part of the estuary, along the beach and into the Cape Vidal reserve. Knowledgeable Zulu guides teach you about flora and fauna and the use of plants in Zulu culture and medicine. Book through Shaka Barker Tours (43 Hornbill St; ☎035 590 1162, ☜shakabarker.co.za; R150 including bike rental; minimum two people).

FISHING

Deep-sea fishing trips (for novices and seasoned anglers) with a skipper, guide, experienced fisherman, bait and tackle supplied. Either tag and release your game fish or take it home to cook. The approximately six-hour trip run by Advantage Tours (☎035 590 1259) costs from R700. Bring your own lunch and refreshments.

HORSERIDING

Bhangazi Horse Safaris (☎035 550 4898, ☜horsesafari.co.za) offers rides through bushland, forests and lakes where you can view wildlife, or along the beach. The half-day trip costs R450.

KAYAKING

Kayaking in the lake system gives an unparalleled experience of the wetland. St Lucia Kayak Safaris (☎035 590 1233, ☜kayaksafaris.co.za) runs half- and full-day outings which cost R275–475, including all gear, transfers to the launch site, a light lunch and refreshments.

LAKE CRUISES

It's well worth going on a lake cruise with St Lucia Safaris (☎035 590 1047, ☜stluciasafaris.com; R170; 2hr), departing from the eastern shore at the jetty next to *Für Elize* (see opposite). You stand a good chance of seeing crocodiles and hippos, as well as pelicans, fish eagles, kingfishers and storks.

WETLAND WILDLIFE TOURS

An outstanding range of tours in the wetland is led by Kian Barker, a qualified zoologist and marine biologist, including the full-day St Lucia World Heritage Tour (R495) and the interesting and unusual Chameleon Night Drive (R325), which goes out in search of the sixteen chameleon species of the St Lucia region (a staggering fourteen of which are endemic). Also recommended is the one-night, two-day Turtle Tour (Nov–Feb; R2250) to watch the annual turtle egg-laying migration at Kosi Bay (see p.426). Book through Shaka Barker Tours (see above).

WHALE-WATCHING

Humpback and southern right whales cruise along the wetland's shore, and in season (June–Nov) you can join a boat excursion to look for them. Book through Advantage Tours & Charters (see above; R850; 2hr); the trips leave from the Advantage office on McKenzie St. There's no jetty down at the beach and launching the boat into the waves is an adventure in itself; if the ocean is choppy, expect to get soaked.

Cape Vidal

Daily: April–Oct 6am–6pm; Nov–March 5am–7pm • R25, plus R35 per vehicle • ☎035 590 9012

Cape Vidal, another popular fishing spot, can only be reached via St Lucia, from where you take a tarred road north (the extension of McKenzie St) for 32km, navigating a narrow land bridge between the lake and the Indian Ocean. En route you'll pass through grassland and wetlands populated by small game, rhino, birdlife and the occasional leopard. There's no public transport to Cape Vidal.

There's enough stunning wilderness at Cape Vidal to keep you chilling out for several days, even if you aren't a keen angler. The sea is only minutes from the KZN Wildlife accommodation and an offshore reef shelters the coast from the high seas, making it safe for **swimming** and providing good opportunities for **snorkelling**: you'll see hard and soft corals, colourful fish and tiny **rock pools** full of snails, crabs, sea cucumbers, anemones and urchins as burly anglers, who use the rocks for casting their lines into the wide ocean, look on you in disbelief.

Whale-watching

Cape Vidal is an excellent place for shore sightings of **humpback whales**, which, in winter, breed off Mozambique not far to the north. In October they move south, drifting on the warm Agulhas current with their calves. If you're lucky you may see these and other whales from the dunes; a **whale-watching tower**, reached through the dune forest south of the restcamp, provides an even higher viewpoint. Eighteen-metre plankton-feeding whale sharks, the largest and gentlest of the sharks, have been sighted off this coast in schools of up to seventy at a time, and manta rays and dolphins are also common.

ACCOMMODATION	**CAPE VIDAL**

There's a small store selling basics and a petrol pump at the beach.

Beach Log Cabins ☎ 035 590 9012, ⊛ kznwildlife .com. Eighteen five-bed and eleven eight-bed Swiss-style log cabins, all of which are en suite and provided with linen and cooking utensils. Minimum charge for three and four people, respectively. **R930**

Bhangazi Complex ☎ 035 590 9012, ⊛ kznwildlife .com. Cabins ranging from six to twenty beds in dormitory rooms which are let out to groups, and there's also a campsite with space for fifty tents in the dune forest near the beach, with ablution facilities. Bookings for the campsite in particular are vital during school holidays and over long weekends. Camping **R400**, cabin **R500**

The western shore

Charter's Creek • R20

Accessible only with your own transport, the **western shore** of Lake St Lucia marks the old seashore, harking back aeons to a time when the ocean level was 2m higher than it is today. Decayed matter from marine animals has created a rich soil that once supported an extensive array of animal life, and although the Big Five were shot out ages ago, **birdlife** and over a hundred species of **butterfly** still flit about. Among the **herbivores** are suni – Africa's smallest antelope – as well as nyala and red duiker. With no dangerous predators apart from **crocodiles** (take care along the shore), the inland bushveld and woodlands are safe for walking without a guide. Drought in recent years has limited the number of visitors permitted in certain areas along the western shore (indeed, unless there is exceptional rainfall the lake could be gone altogether in the next fifteen or twenty years). Currently, only day visitors are allowed at **Charter's Creek**, at the southern end of the lake, while **Fanies Island**, 20km north of Charter's Creek, is closed completely.

False Bay Park

About 20km north of Fanies Island • Daily 6am–6pm • R20 • ☎ 035 562 0425

False Bay Park perches on the western shore of a small, lozenge-shaped waterway connected to Lake St Lucia by a narrow, steep-sided channel known colourfully as "Hell's Gates" (note that it's not possible to launch boats in this part of the lake due to the low water level). Two self-guided hikes, the 8km **Dugandlovu Trail** and the 10km circular **Mpophomeni Trail**, are clearly waymarked. They pass through a variety of terrain, and offer the opportunity of seeing birds and a decent variety of antelope and other small mammals such as jackals, mongooses and warthogs. The shorter 6km **Ingwe Trail** passes alongside the lake.

ARRIVAL AND DEPARTURE	THE WESTERN SHORE

By car You reach False Bay Park via Hluhluwe (see p.411); continue east through the village to a T-junction at the end of the road and follow the signposts for 15km to the False Bay Gate.

ACCOMMODATION

Falaza Game Park ☎ 035 562 2319, ⊛ falaza.co.za. For a touch of luxury, head for this slick tented accommodation in a small reserve, which also boasts a reasonably priced health spa and a pool which the rhino enjoy lounging around. Activities such as guided walks and boat trips, or game drives into Hluhluwe-Imfolozi Park, can be arranged. R1700

Sand Forest Lodge ☎ 035 562 2509, ⊛ sandforest.co.za. A collection of campsites and self-catering cottages, located on a small reserve with antelope, zebra and wildebeest. Meals are available on request. Camping R75, cottage R400

Mkhuze Game Reserve

Daily: April–Oct 6am–6pm; Nov–March 5am–7pm • R25, plus R35 per vehicle • ☎ 035 573 9004

Reached across the Lebombo Mountains, 28km east of **Mkhuze** village on the N2, **Mkhuze Game Reserve** is notable for its varied and highly beautiful countryside, and rich birdlife. The reserve is a major part of the iSimangaliso Wetland Park, connected to the coastal plain by a slender corridor through which the Mkhuze River flows before emptying into Lake St Lucia. It marks the final haul of the coastal plain stretching down the east of the continent from Kenya. The landscape varies from the **Muzi Pans**, wetlands consisting of seasonal flood plains floating with waterlilies, reed beds and swamps, to savanna. Elsewhere you'll come across stands of acacias, and in the south across the Mkhuze River you can wander through the cathedral-like fig forest that echoes to the shriek of trumpeter hornbills.

ARRIVAL AND DEPARTURE	MKHUZE GAME RESERVE

On a tour There's no public transport into Mkhuze, and if you don't have your own vehicle you'll need to join one of the daytime or night-time excursions into the park from Mkhuze village (see below).

By car If you're driving, the easiest way to get to the reserve is to leave the N2 at Mkhuze village and follow the signs along a good dirt road to Emshopi Gate. An alternative route, which leaves the N2 further south, 35km north of Hluhluwe, involves a lot more driving on dirt and doesn't knock much off the distance. Another entry point provides quick access from Sodwana Bay via the new Ophansi Bridge that crosses the Mkhuze River on the eastern side of the reserve. From Sodwana Bay, travel south on the R22 and turn down the D820 access road upon which the bridge is built; it's about a 40min drive from Sodwana Bay to the reserve.

INFORMATION

Reception office 9km from the entrance gate; provides a clear map that shows all routes and distances and gives general information about the park. You can buy fuel at the entrance gate, and there's a shop selling basic supplies and books at reception, but you should stock up on provisions in Mkhuze village before heading out here.

ACCOMMODATION

Ghost Mountain Inn In Mkhuze village, signposted off the N2 ☎ 035 573 1025, ⊛ ghostmountaininn.co.za. An attractive hotel, great for a drink or meal and a dunk in their pool even if you aren't staying. They organize four-hour game drives to Mkhuze (from R535 per person; minimum four people) and guided hikes up Ghost Mountain, which overlooks Mkhuze (3–4hr; R125; minimum two people). R1190

Mantuma 9km into the park in the northern section; book through KZN Wildlife ☎ 035 573 9004. A range of KZN Wildlife accommodation options, the cheapest being two-bed rest huts with shared ablution facilities and a kitchen. There are also larger chalets that sleep two, four or six. The most enticing units, however, are the large two- or four-person safari tents, each with its own ablutions. R400

Nhlonhlela Bush Lodge Overlooking Nhlonhlela Pan between Mantuma and Emshopi Gate; book through KZN Wildlife ☎ 035 573 9004. Four two-bed rooms run by KZN Wildlife, connected by wooden walkways to a

5

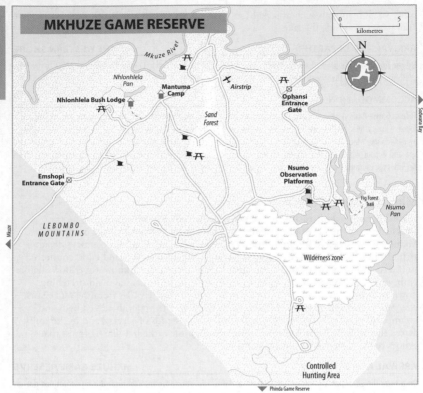

communal kitchen and living area. There's a cook (you bring the ingredients) and a field ranger included in the price. Minimum charge for six people. R2280

Phinda Private Game Reserve Book through & Beyond Africa ☎ 011 809 4300, �🖰 andbeyondafrica .com. A small private game reserve at Mkhuze's southern end, *Phinda* offers good chances of seeing lion, cheetah and both species of rhino. Accommodation is at five opulent lodges in a variety of original styles, from stilted Afro-Japanese timber houses to intimate chalets chiselled into the rock. All provide fine-tuned hospitality of the highest standard, and game drives and walks are accompanied by well-informed expert guides who are as good as any you'll find in South Africa. Rates include all meals and game activities. R7200

CAMPSITE

Emshopi Campsite At the main gate to Mkhuze; book through KZN Wildlife ☎ 033 845 1000, ⍟ kznwildlife.com. A simple, fairly large campsite handily located at the park entrance, with hot-water showers available on site. R150

Maputaland

Also known as **Maputaland**, the extreme northeast section of the Elephant Coast is the remotest tract of South Africa, mostly accessible only along dirt roads that work their tortuous way to the coast. The quickest way of reaching this area is from **Hluhluwe** village, where a tarred road, the **R22**, strikes north for some 150km, passing **Sodwana Bay** and terminating near **Kosi Bay** and the Mozambique border. Another road, 11km north of **Mkhuze** village, snakes north and then east for 133km, eventually connecting with the R22 about 40km south of Kosi Bay. This road gives access to the border village of **Ingwavuma**, home to a Zulu festival and the base for some excellent hikes, as well as the **Ndumo Game Reserve** and **Tembe Elephant Park**, both reserves reaching down from the Mozambique border.

5

Sodwana Bay

Around 80km northeast of Hluhluwe village • Daily 24hr • R20

A tiny scoop in the Zululand Coast, **SODWANA BAY** is the only breach in an almost flawless strand extending 170km from St Lucia to Kosi Bay. It's the fortuitous convergence of the bay (which makes it easy to launch boats), with the world's southernmost coral reefs that makes Sodwana the most popular base in the country for **scuba diving** and the most popular KZN Wildlife resort. Because the continental shelf comes extremely close to shore (near vertical drops are less than 1km away), it offers very deep waters, much loved by anglers who gather here for some of South Africa's best deep-sea **game fishing**, mostly tag and release. The abundance of game fish also makes for some of the best surf fly-fishing in the country.

When there's no one around, Sodwana Bay is paradise, with tepid waters, terrific sandy beaches, relaxed diving and snorkelling, and plenty of accommodation. Over weekends and during school holidays, however, fashion-conscious Jo'burgers tear down in their 4WDs, while thick-set anglers from Gauteng, Free State and Mpumalanga come here and drink themselves into a stupor. Thankfully, government regulations now limit the number of 4WDs using the beach as a car park. A gentler presence from mid-November to February are the leatherback and loggerhead **turtles**, who make their way onto Sodwana's beaches to reproduce, as they've been doing for the last 60,000 years (see box, p.425).

The national park takes in the bay itself, while the desultory collection of shops and an upmarket lodge that pass for the town are 8km to the west, back along the Mbazwana road.

GAME VIEWING AND ACTIVITIES IN MKHUZE

Some 84km of roads traverse Mkhuze, but one of the best ways to see game is to stay put and wait for the animals to come to you. Several **hides** have been erected at artificial watering holes and on the edge of pans, and both of these locations attract plenty of animals, particularly in the drier months.

Mkhuze is among the top spots for **birdwatching** in the country, with an impressive 430 species on record. Some of the prizes include Pels fishing owl and Rudd's apalis, a small, insect-eating bird with a very restricted distribution. Even if you know nothing about birds, you're likely to appreciate one of Africa's most colourful here – the lilac-breasted roller. The two hides at **Nsumo Pan**, in the southern section of the park, apart from overlooking a very beautiful natural waterway, are superbly placed for observing **waterfowl**. Between July and September, if conditions are right, you can see up to five hundred birds on the water at one time, among them flocks of pelicans and flamingos, kingfishers, fish eagles, and countless other species. To arrange a specialist birding guide from the local community, contact one of the guides listed on the website of the Zululand Birding Route (ⓦzbr.co.za; R290 half day, R450 full day).

In terms of other animals, the obvious draw of Mkhuze is its black and white **rhinos**. Of the **predators**, there are no lions, while cheetah and leopard are present but rarely glimpsed; you're more likely to see jackals. You stand a good chance of seeing several types of antelopes, including impala, eland and kudu. Primates such as baboons and vervet monkeys are generally found rustling around in the trees and making a nuisance of themselves on the ground, while at night you could be treated to the eerie call of the thick-tailed bushbaby from the canopy.

KZN Wildlife offers a number of activities, including recommended **night drives** from *Mantuma* (R200). During the day, you can explore Mkhuze on foot with a field ranger on two-hour conducted **walks** (R110) that concentrate on either game or birds. Also good for birding is a guided walk (R130) along the 3km **Mkhuze Fig Forest Trail** – another highlight of the reserve. Sycamore fig forest is one of the rarest types of woodland in South Africa, and the stands of massive trees give the forest a gentle green glow. Monkeys and baboons, which pass through from time to time, pose no threat to anything but your food, although you should keep alert to the possibility of encountering black rhinos or hippos.

5

The Mgobolezeni Trail

The 5km circular **Mgobolezeni trail** winds its way from just across from the park reception through a variety of habitats, including woodland, to the coastal lake that gives the hike its name. Arrows and signs indicate the way – but take care not to get sidetracked down one of the many game paths that crisscross it. The walk takes around three hours and there's no drinkable water along the way, so you should bring refreshment. **Crocodiles** live in the lake, as do **hippos** who leave the water to feed, usually at dusk. If you encounter a hippo on land, treat it with the utmost respect: hippos are responsible for more human deaths than any other African mammal. Avoid getting between a hippo and its line of retreat, which will generally be the most direct route to the safety of the water. If you do disturb one, find a tree to hide behind or, even better, to climb.

Apart from hippos, you may be lucky enough to see some of the other animals that inhabit the dune forest and its surrounds, among them bushbuck, duiker and Tonga squirrels. A trail **booklet** available from the park reception interprets points of interest along the way.

ARRIVAL AND DEPARTURE   SODWANA BAY

By public transport Minibus taxis run to Sodwana Bay from Mbazwana. If you haven't got your own vehicle, note that the place is so spread out that getting around on foot can be a major hassle.

INFORMATION AND TOURS

Tourist facilities The KZN Wildlife office (Mon–Thurs 8am–4.30pm, Fri & Sat 7am–4.30pm, Sun 7am–3pm), park entry gate and a small shop with food and other camping basics, as well as an ATM, are up the hill past the town. Petrol is available at the entry gate.

Tours Guided quad-bike rides are available from an outlet called Off-Road Fun (☏082 785 7704; R200/hr), either within the bay area or, more ambitiously, on a three-hour jaunt to Lake Sibaya (R400). During December and January, when loggerhead and leatherback turtles (see box, p.425) come to nest and lay their eggs on the beach, you can join one of the guided turtle tours from Sodwana Bay. As a limited number of licences are issued each year for these, the operators change from year to year, so enquire locally.

ACCOMMODATION

Most accommodation at Sodwana Bay lies inside the KZN Wildlife conservation area along the bay's beaches. Rates tend to be on the high side because of the lack of competition in the area. If you're staying inside the park at the privately run *Coral Divers* or *Mseni*, you must pay a R70 daily camping fee to KZN Wildlife. *Mseni* includes the fee in its rate; to stay at *Coral Divers*, pay the fee at the KZN Wildlife office.

Coral Divers Sodwana Main Rd ☏035 571 0290, ⓦcoraldivers.co.za. The largest dive outfit at Sodwana Bay is a basic, rather tired divers' haunt with a variety of two-bed safari tents and two-bed cabins with or without their own bathrooms. You can self-cater or pay for half board, and takeaways are available throughout the day. Free transport to and from the beach to coincide with dives and meal times. **R140**

KZN Wildlife Accommodation At the northern end of the reserve ☏035 571 0051. Twenty fully equipped log cabins with either five or eight beds, with minimum charges for three and four people, respectively. There are also a staggering 350 campsites here, and the seasonal population explosion allegedly makes Sodwana Bay the largest campsite in the southern hemisphere. Camping **R400**, cabin **R1155**

DRIVING MAPUTALAND

Your biggest challenge in Maputaland is likely to be getting around. For much of this area, a **4WD** vehicle is essential and it's best to travel in two vehicles as there's nowhere to get repairs done and facilities are poor. It's also essential to carry an inflated spare tyre, jack and wheel spanner, and spare water. Watch out for unattended stray animals and school children wandering onto the roads; never resort to speeding on dirt roads to make up time, and watch out for potholes on all roads.

DIVING AND SNORKELLING IN SODWANA BAY

5

Unless you're a keen angler, the principal reason to come to Sodwana Bay is for the diving off the **coral reefs** that thrive here in the warm waters carried down the coast by the Agulhas current. The sea is clear, silt-free and perfect for spotting some of the 1200 varieties of **fish** that inhabit the waters off northern KwaZulu-Natal, making it second only to the Great Barrier Reef in its richness.

The closest reef to the bay, and consequently the most visited, is **Two Mile Reef**, 2km long and 900m wide, offering excellent dives. Among the others is **Five Mile Reef**, which is further north and is known for its miniature staghorn corals, while beyond that, **Seven Mile Reef** is inhabited by large anemone communities and offers protection to turtles and rays, which may be found resting here.

There's excellent **snorkelling** at Jesser Point, a tiny promontory at the southern end of the bay. Just off here is **Quarter Mile Reef**, which attracts a wide variety of fish, including moray eels and rays. Low tide is the best time to venture out – a sign on the beach indicates daily tide times. You can buy competitively priced snorkels and masks (or rent them for R30 per day) from the dive shop at *Sodwana Bay Lodge*. Here you'll also find a **dive operation** offering various diving courses, diving packages and scuba equipment rental. There is also a dive operator providing similar services at *Coral Divers*.

Mseni Lodge Right on the water's edge, south of the village ☎035 571 0284, ⓦmseni.co.za. The only establishment to have direct access to the beach, this is a comfortable lodge offering en-suite B&B log cabins or self-catering units sleeping five or eight people spread out amid thick coastal forest. There's a restaurant, bar, satellite TV and swimming pool. R1300

Sodwana Bay Lodge Sodwana Main Rd, in the village ☎035 571 6000, ⓦsodwanabaylodge.co.za. Simple yet comfortable reed and thatched en-suite two-bed B&B chalets (insist on getting a renovated one). A poolside bar downstairs has pool tables and a sun deck that attracts both visitors and locals. Rates include half board. R1320

Visagie Lodge 500m beyond Sodwana Bay Lodge, towards the bay ☎035 571 0089, ⓦvisagiecharters .co.za. Basic accommodation in cabins sleeping four or six people, with a restaurant and bar on site. Meals are available on request, as are turtle tours and other activities. R400

EATING

Leatherback's Seafood and Grill Sodwana Bay Lodge (see above). The reasonably priced *Leatherback's* offers decent food, including the best pizzas around and carvery fare such as pork ribs and rack of lamb (mains R55–80). Daily 6.30am–10pm.

Jabu's Takeaways Located in an old caravan parked next to the craft market in the village. A regular hangout for divers, dishing out cheap, filling half-loaves of bread stuffed with fried potatoes, fried egg or curry for around R25. Daily 8am–7pm.

Lake Sibaya

Lake Sibaya, South Africa's largest natural freshwater lake, covers 77 square kilometres and is fringed by white sandy beaches disappearing into dense forest. On a windless day, the lake, 10km due north of Sodwana Bay, appears glassy, azure and flat; the waters are so transparent that when KZN Wildlife take a hippo census they just fly over and count the dark blobs clearly visible from the air. From the margins, timid crocodiles cut the lake surface, exchanging the warmth of the sun for the safety of the water. This is not an unpopulated wilderness: the lake fringes are dotted with traditional African lands and villages. There's an exceptionally easy-going 3km **circular walk** that starts from the viewing platform behind KZN Wildlife's now closed *Baya Camp*. **Birdwatching** can be rewarding (there are two hides), with close on three hundred species present. Needless to say, with crocs and hippos lolling about, swimming in the lake is most unwise.

Mabibi

Daily 6am–6pm • R20, plus R15 per vehicle • ☎035 474 1504

MABIBI is probably one of the most peaceful spots to camp in South Africa, where you can pitch your tent in luxuriant subtropical forest and follow a boardwalk down the

5

duneside to the **sea** – a walk that takes about ten minutes. Outside school holidays, there's a fair chance of having a perfect tropical beach all to yourself; and you won't get the frenetic activity of outboard motors and 4WD vehicles found at Sodwana Bay and other spots to the south – they're banned within the Maputaland Coastal Forest Reserve, which Mabibi falls under. The coast here offers **surf angling** and **snorkelling** matching that at Sodwana Bay, with rich tropical marine life thriving on the coral reefs offshore. A number of mammals live in the forest, but most of them – bushbabies, large-spotted genets and porcupines – only come out after dark.

ARRIVAL AND DEPARTURE   MABIBI

By car One approach to Mabibi is the tarred Kwa-Ngwanase (also called Manguzi) Rd from the N2, some 11km north of Mkhuze. At the Manzengwenya intersection, turn right and follow the (poorly marked) signboards to Mabibi. Because this final 45km from the junction is along gravel and thick sand tracks, a 4WD vehicle, or at least one with high clearance such as a

bakkie (pick-up truck), and competent driving are essential. You can also reach Mabibi on the coastal forest link road (also called Coastal Cashews Rd) from Mbazwana; turn right at the Manzengwenya Rd and follow the signs. If you're staying at *Thonga Beach Lodge*, you'll be collected at the end of the tarred road, beyond the Manzengwenya intersection.

ACCOMMODATION

Campsite Book through Isibindi Africa ☏ 035 474 1473, ⊚ isibindi.co.za. Ten remote and idyllic campsites situated in subtropical forest, perched on a plateau on top of the dunes and sheltered from the wind. A boardwalk leads down to the sea. **R80**

Thonga Beach Lodge ☏ 035 474 1473, ⊚ isibindi .co.za. The luxury Robinson Crusoe-style *Thonga Beach Lodge* offers thatched suites secluded in the coastal dune forest. The lodge has a wellness centre, dive operation, turtle tracking tours and sundowners at Lake Sibaya. Rates include full board. **R2475**

Rocktail Bay

South Africa's most sublime beachstay lies about 20km north of Mabibi along the coast at **ROCKTAIL BAY**, a stretch of sand and sea that's restricted to guests who are prepared to pay for the privilege. Few parts of the South African coastline are as unspoilt as the beaches around here, and although there's no big game to pull in the punters, there's excellent **scuba diving** offshore, and a dive centre with a qualified PADI instructor, a boat and skipper – one of the highlights is diving with pregnant ragged-tooth sharks as they migrate north up the KwaZulu-Natal coast from around late September to May. The **birdwatching** here is excellent; among a number of rare species are the green coucal, grey waxbill, Natal robin and – particularly prized – the palmnut vulture.

Supreme idleness is one of the big attractions of the place, but you can go snorkelling, walk in the coastal forest, join an excursion to a fossilized dune called Black Rock and watch turtles during the summer egg-laying season. **Surf fishing** for kingfish, barracuda, blacktail and the like is another possibility.

ACCOMMODATION   ROCKTAIL BAY

Rocktail Beach Camp Book through Safari & Adventure Co ☏ 011 257 5111, ⊚ safariadventurecompany.com. The comfortable *Rocktail Beach Camp* – seventeen en-suite tent rooms set in the forest a short walk from the beach – is the ideal way to get away from it all. There's no phone,

limited solar electricity, and the last few kilometres are so heavy-going that you leave your vehicle at the Coastal Cashews Farm on the dirt road from Mabibi and get ferried in by 4WD (included in the rate). Rates include full board. **R280**

Ndumo Game Reserve

Daily: April–Sept 6am–6pm; Oct–March 5am–7pm • R40, plus R35 per vehicle • ☏ 035 591 0058

One of the most beautiful of the KwaZulu-Natal reserves, **Ndumo** looks across the flood plain into Mozambique to the north and up to the Lebombo Mountains in the south. Its northern extent hugs the **Usutu River**, which rises in Swaziland and defines

South Africa's border with Mozambique. The turn-off to the reserve is 56km north of Jozini, with the final 15km along a rough gravel track.

No great volume of animals trammel the reserve (nyala, hippo and both species of rhino are among the 62 species here), and they may be more difficult to see than elsewhere. For twitchers, however, Ndumo ranks among the country's top **bird-watching** spots. The staggering 430 different varieties recorded here include the African broadbill, Pels fishing owl and the southern banded snake eagle.

It's possible to **drive** around some areas, one of the highlights being the trip to **Redcliffs**, where there's a picnic site with a towering vantage point offering soaring views across the Usutu River into both Swaziland and Mozambique.

INFORMATION AND TOURS
NDUMO GAME RESERVE

KZN Wildlife operates an education centre on the reserve, 2km from the restcamp office (daily 7am–4pm; ☎ 035 591 0004). They can organize open-topped 4WD outings in the mornings and evenings to the lovely Inyamiti pan, which is inhabited by hippos and crocodiles and receives visits from an array of waterfowl; guided walking trails are also available.

ACCOMMODATION

KZN Wildlife Restcamp ☎ 035 591 0058. A number of campsites and seven well-maintained, two-bed huts perched on a hill, each with a fridge and shared ablutions. A shop near the entrance gate sells basic supplies, but you're better off stocking up en route in Mkhuze village. R660

Ndumu River Lodge Just outside the park ☎ 035 592 8000, ⓦ ndumu.com. A pleasant place to stay, offering en-suite B&B rooms or self-catering chalets. There's also a restaurant and bar on site, and you can fish in the nearby river. Directions are given when you book. R1200

Tembe Elephant Park

☎ 031 267 0144, ⓦ tembe.co.za

The easy-going and remote **Tembe Elephant Park**, on the border with Mozambique, is part-owned by the local Tembe tribe, and access is limited to those staying in the rather pricey accommodation on offer. The park is located on what was once known as the "Ivory Route" along which Zulu ivory merchants once plied their trade, and it is still home to over 220 elephants, including some of the largest in Southern Africa. The park

---

TURTLES

Sea turtles from as far afield as Malindi in Kenya (3500km to the north) and Cape Agulhas (2000km west along the South African coastline) come ashore on the beaches of the northern Elephant Coast every year between October and February to lay their eggs. The turtles have survived virtually unchanged for almost a hundred million years and it's reckoned that loggerhead turtles have been using Maputaland's beaches to lay their eggs for 60,000 years.

It is believed that the turtles are lured onto the shore by a hormone that oozes from the beach, a scent that they follow and which is thought to have been programmed into their subconscious while they were themselves in their eggs. The myopic turtle, whose eyes are adapted to underwater vision, pulls herself along the beach in the dark until she encounters an obstruction such as a bank or a log, where she begins digging a pit using her front flippers until she has scooped out a nest big enough to hold her own volume. She then digs a flask-shaped hole about 50cm deep and lays her eggs into this, a process which takes about ten minutes. The turtle fills the hole with sand using her front flippers, disguising the place where the eggs are stored, and returns to the sea. After about two months the eggs hatch, and the entire clutch of hatched turtles will simultaneously race down the beach. Once in the ocean, the hatchlings swim out to sea where they are carried away by the Agulhas current into the Atlantic or along the Indian Ocean coast. Only one in five hundred will survive to return.

The whole of the northern Elephant Coast is excellent for spotting loggerhead and leatherback turtles, with **Rocktail Bay** probably the best spot of all. As the turtles are easily disturbed, only a few licensed operators are allowed to escort visitors to watch the turtles at night.

5

also contains the other Big Five species, as well as game such as impala and suni antelope, and a wide variety of birds can be found flitting through its sand forests and wetlands.

ARRIVAL AND DEPARTURE   TEMBE ELEPHANT PARK

By car The turn-off to Tembe lies 15km or so further east of Ndumo. You can reach the gate with a normal vehicle, but in the park itself 4WD is necessary – you leave your car at the gate and transfer to the park's own 4WD vehicle.

ACCOMMODATION

Safari tents Accommodation at Tembe is in luxury en-suite safari tents built on raised wooden platforms. The price includes all meals and game drives conducted by knowledgeable guides from the local community, and traditional Tembe dancers come to perform in the evenings on request. **R1600**

Kosi Bay

Kosi Mouth daily 6am–6pm • R20, plus R15 per vehicle • ☏ 035 592 0236

At the northernmost reaches of the KwaZulu-Natal coast, **KOSI BAY** is at the centre of an enthralling area of waterways fringed by forest. Despite the name, this is not a bay at all, but a system of four lakes connected by narrow reed channels, which eventually empty into the sea at Kosi Mouth.

One of the most striking images of Kosi Bay is of mazes of reed fences in the estuary and other parts of the lake system. These are **fish traps**, or kraals, built by local Tonga people, a practice that has been going on for hundreds of years. Custom has made the method of harvesting sustainable due to the fact that trap numbers are strictly controlled; the traps are passed down from father to son and capture only a small fraction of the fish that pass through. To see the fish traps – and the beach – you'll need to travel to Kosi Mouth, a hard-going 20-minute drive for which you'll need 4WD. Note that a permit is required for Kosi Mouth, which you can obtain at the gate.

ACCOMMODATION   KOSI BAY

In addition to KNZ's wildlife's restcamp, a number of locally owned and operated camps have opened in recent times, the proprietors all enthusiastic hosts and knowledgeable guides. Directions to the camps are given when you book, and 4WD transfers from Kwa-Ngwanase (Manguzi) can be arranged for an additional charge.

Hlalanathi Forest Camp ☏ 072 345 6260. A collection of campsites with a communal kitchen (bring your own provisions) and dining area. The main draw is its unique setting in the sand forest at Bhanga Nek. **R80**

★ **Kosi Forest Lodge** Inside the reserve ☏ 035 474 1473, ⊛ isibindiafrica.co.za. Arguably the most dreamy place to stay in KwaZulu-Natal, featuring eight reed-and-thatch suites in a remote landscape of palms, lakes, sand forest and bleached white beaches. There's no electricity, and if you don't have your own 4WD you have to be collected from the Total garage in Kwa-Ngwanase and taken along sandy tracks to the lodge. Activities include guided canoeing trips, reef snorkelling and forest walks; there's a good chance you'll see hippos, crocodiles and marine turtles. The rate is inclusive of all meals and activities. **R3560**

KZN Wildlife Restcamp Inside the reserve on the western shore of Nhlange, the largest of the lakes ☏ 035 592 0236. Two-bed, five-bed (minimum charge for four people) and six-bed cabins, with a small campsite nearby. The price includes the park entry fee. Camping **R385**, cabins **R500**

Thobeka Backpackers 4km north of Kwa-Ngwanase ☏ 072 446 1525, ⊛ kosi.co.za. A delightfully rustic, friendly backpackers hidden away in the forest, with bush camp-style dorms and doubles connected by elevated walkways. A variety of activities is available, including snorkelling, tours into Mozambique, trips to a colourful border market and even courses in bush cooking. Dorm **R110**, double **R300**

Ithala Game Reserve

Daily: March–Oct 6am–6pm; Nov–Feb 5am–7pm • R40, plus R30 per vehicle • ☏ 034 983 2540.

West of Maputaland and close to the Swaziland border, the small **Ithala Game Reserve** is little known, despite being one of the country's most uncrowded and

5

spectacularly scenic places to watch wildlife. Ithala is largely mountainous and the terrain is extremely varied, with numerous cliffs and rock faces contained within a protective basin.

Like the rest of the KwaZulu-Natal game reserves, Ithala is excellent for white **rhinos** and there's plenty of **plains game**, including zebras and giraffes. Of the **predators**, you could, if you're very lucky, encounter brown hyenas, cheetahs and leopards. If you're obsessed with seeing the Big Five, however, Ithala is not the place to visit – lions are notably absent here, even though the other four make periodic appearances. The best idea, then, is to forget the mammal checklist and take a slow drive around the mountains into the valleys and along the watercourses. One of the most rewarding **drives** is along Ngubhu Loop, with a detour to Ngubhu picnic site.

ARRIVAL AND DEPARTURE   ITHALA GAME RESERVE

By car There's no public transport to the park or near it, so driving here is your only option. The entrance gate is just off the R69.

INFORMATION AND TOURS

The camp's reception can provide **information** and **maps**. There are some **self-guided trails** into the wooded mountainside above *Ntshondwe Camp*, which give the chance to stretch your legs if you've spent a morning driving around. **Day and night drives** (R190) in open vehicles can be booked through the restcamp's reception.

ACCOMMODATION

Mbizo Bush Camp ☎ 033 845 1000, ⊛ www .kznwildlife.com. If you want an extremely pared-down bush experience, you can't beat this marvellous bush camp with space for just eight people, shaded by thorn trees and ilala palms, on the banks of the Mbizo River. Expect no frills here – it's cold showers in reed enclosures and cooking over wood fires, the only concession to civilization being a flushing toilet. Minimum charge for six people. R2370

Mhlangeni and Thalu Bush Camps ☎ 033 845 1000, ⊛ www.kznwildlife.com. A wonderful choice for something a bit wilder, these camps, *Thalu* and *Mhlangeni*, are both in beautiful secluded settings and have four (minimum charge for three) or ten (minimum charge for seven) beds respectively. Both are staffed by an attendant and you can make arrangements to have a field ranger take you on walks. R1185

★ **Ntshondwe Camp** ☎ 033 845 1000, ⊛ www .kznwildlife.com. This is one of the best game-reserve restcamps in South Africa, offering extremely comfortable two-, four- and six-bed self-catering chalets with fully equipped kitchens, lounge areas and verandas, as well as two-bed non-self-catering units. Each chalet is surrounded by indigenous bush through which paved walkways weave their way around granite rocks and trees to the main reception area. R675

Ntshondwe Lodge ☎ 033 845 1000, ⊛ www .kznwildlife.com. Next to the restcamp, yet completely secluded, this luxury lodge has three beautifully decorated rooms and a small plunge pool overlooking the reserve. A cook is on hand to prepare the food you bring. R3600

EATING

If you want to self-cater, you'll need to bring supplies – the camp shop specializes in beer and frozen meat and hasn't much by way of fresh food. Louwsburg, signed from the surfaced road along the southern section of the reserve, has a very small general store that's a little better, and, further afield, Vryheid, Pongola and Mkhuze are better still.

Ntshondwe Camp The camp's restaurant serves a surprisingly varied range of foods from *escargot* to steaks – though meat-free meals aren't always on the menu – and a cosy bar whose sun deck looks out over the water hole and across the valleys.

Central Zululand and the Battlefields

Central Zululand – the Zulu heartland – radiates out from the unlovely modern town of **Ulundi**, some 30km west of the Hluhluwe-Imfolozi Park. At the height of its influence in the 1820s and 1830s, under King Shaka, the core of the Zulu state lay

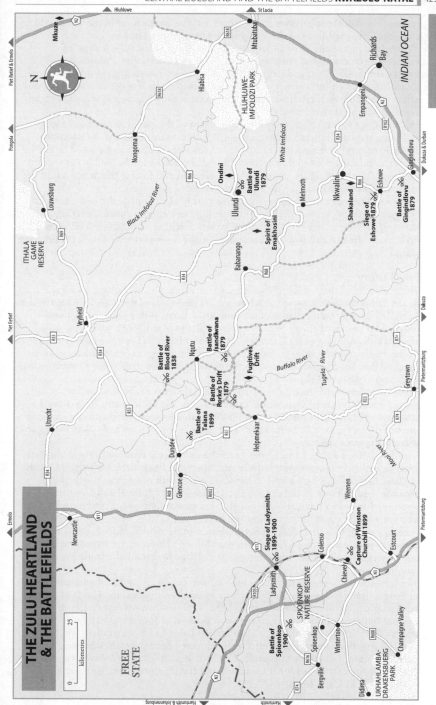

5

between the **Black Imfolozi River** in the north and the **Tugela River** in the south, which discharges into the Indian Ocean roughly 100km north of Durban.

Contained in a relatively small area to the west of the heartland is a series of nineteenth-century **battlefield sites**, where Zulus and Boers, then Zulus and the British, and finally Boers and Brits came to blows. Don't attempt to visit this area on your own: all you'll see is empty veld with a few memorials. Far better is to join a tour with one of the several excellent guides who make it their business to bring the region's dramatic history alive (see box, p.435).

Don't expect to see "tribal" people who conform to the Zulu myth outside theme parks like Shakaland, near Eshowe (see p.434). Traditional dress and the **traditional lifestyle** are largely a nineteenth-century phenomenon, deliberately smashed by the British a century ago when they imposed a poll tax that had to be paid in cash – thus ending Zulu self-sufficiency, generating urbanization and forcing the Africans into the modern industrial economy, where they were needed as workers.

You will find beautiful Zulu crafts in this part of the country, the best examples being in museums such as the little-known but outstanding **Vukani Zulu Cultural Museum** in Eshowe (see opposite). Also worth checking out is the reconstructed royal enclosure of Cetshwayo, the last king of the independent Zulu, at **Ondini**, near Ulundi.

Brief history

The truth behind the Zulus is difficult to separate from the mythology, which was fed by the Zulus themselves as well as white settlers. Accounts of the Zulu kingdom in the 1820s rely heavily on the diaries of the two adventurers, **Henry Fynn** and **Nathaniel Isaacs**, who portrayed King Shaka as a mercurial and bloodthirsty tyrant who killed his subjects willy-nilly for a bit of fun. In a letter from Isaacs to Fynn, uncovered in the 1940s, Isaacs encourages his friend to depict the Zulu kings as "bloodthirsty as you can, and describe frivolous crimes people lose their lives for. It all tends to swell up the work and make it interesting."

A current debate divides historians about the real extent of the **Zulu empire** during the nineteenth century. What we do know is that in the 1820s Shaka consolidated a state that was one of the most powerful political forces on the subcontinent, and that internal dissent to his rule culminated in his assassination by his half-brothers **Dingane and Mhlangana** in 1828.

In the 1830s, pressure from whites exacerbated internal tensions in the Zulu state, and reached a climax when a relatively small party of Boers defeated Dingane's army at **Blood River**. This led to a split in the Zulu state, with one half following **King Mpande**, and collapse threatened when Mpande's sons Mbuyazi and Cetshwayo led opposing forces in a pitched battle for the succession. **Cetshwayo** emerged victorious and successfully set about rebuilding the state, but too late. Seeing a powerful Zulu state as a threat to a confederated South Africa under British control, the British high commissioner, Sir Bartle Frere, delivered a Hobson's choice of an **ultimatum** on the banks of the Tugela River, demanding that Cetshwayo should dismantle his polity or face invasion.

In January 1879, the British army crossed the Tugela and suffered a humiliating disaster at **Isandlwana** – the British army's worst defeat ever at the hands of native armies – only for the tide to turn that same evening when just over a hundred British soldiers repulsed a force of between three- and four thousand Zulus at **Rorke's Drift**. By the end of July, Zulu independence had been snuffed, when the British lured the reluctant (and effectively already broken) Zulus, who were now eager for peace, into battle at **Ulundi**. The British set alight Cetshwayo's capital at **Ondini** – a fire that blazed for four days – and the king was taken prisoner and held in the Castle in Cape Town.

ZULU FESTIVALS

In September and October KwaZulu-Natal is host to three significant Zulu **festivals** that until recently were only attended by the actual participants, though it's now possible to witness these with the Eshowe-based Zululand Eco-Adventures (see p.432). If you're not around in September or October, Zululand Eco-Adventures can arrange for you to attend several lower-key Zulu ceremonies that give an authentic, non-touristy insight into various aspects of Zulu life. These range from *sangoma* healing ceremonies (Wed & Sun), Zulu weddings (Sat & Sun), coming-of-age ceremonies (Sat & Sun) and a visit to a Zulu gospel church (Sun).

THE ROYAL REED DANCE

In the second week of September, the Zulu King hosts a four-day celebration at his royal residence at **Nongoma**. The event is both a rite of passage to womanhood for the young maidens of the Zulu nation, and a chance for them to show off their singing and dancing talents. The festival, known as **Umkhosi woMhlanga** in Zulu, takes its name from the riverbed reeds that play a significant role in Zulu life. Young women carry the reed sticks, which symbolize the power of nature, to the king. According to Zulu mythology, only virgins should take part, and if a woman participant is not a virgin, this will be revealed by her reed stick breaking. A second Reed Dance takes place in the last week of September at the king's other residence in Ingwavuma (see p.420).

KING SHAKA DAY

In honour of King Shaka, a celebration is held yearly on September 24 in **KwaDukuza** (see p.392), Shaka's original homestead and the place where he was murdered in 1828 by his brothers Dingane and Mhlangana. It was Shaka who brought together smaller tribes and formed them into the greatest warrior nation in Southern Africa. Today, the celebration is attended by a who's who of South African Zulu society; there are speeches by the likes of Inkatha Freedom Party leader Chief Mangosuthu Buthelezi, along with music and fantastic displays of warrior dancing, the men decked out in full ceremonial gear and armed with traditional weapons.

SHEMBE FESTIVAL

Held in mid- to late October in **Judea**, near Eshowe, the Shembe Festival is the culmination of weeks of endless rituals, dancing and prayers held throughout KwaZulu-Natal. Some thirty thousand members of the Shembe Church (see p.378) return here every year to meet their leader and celebrate their religion with prayer dances and displays of drumming.

Eshowe

The name **ESHOWE** has an onomatopoeic Zulu derivation, evoking the sound of the wind blowing through the trees. Though visitors generally give the town a miss on the way to the more obvious drama of Ondini and the Battlefields, the place offers a gentle introduction to the Zulu heartland and deserves more than just a passing glance. Apart from its attractive setting, interlacing with the **Dlinza Forest**, the town is home to one of the world's finest collections of Zulu crafts and has a tour operator offering excellent excursions that take you out to experience some authentic Zulu culture and other aspects of life in Zululand that you would otherwise most likely miss.

Vukani Zulu Cultural Museum

Fort Nongqayi, Nongqayi Rd • Mon–Fri 7.30am–4pm, Sat & Sun 9am–4pm • R25 • ☎ 035 474 2281, ⓦ eshowemuseums.org.za

Containing more than three thousand examples of traditional Zulu arts and crafts, this brilliant museum is housed in a purpose-built structure on the grounds of Fort Nongqayi. Guided tours take you through the huge range of **baskets** (a craft at which Zulu culture excels), each made for a specific purpose, the finest of which are the ones by **Reuben Ndwandwe**, arguably the greatest Zulu basket weaver. There are also carvings, beadwork, tapestries and some outstanding ceramics, including works by **Nesta Nala**, one of the leading proponents of the form. Both Ndwandwe and Nala died

5

a few years ago of AIDS. The benchmark examples here allow you to form an idea of the quality of basketry and crafts you'll see for sale as you work your way around Zululand. The museum itself sells baskets and pottery by local artists, which far surpass what's on offer at the on-site crafts shop.

Zululand Historical Museum

Fort Nongqayi, Nongqayi Rd • Mon–Fri 7.30am–4pm, Sat & Sun 9am–4pm • **Zululand Missionary Museum** Mon–Fri 7.30am–4pm, Sat & Sun 9am–4pm • Free • **Phoenix Gallery** same hours • Free • ⓦ www.phoenix-zululand.org

With a collection that's eccentric and informative by turns, but never dull, this is the place to see furniture belonging to **John Dunn**, the only white man to become a Zulu chief; incidentally, he also took 49 wives, so becoming the progenitor of Eshowe's coloured community, many of whom still carry his last name. The museum also exhibits Zulu household artefacts and has displays on Zulu history. Also in the Fort Nongqayi complex are the **Zululand Missionary Museum** in a replica of the fort's chapel, which contains exhibits relating to the Norwegian missionaries who came to this part of South Africa in the nineteenth century; a working **paper mill** where you can see boxes, photo frames, notepads and the like being made from sugar-cane fibre and even elephant dung; and the very touching **Phoenix Gallery**, where drawings and paintings by the male (overwhelmingly black) inmates of Eshowe prison are stark and sometimes shocking expressions of their feelings of alienation and anger.

Dlinza Forest and aerial boardwalk

Off Kangela St on the southwestern side of Eshowe (accessed from the museums complex at Fort Nongqayi) • Daily: May–Aug 7am–5pm, Sept–April 6am–5pm • R25 • ☎ 035 474 4029

A must for birdwatchers, **Dlinza Forest** is also a great place for picnics or strolling along the impressive **Dlinza Forest Aerial Boardwalk**. Wheelchair-friendly, the boardwalk spans 125m and is raised 10m into the air just under the forest canopy, giving visitors a chance to experience a section of the woodland normally restricted to birds. The boardwalk leads to a 20m-high stainless-steel **observation tower**, offering stunning panoramas across the treetops to the Indian Ocean shimmering in the distance. A **visitor information centre** at the foot of the boardwalk provides information about forest ecology. Among the birds you might see here are black sparrowhawks, crowned eagles and spotted ground thrushes, while eighty species of butterfly have also been recorded in the forest.

ARRIVAL AND DEPARTURE ESHOWE

By bus The Durban–Swaziland Baz Bus passes through town, dropping off and picking up passengers at *Zululand*

Backpackers at the *George Hotel*.

TOURS

Tours Based at the *George Hotel*, ★ Zululand Eco-Adventures (☎ 035 474 4919, ⓦ www.eshowe.com) offers tours giving an authentic experience of local Zulu life. It can take you to rural Zulu communities where you'll have the opportunity to attend a variety of Zulu ceremonies (see box, p.430), and see markets and *shebeens* without feeling like you're in a theme park. The company takes an active role in the local community and will take you out to a

school or an orphanage in the morning, where you'll spend an unhurried day with the kids before being picked up again in the afternoon – a rewarding experience for both you and the children, and one that involves only a negligible charge for the transport. Occasionally, **volunteers** are needed to work in various upliftment projects in the Eshowe area; if interested, contact Zululand Eco-Adventures.

ACCOMMODATION

★ **Chase Guest House** About 1.5km along John Ross Highway from the KFC on Main St ☎ 035 474 5491 or ☎ 083 265 9629, ⓦ thechase.co.za. This lovely,

peaceful farm has two large en-suite rooms and endless views of the surrounding sugar-cane fields. On the grounds there are also two smart self-contained units sleeping two, with the option of B&B or self-catering. A pool, tennis court, internet access and very charming hosts add to the appeal. R500

Chennells Guesthouse 36 Pearson Ave ☎035 479 4919, ⓦeshowe.com. Under the same management as the *George Hotel*, this beautiful colonial home built over a century ago boasts a large garden, a swimming pool and very comfortable rooms. The owners throw in some nice touches, such as complimentary sherry in the evenings. R795

Forest View Lodge 52 Addison Rd ☎035 474 1282, ⓔwoodprod@iafrica.com. Pretty wood-and-brick rooms in a quiet neighbourhood, some of which come with their own balconies overlooking a flower-filled garden. There are a few family-friendly self-catering cottages as well. R440

George Hotel 36 Main St ☎035 474 4919, ⓦeshowe .com. This busy hotel in an historic 1906 building is steeped in local history, and is something of a focal point for the town. It offers renovated en-suite rooms, many with their original wooden floors, and an on-site travel agent. R656

Zululand Backpackers Lodge Attached to the George Hotel ☎035 474 4919, ⓦeshowe.com. The cheapest beds in Eshowe, with dorms, doubles and camping. There are also laundry facilities and an attractive deck overlooking Dlinza Forest. Dorm R125, double R350

EATING AND DRINKING

Adam's Outpost In the museum complex at Fort Nongqayi ☎035 474 1787. At *Adams' Outpost*, in a converted settler house, you can get healthy soups, home-made bread and good curries (R50–80) or a good-value Sunday lunch buffet (R85; reservations required). Mon–Fri 7.30am–4pm, Sun 9am–4pm.

★ **Café Zulu** George Hotel ☎035 474 2952. Serves delicious pies, muffins and quiches (R15–20) as well as Italian coffee and tea grown in Zululand. Daily 8am–4pm.

George Hotel The most popular place to eat in Eshowe is the restaurant at the *George Hotel*, where you can get German specialities like schnitzel along with the usual steaks and lamb chops (R70–90). Daily 7–9.30am & 6–9pm.

George Hotel bar For drinking, head to the bar at the *George Hotel*, a friendly meeting place where, if you're lucky, you'll get to taste a beer or two brewed at the on-site Zululand Brewery. Daily noon–midnight.

Ulundi

Some 90km north of Eshowe on the R66

ULUNDI is the former capital of the KwaZulu Bantustan and lies at the centre of the **eMakhosini Valley** (Valley of the Kings). The latter holds a semi-mythical status among Zulu nationalists as the birthplace of the Zulu state and the area where several of its founding fathers lived and are now buried. A memorial to them was erected in 2003, the Spirit of eMakhosini, on a hill 3km up the R34, beyond the junction with the R66 for Ulundi. The circular memorial is surrounded by seven large aluminium horns representing the kings that came before Shaka, while in the centre is an impressive 600-litre bronze traditional beer pot.

The **Battle of Ulundi Memorial**, just outside town on the tarred road to the Cengeni Gate of the Hluhluwe-Imfolozi Park, is the poignant spot marking the final defeat of the Zulus. An understated small stone structure with a silver dome houses a series of plaques listing all the regiments on both sides involved in the last stand of the Zulus on July 4, 1879. The rectangular park around the memorial marks the site of the hollow square formation adopted by the British infantry and supported to devastating effect by seven- and nine-pounder guns.

Ondini Historical Reserve

A few kilometres from Ulundi • Daily 8am–5pm • R20 • ☎035 870 2050

By far the most interesting sight around here is the **Ondini Historical Reserve**, which houses the reconstruction of the royal residence of **King Cetshwayo**, a site museum and a cultural museum. After the decisive Battle of Ulundi, the royal residence at Ondini was razed to the ground and Cetshwayo was captured. Still puzzled by Britain's actions, Cetshwayo wrote to the British governor in 1881 from his exile at the Castle in Cape Town: "I have done you no wrong, therefore you must have some other object in view in invading my land." The *isigodlo*, or **royal enclosure**, has been partially reconstructed with traditional Zulu beehive huts that you can wander round, while the site museum

5

ZULU THEME PARKS

North of Eshowe, the winding R66 leaves behind the softer vistas of the Dlinza Forest, the citrus groves and green seas of cane plantations and looks across huge views of the valleys that figure in the creation mythology of the Zulu nation. In no time you're into thornveld (acacias, rocky *koppies* and aloes) and **theme park** country.

Most accessible of these "Zulu-village hotels" is **Shakaland**, 14km north of Eshowe off the R68 at Norman Hurst Farm, Nkwalini (☏035 460 0912, ⓦwww.shakaland.com). Built in 1984 as the set for the wildly romanticized TV series *Shaka Zulu*, Shakaland is a reconstruction of a nineteenth-century Zulu kraal and quite unrepresentative of how people live today. However, the theme park just about manages to remain on the acceptable side of exploiting ethnic culture, and offers the chance to sample **Zulu food**. **Tours** for day visitors (daily 11am & 4pm; R315) include an audiovisual presentation about the origin of the Zulus, a guided walk around the huts, an explanation of traditional social organization, spear-making, a beer-drinking ceremony and a buffet lunch with traditional food. The highlight, however, is probably one of the best choreographed Zulu **dancing** shows in the country, with the dramatic landscape as the backdrop; it's worthwhile putting up with all the other stuff just to see it.

In a different league, **Simunye Zulu Lodge** (☏035 450 0101, ⓦwww.simunyelodge.co.za), along the D256, off the R34 and 6km north of Melmoth, offers a far more authentic experience of Zulu culture, introducing guests to contemporary ways of life as well as traditional customs. Visitors are conveyed to the camp by horse, ox wagon or 4WD, and get to see dancing, visit a working kraal and meet local people.

There is traditional-style accommodation at both places. Shakaland offers comfortable beehive huts (R1850), with untraditional luxuries such as electricity and en-suite bathrooms. At Simunye you can also choose to sleep in beehive huts, or opt for rondavels at a kraal or stone-and-thatch cottages carved into the cliffside (full board R2100).

has a model showing the full original arrangement. Among the items in the **Cultural Museum** is a major bead collection.

ACCOMMODATION ULUNDI

Muzi Bushcamp ☏035 870 2500, ⓦwww.tintasafaris. co.za. Here you can stay in a traditional Zulu hut, the choice ranging from beehives to grass-and-reed rondavels and more modern concrete huts, most en suite. All the huts are located in a traditional *umuzi* (homestead) with a central fire area for night-time gatherings. The camp offers tours to eMakhosini Valley, the surrounding battlefields and Hluhluwe-Imfolozi Game Park. R600

The Battlefields

Most of the major KwaZulu-Natal Battlefields lie in the northwestern corner of the province, where the Boers first came out of the mountains from the northeast into Zulu territory and inflicted a severe defeat on the Zulus at **Blood River** in 1838, 13km southeast of the tiny town of Utrecht. Some four decades later, the British spoiled for war and marched north to fight a series of battles against the Zulus, the most notable being at **Isandlwana** and **Rorke's Drift** southeast of Dundee.

Twenty years on, Britain again provoked war, this time against the **Boers** of the South African Republic and the Orange Free State to the north and west. In the early stages of the Second Anglo-Boer War (also known as the South African War) the huge, lumbering British machine proved no match for the mobile Boers. At **Ladysmith**, the British endured months of an embarrassing siege, while nearby, at **Spioenkop**, bungling British leadership snatched defeat from the jaws of victory. Although the empire successfully struck back, it took three years to subdue the South African Republic and the Orange Free State, two of the smallest states in the world, after committing half a million troops to the field in an operation that proved to be the costliest campaign since the Napoleonic Wars nearly a century earlier.

If you're only planning to take in one battlefield site, then Isandlwana should be the one, though you really should see Rorke's Drift as well to complete the day; both sites are eerily beautiful.

Isandlwana Battlefield

Off the R68 just over 130km northwest of Eshowe and 70km southeast of Dundee • Mon–Fri 8am–4pm, Sat & Sun 9am–4pm • R20 • ☎ 034 271 8165

On January 22, 1879, the British suffered the most humiliating defeat in their colonial history when virtually their entire force of 1200 men at Isandlwana was obliterated by warriors armed with spears. Dominated by an eerie hill, the **Isandlwana Battlefield** remains unspoilt and unchanged apart from some small homesteads and the graves of those who fell. A small **interpretation centre** houses artefacts and mementos.

The monumental bungling and the scale of the Zulu victory over the British sent shock waves back to London. Following the British ultimatum to the Zulus, three colonial columns were sent to invade Zululand. King Cetshwayo responded by sending a force against each of these. On January 21, 1879, Zulu troops encamped 6km from Isandlwana Hill, where one of the British columns had set up camp. Unaware of the Zulus over the brow, the British commander took a large detachment to support another British force, leaving the men at Isandlwana undefended and unfortified.

BATTLEFIELD GUIDES

Visiting the **Battlefields** with a qualified guide will infinitely enhance the experience. The guides below specialize in different battle sites, usually those closest to their base. Most guides have negotiable fees; expect to pay in the region of R400–700 per person for a day-trip, and many will require you to have your own transport.

The next best thing to hiring a guide is buying an **audio tour** to listen to in your car; these are available from reception at the Talana Museum (see p.437). The late David Rattray's excellent set of CDs *The Day of the Dead Moon*, covering Rorke's Drift and Isandlwana, is available directly from *Fugitive's Drift Lodge* (see p.436). As for reading matter, one of the most authoritative **books** about the Anglo-Boer War is the highly entertaining *Boer War* by Thomas Pakenham (see p.672).

RECOMMENDED GUIDES

Elisabeth Durham ☎ 034 212 1014, ⓦ cheznousbb .com. Informative tours in English and French (R800–1200) of Rorke's Drift, Isandlwana and the route followed by the French Prince Imperial, who fell at Nqutu.

Ron Gold, KwaZulu-Natal Tours ☎ 033 263 1908 or ☎ 083 556 4068, ⓦ kwazulu-natal-tours.com. Gold specializes in the battles of Spioenkop, Willow Grange and Colenso, and the site of Churchill's arrest, offering both half- and full-day tours (R700–1000).

Fugitive's Drift Lodge ☎ 034 642 1843, ⓦ fugitives-drift-lodge.com. David Rattray, the doyen of battlefield guides, was based at this lodge (see p.436) near Rorke's Drift until his untimely murder during a botched robbery. The baton has now been passed to the lodge's other excellent guides, Rob Caskie, Joseph Ndima and George Irwin, who, like Rattray, are great storytellers. Their half-day Isandlwana (departs at 7.30am) and Rorke's Drift (departs at 3pm in winter and 3.15pm in summer) tours cost R910 per person for both battlefields.

Evan Jones ☎ 034 212 4040 or ☎ 082 807 8598, ⓦ battleguide.co.za. Extensive full-day tours of all the Battlefields (from R700 per person) by a guide with a vast repository of knowledge, who breathes life into the battles.

Pat Rundgren ☎ 034 212 4560 or ☎ 082 690 7812, ⓔ gunners@trustnet.co.za. A large, burly man of Scandinavian/Irish descent, Pat provides an alternative perspective on the battles around the Dundee area. Tours cost R390 per person per day, including transport.

Foy Vermaak ☎ 034 642 1925, ⓦ www.pennyf .co.za. Based close to Isandlwana and Rorke's Drift, in which he specializes; he also covers Helpmekaar and Fugitive's Drift. Tour rates are R800 per day for up to four people.

5

Meanwhile, a British scouting party rode to the brow of a hill and was stunned to find the valley filled with some 25,000 Zulu warriors sitting in utter silence. Because of a superstition surrounding the phase of the moon, the Zulus were waiting for a more propitious moment to attack. On being discovered, they rose up and converged on the British encampment using the classic Zulu "horns of the bull" formation to outflank the unprotected British, whom they completely overran.

The British press at the time demonized the Zulus for disembowelling the dead. In fact, the practice had a religious significance for the Zulus, who believed that it released the spirit of the dead. The custom also had a less spiritual significance; a Zulu warrior was required to "wash his spear" (ie kill an enemy) before he was allowed to marry.

Rorke's Drift

Connected by the D30 with Isandlwana, 15km to the east • Field Museum and interpretation centre Mon–Fri 8am–4pm, Sat & Sun 9am–4pm • R20 • ☎ 034 642 1687 • Craft centre Mon–Fri 8am–4pm, Sat & Sun 9am–4pm

The same evening as the Isandlwana battle (see p.435), tattered British honour was restored when a group of British veterans successfully defended the field hospital at **Rorke's Drift**, just across the Buffalo River from the site of the earlier disaster, against four advancing Zulu regiments. Despite Cetshwayo's express orders not to attack Rorke's Drift, three- to four thousand hot-headed young Zulu men were so fired up by the Isandlwana victory and so eager to "wash their spears" – they were part of a reserve force and had not yet seen action – that they launched the assault. For twelve hours spanning January 22 and 23, 1879, just over a hundred British soldiers (many of whom were ill) repulsed repeated attacks by the Zulus and so earned eleven Victoria Crosses – the largest number ever awarded in one battle.

Rorke's Drift is the most rewarding Battlefield to visit on your own, thanks to its excellent **field museum** and interpretation centre. While you're here, it's also worth taking in the **Rorke's Drift ELC Craft Centre**, known for its hand-printed fabrics and tapestries depicting rural scenes.

ACCOMMODATION   THE BATTLEFIELDS

Accommodation around Isandlwana and Rorke's Drift is fairly spread out, most of it in small villages in the area. Many guesthouses offer meals and the owners often double as guides.

BABANANGO

Babanango Lodge Signposted 4km west of Babanango on the R68 ☎ 035 835 0062, ⊛ babanangovalley.co.za. Situated on a Natural Heritage Site deep in a beautiful valley, where you can be taken on walks to explore the veld, rocks and river. With a degree in animal behaviour, the proprietor combines tours of Hluhluwe-Imfolozi Park and ecological topics, including birding and basic tree identification, with Zulu historical sites and the Anglo-Zulu Battlefields. Accommodation is in pleasant en-suite rooms, and there's a swimming pool. Rates include half board. **R1520**

HELPMEKAAR

Penny Farthing Along the R33 south of Rorke's Drift and 30km south of Dundee ☎ 034 642 1925, ⊛ www .pennyf.co.za. Near the minuscule settlement of Helpmekaar, *Penny Farthing* is an historic pioneer farm still furnished with original objects and generations of hunting trophies, set in an area of big open grasslands and hills, crisscrossed with hiking trails. The host Foy Vermaak is a Battlefields guide (see box, p.435) who enjoys fireside chats on the subject, and has a personal collection of memorabilia. **R1100**

NEAR RORKE'S DRIFT

Fugitives' Drift Lodge 9km north of Rorke's Drift along the D31 dirt road ☎ 034 642 1843, ⊛ fugitives-drift-lodge.com. The ultimate Battlefields place to stay, this luxury lodge, located on a huge game farm, overlooks the drift where the few British survivors of Isandlwana fled across the Buffalo River. The colonial-style rooms are in individual cottages that open onto lawns and gardens, and guests eat together in a central dining room among the world's largest Zulu battlefield memorabilia collection. If it's beyond your budget, you can always stay in Dundee and book one of its famous Battlefield tours (see box, p.435). Rates include full board. **R5800**

Dundee

Some 32km west of the Rorke's Drift turn-off, along the R68, **DUNDEE** has little to offer except shops, supermarkets and pharmacies, but does serve as a good base for exploring the surrounding areas.

The Talana Museum

2km outside Dundee on the R33 to Vryheid • Mon–Fri 8am–4.30pm, Sat & Sun 10am–4.30pm • R20 • ☎ 034 212 2654, ⓦ www.talana.co.za

The one thing in Dundee worth seeing is the excellent **Talana Museum**. Under shady blue gums, the museum consists of ten historic whitewashed buildings from the time of the 1899 Battle of Talana Hill, the first engagement of the Anglo-Boer War. The most interesting of these is **Talana House**, which gives information about northern KwaZulu-Natal conflicts including the Anglo-Zulu, Zulu-Boer and Anglo-Boer wars. The displays include weapons and uniforms, but most evocative are the photographs that really personalize the wars and provide fascinating details such as the POW camps Boers were exiled to in far-flung parts of the British Empire, including St Helena and the Far East. Often-neglected aspects of the Anglo-Boer War, including the roles of Africans and Indians, also get some coverage. In a photograph of Indian stretcher-bearers, you may be able to spot the youthful Mohandas Gandhi, who carried wounded British soldiers off the Spioenkop and Colenso Battlefields. Arrangements can be made with the curator for guided tours of the museum and surrounding Battlefields.

ARRIVAL AND DEPARTURE   DUNDEE

By minibus taxi The only public transport to Dundee is minibus taxis, many of which, when coming from the east, require you to change in Vryheid. There are also direct routes to Ladysmith.

INFORMATION

Tourist information Just off Victoria St in Civic Gardens (Mon–Fri 9am–4.30pm; ☎ 034 212 2121, ⓦ tourdundee. co.za). They can recommend local tour guides, and provide information about the various re-enactments staged from time to time to coincide with the anniversaries of famous battles.

ACCOMMODATION

Battlefields Backpackers International 90 Victoria St ☎ 034 212 4040, ⓦ bbibackpackers.co.za. A small hostel offering somewhat cramped but friendly backpackers accommodation in two doubles and two dorms, with a free drink for each new arrival. Worthwhile Battlefield tours are also conducted by owner Evan Jones (see box, p.435). Dorm R140, double R270

Chez Nous 39 Tatham St ☎ 034 212 1014, ⓦ cheznousbb.com. You can stay on a B&B or self-catering basis at Chez Nous, run by gregarious French hostess Elisabeth Durham, who cooks delicious three-course dinners on request, and also leads tours of the Battlefields (see box, p.435). Rooms come in the form of spacious doubles or cottages sleeping up to six. R500

Lennox Cottage 3km east of town on the R68 ☎ 034 218 2201, ⓦ lennox.co.za. Advance booking is essential at the unpretentious and comfortable *Lennox Cottage*, on an organic farm run by former rugby Springbok Dirk Froneman and his wife, Salome, who cooks good dinners. R600

EATING

Phumula Coffee Shop In Pick 'n Pay Centre ☎ 034 212 1897. It's worth dropping by this quirky café for their good breakfasts – ranging from omelettes to smoked kippers and mince on toast (R20–30) – or to sample one of their four different flavours of cappuccino (try marshmallow). Mon–Fri 7.30am–4.30pm, Sat 7.30am–1pm.

Ncome Blood River

The battle of Blood River takes its name from reports that the Ncome River turned red with blood when, on December 16, 1838, Andries Pretorius' band of 470 Voortrekkers barricaded themselves behind their wagons and defeated an army of 10,000 to 15,000 Zulu soldiers commanded by King Dingane. The resulting Zulu casualties numbered in the thousands, according to official counts, while the Voortrekkers suffered nothing

5

more than injuries. Although the event has become a defining moment for Afrikaner nationalists, some historians argue that the number of Zulu dead was most likely inflated by the victors. Today the battlefield is the site of an impressive Boer monument, plus a museum that presents a much more balanced perspective on events.

Blood River Battlefield

48km from Dundee on the way to Vryheid, off the R33 • Daily 8am–4.30pm • R20 • ☎ 034 632 1695

You can't fail to be amazed by the monument at the **Blood River Battlefield**. Of all the Afrikaner quasi-religious shrines across the country, this definitely takes the biscuit, comprising a replica laager of 64 life-size bronze wagons on the site. During the apartheid years, this date was celebrated by Afrikaners as the **Day of the Vow**, a public holiday honouring a supposed covenant made by the Boers with God himself that if he granted them victory, they would hold the day sacred. Afrikaners still visit the monument on this day, but under the new government the public holiday has been recycled as the **Day of Reconciliation**, with Blood River also referred to by its Zulu name, Ncome.

Ncome Monument and Museum Complex

On the eastern side of Ncome Blood River • Daily 8am–4.30pm • Free • ☎ 034 271 8121, ⊕ ncomemuseum.org.za

The **Ncome Monument and Museum Complex**, across the river from the Blood River Monument, does a good job presenting the Zulu side of the conflict, with its horn-shaped design inspired by the Zulu martial formation. Exhibits include a display about battle strategy, and a reed garden relating the importance of river reeds in Zulu life. Taken together with the Boer monument, the museum illustrates the difficulties inherent in South African historical memory.

Ladysmith

LADYSMITH, 61km south of Dundee on the N11, owes its modest fame to one of the worst sieges in British military history nearly a century ago – the best reason to linger is to learn about the Anglo-Boer War at the Ladysmith Siege Museum – and more recently to **Ladysmith Black Mambazo**, the local vocal group that helped Paul Simon revive a flagging career in the mid-1980s.

It's easy enough to walk around Ladysmith's small centre; **Murchison Street** is the main artery running through town, where you'll find banks, the post office and shops.

Ladysmith Siege Museum

Corner of Queen and Murchison sts • Mon–Fri 9am–4pm, Sat 9am–1pm • R11 • ☎ 036 637 2992

The **Ladysmith Siege Museum** is the obvious starting point for any tour of the Anglo-Boer Battlefields. The siege began on November 2, 1899, and lasted 118 days, with twelve thousand British troops suffering the indignity of being pinned down by undisciplined farmers. This compelling little museum tells the story of the war through text and photographs, conveying the appalling conditions during the siege as well as key points in a war that helped shape twentieth-century South Africa, paving the way for its unification. The museum is also a good place to browse books about the war, written from both the British and Boer points of view.

ARRIVAL AND DEPARTURE   LADYSMITH

By bus Greyhound Johannesburg–Durban buses pull in at the Guineafowl Service Station on Murchison St.
By train The train station (☎ 036 271 2020) is 500m east of the town hall on Lyell St, but arrival and departure times during the night make the train an unrealistic option.

INFORMATION AND TOURS

Tourist information At the Siege Museum (Mon–Fri 9am–4pm, Sat 9am–1pm; ☎ 036 637 2992).
Tours Local battlefields tour guide Liz Spiret (☎ 036 637 7702 or ☎ 072 262 9669, ✉ lizs@telkomsa.net) charges R900 for up to four people (you need to have your own transport).

ACCOMMODATION

Budleigh House 12 Berea Rd ⓣ036 635 7700, ⓔslabb12@telkomsa.net. Rooms at this elegant guesthouse are pleasantly decorated, featuring wooden floors and a subtle African feel. There's also a pool and sunny patio on which to enjoy the lovely garden. **R630**

Bullers Rest Lodge 59/61 Cove Crescent ⓣ036 637 6154, ⓦbullersrestlodge.co.za. A smart thatched establishment with cosy, country-style furnishings and a large wooden deck overlooking town. The on-site pub is filled with original battlefield artefacts. Dinners and packed lunches available on request. **R700**

Hunters' Lodge 6 Hunter St ⓣ036 637 2359, ⓔjem@futurenet.co.za. This lovely old home is located in a peaceful neighbourhood and has fifteen en-suite rooms surrounded by a well-manicured garden. Dinners are available on request. **R900**

Royal Hotel 140 Murchison St ⓣ036 637 2176, ⓦroyalhotel.co.za. In the heart of town, this is the hotel that harboured the upper classes during the siege – and was regularly shelled by the Boers. Now a mid-range establishment catering mainly to travelling reps, it's full during the week, which makes booking essential at any time of year. It can be noisy due to traffic. **R935**

EATING

Royal Hotel 140 Murchison St. The restaurant at the *Royal Hotel* was patronized in former times by the more privileged of the besieged, including Frank Rhodes (brother of the more famous Cecil). It is still the best place to eat in town, though the food – mostly pub fare and steaks – is not particularly sophisticated (most mains R60–90).

Spioenkop

35km west of Ladysmith • Spioenkop Battlefield daily 9am–3pm • R20 • ⓣ036 637 2992 • Spioenkop Nature Reserve daily: April–Sept 6am–6pm, Oct–March 5am–7pm • R20 • ⓣ036 488 1578

Spioenkop Battlefield is set in the Spioenkop Nature Reserve. The bloodiest of all the Anglo-Boer War battles, Spioenkop took more British lives than any other and taught the British command that wars fought by means of set-piece battles were no longer viable. After this, the guerrilla-style tactics of modern warfare were increasingly adopted.

Some 1700 British troops took the hill under cover of a mist without firing a shot, but were able to dig only shallow trenches because the surface was so hard. When the mist lifted they discovered that they had misjudged the crest of the hill, but their real failure was one of flawed command and desperately poor intelligence. Had the British reconnoitred properly, they might have discovered that they were facing a motley collection of fewer than 500 Boers with only seven pieces of artillery, and they could have called in their 1600 reserves to relieve them. Despite holding lower ground, the Boers were able to keep the British, crammed eight men per metre into their trenches, pinned down for an entire sweltering midsummer day. Around six hundred British troops perished and were buried where they fell on the so-called "acre of massacre".

Meanwhile the Boers, who were aware of the British reinforcements at the base of the hill, had gradually been drifting off, and, by the end of the day, unbeknownst to the British, there were only 350 Boers left. In the evening the British withdrew, leaving the hill to the enemy.

Today you can stand at the summit of the rocky hill and look out over the desolate battlefield, where small plaques mark out the positions of the two sides. A mass grave marks the final resting place of hundreds of fallen British troops.

ACCOMMODATION — SPIOENKOP

KZN Wildlife Ipika Bush Camp On the slopes of Spioenkop Mountain ⓣ036 488 1578. This simple bush camp consists of just one four-bed safari tent and campsites. There's a minimum charge for three people for the tent. Camping **R128**, safari tent **R610**

Three Tree Hill Lodge Adjoining the reserve ⓣ036 448 1171, ⓦthreetreehill.co.za. Tours of the battlefield and outdoor activities, including wildlife-spotting, can be arranged at this colonially stylish lodge. Each room has its own veranda overlooking the valley, and a spacious two-bedroom suite is available for families. Rates include full board. **R3780**

Free State

AARDVARK EMERGING FROM BURROW

Free State

The Maloti Route, one of South Africa's most scenic drives, skirts the mountainous eastern flank of the Free State, the traditional heartland of conservative Afrikanerdom, which lies landlocked at the centre of the country. If you're driving from Johannesburg to Eastern or Western Cape, the Eastern Highlands, which sweep up to the subcontinent's highest peaks in the Lesotho Drakensberg, are worth the detour. Bloemfontein, the capital, is only worth visiting if you are passing through, but once there you'll find very good guesthouses, restaurants and museums. Closer to Johannesburg, the riverside town of Parys is a pleasant rural escape that long ago was ground zero for a massive meteorite impact.

6

The highlight of the Eastern Highlands is the **Golden Gate National Park**, designated as such for the beauty of the Maloti Mountains, with their stripy red sandstone outcrops. Southeast of Golden Gate you can drive to the Sentinel car park – access point for hikes up to the highest plateaus of the Drakensberg – via the interesting **Basotho Cultural Village**. West of Golden Gate is **Clarens**, by far the nicest of the string of towns along the Lesotho border. In the rest of the province, flat farmlands roll away into kilometres of bright-yellow sunflowers and mauve- and pink-petalled cosmos, with maize and wheat fields glowing under immense blue skies.

Brief history

Intriguing though it sounds, the name "Free State" applies to former redneck country. For nearly 150 years, the only free people in the Free State were its white settlers, who in 1854 were granted independence from Britain in a territory between the Orange and Vaal rivers, where they created a Boer Republic called the **Orange Free State**. The "Orange" part of the name came from the royal Dutch House of Orange. The system of government in the republic, inspired by the US Constitution, was highly democratic – if you were white and male. Women couldn't vote, while Africans had no rights at all, and were even forbidden from owning land. In 1912 the ANC was formed in the Bloemfontein township of Batho, while the Nationalist Party was founded two years later in Bloemfontein itself. In 1914, the Orange Free State became a bastion of apartheid, being the only province to ban anyone of Asian descent from remaining within its borders for longer than 24 hours. Africans fared little better; in 1970, under the grand apartheid scheme, a tiny barren enclave wedged between Lesotho, KwaZulu-Natal and the Free State became QwaQwa, a "homeland" for Southern Sotho people – a result of forced clearances from white-designated areas. The Bantustans have since been reincorporated into South Africa and, after an ANC landslide in Free State province in the 1994 elections, the "Orange" part of the name, with its Dutch Calvinist associations, was dropped.

GOLDEN GATE HIGHLANDS NATIONAL PARK (P.449)

Highlights

❶ Maloti Route A scenic drive skirting the Lesotho border, past massive rock formations, cherry orchards and sandstone farming towns, including the delightful artist town of Clarens. **See p.448**

❷ Basotho vernacular architecture See the decorative adobe huts typical of the Eastern Free State and Lesotho at the Basotho Cultural Village, and spend the night in a comfortable rondavel. **See p.448**

❸ Drakensberg Escarpment Catch some of South Africa's most spectacular mountain views by climbing to the highest point on the escarpment via a chain ladder. **See p.450**

❹ Golden Gate Highlands National Park Hike or drive through this stunning reserve, dominated by the beautiful Maloti Mountains with their stripy red sandstone outcrops. **See p.449**

❺ Parys Tour the remnants of the massive impact dome made by a meteorite two billion years ago, or simply relax in the town centre, shop for antiques, eat vetkoek and paddle down the Vaal River. **See p.454**

HIGHLIGHTS ARE MARKED ON THE MAP ON P.444

Bloemfontein

BLOEMFONTEIN, part of Mangaung municipality, is located at the crossroads of South Africa, which means that many travellers break their journey across the country here. Despite its reputation as the hick capital of South Africa, Bloem (or "flower", as it is lovingly called) is actually quite agreeable, and there's enough diversion for a day or two. The city's surprisingly fine Oliewenhuis Art Museum is set in beautiful gardens, while the unmistakably provincial President Brand Street is lined with handsome, sandstone public buildings paying a pick 'n' mix homage to Mediterranean, British, Renaissance and Classical influences. Bloem is also the seat of the provincial parliament and South Africa's Court of Appeal.

As an overnight stop, the city offers good accommodation at reasonable prices, upmarket shopping centres and a couple of nightlife opportunities. In common with other South African cities, the white population has deserted the city centre. Instead, the suburbs just northwest of the city centre have become the place to shop and hang out. The Loch Logan Waterfront Mall beside the stadium and Westdene's four-storey Mimosa Mall in nearby Kellner Street provide coffee shops, chain restaurants, banks, bookshops and more.

If you're around in August, visit the Castle Granaat Rock Festival at the Oliewenhuis Art Museum, which sees popular South African bands perform in a very family-friendly atmosphere. In October, try to catch the ten-day Manguang African Cultural Festival (🌐macufe.co.za), which fills the city with storytelling, poetry, art, music and dance, and attracts people from all over the country.

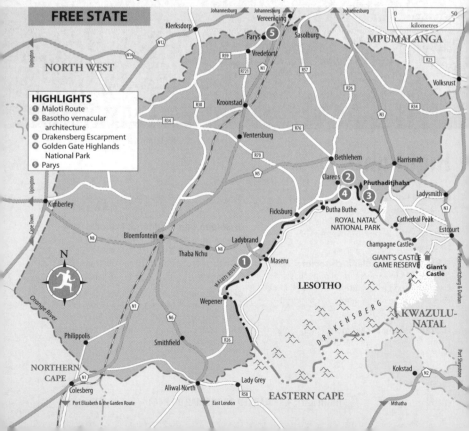

FREE STATE

HIGHLIGHTS
❶ Maloti Route
❷ Basotho vernacular architecture
❸ Drakensberg Escarpment
❹ Golden Gate Highlands National Park
❺ Parys

President Brand Street

For a rewarding stroll in the centre, head down **President Brand Street**, starting at the City Hall at the north end on the corner of Charles Street. Built in 1934, the building was designed in the "new tradition style" by Gordon Leith, a former employee of Sir Herbert Baker, and features large animal skulls above the windows.

South of the City Hall stands the Roman-style Court of Appeal of South Africa, built in 1929. Staring at it from across the road is the imposing sandstone and red-brick Fourth Raadsaal from 1890, the last parliament building of the independent Orange Free State republic (it's now the provincial legislature). Further south on the corner of Selborne Avenue is the Supreme Court, completed in 1906. The Old Presidency, opposite, was built on the site of the home of **Major Henry Warden**, the founder of Bloemfontein. It was built in 1861 in "Scottish baronial style" as the official seat of the head of the republic.

National Museum

36 Aliwal St • Mon–Fri 8am–5pm, Sat 10am–5pm, Sun noon–5.30pm • R5 • ⓦ www.nasmus.co.za

To the east of President Brand Street is the **National Museum**, well worth a visit for its good dinosaur fossil collection, the 260,000-year-old Florisbad human skull and an impressive reconstruction of a turn-of-the-twentieth-century Bloemfontein street.

First Raadsaal

95 St George's St • Mon–Fri 10am–1pm, Sat & Sun 2–5pm • Free • ⓦ www.nasmus.co.za

Bloemfontein's oldest building, the **First Raadsaal** is a small thatched pioneer cottage that was built by Warden (see above) as the town's first school, but used later as an assembly hall for the first parliament. Inside, and in a grander adjacent building, is a dry exhibition on the history of the establishment of Free State.

King's Park

The small **King's Park** gardens are wedged between Loch Logan and the zoo, and are a lovely spot for a picnic, especially when the thousands of roses are in bloom in summer.

Bloemfontein Zoo

Daily: summer 8am–6pm; winter 8am–5pm • R32

Occupying the western half of King's Park, **Bloemfontein Zoo** is a reasonable place to see the Big Five, hippos, tigers and antelope. It's well known for the breeding programme it had in the past for the liger, a cross between a lion and a tiger, no longer on view.

The waterfront and stadium

Built on the opposite site of Loch Logan lake to the zoo, the **Loch Logan Waterfront Mall** boasts shops, cafés, several chain restaurants and a cinema; unfortunately many of its independent waterfront restaurants have closed since the 2010 football World Cup. Connected to the mall is the **Vodacom Stadium**, used mainly for rugby.

National Women's Monument and War Museum

Monument Rd • Mon–Fri 8.30am–4.30pm, Sat 10am–5pm, Sun 2–5pm • R5 • ⓦ anglo-boer.co.za

Just over 2km south of the centre, in an industrial part of town, a sandstone needle pointing skywards marks the **National Women's Monument and War Museum**. This stands as a memorial to the 26,370 Afrikaner women and children who died in British concentration camps during the second Anglo-Boer War. The suffering depicted in the museum isn't an exaggeration, but it is a little heavy-handed. Two cursory panels on

6

WESTDENE

3, 4, ❶, Waverley & Oliewenhuis Art Museum ▲ Naval Hill

■ BARS & CLUBS

Barba's Café	3
Cubaña	1
Moods and Flavours	4
Mystic Boer	2

Freshford
House
Museum

Zoo
Loch
Logan

Loch Logan
Waterfront
Mall

City
Hall

Mangaung
Stadium

Hertzog
Square

National
Museum

Appeal Court

Fourth
Raadsaal

Intercity
Bus Stop

The Old
Presidency

Supreme
Court of Appeal

First
Raadsaal

Minibus
Taxi Rank

Train
Station

■ ACCOMMODATION

Bohemian Guest House	1
Canada House	4
Cherry Tree Cottage	3
City Lodge	6
De Oude Kraal Country Lodge	9
Halevy Heritage Hotel	8
Hobbit Boutique Hotel	2
Kleine Eden Guest House	5
The Urban	7

N

BLOEMFONTEIN

0   500
metres

● RESTAURANTS & CAFÉS

Coco C	4
Karma	2
Seven on Kellner	3
The Terrace	1

▼ National Women's Monument & War Memorial

concentration camps for Africans are a post-apartheid afterthought that at least provide a partial record of the more than 14,000 black South Africans who died incarcerated.

Oliewenhuis Art Museum

16 Harry Smith St, 2km north of the centre off Aliwal St • Mon–Fri 8am–5pm, Sat 10am–5pm, Sun 1–5pm • Free • ⓦ www.nasmus .co.za

The best of Bloemfontein's museums, the Oliewenhuis Art Museum's collection – which includes a surprisingly good range of South African sculpture and painting – is housed in the former residency of South African presidents, a beautifully light, neo-Cape Dutch manor set in large, attractive gardens, surrounded by wild bush traversed by short walking trails. Even if you're not interested in the gallery, it's still worth having tea at the café on the lawn – its trees and fountain make it the most harmonious location in town, and there's art here too, most notably the quirky African Carousel.

Freshford House Museum

31 Kellner St • Mon–Fri 10am–1pm, Sat & Sun 2–5pm • R10 • ⓦ www.nasmus.co.za

To the north of the city centre, just across Nelson Mandela Drive, the Freshford House Museum is a beautifully maintained Edwardian house from 1897, which was designed and inhabited by architect John Edwin Harrisson. The interior has been refurbished impeccably in Victorian and Edwardian style, giving great insight into the daily life of that era.

ARRIVAL AND DEPARTURE   BLOEMFONTEIN

Situated in the centre of the country and along the main route from Johannesburg to Cape Town, Bloemfontein is well connected to all South Africa's major cities as well as to Lesotho.

By bus Translux, Intercape, SA Roadlink and Greyhound buses pull in at the central bus terminal in the tourist complex on Park Rd, 1km south of Loch Logan mall.
Destinations: Cape Town (10 daily; 12hr); Durban (3 daily; 9hr); East London (2 daily; 8hr 30min); Johannesburg (16 daily; 5hr); Maseru Bridge (daily; 2hr); Mossel Bay (daily; 9hr 30min); Pietermaritzburg (3 daily; 8hr); Port Elizabeth (2 daily; 9hr); Pretoria (13 daily; 7hr); Upington (2 weekly; 7hr 30min).
By plane The small airport (☎051 407 2240) is located 10km east of town on the N8; there are pricey SAA flights between here and the major cities, and budget flights to

Johannesburg and Cape Town by Mango. There are no regular shuttle buses from the airport into town, so your only choice is to hail or phone for a taxi, or rent a car. The following agencies are based at the airport: Avis ☎051 433 2331, Budget ☎051 433 1178, Europcar ☎051 433 3511, Hertz ☎051 400 2100.
Destinations: Cape Town (4–5 daily; 1hr 45min); Durban (1–2 daily; 1hr); Johannesburg (5–10 daily ; 1hr).
By train Trains operate from Bloemfontein Station (☎086 000 8888) on Harvey Rd, at the east end of Maitland St.
Destinations: Johannesburg (Wed, Fri & Sun; 7hr); Port Elizabeth (Wed, Fri, Sun; 13hr).

GETTING AROUND

By taxi The taxi rank lies one block west of the train station on Hanger St. The area around the station and the minibus taxi rank is regarded by some residents as the dodgiest in the city centre, but there have been few actual

incidents; stay alert, and avoid the area at night. Fortunately, metered taxis usually gather outside the train and bus stations; alternatively, you can phone for one (Bloem Taxis ☎051 433 3776; GG Taxis ☎051 522 6969).

INFORMATION

Tourist information Inside the tourist complex and bus terminal on Park Rd (Mon–Fri 8am–4.15pm, Sat 8am–

noon; ☎051 405 8489, ⊛mangaung.co.za).

ACCOMMODATION

Bloemfontein's accommodation is cheaper than Cape Town and Johannesburg and is of a high standard. The more central suburbs of Westdene and Waverley, both just north of the centre, are the best areas to stay in. Most places offer breakfast as an extra, since many travellers leave early in the morning for the next, long, leg of the N1. If you are driving through and need a bed for the night, do ring guesthouses in advance, rather than just turning up.

Cherry Tree Cottage 12A Peter Crescent, Waverley ☎051 436 4334 or ☎072 291 0336; map p.446. A peaceful, a/c B&B set in a beautifully landscaped garden and bordering a reserve with resident giraffe. The four bedrooms each have their own separate entrances. R700

Halevy Heritage Hotel Corner Markgraaff and Charles Sts ☎051 403 0600, ⊛halevyheritage.com; map p.446. Well over a century old, the city-centre *Halevy* was built as an inn for theatre-goers and now mainly sees business visitors using its small but well-equipped rooms. R1270

TOLKIEN IN BLOEMFONTEIN

Bloemfontein's biggest surprise is that it's the birthplace of **John Ronald Reuel Tolkien**, author of *The Lord of the Rings* and *The Hobbit*, a fact the city seems curiously reluctant to publicize. Tolkien's father, Arthur, left his native Birmingham to work in the colonies, eventually becoming manager of the Bank of Africa in Bloemfontein. J.R.R. was born in 1892, in a house standing on the corner of West Burger and Maitland streets, a couple of blocks east of President Brand Street. When Arthur Tolkien died three years after J.R.R.'s birth, his wife returned to England with her two infant sons; their house was later torn down to make way for a furniture shop.

6

Hobbit Boutique Hotel 19 President Steyn Ave, Westdene ☏ 051 447 0663, ⓦ hobbit.co.za; map p.446. Inspired by Tolkien's *The Hobbit*, this is the best place to stay in Bloemfontein; a luxurious establishment filled with beautiful and comfortable antique furniture, with teddy bears tucked into every bed under handmade quilts. Excellent three-course dinners are available for guests (phone by lunchtime). Book well in advance. **R1100**
Kleine Eden Guest House 2 Moffett St, Fichardt Park ☏ 051 525 2633, ⓦ kleine-eden.co.za; map p.446. Well-maintained guesthouse with B&B, self-catering and family units. Rooms all have their own entrance and private garden. Breakfast extra. **R650**
The Urban 101 Parfitt St, Park West ☏ 051 444 3142, ⓦ urbanhotel.co.za; map p.446. A slick and surprisingly affordable designer hotel decorated in white, black and red. Rooms are small, functional and stylish, and a decent breakfast is included. **R700**

EATING AND DRINKING

While Bloemfontein is no culinary capital and there are few regional specialities to sample, you can still have a good and inexpensive meal here. You'll also find the usual restaurant chains scattered around the centre and in the shopping malls. Westdene's Second Avenue has a handful of restaurants and is safe to stroll about at night. There's no English-language newspaper so ask a local to translate the Afrikaans-language listings in the *Volksblad* newspaper to find out what's going on in Bloemfontein.

Barba's Café 16 Second Ave, Westdene ☏ 051 430 2542; map p.446. Serves excellent Greek food in buffets or à la carte dining, but is mainly known for its Saturday-night bashes which go on into the small hours. Daily noon–1am.
Cubaña Corner of Second Ave and President Reitz St, Westdene ☏ 051 447 1920; map p.446. A bustling Latino restaurant and bar serving up large portions of decent food. Later on in the evenings, cocktails are served and DJs play Latino music. Wednesday is a rowdy student night. Mon–Sat 8am–2am, Sun 11am–2am.
Karma 87a Kellner St, Westdene ☏ 051 448 8836; map p.446. A beautifully converted house with decorated ceilings and a huge menu, serving tasty breakfasts, burgers, grilled meat and fish, curries and the greasy local *vetkoek* (deep-fried pastry). Mon–Fri 7am–10pm, Sat 7am–3pm, Sun 11am–2pm.
Moods and Flavors 62 Parish Ave, Heidedal ☏ 051 432 4399, ⓦ moodsandflavors.co.za; map p.446. An excellent and rather upmarket jazz bar in a mixed district

east of the centre, with easy-going patrons. Live jazz from all over the country is performed a few times per month; call to find out what's on. People dress up for a really good time here. Daily noon–1am.
Mystic Boer 84 Kellner St, Westdene; map p.446. A great place to down a few tequilas, with pizzas available to snack on, and different music styles and special offers throughout the week. There's live music on Wednesdays. The best place in town for a night out. Mon–Sat 2pm–2am, Sun 5pm–midnight.
Seven on Kellner 7 Kellner St, Westdene ☏ 051 447 7928; map p.446. Upmarket dining in a fine old house, with a short but inventive menu that includes grilled meat and fish as well as pizza. Mon–Fri noon–11pm, Sat 6–11pm.
The Terrace 16 Harry Smith St; map p.446. Tables in the formal gardens of the Oliewenhuis Art Museum, leading onto a nature reserve, make this Bloemfontein's nicest place for afternoon tea and cake. Tues–Sat 9am–5pm, Sun 10am–5pm.

DIRECTORY

Emergencies ☏ 051 404 6225.
Hospitals The main state hospital is Universitas (☏ 051 405 3911), offering a free 24hr emergency ward, but you may wait hours and the level of care is variable. The private hospitals are a better choice: Medi-Clinic, Kellner St ☏ 051 404 6666; Rosepark Hospital, Fichmed Centre, Gustav

Crescent ☏ 051 505 5911.
Pharmacies Dis-Chem, Loch Logan Waterfront mall, First Ave (Mon–Fri 9am–6pm, Sat 9am–5pm, Sun 10am–2pm).
Post office Corner of Oos Burger and Maitland sts (Mon, Tues, Thurs & Fri 8am–4.30pm, Wed 8.30am–4.30pm, Sat 8am–noon).

The Maloti Route

Hugging the Lesotho border for 280km from Phuthaditjhaba (Witsieshoek) in the north to Wepener in the south, the tarred **Maloti Route** offers one of South Africa's most scenic drives, taking you past massive rock formations streaked with red and ochre, cherry orchards and sandstone farming towns. Wedged into a corner between Lesotho and northern KwaZulu-Natal, **Phuthaditjhaba** is the gateway to the Sentinel,

> **HIKING THE DRAKENSBERG AMPHITHEATRE**
>
> The easiest hiking access onto the high **Drakensberg Escarpment** and some of South Africa's most dramatic mountain scenery can be found just southeast of the Golden Gate park. A five-hour return hike leads past two metal ladders to the top of the chunky **Sentinel Peak**, with fantastic views of the Drakensberg amphitheatre and the Tugela waterfall, at 948m the second highest in the world. The starting point is at the Sentinel car park, near the *Witsieshoek Mountain Lodge*, south of Phuthaditjhaba; this can only be reached with private transport.

6

from where it's easy to hike the Drakensberg Escarpment. Not far to the west is the highlight of the region, the **Golden Gate Highlands National Park**, encompassing wide-open mountain country. The park is an easy three- to four-hour drive from Johannesburg, which means you could easily use it as a first- or last-night stop if you're arriving or leaving from Johannesburg and don't want to spend the night in the city. Nearby, the **Basotho Cultural Village** is worth visiting to gain some insight into Basotho traditions. The closest village to the Golden Gate Park is **Clarens**, a centre for arts and crafts and the most attractive of all the villages along the route.

Basotho Cultural Village

20km east of Golden Gate National Park and signposted from the main Rd • Mon–Fri 8.45am–4pm, Sat & Sun 9am–4pm (last tours at 3.30pm) • R60 • ☎ 058 721 0300, ✉ basotho@sac.fs.gov.za

The **Basotho Cultural Village** is a great place to learn about the traditional lives of the Basotho people, who have lived in the vicinity and just across the border in Lesotho for centuries. The main display in the reconstructed village is a courtyard of beautiful Basotho huts, from organic circular sixteenth-century constructions to square huts with tin roofs, bright interior decor and European blankets and utensils. Visitors are taken on a tour run by actors in traditional dress, meeting the chief, sampling traditional beer, hearing musicians play and seeing a traditional healer; you also learn about the curious spiral aloe, plants unique to the Drakensberg.

The views across the surrounding **QwaQwa Nature Park** are awesome, and there's an endless choice of walks and pony rides. The curio shop sells some quality local crafts (look out for raffia mats and baskets and the conical hats unique to this area), and the open-air tea garden serves teas and traditional food.

You can stay the night here in some traditional Basotho rondavel huts with views over the plain (see p.451).

Golden Gate Highlands National Park

300km northeast of Bloemfontein on the R712 • R100/day for hiking, driving through is free • ☎ 058 255 1000, 🌐 sanparks.org/parks/golden_gate

The **Golden Gate Highlands National Park** was designated for its outstanding beauty rather than its wildlife. Although eland, zebra, mountain reedbuck and black wildebeest roam the hillsides, the real attraction here is the unfettered space, eroded sandstone bastions and seamless blue skies. These rocks, grassy plateaus and incised valleys belong to the Drakensberg range (see p.398), characterized here by spectacular yellow and red cliffs and overhangs.

A number of hour-long rambles into the sandstone ravines start from a direction board near the footbridge at the *Glen Reenen Rest Camp*. There aren't many medium-length hikes in the park, the only exception being a sometimes steep and physically challenging half-day walk up Wodehouse Kop, which offers great views. The most strenuous hike, available for groups only, is the demanding two-day circular Rhebok Trail, which reaches the highest and lowest points of the park; hikers need to book the basic overnight

6

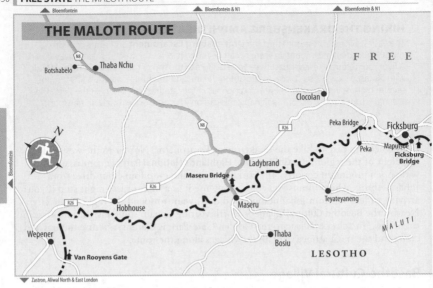

accommodation through South African National Parks (see p.65). In the summer you can swim in a natural waterfall pool close to the *Glen Reenen* campsite; other activities at Golden Gate include horseriding, fossil tours, scenic drives and hiking trails, all arranged via the *Glen Reenen* reception. For those quickly driving through, two asphalted loops signposted off the main road take in fields populated by zebra and antelope, a carcass-strewn vulture feeding spot, and stunning views of the highest peaks of the Drakensberg.

ARRIVAL AND DEPARTURE

BASOTHO CULTURAL VILLAGE

Occasional **minibus taxis** along the R712 between Clarens and Phuthaditjhaba via the Golden Gate Park drop visitors off at the access road to the Basotho Cultural Village, from where it's a 2km walk.

HIKING UP THE DRAKENSBERG ESCARPMENT

South Africa's most spectacular mountain views are from the **Drakensberg Escarpment**, the broad area right at the top of the major peaks, and from the top of the **Amphitheatre**, the grand sweep of mountains dominating the Royal Natal National Park. Both of these require a high level of fitness to reach if approached from KwaZulu-Natal (see p.402) but can be achieved relatively easily via the Free State from the Sentinel car park. A tough ten-hour climb from the Mahai campsite in the Royal Natal National Park (see p.409), or a 2.5-hour walk from the Sentinel car park brings you to the foot of a 30m-high chain ladder leading up an almost vertical face; from the top, you can make the final short onslaught to the highest peak on the escarpment (3278m). Don't be lulled by your apparently easy conquest: it's the Berg's prerogative to have the last word. Always tackle the ladder with enough food, water, clothes and a tent in which to sit out violent storms, and set out early so you have the whole day for the excursion.

For those bitten by the mountain bug, some serious hikes are available, including a two-week trek along the escarpment plateau to Sani Pass in the southern Drakensberg. You can also take in the most dramatic parts of the Berg on a five-day, 62km escarpment traverse, sleeping in caves, from the Sentinel car park to Cathedral Peak in the Natal Drakensberg Park, roughly 40km to the southwest. For any hikes of this nature you'll need a map and the excellent *Best Walks of the Drakensberg* by David Bristow (see p.674), available in most bookshops.

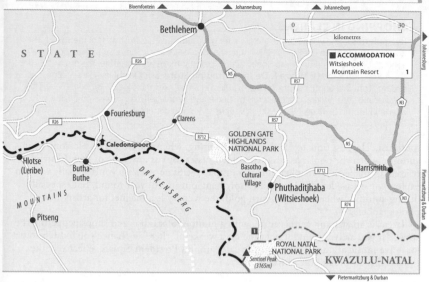

GOLDEN GATE

Golden Gate is almost equidistant from Bloemfontein and Johannesburg (320km to the north on good, tarred roads), and is easily reached from either city. There are no entry gates to the park, which is open 24 hours.

ACCOMMODATION

BASOTHO CULTURAL VILLAGE

Basotho Cultural Village Rest Camp ☎058 721 0300, ✉basotho@sac.fs.gov.za. The newly renovated self-catering rondavels in the beautifully situated museum village offer magnificent views over the plains. **R600**

THE ESCARPMENT

Witsieshoek Mountain Lodge End of the R57 Rd ☎058 713 6361 or ☎073 228 7391, ⓦwitsieshoek. co.za. Currently being upgraded after years of neglect, the lodge is spectacularly set at 2283m above sea level, making it the highest lodge in the country. It has functional rooms in chalets and bungalows, some with excellent views of the mountains. A restaurant and an indoor pool are also planned. **R780**

GOLDEN GATE

The *Golden Gate Hotel* has a restaurant and the rest camp has a basic shop, but otherwise all accommodation is self-catering – and the nearest alternative for food is Clarens, 20km away, which is also the place to head if all accommodation is full at the park (see below).

Glen Reenen Rest Camp ☎012 428 9111 or ☎058 255 1000 on the day, ⓦsanparks.org. In the centre of the park, but unfortunately right beside a road that has truck traffic all night. Camping, rondavels and basic four-bed cottages (R1100) are available. As well as the provisions store, there's also a swimming pool, picnic sites and a filling station. Camping **R145**, rondavel **R635**

Golden Gate Hotel ☎012 428 9111 or ☎058 255 1000 on the day, ⓦsanparks.org. Recently modernized, this is the smartest place to stay in the park, with well-equipped self-catering chalets and comfortable B&B rooms, most with fantastic views. Breakfast and dinner are available on request. **R840**

Highlands Mountain Retreat ☎012 428 9111 or ☎058 255 1000 on the day, ⓦsanparks.org. Away from the crowds, and beautifully located in the foothills off the Oribi Loop Rd, the *Highlands Mountain Retreat* offers luxury family log cabins and double rooms. **R1025**

Clarens

Some 20km west of Golden Gate Highlands National Park lies the tree-fringed village of **CLARENS**, the most appealing of the settlements along the Maloti Route. Founded in 1912, Clarens is especially remarkable for its dressed stone architecture, which glows under the sandstone massif of the Rooiberge (Red Mountains) and the Malotis to the

6

SHOPPING IN CLARENS

The **galleries** in the village centre are great for gifts and souvenirs. Just west of the square, the excellent **Bibliophile** bookshop (313 Church St; Mon–Sat 9am–4.30pm, Sun 10am–3pm) is a good place to stock up on photo books, fiction, Lesotho maps and literature. The most charming shop is the **Di Mezza & De Jager Trading Store** (Sias Oosthuizen Street; Mon–Sat 8.30am–1pm & 2–5pm), signposted as "The Blanket Shop" near the *Maluti Mountain Lodge*. This genuine old-style general dealer's is run by Gertie and Minnie who can advise on quality woollen Basotho blankets (R300–900) in various styles and patterns.

---

southeast. The best time to see the village is spring, when the fruit trees blossom, or in autumn, when the poplar leaves turn golden russet. But at any time of year, Clarens' relaxed air makes it a rare phenomenon in the Free State – a *dorp* you'd actually want to explore, or sip a sidewalk lager and simply hang out in. All year round, but especially during autumn, when the leaves turn gold, the scenery is a magnet for artists and photographers.

Clarens is an arts and crafts centre, with a number of studios and shops peppering the streets. If you arrive around lunchtime on a weekend, there's a chance you'll catch some local live music at one of the streetside cafés around President Square, effectively the town centre in the middle of Main Street.

INFORMATION
CLARENS

Tourist information Market St, just off President Square (☎ 058 256 1813; Mon–Fri 9am–4pm, Sat & Sun 9am–7pm).

Clarens Destinations is a useful accommodation booking and information service (☎ 058 256 1189 or 1542, or ☎ 082 921 8611, ⊛ goclarens.co.za).

ACCOMMODATION

Clarens Inn 93 Van Reenen St ☎ 058 256 1173 or ☎ 082 377 3621, ⊜ schwim@netactive.co.za. The cheapest place to stay, with the choice between a functional dorm, camping, tepees, a very basic honeymoon suite and a range of equally basic self-catering units sleeping up to six people (R150/person). Camping R50, dorm R100, suite R300
Cottage Pie 89 Malherbe St ☎ 058 256 1214 or ☎ 082 853 5947, ⊛ cottagepiebb.co.za. One of the town's best B&Bs with a lovely setting in a lush garden along a stream. There's a garden chalet, and two rooms inside the thatched main house, with excellent breakfasts served on the patio. R640

Maluti Mountain Lodge Steil St, just off the R712 on the northern edge of town ☎ 058 256 1422, ⊛ malutimountainlodge.co.za. One of the most upmarket places to stay, with pleasant rondavels in the garden and comfortable balconied rooms in the lodge, the best of which are mountain-facing. R1000
Red Mountain House President Square ☎ 058 256 1456, ⊛ redmountainhouse.co.za. Centrally situated B&B that has rooms on the upper floor opening onto balconies with views onto the square and the mountains. Rooms have fireplaces and are luxuriously furnished with Persian rugs and Victorian antiques. R970

EATING AND DRINKING

On weekends, when the crowds arrive in town, most restaurants are packed and service is slow – it's best to book in advance or to arrive early if you're hungry.

278 on Main 278 Main St ☎ 082 556 5208, ⊛ 278onmain.co.za. A good variety of sweet and hearty breakfasts, pasta and meat dishes, pancakes and desserts in a quirky interior, at the very end of the row of restaurants in the village. Daily 7.30am–9pm.
★ **Clementines** Church St ☎ 058 256 1616. Booking is essential at Clarens' best restaurant, housed in an atmospheric old tin bus maintenance shed. Try the steaks, a slow-food oxtail stew, or grilled local rainbow trout,

washed down with beer from the Clarens Brewery. There's plenty of space in the garden for romping kids. Tues–Fri noon–3pm & 5.30–11pm, Sat & Sun 10am–3pm & 5.30–11pm.
The Highlander President Square ☎ 058 256 1912. A cosy restaurant with a fire in winter and a terrace for when the weather is fine; it's especially recommended for its home-made pies, pizza, breakfasts and cheesecake. Daily 7.30am–10pm.

Street Caffe & Bruce's Pub Main St The town's busiest restaurant, due to its reasonably priced pizzas, snacks, steaks and salads, and several varieties of local and imported beers on offer. Daily 9am–11pm.

Ficksburg

FICKSBURG, 82km southwest of Clarens, is the centre of South Africa's cherry and asparagus farming. The town's sandstone architecture gives it a pleasant ambience, and it's a good place to make a stop halfway down the Maloti Route. An annual Cherry Festival in the third week of November is the highlight of Ficksburg's calendar; it features a marathon, floats, stalls, a "cherry queen" competition and a popular beer festival.

6

ARRIVAL AND DEPARTURE   FICKSBURG

By minibus taxi Minibus taxis from the Maputsoe border crossing on the eastern edge of town link Ficksburg to Bloemfontein, Johannesburg and other towns.

ACCOMMODATION

Bella Rosa 21 Bloem St ☎051 933 2623. A hugely popular and well-priced pair of Victorian sandstone houses set in a lovely garden, with nicely furnished en-suite rooms. Dinner is available but must be booked. **R460**

Ladybrand

LADYBRAND lies on the main route into Lesotho, just over 50km southwest of Ficksburg. It's one of the few small towns in the Free State that is booming, owing to its proximity of Lesotho's capital, 12km away. Many people working on projects in Lesotho stay in Ladybrand rather than in Maseru because of its calm and family-friendly village atmosphere.

FARMSTAYS AND HORSERIDING AROUND CLARENS

Horseriding is big along the Eastern Highlands. A couple of farms near Clarens – both excellent family destinations – provide outstanding riding onto the Drakensberg Escarpment, from where you can gaze across into Lesotho and view Southern Africa's highest peaks.

The friendly and very Afrikaans *Bokpoort Holiday Farm* (☎058 256 1181, ⊛bokpoort.co.za) has a range of accommodation, from upmarket en-suite chalets with fireplaces and kitchenettes (R700), to self-contained, en-suite "mountain" huts (R250) and dorm beds (R100) in an old sandstone barn. If you're camping (R60), there's a good communal cooking and dining area. Reasonably priced meals, including dinner, can be ordered from the farmhouse kitchen, while a small shop sells basics.

Bokpoort's big draw is the memorable **Western-style riding** in deep, comfortable cowboy saddles on sure-footed horses. Short rides from the farmhouse (R250 for 2hr) take in San rock paintings and swimmable river pools, with the chance of seeing eland, zebra and springbok on the adjoining game farm. One-day riding trails into the mountains on the Lesotho border cost R800 per person (including picnic basket); two- or three-day trails (including meals and overnight stay) cost R2000 per person per day (R1500 in groups of five or more); a 4WD vehicle brings the food and bedding (you sleep on mattresses in a remote mountain hut), and you ride about six hours a day.

High-quality horses and riding are also available at *Schaapplaats Farm Cottages & Ashgar Equestrian Centre* (☎058 256 1176 or ☎083 630 3713, ⊛ashgarhorses.co.za), in the mountains 6km south of Clarens off the R711. An establishment with a more English flavour, this turn-of-the-twentieth-century farm has four self-catering sandstone cottages sleeping two to four people (R200/person). From here you can go on terrific **mountain hikes**, visit Boer War graves and San rock paintings and, of course, ride horses (R250 per person for 2hr). There's also a chance to brush up your equestrian skills, as the owner is a qualified riding teacher. Moreover, there is some game on the farm (zebra, wildebeest, antelope etc), which adds zest to any ride.

The area is certainly fine **horseriding** country, and *Greenock* (see below) offers superlative guided riding in isolated mountains.

ARRIVAL AND DEPARTURE   LADYBRAND

By bus and minibus taxi Minibus taxis and scheduled Intercape buses to and from the Maseru bridge border crossing link to cities and towns across Free State, and to Johannesburg and Durban; not all of them pass Ladybrand, so check the routing in advance.

ACCOMMODATION

Cranberry Cottage 37 Beeton St ☎ 051 924 2290 or ☎ 082 921 1575, ⓦ www.cranberry.co.za. One of the best, and most popular, options in town, offering 34 comfortable country-style B&B rooms (including several self-catering units). There's a gym and spa here, and the owners have reams of information on day-trips and rock-art sites. R820

Greenock & De Hoek ☎ 051 924 2961, ⓦ web.mac .com/africanhorses/greenock_riding. Set in a beautiful valley 7km north of town, the Greenock and De Hoek farms offer riding excursions and accommodation in the form of self-catering rooms, rondavels and log cabins, although you can take plain, well-cooked meals with the friendly hosts (and their pets) for a very reasonable amount. R400

EATING

Duck Pond 37 Beeton St ☎ 051 924 2290. The popular restaurant of the *Cranberry Cottage* serves excellent three-course or à la carte international meals. In summer guests are seated out on the terrace by the duck pond. Daily 5–11pm.

Station Café 1 Princess St, ☎ 051 924 2834. Ladybrand's former train station is now an attractive restaurant with wonderful organic South African dishes, with ingredients sourced from the region. Tues–Sat 8am–4.30pm.

Parys and the Vredefort Dome

The small town of **PARYS**, just off the N1 highway 300km northeast of Bloemfontein and 100km from Johannesburg, makes a good stopover on the long trek across the country, or an interesting day-trip from Jo'burg. The town, with its galleries, antique

---

THE VREDEFORT DOME

Some two billion years ago, an **asteroid** the size of Cape Town's Table Mountain slammed into Earth at a speed of 30,000 kilometres per hour, forming a 300km-wide crater. The impact at **Vredefort**, 10km south of Parys, vaporized the asteroid and part of the Earth's crust, melting, pulverizing and shattering rocks for kilometres around. It also forced rocks beneath the impact area briefly downward before these rebounded, raising and upending rock layers to form a dome structure. Even though the Earth's surface has eroded about 10km since the impact, the weathered **concentric rings** of this dome can still be seen, forming the hills around Parys. The rim of the crater, originally up to 150km away, has not survived the elements, though it's thanks to the downward sagging of the gold-bearing layers around the dome, caused by the impact, that the richest source of gold in the world was preserved from erosion before the first gold diggers discovered these layers in Johannesburg, in 1886.

The dome area is best experienced on a **tour**, which takes in the view of the dome remnants, and tracks down strange melt rock formations. Blast! Talks & Trails, based 2km from Parys at *Otters' Haunt Lodge* (Kopjeskraal Rd, ☎ 056 818184 or ☎ 084 245 2490, ⓦ vdome.co.za), organizes dome walks (2–3hr; R195–295) and drives (rates depend on duration and if you bring your own car). six kilometres from Parys the *Kopjeskraal Country Lodge* (☎ 083 406 0841, ⓦ www.kopjeskraal.co.za/tours.htm) has walks (2hr; R100) and a two-and-a-half-hour 4WD drive (R150/person).

A well-designed new **visitor centre** on the outskirts of Vredefort on the road to Parys has an introductory film, 3D models, and interactive displays about the Vredefort impact, the solar system, meteorites, asteroids, craters and the environmental consequences of impacts. Ask the Parys tourist information office for details (see opposite).

shops, adventure sports and the meandering Vaal River, is pleasant enough, but its main claim to fame is harder to spot, as it's situated near **Vredefort**, the epicentre of a massive meteorite impact some two billion years ago. What remains of the huge 300km-wide crater is now South Africa's most abstract World Heritage Site, as it can only properly be seen from space, but by joining a tour (see opposite) it is possible to get a good idea of what happened and to view what's left of the impact dome, the mass of molten rock that was thrust upwards after the meteorite struck.

Early November is a good time to visit Parys, when outdoor enthusiasts descend on the town for dragon-boat racing, competitions and live music during the annual Dome Adventure Festival (ⓦdomefest.co.za).

6

INFORMATION   PARYS

Tourist information 30 Water St (Mon–Fri 8am–5pm, Sat & Sun 9am–4pm; ☎056 811 4000, ⓦparys.info).

ACCOMMODATION

Art Lovers Guesthouse 89 Breë St ☎056 817 6515, ⓦartloversguesthouse.co.za. Six classically furnished suites with quality sheets, antiques, chandeliers and Persian carpets. No children under 12. **R1100**

Kapstok Guesthouse 55 Kruis St ☎072 885 3288, ⓦkapstok.co.za. "The coat hanger" has several small but comfortable en-suite doubles, as well as two cottages sleeping up to five people (R925). Breakfast extra. **R550**

EATING AND DRINKING

Art Lovers 89 Breë St ☎056 817 6515. Headed by an award-winning chef and set in an art gallery, this restaurant serves delicious South African and international à la carte meals during the week, and a buffet on Sundays. Daily noon–9pm.

Vetkoek Paleis & Kerrie Hys 62 Breë St ☎056 817 6833. Go local and snack on Afrikaner *vetkoek*, deep-fried pastries with various fillings, or a bunny chow curry. Normal breakfasts and pancakes are also served. Mon–Fri 8.30am–6pm, Sat & Sun 8am–2pm.

Gauteng

JOHANNESBURG AT DUSK

Gauteng

Gauteng is South Africa's smallest region, comprising less than two percent of its landmass, yet contributing around forty percent of the GDP. Home to nearly ten million people, Gauteng is almost entirely urban; while the province encompasses a section of the Magaliesberg Mountains to the east and the gold-rich Witwatersrand to the south and west, the area is dominated by the huge conurbation incorporating Johannesburg, Pretoria and a host of industrial towns and townships that surround them. Although lacking the spectacular natural attractions of the Cape Province or Mpumalanga, Gauteng has a subtle physical power. Startling outcrops of rock known as *koppies*, with intriguing and often lucrative geology, are found in the sprawling suburbs and grassy plains of deep-red earth that fringe the cities.

7

The older parts of Johannesburg and Pretoria are gloriously green in summer: both are among the most tree-rich cities on Earth, and Johannesburg, home to ten million of them, is proudly described by locals as the world's largest man-made forest. The ubiquitous jacaranda trees blossom in late spring, turning the suburbs purple.

Gauteng is dominated by **Johannesburg**, whose origins lie in the exploitation of **gold** (Gauteng means "Place of Gold" in Sotho). Although it has grown rapidly since the discovery of gold in 1886 to become the richest metropolis in Africa, it is a hectic city, home to extreme contrasts of wealth and poverty. The city has a reputation among both visitors and South Africans as a place to avoid, but those who acquire a taste for Jo'burg – something you can do in just a few days – are seduced by its energy and vibrancy, unmatched by any other city in South Africa. A highly cosmopolitan city, and the most Africanized in the country, Jo'burg boasts South Africa's most famous townships, its most active and diverse cultural life, some of its best restaurants and the most progressive nightlife.

Some 50km north lies dignified **Pretoria**, the country's administrative capital. Historically an Afrikaner stronghold, today it's a cosmopolitan mix of civil servants, diplomats and students from South Africa and around the world. Smaller and more relaxed than Johannesburg, Pretoria is an important and intriguing destination in its own right, with a range of interesting museums and historic buildings. The new Gautrain rapid rail connection between Jo'burg and Pretoria is nothing less than a transport revolution, finally offering locals and travellers a safe and affordable alternative to the tedious traffic jams on the N1.

Less than an hour from the centre of Jo'burg, the section of the **Magaliesberg Mountains** that extends into Gauteng is a magnet for Johannesburgers desperate to escape the city's hectic tempo. Although the hills can hardly be described as remote and

TOWNSHIP HOUSE IN SOWETO

Highlights

❶ **Downtown Johannesburg** Experience a truly pan-African urban buzz at the heart of the continent's richest city. **See p.466**

❷ **Melville** Hang out with Jo'burg's students and hipsters in one of the city's few places where bars, cafés and decent restaurants line the street. **See p.474**

❸ **The Apartheid Museum, Jo'burg** A powerful, inspiring journey through the South African struggle for freedom. **See p.478**

❹ **Soweto tours** Sample the vibrancy of South Africa's most historically significant township. See p.480

❺ **The big match** Whether it's Chiefs v Pirates or Springboks v All Blacks, sport in Jo'burg is always big news. **See p.491**

❻ **Live music** Make the effort and you'll find that Jo'burg has the best scene in the country. See p.490

❼ **Cradle of Humankind** A series of caves on the fringe of Johannesburg provides vital fossil evidence of human ancestry. **See p.494**

❽ **Voortrekker Monument and The Freedom Park, Pretoria** These two monuments are dramatic tributes to the old and new South Africa. **See p.503**

HIGHLIGHTS ARE MARKED ON THE MAP ON P.461

untamed, you'll find ample opportunities for nature trailing and hiking. As in much of Gauteng, however, the important part lies underground, with a series of caves, underground passages and archeological sites making up the **Cradle of Humankind** World Heritage Site. Most famous of these sites are the **Sterkfontein Caves**, where some of the world's most important discoveries of pre-human primate fossils have been made.

Johannesburg

Back in October 1886, when gold was discovered, what is now **JOHANNESBURG** was an expanse of sleepy, treeless veld. Now it is the economic engine of Africa: a sprawling, infuriating, invigorating home to eight million people, but never the country's seat of government or national political power.

During the apartheid era, Jo'burg was the city in which black resistance and urban culture were most strident – Nelson Mandela and Walter Sisulu formed the country's first black law firm here in 1952, before helping to sow the seeds of liberation – while the democratic era has seen the city become the vanguard of the gradual deracialization of South African society. The country's burgeoning **black elite** and **middle class** are concentrated here, and the city is a giant soup of ethnicities: Zulu and Sotho-speaking blacks, Afrikaners and English-speaking whites predominate, but Jozi culture is also enriched by immigrants from across Africa, as well as sizeable Indian, coloured, Chinese, Greek, Jewish, Portuguese and Lebanese communities. Jo'burg is an unpretentious, loud, ballsy city; outsiders are quickly accepted, and a pervasive social warmth keeps many of its more relaxed citizens – who you'd expect to prefer Cape Town – from leaving.

Even so, there are still astonishing extremes of wealth and poverty here: mansions in verdant **suburbs** are protected by high walls and electrified fences, only a kilometre or two from sprawling **shantytowns** such as the inner-city flatlands of Hillbrow and Yeoville, where hundreds of thousands of immigrants, mostly from Zimbabwe, have formed a teeming ghetto economy, since the formal job market cannot absorb most of them.

The bewildering size of Jo'burg can be daunting for all but the most determined traveller. Some visitors fall into the trap of being too intimidated by the city's reputation to explore, venturing out only to the bland, safe, covered shopping malls and restaurants of the northern suburbs while making hasty plans to move on. However, once you've found a convenient way of getting around, either by car, on the shiny new **Gautrain** trains and buses, or in the company of a tour guide, the history, diversity and crackling energy of the city can quickly become compelling.

The **central business district**, which in the 1990s was all but abandoned by big business fleeing crime and grime, is undergoing a slow rebirth, with crime rates dropping and property investors moving in. New City Improvement Districts have been implemented to oversee the cleaning, sprucing up and guarding of the central areas, most effectively so far in Braamfontein; security guards and cameras can now be seen on many street corners and, as a result, it's now relatively safe to walk around the CBD during the day.

Shopping is Jo'burg's biggest addiction, and the city offers an abundance of superb contemporary African art, fashion and design. And then there are the **townships**, most easily explored on a tour but, in some cases, possible to get to under your own steam.

Jo'burg is also a great place to watch **sport**, with soccer, rugby and cricket teams commanding feverish support. The 2010 Football World Cup was headquartered in the city; the 100,000-seat FNB Stadium (formerly Soccer City) is a proud reminder of the event, and now regularly used for games and concerts.

Brief history

Johannesburg dates back to 1886, when Australian prospector **George Harrison** found the main Witwatersrand gold-bearing reef. Almost immediately, this quiet area of the Transvaal became swamped with diggers from near and far, and a tented city sprang up around the site. The Pretoria authorities were forced to proclaim a township nearby: they chose a useless triangle of land called the Randjeslaagte, which had been left unclaimed by local farmers. **Johan Rissik**, the surveyor, called it Johannesburg, either after himself or Christiaan Johannes Joubert, the chief of mining, or the president of the South African Republic (ZAR), Paul Johannes Kruger.

Mining magnates such as Cecil Rhodes and Barney Barnato possessed the capital necessary to exploit the world's richest gold reef, and their **Chamber of Mines** (a self-regulatory body for mine owners, founded in 1889) attempted to bring some order to the digging frenzy, with common policies on recruitment, wages and working conditions. In 1893, due partly to pressure from white workers, and with the approval

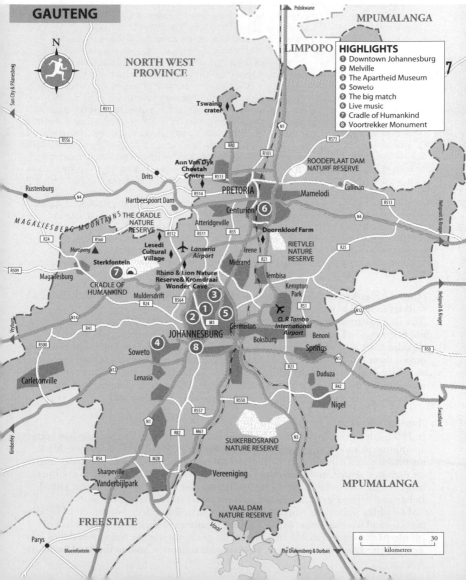

GAUTENG

N

NORTH WEST PROVINCE

MPUMALANGA

LIMPOPO

HIGHLIGHTS
1 Downtown Johannesburg
2 Melville
3 The Apartheid Museum
4 Soweto
5 The big match
6 Live music
7 Cradle of Humankind
8 Voortrekker Monument

7

CRIME AND SAFETY IN JOHANNESBURG

With Johannesburg's extremes of poverty and wealth, its brash, get-ahead culture and the presence of illegal firearms, it's hardly surprising that the city can be a dangerous place. Despite its unenviable reputation, it's important to retain a sense of proportion about potential risks and not to let paranoia ruin your stay. Several hundred thousand foreign football fans visited Johannesburg during the 2010 World Cup, with not a single noteworthy incident. Remember that most crime happens in the outlying townships, and that the vast majority of Jo'burgers are exceedingly friendly; as in all major cities, taking simple precautions (see p.73 and below) is likely to see you through safely.

If you're wandering around **on foot**, the most likely risk of crime is from mugging. Although significant effort has gone into making the riskiest central areas safer – such as the installation of security cameras – remain alert when exploring the central business district (CBD), Braamfontein and Newtown, do your touring in daylight, use busy streets and never be complacent.

Joubert Park, Hillbrow and Berea are regarded as **no-go zones**; Yeoville and Observatory are safer and generally fine if you're confident or have someone to show you around. You're very unlikely to be mugged on the streets of Melville, Parktown or Rosebank. If you want to walk around one of the riskier areas, study maps beforehand (not on street corners), don't walk around with luggage and avoid groups of young men (the main offenders). If you're carrying valuables, make a portion of them easily available, so that muggers are likely to be quickly satisfied. Never resist muggers. You're unlikely to be mugged on **public transport** but, as always, it's wise to stay alert, especially at busy spots such as Park Station and taxi ranks, and to be extra vigilant when getting off minibus taxis. Waiting for buses in the northern suburbs is generally safe.

If you're **driving** around, note that there is a small risk of "smash and grab" theft or carjacking; keep all bags and valuables locked up in the trunk, lock the car doors and keep windows up when driving after dark or when in central areas. Be aware of your surroundings when leaving or returning to your car and entering driveways and always seek out secure – preferably guarded – parking; in Jo'burg this is in ample supply. Although urban legend suggests you can cruise through red light sat night, this is dangerous and illegal; stop, keep a good distance from the car in front and be aware of anyone moving around the car.

Don't expect too much from the **police**, who normally have priorities other than keeping an eye out for tourists. In the city centre and Rosebank, **private guards**, identifiable by their yellow armbands and, stationed on street corners, provide an effective anti-crime presence on the street.

of the ZAR government, the chamber introduced the **colour bar**, which excluded black workers from all but manual labour.

By 1895, Johannesburg's population had soared to over 100,000, many of whom were not Boers and had no interest in the ZAR's independence. Kruger and the burghers regarded these *uitlanders* (foreigners) as a potential threat to their political supremacy, and denied them the vote despite the income they generated for the state's coffers. Legislation was also passed to control the influx of blacks to Johannesburg, and Indians were forcibly moved out of the city into a western location. Before long, large shantytowns filled with blacks and Indians were springing up on the outskirts of Johannesburg.

The Anglo-Boer War
In 1900, during the Anglo-Boer War, Johannesburg fell to the British, who had been attempting to annex the gold-rich area for some time. At the same time, more black townships were established, including **Sophiatown** (1903) in an area previously used for dumping sewage, and **Alexandra** (1905). Bubonic plague erupted on the northern fringes of the city in 1904, providing justification for the authorities to burn several Indian and African locations, including **Newtown**, just west of the centre.

Meanwhile, white mine workers were becoming unionized, and outbreaks of fighting over pay and working hours were a frequent occurrence. Their poorly paid black counterparts were also mobilizing; their main grievance was the ruling that skilled jobs were the preserve of white workers. Resentments came to a head in the **Rand Revolt** of

1922, after the Chamber of Mines, anxious to cut costs, decided to allow blacks into the skilled jobs previously held only by whites. White workers were furious: street battles broke out and lasted for four days. Government troops were called in to restore order and over two hundred men were killed. Alarmed at the scale of white discontent, Prime Minister Jan Smuts ruled that the colour bar be maintained, and throughout the 1920s the government passed laws restricting the movement of blacks.

Populating Soweto

During the 1930s, the township of **Orlando** became established southwest of the city, with accommodation for 80,000 blacks; this was the nucleus around which **Soweto** evolved. By 1945, 400,000 blacks were living in and around Johannesburg – an increase of one hundred percent in a decade. In August 1946, 70,000 African

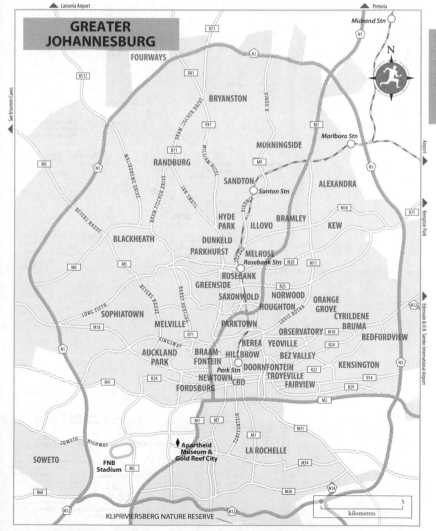

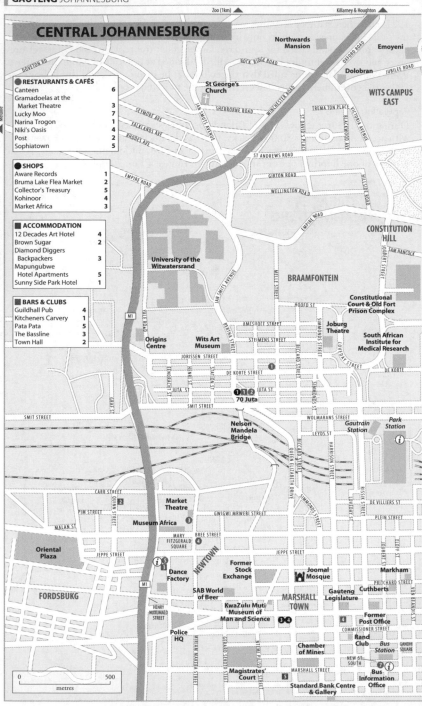

CENTRAL JOHANNESBURG

● RESTAURANTS & CAFÉS

Canteen	6
Gramadoelas at the Market Theatre	3
Lucky Moo	7
Narina Trogon	1
Niki's Oasis	4
Post	2
Sophiatown	5

● SHOPS

Aware Records	1
Bruma Lake Flea Market	2
Collector's Treasury	5
Kohinoor	4
Market Africa	3

■ ACCOMMODATION

12 Decades Art Hotel	4
Brown Sugar	2
Diamond Diggers Backpackers	3
Mapungubwe Hotel Apartments	5
Sunny Side Park Hotel	1

■ BARS & CLUBS

Guildhall Pub	4
Kitcheners Carvery	1
Pata Pata	5
The Bassline	3
Town Hall	2

Mineworkers Union members went on strike over working conditions. The government sent police in, and twelve miners were killed and over a thousand injured.

Forced removals of black residents from Johannesburg's inner suburbs, particularly from Sophiatown, began in 1955. Thousands were dumped far from the city centre, in the new township of Meadowlands, next to Orlando, and Sophiatown was crassly renamed Triomf (triumph). The **ANC** (see p.655) established itself as the most important black protest organization during this period, proclaiming the **Freedom Charter** in Kliptown, Soweto, that year.

During the 1950s, a vigorous black urban culture began to emerge in the townships, and the new *marabi* jazz and its offspring, the jubilant *kwela* pennywhistle style, were played in illegal drinking houses called *shebeens*. This was also the era of *Drum Magazine*, which celebrated a glamorous, sophisticated township zeitgeist, and introduced a host of talented journalists, such as Can Temba and Casey "Kid" Motsisi, to the city and the world. Mbaqanga music emerged later, with its heavy basslines and sensuous melodies capturing the bittersweet essence of life in the townships.

Resistance and democracy

The formation in 1972 of the **Black Consciousness Movement** (BCM) rekindled political activism, particularly among Soweto students. On June 16, 1976, student riots erupted in the township, and the unrest spread nationwide (see p.533). The youth's war against the State escalated in the 1980s, resulting in regular "**states of emergency**", during which the armed forces had permission to do anything they liked to contain revolt. Towards the end of the decade, the government relaxed "petty" apartheid, turning a blind eye to the growth of "grey" areas like Hillbrow – white suburbs where blacks were moving in.

The three years after Nelson Mandela's release in 1990 saw widespread political violence in Gauteng right up until the day before the elections. However, as elsewhere in South Africa, the election on April 27, 1994, went off peacefully. The ANC won comfortably in Gauteng then, and retained their hold in 1999 and 2004. They also carried the province in 2009, despite a growing feeling that the ANC have not totally lived up to their promises. Black South Africans have indeed made steady inroads into positions of influence in business and politics, but, as an increasing number of township dwellers move to the suburbs, Johannesburg's infrastructure has struggled to cope: low-income housing is not being built fast enough, energy supply is wobbling as demand surges, and traffic is often hellish, though the new Gautrain rail network should make a difference along the north–south routes.

The central business district (CBD)

Johannesburg's **CBD**, the grid of streets and tightly packed skyscrapers just to the south of the Witwatersrand Ridge, is the most recognizable part of the city. For a century after the first mining camp was built, on what is now Commissioner Street, the CBD was the core of Jo'burg's buzzing commercial and financial life. Then there was the mass exodus during the crime-ridden 1980s and 1990s, and when the Jo'burg Stock Exchange moved out in 1999 in favour of Sandton, the city centre was all but written off. However, thanks to the gradual regeneration of the area over recent years, a visit to the CBD offers the chance to see buildings and institutions with a fascinating history and get a taste of the bustle, sounds and thrills of a genuinely African city.

The Carlton Centre and around

Commissioner St • Centre and viewpoint daily 9am–7pm • R8, buy tickets on the lower ground • Parking free for tower ticket holders • ☎ 011 308 2876

The **Carlton Centre** is a good place to start exploring the CBD. The complex has a lively shopping mall on the lower and underground floors, but the main attraction is the

GANDHI IN JOHANNESBURG

Although **Mohandas Gandhi** has many strong links with Durban, the South African city he arrived at in 1893, it was the ten years he spent in Johannesburg between 1903 and 1913 that first tested the philosophies for which he is famous. As an advocate, he frequently appeared in the Transvaal Law Courts (now demolished), which stood in what has since been renamed Gandhi Square in downtown Jo'burg. Defending mainly South African Indians accused of breaking the restrictive and racist registration laws, Gandhi began to see practical applications for his concept of **Satyagraha**, soul force, or passive resistance, as a means of defying immoral state oppression.

Gandhi himself was twice imprisoned, along with other passive resisters, in the fort in Braamfontein, on what is now Constitution Hill. On one of these occasions he was taken from his cell to the office of General Jan Smuts to negotiate the prisoners' release, but finding himself at liberty had to borrow the railway fare home from the general's secretary.

Gandhi's ideas found resonance in the non-violent ideals of those who established the **African National Congress** in 1912. Forty years later, only a few years after Gandhi's successful use of Satyagraha to end the British Raj in India, the start of the ANC's Defiance Campaign against the pass laws in 1952 owed much to his principles. MuseuMAfricA (see p.468) contains displays on Gandhi's time in Johannesburg, and he is commemorated with a statue on Gandhi Square.

Top of Africa viewpoint on the fiftieth floor of the Carlton Tower, Africa's tallest building (222m), which offers breathtaking views of the centre of Johannesburg, and shows how the mines, mine dumps and city concrete exist cheek by jowl. Interestingly, the adjacent *Carlton Hotel* was once the best hotel on the continent, but now stands empty after being closed in 1997.

Main Street

Main Street, partially pedestrianized for six blocks west of the regenerated Gandhi Square near the Carlton Centre, is home to the offices of various mining companies and makes for a great introduction to Jo'burg's mining history. Industrial relics such as trains, wooden stampmills and a headgear lift tower have been placed along the road; walk right to the end to see two impressive 1940s Art Deco AngloGold Ashanti office buildings, fronted by a fountain with a beautiful statue of a herd of springboks jumping over a pond.

Gauteng Legislature and around

Corner of Rissik and Market sts

The impressive **Gauteng Legislature** was built in 1915 as the City Hall and is fronted by huge palm trees. Beside it stands the city's daintiest little skyscraper, the ten-storey **Barbican**, built in 1931, which was saved from neglect and destruction when it was renovated in 2010. Directly opposite the Legislature, the former **Rissik Street Post Office** was not as lucky, and its burnt-out shell stands testimony to the indifference of the current city management to its heritage; squatters accidentally set it on fire in 2009 and little has happened since. When this building was completed in 1897 it was the tallest in the city. Neo-Baroque in style, its fourth floor and clock tower were later additions, timed to coincide with the accession of the British king, Edward VII, in 1902.

Rand Club

33 Loveday St • Visits by prior arrangement only, book at least a week in advance • Free if followed by lunch at the club • ☎ 011 870 4268, ✉ catering@randclub.co.za

The grandiose **Rand Club** is where mining magnates, nicknamed Randlords, have come to dine and unwind for over 120 years. Although the club was founded in 1887, the current building was completed in 1904 and is the fourth to occupy the site, as each successive clubhouse was replaced to reflect the members' growing wealth. The impressive hall with its stained-glass dome is surrounded by various dining rooms, a library and the *Main Bar*, home to the longest bar in Africa, which snakes around the room. Non-members can join tours of the building, lunch, dine or drink at the club (all with prior booking). Visitors must observe the dress code: a shirt and smart trousers and shoes for the men, smart casual for the women.

Standard Bank Art Gallery

Frederick St • Mon–Fri 8am–4.30pm, Sat 9am–1pm • Free • ☎ 011 631 1889, ⓦ standardbankgallery.co.za

At the superb **Standard Bank Art Gallery**, changing exhibitions consistently show off some of the best contemporary African art in South Africa. The gallery is especially good at uncovering new talent; keep an eye out for the annual exhibition by the Standard Bank Young Artist Award winner.

Ferreira Mine Stope

5 Simmonds St • Daily 8.30am–5pm • Free

In the Standard Bank's head office, it's possible to take a lift from the main concourse down to the **Ferreira Mine Stope**, an old mine tunnel discovered when the building was being constructed in 1986. The plain rock face you see still bears pick-axe scars, and there's a simple though fascinating display putting the history of Johannesburg in context; look out for the old sepia photographs of the mine and early Jo'burg.

Diagonal Street

Diagonal Street, at the western end of Pritchard Street, lies at the heart of one of the most fascinating areas of the CBD. In the shadow of various concrete and glass behemoths, including the former Johannesburg Stock Exchange, is a street of old two-storey buildings, some of which date back to the 1890s; the lines of washing on the upstairs balconies show that they are still residential. The streets are home to a number of traders and shops peddling traditional medicines (*umuthi*), Sotho blankets and paraffin stoves alongside mobile phones. Though it might not feel so at first, the area is fairly safe, and with businessmen mingling with hawkers it has a very urban-African buzz. At the southern end of the street there are two lovely statues of ANC heroes Walter and Albertina Sisulu.

KwaZulu Muti Museum of Man and Science

14 Diagonal St • Mon–Fri 7.30am–5pm, Sat 7.30am–1pm • Free • ☎ 011 836 4470

If you're feeling brave, take a look at the rather spooky **KwaZulu Muti Museum of Man and Science**, a shop selling all kinds of traditional medicines, often manufactured from the dried animal skins hanging from the ceiling. You might also find yourself brushing against dangling ostrich feet or a pair of monkey skulls.

Newtown

On the western edge of the CBD between Diagonal Street and the M1 motorway flyover, **Newtown** is an area of redevelopment where some of Johannesburg's most vibrant cultural hot spots are found alongside derelict factories and areas of wasteland. The striking Nelson Mandela Bridge provides a swift link to the district from Braamfontein and the northern suburbs. Newtown is a safe place to visit; by day for strolling along the signposted heritage trail (see ⓦ newtown.co.za/heritage), and at night, when the various music and theatre venues are in full swing.

MuseuMAfricA

Mary Fitzgerald Square • Tues–Sun 9am–5pm • Free • ☎ 011 833 5624

At the heart of Newtown is the excellent **MuseuMAfricA**. The sheer size of the museum building – formerly the city's fruit and vegetable market – can make it seem a bit sparse and empty, but in fact the permanent exhibitions and numerous temporary displays are well worth seeing. Most successful is Sounds of the City, which features imaginative re-creations of shacks and *shebeens* in Sophiatown, home to famous musicians such as Hugh Masekela and Miriam Makeba, and which describes the different musical styles that were forged in this township during the 1950s. In a side room, look out for Tried for Treason, an exhibition dedicated to the Treason Trial (1956–61), when 156 people, including Nelson Mandela and many well-known ANC activists of all races, were accused of plotting against the state.

Market Theatre and The Bassline

Theatre Mary Fitzgerald Square, entrance at the eastern end of MuseuMAfricA

The famous **Market Theatre** (see p.491) has been a reliable source of stimulating and often ground-breaking dramatic output over the last thirty years or so. Outside, there's a handful of shops and places to eat and drink. The cultural theme continues south of Jeppe Street, with Jo'burg's best live music venue, The **Bassline** (see p.490), and a dance rehearsal and performing space called the Dance Factory, which is used for the annual Arts Alive Festival (see box, p.493).

South African Breweries (SAB) World of Beer

On the corner of President and Gerard sts • Tues–Sat 10am–6pm • R35 • ☏ 011 836 4900, ⓦ worldofbeer.co.za

The ninety-minute tour of the **South African Breweries (SAB) World of Beer** takes you through six thousand years of brewing history, which begs the question why SAB's ubiquitous end product, the anaemic, fizzy Castle lager, is so disappointing. Still, the reconstructed gold-rush pubs and Sixties *shebeen* are fun, along with the greenhouse where sample crops of barley and hops grow; use your two free beers to wash down a pub lunch on the balcony of the *Tap Room* bar and watch the city rush by.

Police Headquarters and Oriental Plaza

Main Reef Rd

At the infamous Johannesburg **police headquarters**, anti-apartheid activists were detained and tortured, and some fell to their deaths having "jumped" from the tenth floor. After this, it's a pleasant relief to find the remains of the old Indian neighbourhood of **Fordsburg** just further west, where Jeppe Street passes under the M1 flyover. This busy commercial street ends up at the **Oriental Plaza**, a hugely popular, Indian-owned shopping complex, selling everything from fabrics to spices and where haggling is *de rigueur*. This is just about all that remains of Newtown's once-thriving Indian community, most of which was forcibly removed in 1904 to make way for whites.

Johannesburg Art Gallery

Joubert Park • Tues–Sun 10am–5pm • Free • ☏ 011 725 3130, ⓦ joburg.org.za/culture/museums-galleries/jag

On the eastern side of Park Station, **Joubert Park**, named after General Piet Joubert (who lost the South African Republic general election to Paul Kruger in 1893), is the only inner-city green space but largely regarded as a no-go area.

The one sight you can visit here is the **Johannesburg Art Gallery**, housed in an elegant, predominantly nineteenth-century building accessed via King George Street. This is one of the most progressive galleries in the country and regular exhibits include vast wooden sculptures by the visionary Venda artist Jackson Hlungwani that tower up to the ceilings. Elsewhere, there's a very South African mixture of African artworks and artefacts from the ceremonial to the purely decorative, and a range of European paintings, including some minor Dutch Masters. The special exhibitions are usually excellent, too.

Arts on Main and Main Street Life

264 & 286 Fox St • Daily 9am–5pm, bars/restaurants till late (see p.487) • Free • ☏ 011 725 3130, ⓦ mainstreetlife.co.za, ⓦ www.artsonmain .co.za • Best reached from the M2 highway via Joe Slovo Drive (M31); take the R24 Market St exit and follow signs to the right

Just off Main Street in the Maboneng precinct, east of the city centre, two city blocks have been transformed into a hive of cultural activity, and are perhaps the best place to get a taste of the potential of the city centre, and of how Jo'burg is changing for the better. **Arts on Main** is a former warehouse complex that now houses art ateliers and galleries, the LoveJozi T-shirt and clothing shop, an arts bookshop, the *Canteen* restaurant (see p.487) and a rooftop bar; it positively buzzes with people during the excellent **Market on Main** every Sunday, when clothing, accessories and healthy food are for sale. Just 200m down the road, **Main Street Life** is a 1970s industrial building that has been converted into a complex with an exhibition space, apartments, the *12 Decades Hotel* (see p.485), the Bioscope art-house cinema (see p.492), a café, the *Pata Pata* bar (see p.490) and a rooftop bar with great CBD views. The area is safe to visit, even at night, with plenty of security guards around.

The central suburbs

Grouped around the CBD are various suburbs which, given Johannesburg's itinerant population and fast-changing demography, seem to be in a state of constant change. Some, particularly Hillbrow, Berea and Yeoville, were once the "grey areas" of Johannesburg, where apartheid first started to break down in the 1980s. The police turned a blind eye as large numbers of blacks started moving from the townships into these previously all-white areas. Today, most whites have left these neighbourhoods – though they still reside in leafy, residential Observatory, just east of Yeoville – while migrants from all over Africa have flooded in. The hectic street life of Yeoville, Berea and Hillbrow can be very exciting, but you should not venture into these areas at night and should consider going with a street-smart local guide during the day.

Braamfontein

ⓦ braamfontein.org.za

It's not just for the transport facilities at **Park Station** that you might have cause to visit Braamfontein, which starts at the main train station and extends north as far as Empire Road. Helped by its small size and clear physical boundaries, Johannesburg's prime student district is fast reviving after successful city improvement projects, increased policing and security, numerous new artworks and dozens of office-space-to-budget-accommodation conversions. It's a fun place to start exploring the new Johannesburg.

70 Juta

Corner of Juta and De Beer sts • ⓦ 70jutastreet.wordpress.com

This small new development with its fashion boutiques, shops, galleries and café has the hipsters flocking to Braamfontein. Across the street, the historical *Milner Park Hotel* from 1906 is now home to creative companies and the fashionable hangout *Kitchener's Carvery Bar* (see p.490).

Constitution Hill and Old Fort prison complex

Joubert St • Tours of the prisons and court every hour, Mon–Fri & Sun 9am–5pm, Sat 10am–3pm • R30 • ☎ 011 381 3100, ⓦ www .constitutionhill.org.za

Since 2003, **Constitution Hill** has been the home of the Constitutional Court, South Africa's highest court. Its hearings are fascinating for those interested in law or political science: the Court must tread a difficult path between the constitution's array of popular rights and the frustrating realities of a state that is struggling to guarantee them. The Court was built using the bricks of a demolished men's prison and is decorated with over two hundred mostly excellent modern and contemporary South African paintings and sculptures, worth seeing in themselves.

The adjacent **Old Fort prison complex** was built by Paul Kruger during the second Anglo-Boer War to protect against the English and to keep an eye on the gold mine in the village below. The fort was subsequently converted to a prison and used to incarcerate and torture black men during apartheid for breaking racist laws or fighting for their repeal. You can visit the spine-chilling **Number Four prison building**, where Gandhi and Pan-Africanist Congress leader Robert Sobukwe were both held, and the cell where Mandela was kept briefly after his arrest in 1962.

The **Women's Jail**, built in 1910, is a grand Edwardian building that held black and white women prisoners in separate sections. The notorious serial poisoner Daisy de Melker was kept here when she was on death row, but major political leaders such as Winnie Madikizela-Mandela, Albertina Sisulu, Helen Joseph and Ruth First also became familiar with its cells. From the 1950s onward, most of the prison's inmates were pass-law offenders, until the systematic restriction of the movement of black people was repealed in 1986.

Rich in symbolism, the Court and the prison complex provide a subtle but arresting testimony to the country's ongoing transformation, eloquently expressing the pride South Africans have in their new constitution and the democratic principles enshrined therein.

Origins Centre

Yale Rd • Daily 9am–5pm • R75 • ☎ 011 717 1365, ⓦ origins.org.za

On the campus of the University of the Witwatersrand, also known as "Wits", the **Origins Centre** uses a combination of films and exhibits to explain the African origins of humanity before moving on to its main focus: the beliefs, traditions and rock art of the San people (see box, p.406). This is the museum's main strength, and the displays give a useful overview for those intending to explore the San rock-art sites of the Ukhahlamba Drakensberg in KwaZulu-Natal (see p.398).

Wits Art Museum

Corner of Jorissen St and Jan Smuts Ave • Free • ☎ 011 717 1365, ⓦ www.wits.ac.za/wam

Set to open in 2012, the new Wits Art Museum will present the university's art collection, built up over seventy years, which is notable for its extensive collection of art from West and Central Africa.

Hillbrow

Smit Street marks the boundary of Joubert Park with infamous and densely populated **Hillbrow**, dominated by high-rise apartment buildings all crammed with people. Hillbrow has always attracted Jo'burg's new immigrants. Immediately after World War II, the typical immigrant was English, Italian or East European Jewish. These days, Africans from all over the continent are arriving in numbers, giving Hillbrow a uniquely pan-African atmosphere, with music from Lagos to Kinshasa to Harare pumping from the bars, clubs and markets that line the main thoroughfares. Along the many side streets, the scene is distinctly seedy, with drug pushers loitering outside lurid strip joints. The suburb is widely regarded as a no-go area for tourists; your best chance to experience it is with a knowledgeable local such as Timothy Rees-Gibbs (☎078 304 6469), a young member of the Hillbrow police youth desk who, for a donation, will safely take visitors on walks around the district's renovated areas, passing the lovely mock-Tudor Windybrow Theatre on Nugget Street, renovated parks and apartment buildings, as well as some fascinating hijacked high-rise buildings.

The northern suburbs

Safe, prosperous and packed with shops and restaurants, the **northern suburbs** seem a world apart from the CBD and its surrounds. The name is actually a catch-all term for the seemingly endless urban sprawl running over 30km from Parktown, beyond the N1 ring road and into an area known as **Midrand**, which is itself creeping toward the southern edge of Pretoria. With the notable exception of Alexandra, this is a moneyed area, where plush shopping malls are often the only communal meeting points, and the majority of homes use high walls, iron gates and electric fences to advertise how security-conscious a life the owners lead. Despite the often numbing sheen of affluence, however, interesting pockets do exist, such as the centres of the suburbs of Melville, Rosebank and Parkhurst. Most of the suburbs are close to major arterial roads and best explored by car, though the new Gautrain and its bus routes now also offer easy access to some areas.

■ ACCOMMODATION				Tashas	7	Bryanston Organic Market	1
Backpackers' Ritz	6	Ten Bompas	8	Tsunami	6	Everard Read Gallery	4
Claire's of Sandton	3	The Westcliff	10	Wolves	5	Exclusive Books	2/6
The Grace in Rosebank	9					Goodman Art Gallery	8
Premiere Classe Suite Hotel	7	● RESTAURANTS & CAFÉS		■ BAR & CLUB		Hyde Park Corner	2
Sandton Lodge Bryanston	1	Assaggi	3	Hyde Park Bar	1	Kim Sacks Art Gallery	9
Sandton Lodge Inanda	4	Montego Bay	1			Melrose Arch	3
Sandton Lodge Rivonia	2	Moyo	4	● SHOPS		Sandton City Shopping Centre	1
Southern Sun	5	Red Chamber	2	African Craft Market		The Mall of Rosebank	5
				of Rosebank	7		

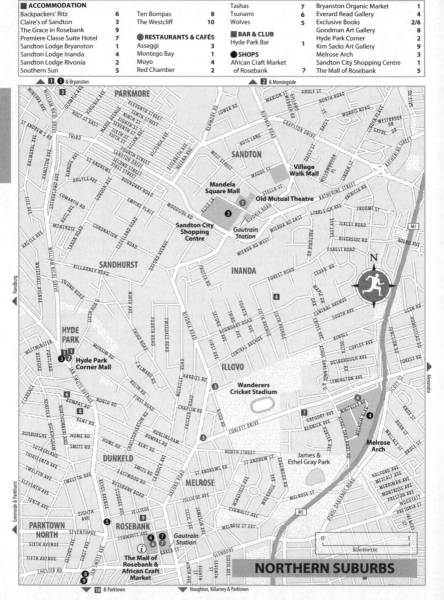

NORTHERN SUBURBS

SIR HERBERT BAKER

South Africa's most famous architect, **Sir Herbert Baker**, was born in Kent, England, in 1862. Apprenticed to his architect uncle in London at the age of 17, Baker attended classes at the Royal Academy and Architectural Association, where he took care to make the contacts he would use so skilfully in later life. By the time he left for the Cape in 1892, Baker was already a convert to the new so-called **Free Style**, which advocated an often bizarre, but roughly historical, eclecticism. The young architect's favourite influences, which would crop up again and again in his work, were Renaissance Italian and medieval Kentish.

Once in the Cape, Baker met **Cecil Rhodes**, and this connection, assiduously cultivated, established him as a major architectural player. The second Anglo-Boer War began in 1899 and Rhodes, assuming eventual British victory, sent Baker off to study the Classical architecture of Italy and Greece, hoping that he would return fully equipped to create a British imperial architecture in South Africa. Baker returned to South Africa deeply influenced by what he had seen, and was summoned by **Lord Alfred Milner**, the administrator of the defeated Transvaal, to fulfil Rhodes' hopes.

Baker took up the challenge enthusiastically, beginning with the homes of the so-called "kindergarten", the young men, mostly Oxford- and Cambridge-educated, whom Milner had imported to bring British-style "good governance" to the defeated territory. The result was the **Parktown mansions**, the opulent houses lining the roads of Johannesburg's wealthiest suburb. In adherence to the architectural creeds he had learnt in England, Baker trained local craftsmen and used local materials for these mansions. He also pioneered the use of local *koppie* stone, lending a dramatic aspect even to unadventurous designs.

Baker's major public commissions were the **St George's Cathedral** in Cape Town, the **South African Institute for Medical Research** in Johannesburg, and the sober, assertive **Union Buildings** in Pretoria, which more than any other building express the British imperial dream – obsessed with Classical precedent, and in a location chosen because of its similarity to the site of the Acropolis in Athens.

Baker left South Africa in 1913 to design the Secretariat in New Delhi, India, returning to England on its completion, where he worked on South Africa House in Trafalgar Square, London. He was knighted in 1923; he died in 1946, and is buried in Westminster Abbey.

Parktown

The first elite residential area in Johannesburg, **Parktown** has retained its upmarket status despite its proximity to Hillbrow (see p.471), which lies just southeast on the other side of Empire Road. The first people to settle in Parktown were Sir Lionel Philips, president of the Chamber of Mines, and his wife Lady Florence. In 1892, seeking a residence that looked onto the Magaliesberg rather than the mine dumps, they had a house built on what was then the Braamfontein farm. The rest of the farm was planted with eucalyptus trees and became known as the Sachsenwald Forest, some of which was given over to the Johannesburg Zoo a few years later. The remaining land was cleared in 1925 to make way for more residential developments.

Johannesburg Zoo

Roughly 2km north of Parktown, off Jan Smuts Ave • Daily 8.30am–5.30pm • R50 • ☎ 011 646 2000, ⓦ jhbzoo.org.za

Johannesburg Zoo is home to about two thousand species, including polar bears, gorillas, rhinos, white lions and red pandas. The zoo is slowly being spruced up, and it remains immensely popular, especially on warm weekends. The café beside the chimp enclosure is an excellent spot for lunch.

Zoo Lake

Opposite the zoo, on the west side of Jan Smuts Ave

The park at **Zoo Lake** is a popular and safe walking and picnic spot that occasionally hosts outdoor performances, including an all-day music event every September during the Arts Alive festival (see box, p.493). You can rent a rowing boat and pootle around

PARKTOWN'S RANDLORD MANSIONS

Parktown's main attraction lies in its distinctive architecture, largely the legacy of Sir Herbert Baker (see box, p.473). Baker's arrival in 1902 heralded a style particular to this district, still evident today in the opulent **mansions** of the Randlords, the rich mine owners, lining the streets. The Parktown & Westcliff Heritage Trust (see p.485) runs regular tours, usually on Saturday afternoons, to some of the notable buildings in Parktown as well as to other districts in Johannesburg; and the Heritage Weekend (second weekend in September), also organized by the Trust, features more tours and special events around the Parktown mansions and city centre.

High walls make viewing the buildings a little tricky on an independent visit, though most now have blue plaques with information outside. A good place to start is the area around Ridge Road, just north of the Randjeslaagte beacon, which marks the northern point of old Johannesburg. The *Sunnyside Park Hotel* here is a massive complex that Lord Alfred Milner used as his governor's residence from 1900. The best of the houses nearby are **Hazeldene Hall**, built in 1902 and featuring cast-iron verandas imported from Glasgow, and **The View**, built in 1897, with carved wooden verandas and an elegant red-brick exterior. To the north of Ridge Road, York Road curves to the left into Jubilee Road, with several palaces on its northern side; the neo-Queen Anne-style **Emoyeni**, at no. 15, built in 1905, is especially striking. At the corner of Jubilee Road and Victoria Avenue stands **Dolobran**, a weird and impressive house, also built in 1905, with a perfect veranda, wonderful red-brick chimneys, red Marseilles roof tiles and hallucinatory stained glass.

Crossing the busy M1 onto Rock Ridge Road, you'll reach the **Northwards Mansion**, built by Sir Herbert Baker in 1904 and home of the Parktown Trust. Unfortunately, there's no access along the road to Baker's own residence at no. 5. On the parallel Sherborne Road, you can see Baker's attractive St George's Church and its rectory, which mix Kentish and Italian features and were built in local rock.

the lake, or sample African cuisine at the lakeside restaurant, which has outdoor and indoor tables and plenty of peaceful, shady nooks in which to eat.

National Museum of Military History

Erlswold Way 22 • Daily 9am–4.30pm • R22 • ☎ 011 646 5513, 🌐 ditsong.org.za/militaryhistory.htm

The **National Museum of Military History**, next to the zoo, has a fascinating collection of intimidating tanks, guns and uniforms, and a display on Umkhonto we Sizwe (MK), the armed wing of the ANC – although the other liberation armies are conspicuous by their absence. The display focuses on the wing's commander, Joe Modise, who became Minister of Defence in the ANC government.

Melville

Together with Parkhurst (see p.476), **Melville** is one of the more relaxed of the northern suburbs. When so many shops and restaurants in Jo'burg are tucked away in soulless malls, it's refreshing to find streets that are pleasant to walk and full of cafés, second-hand bookshops and quirky antique dealers as well as a main drag (Seventh Street) lined with restaurants, bars and clubs for every taste. Melville lost some of its appeal in recent years as restaurants were increasingly replaced by noisy student bars, but new security patrols have been effective in reducing problems.

Melville Koppies

North of Melville • Melville Koppies Central tours every Sun; check website for hours • R30 • ☎ 011 482 4797, 🌐 mk.org.za

The **Koppies** is a pleasant 3km-long hilltop park that is split into three distinct sections that contain hundreds of species of indigenous flora and fauna. Melville Koppies Central is a reserve that can only be visited on tours (starting on Judith Road opposite Marks Park; 3hr) and which is lovingly maintained by volunteers who weed out tons of invasive non-African plants every year. Tours take in the archeological remains of both Stone Age and Iron Age settlements near the top of the hill. Flanking the reserve on

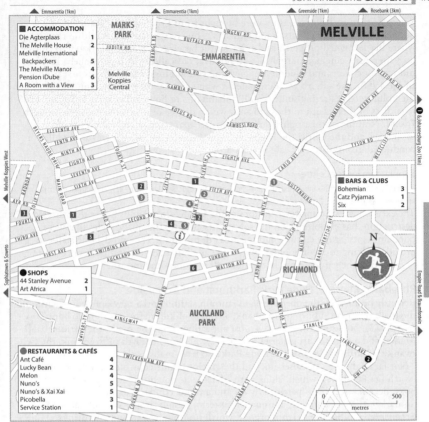

either side, Koppies East and West are public parks that are open daily from dawn until dusk: the main appeal of Melville Koppies East, reached from Zambesi Road, is the hilltop, which offers fantastic views over central Jo'burg and the leafy suburbs. Melville Koppies West has a number of good walking trails – to get there, follow Ayr Road (off Melville's Main Road) which becomes Korea and then Arundel Road, and then turn right into the Third Avenue dead-end.

Emmarentia Park and Dam

Beyers Naude Drive • Daily 8am–5pm • Free • ☎ 011 782 7064

Emmarentia Park, a large spread of green parkland running north and west of the city for several kilometres, contains the beautiful **Johannesburg Botanic Garden** in its northeast corner. Situated beside Emmarentia Dam, a popular lake for paddling and rowing, the garden is noted for its wide-open spaces and routes for joggers, cyclists and walkers which are safe during daylight hours when others are around. Apart from the fields, the botanical gardens have some attractive formal herb and rose gardens that are perfect for picnics. The main field is regularly used for concerts and festivals.

Sophiatown

West of Melville, the suburb of **Sophiatown** is unremarkable architecturally but significant in the history of apartheid – it was here that **Archbishop Trevor Huddleston**, the English cleric who established the Anti-Apartheid Movement, worked in the 1950s.

When he died in 1998, his ashes were brought from London to be scattered in Sophiatown. For many years, Sophiatown was one of the few places within the city where blacks owned property, and as a result it became a creative whirlpool of culture, jazz, literature, cinema, journalism and political radicalism; Miriam Makeba had her musical roots here, and Huddleston gave the young Hugh Masekela his first trumpet. In the 1950s, the suburb was designated a white area by the government, who sent in the bulldozers, scattering some 65,000 inhabitants to Soweto between 1955 and 1960, regardless of their claim to the land and, with a degree of irony, renaming the suburb **Triomf**. Nothing of the original suburb remains apart from two houses, the old orphanage and the Christ the King Anglican church, from where Trevor Huddleston conducted his ministry; it's safe to walk around.

Sophiatown Visitor Centre

Corner of Toby St and Edward Rd • Tues, Wed & Fri 10am–4pm, Thurs 11am–6pm, Sat 11am–3pm • R25; R30 with house tour; R60 with suburb tour • ☎ 011 673 1271, ⓦ www.trevorhuddleston.org

The excellent new **Sophiatown Visitor Centre**, located in a 1930s house that survived destruction, has exhibitions on the suburb, its culture, the music styles that were popular, "tsotsi" gang culture, and the area's destruction. The enthusiastic staff can provide walking tours of Sophiatown when called in advance, and jazz concerts are organized in the garden every last Sunday afternoon of the month.

Rosebank, Melrose, Hyde Park, Parkhurst and Greenside

Recently boosted by the opening of a Gautrain station and a new open-air extension to the mall, the small suburb of **Rosebank**, a couple of kilometres north of Jo'burg Zoo (see p.473), boasts one of the city's most appealing shopping malls, the African Craft Market and a series of art galleries (see p.492). Just to the north of Rosebank, the two swanky suburbs of **Melrose** and **Hyde Park** also have malls as their main focus.

Not far to the west of Rosebank and the gracious but sleepy old suburb of Parktown North lies **Parkhurst**, which, along with Melville, is one of the few northern suburbs to boast decent street life – particularly on and around Fourth Avenue, which is full of upmarket cafés, restaurants, antique and interior design shops. West of Parkhurst is **Greenside**, another hip neighbourhood worth heading to for food and drinks.

Sandton

Some 20km north of the CBD, **Sandton** is the archetypal northern suburb. It is outrageously rich, with plush shopping centres and endless rows of lavish houses. In the 1980s and 1990s, it became the retreat of choice for banks and large corporations fleeing the CBD. A stroll through the connected Sandton City and Nelson Mandela Square shopping centres, complete with a pseudo-Italian piazza crammed with restaurants and cafés, may make you shudder at the ostentation, but with cash to burn you'll have some fun.

At one end of **Nelson Mandela Square** is a large bronze statue of the man himself: sadly, it's a mediocre work, achieving neither a compelling likeness nor any originality of approach.

Alexandra

Soweto-based Imbizo Tours runs tours that combine the main points of interest in Soweto and Alexandra • ☎ 011 838 2667, ⓦ imbizotours.co.za

The contrast between desperately poor **Alexandra**, just east of the M1, and the surrounding suburbs could hardly be greater. When it was founded, this black township was one of the few places where blacks could own property. The sense of ownership and independence helped Alex, as it's commonly known, to avoid the forced removals of former governments. Despite the simple grid design its map suggests, the township is actually a bewildering maze with overcrowded housing and a woeful lack of basic services such as sewerage and water. Half a million people live here in an area of less than eight square kilometres, with immigrants from places such as Mozambique, Malawi and Zimbabwe putting additional pressure on the township's inadequate infrastructure. In 2008, a series of riots was sparked when immigrants were attacked in Alexandra: the riots killed two people and injured forty more, and triggered further **xenophobic violence** elsewhere in the country.

"Exhilarating and precarious" was how Nelson Mandela described Alex when he lived here in the early 1940s after running away from the Eastern Cape to find work in Jo'burg as an articled law clerk. In those days, the township was well known for its gangsters as well as its developing political militancy, which saw **bus boycotts** preventing bus companies from raising their fares, one of the first examples of mass action by blacks achieving political results. Alexandra has long been an ANC stronghold, and paid dearly for it until the collapse of apartheid, with ongoing warfare between Inkatha vigilantes and the ANC in the 1980s leading to one section of Alex being dubbed "Beirut".

While the old spirit of Alex lives on in the bustling streets on the western side of the polluted Jukskei River, the eastern bank is lined with new houses, some built by government funding and others by middle-class blacks looking to improve their quality of life but wanting to remain in the township. Here you can also see the athletes' village built when the 1999 All African Games were held in Johannesburg; named "Tsutsumane" (Shangaan for "runner"), it has since been turned into housing for locals. Not far from here a patch of land has been turned into a **cricket oval**; it's surreal to watch this most colonial of games being played against a backdrop of densely packed township shacks, with the skyscrapers of opulent Sandton peeking over the horizon beyond. While less popular than those of Soweto, tours of Alexandra are safe, authentic and very enjoyable, enabling visitors to learn about township life, just minutes from the malls of Sandton.

7

The eastern and southern suburbs

Among the oldest of the city's suburbs, and for years home to Johannesburg's Jewish and Portuguese communities, the eastern suburb of **Bezuidenhout Valley** (better known as Bez Valley) has changed dramatically in recent years, with whites moving out of much of the old housing to make way for township and immigrant blacks. **Cyrildene**, to the northeast of Bez Valley, has become the city's new Chinatown, with a fascinating collection of Chinese supermarkets, businesses and authentic restaurants along Derrick Avenue.

Most visitors to this area, however, come to **Bruma Lake**, an artificial stretch of water that has proved a disappointing attraction save for its popular and lively flea market (see p.493). Nearby, and safe for walkers, joggers and picnickers, is one of Jo'burg's more accessible green spaces, **Gillooly's Farm**, a park set around a dam. The park is overlooked by a dramatic *koppie* that can be climbed in twenty minutes.

The suburbs immediately **south of the city centre** were traditionally the preserve of the white working class. After the repeal of the Group Areas Act in 1990, blacks started moving in; unusually in contemporary South Africa, many are wealthier than the original residents.

Gold Reef City
15km south of the city centre along the M1 • Tues–Sun 9.30am–5pm • R120 • ☎ 011 248 6800, ⓦ goldreefcity.co.za

Gold Reef City is where old Johannesburg meets Disneyland: a large, gaudy entertainment complex built around the old no. 14 shaft of the Crown Mines. If you can tolerate the tackiness and piped ragtime music, there are some points of interest at what is essentially a theme park, notably the old gold mine itself, into which you can descend 200m and get an inkling of what it's like to work underground. Keep an eye out, too, for the tribal dancing that happens three times a day; the dancers are excellent, even if their routines bear little resemblance to the real thing.

You can wander round the streets filled with period houses, shops and museums, though most are generally disappointing, with the possible exception of those dedicated to early Johannesburg, such as Olthaver and Nourse House. Otherwise, the most enjoyable thing to do in Gold Reef City is to go on one of the thrill rides (all included in the entrance ticket), such as the Raging Rapids water ride and the terrifying Anaconda roller coaster. Various restaurants serve decent though pricey food, but the main focus of this section of Gold Reef City is the vast casino, complete with hundreds of slot machines and various gaming tables.

The Apartheid Museum

Just to the left of the main entrance to the Gold Reef City complex, 15km south of the city centre along the M1 • Tues–Sun 10am–5pm • R30 • ⓦ apartheidmuseum.org

The excellent **Apartheid Museum**, featuring separate entrances for "whites" and "non-whites" (your race is randomly assigned), is truly a world-class museum, delivering a sophisticated visual history that is distressing, inspiring and illuminating. The museum offers a nuanced insight into the deep social damage wrought by apartheid – and by colonial policies that long preceded it – and helps to explain the persistence of poverty and racial tension in the new South Africa. On the other hand, the museum's visual account of the jubilant advent of democracy serves to remind us how miraculous the transition was.

Give yourself plenty of time to view the permanent exhibition of photographs by Peter Magubane of the 1976 Soweto uprising, and don't miss the exhilarating short documentary on the State of Emergency during the mid-1980s, when a wave of mass demonstrations and riots, though violently suppressed, shook the resolve of the regime.

Klipriviersberg Nature Reserve

15km south of the centre on Ormonde Drive, Mondeor • Dawn–dusk • Free • ⓦ www.knra.co.za

Few Jo'burgers know about this undeveloped, unspoilt parkland, just beyond the N12 in the suburb of Mondeor. There are easy valley trails on which you can spot zebras, wildebeest, hartebeest and other wildlife, as well as strenuous uphill hikes rewarded by wonderful views of the city to the north.

Soweto

South Africa's most famous township, **Soweto** (short for South West Townships), is a place of surreal contrasts. The area was home to two Nobel Peace Prize winners, yet suffers one of the highest rates of murder and rape in the world; it is the richest township in South Africa, home to a growing number of millionaires, but has some of the most desperate poverty; it is the most political township, yet has the most nihilistic youth.

Southwest of the city centre, Soweto is huge, stretching as far as the eye can see, with a population estimated at between three and four million. Like any city of that size, it is divided into a number of different suburbs, with middle- and upper-class neighbourhoods among them. At first sight, it appears an endless jumble of houses and shacks, overshadowed by palls of smoke, though parts of it have a villagey feel. Apart from the Hector Pieterson Memorial and Museum, most of Soweto's **tourist highlights** are physically unimpressive, their fame stemming from historical associations. That history, however, is enthralling, not least because here it is told with a perspective and context rarely found in the rest of South Africa. For visitors it means an insight not just into a place much mentioned in 1980s news bulletins for funerals and fighting, but into a way of life most Westerners rarely encounter.

A visit to Soweto with one of the many **tours** (see box, p.480) is the single most popular attraction in Johannesburg. Where once these had a whiff of daring and originality, a

7

VISITING SOWETO

For information, head to the Soweto Tourism Information Centre on Walter Sisulu Square in Kliptown (Mon–Fri 8am–5pm; ☎011 342 4316).

The most common – and convenient – way to visit Soweto is with a **tour operator**. By far the oldest, biggest and slickest operation is Jimmy's Face to Face Tours (☎011 331 6109, Ⓦface2face.co.za). Jimmy pioneered tours into the township, and currently offers three-hour, half-day and night tours, some in combination with the Apartheid Museum. Imbizo Tours (☎011 838 2667 or ☎083 717 8663, Ⓦimbizotours.co.za), run by the irrepressible Mandy Mankazana, provides stiff competition – particularly recommended are her evening *shebeen* crawls lasting up to five hours, depending on your stamina (indicate what kind of company you would like to keep, from politicians to sports fanatics, and Mandy will select an appropriate venue). Another recommended way to experience the township is on the bicycle tours offered by Soweto Bicycle Tours (☎011 936 3444, Ⓦsowetobicycletours.com).

As well as the well-established operators, smaller, more flexible outfits offer imaginative **alternative tours** such as jazz outings, walks around Orlando West and Diepkloof, visits to Sowetan artists or local churches, and homestays with locals. Try Phaphama's language immersion tours (☎011 982 2088, Ⓦphaphama.org) or Past Experiences (☎011 678 3905, Ⓦpastexperiences.co.za); alternatively, your accommodation may well have links to a reliable tour company or you can choose to travel independently using the safe Rea Vaya BRT bus system.

well-trodden tourist trail has developed, and unless you're content to follow the herds of minibuses and coaches around the conventional sights, visiting the same shantytowns and *shebeens*, it's well worth using an operator who mixes the highlights with lesser-known sights. Most outfits are keen for you to "meet the people", though conversations can tend to be strained and lead to your leaving a "donation" or buying local craftwork. While this gets a few tourist dollars directly into the townships, it often leaves visitors feeling pressurized and vulnerable. Ask your guide about the best way to deal with this.

At one time, taking yourself to Soweto would have meant a display of bravado bordering on foolhardiness, but it's now possible to visit the main sights **independently**. In Soweto, residents will stop to greet you or to chat, regardless of your colour. There are surprisingly few criminal incidents affecting tourists, though as ever it pays to remain vigilant; exploring less-visited areas by yourself, or going after dark, isn't recommended for safety reasons. If you want to drive to Soweto, you'll need good navigational skills – the lack of obvious landmarks amid kilometre upon kilometre of boxy little houses can be highly confusing. The new Rea Vaya bus route from the city centre that passes near Vilakazi Street offers a good alternative to taking a minibus taxi to Soweto, which are more confusing than dangerous, as it isn't always easy to ascertain which part of the township they are heading for. Forming a cross with two fingers is the recognized minibus signal indicating that you want to go to "crossroads", which will bring you to the centre of Soweto. From here you can pick up another taxi to whichever sight you want to visit, though even in a taxi you may be let out on one of the main roads and have to walk a little way to reach your target.

Orlando West and Dube

Set in the northern part of Soweto, **Orlando West** and **Dube** qualify as two of its more affluent suburbs, with a number of sights and the greatest concentration of places to eat and drink. **Orlando East**, across Klipspruit Valley from Orlando West, was the first part of Soweto to be established in 1932, and the area is fairly easily accessible by car off the Soweto Highway (M70).

Hector Pieterson Memorial and Museum

8287 Khumalo St, Orlando West • Mon–Fri 10am–5pm, Sat & Sun 10am–4.30pm • R25 • ☎011 536 0611 • Using the Rea Vaya BRT bus from Jo'burg CBD, get off at Boomtown stop, and then walk or take the F4 feeder bus to Vilakazi St

The **Hector Pieterson Memorial and Museum**, opened in 2002, was named after the first student to be killed in the Soweto uprising (see box, below). Dedicated to Pieterson and the other students who died, the museum focuses specifically on the events surrounding and leading up to the Soweto uprising. The startling brutality used in the repression of student activists is depicted in video and pictures, including images from well-known black photographers such as Peter Magubane and Sam Nzima. Interestingly, Hector's sister Antoinette Sithole (see box, below) currently works in the museum.

The Mandela House Museum
Vilakazi St • Mon–Fri 9am–5pm, Sat & Sun 9am–4pm • R60 • ☎ 011 936 7754, ⊛ mandelahouse.com • Use the same Rea Vaya BRT bus stop as for the Pieterson Memorial

Vilakazi Street was once home to Nelson Mandela and Desmond Tutu. **Mandela's bungalow** is where he lived with Winnie in the late 1950s and early 1960s, before his imprisonment on Robben Island, and where Winnie lived until exiled to the Free State (from which she returned to an imposing brick house with high walls and security cameras, just down the road). On his release, Nelson insisted on returning to his old home, but its small size and lack of security proved too much of a strain, and he moved out of Soweto. Tours of the old bungalow mix fascinatingly mundane memorabilia,

7

THE SOWETO UPRISING OF 1976

The **student uprising** that began in Soweto in June 1976 was a defining moment in South African history. The revolt was sparked off by a government ruling that **Afrikaans** should be used on an equal basis with English in black secondary schools. While this was feasible in some rural areas, it was quite impossible in the townships, where neither pupils nor teachers knew the language.

On June 16, student delegates from every Soweto school launched their long-planned mass protest march through the township and a rally at the Orlando football stadium. Incredibly, details of the plan were kept secret from the omnipresent *impimpis* (informers). Soon after the march started, however, the police attacked, throwing tear gas and then firing. The crowd panicked, and demonstrators started throwing stones at the police. The police fired again. Out of this bedlam came the famous photograph of the first student to die, Hector Pieterson, bleeding at the mouth, being carried by a friend, while his sister Antoinette looks on in anguished horror.

The police retreated to Orlando East, and students rushed to collect the injured and dead, erect barricades, and destroy everything they could belonging to the municipal authority, including beer halls. The attacks heightened the antagonism between the youth and many older people who thought that class boycotts were irresponsible, given the students' already dismal employment prospects. Students responded angrily, accusing their elders of apathy in the face of oppression, which they attributed in part to drunkenness. In a society that has traditionally regarded respect for the old as sacrosanct, this was a historic departure and its effects still reverberate throughout South Africa's townships.

In the days following June 16, all Soweto schools were closed indefinitely, thousands of police were stationed throughout the township, and police brutality continued unabated. In the face of worldwide condemnation the government ascribed the violence to Communist agitation, citing as evidence the clenched-fist salutes of the students, though this was really an indication of their support for South Africa's **Black Consciousness Movement**, founded by Steve Biko (see p.340). Meanwhile, rebellion spread to other townships, particularly in Cape Town. In Soweto, schools did not reopen until 1978, by which time many students had abandoned any hope of formal education. Some had left the country to join the military wings of the ANC and PAC, while others stayed at home, forming "street committees" to politicize and police the communities. Others drifted into unemployment.

Now the armed struggle is over, the problems that face the former students of 1976 are manifold. As their parents warned, their lack of qualifications counts against them in the job market, even if June 16 is now a national holiday, during which they are praised for their role in the struggle. The street committees have dissolved, but the guns remain.

including some original furnishings, a collection of Winnie and Nelson's photographs and audiovisual displays describing living conditions in Soweto at the time Mandela lived there.

Regina Mundi Church

Near the junction of Klipspruit Valley (the M10) and Potchefstroom (the M68) rds • The closest Lakeview Rea Vaya BRT bus is near the church

The **Regina Mundi Church** is Soweto's largest Catholic church and was the focus of numerous gatherings in the struggle years. Again, its impact owes more to historical aura than aesthetic appeal, although with so few large buildings in the township it has a certain presence. The caretaker shows visitors around; look out for the bullet holes left in the ceiling by the South African police, and the (black) Madonna and Child painting near the altar.

Kliptown Open Air Museum

Walter Sisulu Square • Mon–Sat 10am–5pm, Sun 10am–4.30pm • Free • The Rea Vaya BRT feeder bus F5 travels from Lakeview to Klipspruitvalley Rd for Sisulu Square

The **Walter Sisulu Square of Dedication** is the site where the ANC's Freedom Charter was proclaimed to thousands in 1955. The square is also home to the **Kliptown Open Air Museum**, on its western side, which explains the history behind the Freedom Charter through photographs, documents and news clippings, and is worth a look once you've finished with the Hector Pieterson and Mandela House museums.

FNB Stadium

Nasrec, Soweto • Tours by appointment only • Mon–Fri at 9am, 10.30am, noon, 1.30pm & 3pm, Sat & Sun at noon & 1.30pm • R80 • ☎ 011 247 5300, ⓦ stadiummanagement.co.za

Positioned halfway between the CBD and Soweto in Nasrec and known as Soccer City during the 2010 Football World Cup, Africa's largest stadium is a beautiful structure, designed by South African architects and built on top of an older football stadium that was used for Mandela's first speech after his release from prison in 1990. With earth colours on the exterior that blend in nicely with the adjacent mine dumps, the interior is larger than you'd expect, with ninety thousand orange seats spread across three tiers. Unlike some other World Cup venues in South Africa, this stadium is no white elephant and regularly fills to capacity for matches, concerts and rallies. If you can't make it to a game, the sixty- to ninety-minute tours of the stadium are very worthwhile, taking in the players' rooms and VIP areas.

ARRIVAL AND DEPARTURE   JOHANNESBURG

BY PLANE

OR Tambo International Airport (☎ 086 727 7888, ⓦ airports.co.za), named after the ANC's greatest leader in exile, lies 20km east of the city centre. On the ground floor of the international arrivals hall there's a tourist information desk (daily 5.30am–10pm; ☎ 011 390 3614) and 24-hour facilities for changing money; ATMs, a post office and an internet café can be found on the first floor.

ONWARD TRANSPORT

Gautrain The fastest and easiest way to get to the city – especially during the dreaded morning and afternoon rush hours – is on the brand-new Gautrain rail link (daily 5.30am–8.30pm; see p.484), which takes fifteen minutes to reach Sandton station (R105), where you can change for trains south to Rosebank and Park stations and north to Pretoria, or use the Gautrain feeder buses to Sandton's hotels.

Buses Alternatively, the Airport Shuttle (☎ 086 1748 8853, ⓦ www.airportshuttle.co.za; R350–1050, R50 extra between 9pm and 5.30am) offers a round-the-clock pick-up and drop-off service from the airport; book a day in advance. Another good bet is the Magic Bus service, which offers door-to-door transfers to the main suburbs (from R300); buy tickets at the company's office (☎ 011 394 6902, ⓦ www.magicbus.co.za) on the ground floor of the domestic Parkade building.

Courtesy buses The more expensive hotels often provide courtesy buses, while most backpacker hostels and some smaller guesthouses or B&Bs offer free pick-ups (which are best booked when making your reservation) and sometimes free drop-offs back to the airport.

Taxis Taking a metered taxi from the airport is convenient and safe, though you should make certain the driver knows where you're going before you set off, and get a quote beforehand. The official ORTIA Taxi Association (☎011 390 1502, ⓦjiata.co.za/ortiata) has a stand next to the tourism office in the arrivals hall where you can book rides. You should pay around R380 to get to central Jo'burg, Rosebank or Sandton, and no more than R450 to reach a far northern or western suburb.

Car rental Standard car rental deals are available from the main companies such as Avis (☎011 394 5433), Budget (☎011 398 0123), EuropCar (☎086 113 1000) and Tempest (☎011 578 0160), which all have offices at both airports and in several city locations. For cheaper deals try Apex Rent-a-Wreck (13 Siemert Rd, CBD, ☎011 402 5150, ⓦrentawreck .co.za) and Comet (meets customers at the airport, ☎011 974 9618, ⓦcometcar.co.za), or book via a broker website like ⓦcarhire.co.za. It's also always worth asking at your accommodation if they have any discount arrangements.

Airline information All of the following airlines have ticket offices at OR Tambo International Airport: Air France ☎086 134 0340; British Airways ☎011 441 800; Lufthansa ☎0861 842 538; KLM ☎011 961 6700; South African Airways ☎011 978 1000, SA Airlink ☎011 395 3579, SA Express ☎011 978 5577. Qantas, 195 Jan Smuts Ave, Parktown North (☎011 441 8550), and Virgin Atlantic, 50 Sixth Rd, Hyde Park (☎011 340 3500), have offices in the city.

LANSERIA AIRPORT

Jo'burg's secondary Lanseria Airport (☎011 367 0300, ⓦwww.lanseria.co.za) is 30km northwest of the city centre and is used by an increasing number of budget airlines. Taxis don't tend to wait at this airport and there's no public transport, so either organize a transfer with your accommodation or call a taxi (see p.385).

Destinations: Bloemfontein (5–10 daily; 1hr); Cape Town (more than 70 daily; 2hr); Durban (more than 50 daily; 1hr); East London (8 daily; 1hr 25min); Hoedspruit (2 daily; 1hr); Kimberley (3–7 daily; 1hr 30min); Nelspruit (4–6 daily; 1hr 50min); Pietermaritzburg (2–4 daily; 1hr); Port Elizabeth (15 daily; 1hr 40min); Richard's Bay (6 daily; 1hr 30min); Umtata (4 daily; 1hr 45min); Upington (2 daily; 1hr 50min).

BY CAR

Toll roads Note that to pay for extensive roadworks over the past years a much-hated electronic road toll system came into effect in 2011 for the N1, N3, N12 and R21 around Jo'burg and up to Pretoria; all vehicles are charged

at about R0.50 per kilometre by automatic toll gantries that span the highways. Visitors are expected to register beforehand via ⓦnra.co.za or to buy a day pass, though details were still vague at time of research.

Rush hour When driving to Pretoria, it's wise to avoid the afternoon rush hour northwards (from 3.30–5pm), when travel time can double to 2hr; this is also when a quick 45min drive to the airport can turn into a two-hour ordeal.

BY BUS AND MINIBUS

Greyhound, Intercape and Translux buses, and minibuses arrive at Park Station in the centre of town. Once notoriously unsafe, Park Station has been significantly improved in recent years, and the main concourse is big, open and secure, with information desks for all the bus companies. That said, it's not a good idea to walk around the surrounding area with a lot of luggage, so you're best off taking the Gautrain or a taxi to your final destination, or arranging a pick-up with your accommodation. Park Station has a number of car rental offices conveniently located on the upper concourse, usually listed under the name "Braamfontein" on their websites.

Destinations: Reithridge (3 daily; 7hr); Bloemfontein (16 daily; 5hr); Cape Town (6 daily; 19hr 30min); Durban (16 daily; 8–11hr); East London (12 daily; 12hr 45min); Kimberley (5 daily; 6hr 30min); King William's Town (3 daily; 12hr 15min); Knysna (daily; 17hr); Kuruman (daily; 7hr); Ladysmith (2 daily; 5hr 45min); Mossel Bay (2 daily; 17hr); Nelspruit (6 daily; 5hr); Newcastle (daily; 5hr); Oudtshoorn (2 daily; 14hr 30min); Pietermaritzburg (16 daily; 7hr); Plettenberg Bay (daily; 17hr 30min); Port Elizabeth (4 daily; 13hr 15min); Pretoria (over 30 daily; 1hr); Umtata (daily; 11hr 30min).

Baz Bus operates services from Johannesburg to Durban via the Drakensberg (5 weekly), stopping at hostels in the city.

Destinations: Durban (8hr); Pietermaritzburg (6hr 30min); Pretoria (1hr); Amphitheatre, Northern Drakensberg (4hr).

BY TRAIN

Gautrain and intercity trains pull in at Park Station in the centre of town (see p.484). The Airport Shuttle (see opposite) can provide a pick-up and drop-off service from Sandton Gautrain station.

Destinations: Bloemfontein (Wed, Fri & Sun; 7hr); Cape Town (1–3 daily; 26hr 15min); Durban (7 weekly; 13–14hr); Kimberley (daily; 8hr 15min); Port Elizabeth (Wed, Fri & Sun; 20hr); Pretoria (more than 30 daily; 45min).

GETTING AROUND

Johannesburg's **public transport** system is undergoing something of a revolution, with the recently launched Gautrain rail and bus network and Rea Vaya rapid bus (BRT) system being very well received by city residents. Currently, Rea Vaya only shuttled to Soweto and back, but the network is set to link up with the Gautrain stations and to expand to the northern suburbs in coming years. However, driving still remains very much the order of the day in Jo'burg, though the CBD and some suburbs, notably Melville, are easily explored on foot. **Private taxis**, which should be booked in advance by telephone (see p.485), are an expensive option in Jo'burg as a simple journey to the CBD from the northern suburbs will cost at least R200.

7

BY CAR

Getting around The best way to explore Johannesburg is still in your own car. Although road signs can be poor and the local drivers pushy, familiarity with a few key roads, careful map reading before you set out or a GPS device makes driving around relatively straightforward. In the city centre, the grid system does make navigation reasonably logical, though it's beset by one-way streets. SatPack (Wsatpacktravel.com) has free downloadable maps of Jo'burg and other destinations in South Africa that you can use on any mobile phone to avoid driving into any no-go zones; they also have a tailor-made itinerary planning service. Avoid driving around the city centre from 4pm to 6pm when rush hour gridlock jams up the streets.

Routes The M1 connects the centre to the northern suburbs, crossing above Newtown on a flyover, through Braamfontein and Parktown, and heading into Houghton and Sandton, eventually turning into the N1 for Pretoria. South of the centre, the M1 is one of the best routes to Soweto. The next artery west of the M1, also useful for heading north, is Oxford Rd, which starts off in Parktown, and becomes Rivonia Rd once it enters Sandton. West again is Jan Smuts Avenue, which passes through Rosebank and Dunkeld before hitting Hyde Park.

Parking If you're travelling into the city centre by car, guarded parking can be found underneath Gandhi Square, in the Carlton Centre parkade on Main St (connected to the Centre via an underground passage) or at the Market Theatre.

BY BUS

Metrobus Most of Jo'burg's municipal Metrobus routes start and end at the main terminus in Gandhi Square, off Eloff St in the city centre. There's a bus information office in the Gandhi Mall on the southern side of Gandhi Square (Mon–Fri 6am–6pm, Sat 8am–1pm; ☎011 375 5555, Wjoburg.org.za/bus), where you can pick up timetables. Buses only run between the suburbs and the centre, so are useless for getting from one suburb to another, unless they both lie on the same route to town. Most buses stop by 6.30pm, though a small number keep going until 9.30pm. At weekends very few routes have services and there are waits of at least an hour between buses. Fares (R7–19, depending on distance) should be paid to the driver; ensure you get a ticket as you may need to show it to a ticket inspector. Useful routes include the #67 to Melville and the #05CD to Rosebank and Sandton.

BRT The new Rea Vaya Bus Rapid Transit (BRT) system (Wreavaya.org.za) is a fast and safe way to get from the CBD to Soweto as it uses dedicated roads and lanes; the high-floor buses only stop at specially designed raised bus stops which are clean, enclosed and well guarded. The network was still under construction at the time of writing, with a new line

from Park Station to Soweto (passing Melville) planned to open next. The first trunk line, the T1 from Ellis Park in the CBD to Thokoza Park in Soweto, has several feeder (F) bus routes, and links up with the C3 inner-city circular route. Handy for tourists, this line links the Johannesburg Art Gallery with the Old Fort on Constitution Hill, the Origins Centre in Braamfontein, Park Station, Rissik St, Newtown and the Carlton Centre, where you can transfer to the T1 to Soweto. Tickets (R7.30 for the trunk route, R4 for the feeder buses and the inner-city circular route) are valid for two hours and can be bought at the stops. Buses on the trunk route run every 5–16 minutes on weekdays from about 5am to 8pm, and every 20–30min on weekends between 6am and 6pm; the inner-city circular route has buses every 15–20min on weekdays from 6am to 8.30pm, and every 15–30min on weekends between 7am and 5.30pm. The Rea Vaya website has handy maps showing the main sights in CBD and Soweto in relation to the bus stops.

Gautrain feeder buses The shiny gold Gautrain feeder buses (Wgautrain.co.za) serve all Gautrain stations except for the airport station (weekdays only; R20, R6 if combined with a train journey); you'll need a pre-loaded Gautrain Gold Card to travel on them. Useful routes include: from Park Station to Parktown, from Rosebank Station to Hyde Park Corner mall and Melrose Arch mall, and from Sandton Station to the Montecasino complex in Fourways. Route information can be found at the stations, the bus stops and online; call ☎010 223 1098 to find out the exact arrival time of the next bus.

BY MINIBUS TAXI

Minibus taxis transport the vast majority of commuters, and cover the widest area. They can be picked up at ranks or hailed mid-route by either raising your forefinger if you're heading into town, pointing downwards if you want to go uptown or pointing towards yourself if you want Park Central Taxi Terminus, where most of the city's minibus taxis terminate. This is a hectic place and can be a little intimidating: be vigilant and discreet with your valuables and you should avoid any problems. Minibuses for Melville leave from rank #1, for Sandton from rank #2 and for Orlando West in Soweto from rank #9. Fares start at R5–8 for short rides.

BY TRAIN

Gautrain The rapid rail network (☎011 4288 7242, Wgautrain.co.za) was completed in 2011 and connects Johannesburg's Park Station to Pretoria via Rosebank and Sandton, with an airport line branching off at Sandton. Security is very tight with guards at stations and on every train car. The system uses Gold Cards (one-off purchase fee R10) that can be purchased and charged with money at stations and used to pay for train travel, as well as on the feeder buses and for parking. Trains run daily from 5.30am to 8pm at intervals of 15 to 30 minutes. The fare from Park Station to Rosebank is R19, to Sandton R21.

Metrorail The city's other suburban train system, Metrorail, has a poor security reputation, very limited services and is best avoided.

INFORMATION AND TOURS

Tourist information Gauteng Tourism's main office is in Newtown at 1 Central Place, Henry Nxumalo St (Mon–Fri 8am–5pm; ☎011 639 1600, ⓦ www.gauteng.net), with another useful kiosk attached to the African Craft Market in Rosebank (daily 9am–5pm). The free maps available from these offices are poor quality, and if you're driving around the city you'll need a GPS device or a detailed street guide such as Mapstudio's *Gauteng Central Street Guide*, available from most bookshops. In Melville (see p.474), the Melville Visitors Centre, corner of Seventh St and First Ave (Mon–Sat 9am–6pm; ☎072 305 0281, ⓦ melvillesa.co.za), has information on accommodation, art and photography exhibitions and crafts for sale.

Tours The Parktown & Westcliff Heritage Trust (☎011 482

BY TAXI

Reliable taxi companies include Maxi Taxis (☎011 648 1212) and Rose Taxi (☎011 403 0000), usually charging fixed rates. Taxis often also wait outside the large hotels and the main Gautrain stations.

3349 from Mon–Fri 9am–1pm, ⓦ parktownheritage.co.za) conducts walking and bus tours (from R80) most Saturday afternoons to various destinations in the city centre and the suburbs. These follow diverse themes and are a good way to acquaint yourself with the more interesting areas of this sprawling city. Tours can be booked directly with the Trust or via ⓦ computicket.com. The travel agency Past Experiences (☎011 478 3647, ⓦ pastexperiences.co.za) offers tailor-made tours of Johannesburg and the archeological sites west of town, and also does regular group tours of the city centre and Soweto; these are fun to join as they often use public transport and the other participants are usually locals rediscovering their city, allowing for interaction with all kinds of Jo'burgers.

ACCOMMODATION

There's plenty of accommodation to be found in Jo'burg's **northern suburbs**, which are the easiest places to stay if you have to rely on public transport. Melville is relatively close to the CBD and offers something many visitors don't expect to find in Johannesburg: a characterful community with cafés, restaurants and bars within safe walking distance of a great number of guesthouses. Rosebank is well located at the heart of the northern suburbs, and has a decent selection of places to eat out or shop. In Sandton there's a wealth of pricey chain hotels aimed at business executives, as well as some lovely large private homes with huge gardens that offer bed and breakfast. It is possible to stay in the townships, where a few guesthouses have opened. The most rewarding option is to stay with locals, something best arranged through an experienced tour operator (see p.above).

CENTRAL SUBURBS

★ **12 Decades Art Hotel** 286 Fox St ☎010 007 0102, ⓦ mainstreetlife.co.za/art-hotel; map pp.464–465. Each room at this hotel on the top floor of the Main St Life building (see p.469) has been designed to reflect a specific decade in the life of Jo'burg. Mining, theatre, apartheid (with race laws printed in the toilet bowl) and the Ponte building are just a few of the themes. **R545**

Brown Sugar 75 Observatory Ave, Observatory Ext 1 ☎011 648 7397, ⓦ brownsugarbackpackers.com; map pp.464–465. A well-known hostel on Observatory Ridge, located in a mansion built for a drug baron and offering accommodation in dorms, rooms and log cabins. Come here for a fast-track introduction to Jo'burg's hedonistic nightlife rather than comfort or chilling out. Dorm **R160**, double **R300**

Diamond Diggers Backpackers 36 Doris St, Kensington ☎011 624 1676, ⓦ diamonddiggers.com; map pp.464–465. Boasting a dramatic view of the inner-city skyline, this cheap but clean and organized lodge is not too far from the airport and downtown Jo'burg. Dorm **R70**, double **R150**

Mapungubwe Hotel Apartments 54 Marshall St, Marshalltown, CBD ☎011 429 2700, ⓦ mapungubwehotel.co.za; map pp.464–465. Set in a former bank near the Anglo American and BHP Billiton offices, the first luxury hotel to open in the city centre for decades has an impressive foyer, stylishly furnished rooms and apartments, and a bar in the old underground bank vaults. **R1290**

NORTHERN SUBURBS

Backpackers' Ritz 1A North Rd (off Jan Smuts Ave), Dunkeld West ☎011 325 7125, ⓦ www.backpackers-ritz.co.za; map p.472. A well-known, busy lodge in a large suburban house halfway between Rosebank and Sandton, with a pool, gardens and travel centre. Dorm **R125**, double **R375**

★ **Claire's of Sandton** 42 Eighth St, Parkmore, Sandton ☎011 784 1639, ⓦ clairesofsandton.co.za; map p.472. Comfortable rooms with great attention to detail, friendly and helpful hosts, and a big pool make this one of the northern suburbs' best guesthouses. Special rates for longer stays. **R880**

7

7

★ **Die Agterplaas** 66 Sixth Ave, Melville ☎011 726 8452, ⊛agterplaas.co.za; map p.475. Just a short walk from Melville's restaurants and cafés, this neat, tasteful guesthouse has rooms with views over the Melville *koppies* from pleasant balconies and more rooms in a house across the road. The famed breakfasts attract non-guests as well. R790

The Grace in Rosebank 54 Bath Ave, Rosebank ☎011 280 7200, ⊛www.thegrace.co.za; map p.472. One of the most luxurious hotels in town, with stylish, sophisticated rooms aimed at business travellers, and a convenient central location. R4510

★ **The Melville House** 59 Fourth Ave, Melville ☎011 726 3503, ⊛themelvillehouse.com; map p.475. One of the best Melville guesthouses, close to cafés and restaurants and genuinely plugged in to what's going on in Jo'burg. The owner is a writer and manages to create a lively, sociable atmosphere that attracts plenty of fellow artists. There's a garden with a small pool too. R880

Melville International Backpackers 37 First Ave, Melville ☎011 482 5797, ⊛melvillebackpackers.co.za; map p.475. A small, relaxed hostel between Melville's Main and 7th sts, with wooden floors, ornate pressed metal ceilings and a pool. Dorm R150, double R450

The Melville Manor 80 Second Ave, Melville ☎011 726 8765, ⊛melvillemanor.co.za; map p.475. In an elegantly restored Victorian house, this welcoming, well-run guesthouse with a pool and a great communal kitchen and dining area is less than a minute's walk from the Melville restaurant strip. R630

★ **Pension iDube** 11 Walton Ave, Auckland Park ☎011 482 4055 or ☎082 682 3799, ⊛pensionidube .co.za; map p.475. A great budget guesthouse with tastefully decorated doubles, a communal kitchen and lounge, a pool and a friendly, easy-going atmosphere, just a few blocks from Melville's cafés and nightlife. R480

Premiere Classe Suite Hotel 62 Corlett Drive, Melrose North ☎011 788 1967, ⊛premiereclasse. co.za; map p.472. A calm, quiet and friendly hotel with comfortable one and two-bedroom suites with fully equipped kitchens and free internet. It's close to the Melrose Arch complex and the Wanderers cricket stadium. Long-term rates available. R600

A Room with a View 1 Tolip St, Melville ☎011 482 5435, ⊛aroomwithaview.co.za; map p.475. A grand and charmingly surreal two-storey Italian-style villa, laid out and decorated in exuberant style, with twelve rooms, an indoor pool, efficient service and plenty of light provided by balconies and skylights. R920

Sandton Lodge Inanda 66 Sixth Ave, Inanda, Sandton ☎011 788 4169, ⊛sandtonlodge.co.za; map p.472. Sleek, modern rooms with flat-screen TVs and large beds in a lovely house backed by a pretty garden with fountains. There are sister lodges in Bryanston and Rivonia. R1300

Ten Bompas 10 Bompas Rd, Dunkeld West ☎011 341 0282, ⊛tenbompas.com; map p.472. One of Jo'burg's most stylish small hotels, with each of its quiet and intimate suites (all with fireplaces and separate living areas) decorated by a different interior designer. Rates include laundry and internet. R3500

★ **The Westcliff** 67 Jan Smuts Ave, Westcliff ☎011 481 6000, ⊛westcliff.co.za; map p.472. The size of a small village, painted pink and built on a high east-facing ridge, the *grande dame* of Jo'burg's upmarket hotels has elegant rooms and suites accented by soft, gentle tones. A main attraction is the bar and infinity pool, which overlook the lush green expanse of the northern suburbs – you can even watch the elephants in the nearby zoo. The cocktails are fantastic. R2515

EASTERN SUBURBS

Africa Rest 10 Church St, Kempton Park ☎011 394 3940, ⊛www.africarest.co.za. A motel and hostel near to the airport with cheap and clean rooms and a free shuttle service. Dorm R80, double R150

Airport En Route 97 Boden Rd, Benoni Small Farms, Benoni ☎011 963 3389, ⊛sa-venues.com/visit/ airportenroute. A tidy, congenial budget lodge located 15 minutes from the airport (pickups from R80) in the famously sleepy suburb where film star Charlize Theron grew up. Accommodation is in cosy, three-bed log cabins, some of which are en suite, and two rooms sleeping up to four people (R550); camping is also available. Camping R80, cabin R300

The Aviator Corner of Kempton and Bosch St, Kempton Park ☎011 921 8300, ⊛signaturelifehotels.com. Just 3km from the airport, this new hotel has everything you need for a stopover: modern rooms, a pool with deckchairs, a decent restaurant, and free transfers to and from the airport and the Rhodesfield Gautrain station. R630

French Guest House 16 Meintjies St, Rhodesfield, Kempton Park ☎011 394 5245, ⊛joburg -frenchguesthouse.com. A simple French-owned guesthouse 8km from the airport but away from the noise, offering a pool, free airport shuttle and French meals. A stone's throw from the Rhodesfield Gautrain station, for cheap transport into the city. R600

★ **Purple Palms** 1 Boompeiper Ave, Birch Acres, Kempton Park ☎011 393 4393, ⊛purplepalms.co.za. Cheerful, organized and exceptionally clean self-catering set-up close to the airport with a small pool, garden, free internet and book exchanges, plus a "day stay" option for short airport stopovers. There's a supermarket within easy walking distance. More luxurious than your average hostel. Dorm R90, double R220

SOWETO

Botle's Guest House 648 Monyane St, Dube Village ☎082 838 1886, ⊛botleguest.co.za. Housed in an unprepossessing brick house, but very comfortable and secure, and just a short trip from Vilakazi St and the Hector Pieterson Memorial. R770

Lebo's Soweto Backpackers 10823a Pooe St, Orlando West ☎011 936 3444, ⓦsowetobackpackers.com. One of the country's few black-owned backpacker hostels, with dorms, singles, doubles and camping. Walking and cycling tours, and volunteer opportunities in Soweto are also available. Camping R80, dorm R120, double R300

Lolo's Guest House 1320 Diepkloof Extension, Diepkloof ☎011 985 9183, ⓔlolosbb@mweb.co.za. A smart and modern guesthouse run by former teacher Mrs Lolo Mabitsela in the historic Diepkloof district. There's a small garden, guarded parking and a conference room;

tailor-made tours, including Soweto bar crawls, can be arranged. R550

Vhavenda Hills B&B 11749 Mampuru St, Orlando West Extension ☎011 936 0411, ⓦsowetobnb.co.za. This tidy, colourful B&B is close to the Soweto tourism district. Satellite TV, laundry service and struggle stories are part of the deal. R600

Zizwe Guesthouse 8108 Ngakane St, Orlando West ☎011 942 2685, ⓔzizwer@telkomsa.net. Close to Mandela's original home in the heart of Soweto, this guesthouse occupies one of the unadorned, flat-roofed buildings typical of the area. Rooms are simply furnished and have their own private bathroom, with use of a shared kitchen. R500

EATING

The wealth, diversity and fast-paced social life of Johannesburg combined with its cosmopolitan nature means that the city has a huge range of places to eat out. Authentic French, Italian, Chinese, Greek and Portuguese restaurants are all found here, and there are increasing numbers of African restaurants, not just township South African but also Congolese, Moroccan, Ethiopian and Cape Malay. Prices are inevitably a bit higher than elsewhere in the country outside Cape Town and the Winelands, and you can blow out in spectacular style, but an average meal out is still good value. The bulk of Jo'burg's restaurants are in the **northern suburbs**; the key places to try are Seventh Street in Melville, the junction of Greenway and Gleneagles in Greenside, and Fourth Avenue in Parkhurst (west of Parktown North). The Melrose Arch complex in Melrose is another congenial place for a meal, with plenty of upmarket restaurants and cafés grouped together around a square. All of Jo'burg's **shopping malls** are well stocked with takeaways and restaurants, frequently unadventurous, bland chains, though some top-notch venues do exist in malls. If you don't fancy heading out even for a takeaway meal, you can make use of a service called **Mr Delivery**, which picks up and delivers meals from a range of reasonable mid-priced eating places: contact them on ⓦmrdelivery.com or ☎011 482 4748 (Melville), ☎011 442 4411 (Rosebank) or ☎011 784 6000 (Sandton).

CBD

There are a few truly original restaurants in Newtown, which is a generally safe area to eat out at night, as well as new venues in Braamfontein and elsewhere.

Canteen 264 Fox St ☎011 334 5947; map pp.464–465. The restaurant in the Arts on Main courtyard is set beside the olive tree garden and has a varied international menu priced around R60 – including some great burgers. Tues & Wed 9am–4pm, Thurs–Sun 9am–1am.

Gramadoelas at the Market Theatre Miriam Makeba St, Newtown ☎011 838 6960; map pp.464–465. A venerable restaurant famous for its authentic Cape and African dishes like *sosaties*, Mopani worms and *umngqusho* (braised beef, beans and maize). The visitors' book is star-studded. Most mains R70–90. Tues–Sat noon–10pm, Sun & Mon 5–10pm.

Guildhall Pub Corner of Market and Harrison sts ☎011 833 1770; map pp.464–465. A wonderful, traditional pub founded in 1888 just after gold was discovered, making it Jo'burg's oldest watering hole. It still looks the part, though nowadays tasty Portuguese food (R25–60) is served along with the beer. Have lunch on the first-floor balcony for rare CBD street views. Mon–Fri 11am–2am, Sat 11am–7pm.

Lucky Moo Gandhi Square ☎011 492 0628,

ⓦluckymoo.co.za; map pp.464–465. This successful city-centre venture serves tasty and affordable (mains R40) Chinese wok dishes to eat in the tiny restaurant, on the terrace outside or to take away. Mon–Fri 9am–5pm, first and last Sat of the month 9am–3pm.

Narina Trogon 81 De Korte St, Braamfontein ☎011 339 6645; map pp.464–465. Named after the eponymous colourful bird, this beautifully designed restaurant has fireplaces, movable glass partitions and an amazing walled-in terrace at the back. The short menu lists innovative international dishes (around R100) and, unusually for Jo'burg, proper freshly squeezed juices. Mon & Tues 7am–4pm, Wed–Fri 7am–10pm, Sat 5–10pm.

Niki's Oasis 138 Bree St, Newtown ☎011 492 1134; map pp.464–465. Local staples such as oxtail, tripe, *potjiekos* (stew) and *pap* (mostly around R70), and regular live jazz. Situated opposite the Market Theatre. Mon–Sat 11.30am–midnight.

Post 70 Juta St, Braamfontein; map pp.464–465. On the corner of the hip Juta Street development, *Post* serves healthy sandwiches, cakes, coffee and home-made lemonade, with large windows and a stack of LPs to select the background music from. Tues–Fri 6.30am–4pm, Sat 8.30am–2pm.

7

★ **Sophiatown** Off Mary Fitzgerald Square, Newtown ☎ 011 836 5999, ⓦ sophiatownbarlounge.co.za; map pp.464–465. This township retro restaurant is popular with chic black Jo'burgers. The excellent food (mains R80–140) includes crocodile, kudu and ostrich, all served to a soundtrack of old- and nu-school Afrojazz and Afropop. Smart but relaxed, it's a perfect place to begin a balmy summer night out. Mon–Wed 10.30am–9pm, Thurs–Sat 10.30–2am, Sun 11.30am–8pm.

ROSEBANK, MELROSE, HYDE PARK AND SANDTON

Assaggi 30 Rudd Rd, Post Office Centre, Illovo ☎ 011 268 13 70; map p.472. Despite the setting in an ugly mall, this is one of Jo'burg's best Italian restaurants, with a new menu every month reflecting the seasonal offer (main courses around R90). Mon 6.30–9pm, Tues–Sat 12.30pm–2pm & 6.30–9pm.

Montego Bay Nelson Mandela Square, Sandton ☎ 011 883 6407; map p.472. Lip-smackingly good seafood – including fresh oysters and sushi – together with slick service. Dishes typically cost R100–130, but can be much more. Daily noon–4pm & 6–11pm.

Moyo Melrose Arch, Melrose ☎ 011 684 1477, ⓦ moyo.co.za; map p.472. In the upmarket Melrose Arch complex, this sleek but slightly touristy venue occupying five floors offers a good variety of African dishes (around R100–150), from ostrich with Ethiopian spices to veggie options such as lentil *bobotie*, along with performances of dance and music. There's another branch at Zoo Lake. Book ahead. Daily 11am–11pm.

Red Chamber Upper Floor, Hyde Park Corner of Mall, Hyde Park ☎ 011 325 604; map p.472. The usual Chinese dishes plus more original creations, such as sizzling ostrich with spring onion, and good Peking duck, served in plusher surroundings than you tend to get in Chinatown. Most mains R60–80. Daily noon–10.30pm.

★ **Tashas** Oxford Rd, The Zone, Mall of Rosebank ☎ 011 447 7972, ⓦ tashascafe.com; map p.472. A wonderfully designed, smash hit restaurant chain with a varied bistro menu listing everything from breakfasts and sandwiches to steaks and Turkish flat bread wraps. Book ahead to be certain of a table. Mon–Wed 7am–6pm, Thurs–Sat 7am–7pm, Sun 7.30am–5pm.

Tsunami The Mall of Rosebank, Rosebank ☎ 011 880 8409, ⓦ tsunamisa.co.za; map p.472. A disastrous name, but this swanky "seafood emporium" has very decent sushi, sashimi and other seafood dishes. Sushi plates are R18–37, much cheaper on Thursdays. Daily noon–11pm.

★ **Wolves** 3 Corlett Drive, Melrose ☎ 011 447 2360, ⓦ wolves.co.za; map p.472. A fantastic little café, halfway between Rosebank and Sandton, serving killer red velvet cake, healthy breakfasts and sandwiches. Drop by on Thursday evenings for the Howl night, with live music by

South African bands. Mon–Wed 7:30am–7pm, Thurs & Fri 7:30am–11.30pm, Sat & Sun 9am–4pm.

GREENSIDE AND PARKHURST

★ **The Attic** 24 Fourth Ave, Parkhurst ☎ 011 880 6102. Capable staff, a casual atmosphere and consistently excellent food make this a Parkhurst favourite. There's meat and fish dishes priced around R150, some vegetarian options and, in season, delicious mussels. Be sure to book ahead or arrive early. Mon 6–10.30pm, Tues–Sun noon–3pm & 6–10.30pm.

Doppio Zero Corner of Barry Herzog and Gleneagles Rd, Greenside ☎ 011 646 8740. Unpretentious and hugely popular Italian place with an eclectic menu. Breakfast is a big draw: the omelettes are exceptional. Most pizzas and pasta dishes are R60–90. Mon & Sun 7am–9pm, Tues–Sat 7am–10.30pm.

Karma Corner of Gleneagles and Greenfield rds, Greenside ☎ 011 646 8555. A stylish modern Indian restaurant specializing in tandooris, with a few contemporary fusion dishes, such as chicken curry with avocados, thrown in for good measure. Mains around R70. Daily noon–3pm & 6–10pm.

Nice on Fourth Corner of 14th St and Fourth Ave, Parkhurst ☎ 011 7886286. One of the best breakfast spots around, though it's good any time of day for sandwiches, salads or cake. Tues–Sun 8am–3pm, dinner by reservation Thurs & Fri 8–11pm.

★ **Odd Café** 116 Greenway, Greenside ☎ 011 486 3631, ⓦ oddcafe.wordpress.com. Slightly odd indeed, this small place rustles up delicious "comfort food with a twist", such as spanakopita spinach pie and Mediterranean sandwiches, for eating inside or on the pavement terrace. Look for the wacky graffiti building. Mon 7am–5pm, Tues–Sat 7am–11pm, Sun 8am–3pm.

MELVILLE

★ **Ant Café** 11 Seventh St ☎ 078 777 8877; map p.475. A classic Melville hangout, *Ant* has delicious crisp thin-crust pizzas (mains R40–100), friendly service, a few comfy chairs on the pavement, and after all these years is still proud to only accept cash. Daily 8am–11pm.

Lucky Bean 16 Seventh St ☎ 011 482 5572, ⓦ luckybeantree.co.za; map p.475. A trendy place at the bottom of the street with comfy sofas for cocktails and an imaginative menu that includes ostrich burger, wild mushroom risotto and springbok pie (mains R60–120). Tues–Fri 11am–10pm, Sat & Sun 10am–11pm.

Melon 9a Seventh St ☎ 011 482 9965, ⓦ melonrestaurant.co.za; map p.475. Gourmet food at affordable prices in one of Melville's better-looking spaces. Enjoy oysters, smoked salmon and asparagus penne (R69) or a large sirloin steak (R98). Daily noon–11pm.

Nuno's 5 Seventh St ☎ 011 482 6990; map p.475. This

popular Portuguese restaurant has chicken *trinchado* and *espetadas* skewers mixed in with more generic pastas and salads (mains R50–90). The outside tables are great for people-watching and there's a relaxed bohemian atmosphere, which continues after dark in the attached Mozambican-themed bar, *Xai Xai*. Daily 8am–midnight.

Picobella 66 Fourth Ave ☎ 011 482 4309; map p.475. A converted villa with a lovely *stoep* (porch) is the best Italian place for miles; pizzas like the one with spicy chicken strips, mushrooms and avocado (R54) are served up in a flash. Daily 8am–10pm.

★ **Service Station** Corner of Ninth St and Rustenburg Rd ☎ 011 726 1701; map p.475. A superbly stylish, daytime-only café-deli housed in a converted garage with appetizing and healthy breakfasts and lunches (both around R50), a pay-by-weight buffet of quiche and salads from 12.30pm, and home-made ice cream. Mon–Fri 8am–6pm, Sat 8am–4.30pm, Sun 8.30am–3.30pm.

BRYANSTON AND MORNINGSIDE

Bistro 277 on Main Cramerview Centre, 277 Main Rd, Bryanston ☎ 011 706 2837. Deep in the northern suburbs but away from the glitzy malls, this long-standing favourite serves excellent traditional French cuisine and South African staples with a French twist, such as pan-fried kudu fillet with roast new potatoes, in pleasant, spacious surroundings (most mains R70–90). Daily noon–2.30pm & 6–10.30pm.

The Codfather 1 First Ave, corner of Rivonia Rd, Morningside ☎ 011 803 2077. Select fresh fish (priced by weight; Cape salmon, for example, is R70 for 250 grams) from the vast displays, then watch as it's scaled, filleted and cooked to order. There's also a sushi bar attached. Daily 10am–11pm.

★ **Fruits and Roots** Hobart corner of Shopping Centre, Grosvenor Rd, Bryanston ☎ 011 463 2928, ⓦ fruitsandroots.co.za. One of the city's top organic, health and wholefood shops, with a great bar-café attached serving diverse vegetarian platters, from crudités and dips to wraps (R20–40). Mon–Fri 8am–6pm, Sat 8am–4pm.

THE EASTERN SUBURBS

The key area for dining in the eastern part of the city is Cyrildene, between Observatory and Bruma, home of the city's new Chinatown.

The Fisherman's Plate 18 Derrick Ave ☎ 011 622 0480. Loud and unpretentious, this is a cult favourite, with Formica-topped tables, no-nonsense lighting and fearsomely flavourful Chinese cuisine. Most dishes are around R60. Tues–Sun noon–2.30pm & 6–9pm.

SOWETO

Soweto tours (see p.480) all stop off for a meal in a local restaurant, bar or *shebeen*, and so long as you're not part of a huge group of tourists, it's not a bad way to meet some locals. If you're heading to Soweto under your own steam or with a local contact, any of the places below are worth checking out and will give you a warm welcome. Commonly, some kind of meat and *pap* is the main dish on offer, often alongside local favourites such as tripe or ox shin.

Chaf-Pozi Corner of Chris Hani Drive and Nicholas St, Diepkloof ☎ 072 629 6640. *Shebeen* chic at the foot of Soweto's iconic Orlando cooling towers; there's both traditional *pap en vleis* (cornmeal and meat) dishes (from R30) and sirloin steak available here – point out your meat of choice at the butchery and it gets grilled on the spot. Daily 10am–10pm.

Nambitha 6877 Vilakazi St, Orlando West ☎ 011 936 9128. Serving mutton curry and other African food (R50–80), along with burgers and fried breakfasts, this restaurant close to Mandela's House Museum is a popular meeting place for a younger crowd with eclectic tastes. Daily noon–11pm.

★ **The Rock** 1987 Vundla Drive, Rockville ☎ 011 986 8182. A massively popular upmarket venue for eating, drinking and dancing, with DJs or live jazz on offer most nights. The roof deck is a wonderful spot to unwind, get an overview of Soweto, and enjoy a sundowner.

Sakhumzi 6980 Vilakazi St, Orlando West ☎ 011 536 1379. Opposite the Mandela House Museum and featuring typical Soweto food in its buffet (R90), this is also the best place in the area to enjoy drinks on the lively streetside terrace. Daily 11am–10pm.

Wandie's Place 618 Makhalemele St, Dube ☎ 011 982 2796, ⓦ www.wandies.co.za. Situated 2km west of Vilakazi St, this was once Soweto's archetypal tourist-friendly *shebeen*, now the area's smartest eating spot, though it retains its popularity with locals. A buffet of local African food costs R110. Daily 10am–11pm.

BARS AND CLUBS

Jo'burg has the country's most racially mixed nightlife. However, the problem for visitors is that the best clubs are far-flung, and there's only one proper nightlife strip, **Melville's Seventh Street**, which is great fun for drinking but can't compete with Cape Town's Long Street (see p.150) if you want to dance. In many parts of the city, particularly the **northern suburbs**, old-school pubs and bars have been replaced by combination café/bar/restaurants, open most hours and commonly located in malls and shopping centres. Irish theme pubs and sports bars are often packed and jovial, if not exactly cutting-edge. Some **Soweto** *shebeens* you can visit during the day (see above); at night, only head to the townships in the company of a guide.

7

7

TOP 5 DRINKS WITH A VIEW

The Rock Soweto, see p.489
The Westcliff Westcliff, see p.486
Guildhall Pub CBD, see p.487

Southern Sun Hyde Park Bar Hyde Park, see below
Main Street Life CBD, see below

CBD

★ **Kitcheners Carvery** Corner of Juta and De Beer sts ☎ 072 947 8508; map pp. 464–465. The well-preserved pub in the century-old former *Milner Hotel* has regular punters propping up the bar during the week, with hip youngsters taking over on Wed–Sat nights, when DJs and bands perform; funk and soul during the week, house and electro at weekends. Daily noon till late.

Pata Pata 286 Fox St, Main St Life; map pp. 464–465. Named after a song by famous local singer Miriam Makeba, this large ground-floor bar has a mix of secondhand furniture to lounge on, and a small stage for live jazz music on Fri & Sat. Daily 7am–2am.

NORTHERN SUBURBS

Bohemian 5 Park Rd, Richmond ☎ 011 482 1725, ⊛ thebo.co.za; map p.475. *The Bo* is a pleasantly seedy pool hall close to Melville with live rock from Thursday to Saturday and half-price pizza on Monday. Popular with students from the nearby residences. Daily 11am–2am.

Catz Pyjamas 12 Main Rd, Melville ☎ 011 726 8596, ⊛ catzpyjamas.co.za; map p.475. A large first-floor bar and food stop that's open 24hrs; it's nothing special during daylight hours, but gets interesting when it fills up in the wee hours with party-minded patrons from nearby clubs.

The Red Room Corner of Beyers Naude and Juice sts, Honeydew ⊛ redroom.co.za; map p.475. A popular rock and indie club far out in the northern suburbs, attracting a varied and interesting crowd of Goths, yuppies and hipsters. Sat 9pm–4am.

★ **Six** 6 Seventh St, Melville; map p.475. One of the more relaxed bars along Melville's nightlife strip, attracting a funky, left-of-centre and/or gay cocktail-drinking crowd. Expect people dancing in any available space as the night proceeds. Daily noon–2am.

Southern Sun Hyde Park Bar First Rd, Hyde Park ☎ 011 341 8080; map p.475. A hotel bar with a difference – this designer bar is perched on top of the Hyde Park mall with excellent sunset views, and is crammed with trendy people downing drinks on weekend nights. Daily 6pm–2am.

LIVE MUSIC

Johannesburg dominates the South African music scene, offering a much wider spectrum of sounds than Cape Town or Durban. Friday and Saturday nights are the busiest times for gigs. Jo'burg is always discovering superb new **jazz** talent, but established artists to look out for include the gifted vocalist Simphiwe Dana, singer-songwriter Vusi Mahlasela, Afro-fusion merchants Freshlyground and trumpeters Marcus Wyatt and Hugh Masakela. Newtown and a couple of venues in the northern suburbs are your best bets for live jazz. **Indie** acts worth catching live include indie-pop hotshots Desmond and the Tutus, Kid of Doom, Us Kids Know, João Orrechia, Black Hotels and BLK JKS. Kwaito, the hugely popular **township-house** genre, is rarely performed live except at major concerts. You might hear some from **hip-hop** artists such as the excellent Hip-Hop Pantsula (HHP), Teargas, Skwatta Kamp or Pitch Black Afro. As for classical music, the Johannesburg Philharmonic Orchestra performs regularly at Linder Auditorium in the Wits University campus (entrance on St Andrews Rd) in Parktown (☎ 011 789 2733, ⊛ www.jpo.co.za). A useful **online gig guide** is provided by ⊛ jhblive.co.za, and tickets are usually available via ⊛ computicket.com.

CBD

Some of the restaurants in Newtown also have live music (see p.487).

★ **The Bassline** 10 Henry Nxumalo St, Newtown ☎ 011 838 9142, ⊛ bassline.co.za; map pp. 464–465. The city's leading live venue by some distance; the hottest local artists across the genres play here, and world-class acts from west and central Africa also stop by. Thursday is reggae night. Guarded parking to the rear, entered below the flyover. Open for events only.

Town Hall 66 Carr St, Newtown ☎ 082 332 5772; map pp. 464–465. A trendy nightspot in the warehouse district west of the M1 flyover. Regular DJ and live music

performances, sometimes spilling over into *The Woods* bar next door. Thurs–Sat 9pm–3am.

NORTHERN AND EASTERN SUBURBS

The Radium Beerhall 282 Louis Botha Ave, Orange Grove ☎ 011 728 3866, ⊛ theradium.co.za. A charmingly shabby Victorian pub – probably the second oldest in town – with live music several nights a week, and Portuguese food on the menu. On the first Sun of every month, don't miss the entertaining eighteen-piece band playing jazz and swing. Daily 10am till late.

Tanz Cafe The Buzz Shopping Centre, Witkoppen Rd, Fourways ☎ 011 658 0277, ⊛ tanzcafe.co.za. Buried deep in suburbia, *Tanz* is another good live music venue with concerts several nights per week; this is a good place to catch new bands. Drivers should stay off the booze – this area is prime bribe-hunting territory for the police on weekend nights. Tues–Sun 7pm–2am.

ENTERTAINMENT

Johannesburg has always offered the best **entertainment** in South Africa: the city draws top performers from all over the world and its audiences are the most sophisticated around. Though newspapers offer some event pointers, the best way to find out what's on is to listen to the local radio stations (see box, p.492) and keep your eyes peeled for roadside posters and leaflets. The *Mail & Guardian* newspaper, published on Fridays, carries decent listings and articles on the main events, while the *Daily Star* newspaper tracks mainstream cinema and theatre. **Tickets** for most events can be booked through Computicket (☎083 915 8000, ⓦcomputicket.com), which also has desks in all Checkers and Shoprite supermarkets and in some malls.

THEATRE, OPERA AND DANCE

The Joburg Theatre in Braamfontein and the Market Theatre in Newtown are Johannesburg's premier venues for theatre and opera productions, but there are several other good venues. Johannesburg dance is undergoing a revival: check out the Dance Factory in Newtown for some of the latest offerings.

Barnyard Theatre Cresta Shopping Centre, Beyers Naude Drive, Cresta ☎011 280 4370. The most central of a popular chain of theatres staging musical tribute shows, theatre and cabaret. On the lower ground floor of Cresta Shopping Centre, ten minutes' drive north of Melville.

The Dance Factory 10 Henry Nxumalo St, Newtown ☎011 833 1347. An interesting but irregular programme of dance by both professionals and township kids in a purpose-built dance studio – check local papers for details.

Joburg Theatre Loveday St, Braamfontein ☎0861 670 670, ⓦjoburgtheatre.com; map pp. 464–465. A good mix of both mainstream and more adventurous theatre, ballet and opera productions at this impressive, four-stage venue. There's safe parking underneath the venue, entered from Simmonds St.

Market Theatre 56 Margaret Mcingana St, Newtown ☎011 832 1641, ⓦmarkettheatre.co.za; pp. 464–465. The venue for some of Johannesburg's finest stage productions and top-grade visiting music acts; also celebrated for its innovative community theatre, and the odd costly epic.

Montecasino Theatre Montecasino, corner of William Nicol Dr and Witkoppen Rd, Fourways ☎011 511 1988, ⓦmontecasino.co.za. Two stages for comedies, musicals and touring shows. The new 1800-seat Teatro at Montecasino (☎011 510 7472) stages large musicals.

Old Mutual Theatre on the Square Nelson Mandela Square, Sandton ☎011 883 8606, ⓦtheatre onthesquare.co.za; map p.472. Lightweight drama, some political theatre and a handful of mainstream music or cultural acts. There are regular free lunchtime concerts on weekdays too.

SPECTATOR SPORT IN JO'BURG

Sport is a major preoccupation anywhere in South Africa, but in Johannesburg it's an obsession. The biggest sport in town is **football**, and there's a passionate rivalry between Jo'burg's two biggest teams, fuelled by the type of scandal, intrigue and mutual loathing that sustains armies of sports reporters. In Jo'burg (and specifically Soweto), you're either a fan of **Kaizer Chiefs** or **Orlando Pirates**, and for decades local derbies have pulled mammoth crowds of seventy thousand. This is where the Chiefs are based, until they move into their very own Amakhosi Stadium, 40km west of Jo'burg. It's worth trying to go to a home game of either team, especially one against Pretoria giants Mamelodi Sundowns. Tickets are cheap, the football can be exciting – if a little chaotic – and the atmosphere is often exhilarating. Crowd violence is very rare, and there is secure parking.

Ellis Park in downtown Jo'burg (☎011 402 8644) is a South African rugby shrine, particularly since the triumph there of the Springboks in the 1995 World Cup. As well as hosting international fixtures it's also home ground to the provincial **Gauteng Lions** team. The best way to get there is to make use of the park-and-ride system that operates for big games, with buses shuttling in from car parks outside the centre.

The major **cricket** games, including five-day test matches, are played at the Wanderers Stadium, off Corlett Drive, Illovo (☎011 788 1008), though if you look carefully at the touring programme for any visiting international teams you may find fixtures scheduled to be played in Soweto or Alexandra.

7

LOCAL RADIO

Given that Jo'burgers spend so much time in their cars, **radio** is huge in Gauteng. If you're in town for a few days it's worth flicking around the airwaves to sample some of the local stations, which will give you a flavour of the city. Not all are in English, of course, but don't let that put you off; the following is a selection of the current favourites.

Highveld Stereo 94.7FM. Endless classic mainstream tracks, soft rock and Celine Dion for the northern suburbs.
JoziFM 105.8FM. A ballsy talk station that broadcasts to Soweto and surrounding areas.
Khaya 95.9FM. For listeners who are too old for YFM, Khaya has a mellower mix of mainstream Afro-pop and smooth jazz, with good information on who's playing live in Johannesburg.
Radio 702 702MW. A well-established local talk-radio station famed for its lively discussion programmes,

excellent presenters and news coverage.
SAfm 104–107FM. A national SABC news and talk station, featuring some very skilled presenters and robust political debate. A fascinating gauge of the political dynamics of the country, though many callers are infuriating or waffly or both.
YFM 99.2FM. *The* station for under-21s. A blistering introduction to the upwardly mobile young black culture of Johannesburg, with wall-to-wall hip-hop and *kwaito*.

CINEMAS

The *Mail & Guardian*, published on Friday, is worth picking up for its cultural supplement with events and cinema listings. Tickets cost R30–50.

★ **Bioscope** 286 Fox St, CBD ☎ 087 830 0445, ⓦ www .thebioscope.co.za. An excellent art-house movie cinema in the Main St Life complex where anything goes: environmental documentaries, Japanese splatter films, foreign film festivals, gay flicks and Asian movie nights that

include food. Don't miss the regular screenings of the hilarious local cult documentary *Unhinged – Surviving Joburg*.
Ster-Kinekor ⓦ www.sterkinekor.com. Cinema complexes in the Rosebank, Sandton and other malls. Their separate Cinema Nouveau brand, with a branch in Rosebank, has art-house films and regular festivals themed by country, which are often free to visit.

SHOPPING

Johannesburg is a magnet for consumers from all over the subcontinent. For visitors, the city is the best place in South Africa to find arts and crafts, with excellent flea markets and galleries offering a plethora of goods, some of very high quality. As the queen of mall culture, Johannesburg is also home to over twenty major malls (typically open daily 8am–6pm), most of which are depressingly anonymous, though the handful listed below are so plush and enormous that they arguably merit visiting in their own right.

MALLS

Hyde Park Corner Jan Smuts Ave, Hyde Park ⓦ hydeparkshopping.co.za; map p.472. A trendy and upmarket mall, awash with haute couture outlets. The excellent Exclusive Books chain has a large branch here, and the restaurants are much better than in other malls.

★ **The Mall of Rosebank** Corner of Baker St and Cradock Ave, Rosebank ⓦ themallofrosebank.co.za; map p.472. One of the city's coolest and least soulless malls, with exclusive boutiques, craft shops, the Sunday crafts market and plenty of outdoor cafés and restaurants in the newly opened pedestrian streets of the adjoining The Zone centre. Right next to the Rosebank Gautrain station.

★ **Melrose Arch** Athol Oaklands Drive, Melrose North ⓦ melrosearch.co.za; map p.472. A beautifully designed city quarter, surrounded by tight security, with European-style streets, plazas, restaurants, bars, hotels and an upmarket mall, all on top of a huge parking garage.

Sandton City Shopping Centre Corner of Sandton Drive and Rivonia Rd, Sandton ⓦ sandtoncity.com; map p.472. Linked to the opulent Nelson Mandela Square shopping centre, this enormous – and expanding – complex has a mind-boggling abundance of shops (including some good bookshops), plus cinemas and African art galleries.

CRAFT SHOPS, MARKETS AND PRIVATE ART GALLERIES

The craft shops, galleries and markets below follow regular shop opening hours unless mentioned otherwise.
44 Stanley Avenue Milpark; map p.475. A deeply hip design and art complex between Braamfontein and Melville, with cafés, restaurants and galleries, and shops selling antiques, furniture and gifts.
African Craft Market of Rosebank The Mall of Rosebank, 50 Bath Ave, Rosebank; map p.472. An

JOHANNESBURG ARTS FESTIVALS

Johannesburg hosts regular festivals in nearly every artistic field. These include:

Arts Alive Festival ⓦartsalive.co.za. Every September. The city's major festival for the performing arts takes place over three weeks at various venues, mainly in Newtown, but also in some townships. Live music dominates, but dance, cabaret and theatre are also well represented. "Jazz on the Lake", on Zoo Lake, is a mainstay of the festival, and always features major South African artists in front of big crowds.
FNB Dance Umbrella Wits Theatre, Braamfontein ☏011 492 0709, ⓦat.artslink.co.za/~arts. Around

ten days during February/March. Africa's largest festival of dance and choreography hosts international companies but also acts as the major national platform for work by South African talent.
Joy of Jazz Festival Newtown ☏011 326 0141, ⓦjoyofjazz.co.za. Late August/early September. A weekend festival that draws the cream of South African jazz, including the likes of Pops Mohamed and Hugh Masekela, along with international guest stars.

---

entertaining two-storey place with an impressive array of cottage-industry crafts and clothes. A floor of the adjoining car park is taken over every Sun (9am–5pm) for a rooftop crafts and food market (ⓦcraft.co.za).
Art Africa 62 Tyrone Ave, Parkview ☏011 486 2052; see p.475. Just west of the zoo, this shop has a very good selection of both innovative and more familiar crafts from South Africa and the region, many ingeniously created out of recycled material.
Bruma Lake Flea Market Bruma Lake, east of the centre; map pp.464–465. A huge, permanent and very popular market of mostly African crafts and souvenirs, mainly mainstream and fairly inexpensive. At weekends, the crowds are entertained with music.
Bryanston Organic Market Culross Rd, off Main Rd, Bryanston ☏011 706 3671, ⓦbryanstonorganicmarket .co.za; map p.472. Right-on collection of stalls selling lovely organic food, unusual home crafts and handmade clothes. Hosted by Michael Mount Waldorf School. Thurs & Sat 9am–3pm.
Everard Read Gallery 6 Jellicoe Ave, Rosebank ☏011 788 4805, ⓦeverard-read.co.za; map p.472. A renowned gallery worth visiting for exhibitions of fine contemporary artists. Their new cylindrical Circa exhibition building offers great views over the leafy suburbs from the roof.
Goodman Art Gallery 163 Jan Smuts Ave, Rosebank ☏011 788 1113, ⓦgoodman-gallery.com; map p.472. The city's leading contemporary gallery, regularly hosting shows by globally renowned South African artists such as William Kentridge, David Goldblatt and Moshekwa Langa.
Kim Sacks Art Gallery 153 Jan Smuts Ave, Rosebank ☏011 447 5804, ⓦkimsacksgallery.blogspot.com; map p.472. A trove of magnificent crafts and traditional art from across Africa. The prices can be hefty, but the quality is consistently exceptional.
M2 Highway market CBD. An informal market stretching underneath this major artery, a few blocks south

of Anderson St. Most stalls specialize in *umuthi* folk medicine, but there are plenty of local crafts as well.
Market Africa Newtown; map pp.464–465. A flea market held next to the Market Theatre every Saturday; rifle through colourful blankets from Mali, Congolese masks and statues, local beadwork animals and objects, and more. Sat 9am–4pm.

BOOKSHOPS

Collector's Treasury CTP House, 244 Commissioner St, CBD ☏011 482 6516; map pp.464–465. For decades, the Treasury has been a book-lover's dream come true, with some two million secondhand books (including lots of Africana) on shelves and in random piles over several floors.
Exclusive Books ⓦexclus1ves.co.za; map p.472. South Africa's biggest and best bookshop chain, with all the latest titles. There are branches in many malls, but the best shops are in Hyde Park Mall (☏011 325 4298), Mandela Square, Sandton (☏011 748 5416), and The Mall of Rosebank (☏011 447 3028).

MUSIC SHOPS

The Musica chain of shops, found in most malls, concentrates on soul and rock import CDs, with small selections of local music. In the CBD there are dozens of small shops selling CDs of South African as well as American sounds.
Aware Records 70 Juta St, Braamfontein ☏083 300 2196, ⓦawareza.tumblr.com; map pp.464–465. A specialist record store selling new and secondhand vinyl and CDs. The owners can help track down anything not available in store.
Kohinoor 54 Market St, CBD ☏011 834 1361; map pp.464–465. Excellent vinyl selection, as well as a range of tapes and CDs. The focus is on jazz, but you'll find all manner of South African styles here, ranging from gospel to *maskanda* and *mbaqanga*. The music section of the shop is downstairs.

7

DIRECTORY

American Express The Zone shopping centre, 177 Oxford Rd, Rosebank (☎011 880 8382); Sandton City Shopping Centre, Sandton Drive (☎011 883 9009).

Banks and exchange All the main shopping malls have banks and exchange offices where you can change money.

Hospitals and ambulance services In any medical emergency, your best bet is to call the private Netcare 911 ambulance service on ☎082 911. Patients are taken to a Netcare private hospital, which will be expensive but more dependable than a public hospital. State-run hospitals with 24hr casualty departments include Johannesburg General Hospital, Parktown (☎011 488 3334/5), and Helen Joseph Hospital, Auckland Park (☎011 489 1011). Private hospitals include Milpark Hospital, Guild St, Parktown (☎011 480 5600), and Morningside Medi-Clinic, off Rivonia Rd in Morningside (☎011 282 5000). Private hospitals are always

the best option, but without proof of medical insurance, a hefty payment will be needed on admission.

Internet access It's very easy to get online in Jo'burg – most malls have at least one internet café.

Post offices Most major suburbs have a centrally located post office. The main poste restante post office is on Jeppe St in the CBD.

Swimming & gyms Public swimming pools around Johannesburg are not always kept in great repair, one exception being the superb, outdoor, heated Olympic-sized Ellis Park pool (Mon–Fri 7am–7pm, Sat–Sun 8am–5pm; ☎011 402 5565). As for gyms, try the chain of Virgin Active gyms around the city (☎086 020 0911, ⓦvirginactive.co.za); some hotels can give you a voucher valid for one visit to the gyms, otherwise you can pay the single-visit fee of R135.

Around Johannesburg

Johannesburgers wanting to get away from it all tend to head northwest towards the **Magaliesberg Mountains**, stretching from Pretoria in the east to Rustenberg in the west. Don't expect to see a horizon of impressive peaks: much of the area is private farmland running across rolling countryside, although there are some impressive *kloofs* (gorges), as well as refreshingly wide vistas. Unprepossessing as the mountain range might be, a series of caves on their southeastern (Johannesburg) side holds some of the world's most important information about human evolution stretching back some 3.5 million years. These caves, including the renowned Sterkfontein Caves, are now protected as part of the **Cradle of Humankind**, one of South Africa's first World Heritage Sites.

The Cradle of Humankind

Covering some 47,000 hectares, the **Cradle of Humankind** is the name given to the area in which a series of dolomitic caves has in the last fifty years or so produced nearly two-fifths of the world's hominid fossil discoveries. Given its accessibility and the richness of the finds, it has now arguably overtaken Tanzania's Olduvai Gorge as Africa's (and therefore the world's) most important paleontological site.

Sterkfontein Caves

Tours daily every half hour 9am–5pm • R120 • R190 in combination with Maropeng museum • ☎011 577 9000, ⓦmaropeng.co.za

The best-known of the Cradle of Humankind sites are the **Sterkfontein Caves**, believed to have been inhabited by pre-human primates who lived here up to 3.5 million years ago. They first came to European attention in 1896, when an Italian lime prospector, Gulgimo Martinaglia, stumbled upon them. Martinaglia was only interested in the bat droppings, and promptly stripped them out, thus destroying the caves' dolomite formation. Archeologist Dr Robert Broom excavated the caves between 1936 and 1951; in 1947, he found the skull of a female hominid (nicknamed "Mrs Ples") that was over 2.5 million years old. In 1995, another archeologist, Ronald Clarke, found "Little Foot", the bones of a 3-million-year-old walking hominid, with big toes that functioned like our thumbs do today. In 1998 an *Australopithecus* skeleton discovered here was the oldest complete specimen known, reckoned to be 3.3 million years old.

7

MRS PLES AND FRIENDS

Embedded in the dolomitic rock within a dozen caves in the area now called the Cradle of Humankind are the fossilized remains of **hominids** that lived in South Africa up to 3.5 million years ago. Samples of fossilized pollen, plant material and animal bones also found in the caves indicate that the area was once a **tropical rainforest** inhabited by giant monkeys, long-legged hunting hyenas and sabre-toothed cats.

Quite when hominids arrived on the scene isn't certain, but scientists now believe that the human lineage split from apes in Africa around five to six million years ago. The oldest identified group of hominids is *Australopithecus*, a bipedal, small-brained form of man. The first *Australopithecus* discovery in South Africa was in 1924, when Professor Raymond Dart discovered the **Taung child** in what is now North West Province. In 1936, australopithecine fossils were first found in the Sterkfontein Caves, and in 1947 Dr Robert Broom excavated a nearly complete skull which he first called *Plesianthropus transvaalensis* ("near-man" of the Transvaal), later confirmed as a 2.6-million-year-old *Australopithecus africanus*. Identified as a female, she was nicknamed "**Mrs Ples**", and for many years she was the closest thing the world had to what is dubbed "**the missing link**".

A number of even older fossils have since been discovered at Sterkfontein and nearby caves, along with evidence of several other genera and species, including *Australopithecus robustus*, dating from between one and two million years ago, and *Homo ergaster*, possibly the immediate predecessor of *Homo sapiens*, who used stone tools and fire.

If you're keen to learn more about this fascinating topic and want to visit some of the caves and dig sites not open to the general public, you could try one of the excellent **tours** offered by Palaeo-Tours (☎082 804 2899, ⊛palaeotours.com) or Past Experiences (☎011 678 3905, ⊛pastexperiences.co.za).

Kromdraai Wonder Cave

Mon–Fri 8am–5pm, Sat & Sun 8am–6pm • Tours depart on the hour • R60 R140 in combination with the Rhino & Lion Nature Reserve • ☎011 957 0106, ⊛wondercave.net • Get here through the Rhino and Lion Nature Reserve – the alternative route is on a longer, rough dirt Rd

The only other cave with open public access is the Kromdraai Wonder Cave, located on the edge of the Rhino and Lion Nature Reserve (see p.below) to the northeast of Sterkfontein. Also mined for lime in the 1890s, this cave hasn't revealed any paleontological finds, and the main focus of attention is the extraordinary stalactites, stalagmites and rimstone pools to be found in a huge underground chamber. Once you've descended into the cave by a lift, carefully placed lighting and marked trails make the experience theatrical and unashamedly commercial.

The Rhino and Lion Nature Reserve

Daily 8am–4pm • R100; R140 in combination with the Kromdraai Wonder Cave • ☎011 957 0106, ⊛rhinolion.co.za

The fourteen-square-kilometre **Rhino and Lion Nature Reserve** is really more a safari park than anything resembling a wilderness game reserve as found in other parts of South Africa, but it is Gauteng's best site for seeing large mammals. The main section of the reserve has white rhino, wildebeest, hartebeest and zebra roaming free, while the Lion and Predator Camp has several large enclosures containing lions, cheetahs and wild dogs. Elsewhere, there's a vulture hide, a series of hippo pools (located opposite the main gate), a breeding centre and an animal crèche where you can pet lion cubs. Visits can also be organized to the nearby **Old Kromdraai Gold Mine**, the second-oldest mine on the Witwatersrand, where you can follow the original mining tunnel 150m into the hillside.

Maropeng Museum

Down the R400 turn-off from the R563, northwest of the Sterkfontein Caves • Daily 9am–5pm • R115; R190 in combination with Sterkfontein Caves • ☎014 577 9000, ⊛www.maropeng.co.za

Housed in a striking building, the Tumulus, half clad in grassy earth to simulate a burial mound, **Maropeng** ("returning to the place of our ancestors" in SeTswana) is an impressive museum dedicated to human origins and evolution. Visitors can take a short underground boat ride into the mists of time, and then browse through some child-friendly interactive displays and other exhibits explaining the history of human development. A room full of original hominid, plant and animal fossils, loaned from various institutions across South Africa, provides a fitting finale.

| ARRIVAL AND DEPARTURE | THE CRADLE OF HUMANKIND |

By car The Cradle of Humankind can only be reliably reached by car: head west out of Johannesburg on the R47 (Hendrik Potgieter Rd) or M5 (Beyers Naude Drive), then follow the N14 until the R563 junction. A few kilometres northwest along the R563 is a right turn which will take you to the Sterkfontein Caves turn-off.

ACCOMMODATION

Cradle Forest Camp Kromdraai Rd ☎011 659 1622, ⓦthecradle.co.za. Cheap but perfectly decent self-catering thatched chalets, just big enough for a couple, set in green surroundings in the small Cradle Nature Reserve. R600

Forum Homini Kromdraai Rd ☎011 668 7000, ⓦforumhomini.com. Set in a private game farm that's home to antelopes and hippos, this award-winning hotel has beautiful "cave chic" rooms overlooking a lake. The fantastic gourmet restaurant *Roots*, which serves set lunches and dinners, is worth the trip alone; plan to spend several hours eating here. Rates include meals. R3500

Maropeng Hotel Off the R400 ☎014 577 9100, ⓦmaropeng.co.za. The chic hotel next to the Maropeng Museum is not cheap, but each of its classy earth-toned rooms has a patio commanding a dramatic Magaliesberg view. R1150

Pretoria

Gauteng's two major cities are just 50km apart, but could hardly be more different. With its graceful government buildings, wide avenues of purple flowering jacarandas, and stolid Boer farming origins, **PRETORIA** – or **TSHWANE** as the metropolitan area is now officially known (see p.500) – was for a long time a staid, sleepy city. However, since the arrival of democracy, the country's capital has become increasingly cosmopolitan, with a substantial diplomatic community living in Arcadia and Hatfield, east of the city centre, and middle-class blacks swelling the ranks of civil servants. Nowadays, most Pretorians are not Afrikaners, but Pedi and Tswana; and thousands of black students studying at the city's several universities have further diluted Pretoria's traditional Afrikaans roots.

Pretoria is close enough to Johannesburg's airport to provide a practical alternative base in Gauteng. It feels safer and is less spread out than Jo'burg (though don't make the blithe assumption that Pretoria is crime-free), there are more conventional sights and the **nightlife** is energetic and fun.

Pretoria's city centre is a compact grid of wide, busy streets, easily and comparatively safe to explore on foot. Its central hub is **Church Square**, where you can see some fascinating architecture; and there are other historic buildings and museums close by. To the north lie the vast **National Zoological Gardens**, while the Arcadia district is the site of the city's famous **Union Buildings**. On the southern fringes of the city is the remarkable **Voortrekker Monument**, and **The Freedom Park**, a memorial that attempts to come to terms with South Africa's past conflicts.

Brief history

Unlike Johannesburg, Pretoria developed at a leisurely pace from its humble origins as a **Boer farming community** on the fertile land around the Apies River. When the city was founded in 1855 by **Marthinus Wessel Pretorius**, who named it after his father, Andries Pretorius, it was intended to be the capital around which the new South African Republic (ZAR) would prosper. Embodying the Afrikaners' conviction that the land they took was God-given, Pretoria's first building was a church. The town was then laid out with streets wide enough for teams of oxen brought in by farmers to make U-turns.

In 1860, the city was proclaimed the capital of the ZAR, the result of tireless efforts

7

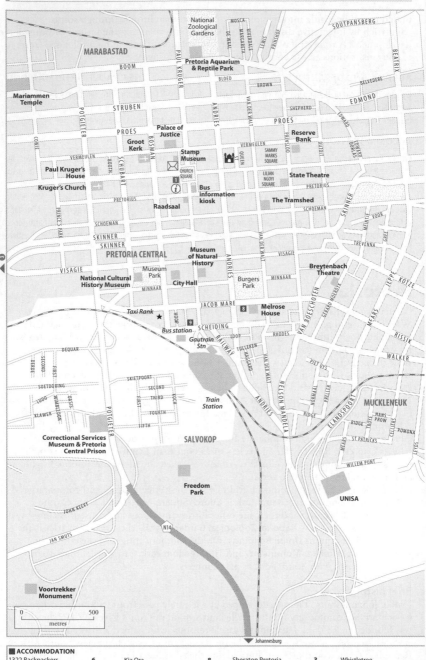

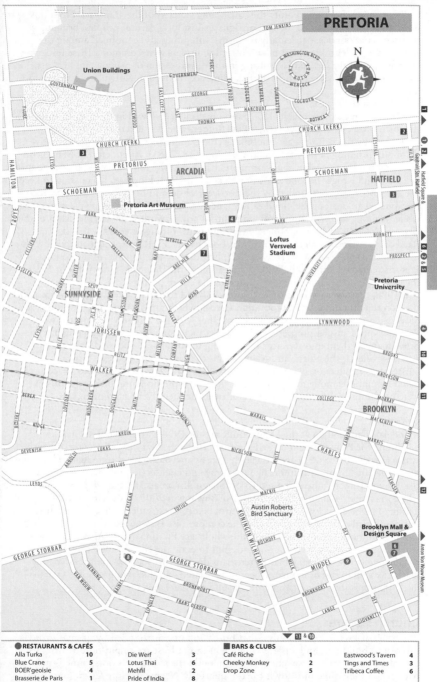

PRETORIA

Union Buildings

Pretoria Art Museum

ARCADIA

HATFIELD

Loftus
Versveld
Stadium

Pretoria
University

SUNNYSIDE

BROOKLYN

Austin Roberts
Bird Sanctuary

Brooklyn Mall &
Design Square

● **RESTAURANTS & CAFÉS**

Alla Turka	**10**	Die Werf	**3**	
Blue Crane	**5**	Lotus Thai	**6**	
BOER'geoisie	**4**	Mehfil	**2**	
Brasserie de Paris	**1**	Pride of India	**8**	
Crawdaddy's	**9**	Tasha's	**7**	

■ **BARS & CLUBS**

Café Riche	**1**	Eastwood's Tavern	**4**	
Cheeky Monkey	**2**	Tings and Times	**3**	
Drop Zone	**5**	Tribeca Coffee	**6**	

by Stephanus Schoeman to unite the squabbling statelets of the Transvaal. From this base, the settlers continued their campaigns against local African peoples, bringing thousands into service, particularly on farms. Infighting also continued among the settlers, and violent skirmishes between faction leaders were common. These leaders bought most of the best land, resulting in the dispossession of many white trekkers, and also in the massacre of most of the animals of the region, particularly its elephants.

The Boer Wars

The British annexed Pretoria in 1877, and investment followed in their wake. Although the town prospered and grew, farmer **Paul Kruger**, who was determined not to be subjugated by the British again, mobilized commandos of Afrikaner farmers to drive them out, resulting in the first Anglo-Boer War (1877–81). After defeat at Majuba on the Natal border, the colonial government abandoned the war and ceded **independence** in 1884. Paul Kruger became ZAR president until 1903. However, his mission to keep the ZAR Boer was confounded by the discovery of **gold** in the Witwatersrand, which precipitated an unstoppable flood of foreigners. Kruger's policy of taxing the newcomers, while retaining the Boer monopoly on political power, worked for a while. Most of the elegant buildings of Church Square were built with mining revenues, while the Raadsaal (parliament) remained firmly in Boer hands. ZAR independence ended with the second Anglo-Boer War (1899–1902), but, despite the brutality of the conflict, Pretoria remained unscathed. With the creation of the **Union of South Africa** in 1910, the city became the administrative capital of the entire country.

In 1928, the government laid the foundations of Pretoria's industry by establishing the **Iron and Steel Industrial Corporation** (Iscor), which rapidly generated a whole series of related and service industries. These, together with the civil service, ensured white Pretoria's quiet, insular prosperity. Meanwhile, increasing landlessness among blacks drove many of them into the city's burgeoning **townships**. Marabastad and Atteridgeville are the oldest, and Mamelodi is the biggest and poorest.

After the introduction of apartheid by the National Party in 1948, Pretoria acquired a hated reputation among the black population. Its supreme court and central prison were notorious as the source of the laws that made their lives a nightmare.

Democracy

Mandela's **inauguration** at the Union Buildings in 1994 was the symbolic new beginning for Pretoria's political redemption. Through the 1990s, the stages of South Africa's revolution could be seen as clearly here as anywhere else: the gradual replacement of the diehards from institutions like the army and civil service, new faces in almost all the old government offices, the return of foreign diplomats and the influx of students.

Pretoria's metropolitan area was renamed **Tshwane** in 2005 by the city council, after a Tswana-Ndebele chief who ruled in the area before Boer settlers arrived. The central business district remains Pretoria, but the compromise is awkward, with most media, and indeed most citizens, still calling the whole city Pretoria. Many Afrikaners resent what they see as a spiteful and costly attempt to erase the city's historic origins from public memory, while many black Pretorians don't see why a post-apartheid, mainly black city should still bear a name deeply associated with racial oppression. It seems likely that the city will lug two names around for years to come.

Church Square

The heart of Pretoria is undoubtedly **Church Square**, surrounded by dramatic and important buildings, and a place where you can at least try to put South Africa's complex history into perspective. It was here that Boer farmers outspanned their oxen when they came into town for the quarterly *Nagmaal* (Holy Communion) of the Dutch Reformed Church, turning the square temporarily into a campsite.

Indeed, nearly every important white meeting, protest or takeover the city has known happened in Church Square; the ZAR Vierkleur ("four colours") flag was lowered here in 1877 to make way for the Union Jack, only to rise again in 1881, after the British eviction from the republic; the British flag flew again in 1900 but was lowered for the last time in 1910; Paul Kruger was proclaimed head of state in the square four times, and thirty thousand people crammed into the square in 1904 for his memorial service. Such historical resonances are viewed differently by Pretoria's black community, and the square's central **statue of Paul Kruger** is for many an unwanted relic of a dismal past.

Raadsaal and the Old Nederlandsche Bank Building
Southwest corner of Church Square

The old **Raadsaal** (parliament) was built in neo-Renaissance style in 1891, and still exudes the bourgeois respectability yearned for by the parliamentarians of the ZAR. Ask the security guard for a peek inside and to look at the room where Paul Kruger spent most of his time during the final stages of the Anglo-Boer War.

Next to the Raadsaal is the **Old Nederlandsche Bank Building**, home of the tourist office (see p.506). Incredibly, it took a gathering of 10,000 people in 1975 and five years of deliberation to reverse a decision to demolish this building and the Raadsaal.

Palace of Justice
Northwest corner of Church Square

Started in 1897 and, half completed, used as a hospital for British troops during the second Anglo-Boer War, the grandiose **Palace of Justice** was home to the Transvaal Supreme Court for many years after its completion in 1902, and was the location of the Rivonia Trial in 1963–64, which saw Nelson Mandela and other leaders of the ANC sentenced to life imprisonment. Restoration work has revealed and repaired the splendid facade and balconies, although the new court is an ugly box sitting squatly in a street behind the Palace.

Queen Street Mosque

A small passageway off Queen Street brings you to the unexpected site of a bright white **mosque**, oriented at an angle to the city grid so as to face Mecca. Pretoria's Muslims, who reportedly got on well with Kruger, acquired the site in 1896, and the current building was constructed in 1927 by Cape artisans. The mosque is now hemmed in by ugly tower blocks, but is somehow all the more indomitable for that.

Lilian Ngoyi Square

Lilian Ngoyi Square is named after the anti-apartheid activist who was one of the leaders of the 1956 Women's March that started on this spot. Until 2006 this was called Strijdom Square, and was the site of a vast and horrific bust of the man himself. Prime minister from 1954 to 1958, **Johannes Gerhardus Strijdom** began the wave of apartheid legislation that peaked under his successor, Hendrik Verwoerd, and was a firm believer in "white supremacy". Dramatically, on May 31, 2001, forty years to the day after the statue was completed, a structural fault (or divine intervention, depending on your point of view) caused it to collapse.

SAFETY IN PRETORIA

While other parts of central Pretoria are fairly safe to walk around if you take the normal precautions, be extra careful when wandering north of Church Square around busy Proes and Struben streets, and also be vigilant in the Sunnyside district, east of the CBD.

Paul Kruger's House and around

60 Church St West • Mon–Fri 8.30am–5.30pm, Sat & Sun 8.30am–5.30pm • Free • ☎ 012 326 9172, ⓦ ditsong.org.za/kruger.htm

Paul Kruger's House was built in 1884 by the English-speaking Charles Clark, described by Kruger as one of his "tame Englishmen", who mixed his cement with milk instead of water. Inside, the **museum** is rather dull, though you may find some interest in Kruger's effects, such as his large collection of spittoons. The *stoep* (veranda) is the most famous feature of the house, for here the old president would sit and chat to any white person who chose to join him. Out at the back is Kruger's private railway coach, built in 1898, which he used during the second Anglo-Boer War.

Opposite is a characteristically grim Reformed church known as **Kruger's Church**. The **Groot Kerk** (Great Church), on the corner of Vermeulen and Bosman streets, is more impressive; its strikingly ornate tower is one of the finest in the country.

Burgers Park

Jacob Maré St • Daily 8am–6pm • Free

Between Andries and Van der Walt streets lies the restful **Burgers Park**, named after ineffective ZAR president Thomas Burgers, who was in office between 1873 and 1877. The well-manicured lawns are ideal for picnics or an afternoon snooze.

Melrose House

275 Jacob Maré St • Tues–Sun 10am–5pm • R9 • ☎ 012 322 2805, ⓦ melrosehouse.co.za

Opposite the park's southern border, you'll find **Melrose House**, an over-decorated Victorian domicile with a wonderful conservatory and interesting exhibitions. The house was built in 1886 for local businessman George Heys, who made his money running mailcoach services. Lord Kitchener used the house during the second Anglo-Boer War, and the treaty of Vereeniging that ended hostilities was signed inside.

Museum of Natural History

432 Paul Kruger St • Daily 8am–4pm • R25 • ☎ 012 322 7632, ⓦ ditsong.org.za/naturalhistory.htm

The grand **Museum of Natural History** is Pretoria's oldest museum and is home to plenty of stuffed animals, bird exhibits, models of dinosaurs and casts of fossil remains. The originals can be viewed by appointment only. This is a good place to come to put the discoveries of the nearby Cradle of Humankind (see p.494) into context: alongside a bronze bust of Robert Broom staring into the three-million-year-old eye sockets of Mrs Ples is an assortment of fossilized discoveries and reconstructions of early hominid life.

City Hall

Paul Kruger St

Forming an architectural ensemble with the Museum of Natural History directly opposite, the **City Hall** was built in 1935 in a mix of Greek and Roman architectural styles. The park in front of the building has a series of fountains and well-tended flowerbeds and statues of the city's founding fathers Andries and Marthinus Pretorius and – added in 2006 – founding grandfather Chief Tshwane.

National Cultural History Museum

149 Visagie St • Daily 8am–4pm • R25 • ☎ 012 324 6082, ⓦ ditsong.org.za/culturalhistory.htm

The permanent exhibitions at the **National Cultural History Museum**, west of the City Hall, are eclectic to the point of being a bit unconnected: they include displays of San rock art, and a room showing work by J.H. Pierneef (1886–1957), one of the country's most famous artists, who is known for his dramatically stylized bushveld landscapes.

National Zoological Gardens

232 Boom St • **Zoo** Daily 8.30am–5.30pm • R55; cableway R10 • **Night tour** Wed, Fri & Sat 6.30pm • R70 • Minimum of eight people • **Camping tour** Fri & Sat 5pm • R100 • ☎ 012 328 3265, ⓦ nzg.ac.za

Pretoria's spacious and recommended **zoo** houses rare species of antelope, a white rhinoceros, and a wide selection of South American as well as African animals. Next door, the **Pretoria Aquarium and Reptile Park** (included in the price) is less impressive, but nonetheless has plenty of beasts, some very weird and highly venomous. A cable-car ride takes you right over the zoo, across the Apies River and to the top of the ridge for fine views of the city. It's well worth trying to book one of the **night tours**, when you'll see some of the zoo's nocturnal creatures, like bats, owls and lions, at their most active; it's also possible to spend the whole night in the zoo on a camping tour.

Mariammen Temple

7th St, Marabastad

The scruffy streets of Marabastad, the city's first "non-white" area, lie to the west of the zoo and, while fascinating, can feel quite intimidating if visiting alone. Don't miss the intricately decorated Hindu **Mariammen Temple** from 1930, right next to the market, which was built in Tamil style with a colourful Gorpuram tower, and is dedicated to the consort of the god Shiva, who protects against infectious diseases.

The Correctional Services Museum

Potgieter St • Tues–Fri 9am–3pm • Free • ☎ 012 314 1766

The chilling **Correctional Services Museum** at Pretoria Central Prison, along the R101 towards Johannesburg, is well worth a visit. You'll see the notorious prison, where many famous political prisoners were held (and many executed), on your right. Be prepared to walk past depressed-looking visiting relatives on your way in. Inside the museum you can see artwork made by prisoners, including a life-size statue of an inmate crawling towards an expressionless prison warder, who has his arms outstretched, ready to correct him. There are also exhibits of knives concealed in Bibles and shoes, files in cakes and so forth. Most alarming by far are the group photos of various forbidding-looking prison warders through the ages, which seem a strange sort of propaganda for the prison service.

The Freedom Park

Salvokop Hill • Guided tours daily 9am, noon & 3pm • R45 • ☎ 012 470 7400, ⓦ www.freedompark.co.za

Freedom Park, which sits atop Salvokop Hill, is punctuated by a sculpture of ascending "reeds" that are dramatically illuminated at night. Started in 2000 in response to the Truth and Reconciliation Commission's (see box, p.662) call for new symbols to resolve past conflicts, and still partly under construction, the park is a courageous and successful attempt to create a memorial that speaks to all sections of post-apartheid society in South Africa. Visits are by guided tour only and take you past **The Wall of Names**, inscribed with the names of 75,000 victims of various South African conflicts, an eternal flame to the unknown soldier, and boulders representing important moments in the history of the country's nine provinces – Gauteng's rock symbolizes the peaceful marches in Soweto, Sharpville, Mamelodi and other townships that were met by police violence.

The Voortrekker Monument

Eeufees Rd • Daily: May–Aug 8am–5pm, Sept–April 8am–6pm • R40 • ☎ 012 326 6770, ⓦ voortrekkermon.org.za

The famous **Voortrekker Monument and Museum**, in stark contrast to The Freedom Park (see above), is very much a symbol of Afrikaner domination in the old South

Africa. The striking, austere block of granite was built in 1940 to commemorate the Boer victory over the Zulu army at Blood River on December 16, 1838 (see p.437), and its symbolism is crushingly heavy-handed. The monument is enclosed by reliefs of ox wagons, with a large statue of a woman standing outside, shaking her fist at imaginary oppressors. Inside, a series of moving reliefs depicts scenes from the Great Trek, and you can climb to the top of the tower for a peek down into the hall, or for dramatic views of the surrounding nature reserve. This has various hiking and mountain-bike trails, leading to lookout points over Pretoria. You can also explore the reserve on horseback (book in advance).

Arcadia and the Union Buildings

In the **Arcadia district**, Pretoria's **Union Buildings**, the headquarters of the South African government, perch majestically on the main hill. Designed by Herbert Baker (see box, p.473) in 1910, allegedly to symbolize the union of Briton and Boer, the lashings of colonnades and lavish amphitheatre seem instead to glorify British imperial self-confidence. Nelson Mandela had an office here after his release from prison, and the buildings were famously the site of his inauguration as president in 1994. This was perhaps the first time their imperialist symbols were transformed, not least by the African praise-singers who delivered their odes from the amphitheatre, proclaiming Mandela as the latest in a long line of African heroes from Shaka to Hintsa, and beyond. Unfortunately, it's not possible to walk around the buildings, but you can view them – and enjoy great views over the city – from the attractive gardens below.

Pretoria Art Museum

Corner of Schoeman and Wessels sts • Tues–Sun 10am–5pm • R6 • ☎ 012 344 1807, ⓦ pretoriaartmuseum.co.za

South of the Union Buildings, the **Pretoria Art Museum** is housed in a modernist pavilion overlooking a park. Inside is a modestly sized but excellent selection of South African and early Dutch-inspired art, some works of "resistance art" by the likes of William Kentridge, and a number of black artists, including Ephraim Ngatane and Gerard Sekoto.

Sunnyside, Loftus Versveld Stadium and Pretoria University

Southeast of the centre, desegregated **Sunnyside** is the central suburb with the strongest African feel, with a lively street life, distinctive old houses and a multitude of cafés – though it's best not to walk around alone here. Esselen Street is the busiest thoroughfare, brimming with bars and street hawkers.

East of Sunnyside is the huge **Loftus Versveld Stadium**, home to Pretoria's hugely popular sporting giants – the Bulls rugby team and the Mamelodi Sundowns football team.

Mapungubwe Museum

In the Old Arts Building on Pretoria University campus • Tues–Fri 10am–4pm • Free • ☎ 012 420 3146

This small but worthwhile **museum** is dedicated to the remarkable archeological finds at Mapungubwe (see p.583), a hilltop fort near the Limpopo River that was the ancient capital of a major southern African kingdom. Among the artefacts on display are a rhinoceros made from thin gold foil, figurines, jewellery and decorated pots, all at least 700 years old.

Hatfield and Brooklyn

Hatfield, beyond Pretoria University, has developed in the last few years into Pretoria's liveliest area, with the trendiest hangouts and nightlife along Burnett Street, where you'll find a plethora of studenty cafés, bars and restaurants.

Anton van Wouw Museum

299 Clark St • Mon–Fri 10am–4pm • Free • ☎ 012 460 7422

To visit the elegant house and **museum** of the acclaimed Dutch-born sculptor, **Anton van Wouw**, you'll need to head southeast of the university to the wealthy suburb of **Brooklyn**. Van Wouw was responsible for most of the brooding effigies of Afrikaner public figures from the 1890s to the 1930s that are scattered around the country, including the Kruger statue in Pretoria's Church Square (see p.500). His most famous work is the Voortrekker Monument (see p.503). The museum, designed by the celebrated architect Norman Eaton in 1938, houses a collection of his smaller pieces. Van Wouw's figures tend to be placed in rural settings, but here you'll find two striking, non-rural pieces, one of a mine worker, the other an accused man standing in the dock. Keep an eye out, too, for *The Guitar Player*, a feisty-looking woman strumming away with a trace of a smile on her face.

UNISA

Travelling south of the centre towards Johannesburg on Elandspoort Road, you can't miss the enormous and head-shakingly ugly **UNISA**, South Africa's largest university, which lurches over the highway to Jo'burg like a renegade ocean liner. Over two hundred thousand students are enrolled here – though most of them study by correspondence.

UNISA Art Gallery

Tues–Fri 10am–4pm • Free • Preller St, Kgorong Building • ☎ 012 429 6255, ⓦ www.unisa.ac.za/gallery

The university's very good **art gallery**, inside the new entrance building, hosts some of Pretoria's most innovative exhibitions of visual and conceptual art, as well as a permanent collection exhibiting young South African talent of all backgrounds.

ARRIVAL AND DEPARTURE — PRETORIA

By plane Johannesburg's OR Tambo International Airport (see p.482) is 55km to the southeast of Pretoria. The Gautrain (see p.482) connects the airport to Pretoria and Hatfield stations, with a change in Sandton, daily between 5.30am and 8.30pm; tickets from the airport to Pretoria or Hatfield stations are R125. The Airport Shuttle (☎ 086 1748 8853, ⓦ airportshuttle.co.za) also goes to Pretoria from OR Tambo airport for around R350. Lanseria Airport (see p.483) is 55km southwest of Pretoria; there's no public transport from here, and a taxi to the city will cost around R400. It's often less expensive to arrange with your accommodation to be collected from the airport. Apart from at the airport (see p.483), car rental offices in Pretoria include Avis, 70 Schoeman St (☎ 012 301 0700); Budget, corner Schoeman and Duncan sts (☎ 086 101 6622); Europcar, Meiring Naude Rd, Brummeria (☎ 086 113 1000); Tempest, 861 Schoeman St (☎ 012 430 2724).

By train Gautrain and Metrorail trains from Johannesburg arrive at Pretoria station, situated just south of the city centre; the Gautrain also serves Hatfield station, with trains running every twelve to twenty minutes between 5.30am and 8.30pm.

By bus Intercity buses stop beside the train station, while minibus taxis from Jo'burg and other destinations arrive nearby at the corner of Jacob Maré and Bosman sts.

Destinations: Aliwal North (3–4 daily; 9hr); Beaufort West (4 daily; 13hr); Bloemfontein (11 daily; 7hr); Cape Town (6 daily; 20hr); Durban (18 daily; 9hr); East London (2 daily; 14hr); George (2 daily; 17hr); Graaff-Reinet (2 daily; 13hr); Harrismith (10 daily; 4hr); Johannesburg (over 30 daily; 1hr); Kimberley (4 daily; 7hr); King William's Town (4 daily; 14hr); Klerksdorp (5 daily; 3hr); Knysna (1 daily; 19hr 30min); Kuruman (daily; 9hr 15min); Ladysmith (daily; 6hr 45min); Mossel Bay (2 daily; 19hr); Nelspruit (5 daily; 6hr); Queenstown (3 daily; 12hr); Umtata (2 daily; 13hr).

GETTING AROUND

By bus Two Gautrain feeder bus lines loop from Pretoria station through the city centre, while the suburbs, malls and embassies in Arcadia, Brooklyn and Menlyn are served by Gautrain buses from Hatfield station. The Gautrain can also be used to travel from Pretoria station to Hatfield. Municipal bus services to other suburbs start along Vermeulen St between Bosman and Andries sts. The driver sells tickets (R10) and has timetables available, otherwise visit the information kiosk in Church Square (☎ 012 358 0839).

By taxi The best local taxi firm is Rixi Taxi (☎ 012 362 6262); alternatively, try Dial-a-Dove Taxi (☎ 012 323 2040).

INFORMATION

Tourist information In the Old Nederlandsche Bank building on Church Square (Mon–Fri 7.30am–4pm; ☎ 012 358 1430, ⊛ tshwanetourism.co.za).

ACCOMMODATION

Besides the many chain hotels, Pretoria has numerous guesthouses dotted around the suburbs, such as Brooklyn and Hatfield, which offer good nightlife and easy access to Loftus Versveld Stadium and the Gautrain station. Backpackers can choose from a reasonable selection of hostels, located in central Pretoria as well as the suburbs. Most offer transfers from the airport, which are among the cheapest you'll find. As with Jo'burg, it's worth booking your first night before you arrive.

1322 Backpackers 1322 Arcadia St, Hatfield ☎ 012 362 3905, ⊛ 1322backpackers.com; map pp.498–499. A very popular hostel near to the embassies and Hatfield's nightlife, with a kitchen, pool and travel desk. Just a short walk from Gautrain's new Hatfield station. Dorm **R110**, double **R270**

Battiss-Zeederberg Guesthouse 3 Fook Island, 92 Twentieth St, Menlo Park ☎ 012 460 7318; map pp.498–499. Very comfortable B&B accommodation in the original home of eccentric Walter Battiss, one of South Africa's greatest twentieth-century artists, with brightly painted floors, unusual decorations and a distinctly Greek feel. **R720**

Brooks Cottage 283 Brooks St, Brooklyn ☎ 012 362 3150, ⊛ brookscottage.co.za; map pp.498–499. An elegant Cape Dutch-style home – a national monument – with smart rooms, satellite TV and breakfast served on the porch overlooking the pool. **R800**

Hotel 224 Corner of Leyds and Schoeman sts ☎ 012 440 5281, ⊛ hotel224.com; map pp.498–499. A characterful and excellent budget hotel, with recently renovated single and double rooms, plus a restaurant and bar attached and safe parking. **R755**

Kia Ora 257 Jacob Maré St ☎ 012 322 4803, ⊛ hostel .myweb.absamail.co.za; map pp.498–499. With a prime location opposite Burgers Park, this friendly hostel is ideal for sightseeing in Pretoria. The dorms and private rooms are clean and comfortable, and there's a congenial bar next door. Dorm **R150**, double **R320**

La Maison 235 Hilda St, Hatfield ☎ 012 430 4341, ⊛ lamaison.co.za; map pp.498–499. A very pleasant guesthouse in a mock castle dating back to 1922, with lovely gardens, six Victorian-styled rooms full of antiques, and an outstanding Portuguese restaurant. **R900**

Osborne House 82 Anderson St, Brooklyn ☎ 012 362 2334, ⊛ osborneguesthouse.com; map pp.498–499. A wonderfully elegant guesthouse in a restored Edwardian manor house with lovely furniture, big windows, wooden floors and a secluded pool with a deck, perfect for breakfasts in the sun. **R1000**

Pretoria Backpackers 425 Farenden St, Clydesdale ☎ 012 343 9754, ⊛ pretoriabackpackers.net; map pp.498–499. A relatively upmarket backpacker place near the Loftus Versveld Stadium, with doubles as well as smallish dorms, spread over two lovely old houses with original features, a relaxing garden *stoep* and a pool. There's also a useful travel centre. Dorm **R120**, double **R320**

Sheraton Pretoria 643 Church St, Arcadia ☎ 012 429 9999, ⊛ sheraton.com/Pretoria; map pp.498–499. This fine five-star hotel boasts all the usual *Sheraton* touches, but most importantly has the best views in town of the Union Buildings. If you can't afford a room with a view, head to the terrace beside *Tiffens Bar & Lounge* for high tea. **R1720**

★ **Ted's Place** 961 Wagon Wheel Ave, Wapadrand ☎ 012 807 2803 or ☎ 083 452 5546, ⊛ teds-place. za.net; map pp.498–499. In the eastern suburbs, close to shops and restaurants. One of the nicest places to stay in Pretoria, this large, elegant hilltop house with a lovely garden offers friendly B&B and enjoyable tours to Pilanesberg and other nearby attractions. **R680**

That's It Guest Home 5 Brecher St, Clydesdale ☎ 012 344 3404, ⊛ thatsit.co.za; map pp.498–499. Near Loftus Versveld Stadium is this neat, un-elaborate, reasonably priced B&B in a family home with four rooms and a relaxing garden and pool. **R730**

Victoria Hotel Corner of Scheiding and Paul Kruger sts ☎ 012 323 6054, ✉ hvic@absamail.co.za; map pp.498–499. The interior of this 1894 building opposite the train station has seen better days, but there's a friendly atmosphere and you can rent rooms for the day, which is handy if you're waiting for bus connections. **R550**

★ **Whistletree Lodge** 1267 Whistletree Drive, Queenswood ☎ 012 333 9915, ⊛ whistletreelodge .com; map pp.498–499. Roughly 7km northeast of the centre, this small boutique hotel is adorned with beautiful antiques, eclectic artwork and stylish furniture, giving the place a refined and luxurious atmosphere. Facilities include a pool, sauna and tennis courts; all rooms have private balconies; and the service is impeccable. **R760**

EATING

As with Pretoria's accommodation, the best restaurants and cafés are found in Hatfield and Brooklyn, although the most atmospheric place to sip an espresso is right in the city centre.

Alla Turka Irene Village Mall, Nellmapius Drive and Van Ryneveld Drive, Irene ☎ 012 662 4314, ⓦ alaturka .co.za; map pp.498–499. A welcoming, radiantly colourful restaurant owned by a Turkish-Lebanese couple. The menu features a medley of Mediterranean flavours (R90–125), and belly dancers perform on Fri & Sat nights for a small performance fee. Daily noon–11pm.

★ **Blue Crane** 156 Melk St, New Muckleneuk ☎ 012 460 7615, ⓦ bluecranerestaurant.co.za; map pp.498–499. A fairly smart restaurant in a unique location, overlooking the lake and the Austin Roberts Bird Sanctuary. The large menu includes lamb shank and ostrich kebabs (mains R90–120). Tues–Sat noon–9.30pm, Sun & Mon noon–2.30pm.

BOER'geoisie Greenlyn Village, Thirteenth St, Menlo Park ☎ 012 460 0264; map pp.498–499. The name says it all – traditional *boerekos* (farmers' food) jazzed up with bistro-cuisine flourishes. The *potjies* (stews) are the house speciality; options include lamb with dumplings. Mains around R80. Mon–Fri noon–3pm & 6–10pm, Sat 6–10pm, Sun noon–3pm.

Brasserie de Paris 381 Aries St, Waterkloof Ridge ☎ 012 460 3583; map pp.498–499. This reproduction of a classic Parisian café has a French-inspired menu, including dishes such as scallop vol-au-vent and steak tartare. Most mains R95–150. Mon–Fri noon–2.30pm & 7–9pm, Sat 7–9.30pm.

Crawdaddy's Corner of Middel and Dey sts, Brooklyn ☎ 012 460 0889, ⓦ crawdaddys.co.za; map pp.498–499. A popular Cajun-themed restaurant, serving chowder and surf-and-turf-style dishes such as prawns and calamari with a meat accompaniment (mains R70–150). Sun–Thurs noon–10.30pm, Fri & Sat noon–11.30pm.

Die Werf 66 Olympus Rd, Faerie Glen ☎ 021 991 1809; map pp.498–499. A farmhouse with several intimate dining rooms, where you can try a hearty selection of home-cooked *boerekos* classics, including *kerrie skaapafval* (curried mutton tripe). Mains R80–100. Tues–Sun 8am–3pm & 6.30–10pm.

Lotus Thai 281 Middel St, Brooklyn ☎ 012 346 6230; map pp.498–499. An elegant, authentic Thai restaurant in the heart of Brooklyn, with stylish, contemporary decor and efficient staff. Plenty of curry and stir-fry dishes (R60–100), as well as sushi. Daily noon–10pm.

Mehfil 1145 Burnett St, Hatfield ☎ 012 362 8080; map pp.498–499. Tasty and well-priced food from North India – the lamb dishes are particularly good. An ideal place for dinner before hitting the bars along Burnett St. Mains around R60. Daily 10.30am–11.30pm.

★ **Pride of India** Groenkloof Plaza, George Storrar Drive, Groenkloof ☎ 012 346 3684; map pp.498–499. Filled with exquisite, imported Indian artefacts and oozing class and confidence, this is the place in town for beautifully prepared North Indian and Goan curries (mostly around R70). Mon–Sat 11.30am–3pm & 5–10pm, Sun 11.30am–3pm.

Tashas Design Square mall, corner of Bronkhorst and Veal sts, Brooklyn ☎ 012 460 2951, ⓦ www .tashas.co.za; pp.498–499. An immensely popular chain bistro with a beautiful, simple design and an extensive menu offering breakfasts, good freshly squeezed juices (rare in South Africa), sandwiches, pasta and cakes; mains cost R50–90. Book ahead or expect to queue. Mon 6.30am–9pm, Tues–Sat 6.30am–10pm, Sun 7.30am–9pm.

BARS AND CLUBS

Most of the city's action is in Hatfield and, to a lesser extent, Brooklyn: the former is where the students hang out, with Hatfield Square being the hub of activity, while Brooklyn attracts an older, more yuppie crowd.

★ **Café Riche** 2 Church Square ☎ 012 328 3173; map pp.498–499. Opened in 1905, this café remains one of the finest in the country, boasting a Continental atmosphere and a quirky events programme, including late-night philosophical discussions (last Fri of the month) and jazz (Sun). Great for Sunday brunch. Daily 6am–midnight.

Cheeky Monkey Burnett St, Hatfield Square ⓦ cheekymonkeybar.co.za; map pp.498–499. The best of the dozen bars on lively Hatfield Square, Cheeky Monkey is often crammed with students downing beer, cocktails or snacks from the in-house restaurant/pizzeria. Daily noon till late.

Drop Zone Burnett St, Hatfield Square ☎ 012 362 6528, ⓦ clubdropzone.co.za; map pp.498–499. A studenty nightclub with plenty of daily drinks specials, live acts, foam parties and loud music that rarely deviates from the mainstream. No under 21s. Daily 8pm till late.

Eastwood's Tavern 391 Eastwood Rd, Arcadia ☎ 012 344 0243; map pp.498–499. An often raucous pub-restaurant near Loftus Versveld Stadium popular with meat- and beer-loving sports fans. Select a raw piece of steak (R60) and cook it yourself in the braai area. Mon–Sat 8am–midnight, Sun 8am–10pm.

★ **Tings and Times** 1065 Arcadia St, Hatfield ☎ 012 430 3176, ⓦ tings.co.za; map pp.498–499. Reggae predominates at this eclectic bar on a quieter street that runs parallel to Burnett St. The best place in town to catch live bands, and there's a menu with pitta bread variations and other snacks. Tues–Sat noon–1.30am.

Tribeca Coffee Design Square mall, Brooklyn ☎ 012 460 3068; map pp.498–499. A trendy hangout full of beautiful people – many of them gay – serving coffee by day and cocktails in the evening. The music is mainly house and electro. Daily 8am–midnight.

ENTERTAINMENT

Pretoria lacks the dynamism and breadth of Johannesburg's arts and music scene, but there's still a fair amount going on. The *Pretoria News* is good for listings for theatre and cinema, while the *Mail & Guardian* covers the visual arts, theatre and major musical events. Computicket (☎ 083 915 8000, ⍵ computicket.com) is the big central ticket outlet for most arts and sports events, with outlets in malls and all Checkers and Shoprite supermarkets.

Breytenbach Theatre 137 Gerard Moerdyk St ☎ 012 440 4834; map pp.498–499. The "Breytie" is a venue for lively student theatre, though it's said to be haunted by the ghosts of those who died there when it was a hospital for Germans.

State Theatre Church St ☎ 012 392 4000, ⍵ www .statetheatre.co.za; map pp.498–499. The city's main venue for theatre, opera and classical concerts. Under the leadership of Hugh Masekela and then Aubrey Sekhabi, it puts on an interesting programme of jazz and black theatre.

DIRECTORY

American Express Brooklyn Mall, Bronkhorst St, Brooklyn ☎ 012 346 2599.

Banks Most banks are around Church Square and along Church St.

Bookshops Exclusive Books have a branch at Brooklyn Mall, Bronkhorst St, Brooklyn (☎ 012 346 5864). Protea Book House, 1067 Burnett St, Hatfield (☎ 012 362 1563), offers a wide range of new and secondhand books.

Embassies and consulates Australia, 292 Orient St, Arcadia (☎ 012 423 6000); Canada, 1103 Arcadia St, Hatfield (☎ 012 422 3000); Ireland, 1st Floor, Southern Life Plaza, 1059 Schoemann St, Arcadia (☎ 012 342 5062); Lesotho, 391 Anderson St, Menlo Park (☎ 012 460 7648); Malawi, 770 Government Ave, Arcadia (☎ 012 342 0146); Mozambique, 529 Edmund St, Arcadia (☎ 012 401 0300); Namibia, 197 Blackwood St, Arcadia (☎ 012 481 9100); Swaziland, 715 Government Ave, Arcadia (☎ 012 344 1910); UK, 255 Hill St, Arcadia (☎ 012 421 7500); US, 877 Pretorius St, Arcadia (☎ 011 431 4000); Zambia, 570 Ziervogel Ave, Arcadia (☎ 012 326 1854); Zimbabwe, 798 Merton Av, Arcadia (☎ 012 342 5125).

Emergencies Private ambulance (Netcare) ☎ 082 911; ambulance & fire ☎ 10177; police ☎ 10111.

Flea market Hatfield Flea Market, 1122 Burnett St (every Sun), is Pretoria's best flea market, with crafts, bric-a-brac and lively banter.

Hospitals Those with 24hr casualty services include Steve Biko Academic Hospital, Voortrekker Rd (☎ 012 354 1590), and Wilgers Hospital, Denneboom Rd (☎ 012 807 8100).

Internet cafés Central Pretoria has plenty of internet cafés, particularly along Church St between Bosman and Schubart sts. In Hatfield, try Videorama, The Fields, 1054 Burnett St (Mon–Fri 9am–10pm, Sat & Sun 10am–10pm).

Pharmacies In virtually every shopping mall; there are also 24hr pharmacies at Wilgers Hospital (see above) and the Muelmed Medi-Clinic, 577 Pretorius St (☎ 012 440 1457).

Post office Church St (Mon, Tues, Thurs & Fri 8am–4.30pm, Wed 8.30am–4.30pm, Sat 8am–noon).

Around Pretoria

The most absorbing sight in the immediate vicinity of Pretoria is **Doornkloof Farm**, the former home of Prime Minister Jan Smuts. Further out, to the east of Pretoria, the mining town of **Cullinan** harks back to the pioneering days of diamond prospecting, while north of the city the **Tswaing meteorite crater** is a great place for a short hike. To the west, **Lesedi Cultural Village** has become a victim of its own popularity, although those impassioned by wildlife conservation should not miss the **De Wildt Cheetah and Wildlife Trust**.

Doornkloof Farm

Irene, signposted 20km south of Pretoria along the R21 • Mon–Fri 9.30am–4.30pm, Sat & Sun 9.30am–5pm • R15 • ☎ 012 667 2917

Doornkloof Farm was the home of **Jan Smuts** for much of his life, including during his periods as prime minister of South Africa. His fairly simple wood-and-corrugated-iron house is now a museum, which does tend toward hagiography but still manages to shed light on one of South Africa's most enigmatic politicians. The massive library on the site reflects Smuts' intellectual range, while numerous mementos confirm his internationalism. Other displays focus on Smuts' role as one of the most successful commanders of Boer forces during the Anglo-Boer Wars. The surrounding farm is part of the museum, and features the pleasant 2.5-kilometre **Oubaas Trail**, leading from the house to the top of a nearby *koppie*, a walk the nature-loving Smuts took every day. Scattered near the house are various pieces of military hardware such as cannon and armoured vehicles – a little incongruously, given the declarations of peace and tranquillity posted along the trail and elsewhere. For refreshment, there's a tearoom next to the house.

Cullinan and the Premier Mine

50km east of Pretoria • **Surface tours** Mon–Fri 10.30am & 2pm, Sat & Sun 10.30am • 2hr • R80 • ☎ 012 734 0081 • **Underground tours** Mon–Fri 10.30am, Sat 7.30am • 4hr • R490 • Booking required • ☎ 012 734 2170, ⓦ diamondtourscullinan.co.za • **Diamond Express train** R175 • ☎ 012 548 4090, ⓦ friendsoftherail.com

Popular with tourist coaches, it was in quaint **Cullinan**'s **Premier Mine**, still worked today, that the world's largest diamond, the 3106-carat **Star of Africa**, was discovered in 1905. Mine enthusiasts can take a surface tour of the mine, or dress in protective clothing and see operations from close up, 760m underground. Otherwise there isn't much to do in Cullinan other than wander around. The best way to visit is on the **Diamond Express** steam-train day-trip organized about once a month by Friends of the Rail, departing from Pretoria's Hermanstad depot at 8.30am and returning at 5.30pm, leaving enough time in Cullinan to wander the streets and have a relaxed lunch.

Tswaing Crater

Onderstepoort Rd, Soshanguve, off the M35 • Daily 7.30am–2pm • R25 • ☎ 012 000 0010, ⓦ ditsong.org.za/tswaing.htm

Tswaing Crater is one of the youngest and best preserved meteorite craters in the world, a 1.4km-wide and 200m-deep depression created around 220,000 years ago. Tswaing means "place of salt" in Tswana, and the rich deposits of salt and soda around the edge of the shallow crater lake have attracted people since ancient times; artefacts up to 150,000 years old have been discovered here. Register at the new visitors' centre on the main road before driving to the car park, from where a pleasant 7km trail crosses the veld to the crater, down to the lake and back; alternatively, park closer to the rim from where it's a short stroll to the crater.

Lesedi Cultural Village

Southwest of Pretoria, off the R512, near Lanseria Airport • Tours daily at 11.30am & 4.30pm • R240 tour only, R390 for the tour plus a meal and dance performance • Accommodation R2020 including tour • ☎ 012 205 1394, ⓦ lesedi.com

Lesedi Cultural Village crams five cultural villages into one bewildering experience, with the Zulu, Pedi, Xhosa, Ndebele and Basotho all represented. Tourists are escorted round the fairly authentic kraals, entertained by a lively display of colourful costumes, singing and dancing, then fed heartily with a traditional African feast in the vividly decorated restaurant. You can also stay the night in a grass hut with a Lesedi family.

Ann van Dyk Cheetah Centre

West of Pretoria, just off the R513 going towards Brits • **Cheetah run and tour** Tues, Thurs, Sat & Sun 8am • R380 • **Tours** Mon, Wed, Fri 8.30am, Tues, Thurs, Sat & Sun 1.30pm • R270 • Book in advance • ☎ 012 504 9906 or ☎ 082 892 0515, ⓦ dewildt.co.za

The **Ann van Dyk Cheetah Centre** is a world-renowned conservation project. The centre's mission is to protect the cheetah by developing predator management policies with farmers, breeding cubs in captivity (over 750 have been raised to date) and then generally transporting them to game reserves. Other endangered animals bred and/or cared for at the centre include African wild dogs, vultures and brown hyenas.

Visitors can get up close and personal with the centre's senior cheetahs, who are utterly relaxed in human company, and there's a tour of the centre and the enclosures housing the other animals. Photographing cheetahs on the run is a big draw, and there's also a cheetah adoption programme if you get passionate about the centre's cause.

North West Province

WILDEBEEST IN MADIKWE GAME RESERVE (P524)

North West Province

South Africa's North West Province is one of the country's least-understood regions – renowned, among tourists at least, for the opulent Sun City resort and the Big Five Pilanesberg National Park, but not much else. Few people venture beyond these attractions to explore this area in greater depth; consequently, it can be curiously rewarding to do so. The old-fashioned hospitality of the myriad little *dorps* scattered throughout the region, and the tranquillity of the endless stretches of grassland and fields of *mielies* (sweetcorn) make a refreshing change after hectic Johannesburg and Pretoria.

North West Province extends west from Gauteng to the Botswana border and the Kalahari Desert. Along the province's eastern flank, essentially separating it from Gauteng, loom the **Magaliesberg mountains**, one hundred times older than the Himalayas and dotted with **holiday** resorts for nature-starved Jo'burgers. The **N4** from Pretoria cuts through the mountains to the main town of the northeastern part of the province, **Rustenburg**, gateway to the windswept **Kgaswane Mountain Reserve**, where you can hike high enough to gaze down onto the shimmering plains beneath. **Groot Marico**, further west along the N4, is a friendly *dorp* with powerful home-brews and laidback people to share them with. Further to the west lies the provincial capital of **Mafikeng** – famed for its siege during the second Anglo-Boer War – while near the Botswana border, **Madikwe Game Reserve** is one of South Africa's undiscovered wildlife gems, a massive Big Five park which sees remarkably few visitors and boasts some superb game lodges.

Brief history

San hunter-gatherers were the province's first inhabitants: they were displaced 500–1000 years ago by cattle-herding Iron-Age peoples from the north, who pitched their first settlements on low ground near watercourses. These settlements developed into stone-walled towns on hilltops; and by 1820, the largest, Karechuenya (near Madikwe), was estimated to have more inhabitants than Cape Town. By the nineteenth century, the dominance of the Rolong, Taung, Tlhaping and Tlokwa clans was established. European observers classified them all as **Tswana**, but it's unclear whether these people regarded themselves as very different from people further east classified as "Sotho".

The outbreak of intense **inter-clan violence** in the early 1800s was due to displacements caused by the expansion of white *trekboers*, and the growing availability of firearms. Victory went to those who made alliances with the new arrivals, whether **Griqua** from the Northern Cape or **Afrikaners** from further south. However, the clans' victories were short-lived and their Griqua and Afrikaner allies soon evicted them from their land and forced them into service. Various mini-states were formed until, in 1860, they were all amalgamated to form the **South African Republic** (ZAR), with Pretoria as its capital.

The first Anglo-Boer War (1877–81) left most of the province unaffected. Of far greater impact was the **second Anglo-Boer War** (1899–1902). As well as the celebrated **siege of Mafikeng**, where British and Tswana forces held out for 217 days against

8

PLACE OF THE LOST CITY, SUN CITY

Highlights

❶ Kgaswane Mountain Reserve High above Rustenburg, in the Magaliesberg mountains, varied trails allow you to hike through savannah, rolling hills, rocky *kloofs* and past sparkling streams. **See p.518**

❷ Sun City Las Vegas meets the bushveld at this unique fantasyland of hotels, slot machines, stage shows, elephant safaris, lush golf courses and a fun-filled water park. **See p.518**

❸ Pilanesberg Park The most accessible Big Five park from Johannesburg and Pretoria, with beautiful landscapes in a former volcano crater, and terrific game viewing. **See p.520**

❹ Groot Marico One of the most characterful of South Africa's tiny *dorps*, or small farming towns, famed for its literary connections and the potency of the local fruit spirit, mampoer. **See p.523**

❺ Madikwe Game Reserve An often-overlooked Big Five reserve in the corner of the province; prepare to be pampered in some of South Africa's classiest wildlife lodges. **See p.524**

HIGHLIGHTS ARE MARKED ON THE MAP ON P.514

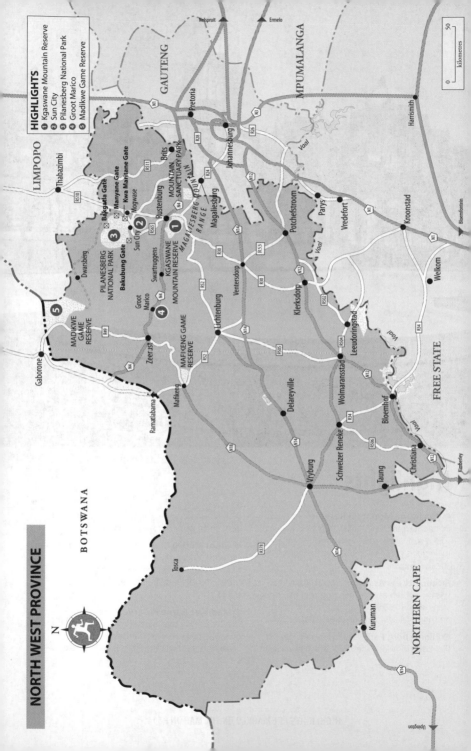

NORTH WEST PROVINCE

HIGHLIGHTS
① Kgaswane Mountain Reserve
② Sun City
③ Pilanesberg National Park
④ Groot Marico
⑤ Madikwe Game Reserve

N

BOTSWANA

LIMPOPO

GAUTENG

MPUMALANGA

FREE STATE

NORTHERN CAPE

Nelspruit
Ermelo
Harrismith
Thabazimbi
Pretoria
Johannesburg
Kroonstad
Bloemfontein
Welkom
Parys
Vredefort
Potchefstroom
Britts
Rustenburg
Magaliesburg
MOUNTAIN
SANCTUARY PARK
MAGALIESBERG MOUNTAIN RANGE
Bakgatla Gate
Manyane Gate
Kwa Maritane Gate
Mogwase
Sun City
Bakubung Gate
PILANESBERG
NATIONAL PARK
Dwarsberg
Swartruggens
Groot Marico
KGASWANE
MOUNTAIN RESERVE
Zeerust
MADIKWE
GAME RESERVE
Gaborone
Ramatlabama
Mafikeng
MAFIKENG GAME RESERVE
Lichtenburg
Ventersdorp
Klerksdorp
Leeudoringstad
Wolmaransstad
Bloemhof
Christiana
Kimberley
Delareyville
Schweizer Reneke
Taung
Vryburg
Tosca
Kuruman
Upington

Vaal

R510
R511
R565
R556
R24
R28
N1
N4
N12
N3
R26
R36
N1
R30
R53
R52
R30
R502
R504
R34
R506
R378
N14
N18
R49
R30
N4
N12

0   50
kilometres

VISITING NORTH WEST PROVINCE

Relentless sun alleviated only by torrential rain makes **summer** in North West Province something of an endurance test: aim to come here in **spring** or **autumn**. For the more adventurous, **camping** in the quiet and timeless veld is especially rewarding in this part of South Africa. **Tourist information** for the province is provided by the North West Parks & Tourism Board (☏ 018 397 1500 or ☏ 086 111 1866, ⊕ tourismnorthwest.co.za); its website has information and links to all of the region's parks. **Malaria** is absent throughout the province.

Afrikaner troops, there were protracted skirmishes up and down the Vaal River. After the British victory, both Afrikaner and Tswana had their lands torched and many were thrown into concentration camps.

The Union Treaty of 1910 left the province, as the western part of the Transvaal, firmly in Afrikaner hands. Its smaller *dorps* soon became synonymous with rural racism, epitomized in the 1980s by the fascistic AWB led by **Eugene Terreblanche**, whose power base was here. In addition, the province played a relatively minor role in the national struggle against apartheid due to the absence of a significant black working class after the migration of many Tswana men to work in the gold mines of the Witwatersrand.

In 1977, the **Bophuthatswana Bantustan** homeland – or "Bop" – was created around Mmabatho in the western part of the province out of the old "native reserves", the poor-quality land into which Tswana had been forced. Far from being a long-awaited "independent" homeland for the blacks in this area, Bop proved to be a confusing amalgamation of enclaves, ruled by the corrupt **Lucas Mangope**, who grew rich on the revenues from **Sol Kerzner**'s casinos in Sun City and Mmabatho and the discovery of platinum. Bophuthatswana's short life came to an end in March 1994, a month before South Africa's elections, when its army mutinied. Mangope called in hundreds of armed AWB neo-fascists to help quell the uprising, but the AWB – and Mangope – were ingloriously defeated.

8

Bojanala Region

Bordering Gauteng, **Bojanala Region** lies in North West Province's northeastern bushveld and is a popular weekend destination for Jo'burgers. One of the more distinctive parts of this largely empty and flat province is the **Magaliesberg mountain range**, which gets its name from the Tswana chief **Mogale** of the Kwena clan. Kwena people lived here from the seventeenth century until 1825, when most of them were forced out by the Ndebele chief **Mzilikazi**. Afrikaner farmers continued the process of eviction, and today the dispossession and expulsion of the Kwena in the Magaliesberg is complete.

Great chunks of the Magaliesberg have been fenced off and turned into time-shares or resorts, but there are oases of unspoilt nature, notably **Kgaswane Mountain Reserve** – accessed from the region's main town, **Rustenburg** – and the **Mountain Sanctuary Park**, both preserved in something like their previous natural state and well stocked with wildlife. (The southeastern Magaliesberg mountains are covered in Chapter 7.)

Further north, occupying an ancient volcanic crater, is the outstanding **Pilanesberg National Park** – the "Big Five" mainstay of Gauteng-based safari operators. If you're in the mood for a fun-in-the-sun water park and some surreal tourist opulence, **Sun City** is worth checking out, if only as a stopover on your way in to Pilanesberg.

Rustenburg

Some 120km northwest of Johannesburg lies the platinum-mining town of **RUSTENBURG**, the oldest town in the former Western Transvaal. With its grid of

CRIME IN RUSTENBURG

Rustenburg is currently experiencing a boom with the development of new platinum reserves, and the new wealth has brought with it a rapid increase in **crime**. The police and security presence on the streets is not as visible as it is in other high-crime cities such as Jo'burg and Durban, and there is a very serious threat of muggings, sometimes involving weapons, when walking around town both during the day and at night. The **Waterfall Mall** is relatively safe, but exercise extreme caution when exploring other areas, particularly around the bus station and main thoroughfares such as **Fatima Bhayat Street**. The **main police station** is on the corner of Beyers Naude Drive and Kruis Street (☎014 590 4111).

prefabricated chain stores and shopping malls, the place is a pretty dreary hymn to misguided town planning and eminently missable. Still, you may end up staying if you're visiting the glorious Kgaswane Mountain Reserve, 7km south of town.

Rustenburg's historic centre is limited to two blocks of Burger Street, from Nelson Mandela Drive to Oliver Tambo Drive. Here you'll find two churches: the old **Anglican church**, dating from 1871, and the 1850 **Dutch Reformed church**. Facing the latter is the graceful 1935 town hall and a **statue of Paul Kruger** by French sculptor Jean Georges Achard, showing the president in his last days in exile in France, sitting grumpily in an armchair. After this quick sightseeing tour, head to the gleaming **Waterfall Mall** (Mon–Fri 9am–6pm, Sat 9am–5pm, Sun 9am–1pm), 5km east of town (follow Nelson Mandela Drive), for the province's best shopping.

ARRIVAL AND DEPARTURE — RUSTENBURG

By bus and minibus taxi None of the major bus companies has scheduled stops in Rustenburg. Long-distance minibus taxis and the daily Bojanala bus (☎014 565 8540, ⓦbojanalabus.co.za) from Mafikeng (3hr, not via Groot Marico) arrive at the terminal at the western end of Nelson Mandela Drive by Beneden St.

Long-distance minibus taxis depart regularly, covering most of the province, including Groot Marico (1hr 30min, take the Zeerust taxi) and Mafikeng (3hr 30min), and also go to Lesotho (daily; 9hr). Bays are clearly marked with destinations, and tickets are available on the buses; it's best to check your options the day before you travel.

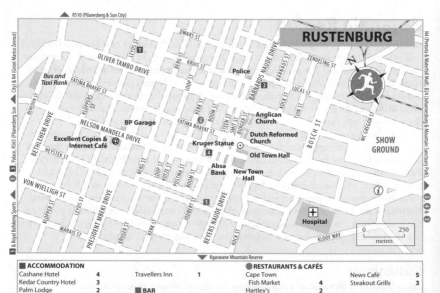

■ ACCOMMODATION		● RESTAURANTS & CAFÉS	
Cashane Hotel	4	Cape Town	4
Kedar Country Hotel	3	Fish Market	
Palm Lodge	2	Hartley's	2
Rainhill Farm	5	Ivory Pot	1
Travellers Inn	1	News Café	5
■ BAR		Steakout Grills	3
Castle Corner	1		

When leaving the bus terminal, avoid its northern section: muggings are common in this area. Car rental is available from Avis at 194 Beyers Naude Drive (☎014 592 9902).

INFORMATION

Tourist information 2km from the centre at the eastern entrance of town, on Kloof Rd, between Nelson Mandela Drive and Fatima Bhayat St (Mon–Fri 8am–4.30pm, Sat 8am–noon; ☎014 597 0904, ✉tidcrust@mweb.co.za).

ACCOMMODATION

You'll get the most out of the area by staying out of town. You can camp at Kgaswane Mountain Reserve (see p.518) and Mountain Sanctuary Park, and there are dozens of rural (and sometimes quite flashy) B&Bs and resorts in the surrounding countryside – you'll find a selection online at ⓦrustenburgaccommodation.co.za. There's safe parking at all the following recommendations.

Cashane Hotel 66 Steen St ☎014 592 8541; map opposite. An ageing but well-kept hotel on six floors, with comfortable, well-equipped rooms and views over town. There's also a good bar and a dull restaurant. R440

Kedar Country Hotel 20km northwest of town in Boshoek, 500m off the R565 to Sun City ☎014 573 3218, ⓦrali.co.za; map opposite. Set amid plentiful game and birdlife, this lovingly restored farmhouse once belonged to President Kruger, who's honoured by a small museum. The simple yet luxurious Afrikaner-style decor makes for a refreshingly tranquil rural getaway, and there's also a swimming pool, plus two suites (R7750) with private plunge pools. R1130

Palm Lodge 99 Beyers Naude Drive ☎014 597 2520; map opposite. A large thatch-roofed complex appearing swankier than it is, with dozens of small, dark rooms, one-bedroom self-catering units, a swimming pool, two bars and a restaurant. R400

Rainhill Farm 4km southwest of town; follow Bethlehem Drive, turn right on Brink St, left on Watsonia Rd, right at the end ☎014 592 8911, ⓦrainhill.co.z; map opposite. Four charming rooms in 1940s chalets decked out with antiques, perfect for families or honeymooners. Catch a minibus taxi to Rustenburg Kloof. R560

★ **Travellers Inn** 99 Leyds St ☎014 592 7658, ⓦtravellersinn.co.za; map opposite. Offering good modern rooms, with a dorm for backpackers. There's a swimming pool, a lovely rustic bar and superb food. Gay and lesbian couples welcome. Dorm R150, double R400

EATING, DRINKING AND NIGHTLIFE

Rustenburg is dominated by fast-food joints: Nelson Mandela Drive and Fatima Bhayat St have plenty, while there are more appealing restaurants at some of the hotels and in the Waterfall Mall (ⓦwaterfallmall.co.za). There are some good spots for traditional African food, including the food stands in and around the bus terminal (although exercise caution in all of these areas day and night).

Cape Town Fish Market Waterfall Mall, 1 Augrabies Ave ☎014 537 3663, ⓦctfm.co.za; map opposite. This quality chain restaurant is one of the best food options in the mall, with good fresh fish dishes, sushi and bento boxes. Daily 11am–11pm.

Castle Corner Heystek St ☎014 592 1108; map opposite. Posh English-style pub with lots of beer on tap, reasonable grub (R50–70) and satellite sports. Local bands provide live music Wed, Fri & Sat nights. Daily noon–10pm.

Hartley's Rainhill Farm (see above) ☎014 594 1992; map opposite. Tranquil, country-style pub and family restaurant. The pub area is called *The Milk Shed*, while *The*

Pack House is the more formal, non-smoking restaurant. The food at both (R50–80) ranges from ribs and steaks to prawns and seafood platters – don't miss the farm's famous orange marmalade. Daily noon–10pm.

Ivory Pot in a small arcade off Fatima Bhayat St; map opposite. Popular restaurant that's excellent for a traditional African lunch – offering various meats served with *pap*, *samp*, beans, rice and vegetables (around R25). Mon–Sat 8am–4pm.

News Cafe Waterfall Mall, Value Mart ☎014 537 3711; map opposite. By day a café with decent meals, by night the best place in town for drinks, occasional live music and maybe even some dancing. Daily 11am–11pm.

DIRECTORY

Banks Absa at Waterfall Mall has a bureau de change.
Emergencies Private ambulance (Netcare) ☎014 568 4338 or ☎082 911; ambulance ☎014 556 2073; fire ☎014 590 3334; police ☎014 590 4111.
Health Doctors and dentists are available at Medicross

Medical Centre, corner of President Mbeki Drive and Von Wielligh St ☎014 592 8562.
Internet Excellent Copies & Internet Café, Nelson Mandela Drive, opposite the BP petrol station.

Kgaswane Mountain Reserve

7km south of Rustenburg • Daily: April–Aug 6am–6pm; Sept–March 5.30am–7.30pm • R20, plus R10 per vehicle • ☎ 014 533 2050, ⓦ tourismnorthwest.co.za/kgaswane

Kgaswane Mountain Reserve spans a spectacular forty-square-kilometre portion of the Magaliesberg and is dotted with rock formations, created by millennia of erosion, areas of dry veld and streams coursing through the valleys. The reserve's unique **flora** includes aloes indigenous to the Magaliesberg and the discreet *frithiapulchra*, a succulent with only its leaf tips exposed, flowering between November and March. The many crags are perfect for predatory **birds**; keep a lookout for the rare black eagle, Martial eagle and Cape vulture, as well as parrots and paradise flycatchers. Kgaswane is also home to eight hundred **antelopes**, representing most of South Africa's species, and also zebras. Predators are few in number and limited to caracal, aardwolf, black-backed jackals and the elusive leopard.

ARRIVAL AND INFORMATION KGASWANE MOUNTAIN RESERVE

By car You'll need your own vehicle to reach the reserve: take the R24 from central Rustenburg towards Johannesburg and turn right at the traffic lights just after the Waterfall Mall (or just before the mall when coming from Jo'burg), and follow the road up the hill, turning left onto the signposted road to the reserve gate. From here, the road winds dramatically up to the visitor centre in a broad valley near the mountaintop. **Visitor centre** In the middle of the park (often closed in winter; check at the gate), stocking useful maps and information on hikes and trails.

ACCOMMODATION

Campsite ☎ 014 533 2050, ⓦ tourismnorthwest.co.za /kgaswane. The visitor centre has sheltered camping and braai facilities that are open year-round; theres no shop so bring all supplies you need. In winter, count on very cold nights. R20

Sun City

R50 • ☎ 011 780 781, ⓦ suncity.co.za

A surreal pocket of high-rise hotels and tinkling gaming machines in the endless bushveld, **SUN CITY** consists of four hotel resorts tightly packed together with golf courses, a water park and various other attractions. When entrepreneur Sol Kerzner began building the vast complex in the 1970s, the area was part of the Bophuthatswana Bantustan and therefore one of the few places in the country where you could **gamble** legally. Thousands visited from "across the border" to sample Kerzner's blend of gaming, topless shows and over-the-top hotels. However, now that gambling is legal in South Africa, Sun City has altered its focus, promoting itself these days as a **family destination** – indeed, if you have kids to entertain, this is an excellent place to bring them. The resort also makes a good base for exploring Pilanesberg National Park.

Cabanas and Waterworld

Cabanas, close to the entrance, is the area that young kids will enjoy most: it has a small zoo, horseriding, a crèche, an aviary with summer flying displays by hawks, falcons and owls, and a crocodile sanctuary, where you can feed the hungry denizens at 4.30pm. Behind it is **Waterworld**, a large artificial lake used for a range of watersports, from parasailing to waterskiing.

> ### EXPLORING KGASWANE
>
> The reserve can be explored on a day or two-night **hike**, or by **bicycle** (bring your own). There are two short trails for day hikes. The two- to three- how 5km **Peglarae Trail** follows a relatively easy path through rocky terrain and takes in most of the reserve's best features and views. Shorter and flatter is the 2km **Vleiramble** to a viewing hut on the *vlei*, popular with birders. Overnight hikes follow the **Rustenburg hiking trail** (19.5km or 23.5km) and last two days and two nights.

Entertainment Centre

The **Entertainment Centre** next to the towering triangle of *Cascades* hotel is the focal point of Sun City, with rows of bleeping slot machines and arcade games, a cinema, upmarket shops, and a concert hall hosting various musical acts and other events. Next to the Entertainment Centre you'll find an aviary, tennis courts, health spa and the renowned Gary Player Golf Course (green fee R765; book well in advance as a waiting list of several months is not uncommon).

Lost City and Valley of the Waves

R100; free if you're staying at one of the hotels • **Valley of the Waves** daily: May–Aug 10am–5pm; closed mid-May to mid-June; Sept–April 9am–6pm • **Palace Tour** 8 daily: 11.30am–4pm; departs from the Welcome Centre • R60

The **Lost City** is the resort's showpiece, separated from the rest of the complex by the vibrating Bridge of Time. Inside is the **Valley of Waves**, a gigantic water park designed to look like a beach, complete with sand, palm trees, three water slides and a machine producing 2m-high breakers suitable for surfing. Deeper into the acres of specially planted rainforest above the Valley, you'll find waterfalls, trickling streams and a network of explorable paths, all interspersed with "remains" of the Lost City.

Overlooking the whole scene is the staggering *Palace of the Lost City* (see p.520); you can pop in for a drink if you're not staying, or join a *Palace* tour for a more thorough look.

Letsatsing Game Reserve

Elephant ride R1600 • Elephant interaction R580 • Quad biking R410 • Clay pigeon shooting R380 • Archery R230 • Drumming and dancing lessons R165

A twenty-minute drive from the Welcome Centre and sandwiched between the golf course, the fenced-off Pilanesberg park and the main road, the small **Letsatsing Game Reserve** lacks dangerous predators and is used exclusively for those participating in Gametrackers' outdoor activities (see p.519). Here, five friendly elephants, orphaned in 1980s Zimbabwe and subsequently domesticated, take visitors on one-hour rides (including snacks and drinks) three times per day; note that joining large groups means less time on the elephants. There's also an elephant interaction programme (includes lunch), where visitors can safely touch, feed and photograph the elephants and chat to the knowledgeable keepers. Other outdoor activities such as quad biking, clay pigeon shooting, archery, drumming and gumboot dancing lessons are held on the far side of the reserve. The Gametrackers desk at the Welcome Centre arranges all transport to the reserve.

8

ARRIVAL AND DEPARTURE   SUN CITY

By car Driving from Pretoria or Jo'burg, follow the N4 past the Brits turn-off, and turn right onto the R556, from where it's roughly 70km. A popular option is to join a day tour from Pretoria or Jo'burg; a large number of operators based in those cities offer trips (see p.485), with prices depending on the target market; expect to pay at least R350–500, plus R200–300 if combined with a short safari at Pilanesberg. There's parking near the Welcome Centre, though when it's busy day visitors use the vast car park by the main gate and hop on the monorail train to the Welcome Centre.

By minibus taxi Regular minibus taxis from Rustenburg to Mogwase pass the Sun City entrance, and daily shuttle buses operated by Ingelosi Tours (R400, return R500; ☎014 557 4488, ⍟ingelositours.co.za, tickets online at ⍟computicket.com) drive from OR Tambo International Airport, Sandton and Pretoria.

INFORMATION AND TOURS

Tourist information Sun City's Welcome Centre (Mon–Thurs & Sun 8am–7pm, Fri & Sat 8am–10pm; ☎014 557 1544) can provide maps, leaflets and details of special offers. There's also an information desk for the North West Parks & Tourism Board (Mon–Fri 8am–4.30pm, Sat & Sun 9am–2pm; ☎014 557 1907).

Tours Gametrackers (☎014 552 5020, ⍟gametrac.co.za) also has a desk at the Welcome Centre where you can book game drives, balloon flights, elephant-back safaris, elephant interaction and other outdoor activities.

ACCOMMODATION

Sun City's hotels are all located within a short distance of each other in the centre of the valley. Rooms can be booked through Sun City Reservations (☎ 011 780 7810, ⓦ suninternational.co.za), but will be considerably cheaper if arranged through a tour company as part of a package, or over the internet. All hotels are enormous – *Cascades*, the smallest, has a mere 243 rooms.

Cabanas ☎ 011 780 7810, ⓦ suninternational.co.za. The cheapest accommodation in Sun City, and close to most of the kids' activities, this is the obvious base for families. The rooms are small and somewhat dated, but the atmosphere is relaxed and there's a good indoor pool and reasonably priced restaurants. R1500

Cascades ☎ 011 780 7810, ⓦ suninternational.co.za. After the *Palace*, this is the resort's most comfortable place to stay, though the rooms and service are bland. Next door to the Entertainment Centre, it's a stylish pyramid-shaped high-rise with tropical decor, a mini rainforest and aviary, and outside lifts offering splendid views. The inviting pool and bar are for residents only. R2500

★ **Palace of the Lost City** ☎ 011 780 7810, ⓦ suninternational.co.za. Like something out of an *Indiana Jones* film, the enormous *Palace* is a fantastically opulent and imaginative hotel, designed as a soaring African jungle palace with towers, domes, extravagant carvings and sculptures. Rooms are large and beautifully furnished, and although a stay here is bank-breakingly expensive (you'll find better value elsewhere), the experience is unforgettable. R4100

Sun City Hotel ☎ 011 780 7810, ⓦ suninternational .co.za. The resort's original hotel houses the main casino, so is a good choice if gambling is your main reason for visiting Sun City. The large, balconied rooms have great views and there are four decent restaurants. R2300

EATING, DRINKING AND NIGHTLIFE

The Entertainment Centre has lots of moderately priced restaurants, snack bars, cafés, a casino and a cinema. For **drinking** and **dancing**, the *Traders* bar and *Silhouette* nightclub (admission free) are on the upper level of the Entertainment Centre, which is where you'll also find an alcohol-free nightclub for teenagers.

Crystal Court Palace of the Lost City. The classically furnished *Crystal Court* hosts two recommended dining experiences: a sumptuous breakfast buffet (R225) and afternoon high tea (R145); otherwise there's a buffet on weekdays and à la carte dining on weekends.

Santorini Cascades Hotel. This chain restaurant, situated beside the lovely pool at *Cascades*, is known for its affordable, tasty Mediterranean food (R75–100) including Greek kleftiko, pitta dishes and pizza.

Pilanesberg Game Reserve

Daily: March, April, Sept & Oct 6am–6.30pm; May–Aug 6.30am–6pm; Nov–Feb 5.30am–7pm • R65, plus R20 per car • ☎ 014 555 1600, ⓦ pilanesberg-game-reserve.co.za

Adjacent to Sun City and home to a huge variety of animals, the **PILANESBERG GAME RESERVE** is North West Province's biggest tourist draw. The artificially created reserve was, until 1979, occupied by farmers and the **Tswana** people, who were unceremoniously evicted when **Operation Genesis** saw over six thousand animals shipped in from all over the country to fill the park. Just two to three hours' drive from Pretoria and Jo'burg, Pilanesberg is definitely the place to come to see some game if you're based in Gauteng and have only limited time in South Africa. Like any other game parks, you'll get the most from your visit if you stay in or near the reserve so that you're in the best position to head out at prime game-viewing time: at dawn, before the day visitors arrive.

Don't let the crowds or the managed nature of the place put you off: the park offers game-viewing thrills aplenty, with a good chance of seeing all of the **Big Five**, along with hippo, brown hyena, giraffe and zebra. The majority of antelope species are here, too, and there's a vast array of birdlife – over 365 species recorded so far. At night, some fantastic creatures emerge, including civet, porcupine and caracal, though you'll be lucky to spot them.

Covering some 650 square kilometres, and with 200km of good-quality tar and gravel roads, you'll need at least a day to do Pilanesberg justice. The reserve is easily explored by car, especially with the official map (for sale at the gates and camp shops). The park's many

beautiful hills – the result of an unusual volcanic eruption that occurred 1200–1300 years ago – are in some ways Pilanesberg's finest feature, though they are often ignored by visitors more interested in scouring their slopes for wildlife. Pilanesberg's natural focus, for visitors and wildlife alike, is the alkaline **Lake Mankwe** ("place of the leopard"), whose goings-on are best observed from several walk-in hides. The various picnic spots and hides dotted around are ideal for breaking the drive – the hides in particular aren't used by many visitors and as a result can be cool, peaceful places to appreciate the natural surroundings. If you're self-driving, don't hesitate to ask the safari jeep drivers for sighting tips; all of them are in radio contact with each other and know exactly what's going on.

ARRIVAL AND DEPARTURE — PILANESBERG GAME RESERVE

By car There are four entrance gates to the reserve; the most commonly used are Manyane, on the eastern side of the reserve near Mogwase, where the park headquarters are located, and Bakubung in the south, just to the west of Sun City off the R565.

By minibus taxi There are frequent minibus taxis running the 54km from Rustenburg to Manyane Gate (ask for Mogwase).

INFORMATION

At the gates At both gates you'll find notice boards for wildlife sightings, useful for tracking down animals on your checklist, as well as the excellent official map and park guidebook explaining the various habitats, enabling you to plan your journey around what you most want to see. The Pilanesberg Centre, an old Cape Dutch building located in the centre of the park, contains a café, gift shop and open-air restaurant with a wonderful terrace overlooking a watering hole usually teeming with less timid wildlife.

Wildlife watching Areas known for popular animals can become congested during daytime; the traffic disappears after dark, when only tour buses on night-game drives are allowed in, making this one of the optimum times to visit the park (although be sure to bring some warm clothes on winter nights).

ACCOMMODATION

Pilanesberg's accommodation ranges from upmarket lodges where game drives are included in the price, to large, resort-style complexes on the fringes of the park, and cheaper, more basic camps outside the boundaries. Bookings for *Bakgatla* and *Manyane* must be made through Golden Leopard Resorts (☎ 014 555 1000, ⓦ goldenleopardresorts.co.za), and those for *Bakubung*, *Kwa Maritane* and *Tshukudu* through Legacy Hotels (☎ 011 806 6888, ⓦ legacyhotels.co.za); both offer ten percent reductions for online bookings. Camping (from R90 per person) is possible at Golden Leopard's resorts. *Bakubung* and *Kwa Maritane* have shuttle buses every other hour to and from Sun City, while all lodges can arrange game drives and guided walks if not included in the rates. Some may insist on two-night stays at weekends.

PILANESBERG TOUR OPERATORS

Rates for normal **safaris** depend on group size (larger groups are cheaper) and whether the tour is scheduled or private. On a scheduled tour, you may be sharing a minibus with up to fifteen other visitors; check also whether lunch and entry fees are included. The special activities organized by Gametrackers and Mankwe can usually be incorporated into trips run by other operators, particularly if you have the flexibility of a private tour. Prices for day-trips from Gauteng average R500–800 per person on a scheduled tour; private tours start at around R1000 for the day. Rates for overnight trips vary according to where you stay; budget on upwards of R3000. While all activities can be booked on arrival, it's best to reserve them in advance either directly or through your lodge to avoid missing out.

Gametrackers Outdoor Adventures Sun City ☎ 014 552 5020, ⓦ gametrac.co.za. Apart from the elephant-back safaris near Sun City (see p.518) you can join spectacular balloon flights over the park (R3500) and day and night game drives (from R395); pick-ups from some of the resorts and lodges around the park are possible.

Mankwe Safaris Manyane Gate ☎ 014 555 7056, ⓦ mankwesafaris.co.za. A concessionaire offering day and night game drives (from R350) plus "Heritage Tours", blending nearby cultural attractions with the Big Five.

Ulysses Tours & Safaris ☎ 012 653 0018, ⓦ ulysses.co.za. A well-regarded and professionally run upmarket outfit based in Pretoria; day-trips to Pilanesberg every Saturday or otherwise on demand, from R900.

Bakgatla Resort Near Bakgatla Gate at the foot of Garamoga Hills ☎ 014 555 1800, ⓦ goldenleopard resorts.com. A large collection of reasonable chalets, safari tents with attached bathrooms and shady verandas, plus a large campsite. There's a decent restaurant and a large pool, too. Camping R160, safari tent R1150, chalet R1550
Bakubung Bush Lodge On the southern edge of the park, just west of Sun City ☎ 011 806 6888, ⓦ legacy hotels.co.za. The highlight at this large, modern lodge is the hippo pool, a stone's throw from the restaurant from where you can see the hippos bathing. The hotel rooms and chalets are pleasant if bland. R3600
Ivory Tree Lodge Near Bakgatla Gate ☎ 011 806 6888, ⓦ legacyhotels.co.za. Luxurious lodge with stylish rooms (with en-suite toilets and showers outside), a health spa, conference centre and a rather hotel-like feel. R2125
Kwa Maritane Bush Lodge ☎ 011 806 6888, ⓦ legacy hotels.co.za. A beautiful, upmarket resort in the park's southeast corner near Pilanesberg Airport. Recently refurbished, it has decent rooms, a good restaurant and a pool with views over the reserve. R3600
Manyane Resort Just outside Manyane Gate ☎ 014 555 1800, ⓦ goldenleopardresorts.com. Low cost and convenience compensate for the distinctly un-bushlike atmosphere of the park's main camp. Stay in thatched chalets with a/c, safari tents or bring a tent or caravan; there's also a bar and restaurant, pool, mini-golf and walking trails. Camping R160, safari tent R684, chalet R990
Tshukudu Bush Lodge 8km from Bakubung Gate within the park ☎ 011 806 6888, ⓦ legacyhotels.co.za. Gaze out at big game at the water hole from your veranda at Pilanesberg's most upmarket and exclusive lodge, attractively located on a hilltop with sweeping views. The six picturesque thatched cottages offer luxury accommodation with sunken baths and roaring log fires; there's also a swimming pool. No children under 12. Rates include full board and game drives. R8700

The Central Region

Thanks to its scrawny and desolate dryness, North West Province's Central Region feels especially remote, and there are not all that many towns worth visiting. **Mmabatho**, once the capital of Bophuthatswana and now incorporated into neighbouring **Mafikeng**, the provincial capital, forces reluctant bureaucratic pilgrimages on people from all over the province. The region's appeal lies elsewhere, in the brooding plains and lush river valleys of **Marico** and the rarely visited game reserves, including **Madikwe** on the Botswana border. And then there are the people themselves: local Tswana and Afrikaners are both short on English but long on hospitality, at least to visitors, a trait best experienced at the village of **Groot Marico**, famed nationwide for its *mampoer* peach brandy and quintessentially laidback spirit.

Groot Marico

GROOT MARICO, a tiny, dusty and characterful *dorp* resting contentedly by the banks of the Marico River, just south of the N4 and 90km west of Rustenburg, gained fame through **Herman Charles Bosman**'s short stories based on his time as a teacher here. In mid-October, Groot Marico hosts the literary Bosman Weekend, drawing fans of one of South Africa's best-loved authors from far and wide. At other times, visit the **Herman Charles Bosman Living Museum** on Fakkel Street (daily 8am–6pm; R10) which includes a re-creation of the school where Bosman taught and provides insight into his life. Nearby, the **Art Factory** on Paul Kruger Street (daily 8am–6pm; free) sells Tswana cultural artefacts and locally made Afrikaner crafts such as wooden pipes, whips and clocks.

Although prone to stultifying heat, particularly in summer, the hills of the Marico district around the town are good for hiking, and when it all gets too much you can make for the river for cool relief. The water of the **Marico Oog** ("Marico Eye"), a spring 20km south of town, is particularly clear and refreshing: festooned with water lilies and surrounded by beautiful dolomitic rocks, it makes a tranquil place for a picnic, and can be paradise for birdwatchers, with over four hundred species recorded here. It's also a favoured spot for scuba divers; contact the town's information centre for more details.

8

8

MAMPOER

According to legend, a Pedi chief by the name of Mampuru introduced the art of distilling peach brandy to the Boers. Named **mampoer** in his honour, the fearsomely strong spirit has inspired locals and visitors alike ever since. Any fruit can be used to make *mampoer*, but peach is the most traditional: until 1878, much of North West Province's farmland grew peach trees solely devoted to this purpose. Things changed with the ZAR government's distilling tax, and the new licensing system introduced in 1894, when thousands of *mampoer* stills were destroyed. A few, however, escaped detection. A local story recounts that one farmer cleaned out his entire drainage system, but made no attempt to conceal his fifteen barrels of *mampoer*. The inspectors found the barrels, split them open and poured the entire contents down the drain. Meanwhile, the canny farmer had his family stationed in the field where the pipe ended up with every container the household possessed, and managed to recover fourteen of the fifteen barrels.

If you want to **sample** and buy *mampoer*, head for Maruthwane Farm, 12km west of Groot Marico on the N4 (open daily 9am–5pm), where you can also see demonstrations of how the stuff is made. In the old days the alcohol content was measured by throwing a chunk of lard into a sample: if it floated halfway, the *mampoer* was perfect. Nowadays, you just hold a match over it – the higher and cleaner the blue flame, the better the brew. Groot Marico's information office organizes *mampoer* tours (half day R150, full day R250; both including farm lunch).

ARRIVAL AND DEPARTURE   GROOT MARICO

By bus The Intercape bus from Johannesburg/Pretoria (daily 3hr/4hr) to Gaborone in Botswana (3hr) drops travellers off along the main road within walking distance of the town centre.

By minibus taxi Minibus taxis travelling along the N4 from Pretoria or Rustenburg to Zeerust or Botswana will stop at the Groot Marico turn-off, a twenty-minute walk north of the village.

INFORMATION

Tourist information Paul Kruger St, next to First National Bank (daily 8am–6pm; ☎ 014 503 0085 or ☎ 083 272 2958, ⓦ marico.co.za), in an enclosure built by Italian POWs in World War II. As well as providing a welter of information on the town and its activities, it also holds the keys to the nearby Bosman museum and Art Factory, and organizes half- and full- day tours which take in a *mampoer* distillery (see above), and can make accommodation bookings.

ACCOMMODATION

Angela's Guest House Between the village and the N4 highway ☎ 014 503 0082, ✉ angela_s@telkomsa.net. Near to town, *Angela's* has four comfortable en-suite rooms and a self-catering cottage set in a lovely garden and orchard, and can organize massage and beauty treatments as well as meals. **R520**

River Still Guest Farm 6km south of the village ☎ 083 2722 958, ⓦ riverstill.co.za. Four small self-catering cottages by the river in a secluded and heavily forested valley, just perfect for birders. Swimming in the river is possible, and there are also canoes for rent and drumming sessions on weekends. **R440**

EATING AND DRINKING

The local guesthouses are your best bet for **a meal**, while the *Groot Marico Bushveld Hotel* on Paul Kruger Street has the pick of the town's **bars**, where white locals, inspired by beer, brandy and their own good humour, have been known to dance traditional Afrikaans two-steps.

Madikwe Game Reserve

R50 · ☎ 018 350 9931, ⓦ madikwe-game-reserve.co.za

Tucked up in the very north of the province near the Botswana border lies the 765-square-kilometre **MADIKWE GAME RESERVE**, one of South Africa's largest wildlife areas. The reserve was established in 1991 from reclaimed farmland, and thanks to **Operation Phoenix**, which saw the reintroduction of over eight thousand animals, Madikwe's largely low-lying plains of woodland and grassland are now amply stocked with the Big Five, plus dozens of other mammals, including cheetah, wild dogs, spotted hyena and most of Southern Africa's plains antelopes. Twitchers won't be disappointed, with some 350 bird species recorded so far; the Marico River, on the eastern border, and the *koppies* scattered all around, are particularly rewarding birding areas.

Long promoted as South Africa's "bijou reserve", the low tourist density so liberally vaunted in the brochures no longer quite rings true given that around **twenty lodges** vie for your trade, although Madikwe does remain one of the least known of South Africa's large wildlife areas. Access is reserved to guests of its lodges and **day visitors**, who must book a package through one of the lodges that includes a **game drive** and lunch; independent day visits are not allowed.

ARRIVAL AND DEPARTURE
MADIKWE GAME RESERVE

By car Road access to Madikwe is normally through Tau Gate, 12km off the R49, although, depending on where you're staying, the reserve can also be approached from the east via Molatedi Gate. Whichever approach you take, you'll need to inform your lodge prior to arrival.

By plane It's possible to fly to the small airport inside the reserve on the two to three daily flights from Johannesburg which take 45 minutes (around R2150); book through the lodges or directly with Madikwe Air (☎011 805 4888, ⓦ madikwecharter.com) or Federal Air (☎011 395 9000, ⓦ fedair.com), who can also arrange private charters. The lodges take care of transport to and from the airport.

ACCOMMODATION

Accommodation rates at all lodges include full board, day and night game drives, and guided bush walks. There is no budget accommodation or camping.

Jaci's Safari Lodge & Tree Lodges ☎083 700 2071, ⓦ madikwe.com. Two exceptional lodges whose sense of style, comfort and laidback luxury are hard to beat. The *Safari Lodge* overlooks a natural water hole on the Marico River and has a natural rock swimming pool nearby, while the *Tree Lodges'* rooms are built around trees several metres off the ground. Children welcome. **R5990**

Madikwe Hills ☎018 365 9904; reservations ☎013 737 6626, ⓦ madikwehills.com. Another gem, this one built around a *koppie* close to the riverbank. Rooms are modern and have views over the veld. There are even better views from the sundowner terrace and its small swimming pool, plus there's a gym, spa, childcare facilities and the food is excellent. **R8500**

Mateya Safari Lodge ☎014 778 9200, ⓦ mateyasafari .com. Experience the ultimate in bush chic at these five luxurious suites, each boasting its own swimming pool, as well as both indoor and outdoor showers. There's a spa and the lodge's excellent food is best sampled on the terrace overlooking the veld. No children under 16. **R11000**

★ **Mosetlha Bush Camp Eco Lodge** ☎011 444 9345, ⓦ thebushcamp.com. Slightly cheaper than Madikwe's other accommodation and offering the most intense wilderness experience. Located in the reserve's centre, there's no perimeter fence here and accommodation is in very simple open-sided log cabins, with no electricity, and hot outdoor showers delivered by an ingenious donkey boiler and bucket system. What it lacks in luxury it makes up for in atmosphere and expertise, with the emphasis placed on game walks as much as drives. **R3390**

Mafikeng

Mafikeng, 25km south of the Ramatlabama border post with Botswana, offers a unique portrait of the vision of apartheid and its deep contradictions. Acting as a shopping and transport hub for the wide area of farmland that surrounds it, it is most famous for Baden-Powell and the Boer siege of 1899–1900 (see box, p.527).

Mafikeng Museum
Martin St • Mon–Fri 8am–4pm, Sat 10am–1pm • Donation • ☎018 381 6102

The town's main attraction is the **Mafikeng Museum**, housed in the impressive former town hall, which was built in 1902, two years after the siege (see p.527) ended. There's a restored steam locomotive outside, in use from 1901 until 1971 when it pulled the Kimberley–Bulawayo Express. Inside, you'll find San hunting weapons and poisons, and a life-size re-creation of a traditional Tswana hut, complete with its trademark enclosed porch. The siege of Mafikeng is given a room of its own, filled with classic British imperial memorabilia, from weaponry to a wonderful collection of photos.

8

Keep an eye out too for the fascinating exhibit on Mafikeng and the railways, which provides evidence of the connection between their spread from Cape Town and Rhodes' mission to colonize Africa.

Mafikeng Game Reserve

On the eastern edge of town • Daily: May–Aug 7.30am–6pm, Sept–April 7.30am–7pm • R25, plus R5 per car • ☎ 018 381 5611, ⓦ tourismnorthwest.co.za/mafikeng_reserve • Two entrances: one 10km east of Mafikeng along the R49 towards Zeerust, the other just 3km from the town centre – go down Shippard St and turn right after the railway bridge (2km) onto Jacaranda St and Aslaagte Gate is straight ahead

The 46-square-kilometre **Mafikeng Game Reserve** is worth a quick drive around for its acacia-strewn bushveld landscape and herbivorous plains game, including white rhino and buffalo. Cooke's Lake, in the reserve's western corner next to town, is reasonably good for waterfowl and mongooses (and the snakes they prey on).

ARRIVAL AND DEPARTURE   MAFIKENG

By bus and minibus taxi None of the major intercity bus companies serves Mafikeng, but Atamelang (☎ 018 381 2680) has a daily service to Johannesburg (3hr), while Bojanala Bus (☎ 014 565 8540) crawls once a day to Rustenburg (3hr). There are minibus taxis to most destinations within the province, as well as two to three daily to Kimberley (5hr). The hassle-free bus and minibus taxi terminal can be found between Victoria and Hatchard sts on the northern side of town.

INFORMATION

Tourist information In the Mafikeng Museum (Mon–Fri 8am–4pm; ☎ 018 381 0067); it seldom has city maps or other useful information.
North West Parks & Tourism Board Headquarters Heritage House, next to Cooke's Lake, 1km south of the centre (Mon–Fri 7.30am–4.30pm; ☎ 018 397 1500, ⓦ www.tourismnorthwest.co.za); for questions about the province's parks and nature reserves.

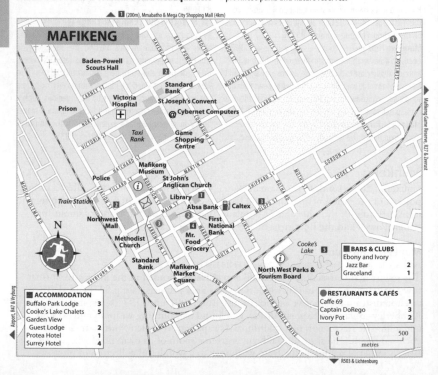

MAFIKENG

THE SIEGE OF MAFIKENG

Mafikeng was **besieged** within three days of the start of the **second Anglo-Boer War** (1899–1902) by generals Snyman and Cronje. **Colonel Robert Baden-Powell** (founder of the Boy Scouts) had the task of defending the town. This he did for 217 days, from October 16, 1899, until May 17, 1900, when relief arrived from Rhodesia and from the south. In the process, Baden-Powell became a British household name and hero, and the exuberant scenes of jubilation in London that greeted news of the relief gave rise to a new word in the English language: **maffick**, which meant to celebrate unduly.

Strategically, Mafikeng was irrelevant to the war; Baden-Powell's real achievement was to distract the six thousand Afrikaners besieging the town from fighting elsewhere. He relied heavily on the **Barolong** people for defence, labour and reconnaissance, but failed to record this either in his dispatches to London or in his memoirs, despite the fact that four hundred Barolong lost their lives during the siege – twice as many as British. Some of the British casualties of the siege are marked by white iron crosses in the town's **cemetery** on Carrington Street, next to the railway sidings. Until the 1980s this was a whites-only cemetery, and today it still commemorates only the Europeans who died during the siege. The Barolong also received far fewer rations, and over one thousand subsequently died of starvation; they received none of the £29,000 raised in Britain for the rehabilitation of Mafikeng. To add insult to injury, not one Barolong was decorated for bravery, in contrast to the plentiful medals dished out to the British regiments, and none of the promises Baden-Powell made about land grants to them was ever kept. An important legacy of the involvement of the black population was the diary of the siege kept by **Sol Plaatje**, one of the first black writers to make an impact on English literature, who was later to become a founder member of the South African Native Congress, forerunner to the ANC.

8

ACCOMMODATION

Buffalo Park Lodge 59 Molopo St, at the corner of Botha Rd ☎018 381 2159, ⓦbuffalolodge.co.za. A family-run place with small, cool and well-kept twin bedrooms with TVs, a good pub-restaurant and a small swimming pool. R560

Cooke's Lake Chalets Cooke's Lake, access on Nelson Mandela Drive ☎018 381 6020. Near the city centre and overlooking the pretty lake with plenty of birdlife, these beautiful two-storey wood-and-thatch chalets are the most attractive places to stay in Mafikeng. R750

Protea Hotel 80 Nelson Mandela Drive ☎018 381 0400, ⓦproteahotels.com. Just north of the centre, Mafikeng's newest and best hotel has comfortable rooms, a good restaurant and cheerful staff. R1150

EATING AND DRINKING

Mafikeng is no culinary paradise, with good food limited to the hotels and fast-food joints scattered across town. Walking around at night is not recommended and, as Mafikeng still lacks a telephone taxi service, unless you have wheels or can find a local to accompany you, nightlife is limited to within a block or two of your hotel.

Caffe 69 Corner of Tillard and Gemsbok sts ☎018 381 0700, ⓦcaffe69.co.za. This relaxed restaurant and bar is the town's main upmarket eating place, with reliably good South African and international dishes, and several beers on tap. Daily noon–11pm.

Ebony and Ivory Jazz Bar Corner of Martin and Station sts. One of the better local bars, with a plush modern interior, an unintimidating atmosphere and nicely mellow jazz and fusion music. Live bands once a month. Daily 10am–10pm.

Ivory Pot 11 Shippard St ☎082 577 8267. Cheap and authentic African meals consisting of meat with *ting* (sour sorghum porridge), *samp* (corn kernels), *pap* or rice, served in a cheerful orange room. Daily noon–9pm.

DIRECTORY

Bank Money exchange at First National Bank, Robinson St.
Hospitals Best is the private Victoria Hospital, Victoria St ☎018 381 2043. The state hospital is Mafikeng Provincial Hospital, south of the centre in Danville ☎018 383 2005.
Internet access Cybernet Computers, Nelson Mandela

Drive, opposite Game Shopping Centre.
Pharmacies and doctors There are several at Game Shopping Centre and Mega City Shopping Mall in Mmabatho.
Police Corner of Tillard and Carrington sts ☎018 387 7500.
Post The post office is on Carrington St.

Mpumalanga

LEOPARD, SABI SANDS RESERVE (P.563)

9

Mpumalanga

Mpumalanga, "the land of the rising sun" to its Siswati- and Zulu-speaking residents, extends east from Gauteng to Mozambique and Swaziland. To many visitors the province is synonymous with the Kruger National Park, the real draw of South Africa's east flank, and one of Africa's best game parks. Kruger occupies most of Mpumalanga's and Limpopo Province's borders with Mozambique, and covers over 20,000 square kilometres – an area the size of Israel or El Salvador. Unashamedly populist, Kruger is the easiest African game park to drive around on your own, with many well-run restcamps for accommodation. On its western border lie a number of private reserves, offering the chance – at a price – to escape the Kruger crush, with well-informed rangers conducting safaris in open vehicles.

Apart from the irresistible magnet of big-game country, Mpumalanga also has some spectacular scenery in the mountainous area known as the **Escarpment**, usually passed through en route to Kruger. The most famous viewpoints – **God's Window**, **Bourke's Luck Potholes** and **Three Rondavels** – are along the lip of the Escarpment, which can be seen on a 156km drive from the lowveld known as the **Panorama Route**. The views of **Blyde River Canyon** are most famous of all and, while you can't drive into the canyon, there are some fabulous hiking and river-rafting opportunities in this area. None of the Escarpment towns merits exploration, but they are fine as night stops.

Jammed between the mountains and Kruger are the former African **Bantustans**, created under apartheid: Lebowa for Sotho-speakers and Gazankulu for Shangaan- and Tsonga-speaking people. Mozambique is a short hop away, there is daily transport to Maputo, and you'll see cars with Mozambique number plates, especially in Nelspruit, the modern capital of Mpumalanga, taking advantage of the superior medical care and shopping. Nelspruit also connects with the road south through **Barberton** to Swaziland.

Descending the Escarpment on one of four mountain passes takes you into the tropical-fruit-growing and bushveld country of the **lowveld**, with impressive views back towards the towering massif of the Escarpment. A number of places close to the **Blydepoort Dam** at the foot of the Blyde River Canyon can be taken in as bushveld breaks on the way to or from Kruger. Closest to this area is the small but growing centre of **Hoedspruit** (actually in Limpopo Province, but covered here because of its proximity to Kruger) with its own airport, a jumping-off point for safaris in the central and northern section of the park, and yielding access to the Manyeleti and Timbabavati

TRADITIONAL FEAST, SHANGANA CULTURAL VILLAGE, P.548

Highlights

❶ Aerial Cable Trail Glide in a harness through the air, over tree tops and the river, on a 1.2km trail near Hazyview. **See p.547**

❷ African meals at the Shangana Cultural Village Here you can sample crocodile and unusual vegetables, cooked over open fires, and watch stirring traditional dances. **See p.548**

❸ Brushing an elephant Enjoy a close encounter grooming an elephant or holding its trunk as you walk together, at the Hazyview Elephant Sanctuary. **See p.547**

❹ Bush breakfasts There's no more satisfying way to round off a couple of hours of game viewing than with a cooked breakfast in the wilds of Kruger. **See box, p.552**

❺ Walking safaris in Kruger It's worth leaving behind the security of a vehicle for the thrill of potential close encounters with animals. **See p.557**

❻ Leopard-spotting The luxury camps in the Sabi Sands Game Reserve offer excellent opportunities to observe leopards. **See p.563**

HIGHLIGHTS ARE MARKED ON THE MAP ON P.532

9

private game reserves. Note that **malaria** (see p.71) is a potential hazard in the lowveld and Kruger, particularly in summer.

The Escarpment

Four hours' drive east of Johannesburg International Airport is one of the city's favoured mountain retreats: the waving grasslands and luxury guesthouses of the Mpumalanga Drakensberg, generally known as the **Escarpment**. While most travellers visit the region purely because of its proximity to the Kruger National Park, it provides

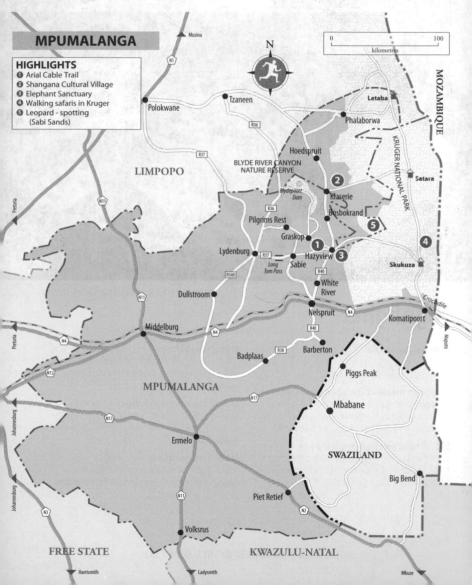

MPUMALANGA

HIGHLIGHTS
1. Arial Cable Trail
2. Shangana Cultural Village
3. Elephant Sanctuary
4. Walking safaris in Kruger
5. Leopard - spotting (Sabi Sands)

some of the most dramatic views in the country, which can be enjoyed with little effort, even if you are simply passing through en route to Kruger. This tour of these highlands, known as the **Panorama Route**, can also be taken as an organized day-trip by numerous tour operators in Nelspruit. The main draw of the Escarpment is the **Blyde River Canyon**, whose dizzying views into one of the world's great gorges appear in countless South African tourist brochures. In addition to a number of viewpoints along the Escarpment lip, the canyon has hiking trails which give access to the flora and (if you're quiet and lucky) fauna of the reserve, including zebra, hippo, kudu and numerous primates – baboons, vervet and samango monkeys and bushbabies.

Dullstroom

Some 209km east of Johannesburg, the R540 branches off the N4 at nondescript **Belfast** and heads into the hills, where the highveld countryside is covered by grasslands, waving tall and green in summer, but turning russet in winter. Unless your passion is fly-fishing, chances are you'll find the crossroads settlement of **DULLSTROOM**, 35km north of Belfast, as unexciting as its name suggests, though it can be a useful place to stop over for a night on your way to Kruger National Park, especially if you're leaving Johannesburg late.

Birds of Prey Rehabilitation Centre

1km outside Dullstroom on the R540 • Daily 9am–4pm • R40 • Demonstrations daily 10.30am & 2.30pm • ☎ 072 378 8562, ⓦ birdsofprey.co.za

The **Birds of Prey Rehabilitation Centre** makes a worthwhile visit and is exclusively devoted to the housing, nourishment and rehabilitation of raptors, with very good flying demonstrations daily. The centre is run by two extremely knowledgeable and witty Englishmen, both called Mark and passionate about the birds they care for.

ARRIVAL AND INFORMATION   DULLSTROOM

By bus Dullstroom is 260km from Johannesburg's OR Tambo airport (2hr 30min–3hr). It is served four times a week on the City to City bus (☎ 015 781 1037), which leaves from Johannesburg Station.

Tourist information Auldstone House, on the main road, Naledi Drive (Mon–Fri 9am–5pm, Sat 9am–4.30pm, Sun 9am–2pm; ☎ 013 254 0254, ⓦ dullstroom.biz).

ACCOMMODATION

Critchley Hackle Lodge Teding van Berkhout St ☎ 013 254 0149, ⓦ critchleyhackle.co.za. A gracious, country-style hotel, offering stone and brick cottages, each with a fireplace, and a veranda with outdoor seating. Facilities include a restaurant, a bar for after-dinner cognac, and there's also a patio for tea and scones. **R2190**

Dullstroom Inn Teding van Berkhout St ☎ 013 254 0071, ⓦ dullstroominn.com. A Victorian country inn, with very reasonably priced floral rooms, though no views.

Its pub gets packed at weekends; if you want a room away from the action, ask for the annexe. **R780**

Old Transvaal Inn 117 Hugenote St ☎ 013 254 0222. A modest and friendly B&B with a fine location and a certain quaintness of style. It is the cheapest stop-over in town; rooms include your own bath and shower, but you'll be cold on winter nights. There's also a pub that serves meals. **R350**

EATING

Dullstroom Inn Signposted just off Teding van Berkhout St ☎ 013 254 0071. Hearty pub food with chalked-up dishes of the day, including vegetarian fare such as a ploughman's lunch and lots of trout (R80). The fireplace and darkish interior make it a great winter or evening choice. Daily 7am–9pm.

Mrs Simpson's 94 Teding van Berkhout St ☎ 013 254 0088. An always busy restaurant for fine dining. Their Dullstroom trout with garlic and almonds (R100), followed by malva pudding, is particularly recommended. Booking

ahead essential. Thurs–Sun 11.30am–3pm.

Pickles & Things 86 Naledi Drive ☎ 013 254 0115. Best place in town for coffee, and fair trade at that, and one of the best-known restaurants, this is a popular, busy place with big breakfasts (R80), home-made bread, and an inviting garden. The deli at the front of the restaurant stocks smoked trout and other delicacies like nougat. Book ahead for dinner. Mon, Wed, Thurs & Sun 7am–5pm, Tues 7am–3pm, Fri & Sat 7am–9pm.

9

Lydenburg

Some 58km north of Dullstroom, humdrum **LYDENBURG** is the site of one of South Africa's major archeological finds; subsequently, the main reason to come here is to visit the museum.

Lydenburg Museum

In the Gustav Klingbiel Nature Reserve, 3km out of town along the R37 to Sabie • Mon–Fri 9am–noon & 2–4.15pm, Sat & Sun 10am–4pm • Free • ☎ 013 235 2213

Replicas of the archeological finds made in Lydenburg are on display here, including the **Lydenburg Heads**, seven beautiful ceramic masks (probably ceremonial) dating back to the fifth century, which are some of the first figurative sculptures in Southern Africa. As well as replicas of these heads (the originals are in the South African Museum in Cape Town), there are excellent displays on human activity in the vicinity over the past million years or so.

Sabie and around

Lying on the R37 beyond Long Tom Pass, **SABIE** (pronounced "Saabie", like the car) is the centre of Mpumalanga's agroforestry industry. It holds the dubious distinction of lying at the heart of South Africa's largest artificial forest, with 450 square kilometres under active cultivation. The extensive pine plantations look monotonous compared to the rich, jungly variety of the remaining pockets of indigenous woodland.

Before the foresters arrived, Sabie made its name as a **gold** centre, with a lucky strike in 1895 at the Klein Sabie Falls. Mining stopped halfway through the twentieth century, and today the gold prospectors have been replaced by escapees from hectic Johannesburg, who make a living here running restaurants, B&Bs and craft shops.

Sabie's slow pace and mildly arty ambience make it a congenial base for exploring the Escarpment. If you don't have your own transport, you can still take advantage of its well-organized backpacker lodge and a raft of adventure activities. Numerous **waterfalls** drop down the slopes outside Sabie. Just 7km from town, down the Old Lydenburg Road, you can visit three of the most impressive: **Bridal Veil**, **Horseshoe** and, appropriately at the end of the road, **Lone Creek Falls**. The loveliest of the three, Lone Creek is reached down a paved path that crosses a river and works its way back to the car park.

Mac Mac Falls

Falls 13km north of the town along the Graskop Rd • R10 • Pools 11km north of town • R10

The most visited of the falls around Sabie are the spectacular 65m **Mac Mac Falls**, named after the many people of Scottish descent who died looking for gold in the area and whose names appear on dozens of tombstones in the vicinity. While you can't swim in the inviting waterfall pool at the base of the falls, there is a river pool at the Mac Mac Pools, 2km before you reach the falls themselves, where there's also a picnic and braai area, and the 3km **Secretary Bird walking trail**.

ARRIVAL AND INFORMATION   SABIE AND AROUND

Sabie is 60km from Nelspruit on a windy road, often slowed down by logging trucks.

By bus Public transport to Sabie is limited to minibus taxis plying the routes from neighbouring towns; otherwise *Sabie Backpackers* runs a reasonably priced shuttle between Nelspruit and Sabie, on request, which takes an hour.

Tourist information There are two information offices in the village, the best of which is on Market Square (Mon–Fri 8am–5pm, Sat 9am–1pm; ☎ 013 767 1833, ⓦ lcbt.co.za).

ACCOMMODATION

Sabie offers a good supply of reasonably priced accommodation, though prices can rise dramatically during South African school holidays.

ADVENTURE ACTIVITIES IN SABIE

With its forest, massive gorge and mountains, the Escarpment offers good opportunities for adventure activities. Among the operators running a range of these is Sabie Xtreme Adventures, based at *Sabie Backpackers Lodge* (see below). The activities on offer include **caving by candlelight** in the Lone Creek Caves, **waterfall abseiling** at the Sabie Falls, whitewater tubing and canyoning.

For **river rafting** in the Blyde River Canyon, one of the largest in the world, Induna Adventures is recommended (☎013 737 8308/1, ⓦindunaadventures.com). Its half-day trip runs either in the morning or afternoon and takes three hours. The company is based in Hazyview, an hour's drive from the Canyon. You can be collected from accommodation in Hazyview, or meet at the *Swadini Forever Resort* at the Canyon itself.

Hillwatering Country House 50 Marula St ☎013 764 1421, ⓦhillwatering.co.za. Renovated 1950s home with four large bedrooms, each with its own veranda, overlooking the Bridal Veil Falls. The reception is warm and breakfast excellent. R800

Merry Pebbles Holiday Resort 2km west from the centre on the Old Lydenburg Rd ☎013 764 2266, ⓦmerrypebbles.co.za. Go for the newer units at this resort, which offers camping as well as self-catering and en-suite chalets. The facilities include a lovely, big heated pool and children's playground. No quad bikes or motorbikes are allowed. Camping R100, chalet R730

Misty Mountain Lodge 24km southwest of Sabie on Long Tom Pass ☎013 764 3377, ⓦmistymountain .co.za. Pleasant B&B units, some with splendid views across pine plantations into the valleys. There's trout fishing on the property, with rods and flies for rent at a nominal

rate; the lodge is also well placed for walks into indigenous forest. You can self-cater or take advantage of the restaurant and pub on the premises. R1070

Sabie Backpackers Lodge 185 Main Rd ☎013 764 2118, ⓦsabiextreme.co.za. A well-run, fun hostel, with camping, dorms and doubles, featuring sturdy beds and warm bedding. There's also accommodation for two in a tree house. Xtreme Adventures, based here, organizes a host of adventure activities (see box above), and the lodge has good weekend packages available, with wall-to-wall adventure activities. Camping R70, dorm R110, double R260

Villa Ticino On the corner of Louis Trichardt and Second sts ☎013 764 2598, ⓦvillaticino.co.za. Hospitable, and often full, Swiss-owned B&B with a terrace looking onto the hills, and a lounge with a pool table. Winter discounts are available, and prices are a bit less if you stay for two nights. R880

EATING AND DRINKING

The Wild Fig Tree On the corner of Main and Louis Trichardt sts. South African dishes and venison (R90) are the speciality at this fairly upmarket restaurant, the best in town, with a wide deck to make the most of the weather. Daily 8am–10pm. R90.

Woodsman Restaurant On the corner of Main and

Mac Mac rds. A licensed restaurant with a beer garden, serving Cypriot Greek food, including vegetarian *meze*, plus local specialities such as ostrich and trout, and slow-cooked lamb (R90). Also good for coffee and snacks on the terrace, or at the cosy fire. Daily 8am–10pm.

Pilgrim's Rest

Hiding in a valley 35km north of Sabie, **PILGRIM'S REST**, an almost too-perfectly restored gold-mining town, is an irresistible port of call for tour buses. With a collection of red-roofed, corrugated-iron buildings, including the characterful *Royal Hotel* brimming with Victoriana, the place is undeniably photogenic. But you can't help feeling there's little substance behind the romanticized gold-rush image, especially when the village nods off after 5pm once the day-trippers have been spirited away. If you do want to visit a real gold mine, you're best off heading to Barberton (see p.544).

Pilgrim's Rest stretches along its one main road and is divided into Uptown and Downtown. Commercialized **Uptown** has the greatest concentration of shops and restaurants and draws the bulk of tourists; **downtown**, just 1km to the west, has a more down-to-earth atmosphere. Apart from souvenir hunting and lingering in the cafés and tea shops, the main activity in Pilgrim's Rest is visiting its handful of **museums**, and the place to absorb the history best is at the old cemetery, where the losses tell their own story.

9

Brief history

Pilgrim's Rest owes its origins to South Africa's first **gold rush**, which predates the uncovering of the great Gauteng seams. In 1873, Alex "Wheelbarrow" Patterson discovered gold here, though his attempts to keep his discovery secret were a total failure, and by the end of the year Patterson had been joined by 1500 diggers frantically working four thousand claims. Far from the pristine little village of today, the **Pilgrim's Rest diggings** were the site of gruelling labour and unhygienic conditions. Many diggers arrived malnourished, suffering from dysentery and malaria after punishing journeys. Those who survived could expect drab lives in tents or, if they struck lucky, more permanent wattle-and-daub huts. In 1896, the diggings were bought up by the Transvaal Gold Mining Estates (TGME), which closed its Beta Mine in 1972, handing Pilgrim's Rest over to the provincial administration. The settlement was declared a historic monument in the 1980s, but mining continues behind the hill to the southwest of town, with functional buildings, cyanide-filled slime dams and great red scars hacked into the hillside, the forest having been bulldozed out of existence.

Diggings Site Museum

Graskop Rd • Guided tours only, daily at 10am, 11am, noon, 2pm & 3pm • R15, buy tickets from the tourist office • **Tourist office** Main St; Uptown; daily 9am–12.45pm, 1.45–4pm; ☎ 013 768 1060, ⓦ pilgrims-rest.co.za

To get a really authentic impression of the gold-mining days, head for the open-air **Diggings Site Museum** on the eastern edge of town, where you can see demonstrations of alluvial gold-panning and get a guided tour around the bleak diggers' huts and the remnants of workings and machinery from the early mining days.

Alanglade House Museum

Main St • Guided tours only, daily 11am & 2pm • R20, buy tickets from the tourist office • **Tourist office** Main St, Uptown; daily 9am–12.45pm, 1.45–4pm; ☎ 013 768 1060, ⓦ pilgrims-rest.co.za

If you want to see how mine owners and managers lived, visit **Alanglade**, the reconstructed home of the former general manager of the mine, just west of the Downtown area. The house has a wonderful collection of early twentieth-century British fashion and decorative arts and reveals a sheltered way of life far removed from either Africa or mining.

ARRIVAL AND INFORMATION   PILGRIM'S REST

By car Pilgrim's Rest is easily accessed by car on the exceptionally winding R532, 41km from Sabie, or on the R535 from Graskop, 17km away.

By minibus taxis There are no scheduled buses; minibus taxis can be found at both Sabie and Graskop.

Tourist information Signposted on the main road, Uptown, close to the *Royal Hotel* (daily 9am–12.45pm, 1.45–4pm; ☎ 013 768 1060, ⓦ pilgrims-rest.co.za); tickets for local museums can be bought here.

ACCOMMODATION

Though Pilgrim's Rest is by far the prettiest of the Escarpment towns, it is primarily set up for day-trippers, thus there's scant accommodation in the town itself.

Crystal Springs Mountain Lodge 10km out of town on the R533 to Lydenburg ☎ 013 768 5000, ⓦ grc-resorts.co.za. A large time-share resort with high-quality cottages available for hire. Each thatched cottage has a deck and Escarpment views, and there's a restaurant and bar on site, plus trampolines, a heated pool, playground, a games room and, for adults, a jacuzzi, sauna and steambath. From the cottages there are well-marked walking trails into a ravine. R1300

★ **District Six Miners' Cottages** Main Rd, Downtown ☎ 013 768 1211 or ☎ 083 271 8262. Self-catering

accommodation, run by the Public Works Department, in authentic two-bedroom 1920s workers' houses, sleeping two to four, with verandas overlooking the town and mountains. You'll need to book ahead during office hours (Mon–Fri 8.30am–4pm), as there's no on-site office. Use the mobile for after-hours reservations. R300

Royal Hotel Main St, Uptown ☎ 013 768 1100, ⓦ royal-hotel.co.za. Atmospheric hotel that dates back to the gold-rush days and brims with luxurious Victoriana, with guests mostly accommodated in restored houses on the main road. A visit to the pub is essential. R950

EATING AND DRINKING

Pilgrim's Rest has a few restaurants and teashops to provide for the daily influx of visitors, all situated along the main road, and all open during the day only, apart from the hotel. Catering for the tourist trade, food is nothing to write home about.

Royal Hotel Uptown. Probably the nicest place in town, where you can take in the historical atmosphere while having a steak and salad or an English breakfast; a visit to the colonial-styled pub is mandatory. Daily 8am–9pm.

Scott's Cafe Uptown, near the *Royal Hotel*. A good, reasonably priced option for lunch serving savoury and sweet pancakes, sandwiches, salads and other light meals. There's a pleasant bar, and curios for sale. Daily 9am–5pm.

Graskop

Some 17km east of Pilgrim's Rest, **GRASKOP** owes its place on the tourist map to *Harrie's Pancake Shop*, which serves much-imitated but rarely rivalled crêpes, and attracts all the tour buses doing the Escarpment viewpoints. The town itself is very ordinary, with timber trucks rumbling heavily through, but its location close to the **Blyde River Canyon** goes some way towards compensating. The growing number of artists here, together with a small gay community, are helping to shift Graskop's lumberjack image. One notable village industry is the **wild African silk** factory and showroom, a couple of doors down from the tourist office in Louis Trichardt Street, which sells a range of products manufactured from the silk of mopane silkworms (indigenous to Botswana).

Big Swing

☎ 013 737 8191 • R320

For adrenaline junkies, Graskop's **Big Swing** is the best of all the big swings on the Escarpment – a 68m free fall done in under three seconds, on one of the world's highest cable gorge swings. After the drop, you "fly free" across the gorge on a 135m highwire "*foefie* slide", 130m above ground, to glimpse the Graskop Falls. It's also possible to swing tandem. Book in advance – they will either pick you up or direct you to the gorge.

INFORMATION | GRASKOP

Tourist information In Spar Supermarket, on the corner of Kerk and Richardson sts (☎ 013 767 1886, ⊛ graskop. co.za).

ACCOMMODATION

★ **Graskop Hotel** On the corner of High and Louis Trichardt sts ☎ 013 767 1244, ⊛ graskophotel.co.za. One of the nicest places to stay on the Escarpment, with a personal and relaxed atmosphere. Though unprepossessing from the outside, it actually has a very stylish interior of retro furniture, African baskets, fabrics and sculptures. The rooms, some of which are in garden wings, are airy and decorated with considerable flair. R760

Graskop Log Cabin Village Oorwinning St ☎ 013 767 1974, ⊛ logcabin.co.za. A self-catering resort right in the centre of town, with a swimming pool, but no views from the log cabins. Cheaper during the week and for longer stays. There are also some pretty corrugated iron "settlers' huts" (⊛ settlersvillage.co.za) with verandas, decorated to look like the photogenic cottages in Pilgrim's Rest. R550

Westlodge B&B 12 Hugenoten St ☎ 013 767 1390/ 1869, ⊛ westlodge.co.za. Bright, spacious rooms and a warm welcome, with a lounge and balcony for guests' exclusive use. The owners will direct you to all the sights. R1250

EATING

Canimambo On the corner of Hoof and Louis Trichardt sts ☎ 013 767 1868. For excellent Portuguese and Mozambican cuisine, with an informal and cheerful atmosphere and a fire in the winter. There is spicy bean stew for vegetarians, while a carnivorous speciality is rump steak done with butter, garlic and whiskey. Daily 9am–9pm.

Harrie's Pancake House Louis Trichardt St. The legendary and well-signposted *Harrie's* serves the best sweet and savoury pancakes in town, and has a nice outdoor terrace, as well as an inside dining room with a roaring log fire in winter. Daily 8.30am–5pm.

9

The Silver Spoon Corner of Louis Trichardt/Kerk sts. *The Silver Spoon* works hard to compete with *Harrie's* for pancakes and waffles, and also offers egg breakfasts, hamburgers, salads and toasted sandwiches. Daily 8am–5pm.

Blyde River Canyon

There are few places in South Africa where you can enjoy such easily accessible and dramatic scenery as that of the colossal **Blyde River Canyon**, weathered out of strata of red rock and dropping sharply away from the Escarpment into the lowveld. The **Blyde River Canyon Nature Reserve** (also known as Blyderivierspoort Nature Reserve) stretches from a narrow tail near Graskop in the south, and broadens into a great amphitheatre partially flooded by the **Blydepoort Dam** about 60km to the north.

The drive along the canyon lip

Viewpoints R25

The views of the canyon are wonderful from both above and below, but the nicest way to take in the vistas is on an easy half-day's drive along the canyon lip. Some 3km north of Graskop, the R534 does a 15km loop past a series of superb **viewpoints**. The road winds through pine plantations until it comes to the turn-off to the **Pinnacle**, a gigantic quartzite column topped with trees, rising out of a ferny gorge. After another 4km the road reaches the sheer drop and lowveld views of **God's Window**, one of the most famous of the viewpoints; it's also one of the most developed, with toilets and curio stalls. The looping road returns to rejoin the R532, which continues north for 28km beyond the turn-off to reach **Bourke's Luck Potholes** at the confluence of the Treur and Blyde rivers – a collection of strange, smoothly scooped formations carved into the rocks by water-driven pebbles. The best view of all lies 14km beyond, at the **Three Rondavels**. The name describes only one small feature of this cinemascope vista: three cylinders in the shape of huts with the meandering Blyde River twisting its way hundreds of metres below. No photograph does justice to the sheer enormity of the view, punctuated by one series of cliffs after another buttressing into the valley.

Three Rondavels to Blydepoort Dam

The 90km **drive** from the Three Rondavels viewpoint to the base of the canyon provides spectacular views of the Escarpment cliffs rising out of the lowveld and is easily incorporated into your itinerary if you're heading to or from Kruger. The drive winds west to join with the R36 and heads north to begin its descent through the Abel Erasmus Pass and then the J.G. Strijdom Tunnel through the mountain, with the wide lowveld plains opening out on the other side. The road takes a wide arching trajectory to circumnavigate the canyon.

Blyde River Canyon Adventure Centre

Daily 8am–5pm • Small entry fee • **Boat Trips** daily at 9am, 11am & 3pm • R100 • ☎ 015 795 5961

To reach the **Blydepoort Dam**, take the R527 once the road splits when you're out of the tunnel, and follow the signposts to a dead end where you'll find the **Blyde River Canyon Adventure Centre** which has interesting displays on local ecology and a useful model of the canyon that helps you get orientated. Most people come here to take a recommended **boat trip** on the dam, which provides great views of the spectacular mountain ravines above and of the formations created by calcium deposits from natural springs. You may catch sight of hippos or crocs in the dam.

ACCOMMODATION	BLYDE RIVER CANYON

BLYDE RIVER CANYON NATURE RESERVE

Forever Blydepoort 5km north of the turn-off to the Three Rondavels lookout ☎ 086 122 6966, ⓦ foreversa .co.za. The only place to stay in the nature reserve is *Forever* *Blydepoort*. The resort has comfortable, self-contained and fully equipped cottages, a swimming pool, supermarket, bottle store and filling station; the atmosphere can feel a little institutionalized, but it's a good place for children. **R950**

9

BLYDEPOORT DAM

Apart from near the dam itself, there is some excellent accommodation in the area between the base of the mountains and Hoedspruit, covered in the lowveld section (see p.549).

Forever Swadini Signposted off the R531 ☎015 795 5141, ⓦ foreversa.co.za/swadini. If you want to stay close to the dam, the best place is *Forever Swadini*, which

has chalets for up to six, for which you pay a flat rate, however many of you there are, and a campsite with stunning scenic surrounds; it's great for kids, and cheap for a group, but has a similar institutional feel to its sister resort on the mountain (see opposite). A number of short trails start from here if you want to explore the environs. Camping R105, chalet R800

The lowveld

South Africa's **lowveld**, wedged between the Mpumalanga section of the Drakensberg and Mozambique, is part of a vast subtropical region of savanna that stretches north through Zimbabwe and Zambia as far as Central Africa. Closely associated at the

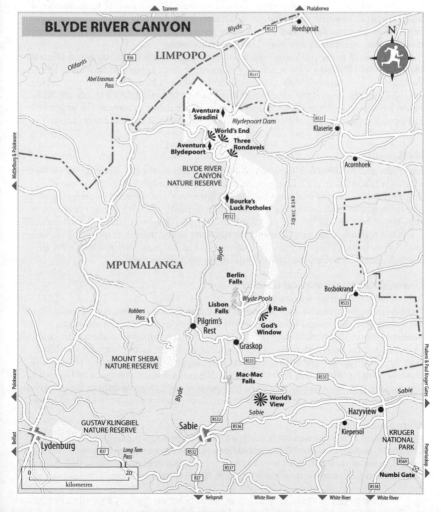

9

HIKING THE PRIME CANYON ROUTE

A guided three-day **Prime Canyon Route** is available with **Hike Africa** (☎084 775 8831, ⓦhikeafrica.co.za), taking in shaded *kloofs*, impressive waterfalls and relaxing pools. You sleep in overnight huts equipped with braai facilities; bring your own hiking gear, including a sleeping bag. The trail costs approximately R100 per day.

---

turn of the last century with fortune-seekers, hunters, gold-diggers and adventurers, these days the South African lowveld's claim to fame is its proximity to the Kruger National Park and the adjacent private game reserves. Although several of the towns on the game park fringes are pleasant enough, most people come here to get into big-game country.

Largest of the lowveld towns, and the capital of Mpumalanga, is **Nelspruit**, accessible by air and bus (including buses from Maputo in Mozambique). East of Nelspruit, the N4 runs close to the southern border of the Kruger, providing easy access to its Malelane and Crocodile Bridge gates; the latter is just 12km north of **Komatipoort**, a humid frontier town on the border with **Mozambique**. From Nelspruit, you can also head 32km south to **Barberton**, an attractive settlement in the hills with strong mining connections, or continue another 41km to **Swaziland**.

The R40 north of the provincial capital passes through **White River**, **Hazyview**, **Klaserie**, **Hoedspruit** and **Phalaborwa**, a series of small towns that act as bases for exploring Kruger. Each town is well supplied with accommodation, and has a Kruger entrance gate nearby; tours are available from some. The closest to Nelspruit and an entry point into the Park, Hazyview is now leader of the pack. Hoedspruit and Phalaborwa actually fall within Limpopo Province, but for the sake of continuity have been included in this chapter.

Nelspruit

Fast-growing **NELSPRUIT**, 358km east of Johannesburg on the N4, grew in the 1890s as a base for traders, farmers and prospectors, but there is little evidence left of these origins. Most of the old buildings have been ripped out and replaced by shopping malls and freeways, and the town has a bustling and prosperous feel. It's a major commercial centre, not only for the lowveld but also for shoppers from Swaziland and Mozambique.

The town also has the best **transport connections** in the province, including air links with Johannesburg, Cape Town and Durban, and to Maputo. Nelspruit also has an excellent hospital and all the facilities and shops you might need.

Lowveld National Botanical Garden

Signposted off the R40 to White River • Daily 8am–5pm • R15

Nelspruit's major attraction is the **Lowveld National Botanical Garden**. Set on the banks of the Crocodile River, the garden comes a close second to Cape Town's Kirstenbosch Gardens (see p.110). Natural waterfalls and walks through rainforest make a pleasant break from the midday heat, with **trees** grouped according to habitat and helpfully identified with labels. The garden specializes in **cycads** from around the world, and there's also a grove of baobabs from South Africa and other African countries. A useful brochure sold at the entrance gate has a map showing the highlights of the garden and the paths through it, and you'll find a tea room open for refreshments, as well as a restaurant with good views.

Chimpanzee Eden

10km out of Nelspruit on the R40 to Barberton • Daily 10am, noon & 2pm • R200 • ☎079 7771514, ⓦjanegoodall.co.za

The Jane Goodall-sponsored **Chimpanzee Eden** is dedicated to the rescue and rehabilitation of chimpanzees. Here you may see chimpanzees on set tours, who have been rescued from terrible conditions in places like Angola and Somalia, re-learning to

9

climb trees, foraging for food in the leaves, carefully grooming each other and establishing troop relationships, though you don't get to touch or interact with them in any way.

ARRIVAL AND DEPARTURE   NELSPRUIT

By plane Flights arrive at the tiny, thatched Kruger Mpumalanga International Airport (KMIA; ☎ 013 753 7500), 20km north of town off the R40 to White River. There is one direct flight a day from Cape Town, on SA Airlink (ⓦ flyairlink.com), six from Johannesburg, including one on Kulula which is the cheapest (ⓦ kulula.com), and two from Durban. Unfortunately, flights to Nelspruit are among the most expensive in the country, and it may work out cheaper to fly into Johannesburg and continue here by car. All the major car rental companies, including Avis (☎ 013 741 1087), have rental desks at the airport. Without hiring a car, your best option for onward travel is a private shuttle: Tina Bohm of Malachite Tours and Transfers (☎ 083 459 4150, ⓦ malachitetours.co.za) meets flights on request and

provides reliable transfers into Nelspruit (or into Kruger and the private reserves, to Hazyview, and onwards from Nelspruit to Mozambique). Otherwise, try reasonably priced Jackson Mahlati (☎ 083 414 0801, ⓔ jacksontransfers @webmail.co.za) who offers the cheapest trip into Nelspruit.
By bus From Johannesburg, the City Bug is the best option (ⓦ citybug.co.za) with four departures daily (approx 6hr), leaving from Pretoria, Johannesburg and OR Tambo Airport, arriving at the BP garage in the Sonpark Centre, Piet Retief St, just south of the city centre. It is way too far to walk to any accommodation from the bus stop; it's best to arrange a taxi beforehand, through Edgars Taxi Service (☎ 072 147 1677), or to get someone from your accommodation to meet you.

INFORMATION

Tourist information Lowveld Tourism (Mon–Fri 7am–6pm, Sat 8am–1.30pm; ☎ 013 755 1988/1989, ⓦ lowveldtourism.com), at the Crossings Centre, corner of the N4 and General Dan Pienaar St, signposted as you hit town from Johannesburg, is the town's main tourist office.

It provides maps and basic information, and arranges accommodation, including bookings for Kruger's restcamps, as well as day-trips with various tour operators. Lowveld Tourism also has a kiosk at the upmarket Riverside Mall, just north of the city centre on the R40.

ACCOMMODATION

Nelspruit's accommodation is largely geared towards business travellers, and none is close to restaurants. Most places have swimming pools to beat the summer heat, outdoor eating areas and tropical gardens. There are also some excellent options a few kilometres out, on farms, and a gorgeous game lodge virtually at the airport.

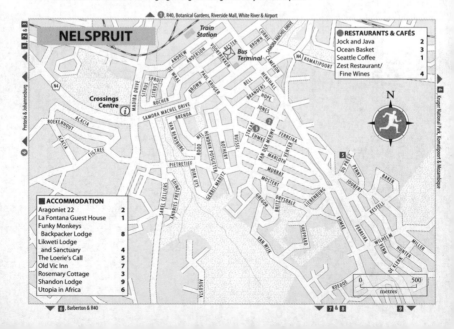

NELSPRUIT

● RESTAURANTS & CAFÉS
Jock and Java   2
Ocean Basket   3
Seattle Coffee   1
Zest Restaurant/ Fine Wines   4

■ ACCOMMODATION
Aragoniet 22   2
La Fontana Guest House   1
Funky Monkeys Backpacker Lodge   8
Likweti Lodge and Sanctuary   4
The Loerie's Call   5
Old Vic Inn   7
Rosemary Cottage   3
Shandon Lodge   9
Utopia in Africa   6

Aragoniet 22 22 Aragoniet St ☎083 631 2136, ⓦaragonietlodge.co.za; map opposite. Spotless, spacious and cheap self-catering or B&B in two garden flats and two rooms, in a convenient location, and attractive mainly for the price. **R500**

Funky Monkeys Backpacker Lodge 102 Van Wijk St ☎013 744 1310, ⓦfunkymonkeys.co.za; map opposite. Popular hostel with a licensed bar, pool table, shady veranda, swimming pool and broadband internet. It offers one- to three-day tours into Kruger and can arrange pick-ups from the town centre or airport. Dorm **R100**, double **R300**

La Fontana Guest House Corner of John Vorster and Besembos rds ☎013 741 3138, ⓦlafontana.co.za; map opposite. Mid-range B&B with six rooms, a relaxed feel and a large pool and garden, in a quiet residential area, with the usual pluses of a/c and television. Mostly used by business travellers. **R550**

★ **Likweti Lodge and Sanctuary** On the R358 between Nelspruit and White River, 5km from KMI airport ☎013 750 8100, ⓦlikweti.co.za; map opposite. Planes are not allowed to fly over Likweti's 1400 acres of rocky outcrops and open plains, which are home to rhino, buffalo, zebra and giraffe. Three types of accommodation are available: the lodge, set on a ridge, faces the sunrise, with supremely comfortable rooms and excellent food (R4250); more modestly, you can stay in one of the three rooms in a bungalow with garden and pool, close to the entrance gate (R1090); or self-cater in a two-storey chalet that sleeps four. **R460**

The Loerie's Call 2 Du Preez St ☎013 744 1251 or ☎083 283 6190, ⓦloeriescall.co.za; map opposite. A modern place with a pool, offering upmarket en-suite rooms with private verandas overlooking the Crocodile River Valley. As it's often fully booked, reserve well ahead. There is also a very good restaurant on site. **R1000**

★ **Old Vic Inn** 12 Impala St, 3km from town ☎013 744 0993 or ☎082 340 1508, ⓦkrugerandmore.co.za; map opposite. Six clean, comfortable doubles, some en suite, and a dorm in a quiet backpacker hostel, with a pool, garden and walks in the adjoining nature reserve. There are also three self-catering units suitable for families. The owners can arrange transport from the centre of town and from the airport, and can organize tours, including to Mozambique and to Kruger. Their in-house tour company is the only backpackers' tour company that will get you a bed right in Kruger Park, at Lower Sabi; the tours are normally run by the owner himself. Dorm **R100**, double **R600**

★ **Rosemary Cottage** 16km west of Nelspruit, off the N4 ☎084 205 9522, ⓦalkmaarrosemarycottage.co.za; map opposite. A charming and comfortable two-bedroom self-catering cottage with a veranda, a veg and herb garden, on a working orange and macadamia nut farm, a 20min drive from Nelspruit. If you opt for B&B, you'll be treated to home-baked bread and preserves. **R700**

Shandon Lodge 1 Saturn St ☎013 744 9934, ⓦshandon.co.za; map opposite. Rooms with private entrances arranged around a swimming pool and tropical garden, in a well-established colonial-style home. The hosts are friendly and provide good food – including picnic hampers for a day out in Kruger – as well as loads of information. **R900**

EATING AND DRINKING

Jock and Java Corner of Ferreira and Van der Merwe sts ☎013 755 4969; map opposite. The first choice for reasonable food (mains R80) in the centre, with a coffee shop, pub, garden setting and safe parking. At night, especially at the weekend, it doubles up as a local party place. Daily 8am till late.

Ocean Basket 17 Ferreira St ☎013 752 7193; map opposite. A reasonably priced fish restaurant in a central and pleasant location, with the benefit of outdoor seating on balmy evenings. If hake and chips (R80), prawns, sole or kingklip with salads don't cut it, steaks are always available. Daily 11am–9.30pm.

Zest Ilanga Mall, N4 West ☎013 742 2217; map opposite. A spoil-yourself restaurant with a French accent and emphasis on attractive plating. Breakfast choices include savoury pancakes, plus hamburgers and wraps for lunch, while the set menus are really popular and good value at R100. Mon–Sat 9am–9.30pm, Sun 11am–3pm.

DIRECTORY

Embassies Mozambique, Bell St ☎013 752 7396.

Emergencies Ambulance ☎013 10177.

HEADING INTO MOZAMBIQUE

Maputo is only 200km from Nelspruit, an easy journey by car on the N4, though there are two toll gates to pass through (R60). The Cheetah Express (☎013 755 1988, R250 one-way) is a **shuttle service** between the two cities – it leaves Nelspruit at 4.30pm (Mon–Sat); the journey takes three hours. Tickets can be purchased from the tourist office at the Crossings Centre (see **opposite**) and **visas** (R750) must be purchased beforehand at the Mozambique Consulate, Ferriera Street opposite Absa Square (☎013 753 2089). You'll need a whole day for this – arrive

9

Hospital Nelspruit Private Hospital ☎ 013 759 0500.
Internet access There is an internet café and wi-fi in the *Mugg & Bean* restaurant at the Crossings Centre.
Pharmacy Chemist Mopani, Crossings Centre (☎ 013 755 5500, out of hours ☎ 082 761 1603).
Post office The main post office, in Voortrekker St, is open

8.30am–4pm. Each shopping centre has a Postnet, easier to use than the post office.
Shopping Adjacent to the casino and provincial parliament, Riverside mall has the best collection of shops in the province, though the Crossings Centre is more central and likely to have most of what you need.

Kruger's southern fringe

The N4 east of Nelspruit roughly follows the progress of the **Crocodile River**, which traces the southern boundary of Kruger National Park. For 58km to the tiny settlement of **Malelane**, the road travels within view of the Crocodile's riverine forest, passing lush, subtropical farmlands and the Dalí-esque formations of granite *koppies*. Some 4km further on, the road turns off to Kruger's **Malelane Gate**, the most convenient entry point for *Berg-en-Dal* restcamp (see p.555). The only blight on the journey is the smoke stacks from the Malelane sugar-cane mill.

ACCOMMODATION   **KRUGER'S SOUTHERN FRINGE**

Buhala Game Lodge 12km east of Malelane Gate ☎ 082 940 8630, ⓦ buhala.co.za. A fabulous guesthouse on a mango, sugar-cane and papaya farm, on the banks of the Crocodile River, with views from a wooden deck across the slow water into Kruger, a swimming pool, and ten a/c elegant doubles. Drives into the park can be arranged from here for around R770 per person, as well as walks in for R450. Golfers stay here too, for the nearby Leopard Creek course. R2800

★ **Kwa Madwala Game Reserve** Signposted off the N4, between Malelane and Crocodile Bridge gates ☎ 082 779 2153, ⓦ kwamadwala.net. A game lodge experience at B&B prices, set in a beautiful area of bushveld, dotted with granite hills and roamed by the Big Five (apart from buffalo). There are three accommodation

options, of which Manyatta Rock Camp offers chalets built into granite outcrops, and has a nice pool and good views, though with farmland and a sugar-processing mill not too far away, it doesn't have a totally wild feeling. Rates include dinner, bed and breakfast; game drives are extra, and self-catering is available for R1000. R3200

Selati 103 2km from Malelane Gate ☎ 013 790 0978 ⓦ selati103.co.za. These functional self-catering garden cottages score high with their location by the park gate, and come with breakfast or dinner available by prior arrangement, including a packed breakfast if you're going early into the park. There is a pool and braai facilities, but stock up with food beforehand. Great for families, or a night-stop if you don't have time to drive into the Park. R700

Barberton

BARBERTON, 36km south of Nelspruit, began its urban existence after **gold** was discovered in 1883. An influx of shopkeepers, hoteliers, barmen, prostitutes, even ministers of religion, soon joined the diggers in the growing frontier town, which consisted of tents, tin, thatch and mud, with nearly every second building functioning

---

KRUGER HORSERIDING

Horseriding in big game country is a fabulous experience. Kwa Madwala Reserve (☎ 082 779 2153, ⓦ kwamadwala.net), 80km east of Nelspruit, offers rides on their massive conservancy, which is home to all of the Big Five except buffalo. A two-hour ride costs R700.

You stand an excellent chance of seeing wild horses with Kaapsehoop Horse Trails (☎ 082 774 5826, ⓦ horsebacktrails.co.za; from R350), in a mountainous, forested area off the N4, 35km west of Nelspruit. Kaapsehoop also offers overnight trails for competent riders. There is also very nice, reasonably priced self-catering accommodation available at the riding centre, with friendly staff and a relaxed vibe (R400).

Riding with Off-Beat Safaris, 13km north of Hoedspruit (☎ 015 793 2422 or ☎ 082 494 1735, ⓦ offbeatsafaris.co.za), is a recommended way to view giraffe, kudu, zebra and wildebeest. They run rides every morning and afternoon for R250.

as a boozing joint. During the fabulous boom of the 1880s the mines slipped out of the grasp of the small-time prospectors and came under the control of the large corporations that still own them today. There are seven working **mines** around Barberton, each with its own entertainment venue for miners only, which means you won't find miners packing out public bars as in the wild days of old.

This is the best place in the country to take an **underground gold-mining tour**, in a working mine, or learn to do gold panning. This attraction aside, Barberton also has a colonial backwater charm, reasonably priced accommodation, a handful of historical sights, tropical vegetation and an attractive setting in a basin surrounded by mountains.

Barberton Museum
36 Pilgrim St • Mon–Fri 9am–4pm, Sat & Sun 9am–1pm & 2–4pm • Free

You can explore the mining history of the town at the **Barberton Museum**, three blocks east of the tourist office. In a well-designed, modern building, the museum has good displays on the fascinating gold-rush era. The museum can provide a map of the town's **Heritage Walk**, on which green and white signposts direct you to some historical houses and monuments, including the worthwhile Belhaven House and Stopforth House.

Umjindi Jewellery Project
Pilgrim St, next to the museum • Mon–Fri 8am–5pm, Sat 8am–2pm

An interesting project that trains people in this gold-producing area to become jewellery designers and makers over three years; some of the work produced is on sale here.

ARRIVAL AND INFORMATION   BARBERTON

By minibus taxi There is no scheduled public transport to Barberton, though from Nelspruit you can take a minibus taxi.
Tourist information Crown St (Mon–Fri 7.30am–4.30pm, Sat 9am–2pm; ☎013 712 2880, ⓦ barberton.co.za).
Activities and tours Barberton Odyssey (☎079 180 1488) can, for a small fee, offer a guided historical walk.

ACCOMMODATION

Aloe Ridge Guest Farm 10km north of Barberton on the R38 ☎082 456 3442, ⓦ aloeridgeguestfarm.com. Peaceful and reasonably priced B&B or self-catering accommodation on an organic farm, with excellent birding opportunities. The three rooms in the main house and two cottages are all furnished with wooden furniture, with cotton bedding, and do not have television. The cottages have patios and children's play areas. R600
Fountain Baths Guest House 48 Pilgrim St ☎013 712 2707, ⓦ fountainbaths.co.za. Central, stalwart establishment with pleasant B&B rooms and self-catering mini-apartments for two to four people, in a tropical garden edging onto Saddleback Hill. R600

Mazwita Bush Camp 17km towards Nelspruit on the R40 ☎082 604 1190, ⓦ mazwita.com. A small game farm with thatched rondavels, wooden walkways and lovely hilly surrounds where you can walk, cycle or drive to view plains game in the bush without predator dangers. R1100
Old Coach Road Guest House and Restaurant 13km north of Barberton on the R38 to Kaapmuiden ☎013 719 9755, ⓦ oldcoachroad.co.za. Comfortable twin and double en-suite rooms, as well as one family unit, at a friendly establishment set in its own peaceful grounds, with a pool, big lawn and monkeys in the trees. The licensed restaurant (eves only) has a terrace looking onto spectacular mountains. R730

HEADING INTO SWAZILAND

The closest and most beautiful route **into Swaziland** from Barberton is through the border crossing at Bulembu (8am–4pm), but the road is poor and should be avoided in the summer unless you're in a 4WD vehicle, though an ordinary car can make it in the winter (dry season). A more practical option, which takes the same time, is to enter Swaziland via the border posts of Ngwenya/Oshoek (7am–10pm) or Jeppe's Reef/Matsamo (7am–8pm), the latter route requiring you to pass through the Kaapmuiden toll gate east of Nelspruit on the N4.

9

EATING AND DRINKING

Co-Co Pan Crown St. Barberton's best place to eat, and the most central, with no frills, is the cheap and friendly *Co-Co Pan*, which serves straightforward hamburgers, steaks and omelettes. Daily 8am–9pm.

Papa's Kitchen 18 Judge St. Your best chance to meet locals over a drink and pub meal is to head for *Papa's Kitchen*, two streets away from the tourist office, which is also known for some knees-up live music. Daily 10am–late.

Victorian Tea Garden Next to the tourist office on Crown St. The pleasant *Victorian Tea Garden*, with a white gazebo straight out of a London park, serves good tea and light snacks outdoors. Mon–Fri 8am–5pm, Sat 8am–1pm.

Kruger's western flank

The **R40** heads north from Nelspruit along the western border of the Kruger National Park, passing through prosperous tropical-fruit-growing farmlands and crowded, poverty-stricken African areas. The only reason you're likely to find yourself heading north along this road from **Hazyview** is to access the private game reserves – **Sabi Sands**, **Manyeleti** or **Timbavati** – that join up with the western flank of Kruger (see p.561), or to reach the **Orpen Gate**, for the rewarding central section of Kruger National Park. Though marked prominently on maps, **Klaserie**, which lies on the border of Mpumalanga and Limpopo Province, is little more than an easily missed petrol station and shop, surrounded by a number of private game farms – poor cousins to the pricier lodges inside the game reserves to the east.

North of the Mpumalanga border, in Limpopo, you'll pass little towns en route to the central section of Kruger National Park and the Manyeleti and Timbavati private game reserves. Coming down the Escarpment along the R36/R527 from the Blyde River viewpoints, you'll encounter a fork in the road after about 75km. The more northerly road leads to the towns of **Hoedspruit**, which is not a desirable destination or place to base yourself, particularly in the area at the foot of the Escarpment, and Klaserie. Much further north and generally reached from Polokwane on the N1, the mining town of **Phalaborwa** is conveniently 2km from the Phalaborwa Gate into central Kruger and the rewarding camps of Letaba and Olifants.

Hazyview

HAZYVIEW, 43km north of Nelspruit, is a service centre for Southern Kruger, with **Phabeni Gate** situated a mere 10km from town. It's the last town to stock up in before reaching the major Paul Kruger Gate into Skukuza, Kruger's "capital", as well as the entrance to the Sabi Sands Reserve. It is a centre too for surrounding farms, with large

---

BARBERTON MINING TOURS AND TRAILS

Barberton offers spectacular gold mining tours down a historical mine, as well as into a commercial, working mine. **Galaxy Gold Mines** offers tours at 8am, 11am and 2pm at the historical Pioneer Mine, 15km out of town (book through Barberton Odyssey ☎079 180 1488; R180; 2hr 30min), for which you will be provided with gum boots, a hard hat and a headlamp, and shown how to pan for gold.

To tour around a **working mine** (R750) you'll need a whole day, and to book beforehand with Galaxy – a minimum of six people is required. During the tour, the Mine Captain takes you 800m underground for four hours, and the next three hours are spent at the gold processing plants above ground.

To get a sense of what the old mines were like, the 2km circular **Fortuna Mine hiking trail**, just south of town, takes you through a disused tunnel built to transport gold-bearing ore to the Fortuna Mine. The trail, which starts at the car park off Crown Street to the south of town, goes through an attractive area of indigenous trees before entering the 600m tunnel (bring a torch and wear proper walking shoes), and once you're through you get good views of Barberton and the De Kaap Valley. Maps are available from the tourist office, but the route is strenuous and the terrain rough.

shopping centres and busy roadside market stalls selling fruit and goods to the surrounding African community. The town is one of the best bases for visitors who want to stay outside the park and do some adventure **activities** and **tours**, as well as view game. Hazyview is spread out, but **Perry's Bridge**, on the corner of the R536 and R40, is a central stop-off with a small complex of luxury shops, craft outlets and restaurants.

The Skyway Trails

R450 • ☎ 082 825 0209 or ☎ 013 737 8374, ⊛ skywaytrails.com

The **aerial cable way**, Skyway Trails, offers three-hour jaunts above the trees, on which you glide from platform to platform over the valley, securely clipped to a stout cable. Helmets and harnesses are provided and the guides are capable and fun. No skills are needed, other than a degree of calmness and a head for heights, and children aged 6–10 can ride with a guide. You meet at *Gecko Lodge*, 3km along on the R536 from Hazyview, where you are kitted up and given a short lesson before being transported to the hilltop where the trail begins. Book in advance.

The Elephant Sanctuary

Brush Down R450 • Trunk in Hand R400 • Elephant ride R750 • ☎ 079 624 9436, ⊛ elephantsanctuary.co.za

At the **Elephant Sanctuary**, 5km from Hazyview on the R536 road to Sabie, you can touch and feed the two orphaned elephants rescued from a culling programme. A variety of programmes offers close encounters with the elephants – the "Brush Down" Programme, where you groom the animals and feel the texture of their skin and ears, combined with "Trunk in Hand" where you walk alongside them, lightly holding their trunks, is recommended. Rides are also available.

ARRIVAL AND DEPARTURE   HAZYVIEW

The shortest and quickest route here from Johannesburg, 421km away, is via the N4 and Nelspruit. No public transport apart from minibus taxis comes into Hazyview, but if you're staying at one of the local backpacker lodges you can arrange to be collected from Nelspruit.

INFORMATION

Big 5 Country Tourism Perry's Bridge (Mon–Sat 8am–5pm, Sun 10am–1pm; ☎ 013 737 8191, ⊛ big5country .co.za). The best information office in Mpumalanga, and can book accommodation, safaris into Kruger Park, adventure activities and transfers. It has created the clearest map of the region and has its own activity booklets, all available at the office, and it also covers the Escarpment. Conveniently, there's an internet café at Perry's Bridge too (Mon–Sat).

ACCOMMODATION

Guesthouses, many of them fairly upmarket, pop up all along the way to Hazyview until you reach the densely populated former Bantustan areas around **Bosbokrand**. Hazyview itself has a wide range of **accommodation**, most of it in farmland strung along the roads radiating out to the neighbouring towns of Sabie (the R536), Graskop (the R535) and White River (the R538), as well as to Kruger's Paul Kruger Gate (the R40).

Bohms Zeederberg Country House 17km from Hazyview, on the R536 ☎ 013 737 8101, ⊛ bohms .co.za. Well-run chalets with an old-fashioned feel, set in subtropical gardens around a swimming pool, with magnificent views and walking trails to the river below. Wheelchair-friendly. **R785**

Bushpackers at Gecko Lodge 3km from Hazyview on the R536 ☎ 013 737 8140 or ☎ 082 342 6598, ⊛ bushpackers.co.za. Situated next to *Gecko Lodge* (see below), with a swimming pool, camping, dorms and doubles, with a funky bar and home-cooked meals. Transfers to and from Nelspruit, and trips of a day or longer into Kruger Park or the Escarpment are also available. Camping **R60**, dorm **R100**, double **R400**

Eagle's Nest Chalets 5km from Hazyview on the R536 Rd to Sabie ☎ 013 737 8434, ⊛ tranquilitylodges .co.za. Twelve well-run self-catering chalets perched on top of a hill, in tropical gardens, with a swimming pool and mini golf. From the R536 take the Kiepersol Rd and wind up 2.2km of dirt road. **R450**

Gecko Lodge 3km from Hazyview on the R536 ☎ 013 737 8374 or ☎ 082 556 6458, ⊛ geckolodge.net. Probably the nicest setting in Hazyview, with lush riverine vegetation and a stream running through the grounds. Rooms are decent and

9

well priced, and there is a pub as well as a restaurant. The lodge is also the starting point for the aerial cable trails. R820
Idle and Wild 6km from Hazyview, on the R536 ☎ 013 737 8173 or ☎ 082 381 7408, ⊛ idleandwild.co.za. This mango farm in a lush valley on the banks of the Sabie River offers two thatched rondavels, a family unit and two honeymoon suites (with their own spa bath) in the lush garden, as well as two en-suite bedrooms in the main house. All have kitchenettes, and there's a jacuzzi, sauna and swimming pool. Quad biking and river rafting on site. R800
Numbi Main Rd ☎ 013 737 7301, ⊛ hotelnumbi.co.za. An old-fashioned, comfortable place, right in the centre,

offering camping, garden suites and hotel rooms. The grounds are shady and the hotel's restaurant serves good steaks. Camping R110, double R890

⭐ **Rissington Inn** 2km south of town, just off the R40 ☎ 013 737 7700, ⊛ www.rissington.co.za. A relaxed and informal place (kids are welcome), with fourteen rooms set in the gardens of a large thatched homestead. Best are the garden suites which have roofless outside showers. There's also a swimming pool and a bar and restaurant. It makes a good transition between "civilization" and being on safari. R1100

EATING AND DRINKING

Kuka Perry's Bridge Centre ☎ 013 737 6957. Sophisticated Afro-chic restaurant and cocktail bar with colourful, modern decor and both indoor and outdoor seating. As well as game and meat dishes, there are good salads. Daily 7am till late.
Shangana Cultural Village 4km out of town on the R535 to Graskop ☎ 013 737 5804/5. Delicious African dinners (from R350; book in advance) cooked in massive pots over an open fire. The menu might include crocodile in spicy peanut sauce and beef and honey-glazed sweet potato, and vegetarians are well catered for. You eat in huts

and are served very graciously by women from the household. The meals are the climax of a tour of the village and an energetic show of dancing, all of which is included in the price.
Summerfields Kitchen 4.5km out of town on the R536 Sabie Rd ☎ 013 737 6500. Lovely setting on a rose farm (though none for picking or sale). Light lunches are served on a wooden deck under cream umbrellas, while dinners feature the likes of lamb cutlets or kudu fillets (R130). Prices are reasonable and there's a kids' menu and play area. Tues–Sat 8am–9pm, Sun & Mon 8am–2pm.

Orpen Gate

After Hazyview, the R40 passes through irrigated farmlands and low hills dotted with bushveld trees. As you approach **Bosbokrand**, 28km to the north, the corridor between the Escarpment and big-game country changes, with the sudden appearance of shantytowns, busy roads, overgrazed lands and dense settlements interspersed with the odd papaya and banana tree. Bosbokrand is also known as **Bushbuck Ridge** (a direct translation from the Afrikaans), the name coming from the hilly finger extending east from the Escarpment – although any bushbucks that might once have wandered here have long since been eaten and displaced by cattle and goats.

Despite the fact that maps indicate little or no habitation in this area, this busy and sometimes hazardous road passes through the former Bantustan of **Lebowa**, where people live crammed at a density six times greater than the provincial average. **Klaserie**, 42km north of Bosbokrand in the middle of game farms, sits poised on the border between Mpumalanga and Limpopo Province. Forty-five kilometres east from here lies **Orpen Gate** into Kruger.

Nyani Shangaan Cultural Village

Along the Orpen Rd, 32km from Orpen Gate · Daily 8am–4pm · Tour R75 · Tour and lunch R150, booked in advance · ☎ 083 512 4865

A worthwhile visit is to the **Nyani Shangaan Cultural Village**. It's a good option for lunch or **overnighting**, with dinner and a display of **traditional dancing** laid on. Unlike some of the more commercialized cultural villages, this is a genuine effort developed by Axon Khosa, a local Shangaan man. He and his extended family take visitors on a tour of the village and offer a **meal**, which is usually a chicken dish with butternut or gem squash, served with wild spinach and groundnuts mixed into *mielie pap*. You need to book in advance; it's also possible to **stay overnight** here (see opposite).

ACCOMMODATION   ORPEN GATE

Nyani Shangaan Cultural Village Along the Orpen Rd, 32km from Orpen Gate ☎083 512 4865. For an authentically Shangaan experience, stay in the cultural village, in a hut with traditional dung floors and thatching that looks untidy by comparison with the safari lodges. The walls are constructed with mud from termite mounds and are beautifully hand decorated with white, orange and black motifs; huts have fold-up mattresses, and there are cold showers and flush toilets. Booking essential, minimum group size is four. R1400

Timbavati Safari Lodge On the Orpen Gate Rd, 13km from Klaserie and 20km from the gate to Kruger itself ☎015 793 0415 or ☎082 362 2922, ⓦtimbavatisafarilodge.com. The pick of the places to stay in the vicinity is *Timbavati Safari Lodge*, which has space for couples or larger groups in thatched Ndebele-styled huts, plus a pool, bar and pleasant outdoor dining with wholesome, hearty dinners under the stars. Walks on the property itself are safe, with the chance of sighting giraffe, zebra and buck. Worthwhile visits to the tribal villages across the road can easily be arranged and staff can organize game drives and adventure activities in the area. R750

Hoedspruit

Lurking in the undulating lowveld, straight up the R40 from Klaserie, with the hazy blue mountains of the Escarpment visible on the distant horizon, is the small but growing service centre of **HOEDSPRUIT**. The town lies at the heart of a concentration of **private game reserves** and lodges, and is a good base for specialist **activities**, such as horseriding and rafting on the Blyde River, visiting animal rehabilitation centres and lazy hot-air ballooning over the bush. Hoedspruit is a significant arrival point for air travellers heading for Kruger, Manyeleti and Timbavati, though it is definitely not a place to base yourself for drives into the park.

Moholoholo Wildlife Rehabilitation Centre

On the R531 between the R40 and R527, about 3km from the tarred turn-off to the Blydepoort Dam • Tours Mon–Sat 9.30am & 3pm, and during school holidays Sun at 3pm • Booking essential • R100 • ☎015 795 5236, ⓦmoholoholo.co.za

At the **Moholoholo Wildlife Rehabilitation Centre**, ex-ranger Brian Jones has embarked on an individual crusade to rescue and rehabilitate injured and abandoned animals, notably raptors, but also lions, leopards and others. Tours are informative and you get to see a lot of endangered animals close up. The centre is part of a wider reserve and both night drives and early-morning walks are offered, and there is also accommodation (see p.550).

Monsoon Gallery

Along the R527, near its junction with the R36 • Daily 8.30am–4.30pm • Free • ☎015 795 5114, ⓦmonsoongallery.com

The **Monsoon Gallery**, 29km west of Hoedspruit, makes a good place to pause on your journey. Its great African arts and crafts shop has an absorbing selection of authentic material, including ironwork and woodcarving from Zimbabwe, superb tapestries from the Karosswerkers factory near Tzaneen, Venda pots and jewellery, and African music CDs and books.

ARRIVAL AND DEPARTURE   HOEDSPRUIT

By plane Daily flights from Johannesburg arrive at Eastgate airport (☎015 793 3681), some 14km south of Hoedspruit. Avis has an office at the airport (☎015 793 2014), and for transfers to game lodges from here, contact Eastgate Safaris (☎015 793 3678 or ☎082 774 9544), though most lodges send their own vehicles to meet guests.

UP IN THE AIR

Hot-air ballooning is a fabulous way to appreciate the landscape, and recommended flights are offered by Sun Catchers (☎087 806 2079, ⓦsuncatchers.co.za; R2600). Conditions have to be perfect, and flights are generally very early in the morning when the weather is at its most stable. They leave from different locations depending on the weather – you'll be advised in good time where to meet your flight. If you are ballooning, you can get accommodation at *Otter's Den*, a small and relaxing camp, on a bush-covered island in the Blyde River; see the Sun Catchers website for more details.

9

By bus City to City (☎015 781 1037) departs Johannesburg Station four times a week for the seven-hour journey to Hoedspruit.

INFORMATION

Hoedspruit itself has a small centre, and you'll find everything you might need in the Kamogelo and Crossings Centre shopping malls on the R527 and R40 respectively, including an internet café at the former and a well-stocked Pick 'n Pay supermarket and ATM at the latter.

ACCOMMODATION

★ **Blue Cottages Country House** ☎015 795 5114, ⓦcountryhouse.co.za. Comfortable suites in a farmhouse filled with African artefacts and fabrics, set in an enticingly cool and colourful tropical garden; more modest, but also beautiful, are the garden cottages. Breakfast is served nearby at *Mad Dogz Café* and you can have a mid-priced dinner served in your garden by candlelight. R1320

Moholoholo Forest Camp 26km from Hoedspruit on the R531 ☎013 795 5236, ⓦmoholoholo.co.za. *Forest Lane,* in the foothills of the Drakensberg Escarpment, is an unshowy safari camp with meals thrown in and plenty of game, including rhino, on the property. R2780

Trackers On the R531 abutting the canyon's cliffs 25km from Hoedspruit ☎015 795 5033 or ☎082 494 4266, ⓦtrackers.co.za. A variety of accommodation – camping, and self-catering or B&B chalets – on a farm with indigenous bushveld vegetation, where you may see zebra and antelope. Bring your own drinks, as you can't buy any here. A botanist living on the farm runs recommended guided walks through the bush. Camping R80, double R500

Zuleika Country House Signposted on the R531 ☎015 795 5064 or ☎072 480 1334, ⓦzuleika.co.za. Situated in a citrus farming area, *Zuleika* doesn't have river frontage, but it has a pretty tropical garden and swimming pool. Its fifteen rooms are all decorated to a high standard, and vary in price depending on whether you self-cater or go for a luxury B&B room with a mountain-facing wooden deck. R1000

Phalaborwa

PHALABORWA ("pal-a-bore-wa"), 74km north of Hoedspruit, gives access to the central and northern part of Kruger Park. It is right at the gate to the park – the closest of any town to the park – and is thus an extremely viable base. With the Transfrontier Park now open it is the last South African town you go through before crossing the efficient Giryondo border post into Mozambique.

The name Phalaborwa means "better than the south", a cheeky sobriquet coined as the town developed on the back of its extensive mineral wealth. During the 1960s, the borders of the park near Phalaborwa suddenly developed a kink, and large copper deposits were found, miraculously, just outside the protected national park area.

But mining actually began at Phalaborwa some time after 200 AD, and the **Masorini Heritage Site**, close to Phalaborwa Gate, is a reconstruction of an iron-smelting village.

ARRIVAL AND DEPARTURE

PHALABORWA

By plane Two SA Airlink (☎015 781 5823, ⓦflyairlink.com) flights arrive daily from Johannesburg (1hr) at Phalaborwa Airport, 5min drive from Kruger's Phalaborwa Gate, off President Steyn St. Unfortunately, this is one of the most expensive flights in the country. There are a number of car rental firms represented at the airport, including Avis (☎015 781 3169) and Budget (☎015 781 5404).

By bus Two buses make the approximately eight-hour trip from Johannesburg: Translux (☎015 781 1037) goes every day via Polokwane, while City to City (same number) takes in Dullstroom, Lydenburg and Hoedspruit, four times a week, and takes nine-and-a-half hours.

INFORMATION

Tourist information Sureturnkey Travel, 73a Sealene St (Mon–Fri 8.30am–5pm, Sat 9–11am; ☎015 781 1037, ⓦphalaborwa.co.za), makes bookings for Kruger, accommodation and car rental. They also have an office at the airport.

ACCOMMODATION

Daan & Zena's 15 Birkenhead St ☎015 781 6049, ⓦdaanzena.co.za. Brightly painted and friendly B&B (self-catering available) in en-suite rooms located in three neighbouring houses, with a/c and TV in each room, and

ACTIVITIES AROUND PHALABORWA

Keen **golfers** shouldn't miss the chance of a round at the signposted **Hans Merensky Country Club,** Copper Road (☏015 781 3931, ⊛hansmerensky.co.za), where it's not unusual to see giraffes and elephants sauntering across the fairways.

You can whet your appetite before heading into Kruger Park with a **sundowner boat trip** with Jumbo River Safaris (booking essential; ☏015 781 6168; R130), which sets out at 3.30pm down the Olifants River, frequently encountering game – including elephants – and guaranteeing sightings of crocs and hippos. Kruger Park's own activities, run from **Phalaborwa Gate** (☏013 735 3547 or 3548), are definitely worth doing, and participants can be collected from their accommodation. Top of the list are the **bush braais** (R575), a combination of a night drive and a braai inside a *boma* at Sable Dam, where you experience all the night sounds of the bush while chomping on your boerewors. Bush breakfasts are organized at the same location, and the price includes entrance to Kruger Park. **Walking safaris** and drives (R550) into the park are also bookable at the gate.

three swimming pools to choose from. R350
Elephant Walk 30 Anna Scheepers St ☏015 781 5860 or ☏082 495 0575, ⊛accommodationphalaborwa. com. A small and friendly hostel and B&B, in a pleasant suburban home with a large garden, 2km from the Kruger gate, with camping facilities and budget tours into Kruger, plus a booking service for Phalaborwa/Kruger activities. Besides dorms and twins, they have four en-suite garden

rooms, and a swimming pool in the garden. Camping R75, dorm R100, B&B R620
Sefapane Lodge Copper St, a 5min drive out of town almost at the gate into Kruger Park ☏015 780 6700, ⊛sefapane.co.za. Relaxed and upmarket accommodation in neat thatched huts in subtropical gardens, with a restaurant, a nice pool and a poolside bar. R1300

EATING AND DRINKING

Sefapane Lodge Copper St, a 5min drive out of town almost at the gate into Kruger Park. The attractive restaurant at this upmarket lodge serves small portions of pricey nouvelle cuisine (mains R110); its sunken bar beside the swimming pool is particularly convivial. Daily 7am–9pm.

★ **Villa Luso** 6 Grosvenor Crescent ☏015 781 5670. Mozambican food, including recommended seafood platters and sole, and tender T-bone steaks (R90). It is relaxed and comfortable with checked tablecloths and nice outdoor seating under thatch. Mon–Sat 7am till late.

Kruger National Park

KRUGER NATIONAL PARK is arguably the emblem of South African tourism, the place that delivers best what most visitors to Africa want to see – scores of elephants, lions and a cast of thousands of other game roaming the savanna. A narrow strip of land hugging the Mozambique border, Kruger stretches across Limpopo Province and Mpumalanga, an astonishing 414km drive from Pafuri Gate in the north to Malelane Gate in the south, all of it along tar, with many well-kept gravel roads looping off to provide routes for game drives.

Kruger is designed for **self-driving** and **self-catering**. Self-driving offers complete flexibility, though the temptation is to drive too much and too fast, leading to fewer sightings. Furthermore, rental cars tend to be low off the ground and aren't as good for game viewing as those used by lodges or tour operators. However, you can hop in a car knowing you'll find supplies at most of the restcamps – indeed self-driving is often the only way of seeing Kruger's animals if you're travelling with young children and want to manage time and food your own way. The park's popularity means that not only are you likely to share animal sightings with other motorists, but that **accommodation** is at a premium, particularly during South African school holidays, when you may not be able to find anything. Book as far in advance as possible.

Outside the public section, big-game country continues in several exclusive and expensive **private wildlife reserves**, clustering on huge tracts of land to the west, often

9

referred to as Greater Kruger. As far as animals are concerned, the private and public areas are joined in an enormous, seamless whole. The three major private reserves are **Sabi Sands** to the south, and **Timbavati** and **Manyeleti**, adjoining the central section of the national park. The private reserves are not places you drive around yourself, and they offer a greater sense of being in the wilderness as there are no tarred roads or buildings away from the lodges, and you will not be sharing your sightings with a bunch of other cars. The safari lodges are luxuriously romantic and beautifully set, and dedicated to finding you wildlife.

But whatever you choose, be sure to relax and don't get too obsessed with seeing the Big Five. Remember that wildlife doesn't imitate TV documentaries: you're most unlikely to see lion-kills (you may not see a lion at all), or huge herds of wildebeest migrating across dusty savanna. The element of luck involved is exactly what makes game spotting so addictive.

Brief history

It's highly questionable whether Kruger National Park can be considered "a pristine wilderness", as it's frequently called, given that people have been living in or around it for thousands of years. **San hunter-gatherers** have left their mark in the form of paintings and engravings at 150 sites so far discovered, and there is evidence of farming cultures at many places in the park.

Around 1000–1300 AD, centrally organized states were building stone palaces and engaging in **trade** that brought Chinese porcelain, jewellery and cloth into the area, but it was the arrival of white **fortune-seekers** in the second half of the nineteenth century that made the greatest impact on the region. African farmers were kicked off their traditional lands in the early twentieth century to create the park, and hunters and poachers made their livelihoods here decimating game populations.

Paul Kruger, former president of the South African Republic, is usually credited with having the foresight to set aside land for wildlife conservation. Kruger figures as a shrewd, larger-than-life character in Afrikaner history, and it was **James Stevenson-Hamilton**, the first warden of the national park, who cunningly put forward Kruger's name in order to soften up Afrikaner opposition to the park's creation. In fact, Stevenson-Hamilton knew that Kruger was no conservationist and was actually an inveterate hunter; Kruger "never in his life thought of animals except as biltong", he

---

WALKS AND GAME DRIVES

Whether you're staying in Kruger or not, you can still join one of the early morning, mid-morning, sunset or night **game drives** organized by the park (R380). Not only are these drives one of the cheapest ways of accessing the park, but the viewing is unsurpassed because of the height of the open vehicles, though you will not get any commentary, especially if you are near the back and can't hear the driver. Drives in smaller, more comfortable vehicles are a little more expensive, but worth it. The drives leave from every camp in the park (book at reception or, even better, when you make your reservation) and, for those staying outside the park, from these entrance gates: Crocodile Bridge (☎013 735 6012), Malelane (☎013 735 6152), Numbi (☎013 735 5133), Paul Kruger (☎013 735 5107), Phabeni (☎013 735 5890) and Phalaborwa (☎013 735 3547/3548).

For those staying inside the park, three-hour **game walks** (R470) are conducted every morning at dawn from each camp, and there are also afternoon walks. Groups are restricted to eight people, so it's worth booking beforehand. No under 12s. **Bush breakfasts and evening braais**, departing from most camps as well as the entry gates, combine a short drive with a meal outdoors (R160). It's probably going to be the only meal for which you'll ever have to sign an indemnity form. Kruger also runs several three-night **wilderness trails** (see box, p.557) in different parts of the park, led by armed rangers – a fabulous way of getting in touch with the wilderness, but one you'll have to book months in advance.

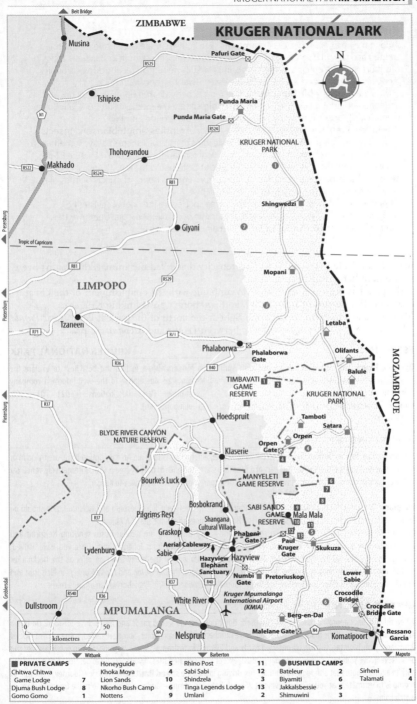

KRUGER NATIONAL PARK

N

ZIMBABWE

Beit Bridge

Musina

Pafuri Gate

Tshipise

Punda Maria

Punda Maria Gate

R525

KRUGER NATIONAL PARK

Thohoyandou

R524

Makhado

R522

R524

R81

Pietersburg

N1

Giyani

Shingwedzi

Tropic of Capricorn

R81

Mopani

LIMPOPO

R529

Pietersburg

Tzaneen

Letaba

R71

R71

Olifants

Phalaborwa

Balule

Phalaborwa Gate

R36

R40

TIMBAVATI GAME RESERVE

Pietersburg

R37

Hoedspruit

KRUGER NATIONAL PARK

BLYDE RIVER CANYON NATURE RESERVE

Tamboti

Satara

Klaserie

Orpen

Orpen Gate

MOZAMBIQUE

Bourke's Luck

MANYELETI GAME RESERVE

Bosbokrand

SABI SANDS GAME RESERVE

Mala Mala

Pilgrims Rest

Shangana Cultural Village

Graskop

Phabeni Gate

Paul Kruger Gate

Skukuza

Groblersdal

R37

Aerial Cableway

Sabie

Hazyview Elephant Sanctuary

Hazyview

Lydenburg

Numbi Gate

Pretoriuskop

Lower Sabie

R540

R37

R40

Kruger Mpumalanga International Airport (KMIA)

Crocodile Bridge

R36

White River

Crocodile Bridge Gate

Dullstroom

MPUMALANGA

Berg-en-Dal

Malelane Gate

N4

Ressano Garcia

0   50
kilometres

N4

Nelspruit

Komatipoort

Witbank

Barberton

Maputo

■ PRIVATE CAMPS		Honeyguide	5	Rhino Post	11	● BUSHVELD CAMPS		Sirheni	1
Chitwa Chitwa		Khoka Moya	4	Sabi Sabi	12	Bateleur	2	Talamati	4
Game Lodge	7	Lion Sands	10	Shindzela	3	Biyamiti	6		
Djuma Bush Lodge	8	Nkorho Bush Camp	6	Tinga Legends Lodge	13	Jakkalsbessie	5		
Gomo Gomo	1	Nottens	9	Umlani	2	Shimuwini	3		

9

KRUGER FLORA AND FAUNA

Among the nearly 150 species of **mammals** seen in the park are cheetah, leopard, lion, spotted hyena, wild dog, black and white rhino, blue wildebeest, buffalo, Burchell's zebra, bushbuck, eland, elephant, giraffe, hippo, impala, kudu, mountain reedbuck, nyala, oribi, reedbuck, roan antelope, sable antelope, tsessebe, warthog and waterbuck.

The staggering 507 **bird species** include raptors, hefty-beaked hornbills, ostriches and countless colourful specimens. The **birders' "big six"** are the saddle-billed stork, kori bustard, martial eagle, lappet-faced vulture, Pel's fishing owl and ground hornbill.

Keep your eyes open and you'll also see a variety of **reptiles**, **amphibians** and **insects** – most rewardingly in the grounds of the restcamps themselves: there's always something to see up the trees, in the bushes or even inside your rondavel. If you spot a miniature ET-like reptile crawling upside down on the ceiling, don't be tempted to kill it; it's an insect-eating gecko and is doing you a good turn. If, however, you have a horror of insects or frogs, stay away from Kruger in the rainy season (Nov–March).

Common among the three-hundred-plus **tree** species are the baobab, cluster fig, knobthorn, Natal mahogany, monkey orange, raisin bush, tamboti, coral tree, fever tree, jackalberry, leadwood, marula, mopane, lala palm and sausage tree.

wrote in a private letter, and it was his tenacity that saved the animals that hadn't been shot out, rather than Kruger's.

The park has been extended into Mozambique with the establishment of the Great Limpopo Transfrontier Park in 2000, and two border posts linking Kruger to Mozambique have been created, one right at the north of the park at Pafuri near *Punda Maria Camp*, the other at Giriyondo, between *Letaba* and *Mopani* camps.

ESSENTIALS

KRUGER NATIONAL PARK

Opening hours Daily: Oct–Mar 5.30am–6.30pm; April, Aug & Sept 6am–6pm; May–July 6am–5.30pm.
Admission R180
Contact information ☎ 012 428 9111, ⊛ sanparks.org/parks/kruger

In Mozambique To find out best how to explore the Mozambican side, speak to the well-informed company Transfrontier Parks Destinations (☎ 021 701 7860, ⊛ dolimpopo.com).

ARRIVAL AND DEPARTURE

Johannesburg is the city with the best connections to Kruger, whether by land or air. An easy option if you are flying in or out of Johannesburg is to see the park as part of a tour that starts and ends in the city (see p.556). Alternatively, rent a car at the airport for the easy five-hour drive to the park; the airport is on the N4 motorway to Kruger.

By plane The three local airports servicing Kruger are Nelspruit (see p.542; for the southern section), Hoedspruit (see p.549; for the central and northern sections) and Phalaborwa (see p.550; for the northern section); each airport has car rental, which you'll need for the remainder of the journey. Unfortunately, flights to airports near Kruger are pricey and there are few special deals. Kulula flies between Johannesburg and Nelspruit, and should be more affordable than SA Airlink.
By bus There are regular buses servicing Nelspruit and Phalaborwa from Johannesburg. Once you have arrived, book one of the many tours on offer at the backpacker lodges: the *Old Vic Inn* and *Funky Monkeys* in Nelspruit and *Elephant Walk* in Phalaborwa can arrange tours.

GETTING AROUND

When driving, only approved roads should be used; don't drive on unmarked roads and never drive off-road. Do buy a Kruger map showing all the marked roads. Roads have numbers rather than names. Some are tarred, some are dirt. Speed limits are 50km/h on tar, 40km/h on untarred roads and 20km/h in restcamps; speed traps operate in some parts of the park. Never leave your car (it's illegal and dangerous), except at designated sites. If you're trying to get from one part of the park to another, note that although it's far more fun driving inside, the **speed limit** makes it a slow journey – the rule of thumb is to estimate that you will be driving at 25km/h between camps – and you're bound to make frequent stops to watch animals.

CHOOSING YOUR ROUTE

The **public section** of Kruger can be divided roughly into three sections, each with a distinct character and terrain. If your time is limited, it's best to choose just one or two areas to explore, but if you're staying for five days or more, consider driving the length of the park slowly, savouring the changes in landscape along the way. The southern, central and northern sections are sometimes referred to as "the circus", "the zoo" and "the wilderness" – sobriquets that carry more than a germ of truth. Each camp is like a small village in a vast area, with *Skukuza* in the south the largest.

The **southern section** has the greatest concentration of game, attracts the highest number of visitors and is the most easily accessible part of the park if you're coming from Johannesburg. The **central section** also offers good game viewing, as well as two of the most attractive camps in the park at *Olifants* and *Letaba*. The further north you go, the thinner both animal populations and visitors become, but it's the **northern section** that really conveys a sense of wilderness, reaching its zenith at the marvellously old-fashioned *Punda Maria* camp.

WHEN TO VISIT

Kruger is rewarding at any time of the year, though each season has its advantages and drawbacks. If you don't like the heat, avoid **high summer** (Dec–Feb), when temperatures are in the mid- to high thirties, with short thunder showers. At this time of the year, everything becomes green, the grass is high, animals are born and birdlife is prolific. There's little rain during the **cooler winter** months of April to August; the vegetation withers over this period, making it easier to spot game. Although daytime temperatures rise to the mid-twenties (days are invariably bright and sunny throughout winter), the nights and early mornings can be very cold, especially in June and July, when you'll definitely need a warm jacket and woolly hat. **September and October** are the peak months for wildlife viewing.

ACCOMMODATION

At most of the fourteen main **restcamps** inside Kruger, the sounds of the African night tend to get drowned out by air conditioning and the merriment of braais and beer. Nearly all camps have swimming pools, electricity, petrol stations, shops (though they don't stock much in the way of fruit or vegetables), restaurants and laundrettes. The restcamps are very pleasant, with walks around the edges, labelled trees to help you identify what you see on drives, and plenty of birds and smaller creatures around the camps themselves. You'll find thatched rondavels, each with an outdoor eating area, facing communally towards each other rather than out towards the views. The best rondavels are on the camp perimeters or directly facing onto rivers.

Just about all restcamps have a **campsite** (with shared kitchen and washing facilities), which provides the park's cheapest accommodation (from R150 per site), but the stands are generally very close together, and you may not get shade. Sites for caravans and camper vans are available wherever there's camping and often have a power point. Most camps have furnished safari tents and huts in configurations usually sleeping two to four people. These are fully equipped, with shared communal kitchens and ablutions. Bungalows, cottages and family cottages sleep two to six people and come in several variations, with fully equipped kitchens and bathrooms. For a couple expect to pay R700–1100 per night for accommodation, depending on facilities and position.

For a more rustic experience, head out to one of the handful of **bushveld camps** (from R1200) away from day-to-day trivialities and the tourist pack. The bushveld camps have accommodation of the same standard as the main restcamps, but accommodate fewer people, and are far smaller. They dispense with shops and restaurants, but are within reasonable reach of the restcamps.

Kruger's restcamps and bushveld camps are administered by SANParks (☎ 012 428 9111, ⓦ sanparks.org/parks/kruger) – the place to book accommodation in advance (though on the day, you can book directly with the camps). If you're planning on staying at the park at any time, particularly over school holidays or weekends, book well ahead as the park is often full. Booking opens thirteen months in advance.

SOUTHERN KRUGER RESTCAMPS

The so-called "circus" is the busiest section of the Kruger, with its hub at *Skukuza*, the biggest of all the Kruger camps, and *Lower Sabie*, one of the most popular. Apart from containing some of the best places for seeing large quantities of game, southern Kruger is also easily reached from Johannesburg along the N4. At peak times of year, the area buzzes with vehicles jostling to get up close anywhere that big cats are sighted – events which always seem to induce bad human behaviour.

Berg-en-Dal In the southwest corner of the park, 12km northwest of Malelane Gate ☎ 013 735 6106/6107; book with SANParks ☎ 012 428 9111, ⓦ sanparks.org /parks/kruger; map p.553. Set attractively among *koppies* in a shallow grassy basin (its Afrikaans name means "hill and dale"), *Berg-en-Dal* is best known for seeing rhino. Built in the 1980s, the camp overlooks the Matjulu stream and dam, and has modern, fully equipped chalets that break

9

with the Kruger tradition of thatched rondavels. The chalets are landscaped among indigenous bushveld vegetation and are widely spaced to provide privacy. Facilities include a beautifully positioned swimming pool, a shop with a good range of food, a licensed restaurant reputed to give excellent service, a snack bar, a filling station and a laundry.

Crocodile Bridge 12km north of Komatiport on N4 ☎013 735 6012; book with SANParks ☎012 428 9111, ⓦ sanparks.org/parks/kruger; map p.553. The least impressive of Kruger's restcamps, and its position at the very southern edge of the park, overlooking sugar-cane farms, does nothing to enhance your bush experience. However, old hands say this is a tremendously underrated camp as there is a high density of general game, and you have an excellent chance of seeing the Big Five. Moreover it is quiet and has a lovely campsite with plenty of big trees for shade. Accommodation includes camping, two-bed permanent tents and en-suite bungalows sleeping two to three, with cooking facilities. Amenities are limited to a laundry and filling station, and a shop selling basic supplies.

★ **Lower Sabie** 35km north of Crocodile Bridge ☎013 735 6056/6057; book with SANParks ☎012 428 9111, ⓦ sanparks.org/parks/kruger; map p.553. Often fully booked and very busy (book 13 months in advance), *Lower Sabie* occupies game-rich country, with an outlook over the Sabie River, which places it among the top three restcamps in the Kruger for animal-spotting. One of its biggest attractions is the large wooden viewing deck

outside the restaurant (open to day visitors) where you can have a snack while often watching elephants crossing the river in front of you. Accommodation includes camping, safari tents, bungalows and guest cottages, some with river views. There's a restaurant, a cafeteria, a shop, a swimming pool, a filling station and a laundry.

Pretoriuskop 9km east of Numbi Gate ☎013 735 5128/5132; book with SANParks ☎012 428 9111, ⓦ sanparks.org/parks/kruger; map p.553. Set in an area of sourveld, characterized by granite outcrops, tall grass and sickle bush favoured by mountain reedbuck, sable and white rhino, the camp is in an area stalked by lions, wild dogs and side-striped jackals. However, given the dense bush, game viewing is disappointing, and all you're likely to spot are larger species such as kudus and giraffes. Accommodation here consists of en-suite cottages and guesthouses, bungalows and cheaper huts, and camping with shared ablution and cooking facilities. The camp has a restaurant, a snack bar, a shop, a laundry, a semi-natural rock swimming pool – one of the most beautiful in Kruger, with a surrounding garden and picnic area – and a filling station. Around the perimeter fence at night, you're almost certain to see patrolling hyenas, waiting for scraps from braais. One feature of the camp is the tame impala which wander freely around.

Skukuza 12km east of Paul Kruger Gate ☎013 735 4152; book with SANParks ☎012 428 9111, ⓦ sanparks.org /parks/kruger; map p.553. Kruger's largest restcamp accommodates over a thousand people, has a conference centre and a large hotel in the offing, and lies at the centre of

---

KRUGER TOUR OPERATORS

There are many **tours** to Kruger, several of which depart from Johannesburg. Prices given below are per person unless otherwise noted, and most include park entry fees, meals and transport to and from Johannesburg. Backpacker hostels in Nelspruit, Hazyview and Phalaborwa also run tours into Kruger at reasonable prices. In addition, in the Nelspruit and Hazyview area are some excellent tour guides who will take you into the Park, or organize trips in Mpumalanga.

Livingstone Trails ☎082 654 9478, ⓦ livingstonetrails.co.za. Four-day trips from Johannesburg, taking in the spectacular Blyde River Canyon, and day and night drives in Kruger Park. You can choose camping (R4000) or bedded accommodation (R5000).

★ **Nguni Africa** ☎082 221 4177, ⓦ nguniafrica .co.za. Extremely knowledgeable and personable guide Andrew Hall, based in Nelspruit, can take you into the Park in a Land Rover, and you'll be sure to spot plenty of game. He also offers airport or lodge transfers and can put together a package for you to see the region.

Outlook Small Group Explorations ☎011 894 5406, ⓦ outlook.co.za. With a long menu of options departing from Jo'burg, you can choose whether to camp (R4400) on a three- day tour, have bedded

accommodation (R7700) on a four-day safari, or do a combo of Kruger and Sabi Sands for five days (R11,000).

Transfrontiers ☎082 388 5884, ⓦ transfrontiers .com. A reputable option if you want to walk in Kruger. On its five-day safaris (R6100), which depart regularly from Jo'burg hostels, you spend two nights in the Timbavati Reserve and two nights in Klaserie. Accommodation is in large tents with proper beds, duvets and pillows, and the guides are knowledgeable and fun. They also do trips into Mozambique.

Wildlife Safaris ☎011 791 4238 or ☎011 792 2080, ⓦ wildlifesaf.co.za. Three-day Kruger trips (R640), which are all in comfortable, en-suite rooms, departing from Johannesburg. Options include trips combining Kruger and KwaZulu-Natal parks, as well as Kruger and a private reserve.

WILDERNESS TRAILS

Undertaken with the guidance of an experienced ranger, Kruger's three-night **wilderness trails** (eight in different areas) pass through landscapes of notable beauty with diverse plant and animal life. However, they don't bring you nearer to game than driving; they're really about getting closer to the vegetation and smaller creatures, though you have a good chance of encountering big game. Groups are limited to eight people staying in the same camp, comprising four rustic, two-bed huts, served by reed-walled showers and flush toilets; simple meals are provided. You walk for five hours in the morning, return to the camp for lunch and a siesta, and go walking again for an hour or two in the evening, returning to sit around a campfire. The trails are heavily subscribed. You can **book** up to thirteen months in advance through SANParks (see p.554). The cost is around R3500 per person, including accommodation and meals. The only trail where you carry your own stuff is the **Olifants River backpack trail**, a guided, three-night trail, following the course of the Olifants River. If you want a more than average possibility of walking into big game, book Sweni or Metsi Metsi trails, while birding is best in the far north on Nyalaland Trail, and the trails that are closest to signs of civilization are Bushmans and Wolhuters near *Berg-en-Dal* in the south.

More expensive and a lot easier to get a booking on are the fabulous two- or three-night walking safaris in a magnificently wild concession near *Skukuza* with Rhino Post Walking Safaris (Ⓦisibindiafrica.co.za) who use *Plains Camp* as their base (see p.563), with the option of a sleep-out in a treehouse, where you spend the night cosily bedded on an elevated platform, able to see the stars and hear the sometimes chilling sounds of the night.

---

the best game-viewing area in the park. Its position is a mixed blessing; although you get large amounts of game, hordes of humans aren't far behind, and cars speeding at animal sightings can chase away the very animals they are trying to see. Accommodation is in a range of en-suite guesthouses, cottages and bungalows, or more cheaply in huts, safari tents and campsites, with shared ablutions and kitchens. *Skukuza* is the hub of Kruger; with its own airport (private airlines and charters only) and car-rental agency, and its sprawling collection of rondavels and staff village, it resembles a small town and all the cars can be irksome. There are two swimming pools, and a deli café with internet facilities, plus a post office, a bank, a filling station and garage, two restaurants, a cafeteria and a really good library (Mon–Fri 8.30am–4pm & 7–9pm, Sat 8.30am–12.45pm, 1.45–4pm & 7–9pm, Sun 8.30am–12.45pm & 1.45–4pm) with a collection of natural history books and exhibits. Golf at *Skukuza* is also a draw, where you'll have to sign an indemnity form in case of bumping into wildlife on the course. Night drives and day drives in open vehicles can be arranged at the main complex – the night drives are excellent, since all the other vehicles are safely tucked up for the night, and you'll have the road to yourself. If you're just driving through Skukuza, rather than staying over, there is a special area designated for day visitors, with its own swimming pool and picnic area.

CENTRAL KRUGER RESTCAMPS

Game viewing can be extremely good in the "zoo", the rough triangle between *Orpen*, *Satara* and *Letaba*, which is reckoned to be one of the global hot spots for lions. At *Olifants* you'll find the Kruger's most dramatically located

camp, with fantastic views into a river gorge, while *Satara* is one of the most popular – its placement is ideal for making sorties into fertile wildlife country. It is estimated that there are about sixty lion prides in this central area, but, even so, you may not be lucky enough to see one.

Balule On the southern bank of the Olifants River, 41km north of *Satara* and 87km from Phalaborwa Gate ☎013 735 6306 or 6307; book with SANParks ☎012 428 9111, Ⓦsanparks.org/parks/kruger; map p.553. A very basic satellite to *Olifants* (11km to the north), *Balule* is one of the few restcamps where two can stay for under R275 without resorting to camping. The restcamp has two sections, one consisting of six rustic three-bed rondavels and another of fifteen camping and caravan sites. Each section has its own communal ablution and cooking facilities. You can forget about a/c; the only electricity is in the fence to keep out lions. Guests have to bring their own crockery, cutlery and utensils, and must report to *Satara* or *Olifants* at least half an hour before the gates close.

Letaba 52km east of Phalaborwa Gate ☎013 735 6636/6637; book with SANParks ☎012 428 9111,

---

TOP 5 ACTIVITIES

Rhino Post Walking Safaris p.563
Birdwatching at Pafuri picnic site p.561
Rhino gazing at Pretoriuskop p.558
Leopard-spotting in the Sabi Sands p.563
Wildlife viewing at Sunset Dam, Lower Sabie p.558

GAME VIEWING AND PICNIC SITES IN SOUTHERN KRUGER

GAME VIEWING

Berg-en-Dal The focus of the camp is the Rhino Trail along the perimeter fence (with Braille facilities), meandering under riverine trees along the Matjulu dam, where there are resident crocodiles and nesting fish eagles. Game includes white rhino, leopards and lions, and plenty of kudu. Some say this is the best camp from which to set out on a morning walk, because of the high likelihood of encountering white rhino, and the pretty scenery.

Crocodile Bridge Try the tarred H4 north and dirt S25 east for elephant, rhino and buffalo. For cheetah, among the best places are the open plains along the S28 Nhola Road. If you're pushing north to *Lower Sabie*, it's worth taking the drive slowly, as this area, dotted with knobthorn and marula trees, is known for its herbivores, which include giraffe, wildebeest, zebra and buffalo, as well as ostrich, warthog and the magnificent black sable antelope. You should also keep your eyes peeled for predators such as lion, cheetah, hyena and jackal.

Lower Sabie The must-drive roads here include the H10 for lion and cheetah, the S130 for white rhino and the H4-1 for leopard. Sunset Dam, just outside *Lower Sabie*, is a favourite sunset spot, where you can get really close to the water, and is worthwhile at any time of day.

Pretoriuskop A decent focus for a day drive is Transport Dam, on the H1-1, a good place to see buffalo and elephant, and there's invariably other game to be found.

Skukuza Most people drive along the Sabie River to *Lower Sabie*, on the H4, one of the best places to see game. The tangled riverine forest, flanked by acacia bush and mixed savanna, is the most fertile and varied in the park. Another great drive is northeast on the H1–2 to Tshokwane picnic site, stopping at Elephant, Jones, Leeupan and Siloweni water holes. The area around *Skukuza* is also one of the best places to see endangered African wild dogs; worth trying is the S114 between Skukuza and Berg-en-Dal, the S1 between Phabeni Gate and Skukuza, and the H11 between Paul Kruger Gate and Skukuza.

PICNIC SITES

One of the park's nicest picnic sites is at **Afsaal**, between *Berg-en-Dal* and *Skukuza* on the H3, a good focus for a day drive. Once here, look out for the African scops-owl which sleeps in a tamboti tree nearly every day – the tree is marked so that you can try to spot the camouflaged bird. There's a shop on site.

Another top picnic spot is **Mlondozi**, north of *Lower Sabie* on the S29, which overlooks a dam from a thatched *lapa*, with some tables and chairs under trees. **Tshokwane** Picnic Site, 40km north of *Lower Sabie* on the H10, is much busier, but you can buy meals here.

ⓦ sanparks.org/parks/kruger; map p.553. *Letaba* is set in *mopane* shrubland along the Letaba River. Old and quite large, the camp is beautifully located on an oxbow curve, and though very few of the rondavels afford a view, the restaurant does have great vistas; you can spend a day just watching herds of buffalo mooching around, elephants drifting past and a host of other plains game. There is the full range of accommodation and the camp offers the usual shopping and laundry facilities, a swimming pool, a vehicle-repair workshop, and an interesting museum, Elephant Hall, with exhibits on the life of elephants, including a display on the Magnificent Seven, bulls with inordinately large tusks that once roamed the area, with six pairs of their tusks on display.

Olifants 80km east of Phalaborwa Gate ☎013 735 6606/6607; book with SANParks ☎012 428 9111, ⓦ sanparks.org/parks/kruger; map p.553. With a terrific setting on cliffs overlooking the braided Olifants River, *Olifants* has a charmingly old-fashioned feel and is reckoned by many

to be the best restcamp in Kruger. It's possible to spend hours sitting on the benches on the covered look-out terrace, gazing into the valley whose airspace is crisscrossed by Bateleur eagles and yellow-billed kites cruising the thermals, while the rushing of the water below creates a hypnotic rhythm. Of the thatched, en-suite rondavels, numbers 1–24 boast superb views overlooking the valley; it's worth booking well in advance to get one of these. There are also more exclusive guesthouses. You can eat at the restaurant or the snack bar, and there's a shop and a laundry. This is also promising country for spotting elephant, giraffe, lion, hyena and cheetah, and you should look out for the tiny klipspringer, a pretty antelope that inhabits rocky terrain which it nimbly negotiates by boulder-hopping. Mountain biking is available only at *Olifants*. Only six people at a time, accompanied by armed field guides, can go on the biking trails (hence it's best to book in advance through *Olifants* directly or SANPark), and the scenery is wonderful. The morning ride costs R440, while the afternoon ride is a bit cheaper and shorter.

GAME-VIEWING TIPS

- The best times of day for game viewing are when it's cooler, during the early morning and late afternoon. Set out as soon as the camp gates open in the morning and go out again as the temperature starts dropping in the afternoon. Take a siesta during the midday heat, just as the animals do, when they head for deep shade where you're less likely to see them.
- It's worth investing in a detailed **map of Kruger** (available at virtually every restcamp) in order to choose a route that includes rivers or pans where you can stop and enjoy the scenery and birdlife while you wait for game to come down to drink, especially in the late afternoon.
- **Driving really slowly** pays off, particularly if you stop often, in which case switch off your engine, open your window and use your senses. Stopping where other cars have already stopped or slowed down is probably the best strategy you could choose.
- Don't embark on overambitious drives from your restcamp. Plan carefully.
- **Binoculars** are a must for scanning the horizon.
- Take **food and drink** with you, and remember you can only use toilets and get out at the **picnic sites**, where there's always boiling water available, braai places powered with gas, and, at some sites, food or snacks for sale.

Orpen and Maroela Right by an entrance gate, 45km east of Klaserie ☎013 735 6355; book with SANParks ☎012 428 9111, ⓦsanparks.org/parks/kruger; map p.553. Recommended mainly if you're arriving late and don't have time to get further into the park before the camp gates close. However, *Orpen* is very good for game viewing, because the substantial Timbavati Private Game Reserve lies to the west, so you're already well into the wilderness once you get here. There's a waterhole right in front of the camp, and animals come and go all the time. The camp is small, peaceful and shaded by beautiful trees; facilities include a petrol station, a shop and a swimming pool overlooking a waterhole, and accommodation is in bungalows and en-suite guest cottages, with communal kitchens. If you want to camp, you'll need to go to the small *Maroela* satellite camping area, overlooking the Timbavati River, approximately 4km from *Orpen*. You must report to *Orpen* reception to check in before going to the campsite, which has electricity.

★ **Satara** 46km due east of Orpen Gate ☎013 735 6306/6307; book with SANParks ☎012 428 9111, ⓦsanparks.org/parks/kruger; map p.553. *Satara* ranks second only to *Skukuza* (92km to the south) in size and the excellence of its game viewing. Set in the middle of flat grasslands, the camp commands no great views, but is preferable to *Skukuza* because it avoids the feeling of suburban boxes on top of each other. Very busy in season, accommodation ranges from camping, through bungalows and cottages arranged around lawned areas shaded by large trees, to secluded guesthouses; besides a shop, petrol station, laundry and an AA vehicle repair workshop, there's also a swimming pool, restaurant and cafeteria, where you can eat in a virtual blizzard of noisy birds. *Satara* itself is usually good for sighting grazers such as buffalo, wildebeest, zebra, kudu, impala and elephant; the night drives are particularly recommended.

Tamboti Turn left 2km after *Orpen* and continue for 1km ☎013 735 6355; book with SANParks ☎012 428 9111, ⓦsanparks.org/parks/kruger; map p.553. Not far from Orpen Gate, *Tamboti* is Kruger's only tented camp. You sleep in tents (from R400) in a tranquil position on the banks of the frequently dry Timbavati River, set among apple leaf trees, sycamore figs and jackalberries. From the tents, elephants can often be seen just beyond the electrified fence, digging in the river bed for moisture,

GAME VIEWING AND PICNIC SITES IN CENTRAL KRUGER

The S100 or **N'wanetsi River Road** is one of the best-known drives in the park, with a stop at N'wanetsi Picnic Site, and beautiful scenery of riverine trees and open acacia savanna. It passes through a variety of terrain, which besides being scenic, means it attracts large herds of buffalo, giraffe, zebra, wildebeest, kudu and waterbuck and, in their wake, big cats. The S100 is one of the best roads to find lions.

Satara Rewarding drives are the Timbavati River Road (S39) and the drive east of Satara along the S100, which snakes along the N'wanetsi River towards the Lebombo Mountains marking the border with Mozambique.

About halfway along the tarred road between Satara and Skukuza, the area around **Tshokwane picnic site** can be good for lions, hence the number of motorists here.

9

hence the camp's popularity (you'll have to book ahead to be sure of getting a place). Each walk-in tent has its own deck overlooking the river, but best of all are numbers 21 and 22, which enjoy the deep shade of large riverine trees, something you'll appreciate in the midsummer heat. The tents have fridges and electric lighting, while all kitchen, washing and toilet facilities are in two shared central blocks (bring your own cooking and eating utensils).

NORTHERN KRUGER RESTCAMPS

You won't find edge-to-edge game in the northern "wilderness", the least visited of Kruger's regions, but you do get a much stronger feeling here of being in the wilds, particularly after you've crossed the Tropic of Capricorn north of *Mopani* camp and hit *Punda Maria* camp, which feels like a real old-time outpost in the bush.

Mopani 42km north of Letaba ☎013 735 6535/6536; book with SANParks ☎012 428 9111, ⊛sanparks.org/parks/kruger; map p.553. *Mopani* is one of the newer camps in Kruger and overlooks the Pioneer Dam. The dam, one of the few water sources in the vicinity, attracts animals to drink and provides an outstanding lookout for a variety of wildlife, including elephant, buffalo and antelope. This is a sprawling place in the middle of monotonous *mopane* scrub, with en-suite accommodation built of rough-hewn stone and thatch (no camping), and a restaurant and a bar with a good view across to the dam. Other facilities include a shop, a laundry and a petrol station; the swimming pool, one of the best in the park, provides cool relief after a long drive.

★ **Punda Maria and Pafuri** 71km beyond *Shingwedzi* ☎013 735 6873; book with SANParks ☎012 428 9111, ⊛sanparks.org/parks/kruger; map p.553. Kruger's northernmost camp is a relaxed, tropical outpost near the Zimbabwe border. To aficionados, this is the real Kruger, the park's wildest and least-visited camp, regarded as unpretentious and peaceful. There's less of a concentration of game up here, but this isn't to say you won't see wildlife (the Big Five all breeze through from time to time). The real rewards of *Punda* are in its landscapes and stunningly varied

vegetation, with a remarkable nine biomes all converging here, which also makes it a paradise for birdwatchers. The landscape around *Punda* has many craggy sandstone cliffs, the hilltops crowned with giant baobabs, some as old as 4000 years. Accommodation is camping, or in safari tents with communal cooking and ablution areas or en-suite fully equipped bungalows. The camp has a very simple restaurant, a small shop, a petrol station, a swimming pool and a bird hide. From Punda Maria you can go on a guided visit to the spectacular historical and archeological site of Thulamela with its majestic location – overlooking the confluence of the Luvuvhu and Limpopo rivers (R250 per person).

Shingwedzi 63km north of Mopani ☎013 735 6806/6807; book with SANParks ☎012 428 9111, ⊛sanparks.org/parks/kruger; map p.553. A fairly large camp featuring a campsite, square, brick huts and a few older, colonial-style whitewashed, thatched bungalows, as well as a cottage and a guesthouse, sited in extensive grounds shaded by *pals* and *mopane* trees. The dining room has a terrace, frequented by starlings and cheeky hornbills jostling to pounce on your food. From the terrace you get a long view down across the usually dry Shingwedzi River. Look out for the weavers' nests with their long, tube-like entrances hanging from the eaves outside reception and the cafeteria. Facilities include a shop, a petrol station and a swimming pool, and night drives are on offer.

Tsendze 10km south of Mopani; book with SANParks ☎012 428 9111, ⊛sanparks.org/parks/kruger; map p.553. One of the quietest and wildest places to camp in the park, with no generators allowed and no facilities other than communal ablution blocks.

BUSHVELD CAMPS

If you want to stay at a bushveld camp, book as early as possible, as demand for the bush experience they offer is pretty high. Note that the camps are out of bounds to anyone not booked in to stay. Most offer game drives during the day and at night.

★ **Bateleur** About 40km southwest of *Shingwedzi* restcamp ☎013 735 6843; book with SANParks ☎012

HIDING OUT IN KRUGER

One of the highlights of Kruger is to do sunset and a sleepover in **Sable Hide** (book at Phalaborwa Gate ☎013 735 3547), next to Sable Dam, about 43km from *Letaba*, close to the Phalaborwa Gate. You may take occupation of the hide thirty minutes before the gate closes; bedding, a braai grid and light are provided at Phalaborwa Gate. Full moon is best to watch animals coming to drink. You can stay in the hide for one night only, and it is hired out exclusively for your group (R415 for two people).

The park's other overnight hide, **Shipandani Hide** (R415), 3km to the south of *Mopani*, is best done in the cooler months, as mosquitoes are bad in the summer; you collect your bedding and lamp from **Mopani**. Set on the Tsendze River, you will hear hippos grunting all night.

Lake Panic, only a twenty-minute drive (7km) from *Skukuza* (see p.556), has one of the best hides in the park, where you'll see herons, kingfishers, ducks, geese, dikkop and African jacanas, as well as hippos and crocodiles.

GAME VIEWING AND PICNIC SITES IN NORTHERN KRUGER

The S52 **Red Rocks Loop** southwest of Shingwedzi is a favoured road for elephant sightings, and if you drive it in the early morning, look out for leopards.

★ **Pafuri picnic site** 46km north of *Punda*. This picnic site should on no account be missed, as it's here that you'll experience the true richness of northern Kruger, and it is rated as the top birding spot in the park. The site is a large area under the shade of massive thorn trees, leadwoods and jackalberry trees on the banks of the Luvuvhu River and is the ultimate place for lunch. An interpretation board gives a fascinating account of human history in the area. There are braai facilities, a constantly boiling kettle to make your own tea, and the attendant can sell you ice-cold canned drinks.

428 9111, ⓦ sanparks.org/parks/kruger; map p.553. Well off the beaten track, in the remote northern section of the park on the banks of the frequently dry Mashokwe stream. The camp has a timber viewing-deck, excellently placed for views of game coming to drink at a seasonally full water hole. The nearby Silver Fish and Rooibosrand dams also attract game as well as birdlife in prodigious quantities. There are three six-bed cottages and four four-bed cottages; each has its own kitchenette and fridge, with electricity provided by solar panels.

★ **Biyamiti** 41km northeast of the Malelane Gate and 26km west of Crocodile Bridge Gate ☎ 013 735 6171; book with SANParks ☎ 012 428 9111, ⓦ sanparks.org /parks/kruger; map p.553. *Biyamiti* lies on the banks of the Mbiyamiti River. Its proximity to the latter is one of the main advantages of this very southerly camp, and the surrounding terrain attracts large numbers of game including lion, elephant and rhinos. There are ten two-bed guest cottages and five one-bed cottages, all with fully equipped kitchens.

Shimuwini About 50km from the Phalaborwa Gate on the Mooiplaas Rd ☎ 013 735 6683; book with SANParks ☎ 012 428 9111, ⓦ sanparks.org/parks /kruger; map p.553. *Shimuwini* lies on the upper reaches of the Shimuwini Dam, which is filled by the Letaba River. Situated in *mopane* and bushwillow country, with sycamore figs along the banks of the river, this peaceful camp is not known for its game but is a perennial favourite among bird-watchers. It's an excellent place for spotting riverine bird species, including fish eagles. Accommodation is in five two-bedroom cottages, nine more elite two-bedroom guest cottages, and one three-bedroom guest cottage.

Sirheni Roughly 54km south of Punda Maria ☎ 013

735 6860; book with SANParks ☎ 012 428 9111, ⓦ sanparks.org/parks/kruger; map p.553. *Sirheni* is on the bank of Sirheni Dam. It's a fine spot for birdwatching, beautifully tucked into riverine forest, with some game also passing through the area. The big pull, however, is its remote bushveld atmosphere in an area that sees few visitors. There are five four-bedroom cottages and ten guest cottages, all en suite and equipped with kitchens. The camp's two bird hides are a great pull.

Talamati About 31km south of Orpen Gate ☎ 013 735 6343; book with SANParks ☎ 012 428 9111, ⓦ sanparks .org/parks/kruger; map p.553. Lying on the banks of the usually dry Nwaswitsontso stream, the mixed bushwillow woodland setting of *Talamati* attracts giraffe, kudu, wildebeest, zebra and predators like lion, hyena and jackal, as well as rhino and sable. Two hides within the perimeter of the camp overlook a water hole, where game viewing can be excellent. The camp has ten comfortable two-bedroom and four smaller one-bedroom cottages arranged in an L-shape along the river in a forest of leadwoods and russet bushwillows.

Tzendze Rustic Camp 7km south of *Mopani* ☎ 013 735 6535 or 6536; book with SANParks ☎ 012 428 9111, ⓦ sanparks.org/parks/kruger; map p.553. The back-to-basics *Tzendze Rustic Camp* caters for those who wish to escape the typical Kruger camp vibe. There is no electricity here – the lighting in the ablutions is from a solar battery system and hot water in the outdoor showers is from gas geysers. There are thirty camping sites (sites 14, 15 and 16 are best; R150 per site), but as each is surrounded by trees and scrub the atmosphere is wild and rustic. The nearest shop is at *Mopani*.

Private reserves – Greater Kruger

Kruger's western flank is comprised of private reserves, whose boundaries with Kruger are unfenced – the whole zone is often referred to as **Greater Kruger**. Within each reserve are a number of gorgeous safari lodges, each on a large tract of land. Some establishments have three different lodges on their properties, each one different in character, and with some price variations.

It's in these private reserves that you'll find utterly luxurious and romantic accommodation, fabulous food and classic safaris on Land Rovers, where you'll see

9

plenty of big game, smaller animals and birds. All lodges follow the same basic formula: full board, with dawn and late-afternoon game drives conducted by a ranger, assisted by a tracker, in open vehicles. Afternoon outings usually turn into night drives following sundowners in the bush. In winter months you'll be given blankets on the vehicle and even hot water bottles in some places, to cope with the cold. Dinners are inevitably lamplit, around a fire, in the open. Several offer bushwalks, usually after breakfast, and most overlook water holes, rivers or plains, so that you can look out for animals during the time you're in camp, when you're not lazing around the pool, making use of the spa or gym facilities or perusing their collection of animal books on gigantic sofas.

The **Sabi Sands reserve** (ⓦsabi.krugerpark.co.za) is one of the best places in the world for seeing leopards and lions. **Sabi Sands South** is the most exclusive of all the game-viewing areas in South Africa, not only because of the superb game, but also because of its proximity to Nelspruit, and by car it's a two- to three-hour easy run to the lodges from KMIA airport. **Sabi Sands North** is cheaper, and the game is good, but access is more difficult. From the R40 you turn east at Acornhoek, travelling along dirt roads through traditional African villages for a couple of hours to reach the lodges. The same goes for **Manyeleti**, north of Sabi Sands. **Timbavati** is the most northerly reserve, accessed from the Orpen Gate road, but easier to reach, with far less travelling on dirt roads, than either Manyeleti or Sabi Sands North.

ACCOMMODATION   PRIVATE RESERVES

Prices are undeniably very steep in the private reserves – you're paying for the African wilderness experience, and for rangers who are dedicated to showing you as much as possible. Prices quoted below include all meals and all game activities. You need to book ahead, and get driving instructions to your camp, as no pop-ins are allowed.

MANYELETI
Honeyguide 4km from Orpen Gate ☎011 341 0282, ⓦhoneyguidecamp.com; map p.553. One of the more reasonably priced camps, and the only one to offer tented accommodation at each of its two locations, *Khoka Moya* which takes children and is contemporary in design, and *Mantobeni*, which has more of a traditional safari camp feel. With a lack of tended gardens, the camps maximize the bush feel, and although they don't have views of a river or a water hole, they make up for it with attentive staff and superb rangers and trackers. Each tent is enormous and has its own bathroom with double showers and basins. The best thing about *Honeyguide* is that there is an imaginative children's programme, and great tolerance of children of all

ages. Rangers will take your kids off your hands and make casts of animal tracks in the bush, teach them about wildlife and in the evenings sit them on cushions around the campfire. Meals are plated, and all beverages, including wine, are included in the price. <u>R7700</u>

TIMBAVATI
Shindzela 33km inside the reserve, accessed from Timbavati Gate ☎015 793 1578, ⓦshindzela.co.za; map p.553. *Shindzela's* draw is its small size, affordability and walking opportunities. It is a twelve-bed unfenced, no-frills tented lodge, with early morning walks of two to four hours, or game drives if you prefer. They also do transfers from Johannesburg. <u>R3200</u>

WILDLIFE IN THE PRIVATE RESERVES

In terms of **wildlife**, if it's leopards you're after, Sabi Sands is best, especially in the south, where they have become quite blasé about people and vehicles. Timbavati is much quieter and wilder than Sabi Sands, and is known for its large herds of buffalo, with plenty of lions and elephants, though it's not good for viewing leopards and cheetah. Timbavati's name is associated with the extraordinary phenomenon of **white lions**, and while you may see some prides carrying the recessive gene which makes them look a little paler, the last sighting of an adult white lion was in 1993 – though a dozen cubs have been born since, but with the high mortality rate, it is not known whether two which were doing well in 2010 have survived. Manyeleti has a good spread of all game, with some stirring landscapes of open grasslands and rocky outcrops, where it borders Kruger. During the apartheid days, Manyeleti was the only part of Kruger black people were allowed in, and consequently is far less developed than the other reserves, with little accommodation, which works to its advantage in that there are fewer vehicles about.

Umlani Close to Orpen Gate, accessed from Orpen Rd ☎021 785 5547, ⓦumlani.com; map p.553. Eight reed-walled huts overlooking the dry Nhlaralumi River, each with an attached open-topped bush shower, heated by a wood boiler (there's no electricity). *Umlani* (meaning "place of rest") isn't fenced off, the emphasis being very much on a bush experience, and windows are covered with flimsy blinds so that you get to hear all the sounds of the night. The decor is simple, as is the food, though it's delicious and you don't end up overstuffed. Altogether, *Umlani* delivers a much more satisfying experience of the wilds than many other places, and offers very good value. R6050

SABI SANDS NORTH

Chitwa Chitwa Game Lodge ☎011 883 1354, ⓦchitwa.co.za; map p.553. Beautifully set on the edge of the largest *pan* (lake) in the Sabi Sands, where you'll definitely see animals coming to drink as well as resident hippos and crocodiles, *Chitwa Chitwa* provides both luxury and the chance to spot big cats, but keeps its rates a bit lower than high-profile neighbours to the south. It's the prettiest of the northern Sabi Sands lodges, and each comfy suite has a fireplace and a view of the water. Two swimming pools allow kids to use one, and adults to enjoy lengths in the other. R10,000

Djuma Game Reserve ☎013 735 5118 or ☎07967 97528, ⓦdjuma.com; map p.553. The best of *Djuma's* camps is *Vuyatela*, combining a hip, contemporary African feel with township art and funky fittings, plus good wildlife spotting. Each five-star suite has its own plunge pool and mini-bar. Moreover, there is a library, gym and wellness centre for massages and beauty treatments. *Djuma* is one of the more socially-minded establishments, with traditional village trips organized during the day between game drives, and they support preschools in Dixi village. R9000

Nkorho Bush Camp ☎013 735 5367, ⓦnkorho.com; map p.553. A small, family-operated outfit in thinly wooded grassland, *Nkorho* scores on affordability. There are six simple chalets with showers, catering to a maximum of sixteen guests. The communal areas comprise an open-air lounge, a bar with a pool table and an African fantasy of a *boma* – constructed from gnarled tree trunks – where evening meals are served around an open fire. The swimming pool overlooks a productive water hole. R5520

SABI SANDS SOUTH

⭐ **Lion Sands** ☎011 484 9911/9916, ⓦlionsands.com; map p.553. The top game lodge at present in Sabi Sands if you want a suite and bathroom, which couldn't, more romantic or beautiful, overlooking the Sabi River. *River Lodge*, with eighteen suites, has plenty of friendly staff to cater to every need, including your own butler who sees to you at your table under the trees next to the river,

combined with terrific game viewing. The food is top-notch, and two swimming pools, heated in winter, are placed right next to the river so you can hang out and watch the hippos. Adjoining *River Lodge* is *Ivory Lodge*, which offers more privacy and exclusivity, and each suite has its own pool. *River Lodge* R11,700, *Ivory Lodge* R19,000

⭐ **Nottens Bush Camp** ☎013 735 5105, ⓦnottens.com; map p.553. Four decades old and still resisting the temptation to expand, this family-run outfit feels as if you are staying on a sociable friend's farm. Meals are served around a fire, or on a massive deck that acts as a viewing platform. The camp houses just eighteen (children over 8 welcome) in large tin-roofed chalets, facing the plain and lit by paraffin oil lamps. The lack of electricity in the bedrooms is meant to bring guests into better contact with the bush. It offers very good value for a five-star game-viewing experience, and has a swimming pool where you can actually do laps, next to the massage room. R7000

Sabi Sabi ☎011 447 7172, ⓦsabisabi.com; map p.553. *Sabi Sabi* has four different lodges, situated in a wildlife-rich area, of which the largest, *Bush Lodge*, can't fail to please if you are looking for more of a hotel experience, with a larger number of guests, than what you'll find at an intimate safari camp. The suites with indoor and outdoor showers all have patios; children are welcomed at *Bush Lodge*, and there are DVDs and TVs to watch if you desire. R13,000

OTHER CONCESSIONS

Tinga Legends Lodge Close to Skukuza, on the banks of the Sabi River ☎011 880 9992, ⓦtinga.co.za; map p.553. *Tinga* guests can be driven around the massive concession where no other vehicles can be seen, as well as on the network of public roads in Kruger. The riverside suites, each with a deck overlooking the water, heated plunge pool and baths where you can gaze at the river, are simply gorgeous. R14,500

⭐ **Rhino Post Walking Safaris and Plains Camp** ☎035 474 1473 or ☎011 467 1886, ⓦisibindiafrica.co.za; map p.553. Two safari camps on this magnificent, wild concession near *Skukuza*, offering different experiences. *Rhino Post Lodge* has eight suites built out of stone, wood and thatch, above a sandy river bed, while *Plains Camp* has four super-comfy safari tents, overlooking a plain that is rarely absent of game. *Plains Camp*, simply furnished in a pioneer style, is marvellously peaceful with a maximum of eight guests, and has been built with no trees cut down or concrete used, and is solar powered. For an ultimate wilderness experience, walk with a superbly informed armed guide to the tree-house overnight camp, which has basic beds under mosquito nets set on high wooden platforms, where you hear all the African night sounds. R5900

Limpopo

BAOBAB TREES

Limpopo

Limpopo Province is considered by many to be South Africa's no-man's-land: a hot, thornbush-covered area caught between the dynamic heartland of Gauteng to the south and, to the north, the Limpopo River, which acts as South Africa's border with Zimbabwe and Botswana. The real highlights of Limpopo are often overshadowed by the busy N1 highway, South Africa's umbilical cord to the rest of the continent, which dissects the province. But this is where you'll find vast open spaces with wildlife galore and breathtaking mountainous landscapes covered in mist, all accessible at lower prices than elsewhere in the country. Culturally, Limpopo also stands out: seven of South Africa's eleven official languages are spoken here, and you stand a good chance of meeting people from the majority of the country's ethnic groupings while travelling around the province. The region is also well endowed with a remarkable and ever-increasing number of wildlife and nature reserves, housing the country's highest population of rhinos and a multitude of elegant species of antelope, and ensuring that there is brilliant game viewing to be had.

The eastern side of the province is lowveld, dominated by the 70km-wide strip of Kruger National Park abutting the Mozambique border. This part of Limpopo is covered, along with Kruger itself, in the preceding chapter. The principal attractions of the rest of the province lie in its three wild and distinctive **mountain escarpments**. The best known of these is the **Drakensberg** Escarpment, making the descent from highveld to lowveld through lush forests in the Letaba to the west of Kruger.

Polokwane, the provincial capital, lies west of the Drakensberg along the N1, while further to the west lies the sedate **Waterberg** massif, a region dedicated to wildlife conservation and offering malaria-free Big Five game viewing. In the north, parallel to the Limpopo River and bisected by the N1, are the subtropical **Soutpansberg Mountains**, and the intriguing and still very independently minded **Venda** region, a homeland during the apartheid era, to the east. North of the Soutpansberg are wide plains dominated by surreal baobab trees, much in evidence along the N1 as it leads to the only border post between South Africa and Zimbabwe, at Beitbridge. Hugging the border to the west, stifling hot Mapungubwe National Park provides a fascinating insight into what is now recognized as Africa's earliest kingdom.

The N1 is, by South African standards, fast and easy, if often busy. It's a **toll road**, with five toll stops along the way from Johannesburg to the border with Zimbabwe costing roughly R20 each time. As regards **public transport**, SA Roadlink, City to City and Translux buses ply the N1 between Johannesburg and the Musina border post, stopping at Polokwane and Makhado. Translux also runs buses between Tzaneen and Johannesburg via Polokwane. In addition, these and other routes are covered by

Highlights

❶ Exploring the Letaba Experience this otherworldly area of lush forests, subtropical tea plantations and upmarket country-house guesthouses, and the quirky, time-warped town of Haenertsburg in its midst. **See p.573**

❷ Horseriding in the Waterberg This mountain range offers some of South Africa's finest wilderness riding and horseback safaris, with outrides among zebra and giraffe, and the occasional rhino tagging along. **See p.576**

❸ Mapungubwe archeology Climb the Hill of Jackals and see the remains of Africa's earliest kingdom, then continue to the fantastic nearby San cave paintings. **See p.583**

❹ Soutpansberg Mountains Spend the night in the mountains watching the magical display of stars above and let the soothing sound of the gushing waterfall gently lull you to sleep. **See p.580**

❺ Venda crafts Explore the remote, simple villages of the mystical Venda region and discover its skilful and distinctive art, pottery and woodcarvings. **See p.583**

HIGHLIGHTS ARE MARKED ON THE MAP ON P.568–569

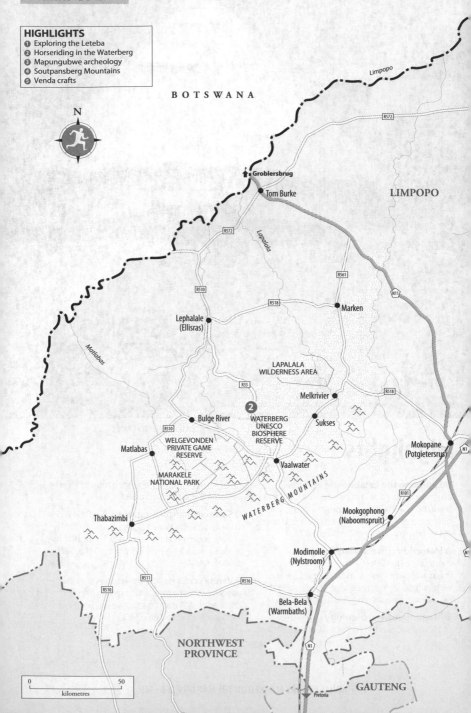

LIMPOPO

N

BOTSWANA

Limpopo

R572

LIMPOPO

Groblersbrug

Tom Burke

R572

Lapalala

R561

R10

R518

N11

Marken

Lephalale
(Ellisras)

LAPALALA
WILDERNESS AREA

Matlabas

R33

Melkrivier

R518

2

WATERBERG
UNESCO
BIOSPHERE
RESERVE

Sukses

Bulge River

R510

Mokopane
(Potgietersrus)

N1

WELGEVONDEN
PRIVATE GAME
RESERVE

Matlabas

Vaalwater

MARAKELE
NATIONAL PARK

R101

Thabazimbi

WATERBERG MOUNTAINS

Mookgophong
(Naboomspruit)

N1

Modimolle
(Nylstroom)

R511

R510

R516

Bela-Bela
(Warmbaths)

NORTHWEST
PROVINCE

N1

GAUTENG

0 — 50
kilometres

Pretoria

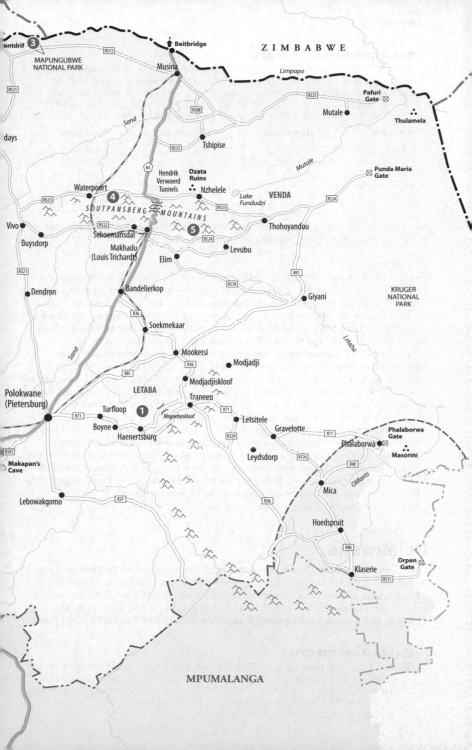

10

NAME CHANGES IN LIMPOPO

What was once known as South Africa's Northern Province was renamed **Limpopo** in 2002, and the capital, Pietersburg, was subsequently renamed **Polokwane**. A number of other towns with "colonial" names have also undergone official name changes, though some of these changes have been taken to court for various political and procedural reasons. Examples of these that you are bound to come across while travelling in the province include:

Old name	New name	Old name	New name
Ellisras	Lephalale	Nylstroom	Modimolle
Louis Trichardt	Makhado	Potgietersrus	Mokopane
Messina	Musina	Warmbaths	Bela-Bela
Naboomspruit	Mookgophong		

---

minibus taxis from any moderately sized town; the best way to find out where they're going and when they depart is to enquire at the taxi rank.

Brief history

The first black Africans arrived in South Africa across the Limpopo River some time before 300 AD. The various movements and migrations, and of course trading, ensured a fluidity in the people who established themselves here, and the historical and cultural ties to the north are, as you might expect, stronger in this region than in other parts of South Africa. Traditional arts and crafts such as **pottery** and **woodcarving** are still an important part of life; and **witchcraft** is still encountered in many places.

The arrival of the **Voortrekkers** in the early nineteenth century brought profound changes to the region. Their route roughly followed that of the N1 today, and brought about the founding of the towns now called Bela-Bela, Modimolle and Polokwane, among others. The Voortrekkers who ventured this far north were determined people, and their conflicts with the local peoples were notoriously bitter. In 1850, at **Makapan's Cave** off the N1 near Mokopane, several thousand Ndebele were starved to death by an avenging Boer commando, while further to the north, in 1867, Venda troops forced the Voortrekkers to abandon the settlement they had established at **Schoemansdal** in the Soutpansberg.

In the twentieth century, the apartheid years saw several large chunks of the province hived off as homeland areas, with Venda becoming notionally independent and Lebowa and Gazankulu self-governing. Today the contrasts between the old homelands and the white farming areas are manifest throughout the province, although in 2009 the province voted overwhelmingly in favour of the ANC.

Polokwane

Lying almost dead centre in the province of which it is the capital, **Polokwane** is the largest city on the Great North Road between Pretoria and the border. It's mostly an administrative and industrial centre, and much of its energy derives from the large volume of traffic moving through the city on the N1. But it does have an excellent museum, and if you're heading towards the lowveld or central Kruger National Park,

---

MALARIA IN LIMPOPO

Parts of Limpopo are **malarial**; you will need to take prophylactics, and exercise caution against mosquitoes if you are travelling in the lowveld, including Kruger National Park, or north of the Soutpansberg Mountains. The Waterberg area was not affected at the time of writing, though it's worth double-checking the current situation with your accommodation or safari provider before you go.

Polokwane is the point to connect with the R71 to Phalaborwa. The clutch of similar-looking one-way streets in the downtown area are all laid out in strict grid pattern, making navigation, especially by car, almost impossible.

Civic Square

At the heart of Polokwane's busy, compact CBD is the **Civic Square**, a park area bounded on two sides by Landros Mare and Thabo Mbeki streets. Streets on either side are abuzz with the bustle from street traders competing with stores and selling anything from top designer gear to Chinese enamelware.

Bakone Malapa Museum

9km southeast of town on the R37 • Mon–Fri 8am–4.30pm, Sat 9am–3.30pm • R7.50

The only sight in town really worth seeing is the open-air **Bakone Malapa Museum**. A simple but genuine project, it succeeds in conveying some of the old way of life of the local Bakone people – a grouping within the Northern Sotho – where many flashier examples have fallen short. A village of huts has been built in the traditional style, and ten people live permanently on site, working on crafts such as pottery and leatherworking through the day. One of them also acts as a guide, and will explain the different activities you see, as well as the architecture, history and legends of the site.

ARRIVAL AND DEPARTURE   POLOKWANE

All intercity buses (5 daily; 4–5hr) pass through the centre of town: Translux and City-to-City stop in front of their ticket office on Thabo Mbeki St, a stone's throw from Civic Square. SA Roadlink buses stop at their ticket office, also on Thabo Mbeki St, directly in front of the *Garden Court* hotel.

By plane Gateway Airport, on the N1 5km north of the city (☎015 288 0122, ⊛gaal.co.za), is served by domestic flights to Johannesburg (SA Airlink ☎015 288 0166, flyairlink.com; Mon–Fri 4 daily, Sat & Sun 2–3 daily; 1hr) and occasional

international connections from neighbouring countries. All the city's car-rental firms are here including Avis (☎015 288 0171), Budget (☎015 288 0169) and Europcar (☎015 288 0097). Taxis are also lined up outside (☎015 297 4493).

By train The train station (☎015 299 6202) is on the northern edge of the city centre, just off the R521 (an extension of Market St). At the time of writing the daily train between Johannesburg and Mussina had been cancelled indefinitely. Check ⊛shosholoza-meyl.co.za for the latest details.

INFORMATION

Tourist information There are two tourist information offices in Polokwane. One is the municipal tourist information service (Mon–Fri 7.30am–5pm, Sat 9am–1pm; ☎015 290 2010) at the Civic Square, which can help with information about the city's accommodation, attractions and transport. The other is Limpopo Tourism and Parks, on the outskirts of town on the western side of

the N1 when coming from Johannesburg (Mon–Fri 8am–4.30pm; ☎015 293 3600, ⊛golimpopo.com), which runs a provincial service and stocks an array of brochures and maps. There is also a helpful budget travellers' tourist agent, SA Tours and Bookings (☎082 375 3870, ⊜satours@mweb.co.za), at *Plumtree Lodge* (see below).

ACCOMMODATION

African Roots Guesthouse 58a Devenish St ☎015 297 0113, ⊛africanroots.info; map p.572. On the corner of Oost St at the eastern edge of the city centre, this is a relaxed, tasteful spot with immaculate and stylish rooms given character by local and foreign works of art selected by the designer proprietors. The breakfast restaurant also serves evening meals on request. Wi-fi throughout. R700

Garden Court On the corner of Thabo Mbeki and Bok St ☎015 291 2030, ⊛southernsun.com; map p.572. Large modern hotel complex, a short walk from Civic Square, and

super convenient if you're catching an early morning inter-city bus. Rooms are predictable but decent enough, and there's a good restaurant and an outdoor pool. Half price at weekends. R1120

Pietersburg Club 122 South St ☎015 291 2900; map p.572. Four blocks from Civic Square, this traditional gentlemen's club has taken the leap into the twenty-first century and now offers comfortable en-suite rooms, some with garden-facing verandas ideal for sipping sundowners. The club also encompasses an excellent restaurant and a

10

10

bizarre remnant from days gone by, a men-only bar. The "members only" sign at the club entrance refers only to residents of Polokwane. Free wi-fi throughout. **R700**

★ **Plumtree Lodge** 138 Marshall St ☎ 015 295 6153, ⊛ plumtree.co.za; map p.572. Not far from the centre, this is one of the city's oldest and most efficiently run lodges, with smart rooms set around a large compound and garden, a poolside bar, and breakfasts to die for. This is probably the friendliest and most comfortable place to stay

in town. Cheaper rates (R595) over the weekend and wi-fi available at reception. **R775**

Victoria Place Guest House 32 Burger St ☎ 015 295 7599, ⊛ victoriaplace.co.za; map p.572. Situated a short walk east of the centre. As the name implies, a Victorian-style guesthouse, consisting of fourteen individualistic en-suite rooms in three separate buildings and a self-catering section across the street. Known especially for its hearty breakfasts. **R760**

EATING

True to its functional role, Polokwane has no shortage of chain restaurants and takeaways. The largest collection of these can be found at the two malls: Savannah Mall and the new upmarket Platinum Park shopping centre, both on the western fringes of the city.

Ambience 34a Rabe St ☎ 015 291 4012; map p.572. Classy, contemporary restaurant serving tasty light meals, including a range of wraps, quiches and salad, as well as a range of less healthy but equally delicious cakes and teatime treats. Seating is also available outside in a pretty garden. Mon–Fri 8am–9pm, Sat 8am–5pm.

Nguni Grill De Wet Drive ☎ 082 314 8788; map p.572. On the corner of Morris St, this is a proper steak house serving weird things like puff adder sausages (not really puff adder but sausages made of minced kidney and liver), grilled tortoise (actually lamb's liver) and lots of other

unusual but tasty meat dishes. Tues–Sat 11am–11pm, Sun 11am–4pm.

Rhapsody's Platinum Park shopping centre ☎ 015 297 1296, ⊛ www.rhapsodys.co.za; map p.572. Part of a national chain of fine dining restaurants, *Rhapsody's* branch in Polokwane specializes in beautiful slow-cooked lamb shank (R195). This is also a great place for breakfast, with about ten different options such as poached eggs served with spinach and hollandaise sauce, and a full-on traditional English fry-up. Mon–Thurs 7am–10.30pm, Fri 7am–11pm, Sat 8am–11pm, Sun 9am–3pm.

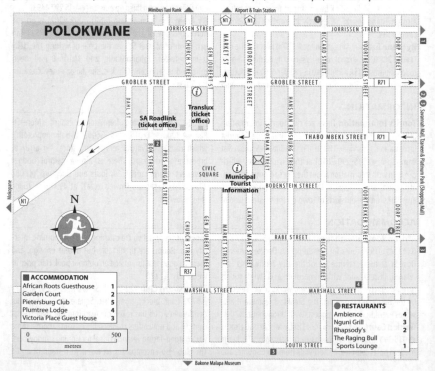

POLOKWANE

■ ACCOMMODATION
African Roots Guesthouse 1
Garden Court 2
Pietersburg Club 5
Plumtree Lodge 4
Victoria Place Guest House 3

● RESTAURANTS
Ambience 4
Nguni Grill 3
Rhapsody's 2
The Raging Bull Sports Lounge 1

The Raging Bull Sports Lounge and Grill 77 Biccard St, opposite ANC headquarters ☎ 015 297 7440; map p.572. A popular sports pub, with televisions in every corner, showing different sporting events simultaneously. With an affordable grill menu, and occasional DJing in the evening which packs out the dancefloor, *Raging Bull* is also the place to head for a fun night out. Mon–Thurs 8am to midnight, Fri & Sat 8am–2am, Sun 8am–4pm.

Letaba

East of Polokwane, the **Letaba** is a forested, lush, mountainous area, contrasting very sharply with the hot lowveld and bushveld abutting it east towards Kruger and west towards Polokwane. It marks the first dramatic rise of the Drakensberg Escarpment as it begins its sweep south through Mpumalanga. The forest begins around the mountain village of **Haenertsburg** and follows two very scenic parallel valleys to Limpopo's second-largest but missable town, **Tzaneen**. The valleys are filled with lakes surrounded by dark pine forests, sparkling rivers, misty peaks and, towards Tzaneen, subtropical crops such as macadamia nuts and avocados. With some very comfortable and beautifully located guesthouses, farm-stalls and tea rooms, hiking trails and trout fishing, the Letaba is in many ways an attractive, less-well-known alternative to Mpumalanga's crowded highlands, although it is gradually making solid inroads onto the tourist route.

10

Haenertsburg

Mellow **Haenertsburg** lies 60km from Polokwane, high on a hillside tucked away behind the R71 as the road winds down into the thickly wooded Magoebaskloof Valleys. Once an old gold-rush village, Haenertsburg has wonderful views over the area known as the Land of the Silver Mist; that is, when it's not covered in a light carpet of mist that gives it its nickname. With no fences or gates to protect private property, the town has an unusual and unmistakable time-warped feel to it – as if existing within an isolated bubble. This is apparently due to the town's many eccentric residents, some of whom are said to use otherworldly powers to protect the town. There's not much more to Haenertsburg that its **main street**, Rissik Street, which is lined with various quaint olde-worlde shops, including a secondhand bookshop, art gallery and antique and curio shops.

INFORMATION   HAENERTSBURG

Tourist information Situated next door to *Pennefather* on Rissik St (ⓦ magoebaskloeftourism.co.za).

ACCOMMODATION

There a plenty of places to stay in the Haenertsburg area, and the two roads to Tzaneen are literally littered with B&B signs. The ones listed below are the most convenient places for visiting the town; accommodation along the two routes is covered on p.575.

BaliWillWill Farm D3 Rd D ☎015 276 2212, ⓔ glmccomb@absamail.co.za; map p.574. 1.5km into the hills west of Haenertsburg, this is a beautiful and peaceful spot – and a working farm – with B&B rooms in the farmhouse and two self-catering flats in an old farm building. There's also a shady area for camping at the back with showers, a kitchen area and a braii. Camping R50, double R440

Glenshiel 2km east of Haenertsburg on the R71 ☎ 015 276 4335, ⓦ glenshiel.co.za; map p.574. *Glenshiel* is one of the finer old country lodges in South Africa, with roaring

---

THE CHANGUION HIKING TRAIL

A 10km circular historical **hiking trail** – the Changuion Trail – runs south of Haenertsburg through beautiful grassland and indigenous afromontane forest, offering stunning panoramic views of the Drakensberg Escarpment. It's well worth setting time aside to do the trail, which takes roughly four hours at a leisurely pace. Look out especially for the blue swallow, Methuens Dwarf gecko and the delicate and rare Wolkberg Zulu butterfly. A map of the route is painted on the wall outside The Elm by the tourist office.

10

fires, deep sofas, antiques and good food. Set in an old farmhouse surrounded by lush pine forests and a number of hiking trails, this is an ideal place to chill out for a couple of days. Free wi-fi throughout. R1320

⭐ **The Pennefather** 105 Rissik St ☎ 015 276 4885, ✉ pennefather@telkomsa.net; map below. The only

option actually within the town itself, and conveniently located for the start of a hiking trail. Named after Haenertsburg's original mining company, *The Pennefather* consists of six historic mining style cottages lining a small courtyard with comfortable self-catering facilities and a small balcony out front. Excellent value. R560

EATING & DRINKING

Picasso's Restaurant. Across from the D Rd junction on R71 just as you leave town 🌐 picassoshaenertsburg .co.za; map below. A large wooden Austrian-style chalet beside the road offering good food, including pancakes, big breakfasts (R42) and delicacies such as Kudu steak served with marula jelly. Easter to mid-Jan Tues–Sat 8.30am–9pm, Sun 8.30am–4pm; rest of the year Tues–Thurs & Sun 8.30am–4.30pm, Fri & Sat 8.30am–9pm.

⭐ **The Red Plate** Rissik St 161 ☎ 083 305 2851 🌐 redplate.co.za; map below. With both indoor and outdoor seating – the latter on a terrace overlooking

downtown Haenertsburg – *The Red Plate* serves excellent food throughout the day including freshly caught trout (R75) and an array of tasty salads, as well as the usual burgers and steaks. Tues & Sun 9am–4.30pm, Wed–Sat 9am–8pm.

Iron Crown Pub and Grill Rissik St, at the entrance to town from the R71; map below. With numerous large TV screens showing simultaneous sporting events from throughout the world, this busy pub is successfully promoted as the town's day-care centre for husbands. Food is primarily standard pub grub including fish and chips and burgers. Tues–Fri 11am–11pm, Sat 10am–11pm, Sun 9am–4pm.

Along the two valley roads to Tzaneen

Just east of Haenertsburg is a turning off the main R71 for the R528 which offers an alternative route to Tzaneen via **Georges Valley Road**. There is, in fact, little to choose between the two options in terms of both distance and stunning scenery. Along the Georges Valley Road lies a memorial to **John Buchan**, author of *The Thirty-Nine Steps*.

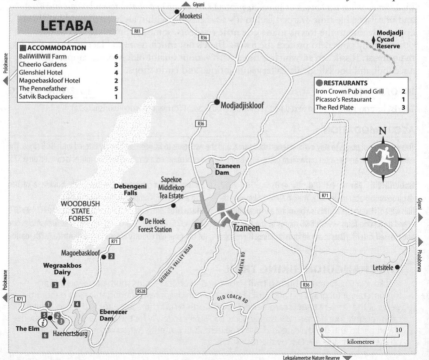

LETABA

■ ACCOMMODATION	
BaliWillWill Farm	6
Cheerio Gardens	3
Glenshiel Hotel	4
Magoebaskloof Hotel	2
The Pennefather	5
Satvik Backpackers	1

● RESTAURANTS	
Iron Crown Pub and Grill	2
Picasso's Restaurant	1
The Red Plate	3

A heavy copper plaque commemorating him at the site was recently stolen but local fans are keen to have it reinstated. Further along, the tranquil **Tzaneen Dam** is an atmospheric spot for swimming and picnicking.

Taking the R71, the Magoebaskloof Valley Road, will lead you through the dramatic **Magoebaskloof Valley**, named after the rogue chief Makgoba, who in 1895 had his head chopped off by native warriors serving under the Boer leader Abel Erasmus. The grand *Magoebaskloof Hotel* (see below) here is the starting point for a number of fairly steep hiking trails, including an attractive 1.5km waterfall walk.

After the turn-off to the Debengeni Falls, the valley becomes broader, the rolling hillsides covered with huge stands of citrus, avocado, kiwi and banana trees, as well as by the rich green texture of tea bushes.

Cheerio Gardens

4km out of Haenertsburg, off the Georges Valley Rd • Free • Tearooms Wed–Sat 9am–5pm, Sun 9am–4pm • ⓦ cheerio.co.za

The tranquil **Cheerio Gardens** stem from the post Boer war era when the new government began the establishment of forestry in the area. The garden was part of the forestry commissioner's estate and today makes a tranquil place for a wander among the mass of pretty cherry trees, and their tearooms – set next to a small pond – are a good place to stop for delicious home-made cakes and scones. The gardens hold an annual Cherry Blossom Festival at the end of September when the garden is at its most colourful. You can also do a spot of trout fishing in the garden's many ponds, and there are also some self-catering cottages here (see below).

Wegraakbos Dairy

4km out of Haenertsburg, off the Georges Valley Rd • Daily 7am–5pm • Tours at 10am, booking essential • R60 • ☎ 071 687 5218

Along the same dirt road as Cheerio Gardens is the tiny **Wegraakbos Dairy**, another wonderful piece of backwoods life. At the dairy, organic cheese is handmade in traditional style over an open fire in a huge copper cauldron with milk from the farm's Brown Swiss cattle. It's a very idyllic setting with geese and duck wandering around freely among the rustic-looking farm buildings. The one-hour tours give you an opportunity to see the cheese being made, amazingly without any electrical or mechanical devices, and afterwards you get a chance to sample the freshly made cheese – some decidedly better than others. If sampling it isn't enough, you can also buy the cheese at a farm stall in front of *Picasso's Restaurant* (see opposite) on weekends.

ACCOMMODATION	**ALONG THE TWO VALLEY ROADS TO TZANEEN**

Cheerio Gardens 4km out of Haenertsburg, off the Georges Valley Rd ☎ 015 276 1804, ⓦ cheerio.co.za. A range of eight different self-catering cottages strategically placed around the Cheerio Gardens, with lots of privacy and beautiful mountain views, some even with private gardens. The comfortable cottages are all former homes of the Thompson family so have loads of character and atmosphere. R525
Magoebaskloof Hotel Magoebaskloof Valley Rd ☎ 015 276 5400, ⓦ magoebaskloof.co.za. This grand hotel boasts what is probably the most spectacular view in the area from its front deck. What the almost identical 68

rooms lack in character is made up for by the creature comforts (pool, DSTV, a choice of two restaurants and a bar) and the breathtaking setting. R1200
Satvik Backpackers Georges Valley Rd, 4km from Tzaneen ☎ 015 307 3920 or ☎ 084 556 2414, ⓦ satvik .co.za. Down a steep dirt track, this is an unusual and appealing backpacker lodge, housed in old workers' shacks, with a range of basic rooms, some self-contained, others sharing a shower block. There's a picturesque waterside bar and braai area, and various walking trails on the vast property, including one going through the indigenous forest. Dorm R100, double R320

Modjadji Cycad Reserve

Daily 7.30am–6pm • R10 • Rondavels R700 • ☎ 15 295 3025, ⓦ www.africanivoryroute.co.za

The area around the rather downbeat village of **MODJADJI**, 32km northeast of Tzaneen off the R36, is the home of the famous **Rain Queen**, the hereditary female monarch of the Modjadji people, who, legend maintains, has the power to make rain – a useful talent in these often parched northern areas – and who provides royal protection of the regal cycad. Currently, there is no queen in post, so to speak, but her royal kraal is up the mist-covered mountainside. At the top of the mountain is the **Modjadji Cycad Reserve**, where a special form of ancient cycad flourishes – the unique Modjadji cycad. The 1300-acre reserve contains some of the world's oldest and largest cycads and incorporates some fine views (often obscured by mist) and various steep but pleasant trails. At the top there are a few facilities, including a souvenir shop and an information centre, which explains a bit more about the cycads and the famous monarch. At the bottom of the mountain, in the reserve, close to the side entrance, are a couple of traditional self-catering rondavels.

Waterberg

Rising out of the plains to the west of the Great North Road, the **Waterberg** was until recently one of the least known of South Africa's significant massifs. During the past decade, however, it has been "discovered" by Johannesburgers, and is now a hugely popular weekend destination. Once an area of lakes and swamps – hence its name – the elevated plateau can often seem as dry as its surrounding northern bushveld, yet it harbours a diversity of vegetation and topography that for years supported extensive farming and cattle-ranching. In recent times, the majority of the old ranches have been converted into private reserves catering either for the hugely lucrative hunting market, or less profitable game viewing, with white rhino often the star attraction, along with giraffe, large antelope and leopard. Today the entire area, some 14,500 square kilometres of both private and publicly owned land, is encompassed by one of the country's foremost conservation projects – the **Waterberg Savanna Biosphere Reserve** (ⓦwaterbergbiosphere.org), designated a biosphere reserve by UNESCO in 2001. It was founded by a close-knit association of landowners who wished to combine wildlife conservation with the benefits of tourism. They have set up an extensive management plan for the area, developing various remarkable tourism initiatives, such as the useful GPS sign boarding that now helps navigation in the tricky area.

As a game-viewing destination, the Waterberg makes a decent alternative to the lowveld areas around Kruger National Park, with the important advantage that malaria isn't present. It has impressive credentials as a vast area of true wilderness, and it is certainly still a lot less commercialized than Kruger. **Vaalwater** – the only settlement of any size – is located at the heart of the biosphere reserve. West of Vaalwater, and also included within the biosphere reserve, are two large game reserves that are home to the Big Five: **Marakele National Park** and the privately owned **Welgevonden** reserve. North of Vaalwater is the highly regarded **Lapalala Wilderness Area**, where the biosphere reserve was originally instigated.

The only reserve you can visit for a game-viewing day-trip under your own steam is Marakele National Park; Lapalala Wilderness Area can be visited with a guide from *Waterberg Cottages* (see p.579). Otherwise, to gain access to the reserves, large or small, you'll almost always be expected to book into accommodation on the reserve itself; as most accommodation in the Waterberg is on reserves, this is generally hard to avoid.

Vaalwater

Black Mamba crafts gallery Mon–Fri 8.30am–5pm, Sat 8.30am–1.30pm, Sun 9.30am–1pm

The small farming town of **Vaalwater** offers the visitor little more than a couple of useful places to stay and eat, and an orientation point on the R33, which connects the N1 at Modimolle with Lephalale. Vaalwater marks the junction between the R33 and the tarred road to Melkrivier and Marken.

COMMUNITY PROJECTS IN THE WATERBERG

There are a number of community projects throughout the Waterberg that have the twofold purpose of providing employment to the many farm labourers who lost their jobs when tobacco farming stopped being lucrative, and providing support for the area's high percentage of HIV/AIDS sufferers by giving them employment when they are well enough to work. The useful **Waterberg Meander brochure** (see p.578) gives a detailed breakdown of community projects that are worth visiting, generally catering towards the tourism trade. You can get the opportunity to see wonderful crafts being made, go on guided tours into traditional homesteads, or on mountain trails past Stone Age settlements and San rock art.

The best of the bunch near Vaalwater is the innovative **Beadle Crafts Workshop** (Mon–Fri 7am–4.30pm, Sat & Sun 9am–4.30pm; ⓦ beadle.co.za), where you will see the colourful and intricate beadwork on leather items such as belts, bracelets and sandals being made. Next to the workshop is a tearoom and a shop where you can buy the goods. The workshop is a short drive north of Vaalwater, towards Melkrivier; coming from Vaalwater, take the first right towards Twenty-Four Rivers, passing the tiny stone, Sir Herbert Baker-designed (see box, p.473), Saint John's church on the southern edge of Triple B Ranch. The workshop is on the northern edge of the ranch (follow the signs), near Horizon Horseback Adventure & Safaris (see p.578).

10

Roughly 1km west of the Village Square along the R33, behind the Spar supermarket, the **Zeederberg Homestead** was the town's first settlement and home to the legendary Zeederberg Stagecoaches that used to crisscross Limpopo and Zimbabwe to service settler outposts. Today, it offers accommodation (see p.579), and the old stagecoach square to the front houses the excellent ★ **Black Mamba crafts gallery**, selling beautiful crafts from throughout southern Africa, and a quality restaurant (see p.579).

Lapalala Wilderness Area

North of Vaalwater; turn left down a dirt road at the Melkrivier junction on the R518 Marken Rd · Guided day-trip R600 · ☎ 014 755 4395, ⓦ lapalala.com

Providing sanctuary for endangered and rare animals, the 244-square-kilometre **Lapalala Wilderness Area** has developed into one of the foremost conservation projects in the country. It was the first private game reserve in South Africa to obtain the highly endangered black rhino and it is now equally well known for its Wilderness School, which introduces some three thousand children a year from all over Africa to the principles and practices of conservation during week-long courses.

To visit Lapalala on day-trips, you must book through *Waterberg Cottages* (see p.579) who organize a guide for R600 per person for a full day packed with adventure, and lunch. For overnight trips your only option is to go through The Ant Collection (ⓦ waterberg.net; see p.578), who run the super-luxurious *Lapalala Bush Camp*.

Marakele National Park

Southwest of Vaalwater · Daily: May–Aug 8am–5pm; Sept–April 8am–6pm · R100 · Sunrise/sunset drive R160 · ☎ 014 777 1745, ⓦ sanparks.org/parks/marakele

In the mountains to the northeast of the mining and hunting town of **Thabazimbi** lies the 670-square-kilometre **Marakele National Park**, reached via a 12km tarred road from Thabazimbi. At its core is the **Kransberg**, a striking assortment of odd-shaped peaks, plateaus and cliffs. The fauna includes tsessebe, roan and sable antelope, red hartebeest and eight hundred breeding pairs of the endangered Cape vulture. Larger game such as elephant, rhino and lion have also been introduced, many from Kruger National Park.

While the park has a great deal of potential, for the moment **day visitors** are restricted to a small area, which includes Kransberg, with its inspiring views. Roads to the accommodation (see p.below) don't require a 4WD, though you'll need one to get around the rest of the reserve. To explore beyond these roads, join one of the excellent two- to three-hour organized sunrise and sunset drives, which meet at the main gate.

Welgevonden Private Game Reserve

25km west of Vaalwater on the tarred road towards Thabazimbi, abutting Marakele • ⓦ welgevonden.org

Privately owned by an association of landowners, the 380-square-kilometre **Welgevonden Private Game Reserve** is managed as one large conservation area, with a strict management plan regulating the number of lodges that can be built and the visitors allowed in the park. This results in some fantastic undisturbed and relatively easy-to-view wildlife throughout the entire area, including the Big Five, a host of antelope and a plethora of colourful birds. All eight commercial lodges in Welgevonden – the rest are private – have their own unique features (check website for a full list) such as bush spas, romantic fireplaces, outdoor showers, and granite swimming pools, and are comfortably kitted out with plush sofas and soft beds. With well-qualified and experienced game guides at hand at all times, there's no question that this is an expensive place to visit, with all-inclusive rates hovering around R3000 per person per day.

ARRIVAL AND INFORMATION   WATERBERG

By minibus taxi The only public transport to Vaalwater is by minibus taxi.

Tourist information Village Square, at the first T-junction as you approach from the east (Mon–Fri 7am–7pm; ☎ 0172 733 3164); also home to an internet café. They stock the useful

Waterberg Meander brochure, which is built up around a series sightseeing routes demarcated by GPS reference points and signboarded throughout the Waterberg area. It's an excellent tool if you get lost – which is not that uncommon. You can also download the brochure on ⓦ waterbergmeander.co.za.

ACCOMMODATION

Based on or next to a reserve, all accommodation in the Waterberg will have different activities on offer, which are worth checking out before you decide where to stay.

THE LAPALALA WILDERNESS AREA

Bush Camp ☎ 014 755 3584, ⓦ waterberg.net. This extremely luxurious tented camp has an unbelievably atmospheric setting, with its safari tents perched on the edge of a hillside overlooking the river valley. Last-minute deals (up to three weeks in advance) reduce rates to R4400. Rates are all-inclusive. **R7200**

MARAKELE NATIONAL PARK

Bontle Camping Site 2km from the main gate ⓦ sanparks.org/parks/marakele. Run by South African National Parks, this is a shaded campsite with fully kitted kitchen and ablution blocks, the obligatory braii area, and the option of a power point. **R270**

Tlopi Tented Camp 17km from the main entrance ⓦ sanparks.org/parks/marakele. A romantic self-catering tented camp on the banks of the Matlabas River, with luxuriously equipped tents sleeping two hovering on stilts over the water's edge. **R915**

WELGEVONDEN PRIVATE GAME RESERVE

Shibula Lodge ☎ 021 882 8206, ⓦ shibulalodge .co.za. A good, friendly option, right in the middle of the

reserve. The lodge overlooks a busy watering hole visited by birds, antelope and the occasional elephant, and has a large family of boisterous and entertaining baboons inhabiting the neighbouring cliffside. You need to book in advance and will be picked up at the main gate. Prices include game drives (and drink and snacks on the game drives) plus all meals. **R6200**

VAALWATER AND AROUND

Ant's Nest and Ant's Hill Off the dirt road to Dorset from Vaalwater ☎ 014 755 3584, ⓦ waterberg.net. Two super-luxurious lodges, offering all-inclusive pampering in the wild including horseriding, game drives, mountain biking, guided game walks and basically everything else your heart might desire, before ending each day with a sundowner at one of the 50-square-kilometre reserve's beautiful viewpoints. Successful breeders of sable antelope and passionate about conservation, the owners are happy to share their vast knowledge and experience. Rates are all-inclusive. **R7200**

★ **Horizon Horseback Adventures & Safaris** Off the Vaalwater–Melkrivier Rd ☎ 014 755 4003, ⓦ ridinginafrica.com. A well-established and highly professional outfit that combines lovely lakeside accommodation in individual chalets and delicious food with loads of fun for horse-lovers: as well as outrides, overnight rides and trips to game areas, activities include cattle-mustering, polocrosse and a cross-country course. Last-minute discounted rates available. Rates are all-inclusive. R5000

Lindani Lindani Reserve ☎ 083 631 5579, ⓦ lindani .co.za. On a 31-square-kilometre reserve halfway between Vaalwater and Marken, *Lindani* comprises eight secluded and attractive thatched self-catering lodges sleeping between four and eighteen people. What makes Lindani unique is the many hiking and mountain-biking trails crisscrossing the reserve, which guests are free to use unsupervised, making this an ideal spot to explore the bush at your own pace. With tranquil picnic spots along rivers and the potential for encountering giraffe and various antelope, it's not surprising this is one of the most popular game lodges in the Waterberg. Minimum stay three nights. R2580

Waterberg Cottages Triple B Ranch ☎ 014 755 4425, ⓦ waterbergcottages.co.za. Pleasant self-catering accommodation in five old farmhouse buildings on the working Triple B Ranch. The ranch is famous for its hardy Bonsmara cattle, which you can learn more about on their farm tours. The unpolluted wide-open skies above also make this an ideal spot for stargazing, hence the offer of brilliant two-hour star tours. R500

Zeederberg Cottages Vaalwater ☎ 014 755 3538, ⓦ zeederbergs.co.za. The only choice in Vaalwater town itself, set around a large, relaxing garden with a pool. The cluster of comfortable self-catering cottages includes a Zulu-style rondavel, and cottages with dorm beds. Guests have access to the kitchen and living room in the main house, and there's free wi-fi at the reception. Dorm R150, double R600

EATING

The only places to eat or go out in Waterberg are in Vaalwater itself, so you'll need to be self-catering or staying at one of the all-inclusive game lodges when away from the town. Vaalwater also houses the Waterberg's only two supermarkets and the area's only banks.

VAALWATER

⭐ **Bush Stop Café** In the Zeederberg Complex. With a fabulous and slightly quirky breakfast and lunch menu, *Bush Stop* dishes up arguably the town's best French toast (served with banana and bacon) and pancakes, and a whole host of weird and wonderful salads, such as a delightful butternut squash salad – when in season. Using only fresh produce and cooking everything themselves from scratch, it would be a shame to miss this place when travelling through Vaalwater. Mon–Fri 8am–5pm, Sat 8am–1.30pm.

La Fleur Across the R33 from Sport on Main by the Village Square. A popular place for home-made ice cream, pizza, coffee and cake, plus also a good option for salads and steak. This is where all the lodge employees hang out on their days off. Mon–Fri 7.30am–10pm, Sat 7.30am–1pm.

Sport on Main Across from the village square on the R33. Still known by many by its old name, *Big 5 Pub and Grill*, this is the place to head to watch sports on TV. It's also a hugely popular pub, open into the wee hours of the morning, and serving up full-on, hearty steaks and burgers. Mon–Sat 8.30am–2am, Sun 10am–4pm.

The far north

The northernmost part of Limpopo Province is a hot, green, undeveloped rural region with much in common with Zimbabwe. Its essential geographical features are the **Limpopo River**, the border between South Africa and Zimbabwe (and, further west, Botswana), and the alluring **Soutpansberg mountain range**, aligned east–west just to the north of the area's main town, Makhado (Louis Trichardt), which is otherwise unremarkable and not worth a stopover.

Perhaps the most distinctive area is the **Venda** region, formerly an "independent" homeland under apartheid. Although economically impoverished, it remains rich in tradition, art and legend. East of the Venda lands is the northern tip of **Kruger National Park**, a less-visited but intriguing part of the park (see p.551); there are two entry gates to the park here, at **Punda Maria** and **Pafuri**.

Both the Limpopo River and the Soutpansberg range lie in the path of the N1 highway, which crosses into Zimbabwe at **Beitbridge**. About 70km west of here, the **Mapungubwe National Park** encompasses a UNESCO World Heritage Iron-Age site which for archeology buffs is probably the area's most enticing attraction.

10

10

The Soutpansberg

The **Soutpansberg**, an impressive range of hills, particularly when approached from the south, attracts sufficient rainfall to create a subtropical climate, and spectacularly lush farms along the southern slopes produce a range of exotic crops such as avocados and macadamia nuts. In other parts, the rocky *kloofs* and green hillsides offer unspoilt mountain retreats, shaded by up to 580 different species of tree, and the home of monkeys, small antelopes, warthogs and some raptors. The uniqueness of the area led to it being designated a UNESCO Biosphere Reserve in 2009, with a similar protection and development status as the Waterberg Biosphere Reserve (see p.576).

The N1 highway bisects the range, passing through missable Makhado, situated in the southern shadow of the mountains, then climbing over a low pass and descending through a pair of tunnels on the northern side. Once over the escarpment, the highway runs north across mostly empty baobab plains to **Musina** and the **Limpopo River**.

ACCOMMODATION   THE SOUTPANSBERG

ALONG THE N1

Along this stretch of the N1, you'll pass a number of hotels and guesthouses that use the lush surroundings to create a mountain-resort-type atmosphere.

★ **Harnham House** 8km north of Makhado on the N1, turn left/west along the scenic Bluegumspoort Rd (look out for the signboard) and follow the dirt road for 6km ☎ 015 517 7260, ⊛ harnhamhouse.co.za. Of the guesthouses hidden in the folds of the Soutpansberg, *Harnham House* is one of the nicest, with rooms in the attractive main house as well as in a lovely remote self-catering cottage overlooking a dam stocked with bream and bass. R500

The Inn on Louis Trichardt 12km north of Makhado ☎ 015 517 7088, ⊛ inn-on-louistrichardt.co.za. One of the best options, with rooms set around pleasant gardens and a pool. There's also an attractive craft shop and tea garden (daily 8am–5pm) in the grounds. R600

AWAY FROM THE N1

Beyond the well-worn N1, you can get deeper into the more remote and wilder parts of the mountains, ideal if you have a couple of days to spare.

Bergpan Eco Resort On the north side of the mountains and east of Waterpoort along the R523 ☎ 015 593 0127, ✉ bergpan@mweb.co.za. Twelve basic self-catering chalets sleeping two in a well-run resort offering tours of the saltpans that gave the mountains their name and a chance to experience salt-making, along with hiking and self-catering cottages. R400

Lajuma Mountain Retreat Along a turn-off on the R522, 46km west of Makhado ☎ 082 875 9482 or ☎ 083 308 7027, ⊛ www.lajuma.com. Situated by the top of Letjume, the highest point of the Soutpansberg, and an ideal spot from which to study the area's unique ecology, *Lajuma* attracts research students from all over the world. Two attractive self-catering thatched chalets perch on the mountainside overlooking a waterfall, and there's a romantic forest cottage tucked into the luxuriant tropical bush. The road up to the retreat can be dicey, at best – if you don't have a 4WD call in advance to be picked up at the gate. R400

★ **Leshiba Wilderness** 36km west of Makhado along the R522, located in a spectacular valley atop the mountain range ☎ 011 726 6347, ⊛ www.leshiba .co.za. A truly unique experience, well worth the long uphill drive (safest in a 4WD). The internationally acclaimed artist Noria Mabasa has used the ruins of old rondavels to create a replica Venda village, alive with sculpted figures that guests can admire when lounging by the pool or enjoying the quirky accommodation – each one different with absolutely no straight lines. R1300

Venda

To the east and north of Makhado lies the intriguing land of the **VhaVenda** people, a culturally and linguistically distinct African grouping known for their mystical legends, political independence and arts and crafts. **Venda** was demarcated as a homeland under the apartheid system in the 1950s, and became one of three notionally independent homelands in South Africa in the late 1970s. Of all the homelands, Venda was one of the least compromised, keeping both its geographic and cultural integrity, and largely being left to mind its own business during the dark years of apartheid. Nowadays, its boundaries have regained their former fuzziness, within Limpopo, but the region has retained its strong, independent identity.

10

VHAVENDA HISTORY AND CULTURE

The people who today call themselves **VhaVenda** are descended from a number of ancient groupings who migrated from the Great Lakes area in east-central Africa in the eleventh and twelfth centuries. Their identity gelled when a group under Chief Dimbanyika arrived at Dzata in the northern Soutpansberg, where a walled fort was later built. From here, they consolidated their power in the region, fending off attack from a number of different African groupings (including the Voortrekkers, whom they drove from their settlement at Schoemansdal in 1867). Although the VhaVenda suffered a reverse at the hands of the Boers in 1898, the onset of the Anglo-Boer War prevented that victory being consolidated.

The **culture** of the VhaVenda is a fascinating one, steeped in mysticism and vivid legend. One pervading theme is water – always an important concern in hot, seasonal climates, but a resource in which Venda is unusually abundant. Lakes, rivers, waterfalls and lush forests all form sacred sites, while legends abound of *zwidutwane*, or water sprites, and snakes who live at the bottom of dark pools or lakes.

Many VhaVenda **ceremonies** and **rituals** still hold great importance, with the most famous being the python, or *domba*, dance performed by young female initiates. Naked but for jewellery and a small piece of cloth around their waists, the teenage girls form a long chain, swaying and shuffling as the "snake" winds around a fire to the sound of a beating drum – another sacred object in Venda – often for hours on end. Your chances of seeing it performed are limited. The genuine thing is most common during spring; Heritage Day around the end of August or the beginning of September is a good time for celebrations.

Aside from a sprinkling of accommodation in Thohoyandou, you'll find almost no tourist-oriented infrastructure whatsoever in Venda, but travelling here can be wonderfully rewarding.

Thohoyandou

THOHOYANDOU isn't a place you'll want to spend time in as it's chaotic and there's nothing to see. It's reached from Makhado by following the R524 70km east, along the southern edge of the Soutpansberg; if you're heading on to Kruger, you'll be thankful that the road bypasses the centre of town. While in the area, check out the fine local crafts at the **Thohoyandou Arts and Crafts Centre** on the R524 on the outskirts of town. **Minibuses** for Makhado use the large taxi rank in front of the shopping mall in town.

INFORMATION

The best place to get info is from one of the established accommodation options such as *Shiluvari Lakeside Lodge* and *Khoroni Hotel*, both of which have lists of tour guides offering trips in the area.

ACCOMMODATION   VENDA

Bougainvilla Lodge Mphephu Drive Unit C 36 & 37 ☏015 962 4064, ⓦbougainvillalodge.com. As the name implies, a bougainvillea-covered place offering simple motel-like rooms – some with a/c – and the option of evening meals if ordered in advance. **R595**

Khoroni Hotel Mphephu St; turn left off the R524 coming from Makhado at the service station, and right at the third set of traffic lights ☏015 962 4600, ⓦkhoroni.co.za. Set in the heart of the downtown area, surrounded by trees, but not far beyond the road and tatty shopping mall. The hotel makes a living through its casino but also has a pool, and decent rooms. It has an impressive record of supporting Venda arts and crafts, with useful maps and tours available. **R780**

The R523 west from Thohoyandou

Along the northern side of the Soutpansberg, through a valley traced by the R523 road between the N1 and Thohoyandou, is the most appealing core of VhaVenda history and legend. This is where you'll find the lush forests, waterfalls and mountains that give Venda its mystical atmosphere.

Driving from Thohoyandou, climb out of town to the north and then west, leaving the suburbs to get among the elevated green scenery which lies enticingly ahead. You'll

TSONGA AND VENDA ARTS AND CRAFTS

The **Venda** and **Tsonga** regions have established a strong reputation in **arts and crafts**. The best known of these are clay pots distinctively marked with angular designs in graphite silver and ochre. Also growing in status are woodcarvings, ranging from abstract to practical, although, while the best of these can be imaginative and bold, many are unfinished and overpriced. You'll also come across tapestries, fabrics, basketwork and painting. Finding your way to these craft villages can be quite an adventure, as they are widely scattered and the roads are poor, so the Ribolla Tourism Association, behind the Swiss mission hospital in Elim (Mon–Fri 8.30am–4.30pm; T 015 556 4262 or T 072 2354543, E ribollata@mweb.co.za), has set up a demarcated **art route** in the area, and hands out free maps of the route. It also has knowledgeable guides to take you around.

pass the **Vondo Dam**, created in the early 1990s and surrounded by pine forests, then climb over the **Thate Vondo Pass**. Over the summit, a small shack marks the entrance to a network of forest roads that take you into the area containing the most important lake in Venda, **Lake Fundudzi**, and the **Sacred Forest**, an area of dense indigenous forest which contains the burial ground of Venda chiefs. In the past you could only look at both from afar, as getting closer was a matter of deep sensitivity and you had to gain permission from the VhaVenda chief. Today, access is unrestricted but there isn't a readily available map showing you the network of roads around the forest, and some of the roads require 4WD; you may be better off joining a **tour** from *Khoroni Hotel* (see opposite) or hooking up with a local guide.

Beyond the crest of the Thate Vondo Pass, the R523 follows the **Nzhelele River** down a valley of scattered but mostly unbroken settlement.

Elim and around

Southeast of Makhado along the R578 lie some areas that used to form part of the self-governing Tsonga homeland of **Gazankulu**. They feature the vibrant roadside action typical of such rural areas – most notably at **ELIM**, a cluster of stalls, minibuses and hoardings on the site of a long-established Swiss mission hospital.

Continuing on the R578 from Elim crossroads, towards the town of **Giyani**, you'll come upon a series of rural arts and crafts workshops (see box above). The traditions and skills in arts and crafts are not dissimilar to what you find in Venda, and most of the workshops and small factories have simple, rural roots, making the trip to see them a worthwhile adventure. *Shiluvari Lakeside Lodge* (see below) can help with guides to arts and crafts workshops in the area, and sells products from many of them in its exquisite and well-stocked crafts boutique.

ACCOMMODATION **ELIM AND AROUND**

★ **Shiluvari Lakeside Lodge** A short way from Elim; turn left at the hospital junction towards Thohoyandou, and follow the signs down a dirt road to the left T 015 556 3406, W shiluvari.com. The peaceful *Shiluvari Lakeside Lodge* has lawns running down to the edge of Albasini Dam and views over the water to the Soutpansberg. The first place in South Africa to gain the prestigious Tourism Fair Trade award, the owners have strong links with the local community and have helped set up the art route that has made visiting this area so popular (see box above). **R1050**

Mapungubwe National Park

Around 60km west of Musina along the R572 road to Pontdrift • Park daily: April–Oct 6.30am–6pm; Sept–March 6am–6.30pm • R100 • Morning and sunset drives (5.30am & 4pm) • R180 • T 015 534 923, W sanparks.org/parks/mapungubwe

The **Mapungubwe National Park** is a UNESCO World Heritage Site, primarily due to its famous Iron-Age site known as the Hill of Jackals, thought to be the site of the first kingdom in Africa. The park is situated at the confluence of the Limpopo and Shashi rivers, where South Africa, Zimbabwe and Botswana meet, and is well worth a detour

10

if you have even the faintest interest in archeology. The park is divided into an eastern and a western side connected only by the main road, with a large plot of private land in between. The main entrance is on the eastern side nearest Musina, which is also where you'll find the Hill of the Jackals and most of the accommodation.

The park offers excellent game viewing with a scenic backdrop of unusual sandstone formations, mopane woodland, riverine forest, and a landscape scattered with otherworldly baobab trees housing wildlife such as elephant, giraffe, white rhino, plus various different antelope, including eland and gemsbok. You can explore the park either in your own car or on three-hour guided morning and sunset drives. If you're lucky, you may spot predators such as lion, leopard and hyenas, and there are over four hundred bird species including kori bustard, tropical boubou and the magnificent pel's fishing owl.

The long-term goal is eventually to develop the park into a tri-border park incorporating Mashatu Reserve in Botswana and the Tuli Circle in Zimbabwe.

Hill of the Jackals

Heritage site tour 7am & 10am from the main gate • R150 • Book at the main gate or on ☎ 015 534 923

The **Hill of the Jackals** – one hour's drive from the main entrance – held a spiritual and mythological importance to local Modimo people long before it was "discovered" in 1932, when a local farmer climbed the dome-shaped granite hill and found various remains, including a tiny one-horned rhinoceros and a bowl, both made out of gold. It is thought that the years 1000–1300 AD were the heyday of a civilization centred at Mapungubwe. Prior to this, the Khoi and San people both left their footprints in the area with numerous sites of important rock art. Most impressive of these is found on land outside the national park (but still within the UNESCO World Heritage Site) at *Kaoxa Bush Camp* (see below).

A new museum is due to open shortly near the national park's main entrance which will exhibit the wonderful treasures of Mapungubwe. Until moved, these items can all be seen at the University of Pretoria (see p.504).

To view the Hill of the Jackals, you need to join a two-hour **Heritage Site Tour**. A knowledgeable guide will talk you through the finds from an archeological dig in front of the hill, before climbing the steps up the hill to where the king and his extended family lived and died.

Kaoxa Bush Camp

☎ 072 536 6297, ⓦ kaoxacamp.com

Nestled in between the eastern and western section of Mapungubwe National Park is a privately owned wilderness area housing **Kaoxa Bush Camp**, a beautiful rustic camp set

---

MAPUNGUBWE AND OTHER ARCHEOLOGICAL SITES

As one of the early melting pots of southern Africa, Limpopo has a number of important **archeological sites** where excavations have helped piece together a picture of the different people who inhabited the land for thousands of years. Some of the most interesting sites are at places where iron was smelted, as the development from what was essentially a Stone-Age culture to an Iron-Age culture, with its associated improvement in tools for cultivation and war, was a vital part of the migration of African tribes into South Africa around 1500 years ago. The presence of slag and other wastes provides the strongest clues – the iron itself seldom survives the processes of erosion. Some of the most revealing excavations have taken place at **Thulamela**, inside Kruger National Park not far from the Punda Maria Gate (see p.551), **Bakone Malapa** cultural village outside Polokwane (see p.571), **Makapan's Cave** near Mokopane (see p.570), **Masorini**, also in the Kruger park, not far from Phalaborwa (see p.550), and the single most important site in Limpopo Province, **Mapungubwe** (Hill of the Jackals), west of Musina (see above).

upon a hillside overlooking the confluence of the Limpopo and Shashi rivers across to Zimbabwe and Botswana. Stretching down to these two rivers, wild animals from Zimbabwe and Botswana are frequent visitors, and signs at the camp make it clear that elephants have right of way. In contrast to the national park, visitors are free to move around independently (after signing lengthy indemnity forms) – on foot or by car. But bearing in mind the many dangerous animals you may encounter, it's a good idea to seek advice before setting off. The only area that you're not allowed to explore by yourself is the amazing rock-art site, which one of the camp staff will take you to.

10

ARRIVAL AND DEPARTURE MAPUNGUBWE NATIONAL PARK

By public transport The only public transport to the park is by non-timetabled minibus taxis.

ACCOMMODATION

Kaoxa Bush Camp Accommodation at the camp comprises three rustic stone cabins with breathtaking views from large front terraces, which compensate for the fact that there's electricity but no a/c (and it gets very hot here). There are also three comfortable furnished safari tents with equally wonderful views. All of the accommodation is self-catering, sharing kitchen and dining facilities. R1190

SAN Parks Accommodation ⓦ sanparks.org/parks /mapungubwe/tourism/accommodation.php. There are a number of different accommodation options within the park, from airy wooden cottages and tented camps to a luxurious stone lodge and a fully equipped campsite, but there are no other facilities so you have to be fully self-sufficient. Check the website for details. R870

Lesotho

FIELDS OF COSMOS, MALEALEA (P.616)

Lesotho

Entirely surrounded by South Africa, the aptly named "mountain kingdom" of Lesotho (pronounced "Lee-su-tu") is proudly independent and very different in character from its dominant neighbour. Whereas the Rainbow Nation next door is, in many respects, distinctly European, laidback Lesotho prides itself on its staunchly African heritage. Few people in the highlands of this fabulously beautiful and rugged land speak English or Afrikaans, though language isn't a barrier when the country's inhabitants – the BASOTHO – count among the most hospitable people in Southern Africa. Another refreshing physical (and psychological) contrast is the almost total absence of fences, which means you can hike into the upland regions at will.

11

Travelling almost anywhere in Lesotho is an adventure: there are no highways or slick city-liner buses here (or, indeed, too many timetables), though the tarred **road network** is good, covered by rickety minibuses held together in some cases by little more than prayers. For the Basotho, **ponies** are the preferred method of transport, particularly in the highlands. You can do the same from pony-trekking lodges all over the country.

Lesotho is one of only a few countries to lie entirely above an altitude of 1000m, earning its nickname of "The Kingdom in the Sky". Even the sandstone **Lesotho lowlands** – which form a crescent along the country's western rim – would be highlands anywhere else. It's here that you'll find all the nation's major towns, including the busily practical capital of **Maseru**, with its very African mix of new glass buildings and dusty streets, which began life as tax-collection centres for the British administration. Lowland attractions include the weavers of **Teya-Teyaneng**, extraordinary caves near **Mateka** rock paintings at **Liphofung**, and the mountain fortress at **Thaba Bosiu**, established by Lesotho's founder, King Moshoeshoe I.

At around 1400m above sea level sandstone gives way to basalt, which forms the bulk of the ruggedly beautiful **Lesotho highlands**. Once up the steep, twisting roads that lead into the mountains you can visit the engineering masterpieces of the **Katse** and **Mohale dams**, ski in the Maloti Mountains, fish from rivers everywhere and, above all, wander through the countryside, dividing your time between remote villages of simple stone-and-thatch huts and the peaceful solitude of the mountains. Three protected areas in particular are worth the effort of getting to: **Ts'ehlanyane National Park** and **Bokong Nature Reserve**, both in the Front Range of the Maloti Mountains and linked by a 39km hiking and horseriding trail, and the exceedingly remote **Sehlabathebe National Park** in the east of the country, offering gloriously rugged hiking terrain.

PONY TREAKKING NEAR MALEALEA (P.616)

Highlights

❶ Pony trekking The ideal way to see Lesotho, following paths from village to village through spectacular mountain scenery and past towering waterfalls; you can also walk alongside while the pony takes your luggage. **See p.598**

❷ Thaba Bosiu The hilltop fortress from which Lesotho's greatest king, Moshoeshoe I, defended his kingdom against attackers offers fabulous views. **See p.601**

❸ Maletsunyane Falls A dramatic 200m waterfall plunging into a vast gorge deep in the remote highland region, reached on foot or by pony. **See p.604**

❹ "Roof of Africa" road The winding road from Butha-Buthe to Sani Pass travels through dramatic mountain passes and valleys, and passes Africa's best ski resort. **See p.612**

❺ Sehlabathebe National Park A lonely mountain reserve with superb hiking. **See p.621**

❻ Highlands Water Project Go on a tour inside Africa's second-highest dam at Katse, visit the power plant at 'Muela and learn about Lesotho's ambitious water project. **See p.610**

HIGHLIGHTS ARE MARKED ON THE MAP ON P.592

11

LESOTHO TRAVEL BASICS

BOOKS AND MAPS

The Morija Museum (see p.614) and some lodges sell books on Lesotho; a number of these also stock a very good 1:250,000 **topographical map** of Lesotho that marks most trails; it's also available from the Department of Lands, Surveys and Physical Planning on Lerotholi Road, near the corner of Constitution Road, in Maseru (☎ 2232 2376; M50). This is also the only place where you can buy the really detailed 1:50,000 maps (M35), essential for serious hiking; plus 1:10,000 maps of Maseru and other towns.

MONEY

Lesotho's currency is the **loti**, plural **maluti** (M), divided into 100 lisenti; the loti is tied to the South African rand (R1=M1). You can also use South African rand throughout Lesotho, but you cannot use or exchange maluti anywhere outside Lesotho (apart from in some border towns such as Ladybrand), so make sure you use them up or exchange them before leaving.

FOOD

The Basotho staple **food** is *papa*, maize meal which is boiled and stirred until it resembles stiff, white mashed potato. An alternative is *nyekoe*, brown beans mixed with sorghum and wheat. Both are fairly bland but filling and usually served with some kind of *nama* (meat) and *moroho* (leafy vegetable – usually spinach or cabbage). On the street, you'll find *dipapata*, delicious steamed bread, and a fried snack called *makoenya* or fat cakes.

PHONE NUMBERS

Lesotho's **country code** is ☎ 266, unless you're calling from South Africa, in which case it's ☎ 09266. There are no **area codes** (numbers given in the guide with area codes are in South Africa). To call collect, dial the international operator on ☎ 109.

PUBLIC HOLIDAYS

January 1 New Year's Day
March 11 Moshoeshoe Day
Good Friday
Easter Monday

May 1 Workers' Day
May 25 Heroes' Day
July 17 King's Birthday
Ascension Day (Thursday)

Lesotho's **winter** runs from May to July, when it often snows in the highlands and sometimes in the lowlands too. Although the days are usually clear and warm, it gets extremely cold at night and ice can make driving hazardous in the highlands, while snowfall blocks even tarred highways for days at a time. **Spring** (Aug–Oct), when the snow melts, is a beautiful time, with new plants sprouting up everywhere. November to January is **summer**, when Lesotho gets most of its rain, often torrential, turning dirt roads into mudslides. Still, when it isn't raining the weather is usually sunny and the landscape is coloured in vivid shades of green. **Autumn** (Feb–April) is one of the best times to visit, as it doesn't usually rain too much and temperatures are moderate. Whatever the time of year, Lesotho can be very cold at night, particularly in the highlands, and prone to rapid weather changes, for which it's always wise to be prepared.

Brief history

Lesotho exists because of the determined efforts of one man, **Moshoeshoe I** (1786–1870), to secure land for his people in the face of intense social upheaval and the insatiable land-hunger of others. Before the arrival of Moshoeshoe's ancestors, around 900 AD, the San inhabited Lesotho unchallenged. Today the San are gone, exterminated in 1873 by the last of many British campaigns against them. However, they left their mark in the country's rock paintings and elements of their tongue in the Sesotho language (including impossible buzzes and clicks), while traces of their vaguely oriental features and paler skin can still be discerned in some Basotho faces.

October 4 Independence Day
December 25 Christmas Day

December 26 Boxing Day

RED TAPE AND VISAS

Visas are not required for most citizens of Western Europe, the Commonwealth (excepting India, Ghana, Nigeria and Pakistan) and the US. If you've travelled through a **yellow fever zone**, you'll need an International Certificate of Vaccination against yellow fever. The standard entry permit is for 14 or 28 days; should you need an extension, visit the Department of Immigration and Passport Services on Assisi Road in Maseru (☎ 2232 3771, ☏ 2231 0538).

ROAD TAX

A "road fund" **fee** of M30 is payable when entering Lesotho by car.

TOUR OPERATORS

Lesotho's tourist infrastructure remains sketchy in some areas, and arranging activities such as pony trekking and visits to the natural parks can be time-consuming, especially without your own transport. If you're short on time, consider an **organized tour**. *Malealea Lodge* (see p.617) in the southwest offers some innovative pony trekking and 4WD combinations, while the *Trading Post Guest House* in Roma (see p.604) is probably the best source of information on 4WD trails. Coming from South Africa, Thaba Tours (☎ 0027 33 701 2888, ☏ thabatours.co.za) specializes in overland trips in Lesotho via Sani Pass, pony trekking, biking and hiking.

WEBSITES

☏ **gov.ls** The Lesotho government's portal with national news and links to its ministries, including the Ministry of Tourism.
☏ **lestimes.com** The *Lesotho Times* newspaper website, doing a good job at presenting "news without fear or favour".
☏ **seelesotho.com** A wealth of information about the history, culture, flora and fauna of Lesotho, plus tips on where to visit and how to get there.

☏ **sesotho.web.za** The first stop if you are interested in learning Sesotho, with guidance in greetings and basic phrases in addition to references for Sesotho publications. There's an online dictionary too.
☏ **visitlesotho.travel** Lesotho's official tourism website has a downloadable map, accommodation and restaurant listings, driving route tips and contact details.

11

The Basotho first settled the fertile plains that today form the Lesotho lowlands and South Africa's Free State, before going on to colonize the mountains. They farmed these plains relatively peacefully for centuries, but by Moshoeshoe's time, tribes from elsewhere had forced thousands of Basotho off their land.

Moshoeshoe became chief in 1820 and established himself on top of a mountain near Butha-Buthe, where he became patron to many refugees in search of safety. However, after a particularly vicious attack on **Butha-Buthe** in 1824, Moshoeshoe decided it was no longer safe and trekked south with his followers in search of a better mountain. He found one at **Thaba Bosiu**, which, though subsequently attacked repeatedly, was never taken. Moshoeshoe earned an almost mythical reputation for wisdom and generosity among ordinary Basotho that survives to this day.

The Europeans in Lesotho

The kingdom was encroached upon by land-hungry Europeans from the 1840s onwards, and the **Orange Free State** government invaded in 1858, their soldiers destroying Morija and then launching a failed attack on Thaba Bosiu. They nonetheless captured plenty of farmland, whose acquisition was sanctioned by a British treaty in 1860. In 1865, the Orange Free State government cited Basotho cattle theft as the pretext for a new conflict, though few could deny Moshoeshoe's bitter assertion that "my great sin is that I possess a good and fertile country". The ensuing **Seqiti War** resulted in the destruction of Basotho crops, forcing Moshoeshoe into a humiliating treaty in 1866 that signed over most of his remaining good land. The war resumed in 1867, and was halted only by the British taking over what was left of the kingdom as the protectorate of **Basotholand** in 1868. The Treaty of Aliwal North in 1869 restored Moshoeshoe's land east of the Caledon but left the rest with the Free State, where it has remained to this day – a loss that still stings.

Moshoeshoe died in 1870 and the British handed Basotholand to the Cape administration a year later, which began taxing its new subjects, establishing a series of hut tax-collection points that have since grown into Lesotho's modest collection of small towns. Discontent turned to open rebellion in 1879, when the Cape government decided to confiscate all Basotho firearms. The result was the **Gun War**, one of few colonial-era conflicts in which the locals came out on top; the prize for the victorious Basotho was the resumption of direct rule from Britain in 1884.

Independence

Along with Bechuanaland and Swaziland, Basotholand rejected incorporation into the union of South Africa in 1910, with **King Letsie II** instead helping found the South African Native National Congress (later the ANC) in 1912. During the following years, the monarchy and chiefs' position declined, partly because British reforms forced their uneasy conversion into a junior arm of the colonial civil service, but also because social changes at

11

LESOTHO

HIGHLIGHTS
1. Pony - trekkking
2. Thaba Bosiu
3. Maletsunyane Falls
4. "Roof of Africa" road
5. Sehlabathebe National Park
6. Highlands Water Project

BORDER POST OPENING TIMES

Monontsa Pass	8am–4pm	Makhaleng Bridge	8am–4pm
Caledonspoort	6am–10pm	Tele Bridge	6am–10pm
Ficksburg Bridge	Open 24hr	Ongeluk's Nek	8am–4pm
Peka Bridge	8am–4pm	Qacha's Nek	6am–10pm
Maseru Bridge	Open 24hr	Ramatseliso's Gate	8am–6pm
Van Rooyen's Gate	6am–10pm	Nkonkoana Gate	8am–4pm
Sephapho's Gate	8am–4pm	Sani Pass	8am–4pm

work in the region, like migration, urbanization and rising education levels, proved too much for them to adapt to. In 1960, when **Moshoeshoe II** was crowned king, independence politics were in full swing, spearheaded by Pan-Africanist Ntsa Mokhele's Basotho Congress Party (BCP), and rivalled by the more conservative Basotho National Party (BNP). After narrowly winning the 1965 elections, the BNP led newly named Lesotho into **independence** on October 4, 1966. However, after losing the 1970 election, prime minister Leabua Jonathan annulled the result, declared a **state of emergency**, and carried on ruling until he was toppled in 1986 by a **military coup** led by Major General Metsing Lekhanya. Lekhanya ordered the **expulsion of the ANC** from Lesotho and signed an agreement that year with apartheid South Africa for the **Lesotho Highlands Water Project** (see box, p.610) – Africa's biggest engineering project to date, aiming to divert much of Lesotho's ample water resources to the thirsty South African province of Gauteng.

In 1990, Lekhanya sent Moshoeshoe II into exile and installed Moshoeshoe's son on the throne as **Letsie III**, but a year later Lekhanya was himself ousted by Major General Phisona, who then gave way to a **democratically elected government** led by Mokhele's BCP in 1993. Letsie stood down in favour of his father in 1995, but Moshoeshoe II died in a car crash the next year, and Letsie regained the throne.

In 1997, the BCP split with Mokhele and most of his cabinet, breaking away to form the Lesotho Congress for Democracy (LCD). The following year Mokhele's health deteriorated and he was forced to step down just before the **1998 elections**, where his successor Pakalitha Mosisili won by a landslide. Opposition parties cried foul amid widespread allegations of **vote-rigging**, and in July and August, crowds gathered outside the Royal Palace in Maseru demanding that the results be overturned – these protests subsequently developed into a **mutiny** by Lesotho Defence Force soldiers. In September, under the flag of a Southern African Development Community (SADC) peacekeeping force, **South African troops** crossed the border, and fierce fighting took place around military bases and at the strategically vital Katse Dam. Meanwhile, thousands of demonstrators protested at what they regarded as South Africa's heavy-handed intervention, and a large number of shops and offices across the country were looted and burned. After the 1998 riots, Lesotho's electoral system was changed to combine majority voting and proportional representation: eighty parliamentary seats to be elected by the first-past-the-post system, forty through proportional representation. Despite some scandals and unrest, subsequent elections passed off with little incident.

Current challenges

Aside from politics, there are some promising economic opportunities for Lesotho. **Mining** is set to bring in significant revenue: since reopening in 2004, the diamond mine at Letseng has discovered three of the world's largest diamonds, and has the potential to provide up to twenty percent of Lesotho's GDP. The government has finalized its **Poverty Reduction Strategy** and continues to attract funding from international donors. And the royalties from the **Lesotho Highlands Water Project** are guaranteed for the foreseeable future.

However, a number of gargantuan challenges remain unanswered. **Poverty** remains entrenched, particularly in the rural areas of the country where the majority rely on small-scale agriculture. It was these areas that were pushed to the brink of emergency in 2007 when Lesotho suffered its worst **drought** in thirty years, resulting in a government appeal for food aid from the international community. **Environmental degradation** remains an issue too, ever visible in the numerous dongas across the country. And economically, Lesotho is still recovering from the massive losses in its textile exports after increased Chinese competition, and suffers very high levels of **unemployment**. Most devastating of all is the scourge of **HIV/AIDS**; the prevalence of the pandemic in Lesotho is one of the highest in the world, and life expectancy for the nation has plummeted to 35 years. The future prospects of the mountain kingdom rest upon whether it can overcome these challenges.

SOME SIMPLE SESOTHO

The Basotho language is **Sesotho**. It can be tricky to speak, as spellings rarely correspond with pronunciation, a legacy of the bizarre nineteenth-century transcription by French missionaries, in which locals take a perverse pride. For more information about Sesotho and tips on learning the language, see ⓦ sesotho.web.za.

BASICS

Yes	*E* ("aye")
No	*E-e* ("ai-ai" as in the ai of hair)
Thank you	*Kea leboha* ("Kiya lee-bowa")
Today	*Kajeno* ("Ka-jen-noo")
Tomorrow	*Hosane* ("Ho-san-nee")
Yesterday	*Moobane* ("Mow-ban-nee")
Where is …?	*E kae …?* ("O kai …")
Where can we stay?	*Nka lula hokae?* ("N-ka dula o kai")
Where are you going?	*U ea kae?* ("Oo ya kai")
Where are you from?	*U tsoa kae?* ("Oo tswa kai")
How much?	*Ke bokae?* ("Ke bo-kai")
I speak Sesotho a little	*Ke bua Sesotho ha nyane* ("Ke boo-a Sesotho han-yaney")

GREETINGS AND RESPONSES

Hello (informal)	*Khotso* ("Khot-so" – literally "peace")
Hello (to one)	*Lumela* ("Do-mela")
…father (used to address any man)	*Ntate* ("N-dar-tay")
…mother (used to address any woman)	*Me* ("Mmeh")
…brother (used to address any boy)	*Abuti* ("A-boo-ti")
…sister (used to address any girl)	*Ausi* ("A-woo-si")
Hello (to many)	*Lumelang* ("Do-melang")
How are you?(formal)	*U phela jooang* ("O pela jwan")
I'm fine (formal)	Ke phela hantle ("Ke pela hank-le") with a clicked *k*
Goodbye (said by person leaving)	*Sala hantle* ("Sala hank-le" – literally "go well")
Goodbye (said by people remaining)	*Tsamaea hantle* ("Ts-my-ya hank-le" – literally "stay well")

ARRIVAL AND DEPARTURE

By plane Lesotho is most comfortably reached by plane from Johannesburg (there are no flights from anywhere else). South African Airlink operates three flights a day to Moshoeshoe I International Airport, 18km southeast of the city, from Monday to Friday and two on the weekends. Taxis and shuttle buses (M50) connect the airport with Maseru.

By bus There are limited bus services from South African cities to Lesotho's main overland border at Maseru Bridge (2km from the capital). Intercape (see p.49) runs a daily service from Cape Town via Bloemfontein and from Durban, while Vaal Maseru (☎0027 18 462 1000, ⓦ vaalmaseru .co.za) has occasional buses from Rustenburg and Klerksdorp in North West Province.

By minibus taxi There are frequent minibus taxis throughout the day from Johannesburg, Bloemfontein and Durban, and less frequently from a host of smaller towns in the Free State and North West Province to various border crossings in Lesotho's western lowlands – particularly Maseru Bridge, Ficksburg Bridge (next to Maputsoe) and Caledonspoort, close to Butha-Buthe, both to the north. All these places have plentiful onward transport connections within Lesotho, with shared taxis shuttling between the border and the nearest towns. It's possible to enter Lesotho from the south via the spectacular Sani Pass by taking a 4WD car or hired transport from Underberg in KwaZulu-Natal (see p.400).

By car Travelling to Lesotho by car, you have a choice of fourteen border crossings. Easiest to reach are the western lowlands crossings, including Maseru Bridge, Ficksburg Bridge and Caledonspoort. The main crossings get very busy with returning migrants on weekends, and it may make sense to take a detour via a smaller crossing. For border opening times, see the map on pp.596–597. If you've rented a car in South Africa, check whether the insurance covers you for Lesotho, especially in winter.

GETTING AROUND

By car Lesotho has a good tarred road network, though you can't avoid dirt (and often boulder-strewn) roads when heading to more out-of-the-way places. The main route from Maseru north is good tar until Oxbow, after which there's potholes all the way to the border at Sani Pass. The Katse dam road from Leribe is tarred, as is the road from Maseru to just beyond Mohale Dam; work to continue it all the way to Thaba-Tseka is almost finished and as the gravel road between Thaba-Tseka and Katse can be handled by saloon cars this makes a big two-day loop from Maseru via Thaba-Tseka and Katse to Leribe possible. The southern route from Maseru is tarred as far as Mphaki, but is passable in an ordinary saloon up to Qacha's Nek. Fuel costs roughly the same as in South Africa; unleaded is readily available in

Maseru, but can be scarce elsewhere. When approaching a police roadblock, be sure to wait at the stop sign until you are waved through. The speed limit is 80km/h, and 50km/h in urban areas. Hitching is much safer than in South Africa and is a good way to get around.

By minibus taxi Inexpensive minibus taxis are often the main form of transport, and run on major routes, at least until early afternoon.

By bus Slower but safer than minibus taxis, and very inexpensive. While there are lots of buses in Lesotho, only one company – the Lesotho Freight and Bus Services Corporation – keeps to a timetable (some of its routes operate in conjunction with other companies). Other buses simply leave when they're full, and as such operate just like minibus taxis.

11

Maseru and the central districts

One of the most convenient entry points from South Africa, and the country's most sophisticated urban centre by far, **Maseru** is a handy first stop for exploring Lesotho, and is the place to fill up on supplies, change money and organize onward transport. Apart from a few elegant colonial sandstone buildings, there's not a great deal to see here. However, if you're in town for a few days there are plenty of excursions into the surrounding countryside, including to **Thaba Bosiu**, the so-called "Mountain of the Night" where the founder of the nation, Moshoeshoe I, ruled for almost fifty years.

Further afield, **Roma** is the country's academic centre, surrounded by beautiful sandstone hills and with a historic Catholic mission. South of Roma, a road ascends into the **central highlands** – one of the most striking drives in the country. At the end of the road, the village of **Semonkong** has a superb lodge, a spectacular waterfall nearby and a wide variety of outdoor activities on offer. Continuing along the A3 east of Roma, the highway heads up into Lesotho's **Central Range**, with the spectacular stretch between the impressive Mohale Dam and unimpressive **Thaba-Tseka** currently being tarred and already accessible for careful saloon drivers.

Maseru

Sprawling **MASERU**, the nation's capital and only big town, spreads east from the Caledon River, which marks the border with South Africa. Maseru was established by the British in 1869 as the administrative centre for newly annexed Basotholand, but Britain put as little effort into developing the town as it did the rest of the country, no doubt expecting it to become just a minor South African town when Basotholand was incorporated into South Africa.

Surrounded by sprawling shantytown suburbs, the city has grown swiftly over recent years, poverty in Lesotho's rural areas having driven people to the capital in search of a better life. Few have found it yet, and the city has a high unemployment rate. Yet Maseru's compact centre has all the marks of an upwardly mobile African city, with slick fashions and mobile phones much in evidence.

Maseru's older buildings, as well as some stylish new ones, are built from well-crafted local **sandstone** – from which the city gets its name – though a number of ugly concrete box buildings diminish the effect and, unfortunately, dominate the skyline. Most of the city's daytime action happens on or around **Kingsway**, the road that runs through town, becoming increasingly downmarket and lively as it heads east towards the cathedral. Compared to most towns and cities in South Africa, Maseru is relatively safe, and as long as you take the **safety precautions** you would in any other African city, you can walk around here comfortably by day. Walking around at night, however, is ill-advised, since the empty streets make wandering tourists fine targets for opportunistic muggers.

Maseru's landmarks

The town's most famous landmarks are a trio of imposing neo-traditional thatched buildings at the west end of Kingsway: the **Basotho Shield**, which houses the tourist office and which – viewed from above – does indeed resemble a shield; the **Basotho Hut**

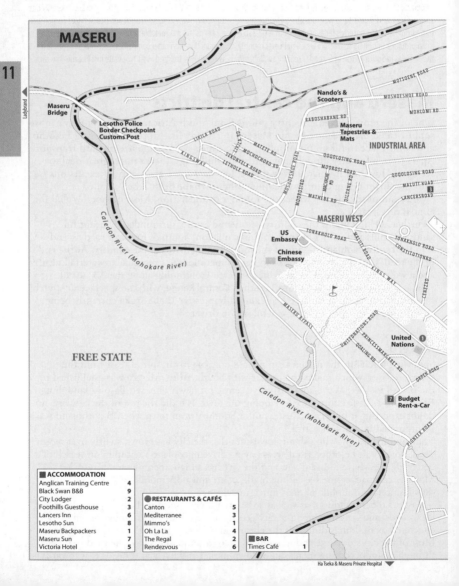

ACCOMMODATION

Anglican Training Centre	4
Black Swan B&B	9
City Lodger	2
Foothills Guesthouse	3
Lancers Inn	6
Lesotho Sun	8
Maseru Backpackers	1
Maseru Sun	7
Victoria Hotel	5

RESTAURANTS & CAFÉS

Canton	5
Mediterranee	3
Mimmo's	1
Oh La La	4
The Regal	2
Rendezvous	6

BAR

Times Café	1

Ha Tseka & Maseru Private Hospital

opposite, and the appropriately shaped **Basotho Hat (Mokorotlo) Building**, housing the well-stocked Lesotho Cooperative Handicrafts shop (see box above). The main part of town lies east of here along Kingsway, though there's not much to see other than a handful of colonial-era buildings: the **Alliance Française** in the former library at the corner with Pioneer Road, the former **Anglican church** next to it, and the 1891 **Resident Commissioner's House** (now a government department), on the left beyond the towering **Post Office** building – evidence of Maseru's intention to create a thoroughly modern capital. Kingsway comes to an end at the traffic circle by the impressively large sandstone **Roman Catholic Cathedral**, where it splits into Main North Road and Main South Road.

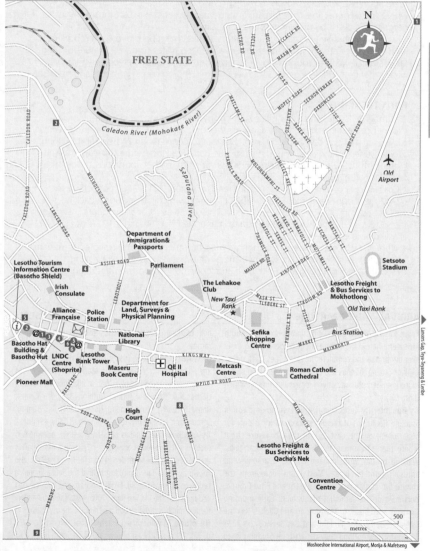

11

HIKING AND PONY TREKKING

Hospitable and almost entirely fenceless, Lesotho is a **hiker's paradise**. It's possible to set off into the hills and walk for as long as you like, with no prospect of an angry farmer yelling at you to get off his land – quite a change from South Africa. In more remote areas, locals get around by pony, and **pony trekking** – which can be arranged at most tourist-oriented lodges and two of the three national parks – is an undoubted highlight of any trip to the country.

HIKING

Always **prepare adequately** before setting out, and bring supplies for at least a day more than you think the hike will take. Be warned that in the highest reaches of the highlands there are very few villages; lovely as this is, it's also risky, so make sure someone knows where you've gone, and don't hike in remote areas on your own. Lesotho's weather is notoriously fickle – be prepared for all eventualities.

Bring enough cash (you can't count on rural banks changing money), a torch, plenty of food (there aren't many stores in remote rural areas), a water container, water-purifying tablets, an all-weather cooker with fuel (don't count on finding firewood), a genuinely waterproof tent, a sleeping mat and a very warm sleeping bag. A compass and map (see p.590) are also invaluable.

PONY TREKKING

A number of lodges and other places offer **pony trekking** (no previous equestrian experience needed) though only a few are well organized, the best being the *Malealea Lodge* (see p.617) and *Semonkong Lodge* (see p.605). Semonkong, Mokhotlong, Bokong, Ts'ehlanyane and the area around the Basotho Pony Trekking Centre (see p.605) are all high up; the others are lower down, with less variable weather conditions, though the terrain is harder on the ponies.

Costs vary according to group size, but tend to average M120–200 per person; for overnights, count on an extra M100–200 per person, which can include a pack horse as well as accommodation. A full-day's ride typically involves six or seven hours (10–15km) in the saddle, so overnight trips can be quite strenuous. Children under 12 are not usually allowed on overnighters.

Wherever you go, make sure you bring a wide-brimmed sunhat, sun protection cream, waterproof gear, swimwear in summer, and a water bottle (and, if you're staying overnight, a sleeping bag and mat, torch and food, though cooking utensils and fuel should be provided).

ARRIVAL AND DEPARTURE

MASERU

From South Africa Buses and minibus taxis from South Africa terminate at the Maseru Bridge border crossing. Walk over the bridge and complete the formalities, then either walk or catch a minibus taxi or a "4 plus 1" (saloon taxi – four passengers plus one driver) for the 2km ride into town (both M4).

By bus Intercity buses from within Lesotho drop you in Stadium Road (not at the bus station, which is only for departures), on the east side of the city centre, from where there are urban minibus taxis and local taxis. Walking by day with luggage is safe, if a somewhat amusing sight for locals. Most buses leave from the chaotic bus station between Market St and Pitso Ground, northeast of the cathedral roundabout. Early morning long-distance buses to Mokhotlong and Qacha's Nek are operated by Lesotho Freight and Bus Services (☎2231 3535); for Mokhotlong they depart from Stadium Road

next to Maseru Mart; to Qacha's Nek they depart from St James.

Destinations Bokong (daily; 7hr 30min); Leribe (8 daily; 2hr); Linakaneng (daily; 8hr); Mafeteng (5 daily; 1hr 30min); Mokhotlong (daily; 7hr); Morija (hourly; 50min); Qacha's Nek (daily; 9hr 30min); Quthing (daily; 3hr 30min); Roma (4 daily; 1hr); Sehong Hong (daily; 8hr 30min); Semonkong (daily; 5hr); Teya-Teyaneng (8 daily; 45min).

By minibus taxi Minibus taxis arriving from elsewhere in Lesotho will drop you at one of several chaotic ranks. Minibus taxis to and from the south depart from the New Taxi Rank (also known as Sefika Taxi Rank), just behind the Sefika Shopping Centre on Moshoeshoe Rd. Minibus taxis to and from the east and north use the Old Taxi Rank, 200m east of the bus station. Regular minibus taxis link both taxi ranks to the city centre.

By plane Moshoeshoe I International Airport (☎2235 0777), 18km southeast of town off Main South Rd (the A2

HANDICRAFTS

Woollen bags, carpets, tapestries and traditional Basotho hats are the most sought-after crafts in Lesotho. The Basotho Hat Building in the city centre is home to the impressive **Lesotho Cooperative Handicrafts shop** (☎ 2232 2523, ✉ lch@basothohat.co.ls; accepts credit cards). Some crafts are also sold in the tourist information centre across the road. You'll find a few more crafts, mostly woven Basotho hats (*mokorotlo*), sold on the pavements around this end of town. Good handicraft outlets on the outskirts of town include **Maseru Tapestries & Mats** (☎ 2231 3975, ✉ maserutapestry@yahoo.com), signposted on Raboshabane Road, in the industrial area, which has handwoven tapestries and carpets; and the similar **Seithati Weavers**, 8km out along the Mafeteng road (☎ 2231 3975, ✇ villageweavers.co.ls).

towards Mafeteng), is served by daily flights from Johannesburg (Mon–Fri 5 daily, Sat & Sun 3 daily; 1hr 10min) by South African Airlink (☎ 2235 0418, ✇ saairlink.co.za). South African Airlink operates a shuttle bus to and from Maseru (☎ 2235 0418; M50), which can pick you up or drop you at a hotel. Private taxis (see below) cost nearer M80. Alternatively, wait for an infrequent minibus taxi at the airport gate. Avis (☎ 2235 0328) and Imperial Car Rental (☎ 2235 0292) have offices at the airport.

11

GETTING AROUND

The city centre is compact and easy to get around on foot, though there are lots of **minibus taxis** running up and down Kingsway and into the suburbs, from just before dawn to around 8pm. At night, **private taxis** are the only option; operators include Luxury Telephone Taxis (☎ 2232 6211), Moonlite Taxis (☎ 2231 2605) and Perfect Taxis (☎ 2232 5222). For **car rental**, head to Avis, at the *Lesotho Sun* (☎ 2231 4325), or Budget Rent-a-Car, at the *Maseru Sun* (☎ 2231 6344); car rental is also available at the airport (see above).

INFORMATION

Tourist information At the west end of Kingsway in the thatched Basotho Shield Building (Mon–Fri 8am–5pm, Sat & Sun 9am–1pm; ☎ 2231 2427, ✇ visitlesotho.travel).

ACCOMMODATION

Maseru is the only place in the country where there's much choice of accommodation, offering everything from camping and grim dorms to luxury suites in plush hotels. The central options, on or near Kingsway, are the most practical if you don't have your own transport.

Anglican Training Centre Corner of Assisi and Lancers rds ☎ 2232 2046; map pp.596–597. Large and fairly institutionalized place reasonably close to Kingsway offering spartan but adequate double rooms with communal showers and toilets. M260

Black Swan B&B 770 Manong Rd, Hillsview ☎ 2231 7700, ✇ blackswan.co.ls; map pp.596–597. Located in a quiet area of town, this hotel has clean and attractive rooms and a small indoor pool set around a tidy compound with a duck pond. M600

City Lodger 212 Moshoeshoe Rd, Maseru West ☎ 2831 7757, ✉ citylodger@gmail.com; map pp.596–597. A boutique guesthouse north of the centre near the industrial area; the elegant rooms with sandstone brick walls are nicely decorated, with sleek bathrooms. M600

Foothills Guesthouse 121 Maluti Rd, Maseru West ☎ 5870 6566; map pp.596–597. This colonial-style, sandstone house offers simple, homely accommodation in a quiet area of town, including six comfortable and spotless rooms and a couple of self-catering chalets. M480

Lancers Inn Kingsway, corner of Pioneer Rd ☎ 2231 2114, ✇ lancersinn.co.ls; map pp.596–597. Maseru's most characterful and pleasant place to stay, set in a very central and attractive sandstone building. There are well-priced and comfortable rondavels and chalets with en-suite bathrooms, a pool and a good beer garden and restaurant, all set in attractive gardens. M845

Lesotho Sun Hilton Rd ☎ 2224 3000, ✇ suninternational.com; map pp.596–597. Maseru's largest and smartest accommodation option, this resort has comfortable (if smallish) rooms with TVs and good views over town, plus loads of sports facilities, health spa, casino, cinema and several good restaurants. M1756

Maseru Backpackers Airport Rd ☎ 2232 5166, ✇ lesothodurhamlink.org; map pp.596–597. The best camping option in Maseru, with clean shower blocks and a well-equipped kitchen, plus very comfortable four-bed rondavels and decent backpacker accommodation in small dormitories. The site, signposted as "Lesotho Durham Link", just beyond the old airport, overlooks the Maqalika Dam, and a range of outdoor activities can be arranged. Camping M50, dorm M110, rondavel M450

Maseru Sun 12 Orpen Rd, Old Europa ☎2231 2434, ⓦ suninternational.com; map pp.596–597. The second of the town's *Sun* hotels, with decent rooms in soothing, well-tended garden surroundings, which are popular with locals in the evenings. There's also a good restaurant and a large, attractive swimming pool. M1225

Victoria Hotel Kingsway ☎2231 3687; map pp.596–597. This plain concrete high-rise towering over Kingsway near the Basotho Hat Building is a prominent landmark in central Maseru, offering comfortable if unremarkable rooms, a bar and an adequate restaurant. M650

EATING AND DRINKING

As you'd expect, Maseru has the best selection of restaurants in Lesotho. Several pricey, upmarket places can be found in the Lesotho and Maseru *Sun* hotels.

Canton Moposo House, Kingsway ☎2231 2003; map pp.596–597. Despite the tacky interior, this is an excellent Chinese restaurant spread across two floors, with a large variety of dishes priced between M50 and M80, and set menus to share; try the eleven-dish menu for M420. Daily 8am–9.30pm.

Mediterranee Pioneer Rd, LNDC Shopping Centre ☎2832 9638; map pp.596–597. Opposite *Lancer's Inn*, this unpretentious pizzeria and coffee shop is popular for its excellent-value pizza, pasta and burgers, all cheap at M20–60, and the DJs playing jazz on Sunday evenings. Daily 7.30am–10pm.

Mimmo's UN Rd, opposite UN House; map pp.596–597. Decent pizzas and filling pasta served in a pleasant setting. It's popular with expats, particularly for lunch on the terrace. Mains from M40–90. Daily noon–10pm.

Oh La La Kingsway, corner of Pioneed Rd; map pp.596–597. With terrace seating in the small park next to the Alliance Française, this rondavel houses the best café in town, with fresh sandwiches (M25), croissants, crepes, pastries and pies, plus good coffee. Mon–Fri 8am–7pm, Sat & Sun 8am–4pm.

The Regal Kingsway ☎2231 3930; map pp.596–597. A stylish dining room and balcony terrace on the first floor of the Basotho Hut, serving very good Indian food as well as some Chinese and European options. The best restaurant in town, yet modestly priced at around M50–90 for a main course. Mon–Sat 10am–3pm & 5.30–9pm.

Rendezvous Lancers Inn, Kingsway ☎2231 2114; map pp.596–597. Lesotho's classiest restaurant (King Letsie is known to dine here regularly), with an African- and French-themed menu and a candlelit atmosphere, and mains priced from M40–100. The outdoor seating is popular at lunchtimes. Daily noon–10pm.

Times Café First floor of LNDC Shopping Centre, Kingsway ☎2231 7705; map pp.596–597. Trendy bar that serves a selection of European food (M40–80, although they don't always have everything on the menu), in addition to coffees and cakes. If you can stand the constant blaring of taxi horns, eat alfresco on the balcony. Daily noon–midnight.

DIRECTORY

Banks and currency exchange The main branches of Standard Lesotho Bank, Nedbank and First National Bank are on Kingsway. The best places for foreign exchange are the Standard Bank on the ground floor of the Lesotho Bank Tower, Kingsway, and Green's Bureau de Change, Kingsway, LNDC Centre, inside the ProCell shop (☎5250 0400; Mon–Fri 8am–5pm, Sat & Sun 8am–1pm), which also changes maloti to rand at 1 percent commission.

Books Maseru Book Centre on Kingsway, just past the Lesotho Bank, has a number of historical and cultural works published by Morija Museum; the craft shop in the Basotho Hat Building also has a selection.

Embassies and consulates Canada, Quadrant Sales Building, Orpen Rd ☎2231 5365; Ireland, Tona-kholo Rd, ☎2231 4068; South Africa, corner Kingsway and Old School Rd, ☎2231 5758; US, 254 Kingsway, ☎221 2666.

Gym The Lehakoe Club, on the corner of Parliament and Moshoeshoe rds (☎2231 7640), offers everything from exercise classes, indoor and outdoor pools, to squash, tennis and a well-equipped gym, all open to non-members.

Hospitals Queen Elizabeth II Hospital, Kingsway (☎2231 2501); Maseru Private Hospital, Thetsane Rd (☎2231 3260).

Internet access Newland Internet Cafe, on Kingsway opposite the Post Office (daily 8am–7pm); Leo Internet Cafe, on Kingsway 200m to the west (Mon–Fri 8am–5pm).

Pharmacy MHS Pharmacy, LNDC Shopping Centre, Kingsway ☎2232 5189.

Police Constitution Rd ☎2231 7262/7623.

Post office Kingsway (Mon–Fri 8am–4.30pm, Sat 8am–noon).

Radio BBC World Service 90.2FM (24hr).

Supermarkets A large, well-stocked Pick 'n Pay supermarket can be found in the Pioneer Mall on Pioneer Rd (Mon–Sat 8am–8pm, Sun 8am–5pm).

Travel agents Flight ticketing and Intercape bus tickets are available through SAA City Centre Maseru Travel, next to the Maseru Book Centre, Kingsway (☎2231 4536, ✉mampek.maserutravel@galileosa.co.za), and Maluti Travel & Tours, next to First National Bank on Kingsway

(☎2232 7172). Intercape bus tickets are sold at the Shoprite supermarket in the LNDC Centre.

Around Maseru

Although you're unlikely to spend much of your time in Lesotho in Maseru itself, there are a number of rewarding places to visit within easy reach of the capital. A little oddly in a country dominated by towering mountains, it is two of the smaller hills, **Thaba Bosiu**, Moshoeshoe I's impregnable hilltop fortress, and nearby **Qiloane**, model for the Basotho hat (*mokorotlo*), which are the most famous, both ranking among the most important historical sites in the country. South of Maseru, the **Qeme Plateau** offers views over the city and surrounding countryside.

Thaba Bosiu

About 20km east of Maseru • Mon–Fri 8am–5pm, Sat 9am–5pm, Sun 9am–1pm • M10

Thaba Bosiu is Lesotho's most important historical sight, a steep mountain with a large flat top that was the capital of the kingdom in the days of Moshoeshoe I. It is a place of great significance to the people of Lesotho, and the burial ground of the country's kings, and as such is well worth a visit.

Moshoeshoe I trekked with his followers from Butha-Buthe to Thaba Bosiu in July 1824 in a bid to settle somewhere far from the warrior clans then terrorizing the flat plains to the north and west, and somewhere that would be extremely hard for anyone to capture. Thaba Bosiu, with its crown of near-vertical cliffs, good grazing and seven

---

TAKING THABA BOSIU

In 1828, the Ngwane were the first to attack Thaba Bosiu, but were decisively beaten, after which they never troubled Moshoeshoe again. **Mzilikhazi**, King of the Ndebele, who later conquered much of modern-day Zimbabwe, tried to take the mountain in 1831, but his men were defeated by a mass of great boulders flung down from the top by the Basotho; Moshoeshoe is reputed to have sent the Ndebele a large number of fat oxen after their defeat, an unprecedented move for a victorious chief – as if to say that he understood that their attack had been inspired by hunger and that he wanted to help them out.

There followed a twenty-year period of relative calm, during which time Moshoeshoe would receive visitors wearing a beautifully tailored dark-blue military uniform, complete with cloak, and offer them tea from a prized china tea service. He allowed the French missionary, **Eugene Casalis**, to establish a mission at the bottom of the mountain in 1837, and employed him as his secretary and interpreter. In 1852 a British punitive force led by the Cape governor, **Sir George Cathcart**, didn't even make it as far as the mountain, instead being attacked a short distance away by Moshoeshoe's well-armed troops, who forced their hasty withdrawal. **Afrikaner forces** fighting for the Orange Free State (OFS) made a brief attempt on Thaba Bosiu in 1858, but came back in 1865 in a more determined manner, armed with heavy artillery, and began steadily shelling the mountain, launching two simultaneous assaults a few days later. Eight men made it to the top, but were seriously wounded as soon as they did so, and speedily retreated back down. A week later, more Afrikaner troops and the OFS president turned up, and another assault was launched. **General Wepener** led his men right to the top of the Khubelu Pass, but he was shot at the top and mortally wounded. The Basotho then mounted a counterattack, and the Afrikaners withdrew. They continued the siege for a month, though, during which time most of the livestock on Thaba Bosiu died of hunger and the Basotho became so short of bullets that they melted down the shells being fired at them to make home-made ones.

Although they won this battle, the Basotho lost the war, and Moshoeshoe signed a humiliating treaty in 1866 that surrendered most of Lesotho's farmland to the OFS. Four years later the old king died and was buried on the top of Thaba Bosiu, and two years after that Lesotho was annexed to the Cape Colony.

or eight freshwater springs on top, fitted the bill perfectly, and despite numerous attacks, the mountain was never taken. The name means "Mountain of the Night", perhaps because, as legend has it, Moshoeshoe first arrived there in the evening, and immediate protective measures took all night to install. A more compelling reason, and the one most Basotho prefer, is that the mountain, which does not look particularly high or impressive by day, seems to grow inexorably as night falls, becoming huge and unconquerable.

Visiting Thaba Bosiu

An official guide from the visitor centre will walk you up the steep **Khubelu Pass** (or "Red Pass"), a cleft in the cliffs marked by two flagpoles, where the Afrikaner General Louw Wepener was killed trying to storm the mountain in 1865 (see box, p.601), and on to the remains of Moshoeshoe's **European house**, built for him by a deserter from the 72nd Seaforth Highlanders, David F. Webber. From here, it's a short walk to the remains of Moshoeshoe's royal court and then to the **royal graveyard**, where the tombs of Moshoeshoe I and most of his successors are marked with simple stone cairns. On the eastern edge of the plateau you get a great view of **Qiloane**, a strange cone-shaped mountain with a large nodule on the top, which was apparently the inspiration for the national headdress, the distinctive Basotho hat.

ARRIVAL AND DEPARTURE	**THABA BOSIU**

By car To get to Thaba Bosiu by car, take Main South Rd from Maseru, turning left at the sign for the National Health Training Centre, just before the Engen petrol station. Follow this road for 10km and turn left at the T-junction for another 3km. Alternatively, follow Main South Rd further towards Roma and follow signs to Thaba Bosiu.

By minibus taxi During the day, frequent minibus taxis run here from Maseru's New Taxi Rank.

INFORMATION

Tourist information At the foot of the mountain (☎ 2235 7207, ✉ touristinfo@ltdc.org.ls). Outside opening hours you're officially not allowed up the mountain, but there's nothing to stop you.

ACCOMMODATION

Mmelesi Lodge ☎ 5886 1116. One of the best-run Basotho-owned lodges in the country, next to the mountain and within walking distance of the visitor centre. It has a plush bar and a pleasant restaurant serving moderately priced meat and fish dishes, a braai area, and comfortable en-suite rondavels at the back. M610

Roma and around

About 30km from Maseru along a good tar road, the mission town of **ROMA** has a beautiful location amid sandstone foothills and is home to the **National University of Lesotho**, which began life in 1945 as Pius XII College, run by the Roman Catholic Church. Between 1964 and 1971 it was the university of all three of the former British southern African protectorates, now Lesotho, Botswana and Swaziland.

A kilometre or so further up the road is **Roma Mission**, most of which was built by French missionaries after 1862. Though grander than its counterpart in Morija, the mission is a little run-down, and there's not much reason to linger.

The road to Semonkong

The road from Roma to Semonkong is one of the most spectacular in Lesotho, with superb views as you climb into the highlands. Where the tarred road turns to gravel at **Moitsupeli**, 18.5km beyond Roma, look ahead towards the twin summits of the appropriately named **Thabana-li-Mele** (Breast Mountains). After the next village of Ha Dinzulu, the road continues to climb, peaking at 2000m at Nkesi's Pass and then dropping down to the village of **RAMABANTA**.

11

By bus and minibus taxi Several buses and many more minibus taxis travel daily between Maseru and Roma, making this one of the busiest public transport routes in the country. Minibus taxis to Roma depart from the New Taxi Rank, by Sefika Shopping Centre, and take 30–45min.

Destinations: Maseru (5 daily; 1hr); Semonkong (4 daily; 4hr).

ACCOMMODATION

ROMA

Trading Post Guest House Signposted off the main road 2km before the centre of Roma, ☎2234 0202, after 5.30pm ☎2234 0267, ⊛tradingpost.co.za. The best accommodation in Roma, built in 1903 as a trading store by John Thomas Thorn, and lived in by his family ever since. This ivy-festooned guesthouse offers luxury rondavels, en-suite doubles and backpacker twin rooms with shared bathrooms in the original sandstone house; plus a self-catering cottage (M500, sleeps six) and camping. Decent meals are available by prior arrangement, there's a small swimming pool, and the family can help arrange activities including pony-trekking in the surrounding hills and walks to nearby dinosaur footprints. Camping M̲6̲0̲, dorm beds M̲1̲0̲0̲, double M̲5̲1̲0̲

RAMABANTA

Ramabanta Trading Post Lodge ☎2234 0202, after 5.30pm ☎2234 0267, ⊛tradingpost.co.za. Sister establishment to the *Trading Post Guest House* (see above), boasts seven lovely en-suite rooms in converted stables, three luxury rondavels sleeping four, backpacker accommodation in three-bed dorms and a campsite. Meals are available and, like the guesthouse in Roma, hikes and pony rides can be arranged, as can 4WD adventures (in your own car) with overnights in villages. Camping M̲6̲0̲, dorm M̲1̲2̲5̲, double M̲5̲0̲0̲

Semonkong and around

Crossing the Makhaleng River and the 3000m-high Thaba Putsoa mountain range from Maseru gets you to the curiously straggly town of **SEMONKONG**. The region was inhabited by the San until 1873, when – after a series of **genocidal campaigns** against them by the British – the last of Lesotho's San were finally exterminated by an expedition led by a certain Colonel Bowker. The town itself began life in the 1880s following the Gun War as a refuge for displaced Basotho from the lowlands. The town offers a few basic stores, plenty of **bars**, and even a post office and bank, though you can't rely on either. If you're here in winter, try to catch the local **horse races** on the last Saturday of every month.

Ketane Falls

From the lodge in Semonkong (see opposite), it's a day's hike or pony trek west (see box opposite) into the pretty Thaba Putsoa mountains to the pristine 120m **Ketane Falls**. The falls are inaccessible by any other means of transport, and the pony trek is considered one of the best in the country. The falls can also be visited on a popular multi-day pony trek from *Malealea Lodge* (see p.617).

Maletsunyane Falls

The dramatic **Maletsunyane Falls** (or Le Bihan Falls, after a French missionary) are a pretty 5km walk downriver from Semonkong. The dramatic falls, the highest single drop in Southern Africa, plunge nearly 200m down a sheer and scary cliff into a swimmable pool, whose mist gives the falls their name: "Smoking Water". There's a steep path down to the bottom, where you can swim or camp. The pool usually freezes by June, but the waterfall keeps going all winter, spraying the surrounding rocks with ice, and forming an impressive ice cage over the pool.

By car The 120km drive from Maseru to Semonkong takes about three hours by private car on asphalt and decent gravel roads – though after heavy rains a 4WD car is necessary.

By bus Lesotho Freight and Bus Services buses leave Maseru twice daily, around 9–10am and 1–2pm, returning around 6–7am and 10–11am; the ride takes around six hours.

ACTIVITIES AROUND SEMONKONG

Working in conjunction with the local community, *Semonkong Lodge* offers a bewildering choice of **outdoor activities**, ranging from short walks through town and along the river in search of bald ibis, to abseiling and adventurous pony treks lasting several days and overnighting in basic huts. Advance bookings are required for overnight rides. Semonkong boasts the longest commercially run **abseil** in the world, a 204m descent down the Maletsunyane Falls (M825). It's an electrifying thirty-minute descent, just metres away from the crashing water. You'll be given training on a small cliff near the lodge before taking the challenge the next day, and receive photos of the experience afterwards.

There is also a variety of **pony treks**, from short jaunts visiting nearby sights to overnight expeditions. As ever, per-person costs work out cheaper in larger groups; the maximum is fifteen people; couples pay M250 per person for a full day's ride. Per-person costs for overnight trips, including the guide and pack horse, are around M870 for one night, M1315 for two nights and M3190 for six nights. For overnight hikes pack horses are optional but recommended; again, as a couple expect to pay around M310 per person for a day and night (M440 with pack horse), or M1120 per person (M1595 with pack horse) for six nights. For day-trips on foot, a guide costs M10 per hour.

11

ACCOMMODATION

Semonkong Lodge 1km south of town beside the Maletsunyane River ☎2700 6037, ⓦplaceofsmoke .co.ls. One of the best lodges in Lesotho, this laidback and well-run place offers en-suite doubles and a dormitory in cosy thatch-and-stone buildings, complete with electricity and hot showers, and with fireplaces in some rooms.

There's also a campsite, a kitchen for self-caterers, a great bar with pool table, balcony and a decent selection of music, and delicious meals (including vegetarian). But the main reason for staying here is for the immense selection of outdoor activities on offer (see box above). Credit cards accepted. Camping M80, dorm M130, double M600

Ha Baroana

About 45km east of Maseru, a few kilometres north of Nazareth village • Daily 8am–5pm • M5

Ha Baroana has what were once some of the finest rock paintings in the country. They are still interesting, with discernible figures of animals, dancers and hunters, but they have been vandalized and washed away by child guides who throw water at them to make them more visible for tourists. The easiest way to get to the paintings is along a difficult dirt road, signposted off the main road. After 3.5km you'll reach the village of Ha Khotso; take the second turning on your right and then continue straight on for another 3km to Ha Baroana. The attractive **visitors' centre** offers a (compulsory) guide to accompany you on the fifteen-minute walk down into the gorge.

MOHALE DAM

About 80km east of Maseru and signposted off the A3, Mohale Dam was completed in 2004 as Phase 1b of the Lesotho Highlands Water Project (see box, p.610). Unlike the astonishing engineering grace of Katse Dam (see p.609), Mohale is little more than an enormous pile of concrete-faced rubble, the highest of its kind in Africa, whose 145m-high barrier holds back almost a billion cubic metres of water. Connected to the Katse Dam by a 32km-long tunnel, its purpose is to feed more water north towards South Africa. A **visitor centre** (Mon–Fri 8am–5pm, Sat & Sun 10am–4pm; ☎2293 6217, ⓔlevotm@lhda.org.ls), with a stunning location overlooking the lake, runs daily **tours** (M10) of the site at 9am and 2pm on weekdays, and either 9am or noon on weekends. The two-hour cruises (M60) on the lake were unfortunately suspended at the time of writing; contact ⓔmohaleboating@ltdc.org.ls or call ☎2293 6432 for more details. The visitor centre is difficult to reach without your own transport but is well signposted: continue 2km beyond Mohale Camp on the A3 and turn left. After 4km turn left again, through a security barrier (where you'll have to register), and continue until you reach the centre.

Thaba-Tseka

The road from Mohale Dam (see p.605) to **THABA-TSEKA** is a dramatic one, peaking in the heart of the Central Range at the 2860m **Mokhoabong Pass**, before descending to the town, which is over 2200m above sea level – although once here there's very little in this 1980s purpose-built administrative centre to detain you. The road was being tarred with help from the Kuwait Fund at time of research, and once finished will make a magnificent Maseru–Katse–Leribe circuit possible.

ARRIVAL AND DEPARTURE   THABA-TSEKA

By bus Lesotho Freight and Bus Services operates three buses daily from Maseru to Thaba-Tseka, leaving the capital at 8.30am, 9am and 9.30am. These continue on to Bokong (next to Katse), Linakaneng and Sehong Hong (a good way along the A4 to Sehlabathebe) respectively, and are as far as you can travel by public transport on those routes.

By car With your own vehicle you could tackle the spectacular road to Mokhotlong and the Sani Pass, but it's not one you should attempt in anything other than a 4WD. The fairly flat gravel road to Katse is suitable for ordinary saloons and there are a number of buses plying the route. There's no road southwest from Thaba-Tseka to Semonkong, though there are hikeable trails.

ACCOMMODATION

Buffalo Hotel 10km east of town along the main road ☎ 2700 7339, ✉ senatentabe@leo.co.ls. A pleasant new hotel with en-suite rooms and rondavels, a restaurant and a bar. Popular with the 4WD crowd crossing Lesotho. **M580**

Mountain Star Lodge Town centre ☎ 2290 0415. A friendly lodge with smallish en-suite rooms with TVs, good basic food in its restaurant – the only one in town – and a lively bar. **M350**

The northern districts

The route north from Maseru right the way round to the **Sani Pass** takes in the best of both Lesotho's lowlands and highlands. The road is tarred all the way to Mokhotlong, and although it's breaking up in places, is fine for 2WD vehicles except in winter. The stretch from Mokhotlong to Sani Pass, and the dramatic winding road down the mighty Drakensberg into South Africa, is dirt, for which 4WD is strongly advised, even if it remains just about passable in a saloon car in good weather.

Kome Cave Village

About 2km from the village of Mateka • M10 • ☎ 5320 0964, ⓦ komecaves.co.ls

Kome Cave Village was once the country's best-kept architectural secret but is now an increasingly popular tourist destination. Seven quaint and inhabited mud dwellings sit under a huge rock overhang, looking more like igloos or West African mud architecture than anything usually found in Southern Africa.

At the modern **visitor centre**, visible on approach from the main road, an obligatory guide accompanies you on the ten-minute walk down to the site, where the ladies living in the huts will happily show you their dwellings and pose for photos.

Teya-Teyaneng

TEYA-TEYANENG (usually abbreviated to "T.Y.") means "place of shifting sands", after the way the nearby river changes its course from time to time. T.Y. is the **crafts capital** of Lesotho, specializing in all manner of weavings (see box opposite), from jerseys to elaborately designed wall hangings.

THE MALOTI–DRAKENSBERG TRANSFRONTIER PROJECT

The **Maloti–Drakensberg Transfrontier Project** (Ⓦmaloti.org.ls) focuses on Lesotho's highland areas bordering South Africa, from near Butha-Buthe in the north clockwise to beyond Qacha's Nek in the south. The project is a hopeful sign that the previously hapless management of the area's roads, tourist facilities and unique but fragile natural areas may soon be a thing of the past. Based on an integrated approach with South Africa, the project focuses on ecological issues and on the area's widespread poverty. The idea is to tackle both aspects by establishing **sustainable tourism** initiatives among local communities, with the emphasis on culture as much as on natural attractions. South African parks and reserves included in the project include Ukhahlamba Drakensberg Park, Royal Natal National Park, Golden Gate Highlands National Park and Ongelurksnek Nature Reserve. During the 20-year project period, it's likely that some of these areas will become **transfrontier parks**. For more information, visit the project coordinator's office in the Ministry of Tourism on the 7th floor of the Post Office building on Kingsway in Maseru (Ⓣ2231 2662).

Leribe (Hlotse)

Some 15km east of Maputsoe, a messy border town opposite Ficksburg in South Africa that's only good for its transport connections, **LERIBE** is a dilapidated but still pleasant little town, officially called **Hlotse** but more commonly known by the name of the surrounding district. It was founded in 1876 by an Anglican missionary, Reverend John Widdicombe, and suffered repeated sieges during the Gun War. Just over 7km south of town, with some effort it's possible to view excellent **dinosaur footprints** at the turn-of-the-twentieth-century **Tsikoane Mission**. To get there, turn off the main road at the white Tsikoane school sign and ask directions to the mission, where you can tip a local to guide you up the steep slope to the rock overhang above the church. Here you'll find a large chunk of rock that fell from the overhang that has dozens of clear three-toed Lesothosaurus footprints of varying sizes; the negative prints can be seen on the overhang ceiling.

Leribe Craft Centre

Mon–Fri 8am–4.30pm, Sat 9.30am–1pm; outside opening hours ask around and someone will open up • Ⓣ2240 0323

The **Leribe Craft Centre**, right by the major intersection on the main road, sells wonderful mohair scarves and shawls (M200–450), blankets and tablemats made by people with disabilities, plus maps and a few books about Lesotho and its history.

THE WEAVING INDUSTRY IN TEYA-TEYANENG

There are four weaving outlets in Teya-Teyaneng, all open daily from 8am to 5pm. The most central is **Setsoto Design** (Ⓣ5808 6312), 300m from the *Blue Mountain Inn* (see p.608), where you can see tapestries being made. A good selection of woven products, crafts and elusive Lesotho postcards is sold in the adjacent shop: expect to pay around M120 for a bag and M1500 for a large tapestry. Credit cards are accepted. Three kilometres south of town, on the left as you come in from Maseru, look for signs to the small showroom of **Hatooa Mose Mosali** (Ⓣ2250 0772), which translates as "women must stand up and work hard". There's a fairly limited range in stock but its catalogue displays some very special wall hangings, which you need to order as they take a week or two to make. A short distance further on, signposted to the right of the main road, the pleasant Anglican St Agnes Mission is home to **Helang Basali Handicrafts** (Ⓣ2250 1546), whose showroom has a limited selection of woven crafts. For the best choice of products, head to **Elelloang Basali Studio** (Ⓣ2250 1520, Ⓦafricancrafts.com/artist/elelloang), about 5km north of town on the road to Leribe (the last building in town, constructed from recycled cans), where you'll find an extensive range of wall hangings, floor rugs, table mats and bags.

11

ARRIVAL AND DEPARTURE

KOME CAVE VILLAGE

By pubic transport Getting to the cave village is easiest via Teya-Teyaneng, where you can pick up fairly regular transport to Mateka; from here it's an easy 30min walk down the hill to Kome.

By car Turn right onto the dirt track behind the football field in Mateka to find signs for the visitor centre; note that driving in a saloon car to Mateka from either Maseru via Lancer's Gap or from Thaba Bosiu via the good gravel road is problematic due to a difficult and steep 30m section between Sefikeng and Mateka.

TEYA-TEYANENG

By car There are two roads from Maseru to Teya-Teyaneng. The most commonly used is the scenic Main North Rd (A1), which takes you through sandstone mountain-studded lowlands. For an alternative, which requires high clearance for a ridiculously short bad stretch on an otherwise perfect asphalt road, follow Main North Rd out of Maseru and turn right after 4km onto the B31, signposted to Sefikeng and Kome Cave Village. This climbs up a steep series of hairpins to Lancer's Gap, an extraordinary ridge with a great gap in

the middle through which the road passes, so named because a Lancers regiment was allegedly ambushed and defeated in it during the Gun War.

By bus and minibus taxi The bus and taxi rank is 100m east of the main highway on the road to Mapoteng. There's plenty of transport to and from Maseru and further north to Leribe and Butha-Buthe, and you rarely have to wait long.

LERIBE

By car The highway from Maseru passes to the south of town, and between the two petrol stations you'll find the main intersection. The road on the left leads up the hill to the town centre.

By bus and minibus taxi The taxi rank is reached along the road branching off at the *Mountain View Hotel*. There's plenty of transport, though if you're heading south it may be quickest to grab a seat on one of the frequent minibuses to Maputsoe and change there. The Lesotho Freight and Bus Services service to Mokhotlong doesn't enter town but stops 100m north of the Caltex garage by the Mount Royal Church.

ACCOMMODATION

TEYA-TEYANENG

Blue Mountain Inn A couple of hundred metres past the post office and its transmitter ☎ 2250 0362, ⊛ skymountainhotels.com. A spacious and well-run hotel with dozens of small and old-fashioned but comfortable chalets, plus a new block with smarter, better-value rooms. It also has a restaurant, serving tasty meals

(M40–70), plus a pizzeria, three bars, a pool and a large lawn with shaded tables. <u>M600</u>

Ka Pitseng Guest House Signposted below the main road as you approach the town from Maseru ☎ 2250 1638. A more modest option than the *Blue Mountain Inn*, with clean rooms and a decent restaurant that serves a Basotho lunch buffet (R50) on Wednesdays. <u>M500</u>

CULTURE AS FASHION: THE BLANKET AND THE HAT

In a region of Africa where **traditional dress** has all but died out, Lesotho stands out as the exception. The **mokorotlo** (Basotho traditional hat) is not widely worn these days, admittedly, though you'll still occasionally see its distinctive cone and bobble in Lesotho. Apparently modelled on the shape of Qiloane Mountain near Thaba Bosiu, and made of woven straw, the *mokorotlo* has become the standard Basotho souvenir, sold in every craft shop, usually for M50 or less.

More prevalent than the *mokorotlo* is the Basotho **blanket**, made from high-quality woven wool and worn all over the country in all seasons. European traders started bringing these from England to Lesotho in the 1860s, though nowadays they are made in South Africa.

The symbols woven into the blankets were originally English design, but acquired significance for the Basotho over time; maize cobs were associated with fertility, for example. Young brides are supposed to wear a blanket around their hips until their first child is conceived, and boys wear different blankets before and after circumcision. The ubiquitous Fraser's Stores, which you find all over the country, first established themselves by selling blankets, and still stock them today; otherwise, the Di Mezza & De Jager Trading Store, just across the border in Clarens (see p.451), is a great place to see different kinds of blankets. Good ones (made of pure wool) cost M400–600, a fortune by local standards.

Although they have always been foreign imports, and are the commodities on which many European trader fortunes have been built, the blankets remain quintessentially Basotho, and a source of national pride.

LERIBE

Mountain View Hotel Just up the road from the main intersection ☎ 2240 0559, ⓦ skymountainhotels.com. A range of rooms in the main building, a glam new extension, and in chalets and rondavels scattered around the pleasant gardens. The restaurant serves tasty meat and fish dishes, and light snacks. There's also a lively bar, which is especially busy at weekends. M600

Naleli Guest House 2km from the centre along the old road north to Butha-Buthe ☎ 2240 0409. The best accommodation and food in town, with a set of nicely furnished rooms that overlook a well-tended garden and terrace. The restaurant serves sandwiches and burgers, and Basotho cuisine on Thursdays. M685

The road to Katse Dam

To the east of Leribe rises the impressive Front Range of the Maloti Mountains. The region is at the heart of Phase 1a of the ambitious **Lesotho Highlands Water Project** (see box, p.610), whose centrepiece is the massive dam and reservoir at **Katse**. The 100km A8 highway built for the dam from Leribe is a remarkable journey almost worth doing for the drive alone, rising steeply up from the lowlands and over the 3090m **Mefika Lisiu Pass**, before reaching the Bokong Nature Reserve.

Bokong Nature Reserve

Just off the A8 · Daily 8am–5pm · M5 · Walk M10 · Guides M20/day · Horses M25/hour, M50/half day, M75/day

Established as part of the Highlands Water Project (see p.610), and a paradise for high-altitude hikers, the highlight of the breathtaking **Bokong Nature Reserve** is the dramatic **Lepaqoa Waterfall**, which freezes in winter to form a column of ice.

The reserve's **entrance** is next to the **visitor centre**, signposted off the highway 1km beyond the pass. Perched dramatically on the edge of a 100m cliff overlooking the Lepaqoa valley, the visitor centre offers a 45-minute walk along a poorly marked footpath to the top of Lepaqoa Waterfall, as well as guides and horses for hire. Particularly recommended is a possible two- to three-day hike along the alpine plateau to Ts'ehlanyane National Park to the north – bring your own camping gear and hire a guide from the visitor centre.

The Katse Dam

Visitor centre Mon–Fri 8am–noon & 1 4pm, Sat & Sun 8am–noon · Tours Mon–Fri 9am & 2pm, Sat & Sun 9am or noon · M10 · ☎ 2291 0377 · **Botanical gardens** Daily 9am–5pm · M10

KATSE village, a former engineers' village overlooking the lake, is drab and boring, with uniform box-like houses. But the massive **dam** below (see box, p.610), which holds back nearly two billion cubic metres of water, really is impressive, even if you aren't usually interested in engineering. To find out more, head for the **visitor centre**, with its bright blue roof, just before the village and dam. The hour-long **tours** take in the tunnels running from inside the dam into the mountainside, as well as the road on top, from where you can look straight down the wall. During initial excavations it was discovered that the bedrock was seismically unstable, so a moveable joint was incorporated into the dam's base, allowing it to flex. Even so, the rapid filling of the reservoir caused a series of minor **earth tremors**. This was all to be expected, said the engineers, but not by the inhabitants of Ha Mapaleng, where a tremor ripped a 30cm-wide, 1.5km-long gash through the village. The local prophetess explained that a huge **underground snake** had been disturbed by the dam's construction and that the entire village would be gobbled up. No one hung around to find out, and the village was eventually relocated 1km away.

Situated in the village and overlooking the dam lake, the **botanical gardens** are beautiful to visit, with several ecosystems represented on the sloping terrain, attracting colourful birds. It's something of a refugee camp for thousands of critically endangered spiral aloes rescued from the construction sites, and a programme to plant seedlings of spiral aloes and montane bamboo is under way.

11

11

THE LESOTHO HIGHLANDS WATER PROJECT

Lesotho's abundance of water but shortage of cash and Gauteng's monetary wealth and water poverty are the facts behind the stunningly ambitious **Lesotho Highlands Water Project** – Africa's largest engineering venture to date. The essence of the project is to dam Lesotho's major south-flowing rivers, then divert the water north through gravity tunnels (the longest in the world) via a hydroelectric power station at 'Muela to the Ash River, north of Clarens in South Africa, from where the water flows into the Vaal and to Gauteng. For this, South Africa pays Lesotho royalties of around R24 million a month.

The treaty formalizing the project was signed in 1986, although without much popular consultation or assessment of the environmental impact. Various compensation arrangements have been put in place for villagers affected by flooding, though not unexpectedly there are grumbles that these promises have not been met.

The project's first phase, which concluded in 2004, was split into two phases. **Phase 1a**, completed in 1997, saw the construction of the 185m-high Katse Dam, an underground hydroelectric plant at 'Muela, tunnels to the Ash River, and all the road infrastructure. Facilities were developed at Liphofung Cave, Katse and the nature reserves as part of this phase, the idea being that local communities would benefit from tourism revenues. **Phase 1b** saw the construction of Mohale Dam on the Senqunyane River, linked to Katse reservoir by tunnel. In 2007, following feasibility studies, the Lesotho Highlands Water Commission confirmed that the preferred site for phase 2 of the project is Polihali in Mokhotlong district, where a dam will be built and water transferred through another tunnel to Katse reservoir.

ARRIVAL AND DEPARTURE   THE ROAD TO KATSE DAM

BOKONG NATURE RESERVE
By minibus taxi The reserve can be reached from Leribe on minibus taxis that run roughly every two hours to Katse; ask to be dropped off at the visitor centre. Minibuses returning from Katse to Leribe are often full when they pass by, so go to nearby Ha Lejone and pick up transport there.

KATSE
By bus and minibus taxi Public transport leaves from the taxi rank at the entrance to Katse village. There are daily buses to Maseru, leaving around 6am, and minibus taxis every two hours or so to Leribe.

ACCOMMODATION

PITSENG
★ **Aloes Guest House** Follow the signs from the A8
☎ 2700 5626, ⓦ aloesguesthouse.com. Dreary Pitseng, on the A8, is notable only for this stylish guesthouse, which offers thatched bungalows set around a grassy compound with a small pool, self-catering facilities or food served upon request. Camping is also available. Quadbikes, pony trekking and guided hikes can be arranged. Camping M̲5̲0̲, bungalow M̲5̲4̲0̲

BOKONG NATURE RESERVE
Reserve accommodation Contact the Booking Office, LHDA Nature Reserves, PO Box 333 Butha-Buthe ☎ 2246 0723 or 2291 3206, ⓔ nature@lhda.org.ls. Camping is possible throughout the reserve, and there are also two stone-and-thatch rondavels close to the falls (each with four single beds) with a shared kitchen and

bathroom. They have gas and bedding, but you need to bring your own food. There are also five large chalets with fabulous views next to the visitor centre, where a basic restaurant serves meals (M25) on request. Advance booking for the restaurant, accommodation and ponies is highly recommended. Camping M̲5̲0̲, rondavels and chalets M̲2̲5̲0̲

KATSE
Orion Katse Lodge Katse village ☎ 2291 0202, ⓦ oriongroup.co.za. The only place to stay in Katse, and undergoing slow renovations to its currently drab rooms. The lodge offers fine views of the reservoir and its impressive birdlife, and a good restaurant serving a decent selection of meals. The hotel can arrange boat cruises (M600–1000), biking, pony trekking and hiking. Dorm M̲4̲0̲0̲, double M̲1̲0̲0̲0̲

Butha-Buthe

BUTHA-BUTHE (or Botha-Bothe, meaning "Lie Down") has a frontier feel – noisy, dirty and dusty – and offers little reason to stay, although it makes a good base for visiting nearby attractions. The town was founded in 1884 because the local chief refused to go to Leribe to pay taxes, necessitating a new tax centre nearer his residence. Butha-Buthe attracted traders from the outset, and is one of few towns in Lesotho with a sizeable Muslim Indian community.

Butha-Buthe Mountain, just east of town, is where Moshoeshoe I had his first stronghold before retreating to Thaba Bosiu in 1824. It's a stiff but not particularly difficult climb and the summit provides tremendous views. You can cut the hiking distance by catching a minibus taxi as far as Ha Mopeli.

ARRIVAL AND DEPARTURE
BUTHA-BUTHE

By minibus taxi There are frequent buses and minibus taxis from the main crossroads in town to Maseru and Katse, and two to three a day to Mokhotlong (7hr), and four daily to Leribe (30min).

ACCOMMODATION

Butha-Buthe Youth Hostel About 3.5km from town in the village of Ha Sechele ☎ 2246 1832. Though tricky to get to, the pleasant IYHF-accredited self-catering hostel, also known as *Ha Thabo Ramakantane*, is set in peaceful surroundings. It's pretty basic and lacks running water or electricity, but there's a kitchen for self-catering, the management is friendly and it's a great place to meet Basotho villagers and hike into the nearby hills. Unless you have a high-clearance vehicle, the only access is on foot: 50m before the Caledonspoort junction, turn right along a small dirt track which is signposted to St Paul's High School. Once past the school bear left and ask for directions; it's about an hour's walk from the town centre. M100

Crocodile Inn Hotel Hospital Rd ☎ 2246 0223, @ crocodile-inn@ilesotho.com. The only central place to stay, the run-down *Crocodile Inn Hotel*, next to the hospital, has shabby en-suite rooms and better rooms in rondavels. There are two bars, which attract dedicated drinkers until well into the morning, and an inexpensive restaurant. M500

Likileng Lodge 1km out of town on the left-hand side of the road heading to Oxbow ☎ 2246 0686, @ fedicsles@leo.co.ls. Probably the best accommodation in town, set in the large LHDA compound and offering clean and functional en-suite rooms, a bar and a restaurant serving tasty meals. M363

Ts'ehlanyane National Park

Daily 8am–5pm • M15, plus M5 per vehicle and M16 if staying overnight • Horses are available for hire by prior arrangement M25/hr, M50/half day, M75/day (minimum age 12) • ☎ 2246 0723 or 2291 3206 • @ nature@lhda.org.ls

A signposted turning 9km southeast of Butha-Buthe leads 32km southeast along good gravel into the western scarp of the Front Range, following a very picturesque valley. Covering 56 square kilometres of extremely rugged hiking terrain at the confluence of the Ts'ehlanyane and Holomo rivers, **Ts'ehlanyane National Park** is intended to protect several areas of ecological importance, particularly the indigenous **Leucosidea sericea woodland** known locally as *Ouhout* or *Che-che* – one of Lesotho's very few forested areas. Equally rare are stands of montane bamboo. **Mammals** present include mainly duikers, baboons and serval cats; there's also the endangered *Metisella syrinx* butterfly, bearded vultures (*lammergeiers*) and ground woodpeckers. The **best time to visit** is in spring, when the small yellow flowers along the riverbanks that give their unpronounceable name to the reserve are in flower. The highlight for hikers and pony trekkers alike is a spectacular 39km trail linking the park with Bokong Nature Reserve to the south (see p.609), with swimming possible in streams along the way.

ACCOMMODATION
TS'EHLANYANE NATIONAL PARK

Maliba Mountain Lodge ☎ 0027 31 702 8791 (South Africa), @ maliba-lodge.com. This new, deluxe private lodge in the national park offers Lesotho's best – and priciest – accommodation in six beautiful thatched suites, each with views of the forest and mountains. The lodge arranges pony trekking, village visits, hiking and other activities. Rates include three meals. M2740

Park Accommodation ☎ 2246 0723 or 2291 3206. Near the park's reception, there's accommodation in a guesthouse, which sleeps six people, or in three-bed dormitories. In addition, for a more rustic experience, there's two self-catering rondavels at the bush camp, which sleep up to four, though there's no electricity. Dorm M50, rondavel M200, guesthouse M350

'Muela

Power plant Tours daily 9am & 2pm • M10 • **Visitor centre** ⊕ 2224 8000

Heading northeast from Butha-Buthe, the A1 road begins to climb into the Maloti Mountains. After 22km, you reach the small settlement of Khukhune where a good tar road on the right leads up to **'MUELA**, an integral part of the Lesotho Highlands Water Project (see box, p.610). Here the water flowing down the delivery tunnel from Katse Reservoir powers an underground hydroelectric station that supplies all of Lesotho with electricity, as well as a small surplus that is sold to South Africa. The real attraction lies underground, and **tours** of the power plant (run by the visitor centre) take you past the three large turbines that power much of Lesotho.

Liphofung Cave Cultural Historical Site

Clearly signposted 3km off the main road north, 7km beyond the 'Muela turn-off • Daily 8am–5pm • M15 • Pony trekking M25/hr, M75/day

11

The **Liphofung Cave Cultural Historical Site** is actually a large sandstone overhang boasting an impressive series of San **rock paintings**, from whose images it gets its name, "Place of the Eland". The site is well worth a visit and is also significant for the Basotho in its role as a hideout for the young Moshoeshoe I. Guided tours of the site start from the visitor centre, where you can also see three traditional Basotho huts. Ponies can be hired from the visitor centre for guided treks, where cultural performances can also be arranged.

ACCOMMODATION — LIPHOFUNG CAVE CULTURAL HISTORICAL SITE

Liphofung Visitor Centre ⊕ 2246 0723. At the site's visitor centre are a couple of delightful self-catering rondavels that each sleep four people. M250

Mamohase Rural Stay B&B Signposted off the main road just south of Liphofung, then 2km down a tough dirt track ⊕ 5805 8438 or 5804 5597, ⊕ mamohaseruralstay.com. A homely set-up, offering local meals in the family dining room and a few beds in thatched rondavels next door, with bucket showers and an outdoor toilet. M500

Oxbow

The A1 into the highlands is one of the most dramatic roads in Lesotho, passing through some particularly striking sandstone cliffs before twisting tortuously up a chain of heart-stopping hairpins into the basalt. Some 20km beyond Liphofung, past **Moteng Pass** (2820m), Oxbow is a string of unremarkable buildings in a narrow valley. In winter, the place is packed out with South Africans looking at snow. Between June and August, **skiing** is the main draw a few kilometres up the road from Oxbow, where AfriSki (see below; ski pass M350/day, equipment rental M295/day) has a fun 2km ski run complete with ski lift and snow-making equipment if the weather doesn't oblige.

ACCOMMODATION — OXBOW

AfriSki Mahlasela Basin ⊕ 0027 58 303 6831 (South Africa), ⊕ afriski.net. About 10km up the road from Oxbow, at 3220m, this incongruous fledgling resort overlooking the ski slope is popular with South Africans in winter. Accommodation ranges from cramped backpacker dorms to very comfortable en-suite rooms. Dorm M150, double M940

New Oxbow Lodge ⊕ 0027 51 933 2247 (South Africa), ⊕ www.oxbow.co.za. The lodge has seen better days but still has perfectly comfortable, warm rooms, a well-stocked bar, and a restaurant serving reasonably priced meals. There's good trout fishing on the Malibamatso River, and wonderful hiking in any direction. M1207

The Roof of Africa route

The scenic road from Oxbow to Mokhotlong is often called "the Roof of Africa route", peaking at **Tlaeeng Pass** (3251m) and passing the ugly **Letseng diamond mine** en route. The road is fully tarred, although the extremes of temperature and heavy mining trucks here have caused damage, and there are numerous potholes. Most transport stops at the small village of **Mapholaneng**, where there's a reasonable restaurant (*Thugela*).

Mokhotlong

Perched on the banks of the scraggly Mokhotlong River, the wind-blown town of **MOKHOTLONG** ("Place of the Bald Ibis") is where the asphalt road from Maseru ends. Mokhotlong was once known as the "Loneliest Place in Africa", and it's easy to see why, since it still gets cut off from the rest of civilization for days or weeks at a time in winter. Mokhotlong began life as a remote police outpost in 1905, and gradually evolved into a trading centre for the region's highlanders, but remained isolated from the rest of Lesotho for years, with radio contact only established in 1947. An airstrip was constructed in 1948 and a rudimentary road link built in the 1950s, but Mokhotlong continued to get the bulk of its supplies by pony from Natal, via Sani, for a long time afterwards. Even today it feels remote, with locals usually riding into town for a shop and a drink on ponies, resplendent in their gumboots and blankets. However, it's the only town of any size in eastern Lesotho and a good place to stock up with supplies if you are using the Sani Top border post.

ARRIVAL AND INFORMATION   MOKHOTLONG

11

By bus and minibus taxi Getting to Mokhotlong is easiest on the daily 7am Lesotho Freight and Bus Services bus from Maseru, taking around 9 hours, and returning at 8am. There are also up to three minibus taxis a day from Butha-Buthe (7hr), and up to three to Sani Top (1hr 30min); the early morning bus from Mokhotlong to Sani Top usually continues down the pass to Underberg, returning in the afternoon;

additionally, *Sani Top Chalet* (see p.404) has a shuttle service between their lodge and the South African border post at the bottom of the pass road; it's a good idea to contact them for the latest transport details. To get from the central bus and minibus taxi stop, it's best to take a taxi (M4).

Bank There's a Standard Lesotho Bank in town with an ATM, but it doesn't change money.

ACCOMMODATION

Farmers' Training Centre 2km north of town, signposted as "FTC" ☎2292 0235. Basic and cheap dorm accommodation with clean rooms but grubby shared bathrooms. The highlight is the pleasant location on the edge of town. No food available. M50

Molumong Guest House 15km southwest of town along the road to Thaba-Tseka, ☎0027 33 702 1774 (South Africa), ⓦmolumonglodge.com. The remotest of Lesotho's lodges is a rustic but characterful 1920s place with fantastic mountain views. The main house is self-catering, with very cosy doubles and a great lounge to relax in. There's also a bunkhouse and a campsite. Only basic supplies are available in the village so come well stocked. The lodge also offers inexpensive pony trekking, and is a good base for hiking. It can be reached on the hourly minibuses from Mokhotlong to Ha Janteau. Camping M80, double M300

Senqu Hotel On the edge of town as you enter on the A1 ☎2292 0330. Very nice rooms (request one with a balcony and a good view), while the old rooms are clean but looking a bit shabby. The restaurant is the best place to eat in town, and there's a bar too. M500

St James Lodge 4km along the road from Mokhotlong to Tsaba-Tseka ☎0027 33 326 1601 (South Africa), ✉stjamesguestlodge@yahoo.com. In the grounds of the St James Mission, this self-catering lodge offers pleasant en-suite rooms, cheaper rondavels with separate bathrooms, and camping. Pony trekking, cultural visits to the village and a church tour are all available. A couple of minibuses run past the mission each day from Mokhotlong. Camping M65, rondavel M300, double M400

Sani and around

The rough gravel road to **SANI** branches off the main road to Mokhotlong 5km before town, and twists its way in spectacular fashion for nearly 60km along the Sehonkong River, peaking at **Kotisephola Pass** (3240m) before dropping to 2895m at **Sani Top**, a few kilometres from the South African border.

At Sani Top there are plenty of rewarding hikes, including a stiff 12km climb up **Thabana Ntlenyana**, at 3482m the highest point in Southern Africa and walkable in a day if you start early. Also tough but stunningly beautiful is the 40km **Top-of-the-Berg** hike to Sehlabathebe National Park, which takes about four days.

The descent from Sani, down the dramatic, hairpin-bend-filled **Sani Pass** into South Africa (see p.402), is only allowed with a 4WD car. In winter, the pass is frequently blocked by snow or ice. Talk of tarring the road has horrified off-road enthusiasts across the subcontinent. **Accommodation** is available just across the border at *Sani Top Chalet* (see p.404).

ARRIVAL AND INFORMATION	SANI AND AROUND

By bus and minibus Getting to Sani is only possible in good weather; if it's been snowing, you can forget it. Some five buses go from Sani to Mokhotlong every day (1hr 30min). On the South Africa side, 4WD tourist vehicles and

minibuses from Underberg run up to Sani (see p.403). **Crossing the border** The border, between *Sani Top Chalet* and Sani Pass, is open daily from 8am to 4pm; the Lesotho side stays open till 5pm to let vehicles through.

The southern districts

The country's **southern districts** can't match the mountains of north and central Lesotho for sheer scale, but they do hold some dramatic countryside that is relatively easy to visit – especially on horseback from the excellent tourist lodges at **Malealea** and **Semonkong**. The nineteenth-century mission town of **Morija** is perhaps the most historic in the country. Morija also has dinosaur footprints in the vicinity, as does **Mohale's Hoek** and, more accessibly, **Quthing**, further south. Moving on northeast past the town of **Qacha's Nek**, the isolated delights of **Sehlabathebe National Park** are so remote as to make visits here a true adventure.

Morija

Set at the foot of the Makhoarane Plateau, 44km from Maseru, the pleasant little town of **MORIJA** houses the country's main museum and Lesotho's oldest building, church and printing press. The town was established in 1833 at Moshoeshoe I's behest as the country's first Christian mission, and granted to three missionaries of the Paris Evangelical Missionary Society.

Lesotho Evangelical Church and around

The large, red-brick **Lesotho Evangelical Church**, with its impressive teak-beamed roof, is usually open on Sundays. Begun in 1847, this is the third church built on the site, using the labour of Pedi economic migrants on their way to Cape Colony, though its tall steeple was only built in 1905. Interestingly, the pillars inside were made from old ships' masts, transported here by ox-cart from Port Elizabeth.

Maeder House

Below the Evangelical Church • Mon–Sat 9am–5pm, Sun 2–5pm

Most of Morija was razed to the ground by Afrikaner troops in 1858, and almost the only building left standing was the historical **Maeder House**, built in 1843. After housing some crafts shops, a new use for the building is currently being sought. During the week you can visit the historic **printing works** next door, which have produced Basotho literature since the 1860s as well as the country's oldest newspaper, *Leselinyana la Lesotho* (Little Light of Lesotho), which has been in almost continual publication since 1863.

Morija Museum and Archives

Main Rd • Mon–Sat 8am–5pm, Sun noon–5pm • M10 • ☎ 2236 0308, ⓦ morijafest.co.ls

The bright-yellow **Morija Museum and Archives** is an excellent reason for coming to town. The exhibits, displayed in a large room and an adjoining hallway, are a stimulating combination of geological and fossil finds, meteorite fragments, ethnographic material and historic items connected with Moshoeshoe (see p.590)and

SANI PASS (P.613) >

> ### ACTIVITIES IN MORIJA
>
> **Pony treks** can be arranged through the *Morija Guest Houses* (see below) or the museum, and range from one-hour jaunts to two-day trips (price negotiable). The best of various **walking trails** from Morija leads to an impressive sets of avian dinosaur footprints on one side of a large rock halfway up the Makhoarane Plateau, 45 minutes beyond the guesthouse. Guides are available for these walks; there are no fixed prices.

his contemporaries. The museum also sells a range of books including the recommended *Guide to Morija* (M15), and can organize tours of the village and surroundings, taking in the church and Maeder House.

In September and October the museum organizes the **Morija Arts and Cultural Festival** (ⓦmorijafest.co.ls), the largest and most significant event of its kind in the country, where traditional music, dancing, horse races and crafts mix with theatre, cinema, sport and children's events.

11

ARRIVAL AND INFORMATION

MORIJA

By bus and minibus taxi Getting to Morija is easy, with buses and minibus taxis running throughout the day from Maseru. There's no bus or taxi rank; most transport drops you outside the post office close to the museum, while buses heading on to Mafeteng and Mohale's Hoek will probably drop you on the highway 1km west of the centre.

Tourist information Morija Museum and Archives also doubles up as the town's tourist information (Mon–Sat 8am–5pm, Sun noon–5pm).

ACCOMMODATION

★ **Morija Guest Houses** ☎2236 0306, ⓦmorijaguesthouses.com. Morija boasts one of Lesotho's most attractive lodgings, set in a dramatic spot right at the top of town; drive up from the museum and follow the white stones. The beautiful thatched house contains several comfortable but thin-walled rooms, plus a fully equipped kitchen, lounge, and veranda with fantastic views over the surrounding area. Just below the guesthouse stand several attractive self-catering Basotho cottages. Meals can be provided by prior arrangement. Backpackers arriving by public transport pay M125 per bed. Camping **M70**, double **M420**

EATING AND DRINKING

Morija Museum Tea Shop The museum's tea shop, in a traditional rondavel in the lovely gardens behind the main building, offers cold drinks and simple Basotho meals; enjoy them sitting on the terrace with valley views. Mon–Sat 9am–4.30pm, Sun 2–4.30pm.

Snack bar You can get drinks and excellent cheap Basotho meals for a very modest M15 in the snack bar attached to the grocer's opposite the post office, a few minutes' walk downhill from the museum.

Malealea

The bustling minibus taxi stop at **Motsekuoa**, 10km south of Morija, marks the turning for the village of **MALEALEA**, one of the best-known places in Lesotho thanks to the hugely popular *Malealea Lodge & Pony Trek Centre* (see opposite). Now a spacious forested compound, set in a spectacular spot in the foothills of the Thaba Putsoa range, the lodge was originally a small trading store established by the British adventurer Mervyn Bosworth-Smith in 1905. It was Bosworth-Smith who wrote the words on the brass plaque at the top of the magnificent Gate of Paradise Pass, 6km before the lodge: "Wayfarer, pause and look upon a gateway of Paradise".

ARRIVAL AND DEPARTURE

MALEALEA

By public transport From Maseru (85km), a daily minibus taxi leaves from the New Taxi Rank at around 11am direct to the gates of *Malealea Lodge*.

By taxi If you miss the bus, jump on any of the hourly taxis to Mafeteng and change at Motsekuoa, where you'll find onward taxis to Malealea five times per day.

DONGAS AND SOIL EROSION IN LESOTHO

One thing you'll quickly notice about Lesotho is that the entire country is virtually **treeless**. Indeed, the country – once the grain basket of the region – is in deep ecological trouble, and acres of irreplaceable topsoil, loosened by decades of over-farming, are washed away down its rivers each year.

The problems began with the expropriation of the best land by the OFS in the 1860s, which forced the Basotho to start farming hilly areas that had previously only been used for winter grazing. This process continues to this day, and you will even see crops being grown at over 2000m in districts like Semonkong and Mokhotlong. Mountains are no substitute for fertile plains, however, and Lesotho has been a net importer of food since the 1920s.

The ecological effect of the unrelenting cultivation of the Lesotho mountains has been devastating. The soil fertility has plummeted and, more seriously, huge quantities of topsoil are simply washed away in each summer's rains. In many places so much topsoil has gone that great ravines called **dongas** have opened up. Though they often look green enough, the remaining soil tends to lie close to the surface rock, making it useless for serious cultivation.

Efforts to slow this process have been under way for some time, most noticeably through the terracing of hillside fields. For one of the best examples of how simply dongas can be reclaimed, ask to be shown the way to the Musi family donga in the village beside the *Malealea Lodge* (see below) – reclamation of the donga began almost two decades ago by Fanuel Musi, and is now carried on by his grandson and wife; donations are appreciated. Ask at the lodge for a guide to take you there.

11

ACCOMMODATION

⭐ **Malealea Lodge & Pony Trek Centre** ☎ 0027 82 552 4215, ⓦ malealea.com. Simple but comfortable accommodation in huts, chalets and rondavels spread out in a pretty forested compound. The lodge is always a lively place; next to the dining room (set meals served at set times) is a great little bar and most evenings guests congregate around an open fire outside. Every afternoon a local choir and band perform for guests, the latter bashing out tunes on home-made instruments. The local community benefits greatly from the lodge through employment and special projects funded by the Malealea Development Trust, and visitors can experience heart-warming hospitality when venturing out. M270

Mafeteng and around

The bustling town of **MAFETENG**, 18km from Van Rooyenshek **border post**, will be the first place you come to in Lesotho if crossing from Wepener in the Free State. It means "the place of Lefeta's people", after the son of a French missionary Emile Rolland, who was the district's first magistrate and was nicknamed Lefeta, or "he who passes", by locals, who regarded him as virtually Basotho except for the fact that he skipped (or "passed by") initiation. Much of the town suffered in the 1998 riots, but the centre has now recovered. The only building of any interest is the **District**

TREKKING FROM MALEALEA

The *Malealea Lodge* (see above) runs a series of **guided pony treks**, from short one-hour jaunts to as many days as your bottom and wallet can stand, with nights in basic huts equipped with gas cookers, kitchen utensils and floor mattresses. Trips can be arranged at short notice. **Costs** vary according to where you go and group size, but count on around M380 for a full day and night, plus M75 for village accommodation, or M10 per hour of hiking. Riders cannot weigh more than 90kg, and luggage is limited to 12.5kg, including food. A good and less pricey alternative to the pony trekking (which can be quite hard on the body if you're not used to it) is simply to **walk** and use a pony as a pack animal. The pony can carry four people's packs, provided they're not excessively heavy.

Short trips include **village walks** and a consultation with a traditional healer (*sangoma*). Longer day-trips, either afoot or in the saddle, go to Botsoela Twin Waterfalls, Pitseng Canyon and its rock pool, San rock paintings, and the Gates of Paradise Pass along Matelile Ridge.

Administrator's office on the main street, worth a quick look for the carved animal heads studding its front wall.

Thabana Morena Plateau

About 20km east of Mafeteng is the impressive **Thabana Morena Plateau**, which makes a good excursion, though you'll need your own transport. Rising above the village of the same name, it rewards those who make the steep hour-long climb with good views of the Free State plains to the west and the Thaba Putsoa range to the east.

ARRIVAL AND DEPARTURE

MAFETENG AND AROUND

By bus As befits a border town, Mafeteng has a very busy bus station where you can easily find transport north to Morija and Maseru, and southeast to Mohale's Hoek,

Quthing and beyond (five buses and numerous minibus taxis daily each way).

ACCOMMODATION

Golden Hotel To the right of the highway from Maseru, just before you enter Mafeteng proper ☎ 2270 0566. The anonymous-looking *Golden Hotel* offers functional en-suite rooms and a dining room serving pizzas and meat dishes. **M360**

Mafeteng Hotel & Restaurant On the south side of town down the small St near the telecommunications

tower. ☎ 2270 0236. Looks like a 1960s airport control tower, but offers pleasant and spacious en-suite rooms, all with satellite TV, plus some cottages in a secluded garden and a good swimming pool. It's a good idea to ask in advance if the disco will be active when you plan to sleep here. Its restaurant may be the best place to eat in town, with a range of moderately priced meat dishes. **M385**

Mohale's Hoek

MOHALE'S HOEK, a short distance from the little-used Makhaleng Bridge borderpost, is a rather bedraggled little town, but it has a decent hotel and some interesting sites in the surrounding hills, including some well-preserved **dinosaur footprints**. Mohale was Moshoeshoe's younger brother, appointed to look after the area by the king as part of his bid to wrest control of the district from chief Moorosi. There are still quite a few of Moorosi's Baphuthi clan here, though, whose language is in some ways closer to Xhosa than Basotho. There's nothing to see or do here apart from the excellent drive, walk or pony trek into the little-visited **Mokhele Mountain Range** (see below).

Mokhele Mountain Range

Ten kilometres east of Mohale's Hoek the beautiful and little-visited **Mokhele Mountain Range** is perfect for a drive, walk or pony trek (ask about treks at the *Mount Maluti Hotel*). To get here, travel a few kilometres south on the main road to the little village of Mesitsaneng; turn left at the signpost for the primary school and head 11km east along a rough dirt track to the historic French **Maphutseng Mission**, in whose roof locals once hid from attacking Boers. When the road bends sharply to the left, branch right down a smaller track and you'll see a plateau a short walk away, where you'll find some **dinosaur footprints** and the remnants of an inscription recording their "discovery" in 1959.

ARRIVAL AND DEPARTURE

MOHALE'S HOEK

By bus and minibus taxi Buses arrive at the busy station in the centre of Mohale's Hoek, while minibus taxis congregate on the main street near the Engen petrol

station – between them and the buses (5/day in both directions) you should be able to find transport heading both north and south throughout the day.

ACCOMMODATION AND EATING

Mount Maluti Hotel ☎ 2278 5224, ⓦ skymountainhotels.com. Comfortable rooms with TVs, plus a bar, tennis court and swimming pool. The hotel

restaurant is the best place to eat in southern Lesotho and offers decent cuisine including superb pizzas fresh from the oven, plus an M65 set evening menu. **M650**

Quthing and around

QUTHING, also known as **Moyeni** ("Place of the Wind"), is a curious split-level town established by the British after the Gun War in 1884. The town itself is messy, though it has an attractive setting beside a river gorge, with views of the surrounding hills improving as you climb to the upper part of town.

Masitise Cave House

A few kilometres west of Quthing • Mon–Fri 8.30am–5pm, Sat & Sun 8.30am–2pm • M10 • ☎ 2700 3259, ⓦ masitisecavehouse.blogspot.com

The **Masitise Cave House** is well worth a visit. This extraordinary house was built into the side of a rock overhang in 1866 by the Swiss missionary D.F. Ellenberger – whose *History of the Basuto: Ancient & Modern*, published in 1912, was the first study of its kind. The house has been converted into a **museum** and contains interesting displays about the history of the Quthing area, the Ellenbergers' fascinating home, and an explanation about the dinosaur footprints in the roof of one of the rooms in the house. To find it, turn off the main road at the "Masitise Primary" sign and follow the rutted road past the church; the curator, Aaron Ntsonyana, will guide you around.

11

Dinosaur footprints

Daily 8am–4pm • M5

The most accessible **dinosaur footprints** in Lesotho are very near the lower section of Quthing. On the road to Mount Moorosi, about 400m from the junction to Quthing town centre, look out for the shed-like building with the thatched **visitor centre** beside it on the left of the road. The shed protects a variety of clearly discernible footprints, and there's also a limited range of handicrafts for sale.

ARRIVAL AND DEPARTURE
QUTHING AND AROUND

By bus and minibus taxi During the day there are always plenty of buses (5 daily) and minibus taxis north towards Maseru, and much more infrequent services northeast towards Qacha's Nek (including a 10am Lesotho Freight and Bus Services bus from Maseru every other day of the week; 7hr). You'll also find minibus taxis heading for the nearby Tele Bridge border post (daily 6am–10pm) where you can pick up transport to Sterkspruit in the Eastern Cape.

ACCOMMODATION

Fuleng Guest House In town, near the first hairpin bend to upper Quthing ☎ 2275 0260. Excellent-value rooms in simple rondavels (although check as they vary in standard), or more luxurious and stylish rooms with TVs. **M342**

Mountain Side Hotel About 100m down the dirt track just beyond Fuleng ☎ 2275 0257. The intimate *Mountain Side Hotel* has mostly adequate rooms. There's a cosy private bar, a friendly public one and a decent restaurant with a tasty fixed menu. **M750**

Villa Maria Guest House Signposted off the main road between Masitise and Quthing town centre ☎ 2275 0364. The pretty sandstone *Villa Maria Mission*, with its twin red spires, is set in peaceful grounds behind the church and has inexpensive accommodation, with clean rooms and communal bathrooms. **M320**

Mount Moorosi and around

Just over 40km beyond Quthing, the small town of **MOUNT MOOROSI** was named after a chief who moved to the region in the 1850s. He was an ally of the San and had several San wives, but made an enemy of the British in the 1870s. British troops attacked his stronghold in 1879, but he held out for eight months until soldiers used scaling ladders on the steep cliffs and finally captured him, after which they cut off and publicly displayed his severed head. **Thaba Moorosi**, where the main battle took place, is 1km or so further along the main road on the right. The site is marked by some stone slabs in which British soldiers sent to catch the chief engraved their names. It's quite a tricky climb, though, so be sure to let someone in Mount Moorosi know where you are going.

Shortly after rounding Thaba Moorosi, the main road leaves the Senqu River and heads swiftly into the highlands through the impressive **Quthing Gorge**, peaking after about 10km at the **Lebelonyane Pass** (2456m), with superb views. A far less used route into the highlands than the northern road to Mokhotlong, the mountain road to Sehlabathebe is ruggedly beautiful, and according to some the most rewarding drive in the country.

ACCOMMODATION   MOUNT MOOROSI AND AROUND

Moorosi Chalets Continue for 4km past Mount Moorosi village, and follow signs another 4km down a gravel road ☎0027 82 824 0883, ⓦmaleleatours.com. Several basic but attractive Basotho huts, en-suite rooms and rondavels run by *Malealea Lodge* (see p.617). It's set in a beautiful valley that's great for pony treks, 4WD trips to Bushman paintings and village stays. There's a kitchen for self-catering, or meals can be provided by prior arrangement. **M240**

Qacha's Nek

Some 34km east of Mphaki at **Sekake**, the road rejoins the southern banks of the Senqu, but deteriorates significantly in quality, though you can still make it with care in an ordinary vehicle. It's a beautiful, undulating drive, though once you reach the approach to **QACHA'S NEK** you'll see the depressingly familiar soil erosion and dongas (see p.617). Named after chief Moorosi's son Ncatya, Qacha's Nek was an area famed for its banditry when the British founded the town in 1888 in an attempt to forestall the kind of trouble they'd experienced with chief Moorosi. Many of the "bandits" were in fact desperate San, hounded from their homes and having no means of survival; this left the British unmoved, and they hunted them to extermination throughout the 1860s and 1870s. Moorosi's Baphuthi people had started moving there in the 1850s, rapidly wiping out all the game, and turning the land over to grazing and cultivation instead. The area has unusually high rainfall, and the weather conditions favour conifers, including a few massive Canadian redwoods, giving Qacha's Nek an atmosphere completely different from most of virtually treeless Lesotho.

There's little to see in town, except the elegant **St Joseph's Church** at its eastern end, but the entire surrounding mountainous countryside is great for **hiking**.

ARRIVAL AND DEPARTURE   QACHA'S NEK

Qacha's Nek is an important border town and there's usually plenty of public transport heading southwest towards Quthing from the Engen garage in the centre of town.

By bus and minibus taxi There's a daily bus to and from Maseru operated by Lesotho Freight and Bus Services; it leaves Maseru at 7am, and Qacha's Nek at 8.30am, and takes up to ten hours. You can hear minibus taxis a mile off, thanks to the cowbells tied to their front. On the other side of the border you'll find transport (roughly hourly) heading for the Eastern Cape town of Matatiele, from where it's easy to find buses and minibus taxis on to Kokstad and beyond.

ACCOMMODATION

Anna's B&B Just past the Central Hotel, near the Farmers' Training Centre ☎2295 0374, ⓔannasb&b @leo.co.ls. This friendly B&B also offers a restaurant and choice of accommodation, either older rooms with shared bath or newer en-suite ones. **M380**

Letloepe Lodge ☎2295 0383, ⓦmalealeatours .com. The town's best accommodation, in an attractive and well-signposted setting at the bottom of the Letloepe cliff on the edge of town, just a few minutes' drive from the border. The lodge offers comfortable en-suite rondavels with TVs, some with their own kitchenettes, and there is a restaurant if you don't want to self-cater. They also have cheaper backpacker accommodation in twin or triple rooms with shared bathrooms (M125). **M420**

Nthatua Hotel The first building on the left as you enter Qacha's Nek on the main road from Quthing ☎2295 0260. A variety of rooms, each more luxurious than the last; all are en suite, and you're also welcome to pitch a tent (M50). All tariffs include a substantial breakfast from a restaurant that also serves lunch and dinner. **M340**

Sehlabathebe National Park

Free • ☎ 2231 2662, ⓦ maloti.org.ls

The oldest nature reserve in the country, **Sehlabathebe National Park** is remote and almost inaccessible, but predictably peaceful and stunningly beautiful. Set on the border with South Africa in the southern reaches of the Drakensberg at an average altitude of 2400m, the park is best known for its prolific birdlife, excellent trout fishing, waterfalls, rock paintings and seemingly endless open spaces just perfect for hiking. There are also a few game animals: baboons, rhebok, eland and the secretive oribi antelope, mongoose, otters, wild cats and jackals. In good weather you probably won't be in any hurry to leave, but at any time of year mist and rain can emerge out of nowhere, even on the finest of days, so come prepared.

ARRIVAL AND DEPARTURE   SEHLABATHEBE NATIONAL PARK

By bus or car To get to the park from the Lesotho side of the border you'll need either a 4WD or to catch the daily Lesotho Freight and Bus Services bus from Qacha's Nek to Sehlabathebe village, just outside the park (departs at noon, returns at 5.30am), which takes four to five hours.
On foot The only other way into the park from the Lesotho side is to hike 40km along the Top-of-the-Berg route from Sani Top. From South Africa, it's a day's walk to the park through the southern section of South Africa's Ukhahlamba Drakensberg Park along a dramatic path starting at Bushman's Nek, 38km from Underberg in KwaZulu-Natal.

INFORMATION

Sehlabathebe Ranger Station Information about the park and hikes. If you want to do some serious hiking, go to the Department of Lands, Surveys and Physical Planning in Maseru (see box, p.590), where you should be able to pick up some detailed maps of the area.

ACCOMMODATION

Camping is permitted anywhere in the park, provided you get a permit from the lodge. Wherever you're staying, you'll need to be self-sufficient in food and bring spare fuel too.

Jonathan's Lodge About 10km from the main gate ☎ 2231 1767 or 5802 8729, ✉ kretha2010@yahoo.com. This twelve-bed lodge was originally built for Lesotho's prime minister, has an adequate kitchen for self-catering and provides bedding and hot-water showers. To be sure of a room, book in advance. Camping **M75**, double **M400**

Sehlabathebe Ranger Station Sehlabathebe village ☎ 2295 0551, ⓦ www.sehlabathebe.com. There are decent dormitory rooms with about 30 beds in total and spotless facilities at this elegant bungalow guesthouse, situated near the entrance gate of the national park. **M120**

11

Swaziland

UMHLANGA REED DANCE

Swaziland

A tiny landlocked kingdom, Swaziland lies in the spanner-like grip of South Africa which surrounds it on three sides, with Mozambique providing its eastern border along the Lubombo Mountains. Although South Africa's influence predominates, Swaziland was a British protectorate from 1903 until its full independence in 1968, and today the country offers an intriguing mix of colonial heritage and homegrown confidence, giving the place a friendlier, more relaxed and often safer feeling than its larger neighbour. Though Swaziland still feels a lot more commercialized than, say, Lesotho, its outstanding scenery, along with its commitment to wildlife conservation, makes it well worth a visit. With a car and a bit of time, you can explore some of the less trampled reserves, make overnight stops in unspoilt, out-of-the-way settlements and, if you time your visit well, take in something of Swaziland's well-preserved cultural traditions.

12

Swaziland is also something of a draw for **backpackers**, with an inexpensive network of minibus Kombi taxis covering all corners of the country, and some good backpacker lodges to boot. There are also plenty of adventure activities on offer – from mountain biking and horseriding to whitewater rafting and tree-top canopy gliding on wires hooked onto sheer rock faces. Swaziland has six **national parks**, between them exemplifying the country's geographical diversity, and all offering good-value accommodation. While not as efficiently run as South African national parks, the Swazi reserves are less officious, and many people warm to their easy-going nature.

Laidback **Mbabane**, the country's tiny capital city, makes a useful base from which to explore the attractive central **eZulwini Valley**, home to the royal palace and the **Mlilwane Wildlife Sanctuary**. With your own transport, or a bit of determination and public transport, you can venture further afield, heading into the highveld of the northwest, and up to the fantastically beautiful **Malolotja Nature Reserve**, with its fabulous hiking country, soaring valleys and cliffs.

Summers are hot, particularly in the eastern lowveld. **Winter** is usually sunny, but nights can be very chilly in the western highveld around the Malolotja Nature Reserve. In summer, rainfall is usually limited to short, drenching storms that play havoc with the smaller untarred roads. Note that Swaziland's eastern lowveld, including Hlane Royal National Park is **malarial** during the summer months (Nov–May). For details on necessary precautions, see p.71.

Brief history

The history of Swaziland dates back to the **Dlamini** clan and their king, **Ngwane**, who crossed the Lubombo Mountains from present-day Mozambique in around 1750. Pushed

WHITE RHINOCEROS

Highlights

❶ **Royal festivals** The spectacular ceremonies of Ncwala and Umhlanga are colourful affirmations of Swazi national identity. **See p.636**

❷ **Malandela's Homestead** A collection of buildings bursting with creativity and enterprise, including the funky performance space and live music venue House on Fire, and Gone Rural, one of the best of Swaziland's many attractive arts and crafts outlets. **See p.637**

❸ **Myxo's cultural tours, KaPhunga** Get a true taste of life in rural Swaziland – this enterprising project allows you to live as part of a village for a few days. **See p.639**

❹ **Malolotja** A wild, rugged and breathtakingly beautiful reserve attracting hundreds of different bird species, with a network of trails perfect for hiking or horseriding. **See p.646**

❺ **Whitewater rafting on the Great Usutu** As action-packed as anything south of the Zambezi – you can paddle a two-man inflatable croc raft down Swaziland's largest river. **See p.641**

❻ **Mkhaya Game Reserve** Swaziland's best wildlife experience, where you can walk with rhino before sleeping in luxurious open-sided cottages in the bush. **See p.641**

HIGHLIGHTS ARE MARKED ON THE MAP ON P.627

CHOOSING THE KING

Swazi monarchs are always men of the **Dlamini** family, and over the course of their reign marry a number of women who are carefully selected from different clans to cement national unity. In theory, the king marries women from increasingly important families as he goes along, which means that the son of the last wife is always a strong contender for the succession. In practice, however, other wives with older sons are also in with a chance, resulting in unrest and power-struggles every time the king dies. After his death, the royal council, or *liqoqo*, selects the new **Queen Mother**, who rules as regent until her son is old enough to take charge. She usually has to work hard to ensure her position against ambitious uncles. The main advantage of this awkward process is that by the time the new king is old enough to rule, he and his mother have generally garnered enough support for him to do so effectively.

into southeast Swaziland by the Ndwandwe people of Zululand, the clan eventually settled at Mhlosheni and then Zombodze in the southwest, where Ngwane reigned precariously, under constant threat of Ndwandwe attack. His grandson, **Sobhuza I**, was forced to flee north from the Ndwandwe, but they in turn were defeated by the Zulu king Shaka in 1819. Sobhuza then established a new capital suitably far from Shaka in the eZulwini Valley, and made peace with the Ndwandwe by marrying the king's daughter.

Sobhuza's power grew as he brought more and more clans under his wing. His alliance with the newly arrived Afrikaners in the 1830s, forged out of mutual fear of the Zulu, was continued by his son **Mswati II** (after whom the Swazi people are named), who stretched his kingdom north to the Sabi River and sent raiding parties as far as the Limpopo River and east to the Indian Ocean.

Europeans arrived in greater numbers throughout the 1880s, after the discovery of gold in neighbouring Transvaal and at Piggs Peak and Forbes Reef in Swaziland. Mswati's son, **Mbandzeni**, granted large chunks of his territory in concessions to the new arrivals, emboldening Britain to ignore his claims to most of the rest, and by the time Swaziland became a protectorate of South Africa in 1894, there was precious little

SISWATI PHRASES

BASICS

Yes	*Yebo* (also a casual greeting)
No	*Cha*
Thank you	*Ngiyabonga*
It's nice/tasty	*Kumnandzi*
Today	*Lamuhla*
Tomorrow	*Kusasa*
Yesterday	*Itolo*

GREETINGS AND RESPONSES

Hello (to one)	*Sawubona*
Hello (to many)	*Sanibona*
How are you?	*Kunjani?*
I'm fine	*Ngikhona*
Goodbye (said by person leaving)	*Sala kahle*
Goodbye (said by person remaining)	*Hamba kahle*

TRAVEL

Where is... ?	*Iphi I... ?*
Where can we stay?	*Singahlala kuphi?*
Where are you going?	*U ya phi?*
How much?	*Malini?*

land left. After their victory in the Second Anglo-Boer War, Britain assumed control of the territory and retained it until 1968.

After World War II the British invested in their protectorate, establishing enormous **sugar plantations** in the northeast, and an **iron-ore mine** at Ngwenya in the highveld (today, the country's major export is sugar). Meanwhile, **Sobhuza II**, who had become king of the Swazis in 1921, concentrated on buying back his kingdom, and had acquired about half of it by the time independence came in 1968. The Swazi aristocracy managed the transition to independence skilfully, with its Imbokodvo party

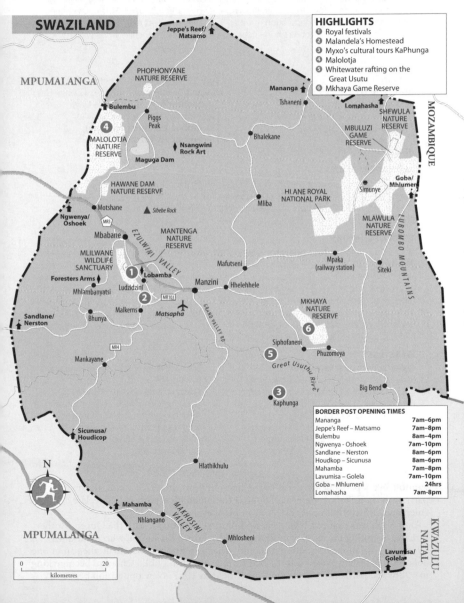

SWAZILAND

HIGHLIGHTS
1. Royal festivals
2. Malandela's Homestead
3. Myxo's cultural tours KaPhunga
4. Malolotja
5. Whitewater rafting on the Great Usutu
6. Mkhaya Game Reserve

BORDER POST OPENING TIMES	
Mananga	7am–6pm
Jeppe's Reef – Matsamo	7am–8pm
Bulembu	8am–4pm
Ngwenya - Oshoek	7am–10pm
Sandlane – Nerston	8am–6pm
Houdkop – Sicunusa	8am–6pm
Mahamba	7am–8pm
Lavumisa – Golela	7am–10pm
Goba – Mhlumeni	24hrs
Lomahasha	7am–8pm

MPUMALANGA

MOZAMBIQUE

KWAZULU-NATAL

Jeppe's Reef/Matsamo

PHOPHONYANE NATURE RESERVE

Mananga

Bulembu

Tshaneni

Lomahasha

SHEWULA NATURE RESERVE

Piggs Peak

Bhalekane

MBULUZI GAME RESERVE

MALOLOTJA NATURE RESERVE

Nsangwini Rock Art

Maguga Dam

HAWANE DAM NATURE RESERVE

Mliba

HLANE ROYAL NATIONAL PARK

Simunye

Goba/Mhlumeni

Motshane

Sibebe Rock

MLAWULA NATURE RESERVE

Ngwenya/Oshoek

MR3

Mbabane

MANTENGA NATURE RESERVE

Mafutseni

Mpaka (railway station)

Siteki

LUBOMBO MOUNTAINS

MLILWANE WILDLIFE SANCTUARY

EZULWINI VALLEY

Lobamba

Manzini

Hhelehhele

Foresters Arms

Ludzidzini

MR101

Mhlambanyatsi

Malkerns

Matsapha

MKHAYA NATURE RESERVE

Sandlane/Nerston

Bhunya

GRAND VALLEY RD

MR4

Mankayane

Siphofaneni

Phuzomoya

Great Usuthu River

Kaphunga

Big Bend

Sicunusa/Houdicop

Hlathikhulu

N

Mahamba

MAKHOSINI VALLEY

Nhlangano

Mhlosheni

MPUMALANGA

Lavumisa/Golela

0   20
kilometres

SWAZILAND TRAVEL BASICS

MONEY

Currency is the **lilangeni** – plural **emalangeni** (E) – which is tied to the South African rand (1 rand = 1 lilangeni). The rand is legal tender in Swaziland, so you won't have to change any money, but note that emalangeni are not convertible outside Swaziland.

PHONES AND PHONE NUMBERS

The **country code** for Swaziland is ☎ 268, followed by the destination number (there are no area codes). The code for phoning out from Swaziland is ☎ 00, followed by the country and area codes and finally the destination number. To arrange a **collect call**, dial ☎ 94.

Swaziland has its own mobile phone network – MTN – which generally works well throughout the country.

PUBLIC HOLIDAYS

January 1	**July 22** (King Sobhuza II's birthday)
Good Friday	**August/September** (Umhlanga Dance Day)
Easter Monday	**September 6** (Independence Day)
April 19 (King Mswati III's birthday)	**December/January** (Ncwala Day)
April 25 (National Flag Day)	**December 25 (Christmas Day)**
May 1 Workers' Day	**December 26 (Boxing Day)**
Ascension Day	

RED TAPE AND VISAS

Nationals of most Commonwealth countries (excluding Bangladesh, India, Pakistan and Sri Lanka), the US, Canada, South Africa, Australia and all EU countries do not require a **visa** if staying sixty days or less. Other nationals must obtain visas before arrival. For details of Swaziland's embassies see p.633.

TOUR OPERATORS

The country's biggest **tour operator** is Swazi Trails (☎ 24162180, ⓦ swazitrails.co.sz), located in the Mantenga Craft Centre (see p.634), offering tours to the royal village and game parks, and whitewater rafting, quad biking, caving and other activities. There are also a handful of smaller local operations, including Taman Tours (☎ 24163370, ⓦ tamantours.com), which runs tours to different parts of Swaziland, and All Out Africa (☎ 24162260, ⓦ alloutafrica.com), which organizes a selection of adventure tours such as river tubing on the Ngwempisi River, and also helps find volunteering opportunities within the country. The tourist office in Mbabane (see p.632) keeps information on other tour guides.

WEBSITES

ⓦ **welcometoswaziland.com** Swaziland's official tourism website is packed with useful information, including hotel listings.

ⓦ **biggameparks.org** Provides information on three of the country's most visited reserves, the Hlane, Mlilwane and Mkhaya parks, with practical information about activities, and an accommodation booking site.

ⓦ **swazi.travel** Hosted by Swazi Trails, with an efficient online accommodation booking service, reams of information about shopping and restaurants, and with details of a range of tours and activities around Swaziland.

12

winning every parliamentary seat in the first elections. In 1973, a radical pan-Africanist party won three seats, prompting Sobhuza to **ban political parties** and declare a state of emergency which technically has been in place ever since.

After Sobhuza's death in 1982, a period of intrigue ensued, with the Queen Mother Dzeliwe assuming the regency until deposed by Prince Bhekimpi, who ruled until 1985, purging all the opposition he could. The current king, **Mswati III**, the son of one of Sobhuza's seventy wives, was recalled from an English public school to become king in 1986, and parliamentary elections were held in 1987. New opposition began to emerge, most notably the **People's United Democratic Movement** (PUDEMO), which has strong support among Swazi workers, though in general Swazis are proud of their distinctive kingdom, and as a result calls for change are tempered by an unwillingness to show disloyalty to the king, or to expose Swaziland to what many see as the predatory ambitions of South Africa.

Thus the maintenance of tradition and appeals to broad nationalism have been key components of Swazi royalty's strategy to retain power. Although Mswati III is sometimes said to favour reform, the authorities have worked hard to keep dissent bottled up, by means of sporadic police repression; opposition leaders have been prevented from speaking freely in the media, and poor turnouts marked the "elections" of 1993, 1998, 2003 and 2008. In 2011, demonstrations triggered by the "Arab Spring", calling for **multi-party democracy** and condemning the government's mismanagement of funds, were stopped in their tracks with the arrest of demonstration organizers. Currently, Swaziland is the only country in Southern Africa not practising multiparty democracy. It seems only a matter of time before it is coerced by the other regional powers into doing so.

ARRIVAL AND DEPARTURE

BORDER CROSSINGS

Crossing the border is usually very straightforward: you simply have to show your passport and pay E50 in road tax per car. There are twelve border posts serving traffic from South Africa, and two crossings into Mozambique. We've listed the most convenient ones below:

Ngwenya/Oshoek (7am–10pm) is the most popular, closest to Johannesburg and the easiest route to Mbabane, only 20km to the east. Can be very busy during holidays and weekends.

Sandlane/Nerston (8am–6pm) is a good alternative 35km further south, and roughly 70km from Johannesburg. Although a longer journey, this road passes through some outstanding scenery.

Houdkop/Sicunusa (8am–6pm) is just off the N2 from Piet Retief in the southwest, which leads to the wonderfully scenic and fast MR4.

Bulembu (8am–4pm), via Piggs Peak in the north, is perhaps the most spectacular crossing in the country, but the bad road makes it a hard journey in an ordinary car.

Jeppe's Reef/Matsamo (7am–8pm) in the north, handy if you're coming in from Kruger Park and Nelspruit.

Lavumisa/Golela (7am–10pm) in the southeast, close to the KwaZulu-Natal coast, is the country's second-busiest crossing, and a popular entry point for through traffic to Kruger National Park.

Mahamba (7am–8pm) in the south, runs lots of traffic from N2/Piet Retief and beyond.

Goba/Mhlumeni (24hr), a busy crossing into Mozambique and the main route for traffic from the southern half of South Africa, so expect lots of lorries on this route.

Lomahasha (7am–8pm), second crossing into Mozambique which passes through Hlane Royal National Park and the scenic Lebombo mountains.

BY PLANE

Swaziland has one international airport, Matsapha (often referred to as "Manzini"), between Mbabane and Manzini. Airlink Swaziland (☎ 25186155, ⱳ flyswaziland .com), a partner of SAA, through whom it can be contacted in South Africa, flies four times daily to and from Johannesburg (1hr). An airport tax fee of E50 is payable when flying out of Matsapha Airport. A new international airport – Sikhusphe – is currently under construction about 50km from Mbabane on the road to Hlane. It may or may not be opened in the near future, depending on whether the strapped government coffers can finance its completion. The general consensus is that it probably won't. For more information, contact Airlink Swaziland.

BY BUS

At the time of writing, the only timetabled bus company connecting South Africa and Swaziland is TransMagnifique (☎ 24049977, ⱳ www.goswaziland.co.sz), which runs a daily bus from Monday to Saturday between Mbabane and Johannesburg (4hr; E500), stopping at Ngwenya, Witbank, Johannesburg Airport and Sandton. Book in advance online. Swazi Cultural Tours (☎ 76044102 or 76426780, ✉ info@swaziculturaltours.com) run a shuttle-bus service to Nelspruit (Mon, Wed, Fri; E350) and St Lucia (Tues & Sat; E380); contact them for further details. A cheaper option is to catch Kombi minibuses (see p.630) which ply the main routes to Swaziland from Johannesburg and Nelspruit nonstop, and depart when they are full.

GETTING AROUND

By car Driving is the best way to see Swaziland; distances are small, all the main tourist sites are near good, tarred roads, and the major gravel roads are in decent condition. Most dirt roads are passable with an ordinary vehicle in dry months. Driving standards, however, leave a lot to be desired – highlighted by the fact that two of the last four ministers of

12

transport have died in road accidents. Also, the general speed limit of 80km/h outside towns is universally ignored and very rarely enforced. For Swazi car rental, see opposite.

By Kombi minibus Swaziland is crisscrossed by a network of Kombi minibus routes that covers almost every corner of the country. The Kombis leave from bus stations in the main towns, when full, and ply the main routes linking the towns, calling at set stops along the way. Kombi travel is cheap – a ticket from Mbabane to Lidwala Backpacker Lodge in the eZulwini Valley costs E6. Ask at the local bus station about the best route to get to your destination. The stations are organized by destination, so all Kombis to, say, Manzini will leave from one corner of the station, and to Big Bend from another. Although buses do tend to get quite packed, they are an efficient way of getting around, and a great way of meeting people.

Mbabane

Tucked in the jumble of granite peaks and valleys that make up the Dlangeni hills, Swaziland's administrative capital, **MBABANE** (pronounced "M-buh-ban"), is small, relaxed and unpretentious, with a population of only about 61,000. The city roughly marks the point where the mountainous Southern African highveld descends briefly into middleveld, before bottoming out further east as dry lowveld.

There's not much to do in Mbabane, but most visitors find it more agreeable than hectic Manzini, especially if you need to stock up on supplies or plan your trip ahead. This is a good base from which to start exploring Swaziland, especially if you're without your own transport: the Mlilwane Wildlife Sanctuary (see p.636) lies not far south, and the royal village of Lobamba (see p.635) makes an easy day-trip – useful if you're here when the *Umhlanga* or *Ncwala* ceremonies take place and everything nearer the village is fully booked.

Mbabane's hilly **centre** is a pleasant jumble of office blocks, markets, malls and shacks that you can very easily explore on foot – which is just as well, as driving here can be stressful without a sound grasp of the street layout and confusing one-way system.

Gwamile Street is the closest the city has to a main street; running south into the central business district (CBD), it's lined in parts by colonial administrative buildings which are attractive to look at, but can only be entered on official business. At the end of Gwamile Street, on the banks of the Mbabane River, lies the daily **Swazi Market** where fresh fruit and vegetable stalls make for a colourful scene.

The main focus of the city centre, however, is the sprawl of shopping malls down the hill from Gwamile Street. Most of Mbabane's main shops, banks and services are located in either the **Swazi Plaza** or the more upmarket **Mall** and **New Mall**.

SIBEBE ROCK TRAILS

About 10km north of Mbabane along the Pine Valley road is Swaziland's most famous geological feature, a huge granite dome called **Sibebe Rock**. Situated among the Mubuluzi Mountains, the area boasts springs you can swim in and a network of trails leading to various breathtaking viewpoints. Rising 300m above the Mubuluzi River Valley, the vast slabs of granite are very steep and dangerous in places, but among the scattered boulders at the summit are Bushman paintings indicating that the rock was inhabited by humans thousands of years ago. While the hard, coarse surface of the granite offers more grip than other types of rock, it can be very dangerous, so a guide is essential for any ascent. The Sibebe Trust (☎ 24046070; E400 for a guide, E25 community fee), is a local community initiative that organizes guided walks in this magical area. You'll find their office – and parking – at the Mubuluzi entrance to the area, at the northern end of Pine Valley road.

For an adrenaline-fuelled ascent up the front face of the rock dome, Swazi Trails (see p.628) offers a challenge they describe as "the steepest walk in the world". They also organize **caving trips** in the same mountain range, which involves a lot of squeezing through narrow spaces and navigation by little more than a head torch and the encouraging words of your guide – it's a memorable adventure for those who don't mind enclosed spaces and a few bumps and scratches.

12

Note that Central Mbabane empties at night, and **muggings** are a risk for those wandering the streets alone. If you're going out after dark, arrange for a taxi to pick you up.

ARRIVAL AND DEPARTURE

By plane Matsapha Airport (☎25186192), 25km southeast of Mbabane, just west of Manzini, is Swaziland's only international airport. There's no public transport from here into Mbabane, so if you haven't arranged a pick-up with your hotel, you'll need to take a taxi (around E150), or rent a car; Avis (☎25186222) and Eurocpar (☎25184393) are located at the airport. There's another Europcar agent at the Engen service station at the junction of the By-Pass Road and Main Road (☎24040459), though Affordable Car Hire (☎24049136 or 76020394) in the Swazi Plaza is cheaper.

By bus and minibus Kombi buses and minibuses from South Africa stop at the main bus station off the Western Distributor Road, beside the Swazi Plaza mall. From here you can catch minibus Kombis to Manzini and Piggs Peak, and local buses within the Mbabane area. Kombis plying the Mbabane–Manzini route leave from the western side of the bus station – this is also where you can rent a private taxi for local travel.

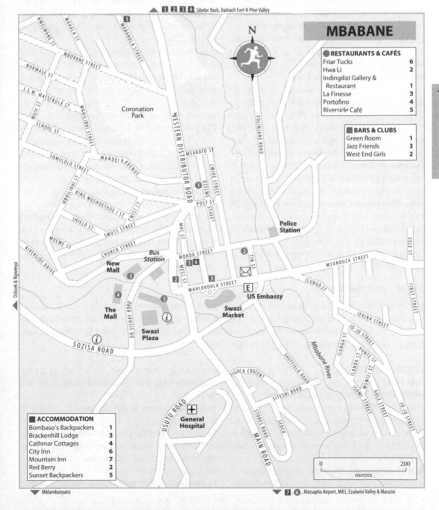

MBABANE

● RESTAURANTS & CAFÉS

Friar Tucks	6
Hwa Li	2
Indingilizi Gallery & Restaurant	1
La Finesse	3
Portofino	4
Riverside Café	5

■ BARS & CLUBS

Green Room	1
Jazz Friends	3
West End Girls	2

■ ACCOMMODATION

Bombaso's Backpackers	1
Brackenhill Lodge	3
Cathmar Cottages	4
City Inn	6
Mountain Inn	7
Red Berry	2
Sunset Backpackers	5

12

GETTING AROUND

Downtown Mbabane is small and easy to explore **by foot**. To head further afield, it's best to take a **taxi**; pre-book with Take Me Home Taxis on ☎ 76068120, or hail one along the main road.

INFORMATION

Tourist office Sozisa Rd (Mon–Thurs 8am–4.45pm, Fri 8am–4pm, Sat 9am–1pm; ☎ 24042531 or ☎ 4090112). Has a good supply of maps, brochures and a list of recommended tour guides. They can also help with hotel bookings (free).

ACCOMMODATION

Mbabane's accommodation is somewhat limited, with only one worthwhile option in the town centre. The rest are a short minibus journey or taxi ride away. If you have your own transport, most establishments in the eZulwini Valley (see opposite) are also close enough to make viable alternatives. All of the places listed below have wi-fi.

Bombaso's Backpackers Lukhalo Rd, 3km north of the centre, off Pine Valley Rd ☎ 24045465, ⓦ bombasos.co.za; map p.631. Funky, young backpackers' place with four- and eight-bed dorms, and three smart doubles sharing facilities. You can pitch a tent in the large garden, which has a pool and great views of Sibebe Rock. There's also a self-catering kitchen, chill-out lounge, various games rooms and a bar. Camping **E50**, dorm **E130**, double **E280**

Brackenhill Lodge Mountain Drive, off Fonteyn Rd ☎ 24042887, ⓦ brackenhillswazi.com; map p.631. Luxurious B&B on a quiet hillside 4.5km north of the city centre. The comfortable rooms are often full so it's a good idea to book in advance. Facilities include a swimming pool, lovely hiking trails and a small breakfast restaurant where dinner is also available when ordered in advance. **E750**

Cathmar Cottages 3km north of Mbabane on Pine Valley Rd ☎ 24043387 or ☎ 24041165, ⓦ visitswazi.com/cathmar; map p.631. A laidback place offering a range of fully equipped self-catering rooms and cottages in a lovely location north of town with views of Sibebe Rock. Facilities include TV and fridge in the cottages, a swimming pool, and breakfast for E60. From **E500**

City Inn Gwamile St ☎ 24042406, ⓦ cityinn.sz; map p.631. The oldest city-centre hotel, offering plain but spacious and tidy en-suite rooms, all carpeted and with TV. It incorporates a small coffee shop where breakfast is served, the popular *Green Room Bar*, and the *Pablo* diner facing the street. As an added bonus, there's free transport to the *Mountain Inn* pool (see below), should you need to cool off. **E580**

Mountain Inn 4km southeast of Mbabane off MR3 ☎ 24042781, ⓦ mountaininn.sz; map p.631. A large, efficient, family-run hotel with sixty spacious rooms and good facilities, including a lovely pool and the *Friar Tuck* restaurant, located on an airy mountainside plot with wonderful views down eZulwini Valley. **E960**

Red Berry Mseni Drive, 3km north of Mbabane, off Pine Valley Rd ☎ 24045217, ⓦ redberrybb.co.sz; map p.631. A smart, modern place with wonderful views of the Pine Valley, encompassing six tidy and fully equipped rooms, and a lovely terrace where breakfast is served. **E720**

Sunset Backpackers Mabandle St, 1km from the town centre ☎ 76752828, ✉ sunsetbackpackers@realnet.co.sz; map p.631. Large backpackers' lodge in a rambling old colonial building with a large garden, offering dorm beds in rooms sleeping four, five, eight and thirty. This is where visiting football teams tend to stay, so it can be both noisy and very busy. **E150**

EATING AND DRINKING

Nightlife in Mbabane is limited during the week and only slightly more lively at weekends. For the best nightlife, however, most locals head out to the eZulwini Valley, especially to *Malandela's* (see p.637) where local and international bands often headline at the House on Fire. Women travellers on their own are likely to encounter some unwanted attention in bars and clubs, but the pestering probably won't be aggressive or persistent.

RESTAURANTS

Friar Tucks Mountain Inn, 4km southeast of the city centre ☎ 24042781; map p.631. Elaborate buffet lunches (E145) during the week, as well as international à la carte meals, such as well-prepared baby chicken (E70), the rest of the time, in an intimate vaulted cellar or outdoors overlooking the pool. Good selection of wine, too. Daily 12.30–3pm & 7–10pm.

Hwa Li Restaurant Prudential Building, Mdada St ☎ 24045986; map p.631. On the ground floor of what's also called Dhlanubeka House, this is a reliable Chinese restaurant serving good-value chow mein, spring rolls and the like. Mon–Sat 11am–9pm.

Indingilizi Gallery & Restaurant 112 Dzeliwe St ☎ 24046213; map p.631. A very pleasant place to come for lunch, situated in the gallery's back garden, and serving light, wholesome dishes at reasonable prices such as omelettes, soups and salads from E25. Mon–Fri 8am–5pm, Sat 8.30am–1pm.

La Finesse New Mall ☎ 24045936; map p.631. A good

restaurant for lunch and dinner, with outdoor seating on a pleasant terrace shaded by large trees, making this the ideal spot on a hot summer's day. The Portuguese/Mozambican/French kitchen excels in seafood dishes such as a delightful fish curry (E75). Mon–Sat 11am–11pm.

Portofino The Mall; map p.631. Downstairs in The Mall, along the central walkway, this is the place to go for Italian ice cream, beautiful cake, good coffee, and well-prepared breakfasts and lunches, all at reasonable prices. Mon–Fri 8am–5.30pm, Sat 8am–5pm, Sun 8.30am–2pm.

Riverside Café Swazi Plaza; map p.631. On the first floor of the Swazi Plaza Mall, overlooking the river and the busy bus station, this café serves excellent-value breakfasts, light lunches and salads as well as more substantial meals such as "chicken liver for chilli addicts" (E30) and peri-peri baby chicken. Mon–Fri 8am–6pm, Sat 8am–2pm.

BARS

Green Room City Inn hotel, Gwamile St; map p.631. The city's most popular bar, packed most nights with both locals and visitors. A popular place for journalists to hang out, so it's good if you want to glean news on happenings in the country.

Jazz Friends Gwamile St ☎24048684; map p.631. Exactly what it says on the tin; a popular, smoky bar frequented by jazz fiends and friends, with music (live or recorded) on most nights.

DIRECTORY

Banks Most banks are found In Gwamile St or in the Swazi Plaza. Branches include First National, Nedbank and Standard. Hours are generally Mon–Fri 8.30am–3.30pm & Sat 8.30–11am.

Bookshops Websters, at 120 Dzeliwe St and in the New Mall, has the best general selection. There is also a CNA newsagent in the Swazi Plaza.

Embassies Mozambique, Princess Drive (☎24043700); South Africa, New Mall (☎24044651); UK Honorary Consulate (☎25516247); US, 7th Floor Central Bank building, Mahlokohla St (☎24046441). Note that the UK's representation in Swaziland is a Pretoria-based consul; for details, see ⊛fco.gov.uk.

Emergencies Fire ☎933; Police ☎999.

Hospitals Mbabane Clinic Service (private), St Michael St (☎24042423); Government Hospital (public), Usutu Rd (☎24042111).

Internet access You can get online at Swazinet, upstairs in the Swazi Plaza.

Pharmacy Mbabane Pharmacy, Gwamile St; Philani Pharmacy, in the Swazi Plaza; and Green Cross, in The Mall.

Post office The main post office is on Mahlokohla St (Mon–Fri 8.30am–4pm, Sat 8.30–11am), and there's a smaller one in the Swazi Plaza.

12

The eZulwini Valley

After passing through Mbabane from the Ngwenya border, the smooth, four-lane **MR3** winds down the steep sides of **Malagwane Hill** in a series of sweeping curves, made hazardous by crawling lorries and reckless minibus taxis. The road then heads off southeast along the eZulwini Valley, but unless you're bound directly for Manzini and beyond, take the turning to the right not long after the foot of the hill onto the older and quieter **MR103** – also known as the eZulwini Valley Road – which links most of the main sights of the **eZulwini Valley** (Place of Heaven). In the 1960s, a succession of casinos, strip joints, hotels and caravan parks sprang up here, catering mainly for South African tourists. When gambling became legal in South Africa in the mid-1990s,

FINE DINING AT FORESTERS ARMS

Just before the small town of Mhlambanyatsi, on the back road to the Sandlane border post – and 27km from Mbabane – the **Foresters Arms hotel and restaurant** (☎24674377, ⊛foresterarms.co.za; E830) is well worth a detour. The hotel is set in a picturesque clearing in the woodland, which can be explored by foot, or on horseback or mountain bike, both of which are available at the hotel, and the rooms are cosy with fireplaces and wonderful mountain views. The main reason to stop here is for the outstanding meals, predominantly made with home-grown and locally sourced produce such as hearty farm-style chicken and corn soup, unusual but mouth-watering tropical salmon, and delicious lamb confit with bean cassoulet. On Sundays, people from all over the country pour in to feast on the hotel's superb buffet lunch (E148) – you'll need to book ahead to be sure of a table.

however, the number of pleasure-seekers dropped; the tourist industry had to start looking beyond the noise of the slot machines and karaoke to the valley's cultural and natural assets, and places such as the **Mantenga Cultural Village** were developed while the royal residences of **Lobamba** and **Ludzidzini**, and **Mlilwane Wildlife Sanctuary**, became more recognized as attractive to visitors. The latter, in particular, is one of Swaziland's main attractions, with its range of accommodation and numerous activities, including hiking trails and game viewing from a mountain bike.

The Mantenga Valley

The first five kilometres or so of the **eZulwini Valley Road** takes you past a strip of glossy, anonymous-looking and hugely overpriced casino hotels. Turning south along Mantenga Drive (signposted to *Mantenga Lodge*) will take you to the much more interesting **Mantenga Valley**, which follows the course of the Lusushwana (or Little Usutu) River. Most prominent in the valley is the twin-peaked **Lugogo Mountain**, also known as "Sheba's Breasts", which featured in H. Rider Haggard's famous adventure novel *King Solomon's Mines*. Further along, on the western horizon, Execution Rock is a stark reminder of the days when murderers and thieves were punished by being forced to jump off the rock to their certain death below. Just beyond the turning to the Mantenga Valley is the **Gables Shopping Centre** which boasts ATMs and banks, a large supermarket, and several good **food** options (see opposite).

Mantenga Craft Centre

Mantenga Drive, less than 1km from the northern turn-off from the eZulwini Valley Rd · Daily 8am–5pm

The **Mantenga Craft Centre** consists of an attractive purpose-built village of craft shops, specializing in more exclusive and individual crafts than found in many other parts of Swaziland, including the beautifully soft Rose Craft mohair fabrics (ⓦswazirosecraft .com), African Fantasy artwork, silver-smithing, and beautiful and quirky carving and sculptures, all sold at fair prices.

12

INFORMATION

THE MANTENGA VALLEY

Tourist information At the southern end of the Craft Centre, the main booking office for Swazi Trails also doubles as the country's best tourist office (daily 8am–5pm; ☎ 24162180, or 76020261 after hours, ⓦ swazitrails.co.sz), which can help you with accommodation booking and trip planning. As the country's leading tour operator, Swazi Trails organize a wide range of cultural and adventure trips including a half-day arts and crafts trail, whitewater rafting (see p.641) and adventure caving.

ACCOMMODATION

Legends Backpacker Lodge Across from Mantenga Craft Centre ☎24161870, ✉legends@mailfly.com. Rather run-down but friendly and tidy, with dorms sleeping six and ten, three doubles, a yard for camping, internet access, and a communal kitchen. It's a great place to base yourself if you're on a tight budget and want easy access to all that the valley has to offer. Camping E50, dorm E100, double E300
Lidwala Backpacker Lodge On the Ezulwini Rd just before the Mantanga Valley turn-off ☎25504951 or 76087706, ⓦlidwala.co.sz. A brilliant backpackers' place on a hillside above the All Out Africa responsible travel company office (see p.628). Comprising of comfortable four- and six- bed dorms, a few en-suite doubles and a grassy bit for camping, there's also a fully kitted kitchen, a packed library and a computer with internet access. Camping E80, dorm E110, double E250

★**Mantenga Lodge** From the Mantenga Craft Centre, continue along a dirt road for about 200m (follow the signs) ☎24161049, ⓦmantengalodge .com. Nestled in between Sheba's Breasts, this is a stunningly located, family-run mid-priced lodge with 36 en-suite rooms, some in cosy chalets on the valley-side, as well as a pool, terrace bar and top-of-the-range restaurant with especially good views of Execution Rock. E640
Timbali Lodge On the eZulwini Valley Rd, 1km after the turn-off from the MR3 ☎24161156, ⓦwww .timbalilodge.co.sz. A former caravan park that has been transformed into a stylish guest lodge with shaded double chalets, self-catering cottages sleeping five, and a large shady area for camping. Camping E80, double E700, cottage E1010

EATING

Boma Restaurant Timbali Lodge (see opposite). Under an enormous, thatched roof with a clean, stylish interior, *Boma* specializes in mouthwatering Swazi-style spring rolls as well as pizza (from E68) from their pizza oven. Daily 10am–10pm.

Calabash Next door to Timbali Lodge ☎ 24161187, ⓦ restaurant-calabash.com. One of Swaziland's best restaurants, serving an excellent range of fresh seafood and specializing in German, Swiss and Austrian dishes such as proper Wiener schnitzel for E79. Fine dining at its best. Daily 10am–10pm.

Kanimambo Gables Shopping Centre ☎ 24163549. Delicious Mozambican food, with lots of spicy seafood dishes such as creamy prawn curry (E55) and fresh fruit juice, plus hugely friendly staff and a Mozambican chef. Tues–Sun noon–9.30pm.

Quartermaine's Pub and Restaurant Gables Shopping Centre ☎ 24163023. Named after a character in *King Solomon's Mines*, *Quartermaine's* serves quality steak-based pub grub from breakfast time onwards, and Swazi burgers for E45. Also has wi-fi (E30/hr). Mon–Fri 9am–11pm, Sat & Sun 8am–11pm.

Mantenga Cultural Village

Daily 6.30am–6pm • E150 • ☎ 24161151, ⓦ www.sntc.org.sz

Mantenga Drive ends at the grand entrance to the tiny **Mantenga Nature Reserve**, only really worth visiting for its cultural village. This open-air living museum replicates a nineteenth-century Swazi homestead with sixteen beehive huts, all built in traditional style using wooden frames joined by leather strips, reed thatch, cow dung and termite-hill earth. Cattle and goats wander about, and there are often demonstrations of traditional activities and crafts. Twice daily (11.15am & 3.15pm) an enchanting thirty-minute traditional music and dance performance takes place in a small open-air arena, telling a story of Swazi soldiers in the Anglo-Boer War, and the love and witchcraft they encounter when they return home.

Although the cultural village is the main attraction of the nature reserve, it's worth finding time to follow the short trail to the scenic 95m **Mantenga Falls** with its pretty **picnic** and **swimming spots**; it's a signposted fifteen-minute walk from the café.

Lobamba

Some 20km south of Mbabane, at the heart of the eZulwini Valley, the small royal village of **LOBAMBA** was originally built in 1830 for King Sobhuza I, and became the royal kraal (residence) of Sobhuza II. The **Houses of Parliament** are situated here, and must be one of the few in the world to have cattle grazing undisturbed in surrounding fields.

National Museum

Next door to the Parliament building • Mon–Fri 8am–4.30pm, Sat & Sun 10am–4pm • E20

A paved road to the north of the MR103 leads to the **National Museum**, which provides a helpful potted history of the country, with displays of cultural artefacts and a mishmash of old photographs of Manzini and Mbabane when they were one-horse towns, and sweaty British administrators in full colonial regalia. The only really interesting item in the natural history wing is a replica of a sixteenth-century head of Krishna that was discovered nearby. It was all that was found of what was a full-bodied statuette and the find has been interpreted as an indication of the high level of trade with the East at the time. Outside the museum stands a life-size re-creation of a traditional Swazi homestead. Remarkably, given their size, these huts are actually portable.

Somhlolo stadium

In front of the Parliament and Museum

Lobamba's **Somhlolo stadium** is the country's venue for major events and football matches, which are usually highly entertaining. For a few emalangeni on a Sunday afternoon, you can treat yourself to genial games of occasional great skill, with a good-humoured and vociferous crowd. Consult the local *Times of Swaziland* for details, or ask locally.

12

12

NCWALA AND UMHLANGA

The most sacred of Swaziland's ceremonies, **Ncwala** celebrates kingship, national unity and the first fruits of the new year. Its timing coincides with the new moon in November, when a group of selected men travel to the ancestral home on the shores of the Indian Ocean to collect foam from the waves. While they are there, the *Ncwala* ceremony begins, with songs and rituals performed until the afternoon of the full moon in December/early January, when the six days of the full *Ncwala* begin. Young Swazi men gather branches of the *lusekwane* tree, from which they build a bower for the king. Warriors gather and sing songs that can only be sung at this time, while the king dances with them. On the sixth day, objects representing the previous year are burnt on a massive bonfire, and prayers are offered to Swazi ancestors. The ceremony ends amid raucous singing, dancing and feasting. Visitors are allowed to attend most of *Ncwala*, but photography is prohibited during certain times (a free permit is also required; contact the Ministry of Information, PO Box 642, Mbabane; ☎ 24040651, ⬛ gov.sz), so be sure to ask first to avoid having your camera smashed.

The **Umhlanga** is a **fertility** or reed **dance** that gets its name from the large reeds brought to the residence of the Queen Mother by young women to repair her kraal, usually in late August or early September. The sixth and seventh days are the most spectacular, when you can watch up to 25,000 young women, dressed in elaborate and carefully coded costumes, sing and dance before the king and Queen Mother at Lobamba, giving the king an opportunity to pick a **new wife**. The former king, Sobhuza II, invariably plucked a new mate from the bevy of young beauties and racked up a total of seventy wives during his lifetime. His successor, Mswati III, now in his forties, has proved a little more restrained with only thirteen wives so far.

Ludzidzini

On the other side of the MR103 from Lobamba, the village of **LUDZIDZINI** is the kraal of the present king, Mswati III, and the Queen Mother. Ludzidzini cannot be visited or even photographed at all except during *Ncwala* (around New Year) and *Umhlanga* (end Aug/early Sept), when permission must be obtained (see box above).

Mlilwane Wildlife Sanctuary

Daily 24hr · E35 · ⬛ biggameparks.org

For many visitors to Swaziland, the highlight of the eZulwini Valley is **Mlilwane Wildlife Sanctuary**, with its relaxed atmosphere and attractive, game-filled plains. The name Mlilwane refers to the "little fire" that sometimes appears when lightning strikes the granite mountains. As well as offering good game viewing and activities, Mlilwane is an easy alternative to staying in Mbabane or on the eZulwini strip. Given its popularity, it's wise to book ahead if you intend to stay overnight.

The reserve holds a special place in the history of wildlife conservation in Swaziland; it was here that Ted Reilly (see box, p.638) first realized his dream of a sanctuary for Swaziland's fast-disappearing **wildlife**. Mlilwane's animals are mainly herbivorous, and include zebra, bountiful numbers of antelope and the sanctuary's emblem, the warthog. There's also the occasional crocodile and hippopotamus, which means you still need to be cautious if viewing the game on foot, bike or horseback.

ARRIVAL AND DEPARTURE
MLILWANE WILDLIFE SANCTUARY

By car To get to Mlilwane, take the turning from the eZulwini Valley Rd, signposted about 1km beyond the turn-off to Ludzidzini. From here, it's 3.5km along a dirt road to the entrance gate, where you pay your entrance fee – if arriving after 6pm entry fees are paid at the main restcamp the following morning. Note that you'll need to show both your entry and accommodation receipts in order to leave the sanctuary again, or they may charge you twice.

By shuttle bus For those who don't have their own transport, there are regular shuttle buses running between *Sondzela* and *Malandela's Homestead* (see opposite).

INFORMATION

Maps The park office, easy to spot in the middle of the main restcamp, can supply laminated maps for cycle and hiking routes for a E10 deposit, or for E20 you can buy a map of the entire sanctuary.

TRAILS AND ACTIVITIES

Guided Guided walks and game drives are available through the park office at the main restcamp. There are also guided mountain-bike tours and horseback trails, both fairly relaxed ways of taking in the park's attractions. For those with a little more horseback experience, various overnight trails involve camping in caves and rustic trail camps in the more remote parts of the reserve. For details, contact Big Game Parks central reservations (see below).

Self-guided Over 40km of road enables you to drive through the park to view game. The best of the self-guided walking trails is the Macobane Hill Trail, a gentle, four-hour hike through the mountains. The more adventurous can climb to the top of Nyonyane, the "Execution Rock", which rises so prominently in the north of the reserve. Whichever route you choose to take, it's important you tell a ranger of your plans before heading out; they keep track of who's out on their own and come out to find you if you're not back by dusk.

ACCOMMODATION

The reserve offers a wide variety of accommodation, which should be booked through Swaziland Big Game Parks Central Reservations (☎ 25283944, ⓦ biggameparks.org), though *Sondzela* (see below) can also be booked directly.

Main Rest Camp About 3.5km from the gate. A host of different (all basic but clean and tidy) accommodation options – self catering as well as B&B – including a campsite, traditional beehive huts and two- and four-person huts, plus a swimming pool. Camping **E70**, huts **E530**

Reilly's Rock Hilltop Lodge On a hilltop about 30min drive from Main Rest Camp. A lovely colonial home full of antiques and hardwood furniture, situated on a hilltop surrounded by woodland and prolific birdlife. With only six rooms, it's more upmarket than a guesthouse but more rustic than a game lodge, and guests here can enjoy fantastic views from the balcony over the Mdzimba Mountains, and wander round the gardens that surround the house. Rates include full board. **E1600**

Sondzela Backpacker Lodge A 15min walk from Main Rest Camp ☎ 25283117. A friendly place firmly established on the backpacking circuit, with dorms, doubles, and comfortable adobe rondavels sleeping two overlooking the valley, all with communal ablution facilities. Camping's also an option (tents only) and there's a lush garden, bar, and a large swimming pool. Camping **E55**, dorm **E95**, double **E240**

12

EATING

You can only buy basic supplies at the Main Rest Camp, so if you've opted for self-catering accommodation it's best to stock up at the Gables Shopping Centre (see p.634) beforehand.

Hippo Haunt At the Main Rest Camp. The only restaurant at Mlilwane serves up some good burgers and chicken-and-chip type fare, including at least one vegetarian option, starting at around E75. There's also a well-stocked bar. The restaurant overlooks an artificially created pond which is home to hippos, crocs and a huge variety of birds, and is a superb place to while away a few hours.

Sondzela Inexpensive breakfast and dinner are available at *Sondzela*, served in front of the campfire. There's only one dish on offer – typical backpacker fare such as chilli con carne – in addition to a vegetarian option.

Malandela's Homestead

1km southeast of the Mahlanya junction, off the MR103 • **Homestead** Daily 9am–11pm (later when there's a performance/live gig) • ☎ 25283448, ⓦ malandelas.com • **Gone Rural** daily 8am–5pm • ☎ 25504936, ⓦ goneruralswazi.com • **House on Fire** Tickets around E50, gigs from 8pm • ☎ 25282110, ⓦ house-on-fire.com • Music festival day ticket E150, whole festival E450 • ☎ 25282110, ⓦ bushfire.co.sz

Malandela's Homestead is situated in the scenic Malkerns Valley, lined with pineapple and sugar-cane fields. Initially just a collection of rustic farm buildings, it has now developed into a lively family-run arts and crafts venue that attracts locals and visitors alike to its top-of-the-range gigs, performances and exhibitions, while its pub and restaurant always seem to be filled to capacity. One of the highlights of the homestead is Gone Rural, one of the most successful and creative **local handicrafts projects** in Swaziland; the colourful and well-designed woven mats and baskets on sale here are made by a huge network of women working from villages all over the country. Next to Gone Rural, the funky **House on Fire** music venue doubles as an art

TED REILLY AND THE SWAZI NATURE CONSERVATION STORY

Swaziland owes the creation and survival of three of its major wildlife sanctuaries – Mlilwane, Mkhaya and Hlane – to **Ted Reilly**, who was born in Mlilwane in 1938, the son of a British Anglo-Boer War soldier who had stayed on. As Reilly was growing up, Swazi wildlife and its natural habitats were coming under serious threat from poachers and commercial farmers. In 1959, Reilly lobbied the colonial government to set aside land for parks, but was defeated by farmers who wanted the land for commercial agriculture. Undeterred, he turned his Mlilwane estate into a park anyway, and set about cultivating a relationship with **King Sobhuza II**. After Swazi independence, Sobhuza became much more powerful, and Reilly's relationship with him lent weight to his nature conservation efforts.

Despite rickety finances, the **Mlilwane Wildlife Sanctuary** opened in 1961, and the restocking and reintroduction of species has continued ever since. Meanwhile, Sobhuza asked Reilly to help stamp out poaching at Hlane. Reilly's tough approach resulted in shootouts with the poachers, earning him the praise of some, but the enmity of many.

Reilly's dependence on royal connections has also generated controversy, and some critics also assert that Reilly subordinates wildlife management principles to the needs of the tourist industry. Reilly's answer to his critics is simply to point to the three game parks his company runs. It's a powerful argument – without Reilly, the parks would not exist. Ted Reilly still lives at Mlilwane and remains active in Swazi conservation.

gallery and amphitheatre-like performance space, and is worth checking out for contemporary African crafts and the exuberant design. With live gigs most weekends, featuring mostly up-and-coming local talent, and the occasional big international act, this is the hottest music venue in Swaziland at the moment. Over the last three days of May, House on Fire is also the venue for the hugely successful **Bush Fire music festival**, with acts like Hugh Masekela, Johnny Clegg and Ladysmith Black Mambazo headlining in the past, and camping on fields next to the homestead. Tickets can be bought via the website.

INFORMATION

MALANDELA'S HOMESTEAD

Tourist information Next door to Gone Rural (daily 8am–5pm; ☎ 25283423); a good array of tourist information leaflets, a few online computers, and wi-fi.

ACCOMMODATION

Malandela's B&B ☎ 25283448, ⊛ malandelas.com. Delightful Afro-chic double rooms built in natural and recycled materials, with lavish breakfasts served on a terrace facing sugar-cane fields and a tranquil garden. It tends to be full when there's a concert happening at House on Fire (see p.637), in which case advance booking is essential. **E440**

EATING AND DRINKING

Malandela's Farmhouse Restaurant ☎ 25283115. Situated under a large thatched roof and offering a European-style menu with good-value à la carte meals including stews, game and fresh fish dishes, plus a fabulous range of salads. The restaurant's outdoor dining area provides excellent views of the adjoining sugar-cane fields and distant mountains. Daily 9.30am–10pm.

Malandela's Pub Adjoining the restaurant, this cosy and homely pub has Guinness on tap and is a popular spot for locals to watch rugby and soccer on cable TV. Mon 11am–11pm, Tues–Sun 10am–11pm.

Along the MR4

The idyllic **Nyanza Farm** (☎ 25283090, ⊛ nyanza.co.sz), situated on the MR4, a few kilometres from the MR103 junction, offers cross-country and mountain horse rides lasting from half an hour to a whole day. It's an appealingly cluttered working farm roamed by dogs, cats, geese, turkeys, peacocks, horses and Jersey cows, and a good place to stay, too (see opposite). Continue on the MR4 a bit further to the **Swazi**

Candles Craft Centre (daily 8am–5pm; ⓦswazicandles.com), which, in addition to a dedicated store producing and selling a bewildering array of brightly patterned wax candles, also encompasses a number of local crafts outlets, including the colourful Baobab Batiks (ⓦbaobab-batik.com) and Kwazi Swazi, selling books, art and a good selection of music.

ACCOMMODATION

★ **Nyanza Cottage** ☏ 25283090 or 76085779, ⓦnyanza.co.sz. Self-catering accommodation in two spacious, rustic, and floorboard-creaking cottages sleeping six at the bottom of a farm track, or in a backpacker lodge which includes a few en-suite double rooms, dorm beds, and facilities for camping outside. Camping E50, dorm E80, double E240, cottage E540

Swaziland Backpackers At the MR103 junction to the Malkerns Valley, 9km west of Manzini ☏ 76085893 or

ALONG THE MR4

76072089, ⓦswazilandbackpackers.co.za. A laidback place with tidy six- and ten-bed dorms, four decent doubles and some pleasant areas outside for camping. Inexpensive breakfasts and dinners are available, and there's also a pool with a pleasant bar. Trips to various attractions, including the game reserves, and activities such as quad biking can be organized. Camping E80, dorm E110, doubles E300

Manzini

MANZINI is Swaziland's largest city and its commercial hub. Almost all of the country's industrial and commercial sector is based in or around here, and the city is dominated by office blocks and malls obscuring its few attractive edifices. With a rising crime rate and an atmosphere far less relaxed than Mbabane, Manzini would be an eminently missable place were it not for its outstanding **market** (Mon–Sat) on the corner of Mhlakuvane and Mancishane streets, which is best on Thursday morning when traders from neighbouring countries come to town. Much of Manzini's market is devoted to fruit and vegetables, household goods and traditional medicines, while an upper section that spills onto the steps below sells **crafts** and **fabrics**. The crafts selection is bigger, more varied and much better value than any other market in Swaziland, while the fabrics – from Zimbabwe, Congo and Mozambique – are hard to find elsewhere in the country.

12

ARRIVAL AND DEPARTURE

By bus Buses from all over the country and South Africa pull in at Manzini's busy main bus station at the end of Louw St, just north of Ngwane St.

MANZINI

By plane Matsapha airport (☏ 25186192) lies 8km west of the city centre; if you're arriving, you'll need to take a taxi into central Manzini.

KAPHUNGA VILLAGE CULTURAL TOURS

An ambitious community tourism project in **KaPhunga** village, about 55km into the mountains southeast of Manzini, provides an excellent off-the-beaten-track opportunity to see the real rural Swaziland. The village is the second-highest settlement in the country and spreads over the top of a mountain rise with absolutely breathtaking views of the valley below – sugar-cane fields galore and the Lebombo Mountains in the distance. Here a young Swazi, Myxo, has built a mini homestead with authentic huts, separate from the main village, so that a certain amount of privacy is allowed both visitors and villagers. You're encouraged to stay at least one night and sleep in the traditional Swazi way, on a mattress on the hut floor. Facilities are fairly basic, but the gorgeous and authentically rustic setting makes this more than adequate. During the day, visitors can join in whatever is going on in the village, such as building projects, farming work, brewing beer or helping at the local primary school. Two-day trips (one night) to KaPhunga, including full board, transport from Manzini and contributions to the village, cost E1050 per person. Extra nights can be arranged. Day-trips including transport and full board cost E950 per person. To book, contact Myxo on ☏ 25058363 or ☏ 76044102, ⓦswaziculturaltours.com.

ACCOMMODATION

With excellent accommodation options available in the eZulwini and Malkerns valleys – both about half an hour's drive away – there's no real reason to stay overnight in Manzini.

The George Hotel Northern end of Ngwane St ☏ 25052260, ⓦ www.tgh.sz; map below. A comfortable business-class hotel with luxurious, spacious en-suite doubles with plush soft carpets, a pool, three restaurants, a bar, and a beauty salon and spa. **E1050**

Matsapha Inn 6km outside town on the MR103, shortly after the Matsapha airport turn-off ☏ 25187482 or 5186888; map below. A good, quiet motel-like option outside the centre, with smart en-suite doubles lining a long corridor, and a bar-restaurant. Convenient for the airport. **E555**

EATING AND DRINKING

Egg Yolk The George Hotel, northern end of Ngwane St; map below. The town's best coffee and also a fine place to eat, selling food prepared at the hotel's posher restaurant, at half the price. Try the Ungcwembe Special – grilled meat served with *pap* and lettuce garnish in a wooden bowl for sharing (E125 for two). Daily 8am–11pm.

Gil Vicente Ilanga Centre, Martins St ☏ 25053874; map below. A popular Portuguese restaurant, which has

long been a fixture in the city and is still going strong. Try the Mozambican peri-peri prawns, or Brazilian *fejoada*. Tues–Sun 8am–midnight.

Mkhulu's Coffee Shop Sandlane St; map below. A busy a/c café serving delicious Continental breakfast, and lunch featuring freshly made bread, plus a delightful selection of home-made cakes and muffins. Mon–Fri 7.30am–5pm, Sat 7.30am–4.30pm.

The south

12

Approaching Swaziland from one of its border crossings in the south is an excellent idea if you're travelling from northern KwaZulu-Natal through to the Kruger National Park or Mpumulanga. The scenery, particularly along the drive between **Mahamba** and Manzini through the **Grand Valley**, is really superb, and the road passes near most of the historical sites of the Swazi royal house. The south is also home to the **Mkhaya Nature Reserve**, Swaziland's most upmarket reserve and a sanctuary for the rare black rhino.

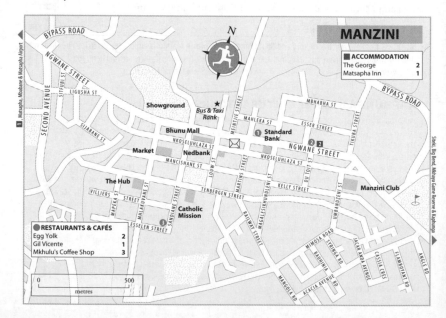

WHITEWATER RAFTING

One of the most exhilarating things you can do in southern Swaziland is to **whitewater raft** on the beautiful Great Usutu River, located in the east of the country near the Mkhaya Nature Reserve. One of the best whitewater rivers in southern Africa, it's also one of the few where you can take a trip in a two-man "croc" raft. The route runs for 15km in summer (a bit less in winter), and crosses over rapids classed in grades two to four. The scenery en route is stunning, but hard to appreciate once you hit the rapids, which leave you paddling like crazy and doing your best not to fall in the water. Trips include pick-ups from various points in the eZulwini Valley and en route to the river, and cost around E850 a person, including a picnic lunch and evening sundowners. Contact Swazi Trails (☎ 24162180, ⓦ swazitrails.co.sz) for bookings and further information.

Mkhaya Game Reserve

35km east of Manzini • Pick up at 10am and 4pm • ☎ 25283944, ⓦ biggameparks.org

Mkhaya Game Reserve is situated along a turn-off from the wonderfully named village of **Phuzumoya** ("drink the wind") in classic lowveld scrubland, filled with acacia and thorn trees. A sanctuary for the rare **black rhino**, Mkhaya also accommodates **white rhino**, **elephant** and numerous antelopes such as nyala, sable and eland. In addition, Mkhaya operates as a refuge where endangered species such **roan antelope** and **tsessebe** are bred. Rubbing shoulders with them, in the reserve section closest to the road, are herds of **Nguni cattle**.

INFORMATION

Essentials You'll need to book your visit to Mkhaya through Swazi Big Game Parks Central Reservations (☎ 25283944, ⓦ biggameparks.org). Day visits cost E545, including lunch. Day visits and overnight stays at Mkhaya must be booked in advance (see above), and you can't tour Mkhaya in your own vehicle, but must arrange to be met at the gate (10am or 4pm) from where you'll drive in convoy to the reserve's ranger base and the starting point of the first game drives – Kombi buses from Manzini to Big Bend stop at the gate; ask for the Phuzamoya shop drop.

MKHAYA GAME RESERVE

12

Game Dives Day visitors are taken on a game drive from the ranger base, and you'll have a high chance of encountering much of the big game. A generous lunch at the main camp is included in the price. For overnighters, morning and evening game drives are included in the accommodation price. Unlike game reserves in South Africa, Mkhaya's experienced Swazi rangers have few qualms about stopping in the middle of a game drive and inviting visitors to get out of the vehicle and walk quite close to white rhino. If you're staying overnight, early-morning game walks can also be organized.

ACCCOMMODATION

Stone Camp The reserve's only camp makes up for the lack of elevation in the reserve with an atmospheric bush setting beside the dry Ngwenyane river bed. Accommodation is offered in seductively luxurious open-plan and open-sided thatched stone huts with en-suite toilets and showers, which give you a wonderful sense of sleeping right in the bush. Beautifully prepared three-course meals are served around a large campfire in the main part of the camp under the shade of a massive sausage tree (its seed pods look like sausages), and staff have been known to treat guests to traditional dancing. **E2520**

The northeast

Northeast Swaziland is dominated by sugar plantations stretching into the distance, shimmering from the constant water spray, wreaking havoc with the water table – and leaving many locals without (hence the need for the new Maguga Dam, see p.646) – but earning the country valuable foreign exchange. Three large tracts of bush – **Hlane**, **Mlawula** and **Mbuluzi** – have been preserved as wildlife and nature reserves, and these are the main attractions for visitors to this region, together with the smaller **Shewula Nature Reserve**. They all form part of the **Lubombo Conservancy**, a grouping of protected land in the **Lubombo Mountains** that runs along Swaziland's eastern border and provides fantastic views of both Swaziland and the western fringes of Mozambique.

SHEWULA MOUNTAIN CAMP

Although isolated and time-consuming to reach, ★ **Shewula Mountain Camp** (booking essential ☎ 76051160, ⓦ shewulacamp.com; E440) is well worth the effort to reach with its spectacular setting at one end of the Lubombo plateau. To get here, take a bumpy dirt road eastwards into the mountains for 16km, from a turn-off 10km north of the Mubuluzi junction on the Manzini-Lomahasha road. Here, the local Shewula community manages a well-run camp with stupendous views west across northeast Swaziland and even, on a clear day, to the skyscrapers of Maputo to the east. It also offers an interesting insight into rural life in Swaziland. Accommodation is in seven rondavels (which sleep up to five people), with bunks or doubles, some with communal ablution facilities, but there's no electricity and cooking in a large kitchen/dining area is done on gas. **Activities** include guided hiking through Shewula Nature Reserve to the Mubuluzi River (E50/person) or a two-hour visit to the nearby village where there's a school for AIDS orphans and a local crafts centre (E40/person). If you don't want to self-cater, meals can be arranged in advance.

The most direct and obvious route to the reserves from Mbabane and Manzini is to follow the signposted and tarred road towards Siteki for 100km and 65km respectively. Turning north roughly 10km before Siteki leads to the reserves listed below.

Mbuluzi Game Reserve

Daily 6am–6pm • E25 for day visitors plus E25 per vehicle staying overnight • ☎ 2383 8861, ⓦ www.mbuluzigamereserve.co.sz

Privately owned and little known, **Mbuluzi** is about 1km off the Manzini–Lomahasha road, and straddles the road to Mlawula Nature Reserve. Set in classic lowveld bush, it encompasses two perennial rivers and riverine forest and some rocky precipices, but dominant in Mbuluzi are the thorn trees. The park has recently been restocked with game, including hippo and giraffe, which you can view in your own vehicle or on a bike. The absence of predators in Mbuluzi also means that you can walk along a network of clearly demarcated **trails**.

ARRIVAL AND DEPARTURE   MBULUZI GAME RESERVE

By minibus kombi Minibus Kombis from Manzini and Simunye to the Lomahasha border stop at the Maphiveni junction, from where it's a 15min hike to the gate.

ACCOMMODATION

Campsite ⓦ www.mbuluzigamereserve.co.sz. The well-equipped campsite is situated in the northern section of the reserve, close to the Mbuluzi River. Facility highlights include a shower block (with hot water) and the obligatory braai area. Book in advance. **E60**

Lodges ⓦ www.mbuluzigamereserve.co.sz. Accommodation at Mbuluzi consists of four privately owned self-catering lodges located – with lots of space between then – in the southern section of the reserve, south of the road to Mlawula. The immensely luxurious lodges are only available when not being used by their owners, and feature creature comforts such as swimming pools, DSTV and a/c. Two of the lodges sleep eight, one is a tented lodge sleeping six, and one lodge sleeps five. Book in advance. **E600**

Mlawula Nature Reserve

Daily 6am–6pm • E25 • ☎ 23838885, ⓦ sntc.org.sz

The largest single protected area in the Lubombo Mountains is the 165-square-kilometre **Mlawula Nature Reserve** south of the Mbuluzi River. The best reason to come to Mlawula is to stay at *Sara Bush Camp* (see opposite), but you can also spend some time exploring a network of self-guided hiking **trails**. As well as climbing into the mountains and onto the plateau at the top of the Lubombo range where unique species of ironwood trees and cycads grow, the trails wend their way around the river heading for caves, a waterfall and a hyena pool, and vary in length from two to eight hours. The bush throughout the reserve is quite dense, however, which largely prevents you from seeing much game. Guides are available to lead you on the hiking trails.

The Mlawula stream and more substantial Mbuluzi River both flow through some spectacular valleys in this reserve, and Stone-Age tools over one million years old have been found along their beds. **Antelope**, **zebra** and **wildebeest** congregate near the water, but so do **crocodiles**, so resist the temptation to swim.

ARRIVAL AND INFORMATION   MLAWULA NATURE RESERVE

By car To get here by car, turn east off the Manzini–Lomahasha Rd at the Maphiveni junction and continue past the Mbuluzi Reserve for a few kilometres until you see a sign pointing to the Mlawula Reserve on your right. There's also a second gate on the eastern side of the reserve, not far from the Mhlumeni/Goba border crossing from Mozambique, on the main road to Siteki.

By minibus Kombi Minibus Kombis from Manzini and Simunye to the Lomahasha border stop at the Maphiveni junction, from where it's a 4km hike to the main Mlawula Nature Reserve gate. Kombis linking the Mhlumeni/Goba border crossing to Siteki stop outside the gate.

Information You can pick up various leaflets at the park gate and a useful map (E10), but no supplies, so stock up beforehand at the nearby supermarket in Simunye.

ACCOMMODATION

Magadzavane Chalets ☎ 23838885, ⓦ sntc.org.sz. A cluster of twenty modern en-suite thatched rondavels near the gate by the Mozambican border, each with a spacious veranda at the front offering fabulous views of the valley. They have electricity so are fully kitted with stove, fridge and TV, and the site also encompasses a pool and restaurant. Book in advance. **E600**

Sara Bush Camp ☎ 23838885, ⓦ sntc.org.sz. A beautiful tented camp, with four large safari tents (sleeping two) on wooden decks perched on the very edge of a cliff overlooking the Mwlawula River and roughly 5km from the main entrance. Each tent has a braai site and its own bathing area, consisting of a tiny perch among the rocks on the cliff edge with a paraffin-boiler shower and galvanized-iron washtub. There's a communal lounge and kitchen area. Book in advance. **E600**

Siphiso campsite ☎ 23838885, ⓦ sntc.org.sz. A shaded site next to the Siphiso River, with a toilet and shower block and braai stands. There's also an area for caravans, and two thatched shelters that are handy should the weather turn nasty. Book in advance. **E60**

Hlane Royal National Park

Daily 6am–6pm • E35 • ⓦ biggameparks.org

Some 67km northeast of Manzini, **Hlane Royal National Park** is the largest of Swaziland's parks. Formerly a private royal hunting ground, the main attraction here is the presence of big game, including **elephant**, **rhino**, **lion** and **leopard**. Hlane has a large population of easy-to-spot elephants and rhino in the northern area of the park, which you can also visit in your own vehicle, and rhino-sighting is virtually guaranteed. Other animals in this section include giraffe, zebra and waterbuck.

Various **southern enclosures** contain lion and leopard, along with some more elephant and rhino. Although the enclosures guarantee lion sightings, the animals are well habituated to vehicles and look completely disinterested in the whole experience Hlane is also home to the largest population of nesting vultures in Africa.

ARRIVAL AND DEPARTURE   HLANE ROYAL NATIONAL PARK

By car The entrance to Hlane is roughly 7km south of Simunye, off the Manzini–Lomahasha Rd.

By Kombis Running between Manzini and Simunye, Kombis stop 300m from the park gate.

TOURS

Guided tours on foot (E150 for 2hr 30min) are available any time during the day from the reception at Main Camp. If you don't have your own transport and you want to go further afield, you can join a guided tour in one of the park's Land Rovers (E230 for 2hr 30min), with sunrise (5.30am) and sunset (4.30pm) tours also available (E255 for 2hr 30min); the sunrise and sunset tours are the most magical, with most sightings; bookings at Main Camp reception.

ACCOMMODATION

Bhubesi Camp 14km from Main Camp along a dirt track ☎ 25283944, ⓦ biggameparks.org. Six self-catering stone cottages overlooking a dry river, and feeling much more remote, though the cottages here have electricity. **E580**

Ndlovu Main Camp ☎ 25283944, ⓦ biggameparks .org. Situated near the gate, with large self-catering thatched cottages that sleep up to eight people and en-suite rondavels sleeping two. There's no electricity at *Ndlovu* (paraffin lamps and gas cooker are provided). Reminiscent of the old Kruger restcamps, the basic – but adequate – accommodation provides a relaxed setting allowing you to focus on the surrounding wildlife. **E530**

Ndlovu Camping Area Main Camp ☎ 25283944, ⓦ biggameparks.org. Open camping ground with plenty of soft grass and trees using a communal kitchen and ablution block (with hot water) and plenty of firewood available in the braai area. **E60**

EATING

Ndlovu restaurant Main Camp. A large thatched restaurant and lounge area, with a wide deck overlooking a nearby watering hole that is home to rhino, and attracts elephant and giraffe. There's a reliable à la carte menu as well as a buffet at dinner time offering the usual gamut of chicken and burgers at surprisingly reasonable prices. Unless there's a large group staying, the wide deck is fairly relaxed, with plenty of trees and shady spots to sit.

The northwest

The highveld of the **northwest** is unquestionably the most beautiful region of Swaziland, with rolling hills perfect for hiking, countless sparkling streams, a sprinkling of waterfalls and some wonderful accommodation.

Most visitors to the northwest are en route to or from Kruger National Park (see p.551), but beautiful **Phophonyane Nature Reserve** is only 64km north of Mbabane and well worth a visit, too. The most spectacular – and rugged – entrance into the country is via the Bulembu road from Barberton in Mpumalanga.

Phophonyane Nature Reserve

40km south of the Matsamo border • Daily 10am–5pm • E20 • ☎ 24371429, ⓦ phophonyane.co.sz

The relaxing, private **Phophonyane Nature Reserve** is situated five slow kilometres away from the road, making it best reached with your own transport (public transport drops off on the main road, entailing a hike to get here). The five-square-kilometre reserve's carefully laid-out **trails** ensure there's plenty to see, including the Phophonyane Waterfall on its northwestern side. The vegetation is subtropical and attracts hundreds of colourful **bird species**, while animals include mongooses, bushbabies, otters and numerous snakes, though all are hard to spot. The **lodge** in the reserve is one of the most beautiful places to stay in Swaziland (see below); if you can't afford to stay, it's still worth stopping here for a short hike and a meal in the thatched restaurant.

ACCOMMODATION   PHOPHONYANE NATURE RESERVE

★ **Phophonyane Nature Reserve** Five secluded two-person safari tents next to the Phophonyane River, with private bathroom facilities in separate huts a few steps up from the tents. There are also family cottages sleeping up to five, with private kitchens and gardens, and two gorgeously romantic beehive huts. The reserve has two pools; one with salt water next to the restaurant, the other blended cleverly into the rocks beside the tumbling river and with a stunning location, looking out onto endless mountains and surrounded by luxuriant vegetation. **E1290**

Nsangwini Rock Art

Komati Valley • E25 • ☎ 76373767 • From the Mbabane–Matsamo Rd follow the Muguga Dam Loop Rd eastwards, following signs down a dirt road turn-off to the east; the hike begins after 7km

A thirty-minute hike down a mountainside trail in the Komati Valley will lead you to a

12

wide expanse of rock art, found in a rock shelter dramatically perched over the Komati River Valley, with breathtaking views of the mountain. The rock art is estimated to be around 4000 years old, and absolutely mind-boggling; you'll find that the longer you look at the rocks, the more you see, including human figures in a trance-like dance holding spears, and the sacred preying mantis. To visit the site you need to hire a guide from the Nsangwini community; they are well informed and will be waiting in a shelter at the start at the hiking trail.

Maguga Dam

On the Maguga Dam Loop Rd, eastwards off the Mbabane–Matsamo Rd • Daily 8am–5pm • Free

The hydroelectric **Maguga Dam** sits snugly in a lowveld dip surrounded on all four sides by the often mist-covered mountains. The dam, primarily constructed to provide water for the vast sugar-cane plantations downstream, was completed in 2002 and filled in 2006. You can ponder the vastness of the construction in the on-site café, while the **information centre**, on a ledge overlooking the dam, gives a full breakdown of the dam's history.

ACCOMMODATON | MAGUGA DAM

Maguga Lodge Next to the Maguga Dam on the Maguga Dam loop road ☎ 24373970, ⓦ magugalodge .com. This scenically located lodge has 33 comfortable en-suite rondavels and a fully kitted campsite. They run relaxing one- hour boat trips on the dam (E100 per person), giving you an opportunity to see the dam's rich birdlife. There's also an outstanding restaurant that overlooks the dam from a large thatched balcony; the Sunday buffet lunch here is especially recommended (E135). Camping **E95**, rondavel **E820**

Malolotja Nature Reserve

Daily 6am–6pm • E28 • ☎ 76133900, ⓦ sntc.org.sz

Swaziland's least touristy park, the easy-going **Malolotja Nature Reserve** offers awesome scenery and some of the finest hiking in Southern Africa. This is a place to come for rugged, wild nature and tranquillity, rather than for game spotting. The mountains here, among the oldest in the world (3.6 billion years old), are covered in grassland and graced by myriad streams and waterfalls, including the 95m-high **Malolotja Falls**.

Nearly three hundred species of **birds** are found in Malolotja, with an impressive colony of the rare bald ibis just by the waterfalls. You'll have to look harder for **game**, although wildebeest, blesbok and zebra are often visible, and there are leopards and elephants lurking somewhere in the gaping tracts of mountain and valley. Malolotja's small network of roads passes some fine viewpoints and picnic sites, but to really savour this park's rugged wilderness and see its waterfalls you'll need to hike, or go by horseback (contact *Hawane Resort*, see opposite). A variety of **trails** is laid out in the reserve, from easy half-day excursions to seven-day marathons, with accommodation available en route (see opposite). **Forbes Reef Gold Mine**, a few kilometres south of the reserve's main entrance on the main tarred road, can be visited alone, but take care on the slippery banks; you can find it using the map you get on arrival at the main entrance.

ARRIVAL AND INFORMATION | MALOLOTJA NATURE RESERVE

By minibus Kombi Minibus Kombis between Mbabane and Piggs Peak stop at the main gate, which is clearly sign-posted on the Mbabane–Matsamo Rd.

Supplies Brochures and maps are available from the reserve's reception building, 500m from the main entrance gate. The reception also houses a nice restaurant (daily 8am–4pm) and there's a curio shop that sells basic provisions, but it's wiser to stock up in Piggs Peak or Mbabane.

Climate If you're on a long hike during the summer, be prepared for hot days; however, temperatures drop dramatically in winter, when the nights can be freezing.

UP IN THE TREES

An alternative way of experiencing the reserve is through **Canopy Tours** (☎76442948, ⓦmalolotjacanopytour.com; E450), which involves gliding on wires between elevated forest platforms while securely kitted out with lots of tackle. You can't really see much wildlife while whooshing along, but there's a good adrenalin kick when stepping off the first platform. Tours last three hours and include a light lunch. Booking is essential; tours start from the reserve's reception building.

ACCOMMODATION

Campsites ☎76133900, ⓦhawane.co.sz. There are eighteen scenic overnight camps scattered around the reserve, all without facilities or water (but with braai areas), for those attempting longer hikes; you'll need to bring all your own equipment. Camps 11 and 12 are near Malolotja Falls. Book in advance. **E50**

Main Restcamp ☎76133900, ⓦhawane.co.sz.

Fifteen tent sites with hot water in a communal bath area, and braai areas, as well as thirteen comfortable log cabins, each sleeping up to eight people. Both are a short walk from the main reception so you can eat at the restaurant there if you don't fancy cooking. Book in advance. Camping **E70**, cabin **E460**

Hawane Dam Nature Reserve

Daily 6am–6pm • E28, or joint ticket with Malolotja

Though technically part of the Malolotja Nature Reserve, **Hawane Dam Nature Reserve** is not directly connected, situated some 12km south of the main gate on the Mbabane road, and on the eastern side of the road. This is a small area around the northern end of the Hawane Dam, designed to protect part of the Black Mbuluzi River wetlands. Hawane's main attraction is its wealth of **birdlife**, and there's an excellent trail for birdwatching.

ACCOMMODATION   HAWANE DAM NATURE RESERVE

Hawane Resort Signposted on the Mbabane Rd down a 1km track, on the opposite side of the main Rd to the dam ☎24424744, ⓦhawane.co.sz. Funky accommodation in quirky triangular adobe chalets sleeping two, and comfortable twin-bed backpacker

accommodation in a nearby converted barn. With large stables housing well-trained horses, this is the place to head if you fancy exploring the attractive surrounding countryside on horseback (E120/hr). Backpackers **E120**, chalet **E966**

EATING

★ **Taste of Africa** Hawane Resort. An outstanding restaurant in a large, character-packed, thatched circular structure, which serves delicious food best defined as

African fusion. Try the seafood-packed Mozambican north-coast soup (E60), coconut crepes (E60), or the delectable honey and cashew-nut ice cream (E85).

Ngwenya Glass factory

On the MR3, west of Motshane • Daily 9am–4pm • ⓦngwenyaglass.co.sz

The Mbabane–Matsamo road meets the fast MR3 between the Ngwenya/Oshoek border post and Mbabane at the small settlement of **Motshane**. A kilometre west of Motshane, along the MR3 towards the border, follow the signs to where one of Swaziland's best-known exports, **Ngwenya glass**, is made. Their products, which range from attractive wine glasses to endless trinkets in the shape of rotund animals, are made from recycled glass and produced by highly skilled workers; it's well worth stopping here just to see them blowing and crafting the glass from the viewing balcony above the roaring furnaces. The adjoining gift shop and **café** are usually swamped by coach-loads of tourists.

12

Contexts

History

Recent fossil finds show that *Homo sapiens* existed along Africa's southern coast over 50,000 years ago. The descendants of these nomadic Stone-Age people – ochre-skinned San hunter-gatherers and Khoikhoi herders (see below) – still inhabited the Western Cape when Europeans arrived in the fifteenth century. By the time of the Dutch settlement at the Cape in the mid-seventeenth century, much of the eastern half of the country was occupied by people who had begun crossing the Limpopo around the time of Christ's birth.

The stage was now set for the complex drama of South Africa's modern history, which in crude terms was a battle for the control of scarce resources between the various indigenous people, African states and the European colonizers. The twentieth century saw the temporary victory of colonialism, the unification of South Africa and the attempts by whites to keep at bay black demands for civil rights, culminating in the implementation of South Africa's most notorious social invention – **apartheid**. Ultimately, it was multiracialism that was victorious and, despite numerous problems, South Africa's lively 2009 elections were proof that democracy was still alive after fifteen years.

The first South Africans

Rock art provides evidence of human culture in the subcontinent dating back nearly 30,000 years and represents Southern Africa's oldest and most enduring artistic tradition. The artists were hunter-gatherers, sometimes called Bushmen, but more commonly **San**. The most direct descendants of the late Stone Age, San people have survived in tiny pockets, mostly in Namibia and Botswana, making theirs the longest-spanning culture in the subcontinent. At one time they probably spread throughout sub-Saharan Africa, having pretty well perfected their **nomadic lifestyle**, which involved an enviable twenty-hour working week spent by the men hunting and the women gathering. This left considerable time for artistic and religious pursuits. People lived in small, loosely connected bands comprising family units and were free to leave and join up with other groups. The concept of private property had little meaning because everything required for survival could be obtained from the environment.

About two thousand years ago, this changed when some groups in northern Botswana laid their hands on fat-tailed sheep and cattle from Northern Africa, thus transforming themselves into herding communities. The introduction of livestock revolutionized social organization, creating the idea of ownership and accumulation. Social divisions developed, and political units became larger and centred around a chief, who had important powers, such as the allocation of pasturage.

These were the first South Africans encountered by Portuguese mariners, who landed along the Cape coast in the fifteenth century. Known as **Khoikhoi** (meaning "men of men"), they were not ethnically distinct from the San, as many anthropologists once believed, but simply represented a distinct social organization. According to current thinking it was possible for Khoi who lost their livestock to revert to being San, and for San to lay their hands on animals to become Khoi, giving rise to the collective term "Khoisan".

30,000 BC	500 BC	500 AD	1488
Hunter-gatherers occupy Cape Peninsula	Khoikhoi sheep herders drift southwards into South Africa, eventually reaching southern coast	Tall Bantu-speaking farmers cross Limpopo River and begin dispersing down South Africa's east coast	Bartholomeu Dias becomes first European to set foot on South African soil at Mossel Bay

Farms and crafts

Around two thousand years ago, tall, dark-skinned people who practised mixed farming – raising both crops and livestock – crossed the Limpopo River into what is today South Africa. These **Bantu-speaking** farmers were the ancestors of South Africa's majority African population, who gradually drifted south, to occupy the entire eastern half of the subcontinent as far as the Eastern Cape, where they were first encountered by Europeans in the sixteenth century.

Apart from having highly developed farming know-how and a far more sedentary life than the Khoisan, the early Bantu speakers were skilled craft workers and knew about mining and smelting metals, including gold, copper and iron, which became an important factor in the extensive network of trade that developed.

The Cape goes Dutch

In the fifteenth century, Portuguese mariners led by **Bartholomeu Dias** became the first Europeans to set foot in South Africa, but it was another 170 years before any European settlement was established here. In 1652, a group of white employees of the **Dutch East India Company**, which was trading between the Netherlands and the East Indies, pulled into Table Bay to set up a refreshment station to resupply company ships.

Despite the view of station commander Jan van Riebeeck that the indigenous Khoi were savages "living without conscience", from the start, the Dutch were dependent on them to provide livestock, which was traded for trinkets. As the settlement developed, Van Riebeeck needed more labour to keep the show going. Much to his annoyance, the bosses back in Holland had forbidden him from enslaving the locals, and refused his request for slaves from elsewhere in the company's empire.

This kicked off the process of colonization of the lands around the fort, when a number of Dutch men were released in 1657 from their contracts to farm as free burghers on land granted by the company. The idea was that they would sell their produce to the company at a fixed price, thereby overcoming the labour shortage. The move sparked the first of a series of Khoikhoi–Dutch wars. Although the first campaign ended in stalemate, the Khoikhoi were ultimately no match for the Dutch, who had the advantages of superior mobility and firepower in horses and guns.

Meanwhile, in 1658, Van Riebeeck established slavery at the Cape via the back door, when he purloined a shipload of slaves from West Africa. The Dutch East India Company itself became the biggest slave owner at the Cape and continued importing slaves, mostly from the East Indies, at such a pace that by 1711 there were more slaves than burghers in the colony. With the help of this ready workforce, the embryonic Cape Colony expanded outwards displacing the Peninsula Khoikhoi, who by 1713 had lost everything. Most of their livestock (nearly fifty thousand head) and most of their land west of the Hottentots Holland Mountains (90km southeast of present-day Cape Town) had been swallowed by the Dutch East India Company. Dispossession and diseases like smallpox, previously unknown in South Africa, decimated their numbers and shattered their social system. By the middle of the eighteenth century, those who remained had been reduced to a condition of miserable servitude to the colonists.

1652	1657	1658	1679
Dutch East India Company establishes supply station at Cape for trade ships sailing to Indies	Company releases indentured labourers to farm as free settlers	First slaves introduced at Cape and within fifty years slaves outnumber settlers	Castle of Good Hope completed

THE TREKBOERS

Like the Khoikhoi, impoverished whites living at the fringes of colonial society had limited options. Many just packed up their wagons and rolled out into the interior, where they lived by the gun, either hunting game or taking cattle from the Khoi by force. Beyond the control of the Dutch East India Company, these nomadic trekboers began to assume a pastoral niche previously occupied by the Khoi. By the turn of the nineteenth century, trekboers had penetrated well into the Eastern Cape, pushing back the Khoi and San in the process.

As their lives became disrupted and living by **traditional** means became impossible, the Khoisan began to prey on the cattle and sheep of the trekboers. The trekboers responded by hunting down the San as vermin, killing the men and often taking women and children as slaves. After the British occupation of the Cape in 1795, the trekboer migration from the Cape

Rise of the Zulus

While in the west of the country trekboers were migrating from the Cape Colony, in the east equally significant movements were under way. Throughout the seventeenth and eighteenth centuries, descendants of the first Bantu-speakers to penetrate into South Africa had been swelling their numbers and had expanded right across the eastern half of the country.

Nowhere was this more marked than in **KwaZulu-Natal**, where, prompted by pressures on grazing land, chiefdoms survived by subduing and absorbing their neighbours. By the early nineteenth century, two chiefdoms, the Ndwandwe and the Mthethwa, dominated eastern South Africa around the Tugela River. During the late 1810s a major confrontation between them ended in the defeat of the Mthethwa. Out of their ruins emerged the **Zulus**, who were to become one of the most powerful polities in Southern Africa. Around 1816, **Shaka** assumed the chieftaincy of the Zulus, whose fighting tactics he quickly transformed.

By 1820, the Zulus had become the dominant regional power and by the middle of the century had established a centralized military state with a forty-thousand-strong standing army. One of the strengths of the system lay in its ability to absorb the survivors of conflict, who became members of the expanding Zulu state. Throughout the 1820s, Shaka sent his armies to invade neighbouring territory. But in 1828, he was stabbed to death by two of his half-brothers, one of whom, Dingane, succeeded him. Dingane continued with his brother's ruthless but devastatingly successful policies and tactics.

The rise of the Zulu state reverberated across Southern Africa and led to the creation of a series of **centralized Nguni states** as well as paving the way for **Boer** expansion into the interior. In a movement of forced migrations known as the **mfecane**, huge areas of the country were laid waste and people across eastern South Africa were driven off their lands. They attempted to survive either in small groups or by banding together to form larger political organizations.

To the north of the Zulu kingdom another Nguni group with strong cultural and linguistic affinities with the Zulus came together under **Sobhuza I** and his son Mswati II, after whom their new state **Swaziland** took its name. In North West Province, a few hundred Zulus under **Mzilikazi** were displaced by Shaka and relocated to Matabeleland, now southwestern Zimbabwe, where they re-established themselves as the **Matabele**

1713	1795	1816–1828	1820s
Khoikhoi dispossessed of livestock by settlers and reduced to servitude	Company goes bust and English becomes official language when British take over	Shaka assumes chieftainship of Zulus and forges militarized regional power in southeast	As defence against Shaka, Nguni states form in Swaziland, Lesotho and Matabeleland

> ## NEW WORD ORDER
>
> In the late nineteenth century, Afrikaans-speaking whites, fighting for an identity, sought to create a "racially pure" culture by driving a wedge between themselves and coloured Afrikaans-speakers. They reinvented **Afrikaans** as a "white man's language", eradicating the supposed stigma of its coloured ties by substituting Dutch words for those with Asian or African roots. In 1925, the dialect of Afrikaans spoken by upper-crust whites became an official language alongside English, and the dialects spoken by coloureds were treated as inferior deviations from correct usage.
>
> For Afrikaner nationalists this wasn't enough, and after the introduction of apartheid in 1948, they attempted to codify perceived racial differences. Under the **Population Registration Act**, all South Africans were classified as white, coloured or African. These classifications became fundamental to what kind of life you could expect. There are numerous cases of families in which one sibling was classified coloured with limited rights and another white with the right to live in comfortable white areas, enjoy superior job opportunities, and be able to send their children to better schools and universities.
>
> With the demise of apartheid, the make-up of residential areas is slowly (very slowly) shifting – and so is the thinking on ethnic terminology. Some people now reject the term "coloured" because of its apartheid associations, and refuse any racial definitions; others, however, proudly embrace the term, as a means of acknowledging their distinct culture, with its slave, East Indies and Khoikhoi roots.

kingdom. In the Drakensberg, on the west flank of KwaZulu-Natal, **Moshoeshoe I** used diplomacy and cunning to establish the territory that became the modern state of **Lesotho**.

The Great Trek

Back in the Cape, many Afrikaners were becoming fed up with British rule. Their principal grievance was the way in which the colonial authorities were tampering with labour relations and destroying what they saw as a divine distinction between blacks and whites. In 1828 a proclamation gave Khoi residents and free blacks equality with whites before the law. The **abolition of slavery** in 1834 was the last straw.

Fifteen thousand Afrikaners (one out of ten living in the colony) left the Cape to escape the meddlesome British. When they arrived in the eastern half of the country, they were delighted to find vast tracts of apparently unoccupied land. In fact, they were merely stumbling into the eye of the **mfecane** storm – areas that had been temporarily cleared either by war parties or by fearful people hiding out to escape detection. As they fanned out further they encountered the Nguni states and a series of battles followed. By the middle of the nineteenth century, descendants of the Dutch had consolidated control and established the two Boer states of the **South African Republic** (now Mpumalanga, North West and Limpopo provinces) and the **Orange Free State** (now Free State), the independence of both of which was recognized by Britain in the 1850s.

The Anglo-Boer War

Despite the benefits it brought, the discovery of gold (see box, opposite) was also one of the principal causes of the **Anglo-Boer War**. Gold-mining had shifted the economic

1820s	1834	1843	1860s
British settlers arrive at Port Elizabeth as bulwark against Xhosa on eastern frontier	Abolition of slavery leads many Boers to leave Cape and establish two republics	British annex Natal, settlers arrive and indentured Indian labourers brought to work cane fields	Discovery of world's biggest diamond deposit at Kimberley

GOLD AND DIAMONDS

In the 1850s Britain wasn't too concerned about the interior of South Africa. Its strategic position aside, South Africa was a chaotic backwater at the butt-end of the empire. Things changed in the 1860s, with the discovery of **diamonds** (the world's largest deposit) around modern-day Kimberley, and even more significantly in the 1880s, with the discovery of **gold** on the Witwatersrand (now Gauteng). Together, these finds were the catalyst that transformed South Africa from a down-at-heel rural society into an urbanized industrial one. In the process great fortunes were made by capitalists like Cecil Rhodes, traditional African society was crushed and the independence of the Boer republics ended.

Although the **Gauteng goldfields** were exceptionally well endowed, they were also particularly difficult to mine, requiring the sinking of deep shafts. Exploiting the mines required costly equipment and cheap labour. Capital quickly flowed in from Western investors eager for profit.

centre of South Africa from the British-controlled Cape to a Boer republic, while at the same time, Britain's European rival, Germany, was beginning to make political and economic inroads in the Boer republics. Britain feared losing its strategic Cape naval base, but perhaps even more important were questions of international finance and the substantial British investment in the mines. London was at the heart of world trade and was eager to see a flourishing gold-mining industry in South Africa, but the Boers seemed rather sluggish about modernizing their infrastructure to assist the exploitation of the mines.

In any case, a number of Britons had for some time seen the unification of South Africa as the key to securing British interests in the subcontinent. To this end, under a wafer-thin pretext, Britain had declared war and subdued the last of the independent African kingdoms by means of the **Zulu War of 1879**. This secured KwaZulu-Natal, bringing all the coastal territories of South Africa under British control. To control the entire subcontinent south of the Limpopo, Britain needed to bring the two Boer republics under the Union flag.

During the closing years of the nineteenth century, Britain demanded that the South African Republic grant voting rights to British miners living there – a demand that, if met, would have meant the end of Boer political control over their own state, since they were outnumbered by the foreigners. The Boers turned down the request and war broke out in October 1899. The British command believed they were looking at a walkover: in the words of **Lord Kitchener**, a "teatime war" that would get the troops home by Christmas.

In fact, the campaign turned into Britain's most expensive since the Napoleonic Wars. During the early stages, the Boers took the imperial power by surprise and penetrated into British-controlled KwaZulu-Natal and the Northern Cape, inflicting a series of humiliating defeats. By June, a reinforced British army was pushing the Boers back, but the Boers fought on for another two years. Lord Kitchener responded with a **scorched-earth policy** that left the countryside a wasteland and thousands of women and children homeless. To house them, the British invented the **concentration camps**, in which 26,370 Boer women and children died. For some Afrikaners, this episode remains a major source of bitterness against the British even today. Less widely publicized were the **African concentration camps** which took 14,000 lives. By 1902, the

1879	1886	1899–1901
Britain declares war on Zulus, suffers humiliating defeat at Isandlwana, but eventually wins	Discovery of gold around Johannesburg	Britain defeats Afrikaners in Anglo-Boer War to gain total hegemony over South Africa

Boers were demoralized, and in May, the Afrikaner republics surrendered their independence in exchange for British promises of reconstruction. By the end of the so-called teatime war, Britain had committed nearly half a million men to the field and lost 22,000 of them. Of the 88,000 Boers who fought, 7000 died in combat. With the two Boer republics and the two British colonies under imperial control, the way was clear for the federation of the **Union of South Africa** in 1910.

Migrant labour and the Bambatha Rebellion

Between the conclusion of the Anglo-Boer War and the unification of South Africa, the mines suffered a **shortage of unskilled labour**. Most Africans still lived by agriculture. To counter this, the government took measures to compel them to supply their labour to the mines. One method was the imposition of **taxes** that had to be paid in coin, thus forcing Africans from subsistence farming and into the cash economy. Responding to one such tax, in 1906 a group of Zulus refused to pay. The authorities declared martial law and dealt mercilessly with the protesters, burning their homes and seizing their possessions. This provoked a full-blown rebellion led by Chief Bambatha, which was ruthlessly put down, at a cost of four thousand rebel lives. Armed resistance by Africans was thus ended for over half a century. After the defeat of the **Bambatha Rebellion**, the number of African men from Zululand working in the Gauteng mines shot up by sixty percent. By 1909, eighty percent of adult males in the territory were away from home, working as migrant labourers. **Migrant labour**, with its shattering effects on family life, became one of the foundations of South Africa's economic and social system, and a basic cornerstone of apartheid.

Kick-starting Afrikanerdom

In a parallel development, large numbers of **Afrikaners** were forced to leave rural areas in the early part of the twentieth century. This was partly a result of the war, but also of overcrowding, drought and pestilence. Many Afrikaners joined the ranks of a swelling poor **white working class** whose members often felt despised by the English-speaking capitalists who commanded the economy, and threatened by lower-paid Africans competing for their jobs.

In 1918 a group of Afrikaners formed the **Broederbond** ("the brotherhood"), a secret society to promote the interest of Afrikaners. It aimed to uplift impoverished members of the **volk** ("people") and to develop a sense of pride in their language, religion and culture. The Broederbond would come to dominate every aspect of the way the country was run for half a century.

During the 1930s, a number of young Afrikaner intellectuals travelled to Europe, where they were inspired by fascism. It was around this time that Afrikaner intellectuals began using the term **apartheid** (pronounced "apart-hate"). Among those kicking their heels in Germany in the 1930s were **Nico Diederichs**, who became a minister of finance under the Afrikaner Nationalist Party; **Hendrik Frensch Verwoerd**, apartheid's leading theorist and prime minister from 1958 to 1966; and **Piet Meyer**, controller of the state broadcasting service, who named his son Izan ("Nazi" spelled backwards – he later claimed this was sheer coincidence).

1910	1912	1913	1918
Boer republics and British colonies merge into Union of South Africa	ANC forms to fight for universal suffrage	Land Act gives whites (20 percent of population) 92 percent of the land	Afrikaner secret society, Broederbond, forms and Nelson Mandela born

In 1939, the Broederbond introduced a scheme that, in the space of a decade, launched ten thousand Afrikaner businesses, some of which are still among the leading players in South Africa's economy.

Africans' claims

Despite having relied on African cooperation for their victory in the Anglo-Boer War and having hinted at enhanced rights for blacks after the war, the British excluded blacks from the cosy federal deal between themselves and the Afrikaners. It wasn't long, in fact, before the white Union government began eroding African rights. In response, a group of middle-class mission-educated Africans formed the **South African Native National Congress** (later to become the ANC) in 1912 to campaign for universal suffrage. In 1914, the leaders went to London to protest against the 1913 **Natives' Land Act**, which confined the black majority to less than ten percent of the land. The trip failed and the Land Act became the foundation for apartheid some 35 years later.

Through the early half of the twentieth century, the ANC remained conservative, unwilling to engage in active protest. In response, a number of alternative mass organizations arose, among them the **Industrial and Commercial Union**, an African trade union founded in 1919, which at its peak in 1928 had gathered an impressive 150,000 members. But in the 1930s it ran out of steam. The first political movement in the country not organized along ethnic lines was the South African Communist Party, founded in 1921 with a multiracial executive. While it never itself gained widespread membership, it became an important force inside the ANC.

Throughout the 1930s, the ANC plodded on with speeches, petitions and pleas, which proved completely fruitless.

Young Turks and striking miners

In 1944, a young hothead named **Nelson Mandela** with friends **Oliver Tambo**, **Walter Sisulu** and **Anton Lembede** formed the **ANC Youth League**. The League's founding manifesto criticized the ANC leadership for being "gentlemen with clean hands". The 1945 annual conference of the ANC adopted a document called "**Africans' Claims in South Africa**", which reflected an emerging politicization. The document demanded **universal franchise** and an end to the **colour bar**, which reserved most skilled jobs for whites.

In 1946 the African Mineworkers' Union launched one of the biggest strikes in the country's history in protest against falling living standards. Virtually the entire Gauteng gold-mining region came to a standstill as 100,000 workers downed tools. Prime Minister Jan Smuts sent in police who forced the workers back down the shafts at gunpoint.

The following year Nelson Mandela took his first step into public life when he was elected general secretary of the ANC.

Winds of change

For years, the white government had been hinting at easing up on segregation, and even Smuts himself, no soft liberal, had reckoned that it would have to end at some point. The relentless influx of Africans into the urban areas was breaking the stereotype of them as rural tribespeople. The government appointed the **Fagan Commission** to

1920s	1930s	1939
Agatha Christie surfs at Muizenberg, Cape Town	Orlando, the nucleus of Soweto, begins evolving	World War splits Afrikaners, with future prime minister John Vorster among those supporting Germany

look into the question of the **pass laws**, which controlled the movement of Africans and sought to keep them out of the white cities unless they had a job.

When the Fagan Commission reported its findings in 1948, it concluded that "the trend to urbanization is irreversible and the pass laws should be eased". While some blacks may have felt heartened by this whiff of reform, this was the last thing many whites wanted to hear. Afrikaner farmers were alarmed by the idea of a labour shortage caused by Africans leaving the rural areas for better prospects in the cities, while white workers feared the prospect of losing jobs to lower-paid African workers.

The National Party comes to power

Against this background of black aspiration and white fears, the Smuts government called a **general election**. The opposition **National Party**, which promoted Afrikaner nationalism, campaigned on a *swart gevaar* or "black peril" ticket, playing on white insecurity and fear. With an eye on the vote of Afrikaner workers and farmers, they promised to reverse the tide of Africans into the cities and to send them all back to the reserves. For white business they made the conflicting promise to bring black workers into the cities as a cheap and plentiful supply of labour.

On Friday May 28, 1948, South Africa awoke to a National Party victory at the polls. Party leader **D.F. Malan** told a group of ecstatic supporters: "For the first time, South Africa is our own. May God grant that it always remains our own. It is to us that millions of barbarous blacks look for guidance, justice and the Christian way of life."

Meanwhile, the **ANC** was driven by its own power struggle. Fed up with the ineffectiveness of the old guard, the Youth League staged a coup, voted in their own leadership with Nelson Mandela on the executive and adopted the League's radical Programme of Action, with an arsenal of tactics that Mandela explained would include "the new weapons of boycott, strike, civil disobedience and non-cooperation".

The 1950s: peaceful protest

During the 1950s, the National Party began putting in place a barrage of laws that would eventually constitute the structure of apartheid. Some early onslaughts on black civil rights included the **Bantu Authorities Act**, which set up puppet authorities to govern Africans in the reserves; the **Population Registration Act**, which classified every South African at birth as "white, native or coloured" (see p.652); the **Group Areas Act**, which divided South Africa into ethnically distinct areas; and the **Suppression of Communism Act**, which made any anti-apartheid opposition (Communist or not) a criminal offence.

The ANC responded in 1952 with the **Defiance Campaign**, aimed at achieving full civil rights for blacks. During the campaign, eight thousand volunteers deliberately broke the apartheid laws and were jailed. The campaign rolled on through 1952 until the police provoked violence in October by firing on a prayer meeting in East London. A riot followed in which two white people were killed, thus appearing to discredit claims that the campaign was non-violent. The government used this pretext to swoop on the homes of the ANC leadership, resulting in the detention and then **banning** of over one hundred ANC organizers. Bannings restricted a person's movement and political activities: a banned person was prohibited from seeing more than one person

1948	1949	1952	1955
National Party wins election and goes full throttle on segregation	Government bans inter-racial marriage and sex, followed by slew of other discriminatory laws	Mandela leads Defiance Campaign against apartheid legislation	Mass non-racial meeting drafts the Freedom Charter, which becomes policy of ANC

THE FREEDOM CHARTER
- The people shall govern.
- All national groups shall have equal rights.
- The people shall share the nation's wealth.
- The land shall be shared by those who work it.
- All shall be equal before the law.
- All shall enjoy equal human rights.

- There shall be work and security for all.
- The doors of learning and culture shall be opened.
- There shall be houses, security and comfort.
- There shall be peace and friendship.

---

at a time or talking to any other banned person; prohibited from entering certain buildings; kept under surveillance; required to report regularly to the police; and could not be quoted or published.

The most far-reaching event of the decade was the **Congress of the People**, held near Johannesburg in 1955. At a mass meeting of three thousand delegates, four organizations, representing Africans, coloureds, whites and Indians, formed a strategic partnership called the Congress Alliance. ANC leader **Chief Albert Luthuli** explained that "for the first time in the history of our multiracial nation its people will meet as equals, irrespective of race, colour and creed, to formulate a freedom charter for all the people of our country". Adopted at the Congress of the People, the Freedom Charter (see box above) became the principal document defining ANC policy.

The government rounded up 156 opposition leaders and charged them with treason. Evidence at the Treason Trial was based on the Freedom Charter, described as a "blueprint for violent Communist revolution". Although all the defendants were acquitted, the four-year trial disrupted the ANC and splits began to emerge. In 1958 a group of Africanists led by the charismatic **Robert Mangaliso Sobukwe** (see p.332) broke away from the ANC to form the **Pan Africanist Congress (PAC)**, arguing that its cooperation with white activists was not in the interests of black liberation.

Sharpeville

On March 21, 1960, Sobukwe and thousands of followers presented themselves without passes to police stations across Gauteng and the Western Cape. At **Sharpeville** police station, south of Johannesburg, the police opened fire, killing 69 and injuring nearly 200. Most were shot in the back.

Demonstrations swept the country on March 27. The next day Africans staged a total stay-away from work and thousands joined a public pass-burning demonstration. The day after that, the government declared a **state of emergency**, rounded up 22,000 people and banned the ANC and PAC. White South Africa panicked as the value of the rand slipped and shares slid. Some feared an imminent and bloody revolution.

Later that month, Prime Minister Hendrik Verwoerd was shot in the head by a half-crazed white farmer. Many hoped that if he died, apartheid would be ditched. But Dr Verwoerd survived, his appetite for apartheid stronger than ever. More than anyone, Verwoerd made apartheid his own and formulated the system of **Bantustans** – notionally independent statelets in which Africans were to exercise their political rights away from the white areas. The aim was to dismantle the black

1958	1960	1961
New prime minister Verwoerd creates ten ethnic "homelands", the cornerstone of Grand Apartheid	Sixty-nine Africans shot dead at anti-pass law protest; government bans anti-apartheid opposition	South Africa leaves Commonwealth and becomes republic; ANC launches armed struggle

majority into several separate "tribal" minorities, none of which on its own could outnumber whites.

In 1961 Nelson Mandela called for a national convention "to determine a non-racial democratic constitution". Instead, Verwoerd appointed one-time neo-Nazi John Vorster as justice minister. A trained lawyer, Vorster eagerly set about passing repressive legislation that circumvented the rule of law.

Nelson Mandela saw the writing on the wall. "The time comes in the life of any nation when there remain only two choices: submit or fight. That time has now come to South Africa. We shall not submit," he told the BBC, before going underground as commander in chief of **Umkhonto we Sizwe** (Spear of the Nation, aka MK), the newly formed armed wing of the ANC. The organization was dedicated to economic and symbolic acts of sabotage and was under strict orders not to kill or injure people. In August 1962 Mandela was captured, tried and with nine other ANC leaders he was handed a **life sentence**.

Apartheid: everything going white

With the leadership of the liberation movement behind bars, the 1960s was the decade in which everything seemed to be going the white government's way. Resistance was stifled, the state grew more powerful, and for white South Africans, businessmen and foreign investors life seemed perfect. For black South Africans, poverty deepened – a state of affairs enforced by apartheid legislation and repressive measures that included bannings, detentions without trial, house arrests and murders of political prisoners.

The ANC was impotent, and resistance by its armed wing MK was virtually nonexistent. But as South Africa swung into the 1970s, the uneasy peace began to fray, prompted at first by deteriorating black living standards, which reawakened industrial action. Trade unions came to fill the vacuum left by the ANC.

The **Soweto uprising** of June 16, 1976, signalled the transfer of protest from the workplace to the townships, as black youths took to the streets in protest against the imposition of Afrikaans as a medium of instruction in their schools. The protest spread across the country and by the following February, 575 people (nearly a quarter of them children) had been killed in the rolling series of revolts that followed.

The government relied increasingly on armed police to impose order. Even this was unable to stop the mushrooming of new liberation organizations, many of them part of the broadly based **Black Consciousness Movement**. As the unrest rumbled on into 1977, the government responded by banning all the new black organizations and detaining their leadership. In September 1977, **Steve Biko** (one of the detained) became the 46th political prisoner to be killed in jail.

The banned organizations were rapidly replaced by new movements and the government never again successfully put the lid on opposition. By the late 1970s business was complaining that apartheid wasn't working any more, and even the government was having its doubts. The growth of the black population was outstripping that of whites; from a peak of 21 percent of the population in 1910, whites now made up only 16 percent. This proportion was set to fall to 10 percent by the end of the century. The sums just didn't add up.

1962	1966–1970s	1970
ANC leadership jailed for treason on Robben Island	About 3.5 million Africans and coloureds forcibly removed from "white" areas	Africans stripped of SA citizenship and assigned to impoverished ethnic "homelands"

Total Strategy

It was becoming clear that the deployment of the police couldn't solve South Africa's problems, and in 1978 defence minister **Pieter Willem (P.W.) Botha** became prime minister in a palace coup. Botha adopted a two-handed strategy, of reform accompanied by unprecedented repression. He devised his so-called **Total Strategy**, which aimed to draw every facet of white society into the fight against the opponents of apartheid. This included military training programmes in white schools, propaganda campaigns, the extension of conscription, and political reforms aimed at co-opting Indians and coloureds.

Despite this, the 1980s saw the growing use of sabotage against the apartheid state. Botha began contemplating reform and moved Nelson Mandela and other ANC leaders from **Robben Island** to Pollsmoor Prison in mainland Cape Town. But he also poured ever-increasing numbers of troops into African townships to stop unrest, while intimidating neighbouring countries. Between 1981 and 1983, the army launched operations into every one of the country's black-ruled neighbours, Angola, Mozambique, Botswana, Zimbabwe, Swaziland and Lesotho.

In 1983 Botha came up with another scheme to shore up apartheid: the so-called New Constitution in which coloureds and Indians would be granted the vote for their own racially segregated – and powerless – chambers. For Africans, apartheid was to continue as usual.

Around the same time, 15,000 **anti-apartheid** delegates met at Mitchell's Plain in Cape Town to form the **United Democratic Front** (UDF), a multiracial umbrella for 575 opposition organizations. The UDF became a proxy for the ANC as two years of strikes, protest and boycotts followed.

Towards the end of the decade, the world watched as apartheid troops and police were regularly shown on TV beating up and shooting unarmed Africans. The Commonwealth condemned the apartheid government, the United States and Australia severed air links and the US Congress passed legislation promoting disinvestment. An increasingly desperate Botha offered to release Mandela "if he renounces violence".

Mandela replied: "I am surprised by the conditions the government wants to impose. I am not a violent man. It was only when all other forms of resistance were no longer open to us that we turned to armed struggle. Let Botha ... renounce violence."

As events unfolded, a subtle shift became palpable: Botha was the prisoner and Mandela held the keys. While black resistance wasn't abating, Botha was now also facing a white right-wing backlash. The ultra-right Conservative Party was winning electoral support and the neo-Nazi Afrikaner Weerstand Beweging (Afrikaner Resistance Movement, aka AWB) was darkly muttering about civil war.

Crisis

In 1986, Botha declared yet another **state of emergency** accompanied by assassinations, mass arrests, detentions, treason trials and torture. Alarmed by the violence engulfing the country, a group of South African businessmen, mostly Afrikaners, flew to Senegal in 1987 to meet an ANC delegation headed by **Thabo Mbeki**. A joint statement pressed for unequivocal support for a negotiated settlement.

1976	1978	1980s
Police shoot dead over 600 during countrywide protests, which start in Soweto schools	Hawkish former defence minister P.W. Botha becomes president	Botha floods townships with troops and sends army into neighbouring countries

In July 1988 Mandela was rushed to Tygerberg Hospital in Cape Town, suffering from tuberculosis. Although he was better by October, the government announced that he wouldn't be returning to Pollsmoor **Prison**. Instead he was moved to a prison warder's cottage at **Victor Verster** (now Groot Drakenstein) Prison just outside Paarl. Outside the prison walls, Botha's policies had collapsed and the army top brass were telling him that there could be no decisive military victory over the anti-apartheid opposition – and that South Africa's undeclared war in Angola was bleeding the treasury dry.

At the beginning of 1989, Mandela wrote to Botha from Victor Verster calling for negotiations. The intransigent Botha found himself with little room to manoeuvre. When he suffered a stroke, his party colleagues moved swiftly to oust him and replaced him with **Frederik Willem (F.W.) De Klerk**.

De Klerk made it clear that he was opposed to majority rule. But he inherited a massive pile of problems that could no longer be ignored: the economy was in trouble and the cost of maintaining apartheid prohibitive; the illegal influx of Africans from the country to the city had become unstoppable; blacks hadn't been taken in by Botha's constitutional reforms, and even South Africa's friends were losing patience. In September 1989, US President George Bush (the elder) told De Klerk that if there wasn't progress on releasing Mandela within six months, he would extend US sanctions.

De Klerk gambled on his ability to outmanoeuvre the opposition. In February 1990, he announced the unbanning of the ANC, the PAC, the Communist Party and 33 other organizations, as well as the **release of Mandela**. On Sunday February 11, at around 4pm, Mandela stepped out of Victor Verster Prison and was driven to City Hall in Cape Town, from where he spoke publicly for the first time in three decades. That May, Mandela and De Klerk signed an agreement in which the government undertook to repeal repressive laws and release political prisoners, while the ANC agreed to suspend the armed struggle. As events moved towards full-blown negotiations it became clear that De Klerk still clung to race-based notions for a settlement: "Majority rule is not suitable for South Africa," he said, "because it will lead to the domination of minorities."

Negotiations

The **negotiating** process, from 1990 to 1994, was fragile, and at many points a descent into chaos looked likely. Obstacles included violence linked to a sinister element in the apartheid security forces who were working behind the scenes to destabilize the ANC; **threats of civil war** from heavily armed right-wingers; and a low-key war of attrition in KwaZulu-Natal between Zulu nationalists of the **Inkatha Freedom Party** and ANC supporters, which had already claimed three thousand lives between 1987 and 1990.

In April 1993 it looked as if it would all fall apart with the **assassination** of Chris Hani, the most popular ANC leader after Mandela. Hani's slaying by a right-wing gunman touched deep fears among all South Africans. A descent into civil war loomed, and for three consecutive nights the nation watched as Mandela appeared on prime-time television appealing for calm. This marked the decisive turning point as it became obvious that only the ANC president could stave off chaos, while De Klerk kept his head down. Pushing his strategic advantage, Mandela called for the immediate setting of an election date. Shortly afterwards the date for elections was set for April 27, 1994.

1983	**1989**	**1989**
Government cracks down further on opposition after formation of ANC-proxy, United Democratic Front	Botha rebuffs Mandela's appeal from prison for negotiations "to avert civil war"	Botha suffers stroke and is replaced by F.W. De Klerk, who unbans ANC

The 1994 election

The election passed peacefully. At the age of 76, Nelson Mandela, along with millions of his fellow citizens, voted for the first time in his life in a national election. On May 2, De Klerk conceded defeat after an ANC landslide, in which they took 62.7 percent of the vote. Of the remaining significant parties, the National Party fared best with 20.4 percent, followed by the Inkatha Freedom Party with 10.5 percent. The ANC was dominant in all of the provinces apart from **Western Cape** and **KwaZulu-Natal**. One of the disappointments for the ANC was its inability to appeal broadly to non-Africans.

For the ANC, the real struggle was only beginning. It inherited a country of 38 million people. Of these it was estimated that six million were unemployed, nine million were destitute, ten million had no access to running water, and twenty million had no electricity. Among adult blacks, sixty percent were illiterate and fewer than fifty percent of black children under 14 went to school. Infant mortality ran at eighty deaths per thousand among Africans, compared with just seven among whites.

The Mandela era

Few people in recorded history have been the subject of such high expectations; still fewer have matched them; Mandela has exceeded them. We knew of his fortitude before he left jail; we have since experienced his extraordinary reserves of goodwill, his sense of fun and the depth of his maturity. As others' prisoner, he very nearly decided the date of his own release; as president, he has wisely chosen the moment of his going. Any other nation would consider itself privileged to have his equal as its leader. His last full year in power provides us with an occasion again to consider his achievement in bringing and holding our fractious land together.

Mail & Guardian, December 24, 1998

South Africa's first five years of democracy are inextricably linked to the towering figure of **Nelson Mandela**. On the one hand, he had to temper the impatience of a black majority that, having finally achieved civil rights, found it hard to understand why economic advancement wasn't following quickly. And on the other, he had to mollify the many fearful whites. The achievements of the government, however, were more uneven than those of its leader.

The overriding theme of the Mandela presidency was that of **reconciliation**. Perhaps the highlight of this policy was in May and June 1995, when the rugby union World Cup was staged in South Africa. **The Springboks**, for many years international pariahs due to their whites-only membership, won, watched by Mandela, sporting Springbok colours – events portrayed in Clint Eastwood's 2009 film *Invictus* (based on a book by John Carlin).

The most significant sideshow of the period was the **Truth and Reconciliation Commission**, set up to examine gross human rights abuses in South Africa between 1960 and 1993 (see box, p.662).

The **New Constitution**, approved in May 1996, ensured that South Africa would remain a parliamentary democracy with an executive president. One of the most progressive constitutions in the world, it incorporated an extensive bill of rights.

Despite the victory of liberal democratic principles, South Africa still displayed a singular lack of the trappings associated with civil society. Crime, sensationalized daily in the media, continued to dog the country. In the closing stages of the ANC's first five years, the police were reporting an average of 52 murders a day, a rape every half hour (including a frightening rise in child rape), and one car theft every nine minutes.

1990	1994
Mandela walks to freedom	Mandela votes in election for first time and becomes president when ANC wins

THE TRUTH AND RECONCILIATION COMMISSION

As you type, you don't know you are crying until you feel and see the tears on your hands.

Chief typist of the transcripts of the TRC hearings
as told to Archbishop Tutu

By the time South Africa achieved **democracy** in 1994, it was internationally accepted that apartheid was, in the words of a UN resolution, "a crime against humanity", and that atrocities had been committed in its name. But no one could have imagined how systematic and horrific these atrocities had been. This emerged at the hearings of the Truth and Reconciliation Commission (TRC), set up to investigate gross abuses of human rights under apartheid. Under the chairmanship of Nobel Peace laureate, Archbishop Desmond Tutu, the commission examined acts committed between March 1960, the date of the Sharpeville massacre, and May 10, 1994, the day of Mandela's inauguration as president.

Evidence was heard from victims and perpetrators under a provision that amnesty would be given in exchange for "full disclosure of all the relevant facts". Unsurprisingly, the commission found that "the South African government was the primary perpetrator of gross human rights abuses in South Africa". It confirmed that from the 1970s to the 1990s the state had been involved in criminal activities including "extra-judicial killings of political opponents". Among the violations it listed were torture, abduction, sexual abuse, incursions across South Africa's borders to kill opponents in exile, and the deployment of hit squads. It also found that the ANC (and a number of other organizations, including the PAC and Inkatha) was guilty of human-rights violations.

There was considerable criticism of the TRC from all quarters. Many felt that justice would have been better served by a Nuremberg-style trial of those guilty of gross violations, but Tutu argued that this would have been impossible in South Africa, given that neither side had won a military victory.

Mr Delivery doesn't

In 1999 **Thabo Mbeki** succeeded Mandela as president of South Africa. A hopeful media dubbed Mbeki "Mr Delivery", believing that this clever, well-educated technocrat would confront poverty and build schools, hospitals and houses – and at the same time create badly needed jobs. Mbeki's business-friendly policies produced healthy **economic growth**, expanded the black middle class and created a small coterie of mega-rich black entrepreneurs. But it did little for the poor fifty percent of the population, and the gulf of inequality became wider than ever.

The poor also bore the brunt of Mbeki's misguided policies on **AIDS**. Holding the view that there was no link between HIV and AIDS, he blocked the provision of **anti-retrovirals** in state hospitals, which contributed to over five million deaths from AIDS-related illnesses and left a million children orphaned.

And like the virus, corruption seemed to be infecting society, the most far-reaching example being the arms deal, in which the ANC government bought military equipment that South Africa's own defence force deemed unsuitable and too expensive. Newspapers alleged that the defence minister at the time was bribed and that a massive donation was paid to the ANC.

While money was squandered on arms, a raft of social problems festered. At the beginning of 2007, eight years after Mbeki assumed power, eight million people were

1999	2003	2007
Thabo Mbeki succeeds Mandela	J.M. Coetzee wins Nobel Prize for Literature	Mbeki replaced as president by Jacob Zuma, at time facing bribery and racketeering charges

living in shacks, millions had no water-borne sewerage and unemployment was running at forty percent. Disquiet at the slow pace of change was growing, and protests erupted on the streets of the townships. In 2005 alone, there were 6000 protests. At the end of 2007 Mbeki was unseated by his party.

His replacement was the controversial former deputy president, **Jacob Zuma**, who was facing charges of bribery, fraud, racketeering, money laundering and tax evasion. A supreme populist, he portrayed himself as the people's president fighting off a conspiracy by an Mbeki-led elite. Miraculously, just two weeks before the April 2009 elections, top-secret recordings surfaced, purporting to prove that former president Mbeki had interfered in the Zuma case and charges against Zuma were dropped.

As expected, the Zuma-led ANC won the poll by a landslide, while the Democratic Alliance (DA), the official opposition, increased its proportion of the vote. Support for the two main parties split down broadly racial lines, with the ANC getting most of its support from Africans and the DA from whites and coloureds.

Given the ANC's overwhelming dominance of South African politics, it perhaps comes as no surprise that South Africa's most significant post-Mandela politics has taken place away from parliament – inside the ANC itself or on the streets.

After the vuvuzelas

For a brief period during 2010, South Africans united in a fever of vuvuzela-blowing euphoria, during the highly successful staging of the **Fifa World Cup**. But there was a return to politics as usual once the visitors had left and the country had returned to work – or not, as in the case of a million public sector workers who staged a three-week strike in August over pay increases and housing allowances. Trade union leader **Zwelinzima Vavi** attacked the ANC for leading South Africa on the path to becoming "a predator state" in which an "elite of political hyenas increasingly controls the state as a vehicle for accumulation".

Vavi's views represented the feelings of millions of South Africa's poor and dispossessed, who, nearly two decades after winning democracy, were still waiting for its economic fruits to be delivered. During Zuma's first two years of tenure, frustration with the ruling party accelerated. There were twice as many service-delivery protests in just 2009 and 2010 than there had been in the previous five Mbeki years.

By 2011, forty percent of South Africa's municipalities had been hit by popular street protests and there were attacks on Zuma from inside his own party. ANC Youth League leader **Julius Malema**, who had helped replace Mbeki with Zuma, now viciously attacked the president as being "worse than Mbeki".

But whether Zuma survives as leader of the ANC is less significant than whether the party can rein in the growing culture of **kleptocracy** in its ranks and meet popular demands; whether it can contain politics within South Africa's hard-won democratic system or whether it is increasingly going to find itself at war with its own supporters.

2009	2010	2011
Charges against Zuma dropped on eve of general election; ANC wins by landslide	SA stages successful football World Cup and unleashes vuvuzela on unsuspecting planet	South Africa joins BRIC (Brazil, Russia, India and China), club of the most important developing nations.

Music

Music from South Africa has a deserved following. The country has some of Africa's most diverse recorded music and its music industry is among the continent's most developed. It doesn't take much effort for an interested listener to encounter anything from indigenous African sounds that have remained largely unchanged for the last two hundred years, to the latest Afropop as well as a variety of white pop styles that would not be out of place anywhere in the Western world.

Gospel

Choral harmony and melody are perhaps black South Africa's greatest musical gifts to the world, and nowhere are they better manifested than in its **churches**. In the mainstream Catholic, Anglican and Methodist denominations a tradition of choral singing has evolved that has taken the style of European classical composers and loosened it up, added rhythm and, as always, some great dance routines.

In the Pentecostal churches, the music is more American-influenced, yet the harmonies and melodies remain uniquely South African and intensely moving. Pentecostal gospel music is the main recorded style; look out for groups like **Lord Comforters**, **Joyous Celebration**, **Pure Magic**, **Lusanda Spiritual Group** and the powerful **Rebecca Malope** (see box below).

Kwaito and hip-hop

South Africa's definitive youth sound, **kwaito**, has been around for nearly two decades. DJs importing dance music in the early 1990s, so the story goes, found white clubs unresponsive to Chicago house. DJs found that black clubbers preferred the records slowed down from 45 to 33rpm.

In an accurate reflection of the depressed and nihilistic mood of township youth culture, *kwaito*'s vibe tends to be downbeat, and the music frequently carries a strong association with gangsterism and explicit sexuality.

Some artists worth looking out for include **Tokollo** (ex-TKZee), **Mzekezeke**, **Kabelo**, the hard-rock-influenced Mandoza, and the matchstick-chewing, gangster-styled **Zola**. **Kalawa Jazmee**, a record label run by Oscar Mdlongwa, aka **DJ Oskido**, has been responsible for several successful *kwaito* groups including **Trompies**, **Bongo Maffin** and the self-consciously retro **Mafikizolo**.

REBECCA MALOPE

Diminutive **Rebecca Malope** is South Africa's biggest-selling music star, enjoying years at the top of the **gospel scene**, with only stadia able to hold her fans, every album going gold or platinum, popular magazines full of her photos, views and story, and everyone knowing the lyrics of her songs. Well, nearly everyone that is, for Rebecca Malope is virtually unknown outside Africa.

The daughter of a Sotho father and Swazi mother, Rebecca was born in Nelspruit, Mpumalanga, in 1969, and soon began singing in the local Assemblies of God church, where her grandfather was a pastor. Her initial recordings were mostly forgettable bubblegum pop. She was spotted in Jo'burg by **Sizwe Zako**, who would become her lynchpin keyboard player. Under his tutelage and, so she says, because of letters from fans pleading that she sing God's songs, Rebecca returned to gospel in 1990, where she has been amply rewarded.

Rebecca's musical formula, engineered by Zako, who also produces, rarely varies. The songs are anthems characterized by swirling keyboards and excellent backing singers, and are delivered in her tremendous, soaring and sometimes husky voice, accompanied by dramatic gestures.

BRENDA FASSIE

Kwaito killed the careers of many of the 1980s pop stars, but the late **Brenda Fassie** managed not only to survive the new music, but to thrive on it. Brenda was South Africa's true pop queen and the one local artist whose music is still pretty much guaranteed to get things going on the dancefloor, wherever you are in the country.

Brenda began her career in the early 1980s as the lead singer for **Brenda and the Big Dudes**, enjoying a string of bubblegum hits, including the classic "Weekend Special", which for years was a South African disco anthem. Her sound mixed *kwaito*, *mbaqanga*, gospel and her own extraordinary persona, earning massive and deserved success.

During the 1990s, while some contemporaries produced comfortable material aimed more at middle-class and middle-aged audiences, Brenda made a point of hanging out with the youth in Soweto and in Hillbrow, Johannesburg's fastest-paced inner-city patch. The result was a lesbian affair that thrilled the tabloids, a bad crack habit, a tendency to lose the plot completely on stage – and the best music she had ever produced.

Tragically, her many demons eventually caught up with her, and after falling into a two-week-long coma, which even saw President Thabo Mbeki coming to her hospital bedside, she died in 2004. Her funeral was a massive media event that witnessed an outpouring of grief exceeding that attending the deaths of most "struggle" veterans.

Local hip-hop artists are more likely than their *kwaito* counterparts to use English, and tend to come from middle-class backgrounds instead of the townships – as a result of which they can afford to spend more on production. Among the notable hip-hopsters are **Skwatta Kamp**, **Optical Illusion**, **Cashless Society**, **Zubz**, **H20** and **Lions of Zion** (who, as their name suggests, blend hip-hop and reggae).

House, rap and reggae

DJ-mixed South African **house** attracts practitioners and fans from all parts of the country's racial and cultural divisions, but it is black DJs such as **DJ Fresh**, **DJ Ready D**, **Glen Lewis**, **DJ Mbuso** and **Oskido** who garner by far the most attention from the local media. The recordings they mix with are almost exclusively from either the UK or France.

South African **rap** has enjoyed sustained popularity since the early 1990s, but has remained almost completely ghettoized within the coloured community of the Western Cape. Heavily influenced by African American rappers, the performers often exude a palpable sense of being "Americans trapped in Africa". Pioneers of the style were the heavily politicized **Prophets of Da City**, several members of which made names for themselves as solo artists after the group's break-up, most notably **Rahim**, **Junior Solela** and **Ishmael**. Other performers who have since come up are **Brasse Van Die Kaap** (who rap in Afrikaans), **Reddy D** and **Godessa**, while Cape Town-based record and production company, African Dope, has enjoyed success with **Teba**, **Funny Carp** and crossover jazz-Latin-hip-hop-funksters **Moodphase5ive**, among others.

What is unusual as regards the place of **Lucky Dube** (who died tragically in 2007 in a hijacking) in the local **reggae** scene is the total lack of successful emulators. An energetic, disciplined and talented live performer, Dube could also deliver a falsetto like Smokey Robinson's, which added a distinct twist to his otherwise familiar roots reggae sound.

Neo-traditional music

As with *kwaito*, the instrumentation in **neo-traditional music** is really just a backdrop to the lyrics and the dance routines. One of its major stars is the Shangaan singer **Thomas Chauke**, perhaps the single bestselling artist in any neo-traditional genre. Hailing from Limpopo Province, he makes heavy use of a drum machine and an electronic keyboard and often picks out some intricate lead-guitar work to complement his vocals.

LADYSMITH BLACK MAMBAZO AND THE ISCATHAMIYA SOUND

The best known of South Africa's many neo-traditional musical genres is Zulu *iscathamiya* (or *mbube*), the distinctive male a cappella choral style made internationally famous by **Ladysmith Black Mambazo**. The style originated among Zulu rural migrants in urban hostels following World War I, and by 1939 the first commercial hit, "Mbube" by Solomon Linda and His Original Evening Birds, had been recorded, eventually selling over 100,000 copies. The song was later reworked as "The Lion Sleeps Tonight", which became a number one hit in both the US and UK.

In 1973, after recording for the SABC for several years, Ladysmith Black Mambazo made their first commercial release, *Amabutho*, for the Gallo label. It quickly sold over 25,000 copies (gold-disc status in South Africa), and since that time the group has recorded over fifty others, most of which have also gone gold. Following their collaboration with him on *Graceland*, Paul Simon produced their *Shaka* Zulu album, which sold 100,000 copies around the world and took *iscathamiya* to the international stage. In 1997, Ladysmith Black Mambazo extended its Afropop credentials with *Heavenly*, an album that featured collaborations with, among other international artists, Dolly Parton. Following the exposure of their song "Inkanyezi Nezazi" in a British TV advertisement for Heinz baked beans, the group went on to sell over a million units in the UK, an all-time record for a South African act.

In Sotho neo-traditional music, the bass lines are good, the shouting is first-class and the accordions can take on an almost Cajun tinge. **Tau Oa Matshela** and **Tau Oa Linare** are some of the groups to look out for.

Zulu neo-trad is pervasive, both in its a cappella form, known as *iscathamiya*, and as a vocal/guitar-based style called *maskanda*. For particularly fine examples of the art, look out for **Phuzekhemisi**, **Shiyani Ncgobo** and the late, great **Mfaz'Omnyama**. Another star of the neo-traditional scene is the queen of Ndebele music, **Nothembi Mkhwebane**. As well as being a talented and veteran performer, Nothembi, who sings and plays electric guitar, is also known for her sensational outfits, decorated with typically intricate Ndebele bead and metalwork.

Jazz

Jazz has been widely popular in South Africa for decades, and you can almost always find performances in Johannesburg, Pretoria or Cape Town on virtually any weekend, and sometimes midweek too. It was **South African jazz** that was the music most associated with the struggle against apartheid, especially after the music's main exponents went into self-imposed exile in the 1960s.

Jazz's roots in the country are much older than this, harking back to the emergence of *marabi* music in Johannesburg's African slums some time after World War I. During World War II, American swing became popular and fused with *marabi* into a new style usually referred to as African jazz. This remained predominant throughout the 1940s and 1950s, and produced the first South African musical exiles in vocalists **Miriam Makeba** and the **Manhattan Brothers**.

The next development was a move in the direction of the American avant-garde, the two early, prime exponents of this in South Africa being the **Jazz Epistles** and the **Blue Notes**. Legislation prohibiting mixed-race public performances caused most of the Epistles to individually leave South Africa in the early 1960s, while the Blue Notes departed en masse in 1964. Some exiled South African jazzers detached themselves from their roots, while others such as **Hugh Masekela** reinterpreted their township influences. Back home, old-style African jazz as performed by the **Elite Swingsters** and **Ntemi Piliso's Alexandra All Stars** remained popular.

In the 1970s and 1980s, various South African strains were fused with funk, soul and rock influences to produce a more accessible, populist brand of jazz, from bands such as **Sakile**, **The Drive** and the **Jazz Ministers**. Following the end of apartheid, the surviving exiles began to trickle back and a new, younger generation of jazz musicians yet again married old local traditions with contemporary international trends.

Over the last two decades a large group of new jazz names has emerged that includes vocalists (**Gloria Bosman, Judith Sephuma, Sibongile Kumalo**), saxophonists (**McCoy Mrubata, Zim Ngqawana**), keyboard players (**Paul Hamner, Themba Mkhize**), guitarists (**Jimmy Dludlu, Selaelo Selota**) and the odd trumpeter (**Prince Lengoasa, Marcus Wyatt**). Although many of the stars of this new generation emulate the smooth style of the Earl Klugh school, there are others whose tastes are considerably more muscular.

Afropop

Afropop is a catch-all category, yet it's arguably where many contemporary South African artists sit most comfortably. Afropop is characterized by a knack for combining local African styles with Western popular influences, the ability to attract a multiracial audience, and the eschewing of computer-generated backing in favour of actual instruments.

Afropop goes back to Miriam Makeba's first American recordings in the early 1960s. More contemporary examples would include Paul Simon's 1987 *Graceland*, a collaboration with Ladysmith Black Mambazo and other local African artists; and the music of **Juluka** and **Savuka**, two bands led in the 1980s and 1990s by Johnny Clegg, whose melding of mainstream pop harmonies with Zulu dance routines and a touch of *mbaqanga* gained great popularity both in South Africa and in France. The music of bubblegum-pop queen **Yvonne Chaka Chaka** from the 1980s and 1990s could also be deemed Afropop. Artists who have subsequently adopted similar formulas include **Jabu Khanyile, Vusi Mahlasela, Ringo and Busi Mhlongo.**

The most successful proponents of the style are Cape Town-based **Freshlyground**, who, because of their broad appeal and engaging sound, were chosen to accompany Shakira in jamming to a billion viewers at the opening and closing ceremonies of the **2010 Fifa World Cup**.

White pop and rock

English-speaking South Africans have successfully replicated virtually every popular Western musical style going back to the late nineteenth century, and some have found fame in the outside world. Among the first and most famous of these are the alternative rockers the **Springbok Nude Girls**, who performed as the opening act for U2 during their 2011 tour of South Africa. Among the country's other international success stories, all of whom relocated overseas, are **Manfred Mann** in the 1960s and more recently **Dave Matthews, Seether, Just Jinger** and **Wonderboom**.

Like South African jazz, **Afrikaans music** is another world unto itself, with a multitude of sub-categories and a long list of heroes and heroines. From the late 1920s until the 1960s American country was its greatest outside influence, but by the early 1970s it looked to the lighter end of foreign pop and in particular Eurodisco. A long line of bouncy Afrikaans pop stars ensued, while a more sober side was represented by the light operatic style of Gé Korsten, probably the single most popular Afrikaans artist of the period.

Following the end of apartheid, a general concern about the future of the Afrikaans language and culture spurred a revival of interest in Afrikaans music. There is undoubtedly more stylistic variety now than ever before: witness the house/disco of **Juanita**, the heavy rock of **Karen Zoid** and **Jackhammer**, the modernized *boeremusiek* of the **Klipwerf Orkes**, and the Neil Diamond-esque songs of **Steve Hofmeyr** (the bestselling Afrikaans music artist). More recent sounds are the punk-rock riffs of **Fokofpolisiekar** and the studied banality of rapper **Jack Parow**.

ENTER DIE ANTWOORD

Die Antwoord (meaning "the answer") was an overnight sensation – an unknown crew from Cape Town that stormed the internet. Rapping in lowlife Cape Flats slang known as zef, they represented the voice of the Mother City's mean streets. That was the story, at least.

Their success was real enough: in February 2010, internet traffic to their website (ⓦdieantwoord.com), which was streaming their debut album o, was so heavy (fifteen million hits) that it crashed. Their signature foul-mouthed lyrics aside, there's nothing crude about their artistry. If you aren't convinced, note the tight machine-gun vocals (likened by Rolling Stone to "Eminem's 'Lose Yourself' on mescaline"), the slick art direction, the careful choreography and the cool Keith Haring-esque graphics on their Enter the Ninja video.

Far from being the band that came in from the Flats, Die Antwoord (frontman Ninja, helium-voiced Yo-landi Vi$$er and DJ Hi-Tek) is the latest surreal vehicle for Waddy Tudor Jones (Ninja), whose previous excursions included hip-hop rig Max Normal and the Constructus Corporation. Jones's history of taking on personas has led detractors to grumble that Die Antwoord "aren't real" (whatever that means in show business), while fans declare him a creative genius. Does it matter? The fact is, Die Antwoord deliver an unmistakably Cape Town sound that cooks.

New wave dance and electronica

Like Afropop, **new wave dance and electronica** is a catch-all phrase, in this case to describe a menagerie of sounds unleashed on South Africa's dancefloors over the past decade, and which have started making their mark in clubs in the US, Britain and the rest of Europe. Local musicians such as **Spoek Mathambo**, **DJ Mujava**, **Culoe De Song**, **Markus Wormstorm** and **Sibot** have been pumping out their blend of local sounds at the world's nightspots – and getting signed up by international labels.

Although global in flavour, the sounds are still distinctly South African, incorporating afro-beat, *kwaito*, *mbaqanga* and anything else that's to hand. Most successful at riding the new wave have been foul-mouthed zef-rappers **Die Antwoord** (see box above).

Discography

In the reviews below, items marked with an asterisk are international releases. Other items are South African releases, issued either by local labels or by the South African operations of international labels.

CROSS-GENRE COMPILATIONS

Various Artists *The Rough Guide to the Music of South Africa* (World Music Network*). Excellent cross section of sounds combining big names with some interesting less-known musicians.

Various Artists *Mzansi Music: Young Urban South Africa* (Trikont*). Fifteen-track collection that captures the city beat of Mzansi's (South Africa's) youth.

Various Artists *Putumayo Presents: South Africa* (Trikont*). An interesting cross section that unlike the other two compilations doesn't restrict itself to black music.

MBAQANGA

Mahlathini and the Mahotella Queens *The Best of Mahlathini and the Mahotella Queens* (Gallo). Perfect introduction to the sound of this most stomping of *mbaqanga* outfits.

Soul Brothers *Igobondela, The Best of The Soul Brothers* and *The Early Years* (Gallo). If *The Best of* whets your appetite, investigate *The Early Years*, a series comprising the classic first twelve albums, recorded in the 1970s and

early 1980s, while *Thul' Ubheke* (2010) showcases them relaxed and at the top of their game.

Various Artists *From Marabi to Disco* (Gallo). A mini-encyclopedia of the development of township musical style from the late 1930s to the early 1980s.

Various Artists *The Indestructible Beat of Soweto Volumes 1–6* (Earthworks*). Superb compilation, mainly featuring 1980s *mbaqanga*.

GOSPEL

Imvuselelo Yase Natali *Izigi* (BMG). One of the most extraordinary gospel acts in South Africa, fronted by the charismatic – and at times plain bizarre – Reverend Makitaza.

IPCC *Ummeli Wethu* (Gallo). An excellent offering from one of South Africa's most popular gospel choirs.

Lusanda Spiritual Group *Abanye Bayawela* (Gallo). The biggest-selling album from a gospel music sensation.

Rebecca Malope *Shwele Baba* (CCP). One of Rebecca's finest albums, with the title track a strong contender for her best-ever song.

Pure Magic *Greatest Hits* (EMI). Simply wonderful melodic gospel-pop, featuring the silky lead vocals of Vuyo Mokoena.

Solly Moholo *Abanye Bayawela Motlhang ke Kolobetswa "Die poppe sal dans"* (CCP). A beautiful release from the country's finest Sotho gospel artist.

Various Artists *Choirs of South Africa* (Roi Music). Stirring gospel anthems delivered by mass choirs with exuberance and power.

Various Artists *Rough Guide to South African Gospel* (Rough Guides*). A comprehensive survey of South African gospel going back to the 1950s.

Various *Joyous Celebration* (Sony, SA). Umpteen albums and still proliferating (they'd hit volume 15 by 2011) of classic gospel.

KWAITO AND HIP-HOP

Bongo Maffin *Bongolution* (Sony Music). A fine release from a popular group which combines Jamaican-style ragga lyrics with *kwaito* beats.

Brenda Fassie *African Princess of Pop* and *Memeza* (CCP). The former is a posthumous survey covering the entire career of South Africa's very own Madonna; the latter, featuring the massive hit "Vul'Ndlela", was Brenda's most commercially successful effort.

H20 *Amanzi'mtoti* (Outrageous Records). Debut album that launched hip-hop duo Siphiwe Norten and Menzi Dludla into Africa.

Kabelo *And the Beat Goes On* (Universal). A monster hit from one of the biggest *kwaito* stars.

Mafikizolo *Sibongile* (Sony Music). Solid melodies, well sung and harmonized (the trio's female vocalist, Sibongile Nkosi, is outstanding).

Makhendlas *Jammer* (CCP). Features two massive hits, "Emenwe" and "Ayeye Aho", from the brother of *kwaito* pioneer Arthur. Makhendlas tragically shot himself immediately after killing a troublesome fan after a gig in late 1998.

Malaika *Malaika* (Sony Music). Hugely successful, this is very much in the style pioneered by Mafikizolo but features even more contemporary African-American influences.

Mandoza *Nakalakala* (CCP). Not only was this album massively popular with African urban youth, the title track has been one of very few *kwaito* recordings to truly cross over into the white pop arena.

M'Du *No Pas No Special* (Sony Music). A popular though somewhat downbeat album from one of *kwaito*'s most enduring stars.

Skwatta Kamp *Khut En Joyn* (Nkull). A fairly relentless first offering from the *enfants terrible* of the local hip-hop scene.

TKZee *Halloween* (BMG). Complete with trademark catchy anthems and R&B-based sounds, this is a solid early (1998) offering from these popular *kwaito* artists.

Trompies *Boostin' Kabelz* (Sony Music). Kicking sounds from one of the coolest *kwaito* acts on the circuit.

Various Artists *Cape of Good Dope Volumes 1 & 2* (African Dope Records). Eclectic mix showcasing the label's performers, including Lions of Zion, Godessa, Moodphase5ive and Max Normal (an earlier incarnation of Die Antwoord's Ninja).

Various Artists *Yizo Yizo Volumes 1–3* (CCP). The soundtrack to South Africa's hippest TV drama, with cuts from virtually every major *kwaito* artist.

Zola *Mdlwembe* (EMI). The first solo album of "Mr Ghetto Fabulous", full of menacing rhythms.

RAP AND REGGAE

Lucky Dube *Prisoner* (Gallo). Dube's reggae album *Prisoner* was at one time South Africa's second bestselling album ever, full of stirring Peter Tosh-style roots tunes.

Prophets of Da City *Ghetto Code* (Universal). South Africa's rap supremos' finest release, full of tough but articulate rhymes and some seriously funky backing tracks, all in true Cape Flats style.

NEO-TRADITIONAL

Amampondo *Drums for Tomorrow* (Melt 2000). South Africa's most famous marimba band deliver a fine and well-produced set here, full of their distinctive Xhosa melodies and powerful polyrhythms.

Ladysmith Black Mambazo *Favourites* (Gallo). A fine greatest hits selection from the group's first decade in the Seventies and early Eighties. *Congratulations South Africa:*

The Ultimate Collection (Wrasse*). This double CD is a mixed bag of Afropop and 1990s *iscathamiya*, including "Inkanyezi Nezazi", which gained the group plenty of new fans after being used in a Heinz baked-beans advert.

Mfaz'Omnyama *Ngisebenzile Mama* (Gallo). The title means "I have been working, Mum", and is amply justified by this superb set, featuring some of the best *maskanda* ever recorded.

Nothembi Mkhwebane *Akanamandl' Usathana* (Gallo). Beautiful guitar-driven sounds from the Ndebele music queen, with a cover showing Nothembi in one of her impressive traditional outfits.

Phuzekhemisi *Ngo 49* (Gallo). Every album recorded by this reigning *maskanda* champion features stunning guitar work, great vocals and murderous bass lines.

Shiyani Ncgobo *Introducing* (Sheer Sound). A very fine *maskanda* album aimed largely at a foreign audience, and thus with far more variety than a domestic offering would feature.

Ringo *Sondelani* (CCP). A superb modern reworking of traditional Xhosa sounds by this bald Capetonian heart-throb, including the hit track "Sondela", which has become one of South Africa's most popular love songs.

Various Artists *Singing in an Open Space* (Rounder*). A survey of Zulu guitar recordings from 1962 to 1982, when the style was still referred to as "Zulu Traditional".

Women of Mambazo *Mamizolo* (Gallo). Beautiful *iscathamiya* melodies and harmonizations, not rendered by the usual male line-up but by a female group led by Nellie Shabalala, the late wife of Ladysmith Black Mambazo leader Joseph Shabalala.

JAZZ

Abdullah Ibrahim *African Marketplace* (Discovery/WEA). Ibrahim's best album – a wistful, nostalgic, other-worldly journey.

Elite Swingsters *Siya Gida* (Universal). A final flowering from these African jazz stalwarts. Lots of great danceable music.

Gloria Bosman *Tranquillity* (Sheer/Limelight*). A young and compelling jazz vocalist, Bosman juggles African and American styles with consummate ease.

Hugh Masekela *Still Grazing* (Universal) and *Black to the Future* (Sony Music). *Still Grazing* is the best available compilation of Masekela's work in the 1960s and 1970s. In the late 1990s Masekela scored a deserved hit with *Black to the Future*, featuring the excellent "Chileshe", an impassioned plea to his countrymen to discard their xenophobia towards African immigrants.

Jimmy Dludlu *Essence of Rhythm* (Universal). Dludlu is the essence of smooth jazz, and is arguably the single most popular representative of what is in turn the most commercially successful jazz style in South Africa today.

Manhattan Brothers *The Very Best of The Manhattan Brothers* (Sterns*). Classic recordings cut between 1948 and 1959 by this seminal vocal quartet, who crossed African-American secular harmonies with indigenous influences.

Miriam Makeba and the Skylarks *Miriam Makeba and the Skylarks* (Teal) and *Welela* (Universal*). *Welela*, from 1989, is probably the finest album by Makeba, who died in

2008 – great songs, wonderfully performed.

Moses Taiwa Molelekwa *Genes and Spirits* (Melt 2000). Fascinating jazz/drum 'n' bass fusion by a talented young pianist, who died tragically in 2001.

Paul Hanmer *Trains to Taung* (Sheer Sound). Constructed around Hanmer's dreamy, acoustic piano-based compositions, this album is now considered a classic.

Robbie Jansen *Nomad Jez* (EMI). Great, if slightly flawed, album from veteran saxophonist Jansen, playing with other luminaries of the local jazz scene.

Sakile *Sakile* (Sony Music). A prime example of the jazz fusion popular in the 1980s, Sakile spawned two major figures in saxophonist Khaya Mahlangu and bass player Sipho Gumede.

Sibongile Khumalo *Ancient Evenings* (Sony Music). Though a classically trained opera singer, Khumalo takes on both jazz and a variety of traditional melodies on this wonderful album.

Various Artists *African Connection Parts I–IV* (Sheer Sound). This series of double-CD compilations from the country's premier independent label provides an accessible survey of South African jazz up to 2004.

Winston Mankunku *Crossroads* (Nkomo/Sheer). Sinuous, upbeat township jazz from the veteran Cape Town saxman.

Zim Ngqawana *Vadzimu* (Sheer Sound). Ngqawana is one of the most revered figures in local jazz, despite also being the very antithesis of the smooth style that currently dominates.

POLITICAL

Mzwakhe Mbuli *Resistance is Defence* (Earthworks*). Great sample of the militant lyricism of the people's poet, including a moving ode to Mandela's release.

Various Artists *South African Freedom Songs* (Making Music Productions). Superb double-CD set documenting the "struggle music" that helped power anti-apartheid resistance.

AFROPOP

Bayete *Umkhaya-Lo* (Polygram). A seminal fusion of South African sounds with laidback soul and funk, spiced with beautifully soothing vocals.

Busi Mhlongo *Urbanzulu* (Melt 2000). An immaculately and expensively produced Zulu *maskanda*-pop classic from

this powerful jazz vocalist.

Freshlyground *Ma'Cheri* (Freeground Records/Sony BMG). Voted Album of the Year at the 2008 SA Music Awards, *Ma'Cheri* showcases the most enduring of South Africa's Afro-popsters.

Johnny Clegg *Best of Juluka/Savuka* (Universal). Born in England, the prolific Clegg mixes white pop harmonies and township rhythms, gaining him a multiracial following in South Africa.

Ladysmith Black Mambazo *Heavenly* (Gallo/Spectrum*). An inspired and commercially successful foray into Afropop, featuring solo versions of various pop classics as well as vocal collaborations with Dolly Parton and Lou Rawls.

Vusi Mahlasela *Silang Mabele* (BMG). Lush harmonies and lilting melodies from this sweet-voiced township balladeer.

Yvonne Chaka Chaka *Bombani* (Teal) and *The Best of Yvonne Chaka Chaka* (Teal, SA). *Bombani* bombed, yet is Yvonne's most intricate and interesting release, mixing a range of traditional styles and featuring wonderful melodies. *The Best of* is pretty much all the 1980s disco-style Yvonne you need.

WHITE POP AND ROCK

Just Jinger *All Comes Around* (BMG). Unexpectedly racking up sales of over 50,000 copies, this classic 1997 release demonstrated that local English rock was far from dead.

Mango Groove *The Best of Mango Groove* (Gallo). Mango Groove's mixture of white pop leavened with a touch of pennywhistle/township jive was briefly – from the late 1980s up to the dawn of democracy – the most commercially successful sound in South African music.

Springbok Nude Girls *Afterlife Satisfaction* (Sony Music). One of South Africa's most popular white bands before they disbanded, here delivering a powerful, if not particularly original, belting rock set.

Various Artists *The Best of SA Pop Vols 1–3* (Gallo). Three double CDs covering all the biggest radio hits of the local English pop scene from the 1960s through to the early 1980s.

AFRIKAANS

Anton Goosen *Bushrock* (Gallo). Goosen is one of South Africa's finest songwriters and performers. His style might best be described as Afrikaans folk rock. *Bushrock* is his one English-language album.

Fokofpolisiekar *Swanesang* (Rhythm Records/The Orchard). One of South Africa's most successful live bands has helped redefine Afrikaner-identity for the post-apartheid generation with its punk-rock-influenced sound, while outraging the conservative establishment, starting

with their name which translates as "fuck off police car".

Johannes Kerkorrel *Ge-Trans-To-Meer* (Gallo-Tusk). The late Kerkorrel was the leading light of the Afrikaans alternative scene of the 1990s, his brand of angst-laden pop also popular in Holland and Belgium.

Steve Hofmeyr *Toeka* (EMI). A smooth pop vocalist, Hofmeyr is the most commercially successful artist in Afrikaans music.

NEW WAVE DANCE AND ELECTRONICA

BLK JKS *Mystery* (Secretly Canadian*). Picked out by *Rolling Stone* magazine in 2009 as "artists to watch", the band (pronounced: "black jacks") went on to perform at the 2010 football World Cup kick-off. *Mystery* features their dizzying excursions across a succession of genres, from indie rock to psychedelia, tinged with traditional South African sounds.

Culoe De Song *We Baba* (Innervisions/!K7 Records*). Described as Deep House for grown-ups, the intoxicating title track of De Song's two-track EP takes its time to reach a lush climax, gradually piling on textures that include an electro beat, looped chanting and animal-like calls.

Die Antwoord *O* (Rhythm Records*). Signature album of the zef rave rap style that brought the trio to the world's attention, featuring their addictive – and plain weird – anthem track *Enter the Ninja*.

Felix Laband *Dark Days Exit* (Compost Records/GoodToGo*). Spacey folk-rock-tinged electronic tone poems spliced with old TV soundtracks as well as jazz and

classical samples to generate chilled, minimalist mindscapes that justify repeated listening.

Goldfish *Perceptions of Pacha* (Pacha Recordings/Finetunes*). Cape Town-based jazz-boogie duo, who weave acoustic sounds into their predominantly electronica-based grooves to crank out one addictively upbeat track after another.

Spoek Mathambo *Mshini Wam* (BBE/!K7 Records*) Fascinating debut solo album from self-styled Afro-futurist, Mathambo, this multi-layered affair features a killer *kwaito* cover version of the Joy Division classic "She's Lost Control".

Various *Zoo City: The Soundtrack* (African Dope). Album issued to accompany the award-winning novel of the same name by Lauren Beukes (see p.674) showcases a number of the contemporary proponents of South African electronica, in its attempt to evoke the gritty atmosphere of Joburg's Hillbrow.

With contributions by Rob Allingham

Books

For a country with a proportionately small reading and book-buying public, South Africa generates a substantial amount of literature, particularly about subjects the literate feel guilty about – namely, politics and history. Titles marked ★ are particularly recommended.

HISTORY, SOCIETY AND ANTHROPOLOGY

Ian Berry *Living Apart*. Superbly evocative and moving photographs spanning the 1950s to 1990s, which chart a compelling vision of the politics of the nation, but at the level of the individual.

Andrew Brown *Street Blues*. Advocate (barrister), police-reserve sergeant and award-winning novelist, Brown paints a gritty, and sometimes witty, picture of life on the beat, tackling the mean streets of Cape Town.

Richard Calland *Anatomy of South Africa: Who Holds the Power?* An incisive dissection of politics and power in South Africa during the first decade of the twenty-first century, from one of the country's most respected commentators.

John Carlin *Playing the Enemy: Nelson Mandela and the Game that made a Nation*. Gripping account of Nelson Mandela's use of the 1995 rugby World Cup to unite a fractious nation in danger of collapsing into civil war. Also published as *Invictus*, the title of the Clint Eastwood film, which starred Matt Damon and Morgan Freeman.

Paul Faber *Group Portrait South Africa: Nine Family Histories*. Fascinating account revealing the complexities of South Africa past and present, through the histories of nine South African families of different races, backgrounds and aspirations. Includes photos and illustrations.

Andrew Feinstein *After the Party: Corruption, the ANC and South Africa's Uncertain Future*. A personal account of how South Africa's government has lost its way, by a former ANC member of parliament. Feinstein resigned in 2001 in protest at the government's cover-up of graft and corruption in negotiating the country's cripplingly expensive arms deal.

Hermann Giliomee and Bernard Mbenga *A New History of South Africa*. A comprehensive, reliable and entertaining illustrated account of South Africa's history.

★ **Peter Harris** *In a Different Time: The Inside Story of the Delmas Four*. Brilliantly told true historical drama about four young South Africans sent on a mission by the ANC-in-exile, which ultimately led them to Death Row. As their defence lawyer, Harris had unique and sympathetic insight into their personalities and motivations. Also published as *A Just Defiance: The Bombmakers, the Insurgents and a Legendary Treason Trial*.

★ **Antjie Krog** *Country of My Skull*. A deeply personal and gripping account of the hearings of the Truth and Reconciliation Commission. Krog, an Afrikaner former-SABC radio journalist and poet, reveals the complexity of horrors committed by apartheid.

★ **J.D. Lewis-Williams** *Discovering Southern African Rock Art* and *Images of Power: Understanding Bushman Rock Art*. Concise books written by an expert in the field, full of drawings and photos. Also worth investigating are the same author's *San Spirituality, Roots, Expression and Social Consequences* and *Stories that Float from Afar: Ancestral Folklore of the San of Southern Africa*.

Hein Marais *Pushed to the Limit*. An assessment of why the privileged classes remain just that with a handful of conglomerates dominating the South African economy and how this relates to Jacob Zuma's rise to power.

★ **Noel Mostert** *Frontiers: The Epic of South Africa's Creation and the Tragedy of the Xhosa People*. An academically solid, brilliantly written history of the Xhosa of the Eastern Cape, and their tragic fate in the frontier wars against the British.

★ **Thomas Pakenham** *The Boer War*. The definitive liberal history of the Anglo-Boer War that reads grippingly like a novel.

Charlene Smith *Robben Island*. Comprehensive and well-written account of Robben Island from prehistoric times to the present, including coverage of its most notorious period – as a prison for opponents of apartheid.

Allister Sparks *First Drafts: South African History in the Making*. A marvellous cross section of incisive writings about South African politics and history during the first decade of the twenty-first century written as he saw it at the time without the benefit of hindsight, by one of the country's most eminent journalists.

Stephen Taylor *The Caliban Shore: The Fate of the Grosvenor Castaways*. Gripping account of the wreck of the *Grosvenor* in the eighteenth century along the Eastern Cape's aptly named Wild Coast. Meticulously researched history, it has the depth and pace of a well-crafted novel as it traces the fates of the survivors.

Desmond Tutu *No Future Without Forgiveness*. The Truth and Reconciliation Commission as described by its chairman. There are better accounts of the hearings, but the book offers essential insight into one of South Africa's most unlikely heroes.

Frank Welsh *A History of South Africa*. Solid scholarship and a strong sense of overall narrative mark this publication as a much-needed addition to South African historiography.

★ **Nigel Worden, Elizabeth van Heyningen and Vivian Bickford-Smith** *Cape Town: The Making of a City*.

The definitive and highly readable illustrated account of the social and political development of South Africa's first city from 1620 to 1899. A companion volume covers the twentieth century.

AUTOBIOGRAPHY AND BIOGRAPHY

J.M. Coetzee *Boyhood: Scenes from Provincial Life* and *Youth*. Two riveting and disquieting accounts of growing up in a provincial town, and the author subsequently finding his way in the world, both in South Africa and London. Coetzee won the 2003 Nobel prize for literature.

★ **Mark Gevisser** *Portraits of Power: Profiles of a Changing South Africa*. Although now well over a decade old, this collection of forty mini-biographies cutting through a cross section of South African society still offers acute insights into a number of the country's significant players.

★ **Sindiwe Magoma** *To My Children's Children*. A fascinating autobiography – initially started so that her family would never forget their roots – that traces Magoma's life from the rural Transkei to the hard townships of Cape Town, and from political innocence to wisdom born of bitter experience.

★ **Nelson Mandela** *Long Walk to Freedom*. The superb bestselling autobiography of the former South African president. Mandela's generosity of spirit and tremendous understanding of the delicate balance between principle and tactics come through very strongly, and the book is wonderfully evocative of his early years and intensely moving about his long years in prison.

Anthony Sampson *Mandela, The Authorised Biography*. Released to coincide with Mandela's retirement from the presidency in 1999, Sampson's authoritative volume competes with *Long Walk to Freedom* in both interest and sheer poundage, offering a broader perspective and sharper analysis than the autobiography.

Chris van Wyk *Shirley, Goodness and Mercy: A Childhood Memoir*. A memoir of growing up in a working-class coloured family in Johannesburg during the apartheid era, with humorous and poignant touches.

THE ARTS

Marion Arnold *Women and Art in South Africa*. Comprehensive, pioneering study of women artists from the early twentieth century to the present.

David Coplan *In Township Tonight: South Africa's Black City Music and Theatre*. Classic, updated in 2008, that traces local music from its indigenous roots through slave orchestras and looks at its humanizing influence in the harsh environment of the townships.

Thorsten Deckler, Anne Graupner, Henning Rasmuss *Contemporary South African Architecture in a Landscape of Transition*. Lavishly illustrated coverage of fifty outstanding architectural projects completed since 1994, all of which, the authors say, display a sense of South African identity.

S. Francis and Rico *Madam and Eve*. Various volumes of witty cartoons conveying the daily struggle between an African domestic worker and her white madam in the northern suburbs of Johannesburg, these cartoons say more about post-apartheid society than countless academic tomes.

Steve Gordon *Beyond the Blues: Township Jazz of the Sixties and Seventies*. Portraits, in words and pictures, of the country's jazz greats such as Kippie Moeketsi, Basil Coetzee and Abdullah Ibrahim (Dollar Brand).

★ **Andy Mason** *What's so Funny?: Under the Skin of South African Cartooning*. Insightful, fascinating and thoroughly collectable wade through the history of South African visual satire from the colonial period, through the apartheid years to the present.

Z.B. Molefe and Mike Mzileni *A Common Hunger to Sing*. Large-format, well-illustrated tribute to the country's black women singers and the obstacles they have overcome.

Ralf-Peter Seippel *South African Photography: 1950–2010*. South Africa's history has provided a rich vein of material for photographers and this volume covers the work of some of the country's most celebrated lensmen, whose work is divided into three periods: apartheid, struggle and freedom.

Paul Weinberg *Then & Now*. Collection by eight photographers, tracing the changes in their subjects and approaches as South Africa moved from apartheid into the present democratic era.

Sue Williamson *South African Art Now*. A survey of South African art from the "Resistance Art" of the 1960s to the present, covering movements, genres and leading artists such as Marlene Dumas and William Kentridge, by one of the country's most influential commentators and an accomplished artist in her own right.

Zapiro *Do You Know Who I am?* In a country where satire is in notoriously short supply, Zapiro is the leading cartoonist, consistently exposing what needs to be exposed. This book is the umpteenth in a series of annual collections, containing work originally published in a number of dailies as well as the *Mail & Guardian* and *Sunday Times*.

TRAVEL WRITING

Richard Dobson *Karoo Moons: A Photographic Journey*. If you need encouragement to explore the desert interior of South Africa, these enticing images should do the trick.

★ **Sihle Khumalo** *Dark Continent, My Black Arse*. Insightful and witty account by a black South African who quit his well-paid job to realize a dream of travelling from the Cape to Cairo by public transport.

Julia Martin *A Millimetre of Dust: Visiting Ancestral Sites*. Sensitively crafted narrative that begins on the Cape Peninsula and takes the author, her husband and two children on a journey to important archeological sites in the Northern Cape, raising ethical, ecological and philosophical questions along the way.

Dervla Murphy *South from the Limpopo: Travels Through South Africa*. A fascinating and intrepid journey – by bicycle – through the new South Africa. The author isn't afraid to explore the complexities and paradoxes of this country.

Paul Theroux *Dark Star Safari*. Theroux's powerful account of his overland trip from Cairo to Cape Town, with a couple of chapters on South Africa, including an account of meeting writer Nadine Gordimer (see Fiction).

SPECIALIST GUIDES

G.M. Branch *Two Oceans*. Don't be put off by the coffee-table format; this is a comprehensive guide to Southern Africa's marine life.

David Bristow *Best Hikes in Southern Africa* and *Best Walks of the Drakensberg*. The South Africa book is a well-written and reliable guide that does your homework for you, selecting the best trails from a confusingly extensive lot. The Drakensberg paperback is indispensable for anyone exploring the massif, with detailed route instructions and informative background about natural history.

Hugh Chittenden (ed) *Robert's Bird Guide*. The definitive reference work on the subcontinent's entire avifauna population: if it's not in Robert's, it doesn't exist. Alas, the weight of this makes it more of a book to consult In a library than on a trip.

Richard D. Estes *Safari Companion: A Guide to Watching African Mammals*. A vital handbook on how to understand African wildlife, with interesting and readable information on the behaviour and social structures of the major species. Highly recommended for anyone wanting to go beyond the checklists.

Brett Hilton-Barber and Lee Berger *The Official Field Guide to the Cradle of Humankind: Sterkfontein, Swartkrans, Kromdraai and Environs World Heritage Site*. Full of photographs and illustrations, this indispensable guide takes you around the World Heritage Sites of the Cradle of Humankind near Jo'burg.

★ **Mike Lundy** *Best Walks in the Cape Peninsula*. Handy, solidly researched guide to some of the peninsula's many walks, and small enough to fit comfortably in a backpack.

L. McMahon and M. Fraser *A Fynbos Year*. Exquisitely illustrated and well-written book about South Africa's unique floral kingdom.

Willie and Sandra Olivier *Hiking Trails of Southern Africa*. Guide to major hikes, from strolls to expeditions lasting several days, throughout South Africa with information and where to get permits. The depth of background, including natural history commentary on each trail, is excellent, but it's less strong on details of terrain and trail conditions.

Colin Paterson-Jones *Best Walks of the Garden Route*. Handy for accessing some of South Africa's premier coastline and forests, away from the ribbon of development along the Garden Route.

Steve Pike *Surfing in South Africa: Swells, Spots and Surf African Culture*. Classic guide, updated in 2008, to everything you need to know about riding the waves along the country's 3000km coastline, written by veteran journalist, surfing aficionado and founder of the definitive surfing website wavescape.co.za.

Ian Sinclair, Phil Hockey and Warwick Tarboton *Sasol Birds of Southern Africa*. Comprehensive volume full of photos geared to the field, with useful pointers to aid quick identification.

Chris and Tilde Stuart *Field Guide to the Mammals of Southern Africa*. One of the best books on this subject, providing excellent background and clear illustrations to help you recognize species.

Braam and Piet van Wyk *Field Guide to the Trees of Southern Africa*. Covering Southern Africa's 900 species, this fully comprehensive guide is more practical to carry than other titles on the subject.

★ **Philip van Zyl** (ed) *John Platter South African Wines*. One of the bestselling titles in South Africa – an annually updated pocket book that rates virtually every wine produced in the country. No aspiring connoisseur of Cape wines should venture forth without it. Also available as a useful, but flawed, iphone app.

FICTION

Tatamkhulu Afrika *The Innocents*. Set in the struggle years, this novel examines the moral and ethical issues of the time from a Muslim perspective.

Mark Behr *The Smell of Apples*. Powerful first novel set in the 1970s recounts the gradual falling of the scales from the eyes of an eleven-year-old Afrikaner boy, whose father is a major-general in the apartheid army.

Lauren Beukes *Zoo City*. Winner in 2011 of the Arthur C. Clarke award for science fiction, this amazing novel is set in an alternative Johannesburg where convicts are sentenced to be "animalled" – to have an animal familiar attached to them. A soundtrack album featuring a compilation of South African electronica tracks intended to evoke the atmosphere of the book has been issued to accompany the book (see Music).

★ **Herman Charles Bosman** *Unto Dust*. A superb collection of short stories from South Africa's master of the genre, all set in the tiny Afrikaner farming district of Groot Marico in the 1930s. The tales share a narrator who, with delicious irony, reveals the passions and foibles of his community.

André Brink *A Chain of Voices*. This hugely evocative tale of eighteenth-century Cape life explores the impact of slavery on one farming family.

★ **Michael Chapman** *Omnibus of a Century of South African Short Stories*. The most comprehensive ever collection of South African tale-telling, starting with San oral stories and working up to twenty-first-century writing, including work by Olive Schreiner, Alan Paton, Es'kia Mphahlele and Ivan Vladislavic.

★ **J.M. Coetzee** *Age of Iron* and *Disgrace*. In a *Mail & Guardian* poll of writers, *Age of Iron* emerged as the finest South African novel of the 1990s. The book depicts a white female classics professor dying from cancer during the political craziness of the 1980s. She is joined by a tramp who sets up home in her garden, and thus evolves a curious and fascinating relationship. But even better is *Disgrace*, a disturbing story of a university professor's fall from grace, set in the Eastern Cape. No writer better portrays the ever-present undercurrents of violence and unease in South Africa.

Achmat Dangor *Bitter Fruit*. From one of the best Cape Town writers, *Bitter Fruit* is the story of the son of two anti-apartheid activists, and of an act of violence and injustice threading two generations, which is resurrected by the Truth and Reconciliation Commission.

Tracey Farren *Whiplash*. Powerful, acclaimed, and by turns relentless and funny, debut novel written in the voice of a Cape Town prostitute coming to terms with her past and present on her own personal walk to freedom.

Damon Galgut *In a Strange Room*. The writer, some say, best placed to fill J.M. Coetzee's literary shoes, Damon Galgut has scooped several literary awards: *In a Strange Room* was shortlisted for the 2010 Man Booker Prize for fiction. Unusually for Galgut, it's set outside South Africa and describes in interchanging first and third person the global travels and relationships of a protagonist named, like the author, Damon. Quirky, beautifully written and highly readable.

Nadine Gordimer *July's People*. This controversial work by Nobel Literature Prize winner Gordimer was first banned by the apartheid regime for being subversive and later temporarily removed from schools by the ANC-governed Gauteng education department for being "deeply racist, superior and patronizing". Published in the 1980s when revolution in South Africa looked increasingly possible, it tells the story of a liberal white family rescued by its gardener July from a political deluge, and taken to his home village for safety.

Lily Herne *Deadlands*. South Africa's street-smart answer to *Twilight* follows the adventures and romance of seventeen-year-old Lele as she navigates the shattered, dystopian and zombie-infested suburbs of a post-apocalyptic Cape Town.

Dan Jacobson *The Trap* and *A Dance in the Sun*. Taut novellas written in the 1950s and published in one volume, skilfully portraying the developing tensions and nuances of the white-versus-black lives of the era.

Shaun Johnson *The Native Commissioner*. Eloquent account of a government official unable to come to terms with the white man's place in Africa. It won its author the 2006 M-Net Award for English fiction.

Fred Khumalo *Seven Steps to Heaven*. Ostensibly a coming-of-age story of two friends and their encounters with sex, *shebeens*, violence and revenge, journalist Khumalo's novel vividly evokes the flavour of South African township life.

★ **Alex La Guma** *A Walk in the Night and Other Stories*. An evocative collection of short stories by this talented political activist/author, set in District Six, the ethnically mixed quarter of Cape Town razed by the apartheid government.

Anne Landsman *The Devil's Chimney*. A stylish and entertaining piece of magical realism set in the Karoo town of Oudtshoorn in the days of the ostrich-feather boom.

Deon Meyer *Thirteen Hours*. The latest offering from South Africa's hottest crime writer is, as usual, a riveting read, but may be uncomfortably close to the bone for some – one thread follows Detective Benny Griessel's quest to find and save the life of an American backpacker on the run from Cape Town gangsters after her travelling companion has been murdered.

Zakes Mda *Ways of Dying*, *His Madonna of Excelsior* and *The Heart of Redness*. The first is a brilliant tale of a professional mourner, full of sly insights into the culture of black South Africa; *Madonna* focuses on a family at the heart of the scandalous case in the Free State in which nineteen people from the small town of Excelsior were charged with sex across the races; while *Heart*, which won the *Sunday Times* Fiction Prize, weaves the historical story of the Eastern Cape cattle killings with a contemporary narrative.

Niq Mhlongo *Dog Eat Dog*. One of the irreverent exponents of post-apartheid literature, Mhlongo has been described as "the voice of the *kwaito* [hip-hop] generation". This novel looks at the life of a student who spends his time bunking classes, picking up girls and playing the system.

Phaswane Mpe *Welcome to Our Hillbrow*. A young black man from the rural areas hits the fleshpots of present-day Hillbrow, where xenophobia, violence and AIDS (from which the author subsequently died) reign.

★ **Es'kia Mphahlele** *Down Second Avenue*. A classic autobiographical novel set in the 1940s in the impoverished township of Alexandra, where Mphahlele grew up as part of a large extended family battling daily to survive.

Mike Nicol *Payback*. Hard-boiled thriller, one of several by established novelist Nicol (who has been compared to Elmore Leonard and Cormac McCarthy), follows a pair of gun-runners drawn back from retirement into Cape Town's dark underworld.

★ **Alan Paton** *Cry, The Beloved Country*. Classic 1948 novel encapsulating the deep injustices of the country, by one of South Africa's great liberals. With tremendous lyricism, the book describes the journey of a black pastor from rural Natal to Johannesburg to rescue his missing son from its clutches.

Kathy Perkins *Black South African Women – An Anthology of Plays*. Ground-breaking collection of ten plays by a wide range of known and unknown playwrights such as Gcina Mhlope, Sindiwe Nagona, Muthal Naidoo and Lueen Conning.

Sol Plaatje *Mhudi*. The first English novel by a black South African writer, *Mhudi* is set in the 1830s, at a time when the Afrikaner Great Trek had just begun. It's the epic tale of a young rural woman who saves her future husband from the raids of the Ndebele, who were then a powerful state in the Marico region.

Linda Rode and Jakes Gerwel *Crossing Over*. Collection of 26 stories by new and emerging South African writers on the experiences of adolescence and early adulthood in a period of political transition.

★ **Olive Schreiner** *Story of an African Farm*. The first-ever South African novel, written in 1883. Though subject to the ideologies of the era, the book nonetheless explores with a genuinely open vision the tale of two female cousins living on a remote Karoo farm.

★ **Ivan Vladislavic** *The Restless Supermarket, The Exploded View* and *Portrait with Keys: Joburg and What-What*. *The Restless Supermarket* is a dark and intricate urban satire from South Africa's most exciting contemporary writer, about Johannesburg's notorious Hillbrow district during the last days of apartheid. *The Exploded View* is a collection of four interlinked pieces, a great follow-up from a writer who's unrivalled at evoking the contradictions and fascinations of Jo'burg, while *Portrait* is not so much a novel as an account, in a series of numbered texts, of the city that inspires Vladislavic's imagination.

Language

South Africa has eleven official languages, all of which have equal status under the law. In practice, however, **English** is the lingua franca that dominates politics, commerce and the media. If you're staying in the main cities and national parks you'll rarely, if ever, need to use any other language. **Afrikaans**, although a language you seldom need to speak, nevertheless remains very much in evidence and you will certainly encounter it on official forms and countless signs, particularly on the road; for this reason we give a comprehensive list of written Afrikaans terms you could come across (see p.678).

Unless you're planning on staying a very long time, there's little point trying to get to grips with the whole gamut of **indigenous African languages**, of which there are nine official ones and several unofficial ones. Having said that, it's always useful to know a few phrases of the local indigenous language, especially greetings – the use of which will always be appreciated even if you aren't able to carry your foray through to a proper conversation (see box, p.680).

The nine official African languages are split into four groups: **Nguni**, which consists of Zulu, Xhosa, siSwati and Ndebele; **Sotho**, which comprises Northern Sotho, Southern Sotho (or Sesotho) and Tswana; **Venda** and **Tsonga**. Most black people speak languages in the first two groups. In common with all indigenous Southern African languages, these operate under very different principles to European languages in that their sentences are dominated by the noun, with which the other words, such as verbs and adjectives, must agree in person, gender, number or case. Known as concordal agreement, this is achieved by supplementing word stems – the basic element of each word – with prefixes or suffixes to change meaning.

The Nguni group, and Southern Sotho, both contain a few **clicks** adopted from San languages, which are difficult for speakers of European languages. In practice, most English-speaking South Africans sidestep the issue altogether and pronounce African names in ways that are often only approximations.

English

South African English is a mixed bag, one language with many variants. Forty percent of whites are mother-tongue English-speakers, many of whom believe that they are (or at least should be) speaking standard British English. In fact, South African English has its own distinct character, and is as different from the Queen's English as is Australian. Its most notable characteristic is its huge and rich vocabulary, with unique words and usages, some drawn from Afrikaans and the indigenous African languages. The hefty *Oxford Dictionary of South African English* makes an interesting browse.

As a language used widely by non-native speakers, there is great **variation in pronunciation** and usage – largely a result of mother-tongue interference from other languages. Take, for example, the sentence "The bad bird sat on the bed", which speakers of some African languages (which don't distinguish between some of the vowel sounds of English) might pronounce as "The bed bed set on the bed". While some English-speaking whites feel that their language is being mangled and misused, linguists argue that it is simply being transformed.

Afrikaans

Broadly speaking, **Afrikaans** is a dialect of Dutch, which became modified on the Cape frontier through its encounter with French, German and English settlers, and is peppered with words and phrases from indigenous tongues as well as African and Asian languages used by slaves. Some historians argue, very plausibly, that Afrikaans was first written in Arabic script in the early nineteenth century by Cape Muslims.

Despite this heritage, the language was used by Afrikaners from the late nineteenth century onwards as a key element in the construction of their racially exclusive ethnic identity. The attempt, in 1976, by the apartheid government to make Afrikaans the medium of instruction in black schools, which led to the Soweto uprising, confirmed the hated status of the language for many urban Africans, which persists to this day.

Contrary to popular belief outside South Africa, the majority of Afrikaans-speakers are not white but coloured, and the language, far from dying out, is in fact understood by more South Africans than any other language. It's the predominant tongue in the Western and Northern Cape provinces, and in the Free State it is the language of the media.

Afrikaans signs

Bed en Ontbyt	Bed and breakfast	**Perron**	Platform (train station)
Dankie	Thank you	**Plaas**	Farm
Derde	Third	**Poskantoor**	Post office
Doeane	Customs	**Regs**	Right
Drankwinkel	Liquor shop	**Ry**	Go
Droe vrugte	Dry fruit	**Sentrum**	Centre
Eerste	First	**Singel**	Crescent
Geen ingang	No entry	**Slaghuis**	Butcher
Gevaar	Danger	**Stad**	City
Grens	Border	**Stadig**	Slow
Hoof	Main	**Stad sentrum**	City/town centre
Hoog	High	**Stasie**	Station
Ingang	Entry	**Straat**	Street
Inligting	Information	**Strand**	Beach
Kantoor	Office	**Swembad**	Swimming pool
Kerk	Church	**Toegang**	Admission
Kort	Short	**Tweede**	Second
Links	Left	**Verbode**	Prohibited
Lughawe	Airport	**Verkeer**	Traffic
Mans	Men	**Versigtig**	Carefully
Mark	Market	**Vierde**	Fourth
Ompad	Detour	**Vrouens**	Women
Pad	Road	**Vrugte**	Fruit
Padwerke voor	Roadworks ahead	**Vyfde**	Fifth
Pastorie	Parsonage		

The Nguni group

Zulu (or isiZulu), the most widely spoken black African language in South Africa, is understood by around twelve million people. It's the mother tongue of residents of the southeastern parts of the country, including the whole of KwaZulu-Natal, the eastern Free State, southern Mpumalanga and Gauteng – as well as South Africa's president, Jacob Zuma. Some linguists believe that Zulu's broad reach could make it an alternative to English as a South African lingua franca. Don't confuse Zulu with **Fanakalo**, which is a pidgin Zulu mixed with other languages. Still sometimes spoken on the mines, it is not popular with most Zulu-speakers, though many white South Africans tend to believe it is.

For all practical purposes, **siSwati**, the language spoken in Swaziland, is almost identical to Zulu, but for historical reasons has developed its own identity. The same applies to **Ndebele**, which shares around 95 percent in common with Zulu. It broke off from Zulu (around the same time as siSwati) when a group of Zulu-speakers fled north to escape the expansionism of the Zulu chief Shaka. Ndebele is now spoken in pockets of Gauteng and North West provinces as well as throughout southern Zimbabwe.

Xhosa (itself an example of a word beginning with a click sound) is Nelson Mandela's mother tongue, which he shares with seven million other South Africans, predominantly in the Eastern Cape. The language is also spoken by Africans in the Western Cape, most of whom are concentrated in Cape Town.

The Sotho group

Northern Sotho dialects, which are numerous and diverse, are spoken by around 2.5 million people in a huge arc of South Africa that takes in the country around the Kruger National Park, around to the Botswana border and south from there to Pretoria.
Southern Sotho, one of the first African languages to be written, is spoken in the Free State, parts of Gauteng, as well as Lesotho and the areas of the Eastern Cape bordering it.
Tswana, also characterized by a great diversity of dialects, is geographically the most widespread language in Southern Africa, and is the principal language of Botswana. In South Africa its dialects are dispersed through the Northern Cape, the Free State and North West provinces.

As with the Nguni languages, the distinctions between the languages in the Sotho group owe more to history, politics and geography than to pure linguistic factors; speakers of some Northern Sotho dialects can understand some dialects of Tswana more readily than they can other Northern Sotho dialects.

Pronouncing place names

The largest number of unfamiliar **place names** that visitors are likely to encounter in South Africa are of Afrikaans origin, followed by names with origins in the Nguni group of languages. Afrikaans and English names are found across the country, while African names tend to be more localized, according to the predominant language in that area. Nguni group pronunciations generally apply in the Eastern Cape, KwaZulu-Natal, parts of Mpumalanga and Swaziland, while Sotho group names will be found in North West Province, Limpopo, the Northern Cape, Free State and parts of Gauteng. Sometimes you'll encounter names with Khoisan derivations, such as "Tsitsikamma" (in which the ts is pronounced as in "tsunami"). The pronunciation tips below are intended as a guide and are neither comprehensive nor definitive.

Afrikaans

In common with other Germanic languages, Afrikaans has a number of consonants that are **guttural**. Apart from these, most consonant sounds will be unproblematic for English-speakers. However, Afrikaans has numerous vowels and diphthongs, which have rough English equivalents but which are frequently spelled in an unfamiliar way – take, for example, the variation in the pronunciation of the letter "e" in the list below.

VOWELS AND DIPHTHONGS

a as in Kakam*a*s	u as in p*u*p	**eu** as in K*eu*rboomstrand	u as in c*u*re
aa as in Br*aa*mfontein	a as in c*a*r	**i** as in Cal*i*tzdorp	e as in ang*e*l
ae as in H*ae*nertsburg	a as in c*a*r but slightly lengthened	**ie** as in D*ie*pwalle	i as in p*i*ck
		o as in B*o*ntebok	o as in c*o*rk, but clipped
aai as in Smitswinkelb*aai*	y as in dr*y*	**oe** as in Bl*oe*mfontein	oo as in b*oo*k
au as in *Au*grabies	o as in bl*o*w	**oo** as in Kl*oo*f	oo as in b*oo*r
ar as in G*ar*ies	u as in b*ur*row	**ou** as in *Ou*drif	o as in wr*o*te
e as in B*o*ntebok	er as in rubb*er*, but clipped	**u** as in W*u*ppertaal	i as in p*i*ck
e as in Clar*e*ns	e as in ang*e*l	**ui** as in Nelspr*ui*t	a as in g*a*te
ee as in Ri*ee*beeck	ee as in b*ee*r	**uu** as in S*uu*rbraak	o as in wr*o*te
ei as in Bloemfont*ei*n	ai as in p*ai*n	**y** as in Vanrhynsdorp	ai as in p*ai*n

BASIC GREETINGS AND FAREWELLS

ENGLISH	AFRIKAANS	NORTHERN SOTHO	SESOTHO
Yes	Ja	Ee	E!
No	Nee	Aowa	Tjhe
Please	Asseblief	Hle.../...hle	(Ka kopo) hle
Thank you	Dankie	Ke a leboga	Ke a leboha
Excuse me	Verskoon my	Tshwarelo	Ntshwaerele
Good morning	Goiemore	Thobela/dumela	Dumela (ng)
Good afternoon	Goeiemiddag	Thobela/dumela	Dumela (ng)
Good evening	Goeinaand	Thobela/dumela	Fonaneng
Goodbye	Totsiens	Sala gabotse/sepele gabotse	Sala(ng) hantle
See you later	Sien jou later	Re tla bonana	Re tla bonana
Until we meet again	Totsiens	Go fihla re kopana gape	Ho fihlela re bonana
How do you do?	Aangename kennis?	Ke leboga go le tseba?	Ke thabela ho o tseb
How are you?	Hoe gaan dit?	Le kae?	O/le sa phela?

CONSONANTS

d as in Suikerbosrand	**t** as in runt	**tj** as in Matjiesfontein	**k** as in key
g as in Magersfontein	guttural ch as in the Scottish loch	**v** as in Nyslvlei	**f** as in fig
		w as in Waterkant	**v** as in vase

Nguni group

The clicks in Nguni languages are the most unfamiliar and difficult sounds for English-speakers to pronounce. The three basic clicks – which, as it happens, occur in the names of three places featured in the Wild Coast of the Eastern Cape (see p.344) – are: the **dental click** (transliterated using "c", as in the Cwebe Nature Reserve) made by pulling the tongue away from the front teeth as one would when expressing disapproval in "tsk tsk"; the **palatal click** (transliterated "q", as in Qholorha Mouth) made by pulling the tongue away from the palate as you would when trying to replicate the sound of a bubbly cork being popped; and the **lateral click** (transliterated "x", as in Nxaxo Mouth), made by pulling away the tongue from the side teeth. To complicate matters, each click can be pronounced in one of three ways (aspirated, nasalized or delayed) and may change when spoken in combination with other consonants.

VOWELS

a as in KwaZulu	a as in father	**o** as in Umkomaas	a as in tall
e as in Cwebe	e as in bend	**u** as in Hluhluwe	u as in put
i as in Kwambonambi	ee as in flee		

CONSONANTS

dl as in Dlinza	aspirated ll as in the Welsh Llewellyn	**ph** as in Mphephu	p as in pass followed by a rapid rush of air
g as in Haga-Haga	hard g as in hug		
hl as in Hluhluwe	aspirated ll as in the Welsh llewellyn (though often pronounced like the shl in shlemiel by English-speakers)	**r** as in Qholorha	guttural ch as in the Scottish loch
		ty as in Idutywa	approximately the initial sound in tube

Sotho group

VOWELS

a as in Thaba	a as in father	**o** as in Mantsebo	o as in bore, but curtailed
e as in Motsekuoa	e as in he	**u** as in Butha	u as in full

TSWANA	XHOSA	ZULU
Ee	Ewe	Yebo
Nnyaa	Hayi	Cha
Tsweetswee	Nceda	Uxolo
Ke a leboga	Enkosi	Ngiyabonga
Intshwarele	Uxolo	Uxolo
Dumela	Molo/bhota	Sawubona
Dumela	Molo/bhoto	Sawubona
Dumela	Molo/bhota	Sawubona
Sala sentle	Nisale kakuhle	Sala kahle
Ke tla go bona	Sobe sibonane	Sizobanana
Go fitlhelela re bonana gape	De sibonane kwakhona	Size sibonane
O tsogile jang?	Kunjani?	Ninjani?
O tsogile jang?	Kunjani?	Ninjani?

CONSONANTS

j as in Ha-Le*j*one	**y** as in *y*es	**ph** as in Ma*ph*utseng	p as in *p*ool
hl as in *Hl*ôtse	aspirated ll as in the Welsh Llewellyn (often pronounced like the shl in *shl*emiel by English-speakers)	**th** as in *Th*aba	t as in *t*ar

Glossary

Words whose spelling makes it hard to guess how to render them have their approximate pronunciation given in italics. Where *gh* occurs in the pronunciation, it denotes the **ch** sound in the Scottish word "loch". Sometimes we've used the letter "r" in the pronunciation even though the word in question doesn't contain this letter; for example, we've given the pronunciation of "Egoli" as "air-gaw-lee". In these instances the syllable containing the "r" is meant to represent a familiar word or sound from English; the "r" itself shouldn't be pronounced.

African In the context of South Africa, an indigenous South African

Aloe Family of spiky indigenous succulents, often with dramatic orange flowers

Apartheid (apart-hate) Term used from the 1940s for the National Party's official policy of "racial separation"

Assegai (assa-guy) Short stabbing spear introduced by Shaka to the Zulu armies

Baai (buy) Afrikaans word meaning "bay"; also a common suffix in place names, eg Stilbaai

Bakkie (bucky) Light truck or van

Bantu (bun-two) Unscientific apartheid term for indigenous black people; in linguistics, a group of indigenous Southern African languages

Bantustan Term used under apartheid for the territories for Africans

Bergie A vagrant living on the slopes of Table Mountain in Cape Town

Black Imprecise term that sometimes refers collectively to Africans, Indians and coloureds, but more usually is used to mean Africans

Boer (boor) Literally "farmer", but also refers to early Dutch colonists at the Cape and Afrikaners

Boland (boor-lunt) Southern part of the Western Cape

Boma An enclosure or palisade

Boy Offensive term used to refer to an adult African man who is a servant

Bundu (approximately boon-doo, but with the vowels shortened) Wilderness or back country

Burgher Literally a citizen, but more specifically members of the Dutch community at the Cape in the seventeenth and eighteenth centuries

Bushman Southern Africa's earliest, but now almost extinct, inhabitants who lived by hunting and gathering

Bushveld Country composed largely of thorny bush

Cape Dutch Nineteenth-century, whitewashed, gabled style of architecture

Ciskei (sis-kye) Eastern Cape region west of the Kei River, declared a "self-governing territory" for Xhosa-speakers in 1972, and now reincorporated into South Africa

Cocopan Small tip truck on rails used to transport gold ore

Coloured Mulattos or people of mixed race

Commandos Burgher military units during the Frontier and Boer wars

Dagga (dugh-a) Marijuana

Dagha (dah-ga) Mud used in indigenous construction

Dassie (dussy) Hyrax

Disa (die-za) One of twenty species of beautiful indigenous orchids, most famous of which is the red disa or "Pride of Table Mountain"

Dominee (dour-min-ee) Reverend (abbreviated to DS)

Donga Dry, eroded ditch

Dorp Country town or village (from Afrikaans)

Drift Fording point in a river (from Afrikaans)

Drostdy (dross-tea) Historically, the building of the landdrost or magistrate

Egoli (air-gaw-lee) Zulu name for Johannesburg (literally "city of gold")

Fanakalo or **fanagalo** (fun-a-galaw) Pidgin mixture of English, Zulu and Afrikaans used to facilitate communication between white foremen and African workers

Fundi Expert

Fynbos (fayn boss) Term for vast range of fine-leafed species that predominate in the southern part of the Western Cape (see p.111)

Girl Offensive term used to refer to an African woman who is a servant

Gogga (gho-gha) Creepy-crawly or insect

Griqua Person of mixed white, Bushman and Hottentot descent

Group Areas Act Now-defunct law passed in 1950 that provided for the establishment of separate areas for each "racial group"

Highveld High-lying areas of Gauteng and Mpumalanga

Homeland See Bantustan

Hottentot Now unfashionable term for indigenous Khoisan herders encountered by the first settlers at the Cape

Impi Zulu regiment

Indaba Zulu term meaning a group discussion and now used in South African English for any meeting or conference

Inkatha (in-ka-ta) Fiercely nationalist Zulu political party, formed in 1928 as a cultural organization

Jislaaik! (yis-like) Exclamation equivalent to "Geez!" or "Crikey!"

Joeys Affectionate abbreviation for Johannesburg

Jol Party, celebration

Kaffir Highly objectionable term of abuse for Africans

Karoo Arid plateau that occupies a large proportion of the South African interior

Khoikhoi (ghoy-ghoy) Self-styled name of South Africa's original herding inhabitants

Kloof (klo-ef; rhymes with "boor") Ravine or gorge

Knobkerrie (the "k" is silent) Wooden club

Kokerboom (both the first and last syllable rhyme with "boor") Quiver tree – a type of aloe found in the Northern Cape

Kopje Dutch spelling of koppie

Koppie Hillock

Kraal Enclosure of huts for farm animals or collection of traditional huts occupied by an extended family

Kramat (crum-mutt) Shrine of a Muslim holy man

Krans (crunce) Sheer cliff face

Laager (lager) A circular encampment of ox wagons, used as fortification by Voortrekkers

Lapa Courtyard of group of Ndebele houses; also used to describe an enclosed area at safari camps, where braais are held

Lebowa (lab-o-a) Now-defunct homeland for North Sotho-speakers

Lekker Nice

Lobola (la-ball-a) Bride price, paid by an African man to his wife's parents

Location Old-fashioned term for segregated African area on the outskirts of a town or farm

Lowveld Low-lying subtropical region of Mpumalanga and Limpopo provinces

Malay Misnomer for Cape Muslims of Asian descent

Matjieshuis (mikeys-hace) Reed hut

Mbaqanga (m-ba-kung-a) A genre of music that originated in Soweto in the 1960s

Mbira (m-beer-a) African thumb piano, often made with a gourd

MK Umkhonto we Sizwe (Spear of the Nation) The armed wing of the ANC, now incorporated into the national army

Mlungu (m-loon-goo) African term for a white person, equivalent to honkie

Moffie (mawf-ee) Gay person

Nek Saddle between two mountains

Nguni (n-goo-nee) Group of southeastern Bantu-speaking people comprising Zulu, Xhosa and Swazi

Nkosi Sikelel 'i Afrika "God Bless Africa", anthem of the ANC and now of South Africa

Nyanga (nyun-ga) Traditional healer

Outspan A place set aside for animals to rest; can also mean to unharness oxen from a wagon

Pass Document that Africans used to have to carry at all times, which essentially rendered them aliens in their own country

Pastorie (puss-tour-ee) Parsonage

Platteland (plutta-lunt) Country districts

Poort Narrow pass through mountains along river course

Pronk (prawnk) Characteristic jump of springbok or impala

Protea National flower of South Africa

Qwaqwa Now-defunct homeland for South Sotho-speakers

Raadsaal (the "d" is pronounced "t") Council or parliament building

Restcamp Accommodation in national parks

Robot Traffic light

Rondavel (ron-daa-vil, with the stress on the middle syllable) Circular building based on traditional African huts

SABC South African Broadcasting Authority

Sangoma (sun-gom-a) Traditional spirit medium and healer

Shebeen (sha-bean) Unlicensed tavern

Shell Ultra City Clean, bright stops along major national roads, with a filling station, restaurant, shop and sometimes a hotel

Sjambok (sham-bok) Rawhide whip

Southeaster Prevailing wind in the Western Cape

Spaza shops (spa-za) Small stall or kiosk

Strandloper Name given by the Dutch to the indigenous people of the Cape; literally beachcomber

Stoep Veranda

Tackie Sneakers or plimsolls

Township Areas set aside under apartheid for Africans

Transkei (trans-kye) Now-defunct homeland for Xhosa-speakers

Trekboer (trek-boor) Nomadic Afrikaner farmers, usually in the eighteenth and nineteenth centuries

Umuthi (oo-moo-tee) Traditional herbal medicine

Velskoen (fel-scoon) Rough suede shoes

Vlei (flay) Swamp

VOC Verenigde Oostindische Compagnie, the Dutch East India Company

Voortrekker (the first syllable rhymes with "boor") Dutch burghers who migrated inland in their ox wagons in the nineteenth century to escape British colonialism

ZAR Zuid Afrikaansche Republiek; an independent Boer republic that included present-day Gauteng, Mpumalanga and Limpopo provinces and which was Britain's main opponent in the Anglo-Boer War

Food and drink

Amarula Liqueur made from the berries of the marula tree

Begrafnisrys (ba-ghruff-niss-racc) Literally "funeral rice"; traditional Cape Muslim dish of yellow rice cooked with raisins

Biltong Sun-dried salted strip of meat, chewed as a snack

Blatjang (blutt-young) Cape Muslim chutney that has become a standard condiment on South African dinner tables

Bobotie (ba-boor-tea) Traditional Cape curried mince topped with a savoury custard and often cooked with apricots and almonds

Boerekos (boor-a-coss) Farm food, usually consisting of loads of meat and vegetables cooked using butter and sugar

Boerewors (boor-a-vorce) Spicy lengths of sausage that are *de rigueur* at braais

Bokkoms Dried fish, much like salt fish

Braai or **braaivleis** (bry-flace) Barbecue

Bredie Cape vegetable and meat stew

Bunny chow Originally a curried takeaway served in a scooped-out half loaf of bread, but now often wrapped in a roti

Cane or cane spirit A potent vodka-like spirit distilled from sugar cane and generally mixed with a soft drink such as Coke

Cap Classique Sparkling wine fermented in the bottle in exactly the same way as Champagne; also called Méthode Cap Classic

Cape gooseberry Fruit of the physalis; a sweet yellow berry

Cape salmon or **geelbek** (ghear-l-beck) Delicious firm-fleshed sea fish (unrelated to northern-hemisphere salmon)

Cape Velvet A sweet liqueur-and-cream dessert beverage that resembles Irish Cream liqueur

Denningvleis (den-ning-flace) Spicy traditional Cape lamb stew

Frikkadel Fried onion and meatballs

Hanepoort (harner-poort) Delicious sweet dessert grape

Kabeljou (cobble-yo) Common South African marine fish, also called kob

Kerrievis (kerry-fiss) See Pickled fish

Kingklip Highly prized deepwater fish caught along the Atlantic and Indian ocean coasts

Koeksister (cook-sister) Deep-fried plaited doughnut, dripping with syrup

Maas or **amasi** or **amaas** Traditional African beverage consisting of naturally soured milk, available as a packaged dairy product in supermarkets

Maaskaas Cottage cheese made from maas

Mageu or **mahewu** or **maheu** (ma-gh-weh) Traditional African beer made from maize meal and water, now packaged and commercially available

Malva Very rich and very sweet traditional baked Cape dessert

Mampoer (mum-poor) Moonshine; homedistilled spirit made from soft fruit, commonly peaches

Melktert (melk-tairt) Traditional Cape custard pie

Mielie Maize

Mielie pap (mealy pup) Maize porridge, varying from a thin mixture to a stiff one that can resemble polenta

Mopani worm (ma-parny) Black spotted caterpillar that is a delicacy among Africans in some parts of the country

Mqomboti (m-qom-booty) Traditional African beer made from fermented sorghum

Musselcracker Large-headed fish with powerful jaws and firm, white flesh

Naartjie (nar-chee) Tangerine or mandarin

Pap (pup) Porridge

Peri-peri Delicious hottish spice of Portuguese origin commonly used with grilled chicken

Perlemoen (pear-la-moon) Abalone

Pickled fish Traditional Cape dish of fish preserved with onions, vinegar and curry; available tinned in supermarkets

Pinotage A uniquely South African cultivar hybridized from Pinot Noir and Hermitage grapes and from which a wine of the same name is made

Potjiekos or potjie (poy-key-kos) Food cooked slowly over embers in a three-legged cast-iron pot

Putu (poo-too) Traditional African *mielie pap* (see p.683) prepared until it forms dry crumbs

Roti A chapati; called rooti in the Western Cape

Rusks Tasty biscuits made from sweetened bread that has been slow-cooked

Salmon trout Freshwater fish that is often smoked to create a cheaper and pretty good imitation of smoked salmon

Salomie Cape version of a roti; unleavened bread

Sambals (sam-bills) Accompaniments, such as chopped bananas, green peppers, desiccated coconut and chutney, served with Cape curries

Samp Traditional African dish of broken maize kernels, frequently cooked with beans

Skokiaan (skok-ee-yan) Potent home-brew

Smoorsnoek (smore-snook) Smoked snoek

Snoek (snook) Large fish that features in many traditional Cape recipes

Sosatie (so-sah-ti) Spicy skewered mince

Spanspek (spon-speck) A sweet melon

Steenbras (ste-en-bruss) A delicious white-fleshed fish

Van der Hum South African naartjie-flavoured liqueur

Vetkoek (fet-cook) Deep-fried doughnut-like cake

Waterblommetjiebredie (vata-blom-a-key-bree-dee) Cape meat stew made with waterlily rhizomes

Witblits (vit-blitz) Moonshine

Yellowtail Delicious darkish-fleshed marine fish

Small print and index

A ROUGH GUIDE TO ROUGH GUIDES

Published in 1982, the first Rough Guide – to Greece – was a student scheme that became a publishing phenomenon. Mark Ellingham, a recent graduate in English from Bristol University, had been travelling in Greece the previous summer and couldn't find the right guidebook. With a small group of friends he wrote his own guide, combining a highly contemporary, journalistic style with a thoroughly practical approach to travellers' needs.

The immediate success of the book spawned a series that rapidly covered dozens of destinations. And, in addition to impecunious backpackers, Rough Guides soon acquired a much broader readership that relished the guides' wit and inquisitiveness as much as their enthusiastic, critical approach and value-for-money ethos.

These days, Rough Guides include recommendations from budget to luxury and cover more than 200 destinations around the globe, as well as producing an ever-growing range of eBooks and apps.

Visit **roughguides.com** to see our latest publications.

Rough Guide credits

Editor: Emma Gibbs
Layout: Ajay Verma
Cartography: Lokamata Sahu
Picture editor: Nicole Newman
Proofreader: Jan McCann
Managing editor: Kathryn Lane
Assistant editor: Jalpreen Kaur Chhatwal
Production: Rebecca Short
Cover design: Nicole Newman, Rhiannon Furbear, Ajay Verma
Photographer: Alex Robinson

Editorial assistant: Lorna North
Senior pre-press designer: Dan May
Design director: Scott Stickland
Travel publisher: Joanna Kirby
Digital travel publisher: Peter Buckley
Reference director: Andrew Lockett
Operations coordinator: Becky Doyle
Operations assistant: Johanna Wurm
Publishing director (Travel): Clare Currie
Commercial manager: Gino Magnotta
Managing director: John Duhigg

Publishing information

This seventh edition published February 2011 by
Rough Guides Ltd,
80 Strand, London WC2R 0RL
11, Community Centre, Panchsheel Park,
New Delhi 110017, India
Distributed by the Penguin Group
Penguin Books Ltd,
80 Strand, London WC2R 0RL
Penguin Group (USA)
375 Hudson Street, NY 10014, USA
Penguin Group (Australia)
250 Camberwell Road, Camberwell,
Victoria 3124, Australia
Penguin Group (NZ)
67 Apollo Drive, Mairangi Bay, Auckland 1310,
New Zealand
Rough Guides is represented in Canada by Tourmaline
Editions Inc. 662 King Street West, Suite 304, Toronto,
Ontario M5V 1M7
Printed in Singapore
© Tony Pinchuck, Barbara McCrea, Donald Reid & Ross
Velton 2012

Maps © Rough Guides
No part of this book may be reproduced in any form
without permission from the publisher except for the
quotation of brief passages in reviews.
704pp includes index
A catalogue record for this book is available from the
British Library
ISBN: 978-1-40538-650-0

Help us update

We've gone to a lot of effort to ensure that the seventh edition of **The Rough Guide to South Africa** is accurate and up-to-date. However, things change – places get "discovered", opening hours are notoriously fickle, restaurants and rooms raise prices or lower standards. If you feel we've got it wrong or left something out, we'd like to know, and if you can remember the address, the price, the hours, the phone number, so much the better.

Please send your comments with the subject line "**Rough Guide South Africa Update**" to @ mail@uk.roughguides .com. We'll credit all contributions and send a copy of the next edition (or any other Rough Guide if you prefer) for the very best emails.

Find more travel information, connect with fellow travellers and book your trip on ⓦ roughguides.com

Tony Pinchuck launched his travels as a schoolboy hitching around South Africa in the 1970s and his explorations of the subcontinent have continued ever since. Now resident in Cape Town, he is production editor on the investigative magazine *noseweek*.

Barbara McCrea was born in Zimbabwe and taught African literature at the University of Natal. She lived in London for fifteen years, working on Rough Guides to Zimbabwe, South Africa and Cape Town, before returning to Southern Africa. She lives with views of whales, surfers and mountains in Cape Town.

Donald Reid was brought up in Glasgow, studied law in Edinburgh and took to the high seas afterwards to avoid the threat of an office. He worked on travel books and magazines in Cape Town and has now settled back in Edinburgh, where he works as a freelance writer.

Ross Velton is the sole author of guidebooks to Orlando and Walt Disney World (for Rough Guides), Haiti and the Dominican Republic, Mali and Cape d'Agde, the world's largest nudist resort, and has contributed to fifteen other Rough Guides. He has written for UK newspapers such as *The Times* and *The Independent* on subjects ranging from cigars in the Dominican Republic to cycling in Montreal.

Acknowledgements

Hilary Heuler: Many thanks to Caitlin Blaser and Rajesh Latchman for a personalized and appreciative introduction to the much-maligned Northern Cape, for ferrying me around Joburg and for generally making my life a thousand times easier (and much more fun). I'd also like to thank the lovely folks at *Sunset Lodge* and Maputaland Tours in St Lucia, whose knowledge of the area was both fascinating and extremely helpful, as well as all the other people along the way whose tips and suggestions have made the book so much better.

Jeroen van Marle: Jeroen would especially like to thank Laura Vercueil of Joburg Tourism, the helpful Gauteng, Clarens, Rustenburg and Maseru tourism offices, the intrepid entrepreneurs at Arts on Main and 70 Juta, Ingrid Jensen at Gautrain, Di Jones and her colleagues at *Malealea Lodge*, Roger Gibson of Wits University's Vredefort Dome Visitor Centre and, as ever, Marta Karwat.

Barbara McCrea: Thanks to our editors, Emma and Kathryn, who got a difficult job done, to Tony Pinchuck for his invaluable and considerable input on the work, to son Gabriel Pinchuck for putting up with the levels of obsessiveness and staying power which Rough Guides demand, and being a cheerful travelling companion, and to the many generous people who have given us

accommodation, meals and information, and made researching fun. And thanks to everyone else in this network of help and support I haven't mentioned by name.

Lone Mouritsen: In Swaziland, Lone would like to thank Patrick Ward for help and advice, and for putting her in touch with Kelly White whose contacts in Swaziland were invaluable and made research planning very easy. A big thank you also goes out to Darron Raw for the latest on adventure tourism plus the low down on the country's tense political situation. In Limpopo, her thanks go out especially to everybody at Horizon Horseback, and Klaus and Bettina at *Plumtree Lodge* in Polokwane. Lastly, she also wants to say thank you to her sister – Mette – for accompanying her on the trip and never moaning about always being on the move.

Tony Pinchuck: Thanks to our editor Emma Gibbs for keeping us on the straight and narrow; to my co-author Barbara McCrea for her vital contribution to the book; to our picture researcher Nicole for her hard work and excellent choice of images; to the City of Cape Town's Kylie Hatton for delivering the goods at a moment's notice; and to all the unmentioned people who had a part in producing this book.

Readers' letters

Thanks to all the readers who have taken the time to write in with comments and suggestions (and apologies if we've inadvertently omitted or misspelt anyone's name):

Christoph Baltzer, Christine Brooks, Debbie Coleman, Tobias Hiddemann, James, Jan Kara, Jim Lambert, Gerolf von Lengeling, Sara Lennard, Isabell McGowen, Keith & Diana Morgan, Chris Myburgh, Alichia Nortje, Emma Norton and Alex Crossman, Paula, Simone Pierk, William Timmermans and Fannia Polet, Esther Premkumar, John Tatam, Gail Walters, Ron Zuiderwijk.

Photo credits

All photos © Rough Guides except the following:
(Key: a-above; b-below/bottom; c-centre; f-far; l-left; r-right; t-top)

p.1 Superstock
p.2 Superstock, Rob Cousins
p.4 Alamy, John Warburton-Lee (tl)
p.5 Corbis, Hoberman Collection
p.9 FLPA, Malcolm Schuyl (t); Robert Harding Picture Library, Yadid Levy (b)
p.10 Getty Images, B. Bahr
p.11 Alamy, Prisma Bildagentur
p.12 Getty Images, Roger de la Harpe
p.13 Alamy, Sean Tilden (t); Corbis, Gideon Mendel (c); Superstock, Ian Trower (b)
p.14 Alamy (c); Robert Harding Picture Library Steve Toon (b); Superstock (t)
p.15 Corbis, Clive Sawyer (b); Keren Su (t)
p.16 Corbis, Niels van Gijn (t); Getty Images, Christopher Thomas (b); Superstock (t)
p.17 Alamy, Africa Media (tl); Robert Harding (tr); Getty Images, Tim Jackson (bl)
p.18 Corbis, Martin Harvey (cl); Frans Lanting (b); Photolibrary (cr); Superstock (t)
p.19 Alamy, AfriPics (t); Corbis, Hoberman Collection (b)
p.20 Alamy, Africa Photobank (c); John Warburton-Lee (t); Bulungula Lodge (b)
p.21 Alamy, Frans Lemmens (r); Getty Images, Roger de la Harpe (t); Bobby Haas (c)
p.22 Alamy, AfriPics (tl); Getty Images, Denny Allen (tr)
p.25 FLPA, Chris and Tilde Stuart (tr); Christian Heinrich (bl); Konrad Wothe (tl); Getty Images, Sami Sarkis (br); Heinrich van den Berg (c)
p.27 Alamy, blickwinkel (c); FLPA, Jurgen & Christine Sohns (br) Michael Krabs (tl); Pete Oxford (bl); Superstock, Nigel Dennis (tr)
p.29 FLPA, Wendy Dennis (b); Getty Images, Shem Compion (cl); Tier Images (cr); Superstock (tl); Dirscherl Reinhard (tr)
p.31 FLPA, MICHAEL KRABS (t); Philip Perry (cr); Getty Images (h); Nigel Dennis (cl)
p.33 FLPA, Richard Du Toit (b); Malcolm Schuyl (t); Getty Images, Heinrich van den Berg (c)
p.35 FLPA, Chris and Tilde Stuart (cl); Winfried Wisniewski (t); Jurgen & Christine Sohns (cr); Getty Images (br); Superstock, Nigel Dennis (bl)
p.37 Alamy, Prisma Bildagentur (br); Sean Tilden (bl); Corbis, Steve Toon (cr); Getty Images, Nigel Dennis (tl); James Hager (tr); Tier Images (cl)
p.39 Corbis, Martin Harvey (t); Krista Kennell (b)
p.41 Alamy, Friedrichsmeirer (b); Getty Images, Karl Beath (t)
p.43 FLPA, Richard Du Toit (b); ImageBroker (t); Christian Heinrich (c); Getty Images, Fabio Chironi (cl); Superstock (cr)
p.45 FLPA (b); Tilde Stuart (tr, c); Getty Images, Steve Toon (tl)
p.82 Superstock, Maisant Ludovic

p.151 Alamy, Jon Arnold
p.162 Alamy, Ariadne Van Zandbergen
p.165 Getty Images, Robert Harding
p.213 Getty Images, Peter Chadwick (tl, b); Nigel Dennis (tr)
p.243 Getty Images, Paul Thompson
p.257 Getty Images, Herman du Plessis (b)
p.262 Superstock, Rob Cousins
p.265 Getty Images, Eric Nathan
p.287 Getty Images, Vittorio Ricci/Flickr RF
p.299 Corbis, Frans Lanting (t); Getty Images, Eric Nathan (b)
p.302 Alamy, LOOK Die Bildagentur der Fotografen
p.305 Alamy, AfriPics (t)
p.313 Getty Images, Roger de la Harpe
p.329 Alamy, Robert Harding (b); Corbis, Steve Toon (t)
p.345 Alamy, Steve Toon
p.363 Getty Images, Peter Pinnock
p.364 Alamy, Michele Burgess
p.387 Getty Images
p.401 AWL Images, Ian Trower
p.427 Alamy, Frans Lemmens (b); Superstock, Herbert Kratky (t)
p.440 Superstock, Nigel Dennis
p.443 Superstock, Micheal Krabs
p.456 Getty Images, Allan Baxter
p.459 Superstock
p.479 Superstock, Giovanni Mereghetti
p.495 Alamy, Africa Media Online (b); Corbis, Jon Hrusa (t)
p.510 Superstock, Heeb Christian
p.513 Getty Images, Eric Nathan
p.521 Superstock (t); Peter Groenendijk (b)
p.528 Corbis, Image Source
p.531 Alamy, AfriPics
p.541 Corbis, Gideon Mendel (tl); Getty Images, Warren Little (tr); Superstock, Walter Bibikow (b)
p.564 Alamy, AfriPics
p.567 Alamy, AfriPics
p.581 Alamy, AfriPics (tr); John Warburton-Lee (b); Getty Images, Piotr Naskrecki (tl)
p.586 Superstock
p.589 Alamy, Gary Cook
p.603 Getty Images, Joe Alblas (t); Superstock (br)
p.615 Getty Images (bl)
p.622 Getty Images
p.625 Superstock
p.645 Getty Images, Ariadne Van Zandbergen (t)
p.648 AWL Images, Ian Trower (b)

Front cover: Burchells zebra, photostaud/Alamy
Back cover: Hole in the Wall on the Wild Coast, Cuan Hansen/Getty (t); Basotho women in traditional dress, Lesotho, Africa Media Online/Alamy (l); Victoria and Alfred Waterfront, Cape Town, Peter Adams/JAI/Corbis (r)

Index

Maps are marked in grey

Maps

Map symbols

The symbols below are used on maps throughout the book

✈	Airport	🕌	Mosque	⊠	Gate	▨	Building
★	Transport stop	✡	Synagogue	⚜	Viewpoint	☐	Market
✉	Post office	♦	Place of interest	⌃	Mountain range	⇄	Church
@	Internet access	ⵉ	Garden	▲	Mountain peak	◯	Stadium
✚	Hospital	⌂	Mountain refuge/lodge	◠	Cave	⬓	Park
ⓘ	Information centre	✂	Battle site	⁝	Hot spring	⊞	Christian cemetery
E	Embassy	∴	Ruins	🜊	Waterfall	☐	Beach
P	Parking	☗	Hide	ⵟ	Lighthouse	▬▬	Wall
🛆	Campsite	♟	Castle	🍇	Vineyards	– –	Ferry
⛽	Fuel/gas station	⛳	Golf course	🏊	Swimming pool	●–•●	Cable car
🚶	Border crossing post	🏛	Monument	⅄	Picnic site	▬▬	Tram line

Listings key

■ Accommodation
● Restaurant/café
■ Bar/club
● Shop

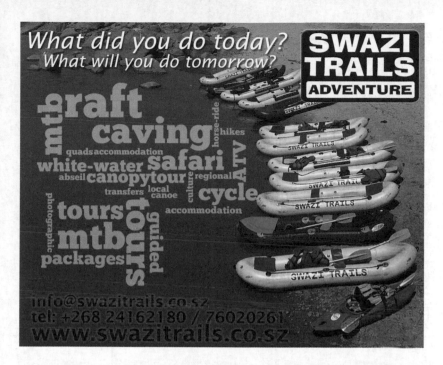